# THE OXFORD Primary School DICTIONARY

Compiled by
A. J. Augarde, Colin Hope, John Butterworth

Illustrations by
Peter Bull

**OXFORD UNIVERSITY PRESS**

**Oxford University Press, Walton Street, Oxford OX2 6DP**

Oxford  New York  Toronto
Delhi  Bombay  Calcutta  Madras  Karachi
Kuala Lumpur  Singapore  Hong Kong  Tokyo
Nairobi  Dar es Salaam  Cape Town
Melbourne  Auckland  Madrid
and associated companies in
Berlin  Ibadan

Oxford is a trade mark of Oxford University Press

British Library Cataloguing in Publication Data
Data available
ISBN 0 19 910335 6 (Hardback-Trade Edition)
ISBN 0 19 910293 7 (Hardback-Educational Edition)
Printed in Great  Britain by The Bath Press, Avon

**OWLS**
OXFORD ENGLISH
DICTIONARY
WORD AND
LANGUAGE
SERVICE

Do you have a query about words, their origin, meaning, use, spelling,
pronunciation, or any other aspect of the English language? Then write to
OWLS at Oxford University Press, Walton Street, Oxford OX2 6DP.

All queries will be answered using the full resources of the
Oxford Dictionary Department.

# Introduction

This is an English language dictionary for children in Elementary schools. It contains all the words you are likely to use at school or at home, and explains what they mean.

English is a rich language. In this dictionary there are words of countless different sorts. There are words to do with maths, words to do with religion, words to do with sport, words for plants, animals, and flowers. There are words that you would use only for special occasions or for writing, and *informal* words such as you would use when talking to your friends. There are some *slang* words, some very old words, and some brand-new ones; and even a few words that you would never use unless you wanted to be deliberately hurtful or offensive. The dictionary tells you when a word has a special kind of meaning, or when it belongs to a certain time or place.

English words are written using an alphabet of twenty-six letters: five of the letters are called *vowels* and the rest are called *consonants*.

**Vowels**: a e i o u (sometimes y)
**Consonants**: b c d f g h j k l m n p q r s t v w x y z

Words are made up of strings of letters, known as *syllables*. A word can have one, two, or many syllables:

Words of **one syllable**: cat, plum, string, go, I
Words of **two syllables**: playing, jelly, open, collect, packet
Words of **three or more syllables**: fortunate (3), everybody (4), parallelogram (5)

Words that stand alone are called *simple* words. But there are many words in English that are formed from other words. Take these examples:

**Simple words**: net, ball, night, fall, under, stand, fork, lift, club
**Compound words**: netball, nightfall, understand
**Hyphenated words**: fork-lift, night-club

The words that are listed in the dictionary are called *headwords* and appear in large, **bold type**. Following each headword is a short paragraph called an *entry*. The main part of the entry is the *definition* – the part that tells you what the word means. The entry also tells you what kind of word it is, how it is used, and how it changes to fit different sentences. If the pronunciation is difficult or unusual, you are shown how to say the word; and, of course, the headword shows you how the word is spelled.

Remember that a dictionary is not a simple answer book. It is a tool. It takes skill, and therefore practice, to use a dictionary properly. If you cannot find a word straight away, don't give up: try searching under different spellings. When you do find your word, read the whole of the entry – or entries – and don't just seize on the first meaning that is given. Only by *exploring* words can you learn to understand them and put them to their full use.

# Dictionary Features

**Headword:** the first word in each entry.

**drape** *verb* (**drapes, draping, draped**)
to hang cloth over something.

**Verb forms:** present tense, present participle, past tense, past participle.

**Pronunciation:** for some difficult words we give a rhyming word, or letters which sound like the headword.

**draught** *noun* (**draughts**)
(rhymes with *craft*)
a current of usually cold air indoors.
**draughty** *adjective*

**Definition:** the meaning of the headword.

USAGE: Do not confuse **draught** with **draft**, which means a rough sketch or plan.

**Usage note:** pointing out words which are easily confused.

**draughts** *noun*
(in America, *checkers*) a game played with 24 round pieces on a chessboard.

**Plural:** all regular and irregular plurals are given.

**draughtsman** *noun* (**draughtsmen**)
**1** someone who makes drawings. **2** a piece used in the game of draughts.

**American equivalent:** where Americans use a different word.

**draw**¹ *verb* (**draws, drawing, drew, drawn**)
**1** to make a picture, diagram, etc. with a pencil, crayon, pen, etc., *I have drawn a map of Britain.* **2** to pull, *She drew her chair up to the table.* **3** to attract, *The fair drew large crowds.* **4** to end a game or contest with the same score on both sides, *They drew 2–2 last Saturday.* **5** to come, *The ship was drawing nearer. The winter is drawing to a close; spring is nearly here.*

**Numbers:** used when a word has more than one meaning.

**Superior numbers:** used with words that have more than one part of speech, or very different meanings.

**draw**² *noun* (**draws**)
**1** an attraction. **2** a raffle or similar competition in which the winner is chosen by chance. **3** a game that ends with the same score on both sides.

**Examples:** how a word is used.

**Part of speech:** noun, verb, adjective, adverb, etc.

**drawbridge** *noun* (**drawbridges**)
a bridge that may be raised or lowered over a moat.

**Illustrations:** adding more information to definitions.

**Adjective forms:** all comparative and superlative forms of adjectives are given.

**Cross-references:** sometimes references are made from one entry to another. Here an irregular verb form is referred to the main entry (**draw**).

**dreary** *adjective* (**drearier, dreariest**)
gloomy; boring.
**drearily** *adverb*, **dreariness** *noun*

**drew** past tense of **draw** *verb*.

**Derivative:** a word with a meaning connected with the headword's meaning.

# Aa

**a** *adjective* (called the *indefinite article*)
1 one; any, *Can you lend me a book?* 2 each; every, *I go there twice a month.*

**aback** *adverb*
**taken aback**, surprised and slightly shocked.

**abacus** *noun* (**abacuses** or **abaci**)
a frame for counting with beads sliding on wires.

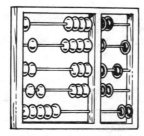

**abandon** *verb* (**abandons, abandoning, abandoned**)
to give up; to leave something without intending to return, *Abandon ship!*

**abbey** *noun* (**abbeys**)
1 a group of buildings where monks or nuns live and work. 2 a community of monks or nuns. 3 a church which is or was part of an abbey, *Westminster Abbey.*

**abbot** *noun* (**abbots**)
the head of an abbey of monks.

**abbreviate** *verb* (**abbreviates, abbreviating, abbreviated**)
to shorten something.

**abbreviation** *noun* (**abbreviations**)
something shortened, especially a word.

**ABC** *noun*
the alphabet, *We know our ABC.*

**abdomen** *noun* (**abdomens**)
1 the part of the body that contains the stomach. 2 the rear part of the body of an insect, spider, etc.
**abdominal** *adjective*

**abide** *verb* (**abides, abiding, abode** or **abided**)
1 to tolerate, *I can't abide noise.*
2 (*old-fashioned use*) to stay, *There were shepherds abiding in the fields.*
**abide by**, to keep a promise, etc.

**able** *adjective* (**abler, ablest**)
1 having the power, skill, or opportunity to do something. 2 skilful, *an able musician.*
**able seaman**, a seaman who is fully trained.
**ability** *noun*, **ably** *adverb*

**-able** *suffix*
that can have a particular action done to it; suitable for a particular purpose, *The wardrobe is nearly too heavy to be movable. Is this fish eatable?*

**abnormal** *adjective*
not normal.
**abnormality** *noun*

**aboard** *adverb*
on a ship or an aircraft.

**abode**[1] *noun* (**abodes**)
the place where someone lives.

**abode**[2] past tense and past participle of **abide**.

**abolish** *verb* (**abolishes, abolishing, abolished**)
to get rid of a law, custom, etc.

**abolition** *noun* (**abolitions**)
(*say* ab-ŏ-lish-ŏn)
abolishing something, especially capital punishment or slavery.
**abolitionist** *noun*

**abominable** *adjective*
1 (*informal*) very bad.
2 causing loathing, *an abominable crime.*
**abominable snowman**, a yeti.

**aborigines** *plural noun*
(*say* ab-er-ij-in-eez)
the people who were the first to live in a country.
**Aborigines**, the people who were the first to live in Australia.
**aboriginal** *adjective* and *noun*

**abortion** *noun* (**abortions**)
the removal of a foetus from a woman's womb before it has developed fully enough to live.

**abound** *verb* (**abounds, abounding, abounded**)
to be plentiful.

**about**[1] *preposition*
1 on the subject of; in connection with, *This film is about the police.* 2 all round, *They ran about the playground. Toys lay about the room.* 3 near to, *She's about five feet tall.*
**about to**, going to, *He was about to sing.*

**about²** *adverb*
1 in various directions or places, *They were running about.* 2 somewhere near by, *There were wild animals about.*

**above¹** *preposition*
1 higher than. 2 more than.
**above-board**, honest.

**above²** *adverb*
at or to a higher place.

**abrasive** *adjective*
that scrapes or grazes.

**abreast** *adverb*
side by side, *They walked three abreast.*
**abreast of something**, keeping up with something, *We must be abreast of modern discoveries.*

**abroad** *adverb*
in or to another country.

**abrupt** *adjective* (**abrupter, abruptest**)
1 sudden, *What caused his abrupt departure?* 2 rather rude because of saying little, *an abrupt reply.*

**abscess** *noun* (**abscesses**)
a swollen place on the body containing pus.

**absence** *noun* (**absences**)
not being in a place, especially not being at school, work, etc.

**absent** *adjective*
not present; away.

**absentee** *noun* (**absentees**)
someone who is not at school, work, etc.
**absenteeism** *noun*

**absent-minded** *adjective*
forgetful; not attentive, *an absent-minded pupil.*
**absent-mindedly** *adverb*

**absolute** *adjective*
1 complete. 2 not restricted, *The king had absolute power.*

**absolutely** *adverb*
1 completely. 2 (*informal*) definitely, '*Are you going to Beth's party?' 'Absolutely!'*

**absorb** *verb* (**absorbs, absorbing, absorbed**)
1 to soak up. 2 to be very interesting to someone, *The book absorbed him.*
**be absorbed in something**, to be giving something all your attention.
**absorbent** *adjective*, **absorption** *noun*

**abstract¹** *adjective*
(*say* ab-strakt)
concerned with ideas, not with things, *Happiness is abstract.*

**abstract²** *verb* (**abstracts, abstracting, abstracted**)
(*say* ăb-**strakt**)
to take away, *Water is abstracted from the river.*

**abstract³** *noun* (**abstracts**)
(*say* ab-strakt)
a summary.

**absurd** *adjective* (**absurder, absurdest**)
ridiculous, *an absurd system.*
**absurdity** *noun*

**abundance** *noun*
plenty, *an abundance of good things.*

**abundant** *adjective*
large in amount.

**abuse¹** *verb* (**abuses, abusing, abused**)
(*say* ă-**bewz**)
1 to misuse. 2 to say unpleasant things about someone.

**abuse²** *noun* (**abuses**)
(*say* ă-**bewss**)
1 misuse of something. 2 unpleasant words said about someone. 3 physical harm done to someone.

**abusive** *adjective*
saying unpleasant things about someone.

**abysmal** *adjective*
(*informal*) very bad, *an abysmal meal. The weather was abysmal.*

**abyss** *noun* (**abysses**)
a hole so deep that it seems to have no bottom.

**academic** *adjective*
1 concerned with learning. 2 not practical.

**academy** *noun* (**academies**)
1 a college or school. 2 a society concerned with art or learning.

**accelerate** *verb* (**accelerates, accelerating, accelerated**)
to move more quickly.
**acceleration** *noun*

**accelerator** *noun* (**accelerators**)
a pedal that you press down to make a motor vehicle go faster.

**accent¹** *noun* (**accents**)
(*say* ak-sĕnt)
1 the way that you pronounce words. 2 the way that people in different parts of a country pronounce words differently, *He has a Yorkshire accent.* 3 pronouncing part of a word more strongly than the rest, *The accent in 'spider' is on the first syllable.* 4 a mark put over a letter to show its pronunciation, *The word 'café' has an accent on the 'e'.*

**accent**² *verb* (**accents, accenting, accented**)
(*say* ăk-**sent**)
to pronounce part of a word more strongly
than the rest.

**accept** *verb* (**accepts, accepting, accepted**)
1 to take something which is offered. 2 to
agree with something, *I accept that idea.*
**acceptance** *noun*

USAGE: Do not confuse **accept** with **except**,
which is a preposition meaning not
including.

**acceptable** *adjective*
1 worth accepting, *an acceptable offer.*
2 satisfactory, *an acceptable standard of
work.*

**access**¹ *noun* (**accesses**)
a way to reach something, *This road is the
only access to the house.*
**give access to something,** to allow something
to be reached, *These stairs give access to
the attic.*

USAGE: Do not confuse **access** with **excess**,
which means too much of something.

**access**² *verb* (**accesses, accessing, accessed**)
(*in Computing*) to gain access to
something, *access a file.*

**accessible** *adjective*
easy to reach.
**accessibility** *noun*

**accession** *noun* (**accessions**)
becoming King or Queen, *a painting of
Edward VII at his accession.*

**accessory** *noun* (**accessories**)
an extra or spare part; things like shoes
and handbags that go with clothes.

**accident** *noun* (**accidents**)
an unexpected event, especially one in
which someone is killed or injured.
**by accident,** not on purpose.

**accidental**¹ *adjective*
not done on purpose, *accidental damage.*
**accidentally** *adverb*

**accidental**² *noun* (**accidentals**)
(*in Music*) a sign which raises or lowers a
note, for instance when the key of the
music changes for a short time only.

**acclaim** *verb* (**acclaims, acclaiming, acclaimed**)
to welcome or applaud someone
enthusiastically.

**acclimatize** *verb* (**acclimatizes, acclimatizing,
acclimatized**)
to get used to, or to make someone or
something become used to a new climate,
environment, etc.
**acclimatization** *noun*

**accommodate** *verb* (**accommodates,
accommodating, accommodated**)
to provide a room or lodging for someone.
**accommodation** *noun*

**accompany** *verb* (**accompanies, accompanying,
accompanied**)
1 to go somewhere with someone. 2 to play
music that supports a singer, etc.
**accompaniment** *noun*, **accompanist** *noun*

**accomplish** *verb* (**accomplishes, accomplishing,
accomplished**)
to do something successfully.
**accomplishment** *noun*

**accomplished** *adjective*
skilful, *an accomplished pianist.*

**accord** *noun*
agreement.
**of your own accord,** without being asked or
told to do something.

**according** *adverb*
**according to someone,** in the opinion of
someone; as stated by someone, *According
to him, we are stupid.*
**according to something,** in a way that suits
something, *Price the apples according to
their size.*

**accordingly** *adverb*
1 consequently; therefore. 2 in a suitable
way.

**accordion** *noun* (**accordions**)
a portable musical instrument like a large
concertina.
**accordionist** *noun*

**account**¹ *noun* (**accounts**)
1 a description or story. 2 an arrangement
to keep money in a bank, etc. 3 a statement
of money owed, spent, or received; a bill.
4 consideration, *Take it into account.*
**on account of,** because of.
**on no account,** certainly not.

**account**² *verb* (**accounts, accounting,
accounted**)
to record how money has been spent.
**account for something,** to make it clear why
something happens.

**accountant** *noun* (accountants)
an expert in preparing and examining financial accounts.
**accountancy** *noun*

**accumulate** *verb* (accumulates, accumulating, accumulated)
to collect; to pile up, *Dark clouds began to accumulate.*
**accumulation** *noun*

**accurate** *adjective*
correct; exact, *an accurate list.*
**accuracy** *noun*

**accuse** *verb* (accuses, accusing, accused)
to say that someone has committed a crime, etc.
**accusation** *noun*

**accustomed** *adjective*
customary, *I sat in my accustomed chair.*
**accustomed to,** being used to, *I am accustomed to having lunch at twelve o'clock.*

**ace** *noun* (aces)
1 the card of highest or lowest value in each suit of a pack of cards. 2 a very skilful person or thing.

**ache**[1] *noun* (aches)
a dull or continuous pain.

**ache**[2] *verb* (aches, aching, ached)
to feel a dull or continuous pain.

**achieve** *verb* (achieves, achieving, achieved)
to accomplish, *She achieved her ambition.*
**achievement** *noun*

**acid**[1] *noun* (acids)
(*in Science*) a substance that contains hydrogen and neutralizes alkalis.
**acidic** *adjective*, **acidity** *noun*

**acid**[2] *adjective*
sour, *This fruit has an acid taste.*
**acid rain,** rain that contains harmful acids because it has absorbed waste gases from the air.

**acknowledge** *verb* (acknowledges, acknowledging, acknowledged)
1 to admit that something is true. 2 to say that you have received a letter, etc. 3 to express thanks for something.
**acknowledgement** *noun*

**acne** *noun*
(*say* **ak**-ni)
inflamed red pimples on someone's face.

**acorn** *noun* (acorns)
the seed of the oak-tree.

**acoustic** *adjective*
(*say* ă-**koo**-stik)
1 of sound or hearing. 2 (of a musical instrument) not using electrical means to make its sound louder, *an acoustic guitar.*

**acoustics** *plural noun*
1 the qualities of a place which make it good or bad for sound, *This hall has bad acoustics.* 2 (*singular noun*) the science of sound.

**acquaint** *verb* (acquaints, acquainting, acquainted)
to tell someone about something, *Acquaint him with the facts.*
**be acquainted with someone,** to know someone slightly.

**acquaintance** *noun* (acquaintances)
someone you know slightly.
**make someone's acquaintance,** to get to know someone.

**acquire** *verb* (acquires, acquiring, acquired)
to obtain.
**acquisition** *noun*

**acquit** *verb* (acquits, acquitting, acquitted)
to decide that someone is not guilty.
**acquittal** *noun*

**acre** *noun* (acres)
(*say* **ay**-ker)
a piece of land measuring 4,840 square yards.

**acrobat** *noun* (**acrobats**)
a person who gives displays of jumping and balancing as entertainment.
**acrobatic** *adjective*, **acrobatics** *plural noun*

**across** *adverb* and *preposition*
1 from one side of a thing to the other, *The table measures 1.5 metres across.* 2 to or on the other side of something, *How can we get across the busy road?*

**act**[1] *noun* (**acts**)
1 an action. 2 a short performance in a programme of entertainment, *a juggling act.* 3 a pretence, *She is only putting on an act.* 4 one of the main parts of a play or opera, *An act can include several scenes.* 5 a law passed by parliament.

**act**[2] *verb* (**acts, acting, acted**)
1 to do something. 2 to have an effect. 3 to take a part in a play, film, etc.

**action** *noun* (**actions**)
1 doing something; something that has been done. 2 a battle; fighting, *He was killed in action.* 3 the part that makes a gun, musical instrument, etc. work.
**out of action**, not working properly.
**take action**, to do something.

**activate** *verb* (**activates, activating, activated**)
to start something working.

**active** *adjective*
1 taking part in activities. 2 functioning, *an active volcano.* 3 of the type of verb in which the subject performs the action, *In 'He hit me' the verb is active; in 'I was hit' the verb is passive.*

**activity** *noun* (**activities**)
1 being active or lively. 2 an action or occupation, *outdoor activities.*

**actor** *noun* (**actors**)
a performer in a play, film, etc.

**actress** *noun* (**actresses**)
a female performer in a play, film, etc.

**actual** *adjective*
real.
**actually** *adverb*

**acupuncture** *noun*
pricking parts of the body with needles to relieve pain or cure disease.

**acute** *adjective* (**acuter, acutest**)
1 sharp, *acute pain.* 2 severe, *an acute shortage of trained staff.*
**acute accent**, the mark ´ put over a letter, as in *café.*
**acute angle**, an angle less than 90 degrees.

**AD** short for *Anno Domini*, used with dates that come after the birth of Jesus, *Columbus reached America in AD 1492.*

**Adam's apple** *noun* (**Adam's apples**)
the lump at the front of a man's neck.

**adapt** *verb* (**adapts, adapting, adapted**)
to become suited to something; to make something suitable for a new purpose, *Can you adapt to your new situation? They adapted the car for driving in the desert.*
**adaptable** *adjective*, **adaptation** *noun*

**adaptor** *noun* (**adaptors**)
a device to connect pieces of electrical or other equipment.

**add** *verb* (**adds, adding, added**)
to put one thing with another.
**add to**, to increase.
**add up**, to make or find a total; (*informal*) to make sense, *Add up the figures. It just doesn't add up – why should he do such a thing?*

**adder** *noun* (**adders**)
a small poisonous snake.

**addict** *noun* (**addicts**)
someone who does or uses something that he or she cannot give up, *a drug addict.*
**addicted** *adjective*, **addiction** *noun*, **addictive** *adjective*

**addition** *noun* (**additions**)
1 the action of adding. 2 something added.
**in addition**, also.
**additional** *adjective*

**additive** *noun* (**additives**)
something added to food, etc. in small amounts.

**address**¹ *noun* (**addresses**)
**1** the details of the place where someone lives, *My address is 29 High Street, Newtown.* **2** a speech.

**address**² *verb* (**addresses, addressing, addressed**)
**1** to write an address on a letter, parcel, etc. **2** to make a speech, remark, etc. to someone, *The judge addressed the prisoner.*

**adenoids** *plural noun*
spongy flesh at the back of your nose, which may hinder breathing.

**adequate** *adjective*
enough; suitable, *an adequate response to the problem.*

**adhere** *verb* (**adheres, adhering, adhered**)
to stick to something.
**someone adheres to something,** someone follows a plan, rule, etc.

**adhesive**¹ *adjective*
causing things to stick together.
**adhesion** *noun*

**adhesive**² *noun* (**adhesives**)
a glue.

**adjacent** *adjective*
near or next, *Her house is adjacent to the shop. We were in an adjacent room.*

**adjective** *noun* (**adjectives**)
a word that describes a noun or adds to its meaning, *Adjectives are words like 'big', 'honest', and 'strange'.*

**adjourn** *verb* (**adjourns, adjourning, adjourned**)
(*say* ă-**jern**)
**1** to break off a meeting, etc. until a later time. **2** to move to another place.
**adjournment** *noun*

**adjudicate** *verb* (**adjudicates, adjudicating, adjudicated**)
(*say* ă-**joo**-di-kayt)
to act as judge in a competition, etc.
**adjudication** *noun*, **adjudicator** *noun*

**adjust** *verb* (**adjusts, adjusting, adjusted**)
to put something into its proper position or order.
**adjuster** *noun*, **adjustment** *noun*

**ad lib**¹ *adjective* and *adverb*
without any rehearsal or preparation.

**ad lib**² *verb* (**ad libs, ad libbing, ad libbed**)
to say or do something without any rehearsal or preparation.

**administer** *verb* (**administers, administering, administered**)
**1** to administrate. **2** to give formally, *He administered the punishment.*

**administrate** *verb* (**administrates, administrating, administrated**)
to manage a business, etc.; to govern.
**administration** *noun*, **administrative** *adjective*, **administrator** *noun*

**admirable** *adjective*
worth admiring; excellent, *an admirable piece of work. This is an admirable place for a holiday.*
**admirably** *adverb*

**admiral** *noun* (**admirals**)
a naval officer of high rank.

**admire** *verb* (**admires, admiring, admired**)
**1** to think someone or something is very good, beautiful, etc. **2** to look at something and enjoy it.
**admiration** *noun*

**admirer** *noun* (**admirers**)
someone who thinks that a particular person or thing is very good, beautiful, etc.

**admission** *noun* (**admissions**)
**1** agreeing or confessing, *He is guilty by his own admission.* **2** entering, *Admission to the show is by ticket only.*

**admit** *verb* (**admits, admitting, admitted**)
**1** to let someone come in. **2** to agree or confess.

**admittance** *noun*
entering, *The sign read: 'No admittance'.*

USAGE: **admission** means entering a public place, usually after paying some money. **admittance** is a more formal word and often refers to entering a place that is private.

**admittedly** *adverb*
as an agreed fact; without denying it, *Admittedly I was teasing the dog, but I didn't expect him to bite.*

**ado** *noun*
fuss; excitement, *There was much ado when the Queen visited our school.*

**adolescence** *noun*
the time between being a child and being an adult.
**adolescent** *noun* and *adjective*

**adopt** *verb* (**adopts, adopting, adopted**)
**1** to take someone into your family and treat him or her as your child. **2** to accept something.
**adoption** *noun*, **adoptive** *adjective*

**adore** *verb* (**adores, adoring, adored**)
to love very much.
**adorable** *adjective*, **adoration** *noun*

**adorn** *verb* (**adorns, adorning, adorned**)
to decorate.
**adornment** *noun*

**adrenalin** *noun*
a hormone that stimulates your nervous system and makes you feel excited.

**adrift** *adverb* and *adjective*
drifting, *The boat was adrift.*

**adult** *noun* (**adults**)
a person or animal that is fully grown.

**adultery** *noun* (**adulteries**)
(*say* ă-dul-ter-i)
being unfaithful to your wife or husband by having another lover.
**adulterer** *noun*, **adulterous** *adjective*

**advance**[1] *noun* (**advances**)
**1** a forward movement. **2** progress. **3** a loan.
**in advance**, beforehand.
**in advance of**, before.

**advance**[2] *verb* (**advances, advancing, advanced**)
to make an advance.

**advanced** *adjective*
**1** far on in progress, life, etc., *an advanced age.* **2** not elementary, *an examination at advanced level.*

**advantage** *noun* (**advantages**)
something useful or helpful.
**take advantage of something**, to use something profitably; to use something unfairly, *Take advantage of our introductory offer! They took advantage of our generosity, and tricked us.*
**to your advantage**, profitable or helpful to you.
**advantageous** *adjective*

**Advent** *noun*
**1** the coming of Jesus. **2** the period before Christmas.

**adventure** *noun* (**adventures**)
**1** an exciting or dangerous experience. **2** taking risks; danger, *He likes adventure.*
**adventurous** *adjective*

**adverb** *noun* (**adverbs**)
a word that tells you how, when, where, or why something happens, *Adverbs are words like 'easily', 'indoors', and 'soon'.*
**adverbial** *adjective*

**adversary** *noun* (**adversaries**)
(*say* ad-ver-să-ri)
an opponent or enemy.

**adverse** *adjective*
unfavourable; harmful, *The drug had adverse effects.*

**adversity** *noun* (**adversities**)
misfortune; trouble.

**advert** *noun* (**adverts**)
(*informal*) an advertisement.

**advertise** *verb* (**advertises, advertising, advertised**)
**1** to praise goods hoping that people will buy them. **2** to make something publicly known, *Have you advertised the concert?*
**advertiser** *noun*

**advertisement** *noun* (**advertisements**)
a public notice that advertises something.

**advice** *noun*
**1** something said to someone to help him or her decide what to do. **2** a piece of information.

**advisable** *adjective*
sensible; worth doing.
**advisability** *noun*

**advise** *verb* (**advises, advising, advised**)
to give someone advice; to recommend something.
**adviser** *noun*, **advisory** *adjective*

USAGE: Do not confuse **advice**, which is a noun, with **advise**, which is a verb.

**advocate**[1] *noun* (**advocates**)
(*say* ad-vŏ-kăt)
a person who speaks in favour of someone or something.

**advocate**[2] *verb* (**advocates, advocating, advocated**)
(*say* ad-vŏ-kayt)
to speak in favour of something.

**aerial**[1] *adjective*
of or by the air or aircraft, *an aerial photograph of our offices.*

**aerial**[2] *noun* (**aerials**)
(in America, *antenna*) a wire, rod, etc. for receiving or transmitting radio or television waves.

**aerobatics** *plural noun*
an exciting display by flying aircraft.
**aerobatic** *adjective*

**aerobics** *plural noun*
exercises which strengthen your heart and lungs.

**aeronautics** *plural noun*
the study of aircraft and flying.
**aeronautic** *adjective*, **aeronautical** *adjective*

**aeroplane** *noun* (**aeroplanes**)
(in America, *airplane*) a flying machine with wings.

**aerosol** *noun* (**aerosols**)
a device that holds a liquid under pressure and lets it out in a fine spray.

**aesthetic** *adjective*
1 concerned with beauty; valuing beauty, *an art critic with high aesthetic values. an aesthetic young poet.* 2 pleasing to look at, *These chairs are aesthetic rather than functional.*

**affair** *noun* (**affairs**)
1 a thing, a matter, or an event. 2 a temporary relationship between two people who are not married to each other. **affairs**, business, *money affairs.*

**affect** *verb* (**affects, affecting, affected**)
to have an effect on; to harm, *The dampness affected her health.*

USAGE: Do not confuse **affect** with **effect**, which is a noun meaning something that happens or an impression.

**affected** *adjective*
1 pretended, *affected interest.* 2 unnatural, *an unpleasant, affected smile.*

**affection** *noun* (**affections**)
love or liking, *I have a great affection for my nephew.*
**affectionate** *adjective*

**afflict** *verb* (**afflicts, afflicting, afflicted**)
to cause someone distress.
**affliction** *noun*

**affluent** *adjective*
(*say* **af**-loo-ĕnt)
rich, *an affluent country.*
**affluence** *noun*

**afford** *verb* (**affords, affording, afforded**)
1 to have enough money to pay for something. 2 to have enough time, etc. to do something.

**afforestation** *noun*
the covering of an area with trees.

**afloat** *adjective* and *adverb*
floating; on a boat, *The boat is afloat. Do you enjoy life afloat?*

**afraid** *adjective*
frightened.
**I'm afraid**, I am sorry; I regret, *I'm afraid I've burnt the cakes.*

**afresh** *adverb*
again; in a new way, *We must start afresh.*

**African**[1] *adjective*
of Africa.

**African**[2] *noun* (**Africans**)
an African person.

**Afrikaans** *noun*
(*say* af-ri-**kahns**)
the language of Afrikaners, developed from Dutch.

**Afrikaner** *noun* (**Afrikaners**)
(*say* af-ri-**kah**-ner)
a South African whose ancestors came from Holland.

**aft** *adverb*
(*say* ahft)
at or towards the back of a ship or aircraft.

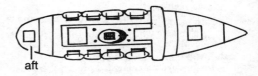

aft

**after**[1] *preposition*
1 later than, *Come after dinner.* 2 in spite of, *After all I've done for him, he never thanked me.* 3 behind, *He came in after me.* 4 pursuing, *Run after him.* 5 in imitation or honour of, *She was named after her aunt.*

**after**[2] *adverb*
1 later, *It came a week after.* 2 behind, *Jill came tumbling after.*

**afternoon** *noun* (**afternoons**)
the time from noon or lunchtime to evening.

**aftershave** *noun* (**aftershaves**)
a pleasant-smelling liquid that men put on their skin after shaving.

**afterwards** *adverb*
at a later time.

**again** *adverb*
1 once more; another time, *Try again.* 2 as before, *You will soon be well again.*
**again and again**, often.

**against** *preposition*
1 touching or hitting, *He leant against the wall.* 2 not on the side of; not in favour of, *Are you against smoking?*

**age**[1] *noun* (**ages**)
1 how old someone or something is. 2 (*especially in plural, informal*) a very long time, *We've been waiting for ages.* 3 a period of history, *the Elizabethan age.* 4 the last part of someone's life, *She had the wisdom that comes with age.*

**age**[2] *verb* (**ages, ageing, aged**)
to become old; to cause to become old.

**aged** *adjective*
1 (*say* ayjd) having the age of, *a girl aged 9.* 2 (*say* **ay**-jid) very old, *an aged man.*

**age-group** *noun* (**age-groups**)
people who are all the same age.

**agency** *noun* (**agencies**)
the office or business of someone who organizes things.

**agenda** *noun* (**agendas**)
(*say* ă-**jen**-dă)
a list of things to be done or discussed, *May I see the agenda for the Parent-Teachers' meeting?*

**agent** *noun* (**agents**)
1 someone who organizes things for other people, *a travel agent.* 2 a spy, *a secret agent.*

**aggravate** *verb* (**aggravates, aggravating, aggravated**)
1 to make something worse. 2 (*informal*) to annoy.
**aggravation** *noun*

**aggression** *noun* (**aggressions**)
starting a war, attack, etc.; being aggressive.
**aggressor** *noun*

**aggressive** *adjective*
1 (of a person) using or likely to use violence. 2 forceful, *an aggressive sales campaign.*

**aggro** *noun*
(*slang*) trouble, especially fighting, *tough young men looking for aggro.*

**agile** *adjective*
moving quickly or easily.
**agility** *noun*

**agitate** *verb* (**agitates, agitating, agitated**)
1 to make someone disturbed or anxious. 2 to campaign for something. 3 to shake something about.
**agitation** *noun*

**agitator** *noun* (**agitators**)
a person who campaigns for something.

**agnostic** *noun* (**agnostics**)
(*say* ag-**nos**-tik)
someone who believes that we cannot know for sure whether there is a God.

**ago** *adverb*
in the past, *She died long ago.*

**agony** *noun* (**agonies**)
severe pain or suffering.
**agonizing** *adjective*

**agree** *verb* (**agrees, agreeing, agreed**)
1 to think the same as someone else. 2 to say that you are willing, *She agreed to go with him.*
**agree with someone,** to suit someone, *Spicy food doesn't agree with her.*
**agree with something,** to match something, *His story doesn't agree with theirs.*

**agreeable** *adjective*
1 willing, *We shall go if you are agreeable.* 2 pleasant, *an agreeable place.*

**agreement** *noun* (**agreements**)
1 agreeing, *Are we in agreement?* 2 an arrangement that people have agreed on.

**agriculture** *noun*
farming.
**agricultural** *adjective*

**aground** *adverb*
stranded on the bottom in shallow water, *The ship ran aground.*

**ah** *interjection*
an exclamation of surprise, pity, admiration, etc.

**ahead** *adverb*
forwards; in front, *Sheila went ahead to show us the way.*

**ahoy** *interjection*
a shout used by seamen to attract someone's attention.

**aid** *noun* (**aids**)
1 help. 2 money, food, etc. sent to another country to help it, *overseas aid.* 3 something that helps, *a hearing aid.*
**in aid of something,** to help something.

**Aids** or **AIDS** *noun*
a disease caused by a virus, that greatly weakens a person's resistance to other diseases.

**ailment** *noun* (**ailments**)
an illness, usually a slight one.
**ailing** *adjective*

**aim**[1] *verb* (**aims, aiming, aimed**)
1 to try or intend to do something. 2 to point a gun, etc. at someone or something. 3 to throw, kick, or shoot something in a particular direction.

**aim**[2] *noun* (**aims**)
1 purpose; intention. 2 pointing a gun, etc.

**aimless** *adjective*
with no aim or purpose, *an aimless life.*
**aimlessly** *adverb*

air¹                                    10

**air¹** *noun* (**airs**)
1 the mixture of gases which surrounds the earth and which everyone breathes. 2 a tune. 3 an appearance or impression of something, *an air of mystery.*
**airs,** haughty, affected behaviour, *He puts on airs.*
**by air,** in an aircraft.
**in the air,** uncertain; spreading about, *All our plans are still in the air. Rebellion was in the air.*
**on the air,** on radio or television.

**air²** *verb* (**airs, airing, aired**)
1 to put clothes, etc. in a warm place to finish drying. 2 to ventilate a room. 3 to express, *He aired his opinions.*

**airborne** *adjective*
1 flying. 2 carried by the air.

**air-conditioning** *noun*
a system for controlling the temperature, purity, etc. of the air in a room or building.
**air-conditioned** *adjective*

**aircraft** *noun* (**aircraft**)
1 an aeroplane or a helicopter, *Two aircraft landed together.*
**aircraft-carrier,** a large ship with a flat deck on which aircraft can take off and land.

**Airedale** *noun* (**Airedales**)
a large rough-haired terrier.

**airfield** *noun* (**airfields**)
a place where aircraft can take off and land.

**air force** *noun* (**air forces**)
a large group of people and aircraft organized for fighting.

**airgun** *noun* (**airguns**)
a gun in which compressed air shoots the bullet.

**air hostess** *noun* (**air hostesses**)
a stewardess in an aircraft.

**airline** *noun* (**airlines**)
a company that provides a regular transport service by aircraft.

**airliner** *noun* (**airliners**)
a large aircraft for carrying passengers.

**airlock** *noun* (**airlocks**)
1 a bubble of air that stops liquid flowing through a pipe. 2 a compartment with airtight doors at each end.

**airmail** *noun*
mail carried by aircraft.

**airman** *noun* (**airmen**)
1 a man who is one of the crew of an aircraft. 2 a man who is a member of an air force.

**airport** *noun* (**airports**)
an airfield, especially one for passengers and cargo.

**air raid** *noun* (**air raids**)
an attack by aircraft.

**airship** *noun* (**airships**)
a large balloon with engines, designed to carry passengers or cargo.

**airstream** *noun* (**airstreams**)
a current of air, especially one that affects the weather.

**airstrip** *noun* (**airstrips**)
a strip of land prepared for aircraft to take off and land.

**airtight** *adjective*
not letting air get in or out.

**airwoman** *noun* (**airwomen**)
1 a woman who is one of the crew of an aircraft. 2 a woman who is a member of an air force.

**airy** *adjective* (**airier, airiest**)
1 with plenty of fresh air. 2 light-hearted; insincere, *airy promises.* 3 light as air.
**airily** *adverb*

**aisle** *noun* (**aisles**)
(rhymes with *mile*)
1 a part at the side of a church. 2 a passage between or beside rows of seats or pews.

**ajar** *adverb* and *adjective*
slightly open, *Leave the door ajar.*

**akela** *noun* (**akelas**)
(*say* ah-**kay**-lă)
an adult leader of a group of Cub Scouts.

**à la carte** *adverb* and *adjective*
(*say* ah-lah-**kart**)
of a meal in a restaurant, etc.: ordered as
separate items from the menu (different
from *table d'hôte*).

**alarm**¹ *verb* (**alarms, alarming, alarmed**)
to make someone frightened or anxious.

**alarm**² *noun* (**alarms**)
**1** a warning sound or signal. **2** being
alarmed, *He cried out in alarm.* **3** an alarm
clock.
**alarm clock,** a clock that can be set to make
a sound to wake a sleeping person.

**alas** *interjection*
(*old-fashioned use*) an exclamation of
sorrow.

**albatross** *noun* (**albatrosses**)
a large sea-bird with very long wings.

**album** *noun* (**albums**)
**1** a book in which you can keep
photographs, stamps, autographs, etc. **2** a
long-playing record; a set of long-playing
records.

**alcohol** *noun*
**1** a colourless liquid made by fermenting
sugar or starch. **2** a drink containing this
liquid, that can make people drunk.

**alcoholic**¹ *adjective*
of or containing alcohol.

**alcoholic**² *noun* (**alcoholics**)
someone who is ill from continually
drinking too much alcohol.
**alcoholism** *noun*

**alcove** *noun* (**alcoves**)
part of a room, etc. where the wall is set
back from the main part.

**ale** *noun* (**ales**)
beer, especially beer that is made, kept,
and served in a traditional way.

**alert**¹ *adjective*
watching for something; ready to act.

**alert**² *noun* (**alerts**)
an alarm.
**on the alert,** on the look-out against danger
or attack.

**A level** *noun* (**A levels**)
the higher standard of examination that is
taken after the GCSE by pupils who want
to go to university.

**algebra** *noun*
(*say* **al**-ji-bră)
mathematics in which letters and symbols
are used to represent numbers.
**algebraic** *adjective*

**alias**¹ *noun* (**aliases**)
(*say* **ay**-li-ăs)
a false or different name.

**alias**² *adverb*
also named, *Muhammad Ali, alias Cassius
Clay.*

**alibi** *noun* (**alibis**)
(*say* **al**-i-by)
**1** evidence that an accused person was not
present when a crime was committed.
**2** (*informal*) an excuse.

**alien**¹ *noun* (**aliens**)
(*say* **ay**-li-ĕn)
someone who is not a citizen of the country
where he or she is living.

**alien**² *adjective*
foreign.
**alien to,** very different from, *Lying was
alien to his nature.*

**alienate** *verb* (**alienates, alienating, alienated**)
to make someone unfriendly, *The politician
alienated his supporters.*
**alienation** *noun*

**alight** *adjective*
on fire; burning, *The bushes were alight.*

**alike**¹ *adjective*
similar; like each other, *Her sisters are
very much alike.*

**alike**² *adverb*
in the same way, *He treats everybody alike.*

**alimentary canal** *noun* (**alimentary canals**)
the tube along which food passes through
the body.

**alimony** *noun*
money paid by someone to his or her wife
or husband after they are separated or
divorced (now called *maintenance* in
Britain).

**alive** *adjective*
living; existing, *Is he alive?*
**alive to something,** aware of something, *She is alive to the dangers.*
**alive with something,** full of living or moving things.

**alkali** *noun* (**alkalis**)
(*say* al-kă-ly)
a substance that neutralizes acids or that combines with acids to form salts.
**alkaline** *adjective*, **alkalinity** *noun*

**all**[1] *adverb*
1 completely, *She was dressed all in white.*
2 very much, *He was all excited.* 3 to each team or competitor, *The score is four goals all.*
**all-clear,** a signal that a danger has passed.
**all in,** (*informal*) exhausted, *I'm all in after that run.*
**all out,** (*informal*) using all your ability, *Go all out to win.*
**all there,** (*informal*) mentally alert; intelligent.
**all the same,** nevertheless; making no difference, *It was raining but I went out all the same. It's all the same to me.*

**all**[2] *noun*
1 everything, *That is all I know.*
2 everyone, *All were agreed.*

**all**[3] *adjective*
the whole number or amount of, *All my books are in the desk.*

### Allah
the Muslim name for God.

**allege** *verb* (**alleges, alleging, alleged**)
(*say* ă-lej)
to say, usually without proof, that someone has done something, *He alleged that I stole the ring.*
**allegation** *noun*, **alleged** *adjective*, **allegedly** *adverb*

**allegiance** *noun* (**allegiances**)
(*say* ă-lee-jăns)
loyalty.

**allegory** *noun* (**allegories**)
a story, poem, etc. which is really about something different from what it seems to be.
**allegorical** *adjective*

**allergic** *adjective*
very sensitive to something, which may make you ill, *He is allergic to pollen, which gives him hay fever.*
**allergy** *noun*

**alley** *noun* (**alleys**)
1 a narrow street or passage. 2 a place where you can play at skittles or tenpin bowling.

**alliance** *noun* (**alliances**)
a friendly connection or association between countries, etc.

**alligator** *noun* (**alligators**)
a kind of crocodile.

**all-in** *adjective*
including or allowing everything, *an all-in price.*

**allot** *verb* (**allots, allotting, allotted**)
to distribute portions, jobs, etc.

**allotment** *noun* (**allotments**)
a small rented piece of ground used for growing vegetables, fruit, or flowers.

**allow** *verb* (**allows, allowing, allowed**)
1 to permit, *Smoking is not allowed.* 2 to give or provide, *She was allowed £10 for books.*

**allowance** *noun* (**allowances**)
a sum of money given regularly to someone.
**make allowances for something,** to be considerate on account of something, *We must make allowances for the fact that he was the youngest in the competition.*

**alloy** *noun* (**alloys**)
a metal formed from a mixture of metals, *Bronze is an alloy of copper and tin.*

**all right**[1] *adjective*
satisfactory; in good condition, *She fixed my bike, so it's all right.*

**all right**[2] *interjection*
yes; I consent, *All right, I'm coming!*

**all-round** *adjective*
in all respects; having all sorts of abilities, *a good all-round athlete.*
**all-rounder** *noun*

**ally** *noun* (**allies**)
(*say* al-I)
1 a country in alliance with another country. 2 a person who helps or cooperates with you.
**allied** *adjective*

**almighty** *adjective*
1 having complete power. 2 (*informal*) very great, *an almighty din.*
**the Almighty,** God.

**almond** *noun* (**almonds**)
(*say* **ah**-mŏnd)
an oval, edible nut.

**almost** *adverb*
in the nearest place or condition to being something; nearly, *I am almost ready.*

**aloft** *adverb*
high up, *The sailors climbed aloft.*

**alone** *adjective* and *adverb*
without any other people or other things.

**along** *preposition* and *adverb*
1 from one end of something to the other.
2 on; onwards, *Move along, please!*
3 accompanying someone, *I have brought my brother along.*

**alongside** *preposition* and *adverb*
next to something.

**aloud** *adverb*
in a voice that can be heard.

**alp** *noun* (**alps**)
a grassy field high up on a mountain, especially in the Alps.
**the Alps,** the range of high mountains in and around Switzerland.

**alphabet** *noun* (**alphabets**)
the letters used in a language, usually arranged in a set order.
**alphabetical** *adjective*, **alphabetically** *adverb*

**alpine** *adjective*
of the Alps.

**already** *adverb*
by or before now, *I've already told you once.*

**Alsatian** *noun* (**Alsatians**)
(*say* al-**say**-shăn)
(in America, *German shepherd*) a large, strong breed of dog, *Alsatians are often used by the police.*

**also** *adverb*
as something or someone extra; besides.

**altar** *noun* (**altars**)
a table or raised surface used in religious ceremonies.

**alter** *verb* (**alters, altering, altered**)
to change, *Has she altered at all?*
**alteration** *noun*

**alternate**[1] *adjective*
(*say* ol-**ter**-năt)
1 every second one, *They work on alternate days.* 2 happening or coming in turns, one after the other, *alternate laughter and tears.*
**alternately** *adverb*

USAGE: Do not confuse **alternate** with **alternative. Alternative** means that you have a choice between two or more things.

**alternate**[2] *verb* (**alternates, alternating, alternated**)
(*say* **ol**-ter-nayt)
to happen, work, etc. in turns; to cause something to happen, etc. in this way.
**alternating current,** electric current that continually reverses its direction.
**alternation** *noun*

**alternative**[1] *adjective*
(*say* ol-**ter**-nă-tiv)
available instead of something else, *We offer an alternative menu for vegetarians.*

USAGE: Do not confuse **alternative** with the adjective **alternate. Alternate** means that first one thing and then the other happens, works, etc.

**alternative**[2] *noun* (**alternatives**)
1 one of two or more possibilities. 2 freedom to choose, *There is no alternative.*

**alternator** *noun* (**alternators**)
a generator that produces alternating current.

**although** *conjunction*
though.

**altitude** *noun* (**altitudes**)
the height of something, especially above sea-level.

**alto** *noun* (**altos**)
1 a contralto. 2 a male singer with a voice higher than a tenor's.

**altogether** *adverb*
1 completely, *He is altogether wrong.* 2 on the whole, *Altogether, it wasn't a bad holiday.*

USAGE: Do not confuse **altogether** with **all together**.

**aluminium** *noun*
a lightweight, silver-coloured metal.

**always** *adverb*
1 all the time; at all times. 2 often, *You are always crying.* 3 whatever happens, *You can always sleep on the floor.*

**am** 1st person singular present tense of **be**.

**a.m.** short for Latin *ante meridiem* which means 'before midday'.

**amalgamate** *verb* (**amalgamates, amalgamating, amalgamated**)
to join together.
**amalgamation** *noun*

**amateur** *noun* (**amateurs**)
(*say* am-ă-ter)
someone who does something as a hobby, without being paid for it.
**amateur** *adjective*

**amateurish** *adjective*
not having or showing skill.

**amaze** *verb* (**amazes, amazing, amazed**)
to surprise someone greatly.
**amazement** *noun*

**ambassador** *noun* (**ambassadors**)
someone sent to a foreign country to represent his or her government.

**amber** *noun*
1 a hard, clear, yellowish substance used for making ornaments. 2 a yellowish colour, especially used in traffic-lights as a signal for caution.

**ambiguous** *adjective*
having more than one possible meaning; uncertain, *His reply was ambiguous.*
**ambiguity** *noun*

**ambition** *noun* (**ambitions**)
1 a strong desire to achieve something. 2 something you want to do very much, *His ambition is to run his own airline.*
**ambitious** *adjective*

**amble** *verb* (**ambles, ambling, ambled**)
to walk slowly.

**ambulance** *noun* (**ambulances**)
a vehicle for carrying sick or injured people.

**ambush**[1] *noun* (**ambushes**)
a surprise attack from a hidden place.

**ambush**[2] *verb* (**ambushes, ambushing, ambushed**)
to attack by surprise from a hidden place.

**amen** *interjection*
a word used at the end of a prayer or hymn, meaning 'may it be so'.

**amend** *verb* (**amends, amending, amended**)
to change or improve something.
**amendment** *noun*

**amenity** *noun* (**amenities**)
a pleasant or useful feature, *The town has many amenities, including a skating-rink.*

**American**[1] *adjective*
of America.

**American**[2] *noun* (**Americans**)
an American person.

**amiable** *adjective*
friendly; good-tempered.
**amiability** *noun*, **amiably** *adverb*

**amicable** *adjective*
friendly.
**amicably** *adverb*

**amid** or **amidst** *preposition*
in the middle of; among, *amid the stress of everyday life. They lived amid the trees.*

**amidships** *adverb*
in the middle of a ship.

**amino acid** *noun* (**amino acids**)
an acid found in proteins.

**ammeter** *noun* (**ammeters**)
an instrument for measuring electric current.

**ammonia** *noun*
a colourless gas or liquid with a strong smell.

**ammunition** *noun*
explosive objects used in fighting, such as bullets, shells, and grenades.

**amnesty** *noun* (**amnesties**)
pardoning people who have broken the law, or letting them out of prison.

**amoeba** *noun* (**amoebas**)
(*say* ă-mee-bă)
a tiny jelly-like creature consisting of one cell.

**among** or **amongst** *preposition*
1 surrounded by; in, *She hid among the bushes.* 2 between, *Let's divide the money among ourselves.*

**amount**[1] *noun* (**amounts**)
a quantity.

**amount**[2] *verb* (**amounts, amounting, amounted**)
to be equal to something, *The bill amounted to £55.*

**ampere** *noun* (**amperes**)
(*say* am-pair)
a unit for measuring the rate of flow of an electric current.

**ampersand** *noun* (**ampersands**)
the sign &, which means 'and', *The ampersand is used in the names of firms like Smith & Co.*

**amphibious** *adjective*
able to live or move both on land and in water.
**amphibian** *noun*

**ample** *adjective* (**ampler, amplest**)
1 large, *This car has an ample boot.* 2 more than enough, *We had ample provisions.*
**amply** *adverb*

**amplifier** *noun* (**amplifiers**)
a device, usually electronic, for making something louder.

**amplify** *verb* (**amplifies, amplifying, amplified**)
1 to make something louder or stronger. 2 to give more details about something.
**amplification** *noun*

**amputate** *verb* (**amputates, amputating, amputated**)
to cut off a diseased leg or arm.
**amputation** *noun*

**amuse** *verb* (**amuses, amusing, amused**)
1 to make someone laugh or smile. 2 to make time pass pleasantly for someone.

**amusement** *noun* (**amusements**)
1 something that amuses. 2 being amused; laughing or smiling.

**amusing** *adjective*
that makes you laugh or smile.

**an** *adjective* (called the *indefinite article*)
a (used instead of *a* when the next word begins with a vowel-sound or a silent h), *Take an apple. You can hire boats for one pound an hour.*

**anaemia** *noun*
(*say* ă-nee-mi-ă)
a poor condition of the blood that makes someone look pale.
**anaemic** *adjective*

**anaesthetic** *noun* (**anaesthetics**)
(*say* an-iss-thet-ik)
a drug or gas that makes you unable to feel pain.
**anaesthesia** *noun*

**anaesthetize** *verb* (**anaesthetizes, anaesthetizing, anaesthetized**)
to give an anaesthetic to a person or an animal.
**anaesthetist** *noun*

**anagram** *noun* (**anagrams**)
a word or phrase made by rearranging the letters of another word or phrase, *'Cart-horse' is an anagram of 'orchestra'.*

**analogue** *adjective*
using something like a clock face to indicate numbers (the opposite of *digital*), *an analogue clock.*

**analogy** *noun* (**analogies**)
comparing two things that are fairly like each other, *an analogy between the human heart and a pump.*
**analogous** *adjective*

**analyse** *verb* (**analyses, analysing, analysed**)
1 to examine something carefully. 2 to divide something into its parts.
**analysis** *noun*, **analytic** *adjective*, **analytical** *adjective*

**analyst** *noun* (**analysts**)
a person who analyses something.

**anarchist** *noun* (**anarchists**)
someone who thinks that governments and laws are bad and should be abolished.
**anarchism** *noun*

**anarchy** *noun*
1 disorder; confusion. 2 lack of government or control.

**anatomy** *noun*
the science or study of how the body is constructed.
**anatomical** *adjective*, **anatomist** *noun*

**ancestor** *noun* (**ancestors**)
a person who lived in the past and was in the same family as someone alive now.
**ancestral** *adjective*, **ancestry** *noun*

**anchor** *noun* (**anchors**)
a heavy object joined to a ship by a chain or rope and dropped to the seabed, etc. to stop the ship from moving.

**anchorage** *noun* (**anchorages**)
a place where ships can stay, held by their anchors.

**ancient** *adjective*
1 of times long past, *ancient history*. 2 very old, *ancient ruins*.
**Ancient Egypt**, Egypt when it was ruled by the Pharaohs.
**Ancient Rome**, Rome, and the empire ruled by it, from early times up to AD 476.

**and** *conjunction*
1 in addition to, *We had buns and lemonade*. 2 so that; as a result, *Work hard and you will pass. Touch that and you'll be burnt*. 3 (*informal*) to, *Go and buy a pen*.

**anemometer** *noun* (**anemometers**)
a device for measuring the speed of the wind.

**anemone** *noun* (**anemones**)
(*say* ă-**nem**-ŏn-i)
1 a small cup-shaped flower. 2 a sea anemone.

**angel** *noun* (**angels**)
1 a messenger or attendant of God. 2 a very kind or beautiful person.
**angelic** *adjective*, **angelically** *adverb*

**anger** *noun*
a strong feeling that you want to quarrel or fight with someone.

**angle**[1] *noun* (**angles**)
1 the space between two lines or surfaces that meet. 2 a point of view, *What is your angle on this?*

**angle**[2] *verb* (**angles, angling, angled**)
1 to put something in a slanting position.
2 to present news, etc. in a particular way, *The report was angled so that the terrorists appeared to have done nothing wrong*.

**angler** *noun* (**anglers**)
someone who fishes with a fishing-rod.

**Anglican**[1] *adjective*
of the Church of England.

**Anglican**[2] *noun* (**Anglicans**)
a member of the Church of England.

**Anglo-Saxon** *noun* (**Anglo-Saxons**)
an English person, especially of the time before the Norman Conquest.

**angry** *adjective* (**angrier, angriest**)
feeling or showing anger.
**angrily** *adverb*

**anguish** *noun*
severe suffering; great sorrow or pain.
**anguished** *adjective*

**angular** *adjective*
1 with sharp corners. 2 bony, *a thin, angular face*.

**animal** *noun* (**animals**)
anything that lives and can move about, *Horses, dogs, birds, fish, bees, and humans are all animals*.

**animate** *verb* (**animates, animating, animated**)
1 to make something lively; to inspire. 2 to make a film by photographing a series of drawings, etc.
**animation** *noun*, **animator** *noun*

**animosity** *noun* (**animosities**)
a feeling of being an enemy towards someone, *There was a lot of animosity in his voice*.

**aniseed** *noun*
a seed with a strong, sweet taste like liquorice.

**ankle** *noun* (**ankles**)
the part of the leg where it is joined to the foot.
**ankle sock**, a short sock just covering the ankle.

**annex** *verb* (**annexes, annexing, annexed**)
(*say* ă-**neks**)
1 to add something to a larger thing. 2 to seize territory.
**annexation** *noun*

**annexe** *noun* (**annexes**)
(*say* an-eks)
a building added to another building.

**annihilate** *verb* (**annihilates, annihilating, annihilated**)
(*say* ă-**ny**-ĭl-ayt)
to destroy.
**annihilation** *noun*

**anniversary** *noun* (**anniversaries**)
a day when you remember something special that happened on the same date in a previous year.

**announce** *verb* (**announces, announcing, announced**)
to make something known; to say something publicly, especially in a broadcast.
**announcer** *noun*

**announcement** *noun* (**announcements**)
something that is made known publicly, especially in a newspaper or on the radio or television.

**annoy** *verb* (**annoys, annoying, annoyed**)
to give someone a feeling of not being pleased.

**annoyance** *noun* (**annoyances**)
**1** the feeling of being annoyed. **2** something that annoys you, *Wasps were a great annoyance at the picnic.*

**annual**[1] *adjective*
**1** happening or coming every year. **2** lasting only one year or season, *annual plants.*
**annually** *adverb*

**annual**[2] *noun* (**annuals**)
**1** a book that comes out once a year. **2** a plant that dies when winter comes.

**anode** *noun* (**anodes**)
the electrode by which electric current enters a device (the opposite of *cathode*).

**anon.** short for **anonymous.**

**anonymous** *adjective*
**1** with a name that is unknown, *an anonymous writer.* **2** by or from someone whose name is unknown, *an anonymous letter.*
**anonymity** *noun*

**anorak** *noun* (**anoraks**)
a thick, warm jacket with a hood.

**anorexia** *noun*
an illness that makes someone not want to eat.
**anorexic** *adjective*

**another**[1] *adjective*
**1** a different, *Find another cup – that one's dirty.* **2** one more, *Take another toffee.*

**another**[2] *pronoun*
another person or thing.

**answer**[1] *noun* (**answers**)
**1** a reply. **2** the solution to a problem.

**answer**[2] *verb* (**answers, answering, answered**)
**1** to give or find an answer to. **2** to respond to a signal, *Answer the telephone.*
**answer back,** to reply cheekily.
**answer for something,** to be responsible for something.

**ant** *noun* (**ants**)
a tiny insect.

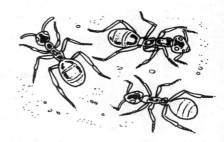

**antagonism** *noun* (**antagonisms**)
being someone's enemy; hatred.
**antagonistic** *adjective*

**antagonize** *verb* (**antagonizes, antagonizing, antagonized**)
to make someone feel you are his or her enemy.

**Antarctic** or **Antarctica** *noun*
the area round the South Pole.

**anteater** *noun* (**anteaters**)
an animal with a long tongue that lives by eating ants.

**antelope** *noun* (**antelope** or **antelopes**)
an animal like a deer, found in Africa and parts of Asia.

**antenna** *noun* (**antennae**)
**1** a feeler on the head of an insect or crustacean. **2** (*plural* **antennas**) an aerial.

**anthem** *noun* (**anthems**)
a religious or patriotic song, usually sung by a choir or group of people.

**anthill** *noun* (**anthills**)
a mound of earth over an ants' nest.

**anthology** *noun* (**anthologies**)
a collection of poems, stories, songs, etc. in one book.

**anthracite** *noun*
a kind of hard coal.

**anthropology** *noun*
the study of human beings and their customs, beliefs, etc.
**anthropological** *adjective*, **anthropologist** *noun*

**anti-** *prefix*
being or used against something or someone, *an anti-tank gun. An anti-Fascist demonstration took place.*

**anti-aircraft** *adjective*
used against aircraft, *anti-aircraft guns.*

**antibiotic** *noun* (**antibiotics**)
a drug like penicillin which destroys bacteria.

**anticipate** *verb* (**anticipates, anticipating, anticipated**)
**1** to do something before the proper time. **2** to do something before someone else does it. **3** to look forward to something.

**anticipation** *noun*
looking forward to doing something.
**in anticipation of something**, expecting that something will happen, *I had taken my umbrella in anticipation of rain.*

**anticlimax** *noun* (**anticlimaxes**)
a disappointing end or result.

**anticlockwise** *adverb* and *adjective*
moving in the opposite direction to clockwise.

**anticyclone** *noun* (**anticyclones**)
an area where air pressure is high, usually causing fine weather.

**antidote** *noun* (**antidotes**)
something which acts against the effects of a poison or disease.

**antifreeze** *noun*
a chemical that is added to water to make it less likely to freeze.

**antipodes** *plural noun*
(*say* an-ti-pŏ-deez)
**the Antipodes**, Australia and New Zealand, seen from the point of view of Britain.

**antiquated** *adjective*
old-fashioned.

**antique** *noun* (**antiques**)
(*say* an-**teek**)
something that is valuable because it is very old.

**anti-Semitic** *adjective*
(*say* an-ti-sim-**it**-ik)
unfriendly or hostile to Jews.
**anti-Semitism** *noun*

**antiseptic** *noun* (**antiseptics**)
a substance that kills germs.

**antler** *noun* (**antlers**)
the branching horn of a deer.

**anus** *noun* (**anuses**)
the opening at the lower end of the intestines, through which solid waste leaves the body.

**anvil** *noun* (**anvils**)
a large block of iron on which a blacksmith hammers metal into shape.

**anxiety** *noun* (**anxieties**)
being worried; something that worries you.

**anxious** *adjective*
**1** worried. **2** eager, *They were anxious to help us.*

**any**[1] *adjective*
**1** one or some, *Have you any wool?* **2** no matter which, *Come any day you like.* **3** every, *Any fool knows that!*

**any**[2] *adverb*
at all; in some degree, *Is it any good?*

**anybody** *noun* and *pronoun*
anyone.

**anyhow** *adverb*
**1** anyway. **2** (*informal*) carelessly, *He does his work anyhow.*

**anyone** *noun* and *pronoun*
any person.

**anything** *noun* and *pronoun*
any thing.

**anyway** *adverb*
whatever happens; whatever the situation may be.

**anywhere** *adverb*
in or to any place.

**apart** *adverb*
**1** away from each other; separately, *Keep your desks apart.* **2** into pieces, *It fell apart.* **3** excluded, *Joking apart, what do you think?*

**apartheid** *noun*
(*say* ă-**part**-hayt)
the policy in South Africa of keeping non-Whites separate from Whites.

**appoint**

**apartment** *noun* (**apartments**)
1 a set of rooms. 2 (*in America*) a flat.

**apathy** *noun*
not being interested.
**apathetic** *adjective*

**ape** *noun* (**apes**)
a monkey without a tail, *Gorillas,
chimpanzees, and orang-utans are apes.*

**aphid** or **aphis** *noun* (**aphids** or **aphides**)
a tiny insect that sucks juices from plants.

**apiece** *adverb*
to, for, or by each, *She gave us an apple
apiece. They cost ten pence apiece. We ate a
cake apiece.*

**apologize** *verb* (**apologizes, apologizing,
apologized**)
to make an apology.

**apology** *noun* (**apologies**)
saying that you are sorry for doing
something wrong.
**an apology for,** a poor specimen of
something, *That was an apology for a meal.*
**apologetic** *adjective*, **apologetically** *adverb*

**apostle** *noun* (**apostles**)
one of the twelve men sent out by Jesus to
tell people about God.

**apostrophe** *noun* (**apostrophes**)
(*say* ă-pos-trŏ-fi)
a punctuation mark ' used to show that
letters have been left out (as in *I can't*) or
with *s* to show who owns something (as in
*the boy's books, the boys' books*) or in the
plurals of letters of the alphabet (as in
*There are two l's in bell*).

**appal** *verb* (**appals, appalling, appalled**)
to shock someone deeply, *The violence
appalled everyone.*

**apparatus** *noun* (**apparatuses**)
1 equipment for a particular experiment,
job, etc. 2 the equipment used for
gymnastics.

**apparent** *adjective*
1 clear; obvious. 2 that appears to be true,
*The apparent reason for his action was not
the real one.*
**apparently** *adverb*

**appeal**[1] *verb* (**appeals, appealing, appealed**)
1 to ask for something that you need, *She
appealed for funds.* 2 to be attractive or
interesting, *Football doesn't appeal to me.*
3 to ask for a decision to be changed, *He
appealed against the prison sentence.*

**appeal**[2] *noun* (**appeals**)
1 asking for something you need.
2 attraction; interest, *Football has little
appeal for him.* 3 the action of asking for a
decision to be changed.

**appear** *verb* (**appears, appearing, appeared**)
1 to come into sight. 2 to seem. 3 to take
part in a play, film, show, etc.

**appearance** *noun* (**appearances**)
1 coming into sight. 2 taking part in a play,
film, show, etc. 3 what someone looks like.
4 what something seems to be.

**appease** *verb* (**appeases, appeasing, appeased**)
to make peaceful or calm, especially by
giving in to demands.
**appeasement** *noun*

**appendicitis** *noun*
an inflammation or disease of the appendix.

**appendix** *noun* (**appendices** or **appendixes**)
1 a small tube leading off from the
intestines. 2 a section added at the end of a
book.

**appetite** *noun* (**appetites**)
desire, especially for food.
**appetizer** *noun*, **appetizing** *adjective*

**applaud** *verb* (**applauds, applauding, applauded**)
to show that you like something, especially
by clapping.
**applause** *noun*

**apple** *noun* (**apples**)
a round fruit with skin that is red, green,
or yellow.
**the apple of your eye,** someone or something
that you love.

**appliance** *noun* (**appliances**)
a device, *household electrical appliances.*

**applicable** *adjective*
1 able to be used, *This law is no longer
applicable.* 2 relevant, *Cross out any
responses which are not applicable.*

**applicant** *noun* (**applicants**)
someone who applies for something.

**application** *noun* (**applications**)
1 a letter etc. asking for something. 2 the
giving of all your attention to something.

**applied** *adjective*
put to practical use, *Cookery is an applied
science.*

**apply** *verb* (**applies, applying, applied**)
1 to put one thing on another, *Apply a
patch to the puncture.* 2 to start using
something.
**apply for something,** to ask for a job, etc.
**apply to someone,** to concern someone, *Her
remarks do not apply to you.*
**apply yourself to something,** to give all your
attention to something.

**appoint** *verb* (**appoints, appointing, appointed**)
1 to choose someone for a job. 2 to arrange
something officially.

**appointment** *noun* (**appointments**)
**1** an arrangement to meet or visit someone. **2** choosing someone for a job. **3** a job or position.

**apposition** *noun*
the placing of a word next to another which it describes, *In 'Elizabeth, our Queen', 'our Queen' is in apposition to 'Elizabeth'*.
**appositional** *adjective*

**appraise** *verb* (**appraises, appraising, appraised**)
to estimate the value or quality of a person or thing.
**appraisal** *noun*

**appreciate** *verb* (**appreciates, appreciating, appreciated**)
**1** to enjoy or value. **2** to understand. **3** to increase in value.
**appreciation** *noun*

**appreciative** *adjective*
enjoying or valuing something, *I enjoy playing to an appreciative audience.*

**apprehension** *noun* (**apprehensions**)
fear; worry.
**apprehensive** *adjective*

**apprentice** *noun* (**apprentices**)
someone who is learning a trade or craft.
**apprenticeship** *noun*

**approach**¹ *verb* (**approaches, approaching, approached**)
**1** to come near to. **2** to go to someone with a request or offer. **3** to tackle a problem, etc.

**approach**² *noun* (**approaches**)
**1** coming near to a place. **2** a request or offer. **3** a way of tackling a problem. **4** a way or road. **5** the final part of an aircraft's flight before landing.

**approachable** *adjective*
(of a person) easy to speak to; friendly.

**appropriate** *adjective*
suitable.

**approval** *noun*
approving someone or something.
**approvals**, stamps received on approval.
**on approval**, received by a customer to examine before buying.

**approve** *verb* (**approves, approving, approved**)
to say or think that someone or something is good or suitable.

**approximate** *adjective*
not exact, *The approximate size of the playground is half an acre.*
**approximately** *adverb*

**approximation** *noun* (**approximations**)
something that is nearly exact.

**apricot** *noun* (**apricots**)
a juicy, orange-coloured fruit with a stone in it.

**April** *noun*
the fourth month of the year.
**April fool**, someone who is fooled on April Fool's Day (1 April).

**apron** *noun* (**aprons**)
**1** a garment worn over the front of your body to protect your clothes. **2** the part of an airfield where aircraft are loaded and unloaded.

**apt** *adjective*
**1** likely, *He is apt to be careless.* **2** suitable, *an apt quotation.* **3** quick at learning, *an apt pupil.*

**aptitude** *noun* (**aptitudes**)
a talent.

**aquarium** *noun* (**aquariums**)
a tank or building in which live fish are displayed.

**aquatic** *adjective*
of, on, or in water, *aquatic sports.*

**aqueduct** *noun* (**aqueducts**)
a bridge that carries water across a valley.

**aqueous** *adjective*
containing or like water, *an aqueous solution.*

**Arab** *noun* (**Arabs**)
a member of a people inhabiting Arabia and other parts of the Middle East and North Africa.
**Arabian** *adjective*

**Arabic** *adjective*
of the Arabs or their language.

**arabic figures** or **arabic numerals** *plural noun*
the figures 1, 2, 3, 4, etc. (compare *Roman numerals*).

**arable** *adjective*
**1** involving the growing of crops, *arable farming.* **2** suitable for ploughing to grow crops on, *arable land.*

**arbitrary** *adjective*
(*say* **ar**-bi-trer-i)
done or chosen at random or without a
proper reason, *an arbitrary decision.*
**arbitrarily** *adverb*

**arbitration** *noun*
settling a quarrel between two people or
two sides.
**arbitrate** *verb*, **arbitrator** *noun*

**arc** *noun* (**arcs**)
**1** a curve. **2** bright light made by an electric
current passing across a gap between two
electrodes.

**arcade** *noun* (**arcades**)
a covered passage or area, especially for
shopping.

**arch**[1] *noun* (**arches**)
a curved part that helps to support a
bridge or building.

**arch**[2] *verb* (**arches, arching, arched**)
to curve.

**archaeology** *noun*
(*say* **ar**-ki-ol-ŏ-ji)
the study of ancient remains.
**archaeological** *adjective*, **archaeologist** *noun*

**archbishop** *noun* (**archbishops**)
a chief bishop.

**archer** *noun* (**archers**)
someone who shoots with a bow and
arrows.
**archery** *noun*

**architect** *noun* (**architects**)
(*say* **ar**-ki-tekt)
someone who designs buildings.

**architecture** *noun*
**1** designing buildings. **2** a style of building,
*Victorian architecture.*

**Arctic** *noun*
the area round the North Pole.

**are** plural and 2nd person singular present
tense of **be.**

**area** *noun* (**areas**)
**1** part of a country, place, etc. **2** the space
occupied by something, *The area of this
room is 20 square metres.*

**arena** *noun* (**arenas**)
(*say* ă-**ree**-nă)
**1** the level space in the middle of a
stadium, etc. **2** the place for a fight or
contest.

**aren't** short for *am not* or *are not.*

**arête** *noun* (**arêtes**)
a sharp ridge on a mountain.

**argue** *verb* (**argues, arguing, argued**)
**1** to quarrel. **2** to give reasons for
something, *She argued that housework
should be shared.*

**argument** *noun* (**arguments**)
**1** a quarrel. **2** a reason given for something.

**aria** *noun* (**arias**)
(*say* **ah**-ri-ă)
a solo in an opera or oratorio.

**arid** *adjective*
dry and barren.
**aridity** *noun*

**arise** *verb* (**arises, arising, arose, arisen**)
**1** to appear; to come into existence.
**2** (*old-fashioned use*) to rise; to stand up.

**aristocracy** (**aristocracies**) *noun*
the people of the highest social rank.

**aristocrat** *noun* (**aristocrats**)
(*say* **a**-ris-tŏ-krat)
a nobleman or noblewoman.
**aristocratic** *adjective*

**arithmetic** *noun*
**1** the science or study of numbers.
**2** calculating with numbers.
**arithmetical** *adjective*

**ark** *noun* (**arks**)
the ship in which Noah and his family
escaped the Flood, according to the Bible.

**arm**[1] *noun* (**arms**)
**1** the part of your body between your
shoulder and your hand. **2** a sleeve.
**3** something shaped like an arm, especially
the side part of a chair.

**arm**² *verb* (**arms, arming, armed**)
   1 to supply with weapons. 2 to prepare for war.
   **armed forces** or **armed services,** the army, navy, and air force.

**armada** *noun* (**armadas**)
   (*say* ar-**mah**-dă)
   a fleet of warships, especially the Spanish Armada which attacked England in 1588.

**armadillo** *noun* (**armadillos**)
   a South American animal whose body is covered with a shell of bony plates.

**armaments** *plural noun*
   weapons.

**armature** *noun* (**armatures**)
   the part of a dynamo that turns and develops electric current.

**armchair** *noun* (**armchairs**)
   a chair with parts on either side to rest your arms on.

**armful** *noun* (**armfuls**)
   as much of something as you can hold by wrapping one or both arms around it, *an armful of hay.*

**armistice** *noun* (**armistices**)
   an agreement to stop fighting in a war or battle.

**armour** *noun*
   a metal covering to protect people or things in battle.
   **armoured** *adjective*

**armpit** *noun* (**armpits**)
   the part underneath the top of your arm.

**arms** *plural noun*
   1 weapons, *Lay down your arms.* 2 a coat of arms.
   **arms race,** the competition between nations in building up supplies of weapons.

**armspan** *noun* (**armspans**)
   the distance across your arms when they are stretched out horizontally and sideways.

**army** *noun* (**armies**)
   1 a large number of people trained to fight on land. 2 a large group, *an army of supporters.*

**aroma** *noun* (**aromas**)
   (*say* ă-**roh**-mă)
   a smell, especially a pleasant one.
   **aromatic** *adjective*

**arose** past tense of **arise.**

**around** *adverb* and *preposition*
   1 round, *They stood around the pond.*
   2 about, *Stop running around.*

**arouse** *verb* (**arouses, arousing, aroused**)
   to rouse.

**arrange** *verb* (**arranges, arranging, arranged**)
   1 to organize. 2 to prepare music for a particular purpose.
   **arrangement** *noun,* **arranger** *noun*

**array** *noun* (**arrays**)
   a display; a series, *an impressive array of books.*

**arrears** *plural noun*
   money that is owing and ought to have been paid earlier.
   **in arrears,** owing money; after the correct time, *He's in arrears with his rent. I'll have to pay the bill in arrears.*

**arrest**¹ *verb* (**arrests, arresting, arrested**)
   1 to use the power of the law to seize someone. 2 to stop something, *arrest the spread of the plague.*

**arrest**² *noun* (**arrests**)
   arresting someone or something.
   **under arrest,** seized by the police, etc.

**arrive** *verb* (**arrives, arriving, arrived**)
   1 to reach the end of a journey; to get somewhere. 2 to come, *The great day arrived.*
   **arrival** *noun*

**arrogant** *adjective*
   unpleasantly proud, with little respect for others.
   **arrogance** *noun*

**arrow** *noun* (**arrows**)
1 a pointed stick shot from a bow. 2 a sign used to show direction or position.

**arsenal** *noun* (**arsenals**)
a place where bullets, shells, etc., and weapons are made or stored.

**arsenic** *noun*
a very poisonous metallic substance.

**arson** *noun*
deliberately setting light to a house, building, etc.

**art** *noun* (**arts**)
1 producing something that is beautiful, especially by painting or drawing; things produced in this way. 2 a subject in which opinion and imagination are more important than exact measurement and calculation, *English and history are arts; chemistry and biology are sciences.* 3 a skill, *the art of sewing.*

**artefact** *noun* (**artefacts**)
an object made by humans, especially one studied by archaeologists.

**artery** *noun* (**arteries**)
a tube carrying blood from the heart to parts of the body.

**artful** *adjective*
skilled at deceiving people.
**artfully** *adverb*

**arthritis** *noun*
(*say* arth-**ry**-tiss)
a disease that makes joints in the body painful and stiff.
**arthritic** *adjective*

**article** *noun* (**articles**)
1 an object; a thing. 2 a piece of writing published in a newspaper or magazine. 3 (*in grammar*) the word 'a' or 'an' (called the *indefinite article*) or the word 'the' (called the *definite article*).

**articulate**[1] *verb* (**articulates, articulating, articulated**)
(*say* ar-**tik**-yoo-layt)
to pronounce clearly.
**articulation** *noun*

**articulate**[2] *adjective*
(*say* ar-**tik**-yoo-lăt)
able to speak clearly and fluently.

**articulated** *adjective*
with parts that are connected by flexible joints, *an articulated lorry.*

**artificial** *adjective*
not natural; made by human beings.
**artificial respiration**, helping someone to start breathing again, especially after an accident.
**artificiality** *noun*, **artificially** *adverb*

**artillery** *noun*
1 large guns. 2 the part of the army that uses large guns.

**artist** *noun* (**artists**)
1 someone who creates art, especially a painter. 2 an entertainer.

**artiste** *noun* (**artistes**)
someone whose job is to entertain people, especially by singing, dancing, or telling stories.

**artistic** *adjective*
1 showing skill and beauty, *an artistic flower arrangement.* 2 of art or artists.

**artistry** *noun*
the skill of an artist, *Look at the artistry of that carving!*

**as**[1] *conjunction*
1 in the way that; how, *Leave it as it is.*
2 when; while, *She slipped as she got off the bus.* 3 because, *Leave him here, as he's grumpy.*
**as ... as**, in the same way; to the same extent that, *It is not as hard as you think.*
**as for**, with regard to, *As for you, you are a fool.*
**as it were**, in some way, *She is, as it were, her own enemy.*
**as well**, also.

**as**[2] *adverb*
equally; similarly, *This is just as easy.*

**as**[3] *preposition*
in the character or role of; like, *He was dressed as a sailor.*

**asbestos** *noun*
a fireproof material that is made up of fine, soft fibres.

**ascend** *verb* (**ascends, ascending, ascended**)
to climb something; to go up.
**ascent** *noun*

**ash**¹ *noun* (**ashes**)
the powder that is left after something has been burned.
**the Ashes,** the prize for which England and Australia play each other at cricket.
**ashy** *adjective*

**ash**² *noun* (**ashes**)
a tree with silvery bark and winged seeds.

**ashamed** *adjective*
feeling shame.
**ashamed of something,** feeling shame because of something.

**ashen** *adjective*
grey; pale, *Her face was ashen.*

**ashore** *adverb*
to or on the shore.

**ashtray** *noun* (**ashtrays**)
a small bowl for cigarette ash.

**Ash Wednesday** *noun* (**Ash Wednesdays**)
the first day of Lent.

**Asian** *adjective*
of Asia.

**aside**¹ *adverb*
to or at one side; away.

**aside**² *noun* (**asides**)
something said on the stage by an actor which the other actors are supposed not to hear.

**ask** *verb* (**asks, asking, asked**)
**1** to speak so as to find out or get something. **2** to invite, *Ask him to the party.*
**ask for it** or **ask for trouble,** (*informal*) to behave in such a way as to get into trouble.

**asleep** *adverb* and *adjective*
sleeping.

**aspect** *noun* (**aspects**)
**1** one part of a problem or situation, *Perhaps the worst aspect of winter is the dark mornings.* **2** the appearance of someone or something. **3** the direction a house, etc. faces, *This room has a southern aspect.*

**asphalt** *noun*
(*say* **ass**-falt)
**1** a sticky black substance like tar. **2** this substance mixed with gravel to surface roads, playgrounds, etc.

**aspirin** *noun* (**aspirins**)
a drug used to relieve pain or reduce fever.

**ass** *noun* (**asses**)
**1** a donkey. **2** a fool.

**assassin** *noun* (**assassins**)
a person who assassinates someone.

**assassinate** *verb* (**assassinates, assassinating, assassinated**)
to murder someone, especially a king, politician, etc.
**assassination** *noun*

**assault**¹ *noun* (**assaults**)
a violent or illegal attack on someone.

**assault**² *verb* (**assaults, assaulting, assaulted**)
to make an assault on someone.

**assemble** *verb* (**assembles, assembling, assembled**)
**1** to bring people together. **2** to put things together.

**assembly** *noun* (**assemblies**)
**1** assembling. **2** people who regularly meet together; a parliament. **3** a regular meeting, such as when everybody in a school meets together.
**assembly line,** a series of workers and machines to assemble the parts of a product.

**assert** *verb* (**asserts, asserting, asserted**)
to declare something.
**assert yourself,** to use firmness or authority.
**assertion** *noun*

**assertive** *adjective*
showing or using firmness or authority.

**assess** *verb* (**assesses, assessing, assessed**)
to decide or test the value of a person or thing.
**assessment** *noun*, **assessor** *noun*

**asset** *noun* (**assets**)
something useful.
**assets,** property.

**assign** *verb* (**assign, assigning, assigned**)
**1** to give or allot. **2** to tell someone to do a task.

**assignment** *noun* (**assignments**)
something that someone has to do, especially a task given to a journalist, or to a student at school or college.

**assist** *verb* (**assists, assisting, assisted**)
to help.
**assistance** *noun*

**assistant** *noun* (**assistants**)
1 someone who helps another person.
2 someone who serves in a shop.

**associate**¹ *verb* (**associates, associating, associated**)
(*say* ă-**soh**-shi-ayt)
1 to put things or ideas naturally or regularly together, *I associate Christmas with ice and snow.* 2 to work together, *Two firms have associated for this project.*

**associate**² *noun* (**associates**)
(*say* ă-**soh**-shi-ăt)
a colleague or companion.

**association** *noun* (**associations**)
1 an organization. 2 associating.

**Association Football** *noun*
a game between two teams of eleven players using a round ball that may only be handled by the goalkeepers.

**assorted** *adjective*
of various sorts; mixed.
**assortment** *noun*

**assume** *verb* (**assumes, assuming, assumed**)
1 to accept, without proof or question, that something is true or sure to happen. 2 to take or put on something, *He assumed an innocent look.*
**assumed,** false, *an assumed name.*
**assumption** *noun*

**assurance** *noun* (**assurances**)
1 being assured; a promise or guarantee.
2 life insurance.

**assure** *verb* (**assures, assuring, assured**)
1 to tell someone something positively, *I can assure you that we will make every effort to help.* 2 to make sure that something will happen.
**assure yourself,** to make yourself feel certain or confident.

**asterisk** *noun* (**asterisks**)
a star-shaped sign * used to draw attention to something.

**asteroid** *noun* (**asteroids**)
one of the small planets found mainly between the orbits of Mars and Jupiter.

**asthma** *noun*
(*say* **ass**-mă)
a disease which makes breathing difficult.
**asthmatic** *adjective* and *noun*

**astonish** *verb* (**astonishes, astonishing, astonished**)
to surprise someone greatly.
**astonishment** *noun*

**astound** *verb* (**astounds, astounding, astounded**)
to amaze or shock someone greatly.

**astride** *adverb*
with one leg on each side of something.

**astrology** *noun*
studying how the planets and stars may affect our lives.
**astrologer** *noun*, **astrological** *adjective*

**astronaut** *noun* (**astronauts**)
someone who travels in a spacecraft.

**astronomical** *adjective*
1 connected with astronomy. 2 extremely large, *The cost was astronomical.*

**astronomy** *noun*
studying the sun, moon, planets, and stars.
**astronomer** *noun*

**at** *preposition*
in a particular place, time, way, or direction.
**at all,** in any way.
**at it,** working at something.
**at once,** immediately; without any delay.

**ate** past tense of **eat.**

**atheist** *noun* (**atheists**)
someone who believes that there is no God.
**atheism** *noun*

**athlete** *noun* (**athletes**)
someone who takes part in, or is good at, athletics.

**athletic** *adjective*
1 of athletics, *an athletic competition.*
2 physically strong.

**athletics** *plural noun*
physical exercises and sports like running and jumping.

**atishoo** *interjection*
the sound of a sneeze.

**atlas** *noun* (**atlases**)
a book of maps.

**atmosphere** *noun* (**atmospheres**)
1 the air around the earth. 2 a feeling,
*There was a happy atmosphere at the
fairground.*
**atmospheric** *adjective*

**atoll** *noun* (**atolls**)
a ring-shaped island of coral in the sea.

**atom** *noun* (**atoms**)
a tiny part of something; the smallest
possible part of a chemical element, *Every
atom has a nucleus at its centre.*
**atom bomb,** an atomic bomb.

**atomic** *adjective*
of atoms; nuclear.
**atomic bomb,** a bomb that uses atomic
energy.
**atomic energy,** energy created by splitting or
joining together the central parts of some
atoms.

**atrocious** *adjective*
(*say* ă-**troh**-shŭs)
awful; terrible.
**atrocity** *noun*

**attach** *verb* (**attaches, attaching, attached**)
to fix or fasten.
**attached to,** fond of.

**attachment** *noun* (**attachments**)
1 something fixed or fastened to a device so
that it can do a special kind of work, *The
garden hose has a car-washing attachment.*
2 fondness or friendship.

**attack**[1] *noun* (**attacks**)
1 an attempt to hurt or harm someone or
something. 2 a sudden illness or pain.

**attack**[2] *verb* (**attacks, attacking, attacked**)
to make an attack; to make an attack on
someone or something.

**attain** *verb* (**attains, attaining, attained**)
to reach or accomplish something, *I have
attained Grade 3 on the violin.*
**attainment** *noun*

**attempt**[1] *verb* (**attempts, attempting, attempted**)
to make an effort to do something.

**attempt**[2] *noun* (**attempts**)
making an effort to do something.

**attend** *verb* (**attends, attending, attended**)
1 to be present somewhere; to go to a
meeting, place, etc. 2 to look after or serve
someone. 3 to give care and thought to
something, *I have some business to
attend to.*

**attendance** *noun* (**attendances**)
1 being present somewhere. 2 the number
of people who are present at a meeting, an
event, etc.

**attendant** *noun* (**attendants**)
someone who helps or goes with another
person.

**attention** *noun*
giving care or thought to someone or
something.
**stand to attention,** to stand with your feet
together and arms straight downwards, as
soldiers do on parade.

**attentive** *adjective*
paying attention.

**attic** *noun* (**attics**)
a room in the roof of a house.

**attitude** *noun* (**attitudes**)
1 the way you think, feel, or behave. 2 the
position of your body.

**attract** *verb* (**attracts, attracting, attracted**)
1 to get someone's attention or interest; to
seem pleasant to someone. 2 to pull
something by an invisible force, *Magnets
attract pins.*
**attraction** *noun*

**attractive** *adjective*
1 getting someone's interest, *an attractive
offer.* 2 (of a person) good-looking.

**auburn** *adjective*
(of hair) reddish-brown.

**auction** *noun* (**auctions**)
a sale when things are sold to the person
who offers the most money for them.
**auctioneer** *noun*

**audible** *adjective*
loud enough to be heard.
**audibility** *noun*

**audience** *noun* (**audiences**)
1 the people who have gathered to see or
hear something. 2 a formal interview with
a king, queen, etc.

**audiovisual** *adjective*
using both sound and pictures to give
information, *Audiovisual aids include
films and video recordings.*

**audition** *noun* (**auditions**)
a test to see if a performer is suitable for a
job or a part in a play, etc.

**auditorium** *noun* (**auditoriums**)
(*say* aw-dit-**or**-i-ŭm)
the part of a building where the audience
sits.

**August** *noun*
the eighth month of the year.

**aunt** *noun* (**aunts**)
1 the sister of your mother or father. 2 your
uncle's wife.

**auntie** or **aunty** *noun* (**aunties**)
(*informal*) an aunt.

**au pair** *noun* (**au pairs**)
(*say* oh-**pair**)
a person from overseas, usually a girl or young woman, who works for a time in someone's home.

**aural** *adjective*
of or using hearing, *an aural comprehension test.*

---

USAGE: Do not confuse **aural** with **oral**, which means spoken, or using your mouth.

---

**au revoir** *interjection*
(*say* oh-rĕ-**vwar**)
French words meaning 'goodbye for now'.

**austere** *adjective*
1 without comfort or luxury. 2 morally strict.
**austerity** *noun*

**Australian** *adjective*
of Australia.

**authentic** *adjective*
genuine, *an authentic signature.*
**authenticity** *noun*

**author** *noun* (**authors**)
the writer of a book, play, poem, etc.
**authorship** *noun*

**authority** *noun* (**authorities**)
1 the right or power to give orders to other people. 2 an organization or person that can give orders to other people. 3 a very knowledgeable person; a book, etc. that gives reliable information.

**authorize** *verb* (**authorizes, authorizing, authorized**)
to give official permission for something.

**autistic** *adjective*
unable to communicate with other people or respond to surroundings.

**autobiography** *noun* (**autobiographies**)
the story of someone's life written by himself or herself.
**autobiographical** *adjective*

**autograph** *noun* (**autographs**)
a person's signature.

**automate** *verb* (**automates, automating, automated**)
to make something work by automation.

**automatic** *adjective*
1 working on its own; not needing continuous attention or control by human beings. 2 done without thinking.
**automatically** *adverb*

**automation** *noun*
(*say* aw-tŏm-**ay**-shŭn)
making processes automatic; using machines instead of people to do jobs.

**automobile** *noun* (**automobiles**)
a motor car.

**autumn** *noun* (**autumns**)
(in America, *fall*) the season when leaves fall off the trees, between summer and winter.
**autumnal** *adjective*

**auxiliary**[1] *adjective*
helping, *auxiliary staff. The yacht has an auxiliary engine.*

**auxiliary**[2] *noun* (**auxiliaries**)
a type of verb that is used in forming parts of other verbs, *In 'I have finished', the auxiliary is 'have'.*

**available** *adjective*
that you can get or use, *Fresh strawberries are available in June.*
**availability** *noun*

**avalanche** *noun* (**avalanches**)
(*say* **av**-ă-lahnsh)
a sudden fall of rocks or snow down the side of a mountain.

**avenue** *noun* (**avenues**)
1 a wide street. 2 a road with trees along both sides.

**average**[1] *noun* (**averages**)
1 the usual or ordinary standard, *Her work is above the average.* 2 the result of adding several quantities together and dividing the total by the number of quantities, *The average of 2, 4, 6, and 8 is 5.*

**average**[2] *adjective*
1 of the usual or ordinary standard.
2 worked out as an average.

**average**[3] *verb* (**averages, averaging, averaged**)
to work out, produce, or amount to an average.

**avert** *verb* (**averts, averting, averted**)
1 to turn something away, *People averted their eyes from the accident.* 2 to prevent something, *The train driver's quick reaction had averted a disaster.*

**aviary** *noun* (**aviaries**)
a place where birds are kept.

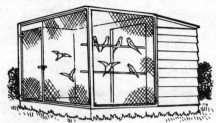

**aviation** *noun*
flying in aircraft.
**aviator** *noun*

**avid** *adjective*
**1** eager, *She is an avid reader.* **2** greedy, *He was avid for fame.*

**avoid** *verb* (**avoids, avoiding, avoided**)
**1** to keep yourself away from someone or something. **2** to find a way of not doing something.
**avoidance** *noun*

**await** *verb* (**awaits, awaiting, awaited**)
to wait for.

**awake**¹ *adjective*
not sleeping.

**awake**² *verb* (**awakes, awaking, awoke, awoken**)
to wake up.

**awaken** *verb* (**awakens, awakening, awakened**)
to wake up.

**award**¹ *noun* (**awards**)
a thing given officially to a person who has done something successful.

**award**² *verb* (**awards, awarding, awarded**)
to give someone an award.

**aware** *adjective*
knowing; realizing, *I was aware of his anger.*
**awareness** *noun*

**awash** *adjective*
with waves or water flooding over it, *The sink has overflowed, and the kitchen floor is awash!*

**away**¹ *adverb*
**1** at or to a distance; not at the place where you usually are. **2** out of existence, *The ice-cream melted away.* **3** continuously; persistently, *He was working away at his sums.*

**away**² *adjective*
played or gained on an opponent's ground, *an away match. an away win.*

**awe** *noun*
fearful or reverent wonder, *The mountains filled him with awe.*

**awed** *adjective*
filled with awe.

**awe-inspiring** or **awesome** *adjective*
causing awe.

**awful** *adjective*
**1** (*informal*) very bad; very great, *I've been an awful fool.* **2** causing fear or horror.
**awfully** *adverb*

**awhile** *adverb*
for a short time.

**awkward** *adjective*
**1** not convenient; difficult to use or deal with. **2** clumsy, *an awkward young man.*

**awoke** past tense of **awake** *verb.*

**awoken** past participle of **awake** *verb.*

**axe**¹ *noun* (**axes**)
a tool for chopping.
**get the axe,** (*informal*) to be dismissed from a job; to be stopped suddenly, *Our project got the axe.*
**someone has an axe to grind,** someone has his or her own reasons for doing something.

**axe**² *verb* (**axes, axing, axed**)
(*informal*) **1** to dismiss someone from a job. **2** to reduce expenses, wages, etc.

**axis** *noun* (**axes**)
**1** a line through the centre of a spinning object. **2** a line dividing something in half.

**axle** *noun* (**axles**)
the rod through the centre of a wheel, on which it turns.

**ay** or **aye** *interjection*
(*say* I)
(*in dialects or old-fashioned use*) yes.

**azalea** *noun* (**azaleas**)
(*say* ă-**zay**-li-ă)
a flowering shrub.

**Aztec** *noun* (**Aztecs**)
one of a native Indian people who lived in Mexico before the Spanish conquest of 1521.

**azure** *adjective*
sky-blue.

# Bb

**babble** *verb* (**babbles, babbling, babbled**)
1 to talk in a silly or meaningless way. 2 to murmur, *a babbling brook*.

**baboon** *noun* (**baboons**)
a large kind of monkey.

**baby** *noun* (**babies**)
a very young child or animal.
**babyish** *adjective*

**babysit** *verb* (**babysits, babysitting, babysat**)
to look after a child while his or her parents are out, *Sally has offered to babysit for us while we go to the show.*

**babysitter** *noun* (**babysitters**)
someone who looks after a child while his or her parents are out.

**bachelor** *noun* (**bachelors**)
a man who is not married.

**back**[1] *noun* (**backs**)
1 the part of your body from your shoulders to your buttocks; the similar part of an animal's body. 2 the part of a thing that faces backwards; the less important side of something, *The back of the house is built of brick, while the front is of stone.* 3 the part of a thing or place that is farthest from the front, *We had to stand at the back of the hall.* 4 a defending player in football, hockey, etc.

**back**[2] *adjective*
placed at the back, *the back row*.

**back**[3] *adverb*
1 backwards; to the place you have come from, *Go back!* 2 to an earlier time, *Put the clock back.* 3 at a distance, *The house stands back from the road*.

**back**[4] *verb* (**backs, backing, backed**)
1 to move backwards. 2 to bet on something. 3 to play or sing music to support a musician or a singer.
**back out**, to withdraw from something.
**back up**, to give someone support or help.

**backache** *noun* (**backaches**)
pain in your back, usually lasting for a long time.

**backbone** *noun* (**backbones**)
the spine.

**background** *noun* (**backgrounds**)
1 the part of a scene, view, etc. that is farthest away from you. 2 the conditions or situation underlying something. 3 a person's experience, education, etc.
**background music**, music used to accompany a film, etc.
**in the background**, not noticeable; not obvious.

**backhand** *noun* (**backhands**)
a stroke in games such as tennis, in which the back of your hand faces your opponent.

**backing** *noun*
1 support, *Our firm will give you financial backing*. 2 material that forms a support or back for something. 3 musical accompaniment, especially for a singer.

**backlash** *noun* (**backlashes**)
a strong, usually angry reaction.

**backlog** *noun* (**backlogs**)
work that should have been finished but still remains to be done.

**backside** *noun* (**backsides**)
(*informal*) the buttocks.

**backstroke** *noun*
a way of swimming on your back.

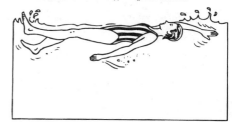

**backward**[1] *adjective*
1 going backwards. 2 not as advanced or developed as others.

**backward**² *adverb*
backwards.

**backwards** *adverb*
1 to or towards the back. 2 in reverse,
*Count backwards from 10 to 1*.
**backwards and forwards,** in one direction and
back again, many times.

**backwater** *noun* (**backwaters**)
a branch of a river that comes to a dead
end.

**backyard** *noun* (**backyards**)
an open area at the back of a house or
similar building.

**bacon** *noun*
smoked or salted meat from the back or
sides of a pig.

**bacteria** *plural noun*
very tiny organisms, *Some bacteria cause
disease*.
**bacterial** *adjective*

**bad** *adjective* (**worse, worst**)
1 not good, *The television picture is bad. All
this drinking is bad for your health.*
2 naughty, *You've been a bad boy!* 3 serious,
*a bad mistake*. 4 decayed, *This meat has
gone bad*. 5 unhealthy; injured, *He had a
bad heart. I've got a bad leg*. 6 unhappy, *I
feel bad about not having phoned her*.
**not bad,** fairly good.

**baddy** *noun* (**baddies**)
(*informal*) a villain, especially in a film.

**badge** *noun* (**badges**)
something that you wear on your clothes to
show people who you are, what school or
club you belong to, etc.

**badger**¹ *noun* (**badgers**)
a grey animal with a white stripe along its
nose, that lives underground, *Badgers hunt
for food at night.*

**badger**² *verb* (**badgers, badgering, badgered**)
to pester, *He badgered me for his pocket
money.*

**badly** *adverb*
in a bad way.
**badly off,** poor.

**badminton** *noun*
a game in which a lightweight object called
a *shuttlecock* is hit backwards and
forwards with rackets across a high net.

**baffle** *verb* (**baffles, baffling, baffled**)
to puzzle someone completely.

**bag**¹ *noun* (**bags**)
a flexible container made of paper, plastic,
cloth, etc.
**bags of something,** (*informal*) plenty of
something, *There's bags of room.*

**bag**² *verb* (**bags, bagging, bagged**)
1 to seize or catch, *I bagged the best seat.*
2 to put something into bags.

**bagel** *noun* (**bagels**)
a hard ring-shaped bread roll.

**baggage** *noun*
luggage.

**baggy** *adjective* (**baggier, baggiest**)
hanging loosely.

**bagpipes** *plural noun*
a musical instrument with air squeezed
out of a bag into a set of pipes.

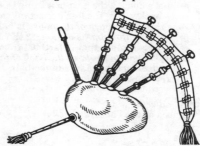

**bail**¹ *noun*
money paid or promised so that an accused
person will not be kept in prison before
coming to trial.

# ballistic missile

**bail**[2] *noun* (**bails**)
one of the two small pieces of wood placed on top of the stumps in cricket.

---

USAGE: Do not confuse **bail**[1] or **bail**[2] with **bale** *noun*. **bale** means a large bundle.

---

**bail**[3] *verb* (**bails, bailing, bailed**)
to scoop water out of a boat.
**bailer** *noun*

**Bairam** *noun* (**Bairams**)
(*say* by-ram)
either of two Muslim festivals, one in the tenth month and one in the twelfth month of the Islamic year.

**Baisakhi** *noun*
a Sikh festival held in April.

**bait**[1] *noun*
food put on a hook or in a trap to catch fish or animals.

**bait**[2] *verb* (**baits, baiting, baited**)
**1** to torment an animal; to tease someone.
**2** to put food on a hook or in a trap, to catch fish or animals.

**bake** *verb* (**bakes, baking, baked**)
**1** to cook in an oven. **2** to make something very hot; to become very hot. **3** to make something hard by heating it.
**baking powder,** a special powder used to make cakes rise.

**baker** *noun* (**bakers**)
someone who makes or sells bread and cakes.
**bakery** *noun*

**balance**[1] *noun* (**balances**)
**1** a device for weighing things, with two containers hanging from a horizontal bar. **2** steadiness, *He lost his balance and fell over.* **3** equality, *We must strike a balance between cost and quality.* **4** the difference between money paid into and money taken out of an account. **5** an amount of money that is owed.

**balance**[2] *verb* (**balances, balancing, balanced**)
to make something steady or equal; to be steady or equal.
**balanced diet,** the right sort and amount of food for good health.

**balcony** *noun* (**balconies**)
**1** a platform sticking out from the outside wall of a building, *A balcony usually has railings around it and can be reached from an upstairs room.* **2** the upstairs part of a cinema or theatre.

**bald** *adjective* (**balder, baldest**)
without any or much hair on your scalp.

**bale**[1] *noun* (**bales**)
a large bundle of hay, straw, cotton, etc., usually tied up tightly.

---

USAGE: Do not confuse **bale** with **bail**[1], a sum of money, or **bail**[2], a piece of wood placed on top of cricket stumps.

---

**bale**[2] *verb* (**bales, baling, baled**)
**bale out,** to jump out of an aircraft with a parachute.

**ball** *noun* (**balls**)
**1** a round object used in many games. **2** something round, *a ball of string.* **3** a grand or formal dance.

**ballad** *noun* (**ballads**)
a simple song or poem, especially one that tells a story.

**ballerina** *noun* (**ballerinas**)
(*say* bal-ĕ-**ree**-nă)
a female ballet-dancer.

**ballet** *noun* (**ballets**)
(*say* **bal**-ay)
a type of entertainment performed on stage, telling a story or expressing an idea in dancing and mime.
**ballet-dancer** *noun*

**ballista** *noun* (**ballistae**)
a type of large catapult used in ancient times for attacking fortified places.

**ballistic missile** *noun* (**ballistic missiles**)
a type of rocket that goes up into the air by its own power but falls freely.

**balloon** *noun* (**balloons**)
1 a small rubber bag inflated with air or gas and used as a toy or for decoration. 2 a large round or pear-shaped bag inflated with a light gas or hot air, so that it can rise into the air. 3 an outline in a strip cartoon containing spoken words.

**ballot** *noun* (**ballots**)
(*say* bal-ŏt)
1 a secret method of voting. 2 a piece of paper on which a vote is made.

**ball-point** or **ball-point pen** *noun* (**ball-points** or **ball-point pens**)
a pen that writes with a tiny ball round which the ink flows.

**ballroom** *noun* (**ballrooms**)
a large room where dances are held.

**balsa** *noun*
(*say* bol-să)
a lightweight wood.

**bamboo** *noun* (**bamboos**)
1 a tall plant with hard hollow stems. 2 a stem of this kind of plant.

**ban** *verb* (**bans, banning, banned**)
to forbid.

**banana** *noun* (**bananas**)
a tropical fruit with yellow skin.

**band**[1] *noun* (**bands**)
1 an organized group of people. 2 a group of musicians. 3 a circular strip of something.

**band**[2] *verb* (**bands, banding, banded**)
to join together in a group.

**bandage** *noun* (**bandages**)
(*say* ban-dij)
a strip of material for binding a wound.

**bandit** *noun* (**bandits**)
an outlaw.

**bandstand** *noun* (**bandstands**)
a platform for a band playing music outdoors.

**bandwagon** *noun* (**bandwagons**)
a wagon for a band playing music in a parade.
**to jump** or **climb on the bandwagon,** to join in something that looks like being successful.

**bandy** *adjective* (**bandier, bandiest**)
having legs that curve outwards at the knees.

**bang**[1] *noun* (**bangs**)
1 a sudden loud noise. 2 a heavy blow or knock.

**bang**[2] *verb* (**bangs, banging, banged**)
1 to hit or shut noisily. 2 to make a loud noise.

**banger** *noun* (**bangers**)
1 (*informal*) a firework that explodes. 2 (*slang*) a sausage. 3 (*slang*) a noisy old car.

**Bangladeshi** *noun* (**Bangladeshis**)
a person from Bangladesh.

**banish** *verb* (**banishes, banishing, banished**)
to punish someone by sending him or her away from a place.
**banishment** *noun*

**banisters** *plural noun*
a handrail with upright supports at the side of a staircase.

**banjo** *noun* (**banjos**)
an instrument like a guitar with a round body.

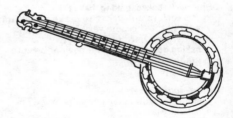

**bank**[1] *noun* (**banks**)
1 a business which looks after people's money. 2 the ground beside a river, canal, lake, etc. 3 a piece of raised or sloping ground. 4 a mass of clouds. 5 a row of lights, switches, etc.
**bank card,** a cheque card.
**bank holiday,** a public holiday.

**bank**[2] *verb* (**banks, banking, banked**)
1 to put money in a bank. 2 to lean over while changing direction, *The plane banked as it turned to land.*
**bank on,** to rely on, *'Will he bring me a present?' 'Don't bank on it.'*
**bank up,** to heap up, *I've banked up the fire.*

**banknote** *noun* (**banknotes**)
a piece of paper money.

**bankrupt** *adjective*
unable to pay your debts.
**bankruptcy** *noun*

**banner** *noun* (**banners**)
a large flag, piece of cloth, etc., carried on
one or two poles in a procession.

**banquet** *noun* (**banquets**)
(*say* bank-wit)
a great feast.

**baptism** *noun* (**baptisms**)
baptizing.

**Baptist** *noun* (**Baptists**)
a Christian who believes that people
should be baptized when they are old
enough to understand baptism.

**baptize** *verb* (**baptizes, baptizing, baptized**)
to receive someone into the Christian
Church in a ceremony in which he or she is
sprinkled with water or immersed in
water, and is usually given Christian
names.

**bar**[1] *noun* (**bars**)
1 a long piece of a hard substance, *a metal
bar*. 2 a counter or room where
refreshments, especially drinks, are
served. 3 one of the small equal sections
into which music is divided, *A waltz has
three beats in a bar*.

**bar**[2] *verb* (**bars, barring, barred**)
1 to fasten with a bar. 2 to prevent someone
from taking part in something.

**barb** *noun* (**barbs**)
a backward-curving point on a fish-hook,
spear, etc.

**barbarian** *noun* (**barbarians**)
an uncivilized, savage person.

**barbaric** *adjective*
very cruel.
**barbarity** *noun*

**barbarous** *adjective*
uncivilized.
**barbarism** *noun*

**barbecue** *noun* (**barbecues**)
1 a party where meat is cooked outdoors.
2 a place or device in which meat is cooked
outdoors.

**barbed wire** *noun*
wire with small spikes on it, used to make
fences.

**barber** *noun* (**barbers**)
a men's hairdresser.

**bar chart** *noun* (**bar charts**)
a diagram showing amounts as bars of
equal width but varying height.

**bar-code** *noun* (**bar-codes**)
a code made up of a series of lines and
spaces, printed on goods, library books,
etc., so that they can be identified by a
computer.

**bard** *noun* (**bards**)
(*old-fashioned use*) a poet or minstrel.

**bare** *adjective* (**barer, barest**)
1 without clothing or covering, *The trees
were bare*. 2 empty or almost empty, *The
cupboard was bare*. 3 that is only just
enough, *the bare necessities of life*.
**barely** *adverb*

**bareback** *adjective* and *adverb*
riding on a horse without a saddle.

**bargain**[1] *noun* (**bargains**)
1 an agreement to buy or sell something.
2 something bought cheaply.

**bargain**[2] *verb* (**bargains, bargaining, bargained**)
to argue over the price of something.
**bargain for something,** to expect something,
*He got more than he bargained for*.

**barge**[1] *noun* (**barges**)
a long flat-bottomed boat used especially
on canals.
**bargee** *noun*

**barge**[2] *verb* (**barges, barging, barged**)
to rush or bump heavily into someone.
**barge in,** to intrude or interrupt rudely,
*Must you barge in while I'm having a
private conversation?*

**baritone** *noun* (**baritones**)
a male singer with a voice between a tenor
and a bass.

**bark**[1] *noun* (**barks**)
1 the sound made by a dog, fox, etc. 2 the
outer covering of a tree's branches or trunk.

**bark**[2] *verb* (**barks, barking, barked**)
1 to make the sound of a dog, fox, etc. 2 to
scrape your skin accidentally on something.

**barley** *noun*
a kind of grain from which malt is made.
**barley sugar,** a sweet made from boiled sugar.

**barman** *noun* (**barmen**)
a man who sells drinks in a bar.

**bar mitzvah** *noun* (**bar mitzvahs**)
a religious ceremony for Jewish boys who are 13.

**barn** *noun* (**barns**)
a building on a farm where grain, hay, etc. is stored.
**barn dance,** a type of country dance, or an informal gathering of people for dancing.

**barnacle** *noun* (**barnacles**)
a shellfish that attaches itself to rocks and the bottoms of ships.

**barnyard** *noun* (**barnyards**)
a farmyard.

**barometer** *noun* (**barometers**)
(*say* bă-**rom**-it-er)
an instrument that measures air pressure, used in forecasting the weather.
**barometric** *adjective*

**baron** *noun* (**barons**)
one of the lowest rank of noblemen.
**baronial** *adjective*

**baroness** *noun* (**baronesses**)
1 a female baron. 2 a baron's wife or widow.

**barrack** *verb* (**barracks, barracking, barracked**)
to jeer at someone.

**barracks** *noun* (**barracks**)
a place where soldiers live.

**barrage** *noun* (**barrages**)
(*say* ba-**rah**z*h*)
1 heavy gunfire. 2 a dam.

**barrel** *noun* (**barrels**)
1 a large cylindrical container with flat ends. 2 the metal tube of a gun, through which the shot is fired.

**barrel-organ** *noun* (**barrel-organs**)
a musical instrument which you play by turning a handle.

**barren** *adjective*
not producing any fruit, children, etc.

**barricade**[1] *noun* (**barricades**)
a barrier, especially one put up quickly to block a street.

**barricade**[2] *verb* (**barricades, barricading, barricaded**)
to block or defend a place by using a barricade.

**barrier** *noun* (**barriers**)
1 a fence, railing, etc. to stop people getting past. 2 an obstacle, *Lack of funds has been a barrier to progress.*

**barrister** *noun* (**barristers**)
a lawyer who is allowed to act on behalf of people in the Crown Courts, High Court, and Appeal Court.

**barrow** *noun* (**barrows**)
1 a small cart. 2 an ancient mound of earth over a grave.

**barter** *verb* (**barters, bartering, bartered**)
to exchange goods for other goods, without using money.

**base**[1] *noun* (**bases**)
1 the lowest part of something; the part on which a thing stands. 2 a basis. 3 a headquarters, especially for the army, navy, or air force. 4 (*in Science*) a substance (such as an alkali) that combines with an acid to form a salt.

**base**² *verb* (**bases, basing, based**)
**base on** or **upon,** to use something as a
basis, *The story is based on actual events.*

**baseball** *noun* (**baseballs**)
1 an American game rather like rounders.
2 the ball used in this game.

**basement** *noun* (**basements**)
a room or rooms below ground level.

**bash**¹ *verb* (**bashes, bashing, bashed**)
(*informal*) to hit hard.
**bash someone up,** (*informal*) to beat
someone up.

**bash**² *noun* (**bashes**)
(*informal*) 1 a hard hit. 2 an attempt, *Have
a bash at it.*

**bashful** *adjective*
shy.

**BASIC** *noun*
a computer language that is designed to be
easy to learn.

**basic** *adjective*
1 forming a base or basis, *a basic
knowledge of French.* 2 most important,
*Food is a basic human need.*
**basically** *adverb*

**basin** *noun* (**basins**)
1 a deep round dish, *a pudding-basin.* 2 a
large container to hold water for washing
in, *a wash-basin.* 3 an enclosed area of
water where ships can stay safely. 4 the
area of land where a river's water comes
from.

**basis** *noun* (**bases**)
1 something to start from or add to, *These
players will be the basis of a new team.*
2 the main principle or ingredient, *You will
be paid on a monthly basis.*

**bask** *verb* (**basks, basking, basked**)
to lie or sit comfortably warming yourself.

**basket** *noun* (**baskets**)
a container, often made of woven strips of
wood.

**basketball** *noun* (**basketballs**)
1 a game in which players try to throw a
ball through a hoop fixed 3 metres above
the ground. 2 the ball used in this game.

**basketful** *noun* (**basketfuls**)
as much of something as you can hold in a
basket, *a basketful of apples.*

**bass**¹ *adjective*
(*say* bayss)
of or forming the lowest sounds in music, *a
bass note.*

**bass**² *noun* (**basses**)
(*say* bayss)
a bass singer, instrument, or part in
written music, *The part is sung by a bass.*

**basset** or **basset hound** *noun* (**bassets** or
**basset hounds**)
a small breed of dog with large, hanging
ears and very short legs.

**bassoon** *noun* (**bassoons**)
a bass woodwind instrument.

**bastard** *noun* (**bastards**)
1 (*informal*) a person, especially an
unpleasant or unfortunate person. 2 a
person whose parents are not married.

**bat**¹ *noun* (**bats**)
a wooden implement used to hit the ball in
cricket, baseball, and other games.
**off your own bat,** without any help from
other people.

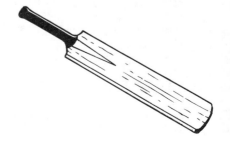

**bat²** *noun* (**bats**)
a flying mammal that looks like a mouse
with wings.

**bat³** *verb* (**bats, batting, batted**)
to use a bat in cricket, etc.

**batch** *noun* (**batches**)
a set of things.

**bated** *adjective*
**with bated breath**, anxiously; hardly daring
to speak.

**bath¹** *noun* (**baths**)
1 a large container for water in which to
wash your whole body. 2 washing your
whole body, *I'd like to have a bath*. 3 the
water used in washing in this way, *Your
bath is getting cold*. 4 (*usually in plural*)
a swimming-bath.

**bath²** *verb* (**baths, bathing, bathed**)
1 to give someone a bath, *Bath the baby*.
2 to have a bath.

**bathe¹** *verb* (**bathes, bathing, bathed**)
1 to go swimming. 2 to wash something
gently.

**bathe²** *noun* (**bathes**)
a swim.

**bathroom** *noun* (**bathrooms**)
a room containing a bath.

**baton** *noun* (**batons**)
a short stick, especially one used to
conduct an orchestra.

**batsman** *noun* (**batsmen**)
someone who uses a bat in cricket, etc.

**battalion** *noun* (**battalions**)
an army unit consisting of two or more
companies.

**batten** *noun* (**battens**)
a strip of wood.

**batter¹** *verb* (**batters, battering, battered**)
to hit hard and often.

**batter²** *noun*
a beaten mixture of flour, eggs, and milk,
for making pancakes, etc.

**battering-ram** *noun* (**battering-rams**)
a heavy pole used to break down gates,
walls, etc.

**battery** *noun* (**batteries**)
1 a portable device for storing and
supplying electricity. 2 a series of cages in
which animals are kept close together on a
farm, *Free-range hens are not kept in
batteries*. 3 a set of devices, especially a
group of large guns.

**battle** *noun* (**battles**)
a fight between large organized forces.

**battlefield** *noun* (**battlefields**)
a place where a battle is or was fought.

**battlements** *plural noun*
the top of a castle wall, usually with
notches through which arrows etc. can be
shot.

**battleship** *noun* (**battleships**)
a heavy warship.

**bawl** *verb* (**bawls, bawling, bawled**)
1 to shout, *'Look out!', he bawled*. 2 to cry
loudly, *The toddler was bawling*.

**bay** *noun* (**bays**)
1 a place where the shore curves inwards.
2 an alcove or compartment.
**at bay**, prevented from coming near
someone, *Keep the enemy at bay*.
**bay window**, a window that sticks out from
the wall of a house.

**bayonet** *noun* (**bayonets**)
a dagger fixed to the muzzle of a rifle.

**bazaar** *noun* (**bazaars**)
1 a sale to raise money for a charity, etc.
2 an oriental market.

**BBC** short for *British Broadcasting
Corporation*.

**BC** short for *before Christ*, used with dates
that come before the birth of Jesus, *Julius
Caesar came to Britain in 55 BC*.

**be** *verb* (*present tense: singular, 1st person* **am**, *2nd person* **are**, *3rd person* **is**, *plural* **are**; *present participle* **being**; *past tense: singular, 1st and 3rd persons* **was**, *2nd person* **were**, *plural* **were**; *past participle* **been**)
1 to exist, *There is a bus-stop at the corner.* 2 to go or come; to visit, *Has the postman been yet? Have you ever been to Africa?* 3 to have a particular description, *She is my teacher. You are very tall.* 4 to become, *She wants to be a scientist.* 5 used to form parts of other verbs, as in *it is coming, he was killed.*

**beach** *noun* (**beaches**)
part of the seashore.

**beacon** *noun* (**beacons**)
a light used as a warning signal.

**bead** *noun* (**beads**)
1 a small piece of something hard with a hole through it, threaded on a string or wire to make a necklace. 2 a small drop of liquid, *beads of sweat.*

**beady** *adjective* (**beadier, beadiest**)
like beads, especially describing eyes that are small and bright.

**beagle** *noun* (**beagles**)
a small hound used for hunting hares.

**beak** *noun* (**beaks**)
the hard, horny part of a bird's mouth.

**beaker** *noun* (**beakers**)
1 a tall drinking-mug. 2 (*in Science*) a glass container for pouring liquids.

**beam**¹ *noun* (**beams**)
1 a long, thick bar of wood or metal. 2 a ray of light or other radiation.

**beam**² *verb* (**beams, beaming, beamed**)
1 to smile very happily. 2 to send out a beam of light, radio waves, etc.

**bean** *noun* (**beans**)
1 a kind of plant with seeds growing in pods. 2 the seed or pod of this kind of plant, eaten as food.

**bear**¹ *verb* (**bears, bearing, bore, born** or **borne**)
1 to carry or support. 2 to have or show, *The letter bore her signature.* 3 to produce, especially to give birth to children, *She was born in 1950. She has borne three sons.* 4 to endure or tolerate, *I can't bear this pain.*
**bearable** *adjective*

USAGE: See the note at **born**.

**bear**² *noun* (**bears**)
a large, heavy, furry animal.

**beard** *noun* (**beards**)
hair on the lower part of a man's face.
**bearded** *adjective*

**bearing** *noun* (**bearings**)
1 the way you behave, walk, stand, etc. 2 the direction or relative position of something.
**your bearings**, knowing where you are in relation to other things, *I have lost my bearings.*

**beast** *noun* (**beasts**)
1 any large four-footed animal. 2 a person you dislike.
**beastly** *adjective*

**beat**¹ *verb* (**beats, beating, beat, beaten**)
1 to hit someone or something often, especially with a stick. 2 to make repeated movements, *Feel your heart beating.* 3 to do better than someone; to overcome. 4 to stir something briskly. 5 to shape or flatten something by hitting it many times.
**beat someone up**, to beat someone violently.

**beat**² *noun* (**beats**)
1 a regular rhythm or stroke, *the beat of your heart.* 2 a strong rhythm in pop music, *This tune has got a beat.* 3 the regular route of a policeman or policewoman.

**Beaufort scale** *noun*
(*say* boh-fert skayl)
a scale for wind-speed ranging from 0 (calm) to 12 (hurricane).

**beauty** *noun* (**beauties**)
**1** a quality that gives delight or pleasure, especially to your senses, *the beauty of the sunset*. **2** a person or thing that has beauty.
**beauty queen**, a woman chosen as the most beautiful in a contest.
**beautiful** *adjective*, **beautifully** *adverb*, **beautify** *verb*

**beaver** *noun* (**beavers**)
a brown, furry, amphibious animal with strong teeth.

**becalmed** *adjective*
unable to sail on because the wind has dropped.

**became** past tense of **become**.

**because** *conjunction*
for the reason that, *We were happy because it was a holiday*.
**because of**, for the reason of; on account of, *He limped because of his bad leg*.

**beckon** *verb* (**beckons, beckoning, beckoned**)
to make a sign to someone asking them to come.

**become** *verb* (**becomes, becoming, became, become**)
**1** to come to be; to start being, *It became darker*. **2** to be suitable for; to look attractive on someone, *That dress becomes you*.
**become of**, to happen to, *What will become of me?*

**bed** *noun* (**beds**)
**1** something for sleeping on; a place to sleep or rest, *I'm going to bed now*. **2** part of a garden where plants are grown. **3** the bottom of the sea or of a river. **4** a flat base; a foundation. **5** a layer of rock.

**bedclothes** *plural noun*
sheets, blankets, etc.

**bedding** *noun*
things for making a bed, such as sheets and blankets.

**bedlam** *noun*
a loud noise or disturbance, *There was bedlam at the playgroup*.

**bedraggled** *adjective*
(*say* bi-**drag**-ŭld)
wet and dirty.

**bedridden** *adjective*
(*say* **bed**-rid-ĕn)
too ill to get out of bed.

**bedroom** *noun* (**bedrooms**)
a room where you sleep.

**bedside** *noun* (**bedsides**)
the space beside a bed, especially the bed of someone who is ill, *He sat by his son's bedside all night*.

**bedspread** *noun* (**bedspreads**)
a covering put over the top of a bed.

**bedstead** *noun* (**bedsteads**)
the framework of a bed.

**bedtime** *noun* (**bedtimes**)
the time when you go to bed or when you ought to go to bed.

**bee** *noun* (**bees**)
a stinging insect that makes honey.

**beech** *noun* (**beeches**)
a tree with smooth bark and glossy leaves.

**beef** *noun*
the meat of an ox, bull, or cow.

**beefburger** *noun* (**beefburgers**)
a hamburger.

**beefeater** *noun* (**beefeaters**)
a guard at the Tower of London.

**beefy** *adjective* (**beefier, beefiest**)
(*informal*) (of a person) big, with strong muscles.

**beehive** *noun* (**beehives**)
a container for bees to live in.

**beeline** *noun*
**make a beeline for something**, to go quickly and directly towards something.

**been** past participle of **be**.

**beer** *noun* (**beers**)
an alcoholic drink made from malt and hops.

**beet** *noun* (**beet** or **beets**)
a plant used as a vegetable or for making sugar.

**beetle** *noun* (**beetles**)
an insect with hard, shiny covers over its wings.

**beetroot** *noun* (**beetroot**)
the crimson root of beet used as a vegetable.

**before**[1] *adverb*
earlier; already, *Have you been here before?*

**before**[2] *preposition*
1 sooner or earlier than, *the day before yesterday.* 2 in front of, *leg before wicket.*

**beforehand** *adverb*
1 earlier, *She had tried to phone me beforehand.* 2 before something happens, *Let me know beforehand if you're going to the meeting.*

**beg** *verb* (**begs, begging, begged**)
1 to ask to be given money, food, etc. 2 to ask seriously or desperately, *He begged me not to tell the teacher.*
**I beg your pardon**, I didn't hear or understand what you said; I apologize.

**began** past tense of **begin**.

**beggar** *noun* (**beggars**)
1 someone who lives by begging.
2 (*informal*) a person, *You lucky beggar!*

**begin** *verb* (**begins, beginning, began, begun**)
to start.

**beginner** *noun* (**beginners**)
someone who is just starting to learn or is still learning a subject.

**beginning** *noun* (**beginnings**)
the start of something.

**begrudge** *verb* (**begrudges, begrudging, begrudged**)
to grudge.

**begun** past participle of **begin**.

**behalf** *noun*
**on behalf of someone**, for someone; done to help someone.
**on behalf of something**, to help a cause.
**on my behalf**, for me.

**behave** *verb* (**behaves, behaving, behaved**)
1 to act in a particular way, *They behaved very badly at the party.* 2 to show good manners, *Why can't you behave?*
**behaviour** *noun*

**behead** *verb* (**beheads, beheading, beheaded**)
to cut off someone's head.

**behind**[1] *adverb*
1 at or to the back, *The others are a long way behind.* 2 staying after other people have gone, *We were left behind when the bus went.* 3 not making good progress; late, *I'm behind with my rent.*

**behind**[2] *preposition*
1 at or to the back of; hidden by, *She hid behind a tree.* 2 not making such good progress as others, *He's behind the rest of the class in French.* 3 supporting, *I am wholeheartedly behind the peace talks.*
**behind someone's back**, without someone knowing or approving.

**behind**[3] *noun* (**behinds**)
a person's bottom, *He kicked me on the behind.*

**beige** *noun* and *adjective*
(*say* bay*zh*)
a fawn colour.

**being** *noun* (**beings**)
1 a creature. 2 existence, *Experience the joy of being.*

**belch**[1] *verb* (**belches, belching, belched**)
1 to let wind noisily out of your stomach through your mouth. 2 to send out smoke, fire, etc.

**belch**[2] *noun* (**belches**)
the act or sound of belching.

**belfry** *noun* (**belfries**)
a tower, or part of a tower, in which bells hang.

**belief** *noun* (**beliefs**)
something you believe.

**believe** *verb* (**believes, believing, believed**)
to think that something is true or that someone is telling the truth.
**believe in something,** to think that something exists; to think that something is good, *Do you believe in ghosts? We believe in sharing our belongings.*
**believable** *adjective,* **believer** *noun*

**bell** *noun* (**bells**)
a device that makes a ringing sound, especially a cup-shaped metal device containing a clapper.
**bell-tent,** a cone-shaped tent.

**bellow** *verb* (**bellows, bellowing, bellowed**)
to roar or shout, *The bull bellowed. 'Quick march!', bellowed the sergeant.*

**bellows** *plural noun*
a device for blowing air into a fire, organ-pipes, etc.

**belly** *noun* (**bellies**)
the abdomen or the stomach.

**belong** *verb* (**belongs, belonging, belonged**)
to have a proper place, *The butter belongs in the fridge.*
**belong to someone,** to be owned by someone, *That pencil belongs to me.*

**belongings** *plural noun*
the things that you own.

**beloved** *adjective*
(*say* bi-**luvd** or bi-**luv**-id)
greatly loved.

**below**[1] *preposition*
lower than, *hitting below the belt.*

**below**[2] *adverb*
at or to a lower place, *I'll have the top bunk; you sleep below.*

**belt** *noun* (**belts**)
1 a strip of material, especially one worn round the waist. 2 a long narrow area, *a belt of rain.*

**bench** *noun* (**benches**)
1 a long seat. 2 a long table for working at.
**the bench,** judges or magistrates.

**bend**[1] *verb* (**bends, bending, bent**)
1 to make or become curved or crooked. 2 to move the top of your body downwards; to stoop.

**bend**[2] *noun* (**bends**)
1 a curve or turn. 2 a sailor's knot.

**beneath** *preposition* and *adverb*
under, *Beneath this soil there is clay.*

**benefactor** *noun* (**benefactors**)
someone who gives money or other help.
**benefaction** *noun*

**benefit** *noun* (**benefits**)
1 advantage; help. 2 money paid by the government to help people who are sick, out of work, earning very little money, etc. 3 a game, concert, etc. to raise money for a particular person or purpose.
**the benefit of the doubt,** being ready to believe that someone is innocent or correct, when you cannot be sure.
**beneficial** *adjective*

**benevolent** *adjective*
kind or helpful.
**benevolence** *noun*

**Bengali** *noun* (**Bengalis**)
1 a person from Bengal, the region to the north-east of India which is divided between India and Bangladesh. 2 a language spoken in Bangladesh and in West Bengal, India.

**bent**[1] *adjective*
1 curved or crooked. 2 (*slang*) dishonest.
**bent on something,** determined to do something.

**bent**[2] *noun*
a liking or talent for something.

**bequeath** *verb* (**bequeaths, bequeathing, bequeathed**)
(rhymes with *breathe*)
to leave someone something in a will.
**bequest** *noun*

**bereaved** *adjective*
left sad because someone has died.
**bereavement** *noun*

**bereft** *adjective*
deprived of something, *bereft of speech.*

**beret** *noun* (**berets**)
(*say* **bair**-ay)
a soft, round, flat cap.

**berry** *noun* (**berries**)
a small, juicy fruit.

**berserk** *adjective*
in or into a frenzy, *The security guards went berserk and fired wildly into the crowd.*

**berth** *noun* (**berths**)
1 a sleeping-place on a ship or train.
2 a place where a ship ties up.

USAGE: Do not confuse **berth** with **birth**, which means being born.

**beside** *preposition*
1 next to; close to, *beside the seaside.*
2 having nothing to do with, *That is beside the point.*
**beside yourself,** very excited or upset, *He was beside himself with grief.*

**besides**<sup>1</sup> *preposition*
in addition to, *Who came besides you?*

**besides**<sup>2</sup> *adverb*
also; in addition to this, *That coat costs too much. Besides, it's the wrong colour.*

**besiege** *verb* (**besieges, besieging, besieged**)
(*say* bi-**seej**)
1 to surround a place with troops. 2 to crowd around someone or something, *The pop star's hotel was besieged by hundreds of fans.*

**best**<sup>1</sup> *adjective*, superlative of **good** and **well**.
most excellent.
**best man,** the bridegroom's main helper at a wedding.
**best seller,** a book that sells in very large numbers.

**best**<sup>2</sup> *noun*
1 the best person or thing, *She was the best at tennis.* 2 the best people or things, *These apples are the best you can buy.* 3 victory, *We got the best of the fight.*

**best**<sup>3</sup> *adverb*
1 in the best way; most. 2 most usefully; most wisely, *He is best ignored.*

**bet**<sup>1</sup> *noun* (**bets**)
1 an agreement that you will pay money, etc. if you are wrong in forecasting the result of a race, etc. 2 the money you risk losing in a bet.

**bet**<sup>2</sup> *verb* (**bets, betting, bet** or **betted**)
1 to make a bet; risk losing money in a bet. 2 (*informal*) to be certain; to predict, *I bet I'm right.*

**betray** *verb* (**betrays, betraying, betrayed**)
1 to be disloyal to a person, cause, etc. 2 to reveal something that should have been kept secret.
**betrayal** *noun*

**better**<sup>1</sup> *adjective*, comparative of **good** and **well**.
1 more excellent. 2 recovered from an illness, *Are you better?*

**better**<sup>2</sup> *noun* (**betters**)
a better person or thing.
**get the better of,** to overcome something; to get an advantage over someone.

**better**<sup>3</sup> *adverb*
1 in a better way. 2 more usefully; more wisely, *We had better leave now, before it's too late.*
**better off,** more wealthy; safer, healthier, etc., *Ask Nick to pay the bill – he's better off than either of us. You'd be better off if you didn't worry so much.*

**better**<sup>4</sup> *verb* (**betters, bettering, bettered**)
1 to improve something, *They did all they could to better matters.* 2 to do better than, *She hopes to better her own record time.*

**between**<sup>1</sup> *preposition*
1 within two or more given limits, *Call on me between Tuesday and Friday.* 2 when comparing; separating, *What is the difference between butter and margarine?* 3 shared among, *Divide these sweets between the children.* 4 connecting two or more people, places, or things, *The train runs between London and Glasgow.*

**between**<sup>2</sup> *adverb*
separating or connecting two or more places, etc., *These two houses do not touch; there is a gap between. The two towns are about fifty miles apart, and there is only one road between.*

**beware** *verb* (*only in the form* **beware**)
be careful, *Beware of pickpockets.*

**bewilder** *verb* (**bewilders, bewildering, bewildered**)
to puzzle someone completely.
**bewilderment** *noun*

**bewitch** *verb* (**bewitches, bewitching, bewitched**)
1 to delight someone very much, *Felicity's beauty bewitched him.* 2 to put a magic spell on someone.

**beyond**<sup>1</sup> *preposition*
1 farther than, *Don't go beyond the end of the street.* 2 outside the range of; too difficult for, *This boat is beyond repair.*

**beyond**<sup>2</sup> *adverb*
farther on, *You can see the next valley and the mountains beyond.*

**bias** *noun* (**biases**)
1 a prejudice. 2 a tendency for a ball to swerve, especially in the game of bowls; a slanting direction.
**biased** *adjective*

**bib** *noun* (**bibs**)
a cloth, etc. put under a baby's chin during meals.

**Bible** *noun* (**Bibles**)
the holy book of Christianity and Judaism.
**biblical** *adjective*

**bicycle** *noun* (**bicycles**)
a two-wheeled vehicle driven by pedals.
**bicycle clip,** a clip to hold your trouser-leg tightly round your ankle when you are cycling.
**bicycle pump,** a pump for putting air into bicycle tyres.

**bid**<sup>1</sup> *noun* (**bids**)
1 offering an amount you will pay for something, especially at an auction. 2 an attempt, *He will make a bid for the world record.*

**bid**<sup>2</sup> *verb* (**bids, bidding, bid**)
to offer an amount of money.

**bide** *verb* (**bides, biding, bided**)
  **bide your time,** to wait.

**big** *adjective* (**bigger, biggest**)
  **1** large. **2** important. **3** elder, *my big sister*.
  **big game,** large animals hunted for sport.

**bigamy** *noun* (**bigamies**)
  the crime of having two or more wives or
  husbands at the same time.
  **bigamist** *noun*, **bigamous** *adjective*

**bike** *noun* (**bikes**)
  (*informal*) a bicycle or motor cycle.

**bikini** *noun* (**bikinis**)
  a woman's two-piece bathing-costume that
  covers very little of her body.

**bile** *noun*
  a bitter greenish-brown fluid, produced in
  the liver, that helps the body to digest fat.

**bilge** *noun* (**bilges**)
  **1** the bottom of a ship. **2** the water that
  collects inside the bottom of a ship.
  **3** (*slang*) nonsense.

**bilingual** *adjective*
  speaking two languages; dealing with two
  languages, *She is bilingual. a bilingual
  dictionary*.

**bill**[1] *noun* (**bills**)
  **1** an account showing how much money is
  owing. **2** the plan for a proposed law. **3** a
  poster. **4** a programme of entertainment,
  *There's a conjuror on the bill*.

**bill**[2] *noun* (**bills**)
  a bird's beak.

**billiards** *noun*
  a game played with long sticks (called *cues*)
  and three balls on a cloth-covered table.

**billion** *noun* (**billions**)
  **1** in America and Britain, a thousand
  millions (1,000,000,000). **2** (*less common*)
  in Britain, a million millions
  (1,000,000,000,000).

**billow**[1] *noun* (**billows**)
  a large wave, *the billows of the sea*.
  **billowy** *adjective*

**billow**[2] *verb* (**billows, billowing, billowed**)
  to rise up or move like waves on the sea,
  *a yacht with billowing sails*.

**billy** or **billycan** *noun* (**billies** or **billycans**)
  a can with a lid, used by campers, etc. for
  making hot drinks or cooking food.

**billy-goat** *noun* (**billy-goats**)
  a male goat.

**bin** *noun* (**bins**)
  a large or deep container.
  **bin-liner,** a bag placed inside a rubbish bin
  to keep it clean.

**binary** *adjective*
  involving sets of two; consisting of two
  parts.
  **binary system,** a system of expressing
  numbers by using the digits 0 and 1 only,
  *In the binary system, 21 is written 10101*.

**bind** *verb* (**binds, binding, bound**)
  **1** to tie up or tie together. **2** to make
  someone do something or promise
  something. **3** to fasten material round
  something. **4** to fasten the pages of a book
  inside a cover.

**bingo** *noun*
  a game played with cards on which
  numbered squares are covered or crossed
  out as the numbers are called out at
  random.

**binoculars** *plural noun*
  a device with lenses for both eyes, for
  making distant objects seem nearer.

**biodegradable** *adjective*
  able to be broken down by bacteria in the
  environment, *a biodegradable
  washing-powder*.

**biography** *noun* (**biographies**)
  the story of a person's life.
  **biographer** *noun*, **biographical** *adjective*

**biology** *noun*
  the science or study of living things.
  **biological** *adjective*, **biologist** *noun*

**biomass** *noun*
  the total amount or weight of living things
  in a particular area.

**bionic** *adjective*
  worked by or containing electronic devices,
  but behaving like a living being, *They
  designed a bionic man*.

**biosphere** *noun*
  the parts of the earth's surface and its
  atmosphere where living things are found.

**birch** *noun* (**birches**)
1 a thin tree with shiny bark and slender branches. 2 a bundle of twigs from this tree, used especially in the past for beating people.

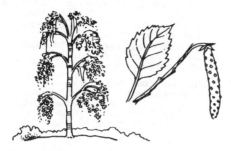

**bird** *noun* (**birds**)
a feathered animal with two wings and two legs.
**bird's-eye view,** a general view of something, especially from above.

**birdseed** *noun*
seeds for caged birds to eat.

**birth** *noun* (**births**)
being born.
**birth certificate,** a document showing where and when you were born.
**birth control,** ways of avoiding making a baby.
**birth rate,** the number of children born in one year for every 1,000 of the population.

USAGE: Do not confuse **birth** with **berth,** which means a sleeping-place, or a place where a ship ties up.

**birthday** *noun* (**birthdays**)
the anniversary of the day you were born.

**birthmark** *noun* (**birthmarks**)
a mark which has been on your body since you were born.

**birthplace** *noun* (**birthplaces**)
where you were born.

**biscuit** *noun* (**biscuits**)
a flat thin piece of crisp baked pastry.

**bisect** *verb* (**bisects, bisecting, bisected**)
to divide something into two equal parts.

**bishop** *noun* (**bishops**)
1 an important clergyman in charge of all the churches in a city or district. 2 a chess-piece shaped rather like a bishop's mitre.

**bison** *noun* (**bison**)
a wild ox.

**bit**[1] *noun* (**bits**)
1 a small piece or amount of something. 2 the part of a horse's bridle that is put into its mouth. 3 the part of a tool that cuts or grips.
**a bit,** slightly, *I'm a bit worried.*
**bit by bit,** gradually.
**bits and pieces,** oddments.

**bit**[2] past tense of **bite** *verb.*

**bitch** *noun* (**bitches**)
1 a female dog, fox, or wolf. 2 (*offensive slang*) a spiteful or unpleasant woman. 3 (*slang*) an unpleasant thing, *That was a bitch of a job!*

**bitchy** *adjective* (**bitchier, bitchiest**)
spiteful, *Stop making bitchy remarks about Sally!*

**bite**[1] *verb* (**bites, biting, bit, bitten**)
1 to cut or take with your teeth. 2 to penetrate, *The tyres bit into the mud.* 3 to accept bait, *The fish are biting.* 4 to sting or hurt, *a biting wind.*
**bite the dust,** to be killed.

**bite**[2] *noun* (**bites**)
1 the act of biting. 2 a mark or spot made by biting, *an insect bite.* 3 a snack.

**bitter** *adjective*
1 not sweet; tasting unpleasant. 2 resentful; envious. 3 very cold, *a bitter wind.*

**black**[1] *adjective* (**blacker, blackest**)
1 of the very darkest colour, like coal or soot. 2 with very dark skin. 3 dismal; not hopeful, *The outlook is black.* 4 very dirty.
**black coffee,** coffee without milk or cream.
**black eye,** an eye with a bruise round it.
**black hole,** (*in Astronomy*) a region in space with such strong gravity that no light escapes.
**black ice,** thin transparent ice on roads.
**black market,** illegal trading.

**black²** *noun* (**blacks**)
1 black colour. 2 a person with very dark skin.

**blackberry** *noun* (**blackberries**)
a sweet black berry.

**blackbird** *noun* (**blackbirds**)
a European song-bird.

**blackboard** *noun* (**blackboards**)
a dark board for writing on with chalk.

**blacken** *verb* (**blackens, blackening, blackened**)
to make or become black.

**blackleg** *noun* (**blacklegs**)
someone who works while other workers are on strike.

**blackmail** *verb* (**blackmails, blackmailing, blackmailed**)
to get money from someone by threatening to reveal something that he or she wants to keep secret.

**blackout** *noun* (**blackouts**)
1 losing consciousness or memory for a short time. 2 a time when lights are kept hidden or turned off.

**blacksmith** *noun* (**blacksmiths**)
someone who makes and repairs things made of iron, especially someone who makes and fits shoes for horses.

**bladder** *noun* (**bladders**)
1 the bag-like part of the body in which urine collects. 2 the inflatable bag inside a football.

**blade** *noun* (**blades**)
1 the sharp part of a knife, sword, axe, etc. 2 the flat, wide part of an oar, propeller, etc. 3 a long narrow leaf, *a blade of grass*.

**blame¹** *verb* (**blames, blaming, blamed**)
to say that someone or something has caused what is wrong, *My brother broke the window but Mum blamed me!*
**he is to blame**, he is the person who caused what is wrong.

**blame²** *noun*
blaming, *I got the blame for what he did.*

**blancmange** *noun* (**blancmanges**)
(*say* blă-**monj**)
a pudding like a jelly made with milk.

**blank¹** *adjective*
1 not written, drawn, or printed on, *blank paper*. 2 without interest or expression, *a blank face*. 3 empty, *When she asked me what was special about today, my mind went blank.*
**blank cartridge**, a cartridge which makes a noise but does not fire a bullet.
**blank verse**, poetry without rhymes.

**blank²** *noun* (**blanks**)
1 an empty space. 2 a blank cartridge.
**draw a blank**, not to get the result you wanted, *I looked for my gloves in the garage, but drew a blank*.

**blanket** *noun* (**blankets**)
a large piece of thick cloth, used as a warm covering for a bed.

**blare** *verb* (**blares, blaring, blared**)
to make a harsh, loud sound.

**blaspheme** *verb* (**blasphemes, blaspheming, blasphemed**)
to talk without respect about sacred things.
**blasphemous** *adjective*, **blasphemy** *noun*

**blast¹** *noun* (**blasts**)
1 a strong rush of wind or air. 2 a loud noise, *a blast of trumpets*.
**blast-off**, the launching of a spacecraft.

**blast²** *verb* (**blasts, blasting, blasted**)
1 to blow something up with explosives. 2 (*informal*) to damn.

**blaze¹** *noun* (**blazes**)
a very bright flame, fire, or light.
**blazes**, (*old-fashioned informal*) hell, *Go to blazes!*

**blaze²** *verb* (**blazes, blazing, blazed**)
1 to burn or shine brightly. 2 to feel very strongly, *He was blazing with anger*.

**blaze³** *verb* (**blazes, blazing, blazed**)
**blaze a trail**, to show the way for others to follow.

**blazer** *noun* (**blazers**)
a kind of jacket, often with a badge on.

**bleach¹** *verb* (**bleaches, bleaching, bleached**)
to make or become white.

**bleach²** *noun* (**bleaches**)
a substance to make things white, to clean things, and to kill germs.

**bleak** *adjective* (**bleaker, bleakest**)
1 bare and cold, *a bleak hillside*. 2 dreary; miserable, *The future looks bleak*.

**bleary** *adjective* (**blearier, bleariest**)
with eyes that do not see clearly.

**bleat**[1] *noun* (**bleats**)
the cry of a lamb, calf, etc.

**bleat**[2] *verb* (**bleats, bleating, bleated**)
to make a bleat.

**bleed** *verb* (**bleeds, bleeding, bled**)
1 to lose blood. 2 to draw blood from someone or an animal. 3 to draw fluid from something, *You will need to bleed the radiators.*

**bleep** *noun* (**bleeps**)
a small, high sound such as some digital watches make.

**blemish** *noun* (**blemishes**)
a flaw or imperfection.

**blend** *verb* (**blends, blending, blended**)
to mix together smoothly or easily.

**bless** *verb* (**blesses, blessing, blessed**)
1 to wish or bring someone happiness. 2 to make or call a person or thing holy.

**blessing** *noun* (**blessings**)
1 being blessed. 2 a short prayer. 3 something you are glad of, *It's a blessing that they are safe.*

**blew** past tense of **blow** *verb*.

**blight** *noun* (**blights**)
1 a plant disease. 2 an evil influence.

**blimey** *interjection*
(*slang*) an exclamation of surprise or annoyance.

**blind**[1] *adjective* (**blinder, blindest**)
1 unable to see. 2 without thought or understanding.
**blind alley**, a road which has one end closed.

**blind**[2] *verb* (**blinds, blinding, blinded**)
to make someone unable to see.

**blind**[3] *noun* (**blinds**)
1 a screen for a window. 2 something used to hide the truth, *His story of having been away on a business trip was just a blind.*

**blindfold**[1] *verb* (**blindfolds, blindfolding, blindfolded**)
to cover someone's eyes with a cloth so that the person cannot see where he or she is, or what is happening.

**blindfold**[2] *noun* (**blindfolds**)
a piece of cloth used to cover someone's eyes so that the person cannot see where he or she is, or what is happening.

**blindfold**[3] *adjective* and *adverb*
with your eyes covered by a cloth.

**blink** *verb* (**blinks, blinking, blinked**)
to shut and open your eyes quickly.

**bliss** *noun*
great happiness.
**blissful** *adjective*, **blissfully** *adverb*

**blister** *noun* (**blisters**)
a swelling like a bubble on your skin.

**blitz** *noun* (**blitzes**)
a sudden, violent attack, especially from aircraft.

**blizzard** *noun* (**blizzards**)
a severe snowstorm.

**bloated** *adjective*
swollen by fat, gas, or liquid.

**blob** *noun* (**blobs**)
a small round mass of something, *blobs of paint.*

**block**[1] *noun* (**blocks**)
1 a solid piece of something. 2 an obstruction. 3 a large building or group of buildings with streets all around it. 4 (*in Australia and New Zealand*) a large plot of land.
**block capitals**, capital letters.
**block graph**, a bar chart on which the bars are divided into equal units (**blocks**).
**block letters**, capital letters.

**block**[2] *verb* (**blocks, blocking, blocked**)
1 to obstruct, *Tall buildings blocked our view.* 2 to stop up, *Leaves blocked the drain.*

**blockade** *noun* (**blockades**)
a kind of siege, especially of a port.

**blockage** *noun* (**blockages**)
1 something that stops up a pipe, etc. 2 an obstructed condition, *Roadworks caused blockages in the traffic.*

**blond** or **blonde** *adjective* (**blonder, blondest**)
fair-haired.

**blonde** *noun* (**blondes**)
a fair-haired girl or woman.

**blood** *noun*
1 the red liquid that flows through veins and arteries. 2 your ancestors, *She has noble blood.*
**blood donor**, someone who gives some blood for use in transfusions.
**in cold blood**, deliberately and cruelly.

**bloodhound** *noun* (**bloodhounds**)
a large breed of dog used to track people by their scent.

**bloodshed** *noun*
the killing and injuring of people.

**bloodshot** *adjective*
having eyes streaked with red.

**bloodstream** *noun*
the blood flowing round the body.

**bloodthirsty** *adjective* (**bloodthirstier, bloodthirstiest**)
eager to kill; involving a lot of killing, *a bloodthirsty film*.

**bloody** *adjective* (**bloodier, bloodiest**)
1 involving bloodshed. 3 (*slang*) damned; very great, *You're a bloody fool*.
**bloody-minded**, deliberately awkward or not helpful.

**bloom** *noun* (**blooms**)
a flower.
**in bloom**, flowering.

**blossom**[1] *noun* (**blossoms**)
1 a flower, especially on a fruit-tree. 2 a mass of flowers on a fruit-tree, etc.

**blossom**[2] *verb* (**blossoms, blossoming, blossomed**)
1 to produce flowers. 2 to develop into something, *She blossomed into a fine singer*.

**blot**[1] *noun* (**blots**)
1 a spot or blob of ink. 2 a flaw or fault.

**blot**[2] *verb* (**blots, blotting, blotted**)
1 to make a blot on something. 2 to dry with blotting-paper.
**blot out**, to delete or obscure.
**blot your copybook**, to spoil your good reputation.

**blotch** *noun* (**blotches**)
an untidy patch of colour.
**blotchy** *adjective*

**blotting-paper** *noun*
thick, soft paper for soaking up ink, etc.

**blouse** *noun* (**blouses**)
a piece of women's clothing like a shirt.

**blow**[1] *verb* (**blows, blowing, blew, blown**)
1 to move in or with a current of air, *Her hat blew off*. 2 to push air from your mouth or nose, *He blew on his tea to cool it*. 3 to make something by blowing, *Let's blow bubbles*. 4 to make a sound by blowing, *Blow the whistle*. 5 to melt with too strong an electric current, *A fuse has blown*.
**blow up**, to destroy by an explosion; to explode; to inflate, *Guerrillas blew up the radio station. The store of dynamite blew up. Blow up your bike's tyres*.
**blow you**, I do not care what happens to you, *Blow you, Jack, I'm all right*.

**blow**[2] *noun* (**blows**)
1 a hard knock or hit. 2 a shock; a disaster, *His death was a great blow. a major blow for the space programme*. 3 the action of blowing.
**blow-lamp** or **blow-torch**, a device for directing an intense flame at something.

**blue**[1] *noun*
a colour like the colour of a cloudless sky.
**out of the blue**, with no warning, *Out of the blue, my friend Martin turned up*.

**blue**[2] *adjective* (**bluer, bluest**)
1 blue in colour. 2 miserable; depressed. 3 obscene, *blue jokes*.

**bluebell** *noun* (**bluebells**)
a blue wild flower.

**bluebottle** *noun* (**bluebottles**)
a large fly.

**blueprint** *noun* (**blueprints**)
a detailed plan.

**blues** *noun*
a type of song or tune that is often sad.
**the blues**, a very sad feeling.

**bluff**[1] *verb* (**bluffs, bluffing, bluffed**)
to deceive someone by pretending, especially by pretending to be able to do something.

**bluff**² *noun* (**bluffs**)
something that someone pretends in order to deceive someone else; a threat that someone makes but is unlikely to carry out, *He said he'd report us, but that was just a bluff.*
**call someone's bluff**, to challenge someone to do what he or she has threatened to do, because you think that he or she will not or cannot do it.

**blunder** *noun* (**blunders**)
a foolish mistake.

**blunt** *adjective* (**blunter**, **bluntest**)
1 not sharp. 2 not tactful.

**blur** *verb* (**blurs**, **blurring**, **blurred**)
to make or become unclear or smeared.

**blurb** *noun* (**blurbs**)
a description that praises something, especially a book.

**blush** *verb* (**blushes**, **blushing**, **blushed**)
to become red in the face, especially when you are embarrassed.

**bluster** *verb* (**blusters**, **blustering**, **blustered**)
1 to blow in gusts. 2 to talk threateningly.
**blustery** *adjective*

**BMX** *noun* (**BMXs**)
1 a kind of bicycle-racing on a dirt-track. 2 a kind of bicycle with small wheels, used especially for dirt-track racing.

**boa** or **boa constrictor** *noun* (**boas** or **boa constrictors**)
a large South American snake that crushes its prey.

**boar** *noun* (**boars**)
1 a wild pig. 2 a male pig.

**board**¹ *noun* (**boards**)
1 a flat piece of wood. 2 a flat piece of wood set up for a particular purpose, *a dart-board. a notice-board.* 3 daily meals supplied in return for money or work, *board and lodging.* 4 a committee.
**board-game**, a game played on a board, such as chess or draughts.
**on board**, aboard.

**board**² *verb* (**boards**, **boarding**, **boarded**)
1 to go on to a ship, aircraft, etc. 2 to give or get meals and accommodation.
**board over** or **up**, to cover something with boards.

**boarder** *noun* (**boarders**)
1 a child that lives at a boarding-school during the term. 2 a lodger.

**boarding-house** *noun* (**boarding-houses**)
a house where people lodge.

**boarding-school** *noun* (**boarding-schools**)
a school in which children live during the term.

**boast** *verb* (**boasts**, **boasting**, **boasted**)
to be proud, especially in talking.
**boastful** *adjective*, **boastfully** *adverb*

**boat** *noun* (**boats**)
a device built to float and travel on water.
**boat people**, refugees who leave their country by sea.
**in the same boat**, in the same situation; having the same difficulties.

**boating** *noun*
going out in a boat, especially a rowing-boat.

**bob** *verb* (**bobs**, **bobbing**, **bobbed**)
to move quickly, especially up and down.

**bobble** *noun* (**bobbles**)
a small round ornament, often made of wool.

**bob-sled** or **bob-sleigh** *noun* (**bob-sleds** or **bob-sleighs**)
a big sledge with two sets of runners.

**bodice** *noun* (**bodices**)
the upper part of a woman's dress.

**bodily**¹ *adjective*
concerned with your body, *bodily functions.*

**bodily**² *adverb*
so as to move the whole of someone or something, *He was picked up bodily and bundled into the gangsters' car.*

**body** *noun* (**bodies**)
1 the flesh, bones, etc. of a person or animal. 2 a corpse. 3 the main part of something. 4 a group of people, things, etc. 5 a distinct object or piece of matter, *Stars and planets are heavenly bodies.*
**body-building**, making your body strong and muscular by doing things like lifting heavy weights, doing exercises, and eating special foods.
**body scanner**, a machine which uses X-rays to make pictures of the inside of the whole body.

**bodyguard** *noun* (**bodyguards**)
a guard to protect someone's life.

**bog** *noun* (**bogs**)
1 an area of wet, spongy ground. 2 (*slang*) a lavatory.
**boggy** *adjective*

**bogus** *adjective*
not genuine.

**boil**[1] *verb* (**boils, boiling, boiled**)
1 to make or become hot enough to bubble and give off vapour. 2 to cook or wash something in water that is bubbling and giving off steam.
**be boiling,** to be very hot.

**boil**[2] *noun* (**boils**)
1 an inflamed spot on the skin.
2 boiling-point, *Bring the milk to the boil.*

**boiler** *noun* (**boilers**)
a container in which water is heated or clothes are boiled.
**boiler suit,** overalls.

**boiling-point** *noun* (**boiling-points**)
the temperature at which something boils.

**boisterous** *adjective*
noisy and lively.

**bold** *adjective* (**bolder, boldest**)
1 brave. 2 impudent. 3 clear; easy to see.

**bollard** *noun* (**bollards**)
1 a short, thick post to direct or keep out traffic. 2 a short, thick post on a ship, quay, etc. to which ropes are attached.

**bolster**[1] *noun* (**bolsters**)
a long pillow.

**bolster**[2] *verb* (**bolsters, bolstering, bolstered**)
to raise or increase something, *Her success bolstered her confidence.*
**bolster up,** to support someone; to help something that is weak.

**bolt**[1] *noun* (**bolts**)
1 a sliding bar for fastening a door. 2 a thick metal pin for fastening things together. 3 a sliding bar that opens and closes the breech of a rifle. 4 a flash of lightning.
**a bolt from the blue,** a surprise, usually unpleasant.

**bolt**[2] *verb* (**bolts, bolting, bolted**)
1 to fasten with a bolt. 2 to run away, *The horse bolted.* 3 to swallow food quickly.

**bomb**[1] *noun* (**bombs**)
a device that explodes.
**the bomb,** nuclear weapons.

**bomb**[2] *verb* (**bombs, bombing, bombed**)
to attack with bombs.

**bombard** *verb* (**bombards, bombarding, bombarded**)
1 to attack with gunfire. 2 to direct a large number of questions, complaints, etc. at someone.
**bombardment** *noun*

**bomber** *noun* (**bombers**)
1 an aircraft built to drop bombs. 2 a person who uses bombs, especially a terrorist.

**bond** *noun* (**bonds**)
1 something that binds, restrains, or unites. 2 a document stating an agreement.

**bondage** *noun*
being a slave.

**bone** *noun* (**bones**)
one of the hard pieces of a skeleton.
**have a bone to pick with someone,** to want to argue with someone about something.

**bonfire** *noun* (**bonfires**)
an outdoor fire to burn rubbish or celebrate something.

**bonnet** *noun* (**bonnets**)
1 (in America, *hood*) the hinged cover over a car engine. 2 a round hat usually tied under someone's chin.

**bonus** *noun* (**bonuses**)
an extra payment or benefit in addition to what you get or expect.

**bony** *adjective* (**bonier, boniest**)
1 thin. 2 with big bones.

**boo** *verb* (**boos, booing, booed**)
to show disapproval by shouting 'boo'.

**booby** *noun* (**boobies**)
a stupid or childish person.
**booby prize,** a prize given to someone who comes last in a contest.
**booby trap,** something designed to hit or injure someone when he or she does not expect it.

**book**[1] *noun* (**books**)
a set of sheets of paper, usually with printing or writing on, fastened together inside a cover.

**book**[2] *verb* (**books, booking, booked**)
1 to reserve a place in a theatre, hotel, train, etc. 2 to record something in a book or list. 3 to write down the name of someone who has broken a rule or the law, *The referee booked him for swearing.*
**book someone in,** to reserve a room for someone in a hotel, etc.

**bookcase** *noun* (**bookcases**)
a piece of furniture designed to hold books.

**bookkeeping** *noun*
recording details of buying, selling, etc.

**booklet** *noun* (**booklets**)
a small book.

**bookmaker** *noun* (**bookmakers**)
a person whose business is taking bets, especially bets made on horse-races.

**bookmark** *noun* (**bookmarks**)
something to mark a place in a book.

**boom**[1] *verb* (**booms, booming, boomed**)
1 to make a deep, hollow sound, *The guns boomed continually.* 2 to be prosperous, *Business is booming.*

**boom**[2] *noun* (**booms**)
1 a booming sound. 2 prosperity; growth. 3 a long pole at the bottom of a sail to keep it stretched. 4 a long pole carrying a microphone, etc.

**boomerang** *noun* (**boomerangs**)
a curved stick, used in Australia as a weapon, which is thrown at its target and comes back to the thrower if it misses.

**boost** *verb* (**boosts, boosting, boosted**)
to increase the power, value, or reputation of a person or thing.

**booster** *noun* (**boosters**)
1 something that increases the power of a system, expecially a radio or television transmitter. 2 an additional engine or rocket for a spacecraft, etc. 3 an additional dose of a vaccine.

**boot** *noun* (**boots**)
1 a shoe that covers the ankle or leg. 2 (in America, *trunk*) the compartment for luggage in a car.
**the boot is on the other foot,** the situation has been reversed.

**booth** *noun* (**booths**)
a small enclosure for telephoning, voting, etc.

**border** *noun* (**borders**)
1 a boundary, *the Scottish border.* 2 an edge, *There is a black border around the poster.* 3 a flower-bed.

**borderline** *noun* (**borderlines**)
a boundary.

**bore**[1] *verb* (**bores, boring, bored**)
1 to drill a hole. 2 to make someone feel tired and uninterested, *The politician bored the audience.*

**bore**[2] *noun* (**bores**)
1 a person who makes you feel tired and uninterested. 2 something uninteresting or annoying.
**boredom** *noun*

**bore**[3] past tense of **bear** *verb.*

**born** or **borne** past participle of **bear** *verb.*

USAGE: **born** is used in sentences such as *Their son was born on the 17th of December. Their second child will have been born by now.* **borne** is used in sentences like *She has borne three children.*

**borough** *noun* (**boroughs**)
(*say* **bu**-rŏ)
an important town or district.

**borrow** *verb* (**borrows, borrowing, borrowed**)
to be lent something.

**Borstal** *noun* (**Borstals**)
a place where, in the past, young people who had broken the law were sent.

**bosom** *noun* (**bosoms**)
a person's breast.

**boss** *noun* (**bosses**)
(*informal*) a person who controls a business, workers, etc.

**bossy** *adjective* (**bossier, bossiest**)
fond of ordering people about.

**botany** *noun*
the study of plants.
**botanical** *adjective*, **botanist** *noun*

**both**[1] *adjective* and *pronoun*
the two; not only one, *Are both films good? Both are interesting.*

**both**[2] *adverb*
**both ... and,** not only ... but also, *This house is both small and ugly.*

**bother**[1] *verb* (**bothers, bothering, bothered**)
1 to cause someone trouble or worry. 2 to take trouble about something; to be concerned. 3 (*informal*) damn!, *Oh, bother! I've forgotten my coat.*

**bother**[2] *noun* (**bothers**)
   trouble or worry.

**bottle**[1] *noun* (**bottles**)
   a narrow-necked container for liquids.

**bottle**[2] *verb* (**bottles, bottling, bottled**)
   to put something in a bottle or bottles.

**bottle bank** *noun* (**bottle banks**)
   a container in which used glass bottles and
   jars are collected for recycling.

**bottleneck** *noun* (**bottlenecks**)
   a place where something, especially traffic,
   cannot flow freely.

**bottom** *noun* (**bottoms**)
   **1** the base of something. **2** the farthest part
   of something, *Go to the bottom of the
   garden.* **3** a person's buttocks.

**bottomless** *adjective*
   **1** very deep. **2** inexhaustible, *a bottomless
   purse.*

**bough** *noun* (**boughs**)
   (rhymes with *cow*)
   a branch of a tree.

**bought** past tense and past participle of **buy**
   *verb.*

**boulder** *noun* (**boulders**)
   a large smooth stone.

**bounce**[1] *verb* (**bounces, bouncing, bounced**)
   **1** to spring back when thrown against
   something. **2** to make a ball, etc. bounce.
   **3** to move to and fro; to jump about. **4** (of a
   cheque) to be sent back by a bank because
   it is worthless.

**bounce**[2] *noun* (**bounces**)
   **1** the action of bouncing. **2** liveliness.
   **bouncy** *adjective*

**bouncing** *adjective*
   big and healthy, *a bouncing baby.*

**bound**[1] past tense and past participle of **bind**
   *verb.*

**bound**[2] *adjective*
   **bound for,** travelling towards, *This train is
   bound for London.*
   **bound to,** certain to; obliged to, *He is bound
   to come.*
   **bound up with,** closely connected with, *His
   illness is bound up with smoking.*

**bound**[3] *verb* (**bounds, bounding, bounded**)
   to leap; to run with leaping steps.

**bound**[4] *noun* (**bounds**)
   a bounding movement.

**boundary** *noun* (**boundaries**)
   **1** a line that marks a limit. **2** a hit to the
   outer edge of a cricket field.

**bounds** *plural noun*
   a boundary, *beyond the bounds of common
   sense.*
   **out of bounds,** where you are not allowed to
   go, *The teachers' car park is out of bounds
   to pupils.*

**bouquet** *noun* (**bouquets**)
   (*say* boo-**kay** or boh-**kay**)
   a bunch of flowers.

**bout** *noun* (**bouts**)
   (*say* bowt)
   **1** a period of illness, *I've just had a bout of
   flu.* **2** a contest at boxing or wrestling.

**boutique** *noun* (**boutiques**)
   (*say* boo-**teek**)
   a small shop, especially one that sells
   fashionable clothes.

**bow**[1] *noun* (**bows**)
   (rhymes with *go*)
   **1** a knot made with loops. **2** the stick used
   for playing a violin, cello, etc. **3** a device for
   shooting arrows.
   **bow-legged,** bandy.
   **bow-tie,** a necktie tied in a bow.

**bow**[2] *noun* (**bows**)
   (rhymes with *cow*)
   the front part of a ship.

**bow**[3] *noun* (**bows**)
   (rhymes with *cow*)
   bowing your body, *The waiter gave a bow.*

**bow**[4] *verb* (**bows, bowing, bowed**)
   (rhymes with *cow*)
   to bend your body forwards to show respect
   or submission, *He bowed to the Queen.*

**bowels** *plural noun*
   the intestines.

**bowl**[1] *noun* (**bowls**)
   **1** a deep, round dish. **2** the rounded part of
   a spoon, etc. **3** a wooden or hard rubber ball
   used in the game of bowls.

**bowl**[2] *verb* (**bowls, bowling, bowled**)
   (*in cricket*) **1** to send a ball towards a
   batsman. **2** to get a batsman out by hitting
   the wicket with the ball.

**bowler** *noun* (**bowlers**)
   **1** someone who bowls in cricket. **2** a hard
   felt hat with a rounded top.

**bowling** *noun*
   **1** the game of bowls. **2** the game of
   knocking down skittles with a ball. **3** the
   action of throwing a cricket ball.

**bowls** *plural noun*
a game played by rolling heavy balls towards a target.

**box**¹ *noun* (**boxes**)
1 a container made of wood, cardboard, etc. 2 a compartment in a theatre, lawcourt, etc., *witness-box*. 3 a hut or shelter, *sentry-box*. 4 a slap on the ear. 5 an evergreen shrub.
**box number,** a number to show where answers should be sent to a newspaper advertisement, etc.
**box-office,** a place where you can book seats for a theatre, cinema, etc.
**the box,** (*informal*) television.

**box**² *verb* (**boxes, boxing, boxed**)
1 to fight with fists. 2 to put into a box.

**boxer** *noun* (**boxers**)
1 someone who boxes. 2 a breed of dog that looks like a bulldog.

**Boxing Day** *noun* (**Boxing Days**)
the first weekday after Christmas Day.

**boy** *noun* (**boys**)
1 a young male person. 2 a son, *My boy's just learned to sail.*
**boyhood** *noun,* **boyish** *adjective*

**boycott** *verb* (**boycotts, boycotting, boycotted**)
to refuse to have anything to do with, *They boycotted the buses when the fares went up.*

**boyfriend** *noun* (**boyfriends**)
a girl's or woman's regular male friend or lover.

**bra** *noun* (**bras**)
(*informal*) a brassière.

**brace** *noun* (**braces**)
1 a device for holding something in place. 2 a wire device for straightening your teeth.
**braces** (in America, *suspenders*) straps worn over your shoulders to hold trousers up.

**bracelet** *noun* (**bracelets**)
an ornament worn round the wrist.

**bracken** *noun*
1 a large fern. 2 a mass of large ferns.

**bracket** *noun* (**brackets**)
1 a mark used in pairs to enclose words or figures, *There are round brackets ( ) and square brackets [ ].* 2 a support attached to a wall, etc., *Shelves can be fixed on brackets.*

**brag** *verb* (**brags, bragging, bragged**)
to boast.

**braid** *noun* (**braids**)
1 a plait. 2 a decorative band of cloth.

**braille** *noun*
a system of writing or printing which blind people can read by touch.

**brain** *noun* (**brains**)
1 the part inside the top of the head that controls the body. 2 the mind or intelligence, *They haven't much brain.*

**brainy** *adjective* (**brainier, brainiest**)
intelligent, *She's the brainiest child in the school.*

**brake** *noun* (**brakes**)
a device for stopping or slowing down something.

**bramble** *noun* (**brambles**)
a blackberry bush or a prickly bush like it.

**branch**¹ *noun* (**branches**)
1 a part that sticks out from the trunk of a tree. 2 part of a railway, river, road, etc. that leads off from the main part. 3 part of a large organization.

**branch**² *verb* (**branches, branching, branched**)
to form a branch.
**branch out,** to start something new.

**brand**¹ *noun* (**brands**)
1 a particular kind of goods, *a cheap brand of tea.* 2 a mark made by branding, *Brands are used on cattle to show who owns them.*

**brand**² *verb* (**brands, branding, branded**)
to mark cattle, sheep, etc. with a hot iron.

**brandish** *verb* (**brandishes, brandishing, brandished**)
to wave something about.

**brand-new** *adjective*
completely new.

**brandy** *noun* (**brandies**)
a kind of strong alcoholic drink.

**brass** *noun* (**brasses**)
1 an alloy made from copper and zinc.
2 wind instruments made of brass, such as trumpets and trombones.
**brass band,** a group of people playing brass wind instruments.
**brass-rubbing,** making a picture by rubbing a piece of paper laid over a brass memorial tablet on a tomb; a picture made in this way.

**brassière** *noun* (**brassières**)
(*say* braz-i-er)
a piece of underwear worn by women to support their breasts.

**brassy** *adjective* (**brassier, brassiest**)
1 coloured like brass. 2 loud and harsh, *a brassy laugh.* 3 impudent and showy, *a wealthy but brassy young man.*

**brave**[1] *adjective* (**braver, bravest**)
not afraid; ready to face danger, pain, etc.
**bravery** *noun*

**brave**[2] *noun* (**braves**)
a Native American warrior.

**brawl** *noun* (**brawls**)
a noisy quarrel or fight.

**brawn** *noun*
1 muscular strength. 2 a food made of cold pork or veal pressed in a mould.

**brawny** *adjective* (**brawnier, brawniest**)
having strong muscles.

**bray** *verb* (**brays, braying, brayed**)
to make a noise like a donkey.

**brazen** *adjective*
1 made of brass. 2 shameless, *brazen impudence.*

**brazier** *noun* (**braziers**)
(*say* bray-zi-er)
a metal container holding hot coals.

**breach** *noun* (**breaches**)
1 the breaking of an agreement, rule, etc.
2 a gap.

**bread** *noun*
1 food made by baking flour and water, usually with yeast. 2 (*slang*) money.

**breadth** *noun* (**breadths**)
width.

**breadwinner** *noun* (**breadwinners**)
someone who earns the money for a family.

**break**[1] *verb* (**breaks, breaking, broke, broken**)
1 to divide into two or more pieces by hitting, pressing, etc. 2 to stop working properly, *My watch has broken.* 3 to stop or end, *She broke her silence.* 4 to fail to keep a promise, law, etc. 5 to change, *After a sunny week, the weather broke.* 6 (of waves) to fall and scatter, *The waves were breaking over the rocks.* 7 to go suddenly or with force, *They broke through the enemy's defences.* 8 (of a boy's voice) to become deeper, when a boy is around 14 years old. 9 to get or come, *break away. break loose. break open.*
**break a record,** to do better than anyone has done before.
**break down,** to stop working properly; to collapse, *The machine broke down. The peace talks broke down.*
**break off,** to detach something; to stop, *We broke off, and restarted work an hour later.*
**break out,** to start suddenly.
**break the news,** to make something known.
**break up,** to split up; to reach the end of a school term, *Emma and her boyfriend have broken up. We break up next Friday.*

**break**[2] *noun* (**breaks**)
1 a broken place; a gap. 2 a sudden dash.
3 a short rest from work. 4 (*informal*) a piece of luck; a fair chance, *Give me a break.*
**break of day,** dawn.

**breakable** *adjective*
easily broken, *Be careful with that box — there are breakable things in it.*

**breakage** *noun* (**breakages**)
a broken thing, *All breakages must be paid for.*

**break-dancing** *noun*
a style of energetic dancing in which the dancers often spin round on their backs, elbows, or heads.

**breakdown** *noun* (**breakdowns**)
1 a collapse or failure, *a nervous breakdown.* 2 dividing something up into parts to make it easier to understand, *a breakdown of the accounts.*

**breaker** *noun* (**breakers**)
a wave breaking on the shore.

**breakfast** *noun* (**breakfasts**)
the first meal of the day.

**breakneck** *adjective*
dangerously fast, *He drove at breakneck speed.*

**breakthrough** *noun* (**breakthroughs**)
an important advance or achievement.

**breakwater** *noun* (**breakwaters**)
a wall built out into the sea to protect a harbour or coast against heavy waves.

**breast** *noun* (**breasts**)
1 one of the parts of a woman's body where milk is produced. 2 a person's or animal's chest.
**breast-stroke**, a way of swimming on your chest.

**breath** *noun* (**breaths**)
(*say* breth)
the air that someone breathes.
**out of breath**, panting.
**take someone's breath away**, to surprise or delight someone.

**breathalyser** *noun* (**breathalysers**)
a device to measure the amount of alcohol in someone's breath.
**breathalyse** *verb*

**breathe** *verb* (**breathes, breathing, breathed**)
(*say* bree*th*)
1 to take air into your lungs through your nose or mouth and send it out again. 2 to speak, *Don't breathe a word of this.*

USAGE: Do not confuse **breathe** with **breath**, which is a noun.

**breather** *noun* (**breathers**)
a pause for rest, *Let's have a breather.*

**breathless** *adjective*
short of breath.

**breathtaking** *adjective*
surprising or delightful.

**bred** past tense and past participle of **breed** *verb*.

**breech** *noun* (**breeches**)
the part of a gun barrel where the bullets are put in.

**breeches** *plural noun*
(*say* brich-iz)
trousers, especially trousers that fit tightly at the knee.

**breed**¹ *verb* (**breeds, breeding, bred**)
1 to produce offspring. 2 to keep animals so as to get young ones from them. 3 to create, *Poverty breeds illness.* 4 to train and produce, *Hollywood breeds film stars.*

**breed**² *noun* (**breeds**)
a variety of similar animals, *a Scottish Fold is a breed of cat.*

**breeder** *noun* (**breeders**)
someone who breeds animals.
**breeder reactor**, a nuclear reactor that creates more radioactive material than it uses.

**breeze** *noun* (**breezes**)
a gentle wind.
**breezy** *adjective*

**breeze-block** *noun* (**breeze-blocks**)
a lightweight building-block made of cinders and cement.

**brethren** *plural noun*
(*old-fashioned use*) brothers.

**brevity** *noun*
being brief or short.

**brew** *verb* (**brews, brewing, brewed**)
1 to make beer or tea. 2 to start or develop, *Trouble is brewing.*

**brewery** *noun* (**breweries**)
a place where beer is made.
**brewer** *noun*

**briar** *noun* (**briars**)
a brier.

**bribe**¹ *noun* (**bribes**)
money or a gift offered to someone to influence him or her.

**bribe**² *verb* (**bribes, bribing, bribed**)
to give someone a bribe.
**bribery** *noun*

**brick** *noun* (**bricks**)
1 a small, hard block of baked clay, etc. used in building. 2 a rectangular block of something, *a brick of ice-cream.*

**bricklayer** *noun* (**bricklayers**)
a worker who builds with bricks.

**bride** *noun* (**brides**)
a woman on her wedding-day.
**bridal** *adjective*

**bridegroom** *noun* (**bridegroom**)
a man on his wedding-day.

**bridesmaid** *noun* (**bridesmaids**)
a girl or unmarried woman who attends the bride at a wedding.

**bridge** *noun* (**bridges**)
1 a structure built over a river, railway, or road, to allow people to cross it. 2 the high platform above a ship's deck, from where the ship is controlled. 3 the bony upper part of your nose. 4 a card-game rather like whist.

**bridle** *noun* (**bridles**)
the part of a horse's harness that controls its head.
**bridle-path**, **bridle-road**, or **bridle-way**, a path suitable for horses but not vehicles.

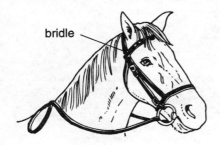

bridle

**brief**[1] *adjective* (**briefer**, **briefest**)
lasting a short time.
**in brief**, in a few words.

**brief**[2] *noun* (**briefs**)
instructions and information, especially given to a barrister.

**briefcase** *noun* (**briefcases**)
a flat case for documents, papers, etc.

**briefs** *plural noun*
very short knickers or underpants.

**brier** *noun* (**briers**)
1 a thorny bush, especially a wild rose-bush. 2 a hard root used especially for making tobacco-pipes.

**brigade** *noun* (**brigades**)
1 an army unit usually consisting of three battalions. 2 a group of people in uniform, *the fire brigade*.

**brigadier** *noun* (**brigadiers**)
an officer who commands a brigade and is higher in rank than a colonel.

**brigand** *noun* (**brigands**)
an outlaw, expecially one who robs travellers in wild country.

**bright** *adjective* (**brighter**, **brightest**)
1 giving a strong light; shining. 2 clever, *He's a bright lad*. 3 cheerful.

**brighten** *verb* (**brightens**, **brightening**, **brightened**)
to make or become bright.

**brilliant** *adjective*
1 very bright. 2 very clever. 3 (*informal*) really good or enjoyable, *That was a brilliant film!*
**brilliance** *noun*

**brim** *noun* (**brims**)
1 the edge round the top of a container. 2 the projecting edge of a hat.

**brimming** *adjective*
full.
**brimming over**, overflowing.

**brine** *noun*
salt water.

**bring** *verb* (**brings**, **bringing**, **brought**)
to make someone or something come; to lead or carry here.
**bring about**, to cause something to happen.
**bring off**, to achieve something.
**bring round**, to make someone conscious again after he or she has fainted.
**bring up**, to look after and educate a child.

**brink** *noun* (**brinks**)
the edge of a steep or dangerous place.

**brisk** *adjective* (**brisker**, **briskest**)
quick and lively.

**bristle** *noun* (**bristles**)
a short, stiff hair.
**bristly** *adjective*

**British** *adjective*
of Great Britain.

**Briton** *noun* (**Britons**)
someone born in Great Britain.

**brittle** *adjective* (**brittler**, **brittlest**)
likely to break or snap.

**broad** *adjective* (**broader**, **broadest**)
1 wide. 2 complete; full, *in broad daylight*. 3 not detailed, *a broad outline*.
**broad bean**, a large flat bean.

**broadcast**[1] *noun* (**broadcasts**)
a radio or television programme.

**broadcast**[2] *verb* (**broadcasts**, **broadcasting**, **broadcast**)
to transmit or take part in a radio or television programme.
**broadcaster** *noun*

**broaden** *verb* (**broadens**, **broadening**, **broadened**)
to make something broader; to become broader.

**broad-minded** *adjective*
tolerant, especially in moral matters.

**broadside** *noun* (**broadsides**)
firing by all the guns on one side of a ship.

**brochure** *noun* (**brochures**)
a pamphlet containing information, especially about a place.

**brogue** *noun* (**brogues**)
1 a strong kind of shoe. 2 a strong accent, *He spoke with an Irish brogue*.

**broil** *verb* (**broils**, **broiling**, **broiled**)
1 to cook on a fire or grid. 2 to make something or someone very hot; to be very hot.

**broke**[1] past tense of **break** *verb*.

**broke**[2] *adjective*
(*informal*) bankrupt.

**broken**[1] past participle of **break** *verb*.

**broken**[2] *adjective*
badly spoken, *The visitor spoke in broken English.*
**broken-hearted,** very sad.
**broken home,** a home where the parents have separated.

**broker** *noun* (**brokers**)
someone who buys and sells things for other people.

**bronchitis** *noun*
(*say* brong-**ky**-tiss)
a disease of the lungs.

**bronze** *noun*
1 an alloy of copper and tin. 2 a yellowish-brown colour.
**bronze medal,** a medal made of bronze, usually awarded as the third prize.

**Bronze Age** *noun*
the time in history when tools and weapons were made of bronze.

**brooch** *noun* (**brooches**)
(rhymes with *coach*)
an ornament pinned on to clothes.

**brood**[1] *noun* (**broods**)
young birds that were hatched together.

**brood**[2] *verb* (**broods, brooding, brooded**)
1 to sit on eggs to hatch them. 2 to keep thinking about something, especially resentfully.

**broody** *adjective* (**broodier, broodiest**)
1 (of a hen) wanting to hatch her eggs.
2 thinking constantly about something, especially resentfully. 3 (*informal*) (of a woman) wanting to have a baby.

**brook** *noun* (**brooks**)
a small stream.

**broom** *noun* (**brooms**)
1 a brush with a long handle, for sweeping. 2 a shrub with yellow, white, or pink flowers.

broom 1

**broomstick** *noun* (**broomsticks**)
1 the handle of a broom. 2 a broom ridden upon by witches in stories.

**broth** *noun* (**broths**)
a thin soup.

**brother** *noun* (**brothers**)
a man or boy who has the same parents as another person.
**brotherly** *adjective*

**brother-in-law** *noun* (**brothers-in-law**)
the brother of your husband or wife; the husband of your sister.

**brought** past tense and past participle of **bring**.

**brow** *noun* (**brows**)
1 the forehead. 2 an eyebrow. 3 the top of a hill or the edge of a cliff.

**brown** *adjective* (**browner, brownest**)
1 of the colour of earth or toast, *Brown bread is often made from wholemeal flour.*
2 suntanned.

**Brownie** *noun* (**Brownies**)
a junior Guide.
**brownie,** (*in America*) a small chocolate cake with nuts.

**browse** *verb* (**browses, browsing, browsed**)
1 to feed on grass or leaves. 2 to read or look at something casually.

**bruise**[1] *noun* (**bruises**)
a dark mark on skin made by hitting it.

**bruise**[2] *verb* (**bruises, bruising, bruised**)
to give someone a bruise; to get a bruise.

**brunette** *noun* (**brunettes**)
a woman with dark brown or black hair.

**brush**[1] *noun* (**brushes**)
1 a device for sweeping, scrubbing, painting, etc. 2 a fox's bushy tail.

**brush**[2] *verb* (**brushes, brushing, brushed**)
1 to use a brush on something, *Have you brushed your hair?* 2 to touch someone or something gently.
**brush something up,** to refresh your knowledge of something.

**Brussels sprout** *noun* (**Brussels sprouts**)
a small green vegetable.

**brutal** *adjective*
coarse and cruel.
**brutality** *noun*, **brutalize** *verb*, **brutally** *adverb*

**brute** *noun* (**brutes**)
1 a brutal person. 2 an animal.

**bubble** *noun* (**bubbles**)
1 a thin transparent ball of liquid filled with air or gas. 2 a small ball of air in a liquid or a solid.
**bubble gum,** chewing-gum that you can blow up into bubbles.

**bubbly** *adjective* (**bubblier, bubbliest**)
1 full of bubbles, *Soda water is bubbly.*
2 lively, *a girl with a bubbly personality.*

**buccaneer** *noun* (**buccaneers**)
a pirate.

**buck**[1] *noun* (**bucks**)
a male deer, rabbit, or hare.

**buck**[2] *verb* (**bucks, bucking, bucked**)
(of a horse) to jump with the back arched.
**buck up,** (*informal*) to hurry.

**bucket** *noun* (**buckets**)
a container with a handle, for carrying liquids, etc.

**bucketful** *noun* (**bucketfuls**)
as much of something as you can carry in a bucket.

**buckle**[1] *noun* (**buckles**)
a fastener for a belt or strap.

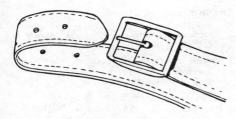

**buckle**[2] *verb* (**buckles, buckling, buckled**)
1 to fasten with a buckle. 2 to crumple, *His knees buckled.*
**buckle down,** to start work, *I must buckle down to this job.*

**bud** *noun* (**buds**)
a flower or leaf before it has opened.

**Buddhism** *noun*
(*say* **buud**-izm)
a religion that started in Asia and follows the teachings of Buddha.
**Buddhist** *noun*

**budding** *adjective*
developing well, *a budding singer.*

**budge** *verb* (**budges, budging, budged**)
to move slightly, *This door is stuck – it won't budge.*

**budgerigar** *noun* (**budgerigars**)
(*say* **bud**-jer-i-gar)
an Australian bird often kept as a pet in a cage.

**budget**[1] *noun* (**budgets**)
1 the money available for a particular purpose. 2 a plan for spending money wisely.

**budget**[2] *verb* (**budgets, budgeting, budgeted**)
to plan a budget.

**budgie** *noun* (**budgies**)
(*informal*) a budgerigar.

**buff** *adjective*
of a dull yellow colour.

**buffalo** *noun* (**buffalo** or **buffaloes**)
a wild ox.

**buffer** *noun* (**buffers**)
1 something that softens a blow, especially a device on a railway engine or wagon or at the end of a railway line. 2 (*in Computing*) a memory in which data can be stored temporarily, especially while being sent from one device to another.

**buffet** *noun* (**buffets**)
(*say* **buu**-fay)
1 a refreshment counter. 2 a meal where guests serve themselves.

**bug**[1] *noun* (**bugs**)
1 an insect. 2 (*informal*) a germ or microbe. 3 (*informal*) a secret hidden microphone. 4 a fault in something, especially a computer program.

**bug**[2] *verb* (**bugs, bugging, bugged**)
1 (*informal*) to fit with a secret hidden microphone. 2 (*slang*) to annoy.

**bugle** *noun* (**bugles**)
(*say* **byoo**-gŭl)
a brass instrument like a small trumpet.
**bugler** *noun*

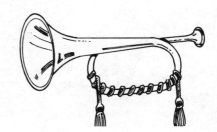

**build**[1] *noun* (**builds**)
the shape of a person's body, *of slender build*.

**build**[2] *verb* (**builds, building, built**)
to make something by putting parts together.
**build in,** to include, *a sink unit with cupboards built in*.
**build up,** to accumulate or increase; to cover an area with buildings; to make stronger or more famous, *A backlog of work has built up. All the fields around the village have been built up. Exercise regularly to build up your health*.

**builder** *noun* (**builders**)
someone who puts up buildings.

**building** *noun* (**buildings**)
1 constructing houses, etc. 2 something built, such as a house or a block of flats.

**building society** *noun* (**building societies**)
an organization that lends money to people who want to buy houses.

**built-in** *adjective*
being a permanent part of a building; included, *built-in kitchen units. The hire-purchase agreement has built-in insurance*.

**built-up** *adjective*
densely covered with houses and other buildings, *a built-up area*.

**bulb** *noun* (**bulbs**)
1 a glass globe with a wire inside to produce electric light. 2 something that looks like an onion, planted in the ground to produce daffodils, tulips, etc.

**bulge**[1] *noun* (**bulges**)
a swelling.
**bulgy** *adjective*

**bulge**[2] *verb* (**bulges, bulging, bulged**)
to swell.

**bulk** *noun* (**bulks**)
1 the size of something, especially when it is large. 2 the majority, *The bulk of the work is done*.
**in bulk,** in large quantities.
**bulky** *adjective*

**bull** *noun* (**bulls**)
a male animal (used in speaking of cattle, elephants, or whales).

**bulldog** *noun* (**bulldogs**)
a breed of dog with a short, thick neck.

**bulldozer** *noun* (**bulldozers**)
a heavy vehicle with tracks, with a wide metal blade in front, used to clear or flatten land.
**bulldoze** *verb*

**bullet** *noun* (**bullets**)
a small lump of metal shot from a rifle or pistol.

**bulletin** *noun* (**bulletins**)
an announcement of news.

**bulletproof** *adjective*
able to stop bullets.

**bullfight** *noun* (**bullfights**)
a contest between men and bulls, done as a public entertainment.
**bullfighter** *noun*, **bullfighting** *noun*

**bullion** *noun*
bars of gold or silver.

**bullock** *noun* (**bullocks**)
a young bull.

**bull's-eye** *noun* (**bull's-eyes**)
1 the centre of a target. 2 a hard peppermint sweet.

**bully**[1] *verb* (**bullies, bullying, bullied**)
1 to hurt or frighten a weaker person. 2 to start play in hockey, *bully off*.

**bully**[2] *noun* (**bullies**)
1 someone who bullies people. 2 starting play in hockey.

**bulrush** *noun* (**bulrushes**)
a tall rush with a soft, thick head.

**bulwark** *noun* (**bulwarks**)
(*say* **buul**-werk)
a defending wall; a defence, *a bulwark against inflation*.
**bulwarks,** a ship's side above the level of the deck.

**bum** *noun* (**bums**)
(*slang*) **1** a person's bottom. **2** (*in America*) a
tramp.

**bumble-bee** *noun* (**bumble-bees**)
a large bee.

**bump**[1] *verb* (**bumps, bumping, bumped**)
**1** to knock against something. **2** to move
along with jolts, *The cart bumped along the
road.*
**bump into someone,** (*informal*) to meet
someone unexpectedly.
**bump someone off,** (*slang*) to kill someone.

**bump**[2] *noun* (**bumps**)
**1** the action of bumping. **2** a swelling or
lump.
**bumpy** *adjective*

**bumper**[1] *noun* (**bumpers**)
**1** a bar along the front or back of a motor
vehicle to protect it in collisions. **2** a ball in
cricket that bounces high.

**bumper**[2] *adjective*
unusually large; excellent, *a bumper crop
of potatoes.*

**bun** *noun* (**buns**)
**1** a small cake. **2** a round bunch of hair at
the back of a woman's head.

**bunch** *noun* (**bunches**)
a number of things joined or tied together,
*a bunch of bananas.*

**bundle**[1] *noun* (**bundles**)
a number of things tied or wrapped
together.

**bundle**[2] *verb* (**bundles, bundling, bundled**)
**1** to tie or wrap things up together. **2** to put
hurriedly or carelessly, *They bundled him
into a taxi.*

**bung**[1] *verb* (**bungs, bunging, bunged**)
(*slang*) to throw, *Bung that pencil over
here.*
**bunged up,** (*informal*) blocked.

**bung**[2] *noun* (**bungs**)
a stopper, *Put the bung in that barrel.*

**bungalow** *noun* (**bungalows**)
a house without any upstairs rooms.

**bungle** *verb* (**bungles, bungling, bungled**)
to do something unsuccessfully or clumsily.
**bungler** *noun*

**bunk** *noun* (**bunks**)
a bed like a shelf, as on a ship.
**bunk beds,** two single beds, joined one
above the other.
**do a bunk,** (*slang*) to run away.

**bunker** *noun* (**bunkers**)
**1** a container for storing fuel. **2** a sand-filled
hollow made as an obstacle on a
golf-course. **3** an underground shelter.

**bunny** *noun* (**bunnies**)
(*informal*) a rabbit.

**Bunsen burner** *noun* (**Bunsen burners**)
a device that uses gas to make a flame for
scientific experiments, etc.

**buoy** *noun* (**buoys**)
(*say* boi)
an anchored floating object used to mark a
channel, shallow water, etc.

**buoyant** *adjective*
**1** able to float. **2** cheerful, *He was in a
buoyant mood.*
**buoyancy** *noun*

**bur** *noun* (**burs**)
part of a plant that clings to your clothes or
hair.

**burden** *noun* (**burdens**)
**1** a heavy load. **2** something hard to put up
with.
**burdensome** *adjective*

**bureau** *noun* (**bureaux**)
(*say* **bewr**-oh)
**1** a writing-desk. **2** an office or department,
*They will tell you at the Information
Bureau.*

**burette** *noun* (**burettes**)
(*in Science*) a tube with a tap at one end,
used for measuring exact amounts of liquid.

**burglar** *noun* (**burglars**)
someone who breaks into a building to
steal things.
**burglary** *noun*, **burgle** *verb*

**burial** *noun* (**burials**)
burying someone.

**burly** *adjective* (**burlier, burliest**)
big and strong.
**burliness** *noun*

**burn**[1] *verb* (**burns, burning, burnt or burned**)
**1** to damage or destroy something with fire
or heat. **2** to be damaged or destroyed by
fire or heat. **3** to be on fire. **4** to feel very
hot.
**burn up,** to destroy or be destroyed by
burning.

**burn**[2] *noun* (**burns**)
**1** an injury caused by fire or heat. **2** the
firing of a spacecraft's rocket.

**burn**[3] *noun* (**burns**)
(*in Scotland*) a small stream.

**burner** *noun* (**burners**)
the part of a lamp or cooker that shapes
the flame.

**burning** *adjective*
**1** intense, *a burning desire.* **2** hotly
discussed, *a burning question.*

**butterfly**

**burp**[1] *noun* (**burps**)
(*informal*) a belch.

**burp**[2] *verb* (**burps, burping, burped**)
(*informal*) to belch.

**burrow**[1] *noun* (**burrows**)
a hole dug by a rabbit, fox, etc.

**burrow**[2] *verb* (**burrows, burrowing, burrowed**)
1 to dig a burrow. 2 to dig or search deeply,
*He burrowed in his pockets.*

**burst**[1] *verb* (**bursts, bursting, burst**)
1 to break apart. 2 to start something
suddenly, *He burst out laughing and she
burst into tears.* 3 to be very full, excited,
etc., *bursting with energy.*
**burst in,** to rush in.

**burst**[2] *noun* (**bursts**)
1 a split, *There's a burst in one of the pipes.*
2 something short and forceful, *a burst of
gunfire.*

**bury** *verb* (**buries, burying, buried**)
to put a person or thing under the ground.
**bury the hatchet,** to stop quarrelling or
fighting.

**bus** *noun* (**buses**)
a large vehicle for passengers to travel in.
**bus-stop,** a place where a bus regularly
stops.

**bush** *noun* (**bushes**)
a plant like a small tree with many stems
or branches.
**the bush,** wild land, especially in Australia
or Africa.
**bushy** *adjective*

**busily** *adverb*
in a busy way.

**business** *noun* (**businesses**)
(*say* biz-niss)
1 a person's occupation, *My business is
publishing.* 2 a person's concerns or
responsibilities, *Mind your own business.*
3 serious work or discussion, *We had better
get down to business.* 4 an affair or subject,
*I am tired of the whole business.* 5 buying
and selling, *She has made a career in
business.* 6 a shop or firm.

**businesslike** *adjective*
efficient and practical.

**busker** *noun* (**buskers**)
someone who entertains in the street,
especially by playing music.

**bust**[1] *noun* (**busts**)
1 a woman's bosom. 2 a sculpture of a
person's head and shoulders.

**bust**[2] *adjective*
(*informal*) 1 broken or burst. 2 bankrupt.

**bustle** *verb* (**bustles, bustling, bustled**)
to hurry or be very busy.

**busy** *adjective* (**busier, busiest**)
1 doing a lot; having much to do. 2 full of
activity, *a busy street.* 3 (of a telephone
line) already being used.

**busybody** *noun* (**busybodies**)
someone who interferes.

**but**[1] *conjunction*
however; nevertheless, *I wanted to go but I
couldn't.*

**but**[2] *preposition*
except, *There's no one here but me.*

**butane** *noun*
(*say* bew-tayn)
a gas used as fuel.

**butcher** *noun* (**butchers**)
1 someone who cuts up meat and sells it.
2 a cruel murderer.

**butchery** *noun* (**butcheries**)
needless or cruel killing.

**butler** *noun* (**butlers**)
a male servant in charge of other servants.

**butt**[1] *noun* (**butts**)
1 the thicker end of a weapon or tool. 2 a
large barrel. 3 someone who is often
ridiculed, *Why is he always the butt of your
jokes?*

**butt**[2] *verb* (**butts, butting, butted**)
1 to hit someone or something with your
head. 2 to place the edges of things
together.
**butt in,** to interrupt or intrude.

**butter** *noun*
a fatty yellow food made from cream.

**buttercup** *noun* (**buttercups**)
a yellow wild flower.

**butter-fingers** *noun* (**butter-fingers**)
someone who often drops things.

**butterfly** *noun* (**butterflies**)
1 an insect with large white or coloured
wings. 2 a swimming stroke in which you
raise both arms together.

**butterscotch** *noun* (**butterscotches**)
a kind of hard toffee.

**buttocks** *plural noun*
the part of the body on which a person sits.

**button**[1] *noun* (**buttons**)
1 a fastener sewn on clothes. 2 a small knob, *She pressed the button to ring the bell.*

**button**[2] *verb* (**buttons, buttoning, buttoned**)
**button up,** to fasten something with a button or buttons; to be fastened in this way, *Button up your coat. This jacket buttons up at the front.*

**buttonhole**[1] *noun* (**buttonholes**)
1 a slit for a button to pass through. 2 a flower worn on a lapel.

**buttonhole**[2] *verb* (**buttonholes, buttonholing, buttonholed**)
to stop someone so that you can talk to him or her.

**buttress** *noun* (**buttresses**)
a support built against a wall.

**buy**[1] *verb* (**buys, buying, bought**)
1 to get something by paying for it, *I bought these sweets yesterday.* 2 (*slang*) to accept; to believe, *Nobody will buy that excuse.*
**buyer** *noun*

**buy**[2] *noun* (**buys**)
a purchase.

**buzz**[1] *noun* (**buzzes**)
1 a vibrating humming sound. 2 (*informal*) a pleasant, exciting feeling, *I really get a buzz from cycling.*

**buzz**[2] *verb* (**buzzes, buzzing, buzzed**)
to make a buzz.
**buzz off,** (*slang*) to go away.
**buzzer** *noun*

**buzzard** *noun* (**buzzards**)
a bird of prey like a large hawk.

**by**[1] *preposition*
1 near; beside, *Sit by me.* 2 through; along, *You can reach it by the path.* 3 using; by means of, *cooking by gas.* 4 before, *Do your homework by tomorrow.* 5 past, *She went by the window.* 6 during, *They came by night.* 7 according to, *Don't judge by appearances.*
**by the way,** incidentally; on a different subject.

**by**[2] *adverb*
1 past, *I can't get by.* 2 for future use, *Put some money by for the holidays.*
**by and by,** soon; later on, *We'll pass Hyde Park by and by – in fact, there it is now. By and by, Algy turned up.*
**by and large,** on the whole.

**bye** *noun* (**byes**)
a run scored in cricket when the batsman has not touched the ball.

**bye-bye** *interjection*
(*informal*) goodbye.

**by-election** *noun* (**by-elections**)
an election when an MP has died or resigned.

**bygone** *adjective*
belonging to the past, *bygone farming methods.*

**by-law** *noun* (**by-laws**)
a law which only applies to a particular town, district, etc.

**bypass** *noun* (**bypasses**)
1 a road that takes traffic past a congested area. 2 an alternative passage for blood to circulate through while a surgeon is operating on someone's heart.

**by-product** *noun* (**by-products**)
something produced while something else is being made, *Tar and coke are by-products of making gas from coal.*

**bystander** *noun* (**bystanders**)
someone standing near but taking no part when something happens.

# Cc

**C** 1 short for **centigrade**. 2 100 in Roman numerals.

**CAB** short for *Citizens' Advice Bureau*.

**cab** *noun* (**cabs**)
1 a taxi. 2 a compartment for the driver of a lorry, bus, train, or crane.

**cabaret** *noun* (**cabarets**)
(*say* kab-ă-ray)
an entertainment, especially performed in a restaurant or night-club.

**cabbage** *noun* (**cabbages**)
a round, green vegetable.

**cabin** *noun* (**cabins**)
1 a hut or shelter. 2 a compartment in a ship, aircraft, etc. 3 a driver's cab.

**cabinet** *noun* (**cabinets**)
1 a cupboard with drawers or shelves. 2 the group of chief ministers who control the government, *The Prime Minister chose a new cabinet.*

**cable** *noun* (**cables**)
1 thick rope, wire, or chain. 2 a telegram sent overseas.
**cable-car**, a kind of tram pulled by a moving wire rope, carrying people up steep hills.
**cable television**, a television system in which programmes are transmitted by wire instead of through the air.

**cackle** *noun* (**cackles**)
1 the clucking of a hen. 2 a loud, silly laugh. 3 stupid chattering.

**cactus** *noun* (**cacti**)
a fleshy plant that grows in hot, dry places.

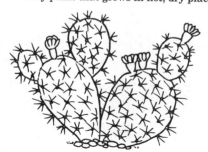

**caddie** *noun* (**caddies**)
someone who helps a golfer by carrying the clubs.

**caddy** *noun* (**caddies**)
a small container for tea-leaves.

**cadet** *noun* (**cadets**)
a young person being trained for the armed forces or the police.

**cadge** *verb* (**cadges, cadging, cadged**)
to get something by begging for it.

**café** *noun* (**cafés**)
(*say* kaf-ay)
a small restaurant.

**cafeteria** *noun* (**cafeterias**)
(*say* kaf-ĕ-teer-i-ă)
a café where the customers serve themselves from a counter.

**caffeine** *noun*
a drug found in tea and coffee which keeps you awake and makes you feel active.

**caftan** *noun* (**caftans**)
a long, loose jacket or dress, with wide sleeves.

**cage** *noun* (**cages**)
a container made of bars or wires, in which birds or animals are kept.

**cagey** *adjective* (**cagier, cagiest**)
(*informal*) cautious about giving information.

**cagoule** *noun* (**cagoules**)
a lightweight waterproof jacket.

**cake** *noun* (**cakes**)
1 a baked mixture of flour, eggs, butter, etc. 2 a flat, round lump of something, *a cake of soap. We ate fish cakes.*
**have your cake and eat it**, to enjoy two alternative good things of which you can usually only have one.
**something is a piece of cake**, (*informal*) something is very easy.

**caked** *adjective*
covered with dried mud, etc.

**calamine** *noun*
a pink powder used to make a soothing liquid to put on your skin.

**calamity** *noun* (**calamities**)
a disaster.
**calamitous** *adjective*

**calcium** *noun*
a greyish-white element contained in teeth, bones, and lime.
**calcium carbonate,** a white mineral which occurs in nature as chalk, marble, and limestone.

**calculate** *verb* (**calculates, calculating, calculated**)
1 to work out something. 2 to plan or intend something.
**calculation** *noun*

**calculator** *noun* (**calculators**)
a machine for doing sums.

**calendar** *noun* (**calendars**)
something that shows the dates of the month or year.

**calf**[1] *noun* (**calves**)
a young cow, whale, seal, etc.

**calf**[2] *noun* (**calves**)
the back part of the leg below the knee.

**calico** *noun*
cotton cloth.

**call**[1] *verb* (**calls, calling, called**)
1 to shout. 2 to telephone. 3 to tell someone to come to you. 4 to make a visit. 5 to name someone or something, *The cat is called Fluffy.* 6 to describe as, *I call that a swindle.* 7 to wake someone up.
**call it a day,** to decide that you have done enough work for one day, and stop working.
**call someone names,** to insult someone.
**call someone up,** to make someone join the armed forces.

**call**[2] *noun* (**calls**)
1 a shout or cry. 2 a short visit. 3 telephoning someone. 4 a request or invitation.
**call-box,** an enclosed place containing a telephone for the public to use.

**calling** *noun* (**callings**)
a profession or trade.

**callipers** *plural noun*
a device for measuring the width of tubes or of round objects.

**callous** *adjective*
not caring about other people's feelings; cruel.

**calm** *adjective* (**calmer, calmest**)
1 quiet and still, *a calm sea.* 2 not excited or agitated, *Please keep calm.*
**calmly** *adverb*, **calmness** *noun*

**calorie** *noun* (**calories**)
a unit for measuring an amount of heat or the energy produced by food.
**calorific** *adjective*

**calves** plural of **calf.**

**calypso** *noun* (**calypsos**)
a West Indian folk-song which is made up as the singer sings it.

**camcorder** *noun* (**camcorders**)
a video camera and sound recorder in one machine.

**came** past tense of **come.**

**camel** *noun* (**camels**)
a large animal with a long neck and one or two humps on its back, *Arabian camels have one hump, and Bactrian camels have two.*

**camera** *noun* (**cameras**)
a device for taking photographs, films, or television pictures.
**cameraman** *noun*

**camouflage** *noun*
(*say* **kam**-ŏ-flahzh)
a way of hiding things by making them look like part of their surroundings.

**camp**[1] *noun* (**camps**)
a place where people live in tents, huts, etc. for a short time.

**camp**[2] *verb* (**camps, camping, camped**)
to have a holiday in a camp; to make a camp, *Let's camp here for the night.*
**camper** *noun*

**campaign**[1] *noun* (**campaigns**)
1 a planned series of actions, especially to arouse interest in something, *a campaign for human rights.* 2 a series of battles in one area or with one aim.

**campaign**[2] *verb* (**campaigns, campaigning, campaigned**)
to carry out a planned series of actions, especially to arouse interest in something, *They are campaigning to stop the destruction of the rain forest.*

**campsite** *noun* (**campsites**)
a place for camping.

**campus** *noun* (**campuses**)
the buildings of a college or university and the land around them.

**can**[1] *verb* (*present tense* **can**; *past tense* **could**)
**1** to be able to do something; to know how to do something, *Can you lift this stone?*
**2** (*informal*) to be allowed to do something, *Can I go home?*

**can**[2] *verb* (**cans, canning, canned**)
to put in a can or cans.
**canned music,** recorded music.
**cannery** *noun*

**can**[3] *noun* (**cans**)
a metal container for food, drink, etc.
**can bank,** a place where used cans are collected for recycling.
**can-opener,** a tool for opening cans.

**Canadian** *adjective*
of Canada.

**canal** *noun* (**canals**)
**1** an artificial waterway. **2** a tube in a human's or animal's body, *The semicircular canals in your ears help you balance.*

**canary** *noun* (**canaries**)
a small yellow bird that sings.

**cancel** *verb* (**cancels, cancelling, cancelled**)
**1** to say that something planned will not be done or not take place. **2** to stop an order for something. **3** to mark a stamp, ticket, etc. so that it cannot be used again.
**cancel out,** to stop the effect of one another, *The arguments cancelled each other out.*
**cancellation** *noun*

**cancer** *noun* (**cancers**)
**1** a disease in which a harmful growth forms in your body. **2** a harmful growth in your body.

**candidate** *noun* (**candidates**)
**1** someone who wants to be elected or chosen for a particular job, position, etc.
**2** someone taking an examination.

**candle** *noun* (**candles**)
a stick of wax with a wick through it, giving light when burning.

**candlelight** *noun*
light given by a candle or candles.

**candlestick** *noun* (**candlesticks**)
a holder for a candle or candles.

**candy** *noun* (**candies**)
sweets; a sweet.

**candyfloss** *noun*
a fluffy mass of sugar that has been spun into fine threads.

**cane**[1] *noun* (**canes**)
**1** the stem of a reed or tall grass; a thin stick. **2** a thin stick used to beat someone.

**cane**[2] *verb* (**canes, caning, caned**)
to beat someone with a cane.

**canine**[1] *adjective*
of dogs.
**canine tooth,** a pointed tooth.

**canine**[2] *noun* (**canines**)
**1** a dog. **2** a canine tooth.

**cannibal** *noun* (**cannibals**)
**1** a person who eats human flesh. **2** an animal that eats animals of its own kind.
**cannibalism** *noun*

**cannon** *noun* (**cannon** or **cannons**)
a large, heavy gun.

**cannonball** *noun* (**cannonballs**)
a large ball fired from a cannon.

**cannot**
can not, *I cannot swim.*

**canoe**[1] *noun* (**canoes**)
a narrow, lightweight boat.

**canoe**[2] *verb* (**canoes, canoeing, canoed**)
to travel in a canoe.
**canoeist** *noun*

**canopy** *noun* (**canopies**)
an overhanging cover.

**can't** short for *can not*.

**canteen** *noun* (**canteens**)
**1** a restaurant for workers in a factory, office, etc. **2** a box containing a set of cutlery. **3** a soldier's or camper's water-flask or set of eating utensils.

**canter** *verb* (**canters, cantering, cantered**)
to go at a gentle gallop.

**canton** *noun* (**cantons**)
each of the districts into which Switzerland is divided.

**canvas** *noun* (**canvases**)
**1** strong, coarse cloth. **2** a piece of this kind of cloth for painting on. **3** a painting.

**canvass** *verb* (**canvasses, canvassing, canvassed**)
to visit people to ask for votes, opinions, etc.

USAGE: do not confuse **canvass** with **canvas,** which means a kind of material.

**canyon** *noun* (**canyons**)
a deep valley, usually with a river running
through it.

**cap**[1] *noun* (**caps**)
1 a soft hat without a brim but often with a
peak. 2 being chosen to be in a particular
sports team, *He got his cap in the first
eleven*. 3 a cover or top. 4 something that
makes a bang when it is fired in a toy
pistol.

**cap**[2] *verb* (**caps, capping, capped**)
1 to cover something, *snow-capped
mountains*. 2 to do better than something,
*Can you cap that joke?*

**capable** *adjective*
able to do something.
**capability** *noun*, **capably** *adverb*

**capacitor** *noun* (**capacitors**)
a device that stores an electric charge.

**capacity** *noun* (**capacities**)
1 ability, *He has a great capacity for work.*
2 the amount that something can hold.
3 the position someone occupies, *in my
capacity as your teacher*.

**cape**[1] *noun* (**capes**)
a piece of high land sticking out into the
sea.

**cape**[2] *noun* (**capes**)
a cloak.

**caper**[1] *verb* (**capers, capering, capered**)
to jump about playfully.

**caper**[2] *noun* (**capers**)
1 jumping about playfully. 2 (*slang*) an
activity or adventure.

**capital**[1] *adjective*
(*old-fashioned informal*) excellent.
**capital city**, the most important city in a
country.
**capital letter**, a large letter of the kind used
at the start of a name or a sentence, *A, B,
C, etc. are capital letters.*
**capital punishment**, punishing people by
killing them.

**capital**[2] *noun* (**capitals**)
1 a capital city. 2 a capital letter. 3 money
or property that can be used to make more
wealth. 4 the top part of a pillar.

**capitalist** *noun* (**capitalists**)
(*say* **kap**-i-tă-list)
someone who uses his wealth to make
more wealth; a very rich person.
**capitalism** *noun*

**capsize** *verb* (**capsizes, capsizing, capsized**)
to overturn a boat in the water.

**capsule** *noun* (**capsules**)
1 a hollow pill containing medicine. 2 a
small spacecraft or pressurized cabin.

**captain** *noun* (**captains**)
1 someone in command of a ship, aircraft,
sports team, etc. 2 an officer in the army or
navy.

**caption** *noun* (**captions**)
1 the words printed with a picture to
describe it. 2 a heading in a newspaper or
magazine.

**captivating** *adjective*
charming and attractive.

**captive**[1] *noun* (**captives**)
a prisoner.

**captive**[2] *adjective*
imprisoned; unable to escape, *to be held
captive. The captive rabbit struggled to get
free.*
**captivity** *noun*

**captor** *noun* (**captors**)
someone who has captured a person or
animal.

**capture**[1] *verb* (**captures, capturing, captured**)
1 to catch or imprison an animal or person.
2 (*in Computing*) to put data into a form
that a computer can accept.

**capture**[2] *noun*
1 the action of capturing or imprisoning an
animal or person. 2 (*in Computing*) the
putting of data into a form that a computer
can accept.

**car** *noun* (**cars**)
1 a motor car. 2 a railway carriage, *a
dining-car*.
**car-boot sale**, an outdoor sale where people
sell things which they have brought by car.
**car phone**, a mobile telephone fitted to a car.

**caramel** *noun* (**caramels**)
1 burnt sugar used to give a sweet taste to
food. 2 a sweet made from butter, milk, and
sugar.

**carat** *noun* (**carats**)
1 a measure of weight for precious stones.
2 a measure of the purity of gold.

**Caribbean**

**caravan** *noun* (**caravans**)
**1** (in America, *trailer*) a small house on wheels, used for living in, especially by gypsies or by people on holiday. **2** a company of people travelling together, especially across a desert.

**carbohydrate** *noun* (**carbohydrates**)
a compound of carbon, oxygen, and hydrogen, *Sugar and starch are carbohydrates.*

**carbon** *noun*
**1** an element found in charcoal, graphite, diamonds, etc. **2** a carbon copy or carbon paper.
**carbon copy,** a copy made with carbon paper; an exact copy, *The attack was a carbon copy of one carried out last month.*
**carbon dioxide,** a colourless gas made by humans and animals breathing.
**carbon monoxide,** a colourless, poisonous gas found especially in the exhaust of motor cars etc.
**carbon paper,** thin coated paper put between sheets of paper to make a copy on the bottom sheet of what is typed or written on the top sheet.

**carburettor** *noun* (**carburettors**)
a device for mixing fuel and air in an internal-combustion engine.

**carcass** *noun* (**carcasses**)
the dead body of an animal or bird.

**card** *noun* (**cards**)
**1** a small, usually oblong, piece of stiff paper. **2** a playing-card. **3** cardboard. **4** a small, oblong piece of plastic issued by a bank, building society, etc., to each individual customer, giving details of his or her account; a cheque card.
**cards,** a game with playing-cards.
**something is on the cards,** something is likely or possible.

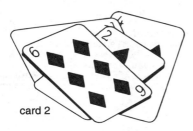
card 2

**cardboard** *noun*
thick, stiff paper.

**cardigan** *noun* (**cardigans**)
a knitted jacket.

**cardinal** *noun* (**cardinals**)
one of the leading priests in the Roman Catholic Church.

**cardinal number** *noun* (**cardinal numbers**)
a number for counting things; 1, 2, 3, etc. (compare *ordinal number*).

**cardphone** *noun* (**cardphones**)
a public telephone that needs a special plastic card (a *phonecard*) to make it work.

**care**[1] *noun* (**cares**)
**1** worry; trouble, *She was free from care.*
**2** serious thought or attention; caution, *Take more care with your homework.*
**3** protection; supervision, *Leave the child in my care.*
**care of ... ,** at the address of ... , *Write to him care of his friend.*
**take care,** to be careful.
**take care of,** to look after; to deal with, *Please could you take care of the cat while I'm away? That cheque will take care of the gas bill.*

**care**[2] *verb* (**cares, caring, cared**)
to feel interested or concerned.
**care for,** to look after; to be fond of, *He cared for his wife when she was ill. I don't care for peanuts.*

**career**[1] *noun* (**careers**)
a job or profession; a way of earning a living or making progress.

**career**[2] *verb* (**careers, careering, careered**)
to rush along wildly.

**carefree** *adjective*
without worries or responsibilities.

**careful** *adjective*
**1** giving serious thought and attention to something, *She is a careful worker.*
**2** avoiding damage or danger, *a careful driver. Be careful with that knife!*
**carefully** *adverb*

**careless** *adjective*
not careful.
**carelessly** *adverb*, **carelessness** *noun*

**caress** *noun* (**caresses**)
(*say* kă-**ress**)
a gentle, loving touch.

**caret** *noun* (**carets**)
a mark (ʌ) showing where something is to be inserted in writing or printing.

**caretaker** *noun* (**caretakers**)
someone who looks after a school, block of flats, etc.

**cargo** *noun* (**cargoes**)
goods carried in a ship or aircraft.

**Caribbean** *adjective*
(*say* ka-ri-**bee**-ăn)
of the West Indies.

**caricature** *noun* (**caricatures**)
an amusing or exaggerated picture or
description of someone.

**carnation** *noun* (**carnations**)
a garden flower with a sweet smell.

**carnival** *noun* (**carnivals**)
a festival, usually with a procession of
people in fancy dress.

**carnivore** *noun* (**carnivores**)
an animal that eats meat.
**carnivorous** *adjective*

**carol** *noun* (**carols**)
a hymn, especially a Christmas hymn.
**caroller** *noun*, **carolling** *noun*

**carp** *noun* (**carp**)
a freshwater fish.

**carpenter** *noun* (**carpenters**)
someone who makes things, especially
parts of buildings, out of wood.

**carpentry** *noun*
the work of a carpenter; things made by a
carpenter.

**carpet** *noun* (**carpets**)
a thick, soft covering for a floor.

**carriage** *noun* (**carriages**)
1 one of the separate parts of a train where
passengers sit. 2 a passenger vehicle pulled
by horses. 3 carrying goods from one place
to another; the cost of carrying goods,
*Carriage is extra.*

**carrier** *noun* (**carriers**)
someone or something that carries things.
**carrier-bag**, a large bag for holding
shopping, etc.
**carrier-pigeon**, a pigeon used to carry
messages.

**carrot** *noun* (**carrots**)
an orange-coloured vegetable.

**carry** *verb* (**carries, carrying, carried**)
1 to support the weight of something. 2 to
take something from one place to another.
3 to have with you, *He is carrying a gun.*
4 to go a long distance, *Sound carries in the
mountains.*
**carried away**, very excited.
**carry on**, to continue; to manage; (*informal*)
to behave excitedly or strangely, *The firm
can't carry on with so little money. Stop
carrying on!*
**carry out**, to put something into practice,
*The plan has been carried out successfully.*

**cart**[1] *noun* (**carts**)
a small vehicle for carrying loads.
**put the cart before the horse**, to do things in
the wrong order.

**cart**[2] *verb* (**carts, carting, carted**)
1 to carry something in a cart. 2 (*informal*)
to carry or transport something heavy or
tiring, *I've been carting these books around
the school all afternoon.*

**Cartesian coordinates** *plural noun*
coordinates that are measured from
straight lines (one horizontal and one
vertical) that cross.

**cart-horse** *noun* (**cart-horses**)
a large, heavy horse.

**cartilage** *noun*
(*say* **kar-tĭ-lij**)
tough, flexible tissue attached to a bone.

**carton** *noun* (**cartons**)
a lightweight cardboard box.

**cartoon** *noun* (**cartoons**)
1 an amusing drawing. 2 a series of
drawings telling a story. 3 an animated
film.
**cartoonist** *noun*

**cartridge** *noun* (**cartridges**)
1 the case containing the explosive for a
bullet or shell. 2 a container holding film to
be put into a camera, ink to be put into a
pen, etc. 3 the device on a record-player
that holds the stylus.
**cartridge paper**, strong white paper.

**cartwheel** *noun* (**cartwheels**)
1 the wheel of a cart. 2 a somersault done
sideways, with your arms and legs spread
wide.

**carve** *verb* (**carves, carving, carved**)
1 to cut something carefully or artistically.
2 to cut meat into slices.

**cascade** *noun* (**cascades**)
a waterfall.

**case**[1] *noun* (**cases**)
1 a container. 2 a suitcase.

**case**² *noun* (**cases**)
1 an example of something existing or happening, *four cases of chicken-pox*.
2 something investigated by the police or by a lawcourt, *a case of murder*. 3 the facts or arguments used to support something, *She made a good case for equality*. 4 the form of a word that shows how it is related to other words, *Fred's is the possessive case of Fred*.
**in any case**, anyway.
**in case**, because something may happen, *Take an umbrella in case it rains*.

**cash**¹ *noun*
1 money in coins and banknotes.
2 immediate payment for goods, *Do you want cash or hire-purchase?*
**cash and carry**, a place where you buy large quantities or big things that you take away with you.
**cash dispenser**, a machine from which customers of a bank, etc. can get money, and information about their accounts.
**cash on delivery**, paying for goods when they are delivered.
**cash register**, a device that records and stores money received in a shop.

**cash**² *verb* (**cashes, cashing, cashed**)
to change a cheque, etc. into coins and banknotes.
**cash in on something**, (*informal*) to take advantage of something.

**cashier** *noun* (**cashiers**)
someone in charge of the money in a bank, office, or shop.

**cashpoint** *noun* (**cashpoints**)
a cash dispenser.

**cask** *noun* (**casks**)
a barrel.

**casket** *noun* (**caskets**)
a small box for jewellery, etc.

**casserole** *noun* (**casseroles**)
1 a covered dish in which food is cooked.
2 food cooked in a dish of this kind.

**cassette** *noun* (**cassettes**)
a small sealed case containing recording tape, film, etc.
**cassette recorder**, a tape recorder that uses cassettes.

**cast**¹ *verb* (**casts, casting, cast**)
1 to throw. 2 to shed or throw off. 3 to make a vote. 4 to make something of metal or plaster in a mould. 5 to choose the performers for a play, film, etc.
**cast off**, to untie a boat; (*in Knitting*) to take stitches off your knitting-needle.
**cast on**, (*in Knitting*) to put stitches on to your knitting-needle.

**cast**² *noun* (**casts**)
1 a shape made by pouring liquid metal or plaster into a mould. 2 all the performers in a play, film, etc.

**castanets** *plural noun*
two pieces of wood, ivory, etc. held in one hand and clapped together to make a clicking sound, usually for Spanish dancing.

**castaway** *noun* (**castaways**)
a shipwrecked person.

**castle** *noun* (**castles**)
1 a large, old building made to protect people in it from attack. 2 a piece in chess, also called a *rook*.

**castor** *noun* (**castors**)
(*say* **kah**-ster)
a small wheel on the leg of a table, chair, etc.
**castor sugar**, finely-ground white sugar.

**casual** *adjective*
1 not deliberate or planned, *a casual remark*. 2 informal; suitable for leisure time, *casual clothes*. 3 not regular or permanent, *casual work*.
**casually** *adverb*

**casualty** *noun* (**casualties**)
someone killed or injured in war or in an accident.

**cat** *noun* (**cats**)
1 a small furry animal, usually kept as a pet and known for catching mice. 2 a lion, tiger, leopard, etc. 3 (*informal*) a spiteful girl or woman.
**let the cat out of the bag**, to reveal a secret.

**catalogue** *noun* (**catalogues**)
a list, especially of goods for sale.

**catalyst** *noun* (**catalysts**)
(*say* **kat**-ă-list)
1 something that starts or speeds up a chemical reaction. 2 something or someone that starts or speeds up change, *The Archduke's assassination was the catalyst that sparked off the war*.

**catamaran** *noun* (**catamarans**)
a boat with two hulls fixed side by side.

**catapult** *noun* (**catapults**)
(in America, *slingshot*) a device for
shooting pellets, small stones, etc.

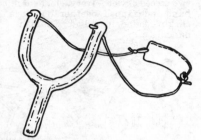

**catastrophe** *noun* (**catastrophes**)
(*say* kă-**tas**-trŏ-fi)
a great or sudden disaster.
**catastrophic** *adjective*

**catch**¹ *verb* (**catches, catching, caught**)
**1** to get hold of someone or something; to
stop or intercept something. **2** to surprise
or detect someone, *He was caught in the
act.* **3** to get an illness, *She caught a cold.*
**4** to be in time to get on a bus or train. **5** to
hear or understand. **6** to become entangled;
to cause something to be entangled, *I
caught my sleeve on a bramble.*
**catch fire,** to start burning.
**catch on,** (*informal*) to become popular; to
understand, *a fashion that is catching on.
Hasn't he caught on yet?*
**catch someone out,** to show that someone is
wrong or mistaken.
**catch up,** to get level.

**catch**² *noun* (**catches**)
**1** catching something. **2** something caught
or worth catching, *a large catch of fish.*
**3** a hidden difficulty. **4** a device for
fastening a door, window, etc.

**catching** *adjective*
(of a disease) easily caught, and liable to
spread quickly.

**catchment area** *noun* (**catchment areas**)
(*in Geography*) an area from which water
drains into a river or a reservoir.

**catch-phrase** *noun* (**catch-phrases**)
a phrase that is very popular.

**catchy** *adjective* (**catchier, catchiest**)
easy to remember; soon becoming popular,
*a catchy tune.*

**category** *noun* (**categories**)
a group or division of people or things, *The
competition had three categories: fiction,
non-fiction, and poetry.*

**cater** *verb* (**caters, catering, catered**)
to provide food or entertainment.
**caterer** *noun*

**caterpillar** *noun* (**caterpillars**)
a long, creeping creature that turns into a
butterfly or moth.

**cathedral** *noun* (**cathedrals**)
a large, important church having a bishop
as its chief priest.

**Catherine wheel** *noun* (**Catherine wheels**)
a wheel-shaped firework that spins round.

**cathode** *noun* (**cathodes**)
the electrode by which electric current
leaves a device (the opposite of *anode*).

**Catholic**¹ *adjective*
**1** of the Roman Catholic church. **2** of all
Christians, *The Holy Catholic Church.*

**Catholic**² *noun* (**Catholics**)
a Roman Catholic.

**catkin** *noun* (**catkins**)
a tiny flower hanging down from a willow,
hazel, etc.

**Cat's-eye** *noun* (**Cat's-eyes**)
(*trademark*) each of a line of devices
containing small pieces of glass or plastic
that reflect the lights of vehicles, set in the
middle of a road or along its edge to help
drivers see their way at night.

**cattle** *plural noun*
cows and bulls.

**caught** past tense and past participle of **catch**
*verb.*

**cauldron** *noun* (**cauldrons**)
a large, round, iron cooking-pot used
especially by witches in stories.

**cauliflower** *noun* (**cauliflowers**)
a kind of cabbage with a large head of
white flowers.

**cause**¹ *noun* (**causes**)
**1** what makes something happen; a reason,
*You have no cause for complaint.* **2** a
purpose for which people work, *She worked
all her life for the cause of justice.* **3** an
organization or charity, *This collection is
for a good cause.*

**cause**² *verb* (**causes, causing, caused**)
to make something happen.

**caution** *noun* (**cautions**)
**1** being careful. **2** a warning.

**cautious** *adjective*
careful.
**cautiously** *adverb*

**Cavalier** *noun* (**Cavaliers**)
a supporter of King Charles I in the
English Civil War.

**cavalry** *noun*
soldiers who fight on horseback or in armoured vehicles.

**cave**[1] *noun* (**caves**)
a large hole in the side of a hill or cliff, or under the ground.

**cave**[2] *verb* (**caves, caving, caved**)
to explore caves.
**cave in,** to collapse.

**caveman** *noun* (**cavemen**)
a man who lived in a cave in prehistoric times.

**cavern** *noun* (**caverns**)
a cave, especially a deep or dark cave.

**cavewoman** *noun* (**cavewomen**)
a woman who lived in a cave in prehistoric times.

**cavity** *noun* (**cavities**)
a hollow or hole.

**CD** short for **compact disc**.

**CD-ROM** short for *compact disc read-only memory*, a system for storing information to be displayed on a VDU screen.

**cease** *verb* (**ceases, ceasing, ceased**)
to stop.
**cease-fire,** an agreement to stop firing guns, made between people who are fighting a war.

**ceaseless** *adjective*
never-ending.

**cedar** *noun* (**cedars**)
an evergreen tree with hard, sweet-smelling wood.

**ceiling** *noun* (**ceilings**)
(*say* **see-**ling)
1 the flat surface that covers the top of a room. 2 the highest limit that something can reach.

**celebrate** *verb* (**celebrates, celebrating, celebrated**)
to do something to show that a day or an event is important.
**celebrated,** famous.
**celebration** *noun*

**celebrity** *noun* (**celebrities**)
a famous person, *a TV celebrity.*

**celery** *noun*
a vegetable with crisp white or green stems.

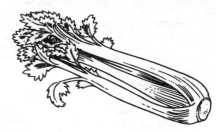

**cell** *noun* (**cells**)
1 a small room, especially in a prison. 2 a very tiny part of a living creature or plant. 3 a device for producing electric current chemically.

**cellar** *noun* (**cellars**)
an underground room.

**cello** *noun* (**cellos**)
(*say* **chel-**oh)
a musical instrument with strings, like a very large violin, placed between the knees of the player.

**cellular** *adjective*
1 of cells; made of cells, *the cellular structure of living things.* 2 using a network of radio stations to allow messages to be sent over a wide area, *a cellular telephone.*

**celluloid** *noun*
a transparent plastic.

**cellulose** *noun*
tissue that forms the main part of all plants and trees.

**Celsius** *adjective*
using a scale for measuring temperature that gives 0 degrees for freezing water and 100 degrees for boiling water.

**Celt** *noun* (**Celts**)
(*say* kelt)
one of the people who lived in Britain before the Romans came.

**Celtic** *adjective*
(*say* **kel-**tik)
of the Celts; of the people descended from them and now living in Wales, Scotland, and Ireland, *a Celtic language.*

**cement** *noun*
1 a mixture of lime and clay used in building to make floors, join bricks together, etc. 2 a strong glue.

**cemetery** *noun* (**cemeteries**)
(*say* sem-ĕ-tri)
a place where dead people are buried.

**censor**¹ *noun* (**censors**)
someone who looks at films, books, letters, etc. and removes anything that he or she thinks may be harmful.
**censorship** *noun*

**censor**² *verb* (**censors, censoring, censored**)
to look at films, books, letters, etc. as your official job, removing anything that you think may be harmful.

**censure** *noun*
criticizing or disapproving of something.

**census** *noun* (**censuses**)
an official count or survey of population, traffic, etc.

**cent** *noun* (**cents**)
1 a coin, *100 cents make a dollar in the United States, Canada, and Australia.* 2 a very small amount of money, *I haven't a cent.*

**centenary** *noun* (**centenaries**)
the hundredth anniversary of something.

**centigrade** *adjective*
a non-technical word for **Celsius**.

**centimetre** *noun* (**centimetres**)
one-hundredth of a metre, about four-tenths of an inch.

**centipede** *noun* (**centipedes**)
a small, long creature with many legs.

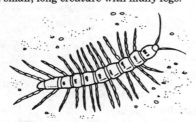

**central** *adjective*
1 of or at the centre. 2 most important, *She will have a central role in our plans.*
**central heating**, a system of heating a building by sending hot water, hot air, or steam around the building in pipes.
**centralize** *verb*, **centrally** *adverb*

**centre** *noun* (**centres**)
1 the middle of something. 2 an important place, *the centre of the country's steel industry.* 3 a place where particular things happen, *a shopping centre. a leisure centre.*
**centre of gravity**, the point in an object around which its mass is perfectly balanced.

**centre-forward** *noun* (**centre-forwards**)
the middle player in the front line of a team in football or hockey.

**centrifugal** *adjective*
moving away from the centre; using centrifugal force, *a centrifugal pump.*
**centrifugal force**, a force that appears to make something revolving move out from the centre.

**centurion** *noun* (**centurions**)
an officer in the ancient Roman army, originally commanding a hundred men.

**century** *noun* (**centuries**)
1 one hundred years. 2 a hundred runs scored by one batsman in an innings at cricket.

**ceramic** *adjective*
of pottery.

**ceramics** *plural noun*
the art of making pottery.

**cereal** *noun* (**cereals**)
1 a grass that produces seeds which are used as food, *Cereals include wheat, barley, oats, maize, and rye.* 2 a breakfast food made from seeds of this kind.

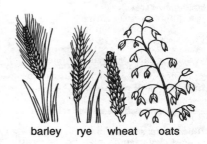

barley    rye    wheat    oats

**ceremony** *noun* (**ceremonies**)
(*say* se-ri-mŏ-ni)
the solemn actions carried out at a wedding, funeral, or other important occasion.
**ceremonial** *adjective*

**certain** *adjective*
1 sure, *I am certain of that.* 2 without doubt, *It is not certain that he was the thief.*
**a certain person** or **thing**, someone or something that is known but not named or described.
**for certain**, for sure.
**make certain**, to make sure.
**certainly** *adverb*

**certainty** *noun* (**certainties**)
1 something that is sure to happen. 2 being sure.

**certificate** *noun* (**certificates**)
an official document that can be used to prove something, *a birth certificate. a savings certificate.*

**certify** *verb* (**certifies, certifying, certified**)
to declare something officially, especially that someone is insane.

**CFC** short for *chlorofluorocarbon*,
a chemical used in refrigerators and aerosols, thought to be harmful to the ozone layer.

**chaffinch** *noun* (**chaffinches**)
a small bird.

**chain** *noun* (**chains**)
1 a row of metal rings fastened together. 2 a line of people. 3 a connected series of things, *a chain of events*.
**chain letter,** a letter that you are asked to copy and send to several other people, who do the same.
**chain reaction,** a series of happenings, one causing another.
**chain saw,** a saw with teeth on a loop of chain driven round by a motor.
**chain store,** one of a series of large shops owned by one company.

**chair** *noun* (**chairs**)
1 a seat, usually with a back, for one person. 2 the person who is in control of a meeting.
**chair-lift,** a set of seats hanging from a moving cable, carrying people up a mountain etc.

**chairman** or **chairperson** *noun* (**chairmen** or **chairpersons**)
the person who is in control of a meeting.

**chalet** *noun* (**chalets**)
(*say* **shal**-ay)
a small house, usually built of wood.

**chalk** *noun* (**chalks**)
1 a kind of soft white rock. 2 a soft white stick of a similar rock, used for writing on blackboards, etc.
**chalky** *adjective*

**challenge**¹ *verb* (**challenges, challenging, challenged**)
to ask someone to do something difficult, have a contest, etc.
**challenger** *noun*

**challenge**² *noun* (**challenges**)
something difficult that you have to do, or that you ask someone to do, *I accept the challenge*.

**chamber** *noun* (**chambers**)
1 (*old-fashioned use*) a room. 2 a hall used for meetings of a parliament, etc.
**chamber music,** music for a small group of players.
**chamber-pot,** a round container for urine, etc., used in the past, usually in a bedroom.

**champagne** *noun*
(*say* sham-**payn**)
a bubbly French wine.

**champion** *noun* (**champions**)
1 the best person in a sport, competition, etc. 2 someone who supports a cause by fighting, speaking, etc., *Martin Luther King was a champion of human rights*.

**championship** *noun* (**championships**)
a contest to decide who is the best player, competitor, etc.

**chance** *noun* (**chances**)
1 a possibility; an opportunity, *This is your only chance.* 2 a risk, *Take a chance.* 3 the way things happen accidentally, *It was pure chance that we met.*
**by chance,** accidentally; without any planning, *By chance, I caught a glimpse of what he was writing. We found the place by chance.*

**chancel** *noun* (**chancels**)
the part of a church round the altar.

**chancellor** *noun* (**chancellors**)
1 an important government or legal official. 2 the chief minister of the government in some European countries, *the German Chancellor spoke.*
**Chancellor of the Exchequer,** the minister in charge of a country's finances.

**chandelier** *noun* (**chandeliers**)
(*say* shan-dĕ-**leer**)
a hanging support for several lights.

**change**¹ *verb* (**changes, changing, changed**)
1 to make something or someone different; to become different. 2 to exchange, *I changed my car for a van.* 3 to give coins or notes of small values in exchange for other money, *Can you change a £5 note?* 4 to go from one train, bus, etc. to another, *Change at Didcot for Oxford.*

**change**$^2$ *noun* (**changes**)
1 changing. 2 the money that you get back when you give more money than is needed to pay for something. 3 a fresh set of clothes. 4 a variation in your routine, *Let's walk home for a change.*

**changeable** *adjective*
likely to change; often changing, *changeable weather.*

**channel** *noun* (**channels**)
1 a stretch of water joining two seas, *The English Channel is between Britain and France.* 2 a broadcasting wavelength. 3 a way for water to flow along. 4 the part of a river, sea, etc. that is deep enough for ships.

**chant**$^1$ *noun* (**chants**)
a tune, especially one that is often repeated.

**chant**$^2$ *verb* (**chants, chanting, chanted**)
to say or call words in a rhythm; to sing, *They chanted a psalm.*

**chaos** *noun*
(*say* **kay**-oss)
complete disorder, *The room was in chaos.*
**chaotic** *adjective*

**chap** *noun* (**chaps**)
(*informal*) a man or boy.

**chapatti** *noun* (**chapattis**)
a flat, thin cake of bread made without yeast, eaten with Indian food.

**chapel** *noun* (**chapels**)
1 a place within a church or belonging to a large house, a school, etc., used for Christian worship. 2 a small church, especially one used by Protestant worshippers.

**chapped** *adjective*
with rough, cracked skin.

**chapter** *noun* (**chapters**)
a section of a book.

**char** *verb* (**chars, charring, charred**)
to scorch; to blacken with fire.

**character** *noun* (**characters**)
1 the characteristics of a person or thing. 2 a person, especially in a story or play.

**characteristic**$^1$ *noun* (**characteristics**)
something that makes a person or thing noticeable or different from others.

**characteristic**$^2$ *adjective*
typical.

**characterize** *verb* (**characterizes, characterizing, characterized**)
1 to be a characteristic of something, *the stony beaches that characterize the south coast.* 2 to describe the character of someone, *The play characterized him as boastful.*

**charades** *plural noun*
(*say* shă-**rahdz**)
a game in which people have to guess a word from other people's acting.

**charcoal** *noun*
a black substance made by burning wood slowly.

**charge**$^1$ *noun* (**charges**)
1 the price asked for something. 2 accusing someone of a crime. 3 rushing to attack. 4 the amount of explosive needed to fire a gun, etc. 5 electricity in something.
**in charge of,** deciding what shall happen to a person or thing; controlling.

**charge**$^2$ *verb* (**charges, charging, charged**)
1 to ask a particular price. 2 to accuse someone of committing a crime. 3 to rush to attack someone or something.

**chariot** *noun* (**chariots**)
a horse-drawn vehicle with two wheels, used in ancient times for fighting, racing, etc.
**charioteer** *noun*

**charisma** *noun*
(*say* kă-**riz**-mă)
the quality that makes someone special, popular, influential, etc.
**charismatic** *adjective*

**charity** *noun* (**charities**)
1 giving money, help, etc. to other people. 2 an organization to help those in need.
**charitable** *adjective*

**charm**$^1$ *noun* (**charms**)
1 attractiveness. 2 a magic spell. 3 something small worn or carried for good luck.

**charm**$^2$ *verb* (**charms, charming, charmed**)
1 to give pleasure or delight to someone; to attract. 2 to put a spell on; to bewitch.

**chart** *noun* (**charts**)
1 a large map. 2 a diagram, list, etc. giving information in an orderly way.
**the charts,** (*informal*) a list of the records that are most popular.

**charter**$^1$ *noun* (**charters**)
1 an official document giving someone rights, etc. 2 hiring an aircraft, vehicle, etc.
**charter flight,** a flight by a hired aircraft.

**charter**$^2$ *verb* (**charters, chartering, chartered**)
1 to hire an aircraft, vehicle, etc. 2 to give a charter to someone.

**charwoman** *noun* (**charwomen**)
(*old-fashioned use*) a woman paid to clean
a house, office, etc.

**chase** *verb* (**chases, chasing, chased**)
to go quickly to try to catch up with
someone or something.

**chasm** *noun* (**chasms**)
(*say* **ka**-zŭm)
a deep opening in the ground.

**chassis** *noun* (**chassis**)
(*say* **shass**-i)
the frame of a vehicle, etc. on which the
body is put.

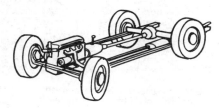

**chat**[1] *noun* (**chats**)
a friendly or informal talk with someone.
**chatty** *adjective*

**chat**[2] *verb* (**chats, chatting, chatted**)
to have a friendly or informal talk.
**chat up**, to talk to someone in a friendly
way because you are attracted to him or
her, *Jane was trying to chat up Simon at
the party last night.*

**chatter** *verb* (**chatters, chattering, chattered**)
**1** to talk quickly or stupidly; to talk too
much. **2** to make a rattling noise.

**chauffeur** *noun* (**chauffeurs**)
(*say* **shoh**-fer)
someone who is paid to drive a car.

**chauvinism** *noun*
(*say* **shoh**-vin-izm)
**1** being too proud of being a man. **2** being
too patriotic.
**chauvinist** *noun and adjective*

**cheap** *adjective* (**cheaper, cheapest**)
**1** low in price; not expensive. **2** inferior.

**cheat**[1] *verb* (**cheats, cheating, cheated**)
**1** to trick someone. **2** to try to do well in an
examination, game, etc. by breaking the
rules.

**cheat**[2] *noun* (**cheats**)
someone who cheats.

**check**[1] *verb* (**checks, checking, checked**)
**1** to make sure that something is correct or
in good condition. **2** to make something
stop or go slower.
**check in**, to sign your name to show you
have arrived at a hotel; to show your ticket
at an airport.
**check on** or **up on something**, to look at
something and see whether it is correct or
suitable.
**check out**, to pay your bill and leave a hotel;
to check on something.

**check**[2] *noun* (**checks**)
**1** checking something. **2** the situation in
chess when a king may be taken. **3** a
pattern of squares.

USAGE: Do not confuse **check** with **cheque**,
which means a piece of paper telling your
bank to pay money out of your account.

**checkmate** *noun* (**checkmates**)
the winning situation in chess.

**checkout** *noun* (**checkouts**)
the place where you pay in a supermarket
or a large shop.

**check-up** *noun* (**check-ups**)
a careful check or examination.

**Cheddar** *noun*
a kind of cheese.

**cheek**[1] *noun* (**cheeks**)
**1** the side of the face below the eye.
**2** impudence.

**cheek**[2] *verb* (**cheeks, cheeking, cheeked**)
to be cheeky to someone.

**cheeky** *adjective* (**cheekier, cheekiest**)
impudent.
**cheekily** *adverb*, **cheekiness** *noun*

**cheer**[1] *noun* (**cheers**)
a shout of pleasure; a shout praising or
encouraging someone.

**cheer**[2] *verb* (**cheers, cheering, cheered**)
**1** to give a cheer. **2** to comfort or encourage
someone.
**cheer up**, to make someone cheerful; to
become cheerful.

**cheerful** *adjective*
happy; contented.

**cheerio** *interjection*
(*informal*) goodbye.

**cheese** *noun* (**cheeses**)
a solid food made from milk curds.
**cheesy** *adjective*

**cheetah** *noun* (**cheetahs**)
a large, spotted animal of the cat family, that can run very fast.

**chef** *noun* (**chefs**)
(*say* shef)
the chief cook in a hotel or restaurant.

**chemical**[1] *adjective*
of or produced by chemistry.

**chemical**[2] *noun* (**chemicals**)
a substance used in or obtained by chemistry.

**chemist** *noun* (**chemists**)
1 someone who makes or sells medicines. 2 an expert in chemistry.

**chemistry** *noun*
1 the way that substances combine and react with one another. 2 studying these combinations, reactions, etc.

**cheque** *noun* (**cheques**)
1 a written instruction to a bank to pay money out of your account. 2 the form you write this instruction on.
**cheque-book,** a number of blank cheques fastened together.
**cheque card,** a card that guarantees that your cheques will be paid.

USAGE: Do not confuse **cheque** with **check** *noun*, which means the action of making sure that something is correct or in good condition.

**chequered** *adjective*
marked with a pattern of squares.

**cherish** *verb* (**cherishes, cherishing, cherished**)
1 to protect lovingly. 2 to be fond of.

**cherry** *noun* (**cherries**)
a small, round fruit with a stone.

**chess** *noun*
a game for two players with sixteen pieces each (called **chessmen**) on a board of 64 squares (called a **chessboard**).

**chest** *noun* (**chests**)
1 a big, strong box. 2 the front part of your body between your neck and your waist.
**chest of drawers,** a piece of furniture with drawers.
**get something off your chest,** (*informal*) to say something that you are anxious to say.

**chestnut** *noun* (**chestnuts**)
1 a hard brown nut. 2 the tree that produces this kind of nut. 3 (*informal*) an old joke or story.

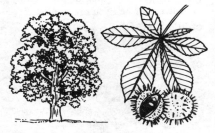

**chew** *verb* (**chews, chewing, chewed**)
to grind food between your teeth.
**chewy** *adjective*

**chewing-gum** *noun*
a sticky flavoured substance for chewing.

**chic** *adjective*
(*say* sheek)
stylish and elegant.

**chick** *noun* (**chicks**)
a very young bird, especially a very young chicken.

**chicken**[1] *noun* (**chickens**)
1 a young hen. 2 a hen's flesh used as food.

**chicken**[2] *adjective*
(*informal*) afraid; cowardly.

**chicken**[3] *verb* (**chickens, chickening, chickened**)
**chicken out,** (*informal*) to stop or withdraw because you are afraid.

**chicken-pox** *noun*
a disease that produces red spots on your skin.

**chief**[1] *noun* (**chiefs**)
1 a leader, *a Native American chief.* 2 the most important person, *Who is chief of your department?*

**chief**[2] *adjective*
most important.

**chiefly** *adverb*
1 most importantly, *Chiefly, you must avoid being seen.* 2 mainly, *The cake is made chiefly of flour.*

**chieftain** *noun* (chieftains)
the chief of a tribe, clan, band of robbers, etc.

**chilblain** *noun* (chilblains)
a sore, usually on a hand or foot, caused by cold weather.

**child** *noun* (children)
1 a young person; a boy or girl. 2 someone's son or daughter.
**child labour,** sending children out to work.

**childhood** *noun* (childhoods)
the time when you are a child.

**childish** *adjective*
1 suitable for children, *a childish game.*
2 immature, *Don't be childish!*

**child-minder** *noun* (child-minders)
a person who is paid to look after children while their parents are out at work.

**childproof** *adjective*
not able to be opened or operated by small children, *The car has childproof door-locks.*

**chill**[1] *noun* (chills)
1 coldness. 2 an illness that makes you shiver.

**chill**[2] *verb* (chills, chilling, chilled)
to make something or someone cold.

**chilly** *adjective* (chillier, chilliest)
1 slightly cold. 2 unfriendly.
**chilliness** *noun*

**chime**[1] *noun* (chimes)
a sound made by a bell.

**chime**[2] *verb* (chimes, chiming, chimed)
to ring, *The clock chimes every quarter-hour.*

**chimney** *noun* (chimneys)
a tall pipe or structure that carries away smoke from a fire.

**chimney-pot** *noun* (chimney-pots)
the piece of pipe at the top of a chimney.

**chimney-sweep** *noun* (chimney-sweeps)
someone who cleans the soot out of chimneys.

**chimpanzee** *noun* (chimpanzees)
an African ape.

**chin** *noun* (chins)
the part of the face under the mouth.

**china** *noun*
thin, delicate pottery.

**Chinese**[1] *adjective*
of China.

**Chinese**[2] *noun* (Chinese)
1 the Chinese language. 2 a Chinese person.

**chink** *noun* (chinks)
1 a narrow opening, *He looked through a chink in the curtains.* 2 a clinking sound, *They heard the chink of coins.*

**chip**[1] *noun* (chips)
1 a small piece of something. 2 a place where a small piece has been knocked off something. 3 a small piece of potato that is fried. 4 a small counter used in games. 5 a silicon chip.
**to have a chip on your shoulder,** to have a grievance; to be ready to quarrel or fight, *He's got a chip on his shoulder about wealthy people.*

**chip**[2] *verb* (chips, chipping, chipped)
1 to knock small pieces off something. 2 to cut a potato into chips.

**chirp** *verb* (chirps, chirping, chirped)
to make short, sharp sounds like a small bird.

**chirpy** *adjective* (chirpier, chirpiest)
(*informal*) lively and cheerful.

**chisel**[1] *noun* (chisels)
a tool with a sharp end for shaping wood, stone, etc.

**chisel**[2] *verb* (chisels, chiselling, chiselled)
1 to shape or cut with a chisel. 2 (*slang*) to swindle.
**chiseller** *noun*

**chivalrous** *adjective*
courteous; helping people who are less strong than yourself, *a chivalrous knight.*
**chivalry** *noun*

**chlorine** *noun*
a chemical used to disinfect water, etc.
**chlorinate** *verb*, **chlorination** *noun*

**chlorophyll** *noun*
the substance that makes plants green.

**choc** *noun* (chocs)
(*informal*) a chocolate.

**choc-ice** *noun* (choc-ices)
an ice-cream covered with chocolate.

**chock-a-block** or **chock-full** *adjective* and *adverb*
completely full.

**chocolate** *noun* (**chocolates**)
1 a sweet, brown food. 2 a sweet made of or covered with this substance. 3 a sweet powder used for making drinks; a drink made of it.

**choice** *noun* (**choices**)
1 choosing. 2 the power to choose between things. 3 what you have chosen.

**choir** *noun* (**choirs**)
an organized group of singers, especially in a church.
**choirboy** *noun*

**choke**[1] *verb* (**chokes, choking, choked**)
1 to stop someone breathing properly. 2 to be unable to breathe properly. 3 to block up something.

**choke**[2] *noun* (**chokes**)
a device in a motor vehicle to control the amount of air mixed with the petrol.

**cholera** *noun*
(*say* kol-er-ă)
an infectious disease that is often fatal.

**cholesterol** *noun*
(*say* kŏ-**less**-tĕ-rol)
a substance found in all the cells of your body that helps to carry fat and that is thought to be bad for your arteries if you have too much of it.

**choose** *verb* (**chooses, choosing, chose, chosen**)
1 to decide to take one person or thing instead of another. 2 to make a decision about something.

**choosy** *adjective* (**choosier, choosiest**)
(*informal*) 1 hard to please, *That cat is getting choosy – she won't eat ordinary cat-food.* 2 careful and cautious when making a choice.

**chop**[1] *verb* (**chops, chopping, chopped**)
to cut or hit something with a heavy blow.

**chop**[2] *noun* (**chops**)
1 a chopping blow. 2 a small, thick slice of meat.
**get the chop**, (*slang*) to be dismissed or killed.

**chopper** *noun* (**choppers**)
1 a small axe. 2 (*informal*) a helicopter.

**choppy** *adjective* (**choppier, choppiest**)
full of small waves, *a choppy sea*.

**chopsticks** *plural noun*
a pair of thin sticks used for eating Chinese or Japanese food.

**choral** *adjective*
(*say* kor-ăl)
of or for a choir or chorus.

**chord** *noun* (**chords**)
(*say* kord)
a number of musical notes sounded together.

USAGE: Do not confuse **chord** with **cord**, which means a piece of thin rope.

**chore** *noun* (**chores**)
(*say* chor)
a hard job; a regular task, *household chores*.

**chorus** *noun* (**choruses**)
(*say* kor-ŭs)
1 a group of people singing or speaking together. 2 music sung by a group of people. 3 the words repeated after every verse of a song or poem.

**chose** past tense of **choose**.

**chosen** past participle of **choose**.

**christen** *verb* (**christens, christening, christened**)
to baptize someone.
**christening** *noun*

**Christendom** *noun*
(*old-fashioned use*) all Christian people or countries.

**Christian**[1] *noun* (**Christians**)
someone who believes in Christ.
**Christianity** *noun*

**Christian**[2] *adjective*
of Christ or Christians.
**Christian name**, a name that someone has besides his or her surname.

**Christmas** *noun* (**Christmases**)
the time of celebrating Jesus's birthday on 25 December or the days around it.
**Christmas pudding**, a rich pudding eaten at Christmas.
**Christmas tree**, an evergreen or artificial tree decorated at Christmas.

**chromatic** *adjective*
of colours.
**chromatic scale**, a musical scale going up or down in semitones.

**chromatography** *noun*
the separation of a mixture into the substances of which it is made, by passing it over a material that absorbs the substances at different speeds so that they appear as layers, often of different colours.

**chrome** *noun*
a shiny, silvery metal.

**chromium** *noun*
chrome.

**chromosome** *noun* (**chromosomes**)
the part of an animal cell that carries genes.

**chronic** *adjective*
1 lasting for a long time, *a chronic disease.*
2 (*informal*) very bad, *a chronic joke.*
**chronically** *adverb*

**chronicle** *noun* (**chronicles**)
a record of events.

**chronological** *adjective*
in the order in which things happen.
**chronologically** *adverb*

**chronology** *noun*
the arrangement of events in the order in
which they happened, especially in history
or geology.

**chrysalis** *noun* (**chrysalises**)
(*say* **kris-ă-lis**)
the cover a caterpillar makes round itself
before it turns into a butterfly or moth.

**chrysanthemum** *noun* (**chrysanthemums**)
a garden flower that blooms in autumn.

**chubby** *adjective* (**chubbier, chubbiest**)
plump, *a chubby baby.*

**chuck** *verb* (**chucks, chucking, chucked**)
(*informal*) to throw.

**chuckle¹** *verb* (**chuckles, chuckling, chuckled**)
to laugh quietly.

**chuckle²** *noun* (**chuckles**)
a quiet laugh.

**chug** *verb* (**chugs, chugging, chugged**)
to move with the sound of a slow-running
engine.

**chum** *noun* (**chums**)
(*informal*) a friend.
**chummy** *adjective*

**chunk** *noun* (**chunks**)
a thick lump.
**chunky** *adjective*

**church** *noun* (**churches**)
1 a building where Christians worship.
2 Christian worship, *Do you go to church?*
**Church**, a group or organization of
Christians, *the Church of England. the
Free Church.*

**churchyard** *noun* (**churchyards**)
the ground round a church, usually used as
a graveyard.

**churn¹** *noun* (**churns**)
1 a large container for milk. 2 a machine
for making butter.

**churn²** *verb* (**churns, churning, churned**)
1 to make butter in a churn. 2 to stir
something vigorously.
**churn out**, to produce large quantities of
something.

**chute** *noun* (**chutes**)
(*say* shoot)
a steep channel for people or things to slide
down.

**chutney** *noun*
a strong-tasting mixture of fruit, peppers,
etc., eaten with meat.

**cider** *noun*
an alcoholic drink made from apples.

**cigar** *noun* (**cigars**)
a roll of compressed tobacco-leaves for
smoking.

**cigarette** *noun* (**cigarettes**)
a small, thin roll of shredded tobacco in
thin paper for smoking.

**cinder** *noun* (**cinders**)
a small piece of coal, wood, etc. partly
burned.

**cine camera** *noun* (**cine cameras**)
a camera used for taking moving pictures
on film.

**cinema** *noun* (**cinemas**)
a place where people go to see films.

**cinnamon** *noun*
a yellowish-brown spice.

**circle¹** *noun* (**circles**)
1 a round, flat shape; the shape of a coin or
wheel, *The edge of a circle is always the
same distance from the centre.* 2 something
like a circle. 3 a balcony in a cinema or
theatre. 4 a number of people with similar
interests, *She belongs to a writers' circle.*

**circle²** *verb* (**circles, circling, circled**)
1 to move in a circle, *Vultures circled
overhead.* 2 to go round something, *The
space probe circled Mars.*

**circuit** *noun* (**circuits**)
(*say* **ser**-kit)
1 a circular line or journey. 2 a racecourse.
3 the path of an electric current.
**circuit-breaker**, an automatic device for
stopping the flow of current in an electric
circuit.

**circular¹** *adjective*
like a circle; round.

**circular²** *noun* (**circulars**)
a letter, advertisement, etc. sent to a lot of people.

**circulate** *verb* (**circulates, circulating, circulated**)
1 to move around and come back to the beginning, *Blood circulates in the body.* 2 to send something to people, *Has the announcement been circulated?*

**circulation** *noun* (**circulations**)
1 the movement of blood around your body. 2 the number of copies of each issue of a newspaper, etc. that are sold.

**circumference** *noun* (**circumferences**)
the line or distance round something, especially round a circle.

**circumstance** *noun* (**circumstances**)
a fact, condition, event, etc. connected with someone or something, *He won under difficult circumstances.*

**circus** *noun* (**circuses**)
an entertainment with clowns, acrobats, animals, etc., usually performed in a big tent.

**cistern** *noun* (**cisterns**)
a water-tank.

**citizen** *noun* (**citizens**)
1 someone born in a city or country, or living there. 2 someone who has full rights in a country.
**citizenship** *noun*

**citric acid** *noun*
a weak acid found in fruits like lemons and limes.

**citrus** *adjective*
of fruits like oranges, lemons, and grapefruit.

**city** *noun* (**cities**)
a large, important town.
**city-state,** (*in History*) a large town which, with the country area around it, was an independent state.

**civic** *adjective*
of a city, citizens, or their council.

**civil** *adjective*
1 of citizens. 2 of the people who are not in the armed forces. 3 polite.
**civil engineering,** designing and making roads, bridges, and large buildings.
**civil rights,** the rights of citizens, especially to have freedom, equality, and the right to vote.
**civil service,** the people who organize the running of a country.
**civil war,** a war fought between groups of people of the same country, such as the English Civil War (1642–51) or the American Civil War (1861–65).

**civilian** *noun* (**civilians**)
someone who is not in the armed forces.

**civilization** *noun* (**civilizations**)
1 making or becoming civilized. 2 a civilized condition or society.

**civilize** *verb* (**civilizes, civilizing, civilized**)
to improve someone's behaviour, manners, education, etc.

**clad** *adjective*
clothed, *a knight clad in armour.*

**claim¹** *verb* (**claims, claiming, claimed**)
1 to ask for something that you think belongs to you. 2 to state or assert.

**claim²** *noun* (**claims**)
1 claiming. 2 something claimed, especially a piece of ground claimed or given for mining, etc.

**claimant** *noun* (**claimants**)
someone who asks for something that he or she thinks should be given to him or her, especially benefit payments.

**clam** *noun* (**clams**)
a large shellfish.

**clamber** *verb* (**clambers, clambering, clambered**)
to climb with difficulty, *We clambered up the muddy slope.*

**clammy** *adjective* (**clammier, clammiest**)
damp and cold or slimy.

**clamp¹** *noun* (**clamps**)
a device for holding things together.

**clamp²** *verb* (**clamps, clamping, clamped**)
to fix with a clamp.
**clamp down on something,** to stop or try to stop something.

**clan** *noun* (**clans**)
a group sharing the same ancestor, *The Scottish clans include the Campbells and the MacDonalds.*

**clang** *verb* (**clangs, clanging, clanged**)
to make a loud ringing sound.

**clanger** *noun* (**clangers**)
(*slang*) a blunder.
**drop a clanger,** to make a blunder.

**clank** *verb* (**clanks, clanking, clanked**)
to make a loud sound like heavy pieces of metal banging together.

**clap¹** *verb* (**claps, clapping, clapped**)
to make a noise by hitting the palms of your hands together, especially as applause.

**clap²** *noun* (**claps**)
1 clapping, especially as applause, *Give our winning team a good clap!* 2 a sudden sharp noise, *a clap of thunder.*

**cleanse**

**clapper** *noun* (**clappers**)
the loose piece inside a bell which makes it
ring when the bell is moved.
**like the clappers**, (*slang*) very quickly or very
hard.

**clarify** *verb* (**clarifies, clarifying, clarified**)
to make something clear.
**clarification** *noun*

**clarinet** *noun* (**clarinets**)
a woodwind instrument.
**clarinettist** *noun*

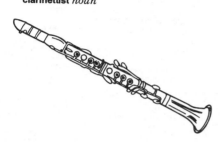

**clarity** *noun*
clearness, *Speak with clarity.*

**clash**¹ *verb* (**clashes, clashing, clashed**)
**1** to make a loud sound like cymbals
banging together. **2** to happen
inconveniently at the same time, *I missed
one of those programmes because they
clashed.* **3** to come into conflict, *Gangs of
rival supporters clashed outside the
stadium.*

**clash**² *noun* (**clashes**)
**1** a clashing sound. **2** a conflict.

**clasp**¹ *verb* (**clasps, clasping, clasped**)
to hold someone or something tightly.

**clasp**² *noun* (**clasps**)
**1** a device for fastening things. **2** a grasp.

**class**¹ *noun* (**classes**)
**1** a group of similar people, animals, or
things. **2** a system of different ranks in
society. **3** a group of children, students, etc.
who are taught together. **4** (*informal*)
elegant appearance or behaviour, *That
actress has really got class.*

**class**² *verb* (**classes, classing, classed**)
to put things in classes or groups.

**classic**¹ *adjective*
generally agreed to be excellent or
important.

**classic**² *noun* (**classics**)
a book, film, writer, etc. that is generally
agreed to be excellent or important.
**classics**, Greek and Latin language or
literature.

**classical** *adjective*
**1** of Greek or Roman literature, etc.
**2** serious or conventional, *classical music.*

**classified** *adjective*
**1** put into classes or groups. **2** officially
secret, *classified information.*
**classified advertisements**, small
advertisements arranged in subjects.

**classify** *verb* (**classifies, classifying, classified**)
to put things in classes or groups.
**classification** *noun*

**classmate** *noun* (**classmates**)
someone in the same class at school, etc.

**classroom** *noun* (**classrooms**)
a room where a class is taught.

**clatter**¹ *noun*
a rattling or annoying noise.

**clatter**² *verb* (**clatters, clattering, clattered**)
to make a rattling or annoying noise.

**clause** *noun* (**clauses**)
**1** part of a contract, treaty, law, etc. **2** (*in
grammar*) part of a sentence with its own
verb, *There are two clauses in 'I'm wearing
the T-shirt which you gave me'.*

**claw**¹ *noun* (**claws**)
one of the hard, sharp nails that some
birds and other animals have on their feet.

**claw**² *verb* (**claws, clawing, clawed**)
to grasp or scratch with a claw or hand.

**clay** *noun*
a sticky kind of earth, *Clay is used for
making bricks and pottery.*
**clayey** *adjective*

**clean**¹ *adjective* (**cleaner, cleanest**)
**1** without any dirt or stains. **2** fresh; not yet
used, *a clean page.* **3** not rude or obscene,
*clean jokes.* **4** honest; honourable, *a clean
fight.*
**cleanliness** *noun*, **cleanly** *adjective and
adverb*, **cleanness** *noun*

**clean**² *verb* (**cleans, cleaning, cleaned**)
to make something clean.

**clean**³ *adverb*
(*informal*) completely, *I clean forgot.*
**clean bowled**, bowled out in cricket without
your bat touching the ball.
**clean-shaven**, without a beard or moustache.

**cleaner** *noun* (**cleaners**)
**1** someone who cleans rooms, etc.
**2** something used for cleaning.
**the cleaners**, a firm which cleans clothes, etc.

**cleanse** *verb* (**cleanses, cleansing, cleansed**)
(*say* klenz)
**1** to clean. **2** to make something or someone
pure.
**cleanser** *noun*

**clear**[1] *adjective* (**clearer, clearest**)
1 easy to understand, see, or hear, *a clear voice*. 2 free from obstacles or unwanted things, *The table is clear*.
**clearly** *adverb*

**clear**[2] *adverb*
1 clearly, *Speak loud and clear*.
2 completely, *He got clear away*. 3 at a distance from something, *Stand clear of the gates*.

**clear**[3] *verb* (**clears, clearing, cleared**)
1 to make or become clear. 2 to show or check that someone is innocent or reliable. 3 to jump over something without touching it.
**clear off**, (*informal*) to go away.
**clear out**, to empty or tidy something; (*informal*) to go away.
**clear up**, to make things tidy.

**clearance** *noun* (**clearances**)
1 clearing something. 2 getting rid of unwanted goods. 3 the space between two things.

**clearing** *noun* (**clearings**)
an open space in a forest.

**clef** *noun* (**clefs**)
a sign that shows the pitch of a stave in music.

**clench** *verb* (**clenches, clenching, clenched**)
to close your teeth or fingers tightly.

**clergy** *plural noun*
people who have official permission to conduct services in a Christian church.

**clergyman** *noun* (**clergymen**)
a male member of the clergy.

**clerical** *adjective*
1 of or done by clerks. 2 of the clergy.

**clerk** *noun* (**clerks**)
(*say* klark)
someone employed to keep records and accounts, deal with papers in an office, etc.

**clever** *adjective* (**cleverer, cleverest**)
quick to learn and understand things; skilful.

**cliché** *noun* (**clichés**)
(*say* klee-shay)
a phrase or idea that is used too often.

**click** *noun* (**clicks**)
a short, sharp sound, *She heard a click as someone turned on the light*.

**client** *noun* (**clients**)
someone who gets help or advice from a lawyer, architect, accountant, etc.; a customer.

**cliff** *noun* (**cliffs**)
a steep rock-face, especially on the coast.

**cliffhanger** *noun* (**cliffhangers**)
something like a story or a sports match that is exciting because you do not know how it will finish.

**climate** *noun* (**climates**)
the normal weather in a particular area.
**climatic** *adjective*

**climax** *noun* (**climaxes**)
the most important part of a story, series of events, etc.
**climactic** *adjective*

**climb** *verb* (**climbs, climbing, climbed**)
1 to go up or down something. 2 to grow upwards. 3 to rise.
**climb down**, to admit that you have been wrong.
**climber** *noun*

**cling** *verb* (**clings, clinging, clung**)
to hold on tightly, *The child clung to its mother*.

**cling film** *noun*
(*trademark*) a thin, clear plastic material that sticks to itself easily and is used especially for wrapping food.

**clinic** *noun* (**clinics**)
a place where people see doctors, etc. for treatment or advice.

**clink** *verb* (**clinks, clinking, clinked**)
to make a short ringing sound.

**clip**[1] *noun* (**clips**)
a fastener for keeping things together.

**clip**[2] *verb* (**clips, clipping, clipped**)
1 to fasten with a clip. 2 to cut something with shears or scissors.
**clippers** *noun*

**clipboard** *noun* (**clipboards**)
a board that you can carry around, with a clip at the top to hold papers.

**clipper** *noun* (**clippers**)
an old type of fast sailing-ship.

**clipping** *noun* (**clippings**)
a piece cut off or out, especially from a newspaper or magazine.

**cloak** *noun* (**cloaks**)
a piece of clothing, usually without sleeves, that hangs loosely from your shoulders.

**cloakroom** *noun* (**cloakrooms**)
1 a place where you can leave coats, hats, luggage, etc. 2 a lavatory.

**clobber** *verb* (**clobbers, clobbering, clobbered**)
(*slang*) to hit someone hard.

**clock** *noun* (**clocks**)
a device that shows what the time is.

**clockwise** *adverb* and *adjective*
moving round a circle in the same direction as a clock's hands.

**clockwork** *adjective*
worked by a spring which you wind up.

**clog**[1] *verb* (**clogs, clogging, clogged**)
to block something up.

**clog**[2] *noun* (**clogs**)
a shoe with a wooden sole.

**cloister** *noun* (**cloisters**)
a covered path round a courtyard or along the side of a cathedral, monastery, etc.

**clone**[1] *noun* (**clones**)
an animal or plant made from the cells of another animal or plant.

**clone**[2] *verb* (**clones, cloning, cloned**)
to produce a clone.

**close**[1] *adjective* (**closer, closest**)
(*say* klohss)
1 near. 2 careful; detailed, *with close attention.* 3 tight; with little empty space, *a close fit.* 4 in which competitors are nearly equal, *a close race.* 5 stuffy, *It's very close in this room.*
**closely** *adverb*, **closeness** *noun*

**close**[2] *adverb* (**closer, closest**)
(*say* klohss)
closely, *Follow close behind.*

**close**[3] *noun* (**closes**)
(*say* klohss)
1 a dead end. 2 an enclosed area, especially round a cathedral.

**close**[4] *verb* (**closes, closing, closed**)
(*say* klohz)
1 to shut. 2 to end.
**close in,** to get nearer or shorter, *The police closed in around the house. The evenings close in as winter gets nearer.*

**close-up** *noun* (**close-ups**)
(*say* **klohss**-up)
a photograph or film taken at short range.

**closure** *noun* (**closures**)
(*say* **kloh**-*zh*er)
the closing of something.

**clot**[1] *noun* (**clots**)
1 a mass of blood, cream, etc. that has nearly become solid. 2 (*informal*) a stupid person.

**clot**[2] *verb* (**clots, clotting, clotted**)
to form into clots.

**cloth** *noun* (**cloths**)
1 material woven from wool, cotton, nylon, etc. 2 a piece of this material. 3 a tablecloth.

**clothe** *verb* (**clothes, clothing, clothed**)
to put clothes on.

**clothes** *plural noun*
things worn to cover your body.
**clothes-line,** a line on which clothes are hung to dry or air.
**clothes-peg,** a device to hold clothes on a clothes-line.

**clothing** *noun*
clothes.

**cloud**[1] *noun* (**clouds**)
a mass of water-vapour, smoke, dust, etc. floating in the air.
**cloudless** *adjective*

**cloud**[2] *verb* (**clouds, clouding, clouded**)
to fill or obscure with clouds, *The sky clouded over.*

**cloudy** *adjective* (**cloudier, cloudiest**)
1 full of clouds. 2 hard to see through, *a cloudy liquid.*

**clout** *verb* (**clouts, clouting, clouted**)
to give someone or something a hard blow.

**clove** *noun* (**cloves**)
the dried bud of a tropical tree, used to flavour apple-pies, etc.

**clove-hitch** *noun* (**clove-hitches**)
a knot for fixing a rope to a pole, etc.

**clover** *noun*
a small wild plant, usually with three leaves, *A clover-leaf is like three small leaves joined together.*

**clown**[1] *noun* (**clowns**)
1 someone in a circus who makes people laugh. 2 an amusing person.

**clown**[2] *verb* (**clowns, clowning, clowned**)
to behave like a clown.

**club**[1] *noun* (**clubs**)
1 a heavy stick. 2 a stick for playing golf. 3 a group of people who meet together because they are interested in the same thing. 4 a playing-card with a black clover-leaf printed on it.

**club**[2] *verb* (**clubs, clubbing, clubbed**)
to hit with a heavy stick.
**club together,** to join with other people in doing something, especially raising money.

**cluck** *verb* (**clucks, clucking, clucked**)
to make a noise like a hen.

**clue** *noun* (**clues**)
something that helps you to solve a puzzle or a mystery.
**not have a clue,** to be ignorant or helpless.

**clueless** *adjective*
(*informal*) stupid; having no idea of how to do something.

**clump** *noun* (**clumps**)
a cluster of trees.

**clumsy** *adjective* (**clumsier, clumsiest**)
likely to knock things over, drop things, or
do something stupid.
**clumsily** *adverb*, **clumsiness** *noun*

**clung** past tense and past participle of **cling**.

**cluster** *noun* (**clusters**)
a group of people or things close together.

**clutch**[1] *verb* (**clutches, clutching, clutched**)
to grasp or snatch at something.

**clutch**[2] *noun* (**clutches**)
1 a tight grasp. 2 a device for disconnecting
the engine of a motor vehicle from its gears
and wheels.

**clutch**[3] *noun* (**clutches**)
a set of eggs in a nest.

**clutter**[1] *verb* (**clutters, cluttering, cluttered**)
to make something untidy or confused.

**clutter**[2] *noun*
a lot of things left around untidily.

**cm** short for **centimetre** or **centimetres**.

**Co.** short for **company**.

**c/o** short for **care of**.

**coach**[1] *noun* (**coaches**)
1 a comfortable bus, usually with one deck,
used for long journeys. 2 a carriage of a
railway train. 3 a carriage pulled by horses.
4 an instructor in athletics, sports, etc.

**coach**[2] *verb* (**coaches, coaching, coached**)
to instruct or train someone in athletics,
sports, etc.

**coal** *noun*
a hard, black mineral used as fuel.

**coarse** *adjective* (**coarser, coarsest**)
1 not delicate or smooth. 2 rough, *coarse
humour.*

**coast**[1] *noun* (**coasts**)
the seashore and the land close to it.
**coastal** *adjective*, **coastline** *noun*

**coast**[2] *verb* (**coasts, coasting, coasted**)
to ride downhill without using power, *They
stopped pedalling and coasted down the
slope.*

**coastguard** *noun* (**coastguards**)
someone whose job is to keep watch on
coasts, prevent smuggling, etc.

**coat**[1] *noun* (**coats**)
1 a piece of clothing with sleeves, worn over
other clothes. 2 a coating, *a coat of paint.*
**coat-hanger,** a shaped piece of wood, wire, or
plastic for hanging a piece of clothing on.
**coat of arms,** a design on a shield, etc.
representing a family, town, etc.

**coat**[2] *verb* (**coats, coating, coated**)
to cover with a coating.

**coating** *noun* (**coatings**)
a covering; a layer.

**coax** *verb* (**coaxes, coaxing, coaxed**)
to persuade someone gently or patiently.

**cobalt** *noun*
a silvery-white metal.

**cobble** *noun* (**cobbles**)
a cobble-stone.

**cobbled** *adjective*
paved with cobble-stones.

**cobbler** *noun* (**cobblers**)
someone who mends shoes.
**cobblers,** (*slang*) nonsense.

**cobble-stone** *noun* (**cobble-stones**)
a smooth, round stone, *Streets used to be
paved with cobble-stones.*

**cobra** *noun* (**cobras**)
(*say* **koh**-brǎ)
a poisonous snake.

**cobweb** *noun* (**cobwebs**)
a thin, sticky net spun by a spider to trap
insects.

**cock**[1] *noun* (**cocks**)
a male bird, especially a male fowl.

**cock**[2] *verb* (**cocks, cocking, cocked**)
1 to turn something upwards or in a
particular direction, *He cocked his eye at
me.* 2 to make a gun ready to fire.

**cockerel** *noun* (**cockerels**)
a young male fowl.

**cocker spaniel** *noun* (**cocker spaniels**)
a kind of small spaniel.

**cockle** *noun* (**cockles**)
an edible shellfish.

**cockney** *noun* (**cockneys**)
1 someone born in London, especially in
east London. 2 a kind of English spoken by
cockneys.

**cockpit** *noun* (**cockpits**)
the place for the pilot in an aircraft.

**cockroach** *noun* (**cockroaches**)
a dark brown insect.

**cocky** *adjective* (**cockier, cockiest**)
(*informal*) conceited; cheeky.

**cocoa** *noun* (**cocoas**)
1 a hot drink that tastes of chocolate. 2 the
powder from which you make this drink.

**coconut** *noun* (**coconuts**)
a large, round nut that grows on palm
trees, *Coconuts contain a sweet white
lining and a milky juice.*

**cocoon** *noun* (**cocoons**)
the covering round a chrysalis.

**cod** *noun* (**cod**)
a large, edible sea-fish.

**code**[1] *noun* (**codes**)
**1** a set of signs, letters, etc. for sending messages secretly or quickly. **2** a set of rules, *the Highway Code.*

**code**[2] *verb* (**codes, coding, coded**)
**1** to change a message into signs, letters, etc. so that its meaning is secret. **2** to put something into a form that can be accepted by a computer, *The data is coded and entered.*

**coeducation** *noun*
educating boys and girls together.
**coeducational** *adjective*

**coffee** *noun* (**coffees**)
**1** a hot drink made from the roasted and crushed beans of a tropical shrub. **2** the powder from which you make this drink.

**coffin** *noun* (**coffins**)
the long box in which a corpse is buried or cremated.

**cog** *noun* (**cogs**)
one of a number of pieces sticking out from the edge of a wheel and allowing it to drive another wheel.
**cog-wheel,** a wheel with cogs.

**cohort** *noun* (**cohorts**)
in the ancient Roman army, any one of the ten parts of a legion.

**coil**[1] *noun* (**coils**)
a circle or spiral of rope, wire, etc.

**coil**[2] *verb* (**coils, coiling, coiled**)
to wind something into circles or spirals.

**coin**[1] *noun* (**coins**)
a piece of metal money.

**coin**[2] *verb* (**coins, coining, coined**)
**1** to manufacture money. **2** to invent a new word.

**coinage** *noun* (**coinages**)
**1** coining. **2** coins; a system of money. **3** a new word.

**coincide** *verb* (**coincides, coinciding, coincided**)
to happen at the same time as something else, *The end of term coincides with my birthday.*

**coincidence** *noun* (**coincidences**)
the way that two things can happen accidentally at the same time; a case of this happening.

**coke** *noun*
a solid fuel made out of coal.

**cola** *noun*
a sweet, brown, fizzy drink.

**colander** *noun* (**colanders**)
(*say* kul-ăn-der)
a strainer for vegetables, etc.

**cold**[1] *adjective* (**colder, coldest**)
**1** not hot or warm. **2** not kind or emotional.
**cold cream,** ointment for cleaning or softening the skin.
**cold war,** a situation where nations are enemies without actually fighting.
**give someone the cold shoulder,** to be unfriendly to someone.
**coldly** *adverb*, **coldness** *noun*

**cold**[2] *noun* (**colds**)
**1** cold weather or temperature. **2** an illness that makes your nose run, gives you a sore throat, etc.

**cold-blooded** *adjective*
**1** having blood that changes temperature according to the surroundings. **2** ruthless.

**coleslaw** *noun*
a salad made of chopped cabbage covered in mayonnaise.

**collaborate** *verb* (**collaborates, collaborating, collaborated**)
to work with someone on a job; to help, *He was said to have collaborated with the enemy.*
**collaboration** *noun*, **collaborator** *noun*

**collage** *noun* (**collages**)
(*say* kol-ah*zh* or kol-ah*zh*)
a picture made by fixing small objects to a surface.

**collapse** *verb* (**collapses, collapsing, collapsed**)
**1** to fall to pieces; to break. **2** to become very weak or ill.

**collapsible** *adjective*
that can be folded up, *a collapsible table.*

**collar** *noun* (**collars**)
**1** the part of a garment that goes round your neck. **2** a band that goes round the neck of a dog, cat, horse, etc.

**collate** *verb* (**collates, collating, collated**)
to collect and arrange something in an organized way, *Collate the results, showing them on a graph.*

**colleague** *noun* (**colleagues**)
someone that you work with.

**collect** *verb* (**collects, collecting, collected**)
1 to get things together from various places, especially as a hobby, *She collects stamps; I collect coins.* 2 to go and get someone or something.
**collector** *noun*

**collection** *noun* (**collections**)
1 things you have collected as a hobby. 2 money given by people at a meeting, church service, etc.

**collective** *adjective*
including or using many or all people or things.
**collective noun**, a singular noun that is a name for a group of things or people, *In 'a pack of dogs', 'pack' is a collective noun.*

**college** *noun* (**colleges**)
a place where people can continue learning something after they have left school.

**collide** *verb* (**collides, colliding, collided**)
to crash into something, *The bicycle collided with the car.*
**collision** *noun*

**collie** *noun* (**collies**)
a breed of dog with a long, pointed muzzle and long hair.

**colloquial** *adjective*
suitable for conversation but not for formal speech or writing, *'Chuck' is a colloquial word for 'throw'.*

**colon** *noun* (**colons**)
a punctuation mark (:), *Colons are often used to introduce lists like this: red, blue, green.*

**colonel** *noun* (**colonels**)
(*say* **ker-nĕl**)
an army officer, usually in charge of a regiment.

**colonial** *adjective*
of colonies.

**colonist** *noun* (**colonists**)
a person who settles in a place and lives in a colony there, *seventeenth-century colonists in America.*

**colony** *noun* (**colonies**)
1 a country controlled by another country. 2 a group of people or animals living together.

**colossal** *adjective*
huge; great.

**colour**[1] *noun* (**colours**)
1 the effect produced by rays of light of a particular wavelength, *Red, blue, and yellow are colours.* 2 the use of all colours, not just black and white, *Is this film in colour?* 3 the colour of someone's skin. 4 a substance used to give colour to things. 5 the special flag of a ship or regiment.

**colour**[2] *verb* (**colours, colouring, coloured**)
1 to give something a colour or colours. 2 to change or exaggerate something. 3 to blush.
**colouring** *noun*

**colour-blind** *adjective*
unable to see or distinguish between some colours.

**coloured** *adjective*
1 having a particular colour. 2 with a very dark skin.

USAGE: The word **coloured**, used to describe people, is often considered to be insulting; it is better to use **black**.

**colourful** *adjective*
full of colour; lively, *a colourful story of life in 18th-century Cornwall.*

**colourless** *adjective*
1 without colour, *Many gases are colourless.* 2 uninteresting, *a colourless town.*

**colt** *noun* (**colts**)
a young male horse.

**column** *noun* (**columns**)
1 a pillar. 2 something long and narrow. 3 a vertical part of a page, *Newspapers are printed in columns.* 4 a regular feature in a newspaper, *a gossip column.*
**columnist** *noun*

**coma** *noun* (**comas**)
(*say* **koh-mă**)
an unnatural deep sleep.

**comb**[1] *noun* (**combs**)
1 a device for making hair tidy. 2 the red, fleshy crest on a fowl's head.

**comb**[2] *verb* (**combs, combing, combed**)
1 to tidy with a comb. 2 to search carefully.

**combat**[1] *noun* (**combats**)
a fight or contest.
**combatant** *noun*

**combat**[2] *verb* (**combats, combating, combated**)
to struggle against something.

**combination** *noun* (**combinations**)
1 combining. 2 a series of numbers or letters used to open a combination lock.
**combination lock,** a lock that is opened by setting a dial or dials to positions shown by numbers or letters.

**combine**[1] *verb* (**combines, combining, combined**)
(*say* kŏm-**byn**)
to join or mix together.

**combine**[2] *noun* (**combines**)
(*say* kom-**byn**)
a group of people combining in business.
**combine harvester,** a machine that reaps and threshes grain.

**combustion** *noun*
the process of burning.

**come** *verb* (**comes, coming, came, come**)
1 to move towards a person or place, *Come here!* 2 to arrive; to reach a place, *Has that letter come yet?* 3 to become, *Dreams can come true.* 4 to occur, *It comes on the next page.* 5 to amount, *The bill came to £10.*
**come about,** to happen.
**come across someone,** to meet someone.
**come by something,** to get something.
**come round** or **come to,** to become conscious, after being unconscious.

**comeback** *noun* (**comebacks**)
a return to the success that someone had at an earlier time, *Some pop stars have had several comebacks.*

**comedian** *noun* (**comedians**)
someone who entertains people by making them laugh.

**comedy** *noun* (**comedies**)
1 a play, film, etc. that makes people laugh.
2 humour.

**comet** *noun* (**comets**)
an object moving across the sky with a bright tail of light.

**comfort**[1] *noun*
freedom from worry or pain.

**comfort**[2] *verb* (**comforts, comforting, comforted**)
to give someone comfort.

**comfortable** *adjective*
1 pleasant to use or wear, *a comfortable chair.* 2 free from worry or pain, *The nurse made the patient comfortable.*
**comfortably** *adverb*

**comic**[1] *adjective*
making people laugh.
**comic strip,** a series of drawings telling a funny story or a story in several parts.
**comical** *adjective*, **comically** *adverb*

**comic**[2] *noun* (**comics**)
1 a comedian. 2 a paper full of comic strips.

**coming**[1] *noun* (**comings**)
arrival, *comings and goings.*

**coming**[2] *adjective*
future, *in the coming years.*

**comma** *noun* (**commas**)
a punctuation mark (,) used to mark a pause in a sentence or to separate items in a list.

**command**[1] *noun* (**commands**)
1 telling someone to do something.
2 authority; control, *He is in command of these soldiers.* 3 skill or ability, *She has a good command of Spanish.*

**command**[2] *verb* (**commands, commanding, commanded**)
1 to tell someone to do something. 2 to be in charge of, *A centurion commanded a hundred soldiers.*
**commandant** *noun*, **commander** *noun*

**commandment** *noun* (**commandments**)
a sacred command, especially one of the Ten Commandments of Moses.

**commando** *noun* (**commandos**)
a soldier trained for making dangerous raids.

**commemorate** *verb* (**commemorates, commemorating, commemorated**)
to be a celebration or reminder of some past event, person, etc.
**commemoration** *noun*, **commemorative** *adjective*

**commence** *verb* (**commences, commencing, commenced**)
to begin.
**commencement** *noun*

**commend** *verb* (**commends, commending, commended**)
to praise, *He was commended for bravery.*
**commendable** *adjective*, **commendation** *noun*

**comment** *noun* (comments)
a remark or opinion.

**commentary** *noun* (commentaries)
a description of an event, especially while
it is happening.

**commentator** *noun* (commentators)
a person who gives a commentary on
events, especially sports.
**commentate** *verb*

**commerce** *noun*
trade.

**commercial**[1] *adjective*
1 connected with trade. 2 intended to make
a profit, *a commercial design studio.*
3 financed by advertisements, *commercial
radio.*
**commercial traveller**, someone employed to
travel around and get orders for goods from
shops, etc.
**commercially** *adverb*

**commercial**[2] *noun* (commercials)
an advertisement, especially on television
or radio.

**commercialized** *adjective*
altered so as to make money, or more
money than before, usually with a loss of
quality, *A lot of Greek holiday resorts are
becoming very commercialized.*

**commit** *verb* (commits, committing, committed)
1 to do something, *She committed the
crime.* 2 to put a person or thing into a
particular place, *He was committed to
prison.*
**to commit yourself**, to promise or decide to do
something.
**commitment** *noun*

**committee** *noun* (committees)
a group of people appointed to organize or
discuss something.

**commodity** *noun* (commodities)
a product that is bought and sold,
especially a mineral or a farm product.

**common**[1] *adjective* (commoner, commonest)
1 ordinary; usual; happening often, *The
dandelion is a common plant.* 2 of all or
most people, *It was common knowledge.*
3 shared, *Music was their common interest.*
4 vulgar.
**Common Market**, a group of European
countries that share some of their laws and
that trade freely together; the European
Community.

**common**[2] *noun* (commons)
a piece of land that anyone can use.

**commonplace** *adjective*
ordinary, *a commonplace remark about the
weather.*

**common-room** *noun* (common-rooms)
an informal room for teachers or pupils at
a school, college, etc.

**commonwealth** *noun* (commonwealths)
a group of countries cooperating together.
**the Commonwealth**, an association of Britain
and various other countries, such as
Canada, Australia, and New Zealand.

**commotion** *noun* (commotions)
an uproar.

**communal** *adjective*
shared by several people.

**commune** *noun* (communes)
a group of people sharing a home, food, etc.

**communicate** *verb* (communicates,
communicating, communicated)
to pass news, information, opinions, etc. to
other people.
**communicative** *adjective*

**communication** *noun* (communications)
1 communicating. 2 something
communicated; a message. 3 a way of
communicating, *Communications include
radio, television, and telephones.*
**communication cord**, a cord or chain inside a
train that you can pull to stop the train in
an emergency.

**communion** *noun* (communions)
religious fellowship.
**Communion**, the Christian ceremony in
which holy bread and wine are given to
worshippers.

**communism** *noun*
a system where property is shared by the
community.
**Communism**, a political system where the
state controls property, production, trade,
etc.; belief in this sort of system.

**Communist** *noun* (Communists)
someone who believes in Communism.

**community** *noun* (communities)
the people living in one area.
**community charge**, a tax to pay for local
services such as refuse collection (replaced
in 1993 by *council tax*).

**commuter** *noun* (commuters)
someone who regularly travels to work,
especially by train or bus.
**commute** *verb*

**compact**[1] *adjective*
small and neat.

**compact**[2] *noun* (compacts)
a small, flat container for face-powder.

**compact disc** *noun* (**compact discs**)
a smooth plastic disc on which digital signals are recorded, and from which the signals are read by a laser beam, *a recording of Beethoven on compact disc.*
**compact-disc player,** a device for reproducing sound recorded on a compact disc.

**companion** *noun* (**companions**)
1 a friend who is with you, or who shares something with you. 2 (in book titles) a reference book, *A Companion to the Lake District.*
**companionship** *noun*

**company** *noun* (**companies**)
1 a group of people doing something together. 2 having people with you, *I am lonely: I need company.* 3 (*informal*) visitors, *We've got company.* 4 an army unit consisting of two or more platoons.

**comparable** *adjective*
(*say* **kom-per-ă-bŭl**)
similar.

**comparative**¹ *noun* (**comparatives**)
the form of a word that expresses 'more', *The comparative of 'big' is 'bigger'; the comparative of 'bad' is 'worse'.*

**comparative**² *adjective*
using or connected with comparisons.
**comparatively** *adverb*

**compare** *verb* (**compares, comparing, compared**)
to work out or say how things are similar, *Compare your answers.*
**compare with,** to be similar to; to be as good as, *How does his car compare with ours? Our football pitch cannot compare with Wembley Stadium.*

**comparison** *noun* (**comparisons**)
the action of comparing.

**compartment** *noun* (**compartments**)
a part or division of something, especially of a railway carriage.

**compass** *noun* (**compasses**)
an instrument that shows you where north is.
**compasses** or **pair of compasses,** a device for drawing circles.

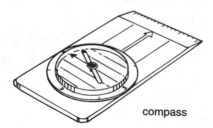

compass

**compassion** *noun*
pity; mercy.
**compassionate** *adjective*

**compatible** *adjective*
1 able to live or exist together without trouble. 2 (*in Computing*) able to be used together, *This computer and that printer are compatible.*

**compel** *verb* (**compels, compelling, compelled**)
to force someone to do something.

**compensate** *verb* (**compensates, compensating, compensated**)
to give someone something to make up for a loss, injury, etc.
**compensation** *noun*

**compère** *noun* (**compères**)
(*say* **kom-pair**)
someone who introduces the performers in a show or broadcast.

**compete** *verb* (**competes, competing, competed**)
to take part in a competition.

**competent** *adjective*
able to do a particular thing, *He is not competent to teach French.*
**competence** *noun*

**competition** *noun* (**competitions**)
a game, race, etc. in which you try to do better than other people.
**competitive** *adjective*, **competitor** *noun*

**compile** *verb* (**compiles, compiling, compiled**)
to collect and arrange information, quotations, etc., *She compiled an anthology of poetry.*
**compilation** *noun*, **compiler** *noun*

**complacent** *adjective*
satisfied with the way you are, with what you do, etc., and not worried about what is wrong with your situation, *Nobody should be complacent about wasting resources.*

**complain** *verb* (**complains, complaining, complained**)
to say that you are not pleased about something.

**complaint** *noun* (**complaints**)
1 complaining. 2 an illness.

**complement** *noun* (**complements**)
1 the amount needed to fill or complete something, *This ship has a full complement of sailors.* 2 a word or words used after a verb to complete the meaning, *In 'She is brave' and 'He was made king', the complements are 'brave' and 'king'.*
**complementary** *adjective*

USAGE: Do not confuse **complement** with **compliment**, which means words or actions that show approval.

**complete**[1] *adjective*
1 having all its parts, *a complete jigsaw puzzle.* 2 finished, *The work is complete.* 3 in every way, *It came as a complete surprise.*
**completely** *adverb*

**complete**[2] *verb* (**completes, completing, completed**)
to make something complete.
**completion** *noun*

**complex**[1] *adjective*
complicated.
**complexity** *noun*

**complex**[2] *noun* (**complexes**)
1 a group of related things, especially a group of buildings. 2 a fixed idea or set of attitudes.

**complexion** *noun* (**complexions**)
the colour or appearance of your skin, especially of your face.

**complicated** *adjective*
1 made of a lot of different parts. 2 difficult.

**complication** *noun* (**complications**)
1 a complicated situation or condition. 2 a difficulty, especially a new one.

**compliment** *noun* (**compliments**)
words or actions that show you approve of a person or thing.
**complimentary** *adjective*

USAGE: Do not confuse **compliment** with **complement**, which means the amount needed to complete something, or the words after a verb.

**component** *noun* (**components**)
a part, especially of a machine.

**compose** *verb* (**composes, composing, composed**)
1 to write music. 2 to make or build up something.
**composer** *noun*

**composition** *noun* (**compositions**)
1 composing. 2 a piece of music. 3 an essay.

**compost** *noun*
manure made of decayed leaves, grass, etc.

**compound**[1] *adjective*
made of two or more parts or ingredients.

**compound**[2] *noun* (**compounds**)
1 a compound substance, *Water is a compound of hydrogen and oxygen.* 2 a fenced area containing buildings.

**comprehend** *verb* (**comprehends, comprehending, comprehended**)
1 to understand. 2 to include.

**comprehension** *noun* (**comprehensions**)
1 understanding. 2 an exercise that tests or helps your understanding of a language.

**comprehensive**[1] *adjective*
including all or many kinds of people or things.
**comprehensive school,** a secondary school for all or most of the children in an area.

**comprehensive**[2] *noun* (**comprehensives**)
a comprehensive school.

**compress** *verb* (**compresses, compressing, compressed**)
1 to press or squeeze together. 2 to get something into a small space.
**compression** *noun*, **compressor** *noun*

**comprise** *verb* (**comprises, comprising, comprised**)
to include; to consist of.

USAGE: Do not use **comprise** with 'of'. It is incorrect to say *The group was comprised of twenty men;* the correct way to say this is: *The group was composed of twenty men.*

**compromise**[1] *noun* (**compromises**)
(*say* kom-prŏ-myz)
settling a dispute by accepting less than you wanted.

**compromise**[2] *verb* (**compromises, compromising, compromise**)
(*say* kom-prŏ-myz)
to accept less than you wanted in order to settle a dispute.

**compulsory** *adjective*
that must be done, *The wearing of seat-belts is compulsory;* not voluntary, *compulsory military service.*

**compute** *verb* (**computes, computing, computed**)
to calculate.
**computation** *noun*

**computer** *noun* (**computers**)
a machine that quickly and automatically does calculations, solves problems, etc.
**computer science,** the study of how computers work and are used.
**computer virus,** a program written deliberately to disrupt the working of a computer system.

**computerize** *verb* (**computerizes, computerizing, computerized**)
to equip with computers; to do something by computer, *Has your office been computerized yet? a computerized booking.*

**comrade** *noun* (**comrades**)
a friend or companion.
**comradeship** *noun*

**con** *verb* (**cons, conning, conned**)
(*slang*) to swindle.

**concave** *adjective*
curved like the inside of a circle or ball.

**conceal** *verb* (**conceals, concealing, concealed**)
to hide.
**concealment** *noun*

**conceit** *noun*
vanity; pride.
**conceited** *adjective*

**conceive** *verb* (**conceives, conceiving, conceived**)
1 to become pregnant. 2 to form an idea, plan, etc.

**concentrate** *verb* (**concentrates, concentrating, concentrated**)
1 to give your full attention to something; to think hard about one thing. 2 to bring or come together in one place. 3 to make a liquid stronger by removing water, etc. from it.

**concentration** *noun* (**concentrations**)
1 giving your full attention to something. 2 condensing a liquid. 3 the strength of a liquid, etc., *Test the effect of acid in different concentrations.*
**concentration camp,** a place where political prisoners, etc. are held.

**concentric** *adjective*
having the same centre.

**concept** *noun* (**concepts**)
an idea.

**conception** *noun* (**conceptions**)
1 conceiving. 2 an idea.

**concern**[1] *verb* (**concerns, concerning, concerned**)
1 to be important or interesting to someone. 2 to be about a particular subject, *This story concerns a shipwreck.* 3 to worry someone.

**concern**[2] *noun* (**concerns**)
1 something that concerns you. 2 a business.

**concerning** *preposition*
on the subject of; in connection with.

**concert** *noun* (**concerts**)
a musical entertainment.

**concertina** *noun* (**concertinas**)
a portable musical instrument that you squeeze to push air past reeds.

**concerto** *noun* (**concertos**)
(*say* kŏn-**cher**-toh)
a piece of music for one instrument and an orchestra.

**concession** *noun* (**concessions**)
something that someone lets you have or do, *As a special concession, parents may park in the teachers' car park on Sports Day.*

**concise** *adjective*
brief; giving a lot of information in a few words.

USAGE: Do not confuse **concise** with **precise**, which means exact.

**conclude** *verb* (**concludes, concluding, concluded**)
1 to end. 2 to decide, *The jury concluded that he was not guilty.*

**conclusion** *noun* (**conclusions**)
1 an ending. 2 a decision.
**in conclusion,** lastly.

**concrete**[1] *noun*
cement mixed with gravel, etc. and used in building.

**concrete**[2] *adjective*
that can be touched or felt; definite, *We must have concrete evidence.*

**concussion** *noun*
an injury to the brain caused by a hard knock.

**condemn** *verb* (**condemns, condemning, condemned**)
1 to say that you strongly disagree with something. 2 to convict or sentence a criminal, *He was condemned to death.* 3 to declare that houses, etc. are not fit to be used.
**condemnation** *noun*

**condense** *verb* (**condenses, condensing, condensed**)
1 to make liquid, etc. stronger or thicker, *condensed milk*. 2 to make something smaller or shorter, *a condensed report*. 3 to change into water or other liquid, *Steam condenses on cold windows*.
**condensation** *noun*, **condenser** *noun*

**condition**[1] *noun* (**conditions**)
1 the character or state of a person or thing; how someone or something is, *This bike is in good condition*. 2 being physically fit, *Get in condition*. 3 something that must happen if something else is to happen, *Learning to swim is a condition of going sailing*.
**on condition** or **on condition that**, only if.

**condition**[2] *verb* (**conditions, conditioning, conditioned**)
1 to put something into a proper condition. 2 to train or accustom, *They have been conditioned to obey unquestioningly*.

**condom** *noun* (**condoms**)
a rubber sheath to cover a man's penis, used as a contraceptive and as protection against disease.

**conduct**[1] *verb* (**conducts, conducting, conducted**)
(*say* kŏn-**dukt**)
1 to lead or guide. 2 to organize or manage something. 3 to direct the performance of an orchestra, etc. 4 to allow electricity, heat, etc. to pass along, *Copper conducts electricity well*.

**conduct**[2] *noun*
(*say* **kon**-dukt)
behaviour.

**conduction** *noun*
the conducting of electricity, heat, etc., *Heat can be transferred by conduction, convection, or radiation*.

**conductor** *noun* (**conductors**)
1 someone who sells tickets on a bus, etc. 2 someone who conducts an orchestra, etc. 3 something that conducts electricity, heat, etc.

**conductress** *noun* (**conductresses**)
a female bus-conductor.

**cone** *noun* (**cones**)
1 an object which is circular at one end and pointed at the other end. 2 an ice-cream cornet. 3 the fruit of a pine, fir, or cedar.

**confectioner** *noun* (**confectioners**)
someone who makes or sells sweets.
**confectionery** *noun*

**confer** *verb* (**confers, conferring, conferred**)
1 to give someone a title, honour, etc. 2 to have a discussion.

**conference** *noun* (**conferences**)
a meeting for discussion.

**confess** *verb* (**confesses, confessing, confessed**)
to admit that you have done something wrong.

**confession** *noun* (**confessions**)
1 an act of admitting that you have done wrong, *The burglar made a confession of all his crimes*. 2 (*in the Roman Catholic Church*) an act of telling a priest that you have sinned.

**confetti** *plural noun*
tiny bits of coloured paper thrown at a bride and bridegroom.

**confide** *verb* (**confides, confiding, confided**)
to tell someone a secret.
**confide in someone**, to trust someone; to talk to someone about something secret.

**confidence** *noun*
1 trust; faith. 2 believing that you are right or that you can do something.
**in confidence**, as a secret.
**confidence trick**, swindling someone after persuading him or her to trust you.

**confident** *adjective*
showing or feeling confidence.

**confidential** *adjective*
1 that should be kept secret, *This information is confidential*. 2 trusted to keep secrets, *a confidential secretary*.
**confidentially** *adverb*

**confine** *verb* (**confines, confining, confined**)
1 to restrict something. 2 to keep someone in a place.
**confinement** *noun*

**confirm** *verb* (**confirms, confirming, confirmed**)
1 to prove that something is true. 2 to make something definite, *Please write to confirm your booking.* 3 to make someone a full member of the Christian Church.
**confirmation** *noun*

**confiscate** *verb* (**confiscates, confiscating, confiscated**)
to take something away from someone as a punishment.
**confiscation** *noun*

**conflict**[1] *noun* (**conflicts**)
(*say* kon-flikt)
a fight, struggle, or disagreement.

**conflict**[2] *verb* (**conflicts, conflicting, conflicted**)
(*say* kŏn-**flikt**)
to disagree; not to match or fit with something else, *Their ideas conflicted.*

**conform** *verb* (**conforms, conforming, conformed**)
to follow accepted rules, other people's wishes, etc., *He always conforms with school rules.*
**conformist** *noun*, **conformity** *noun*

**confront** *verb* (**confronts, confronting, confronted**)
1 to come face to face with someone, *The armies confronted each other.* 2 to face up to something, *confront a problem.* 3 to challenge someone, *Difficult decisions confront us.*
**confrontation** *noun*

**confuse** *verb* (**confuses, confusing, confused**)
1 to make someone puzzled or muddled. 2 to mistake one thing for another.
**confusion** *noun*

**congested** *adjective*
crowded; too full of something, *roads congested with traffic.*
**congestion** *noun*

**congratulate** *verb* (**congratulates, congratulating, congratulated**)
to tell someone how pleased you are about something that has happened to him or her, or that he or she has done.
**congratulations** *plural noun*

**congregation** *noun* (**congregations**)
the people who take part in a church service.

**congress** *noun* (**congresses**)
a conference.
**Congress**, the parliament or government of the USA.

**congruent** *adjective*
(*in Mathematics*) having exactly the same shape and size, *The two triangles are congruent.*
**congruence** *noun*

**conical** *adjective*
shaped like a cone.

**conifer** *noun* (**conifers**)
(*say* kon-i-fer)
an evergreen tree that bears cones.
**coniferous** *adjective*

**conjugate** *verb* (**conjugates, conjugating, conjugated**)
to give the different forms of a verb.
**conjugation** *noun*

**conjunction** *noun* (**conjunctions**)
a joining word, *Conjunctions are words like 'and', 'but', and 'whether'.*

**conjure** *verb* (**conjures, conjuring, conjured**)
to perform tricks that look like magic.
**conjurer** *noun*

**conker** *noun* (**conkers**)
a hard, shiny, brown nut that grows on a horse-chestnut tree.
**conkers**, a game played with conkers threaded on pieces of string.

**connect** *verb* (**connects, connecting, connected**)
1 to join together. 2 to put or go naturally together.
**connection** *noun*, **connective** *adjective*, **connector** *noun*

**conning-tower** *noun* (**conning-towers**)
the part on top of a submarine, containing the periscope.

**conquer** *verb* (**conquers, conquering, conquered**)
to defeat; to overcome, *He managed to conquer his fear.*
**conqueror** *noun*

**conquest** *noun* (**conquests**)
conquering someone.

**conscience** *noun*
(*say* kon-shĕns)
knowing what is right or wrong.

**conscientious** *adjective*
(*say* kon-shee-**en**-shŭs)
1 careful and honest, *conscientious work.*
2 guided by your conscience, *He was a conscientious objector to joining the army.*
**conscientiously** *adverb*

**conscious** *adjective*
(*say* **kon**-shŭs)
1 awake. 2 aware of something, *Are you conscious of the danger you are in?*
**consciously** *adverb*, **consciousness** *noun*

**conscript**[1] *verb* (**conscripts, conscripting, conscripted**)
(*say* kŏn-**skript**)
to make someone join the armed forces.
**conscription** *noun*

**conscript**[2] *noun* (**conscripts**)
(*say* kŏn-skript)
a person who has been made to join the armed forces.

**consecutive** *adjective*
following one after another.

**consensus** *noun*
1 the agreement of everyone, *Can we reach a consensus on this issue?* 2 the opinion of most people, *There was a consensus that the law should be changed.*

**consent**[1] *noun*
agreement or permission.

**consent**[2] *verb* (**consents, consenting, consented**)
to agree; to permit something.

**consequence** *noun* (**consequences**)
1 something which happens because of an event or action, *His illness was the consequence of smoking.* 2 importance, *It is of no consequence.*
**consequences**, a game in which a story is constructed by two or more people.
**consequently** *adverb*

**conservation** *noun*
preventing something, especially your natural surroundings, from being changed or spoilt.
**conservationist** *noun*

**conservative**[1] *adjective*
that does not like changes; tending to conserve things.
**Conservative**, of Conservatives.
**conservatism** *noun*

**conservative**[2] *noun* (**conservatives**)
a conservative person.
**Conservative**, someone who supports the Conservative Party, a British political party that favours private enterprise and conserving existing institutions.

**conservatory** *noun* (**conservatories**)
a room with glass walls and a glass roof, usually built on to the back of a house, where plants can be grown.

**conserve** *verb* (**conserves, conserving, conserved**)
to prevent something being changed or spoilt.

**consider** *verb* (**considers, considering, considered**)
1 to think carefully about or give attention to something. 2 to have an opinion; to believe, *We consider that people should be allowed to follow their own religion. I consider her attractive.*

**considerable** *adjective*
large; important.
**considerably** *adverb*

**considerate** *adjective*
kind and thoughtful.

**consideration** *noun* (**considerations**)
1 careful thought or attention. 2 being considerate. 3 something that needs careful thought; a reason, *Money is a major consideration in this plan. Good weather was the main consideration for choosing a holiday abroad.*

**considering** *preposition*
in view of; with regard to, *This car runs well, considering its age.*

**consist** *verb* (**consists, consisting, consisted**)
**consist of**, to be made of.

**consistency** *noun* (**consistencies**)
1 thickness, especially of a liquid. 2 being consistent.

**consistent** *adjective*
1 matching or agreeing with something; reasonable. 2 (of a person) always acting in the same way.
**consistently** *adverb*

**consolation** *noun* (**consolations**)
comfort or sympathy given to someone.
**consolation prize**, a prize given to someone who does not win a main prize.

**console** *verb* (**consoles, consoling, consoled**)
to give someone comfort or sympathy.

**consonant** *noun* (**consonants**)
a letter that is not a vowel, *In 'table', the consonants are t, b, and l.*

**conspicuous** *adjective*
noticeable; remarkable.

**conspiracy** *noun* (**conspiracies**)
plotting to do something evil or illegal.
**conspirator** *noun*, **conspire** *verb*

**constable** *noun* (**constables**)
an ordinary member of the police.

**contend**

**constant**[1] *adjective*
1 not changing; continual. 2 (of a person) faithful.
**constancy** *noun*, **constantly** *adverb*

**constant**[2] *noun* (**constants**)
(*in Science and Mathematics*) a number or quantity that does not change.

**constellation** *noun* (**constellations**)
a group of stars.

**constipated** *adjective*
unable to empty the bowels easily or regularly.
**constipation** *noun*

**constituency** *noun* (**constituencies**)
a district that elects a Member of Parliament.

**constituent** *noun* (**constituents**)
1 a part of something. 2 someone who lives in the district of a particular Member of Parliament.
**constituent** *adjective*

**constitute** *verb* (**constitutes, constituting, constituted**)
to form or make up something, *the states that constitute the USA.*

**constitution** *noun* (**constitutions**)
1 the principles or laws by which a country is governed. 2 the condition or health of someone's body.
**constitutional** *adjective*

**construct** *verb* (**constructs, constructing, constructed**)
to build.

**construction** *noun* (**constructions**)
1 building. 2 something built.

**constructive** *adjective*
helpful, *constructive criticism.*

**consul** *noun* (**consuls**)
1 an official representative of one country, living in another country. 2 in Ancient Rome, an elected chief ruler.

**consult** *verb* (**consults, consulting, consulted**)
to go to a person, book, etc. for information, advice, etc., *Consult your dictionary for help with spelling.*
**consultation** *noun*

**consultant** *noun* (**consultants**)
1 a person who provides professional advice. 2 a senior hospital doctor.

**consume** *verb* (**consumes, consuming, consumed**)
1 to eat or drink something. 2 to destroy, *The building was consumed by fire.* 2 to use up something.

**consumer** *noun* (**consumers**)
someone who buys or uses goods, services, etc.

**consumption** *noun*
eating, drinking, or using up something, *The consumption of oil has increased.*

**contact**[1] *noun* (**contacts**)
1 touching someone or something. 2 communication. 3 a person to communicate with.
**contact lens**, a small lens worn against your eyeball instead of spectacles.

**contact**[2] *verb* (**contacts, contacting, contacted**)
to get in touch with someone.

**contagious** *adjective*
(*say* kŏn-**tay**-jŭs)
caught by contact with infected people or things, *a contagious disease.*

**contain** *verb* (**contains, containing, contained**)
to have something inside; to include, *This book contains a great deal of information.*

**container** *noun* (**containers**)
something designed to contain things, especially a large box-shaped container for transporting goods by sea.
**container lorry**, a large, usually articulated lorry that carries a container for goods.

**contaminate** *verb* (**contaminates, contaminating, contaminated**)
to make something dirty, impure, diseased, etc.
**contamination** *noun*

**contemplate** *verb* (**contemplates, contemplating, contemplated**)
1 to look at something. 2 to think about something. 3 to intend or plan to do something.
**contemplation** *noun*

**contemporary** *adjective*
1 belonging to the same period, *Florence Nightingale was contemporary with Queen Victoria.* 2 modern; up-to-date, *We like contemporary furniture.*

**contempt** *noun*
a feeling of despising someone.
**contemptible** *adjective*

**contemptuous** *adjective*
despising someone.

USAGE: Do not confuse **contemptuous**, which describes a person's attitude, with **contemptible**, which describes someone or something that is despised.

**contend** *verb* (**contends, contending, contended**)
1 to struggle or compete. 2 to maintain or declare, *We contend that the company was guilty of negligence.*
**contender** *noun*

**content**[1] *noun*
  (*say* **kon**-tent)
  1 the contents of something. 2 the amount
  of a substance found in something, *milk*
  *with a low fat content.*

**content**[2] *adjective*
  (*say* kŏn-**tent**)
  contented, *Are you content with your wages?*
  **contentment** *noun*

**contented** *adjective*
  (*say* kŏn-**tent**-id)
  happy; satisfied.
  **contentedly** *adverb*

**contents** *plural noun*
  (*say* **kon**-tents)
  what something contains.

**contest**[1] *noun* (**contests**)
  (*say* **kon**-test)
  a competition.

**contest**[2] *verb* (**contests, contesting, contested**)
  (*say* kŏn-**test**)
  to compete; to argue about something,
  *After her death, relatives contested her will.*

**contestant** *noun* (**contestants**)
  (*say* kŏn-**test**-ănt)
  someone in a contest.

**context** *noun* (**contexts**)
  the words that come before or after a
  particular word or phrase and help to fix
  its meaning.

**continent** *noun* (**continents**)
  one of the main masses of land in the
  world, *The continents are Africa,*
  *Antarctica, Asia, Australia, Europe, North*
  *America, and South America.*
  **the Continent**, the mainland of Europe, not
  including the British Isles.
  **continental** *adjective*

**continual** *adjective*
  1 happening often, *his continual coughing.*
  2 continuous.
  **continually** *adverb*

**continue** *verb* (**continues, continuing, continued**)
  to go on doing something.
  **continuation** *noun*

**continuous** *adjective*
  going on all the time; without a break, *a*
  *continuous line.*
  **continuity** *noun*, **continuously** *adverb*

USAGE: Do not confuse **continuous** with
**continual**, which sometimes has the same
meaning, but more usually means
happening often but with breaks in
between.

**contour** *noun* (**contours**)
  1 an outline. 2 a line on a map joining
  points that are the same height above
  sea-level.

**contra-** *prefix*
  against.

**contraception** *noun*
  preventing women from becoming
  pregnant.

**contraceptive** *noun* (**contraceptives**)
  something that is used to prevent women
  from becoming pregnant.

**contract**[1] *noun* (**contracts**)
  (*say* **kon**-trakt)
  a formal agreement.

**contract**[2] *verb* (**contracts, contracting,**
  **contracted**)
  (*say* kŏn-**trakt**)
  1 to make or become smaller, *Heated metal*
  *contracts as it cools.* 2 to make a contract.
  3 to get an illness, *She contracted*
  *pneumonia.*
  **contraction** *noun*

**contractor** *noun* (**contractors**)
  a company or firm that does an agreed
  piece of work for someone else, especially
  in the building industry, *We have employed*
  *a contractor to install all the windows in*
  *the new office.*

**contradict** *verb* (**contradicts, contradicting,**
  **contradicted**)
  to say that something is not true or that
  someone is wrong.
  **contradiction** *noun*, **contradictory** *adjective*

**contralto** *noun* (**contraltos**)
  a female singer with a low voice.

**contraption** *noun* (**contraptions**)
  a device or machine that looks strange.

**contrary**[1] *adjective*
  1 (*say* **kon**-tră-ri) opposite; unfavourable.
  2 (*say* kŏn-**trair**-i) obstinate; awkward.

**contrary**[2] *noun* (**contraries**)
  (*say* **kon**-tră-ri)
  the opposite.
  **on the contrary**, the opposite is true.

**contrast**[1] *noun* (**contrasts**)
  (*say* **kon**-trahst)
  1 the action of contrasting. 2 a clear
  difference. 3 the amount of difference
  between colours or tones.

**contrast**[2] *verb* (**contrasts, contrasting,**
  **contrasted**)
  (*say* kŏn-**trahst**)
  1 to show that two things are clearly
  different. 2 to be clearly different.

**contribute** *verb* (**contributes, contributing, contributed**)
1 to give money, help, etc. to a cause, fund, etc. 2 to help to cause something, *His tiredness contributed to the accident.* 3 to write something for a magazine, newspaper, etc.
**contribution** *noun*, **contributor** *noun*

**contrivance** *noun* (**contrivances**)
a device or machine.

**contrive** *verb* (**contrives, contriving, contrived**)
1 to invent, *a tunnelling machine contrived by a Victorian engineer.* 2 to plan cleverly, *She contrived to be there at the same time as him.*

**control**[1] *verb* (**controls, controlling, controlled**)
to be able to make someone or something do what you want.
**controller** *noun*

**control**[2] *noun* (**controls**)
1 making someone or something do what you want; authority. 2 a way of making someone or something do what you want.
**control tower**, the building at an airport where people control air traffic by radio.
**in control**, controlling.

**controversial** *adjective*
that causes a controversy.

**controversy** *noun* (**controversies**)
(*say* kon-trŏ-ver-si or kŏn-trov-er-si)
a long argument or disagreement.

**conundrum** *noun* (**conundrums**)
a riddle.

**convalescent** *adjective*
recovering from an illness.
**convalescence** *noun*

**convection** *noun*
heating by air, liquid, etc. that moves.
**convector** *noun*

**convenience** *noun* (**conveniences**)
1 being convenient. 2 something that is useful, *The house has every modern convenience, such as central heating, a fitted kitchen, built-in cupboards, etc.* 3 a public lavatory.
**at your convenience**, as it suits you.
**convenience foods**, foods that are easy to use and usually have been partly prepared in a factory.

**convenient** *adjective*
easy to use or reach.
**conveniently** *adverb*

**convent** *noun* (**convents**)
a place where nuns live and work.

**convention** *noun* (**conventions**)
an accepted way of doing things.

**conventional** *adjective*
1 done in the accepted way; traditional. 2 not nuclear, *conventional weapons.*
**conventionally** *adverb*

**converge** *verb* (**converges, converging, converged**)
1 to come together, *The two roads converge.* 2 to approach from different directions, *Thousands of fans converged on the football ground.*

**conversation** *noun* (**conversations**)
talking; a talk between two or several people.
**conversational** *adjective*

**converse**[1] *verb* (**converses, conversing, conversed**)
(*say* kŏn-**verss**)
to talk, *They conversed in low voices.*

**converse**[2] *noun*
(*say* kon-**verss**)
the opposite, *The converse is true.*

**conversion** *noun* (**conversions**)
the act of converting.

**convert**[1] *verb* (**converts, converting, converted**)
(*say* kŏn-**vert**)
1 to change. 2 to make someone change his or her beliefs. 3 to kick a goal after scoring a try in Rugby football.
**converter** *noun*, **convertible** *adjective*

**convert**[2] *noun* (**converts**)
(*say* kon-**vert**)
someone who has changed his or her beliefs.

**convex** *adjective*
curved like the outside of a circle or ball.

**convey** *verb* (**conveys, conveying, conveyed**)
1 to transport. 2 to communicate a message, idea, etc.

**conveyor belt** *noun* (**conveyor belts**)
a belt, chain, etc. carrying goods in a factory, etc.

**convict**[1] *noun* (**convicts**)
(*say* **kon**-vikt)
a criminal in prison.

**convict**$^2$ *verb* (**convicts, convicting, convicted**)
(*say* kŏn-**vikt**)
to prove or declare that someone is guilty of a crime.

**conviction** *noun* (**convictions**)
1 being convicted of a crime. 2 being convinced of something.

**convince** *verb* (**convinces, convincing, convinced**)
to persuade.

**convoy** *noun* (**convoys**)
a group of ships, lorries, etc. travelling together.

**cook**$^1$ *verb* (**cooks, cooking, cooked**)
to make food ready to eat by heating it.
**cook up**, (*informal*) to invent, *They cooked up a plan to make a lot of money easily.*

**cook**$^2$ *noun* (**cooks**)
someone who cooks.

**cooker** *noun* (**cookers**)
a device for cooking food; an oven.

**cookery** *noun*
the action or skill of cooking food.

**cool**$^1$ *adjective* (**cooler, coolest**)
1 not warm; fairly cold. 2 not emotional or excited; calm. 3 fashionable, *He's only wearing those sun-glasses in order to look cool.*
**coolly** *adverb*, **coolness** *noun*

**cool**$^2$ *verb* (**cools, cooling, cooled**)
to make someone or something cool; to become cool.
**cooler** *noun*

**coop** *noun* (**coops**)
a cage for poultry.

**cooped up** *adjective*
having to stay in a place which is too small or in which you feel trapped, *We were cooped up in the airliner for two hours, waiting for permission to take off.*

**cooperate** *verb* (**cooperates, cooperating, cooperated**)
to work helpfully with other people.
**cooperation** *noun*, **cooperative** *adjective*

**coordinate**$^1$ *verb* (**coordinates, coordinating, coordinated**)
(*say* koh-or-din-ayt)
to get people or things working properly together.
**coordination** *noun*, **coordinator** *noun*

**coordinate**$^2$ *noun* (**coordinates**)
(*say* koh-or-din-ăt)
a quantity used to fix the position of something, *The coordinates of point P are (4,2).*

**coot** *noun* (**coots**)
a water-bird with a horny white plate on its forehead.

**cop**$^1$ *verb* (**cops, copping, copped**)
(*slang*) to get or receive something.
**cop it**, to get into trouble.

**cop**$^2$ *noun* (**cops**)
(*slang*) a policeman.
**not much cop**, not very good.

**cope** *verb* (**copes, coping, coped**)
to deal with something successfully, *How did you cope with your homework?*

**copper**$^1$ *noun*
1 a reddish-brown metal, *Copper is used for making wire, coins, etc.* 2 a reddish-brown colour. 3 a coin made of copper or bronze.
**copper beech**, a beech-tree with copper-coloured leaves.
**copper sulphate**, blue-green crystals that are a compound of copper and sulphur.
**coppery** *adjective*

**copper**$^2$ *noun* (**coppers**)
(*slang*) a policeman.

**copulate** *verb* (**copulates, copulating, copulated**)
(*say* kop-yoo-layt)
to have sexual intercourse.
**copulation** *noun*

**copy**$^1$ *noun* (**copies**)
1 something made to look exactly like something else. 2 something written out a second time. 3 one newspaper, magazine, book, etc., *We each have a copy of 'Alice in Wonderland'.*

**copy**$^2$ *verb* (**copies, copying, copied**)
1 to make a copy of something. 2 to do exactly the same as someone else.
**copier** *noun*, **copyist** *noun*

**coral** *noun*
a hard substance made of the skeletons of tiny sea-creatures, *Coral is usually red, pink, or white.*

**cord** *noun* (**cords**)
thin rope; a piece of thin rope.

USAGE: Do not confuse **cord** with **chord**, which means a number of musical notes sounded together.

**cordial**$^1$ *adjective*
warm and friendly, *a cordial welcome.*
**cordiality** *noun*, **cordially** *adverb*

**cordial**$^2$ *noun* (**cordials**)
a sweet drink.

**corduroy** *noun*
(*say* **kor**-der-oi)
thick cotton cloth with raised lines across it.

**core** *noun* (**cores**)
the part in the middle of something.

**corgi** *noun* (**corgis**)
a small breed of dog with short legs and large, upright ears.

**cork** *noun* (**corks**)
1 the lightweight bark of a kind of oak-tree.
2 a piece of this bark used to close a bottle.

**corkscrew** *noun* (**corkscrews**)
1 a device for removing corks from bottles.
2 a spiral.

**cormorant** *noun* (**cormorants**)
a large black sea-bird.

**corn**[1] *noun*
grain, *a field of corn*.

**corn**[2] *noun* (**corns**)
a small, hard lump on your toe or foot.

**corned** *adjective*
preserved with salt, *corned beef*.

**corner**[1] *noun* (**corners**)
1 the point where two lines, roads, or walls meet. 2 a kick from the corner of a football field; a hit from the corner of a hockey field.

**corner**[2] *verb* (**corners, cornering, cornered**)
1 to trap someone, *The police cornered the escaped prisoner*. 2 to go round a corner, *His car cornered badly*.

**cornet** *noun* (**cornets**)
1 a small edible container for ice-cream. 2 a musical instrument rather like a trumpet.

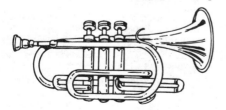

**cornfield** *noun* (**cornfields**)
a field where corn grows.

**cornflakes** *plural noun*
toasted maize flakes eaten for breakfast.

**cornflour** *noun*
(in America, *cornstarch*) fine flour used for making milk puddings, etc.

**cornflower** *noun* (**cornflowers**)
a blue wild flower.

**Cornish** *adjective*
of Cornwall.
**Cornish pasty,** a small pie containing meat and vegetables.

**corny** *adjective* (**cornier, corniest**)
(*informal*) repeated so often that people are bored, *corny jokes*.

**coronation** *noun* (**coronations**)
the crowning of a king or queen.

**coroner** *noun* (**coroners**)
an official who holds an inquiry into the cause of an unnatural death.

**corporal**[1] *noun* (**corporals**)
a soldier just below sergeant in rank.

**corporal**[2] *adjective*
of the human body.
**corporal punishment,** beating or whipping someone.

**corporation** *noun* (**corporations**)
a group of people elected to govern a town.

**corps** *noun* (**corps**)
(*say* kor)
1 a large unit of soldiers. 2 a special army unit, *He is in the Medical Corps*.

USAGE: Do not confuse **corps** with **corpse**, which is the next word in this dictionary.

**corpse** *noun* (**corpses**)
a dead body.

**corpuscle** *noun* (**corpuscles**)
(*say* kor-pus-ŭl)
one of the red or white cells in the blood.

**corral** *noun* (**corrals**)
(*say* kŏ-rahl)
an enclosure for horses, cattle, etc.

**correct**[1] *adjective*
1 true; accurate; without any mistakes, *Your sums are all correct*. 2 proper, *Is that the correct way to talk to your parents?*
**correctly** *adverb*, **correctness** *noun*

**correct**[2] *verb* (**corrects, correcting, corrected**)
to make something correct; to mark the mistakes in something.
**correction** *noun*

**correspond** *verb* (**corresponds, corresponding, corresponded**)
1 to agree with; to match, *Your story corresponds with what I heard*. 2 to exchange letters with someone.

**correspondence** *noun*
1 similarity; agreement. 2 letters; writing letters. 3 letters sent or received.

**correspondent** *noun* (**correspondents**)
1 someone who writes letters to you. 2 someone employed to send news or articles to a newspaper, etc.

**corridor** *noun* (**corridors**)
1 a long, narrow way from which doors open into rooms or compartments. 2 a permitted route, *an air corridor*.

**corrie** *noun* (**corries**)
a deep bowl-shaped hollow on the side of a mountain.

**corrode** *verb* (**corrodes, corroding, corroded**)
to wear away by rust, chemical action, etc.
**corrosion** *noun*, **corrosive** *adjective*

**corrugated** *adjective*
shaped into folds or ridges, *corrugated iron*.

**corrupt** *adjective*
1 wicked. 2 liable to give or accept bribes.
**corruption** *noun*

**corset** *noun* (**corsets**)
a tight piece of underwear worn round the hips and waist.

**cosine** *noun* (**cosines**)
in a right-angled triangle, a number linked with one of the acute angles, equal to the length of the side next to the angle divided by the length of the longest side (the *hypotenuse*).

**cosmetics** *plural noun*
substances for making your skin or hair look beautiful or different, *Lipstick and face-powder are cosmetics*.

**cosmic** *adjective*
(*say* **koz**-mik)
of the universe.
**cosmic rays**, very strong radiation from outer space.

**cosmonaut** *noun* (**cosmonauts**)
an astronaut.

**cost**[1] *noun* (**costs**)
the price of something.
**at all costs**, or **at any cost**, no matter what the cost or difficulty may be.
**cost of living**, the average amount each person in a country spends on food, clothing, and housing.

**cost**[2] *verb* (**costs, costing, cost**)
to have a certain price, *That book cost £5 last year*.

**costly** *adjective* (**costlier, costliest**)
expensive.

**costume** *noun* (**costumes**)
clothes, especially for a particular purpose or of a particular period.

**cosy**[1] *adjective* (**cosier, cosiest**)
warm and comfortable.

**cosy**[2] *noun* (**cosies**)
a cover put over a teapot or boiled egg to keep it hot.

**cot** *noun* (**cots**)
a baby's bed with high sides.

**cottage** *noun* (**cottages**)
a small house, especially in the country.
**cottage pie**, minced meat covered with mashed potato and baked.

**cotton** *noun*
1 a soft white substance covering the seeds of a tropical plant. 2 thread made from this substance. 3 cloth made from cotton thread.

**couch** *noun* (**couches**)
a long, soft seat, usually with one end raised; a sofa.
**couch potato**, (*slang*) a person who spends too much time watching television.

**cough**[1] *verb* (**coughs, coughing, coughed**)
(*say* kof)
to push air suddenly out of your lungs.
**cough up**, (*slang*) to give someone money, information, etc., *Where's my change? Cough it up!*

**cough**[2] *noun* (**coughs**)
(*say* kof)
1 the action or sound of coughing. 2 an illness which makes you cough frequently.

**could** past tense of **can**[1] *verb*.

**couldn't** short for *could not*.

**council** *noun* (**councils**)
a group of people chosen or elected to organize or discuss something, especially to plan the affairs of a town; a corporation.
**council house**, a house owned and let by a council.
**council tax**, a tax paid to the local council by owners of houses.
**councillor** *noun*

USAGE: Do not confuse **council** with **counsel**, which is the next word in this dictionary.

**counsel**[1] *noun* (**counsels**)
1 advice. 2 the barrister or barristers involved in a case in a lawcourt.

**counsel**[2] *verb* (**counsels, counselling, counselled**)
to give advice to someone.
**counsellor** *noun*

**count**[1] *verb* (**counts, counting, counted**)
1 to use numbers to find out how many people or things there are in a place. 2 to say numbers in their proper order. 3 to include someone or something in a total, *There are 30 in the class, not counting the teacher.* 4 to have a particular value or importance, *Qualifications must count for something.*
**count down,** to make a count-down.
**count on,** to rely on.

**count**[2] *noun* (**counts**)
1 counting; a total. 2 one of the things that someone is accused of, *He was found guilty on all counts.*

**count**[3] *noun* (**counts**)
a foreign nobleman.

**countable** *adjective*
that can be counted.
**countable noun,** a type of noun which is the name of something that can be counted, and which is used with 'a' and 'many', *'Dog', 'house', and 'dictionary' are countable nouns.*

**count-down** *noun* (**count-downs**)
counting backwards, especially before launching a rocket, etc.

**countenance** *noun* (**countenances**)
someone's face; the expression on someone's face.

**counter** *noun* (**counters**)
1 a long table where customers are served in a shop, restaurant, bank, etc. 2 a small, round, flat piece of plastic, etc. used in games, especially board games.

**counterfeit** *adjective*
(*say* kown-ter-fit)
copied so as to deceive or swindle people, *counterfeit money.*

**countess** *noun* (**countesses**)
the wife or widow of a count or earl; a female earl.

**countless** *adjective*
too many to count; very many.

**country** *noun* (**countries**)
1 part of the world where a nation of people lives. 2 the countryside. 3 the people who live in a country.

**countryman** *noun* (**countrymen**)
1 a man who lives in the countryside. 2 someone who lives in the same country as yourself.

**countryside** *noun*
an area with fields, woods, villages, etc., away from towns.

**county** *noun* (**counties**)
one of the areas that a country is divided into, *Kent, Leicestershire, and Norfolk are counties of England.*

**couple**[1] *noun* (**couples**)
two people or things.

**couple**[2] *verb* (**couples, coupling, coupled**)
to join things together.
**coupling** *noun*

**coupon** *noun* (**coupons**)
a piece of paper that gives you the right to receive or do something.

**courage** *noun*
being courageous.

**courageous** *adjective*
not afraid; ready to face danger, pain, etc.

**courgette** *noun* (**courgettes**)
(in America, *zucchini*) a kind of vegetable like a small marrow.

**courier** *noun* (**couriers**)
(*say* koor-i-er)
1 someone who carries a message. 2 someone employed to guide and help holiday-makers, especially abroad.

**course** *noun* (**courses**)
1 the direction in which something goes, *the ship's course.* 2 a series of lessons, exercises, etc. 3 part of a meal, *the meat course.* 4 a racecourse. 5 a golf-course.
**in due course,** eventually; at the expected time.
**in the course of,** during.
**of course,** naturally; certainly, *Of course they will help us. 'Will you help us?' 'Of course!'*

**court**[1] *noun* (**courts**)
1 a lawcourt. 2 an enclosed place for games like tennis or netball. 3 a courtyard. 4 the place where a king or queen lives. 5 the people who are usually at a king's or queen's court.

**court**[2] *verb* (**courts, courting, courted**)
to try to get someone's love or support.
**courtship** *noun*

**court-card** *noun* (**court-cards**)
the king, queen, or jack in a pack of playing-cards.

**courteous** *adjective*
(*say* ker-ti-ŭs)
polite.
**courteously** *adverb*, **courtesy** *noun*

**court martial** *noun* (**courts martial**)
1 a court for trying offenders against military law. 2 a trial in this court.

**courtyard** *noun* (**courtyards**)
a space surrounded by walls or buildings.

**cousin** *noun* (**cousins**)
a child of your uncle or aunt.

**cove** *noun* (**coves**)
a small bay.

**cover**[1] *verb* (**covers, covering, covered**)
1 to put one thing over or round another; to hide. 2 to travel a certain distance, *We covered ten miles a day.* 3 to deal with or include, *This book covers stamp-collecting.* 4 to be enough money for something, *£2 will cover my fare.* 5 to aim a gun at or near someone, *I've got you covered.*
**cover up**, not to let anyone know about something wrong or illegal.
**coverage** *noun*

**cover**[2] *noun* (**covers**)
1 something used for covering something else; a lid, wrapper, envelope, etc.
2 something that hides or shelters you.

**coverage** *noun*
the amount of time or space given to reporting an event on radio, on television, or in a newspaper.

**cover-up** *noun* (**cover-ups**)
the act of hiding something that is wrong or illegal, *There has been a cover-up of the accident at the chemical plant.*

**cow** *noun* (**cows**)
a female animal kept by farmers for its milk and beef.

**coward** *noun* (**cowards**)
someone who is not brave.
**cowardice** *noun*, **cowardly** *adjective*

**cowboy** *noun* (**cowboys**)
1 a man who rides round looking after the cattle on a large farm in America.
2 (*informal*) a person who uses dishonest methods in business etc., *Those cowboys who put in the double glazing never sealed the gaps around the window-frames!*

**cowslip** *noun* (**cowslips**)
a wild plant that has yellow flowers in spring.

**cox** *noun* (**coxes**)
someone who steers a boat.

**coxswain** *noun* (**coxswains**)
(*say* kok-swayn *or* kok-sŭn)
a cox.

**coy** *adjective*
shy; pretending to be shy or modest.
**coyly** *adverb*, **coyness** *noun*

**crab** *noun* (**crabs**)
a shellfish with ten legs.

**crab-apple** *noun* (**crab-apples**)
a small, sour apple.

**crack**[1] *noun* (**cracks**)
1 a sudden sharp noise, *the crack of a pistol shot.* 2 a sudden knock, *a crack on the head.* 3 a line on the surface of something where it has broken but not come completely apart; a narrow gap, *There's a crack in this cup.*

**crack**[2] *verb* (**cracks, cracking, cracked**)
1 to make a crack in something; to get a crack, *The plate has cracked.* 2 to make a sudden sharp noise. 3 to tell a joke, *He cracked some old jokes.*
**get cracking**, (*informal*) to get busy; to start some work.

**cracker** *noun* (**crackers**)
1 a paper tube which bangs when two people pull it apart, *Crackers often contain toys, paper hats, and riddles.* 2 a thin biscuit.

**crackle** *verb* (**crackles, crackling, crackled**)
to make small cracking sounds, *The fire crackled in the grate.*

**crackling** *noun*
the hard skin of roast pork.

**cradle**[1] *noun* (**cradles**)
1 a cot for a baby. 2 a supporting frame.

**cradle**[2] *verb* (**cradles, cradling, cradled**)
to hold gently.

**craft** *noun* (**crafts**)
1 a job which needs skill with the hands; a skill. 2 a boat. 3 cunning; trickery.

**craftsman** *noun* (**craftsmen**)
someone who is good at a craft.
**craftsmanship** *noun*

**crafty** *adjective* (**craftier, craftiest**)
cunning; clever.
**craftily** *adverb*, **craftiness** *noun*

crease<sup>2</sup>

**crag** *noun* (**crags**)
a steep piece of rough rock.
**craggy** *adjective*

**cram** *verb* (**crams, cramming, crammed**)
1 to push a lot of things into a space. 2 to fill something very full. 3 to teach someone a lot, or study very hard, for an examination.
**crammer** *noun*

**cramp**<sup>1</sup> *noun* (**cramps**)
pain caused by a muscle tightening suddenly.

**cramp**<sup>2</sup> *verb* (**cramps, cramping, cramped**)
1 to keep someone or something in a very small space. 2 to hinder someone's freedom, growth, etc.

**crane**<sup>1</sup> *noun* (**cranes**)
1 a machine for lifting and moving heavy objects. 2 a large bird with long legs and neck.

**crane**<sup>2</sup> *verb* (**cranes, craning, craned**)
to stretch your neck so that you can see something.

**crane-fly** *noun* (**crane-flies**)
an insect with long, thin legs.

**crank**<sup>1</sup> *noun* (**cranks**)
1 an L-shaped rod used to turn or control something. 2 a person with strange or fanatical ideas.
**cranky** *adjective*

**crank**<sup>2</sup> *verb* (**cranks, cranking, cranked**)
to turn something by using an L-shaped rod, *I had to crank the car's engine to get it to start.*

**cranny** *noun* (**crannies**)
a crevice; a narrow hole or space.

**crash**<sup>1</sup> *noun* (**crashes**)
1 the loud noise of something falling or breaking. 2 a violent collision or fall.

**crash**<sup>2</sup> *verb* (**crashes, crashing, crashed**)
1 to make or have a crash. 2 to move with a loud noise, *The elephants crashed through the jungle.*

**crash-helmet** *noun* (**crash-helmets**)
a padded helmet worn by motor-cyclists, etc.

**crash-landing** *noun* (**crash-landings**)
an emergency landing of an aircraft, which usually damages it.

**crate** *noun* (**crates**)
a container in which goods are transported.

**crater** *noun* (**craters**)
1 the mouth of a volcano. 2 a hole in the ground made by a bomb, etc.

**crave** *verb* (**craves, craving, craved**)
to desire something strongly.

**crawl**<sup>1</sup> *verb* (**crawls, crawling, crawled**)
1 to move on your hands and knees. 2 to move slowly. 3 to be full of or covered with insects, etc., *This room's crawling with cockroaches.*

**crawl**<sup>2</sup> *noun*
1 a crawling movement. 2 a swimming stroke with the arms hitting the water alternately.

**crayon** *noun* (**crayons**)
a pencil, chalk, etc. for making coloured drawings or writing.

**craze** *noun* (**crazes**)
an enthusiastic and brief interest in something.

**crazy** *adjective* (**crazier, craziest**)
mad.
**crazy paving,** paving made of odd pieces of stone fitted together.
**crazily** *adverb*, **craziness** *noun*

**creak**<sup>1</sup> *noun* (**creaks**)
a sound like the noise made by a stiff door-hinge.
**creaky** *adjective*

**creak**<sup>2</sup> *verb* (**creaks, creaking, creaked**)
to make a creak.

**cream** *noun*
1 the richest part of milk. 2 a yellowish-white colour. 3 a food containing or looking like cream, *chocolate cream.* 4 a substance that looks like cream, *face-cream.*
**creamy** *adjective*

**crease**<sup>1</sup> *noun* (**creases**)
1 a line made in something by folding, pressing, or squashing it. 2 a line on a cricket pitch showing where a batsman should stand.

**crease**<sup>2</sup> *verb* (**creases, creasing, creased**)
to make a crease or creases in something.

**create** *verb* (**creates, creating, created**)
to make something that no one else has made or can make.
**creation** *noun*, **creative** *adjective*, **creativity** *noun*

**creative** *adjective*
1 able to create things, *a creative pastime.*
2 showing imagination and thought as well as skill, *You don't have to do something that has been done before; be creative!*

**creator** *noun* (**creators**)
someone who creates something.
**the Creator**, God.

**creature** *noun* (**creatures**)
a living animal or person.

**crèche** *noun* (**crèches**)
(*say* kresh)
a place where babies or small children are looked after while their parents are busy.

**credibility** *noun*
being credible.
**credibility gap**, a difference noted between what particular people say and what is true.

**credible** *adjective*
that you can believe; trustworthy.
**credibly** *adverb*

USAGE: Do not confuse **credible** with **creditable**, which means deserving praise.

**credit**[1] *noun*
1 honour; approval, *Give her credit for her honesty.* 2 trusting someone to pay for something later on, *Do you want cash now or can I have it on credit?* 3 an amount of money in someone's account at a bank, etc.
**credits** or **credit titles**, the list of people who have helped to produce a film, television programme, etc.
**something does you credit**, something that you have done is good and you deserve praise for it, *Your topic work does you credit.*

**credit**[2] *verb* (**credits, crediting, credited**)
1 to believe, *Can you credit that?* 2 to enter something as a credit in an account, *We will credit you with £50.*

**creditable** *adjective*
deserving praise.
**creditably** *adverb*

USAGE: Do not confuse **creditable** with **credible**, which means trustworthy.

**credit card** *noun* (**credit cards**)
a card allowing someone to buy goods on credit.

**creditor** *noun* (**creditors**)
someone that you owe money to.

**creed** *noun* (**creeds**)
a set or statement of beliefs.

**creek** *noun* (**creeks**)
1 a narrow inlet. 2 (*in Australia, New Zealand, or America*) a small stream.
**up the creek**, (*slang*) in trouble.

**creep**[1] *verb* (**creeps, creeping, crept**)
1 to move along close to the ground. 2 to move quietly or secretly. 3 to come gradually, *Doubt crept into her mind.*

**creep**[2] *noun* (**creeps**)
1 a creeping movement. 2 (*slang*) an unpleasant person, especially someone who behaves like a slave or servant to someone else.
**give someone the creeps**, (*informal*) to make someone feel afraid or very uncomfortable.

**creeper** *noun* (**creepers**)
a plant that grows close to the ground or to walls, etc.

**creepy** *adjective* (**creepier, creepiest**)
that gives you the creeps; weird.

**cremate** *verb* (**cremates, cremating, cremated**)
to burn a corpse to ashes.
**cremation** *noun*

**crematorium** *noun* (**crematoria**)
(*say* krem-ă-**tor**-i-ŭm)
a place where corpses are cremated.

**creosote** *noun*
(*say* **kree**-ŏ-soht)
a brown, oily liquid used to prevent wood from rotting.

**crêpe** *noun* (**crêpes**)
(*say* krayp)
1 cloth, paper, etc. with a wrinkled surface.
2 a kind of thin French pancake.

**crept** past tense and past participle of **creep** *verb*.

**crescendo** *noun* (**crescendos**)
(*say* kri-**shen**-doh)
music that gets gradually louder.

**crescent** *noun* (**crescents**)
1 a narrow curved shape, pointed at both ends, *The new moon is a crescent.* 2 a curved street.

**cress** *noun*
a green plant used in salads and sandwiches.

**crest** *noun* (**crests**)
1 a tuft of hair, feathers, or skin on an animal's head. 2 the top of a hill, wave, etc.

**crevasse** *noun* (**crevasses**)
a deep crack in a glacier.

**crevice** *noun* (**crevices**)
a crack in rock or in a wall, etc.

**crew** *noun* (**crews**)
the people who work on a ship, aircraft, etc.

**crib**[1] *noun* (**cribs**)
1 a baby's cot. 2 a framework containing fodder for animals. 3 a translation of a foreign book. 4 something copied. 5 (*locally in Australia and New Zealand*) a small house. 6 (*in Australia*) a light meal; a snack.

**crib**[2] *verb* (**cribs, cribbing, cribbed**)
to copy someone else's work.

**cricket**[1] *noun*
a game played outdoors by two teams with a ball, two bats, and two wickets.
**cricketer** *noun*

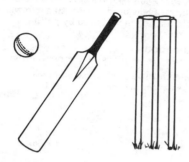

**cricket**[2] *noun* (**crickets**)
an insect like a grasshopper.

**cried** past tense and past participle of **cry** *verb*.

**crime** *noun* (**crimes**)
an action that breaks the law.

**criminal**[1] *noun* (**criminals**)
someone who has committed one or more crimes.

**criminal**[2] *adjective*
of crime or criminals.

**crimson** *adjective*
dark red.

**crinkle** *verb* (**crinkles, crinkling, crinkled**)
to crease or wrinkle.
**crinkly** *adjective*

**cripple**[1] *noun* (**cripples**)
someone who cannot walk properly.

**cripple**[2] *verb* (**cripples, crippling, crippled**)
1 to make someone a cripple. 2 to damage something seriously.

**crisis** *noun* (**crises**)
(*say* **kry-sis**)
an important, dangerous, or very difficult time or situation.

**crisp**[1] *adjective* (**crisper, crispest**)
1 very dry so that it breaks easily. 2 firm and fresh, *a very crisp apple*. 3 frosty. 4 quick and precise, *crisp movements*.

**crisp**[2] *noun* (**crisps**)
(in America, *potato chip*) a very thin fried slice of potato, usually sold in packets.

**criss-cross** *adjective* and *adverb*
with crossing lines.

**critic** *noun* (**critics**)
1 a person who criticizes someone or something. 2 someone who gives opinions on books, plays, films, music, etc.

**critical** *adjective*
1 criticizing. 2 of critics or criticism. 3 of or at a crisis; very serious.
**critically** *adverb*

**criticism** *noun* (**criticisms**)
(*say* **krit-i-si-zŭm**)
what a critic says; the work of a critic.

**criticize** *verb* (**criticizes, criticizing, criticized**)
(*say* **krit-i-syz**)
to say that someone or something is bad, unsatisfactory, etc.

**croak** *noun* (**croaks**)
a deep, hoarse sound, like that of a frog.

**crochet** *noun*
(*say* **kroh-shay**)
a kind of needlework done with a hooked needle.

**crock** *noun* (**crocks**)
(*informal*) an old or worn-out person or thing.

**crockery** *noun*
cups, saucers, plates, etc.

**crocodile** *noun* (**crocodiles**)
a large reptile living in hot countries, with a thick skin, long tail, and huge jaws.
**crocodile tears**, sorrow that is not sincere.

**crocus** *noun* (**crocuses**)
a small spring flower, *Crocuses are yellow, purple, or white.*

**croft** *noun* (**crofts**)
a small farm in Scotland.
**crofter** *noun*

**croissant** *noun* (**croissants**)
(*say* **krwa**-sahn)
a crescent-shaped roll of rich pastry, first made in France and usually eaten for breakfast.

**crook**[1] *noun* (**crooks**)
1 someone who cheats or robs people; a criminal. 2 a shepherd's stick with a curved end.

**crook**[2] *verb* (**crooks, crooking, crooked**)
to bend, *She crooked her finger.*

**crooked** *adjective*
(*say* **kruuk**-id)
1 bent; twisted; not straight. 2 (*informal*) dishonest.

**croon** *verb* (**croons, crooning, crooned**)
to sing softly or sentimentally.
**crooner** *noun*

**crop**[1] *noun* (**crops**)
1 something grown for food, *a good crop of wheat.* 2 a riding-whip with a loop instead of a lash.

**crop**[2] *verb* (**crops, cropping, cropped**)
1 to cut or bite off the top of something, *The sheep cropped the grass.* 2 to produce a crop.
**crop up**, to happen or appear unexpectedly.

**cross**[1] *noun* (**crosses**)
1 a mark or shape like + or ×. 2 an upright post with another post across it, used in ancient times for crucifixions. 3 a mixture of two different things.
**the Cross**, the cross on which Jesus was crucified, used as a symbol of Christianity.

**cross**[2] *verb* (**crosses, crossing, crossed**)
1 to go across something. 2 to draw one or more lines across something. 3 to make the sign or shape of a cross with something, *Cross your fingers for good luck.*
**cross something out**, to draw a line across something because it is unwanted, wrong, etc.

**cross**[3] *adjective*
1 angry; bad-tempered. 2 going from one side to another, *cross winds.*
**crossly** *adverb*, **crossness** *noun*

**crossbar** *noun* (**crossbars**)
a horizontal bar, especially between two upright bars.

**crossbow** *noun* (**crossbows**)
a kind of bow used for shooting arrows, held like a gun and fired by pulling a trigger (compare *longbow*).

**cross-country** *adjective*
across the countryside, *a cross-country race.*

**cross-examine** *verb* (**cross-examines, cross-examining, cross-examined**)
to question someone carefully, especially in a lawcourt.
**cross-examination** *noun*

**cross-eyed** *adjective*
with eyes that look or seem to look in different directions.

**crossing** *noun* (**crossings**)
a place where people can cross a road, railway, etc.

**cross-legged** *adverb* and *adjective*
with legs crossed.

**crossroads** *noun* (**crossroads**)
a place where two or more roads cross one another.

**cross-section** *noun* (**cross-sections**)
1 a drawing of something as if it has been cut through. 2 a typical sample.

**crosswise** *adverb* and *adjective*
with one thing crossing another.

**crossword** *noun* (**crosswords**)
a puzzle in which you have to guess words from clues and write them on a chequered square or diagram.

**crotchet** *noun* (**crotchets**)
(*say* **kroch**-it)
(in America, *quarter note*) a musical note equal to half a minim, written ♩.

**crouch** *verb* (**crouches, crouching, crouched**)
to lower your body, with your arms and legs bent.

**crow**[1] *noun* (**crows**)
a large black bird.
**as the crow flies**, in a straight line.

**crow**<sup>2</sup> *verb* (**crows, crowing, crowed**)
1 to make a noise like a cock. 2 to boast; to be proudly triumphant.

**crowbar** *noun* (**crowbars**)
an iron bar used as a lever.

**crowd**<sup>1</sup> *noun* (**crowds**)
a large number of people in one place.

**crowd**<sup>2</sup> *verb* (**crowds, crowding, crowded**)
1 to make a crowd. 2 to cram; to fill uncomfortably full, *The town is crowded with tourists in summer.*

**crown**<sup>1</sup> *noun* (**crowns**)
1 an ornamental head-dress worn by a king or queen. 2 the king or queen, *This land belongs to the crown.* 3 the highest part of something, *the crown of the road.*

**crown**<sup>2</sup> *verb* (**crowns, crowning, crowned**)
1 to make someone a king or queen. 2 to form or decorate the top of something. 3 to reward; to end something successfully, *Their efforts were crowned with success.*

**crow's-nest** *noun* (**crow's-nests**)
a look-out position at the top of a ship's mast.

**crucial** *adjective*
(*say* **kroo**-shăl)
most important.

**crucifix** *noun* (**crucifixes**)
a model of the Cross or of Jesus on the Cross.

**crucify** *verb* (**crucifies, crucifying, crucified**)
to execute someone by nailing him or her to a cross.
**crucifixion** *noun*

**crude** *adjective* (**cruder, crudest**)
1 natural; not refined, *crude oil.* 2 rough; not finished properly, *a crude hut.* 3 vulgar; rude, *crude jokes.*

**cruel** *adjective* (**crueller, cruellest**)
1 pleased at, or not caring about, the pain and suffering of others, *a cruel tyrant.* 2 causing pain and suffering, *a cruel war.*
**cruelly** *adverb*, **cruelty** *noun*

**cruise**<sup>1</sup> *noun* (**cruises**)
a sailing holiday, especially visiting various places.

**cruise**<sup>2</sup> *verb* (**cruises, cruising, cruised**)
1 to sail or travel at a slow or moderate speed. 2 to have a cruise on a ship or yacht.

**cruiser** *noun* (**cruisers**)
1 a fast warship. 2 a large motor boat.

**crumb** *noun* (**crumbs**)
a tiny piece of bread, cake, etc.

**crumble** *verb* (**crumbles, crumbling, crumbled**)
to break or fall into small pieces.
**crumbly** *adjective*

**crumpet** *noun* (**crumpets**)
a soft, flat cake of yeast mixture, eaten toasted with butter.

**crumple** *verb* (**crumples, crumpling, crumpled**)
to make or become very creased.

**crunch**<sup>1</sup> *noun* (**crunches**)
the noise made by chewing hard food, walking on gravel, etc.
**the crunch**, (*informal*) a crucial event; a crisis.
**crunchy** *adjective*

**crunch**<sup>2</sup> *verb* (**crunches, crunching, crunched**)
to make a crunch; to chew or crush something with a crunch.

**crusade** *noun* (**crusades**)
1 a military expedition made in the Middle Ages to Palestine. 2 a campaign against something that you think is bad.
**crusader** *noun*

**crush**<sup>1</sup> *verb* (**crushes, crushing, crushed**)
1 to press something so that it gets broken or harmed. 2 to defeat.

**crush**<sup>2</sup> *noun* (**crushes**)
1 a crowd; a crowded situation. 2 a fruit-flavoured drink.

**crust** *noun* (**crusts**)
1 the hard outside part of something, especially of a loaf. 2 the rocky outer part of the planet Earth.
**crustal** *adjective*

**crustacean** *noun* (**crustaceans**)
(*say* krus-**tay**-shăn)
a shellfish.

**crutch** *noun* (**crutches**)
a long walking-stick that fits under a lame person's arm.

**cry**<sup>1</sup> *verb* (**cries, crying, cried**)
1 to shout. 2 to let tears fall from your eyes.
**cry off**, to change your mind and not do something you were going to do, *Brian was going to come with us on our cycling holiday, but he cried off at the last minute.*
**cry out for something**, to need something urgently, *The front door is crying out for a coat of paint.*

**cry**<sup>2</sup> *noun* (**cries**)
1 a loud shout. 2 a period of weeping.

**crypt** *noun* (**crypts**)
a room underneath a church.

**crystal** *noun* (**crystals**)
1 a transparent, colourless mineral, rather like glass. 2 a small solid piece of a substance with a symmetrical shape, *crystals of snow and ice.*
**crystal ball**, a glass ball used in crystal-gazing.
**crystal-gazing**, looking into a glass ball to try to see the future.
**crystalline** *adjective*

**crystallize** *verb* (**crystallizes, crystallizing, crystallized**)
to form into crystals.

**cub** *noun* (**cubs**)
a young lion, tiger, fox, bear, etc.
**Cub**, a junior Scout.

**cubby-hole** *noun* (**cubby-holes**)
a small compartment; a snug place.

**cube**[1] *noun* (**cubes**)
1 something that has six square sides, *Dice and sugar-lumps are cubes.* 2 the result of multiplying something by itself twice, *The cube of 3 is 3 × 3 × 3 = 27.*
**cube root**, what gives a particular number if it is multiplied by itself twice, *The cube root of 8 is 2.*

**cube**[2] *verb* (**cubes, cubing, cubed**)
1 to multiply a number by itself twice, *4 cubed is 4 × 4 × 4 = 64.* 2 to cut something into small cubes.

**cubic** *adjective*
of or shaped like a cube.
**cubic foot, cubic metre, etc.**, the volume of a cube with sides that are one foot, metre, etc. long.

**cubicle** *noun* (**cubicles**)
a small division of a room, especially one where swimmers, etc. change their clothes.

**cuboid** *noun* (**cuboids**)
a structure with six rectangular sides.

**cuckoo** *noun* (**cuckoos**)
a bird that makes a sound like 'cuck-oo', *Cuckoos lay their eggs in other birds' nests.*

**cucumber** *noun* (**cucumbers**)
a long green vegetable, eaten raw.

**cud** *noun*
half-digested food that a cow, etc. brings back from its first stomach to chew again.

**cuddle** *verb* (**cuddles, cuddling, cuddled**)
to put your arms closely round a person or animal that you love.
**cuddly** *adjective*

**cue**[1] *noun* (**cues**)
something said or done that acts as a signal for an actor, etc. to say or do something, *Your cue is: 'Here's the detective!'*

**cue**[2] *noun* (**cues**)
a long stick used to strike the ball in billiards or snooker.

**cuff**[1] *noun* (**cuffs**)
1 the end of a sleeve that fits round the wrist. 2 hitting someone with your hand.

**cuff**[2] *verb* (**cuffs, cuffing, cuffed**)
to hit someone with your hand.

**cul-de-sac** *noun* (**cul-de-sacs**)
a dead end.

**culminate** *verb* (**culminates, culminating, culminated**)
to reach the highest or last point, *a long struggle that culminated in victory.*
**culmination** *noun*

**culprit** *noun* (**culprits**)
the person who has done wrong.

**cult** *noun* (**cults**)
a religion; being devoted to someone or something, *the cult of money.*

**cultivate** *verb* (**cultivates, cultivating, cultivated**)
1 to use land to grow crops. 2 to try to make something grow or develop.
**cultivated**, (of a person) with good manners and education.
**cultivation** *noun*, **cultivator** *noun*

**culture** *noun* (**cultures**)
1 development of the mind, body, arts, music, etc. 2 customs and traditions, *Celtic culture.*
**cultural** *adjective*, **cultured** *adjective*

**cunning** *adjective*
clever at deceiving people.

**cup**[1] *noun* (**cups**)
1 a small container from which you drink liquid, *Cups usually have handles and are used with saucers.* 2 an ornamental cup given as a prize.

**cup**[2] *verb* (**cups, cupping, cupped**)
to put into the shape of a cup, *She cupped her hands.*

**cupboard** *noun* (**cupboards**)
(*say* kub-erd)
a recess or piece of furniture with a door, in which things may be stored.

**cupful** *noun* (**cupfuls**)
as much as a cup will hold.

**curate** *noun* (**curates**)
(*say* kewr-ăt)
a clergyman who helps a vicar.

**curator** *noun* (**curators**)
(*say* kewr-ay-ter)
someone in charge of a museum, art
gallery, etc.

**curb** *verb* (**curbs, curbing, curbed**)
to restrain, *Curb your anger.*

**curd** *noun* (**curds**)
a thick substance formed when milk turns
sour.

**curdle** *verb* (**curdles, curdling, curdled**)
to form into curds.
**curdle someone's blood,** to horrify or terrify
someone.

**cure¹** *verb* (**cures, curing, cured**)
1 to get rid of someone's illness. 2 to stop
something bad. 3 to treat something so as
to preserve it, *Fish can be cured in smoke.*

**cure²** *noun* (**cures**)
something that cures a person or thing,
*They are trying to find a cure for cancer.*

**curfew** *noun* (**curfews**)
a time or signal after which people must
stay indoors until the next day.

**curiosity** *noun* (**curiosities**)
1 being curious. 2 something strange.

**curious** *adjective*
1 wanting to find out about things.
2 strange; unusual.
**curiously** *adverb*

**curl¹** *noun* (**curls**)
a curve or coil, especially of hair.

**curl²** *verb* (**curls, curling, curled**)
to form into curls.
**curl up,** to sit or lie with your knees drawn
up.

**curler** *noun* (**curlers**)
a device for curling the hair.

**curly** *adjective* (**curlier, curliest**)
full of curls; curling, *She had curly hair.*

**currant** *noun* (**currants**)
1 a small, black, dried grape. 2 a small,
round, juicy berry; the bush that produces
this berry.

USAGE: Do not confuse **currant** with
**current,** which means a movement of water,
air, or electricity.

**currency** *noun* (**currencies**)
1 money, *foreign currency.* 2 the general
use of something, *Those words have no
currency now.*

**current¹** *noun* (**currents**)
a movement of water, air, or electricity.

USAGE: Do not confuse **current** with
**currant,** which means a dried grape, a kind
of berry, or a berry-bush.

**current²** *adjective*
happening or used now.
**currently** *adverb*

**curriculum** *noun* (**curricula**)
a course of study.

**curry¹** *noun* (**curries**)
food cooked with spices that make it taste
hot.

**curry²** *verb* (**curries, currying, curried**)
to groom a horse.
**curry favour,** to try to get someone's favour
or approval.

**curse¹** *noun* (**curses**)
1 a call or prayer for someone to be harmed
or killed. 2 something very unpleasant.
3 an angry word or words.

**curse²** *verb* (**curses, cursing, cursed**)
to make a curse; to use a curse against
someone.
**be cursed with something,** to suffer because
of something.

**cursor** *noun* (**cursors**)
a movable indicator (often a flashing light)
on a VDU screen.

**curtain** *noun* (**curtains**)
1 a piece of cloth hung at a window or door.
2 the large cloth screen hung at the front of
a stage.

**curtsy¹** *noun* (**curtsies**)
putting one foot behind the other and
bending the knees, a mark of respect made
by women, *The girl made a curtsy to the
Queen.*

**curtsy²** *verb* (**curtsies, curtsying, curtsied**)
to make a curtsy.

**curvature** *noun* (**curvatures**)
curving, *the curvature of the earth.*

**curve¹** *noun* (**curves**)
a line that bends smoothly.

**curve²** *verb* (**curves, curving, curved**)
to put something in a curve; to be in a
curve, *The river curved gently.*

**cushion¹** *noun* (**cushions**)
a bag, usually of cloth, filled with soft material so that it is comfortable to sit on or rest against.

**cushion²** *verb* (**cushions, cushioning, cushioned**)
1 to supply with cushions, *cushioned seats*. 2 to protect from shock or harm, *People should not be cushioned from the truth.*

**custard** *noun*
a thick, sweet, yellow liquid eaten with puddings.

**custom** *noun* (**customs**)
1 the usual way of doing things, *It is the custom to go on holiday in the summer.* 2 regular business from customers.
**customs**, taxes paid on goods brought into a country; the place at a port, airport, etc. where officials examine your luggage.

**customary** *adjective*
usual, *It is customary to thank your host.*
**customarily** *adverb*

**customer** *noun* (**customers**)
someone who uses a shop, bank, business, etc.

**customize** *noun* (**customizes, customizing, customized**)
to alter something, especially a vehicle that normally would look like many others, to make it look unusual and different, *a customized Mini with a lowered roof.*

**cut¹** *verb* (**cuts, cutting, cut**)
1 to use a knife, axe, scissors, etc. to divide, separate, or shape something. 2 to make something shorter or smaller; to remove part of something, *They are cutting all their prices.* 3 to divide a pack of playing-cards. 4 to hit a ball with a chopping movement. 5 to go sideways or across something, *The driver cut the corner.* 6 to stay away from something deliberately, *She cut her music lesson.*
**cut and dried**, already decided.
**cut a record**, to make a record of a tune, a song, etc.
**cut a tooth**, to have a new tooth coming.
**cut off**, to interrupt; to isolate, *She cut me off before I had finished what I was saying. We were nearly cut off by the tide.*
**cut out**, to shape something by cutting; (*informal*) to stop doing something, *Cut out the joking!*
**cut short**, to stop something before it should end.

**cut²** *noun* (**cuts**)
1 cutting; the result of cutting. 2 a small wound. 3 (*slang*) a share, *I want a cut of the profits.*

**cute** *adjective* (**cuter, cutest**)
(*informal*) 1 attractive. 2 clever.

**cutlass** *noun* (**cutlasses**)
a short sword with a wide curved blade.

**cutlery** *noun*
knives, forks, and spoons.

**cutlet** *noun* (**cutlets**)
a thick slice of meat.

**cut-out** *noun* (**cut-outs**)
something cut out of paper, cardboard, etc.

**cut-price** *adjective*
sold at a reduced price, *a cut-price pack of eight toilet rolls.*

**cutter** *noun* (**cutters**)
1 a person or thing that cuts. 2 a sailing-ship with one mast.

**cutting** *noun* (**cuttings**)
1 a clipping. 2 a piece cut off a plant to grow as a new plant. 3 a steep-sided passage cut through high ground for a railway or road.

**cycle¹** *noun* (**cycles**)
1 a bicycle. 2 a series of events that are regularly repeated, *Rainfall is part of the water cycle.*

**cycle²** *verb* (**cycles, cycling, cycled**)
to ride a bicycle.
**cyclist** *noun*

**cyclone** *noun* (**cyclones**)
a wind rotating round a calm central area, especially a violent wind of this kind.
**cyclonic** *adjective*

**cygnet** *noun* (**cygnets**)
(*say* **sig**-nit)
a young swan.

**cylinder** *noun* (**cylinders**)
1 an object with straight sides and circular ends. 2 part of an engine in which a piston moves.

**cylindrical** *adjective*
shaped like a cylinder.

**cymbal** *noun* (**cymbals**)
a round, slightly hollowed metal plate that is hit to make a ringing sound, *The drummer clashed the cymbals together.*

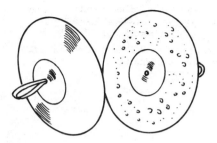

**cynic** *noun* (**cynics**)
(*say* **sin**-ik)
someone who doubts that anything can be good.
**cynical** *adjective*, **cynically** *adverb*, **cynicism** *noun*

**cypress** *noun* (**cypresses**)
an evergreen tree with dark leaves.

# Dd

**dab¹** *noun* (**dabs**)
a gentle touch with something soft.

**dab²** *verb* (**dabs, dabbing, dabbed**)
to touch gently with something soft, *I dabbed my eyes with a handkerchief.*

**dabble** *verb* (**dabbles, dabbling, dabbled**)
1 to splash something about in water. 2 to do something as a hobby, *He is a scientist, but he dabbles in music.*

**dachshund** *noun* (**dachshunds**)
(*say* **daks**-huund or **daks**-huunt)
a small breed of dog with a long body and very short legs.

**dad** *noun* (**dads**)
(*informal*) father.

**daddy** *noun* (**daddies**)
(*informal*) father.

**daddy-long-legs** *noun* (**daddy-long-legs**)
a crane-fly.

**daffodil** *noun* (**daffodils**)
a yellow flower that grows from a bulb.

**daft** *adjective* (**dafter, daftest**)
silly; mad.

**dagger** *noun* (**daggers**)
a pointed knife with two sharp edges, used as a weapon.

**dahlia** *noun* (**dahlias**)
(*say* **day**-li-ă)
a garden plant with brightly-coloured flowers.

**daily** *adjective*
happening every day; done every day.

**dainty** *adjective* (**daintier, daintiest**)
delicate, pretty, and small.
**daintily** *adverb*, **daintiness** *noun*

**dairy** *noun* (**dairies**)
a place where milk, butter, cheese, etc. are made or sold.
**dairy farm,** a farm that produces mainly milk, butter, and cheese.

**daisy** *noun* (**daisies**)
a small flower with white petals and a yellow centre.

**daisy wheel** *noun* (**daisy wheels**)
a small round device like a many-pointed star, with the raised shape of an a, b, c, etc. on each of the points, used in some typewriters and computer printers.

**dale** *noun* (**dales**)
a valley, *the Yorkshire Dales.*

**Dalmatian** *noun* (**Dalmatians**)
a large breed of dog that is white with black or brown spots.

**dam**[1] *noun* (**dams**)
a wall built to hold water back, especially across a river to make a reservoir.

**dam**[2] *verb* (**dams, damming, dammed**)
to hold water back with a dam.

**damage**[1] *verb* (**damages, damaging, damaged**)
to injure; to harm.

**damage**[2] *noun*
injury; harm.

**damages** *plural noun*
money paid to someone to make up for an injury or loss.

**Dame** *noun* (**Dames**)
the title of a lady who has been given the equivalent of a knighthood.
**dame,** a comic middle-aged woman in a pantomime, usually played by a man.

**damn** *verb* (**damns, damning, damned**)
1 to curse, *Damn this awful weather!* 2 to condemn, *His book was damned by the critics.*
**damn!,** a swear-word.

**damned** *adjective*
(*informal*) hateful; annoying.

**damp** *adjective* (**damper, dampest**)
slightly wet; not quite dry.
**damp course,** a layer of material in a wall to stop dampness rising up the wall.
**dampness** *noun*

**damson** *noun* (**damsons**)
a small purple plum.

**dance**[1] *verb* (**dances, dancing, danced**)
to move about in time to music.
**dancer** *noun*

**dance**[2] *noun* (**dances**)
1 a piece of music or set of movements for dancing. 2 a party or gathering where people dance.

**dandelion** *noun* (**dandelions**)
a yellow wild flower with a thick stalk and jagged leaves.

**dandruff** *noun*
tiny white flakes of dead skin in a person's hair.

**Dane** *noun* (**Danes**)
a Danish person.

**danger** *noun* (**dangers**)
something that is dangerous.

**dangerous** *adjective*
likely to kill or harm you.

**dangle** *verb* (**dangles, dangling, dangled**)
to hang or swing loosely.

**Danish** *adjective*
of Denmark.

**dappled** *adjective*
marked with patches or spots of different colours, *a dappled horse.*

**dare** *verb* (**dares, daring, dared**)
1 to be brave enough or rude enough to do something, *I daren't dive in. How dare you call your aunt an old cow!* 2 to challenge someone to do something brave, *I dare you to climb that tree.*

**daredevil** *noun* (**daredevils**)
a reckless or brave person.

**daring** *adjective*
not afraid to take risks; brave, *a daring plan to rescue the hostages.*

**dark**[1] *adjective* (**darker, darkest**)
1 with little or no light, *a dark night.* 2 not light in colour, *a dark green coat.*
**dark horse,** a person about whom you know little but who you think might do something unexpected and impressive.
**darkly** *adverb,* **darkness** *noun*

**dark**[2] *noun*
1 absence of light, *Cats can see in the dark.*
2 sunset, *She went out after dark.*

**darken** *verb* (**darkens, darkening, darkened**)
to make something dark; to become dark.

**darkroom** *noun* (**darkrooms**)
a room kept dark for processing photographs.

**darling** *noun* (**darlings**)
someone who is loved very much.

**darn** *verb* (**darns, darning, darned**)
to mend a hole by sewing across it.

**dart** *noun* (**darts**)
an object with a sharp point, thrown at a dartboard in the game of **darts**.

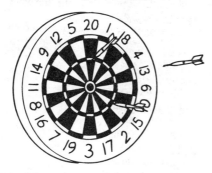

**dartboard** *noun* (**dartboards**)
a round target at which you throw darts.

**dash**¹ *noun* (**dashes**)
1 a short line (—) used in writing or printing. 2 a rush; a hurry.

**dash**² *verb* (**dashes, dashing, dashed**)
1 to rush. 2 to throw something violently; to shatter, *The ship was dashed against the rocks.*

**dashboard** *noun* (**dashboards**)
a panel with dials and controls in front of the driver of a car, aircraft, etc.

**data** *plural noun*
(*say* **day**-tă)
information.

USAGE: The singular form of **data** is **datum**, but it is not often used.

**database** *noun* (**databases**)
a store of information held in a computer.

**date**¹ *noun* (**dates**)
1 the day of the month, or the year, when something happens. 2 an appointment to meet someone. 3 a small, sweet, brown fruit that grows on a palm tree.

**date**² *verb* (**dates, dating, dated**)
1 to give a date to something. 2 to have existed from a particular time, *The church dates from 1684.* 3 to seem old-fashioned, *Some clothes styles date very quickly.*

**daughter** *noun* (**daughters**)
a girl or woman who is the child of a particular person.

**dawdle** *verb* (**dawdles, dawdling, dawdled**)
to go or act too slowly.

**dawn** *noun* (**dawns**)
the time when the sun rises.

**day** *noun* (**days**)
1 the 24 hours between midnight and the next midnight. 2 the light part of the day.

**daybreak** *noun*
the first light of day.

**day-dream** *verb* (**day-dreams, day-dreaming, day-dreamed**)
to have pleasant dream-like thoughts.

**daylight** *noun*
1 the light of day. 2 dawn, *We must start before daylight.*

**day-to-day** *adjective*
ordinary; happening every day, *the routine of day-to-day life.*

**daze** *noun*
**in a daze,** unable to think or see clearly.

**dazed** *adjective*
unable to think or see clearly.

**dazzle** *verb* (**dazzles, dazzling, dazzled**)
to make someone dazed with bright light.

**de-** *prefix*
removing something, *Lorries spread salt and grit to de-ice the roads.*

**dead** *adjective*
1 not alive; not lively or active, *This place is really dead at the weekend.* 2 complete; sure, *a dead loss.*
**dead end,** a street or passage with an opening at only one end.
**dead heat,** a race in which two or more winners finish exactly together.

**deaden** *verb* (**deadens, deadening, deadened**)
to make pain, noise, etc. weaker.

**deadline** *noun* (**deadlines**)
a time-limit.

**deadlock** *noun*
a situation in which people cannot agree.

**deadly** *adjective* (**deadlier, deadliest**)
likely to kill, *deadly poison. a deadly weapon.*

**deadpan** *adjective*
(*informal*) with an expressionless face or manner, *He was an expert in deadpan humour.*

**deaf** *adjective* (**deafer, deafest**)
unable or unwilling to hear.
**deafness** *noun*

**deafen** *verb* (**deafens, deafening, deafened**)
to be very loud, *a deafening noise.*

**deal**[1] *verb* (**deals, dealing, dealt**)
1 to hand out something. 2 to trade, *He deals in scrap metal.* 3 to give out cards for a card-game.
**deal with,** to be concerned with something; to do something that needs doing, *This book deals with cacti. Various jobs need to be dealt with.*
**dealer** *noun*

**deal**[2] *noun* (**deals**)
1 an agreement; a bargain. 2 someone's turn to give out cards for a card-game. 3 sawn fir or pine wood.
**a good deal** or **a great deal,** a large amount.

**dean** *noun* (**deans**)
1 an important clergyman in a cathedral, etc. 2 an important official in a college or university.
**deanery** *noun*

**dear** *adjective* (**dearer, dearest**)
1 loved very much. 2 the usual way of beginning a letter, *Dear Sir. Dear John.* 3 expensive.

**death** *noun* (**deaths**)
dying; the end of life.
**deathly** *adjective*

**debate**[1] *noun* (**debates**)
a discussion, especially in public.

**debate**[2] *verb* (**debates, debating, debated**)
to have a debate; to discuss something.
**debatable** *adjective*

**debris** *noun*
(*say* deb-ree)
scattered fragments; wreckage, *The debris of the crashed airliner was spread over a wide area.*

**debt** *noun* (**debts**)
(*say* det)
something that you owe someone.

**debtor** *noun* (**debtors**)
(*say* det-er)
someone who owes you money.

**debug** *verb* (**debugs, debugging, debugged**)
(*informal*) 1 to remove faults from a computer program. 2 to remove listening devices from a room.

**début** *noun* (**débuts**)
(*say* day-bew or day-boo)
someone's first public appearance.

**decade** *noun* (**decades**)
ten years, *The war lasted for a decade.*

**decaffeinated** *adjective*
with most of the caffeine removed, *Many people prefer decaffeinated coffee.*

**decant** *verb* (**decants, decanting, decanted**)
to pour a liquid from one container into another without disturbing any solid matter that was in the first container.

**decathlon** *noun* (**decathlons**)
an athletic contest consisting of ten events.

**decay**[1] *verb* (**decays, decaying, decayed**)
to go bad; to rot.

**decay**[2] *noun*
decaying; the result of decaying.

**deceased** *adjective*
(*say* di-seest)
dead, *His book describes his deceased aunt.*

**deceit** *noun*
(*say* di-seet)
deceiving someone.
**deceitful** *adjective*, **deceitfully** *adverb*

**deceive** *verb* (**deceives, deceiving, deceived**)
(*say* di-seev)
to make someone believe something that is not true.

**December** *noun*
the last month of the year.

**decent** *adjective*
1 respectable, *Not many of his jokes are decent.* 2 proper; suitable, *earn a decent wage.*
**decency** *noun*, **decently** *adverb*

**deception** *noun*
deceiving someone.

**deceptive** *adjective*
misleading, *Appearances are often deceptive.*

**decibel** *noun* (**decibels**)
a unit for measuring the loudness of sound.

**decide** *verb* (**decides, deciding, decided**)
1 to make up your mind; to make a choice. 2 to settle a contest or argument.
**decidedly** *adverb*

**deciduous** *adjective*
losing its leaves in autumn, *a deciduous tree.*

**decimal**[1] *adjective*
using tens or tenths.
**decimal fraction,** a fraction with tenths
shown as numbers after a dot ($\frac{3}{10}$ is 0.3;
$1\frac{1}{2}$ is 1.5).
**decimal point,** the dot in a decimal fraction.
**decimalization** *noun*, **decimalize** *verb*

**decimal**[2] *noun* (**decimals**)
a decimal fraction.

**decipher** *verb* (**deciphers, deciphering,
deciphered**)
(*say* di-**sy**-fer)
**1** to decode something. **2** to work out the
meaning of something written badly.

**decision** *noun* (**decisions**)
what you have decided.

**decisive** *adjective*
**1** that settles or ends something, *a decisive
battle.* **2** determined; resolute, *a decisive
person.*
**decisively** *adverb*

**deck** *noun* (**decks**)
**1** a floor on a ship or bus. **2** the part of a
record-player where the record is put for
playing.
**deck-chair,** a folding chair with a seat of
canvas or plastic material.

**declaration** *noun* (**declarations**)
the act of saying something clearly or
firmly; an official statement, *The American
Declaration of Independence was made in
1776.*

**declare** *verb* (**declares, declaring, declared**)
**1** to say something clearly or firmly. **2** to
end a cricket innings before all the
batsmen are out.
**declare war,** to say that you have started a
war against someone.

**decline** *verb* (**declines, declining, declined**)
**1** to become weaker or smaller. **2** to refuse
something. **3** to give the grammatical cases
of a word, especially in Latin.

**decode** *verb* (**decodes, decoding, decoded**)
to find the meaning of something written
in code.

**decompose** *verb* (**decomposes, decomposing,
decomposed**)
to decay; to rot.
**decomposition** *noun*

**decompression** *noun*
reducing pressure; reducing the air
pressure on someone who has been in
compressed air.

**decontaminate** *verb* (**decontaminates,
decontaminating, decontaminated**)
to remove contamination from something,
*All vehicles coming away from the wrecked
nuclear power station at Chernobyl had to
be decontaminated.*

**decorate** *verb* (**decorates, decorating, decorated**)
**1** to make something look more beautiful or
colourful. **2** to give someone a medal.
**decorative** *adjective*

**decoration** *noun* (**decorations**)
**1** things like paint, ornaments, carpets,
and pictures that make a place look more
beautiful. **2** making something look more
beautiful or colourful. **3** a medal.

**decorator** *noun* (**decorators**)
a person whose job is to paint rooms and
buildings and to put up wallpaper.

**decoy** *noun* (**decoys**)
(*say* **dee**-koi or di-**koi**)
something used to tempt a person or
animal into a trap.

**decrease**[1] *verb* (**decreases, decreasing,
decreased**)
(*say* di-**kreess**)
to make something or a group of people
smaller or fewer; to become smaller or
fewer.

**decrease**[2] *noun* (**decreases**)
(*say* **dee**-kreess)
the amount by which something decreases.

**decree**[1] *noun* (**decrees**)
an official order or decision.

**decree**[2] *verb* (**decrees, decreeing, decreed**)
to make a decree.

**decrepit** *adjective*
old and weak.

**dedicate** *verb* (**dedicates, dedicating, dedicated**)
**1** to devote, *She dedicated her life to
nursing.* **2** to mention someone's name at
the beginning of a book, etc., as a sign of
friendship or thanks.
**dedication** *noun*

**deduce** *verb* (**deduces, deducing, deduced**)
to work out something by reasoning.

USAGE: Do not confuse **deduce** with
**deduct**, which is the next word in this
dictionary.

**deduct** *verb* (**deducts, deducting, deducted**)
to subtract part of something.
**deductible** *adjective*

**deduction** *noun* (**deductions**)
1 something worked out by reasoning.
2 something subtracted.

**deed** *noun* (**deeds**)
1 something special that someone has done.
2 a legal document.

**deep** *adjective* (**deeper, deepest**)
1 going down a long way from the top, *deep sea*. 2 wide, *a deep book-shelf*. 3 measured from top to bottom or from front to back, *a hole two metres deep*. 4 intense; strong, *deep feelings*.
**deepen** *verb*, **deeply** *adverb*

**deep-freeze** *noun* (**deep-freezes**)
a kind of refrigerator that freezes food quickly and keeps it at a very low temperature.

**deer** *noun* (**deer**)
a fast-running, graceful animal with four legs.

**deface** *verb* (**defaces, defacing, defaced**)
to spoil the appearance of something.

**default** *noun* (**defaults**)
(*in Computing*) what a computer does if you do not give it instructions to do something different, *The default is to save the data on the disk on which the last save was made*.

**defeat**[1] *verb* (**defeats, defeating, defeated**)
to beat someone in a game or battle.

**defeat**[2] *noun* (**defeats**)
a lost game or battle.

**defecate** *verb* (**defecates, defecating, defecated**)
to get rid of faeces from the body.
**defecation** *noun*

**defect**[1] *noun* (**defects**)
(*say* dee-fekt)
a flaw.

**defect**[2] *verb* (**defects, defecting, defected**)
(*say* di-fekt)
to desert a country or cause; to join the enemy.
**defection** *noun*, **defector** *noun*

**defective** *adjective*
having flaws or faults.

---

USAGE: Do not confuse **defective** with **deficient**, which means lacking something.

---

**defence** *noun* (**defences**)
1 the action of defending. 2 something that defends.
**defenceless** *adjective*

**defend** *verb* (**defends, defending, defended**)
1 to protect, especially from attack. 2 to try to prove that a defendant is innocent.
**defender** *noun*, **defensible** *adjective*

**defendant** *noun* (**defendants**)
a person accused of something in a lawcourt.

**defensive** *adjective*
1 that defends. 2 (of a person) seeming to expect criticism, and eager to avoid it.

**defer** *verb* (**defers, deferring, deferred**)
to postpone, *She deferred her departure*.
**deferment** *noun*

**defiance** *noun*
the action of defying.
**defiant** *adjective*, **defiantly** *adverb*

**deficiency** *noun* (**deficiencies**)
a shortage; a lack.
**deficient** *adjective*

**deficit** *noun* (**deficits**)
(*say* def-i-sit)
the amount by which a sum of money is too small.

**defile** *verb* (**defiles, defiling, defiled**)
to make a thing dirty or impure.

**define** *verb* (**defines, defining, defined**)
1 to explain what a word means. 2 to show clearly what something is, *First define the problem*.

**definite** *adjective*
fixed or certain; exact, *Can you be definite about that? Choose a definite date for your holiday*.

**definitely** *adverb* and *interjection*
certainly.

**definition** *noun* (**definitions**)
something defined, especially what a word means.

**deflate** *verb* (**deflates, deflating, deflated**)
1 to let air out of a tyre, balloon, etc. 2 to make someone less proud or confident. 3 to lower or reverse economic inflation.
**deflation** *noun*, **deflationary** *adjective*

**deflect** *verb* (**deflects, deflecting, deflected**)
to make something turn aside.
**deflection** *noun*

**deforestation** *noun*
the loss of trees from an area.

**deformed** *adjective*
not properly or naturally shaped.
**deformation** *noun*, **deformity** *noun*

**defrost** *verb* (**defrosts, defrosting, defrosted**)
1 to remove ice or frost from a refrigerator, windscreen, etc. 2 to unfreeze frozen food.

**deft** *adjective* (**defter, deftest**)
skilful and quick.
**deftly** *adverb*

**defuse** *verb* (**defuses, defusing, defused**)
1 to remove the fuse from a bomb,
explosive, etc. 2 to make a situation less
dangerous.

**defy** *verb* (**defies, defying, defied**)
1 to say or show that you will not obey. 2 to
challenge, *I defy you to do that.* 3 to prevent
something being done, *The door defied all
attempts to open it.*

**degenerate** *verb* (**degenerates, degenerating,
degenerated**)
to become worse or lower in standard, *The
game degenerated into a succession of fouls.*
**degeneration** *noun*

**degrade** *verb* (**degrades, degrading, degraded**)
to humiliate someone.
**degradation** *noun*

**degree** *noun* (**degrees**)
1 a unit for measuring temperature, *Water
boils at 100 degrees centigrade, or 100°C.*
2 a unit for measuring angles, *There are 90
degrees (90°) in a right angle.* 3 extent, *to
some degree.* 4 an award to someone at a
university, college, etc. who has
successfully finished a course, *She has
a degree in English.*

**dehydrated** *adjective*
with all its moisture removed, *dehydrated
potato.*
**dehydration** *noun*

**de-ice** *verb* (**de-ices, de-icing, de-iced**)
to remove ice from a windscreen, etc.
**de-icer** *noun*

**deity** *noun* (**deities**)
(*say* **dee**-i-ti or **day**-i-ti)
a god.

**dejected** *adjective*
sad; gloomy.
**dejection** *noun*

**delay**[1] *verb* (**delays, delaying, delayed**)
1 to make someone or something late. 2 to
postpone something.

**delay**[2] *noun* (**delays**)
delaying, *Do it without delay.*

**delegate**[1] *noun* (**delegates**)
(*say* **del**-i-găt)
a representative.

**delegate**[2] *verb* (**delegates, delegating, delegated**)
(*say* **del**-i-gayt)
to choose or send someone as a delegate.
**delegation** *noun*

**delete** *verb* (**deletes, deleting, deleted**)
to cross something out; to erase something.
**deletion** *noun*

**deliberate**[1] *adjective*
(*say* di-**lib**-er-ăt)
1 done on purpose, *It was a deliberate
insult.* 2 slow and careful, *a slow, deliberate
way of talking.*
**deliberately** *adverb*

**deliberate**[2] *verb* (**deliberates, deliberating,
deliberated**)
(*say* di-**lib**-er-ayt)
to discuss or think carefully.
**deliberation** *noun*

**delicacy** *noun* (**delicacies**)
1 being delicate. 2 a delicious food.

**delicate** *adjective*
1 fine; soft; fragile, *as delicate as a spider's
web.* 2 becoming ill easily, *a delicate child.*
3 using or needing great care, *delicate
peace negotiations.*
**delicately** *adverb*

**delicatessen** *noun* (**delicatessens**)
a shop that mainly sells cooked or
prepared foods, especially foreign foods.

**delicious** *adjective*
tasting or smelling very pleasant.
**deliciously** *adverb*

**delight**[1] *verb* (**delights, delighting, delighted**)
to please someone greatly.

**delight**[2] *noun* (**delights**)
great pleasure.
**delightful** *adjective*, **delightfully** *adverb*

**delinquent** *noun* (**delinquents**)
someone, especially a young person, who
breaks the law.
**delinquency** *noun*

**delirious** *adjective*
1 affected with delirium. 2 extremely
excited or enthusiastic.
**deliriously** *adverb*

**delirium** *noun* (**deliriums**)
the confused state of mind of people who
are drunk or who have a high fever.

**deliver** *verb* (**delivers, delivering, delivered**)
1 to bring things like letters, milk, or
newspapers to someone's house. 2 to give a
speech, etc. 3 to help with the birth of a
baby. 4 to rescue.
**deliverance** *noun*, **delivery** *noun*

**delphinium** *noun* (**delphiniums**)
a garden plant with tall, usually blue,
flowers.

**delta** *noun* (**deltas**)
the area (usually triangular) between the
branches of a river at its mouth.
**delta wing,** a triangular swept-back wing on
an aircraft.
**delta-winged,** with triangular swept-back
wings.

**delude** *verb* (**deludes, deluding, deluded**)
to make someone believe something that is
not true, *I had been deluded into thinking
that everything was going well.*

**deluge**¹ *noun* (**deluges**)
1 a large flood. 2 a heavy fall of rain.
3 something coming in great numbers, *a
deluge of questions.*

**deluge**² *verb* (**deluges, deluging, deluged**)
to fall in a deluge on someone, *He was
deluged with questions.*

**delusion** *noun* (**delusions**)
a false belief or opinion; a false belief that
is a sign of mental illness.

USAGE: Do not confuse **delusion** with
**illusion,** which means an imaginary thing.

**de luxe** *adjective*
of very high quality, *de luxe, gold-plated
bath-taps.*

**demand**¹ *verb* (**demands, demanding, demanded**)
to ask for something firmly or forcefully.

**demand**² *noun* (**demands**)
1 something demanded. 2 a desire to have
something, *There's a great demand for old
furniture.*
**in demand,** wanted; popular.

**demanding** *adjective*
1 asking for many things, *Toddlers can be
very demanding.* 2 needing skill or effort,
*She has a demanding job.*

**demerara** *noun*
(*say* dem-er-**air**-ă)
light-brown cane sugar.

**demist** *verb* (**demists, demisting, demisted**)
to remove condensation from a windscreen,
etc.

**demo** *noun* (**demos**)
(*informal*) a demonstration.

**democracy** *noun* (**democracies**)
1 government by leaders who have been
chosen by the people. 2 a country governed
in this way.

**democrat** *noun* (**democrats**)
a person who believes in or supports
democracy.
**Democrat,** a supporter of the American
Democratic Party.

**democratic** *adjective*
of or connected with democracy.
**Democratic Party,** one of the two main
political parties of the USA.
**democratically** *adverb*

**demolish** *verb* (**demolishes, demolishing,
demolished**)
to knock something down and break it up.
**demolition** *noun*

**demon** *noun* (**demons**)
1 a devil. 2 a fierce or forceful person.

**demonstrate** *verb* (**demonstrates,
demonstrating, demonstrated**)
1 to show something, *She has clearly
demonstrated her ability.* 2 to take part in a
demonstration.
**demonstrator** *noun*

**demonstration** *noun* (**demonstrations**)
1 showing how to do or work something.
2 a march, meeting, etc. to show everyone
what you think about something, *a
demonstration against the new motorway.*

**demoralize** *verb* (**demoralizes, demoralizing,
demoralized**)
to make someone lose confidence or
courage.
**demoralization** *noun*

**demote** *verb* (**demotes, demoting, demoted**)
to reduce someone to a lower rank, *The
sergeant was demoted to the rank of a
private.*

**den** *noun* (**dens**)
1 a lair, *a lion's den.* 2 a place where
something illegal happens, *a gambling den.*
3 a hiding-place, especially for children.

**denial** *noun* (**denials**)
denying or refusing something.

**denim** *noun* (**denims**)
strong cotton cloth, *Jeans are made out of
denim.*
**denims,** (*informal*) trousers or overalls
made of this cloth.

**denominator** *noun* (**denominators**)
the number below the line in a fraction, *In
$\frac{1}{4}$ the 4 is the denominator.*

**denote** *verb* (**denotes, denoting, denoted**)
to indicate; to mean, *A tick denotes that the goods have been checked.*

**denounce** *verb* (**denounces, denouncing, denounced**)
to speak against something; to accuse someone.
**denunciation** *noun*

**dense** *adjective* (**denser, densest**)
1 thick, *The fog was getting denser.*
2 packed close together, *dense forest.*
3 (*informal*) stupid.
**densely** *adverb*

**density** *noun* (**densities**)
1 thickness. 2 (*in Science*) the mass of something per unit of volume, *Water has greater density than air.*

**dent** *noun* (**dents**)
an impression or hollow made in a surface by hitting it.

**dental** *adjective*
of teeth or dentists.

**dentist** *noun* (**dentists**)
a person who cares for other people's teeth.
**dentistry** *noun*

**denture** *noun* (**dentures**)
a set of false teeth.

**deny** *verb* (**denies, denying, denied**)
to say that something is not true; to refuse, *The prisoners were denied light and exercise.*

**deodorant** *noun* (**deodorants**)
something that removes unwanted smells.
**deodorize** *verb*

**depart** *verb* (**departs, departing, departed**)
to go away; to leave.
**departure** *noun*

**department** *noun* (**departments**)
part of a big organization.
**department store**, a large shop that sells many kinds of goods.

**depend** *verb* (**depends, depending, depended**)
**depend on** or **upon someone**, to rely on someone, *He depended on them for help.*
**depend on** or **upon something**, to be decided by something else, *Whether we can picnic depends on the weather.*

**dependable** *adjective*
that you can depend upon; reliable, *a dependable helper.*

**dependant** *noun* (**dependants**)
a person who depends on another, *We have two dependants, a son and a daughter.*

**dependent** *adjective*
depending, *He was dependent on her wages.*
**dependence** *noun*

**depict** *verb* (**depicts, depicting, depicted**)
1 to paint or draw. 2 to describe.

**deplorable** *adjective*
extremely bad; shocking, *a deplorable lack of tact.*
**deplorably** *adverb*

**deplore** *verb* (**deplores, deploring, deplored**)
to be very upset or annoyed by something.
**deplorable** *adjective*

**deport** *verb* (**deports, deporting, deported**)
to send someone out of a country.
**deportation** *noun*

**deposit** *noun* (**deposits**)
1 an amount of money paid into a bank. 2 a first payment for something. 3 a layer of solid matter in or on the earth.
**deposition** *noun*

**depot** *noun* (**depots**)
(*say* dep-oh)
1 a place where things are stored; a place where buses, trains, etc. are kept when they are not in use. 2 the headquarters of an army regiment.

**depress** *verb* (**depresses, depressing, depressed**)
to make someone very sad.

**depressed** *adjective*
1 very sad. 2 having economic difficulties, *a depressed area with high unemployment.*

**depression** *noun* (**depressions**)
1 a great sadness. 2 an area of low air pressure which may bring rain. 3 a long period when there is less trade and business than usual and many people have no work. 4 a shallow hollow in the ground.

**deprive** *verb* (**deprives, depriving, deprived**)
to take something away from someone, *Prisoners are deprived of their freedom.*
**deprivation** *noun*

**depth** *noun* (**depths**)
how deep something is, *the depth of the river.*
**in depth**, thoroughly.

**deputy** *noun* (**deputies**)
a substitute or chief assistant for someone.
**deputize** *verb*

**derail** *verb* (**derails, derailing, derailed**)
to cause a train to leave the track.

**derby** *noun* (**derbies**)
a sporting event between two teams from the same city or area.

**derelict** *adjective*
(*say* de-rĕ-likt)
abandoned, *a derelict ship*; ruined, *a derelict house with crumbling walls.*

**derision** *noun*
scorn, *They treated him with derision.*
**deride** *verb*, **derisive** *adjective*, **derisory** *adjective*

**derivation** *noun* (**derivations**)
where a word comes from, *Do you know the derivation of the word 'tragedy'?*

**derive** *verb* (**derives, deriving, derived**)
to obtain a thing from another person or thing, *The word 'tragedy' is derived from Greek.*
**derivation** *noun*, **derivative** *adjective and noun*

**derrick** *noun* (**derricks**)
1 a machine for hoisting things. 2 a tower that holds the drill when a well is being drilled.

derrick 2

**derv** *noun*
diesel fuel for lorries, etc. (from the first letters of the words 'diesel-engined road vehicles').

**descant** *noun* (**descants**)
a tune sung or played above another tune.
**descant recorder,** a high-pitched recorder.

**descend** *verb* (**descends, descending, descended**)
to go down.
**be descended from someone,** to be in the same family as someone but living at a later time than him or her.
**descent** *noun*

**descendant** *noun* (**descendants**)
a person who is in the same family as you, was born after you, and is your child, or a child of your child, etc.

**describe** *verb* (**describes, describing, described**)
to say what someone or something is like.
**description** *noun*, **descriptive** *adjective*

**desert**[1] *noun* (**deserts**)
(*say* dez-ert)
a large area of very dry, often sandy, land.
**desert island,** an island where nobody lives, especially one in the tropics.

USAGE: Do not confuse **desert** with **dessert**, which means food eaten at the end of a meal.

**desert**[2] *verb* (**deserts, deserting, deserted**)
(*say* di-**zert**)
to abandon someone; to leave something without intending to return.
**desertion** *noun*

**deserter** *noun* (**deserters**)
someone who leaves the armed forces without permission.

**deserts** *plural noun*
(*say* di-**zerts**)
what someone deserves, *He got his just deserts.*

**deserve** *verb* (**deserves, deserving, deserved**)
to have a right to something; to be worthy of something.
**deservedly** *adverb*

**design**[1] *noun* (**designs**)
1 a plan or pattern for something. 2 the way that something is made or planned; an arrangement or pattern.

**design**[2] *verb* (**designs, designing, designed**)
to draw a design; to plan a building, machine, etc.
**designer** *noun*

**designate** *verb* (**designates, designating, designated**)
to mark or describe as something particular, *The river was designated as the boundary.*

**desirable** *adjective*
1 worth having, *a desirable house.* 2 worth doing; advisable, *It is desirable for you to come with us.*
**desirability** *noun*

**desire** *verb* (**desires, desiring, desired**)
to want something very much.
**desirous** *adjective*

**desk** *noun* (**desks**)
1 a kind of table for writing or reading at. 2 a counter behind which a receptionist, cashier, etc. sits.

**desktop** *adjective*
small enough to be put on top of someone's desk, *a desktop computer.*
**desktop publishing,** using a desktop computer and printer to arrange words and pictures so that they are ready to be made into a book.

**desolate** *adjective*
1 having nobody living there, *a desolate island.* 2 sad; lonely.
**desolation** *noun*

**despair** *noun*
a feeling of hopelessness.

**despatch** *noun* (**despatches**) and *verb* (**despatches, despatching, despatched**)
dispatch.

**desperate** *adjective*
1 violent; dangerous, *a desperate criminal.*
2 hopeless; extremely bad, *a desperate situation.*
**desperately** *adverb*, **desperation** *noun*

**despise** *verb* (**despises, despising, despised**)
to think someone is inferior or worthless.
**despicable** *adjective*

**despite** *preposition*
in spite of.

**dessert** *noun* (**desserts**)
(*say* di-**zert**)
food eaten at the end of a meal.

USAGE: Do not confuse **dessert** with **desert**, which means an area of very dry land.

**dessertspoon** *noun* (**dessertspoons**)
a medium-sized spoon used for eating puddings, etc.

**destination** *noun* (**destinations**)
the place you are travelling to.

**destined** *adjective*
intended; fated, *They felt they had been destined to meet.*

**destiny** *noun* (**destinies**)
fate, *His destiny was to die alone.*

**destroy** *verb* (**destroys, destroying, destroyed**)
to ruin or put an end to something.
**destruction** *noun*, **destructive** *adjective*

**destroyer** *noun* (**destroyers**)
a fast warship.

**detach** *verb* (**detaches, detaching, detached**)
to unfasten; to separate, *His section had become detached from the rest of the platoon.*
**detachable** *adjective*, **detachment** *noun*

**detached** *adjective*
not prejudiced; not involved, *a detached observer.*
**detached house**, a house not joined to another.

**detail** *noun* (**details**)
1 a tiny part of something. 2 a small piece of information.
**in detail**, describing or covering each part fully.

**detain** *verb* (**detains, detaining, detained**)
1 to keep someone at a place. 2 to keep someone waiting.

**detect** *verb* (**detects, detecting, detected**)
to discover.
**detectable** *adjective*, **detection** *noun*, **detector** *noun*

**detective** *noun* (**detectives**)
a person who investigates crimes.

**detention** *noun* (**detentions**)
being made to stay in a place, especially being made to stay late in school as a punishment.

**deter** *verb* (**deters, deterring, deterred**)
to put someone off doing something.

**detergent** *noun* (**detergents**)
a kind of washing powder or liquid.

**deteriorate** *verb* (**deteriorates, deteriorating, deteriorated**)
to become worse in condition or quality, *Paintwork deteriorates when it is exposed to the weather.*
**deterioration** *noun*

**determined** *adjective*
with your mind firmly made up.
**determination** *noun*

**deterrent** *noun* (**deterrents**)
something that may deter people, especially a nuclear weapon.
**deterrence** *noun*

**detest** *verb* (**detests, detesting, detested**)
to hate, *She detested noise.*
**detestable** *adjective*, **detestation** *noun*

**detonate** *verb* (**detonates, detonating, detonated**)
to set off an explosion.
**detonation** *noun*, **detonator** *noun*

**detour** *noun* (**detours**)
a route used instead of the normal route.

**deuce** *noun*
a tennis score when both sides have 40 points.

**devastate** *verb* (**devastates, devastating, devastated**)
to ruin or destroy something; to make a place impossible to live in.
**devastation** *noun*

**devastated** *adjective*
very shocked and upset, *I was absolutely devastated to hear that he had lost his job.*

**develop** *verb* (**develops, developing, developed**)
1 to make or become bigger or better. 2 to put up new buildings on a piece of land, *Several fields have been developed in the last year.* 3 to treat photographic film with chemicals so that pictures can be seen.
**developing country**, a poor country that is building up its industry and trying to improve its people's living conditions.

**development** *noun* (**developments**)
1 something that has happened, *Have there been any further developments in the situation since I last saw you?* 2 putting up new buildings; a group of these buildings, *Extensive development has taken place around the village. New developments surround the old town.*

**device** *noun* (**devices**)
something made for a particular purpose.
**leave someone to his or her own devices**, to
leave someone to do as he or she likes,
without help or advice.

USAGE: Do not confuse **device**, which is a
noun, with **devise**, which is a verb meaning
to invent or plan something.

**devil** *noun* (**devils**)
an evil spirit or person.
**devilish** *adjective*, **devilry** *noun*

**devious** *adjective*
1 using unfair and dishonest methods; not
showing what he or she intends to do, *They
thought up a devious plan to remove the
President from power. He's devious, and
you can't trust him.* 2 not direct, *The coach
took us around North London by a devious
route, trying to avoid traffic jams.*

**devise** *verb* (**devises, devising, devised**)
to invent something; to plan something, *We
devised a way of keeping out burglars.*

**devolution** *noun*
giving authority to a more local
organization or person, especially handing
over responsibility for government.

**devote** *verb* (**devotes, devoting, devoted**)
to give something or yourself completely,
*They devote all their free time to sport.
Albert Schweitzer devoted himself to
helping the sick.*
**devotee** *noun*, **devotion** *noun*

**devoted** *adjective*
1 loving and loyal, *a devoted parent.* 2 very
enthusiastic, *He's a devoted supporter of
the local football team.*
**devotedly** *adverb*

**devour** *verb* (**devours, devouring, devoured**)
to eat or swallow something greedily.

**dew** *noun*
tiny drops of water that form during the
night on surfaces out of doors.
**dewy** *adjective*

**dhoti** *noun* (**dhotis**)
(*say* **doh**-ti)
a long piece of cloth worn by Hindu men
around the lower part of their body.

**diabetes** *noun*
(*say* dy-ă-**bee**-teez)
a disease in which there is too much sugar
in a person's blood.
**diabetic** *adjective* and *noun*

**diabolical** *adjective*
like a devil, *diabolical cruelty.*

**diagnose** *verb* (**diagnoses, diagnosing,
diagnosed**)
to find out what disease someone has, *The
doctor diagnosed appendicitis.*
**diagnosis** *noun*, **diagnostic** *adjective*

**diagonal** *noun* (**diagonals**)
a straight line joining opposite corners of a
rectangle.
**diagonally** *adverb*

**diagram** *noun* (**diagrams**)
a picture or plan that explains something.

**diagrammatic** *adjective*
in the form of a diagram, *diagrammatic
information.*

**dial**[1] *noun* (**dials**)
a circular piece of plastic, card, etc. with
numbers or letters round it, *Clocks and
watches have dials.*

**dial**[2] *verb* (**dials, dialling, dialled**)
to telephone a number by turning a
telephone dial or by pressing keys.

**dialect** *noun* (**dialects**)
the way people speak in a particular
district.

**dialogue** *noun* (**dialogues**)
a conversation.

**diameter** *noun* (**diameters**)
1 the width of a circle. 2 a line drawn from
one side of a circle to the other, passing
through the centre.

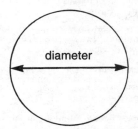

**diamond** *noun* (**diamonds**)
1 a very hard jewel that looks like clear
glass. 2 a shape which has four equal sides
but which is not a square. 3 a playing-card
with a red diamond shape on it.

**diaphragm** *noun* (**diaphragms**)
(*say* **dy**-ă-fram)
1 the muscular part inside the body
between the chest and the abdomen, used
in breathing. 2 a thin sheet or membrane
that keeps things apart.

**diarrhoea** *noun*
(*say* dy-ă-**ree**-ă)
too frequent emptying of waste matter that
is too watery, from the bowels.

**diary** *noun* (**diaries**)
a book where you can write down what happens each day.

**dice** *plural noun*
small cubes marked with dots (1 to 6) on their sides, used in games.

USAGE: The correct singular form of **dice** is **die**.

**dictate** *verb* (**dictates, dictating, dictated**)
1 to speak or read something aloud for someone else to write down. 2 to tell someone what to do; to give orders.
**dictation** *noun*

**dictator** *noun* (**dictators**)
a ruler who has unlimited power.
**dictatorial** *adjective*, **dictatorship** *noun*

**dictionary** *noun* (**dictionaries**)
a book where you can find out what a word means and how to spell it, *Dictionaries usually give words in alphabetical order.*

**did** past tense of **do**.

**diddle** *verb* (**diddles, diddling, diddled**)
(*informal*) to cheat someone, *We've been diddled! He's charged us £10 too much.*

**didn't** short for *did not*.

**die**¹ *verb* (**dies, dying, died**)
to stop living; to come to an end, *The company ran out of money, and died.*

**die**² *noun* (**dice**)
one of a set of dice.

**diesel** *noun* (**diesels**)
1 an internal-combustion engine that works by burning oil. 2 fuel for this kind of engine.

**diet** *noun* (**diets**)
1 special meals that someone eats to be healthy or to lose weight. 2 the food you normally eat.

**differ** *verb* (**differs, differing, differed**)
1 to be different. 2 to disagree, *The two writers differ on this point.*

**difference** *noun* (**differences**)
how different something is from something else.

**different** *adjective*
unlike; not the same, *Her hat is different from mine.*
**differently** *adverb*

**differential** *noun* (**differentials**)
1 a difference in wages. 2 a differential gear.
**differential gear,** a system of gears that allows a vehicle's driving wheels to turn at slightly different speeds when going round corners.

**difficult** *adjective*
not easy.

**difficulty** *noun* (**difficulties**)
1 not being easy; trouble, *I had difficulty in climbing up the slippery slope.* 2 something that causes a problem, *We faced many difficulties when travelling across Africa.*

**diffuse** *verb* (**diffuses, diffusing, diffused**)
1 to spread something widely or thinly, *diffused lighting.* 2 to mix slowly, *diffusing gases.*
**diffusion** *noun*

**dig**¹ *verb* (**digs, digging, dug**)
1 to move soil; to make a hole in the ground. 2 to poke, *He dug me in the ribs.*
**digger** *noun*

**dig**² *noun* (**digs**)
1 a place where archaeologists are looking for ancient remains. 2 a sharp thrust or poke, *She gave me a dig in the ribs with her elbow.* 3 an unpleasant remark, *What he said was clearly a dig at me.*

**digest** *verb* (**digests, digesting, digested**)
to soften and change food in the stomach and intestine so that the body can absorb its goodness.
**digestible** *adjective*, **digestion** *noun*

**digestive** *adjective*
connected with the digesting of food.
**digestive system,** the parts of the body used in digesting food.

**digit** *noun* (**digits**)
(*say* dij-it)
any of the numbers from 0 to 9.

**digital** *adjective*
1 of or using digits. 2 of a type of clock or watch that shows the time with a row of figures, not on a dial (compare *analogue*). 3 (of a computer or a recording system) recording data or sound as a series of binary digits.

**dignified** *adjective*
having dignity.

**dignity** *noun* (**dignities**)
1 a serious or noble manner. 2 a high rank.

**digs** *plural noun*
(*informal*) a room or rooms where you live in someone else's house, and for which you pay.

**dike** *noun* (**dikes**)
1 an embankment. 2 a ditch.

**dilemma** *noun* (**dilemmas**)
a difficult choice.

**dilute** *verb* (**dilutes, diluting, diluted**)
to make a liquid weaker by mixing it with water.
**dilution** *noun*

**dim** *adjective* (**dimmer, dimmest**)
not bright.
**dimly** *adverb*

**dimension** *noun* (**dimensions**)
measurement; size.
**dimensional** *adjective*

**diminish** *verb* (**diminishes, diminishing, diminished**)
to make something smaller; to become smaller.

**dimple** *noun* (**dimples**)
a small hollow on the skin.

**din** *noun*
a loud noise.

**dine** *verb* (**dines, dining, dined**)
to have dinner.
**diner** *noun*

**dinghy** *noun* (**dinghies**)
(*say* **ding**-i)
a small boat.

**dingy** *adjective* (**dingier, dingiest**)
(*say* **din**-ji)
shabby; dirty-looking.

**dinner** *noun* (**dinners**)
the main meal of the day.

**dinosaur** *noun* (**dinosaurs**)
a large prehistoric animal.

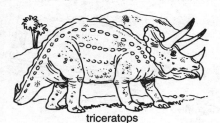

triceratops

**diode** *noun* (**diodes**)
an electronic device that allows an electric current to flow in one direction only and has two places where you can connect wires to it.

**dioxide** *noun* (**dioxides**)
an oxide with two atoms of oxygen and one atom of another element, *carbon dioxide*.

**dip**[1] *verb* (**dips, dipping, dipped**)
1 to put something down or go down, especially into a liquid, *Dip the brush in the paint. The farmer is dipping his sheep to protect them from parasites.* 2 to alter the beam of a vehicle's headlights so that people in front of the vehicle are not dazzled.
**dip into a book,** to read small parts of a book from time to time.

**dip**[2] *noun* (**dips**)
1 dipping. 2 a slope downward. 3 a quick swim. 4 a creamy mixture into which you dip biscuits, etc. before eating them.

**diphtheria** *noun*
(*say* dif-**theer**-i-ă)
a serious disease of the throat.

**diploma** *noun* (**diplomas**)
a certificate awarded for skill in a particular subject.

**diplomacy** *noun*
keeping friendly with other nations or other people.
**diplomat** *noun*, **diplomatic** *adjective*, **diplomatically** *adverb*

**dire** *adjective* (**direr, direst**)
1 urgent, *The refugees are in dire need of food and shelter.* 2 causing fear of what will happen, *dire warnings of disaster.*
3 (*informal*) very bad, *His latest record's really dire.*
**in dire straits,** in a very bad situation, *We were in dire straits, with no money and nowhere to live.*

**direct**[1] *adjective*
1 as straight or quick as possible.
2 straightforward; frank.
**direct current,** electric current flowing only in one direction.
**direct object,** the word that receives the action of a verb, *In 'she hit him', the direct object is 'him'.*
**direct speech,** someone's words written down exactly in the way they were said, instead of being given in an altered, reported form (**indirect speech**), *'I am sure' is direct speech; 'He said that he was sure' is indirect speech.*
**directly** *adverb*, **directness** *noun*

**direct**[2] *verb* (**directs, directing, directed**)
1 to show someone the way. 2 to control; to manage.
**director** *noun*

**direction** *noun* (**directions**)
1 the way you go to get somewhere.
2 directing something.
**directions,** information on how to use or do something.
**directional** *adjective*

**director** *noun* (**directors**)
1 a person who is in charge of something, especially one of a group of people managing a company. 2 a person who decides how a film or play should be made or performed.

**directory** *noun* (**directories**)
a list of people or businesses with their telephone numbers, addresses, etc.

**dirt** *noun*
mud; dust; anything that is not clean.
**dirt-track,** a racing-track made of cinders, earth, etc.

**dirty** *adjective* (**dirtier, dirtiest**)
1 not clean. 2 rude; obscene, *Someone has written dirty words on the wall.* 3 unfair; mean, *It was a dirty trick to steal my sweets.*
**dirtily** *adverb*, **dirtiness** *noun*

**dis-** *prefix*
1 showing the opposite of something, as in *dishonest.* 2 showing that something has been taken away or apart, as in *disarm* or *dismantle.*

**disability** *noun* (**disabilities**)
something that prevents someone from using his or her body in the usual way.

**disable** *verb* (**disables, disabling, disabled**)
1 to make someone unable to use his or her body properly. 2 to make something unable to work, *The telephone system had been disabled by the earthquake.*

**disabled** *adjective*
having a disease or injury that makes it difficult for someone to use his or her body in the usual way.

**disadvantage** *noun* (**disadvantages**)
something that hinders you; a difficulty.
**be at a disadvantage,** to be hindered by something, *He was at a disadvantage because he had missed a term's work while he was ill.*
**disadvantaged** *adjective*

**disagree** *verb* (**disagrees, disagreeing, disagreed**)
1 to have or express a different opinion from someone else. 2 to have a bad effect on someone, *Rich food disagrees with me.*
**disagreement** *noun*

**disagreeable** *adjective*
1 unpleasant, *a disagreeable task.*
2 bad-tempered.

**disappear** *verb* (**disappears, disappearing, disappeared**)
to stop being visible; to vanish.
**disappearance** *noun*

**disappoint** *verb* (**disappoints, disappointing, disappointed**)
to fail to do what someone hopes for.
**disappointing** *adjective*, **disappointment** *noun*

**disapprove** *verb* (**disapproves, disapproving, disapproved**)
not to approve of someone or something.
**disapproval** *noun*, **disapproving** *adjective*, **disapprovingly** *adverb*

**disarm** *verb* (**disarms, disarming, disarmed**)
1 to reduce the size of your army, air force, etc. 2 to take away someone's weapons.
**disarmament** *noun*

**disaster** *noun* (**disasters**)
a very bad accident or misfortune.
**disastrous** *adjective*, **disastrously** *adverb*

**disc** *noun* (**discs**)
1 any round, flat object. 2 a round, flat piece of plastic on which sound or data is recorded.
**disc brake,** a brake using pads of fireproof material pressing against a flat plate.
**disc jockey,** someone who introduces and plays records.
**disc parking,** parking in which vehicles display a disc or card that shows the time of parking.

**discard** *verb* (**discards, discarding, discarded**)
to get rid of something.

**discharge** *verb* (**discharges, discharging, discharged**)
1 to release someone. 2 to send something out, *Vehicles must not discharge excessive smoke.*

**disciple** *noun* (**disciples**)
a follower of a political or religious leader, especially one of Jesus's first twelve followers.

**discipline** *noun*
orderly and obedient behaviour.

**disclose** *verb* (**discloses, disclosing, disclosed**)
to reveal.
**disclosure** *noun*

**Discman** *noun* (**Discmans**)
(*trademark*) a portable stereo compact-disc player.

**disco** *noun* (**discos**)
(*informal*) **1** a discotheque. **2** music of the kind played in discotheques.

**discolour** *verb* (**discolours, discolouring, discoloured**)
to spoil or change the colour of something.

**discomfort** *noun*
being uncomfortable.

**disconnect** *verb* (**disconnects, disconnecting, disconnected**)
to break a connection; to detach something.
**disconnection** *noun*

**discontented** *adjective*
not contented; dissatisfied.
**discontent** *noun*, **discontentedly** *adverb*

**discotheque** *noun* (**discotheques**)
(*say* dis-kŏ-tek)
**1** a place or party where records are played for dancing. **2** the equipment for playing records for dancing.

**discount** *noun* (**discounts**)
an amount by which a price is reduced.

**discourage** *verb* (**discourages, discouraging, discouraged**)
**1** to take away someone's enthusiasm or confidence, *Don't get discouraged: try again.* **2** to try to persuade someone not to do something, *You should discourage him from going out in the rain.*
**discouragement** *noun*, **discouraging** *adjective*

**discover** *verb* (**discovers, discovering, discovered**)
**1** to find something. **2** to find something out, *We only discovered the truth later.*
**discoverer** *noun*, **discovery** *noun*

**discreet** *adjective* (**discreeter, discreetest**)
being careful in what you say and do, especially when you have a secret to keep.
**discreetly** *adverb*

**discriminate** *verb* (**discriminates, discriminating, discriminated**)
**1** to notice the differences between things; to prefer one thing to another. **2** to treat people differently or unfairly because of their race, sex, or religion.
**discrimination** *noun*, **discriminatory** *adjective*

**discus** *noun* (**discuses**)
(*say* dis-kŭss)
a thick, heavy disc thrown in an athletic contest.

**discuss** *verb* (**discusses, discussing, discussed**)
(*say* dis-kuss)
to talk with other people about a subject.
**discussion** *noun*

**disease** *noun* (**diseases**)
an illness; sickness, *measures to combat disease.*
**diseased** *adjective*

**disembark** *verb* (**disembarks, disembarking, disembarked**)
to get out of a boat or an aircraft; to unload something from a boat or an aircraft.

**disgrace**[1] *noun*
**1** shame, *It's no disgrace to be poor.* **2** a person or thing that causes shame or disapproval, *The slums are a disgrace.*
**in disgrace**, disapproved of, *He is in disgrace for telling lies.*
**disgraceful** *adjective*, **disgracefully** *adverb*

**disgrace**[2] *verb* (**disgraces, disgracing, disgraced**)
to cause disgrace to someone or something.

**disguise**[1] *verb* (**disguises, disguising, disguised**)
to make someone or something look different so as to deceive people.

**disguise**[2] *noun* (**disguises**)
something used for disguising.

**disgust**[1] *noun*
a strong feeling of dislike.

**disgust**[2] *verb* (**disgusts, disgusting, disgusted**)
to cause disgust, *His manners disgusted us.*
**disgusted** *adjective*

**disgusting** *adjective*
causing a strong feeling of dislike.
**disgustingly** *adverb*

**dish** *noun* (**dishes**)
**1** a plate or bowl for food. **2** food served on a dish.

**dishcloth** *noun* (**dishcloths**)
a cloth for washing or drying dishes, cups, etc.

**dishevelled** *adjective*
untidy in appearance, *dishevelled hair.*

**dishonest** *adjective*
not honest.
**dishonesty** *noun*

**dishwasher** *noun* (**dishwashers**)
1 a machine for washing crockery, cutlery, etc. 2 a person whose job is to wash crockery, cutlery, etc.

**disinfect** *verb* (**disinfects, disinfecting, disinfected**)
to treat something to destroy germs.
**disinfectant** *noun*

**disintegrate** *verb* (**disintegrates, disintegrating, disintegrated**)
to break up into small pieces.
**disintegration** *noun*

**disinterested** *adjective*
not prejudiced; not favouring one side more than the other, *We will need to find a disinterested person to judge the competition.*

USAGE: Do not confuse **disinterested** with **uninterested**, which means that you are bored by something or do not want to know anything about it.

**disk** *noun* (**disks**)
a disc, especially one used to store computer data.

**dislike**[1] *noun* (**dislikes**)
a feeling of not liking someone or something.

**dislike**[2] *verb* (**dislikes, disliking, disliked**)
not to like someone or something.

**dislocate** *verb* (**dislocates, dislocating, dislocated**)
1 to dislodge a bone from its proper place in the body. 2 to disrupt, *The fog dislocated rail services.*
**dislocation** *noun*

**dislodge** *verb* (**dislodges, dislodging, dislodged**)
to move something from its place.

**disloyal** *adjective*
not loyal.

**dismal** *adjective*
gloomy.
**dismally** *adverb*

**dismantle** *verb* (**dismantles, dismantling, dismantled**)
to take something to pieces.

**dismay** *noun*
discouragement or despair.
**dismayed** *adjective*

**dismiss** *verb* (**dismisses, dismissing, dismissed**)
1 to send someone away, and especially to stop employing them. 2 to reject an idea, etc., *The teacher dismissed our suggestion.* 3 to get a batsman out in cricket.
**dismissal** *noun*

**dismount** *verb* (**dismounts, dismounting, dismounted**)
to get off a horse or bicycle.

**disobey** *verb* (**disobeys, disobeying, disobeyed**)
not to obey.
**disobedience** *noun*, **disobedient** *adjective*

**disorder** *noun* (**disorders**)
1 confusion; disturbance. 2 an illness.
**disorderly** *adjective*

**dispatch**[1] *noun* (**dispatches**)
a report or message.

**dispatch**[2] *verb* (**dispatches, dispatching, dispatched**)
1 to send a person or thing off somewhere. 2 to kill.

**dispense** *verb* (**dispenses, dispensing, dispensed**)
1 to distribute. 2 to prepare medicine.
**dispense with**, to do without something.

**dispenser** *noun* (**dispensers**)
a device that distributes something, *There is a soap dispenser above each wash-basin.*

**disperse** *verb* (**disperses, dispersing, dispersed**)
to scatter, *The police dispersed the crowd.*
**dispersal** *noun*, **dispersion** *noun*

**displace** *verb* (**displaces, displacing, displaced**)
1 to dislodge something; to move someone from his or her place. 2 to take the place of someone or something.

**displacement** *noun*
1 displacing. 2 the amount of water displaced by a ship, etc. floating in it.

**display**[1] *verb* (**displays, displaying, displayed**)
to show something; to arrange something so that it can be clearly seen.

**display**[2] *noun* (**displays**)
1 the displaying of something; an exhibition. 2 the showing of information on a VDU screen.

**displease** *verb* (**displeases, displeasing, displeased**)
to annoy.
**displeasing** *adjective*, **displeasure** *noun*

**disposable** *adjective*
made to be thrown away after it has been used, *a disposable towel.*

**disposal** *noun*
getting rid of something.
**at your disposal**, for you to use; ready for you.

**dispose** *verb* (**disposes, disposing, disposed**)
to make someone willing or ready to do something, *I am not disposed to help him*.
**dispose of**, to get rid of.

**disposition** *noun* (**dispositions**)
a person's character or qualities.

**disprove** *verb* (**disproves, disproving, disproved**)
to prove that something is not true.

**dispute** *noun* (**disputes**)
a quarrel or disagreement.

**disqualify** *verb* (**disqualifies, disqualifying, disqualified**)
to remove someone from a race or competition because he or she has broken the rules.
**disqualification** *noun*

**disregard** *verb* (**disregards, disregarding, disregarded**)
to ignore, *She disregarded my feelings*.

**disrespect** *noun*
lack of respect.
**disrespectful** *adjective*, **disrespectfully** *adverb*

**disrupt** *verb* (**disrupts, disrupting, disrupted**)
to put into disorder, *Floods disrupted traffic*.
**disruption** *noun*, **disruptive** *adjective*

**dissatisfied** *adjective*
not satisfied.
**dissatisfaction** *noun*

**dissect** *verb* (**dissects, dissecting, dissected**)
to cut something up so as to examine it.
**dissection** *noun*

**dissolve** *verb* (**dissolves, dissolving, dissolved**)
to mix something with a liquid so that it becomes part of the liquid.

**dissuade** *verb* (**dissuades, dissuading, dissuaded**)
to persuade someone not to do something, *I will dissuade him from giving up his job*.

**distance** *noun* (**distances**)
the amount of space between two places.
**in the distance**, far away.

**distant** *adjective*
1 far away. 2 not friendly or sociable.

**distil** *verb* (**distils, distilling, distilled**)
to purify a liquid by boiling it and condensing the vapour.

**distillery** *noun* (**distilleries**)
a place where spirits such as whisky are produced.
**distiller** *noun*

**distinct** *adjective*
1 easily heard or seen; definite, *a distinct improvement*. 2 clearly separate or different, *A rabbit is distinct from a hare*.
**distinctly** *adverb*

**distinction** *noun* (**distinctions**)
1 a difference. 2 excellence; honour. 3 an award for excellence.

**distinctive** *adjective*
that distinguishes one thing from another.

**distinguish** *verb* (**distinguishes, distinguishing, distinguished**)
1 to mark or notice the differences between things. 2 to see or hear something clearly.

**distinguished** *adjective*
1 famous, *a distinguished historian*.
2 having dignity, *a distinguished-looking lady*.

**distort** *verb* (**distorts, distorting, distorted**)
1 to change something into an abnormal shape, *His face was distorted with anger*.
2 to change something so that it is untrue, *Newspapers sometimes distort the facts*.
**distorted** *adjective*, **distortion** *noun*

**distract** *verb* (**distracts, distracting, distracted**)
to take someone's attention away from something, *Don't distract me from my work*.
**distracting** *adjective*, **distraction** *noun*

**distress** *noun*
great sorrow, pain, or trouble.
**distressing** *adjective*, **distressingly** *adverb*

**distribute** *verb* (**distributes, distributing, distributed**)
1 to deal or share out, *The teacher distributed textbooks to the class*. 2 to sell or deliver goods to customers. 3 spread or scatter around, *She distributed the seed over the soil*.
**distribution** *noun*, **distributive** *adjective*

**distributor** *noun* (**distributors**)
1 someone who distributes goods. 2 a device that passes current to the sparking-plugs of an internal-combustion engine.

**district** *noun* (**districts**)
part of a town or country.

**distrust** *noun*
lack of trust; suspicion.
**distrustful** *adjective*

**disturb** *verb* (**disturbs, disturbing, disturbed**)
1 to spoil someone's peace or rest; to worry someone. 2 to dislodge something.
**disturbance** *noun*

**disused** *adjective*
no longer used, *a disused warehouse*.

**ditch** *noun* (**ditches**)
a narrow trench to hold or carry away water.

**dither** *verb* (**dithers, dithering, dithered**)
to hesitate, *If you're going to cross the road, wait till there is no traffic, then cross; don't dither*.

**ditto** *noun*
the same as before, *Twenty bottles of red wine, £60; ditto white, £70.*

USAGE: Ditto marks (") are sometimes used in lists, bills, etc., to show where something is repeated.

**divan** *noun* (**divans**)
a bed or couch without back or sides.

**dive** *verb* (**dives, diving, dived**)
1 to go into water head first. 2 to go under water. 3 to move downwards quickly, *The aeroplane dived.*

**diver** *noun* (**divers**)
1 a swimmer who dives. 2 someone who works under water in a special suit called a **diving-suit**. 3 a bird that dives.

**diverse** *adjective*
varied; of several different kinds.
**diversify** *verb*, **diversity** *noun*

**diversion** *noun* (**diversions**)
a different way for traffic to go while the usual road is temporarily closed.

**divert** *verb* (**diverts, diverting, diverted**)
1 to change the direction of something. 2 to entertain or amuse someone.

**divide** *verb* (**divides, dividing, divided**)
1 to separate or break into smaller parts; to share out, *We divided the money between us.* 2 (*in Mathematics*) to find out how many times one number is contained in another, *Six divided by two equals three (6 ÷ 2 = 3).*

**dividend** *noun* (**dividends**)
1 (*in Mathematics*) an amount to be divided. 2 a share of a business's profit.

**divider** *noun* (**dividers**)
a partition.
**dividers**, a pair of compasses for measuring distances.

**divine**¹ *adjective* (**diviner, divinest**)
1 of God; coming from God. 2 like a god. 3 (*informal*) excellent; extremely beautiful.
**divinely** *adverb*, **divinity** *noun*

**divine**² *verb* (**divines, divining, divined**)
to find hidden water, metal, etc. by holding a Y-shaped stick called a **divining-rod**.

**division** *noun* (**divisions**)
1 dividing, especially in mathematics. 2 something that divides. 3 a part of something. 4 an army unit made up of two or more brigades.
**divisible** *adjective*

**divorce**¹ *noun* (**divorces**)
the legal ending of a marriage.

**divorce**² *verb* (**divorces, divorcing, divorced**)
to end a marriage to someone by legal means, *She divorced her husband.*
**divorced** *adjective*, **divorcee** *noun*

**Diwali** *noun*
(*say* di-**wah**-li)
a Hindu festival held in October or November.

**DIY** short for **do-it-yourself**.

**dizzy** *adjective* (**dizzier, dizziest**)
giddy and feeling confused.
**dizzily** *adverb*, **dizziness** *noun*

**DJ** short for **disc jockey**.

**do** *verb* (**does, doing, did, done**)
1 to perform an action; to carry out something, *I have done my job.* 2 to deal with something; to solve a problem, *I can't do this sum.* 3 to be suitable or enough, *This room will do for two people.* 4 to manage or progress; to get on, *She is doing well at school.* 5 (*informal*) to swindle, *I'm afraid you've been done.* 6 used in questions like *Do you want this?* and in statements with 'not' like *I do not want it.*
**someone could do with something**, someone needs or wants something, *I could do with a bath.*
**do away with**, to get rid of or kill.
**do something up**, to fasten something, *Do up your coat.*
**do without something**, to manage without having something.

**Dobermann** *noun* (**Dobermanns**)
a large, muscular breed of dog, often kept to protect people or buildings.

**docile** *adjective*
willing to obey, *a docile cart-horse.*

**dock**¹ *noun* (**docks**)
1 a place where ships are loaded, unloaded, or repaired. 2 a place for the prisoner in a criminal court. 3 a weed with broad leaves.

**dock**² *verb* (**docks, docking, docked**)
1 to come into a dock. 2 to join two spacecraft together in orbit.

**dock**³ *verb* (**docks, docking, docked**)
to cut an animal's tail short; to take money away from someone's pay, *Your wages will be docked if you are late for work.*

**docker** *noun* (**dockers**)
a labourer in a dockyard.

**dockyard** *noun* (**dockyards**)
an area with docks and equipment for building or repairing ships.

**doctor** *noun* (**doctors**)
a person trained to heal sick people.

**doctrine** *noun* (**doctrines**)
a religious or political belief.
**doctrinal** *adjective*

**document** *noun* (**documents**)
something important written or printed.
**documentation** *noun*

**documentary** *noun* (**documentaries**)
a film or a television programme showing real events or situations.

**doddery** *adjective*
shaking or unsteady because of being old, *a doddery old man.*

**doddle** *noun*
(*informal*) something that is very easy to do, *You could pass the test – it's a doddle!*

**dodge**¹ *verb* (**dodges, dodging, dodged**)
to move quickly to avoid someone or something.

**dodge**² *noun* (**dodges**)
**1** a dodging movement. **2** a trick; a clever way of doing something.

**dodgem** *noun* (**dodgems**)
a small electrically-driven car at a fair, which you have to drive around an enclosure, dodging other cars.

**dodgy** *adjective* (**dodgier, dodgiest**)
(*informal*) **1** not safe; involving risk, *a dodgy plan.* **2** dishonest or unreliable, *a dodgy trader.*

**doe** *noun* (**does**)
a female deer, rabbit, or hare.

**does** 3rd singular present tense of **do**, *She does what she likes.*

**doesn't** short for *does not*, *He doesn't understand.*

**dog** *noun* (**dogs**)
a four-legged animal that barks, often kept as a pet.

**dog-eared** *adjective*
(of a book) having the corners of its pages turned down through use.

**dogged** *adjective*
(*say* **dog**-id)
not giving up in spite of difficulties; obstinate.
**doggedly** *adverb*

**dogsbody** *noun* (**dogsbodies**)
someone who does boring, hard, or unpleasant work.

**doings** *plural noun*
(*informal*) things, *Get your doings together, and let's get going!*

**do-it-yourself** *adjective*
that an amateur handyman can make or use, *a do-it-yourself kit for making a dinghy.*

**Dolby** *noun*
(*trademark*) an electronic system used when recording sound to reduce hissing noises.

**doldrums** *plural noun*
the parts of the ocean, near the equator, where there is little or no wind.
**in the doldrums**, not active; bored and sad.

**dole** *noun*
(*informal*) money paid to an unemployed person, *They're on the dole.*

**doll** *noun* (**dolls**)
a toy model of a baby or person.
**doll's house**, a tiny toy house.

**dollar** *noun* (**dollars**)
a unit of money in the United States, Canada, Australia, New Zealand, and some other countries, *100 dollars is written $100.*

**dollop** *noun* (**dollops**)
(*informal*) a shapeless lump of something soft, *a dollop of mashed potato.*

**dolly** *noun* (**dollies**)
(*informal*) a doll.
**dolly mixture**, a mixture of tiny sweets.

**dolphin** *noun* (**dolphins**)
a sea-animal like a small whale.

**domain** *noun* (**domains**)
an area ruled by one person.

**dome** *noun* (**domes**)
a roof shaped like the top half of a ball, *the dome of St Paul's Cathedral.*

**domestic** *adjective*
1 connected with the home, *Domestic science includes subjects like cookery and needlework.* 2 tame, *Cats and dogs are domestic animals.*
**domesticate** *verb*, **domesticity** *noun*

**domesticated** *adjective*
1 trained to live with people, *Dogs are domesticated animals.* 2 enjoying household work and home life, *He has become quite domesticated since he got married.*

**dominant** *adjective*
1 most powerful or important. 2 highest; towering, *the dominant landmark of the Telecom Tower.*
**dominance** *noun*

**dominate** *verb* (**dominates, dominating, dominated**)
to be dominant.
**domination** *noun*

**dominion** *noun* (**dominions**)
1 rule; authority. 2 an area ruled by a king, etc.

**domino** *noun* (**dominoes**)
a small, flat, oblong piece of wood or plastic with dots (1 to 6) or a blank space at each end, used in the game of **dominoes**.

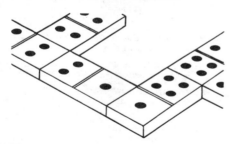

**donate** *verb* (**donates, donating, donated**)
to give something, especially money, to a charity or an organization.
**donation** *noun*

**done** past participle of **do**.

**donkey** *noun* (**donkeys**)
an animal that looks like a small horse with long ears.

**donor** *noun* (**donors**)
someone who gives something, *a blood donor.*

**don't** short for *do not, Don't cycle on the pavement.*

**don't-know** *noun* (**don't-knows**)
someone who has not made up his or her mind about a particular question.

**doodle**[1] *noun* (**doodles**)
a drawing or scribble done absent-mindedly.

**doodle**[2] *verb* (**doodles, doodling, doodled**)
to make a doodle.

**doom**[1] *noun*
ruin; death.
**doom and gloom**, unpleasant or gloomy things, news, etc., *The newspapers always seem to be full of doom and gloom nowadays.*

**doom**[2] *verb* (**dooms, dooming, doomed**)
to destine something or someone to suffer damage, harm, or death, *The plan was doomed to fail. Many rain-forest animals could be doomed to extinction.*
**doomed** *adjective*

**door** *noun* (**doors**)
something that opens and closes the entrance to a room, building, cupboard, etc.

**doorstep** *noun* (**doorsteps**)
the step or piece of ground outside a door.

**doorway** *noun* (**doorways**)
the opening which a door fits.

**dope** *noun* (**dopes**)
(*informal*) 1 a narcotic drug. 2 a fool. 3 information.

**dopey** *adjective* (**dopier, dopiest**)
(*informal*) 1 half asleep. 2 stupid.

**dormitory** *noun* (**dormitories**)
a room for several people to sleep in.
**dormitory town** or **suburb**, a place from which people regularly travel to work elsewhere.

**DOS** short for *disk operating system,* a computer program that allows you to work with data on a computer disk.

**dose** *noun* (**doses**)
an amount of medicine taken at one time.

**dossier** *noun* (**dossiers**)
(*say* **doss**-i-er or **doss**-i-ay)
a set of pieces of information about a person, event, etc.

**dot**[1] *noun* (**dots**)
a tiny spot.

**dot**[2] *verb* (**dots, dotting, dotted**)
to mark with dots.

**dotty** *adjective* (**dottier, dottiest**)
(*informal*) stupid or slightly mad.
**dottiness** *noun*

**double**[1] *adjective*
1 twice as much; twice as many, *a double portion of pudding.* 2 having two of something, *a double-barrelled shotgun.* 3 suitable for two people, *a double bed.*
**double bass,** a musical instrument with strings, like a large cello.
**double-decker,** a bus with two floors, one above the other.
**double glazing,** windows with two layers of glass to keep noise out and heat in.
**doubly** *adverb*

**double**[2] *verb* (**doubles, doubling, doubled**)
1 to make something twice as big; to become twice as big. 2 to fold something. 3 to run quickly.

**double**[3] *noun* (**doubles**)
1 twice the amount, cost, etc., *You could pay double for this carpet elsewhere.* 2 someone who looks exactly like someone else.

**double-cross** *verb* (**double-crosses, double-crossing, double-crossed**)
to trick or betray someone whom you are supposed to be helping.

**doubt**[1] *noun* (**doubts**)
not feeling sure about something.
**doubtful** *adjective,* **doubtless** *adverb*

**doubt**[2] *verb* (**doubts, doubting, doubted**)
not to feel sure about something, *I doubt whether he is telling the truth. Is he telling the truth? I doubt it.*

**dough** *noun*
1 a thick mixture of flour and water used for making bread, buns, etc. 2 (*slang*) money.
**doughy** *adjective*

**doughnut** *noun* (**doughnuts**)
a round bun that has been fried and covered with sugar.

**dove** *noun* (**doves**)
1 a kind of pigeon. 2 a peaceful person.

**dovetail**[1] *noun* (**dovetails**)
a wedge-shaped joint used to join two pieces of wood together.

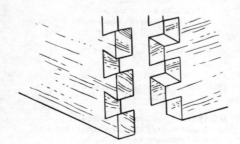

**dovetail**[2] *verb* (**dovetails, dovetailing, dovetailed**)
1 to join two pieces of wood with a dovetail. 2 to fit neatly together, *My plans dovetailed with hers.*

**dowel** *noun* (**dowels**)
a headless wooden or metal pin for holding together two pieces of wood, stone, etc.

**down**[1] *adverb* and *preposition*
1 to or in a lower place, *Run down the hill.* 2 along, *Go down to the shops.*

**down**[2] *noun*
very soft feathers or hair, *Ducks are covered with down.*
**downy** *adjective*

**down**[3] *noun* (**downs**)
a grass-covered hill, *the South Downs.*
**downland** *noun*

**down**[4] *noun* (**downs**)
**have a down on someone,** to have a prejudice or grudge against someone.

**downfall** *noun* (**downfalls**)
1 ruin; ceasing to have fortune or power. 2 a heavy fall of rain, snow, etc.

**downhill** *adverb*
down a slope.
**going downhill,** getting worse in quality or condition, *Journalism is going downhill.*

**downpour** *noun* (**downpours**)
a time when rain falls heavily.

**downright** *adjective* and *adverb*
thorough; thoroughly, *That's a downright swindle. I felt downright angry about it.*

**downstairs** *adverb* and *adjective*
to or on a lower floor.

**downstream** *adverb*
in the direction that a river or stream flows.

**downward** or **downwards** *adverb*
towards a lower place.

**doze** *verb* (**dozes, dozing, dozed**)
to sleep lightly.
**dozy** *adjective*

**dozen** *noun* (**dozens**)
a set of twelve.
**dozens of,** (*informal*) lots of.

**Dr** short for **Doctor.**

**drab** *adjective* (**drabber, drabbest**)
1 not colourful, *drab clothes.* 2 boring, *He lived a drab existence.*

**draft**[1] *noun* (**drafts**)
a rough sketch or plan.

USAGE: Do not confuse **draft** with **draught,** which means a current of air.

**draft**[2] *verb* (**drafts, drafting, drafted**)
to make a draft.

**drawing**

**drag**[1] *verb* (**drags, dragging, dragged**)
1 to pull something heavy along. 2 to search a river, lake, etc. with nets and hooks.

**drag**[2] *noun*
(*informal*) something that hinders or annoys you, *Having to take him everywhere is a drag.*

**dragon** *noun* (**dragons**)
a fierce monster in stories.

**dragonfly** *noun* (**dragonflies**)
an insect with a long body and two pairs of transparent wings.

**drain**[1] *noun* (**drains**)
1 a pipe, ditch, etc. for taking away water or sewage. 2 something that uses up your strength, *Looking after her friend's children has been a real drain on her.*
**something has gone down the drain,** something has been lost or wasted, *If we can't go on holiday, all our planning will have gone down the drain.*

**drain**[2] *verb* (**drains, draining, drained**)
1 to get rid of water with drains. 2 to flow or trickle away. 3 to empty liquid out of a container, *He drained his glass.* 4 to exhaust, *drained of strength.*
**draining-board,** a sloping surface beside a sink where washed dishes, etc. are placed.
**drainage** *noun*

**drake** *noun* (**drakes**)
a male duck.

**drama** *noun* (**dramas**)
1 a play. 2 writing or performing plays. 3 a series of exciting events.
**dramatics** *noun*

**dramatic** *adjective*
1 of drama. 2 exciting; impressive, *A dramatic change has taken place.*

**dramatist** *noun* (**dramatists**)
someone who writes plays.

**dramatize** *verb* (**dramatizes, dramatizing, dramatized**)
1 to make something into a play. 2 to exaggerate.
**dramatization** *noun*

**drank** past tense of **drink** *verb*.

**drape** *verb* (**drapes, draping, draped**)
to hang cloth over something.

**drastic** *adjective*
having a strong or violent effect.
**drastically** *adverb*

**draught** *noun* (**draughts**)
(rhymes with *craft*)
a current of usually cold air indoors.
**draughty** *adjective*

USAGE: Do not confuse **draught** with **draft**, which means a rough sketch or plan.

**draughts** *noun*
(in America, *checkers*) a game played with 24 round pieces on a chessboard.

**draughtsman** *noun* (**draughtsmen**)
1 someone who makes drawings. 2 a piece used in the game of draughts.

**draw**[1] *verb* (**draws, drawing, drew, drawn**)
1 to make a picture, diagram, etc. with a pencil, crayon, pen, etc., *I have drawn a map of Britain.* 2 to pull, *She drew her chair up to the table.* 3 to attract, *The fair drew large crowds.* 4 to end a game or contest with the same score on both sides, *They drew 2–2 last Saturday.* 5 to come, *The ship was drawing nearer. The winter is drawing to a close; spring is nearly here.*

**draw**[2] *noun* (**draws**)
1 an attraction. 2 a raffle or similar competition in which the winner is chosen by chance. 3 a game that ends with the same score on both sides.

**drawback** *noun* (**drawbacks**)
a disadvantage.

**drawbridge** *noun* (**drawbridges**)
a bridge that may be raised or lowered over a moat.

**drawer** *noun* (**drawers**)
a sliding container in a piece of furniture.

**drawing** *noun* (**drawings**)
something drawn with a pencil, crayon, etc.
**drawing-pin,** (in America, *thumbtack*) a short pin with a large flat top.
**drawing-room,** a sitting-room.

**drawl** *verb* (**drawls, drawling, drawled**)
to speak very slowly or lazily.

**dread**[1] *noun*
terror.

**dread**[2] *verb* (**dreads, dreading, dreaded**)
to fear something very much.

**dreadful** *adjective*
awful.
**dreadfully** *adverb*

**dreadlocks** *plural noun*
hair in long tightly-curled ringlets, worn
especially by Rastafarians.

**dream**[1] *noun* (**dreams**)
1 things that you seem to see while you are
asleep. 2 something imagined; an ambition
or ideal.
**dreamy** *adjective*

**dream**[2] *verb* (**dreams, dreaming, dreamt or
dreamed**)
1 to have a dream or dreams. 2 to have an
ambition, *She dreams of being a
ballet-dancer.* 3 to think something may
happen, *I never dreamt she would leave.*

**dreary** *adjective* (**drearier, dreariest**)
gloomy; boring.
**drearily** *adverb*, **dreariness** *noun*

**dredge** *verb* (**dredges, dredging, dredged**)
to drag up something, especially mud from
the bottom of a river or the sea.
**dredger** *noun*

**drench** *verb* (**drenches, drenching, drenched**)
to soak, *They got drenched in the rain.*

**dress**[1] *noun* (**dresses**)
1 a garment with a skirt and blouse
together. 2 clothes; costume, *fancy dress.*
**dress rehearsal,** a rehearsal at which the
actors in a play wear their costumes.

**dress**[2] *verb* (**dresses, dressing, dressed**)
1 to put clothes on. 2 to put a bandage on a
wound. 3 to prepare food for cooking or
eating.

**dresser** *noun* (**dressers**)
a sideboard with shelves at the top.

**dressing** *noun* (**dressings**)
1 a sauce of oil, vinegar, etc. for a salad. 2 a
covering for a wound; a plaster.

**dressing-gown** *noun* (**dressing-gowns**)
(in America, *bathrobe*) a loose garment
worn over pyjamas, etc.

**dressmaker** *noun* (**dressmakers**)
a person whose job is to make clothes for
women.

**drew** past tense of **draw** *verb.*

**dribble** *verb* (**dribbles, dribbling, dribbled**)
1 to let saliva trickle out of your mouth. 2 to
kick a ball as you run along, so that the
ball stays close to your feet.

**dried** past tense and past participle of **dry** *verb.*

**drier** *noun* (**driers**)
something that dries hair, laundry, etc.

**drift**[1] *verb* (**drifts, drifting, drifted**)
1 to be carried gently along by water or air.
2 to move or live aimlessly.

**drift**[2] *noun* (**drifts**)
1 a drifting movement. 2 a mass of snow or
sand piled up by the wind. 3 the general
meaning of a speech, etc., *I don't follow
your drift.*

**driftwood** *noun*
wood washed ashore from the sea.

**drill**[1] *noun* (**drills**)
1 a tool for making holes, *an electric drill.*
2 repeated exercises in military training,
gymnastics, etc. 3 a procedure or routine.

**drill**[2] *verb* (**drills, drilling, drilled**)
1 to make a hole with a drill. 2 to do
repeated exercises, *Watch the soldiers
drilling.*

**drink**[1] *verb* (**drinks, drinking, drank, drunk**)
1 to swallow liquid. 2 to drink alcoholic
drinks, *Don't drink and drive.*
**drinkable** *adjective*, **drinker** *noun*

**drink**[2] *noun* (**drinks**)
1 a liquid for drinking. 2 a drink that
contains alcohol.

**drip**[1] *noun* (**drips**)
a falling drop of liquid.

**drip**[2] *verb* (**drips, dripping, dripped**)
1 to fall in drops. 2 to let liquid fall in
drops, *The tap was dripping.*
**drip-dry clothes,** clothes that do not need
ironing.

**dripping** *noun*
solidified fat which has come from roasting
meat.

**drive**[1] *verb* (**drives, driving, drove, driven**)
to make something or someone move; to
make someone go into a particular state,
*That child will drive me mad!*
**be driving at something,** to be trying to say
something, *What is he driving at?*
**driver** *noun*

**drive**[2] *noun* (**drives**)
1 a journey in a vehicle. 2 energy;
enthusiasm. 3 a road, especially one
leading to a large house. 4 a powerful
stroke in cricket, golf, tennis, etc.

**drive-in** *adjective*
that you can use without getting out of your car, *a drive-in bank. a drive-in cinema.*

**drizzle** *noun*
gentle rain.

**drone**[1] *verb* (**drones, droning, droned**)
1 to make a low humming sound. 2 to talk in a boring voice.

**drone**[2] *noun* (**drones**)
1 a droning sound. 2 a male bee.

**drool** *verb* (**drools, drooling, drooled**)
to let saliva run out of your mouth.
**drool over,** to look at something with great pleasure, *He's been drooling over car catalogues all afternoon.*

**droop** *verb* (**droops, drooping, drooped**)
to hang down weakly.

**drop**[1] *noun* (**drops**)
1 a tiny amount of liquid. 2 a fall; a decrease, *a drop in prices.*
**droplet** *noun*

**drop**[2] *verb* (**drops, dropping, dropped**)
1 to fall. 2 to let something fall.
**drop in,** to visit someone.
**drop out,** to stop taking part in something.

**drought** *noun* (**droughts**)
(rhymes with *out*)
a long period of dry weather.

**drove** past tense of **drive** *verb*.

**drown** *verb* (**drowns, drowning, drowned**)
1 to die because of being under water and unable to breathe. 2 to kill someone or an animal by forcing them to stay under water, stopping them from breathing. 3 to make so much noise that another sound cannot be heard.

**drowsy** *adjective* (**drowsier, drowsiest**)
sleepy.
**drowsily** *adverb*, **drowsiness** *noun*

**drug**[1] *noun* (**drugs**)
1 a substance that kills pain or cures a disease. 2 a substance that affects your senses or your mind, *Heroin is a harmful drug.*

**drug**[2] *verb* (**drugs, drugging, drugged**)
to use a drug to make someone unconscious.

**Druid** *noun* (**Druids**)
a priest of the religion that existed before Christianity in Britain, Gaul (now France), and Ireland.

**drum**[1] *noun* (**drums**)
1 a musical instrument made of a cylinder with a thin sheet of material such as skin stretched over one end or both ends. 2 a cylindrical container, *an oil drum.*

drum[1] 1

**drum**[2] *verb* (**drums, drumming, drummed**)
1 to play a drum or drums. 2 to tap or thump on something, *He drummed his fingers on the table.*
**drum up,** to get something by vigorous effort, *He's drumming up money for a new playground.*
**drummer** *noun*

**drumstick** *noun* (**drumsticks**)
1 a stick used for hitting a drum. 2 the lower part of a roast leg of chicken, etc.

**drunk**[1] *adjective*
excited, helpless, etc. through drinking too much alcohol.

**drunk**[2] *noun* (**drunks**)
someone who is drunk.
**drunkard** *noun*

**drunk**[3] past participle of **drink** *verb*.

**dry**[1] *adjective* (**drier, driest**)
1 not wet; not damp. 2 boring; dull, *a dry book.*
**dry dock,** a dock which can be emptied of water, for repairing ships.
**dry ice,** carbon dioxide frozen solid.
**drily** *adverb*, **dryness** *noun*

**dry**[2] *verb* (**dried, drying**)
to make or become dry.
**dry up,** to become dry; to make something dry.
**dry up!** (*informal*) stop talking!

**dry-clean** *verb* (**dry-cleans, dry-cleaning, dry-cleaned**)
to clean clothes without using water.
**dry-cleaning** *noun*, **dry-cleaner** *noun*

**dryer** *noun* (**dryers**)
a drier.

**dual** *adjective*
double.
**dual carriageway,** a road with at least four lanes, with two or more in each direction.

USAGE: Do not confuse **dual** with **duel,** which is a noun meaning a fight between two people.

**dub** *verb* (**dubs, dubbing, dubbed**)
**1** to change or add new sound to the sound on a film or magnetic tape. **2** to give someone a name or title.

**duchess** *noun* (**duchesses**)
a duke's wife or widow.

**duck**[1] *noun* (**ducks**)
**1** a web-footed bird with a flat beak. **2** a batsman's score of nought at cricket.
**duckbill** or **duck-billed platypus,** a platypus.

duck[1] 1

**duck**[2] *verb* (**ducks, ducking, ducked**)
**1** to bend down quickly to avoid something. **2** to get under water quickly; to push someone under water quickly.

**duckling** *noun* (**ducklings**)
a young duck.

**duct** *noun* (**ducts**)
a tube or channel.

**dud** *noun* (**duds**)
(*slang*) something that is useless or that fails to work, *The firework was a dud.*

**due**[1] *adjective*
**1** expected, *The train is due in five minutes.* **2** owing; to be paid, *Your subscription is due.*
**in due course,** eventually; at the expected time.

**due**[2] *adverb*
directly, *The camp is due north.*
**due to,** because of, *His lateness was due to an accident.*

**duel** *noun* (**duels**)
a fight between two people, especially with pistols or swords.

USAGE: Do not confuse **duel** with **dual,** which is an adjective meaning double.

**duet** *noun* (**duets**)
a piece of music for two players or two singers.

**duff**[1] *noun* (**duffs**)
a boiled pudding.

**duff**[2] *adjective*
(*slang*) useless; bad, *He sold me a duff car.*

**duff**[3] *verb* (**duffs, duffing, duffed**)
**duff up,** (*slang*) to beat someone up.

**duffle-coat** *noun* (**duffle-coats**)
a thick overcoat with a hood.

**dug** past tense and past participle of **dig** *verb.*

**dugout** *noun* (**dugouts**)
**1** an underground shelter. **2** a canoe made by hollowing out a tree-trunk.

**duke** *noun* (**dukes**)
a very high-ranking nobleman.

**dull** *adjective* (**duller, dullest**)
**1** not bright; gloomy, *a dull day.* **2** not sharp, *a dull pain.* **3** stupid, *a dull boy.* **4** boring, *a dull programme.*
**dully** *adverb,* **dullness** *noun*

**duly** *adverb*
rightly; as expected, *Having promised to come, they duly arrived.*

**dumb** *adjective* (**dumber, dumbest**)
**1** unable to speak; silent. **2** (*informal*) stupid.

**dumbfounded** *adjective*
unable to say anything because you are so astonished.

**dummy** *noun* (**dummies**)
**1** something made to look like a person or thing; an imitation. **2** an imitation teat for a baby to suck.

**dump**[1] *noun* (**dumps**)
**1** a place where something, especially rubbish, is left or stored. **2** (*informal*) an unpleasant place.

**dump**[2] *verb* (**dumps, dumping, dumped**)
**1** to get rid of something you don't want. **2** to put something down carelessly.

**dumpling** *noun* (**dumplings**)
a lump of boiled or baked dough.

**dune** *noun* (**dunes**)
a mound of loose sand shaped by the wind.

**dungarees** *plural noun*
trousers with a piece in front covering your chest, held up by straps over your shoulders.

**dungeon** *noun* (**dungeons**)
(*say* **dun**-jŏn)
an underground prison-cell.

**duo** *noun* (**duos**)
a pair of people, especially playing music.

**duplicate**[1] *noun* (**duplicates**)
(*say* dew-pli-kăt)
something exactly the same as something else.

**duplicate**[2] *verb* (**duplicates, duplicating, duplicated**)
(*say* dew-pli-kayt)
to make a duplicate of something; to be a duplicate.
**duplication** *noun*, **duplicator** *noun*

**durable** *adjective*
lasting; strong.
**durability** *noun*

**duration** *noun* (**durations**)
the time something lasts.

**during** *preposition*
while something else is going on.

**dusk** *noun*
twilight in the evening.

**dust**[1] *noun*
tiny particles of dry earth or other material.

**dust**[2] *verb* (**dusts, dusting, dusted**)
1 to clear dust away. 2 to sprinkle with dust or powder.
**duster** *noun*

**dustbin** *noun* (**dustbins**)
a container for household rubbish.

**dustman** *noun* (**dustmen**)
a person whose job is to empty dustbins.

**dustpan** *noun* (**dustpans**)
a pan into which dust is brushed from the floor, etc.

**dusty** *adjective* (**dustier, dustiest**)
1 covered with dust. 2 like dust.

**Dutch** *adjective*
of Holland.
**Dutch elm disease,** a disease that kills elms.
**Dutchman** *noun*, **Dutchwoman** *noun*

**dutiful** *adjective*
doing your duty; obedient.
**dutifully** *adverb*

**duty** *noun* (**duties**)
1 what you ought to do or must do. 2 a kind of tax.

**duty-free** *adjective*
having no tax charged on it by the customs authorities, *Duty-free goods can be bought at airports and on ships and airliners.*

**duvet** *noun* (**duvets**)
(*say* doo-vay)
a kind of quilt used instead of other bedclothes.

**dwarf**[1] *noun* (**dwarfs**)
a very small person or thing.

**dwarf**[2] *verb* (**dwarfs, dwarfing, dwarfed**)
to make something seem very small, *The new skyscraper dwarfs all the buildings around it.*

**dwell** *verb* (**dwells, dwelling, dwelt**)
to live somewhere.
**dwell on something,** to think or talk about something for a long time.
**dweller** *noun*, **dwelling** *noun*

**dwindle** *verb* (**dwindles, dwindling, dwindled**)
to get smaller gradually.

**dye**[1] *verb* (**dyes, dyeing, dyed**)
to colour something by putting it in a special liquid.

**dye**[2] *noun* (**dyes**)
something used to dye fabrics, hair, etc.

**dying** present participle of **die**[1] *verb*.

**dyke** *noun* (**dykes**)
a dike.

**dynamic** *adjective*
energetic; active.

**dynamite** *noun*
1 a powerful explosive. 2 (*informal*) something very exciting, dangerous, etc., *Just wait till we publish that story – it's dynamite!*

**dynamo** *noun* (**dynamos**)
a machine that makes electricity.

**dynasty** *noun* (**dynasties**)
(*say* din-ă-sti)
a series of kings or queens of the same family.

**dyslexia** *noun*
(*say* dis-lek-si-ă)
a problem in reading and spelling, caused by difficulty in recognizing the shapes of letters in the alphabet.
**dyslexic** *adjective*

**dystrophy** *noun*
(*say* dis-trŏ-fi)
a disease that severely weakens your muscles, *muscular dystrophy.*

# Ee

**each¹** *adjective*
every, *Each child had a cake.*

**each²** *pronoun*
every one, *Each of you may have a sweet.*
**each other,** said of something done by each
of two or more people to the other one or
other ones, *They were yelling at each other.*

**eager** *adjective*
strongly wanting to do something;
enthusiastic.
**eagerly** *adverb*, **eagerness** *noun*

**eagle** *noun* (**eagles**)
a large bird of prey with very good eyesight.

**ear¹** *noun* (**ears**)
**1** the part of the head that you hear with.
**2** hearing ability, *She has a good ear for
music.*

**ear²** *noun* (**ears**)
the cluster of seeds at the top of a stalk of
corn.

**eardrum** *noun* (**eardrums**)
a membrane in the ear that vibrates when
sound reaches it.

**earl** *noun* (**earls**)
a British nobleman.

**early** *adverb* and *adjective* (**earlier, earliest**)
**1** before the usual or correct time. **2** near
the beginning.
**earliness** *noun*

**earmark** *verb* (**earmarks, earmarking, earmarked**)
to decide that something shall be used for a
particular purpose, *Funds have been
earmarked for setting up a computer room.*

**earn** *verb* (**earns, earning, earned**)
to get something by working for it or as a
reward.

**earnest** *adjective*
serious; determined.
**in earnest,** seriously.
**earnestly** *adverb*

**earnings** *plural noun*
money that is earned.

**earphones** *plural noun*
a device for listening to recorded or
broadcast sound that fits over or into your
ears.

**earring** *noun* (**earrings**)
an ornament that hangs from your ear.

**earth** *noun* (**earths**)
**1** the planet that we live on. **2** soil; the
ground. **3** the hole where a fox or badger
lives. **4** connection to the ground to
complete an electric circuit.
**on earth,** at all, *Why on earth did you say
that?*
**cost the earth,** (*informal*) to cost a huge
amount of money.
**earthly** *adjective*, **earthy** *adjective*

**earthenware** *noun*
crockery made of baked clay.

**earthquake** *noun* (**earthquakes**)
a sudden violent shaking of the ground.

**earthworm** *noun* (**earthworms**)
a small wriggling creature that lives in the
soil.

**earwig** *noun* (**earwigs**)
an insect with a pair of small claw-like
parts at the end of its body.

**ease¹** *noun*
relief or freedom from difficulty or
discomfort.
**at ease,** comfortably; (*in the army*) standing
with legs apart and hands behind the back.

**ease**[2] *verb* (**eases, easing, eased**)
1 to give ease to someone; to decrease pain, etc. 2 to make something easy. 3 to move something slowly and carefully.

**easel** *noun* (**easels**)
a stand for holding a blackboard or a painting.

**easily** *adverb*
1 with ease. 2 without doubt; very possibly, *He could easily be lying.*

**east**[1] *noun*
the area where the sun rises.

**east**[2] *adjective*
1 coming from the east, *an east wind.* 2 situated in the east, *the east coast.*
**easterly** *adjective*, **eastern** *adjective*

**east**[3] *adverb*
towards the east.
**eastward** *adjective* and *adverb*, **eastwards** *adverb*

**Easter** *noun*
the day or period when the resurrection of Jesus is remembered.
**Easter egg**, a sweet artificial egg eaten at or near Easter.

**easy**[1] *adjective* (**easier, easiest**)
1 able to be done or understood without any trouble. 2 comfortable; giving ease, *an easy chair.*
**easiness** *noun*

**easy**[2] *adverb* (**easier, easiest**)
with ease; comfortably, *Take it easy.*
**stand easy**, (*in the army*) to stand in a more relaxed way than when standing 'at ease'.

**easygoing** *adjective*
calm and tolerant.

**eat** *verb* (**eats, eating, ate, eaten**)
1 to take food into the mouth and swallow it. 2 to use up something; to destroy something, *The sea air has eaten away the ironwork.*

**eatable** *adjective*
fit to be eaten.

**eaves** *plural noun*
the overhanging edges of a roof.

**ebb**[1] *noun*
the tide when it is going out.
**at a low ebb**, in a low or weak condition.

**ebb**[2] *verb* (**ebbs, ebbing, ebbed**)
1 to go down, *The tide was ebbing.* 2 to weaken or lessen, *His strength ebbed away.*

**ebony** *noun* (**ebonies**)
1 a hard black wood, *The black keys on a piano are often made of ebony.* 2 a deep black colour.

**EC** short for **European Community**.

**eccentric** *adjective*
(*say* ik-**sen**-trik)
1 behaving strangely. 2 not always at the same distance from the centre; (of a pivot, hub, etc.) not placed in the centre, *The spacecraft was in an eccentric orbit.*
**eccentric** *noun*, **eccentricity** *noun*

**echo**[1] *noun* (**echoes**)
a sound that is heard again as it bounces off something.

**echo**[2] *verb* (**echoes, echoing, echoed**)
1 to make an echo. 2 to repeat a sound or saying.

**éclair** *noun* (**éclairs**)
(*say* ay-**klair**)
a finger-shaped cream bun with chocolate on top.

**eclipse** *noun* (**eclipses**)
1 a time when the moon comes between the sun and the earth, so that all or part of the sun is hidden. 2 a time when the earth comes between the sun and the moon, so that all or part of the moon is in shadow.

**ecological** *adjective*
of ecology, *The oil spillage was an ecological disaster.*

**ecology** *noun*
(*say* ee-**kol**-ŏ-ji)
the science concerned with living creatures and plants studied in their surroundings.
**ecologist** *noun*

**economic** *adjective*
(*say* eek-ŏ-**nom**-ik or ek-ŏ-**nom**-ik)
1 of economics. 2 profitable, *It is not normally economic to extract drinking-water from the sea.*

**economical** *adjective*
(*say* eek-ŏ-**nom**-ik-ăl)
careful in using money, goods, etc.; not wasteful, *an economical car.*
**economically** *adverb*

**economics** *noun*
(*say* eek-ŏ-**nom**-iks or ek-ŏ-**nom**-iks)
the study of how money is used and how goods, etc. are made, sold, and used.

**economist** *noun* (**economists**)
(*say* i-**kon**-ŏ-mist)
an expert in economics.

**economize** *verb* (**economizes, economizing, economized**)
(*say* i-**kon**-ŏ-myz)
to be economical.

**economy** *noun* (**economies**)
(*say* i-**kon**-ŏ-mi)
**1** being economical; a way of saving money.
**2** managing the money, goods, etc. used by
a community or household, *domestic
economy.*

**ecosystem** *noun* (**ecosystems**)
a group of plants and animals that are
connected because of where or how they
live.

**ecstasy** *noun* (**ecstasies**)
a feeling of great delight or joy.
**ecstatic** *adjective*

**eczema** *noun*
(*say* **ek**-si-mă)
a skin disease causing rough, itching
patches.

**edge**¹ *noun* (**edges**)
**1** the part along the side or end of
something. **2** the sharp part of a knife, axe,
etc.
**on edge,** nervous; irritable.

**edge**² *verb* (**edges, edging, edged**)
**1** to move slowly, *She edged towards the
door.* **2** to give something an edge.

**edgeways** *adverb*
with the edge outwards or forwards.
**not get a word in edgeways,** not to be able to
interrupt a talkative person.

**edgy** *adjective* (**edgier, edgiest**)
tense and easily annoyed.

**edible** *adjective*
not poisonous; eatable.

**edit** *verb* (**edits, editing, edited**)
**1** to get a newspaper, magazine, etc. ready
for publishing. **2** to put a film,
tape-recording, etc. in the order you want.

**edition** *noun* (**editions**)
**1** the form in which something is
published, *a paperback edition.* **2** all the
copies of a newspaper, book, etc. issued at
the same time, *the first edition.*

**editor** *noun* (**editors**)
someone who edits, especially the main
person responsible for a newspaper,
magazine, etc.

**editorial** *noun* (**editorials**)
a newspaper article giving the editor's
opinion on current affairs.

**educate** *verb* (**educates, educating, educated**)
to give someone knowledge or skill.
**educator** *noun*

**education** *noun*
the process of training people's minds and
abilities so that they can learn things and
develop skills; the training that is given to
someone, *She has had a good education.*
**educational** *adjective*

**EEC** short for **European Economic Community.**

**eel** *noun* (**eels**)
a long fish that looks like a snake.

**eerie** *adjective* (**eerier, eeriest**)
frighteningly strange; weird.
**eerily** *adverb,* **eeriness** *noun*

**effect** *noun* (**effects**)
**1** something that happens because of
something else, *The drink had a strange
effect on Alice.* **2** a general impression, *The
lights made a cheerful effect.* **3** a sound
effect.

USAGE: Do not confuse **effect** with **affect,**
which is a verb meaning to have an effect
on or to harm.

**effective** *adjective*
producing an effect; impressive.
**effectively** *adverb,* **effectiveness** *noun*

**effeminate** *adjective*
(*say* i-**fem**-in-ăt)
having some of the characteristics of a
woman, *an effeminate man.*

**effervescent** *adjective*
(*say* ef-er-**vess**-ĕnt)
fizzing, *an effervescent drink.*
**effervescence** *noun*

**efficient** *adjective*
doing work well; effective.
**efficiency** *noun,* **efficiently** *adverb*

**effort** *noun* (**efforts**)
**1** hard work; using energy. **2** an attempt.
**effortless** *adjective*

**e.g.**
for example, *He teaches many subjects, e.g.
music, geography, and maths.*

**egg**[1] *noun* (**eggs**)
1 an oval or round object with a thin shell, laid by birds, insects, fishes, etc., in which their offspring develop. 2 a hen's or duck's egg used as food.

**egg**[2] *verb* (**eggs, egging, egged**)
egg on, to encourage someone, usually to do something bad.

**Egyptian** *adjective*
of Egypt.

**eh** *interjection*
(*say* ay)
an exclamation of surprise or doubt.

**Eid** *noun*
(*say* eed)
a Muslim festival held at the end of Ramadan.

**eiderdown** *noun* (**eiderdowns**)
(*say* I-der-down)
a quilt.

**eight** *noun* (**eights**)
the number 8, one more than seven.
**eighth** *adjective* and *noun*

**eighteen** *noun* (**eighteens**)
the number 18, one more than seventeen.
**eighteenth** *adjective* and *noun*

**eighty** *noun* (**eighties**)
the number 80, eight times ten.
**eightieth** *adjective* and *noun*

**either**[1] *adjective* and *pronoun*
(*say* I-ther or ee-ther)
1 one of two, *Either team can win.* 2 both of two, *Put chairs at either end of the table.*

**either**[2] *adverb*
also; similarly, *If you won't play, I won't either.*

**either**[3] *conjunction*
either ... or, one thing or another, but not both, *You can choose either red or blue. Either come in or go out.*

**eject** *verb* (**ejects, ejecting, ejected**)
1 to send something out forcefully. 2 to make someone leave a place.
ejector seat, a seat that throws a pilot clear of his or her aircraft in an emergency, so that he or she can come down safely by parachute.
**ejection** *noun*

**elaborate**[1] *adjective*
(*say* i-lab-er-ăt)
complicated; carefully planned.

**elaborate**[2] *verb* (**elaborates, elaborating, elaborated**)
(*say* i-lab-er-ayt)
to describe or work out something in detail.
**elaboration** *noun*

**elastic**[1] *adjective*
that goes back to its normal shape after being stretched or squeezed, *Elastic bands are made of rubber.*
**elasticity** *noun*

**elastic**[2] *noun*
elastic material or cord.

**elated** *adjective*
delighted.
**elation** *noun*

**elbow**[1] *noun* (**elbows**)
the joint in the middle of your arm.
elbow-grease, (*informal*) vigorous rubbing or polishing.

**elbow**[2] *verb* (**elbows, elbowing, elbowed**)
to push with your elbow or elbows, *She elbowed me aside and took my place in the queue. I elbowed my way to the front of the crowd.*

**elder**[1] *adjective*
older, *his elder brother.*

**elder**[2] *noun* (**elders**)
a tree with white flowers and black berries.
**elderberry** *noun*

**elderly** *adjective*
rather old.

**eldest** *adjective*
oldest, *my eldest sister.*

**elect** *verb* (**elects, electing, elected**)
to choose someone by voting.

**election** *noun* (**elections**)
1 the action of electing. 2 a time when someone is elected, especially to be a Member of Parliament.

**elector** *noun* (**electors**)
someone who votes in an election.
**electoral** *adjective*, **electorate** *noun*

**electric** *adjective*
of or worked by electricity.
electric chair, a chair which electrocutes criminals.
**electrical** *adjective*, **electrically** *adverb*

**electrician** *noun* (**electricians**)
someone whose job is to deal with electrical equipment.

**electricity** *noun*
a kind of energy used for lighting, heating, and making machines work.

**electrify** *verb* (**electrifies, electrifying, electrified**)
**1** to charge something with electricity. **2** to make something work with electricity. **3** to excite or startle someone, *Her acting electrified the audience.*
**electrification** *noun*

**electrocute** *verb* (**electrocutes, electrocuting, electrocuted**)
to kill someone by electricity.
**electrocution** *noun*

**electrode** *noun* (**electrodes**)
a conductor through which electricity enters or leaves something.

**electrolysis** *noun*
the breaking up of a substance by passing electricity through it, *Water can be broken down into oxygen and hydrogen by electrolysis.*

**electromagnet** *noun* (**electromagnets**)
a magnet worked by electricity.
**electromagnetic** *adjective*

**electron** *noun* (**electrons**)
a particle of matter that is smaller than an atom, has a negative electric charge, and carries electricity.

**electronic** *adjective*
using devices such as transistors, silicon chips, diodes, etc., which are worked by electrons.
**electronic mail,** the use of a computer system to send or receive messages over long distances.
**electronic music,** music made by instruments such as synthesizers.
**electronically** *adverb*, **electronics** *noun*

**electrostatic** *adjective*
of or connected with static electricity, *an electrostatic charge.*

**elegant** *adjective*
tasteful; smart, *elegant clothes.*
**elegance** *noun*, **elegantly** *adverb*

**element** *noun* (**elements**)
**1** (*in Science*) a substance that cannot be split up into simpler substances, *Copper, oxygen, and sulphur are elements.* **2** a part of something. **3** a principle, *Learn the elements of algebra.* **4** the wire or coil that gives out heat in an electric heater, cooker, etc.
**be in your element,** to be in a situation that you like, or doing something that you enjoy, *I'm in my element when talking about bicycles.*
**the elements,** the weather, especially bad weather.

**elementary** *adjective*
dealing with the first or simplest stages of something; easy, *elementary arithmetic.*

**elephant** *noun* (**elephants**)
a very big animal with a trunk, tusks, and large ears.

**elevate** *verb* (**elevates, elevating, elevated**)
to lift something up; to put something high up.
**elevation** *noun*, **elevator** *noun*

**eleven** *noun* (**elevens**)
**1** the number 11, one more than ten. **2** a team of eleven people in cricket, hockey, etc.
**eleventh** *adjective* and *noun*

**elevenses** *plural noun*
(*informal*) a snack or drink in the middle of the morning.

**elf** *noun* (**elves**)
a small or mischievous fairy.

**eligible** *adjective*
qualified or suitable for something; being a suitable person to marry, *an eligible bachelor.*
**eligibility** *noun*

USAGE: Do not confuse **eligible** with **legible**, which means clear enough to read.

**eliminate** *verb* (**eliminates, eliminating, eliminated**)
to get rid of someone or something.
**elimination** *noun*

**élite** *noun* (**élites**)
a group of people who are thought of as better than others in some way and are given special advantages because of this.

**Elizabethan** *adjective*
of the time of Queen Elizabeth I (1558–1603).

**elk** *noun* (**elk** or **elks**)
a large kind of deer.

**ellipse** *noun* (**ellipses**)
an oval.

**elliptical** *adjective*
**1** oval-shaped. **2** with some words left out, *'One moment, please' is an elliptical sentence.*

**elm** *noun* (**elms**)
a tall tree with rough leaves.

**elocution** *noun*
speaking clearly.

**elongated** *adjective*
lengthened.
**elongation** *noun*

**eloquence** *noun*
speaking effectively or skilfully.
**eloquent** *adjective*

**else** *adverb*
besides; instead, *Nobody else knows.*
**or else**, otherwise; (*informal*) or there will be trouble, *Give me the money or else!*

**elsewhere** *adverb*
somewhere different.

**elude** *verb* (**eludes, eluding, eluded**)
to avoid being caught by someone; to escape from someone.

**elusive** *adjective*
difficult to find, catch, remember, or describe, *an elusive scent. Deer are elusive animals.*

**elves** plural of **elf**.

**E-mail** short for **electronic mail**.

**emancipate** *verb* (**emancipates, emancipating, emancipated**)
to set someone free.
**emancipation** *noun*

**embankment** *noun* (**embankments**)
a wall or mound of earth to hold back water or to support a road or railway.

**embark** *verb* (**embarks, embarking, embarked**)
to go on board a ship.
**embark on** or **upon**, to begin something.
**embarkation** *noun*

**embarrass** *verb* (**embarrasses, embarrassing, embarrassed**)
to make someone feel shy or awkward.
**embarrassment** *noun*

**embassy** *noun* (**embassies**)
the building where an ambassador lives and works.

**embedded** *adjective*
fixed firmly into something.

**embers** *plural noun*
small pieces of burning coal or wood in a dying fire.

**emblem** *noun* (**emblems**)
a symbol, *The dove is an emblem of peace.*

**embrace** *verb* (**embraces, embracing, embraced**)
**1** to put your arms round someone; to hug someone. **2** to include something.

**embroider** *verb* (**embroiders, embroidering, embroidered**)
to decorate cloth with sewn designs or pictures.
**embroidery** *noun*

**embryo** *noun* (**embryos**)
a baby or young animal before it is born.
**embryonic** *adjective*

**emerald** *noun* (**emeralds**)
**1** a green jewel. **2** a bright green colour.

**emerge** *verb* (**emerges, emerging, emerged**)
to come out; to appear.
**emergence** *noun*

**emergency** *noun* (**emergencies**)
a sudden dangerous or serious event or situation.

**emery-paper** *noun*
a gritty paper like sandpaper.

**emigrate** *verb* (**emigrates, emigrating, emigrated**)
to go and live in another country.
**emigrant** *noun*, **emigration** *noun*

USAGE: Do not confuse **emigrate** with **immigrate**, which means to come into a country to live there.

**eminent** *adjective*
**1** famous, *an eminent scientist.*
**2** outstanding, *She is known for her eminent kindness.*
**eminence** *noun*

**emission** *noun* (**emissions**)
the action of sending something out; something that is sent out, especially pollution, *There will be stricter controls on vehicles' exhaust emissions.*

**emit** *verb* (**emits, emitting, emitted**)
to send something out, *The volcano emitted smoke and lava.*

**emotion** *noun* (**emotions**)
1 a strong feeling, *Fear and hate are dangerous emotions.* 2 being excited or upset, *Her voice trembled with emotion.*

**emotional** *adjective*
1 connected with strong feelings, *The missing child's parents have been under great emotional stress.* 2 having or expressing strong feelings, *They said an emotional farewell and wept a lot.*
**emotionally** *adverb*

**emperor** *noun* (**emperors**)
a man who rules an empire.

**emphasis** *noun* (**emphases**)
special importance given to something.
**emphatic** *adjective*, **emphatically** *adverb*

**emphasize** *verb* (**emphasizes, emphasizing, emphasized**)
to give emphasis to something.

**empire** *noun* (**empires**)
a group of countries ruled by one person or group of people, *the Roman Empire.*

**employ** *verb* (**employs, employing, employed**)
1 to pay someone to work for you. 2 to use something.

**employee** *noun* (**employees**)
(*say* im-**ploi**-ee)
someone who is employed by someone else.

**employer** *noun* (**employers**)
someone who employs people.

**employment** *noun*
1 employing someone; being employed.
2 a job.

**empress** *noun* (**empresses**)
1 a female emperor. 2 the wife of an emperor.

**empties** *plural noun*
(*informal*) empty bottles, boxes, etc.

**empty**¹ *adjective* (**emptier, emptiest**)
with nothing inside or on it.
**emptiness** *noun*

**empty**² *verb* (**empties, emptying, emptied**)
to make something empty; to become empty.

**emu** *noun* (**emus**)
(*say* **ee**-mew)
a large Australian bird rather like an ostrich.

**emulsion** *noun* (**emulsions**)
1 a creamy liquid. 2 a kind of paint.

**enable** *verb* (**enables, enabling, enabled**)
to make something possible for someone, *This calculator enables you to multiply and divide.*

**enamel** *noun* (**enamels**)
1 a shiny, glassy substance for coating metal, pottery, etc. 2 a hard, shiny paint.
3 the hard, shiny surface of teeth.

**encamp** *verb* (**encamps, encamping, encamped**)
to settle in a camp.
**encampment** *noun*

**enchant** *verb* (**enchants, enchanting, enchanted**)
1 to delight someone. 2 to put a magic spell on someone.
**enchantment** *noun*, **enchantress** *noun*

**enchanting** *adjective*
that delights someone, *She has an enchanting smile.*
**enchantingly** *adverb*

**encircle** *verb* (**encircles, encircling, encircled**)
to surround, *a pond encircled by trees.*

**enclose** *verb* (**encloses, enclosing, enclosed**)
1 to put something in a box, envelope, etc.
2 to put a fence, wall, etc. round something.
**enclosure** *noun*

**encore** *noun* (**encores**)
an extra item performed at a concert, show, etc. after the applause.

**encounter** *verb* (**encounters, encountering, encountered**)
to come across someone or something unexpectedly.

**encourage** *verb* (**encourages, encouraging, encouraged**)
to give someone confidence or hope; to support something.
**encouragement** *noun*

**encyclopaedia** or **encyclopedia** *noun*
(**encyclopaedias** or **encyclopedias**)
a book or set of books containing all sorts
of information.
**encyclopaedic, encyclopedic** *adjective*

**end**[1] *noun* (**ends**)
1 the last part of something; the point
where something stops. 2 the part that is
left after something has been used, *a
cigarette end*. 3 an aim or purpose.
**make ends meet,** to spend no more money
than you earn.
**no end,** (*informal*) very many; a great deal.
**on end,** upright; continuously, *His hair
stood on end. She spoke for two hours on
end.*

**end**[2] *verb* (**ends, ending, ended**)
to finish.

**endanger** *verb* (**endangers, endangering,
endangered**)
to put someone or something in a
dangerous situation, *The destruction of the
rain forests is endangering many rare
species.*

**endeavour** *verb* (**endeavours, endeavouring,
endeavoured**)
to try, *He endeavoured to please her.*

**ending** *noun* (**endings**)
the last part of something.

**endless** *adjective*
1 never stopping, *endless patience*. 2 with
the ends joined to make a continuous strip,
*an endless belt*.
**endlessly** *adverb*

**endothermic** *adjective*
(of a chemical reaction) taking in heat.

**endure** *verb* (**endures, enduring, endured**)
1 to bear or put up with pain, suffering, etc.
2 to continue; to last.
**endurance** *noun*

**enemy** *noun* (**enemies**)
someone who hates you or wants to harm
you.
**the enemy,** the nation or army that is at
war with your country.

**energetic** *adjective*
1 full of energy, *an energetic puppy*. 2 done
with energy, *an energetic dance*.
**energetically** *adverb*

**energy** *noun* (**energies**)
1 strength to do things; liveliness. 2 the
ability to do work, *electrical energy*.

**enforce** *verb* (**enforces, enforcing, enforced**)
to make people obey a law, order, etc.
**enforceable** *adjective*, **enforcement** *noun*

**engage** *verb* (**engages, engaging, engaged**)
1 to occupy or use. 2 to employ someone, *He
engaged an assistant*. 3 to start a battle
against someone. 4 to interlock.
**engage in something,** to take part in
something.

**engaged** *adjective*
1 having promised to marry someone.
2 already being used, *Her telephone
number is engaged.*

**engagement** *noun* (**engagements**)
1 being engaged. 2 an appointment to meet
someone or do something. 3 a battle.
**engagement ring,** a ring that you give to
someone you have promised to marry.

**engine** *noun* (**engines**)
1 a motor. 2 a vehicle that pulls a railway
train.

**engineer** *noun* (**engineers**)
an expert in engineering.

**engineering** *noun*
designing, building, or controlling engines,
machines, bridges, docks, etc.

**English**[1] *adjective*
1 of England. 2 of or in the English
language.
**Englishman** *noun*, **Englishwoman** *noun*

**English**[2] *noun*
the language of England.

**engrave** *verb* (**engraves, engraving, engraved**)
to carve lines, words, etc. on a hard surface.
**engraver** *noun*

**engrossed** *adjective*
with all your attention taken up, *I was
engrossed in my work.*

**engulf** *verb* (**engulfs, engulfing, engulfed**)
to swallow up; to swamp, *a coastal village
was engulfed by the sea.*

**enhance** *verb* (**enhances, enhancing, enhanced**)
to add to a thing's value or attractiveness,
*The school show was enhanced by the
wonderful costumes.*
**enhancement** *noun*

**enjoy** *verb* (**enjoys, enjoying, enjoyed**)
to get pleasure from something.
**enjoyable** *adjective*, **enjoyment** *noun*

**enlarge** *verb* (**enlarges, enlarging, enlarged**)
to make something bigger.
**enlargement** *noun*

**enlist** *verb* (**enlists, enlisting, enlisted**)
to join the armed forces; to bring someone
into the armed forces.
**enlistment** *noun*

**enmity** *noun* (**enmities**)
being someone's enemy; hatred, *The
argument caused enmity between them.*

**enormous** *adjective*
huge.
**enormously** *adverb*

**enough** *adjective*, *noun*, and *adverb*
as much or as many as required.

**enquire** *verb* (**enquires, enquiring, enquired**)
to ask, *He enquired if I was well.*
**enquiry** *noun*

**enrage** *verb* (**enrages, enraging, enraged**)
to make a person or an animal very angry.
**enraged** *adjective*

**enrich** *verb* (**enriches, enriching, enriched**)
to make richer.
**enrichment** *noun*

**enrol** *verb* (**enrols, enrolling, enrolled**)
to make or become a member of a society,
class, etc.
**enrolment** *noun*

**ensemble** *noun* (**ensembles**)
(*say* ahn-**sahmbl**)
1 a group of things that go together. 2 a
group of musicians.

**ensue** *verb* (**ensues, ensuing, ensued**)
to happen afterwards; to follow.

**en suite** *adverb*
(*say* on **sweet**)
forming a single unit, *a double room with a
bathroom en suite.*

**ensure** *verb* (**ensures, ensuring, ensured**)
to make sure.

USAGE: Do not confuse **ensure** with **insure**,
which means to protect yourself or your
goods with insurance.

**entangle** *verb* (**entangles, entangling, entangled**)
to tangle.
**entanglement** *noun*

**enter** *verb* (**enters, entering, entered**)
1 to come or go in. 2 to write something in a
list, book, etc.; to put something into a
computer, *Enter the data.* 3 to enrol; to go
in for a contest, examination, etc.

**enterprise** *noun* (**enterprises**)
1 being enterprising. 2 a task or project,
especially one that needs courage.

**enterprising** *adjective*
adventurous; courageous.

**entertain** *verb* (**entertains, entertaining,
entertained**)
1 to amuse someone. 2 to have people as
guests and give them food and drink.
**entertainer** *noun*, **entertainment** *noun*

**enthusiasm** *noun* (**enthusiasms**)
a strong liking for, or interest in, someone
or something.

**enthusiast** *noun* (**enthusiasts**)
a person who has an enthusiasm for
something, *a football enthusiast.*

**enthusiastic** *adjective*
full of enthusiasm, *She is very enthusiastic
about her new hobby.*
**enthusiastically** *adverb*

**entire** *adjective*
whole, *The entire class went on an outing.*
**entirely** *adverb*, **entirety** *noun*

**entitle** *verb* (**entitles, entitling, entitled**)
to give you a right to something, *You are
entitled to three attempts at the
examination.*
**entitled,** having the title, *a book entitled
'Oliver Twist'.*

**entrance**¹ *noun* (**entrances**)
(*say* en-**trănss**)
1 the way into a place. 2 the act of entering,
*The actor made a grand entrance.*

**entrance**² *verb* (**entrances, entrancing,
entranced**)
(*say* in-**trahnss**)
to enchant.

**entrant** *noun* (**entrants**)
someone who goes in for a contest,
examination, etc.

**entreat** *verb* (**entreats, entreating, entreated**)
to ask someone seriously or desperately.
**entreaty** *noun*

**entrust** *verb* (**entrusts, entrusting, entrusted**)
to trust someone with something; to give
someone a thing to look after, *She
entrusted her necklace to me.*

**entry** *noun* (**entries**)
1 an entrance. 2 something written in a
list, diary, etc.

**envelop** *verb* (**envelops, enveloping, enveloped**)
(*say* in-**vel**-ŏp)
1 to wrap something up. 2 to cover someone
or something completely, *a mountain
enveloped in mist.*

**envelope** *noun* (**envelopes**)
(*say* **en**-vĕ-lohp or **on**-vĕ-lohp)
a wrapper or covering, especially for a
letter.

**envious** *adjective*
feeling envy.
**enviously** *adverb*

**environment** *noun* (**environments**)
surroundings, especially as they affect
people and other living things, *Some
animals and plants can die out if their
environment is damaged.*
**environmental** *adjective*

**equipment**

**environmentalist** *noun* (**environmentalists**)
a person who wants to protect or improve the environment.

**envy**[1] *noun*
a discontented feeling you have when you want something that someone else has got.

**envy**[2] *verb* (**envies, envying, envied**)
to feel envy about someone.

**enzyme** *noun* (**enzymes**)
a chemical substance that causes changes such as digestion.

**epic** *noun* (**epics**)
1 a heroic story or poem. 2 a very exciting and impressive film.

**epidemic** *noun* (**epidemics**)
a disease spreading quickly through a community.

**epilepsy** *noun*
a nervous disorder that makes a person's body move uncontrollably, and can make the person become unconscious.
**epileptic** *adjective* and *noun*

**epilogue** *noun* (**epilogues**)
(*say* ep-i-log)
words written or spoken at the end of something, especially a story or a play.

**episode** *noun* (**episodes**)
1 an incident in a series of events. 2 one programme in a radio or television serial.

**epistle** *noun* (**epistles**)
**the Epistles,** the letters written by Jesus's apostles that are books in the New Testament.

**epitaph** *noun* (**epitaphs**)
the words written on a tomb.

**epoch** *noun* (**epochs**)
(*say* ee-pok)
an era.
**epoch-making,** very important.

**equal**[1] *adjective*
the same in amount, size, value, etc.
**be equal to something,** to be able to do something, *He was equal to the task.*
**equality** *noun*, **equally** *adverb*

**equal**[2] *noun* (**equals**)
a person or thing that is equal to another, *Nobody was Samson's equal.*

**equal**[3] *verb* (**equals, equalling, equalled**)
to be the same in amount, size, value, etc.

**equalize** *verb* (**equalizes, equalizing, equalized**)
to make things equal.

**equalizer** *noun* (**equalizers**)
a goal, etc. that makes the score equal.

**equation** *noun* (**equations**)
(*say* i-**kway**-zhŏn)
(*in Mathematics*) a statement that two amounts are equal, *In the equation* $x + 1 = 3$, x *equals 2.*

**equator** *noun*
(*say* i-**kway**-ter)
an imaginary line round the earth at an equal distance from the North and South Poles.
**equatorial** *adjective*

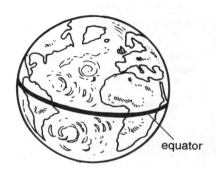

equator

**equestrian**[1] *adjective*
connected with horse-riding, *an equestrian event.*

**equestrian**[2] *noun* (**equestrians**)
a person who rides a horse.

**equidistant** *adjective*
at an equal distance, *The centre of a circle is equidistant from all the points around its circumference.*

**equilateral** *adjective*
(*say* ee-kwi-**lat**-er-ăl)
having all sides equal, *an equilateral triangle.*

**equilibrium** *noun* (**equilibria**)
(*say* ee-kwi-**lib**-ri-ŭm)
balance; being balanced.

**equinox** *noun* (**equinoxes**)
each of the two times in the year when the day and night are of equal length (about 22 September and 20 March).

**equip** *verb* (**equips, equipping, equipped**)
to supply someone or something with what is needed, *Are you equipped for mountaineering?*

**equipment** *noun*
the things needed for a particular purpose.

**equivalent** *adjective*
equal in value, importance, meaning, etc.
**equivalent fractions,** fractions that have the
same value, $\frac{1}{2}$, $\frac{4}{8}$ *and* $\frac{5}{10}$ *are equivalent
fractions.*
**equivalence** *noun*

**er** *interjection*
a sound made by someone who hesitates
while speaking.

**era** *noun* (**eras**)
(*say* **eer**-ă)
a period in history.

**erase** *verb* (**erases, erasing, erased**)
**1** to rub out something. **2** to wipe out a
recording on magnetic tape.
**eraser** *noun*

**erect**[1] *adjective*
vertical; standing on end.

**erect**[2] *verb* (**erects, erecting, erected**)
**1** to build. **2** to make something erect.
**erection** *noun*

**ermine** *noun* (**ermine**)
**1** a kind of weasel with brown fur in
summer and white fur in winter. **2** this
white fur.

**erode** *verb* (**erodes, eroding, eroded**)
to wear away, *Water eroded the rocks.*

**erosion** *noun*
wearing something away, especially the
destruction and removal of rock by the
action of water or wind.

**errand** *noun* (**errands**)
a short journey to take a message, fetch
goods, etc.

**erratic**[1] *adjective*
(*say* i-**rat**-ik)
not reliable or regular.
**erratically** *adverb*

**erratic**[2] *noun* (**erratics**)
a large piece of rock brought from far away
by a glacier.

**error** *noun* (**errors**)
a mistake.
**in error,** by mistake; mistaken.
**erroneous** *adjective*

**erupt** *verb* (**erupts, erupting, erupted**)
**1** to burst out. **2** (of a volcano) to shoot out
lava, etc.
**eruption** *noun*

**escalate** *verb* (**escalates, escalating, escalated**)
to get or make gradually greater or more
serious, *The riots escalated into a war.*
**escalation** *noun*

**escalator** *noun* (**escalators**)
a staircase with an endless line of steps
moving up or down.

**escape**[1] *verb* (**escapes, escaping, escaped**)
**1** to get free; to get away. **2** to avoid
something, *He escaped punishment.*

**escape**[2] *noun* (**escapes**)
**1** escaping. **2** a way to escape from
something.

**escort**[1] *noun* (**escorts**)
(*say* **ess**-kort)
**1** a person who accompanies someone,
especially to give protection. **2** a group of
ships, aircraft, etc. accompanying someone
or something.

**escort**[2] *verb* (**escorts, escorting, escorted**)
(*say* i-**skort**)
to act as an escort to someone or something.

**Eskimo** *noun* (**Eskimos** or **Eskimo**)
one of the people who live in very cold
parts of North America, Greenland, and
Russia.

USAGE: The official name of the people
who live in the far north of North America
is **Inuit.**

**especially** *adverb*
chiefly; more than anything else, *I like
buns, especially cream buns.*

**espionage** *noun*
(*say* **ess**-pi-ŏn-ah*zh*)
spying.

**esplanade** *noun* (**esplanades**)
a flat area for walking, especially by the
sea.

**Esq.** short for **Esquire.**

**Esquire** *noun*
an old-fashioned title put after a man's
name in addressing formal letters, etc., *To
Sam Browne, Esquire.*

**-ess** *suffix*
used to make feminine forms of words, *A
lioness is a female lion. She is the
manageress of a shoe-shop.*

**essay** *noun* (**essays**)
a short piece of writing about a particular subject.

**essence** *noun* (**essences**)
**1** the most important quality or ingredient of something. **2** a concentrated liquid, *vanilla essence.*

**essential**[1] *adjective*
that you must have or do.
**essentially** *adverb*

**essential**[2] *noun* (**essentials**)
an essential thing.

**establish** *verb* (**establishes, establishing, established**)
to start a business, government, relationship, etc.

**establishment** *noun* (**establishments**)
**1** establishing something. **2** a place where business is carried on; an organization.
**the Establishment,** people in positions of power and influence.

**estate** *noun* (**estates**)
**1** an area of land with lots of houses or factories on it. **2** a large area of land belonging to one person. **3** everything that a person owns when he or she dies.

**estate agent** *noun* (**estate agents**)
someone whose business is selling or letting buildings and land.

**estate car** *noun* (**estate cars**)
(in America, *station wagon*) a car with a door or doors at the back, and rear seats that can be removed or folded away.

**esteem** *verb* (**esteems, esteeming, esteemed**)
to think that a person or thing is excellent.

**estimate**[1] *noun* (**estimates**)
(*say* **ess**-ti-măt)
a calculation or guess about the amount or value of something.

**estimate**[2] *verb* (**estimates, estimating, estimated**)
(*say* **ess**-ti-mayt)
to make an estimate.
**estimation** *noun*

**estuary** *noun* (**estuaries**)
(*say* **ess**-tew-er-i)
the mouth of a large river where it flows into the sea.

**etc.** short for **et cetera.**

**et cetera** and other similar things; and so on.

**etch** *verb* (**etches, etching, etched**)
to make a picture by engraving on a metal plate with an acid.
**etching** *noun*

**eternal** *adjective*
lasting for ever; not ending or changing.
**eternally** *adverb*, **eternity** *noun*

**ether** *noun*
(*say* **ee**-ther)
a colourless liquid made from alcohol, used as an anaesthetic or a solvent.

**ethnic** *adjective*
of a national, racial, or tribal group, *an ethnic minority.*

**etymology** *noun* (**etymologies**)
**1** the study of words and where they come from. **2** a description of where a word came from and how it developed.

**eucalyptus** *noun* (**eucalyptuses**)
(*say* yoo-kă-**lip**-tŭs)
an evergreen tree from which an oil is obtained.

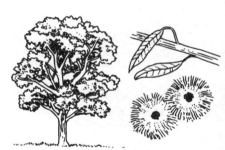

**euphemism** *noun* (**euphemisms**)
a word or phrase which is used instead of an impolite or less tactful one, *'Pass away' is a euphemism for 'die'.*
**euphemistic** *adjective*

**European**[1] *adjective*
of Europe.
**European Community** or **European Economic Community,** a group of countries in Europe that trade freely together.

**European**[2] *noun* (**Europeans**)
a European person.

**euthanasia** *noun*
(*say* yooth-ăn-**ay**-zi-ă)
causing someone to die gently and painlessly when he or she is suffering from an incurable disease.

**evacuate** *verb* (**evacuates, evacuating, evacuated**)
to move people away from a dangerous place.
**evacuation** *noun*, **evacuee** *noun*

**evade** *verb* (**evades, evading, evaded**)
to avoid.
**evasion** *noun*, **evasive** *adjective*

**evaluate** *verb* (**evaluates, evaluating, evaluated**)
to estimate the value of something.
**evaluation** *noun*

**evangelist** *noun* (**evangelists**)
someone who tells people about the Christian gospel.
**evangelical** *adjective*, **evangelism** *noun*

**evaporate** *verb* (**evaporates, evaporating, evaporated**)
1 to change from liquid into steam or vapour. 2 to remove moisture by heating a liquid.
**evaporated milk,** milk that has been thickened by evaporating water from it.
**evaporation** *noun*

**eve** *noun* (**eves**)
the day or evening before an important day, *Christmas Eve*.

**even**[1] *adjective*
1 equal, *Our scores were even.* 2 smooth; level, *He has an even temper.* 3 (*in Mathematics*) that can be divided exactly by two, *Six and fourteen are even numbers.*
**get even with someone,** to take revenge on someone, *I'll get even with him.*
**evenly** *adverb*, **evenness** *noun*

**even**[2] *verb* (**evens, evening, evened**)
to make something even; to become even.

**even**[3] *adverb*
1 so much as, *You haven't even started your work!* 2 still more so, *I ran fast, but Nick ran even faster.* 3 remarkably enough, *She even ignored her mother.*
**even if,** although.
**even now,** at this moment.
**even so,** nevertheless.

**evening** *noun* (**evenings**)
the time at the end of the day before most people go to bed.
**evening dress,** formal clothes worn to evening parties, etc.

**event** *noun* (**events**)
1 something that happens, especially something important. 2 an item in an athletics contest.
**at all events** or **in any event,** anyway.

**eventful** *adjective*
full of happenings, especially remarkable or exciting ones, *an eventful journey across the USA by bicycle.*

**eventual** *adjective*
happening at last or as a result, *Many failures preceded his eventual success.*

**eventually** *adverb*
1 finally, *Eventually, after many failures, he succeeded.* 2 sooner or later, *Don't worry, we'll get there eventually.*

**ever** *adverb*
1 at any time, *It's the best present I've ever had.* 2 always, *ever hopeful.* 3 (*informal*) at all, *Why ever didn't you tell me?*
**ever so** or **ever such,** (*informal*) very much, *I'm ever so pleased. She's ever such a nice girl.*

**evergreen**[1] *adjective*
having green leaves all through the year, *evergreen trees.*

**evergreen**[2] *noun* (**evergreens**)
an evergreen tree.

**everlasting** *adjective*
eternal.

**every** *adjective*
all the people or things of a particular kind; each, *Every child should learn to swim.*
**every bit as ... as,** exactly as good, bad, etc. as someone or something.
**every other day, week, etc.,** each alternate one; every second one.

**everybody** *pronoun*
everyone.

**everyday** *adjective*
happening or used every day; ordinary, *an everyday occurrence.*

**everyone** *pronoun*
every person; all people, *Everyone likes her.*

**everything** *pronoun*
1 all things; all, *Everything you need is here.* 2 the only or most important thing, *Beauty is not everything.*

**everywhere** *adverb*
in all places.

**evict** *verb* (**evicts, evicting, evicted**)
to make someone move out of a house.
**eviction** *noun*

**evidence** *noun*
anything that gives people reason to believe something.
**in evidence,** clearly seen.

**evident** *adjective*
obvious, *It is evident that he is lying.*
**evidently** *adverb*

**evil**[1] *adjective*
wicked; harmful.
**evilly** *adverb*

**evil**[2] *noun* (**evils**)
something evil; a sin.

**evolution** *noun*
(*say* ee-vŏ-**loo**-shŏn)
**1** gradual change into something different.
**2** the development of animals and plants from earlier or simpler forms of life.
**evolutionary** *adjective*

**evolve** *verb* (**evolves, evolving, evolved**)
to develop gradually or naturally.

**ewe** *noun* (**ewes**)
(*say* yoo)
a female sheep.

**ex-** *prefix*
that used to be, *She still keeps in touch with her ex-husband.*

**exact** *adjective*
**1** correct. **2** giving all the details, *an exact description.*
**exactly** *adverb*, **exactness** *noun*

**exaggerate** *verb* (**exaggerates, exaggerating, exaggerated**)
to make something seem bigger, better, worse, etc. than it really is.
**exaggeration** *noun*

**exalt** *verb* (**exalts, exalting, exalted**)
**1** to make higher or greater. **2** to praise someone highly.

**exam** *noun* (**exams**)
(*informal*) an examination.

**examination** *noun* (**examinations**)
**1** a test of someone's knowledge or skill.
**2** a close inspection of something.

**examine** *verb* (**examines, examining, examined**)
to make an examination of someone or something.

**examiner** *noun* (**examiners**)
a person who sets and marks an examination to test students' knowledge.

**example** *noun* (**examples**)
**1** a single thing or event that shows what a group of things or a kind of event is like.
**2** a person or thing that you should copy or learn from.
**for example**, as an example.

**exasperate** *verb* (**exasperates, exasperating, exasperated**)
to make someone very annoyed.
**exasperation** *noun*

**excavate** *verb* (**excavates, excavating, excavated**)
to make or uncover by digging.
**excavation** *noun*, **excavator** *noun*

**exceed** *verb* (**exceeds, exceeding, exceeded**)
**1** to be greater than something else. **2** to do more than you need or ought to do, *The driver was exceeding the speed limit.*

**exceedingly** *adverb*
extremely; very much.

USAGE: Do not confuse **exceedingly** with **excessively**, which means too much or too greatly.

**excel** *verb* (**excels, excelling, excelled**)
**excel at something**, to be very good at something.

**excellent** *adjective*
very good; of the best kind.
**excellence** *noun*

**except** *preposition*
not including; apart from, *Everyone got a prize except me.*

USAGE: Do not confuse **except** with **accept**, which is a verb meaning to take something which is offered, or to agree with something.

**exception** *noun* (**exceptions**)
**1** something that does not follow the normal rule. **2** something not included.
**take exception to something**, to be offended by something.

**exceptional** *adjective*
unusual, *She has exceptional skill.*
**exceptionally** *adverb*

**excerpt** *noun* (**excerpts**)
a piece taken from a book, play, film, etc.

**excess** *noun* (**excesses**)
too much of something, *We have an excess of food.*

USAGE: Do not confuse **excess** with **access**, which means a way to reach something.

**excessive** *adjective*
too much or too great.
**excessively** *adverb*

USAGE: Do not confuse **excessively** with **exceedingly**, which means extremely or very much.

**exchange**[1] *verb* (**exchanges, exchanging, exchanged**)
to give something and receive something else for it.

**exchange**[2] *noun* (**exchanges**)
1 exchanging. 2 a place where telephone lines are connected to each other when a call is made. 3 a place where company shares, etc. are bought and sold.
**exchange programme,** an arrangement in which groups of pupils from two schools, usually in different countries, each go for a while to the other school.

**excite** *verb* (**excites, exciting, excited**)
1 to make someone feel strongly. 2 to make someone lively, active, etc.
**excitable** *adjective*, **excitedly** *adverb*

**excitement** *noun* (**excitements**)
1 being excited. 2 something that excites you.

**exclaim** *verb* (**exclaims, exclaiming, exclaimed**)
to shout or cry out.

**exclamation** *noun* (**exclamations**)
1 exclaiming. 2 a word or phrase that expresses surprise, pain, delight, etc.
**exclamation mark,** the punctuation mark '!' placed after an exclamation.

**exclude** *verb* (**excludes, excluding, excluded**)
to shut or keep someone or something out.
**exclusion** *noun*

**exclusive** *adjective*
1 that excludes. 2 not allowing many people to be involved, *an exclusive club.*
**exclusively** *adverb*

**excrete** *verb* (**excretes, excreting, excreted**)
to pass waste matter out of your body.
**excrement** *noun*, **excretion** *noun*, **excretory** *adjective*

**excursion** *noun* (**excursions**)
a short journey made for pleasure.

**excuse**[1] *noun* (**excuses**)
(*say* iks-**kewss**)
a reason given to explain why something wrong has been done.

**excuse**[2] *verb* (**excuses, excusing, excused**)
(*say* iks-**kewz**)
1 to forgive. 2 to allow someone not to do something, or to leave a room, etc., *Please may I be excused from swimming?*
**excuse me,** a polite apology for interrupting, disagreeing, etc.
**excusable** *adjective*, **excusably** *adverb*

**execute** *verb* (**executes, executing, executed**)
1 to kill someone as a punishment. 2 to perform or produce something, *She executed a perfect somersault on the trampoline.*
**execution** *noun*, **executioner** *noun*

**executive** *noun* (**executives**)
a senior person in a business or government organization.

**exempt** *adjective*
not having to do something, *Old people are sometimes exempt from paying bus fares.*
**exemption** *noun*

**exercise**[1] *noun* (**exercises**)
1 using your body to make it strong and healthy. 2 a piece of work done for practice.
**exercise book,** a book for writing in.

**exercise**[2] *verb* (**exercises, exercising, exercised**)
1 to do exercises. 2 to give exercise to an animal, etc. 3 to use something, *You will have to exercise patience.*

USAGE: Do not confuse **exercise** with **exorcize**, which means to get rid of an evil spirit.

**exert** *verb* (**exerts, exerting, exerted**)
to use power, influence, etc., *He exerted all his strength to bend the bar.*
**exert yourself,** to make an effort.
**exertion** *noun*

**exhale** *verb* (**exhales, exhaling, exhaled**)
to breathe out; to send out something with your breath.
**exhalation** *noun*

**exhaust**[1] *noun* (**exhausts**)
1 the waste gases from an engine. 2 the pipe these gases are sent out through.

**exhaust**[2] *verb* (**exhausts, exhausting, exhausted**)
1 to make someone very tired. 2 to use up something completely.
**exhaustion** *noun*

**exhibit**[1] *verb* (**exhibits, exhibiting, exhibited**)
to display something in public.
**exhibitor** *noun*

**exhibit**[2] *noun* (**exhibits**)
something displayed in public.

**exhibition** *noun* (**exhibitions**)
a collection of things arranged for people to look at.

**exile**[1] *verb* (**exiles, exiling, exiled**)
to banish someone.

**exile**[2] *noun* (**exiles**)
1 a banished person. 2 having to live away
from your own country, *He was in exile for
ten years.*

**exist** *verb* (**exists, existing, existed**)
1 to be; to be real, *Do ghosts exist?* 2 to stay
alive, *They existed on biscuits and water.*

**existence** *noun* (**existences**)
1 existing or being. 2 staying alive, *a
struggle for existence.*

**exit**[1] *noun* (**exits**)
1 the way out of a building. 2 going off the
stage, *The actress made her exit.*

**exit**[2] *verb* (**exits, exiting, exited**)
to leave the stage, *Joseph exits.*
**exit** ( *plural* **exeunt**), he or she leaves the
stage, *Exit Hamlet.*

**exorcize** *verb* (**exorcizes, exorcizing, exorcized**)
to get rid of an evil spirit.
**exorcism** *noun*, **exorcist** *noun*

USAGE: Do not confuse **exorcize** with
**exercise**, which means to do exercises, to
give exercise to an animal, etc., or to use
something.

**exothermic** *adjective*
(of a chemical reaction) giving out heat.

**exotic** *adjective*
unusual; foreign.

**expand** *verb* (**expands, expanding, expanded**)
to make or become larger.
**expansion** *noun*

**expanse** *noun* (**expanses**)
a wide area.

**expect** *verb* (**expects, expecting, expected**)
1 to think that something will probably
happen or that someone will come, *We
expected it would rain.* 2 to think that
something ought to happen, *She expects us
to be obedient.* 3 to be pregnant, *She is
expecting.*

**expectant** *adjective*
1 pregnant, *an expectant mother.* 2 full of
expectation or hope.
**expectantly** *adverb*

**expectation** *noun* (**expectations**)
1 hopefully expecting something.
2 something you hope to get.

**expecting** *adjective*
pregnant, *an expecting mother.*

**expedition** *noun* (**expeditions**)
a journey made in order to do something,
*a climbing expedition.*

**expel** *verb* (**expels, expelling, expelled**)
1 to send or force something out, *This fan
expels stale air.* 2 to make someone leave a
school, country, etc., *He was expelled for
bullying.*

**expenditure** *noun*
spending, *We must reduce our expenditure.*

**expense** *noun* (**expenses**)
1 cost. 2 the spending of money, time, etc.
**expenses**, money used or claimed for
something particular, *travelling expenses.*

**expensive** *adjective*
costing a lot of money.

**experience**[1] *noun* (**experiences**)
1 what you learn from doing and seeing
things. 2 something that has happened to
you.

**experience**[2] *verb* (**experiences, experiencing,
experienced**)
to have something happen to you, *This is
the warmest summer I have ever
experienced.*

**experienced** *adjective*
having much experience; skilled and
knowledgeable.

**experiment**[1] *noun* (**experiments**)
a test made in order to study what
happens.
**experimental** *adjective*, **experimentally** *adverb*

**experiment**[2] *verb* (**experiments, experimenting,
experimented**)
to carry out experiments.
**experimentation** *noun*, **experimenter** *noun*

**expert**[1] *adjective*
skilful; knowledgeable.

**expert**[2] *noun* (**experts**)
someone who has skill or special
knowledge in a particular subject.

**expertise** *noun*
the knowledge or skill that an expert has.

**expire** *verb* (**expires, expiring, expired**)
1 to come to an end; to stop being usable,
*Your TV licence has expired.* 2 to die.
**expiry** *noun*

**explain** *verb* (**explains, explaining, explained**)
1 to make something clear to someone else.
2 to show why something happens.
**explanation** *noun*, **explanatory** *adjective*

**explode** *verb* (**explodes, exploding, exploded**)
1 to burst or suddenly release energy with
a loud bang. 2 to set off a bomb. 3 to
increase suddenly or quickly.

**exploit**[1] *noun* (**exploits**)
(*say* **eks**-ploit)
a brave or exciting deed.

**exploit²** *verb* (**exploits, exploiting, exploited**)
(*say* iks-**ploit**)
1 to use or develop resources. 2 to use something or someone selfishly.
**exploitation** *noun*

**explore** *verb* (**explores, exploring, explored**)
1 to travel through a country, etc. in order to learn about it. 2 to examine something.
**exploration** *noun*, **exploratory** *adjective*, **explorer** *noun*

**explosion** *noun* (**explosions**)
1 the exploding of a bomb, etc. 2 a sudden or quick increase, *the population explosion.*

**explosive¹** *adjective*
likely to explode; able to cause an explosion.
**explosively** *adverb*

**explosive²** *noun* (**explosives**)
an explosive substance.

**export¹** *verb* (**exports, exporting, exported**)
(*say* iks-**port**)
to send goods abroad to be sold.
**exporter** *noun*

**export²** *noun* (**exports**)
(*say* **eks**-port)
something that is sent abroad to be sold.

**expose** *verb* (**exposes, exposing, exposed**)
1 to reveal or uncover something. 2 to show that someone has done wrong; to make someone's crimes known. 3 to let light reach a film in a camera, so as to take a picture.

**exposure** *noun* (**exposures**)
1 revealing or uncovering; being uncovered and being harmed by the weather, *The mountaineers were suffering from exposure.* 2 letting light reach a film in a camera; a section of film used for making one picture, *This film has 24 exposures.*

**express¹** *adjective*
going or sent very quickly, *an express train. an express letter.*

**express²** *noun* (**expresses**)
a fast train, stopping at few stations.

**express³** *verb* (**expresses, expressing, expressed**)
to put an idea or feeling into words.

**expression** *noun* (**expressions**)
1 the look on a person's face. 2 a word or phrase. 3 a way of speaking, playing music, etc. that conveys feelings.
**expressionless** *adjective*, **expressive** *adjective*

**expulsion** *noun* (**expulsions**)
expelling or being expelled.

**exquisite** *adjective*
very delicate or beautiful.
**exquisitely** *adverb*

**extend** *verb* (**extends, extending, extended**)
1 to stretch out. 2 to make something longer or larger. 3 to offer or give, *Extend a welcome to your friends.*

**extension** *noun* (**extensions**)
1 extending. 2 something added on, *You will need an extension for the drill's power cable. We are building an extension at the back of the house.* 3 an extra telephone in an office, house, etc.

**extensive** *adjective*
wide or large, *extensive gardens.*
**extensively** *adverb*

**extent** *noun* (**extents**)
1 the area or length of something. 2 amount or level, *The extent of the damage was enormous.*

**exterior** *noun* (**exteriors**)
the outside of something.

**exterminate** *verb* (**exterminates, exterminating, exterminated**)
to destroy or kill.
**extermination** *noun*

**external** *adjective*
outside.
**externally** *adverb*

**extinct** *adjective*
1 not existing any more, *The dodo is an extinct bird.* 2 not active, *an extinct volcano.*
**extinction** *noun*

**extinguish** *verb* (**extinguishes, extinguishing, extinguished**)
to put out a fire or light.
**extinguisher** *noun*

**extra¹** *adjective*
more than usual; added, *There is an extra charge for taking a bicycle on the train.*

**extra²** *noun* (**extras**)
1 an extra person or thing. 2 someone acting as part of the crowd in a film or play. 3 a run in cricket scored without the bat hitting the ball.

**extra-** *prefix*
1 more than usual, *Today was an extra-special day.* 2 outside of something, *People with extra-sensory perception can sense things that ordinary people cannot.*

**extract¹** *noun* (**extracts**)
(*say* **eks**-trakt)
1 a piece taken from a book, play, film, etc. 2 something obtained from something else, *a plant extract.*

**fabulous**

**extract**[2] *verb* (**extracts, extracting, extracted**)
(*say* iks-**trakt**)
to remove; to take something out of
something else.
**extraction** *noun*, **extractor** *noun*

**extraction** *noun*
1 taking something out, *the extraction of a
tooth.* 2 the place or people that you come
from, *She is of Indian extraction.*

**extraordinary** *adjective*
unusual; very strange.
**extraordinarily** *adverb*

**extraterrestrial**[1] *noun* (**extraterrestrials**)
a living thing from somewhere outside the
planet Earth.

**extraterrestrial**[2] *adjective*
existing beyond the planet Earth,
*extraterrestrial worlds.*

**extravagant** *adjective*
spending too much; stupidly wasteful, *an
extravagant use of resources.*
**extravagance** *noun*, **extravagantly** *adverb*

**extreme**[1] *adjective*
1 very great or strong, *extreme cold.*
2 farthest away, *the extreme north.*
**extremity** *noun*

**extreme**[2] *noun* (**extremes**)
1 something very great, strong, or far
away. 2 either end of something.
**in the extreme**, extremely.
**to extremes**, to extreme or unreasonable
behaviour, *He was driven to extremes.*

**extremely** *adverb*
as much or as far as possible; very much.

**exuberant** *adjective*
very cheerful or lively.
**exuberance** *noun*

**exult** *verb* (**exults, exulting, exulted**)
to rejoice; to be very pleased about a
victory, *The emperor exulted over his
defeated enemy.*
**exultant** *adjective*, **exultation** *noun*

**eye**[1] *noun* (**eyes**)
1 the part of the head used for seeing. 2 the
small hole in a needle.

**eye**[2] *verb* (**eyes, eyeing, eyed**)
to look at someone or something closely.

**eyeball** *noun* (**eyeballs**)
the ball-shaped part of the eye.

**eyebrow** *noun* (**eyebrows**)
a curved fringe of hair growing above your
eye.

**eyelash** *noun* (**eyelashes**)
one of the short hairs that grow on an
eyelid.

**eyelid** *noun* (**eyelids**)
the upper or lower cover of the eyeball.

**eye-opener** *noun* (**eye-openers**)
(*informal*) something that surprises or
shocks you, *Hearing about the number of
homeless people was an eye-opener for me.*

**eyepiece** *noun* (**eyepieces**)
the lens of a telescope, microscope, etc. that
you put to your eye.

**eyesight** *noun*
the ability to see.

**eyesore** *noun* (**eyesores**)
something ugly to look at, *That scrapyard
is an eyesore.*

**eyewitness** *noun* (**eyewitnesses**)
someone who actually saw an accident,
crime, etc.
**eyewitness account**, a description of
something that happened, made by
someone who saw it happen.

# Ff

**F** short for **Fahrenheit.**

**fable** *noun* (**fables**)
a story which teaches a lesson connected
with right and wrong, *Many fables are
about animals.*

**fabric** *noun* (**fabrics**)
cloth.

**fabricate** *verb* (**fabricates, fabricating, fabricated**)
1 to make something, especially in a
factory. 2 to invent a story, etc., *He
fabricated an excuse.*

**fabulous** *adjective*
1 incredibly great, *fabulous wealth.*
2 (*informal*) wonderful; marvellous.
3 spoken of or described in myths, *Dragons
are fabulous creatures.*

**face**¹ *noun* (**faces**)
1 the front part of your head. 2 the look on a person's face, *She had a sour face.* 3 the front of something, *Put the cards face down.* 4 a surface, *A cube has six faces.*
**face to face**, looking directly at someone.
**in the face of something**, in spite of something.
**facial** *adjective*

**face**² *verb* (**faces, facing, faced**)
1 to look in a certain direction; to have the front in a particular direction, *The church faces the school.* 2 to meet or deal with someone or something confidently or bravely, *You will have to face the facts.*

**facet** *noun* (**facets**)
  (*say* **fass**-it)
1 one aspect or view of something. 2 one side of a many-sided object like a diamond.

**facetious** *adjective*
  (*say* fă-**see**-shŭs)
trying to be funny when you should not.
**facetiously** *adverb*

**facilitate** *verb* (**facilitates, facilitating, facilitated**)
to make something easier, *Computerization greatly facilitated the work of the Post Office.*

**facility** *noun* (**facilities**)
  (*say* fă-**sil**-ĭ-ti)
1 something that helps you to do things, *The youth club has facilities for dancing and sport.* 2 easiness.

**fact** *noun* (**facts**)
something that is true or certain.
**as a matter of fact** or **in fact**, really.
**the facts of life**, (*informal*) knowledge of how humans have sex and produce babies.

**factor** *noun* (**factors**)
1 something that helps to bring about a result or situation, *Good publicity was a major factor in our firm's success.* 2 a number by which a larger number can be divided exactly, *2 and 3 are factors of 6.*

**factory** *noun* (**factories**)
a large building where machines are used to make things.
**factory farm**, a farm operated like a factory.

**factual** *adjective*
based on fact; real.
**factually** *adverb*

**fad** *noun* (**fads**)
1 a craze, *The fad for jogging has largely died away.* 2 someone's particular like or dislike, *He has a fad about what food he will and will not eat.*

**fade** *verb* (**fades, fading, faded**)
1 to lose colour, freshness, or strength. 2 to disappear gradually. 3 to make a sound, etc. become gradually weaker or stronger.

**faeces** *plural noun*
  (*say* **fee**-seez)
solid waste that is sent out of the body.

**fag** *noun* (**fags**)
(*informal*) 1 a cigarette. 2 something that is tiring or boring to do.

**fagged** or **fagged out** *adjective*
(*informal*) very tired.

**faggot** *noun* (**faggots**)
a ball of baked chopped liver.

**Fahrenheit** *adjective*
  (*say* fa-**rĕn**-hyt)
using a scale for measuring temperature that gives 32 degrees for freezing water and 212 degrees for boiling water.

**fail**¹ *verb* (**fails, failing, failed**)
1 to try to do something but not be able to do it. 2 to become weak or useless; to come to an end, *The batteries are failing. The crops failed.* 3 not to do something, *He failed to warn me.*

**fail**² *noun* (**fails**)
not being successful in an examination, etc., *She has five passes and one fail.*
**without fail**, definitely, *I'll be there without fail.*

**failing** *noun* (**failings**)
a fault or weakness.

**failure** *noun* (**failures**)
1 not being successful. 2 someone or something that has failed.

**faint**¹ *adjective* (**fainter, faintest**)
1 weak; not clear or distinct. 2 nearly unconscious; exhausted.
**faintly** *adverb*, **faintness** *noun*

**faint**² *verb* (**faints, fainting, fainted**)
to become unconscious for a short time.

**faint-hearted** *adjective*
lacking in courage and confidence.

**fair**¹ *adjective* (**fairer, fairest**)
1 right or just; honest, *It's not fair! Fair trading.* 2 light in colour, *fair hair.* 3 moderate; quite good, *a fair number of offers. I've got a fair idea of what is needed.* 4 fine; favourable, *fair weather.*
**fair copy**, a neat, correct copy.
**fairness** *noun*

**fair**² *noun* (**fairs**)
1 a group of outdoor entertainments like roundabouts, sideshows, and stalls. 2 an exhibition or market.

**fairground** *noun* (**fairgrounds**)
the place where a fair is held.

**fairly** *adverb*
1 honestly; justly. 2 moderately; quite, *It is fairly hard*.

**fairy** *noun* (**fairies**)
an imaginary small creature who can do magic.
**fairy godmother,** someone who helps you by magic.
**fairy story** or **fairy tale,** a story about fairies; an unbelievable story.
**fairyland** noun

**faith** *noun* (**faiths**)
1 strong belief or trust. 2 a religion.
**in good faith,** honestly; trustingly.
**faithless** *adjective*

**faithful** *adjective*
reliable; trustworthy.
**faithfully** *adverb*, **faithfulness** *noun*

**fake**[1] *noun* (**fakes**)
a copy of something made to deceive people.

**fake**[2] *verb* (**fakes, faking, faked**)
1 to make something that looks real so as to deceive people. 2 to pretend, *He faked illness in order to miss games*.
**faker** *noun*

**falcon** *noun* (**falcons**)
a small kind of hawk.
**falconry** *noun*

**fall**[1] *verb* (**falls, falling, fell, fallen**)
1 to come down; to drop down, especially suddenly. 2 to decrease, *Prices have fallen*. 3 to be captured or overthrown, *The city fell after a long siege*. 4 to die in battle. 5 to happen, *Silence fell*. 6 to become, *She has fallen ill*. 7 to come or be directed at, *His glance fell on me*.
**fall back,** to retreat.
**fall back on,** to use for support or in an emergency.
**fall down,** to fail.
**fall for,** to be attracted or convinced by.
**fall in,** to collapse; to take your place in a military line.
**fall out,** to quarrel; to leave your place in a military line.
**fall through,** to fail.

**fall**[2] *noun* (**falls**)
1 the action of falling. 2 (*in America*) autumn.
**falls,** a waterfall.

**fallacy** *noun* (**fallacies**)
a false idea or belief.
**fallacious** *adjective*

**fall-out** *noun*
radioactive dust etc. from a nuclear explosion, especially when carried by the wind.

**fallow** *adjective*
ploughed but not sown with crops, *The field was left fallow every three years*.

**false** *adjective* (**falser, falsest**)
1 untrue; incorrect. 2 artificial; faked, *false teeth. The so-called Hitler diaries proved to be false*. 3 treacherous; deceitful.
**falsely** *adverb*, **falseness** *noun*, **falsity** *noun*

**falsehood** *noun* (**falsehoods**)
a lie.

**falter** *verb* (**falters, faltering, faltered**)
to hesitate when you move or speak.

**fame** *noun*
being famous.
**famed** *adjective*

**familiar** *adjective*
1 well-known; often seen or experienced, *a familiar sight*. 2 knowing something well, *Are you familiar with Shakespeare's plays?* 3 very friendly.
**familiarity** *noun*, **familiarly** *adverb*

**family** *noun* (**families**)
1 parents and their children, sometimes including grandchildren and other relations. 2 a group of things that are alike in some way.
**family planning,** deciding how many babies to have and when to have them; birth control.
**family tree,** a diagram showing how people in a family are related.

**famine** *noun* (**famines**)
a very bad shortage of food.

**famished** *adjective*
very hungry.

**famous** *adjective*
known to a lot of people; very well known, *a famous scientist*.

# fan¹

**fan¹** *noun* (**fans**)
a device for making the air move about, so
as to cool people or things.

**fan²** *noun* (**fans**)
an enthusiast, *a football fan*.

**fan³** *verb* (**fans, fanning, fanned**)
to send a draught of air at something, *She
fanned her face with her hand*.
**fan out**, to spread out.

**fanatic** *noun* (**fanatics**)
(*say* fă-nat-ik)
someone who is too enthusiastic about
something.
**fanatical** *adjective*, **fanatically** *adverb*

**fan belt** *noun* (**fan belts**)
a belt driving the fan that cools a vehicle's
radiator.

**fanciful** *adjective*
1 existing only in someone's imagination,
*the fanciful idea of riding a bicycle to the
North Pole*. 2 unusual, *a fanciful design of
wallpaper*.

**fancy¹** *adjective* (**fancier, fanciest**)
decorated; not plain, *fancy cakes*.
**fancy dress**, unusual costume worn to
parties, dances, etc.

**fancy²** *verb* (**fancies, fancying, fancied**)
1 to want or desire something, *I fancied an
ice-cream*. 2 to imagine or think of
something, *Just fancy him riding a horse!*
**fancy yourself**, to be conceited.

**fancy³** *noun* (**fancies**)
1 imagination. 2 a liking or desire for
something.

**fanfare** *noun* (**fanfares**)
a short piece of loud music on trumpets.

**fang** *noun* (**fangs**)
a long, sharp tooth.

**fantastic** *adjective*
1 strange; ridiculous. 2 (*informal*)
marvellous; excellent.
**fantastically** *adverb*

**fantasy** *noun* (**fantasies**)
something imaginary or fantastic.

**far¹** *adverb* (**farther, farthest**)
1 a long way, *We didn't go far*. 2 much,
*She's a far better singer than I am*.
**far and wide**, over a large area.
**so far**, up to now.

**far²** *adjective* (**farther, farthest**)
distant; opposite, *on the far side of the
river*.
**a far cry**, very different, *Conditions here are
a far cry from what you are used to*.
**Far East**, the countries of east Asia, such as
China and Japan.

**far-away** *adjective*
1 distant, *far-away places*. 2 looking a long
way away, *a lean, tanned cowboy with
far-away eyes*.

**farce** *noun* (**farces**)
1 a ridiculous comedy. 2 ridiculous events.
**farcical** *adjective*

**fare¹** *noun* (**fares**)
the money you pay to travel on a bus,
train, ship, aircraft, etc.

**fare²** *verb* (**fares, faring, fared**)
to get on; to progress, *How did you fare in
your exam?*

**farewell** *interjection*
goodbye.

**far-fetched** *adjective*
unlikely; difficult to believe.

**farm¹** *noun* (**farms**)
1 an area of land where someone grows
crops and keeps animals for food. 2 the
buildings on land of this kind. 3 a
farmhouse.

**farm²** *verb* (**farms, farming, farmed**)
1 to grow crops and raise animals for food.
2 to use land for growing crops, *They farm
a hundred acres in Shropshire*.

**farmer** *noun* (**farmers**)
someone who owns or looks after a farm.

**farmhouse** *noun* (**farmhouses**)
the house where a farmer lives.

**farmyard** *noun* (**farmyards**)
the enclosed area around farm buildings.

**farther** *adverb* and *adjective*
at or to a greater distance; more distant,
*She lives farther from the school than I do*.

**farthest** *adverb* and *adjective*
at or to the greatest distance; most distant.

**farthing** *noun* (**farthings**)
an old British coin that was worth a
quarter of a penny.

**fascinate** *verb* (**fascinates, fascinating, fascinated**)
to be very attractive or interesting to someone.
**fascination** *noun*

**Fascism** *noun*
(*say* **fash**-iz-ŭm)
a dictatorial type of government; a belief in this type of government.
**Fascist** *noun* and *adjective*

**fashion**¹ *noun* (**fashions**)
1 the style of clothes or other things that most people like at a particular time. 2 a way of doing something.

**fashion**² *verb* (**fashions, fashioning, fashioned**)
to make something in a particular shape or style.

**fashionable** *adjective*
1 following the fashion, *fashionable young people.* 2 popular amongst smart people, *a fashionable drink.*
**fashionably** *adverb*

**fast**¹ *adjective* (**faster, fastest**)
1 rapid; quick, *He's a fast runner.* 2 firmly fixed, *Make the boat fast.* 3 showing a time later than the correct time, *Your watch is fast.* 4 that does not fade, *fast colours.*

**fast**² *adverb*
1 quickly. 2 firmly.
**fast asleep**, deeply asleep.

**fast**³ *verb* (**fasts, fasting, fasted**)
to go without food.

**fasten** *verb* (**fastens, fastening, fastened**)
to join one thing firmly to another.
**fastener** *noun*, **fastening** *noun*

**fat**¹ *noun* (**fats**)
1 the white, greasy part of meat. 2 an oily or greasy substance used in cooking, *Butter, margarine, and lard are fats.* 3 an energy-rich food, *Milk, cheese, and cream contain fat.*
**the fat of the land**, the best food.

**fat**² *adjective* (**fatter, fattest**)
1 with a very thick, round body, *a fat man.* 2 thick, *a fat book.* 3 full of fat, *fat bacon.*

**fatal** *adjective*
that causes death or disaster, *a fatal accident.*
**fatality** *noun*, **fatally** *adverb*

**fate** *noun* (**fates**)
1 the power that makes things happen. 2 what has to happen and cannot be altered; what happens to someone in the end.

**father** *noun* (**fathers**)
a male parent.

**father-in-law** *noun* (**fathers-in-law**)
the father of your husband or wife.

**fathom**¹ *noun* (**fathoms**)
a unit of 6 feet, used in measuring the depth of water.

**fathom**² *verb* (**fathoms, fathoming, fathomed**)
to understand, *I can't fathom how you did it.*

**fatigue** *noun*
(*say* fă-**teeg**)
1 tiredness. 2 weakness in metals, etc. caused by repeated stress.
**fatigued** *adjective*

**fatten** *verb* (**fattens, fattening, fattened**)
to make or become fat.

**fattening** *adjective*
likely to make you fat, *Cakes with a lot of sugar and cream in them are fattening.*

**fatty** *adjective* (**fattier, fattiest**)
1 like fat. 2 full of fat, *fatty meat.*

**fault**¹ *noun* (**faults**)
something wrong that spoils a person or thing; a flaw or mistake.
**at fault**, wrong; responsible for a mistake, *The fuel system was at fault. We don't know who was at fault.*
**faultless** *adjective*

**fault**² *verb* (**faults, faulting, faulted**)
to find faults in something.

**faulty** *adjective* (**faultier, faultiest**)
having a fault or faults; wrong.

**fauna** *noun*
(*say* **faw**-nă)
the animals of an area, or of a period in the past.

**favour**¹ *noun* (**favours**)
1 something kind that you do for someone, *Will you do me a favour?* 2 approval; goodwill.
**in favour of someone or something**, liking or supporting someone or something.
**in your favour**, to your advantage.

**favour**² *verb* (**favours, favouring, favoured**)
1 to like or support someone or something. 2 to be kinder to one person than to others, *You favour her and not me.*

**favourable** *adjective*
helpful; approving.
**favourably** *adverb*

**favourite**¹ *adjective*
that is liked most, *my favourite book.*

**favourite**² *noun* (**favourites**)
a person or thing that someone likes most.

**favouritism** *noun*
unfairly being kinder to one person than to others.

**fawn** *noun* (**fawns**)
1 a young deer. 2 a light brown colour.

**fax**[1] *noun* (**faxes**)
1 the process of sending copies of documents by electronic means, using the same wires as the telephone system. 2 a copy made by this process.

**fax**[2] *verb* (**faxes, faxing, faxed**)
to send a copy of something by fax.

**fear**[1] *noun* (**fears**)
a feeling that something unpleasant may happen to you.
**for fear of something,** because of the risk of something.
**fearless** *adjective*, **fearlessly** *adverb*

**fear**[2] *verb* (**fears, fearing, feared**)
1 to be afraid of someone or something. 2 to be anxious or sad about something.

**fearful** *adjective*
1 frightened. 2 awful.
**fearfully** *adverb*

**fearsome** *adjective*
frightening.

**feast**[1] *noun* (**feasts**)
a large, splendid meal.

**feast**[2] *verb* (**feasts, feasting, feasted**)
to have a large, splendid meal.
**feast your eyes on something,** to look at something and enjoy it, *Feast your eyes on these pictures.*

**feat** *noun* (**feats**)
a brave or clever deed.

**feather** *noun* (**feathers**)
one of the very light coverings that grow from a bird's skin.
**feathery** *adjective*

**feature**[1] *noun* (**features**)
1 any part of the face, *He has rugged features.* 2 an important or noticeable part of something; a characteristic. 3 a long or important film, broadcast programme, or newspaper article.

**feature**[2] *verb* (**features, featuring, featured**)
to make something an important or noticeable part of something; to be an important or noticeable part of something, *Sport features a lot in the Sunday papers.*

**February** *noun*
the second month of the year.

**fed** past tense and past participle of **feed** *verb*.

**federal** *adjective*
of a system in which several states are ruled by a central government but make some of their own laws.
**federation** *noun*

**fed up** *adjective*
discontented; very annoyed.

**fee** *noun* (**fees**)
a payment, charge, or subscription.

**feeble** *adjective* (**feebler, feeblest**)
weak.
**feebly** *adverb*

**feed**[1] *verb* (**feeds, feeding, fed**)
1 to give food to a person or animal. 2 to eat, *Sheep feed on grass.* 3 to supply something to a machine, etc.
**feeder** *noun*

**feed**[2] *noun* (**feeds**)
1 a meal. 2 food for animals.

**feedback** *noun*
1 a response, *Is there any feedback from our customers?* 2 something being returned to where it came from, especially a signal in an electronic device.

**feel** *verb* (**feels, feeling, felt**)
1 to touch something to find out what it is like. 2 to experience something; to have a feeling.
**feel like something,** to want something.

**feeler** *noun* (**feelers**)
1 a long, thin part that sticks out from an insect's body, used for feeling. 2 a cautious question, suggestion, etc. to test people's reaction, *I put out feelers to see what they thought of my plan.*

**feeling** *noun* (**feelings**)
1 a mental or physical experience; what you feel. 2 the power to feel things. 3 sympathy or understanding, *He shows no feeling for my suffering.* 4 someone's opinion.

**feet** plural of **foot**.

**feline** *adjective*
belonging to the cat family; like a cat, *The dancer moved with feline grace.*

**fell**[1] *verb* (**fells, felling, felled**)
1 to cut down a tree. 2 to knock someone down.

**fell**[2] *noun* (**fells**)
a piece of wild, hilly country in the north of England; a hill, *Kirk Fell is at the head of Wasdale.*

**fell**[3] past tense of **fall** *verb*.

**fertile**

**fellow**[1] *noun* (**fellows**)
　**1** a friend or companion; someone who belongs to the same group. **2** (*informal*) a man or boy, *He's a good fellow.*

**fellow**[2] *adjective*
　of the same group, class, kind, etc., *Her fellow teachers supported her.*

**fellowship** *noun* (**fellowships**)
　**1** friendship. **2** a group of friends; a society.

**felt**[1] *noun*
　thick woollen material.
　**felt-tip** or **felt-tipped pen**, a pen with a tip made of felt or fibre.

**felt**[2] past tense and past participle of **feel**.

**female**[1] *adjective*
　of the sex that gives birth to offspring, *Women, girls, cows, and hens are all female.*

**female**[2] *noun* (**females**)
　a female person or animal.

**feminine** *adjective*
　**1** of or like women; suitable for women. **2** (*in grammar*) having a grammatical form suitable for the names of females or for words linked with these, *a feminine noun.*
　**femininity** *noun*

**feminist** *noun* (**feminists**)
　a supporter of women's claims to be given rights equal to those of men.
　**feminism** *noun*

**fen** *noun* (**fens**)
　a low-lying area of marshy or flooded land.

**fence**[1] *noun* (**fences**)
　**1** a barrier round a garden, field, etc. or beside a road, railway, etc., *Fences are usually made of wood or posts and wire.* **2** (*slang*) someone who buys stolen goods and sells them again.
　**sit on the fence**, to avoid committing yourself to either side in a contest, argument, etc.

**fence**[2] *verb* (**fences, fencing, fenced**)
　**1** to put a barrier round or along something. **2** to fight with thin swords called *foils*, as a sport.
　**fencer** *noun*, **fencing** *noun*

**fend** *verb* (**fends, fending, fended**)
　**fend for yourself**, to take care of yourself.
　**fend off**, to keep a person or thing away from yourself.

**fender** *noun* (**fenders**)
　**1** a low guard placed round a grate to stop coal from rolling into the room.
　**2** something hung over the side of a boat to protect it from knocks.

fender 2

**ferment**[1] *verb* (**ferments, fermenting, fermented**)
　(*say* fer-**ment**)
　to bubble and change chemically by the action of a substance like yeast.
　**fermentation** *noun*

**ferment**[2] *noun*
　(*say* **fer**-ment)
　**1** fermenting. **2** an excited or agitated condition, *The crowd was in a ferment.*

**fern** *noun* (**ferns**)
　a plant with feathery leaves and no flowers.

**ferocious** *adjective*
　fierce; savage; cruel.
　**ferociously** *adverb*, **ferocity** *noun*

**ferret**[1] *noun* (**ferrets**)
　a small animal used for catching rabbits and rats.

**ferret**[2] *verb* (**ferrets, ferreting, ferreted**)
　**1** to hunt with ferrets. **2** to search or rummage.

**ferry**[1] *verb* (**ferries, ferrying, ferried**)
　to carry people or things across a river, channel, etc.

**ferry**[2] *noun* (**ferries**)
　a ship or aircraft used for carrying people or things across a river, channel, etc.

**fertile** *adjective*
　**1** producing good crops. **2** able to produce offspring.
　**fertility** *noun*

**fertilize** *verb* (**fertilizes, fertilizing, fertilized**)
to make fertile.
**fertilization** *noun*

**fertilizer** *noun* (**fertilizers**)
a substance added to the soil to make it
more fertile.

**fervent** *adjective*
very enthusiastic; passionate, *a fervent
supporter of reform. a fervent plea.*
**fervently** *adverb*, **fervour** *noun*

**festival** *noun* (**festivals**)
a time when people arrange special
celebrations, performances, etc.

**festive** *adjective*
of or suitable for a festival; joyful.
**festivity** *noun*

**festoon** *verb* (**festoons, festooning, festooned**)
to decorate a place with curved chains of
flowers, ribbons, etc.

**fetch** *verb* (**fetches, fetching, fetched**)
**1** to go and get someone or something. **2** to
be sold for a particular price, *The bookcase
fetched £20.*

**fête** *noun* (**fêtes**)
(*say* fayt)
an outdoor entertainment with stalls and
sideshows.

**fetlock** *noun* (**fetlocks**)
the part of a horse's leg above and behind
its hoof.

**fetters** *plural noun*
chains round a prisoner's ankles.

**feud** *noun* (**feuds**)
a long-lasting quarrel or feeling of hatred.

**feudal** *adjective*
of the medieval system in which people
could farm land in exchange for work done
for the owner.
**feudalism** *noun*

**fever** *noun* (**fevers**)
**1** an unusually high body-temperature,
usually with an illness. **2** excitement;
agitation.
**fevered** *adjective*, **feverish** *adjective*,
**feverishly** *adverb*

**few**[1] *adjective* (**fewer, fewest**)
not many.

**few**[2] *noun*
a small number of people or things.
**a good few** or **quite a few,** a fairly large
number.

**fez** *noun* (**fezzes**)
a round, flat-topped hat with a tassel, worn
especially by Muslim men.

**fiancé** *noun* (**fiancés**)
(*say* fee-**ahn**-say)
a man engaged to be married.

**fiancée** *noun* (**fiancées**)
(*say* fee-**ahn**-say)
a woman engaged to be married.

**fiasco** *noun* (**fiascos**)
(*say* fi-**ass**-koh)
a complete failure, *The party turned into a
fiasco.*

**fib** *noun* (**fibs**)
a lie, usually about something
unimportant.
**fibber** *noun*

**fibre** *noun* (**fibres**)
(*say* **fy**-ber)
**1** a very thin thread. **2** a substance made
up of thin threads.
**fibre optics,** the use of thin, flexible threads
of glass or other material that lets light
through, to carry signals in the form of
flashes of light.
**fibrous** *adjective*

**fibreglass** *noun*
a kind of plastic containing glass fibres,
used in building, etc.

**fickle** *adjective*
often changing; (of a person) not loyal.

**fiction** *noun* (**fictions**)
**1** writings about events that have not
really happened; stories and novels.
**2** something imagined or untrue.
**fictional** *adjective*, **fictitious** *adjective*

**fiddle**[1] *noun* (**fiddles**)
(*informal*) **1** a violin. **2** a swindle.

**fiddle**[2] *verb* (**fiddles, fiddling, fiddled**)
**1** (*informal*) to play the violin. **2** to play
about with something with your fingers.
**3** (*informal*) to swindle; to get or change
something dishonestly.
**fiddler** *noun*

**fiddling** *adjective*
annoyingly unimportant, *The job involves
a lot of fiddling details.*

**fiddly** *adjective*
(*informal*) small and awkward to handle, use, or do.

**fidelity** *noun*
(*say* fi-del-i-ti)
**1** being faithful. **2** the exactness with which sound is reproduced.

**fidget** *verb* (**fidgets, fidgeting, fidgeted**)
to move about restlessly.
**fidgety** *adjective*

**field**¹ *noun* (**fields**)
**1** a piece of land with crops or grass growing on it, usually surrounded by a hedge or fence. **2** an area, especially where something happens, *an important development in the field of science.* **3** a battlefield. **4** those taking part in a race, hunt, etc.

**field**² *verb* (**fields, fielding, fielded**)
**1** to stop or catch the ball in cricket, etc. **2** to be in the team that is not batting in cricket, etc.
**fielder** *noun*, **fieldsman** *noun*

**Field Marshal** *noun* (**Field Marshals**)
an army officer of the highest rank.

**fieldwork** *noun*
practical work or research done in various places, not in a school, library, laboratory, etc., *We went to the coast to do some geography fieldwork.*

**fiend** *noun* (**fiends**)
(*say* feend)
a devil.
**fiendish** *adjective*, **fiendishly** *adverb*

**fierce** *adjective* (**fiercer, fiercest**)
angry and violent or cruel.
**fiercely** *adverb*, **fierceness** *noun*

**fiery** *adjective* (**fierier, fieriest**)
**1** full of flames or heat. **2** very emotional; easily made angry, *He had a fiery temper.*

**fiesta** *noun* (**fiestas**)
(*say* fee-est-ā)
a festival in a Spanish-speaking country.

**fife** *noun* (**fifes**)
a small, shrill flute.

**fifteen** *noun* (**fifteens**)
**1** the number 15, one more than fourteen. **2** a team in Rugby Union football.
**fifteenth** *adjective* and *noun*

**fifth** *adjective*
next after the fourth.

**fifty** *noun* (**fifties**)
the number 50, five times ten.
**fiftieth** *adjective* and *noun*

**fifty-fifty** *adjective* and *adverb*
shared equally between two people or groups, *We have fifty-fifty shares in the fireworks. Let's split the sweets fifty-fifty.*

**fig** *noun* (**figs**)
a small, soft fruit full of small seeds.

**fight**¹ *noun* (**fights**)
**1** a struggle against someone, using hands, weapons, etc. **2** an attempt to overcome or destroy something, *the fight against poverty.*

**fight**² *verb* (**fights, fighting, fought**)
**1** to struggle against someone. **2** to try to stop something, *They fought the fire.*
**fighter** *noun*

**figurative** *adjective*
using words in ways that are different from their usual meanings, *'He is up to his ears in debt' is a figurative use of the phrase 'up to his ears'.*

**figure**¹ *noun* (**figures**)
**1** one of the signs we use for numbers, such as 1, 2, and 3. **2** the shape of someone's body. **3** a diagram or illustration. **4** a pattern or shape, *a figure of eight.*
**figure of speech**, a special way of using words that makes someone's speech or writing interesting, such as a metaphor or a simile.
**figures**, arithmetic, *Are you good at figures?*

**figure**² *verb* (**figures, figuring, figured**)
**1** to appear or take part in something, *His name does not figure in the list of entrants.* **2** to imagine, *I figure he'll turn up later.* **3** to work out, *We figured that we had enough money for the holiday.*

**filament** *noun* (**filaments**)
a thread or thin wire.

**file**[1] *noun* (**files**)
1 a metal tool with a rough surface that is rubbed on things to make them smooth. 2 a folder, box, etc. to keep papers in. 3 a line of people one behind the other. 4 (*in Computing*) a collection of data that has been given a particular name.

**file**[2] *verb* (**files, filing, filed**)
1 to make something smooth with a file. 2 to put something in a collection of documents. 3 to walk one behind the other.

**filings** *plural noun*
tiny pieces of metal.

**fill**[1] *verb* (**fills, filling, filled**)
1 to make something full; to become full. 2 to put a filling in a tooth.
**fill in,** to complete a document; to act as a substitute, *Fill in this form. I'll fill in for Sam while he's on holiday.*
**fill up,** to fill something completely.
**filler** *noun*

**fill**[2] *noun* (**fills**)
enough to fill a person or thing, *Eat your fill.*

**fillet** *noun* (**fillets**)
a piece of fish or meat without bones.

**filling** *noun* (**fillings**)
something used to fill a hole or gap, especially a piece of metal put in a tooth to replace a decayed part.

**filling-station** *noun* (**filling-stations**)
a place where petrol is sold.

**filly** *noun* (**fillies**)
a young mare.

**film**[1] *noun* (**films**)
1 a moving picture that tells a story, such as those shown in cinemas. 2 a roll or piece of thin plastic, etc. put in a camera for taking photographs. 3 a very thin layer of something.
**filmy** *adjective*

**film**[2] *verb* (**films, filming, filmed**)
to make a film of something.

**filter**[1] *noun* (**filters**)
1 a device for removing dirt or other unwanted things from liquid, gas, etc. which passes through it. 2 a system allowing part of a stream of traffic to move in a particular direction while the rest of the stream is held up.

**filter**[2] *verb* (**filters, filtering, filtered**)
1 to pass through a filter. 2 to move gradually, *They filtered into the hall.* 3 to move in a particular direction while other traffic is held up.
**filtration** *noun*

**filth** *noun*
disgusting dirt.
**filthy** *adjective*

**fin** *noun* (**fins**)
1 one of the thin, flat parts sticking out from a fish's body and helping it to swim. 2 a thin, flat part sticking out on the outside of an aircraft, rocket, car, etc.

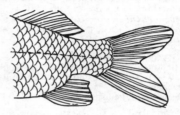

**final**[1] *adjective*
1 coming at the end; last. 2 that puts an end to argument or doubt, *I say you must not go, and that's final!*
**finality** *noun*, **finally** *adverb*

**final**[2] *noun* (**finals**)
the last of a series of contests.
**finalist** *noun*

**finale** *noun* (**finales**)
(*say* fin-ah-li)
the last part of a show, piece of music, etc.

**finance**[1] *noun*
the use or management of money.
**financial** *adjective*

**finance**[2] *verb* (**finances, financing, financed**)
to supply money for something, *How will you finance your expedition?*
**financier** *noun*

**finch** *noun* (**finches**)
a small bird with a short, thick beak.

**find** *verb* (**finds, finding, found**)
1 to see or get something. 2 to learn or experience something, *He found that digging is hard work.*
**find fault,** to think or say that someone or something is not satisfactory.
**find out,** to come to know something for the first time; to catch someone doing something wrong.
**finder** *noun*

**findings** *plural noun*
things you have found out.

**fine**[1] *adjective* (**finer, finest**)
1 dry and sunny; bright, *fine weather*.
2 very thin; delicate, *fine material*.
3 excellent, *a fine picture*.
**finely** *adverb*

**fine**[2] *noun* (**fines**)
money which has to be paid as a
punishment.

**fine**[3] *verb* (**fines, fining, fined**)
to make someone pay money as a
punishment.

**finger**[1] *noun* (**fingers**)
1 one of the separate parts of your hand.
2 a narrow piece of something, *fish fingers*.

**finger**[2] *verb* (**fingers, fingering, fingered**)
to touch and feel something with your
fingers.

**fingernail** *noun* (**fingernails**)
the hard covering at the end of a finger.

**fingerprint** *noun* (**fingerprints**)
a mark made by the tip of a person's finger,
*Detectives identified the criminal by his
fingerprints*.

**finicky** *adjective*
1 very fussy, *She has always been finicky
about what she eats*. 2 small and awkward
to handle, use, or do.

**finish**[1] *verb* (**finishes, finishing, finished**)
to come to an end; to bring something to an
end.

**finish**[2] *noun* (**finishes**)
the end of something.

**Finn** *noun* (**Finns**)
a Finnish person.

**Finnish** *adjective*
of Finland.

**fiord** *noun* (**fiords**)
(*say* fi-**ord**)
an inlet of the sea between high cliffs,
*There are many fiords in Norway*.

**fir** *noun* (**firs**)
an evergreen tree with leaves like needles.

**fire**[1] *noun* (**fires**)
1 burning; the heat and bright light that
come from burning things. 2 coal, wood,
etc. burning in a grate or furnace to give
heat. 3 a device using electricity, gas, etc.
to give heat, *Switch on the electric fire*.
4 the shooting of guns.
**fire-drill**, practising what to do if a building
etc. is on fire.
**fire-escape**, a special staircase or ladder by
which you can leave a building that is on
fire.

**fire extinguisher,** a device containing a
substance that puts out fires, such as
water, and a means of sending this
towards the fire.
**fire-guard,** a protective screen, usually made
of wire mesh, placed in front of a fireplace.
**fire hazard,** something that is likely to catch
fire or to burn easily, *Petrol is a fire
hazard*.
**fire hydrant,** (in America, *fire-plug*) a place
in the street where fire-fighters can
connect hoses to the water main.
**on fire,** burning.
**set fire to something,** to start something
burning.

**fire**[2] *verb* (**fires, firing, fired**)
1 to start something burning. 2 to bake
pottery, bricks, etc. in an oven. 3 to shoot a
gun. 4 (*slang*) to dismiss someone from his
or her job.

**firearm** *noun* (**firearms**)
a small gun; a rifle or pistol.

**fire brigade** *noun* (**fire brigades**)
(in America, *fire department*) a team of
people organized to fight fires.

**fire-engine** *noun* (**fire-engines**)
a large vehicle that carries firemen and
equipment to fight fires.

**fire-fighter** *noun* (**fire-fighters**)
a member of a fire brigade.

**fireman** *noun* (**firemen**)
a man who is a member of a fire brigade.

**fireplace** *noun* (**fireplaces**)
the part of a room where the fire and
hearth are.

**fireproof** *adjective*
that can stand great heat and does not
burn, *Asbestos is a fireproof substance*.

**fireside** *noun* (**firesides**)
the part of a room near the fire.

**fire station** *noun* (**fire stations**)
the headquarters of a fire brigade.

**firewood** *noun*
wood suitable for fuel.

**firework** *noun* (**fireworks**)
a cardboard or paper tube containing
chemicals that burn attractively or noisily.

**firm**[1] *noun* (**firms**)
a business, *She works for a clothing firm.*

**firm**[2] *adjective* (**firmer, firmest**)
1 fixed or solid so that it will not move.
2 definite; not likely to change.
**firmly** *adverb*, **firmness** *noun*

**first**[1] *adjective*
1 coming before all others. 2 the most
important, *He plays in the First Eleven.*
**firstly** *adverb*

**first**[2] *adverb*
before everything else.

**first**[3] *noun*
a person or thing that is first.
**at first,** at the beginning; to start with.

**first aid** *noun*
treatment given to an injured person
before a doctor comes.

**first-class** *adjective*
1 in or of the best seats in a train, aircraft,
etc. 2 sent by or being the fastest postal
service, *a first-class letter. first-class post.*
3 excellent.

**first floor** *noun* (**first floors**)
the next floor above the ground floor.

**firsthand** *adjective and adverb*
got directly, rather than from other people
or from books, *firsthand information.*

**first-rate** *adjective*
excellent.

**fish**[1] *noun* (**fish or fishes**)
an animal that always lives and breathes
in the water.
**fish cake,** a small cake of mashed fish and
potato.
**fish finger,** a small, oblong cake of mashed
fish covered in breadcrumbs.

**fish**[2] *verb* (**fishes, fishing, fished**)
1 to try to catch fish. 2 to search for
something; to try to get something, *He is
only fishing for praise.*
**fish out** or **fish up,** to pull out something.

**fisherman** *noun* (**fishermen**)
someone who tries to catch fish.

**fishmonger** *noun* (**fishmongers**)
a shopkeeper who sells fish.

**fishy** *adjective* (**fishier, fishiest**)
1 smelling or tasting of fish. 2 (*informal*)
suspicious; doubtful, *a fishy story.*

**fission** *noun*
(*say* fish-ŏn)
splitting something, especially splitting the
central part of an atom.

**fist** *noun* (**fists**)
a tightly closed hand.

**fit**[1] *adjective* (**fitter, fittest**)
1 suitable; good enough, *a meal fit for a
king.* 2 healthy; strong, *Keep fit with
exercises.* 3 ready; likely, *I'm fit to collapse.*
**see fit** or **think fit to do something,** to decide or
choose to do something.
**fitness** *noun*

**fit**[2] *verb* (**fits, fitting, fitted**)
1 to be the right size and shape. 2 to put
something into place. 3 to be suited to
something, *Her speech fitted the occasion
perfectly.*
**fit in,** to be suitable or agreeable.
**fitter** *noun*

**fit**[3] *noun* (**fits**)
1 a sudden illness, especially one that
makes you move violently or become
unconscious. 2 (*informal*) an outburst, *a fit
of rage.*
**by** or **in fits and starts,** not regularly; in short
bursts.

**fit**[4] *noun* (**fits**)
the way something fits, *This coat is a good
fit.*

**fitted** *adjective*
made to fit something exactly, *This room
has a fitted carpet.*

**fitting** *adjective*
suitable; proper.

**five** *noun* (**fives**)
the number 5, one more than four.

**fiver** *noun* (**fivers**)
(*informal*) a five-pound note; £5.

**fives** *noun*
a game in which a ball is hit with gloved
hands or a bat against the walls of a court.

**fix**[1] *verb* (**fixes, fixing, fixed**)
1 to join something firmly to something
else; to put something where it will not
move. 2 to decide or settle, *We have fixed
a date for the party.* 3 (*informal*) to mend,
*She's fixing my bike.*
**fix up,** to arrange or organize something.

**fix**[2] *noun* (**fixes**)
1 (*informal*) an awkward situation, *I'm in
a fix.* 2 finding the position of something,
especially by using a compass.

**fixture** *noun* (**fixtures**)
1 something fixed in its place. 2 a sports
event, race, etc. planned for a particular
day.

**flash**²

**fizz** *verb* (**fizzes, fizzing, fizzed**)
1 to make a hissing, spluttering sound. 2 to produce a lot of small bubbles, *The soda water fizzed as I poured it out.*
**fizzy** *adjective*

**fizzle** *verb* (**fizzles, fizzling, fizzled**)
to make a small hissing sound.
**fizzle out**, to end in a disappointing or unsuccessful way.

**flab** *noun*
(*informal*) unwanted fat on someone's body, *You'll have to get rid of some of the flab you put on over Christmas!*

**flabbergasted** *adjective*
(*informal*) extremely surprised.

**flabby** *adjective* (**flabbier, flabbiest**)
fat and soft; not firm.

**flag**¹ *noun* (**flags**)
1 a piece of material with a coloured pattern or shape on it, used as a sign or signal. 2 a small piece of paper that looks like a flag, especially sold in aid of charity.

**flag**² *noun* (**flags**)
a flat slab of paving stone.

**flag**³ *verb* (**flags, flagging, flagged**)
1 to become weak; to droop. 2 to signal with a flag, *The ships flagged messages to each other.*

**flagpole** *noun* (**flagpoles**)
a pole to which a flag is attached.

**flagship** *noun* (**flagships**)
a ship that carries the naval officer in charge of a fleet of ships.

**flagstaff** *noun* (**flagstaffs**)
a flagpole.

**flagstone** *noun* (**flagstones**)
a flat slab of paving stone.

**flake**¹ *noun* (**flakes**)
1 a very light, thin piece of something. 2 a piece of falling snow.
**flaky** *adjective*

**flake**² *verb* (**flakes, flaking, flaked**)
to come off in light, thin pieces.
**flake out**, (*informal*) to faint or fall asleep.

**flame**¹ *noun* (**flames**)
fire that is shaped like a tongue; a quantity of burning gas.

**flame**² *verb* (**flames, flaming, flamed**)
to produce flames.

**flamenco** *noun* (**flamencos**)
(*say* flă-**men**-koh)
a Spanish gypsy style of dancing or singing.

**flamingo** *noun* (**flamingos**)
a long-legged wading bird with pinkish feathers.

**flan** *noun* (**flans**)
a pie without any pastry on top.

**flank** *noun* (**flanks**)
the side of something.

**flannel** *noun* (**flannels**)
1 a piece of soft cloth used for washing yourself. 2 a kind of soft material, *These trousers are made of flannel.*

**flap**¹ *noun* (**flaps**)
1 a part that hangs down from one edge of something, usually to cover an opening, *Stick down the flap of the envelope.* 2 the action or sound of flapping. 3 (*informal*) a panic or fuss, *Don't get in a flap.*

**flap**² *verb* (**flaps, flapping, flapped**)
1 to move up and down or from side to side, *The bird flapped its wings. The yacht's sail was flapping.* 2 (*informal*) to panic or fuss.

**flapjack** *noun* (**flapjacks**)
a thick, sweet biscuit made with oats.

**flare**¹ *noun* (**flares**)
1 a sudden, bright flame. 2 a bright light used as a signal. 3 a gradual widening, especially in skirts or trousers.

**flare**² *verb* (**flares, flaring, flared**)
1 to burn with a sudden, bright flame. 2 to become angry suddenly. 3 (of skirts or trousers) to get gradually wider.

**flash**¹ *noun* (**flashes**)
1 a sudden, bright burst of light. 2 a device for making a brief, bright light by which to take photographs. 3 a sudden display of anger, wit, etc. 4 a short item of news.
**in a flash**, immediately; very quickly.

**flash**² *verb* (**flashes, flashing, flashed**)
1 to make a sudden, bright burst of light. 2 to appear suddenly; to move quickly, *The train flashed past.*

**flashback** *noun* (**flashbacks**)
going back in a film or story to something that happened earlier, *The hero's childhood was shown in flashbacks.*

**flashy** *adjective* (**flashier, flashiest**)
unpleasantly showy and bright.

**flask** *noun* (**flasks**)
1 a bottle with a narrow neck. 2 a vacuum flask.

**flat**¹ *adjective* (**flatter, flattest**)
1 with no curves or bumps; smooth and level. 2 spread out; lying at full length, *Lie flat on the ground.* 3 uninteresting; boring, *a flat voice.* 4 complete; not changing, *a flat refusal.* 5 not fizzy, *This beer is flat.* 6 below the proper musical pitch, *The clarinet was flat.* 7 punctured; with no air inside, *a flat tyre.* 8 (of feet) without the normal arch.
**flat out,** as fast as possible.
**flatly** *adverb,* **flatness** *noun*

**flat**² *noun* (**flats**)
1 (in America, *apartment*) a set of rooms for living in, usually on one floor of a building. 2 the note that is a semitone below a particular musical note; the sign (♭) that indicates this.

**flatten** *verb* (**flattens, flattening, flattened**)
to make something flat; to become flat.

**flatter** *verb* (**flatters, flattering, flattered**)
1 to praise someone more than he or she deserves. 2 to make someone seem better or more attractive than he or she really is, *The artist has flattered his subject.*
**flatterer** *noun,* **flattery** *noun*

**flaunt** *verb* (**flaunts, flaunting, flaunted**)
to display something too proudly.

**flavour**¹ *noun* (**flavours**)
the taste and smell of something.

**flavour**² *verb* (**flavours, flavouring, flavoured**)
to give something a particular taste and smell.
**flavouring** *noun*

**flaw** *noun* (**flaws**)
something that makes a person or thing imperfect, *The diamond had a flaw.*
**flawed** *adjective,* **flawless** *adjective*

**flax** *noun*
a plant that produces fibres from which cloth is made and seeds from which oil is made.

**flea** *noun* (**fleas**)
a small insect without wings that sucks blood.

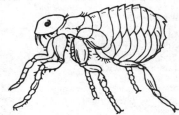

**flee** *verb* (**flees, fleeing, fled**)
to run away, *When he saw the policeman, he fled.*

**fleece**¹ *noun* (**fleeces**)
the wool that covers a sheep's body.
**fleecy** *adjective*

**fleece**² *verb* (**fleeces, fleecing, fleeced**)
1 to shear a sheep. 2 to swindle someone.

**fleet** *noun* (**fleets**)
a number of ships, aircraft, or vehicles, owned by one country or company.

**fleeting** *adjective*
very brief, *I caught a fleeting glimpse of him.*

**flesh** *noun*
the soft substance between the skin and bones of people and animals.
**fleshy** *adjective*

**flew** past tense of **fly** *verb.*

**flex**¹ *noun* (**flexes**)
flexible insulated wire for electric current.

**flex**² *verb* (**flexes, flexing, flexed**)
to move your muscles; to bend your arms, legs, etc.

**flexible** *adjective*
1 easy to bend. 2 easy to change or adapt, *Our working hours are flexible.*
**flexibility** *noun*

**flick**¹ *noun* (**flicks**)
a quick, light hit or movement.

**flick**² *verb* (**flicks, flicking, flicked**)
to hit or move with a flick.

**flicker** *verb* (**flickers, flickering, flickered**)
to burn or shine unsteadily.

**flight**¹ *noun* (**flights**)
1 flying. 2 a journey in an aircraft, rocket, etc. 3 a group of flying birds, aircraft, etc. 4 a series of stairs. 5 the feathers or fins on a dart or arrow.

**flight**² *noun* (**flights**)
running away; an escape.

**flimsy** *adjective* (**flimsier, flimsiest**)
light and thin; fragile, *flimsy fabric. a flimsy folding table.*

**flinch** *verb* (**flinches, flinching, flinched**)
1 to feel or show fear. 2 to wince.

**fling** *verb* (**flings, flinging, flung**)
to throw something violently or carelessly, *He flung his shoes under the bed.*

**flint** *noun* (**flints**)
1 a very hard kind of stone. 2 a piece of this stone or hard metal used to produce sparks.
**flinty** *adjective*

**flip** *verb* (**flips, flipping, flipped**)
to flick.

**flippant** *adjective*
not showing proper seriousness, *Don't be flippant about his illness.*

**flipper** *noun* (**flippers**)
1 a limb that water-animals use for swimming. 2 a device that you wear on your feet to help you swim.

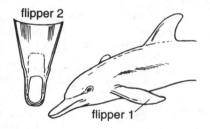
flipper 2
flipper 1

**flirt** *verb* (**flirts, flirting, flirted**)
to behave towards someone as though you wanted to gain his or her love, to amuse yourself.
**flirtation** *noun*

**flit** *verb* (**flits, flitting, flitted**)
to fly or move lightly and quickly, *A moth flitted across the room .*

**float**[1] *verb* (**floats, floating, floated**)
1 to stay or move on the surface of a liquid or in the air. 2 to make something stay on the surface of a liquid.

**float**[2] *noun* (**floats**)
1 a device designed to rest on the surface of a liquid. 2 a vehicle used for delivering milk. 3 a vehicle carrying a display in a parade, etc. 4 a small amount of money kept for paying small bills or giving change.

**flock**[1] *noun* (**flocks**)
a group of sheep, goats, or birds.

**flock**[2] *verb* (**flocks, flocking, flocked**)
to gather in a large crowd; to move in a large crowd.

**flog** *verb* (**flogs, flogging, flogged**)
1 to beat someone severely with a whip or stick. 2 (*slang*) to sell, *He flogged me his watch .*

**flood**[1] *noun* (**floods**)
1 a large amount of water spreading over a place that is usually dry. 2 a great amount of something, *a flood of requests.* 3 the tide when it is coming in.
**flood-plain,** the flat area beside a river that becomes covered with water when the river floods.

**flood**[2] *verb* (**floods, flooding, flooded**)
1 to cover something with a large amount of water. 2 (of a river) to flow over its banks. 3 to arrive in large amounts, *Letters flooded in .*

**floodlight** *noun* (**floodlights**)
a lamp that makes a broad, bright beam.
**floodlit** *adjective*

**floor**[1] *noun* (**floors**)
1 the part of a room that people walk on. 2 all the rooms on the same level in a building, *Her office is on the top floor.*

**floor**[2] *verb* (**floors, flooring, floored**)
1 to put a floor into a building. 2 to knock someone down. 3 to baffle someone, *Some of the exam questions floored everyone.*

**floorboard** *noun* (**floorboards**)
one of the boards forming the floor of a room.

**flop**[1] *verb* (**flops, flopping, flopped**)
1 to fall or sit down suddenly. 2 to flap or droop. 3 (*informal*) to be a failure.

**flop**[2] *noun* (**flops**)
1 the movement or sound of sudden falling or sitting down. 2 (*informal*) a failure.

**floppy** *adjective* (**floppier, floppiest**)
hanging loosely or heavily, *a dog with floppy ears. a floppy T-shirt.*

**floppy disk** *noun* (**floppy disks**)
a round, flat piece of magnetic material, used with computers to store information.

**flora** *noun*
(*say* **flor-ă**)
the plants of a particular area or period.

**floral** *adjective*
of flowers, *a floral display.*

**florist** *noun* (**florists**)
a shopkeeper who sells flowers.

**flounder** *verb* (**flounders, floundering, floundered**)
to move or behave awkwardly or helplessly, *I was floundering, trying desperately to think of an answer.*

**flour** *noun*
a white or brown powder made from corn and used for making bread, cakes, pastry, etc.
**floury** *adjective*

**flourish** *verb* (**flourishes, flourishing, flourished**)
1 to grow or develop strongly; to be successful, *Her business flourished, and gained a large share of the market.* 2 to wave something about.

**flow**[1] *verb* (**flows, flowing, flowed**)
1 to move along smoothly like a river. 2 to hang loosely, *flowing hair.*

**flow**[2] *noun* (**flows**)
1 a flowing movement or mass. 2 the tide when it is coming in, *ebb and flow.*
**flow chart,** a diagram with special shapes connected by lines showing the order in which a series of actions or processes happen, especially a diagram of a computer program.

**flower**[1] *noun* (**flowers**)
1 the part of a plant from which seed or fruit develops, *Most flowers have coloured petals.* 2 a plant that has this kind of part.
**in flower,** producing flowers.
**flowery** *adjective*

**flower**[2] *verb* (**flowers, flowering, flowered**)
to produce flowers.

**flowerpot** *noun* (**flowerpots**)
a pot in which plants are grown.

**flowery** *adjective*
1 decorated with flowers, or pictures of them, *flowery wallpaper.* 2 sounding very grand, *a flowery style of writing.*

**flown** past participle of **fly** *verb.*

**flu** *noun*
influenza.

**fluctuate** *verb* (**fluctuates, fluctuating, fluctuated**)
to rise and fall irregularly.
**fluctuation** *noun*

**flue** *noun* (**flues**)
a pipe that takes smoke and fumes away from a stove, a central-heating boiler, etc.

**fluent** *adjective*
skilful at speaking, especially at speaking a foreign language.
**fluency** *noun*, **fluently** *adverb*

**fluff** *noun*
1 a light, soft substance that comes off blankets, cloth, etc. 2 fine and soft hair, fur, or feathers, *The ducklings were like little balls of yellow fluff.*
**fluffy** *adjective*

**fluid** *noun* (**fluids**)
a substance that flows easily; any liquid or gas.

**fluke** *noun* (**flukes**)
1 an unexpected piece of good luck that makes you able to do something you thought you could not do. 2 one of the flat halves of a whale's tail.

**flung** past tense and past participle of **fling.**

**fluorescent** *adjective*
creating light from radiation, *a fluorescent lamp.*
**fluorescence** *noun*

**fluoridation** *noun*
adding fluoride to drinking-water.

**fluoride** *noun*
a chemical that is thought to help prevent tooth-decay.

**flush**[1] *verb* (**flushes, flushing, flushed**)
1 to blush. 2 to clean or remove something with a fast flow of liquid.

**flush**[2] *adjective*
1 level; without any part sticking out, *The doors are flush with the walls.* 2 (*slang*) having plenty of money.

**flustered** *adjective*
nervous and confused.

**flute** *noun* (**flutes**)
a musical instrument consisting of a long pipe with holes that are covered by fingers or keys.

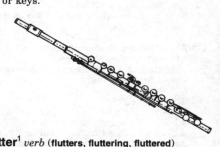

**flutter**[1] *verb* (**flutters, fluttering, fluttered**)
1 to move with a quick flapping of wings, *A butterfly fluttered in through the open window.* 2 to move or flap quickly and irregularly, *The flags fluttered in the breeze.*

**flutter**[2] *noun* (**flutters**)
1 a fluttering movement. 2 a nervously excited condition, *Mum was in a flutter about the flight to Spain.* 3 (*informal*) a small bet.

**fly**[1] *verb* (**flies, flying, flew, flown**)
1 to move through the air with wings or in an aircraft, *I have flown from London to Paris.* 2 to wave in the air, *Flags were flying.* 3 to make something move through the air, *They flew model aircraft.* 4 to move quickly, *Time flies.*

**fly**[2] *noun* (**flies**)
1 a small flying insect with two wings. 2 a real or artificial insect used as bait in fishing.
**fly-fishing**, fishing with a real or artificial insect as bait.

**fly**[3] *noun* (**flies**)
the front opening of a pair of trousers.

**flying saucer** *noun* (**flying saucers**)
a saucer-shaped flying object, believed to come from a planet other than Earth.

**flyleaf** *noun* (**flyleaves**)
a blank page at the beginning or end of a book.

**flyover** *noun* (**flyovers**)
(in America, *overpass*) a bridge that carries one road over another.

**flywheel** *noun* (**flywheels**)
a heavy wheel fixed to a turning part of a machine and helping it to run smoothly.

**foal** *noun* (**foals**)
a young horse.

**foam**[1] *noun*
1 froth. 2 a spongy substance made of rubber or plastic.
**foamy** *adjective*

**foam**[2] *verb* (**foams, foaming, foamed**)
to froth.

**focus**[1] *noun* (**focuses** or **foci**)
1 the distance at which something appears most clear to an eye or a lens. 2 the point at which rays, etc. meet. 3 the most important or interesting part of something.
**in focus**, appearing clearly.
**out of focus**, not appearing clearly.
**focal** *adjective*

**focus**[2] *verb* (**focuses, focusing, focused**)
1 to use or adjust a lens so that objects appear clearly. 2 to concentrate, *She focused her attention on the problem.*

**fodder** *noun*
food for horses and farm animals.

**foe** *noun* (**foes**)
(*old-fashioned use*) an enemy.

**foetus** *noun* (**foetuses**)
(*say* **fee-tŭs**)
a developing embryo.
**foetal** *adjective*

**fog** *noun* (**fogs**)
thick mist.
**foggy** *adjective*

**foghorn** *noun* (**foghorns**)
a loud horn for warning ships in fog.

**fogy** *noun* (**fogies**)
a dull person with old-fashioned ideas.

**foil**[1] *noun* (**foils**)
1 a very thin sheet of metal. 2 a person or thing that makes another look better in comparison.

**foil**[2] *noun* (**foils**)
a thin sword used in fencing.

**foil**[3] *verb* (**foils, foiling, foiled**)
to frustrate, *We foiled his evil plan.*

**fold**[1] *verb* (**folds, folding, folded**)
1 to bend or move so that one part lies on another part. 2 to blend one ingredient into another.
**folding**, made so that it can be folded to take up less space, *a folding chair.*
**fold your arms**, to wrap your arms round each other and hold them in front of your body.

**fold**[2] *noun* (**folds**)
a line where something is folded.

**fold**[3] *noun* (**folds**)
an enclosure for sheep.

**-fold** *suffix*
multiplied by the stated number of times, *a fourfold increase in profits. The number of pupils has risen threefold.*

**folder** *noun* (**folders**)
a folding cover for loose papers, *Keep your homework in this folder.*

**foliage** *noun*
the leaves of a tree or plant.

**folk** *plural noun*
people; ordinary people, especially those who live in the country.
**folk-dance**, a traditional dance of a country or a group of people.
**folk-song**, a traditional song of a country or a group of people.

**folklore** *noun*
old beliefs and legends.

**follow** *verb* (**follows, following, followed**)
1 to come or go after. 2 to do a thing after something else. 3 to take someone or something as a guide or example. 4 to support or take an interest in a pastime, sports team, etc., *Which football team do you follow?* 5 to understand, *Do you follow me?* 6 to result, *Who knows what trouble may follow?*
**follow up**, to follow one thing with another; to do more work, research, etc. on something.

**follower** *noun* (**followers**)
a person who follows or supports a religion, a leader, a political party, etc.

**following** *preposition*
1 after, *Following the motor-cycle outriders came the president's car.* 2 as a result of, *Following our visit to Devon, we have decided to go there for our next holiday.*

**fond** *adjective* (**fonder, fondest**)
1 loving, *fond embraces.* 2 foolishly optimistic, *fond hopes.*
**fond of**, liking very much, *I'm fond of trifle.*
**fondly** *adverb*, **fondness** *noun*

**font** *noun* (**fonts**)
a basin to hold water for baptism in a church.

**food** *noun* (**foods**)
anything that a plant or animal can take into its body to make it grow or give it energy.
**food-chain**, a series of plants and animals, each of which serves as food for the next one.
**food-web**, a number of connected food-chains in an area.

**fool**¹ *noun* (**fools**)
1 a stupid or disliked person. 2 a jester or clown, *Stop playing the fool.* 3 a pudding made of fruit mixed with custard or cream.

**fool**² *verb* (**fools, fooling, fooled**)
1 to behave like a fool. 2 to trick or deceive someone.
**fool about** or **fool around**, to behave stupidly.

**foolhardy** *adjective* (**foolhardier, foolhardiest**)
reckless.
**foolhardiness** *noun*

**foolish** *adjective*
stupid.
**foolishly** *adverb*, **foolishness** *noun*

**foolproof** *adjective*
easy to use or do correctly.

**foot** *noun* (**feet**)
1 the lower part of a leg. 2 the lowest part of something, *at the foot of the hill.* 3 a measure of length, 12 inches or about 30 centimetres.
**on foot**, walking.

**football** *noun* (**footballs**)
1 a game played by two teams which try to kick an inflated ball into their opponents' goal. 2 the ball used in this game.
**football pool**, a way of gambling on the results of football matches.
**footballer** *noun*

**foothill** *noun* (**foothills**)
a low hill near the bottom of a mountain or range of mountains.

**foothold** *noun* (**footholds**)
1 a place to put your foot when climbing, etc. 2 a firm position, *Winning the first three matches has given us a strong foothold in the championship.*

**footing** *noun*
1 having your feet placed on something; what your feet are standing on, *He lost his footing and fell down.* 2 a position or status, *We are on a friendly footing with that country.*

**footlights** *plural noun*
a row of lights along the front of the stage in a theatre.

**footnote** *noun* (**footnotes**)
a note printed at the bottom of a page.

**footpath** *noun* (**footpaths**)
a path for people to walk along.

**footprint** *noun* (**footprints**)
a mark made by a foot or shoe.

**footsteps** *plural noun*
the sound or marks your feet make when you walk or run.
**follow in someone's footsteps**, to do as someone did before you.

**for**¹ *preposition*
1 intended to be received or used by, *This letter is for you.* 2 towards; in the direction of, *They set out for home.* 3 in order to have or get, *Go for a walk.* 4 as far as; as long as, *We've been waiting for hours.* 5 at the price of, *She bought it for £2.* 6 instead of; in place of, *New lamps for old!* 7 because of, *He was punished for swearing.* 8 concerning; in respect of, *She has a good ear for music.* 9 in defence or support of, *Are you for or against the government?* 10 in spite of, *For all his wealth, he is bored.*
**for ever**, always.

**for**[2] *conjunction*
because; since, *Don't go, for I have something to tell you.*

**forbid** *verb* (**forbids, forbidding, forbade, forbidden**)
1 to tell someone not to do something. 2 not to allow something.

**forbidding** *adjective*
looking stern or unfriendly.

**force**[1] *noun* (**forces**)
1 strength; power. 2 (*in Science*) an influence that can be measured and that tends to cause things to move. 3 an organized group of police, soldiers, etc. 4 being active or effective, *Is that law still in force?*
**the forces,** the army, navy, and air force.

**force**[2] *verb* (**forces, forcing, forced**)
1 to use your power or strength to make someone do something. 2 to break something open.

**forceful** *adjective*
strong and effective, *a forceful speaker.*
**forcefully** *adverb*

USAGE: See the note at **forcible**.

**forceps** *noun* (**forceps**)
(*say* for-seps)
pincers used by a dentist, surgeon, etc.

**forcible** *adjective*
done by force.
**forcibly** *adverb*

USAGE: **forcible** can also mean strong and vigorous, but the more usual word for this is **forceful**.

**ford** *noun* (**fords**)
a shallow place where you can wade or drive across a river.

**fore**[1] *adjective*
at or towards the front.

**fore**[2] *noun*
**to the fore,** to or at the front; in a leading position, *Our firm has always been to the fore in using new technology.*

**forecast**[1] *verb* (**forecasts, forecasting, forecast or forecasted**)
to say what you think is going to happen before it happens.

**forecast**[2] *noun* (**forecasts**)
saying what you think is going to happen before it happens, especially what the weather is going to be.

**forecourt** *noun* (**forecourts**)
an open space in front of a petrol station or large building, *Parking is not allowed on the hotel forecourt.*

**forefathers** *plural noun*
ancestors.

**forefinger** *noun* (**forefingers**)
the finger next to your thumb.

**foregone** *adjective*
**foregone conclusion,** an inevitable or obvious result.

**foreground** *noun* (**foregrounds**)
the part of a scene, view, etc. that is nearest to you.

**forehead** *noun* (**foreheads**)
(*say* fo-rid or for-hed)
the part of your face above your eyebrows.

**foreign** *adjective*
1 of or in another country. 2 strange; unnatural, *Lying is foreign to her.*

**foreigner** *noun* (**foreigners**)
a person from another country.

**foreman** *noun* (**foremen**)
someone in charge of a group of other workers.

**foremost** *adjective*
most important.

**forename** *noun* (**forenames**)
a name that someone has besides his or her surname.

**foresee** *verb* (**foresees, foreseeing, foresaw, foreseen**)
to know what is going to happen before it happens; to expect something, *He foresaw trouble from the prisoners.*
**foreseeable** *adjective*, **foresight** *noun*

**forest** *noun* (**forests**)
a lot of trees growing together.
**forested** *adjective*, **forester** *noun*

**forestry** *noun*
planting forests and looking after them.

**foretell** *verb* (**foretells, foretelling, foretold**)
to predict, *She foretold their defeat.*

**forever** *adverb*
continually, *He is forever complaining.*

**forfeit**[1] *verb* (**forfeits, forfeiting, forfeited**)
to lose something as a penalty.

**forfeit**[2] *noun* (**forfeits**)
something that you lose or have to pay as a penalty.
**forfeits,** a game in which people have to do ridiculous things as penalties.

**forgave** past tense of **forgive**.

**forge**[1] *noun* (**forges**)
a place where metal is heated and shaped; a blacksmith's workshop.

**forge**[2] *verb* (**forges, forging, forged**)
1 to shape metal by heating and
hammering. 2 to copy something so as to
deceive people, *These ten-pound notes are
forged.*

**forge**[3] *verb* (**forges, forging, forged**)
**forge ahead,** to get ahead by making a
strong effort.

**forgery** *noun* (**forgeries**)
copying something so as to deceive people;
a copy made to deceive people, *That's not
the real painting; it's a forgery!*

**forget** *verb* (**forgets, forgetting, forgot, forgotten**)
1 to fail to remember, *I forgot my
homework.* 2 to stop thinking about
something, *We have forgotten our quarrels.*
**forget yourself,** to behave rudely or
thoughtlessly.

**forgetful** *adjective*
tending to forget things.
**forgetfulness** *noun*

**forget-me-not** *noun* (**forget-me-nots**)
a small blue flower.

**forgive** *verb* (**forgives, forgiving, forgave,
forgiven**)
to stop being angry with someone about
something, *I forgave him when he
explained.*
**forgiveness** *noun*

**fork**[1] *noun* (**forks**)
1 a small device with prongs for lifting food
to your mouth. 2 a large device with prongs
used for digging or lifting things. 3 a place
where a road, river, etc. divides into two or
more parts.

**fork**[2] *verb* (**forks, forking, forked**)
1 to dig or lift with a fork. 2 to divide into
two or more branches, *Go left where the
road forks.*
**fork out,** (*informal*) to pay out money.

**fork-lift truck** *noun* (**fork-lift trucks**)
a truck with two metal bars at the front for
lifting and moving heavy loads.

**forlorn** *adjective*
unhappy; not cared for.

**form**[1] *noun* (**forms**)
1 a class in school. 2 the shape, appearance,
or condition of something, *The dark form of
a tree stood out against the sunset.* 3 the
way in which something exists; a kind of
thing, *Ice is a form of water.* 4 a long seat
without a back. 5 a printed paper with
spaces where you give answers.

**form**[2] *verb* (**forms, forming, formed**)
1 to shape or construct something; to create
something. 2 to develop, *Icicles formed.*

**formal** *adjective*
1 strictly following the accepted rules or
customs, *You will receive a formal
invitation to the wedding.* 2 ceremonial,
*The formal opening of the bridge takes
place tomorrow.*
**formally** *adverb*

USAGE: Do not confuse **formal** with the
adjective **former**, which means earlier or of
past times.

**formality** *noun* (**formalities**)
1 formal behaviour. 2 something done to
obey a rule or custom.

**format**[1] *noun* (**formats**)
1 the shape and size of a book, a magazine,
etc. 2 the way something is arranged, *What
will the format of the lesson be?*

**format**[2] *verb* (**formats, formatting, formatted**)
(*in Computing*) to prepare a computer disk
to take data, including removing old data
from it.

**formation** *noun* (**formations**)
1 the action of forming something.
2 something formed, *formations of rock.* 3 a
special pattern or arrangement, *flying in
formation.*

**former**[1] *noun*
**the former,** the first of two people or things
just mentioned, *Brown and Jones came in;
the former looked happy.*

**former**[2] *adjective*
earlier; of past times, *in former days.*
**formerly** *adverb*

USAGE: Do not confuse **former** with **formal**,
which means strictly following the
accepted rules, or ceremonial.

**formidable** *adjective*
(*say* **for**-mid-ă-bŭl)
frightening; very difficult to deal with or
do, *a formidable task.*
**formidably** *adverb*

**formula** *noun* (**formulas** or **formulae**)
1 a set of chemical symbols showing what a substance consists of, *$H_2O$ is the formula for water.* 2 a rule or statement expressed in symbols or numbers. 3 a list of what is needed for making something.

**formulate** *verb* (**formulates, formulating, formulated**)
to express something clearly and exactly, *They formulated a plan.*
**formulation** *noun*

**forsake** *verb* (**forsakes, forsaking, forsook, forsaken**)
to abandon, *She forsook her children.*

**fort** *noun* (**forts**)
a fortified building.

**forth** *adverb*
forwards; onwards.

**fortify** *verb* (**fortifies, fortifying, fortified**)
1 to make a place strong against attack. 2 to strengthen something, *A good breakfast will fortify you for the day's work.*
**fortification** *noun*

**fortnight** *noun* (**fortnights**)
two weeks.
**fortnightly** *adverb* and *adjective*

**fortress** *noun* (**fortresses**)
a large fort; a fortified town.

**fortunate** *adjective*
lucky.
**fortunately** *adverb*

**fortune** *noun* (**fortunes**)
1 luck; chance. 2 a lot of money.
**fortune-teller,** someone who tells you what will happen to you in the future.

**forty** *noun* (**forties**)
the number 40, four times ten.
**forty winks,** a short sleep.
**fortieth** *adjective* and *noun*

**forward**[1] *adjective*
1 going forwards; placed in the front, *a forward party of trained troops.* 2 having made more than normal progress; clever. 3 too eager or bold.

**forward**[2] *adverb*
forwards.

**forward**[3] *noun* (**forwards**)
a player in the front line of a team at football, hockey, etc.

**forwards** *adverb*
to or towards the front; in the direction you are facing.

**fossil** *noun* (**fossils**)
the remains of a prehistoric animal or plant that has been in the ground for a very long time and become hard like rock.
**fossil fuel,** fuel such as coal, oil, etc., that was formed from living things a very long time ago.
**fossilized** *adjective*

**foster** *verb* (**fosters, fostering, fostered**)
to bring up someone else's child as if he or she were your own.
**foster-child** *noun*, **foster-mother** *noun*

**fought** past tense and past participle of **fight** *verb.*

**foul**[1] *adjective* (**fouler, foulest**)
1 disgusting; filthy. 2 unfair; breaking the rules.
**foully** *adverb*, **foulness** *noun*

**foul**[2] *noun* (**fouls**)
an action that breaks the rules of a game.

**found**[1] *verb* (**founds, founding, founded**)
1 to get something started; to establish something, *She founded a hospital.* 2 to base, *This novel is founded on fact.*

**found**[2] past tense and past participle of **find.**

**foundation** *noun* (**foundations**)
1 the solid base on which a building is built. 2 a base or basis. 3 the beginning of something.

**founder**[1] *noun* (**founders**)
someone who founds something, *Guru Nanak was the founder of the Sikh religion.*

**founder**[2] *verb* (**founders, foundering, foundered**)
to fill with water and sink, *The ship foundered.*

**foundry** *noun* (**foundries**)
a place where metal or glass is made or moulded.

**fountain** *noun* (**fountains**)
a device that makes water shoot up into
the air.

**fountain pen** *noun* (**fountain pens**)
a pen that can be filled with a supply of ink.

**four** *noun* (**fours**)
the number 4, one more than three.
**on all fours**, crouching on hands and knees.

**fourteen** *noun* (**fourteens**)
the number 14, one more than thirteen.
**fourteenth** *adjective* and *noun*

**fourth** *adjective*
next after the third.
**fourthly** *adverb*

**fowl** *noun* (**fowls**)
a bird that is kept for its eggs or meat.

**fox** *noun* (**foxes**)
a wild animal that looks like a small dog
with a long, furry tail.
**foxy** *adjective*

**foxglove** *noun* (**foxgloves**)
a tall plant with flowers like the fingers of
gloves.

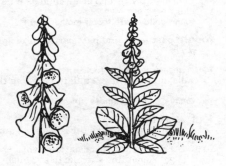

**foyer** *noun* (**foyers**)
(*say* **foi**-ay)
the entrance hall of a cinema, theatre,
hotel, etc.

**fraction** *noun* (**fractions**)
1 a number that is not a whole number, $\frac{1}{2}$
*and* $\frac{3}{5}$ *are fractions.* 2 a tiny part of
something, *You have heard only a fraction
of what happened.*
**fractional** *adjective*, **fractionally** *adverb*

**fracture**[1] *verb* (**fractures, fracturing, fractured**)
to break something, especially to break
a bone.

**fracture**[2] *noun* (**fractures**)
the breaking of something, especially
a bone.

**fragile** *adjective*
(*say* **fra**-jyl)
easy to break or damage.
**fragility** *noun*

**fragment** *noun* (**fragments**)
1 a small piece broken off something, *a
fragment of rock.* 2 a small part, *She
overheard fragments of conversation.*
**fragmentary** *adjective*, **fragmentation** *noun*,
**fragmented** *adjective*

**fragrant** *adjective*
(*say* **fray**-gränt)
with a sweet or pleasant smell.
**fragrance** *noun*

**frail** *adjective* (**frailer, frailest**)
weak; fragile.
**frailty** *noun*

**frame**[1] *noun* (**frames**)
1 something that fits round the outside of a
picture. 2 a rigid structure that supports
something, *I've broken the frame of my
glasses. This bicycle has a light frame.* 3 a
human body, *He has a small frame.*
**frame of mind**, the way you think or feel for
a while, *Wait till he's in a better frame of
mind.*

**frame**[2] *verb* (**frames, framing, framed**)
1 to put a frame on or around. 2 to form or
construct, *They were framing new laws.*
3 (*slang*) to make an innocent person seem
to be guilty.

**frame-up** *noun* (**frame-ups**)
(*slang*) making an innocent person seem to
be guilty.

**framework** *noun* (**frameworks**)
1 a frame supporting something. 2 a basic
plan or system.

**franc** *noun* (**francs**)
a unit of money in France, Belgium, and
some other countries.

**franchise** *noun* (**franchises**)
1 the right to vote in elections. 2 a licence
to sell a firm's goods or services in a
certain area.

**frank**[1] *adjective* (**franker, frankest**)
honest; making your thoughts and feelings
clear to people.
**frankly** *adverb*, **frankness** *noun*

**frank**[2] *verb* (**franks, franking, franked**)
to mark something with a postmark.

**frankfurter** *noun* (**frankfurters**)
a type of smoked sausage first made in
Frankfurt, Germany.

**frantic** *adjective*
wildly agitated or excited.
**frantically** *adverb*

**fretwork**

**fraud** *noun* (**frauds**)
1 a swindle; dishonesty. 2 someone who is not what he or she pretends to be.
**fraudulent** *adjective*

**frayed** *adjective*
worn and ragged at the edge, *Your shirt collar is frayed.*

**freak** *noun* (**freaks**)
1 a very strange or abnormal person, animal, or thing. 2 someone who is very enthusiastic about a particular thing, *She is a fitness freak.*
**freakish** *adjective*

**freckle** *noun* (**freckles**)
a small brown spot on the skin.
**freckled** *adjective*

**free**[1] *adjective* (**freer, freest**)
1 able to do what you want to do or go where you want to go. 2 not costing anything, *a free ride.* 3 available; not being used or occupied, *His afternoons are free.* 4 generous, *She is very free with her money.*
**free of something,** not having something; not affected by something, *The roads are free of ice.*
**do something of your own free will,** to do something without being asked, told, or forced to do it.
**freely** *adverb*

**free**[2] *verb* (**frees, freeing, freed**)
to make someone or something free.

**freedom** *noun*
being free; independence.

**freehand** *adjective and adverb*
without using any help (such as compasses) when drawing, *Draw a circle freehand.*

**free-range** *adjective*
(of animals) allowed to roam freely to find their food; (of food) produced by animals kept in this way, *free-range eggs.*

**freestyle** *adjective*
in which any style of swimming, wrestling, etc. can be used, *a freestyle race.*

**free-wheel** *verb* (**free-wheels, free-wheeling, free-wheeled**)
to ride on a bicycle without pedalling.

**freeze** *verb* (**freezes, freezing, froze, frozen**)
1 to turn into ice or another solid; to become covered with ice, *The pond froze last night.* 2 to make or be very cold, *My hands are frozen.* 3 to keep wages, prices, etc. at a fixed level. 4 suddenly to stand completely still.

**freezer** *noun* (**freezers**)
a large refrigerator for keeping food very cold, *You can keep food in freezers for months.*

**freezing-point** *noun* (**freezing-points**)
the temperature at which a liquid freezes.

**freight** *noun*
(*say* frayt)
1 goods carried in a ship or aircraft. 2 the cost of transporting something.

**freighter** *noun* (**freighters**)
a ship or aircraft carrying mainly goods.

**French** *adjective*
of France.
**French fries,** thin potato chips.
**French horn,** a brass musical instrument made of a tube that goes round in a circle.
**French window,** a long window that serves as a door, opening on to a garden or balcony.
**Frenchman** *noun*, **Frenchwoman** *noun*

**frenzy** *noun* (**frenzies**)
wild excitement; madness.
**frenzied** *adjective*, **frenziedly** *adverb*

**frequency** *noun* (**frequencies**)
1 being frequent. 2 how often something happens. 3 the number of to-and-fro movements made each second by a wave of sound, light, etc.
**frequency polygon,** a graph made by connecting the middle points of the tops of a histogram's columns.

**frequent**[1] *adjective*
(*say* **free**-kwĕnt)
happening often.
**frequently** *adverb*

**frequent**[2] *verb* (**frequents, frequenting, frequented**)
(*say* fri-**kwent**)
to be in or go to a place often, *They frequented the youth club.*

**fresh** *adjective* (**fresher, freshest**)
1 not old, tired, or used, *fresh bread.* 2 not tinned or preserved, *fresh fruit.* 3 cool and clean, *fresh air.* 4 not salty, *fresh water.*
**freshly** *adverb*, **freshness** *noun*

**freshen** *verb* (**freshens, freshening, freshened**)
to make something fresh; to become fresh.

**freshwater** *adjective*
of fresh water; living in rivers or lakes, *freshwater fish.*

**fret** *verb* (**frets, fretting, fretted**)
to worry or be upset about something.
**fretful** *adjective*, **fretfully** *adverb*

**fretsaw** *noun* (**fretsaws**)
a very narrow saw used for making fretwork.

**fretwork** *noun*
1 the skill of cutting decorative patterns in wood. 2 wood cut in this way.

**friar** *noun* (**friars**)
a religious man who has vowed to live a life of poverty.
**friary** *noun*

**friction** *noun*
1 the rubbing of one thing against another.
2 disagreement; quarrelling.
**frictional** *adjective*

**Friday** *noun* (**Fridays**)
the sixth day of the week.

**fridge** *noun* (**fridges**)
a refrigerator.

**friend** *noun* (**friends**)
1 someone you like who likes you. 2 a helpful or kind person.
**make friends**, to become someone's friend.
**friendless** *adjective*

**friendly** *adjective* (**friendlier, friendliest**)
behaving like a friend; kind and helpful.
**friendliness** *noun*

**friendship** *noun* (**friendships**)
being friends.

**frieze** *noun* (**friezes**)
(*say* freez)
a strip of designs or pictures along the top of a wall.

**frigate** *noun* (**frigates**)
a fast warship.

**fright** *noun* (**frights**)
1 sudden, great fear. 2 (*informal*) a person or thing that looks ridiculous.

**frighten** *verb* (**frightens, frightening, frightened**)
to cause someone fright or fear.

**frightful** *adjective*
awful.
**frightfully** *adverb*

**frill** *noun* (**frills**)
1 a decorative edging, usually pleated, on a dress, curtain, etc. 2 an unnecessary extra, *a simple life with no frills.*
**frilled** *adjective*, **frilly** *adjective*

**fringe** *noun* (**fringes**)
1 a decorative edging for fabric, with many threads hanging down loosely. 2 a straight line of short hair hanging down over your forehead. 3 the edge of something, *He stood on the fringe of the crowd.*
**fringed** *adjective*

**frisk** *verb* (**frisks, frisking, frisked**)
1 to jump or run around playfully. 2 to search someone by moving your hands over his or her clothes.

**frisky** *adjective* (**friskier, friskiest**)
playful; lively.
**friskily** *adverb*, **friskiness** *noun*

**fritter**[1] *noun* (**fritters**)
a slice of fruit, meat, etc. fried in batter.

**fritter**[2] *verb* (**fritters, frittering, frittered**)
**fritter away**, to waste something gradually; to spend money or time on trivial things, *He frittered away his money.*

**frivolous** *adjective*
1 not behaving seriously, *Don't be frivolous! This is an important matter.* 2 trivial, *frivolous pleasures.*
**frivolity** *noun*, **frivolously** *adverb*

**frizzy** *adjective* (**frizzier, frizziest**)
tightly curled, *She has frizzy hair.*

**fro** *adverb*
**to and fro**, backwards and forwards.

**frock** *noun* (**frocks**)
a girl's or woman's dress.

**frog** *noun* (**frogs**)
a small jumping animal that can live both in water and on land.
**have a frog in your throat**, to be hoarse.

**frogman** *noun* (**frogmen**)
a swimmer equipped with flippers and breathing apparatus for swimming under water.

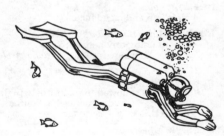

**frolic**[1] *noun* (**frolics**)
a lively, cheerful game or pastime.
**frolicsome** *adjective*

**frolic**[2] *verb* (**frolics, frolicking, frolicked**)
to spend time in lively, cheerful games or pastimes.

**from** *preposition*
1 out of, *She comes from London.*
2 measured with reference to, *We are a mile from home.* 3 starting at, *Recite the poem from the beginning.* 4 because of, *I suffer from headaches.* 5 as opposed to, *Can you tell margarine from butter?*

**front** *noun* (**fronts**)
1 the part of a person or thing that faces forwards; the most important side of something, *The front of the house is blue.* 2 the part of a thing or place that is farthest forward, *Go to the front of the class.* 3 a road or promenade along the seashore. 4 the place where fighting is happening in a war, *More troops were moved to the front.* 5 the forward edge of an advancing mass of hot or cold air.
**in front**, at or near the front.
**frontal** *adjective*

**frontier** *noun* (**frontiers**)
the boundary between two countries or regions.

**frost**[1] *noun* (**frosts**)
1 powdery ice that forms on things in freezing weather. 2 weather with a temperature below freezing-point.
**frosty** *adjective*

**frost**[2] *verb* (**frosts, frosting, frosted**)
to cover something with frost or frosting.
**frosted glass**, glass that has a rough surface so that you cannot see through it.

**frost-bite** *noun*
harm done to the skin by very cold weather.
**frost-bitten** *adjective*

**frosting** *noun*
icing for cakes.

**froth**[1] *noun*
a white mass of tiny bubbles on or in a liquid.
**frothy** *adjective*

**froth**[2] *verb* (**froths, frothing, frothed**)
to form a froth.

**frown**[1] *verb* (**frowns, frowning, frowned**)
to wrinkle your forehead because you are angry or worried.

**frown**[2] *noun* (**frowns**)
wrinkling your forehead, or your expression when you have a wrinkled forehead because you are angry or worried.

**froze** past tense of **freeze**.

**frozen** past participle of **freeze**.

**frugal** *adjective*
(*say* **froo-găl**)
1 very economical and careful, *a frugal housekeeper.* 2 costing little money, *a frugal meal.*
**frugality** *noun*

**fruit** *noun* (**fruit or fruits**)
1 the seed-container that grows on a tree or plant and is often used as food, *Apples, oranges, and bananas are fruit.* 2 the result of doing something, *He lived to see the fruits of his efforts.*
**fruit salad**, a mixture of raw fruit cut up for eating.
**fruity** *adjective*

**fruitful** *adjective*
1 successful; having good results, *Their talks were fruitful.* 2 producing fruit.
**fruitfully** *adverb*

**fruitless** *adjective*
unsuccessful; having no results.
**fruitlessly** *adverb*

**frustrate** *verb* (**frustrates, frustrating, frustrated**)
to prevent someone from doing something; to disappoint someone.
**frustration** *noun*

**fry** *verb* (**fries, frying, fried**)
to cook something in very hot fat.

**frying-pan** *noun* (**frying-pans**)
a shallow pan in which things are fried.
**out of the frying-pan into the fire**, from a bad situation to something worse.

**fudge** *noun*
a soft sweet made with milk, sugar, butter, etc.

**fuel**[1] *noun* (**fuels**)
something that is burnt to make heat or power, *Coal and oil are fuels.*

**fuel**[2] *verb* (**fuels, fuelling, fuelled**)
to supply something with material to burn to make heat or power.

**fug** *noun* (**fugs**)
(*informal*) a stuffy atmosphere in a room.
**fuggy** *adjective*

**fugitive** *noun* (**fugitives**)
(*say* **few-ji-tiv**)
a person who is running away from something.

**fugue** *noun* (**fugues**)
(*say* **fewg**)
a piece of music in which themes are repeated in a pattern.

**-ful** *suffix*
full of, *a trustful dog. They sang a joyful song.*

**fulcrum** *noun* (**fulcra** or **fulcrums**)
the point on which a lever rests.

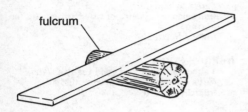

fulcrum

**fulfil** *verb* (**fulfils, fulfilling, fulfilled**)
to accomplish something; to do what is required.
**fulfilment** *noun*

**full**[1] *adjective*
1 containing as much or as many as possible, *The cinema was full.* 2 having many people or things, *full of ideas.*
3 complete, *the full story.* 4 the greatest possible, *Full speed ahead!* 5 fitting loosely; with many folds, *a full skirt.*
**in full,** not leaving out anything.
**to the full,** completely; thoroughly.
**fullness** *noun,* **fully** *adverb*

**full**[2] *adverb*
completely; very, *You knew full well what I wanted.*

**full moon** *noun* (**full moons**)
the moon when you can see the whole of it as a bright circle.

**full stop** *noun* (**full stops**)
the dot used as a punctuation mark at the end of a sentence or after the letters of some abbreviations.

**full-time** *adjective* and *adverb*
of or for all the normal working hours of the day, *a full-time job. She works full-time.*

**fumble** *verb* (**fumbles, fumbling, fumbled**)
to hold or handle something clumsily.

**fume** *verb* (**fumes, fuming, fumed**)
1 to give off strong-smelling smoke or gas.
2 to be very angry.

**fumes** *plural noun*
strong-smelling smoke or gas.

**fun** *noun*
amusement; enjoyment.
**make fun of,** to make people laugh at someone; to make a person or thing seem ridiculous.

**function**[1] *noun* (**functions**)
1 what someone or something does or ought to do, *The function of a doctor is to cure sick people.* 2 an important event, party, etc., *The Queen attends many functions.*
3 any of the basic operations of a computer, calculator, etc. 4 (*in Mathematics*) a relation between numbers, *The function of adding 2 makes 5 into 7, 6 into 8, etc.*

**function**[2] *verb* (**functions, functioning, functioned**)
to work properly, *These scissors won't function.*

**functional** *adjective*
1 working properly, *The machine is fully functional again.* 2 practical, *a car with a simple, functional design.*
**functionally** *adverb*

**fund** *noun* (**funds**)
money collected or kept for a special purpose, *They started a fund for refugees.*

**fundamental** *adjective*
basic.
**fundamentally** *adverb*

**funeral** *noun* (**funerals**)
the ceremony when a corpse is buried or burnt.

**fungus** *noun* (**fungi**)
a plant without leaves or flowers, growing on other plants or on decayed material, *Mushrooms and toadstools are fungi.*

**funk** *verb* (**funks, funking, funked**)
(*informal*) to be afraid of doing something.

**funnel** *noun* (**funnels**)
1 a chimney on a ship or steam-engine. 2 a tube with one very wide end to help you pour things into bottles or other containers.

**funny** *adjective* (**funnier, funniest**)
1 that makes you laugh or smile, *a funny joke.* 2 strange; odd, *a funny smell.*
**funny bone,** part of your elbow which gives you a strange tingling feeling if it is hit.
**funnily** *adverb*

**fur** *noun* (**furs**)
1 the soft hair that covers some animals.
2 animal skin with the hair on it, used for clothing; fabric that looks like animal skin with hair on it.

**furious** *adjective*
very angry; raging.
**furiously** *adverb*

**furl** *verb* (**furls, furling, furled**)
to roll up and fasten a sail, flag, or umbrella.

**furlong** *noun* (**furlongs**)
one-eighth of a mile, 220 yards or about 201 metres.

**furnace** *noun* (**furnaces**)
a device in which great heat can be produced for making glass, heating metals, etc.

**furnish** *verb* (**furnishes, furnishing, furnished**)
to provide furniture for a place.

**furniture** *noun*
tables, chairs, beds, cupboards, and other movable things that you need inside a house, school, office, etc.

**furrow** *noun* (**furrows**)
**1** a long cut in the ground made by a plough. **2** a deep wrinkle on the skin.

**furry** *adjective* (**furrier, furriest**)
**1** like fur, *A furry mould was growing on the bread.* **2** covered with fur, *Rabbits are furry animals.*

**further**[1] *adverb* and *adjective*
**1** at or to a greater distance; more distant, *I can't walk any further.* **2** more, *We need further information.*

**further**[2] *verb* (**furthers, furthering, furthered**)
to help something progress, *We want to further the cause of peace.*

**further education** *noun*
education for people above school age.

**furthermore** *adverb*
also; moreover.

**furthest** *adverb* and *adjective*
at or to the greatest distance; most distant.

**furtive** *adjective*
cautious, as though you were about to do something wrong, *He gave a furtive glance around the shop, then slipped some sweets into his pocket.*

**fury** *noun* (**furies**)
wild anger; a rage.

**fuse**[1] *noun* (**fuses**)
a safety device containing a short piece of wire that melts if too much electricity passes through it.

**fuse**[2] *noun* (**fuses**)
a device for setting off an explosive.

**fuse**[3] *verb* (**fuses, fusing, fused**)
**1** to stop working because a fuse has melted, *The lights have fused.* **2** to blend together, especially through melting.

**fuselage** *noun* (**fuselages**)
(*say* **few**-ze-lahzh)
the body of an aircraft, *Wings and tail are fitted to the fuselage.*

**fusion** *noun*
(*say* **few**-zhŏn)
**1** the action of blending or joining together. **2** the joining together of the central parts of atoms, usually releasing energy.

**fuss**[1] *noun* (**fusses**)
unnecessary excitement or worry about something that is not important.
**make a fuss of someone,** to treat someone with much kindness and attention.

**fuss**[2] *verb* (**fusses, fussing, fussed**)
to be unnecessarily excited or worried about something that is not important.

**fussy** *adjective* (**fussier, fussiest**)
**1** fussing; inclined to make a fuss. **2** full of unnecessary details or decorations.
**fussily** *adverb*, **fussiness** *noun*

**futile** *adjective*
(*say* **few**-tyl)
useless; having no result.
**futility** *noun*

**future** *noun*
**1** the time that will come. **2** what is going to happen in the time that will come.
**future tense,** the form of a verb that shows that something is going to happen in the time that will come, *In English, the future tense uses 'will' and 'shall' in front of the verb.*
**in future,** from now onwards.

**fuzz** *noun*
short, fine, soft hair, *The baby rabbit was like a small ball of grey fuzz.*

**fuzzy** *adjective* (**fuzzier, fuzziest**)
**1** blurred; not clear. **2** covered in short, fine, soft hair.
**fuzzily** *adverb*, **fuzziness** *noun*

# Gg

**g** short for **gram** or **grams**.

**gabardine** *noun* (**gabardines**)
a coat made of a smooth, heavy, hard-wearing cotton or woollen cloth.

**gabble** *verb* (**gabbles, gabbling, gabbled**)
to talk so quickly that it is difficult for people to understand what you are saying.

**gable** *noun* (**gables**)
the three-sided part of a wall between two sloping roofs.
**gabled** *adjective*

**gadget** *noun* (**gadgets**)
(*say* gaj-it)
a small, useful device, *a gadget for opening tins.*
**gadgetry** *noun*

**Gaelic** *noun*
(*say* gay-lik (in Ireland) or gal-ik (in Scotland))
a Celtic language that is spoken in some parts of Ireland and Scotland.

**gag**[1] *verb* (**gags, gagging, gagged**)
to put something over someone's mouth so that he or she cannot speak.

**gag**[2] *noun* (**gags**)
1 something put over someone's mouth to stop him or her from speaking. 2 a joke.

**gaiety** *noun*
being cheerful; amusement.

**gaily** *adverb*
in a cheerful way.

**gain**[1] *verb* (**gains, gaining, gained**)
to get something that you did not have before.
**gain on** or **gain upon,** to come closer to someone or something you are chasing.

**gain**[2] *noun* (**gains**)
something you have got that you did not have before; profit.

**gala** *noun* (**galas**)
(*say* gah-lă)
1 a festival. 2 a series of sports contests, especially in swimming.

**galaxy** *noun* (**galaxies**)
(*say* gal-ăk-si)
a very large group of stars, *You can see three galaxies without a telescope.*
**galactic** *adjective*

**gale** *noun* (**gales**)
a very strong wind.

**gallant** *adjective*
1 brave. 2 polite and helpful, especially towards women.
**gallantly** *adverb*, **gallantry** *noun*

**galleon** *noun* (**galleons**)
a large Spanish sailing-ship used from the 15th to the 17th century.

**gallery** *noun* (**galleries**)
1 a platform sticking out from the inside wall of a building. 2 the highest set of seats in a cinema or theatre. 3 a long room or passage. 4 a building or room where works of art are displayed.

**galley** *noun* (**galleys**)
1 an ancient type of long ship propelled by oars. 2 the kitchen in a ship.

**gallon** *noun* (**gallons**)
a measure of liquid, 8 pints or about $4\frac{1}{2}$ litres.

**gallop**[1] *noun* (**gallops**)
1 the fastest pace a horse can go. 2 a fast ride on a horse.

**gallop**[2] *verb* (**gallops, galloping, galloped**)
to ride at the fastest pace a horse can go, *The cowboys galloped away.*

**gallows** *noun*
a framework on which criminals were hanged.

**Gallup poll** *noun* (**Gallup polls**)
questioning a number of people so as to estimate how many people think in a certain way, *A Gallup poll showed that 60% of people were in favour of a ban on smoking.*

**galore** *adjective*
in large amounts, *There was food galore at the party.*

**galvanize** *verb* (**galvanizes, galvanizing, galvanized**)
1 to coat iron with zinc to protect it from rust. 2 to stimulate or shock someone into doing something.

**gamble** *verb* (**gambles, gambling, gambled**)
1 to play a game for money. 2 to take great risks, *He is gambling with his life.*
**gambler** *noun*

**game**[1] *noun* (**games**)
1 something that you can play, usually with rules, *Football, chess, and ludo are games.* 2 one section of a long game like tennis or whist, *In tennis, you must win at least 6 games to win a set.* 3 a trick or scheme, *What's his game, I wonder?* 4 wild animals or birds hunted for sport or food, *Some people shoot game like pheasants or partridges.*
**game-bird,** a wild bird that is hunted for sport or food.
**the game is up,** a swindle or secret has been revealed.

**game**[2] *adjective*
1 able and willing to do something, *He's game for all kinds of tricks.* 2 brave.
**gamely** *adverb*

**gamekeeper** *noun* (**gamekeepers**)
someone who protects game-birds and animals, especially from poachers.

**gammon** *noun*
a kind of ham or thick bacon.

**gander** *noun* (**ganders**)
a male goose.

**gang** *noun* (**gangs**)
1 a group of young people who go about together. 2 a group of people who work together, *a gang of railwaymen.* 3 a group of gangsters.

**gangplank** *noun* (**gangplanks**)
a plank for walking on to or off a ship.

**gangster** *noun* (**gangsters**)
a violent criminal.

**gangway** *noun* (**gangways**)
1 a gap left for people to move along between rows of seats or through a crowd. 2 a gangplank or other structure for getting on or off a ship.

**gaol**[1] *noun* (**gaols**)
(*say* jayl)
a prison.
**gaoler** *noun*

USAGE: Do not confuse **gaol** with **goal**, which means the posts on a sports field, or a point scored in sports, or something that you try to do.

**gaol**[2] *verb* (**gaols, gaoling, gaoled**)
to put someone in prison.

**gap** *noun* (**gaps**)
an opening or break in something; an interval in time or space.

**gape** *verb* (**gapes, gaping, gaped**)
1 to open your mouth wide. 2 to stare in amazement.

**garage** *noun* (**garages**)
(*say* ga-rah*zh* or ga-rij)
1 a building in which motor vehicles are kept or repaired. 2 a place where petrol is sold.

**garbage** *noun*
rubbish.

**garden** *noun* (**gardens**)
a piece of ground where flowers, fruit, or vegetables are grown.
**garden plant,** a plant of the sort grown in gardens, not wild.
**gardener** *noun*, **gardening** *noun*

**gargle** *verb* (**gargles, gargling, gargled**)
to wash your throat by moving liquid around inside it, without swallowing.

**gargoyle** *noun* (**gargoyles**)
an ugly or amusing carving on a building, especially one of a head that sticks out from a gutter and sends out rainwater through its mouth.

**garland** *noun* (**garlands**)
a wreath of flowers for decoration.

**garlic** *noun*
a plant rather like an onion, with a strong-smelling bulb used for flavouring.

**garment** *noun* (**garments**)
something you wear; a piece of clothing.

**garnish** *verb* (**garnishes, garnishing, garnished**)
to decorate food.

**garrison** *noun* (**garrisons**)
troops who defend a town or fort.

**garter** *noun* (**garters**)
a band of elastic to hold up a sock or stocking.

**gas**[1] *noun* (**gases**)
1 a substance like air, *Oxygen and hydrogen are gases.* 2 a gas that burns and is used for heating or cooking, *Gas is used for gas cookers and gas fires.* 3 (*in America, informal*) petrol.
**gas ring**, a pipe with holes from which gas flows for cooking on.
**gaseous** *adjective*

**gas**[2] *verb* (**gasses, gassing, gassed**)
to overcome or harm someone with a poisonous gas.

**gash** *noun* (**gashes**)
a long, deep cut or wound.

**gasket** *noun* (**gaskets**)
a flat ring or strip of soft material for sealing a joint between metal surfaces.

**gasoline** *noun*
(*in America*) petrol.

**gasometer** *noun* (**gasometers**)
(*say* gas-om-it-er)
a large, round tank in which gas is stored.

**gasp** *verb* (**gasps, gasping, gasped**)
1 to breathe quickly and noisily when you are tired, ill, or astonished. 2 to say something or to speak in a breathless way, *'Is this the right train for London?', he gasped.*

**gastric** *adjective*
of the stomach, *gastric juices.*

**gastro-enteritis** *noun*
an illness in which your stomach and intestines become inflamed.

**gate** *noun* (**gates**)
1 something that opens and closes the entrance to a garden, field, etc. 2 a barrier used to control the flow of water, *a lock-gate.* 3 a place where you wait before you get on an aircraft, etc. 4 the number of people attending a football match, etc.

**gateau** *noun* (**gateaux**)
(*say* gat-oh)
a rich cake, usually made in several layers with cream in between.

**gateway** *noun* (**gateways**)
1 an opening containing a gate. 2 a way to reach something, *the gateway to success.*

**gather** *verb* (**gathers, gathering, gathered**)
1 to come together; to bring things or people together. 2 to collect or pick fruit, nuts, berries, etc. 3 to understand, decide, or learn, *I gather that you are on holiday.*
**gather speed**, to get faster gradually.

**gathering** *noun* (**gatherings**)
an assembly or meeting of people; a party.

**gaudy** *adjective* (**gaudier, gaudiest**)
too showy and bright.

**gauge**[1] *noun* (**gauges**)
(*say* gayj)
1 one of the standard sizes of something. 2 the distance between a pair of railway lines. 3 a measuring instrument, *a pressure gauge.*

**gauge**[2] *verb* (**gauges, gauging, gauged**)
1 to measure. 2 to estimate; to judge, *Try to gauge how many people are likely to respond.*

**gaunt** *adjective*
1 (of a person) thin and looking ill or tired. 2 (of a place) grim and desolate.

**gauntlet** *noun* (**gauntlets**)
a glove with a wide covering for the wrist.

**gauze** *noun*
thin, net-like material of wire, silk, cotton, etc.

**gave** past tense of **give**.

**gay** *adjective* (**gayer, gayest**)
1 cheerful. 2 brightly coloured. 3 (*informal*) homosexual.

**gaze**[1] *verb* (**gazes, gazing, gazed**)
to look at something or someone for a long time, *He gazed at the sunset.*

**gaze**[2] *noun* (**gazes**)
a long, steady look.

**gazelle** *noun* (**gazelles**)
a small antelope.

**gazump** *verb* (**gazumps, gazumping, gazumped**)
(*informal*) to raise the price of a house after accepting an offer from someone.

**GCSE** short for **General Certificate of Secondary Education.**

**gear** *noun* (**gears**)
1 equipment; clothes, *mountaineering gear.* 2 a set of toothed wheels working together in a machine, especially those transmitting power from an engine to the wheels of a vehicle.
**in gear**, with the gears connected.
**out of gear**, with the gears not connected.

**gee** *interjection*
1 a command to a horse to go on or go faster. 2 an exclamation of surprise, disappointment, etc.

**geese** plural of **goose**.

**Geiger counter** *noun* (**Geiger counters**)
a device that detects and measures radioactivity.

**gel** *noun* (**gels**)
a jelly-like substance, especially one used on your hair to give it a particular style.

**gelatine** *noun*
a clear, tasteless substance used to make jellies, etc.
**gelatinous** *adjective*

**gelding** *noun* (**geldings**)
a male horse that has been neutered.

**gem** *noun* (**gems**)
1 a jewel. 2 a very valuable or beautiful thing.

**gender** *noun* (**genders**)
(*say* **jen**-der)
the group in which a noun or pronoun belongs in some languages, *The gender of 'he' is masculine, the gender of 'she' is feminine, and the gender of 'it' is neuter.*

**gene** *noun* (**genes**)
(*say* jeen)
one of the factors in your body that controls what characteristics you inherit from your parents.

**genealogy** *noun* (**genealogies**)
the study of the history of families; a list of the people who are or were members of a particular family.

**general**[1] *adjective*
1 of or concerning all or most people or things, *general knowledge.* 2 not detailed; not specialized, *a general education.*
**General Certificate of Secondary Education,** an examination for pupils in secondary schools.
**general election,** electing Members of Parliament for the whole country.
**general practitioner,** a doctor who is not a specialist or consultant.
**in general,** usually.

**general**[2] *noun* (**generals**)
a high-ranking army officer.

**generalize** *verb* (**generalizes, generalizing, generalized**)
to talk about general things, not particular things; to state principles, *Some young people are safe drivers and some are not; you can't generalize.*
**generalization** *noun*

**generally** *adverb*
usually.

**generate** *verb* (**generates, generating, generated**)
to produce or create something, *Electricity is usually generated in a power station.*
**generator** *noun*

**generation** *noun* (**generations**)
1 generating something. 2 a single stage in a family, *Three generations were included: grandparents, parents, and children.* 3 all the people born about the same time, *His generation grew up during the war.*
**generation gap,** parents and children failing to understand or communicate with each other.

**generous** *adjective*
ready to give or share what you have.
**generosity** *noun*, **generously** *adverb*

**genetic** *adjective*
(*say* ji-**net**-ik)
of genes.
**genetically** *adverb*

**genetics** *noun*
the science that examines how the characteristics of living things are passed on to their offspring by means of genes.

**genial** *adjective*
kind, pleasant, and cheerful, *a genial host. His genial smile made us feel welcome.*
**genially** *adverb*

**genie** *noun* (**genies**)
a magical being in stories who can make your wishes come true, *The genie appeared whenever Aladdin rubbed the lamp.*

**genitals** *plural noun*
the parts of the body used for sexual intercourse.

**genius** *noun* (**geniuses**)
an unusually clever person.

**gent** *noun* (**gents**)
(*old-fashioned slang*) a gentleman; a man.
**the Gents,** (*informal*) a lavatory for men.

**gentle** *adjective* (**gentler, gentlest**)
kind and quiet; not rough or severe.
**gentleness** *noun*, **gently** *adverb*

**gentleman** *noun* (**gentlemen**)
1 a man, *Good evening, ladies and gentlemen!* 2 a well-mannered or honest man, *He's a real gentleman.*
**gentlemanly** *adverb*

**genuine** *adjective*
real; not faked or pretending, *This diamond is genuine. Is she the genuine Duchess?*
**genuinely** *adverb*

**genus** *noun* (**genera**)
 (*say* jee-nŭs)
 a group of similar animals or plants.

**geography** *noun*
 the science or study of the world and its
 climate, peoples, and products.
 **geographer** *noun*, **geographical** *adjective*,
 **geographically** *adverb*

**geology** *noun*
 (*say* ji-ol-ŏ-ji)
 the science or study of the earth's crust, its
 rocks, etc.
 **geological** *adjective*, **geologically** *adverb*,
 **geologist** *noun*

**geometry** *noun*
 the science or study of lines, angles,
 surfaces, and solids.
 **geometric** *adjective*, **geometrical** *adjective*,
 **geometrically** *adverb*

**geranium** *noun* (**geraniums**)
 (*say* jĕ-ray-ni-ŭm)
 a plant with red, pink, or white flowers
 that is often grown in a pot.

**gerbil** *noun* (**gerbils**)
 (*say* jer-bil)
 a small, brown, mouse-like animal with
 long back legs, *Gerbils are often kept as
 pets.*

**germ** *noun* (**germs**)
 a tiny living thing, especially one that
 causes a disease.

**German** *adjective*
 of Germany.
 **German measles**, a disease caught by
 contact with infected people, that gives you
 a cough, a sore throat, and red spots, and
 that can harm an unborn baby if its
 mother catches the disease.

**Germanic** *adjective*
 belonging to the group of languages that
 includes English, German, Dutch, Danish,
 Swedish, and Norwegian.

**germinate** *verb* (**germinates**, **germinating**,
 **germinated**)
 to start growing and developing.
 **germination** *noun*

**gestation** *noun*
 (*in Science*) the time when a foetus is
 growing in its mother's womb, *Elephants
 have a long period of gestation.*

**gesticulate** *verb* (**gesticulates**, **gesticulating**,
 **gesticulated**)
 to make movements with your hands and
 arms while you are talking.

**gesture** *noun* (**gestures**)
 (*say* jes-cher)
 a movement or action which expresses
 what you feel.

**get** *verb* (**gets**, **getting**, **got**)
 **1** to become, *Are you getting angry?* **2** to
 obtain or receive something, *I got a new
 bike yesterday.* **3** to reach a place, *We'll get
 there by midnight.* **4** to put or move, *I can't
 get my shoe on.* **5** to prepare, *Shall I get the
 tea?* **6** to persuade or order, *Get him to
 wash up.* **7** (*informal*) to understand, *Do
 you get what I mean?*
 **get by**, to manage.
 **get off**, to stop riding on a bus, horse, etc.;
 to avoid being punished.
 **get on**, to start riding on a bus, horse, etc.;
 to make progress; to be friendly with
 someone.
 **get on with**, to work at something.
 **get out of**, to avoid something.
 **get over**, to recover from an illness, shock,
 etc.
 **get through to someone**, (*informal*) to make
 someone understand something, *I've tried
 to explain, but I just can't get through to
 him.*
 **get your own back**, to have your revenge.
 **have got to**, must.

**getaway** *noun* (**getaways**)
 an escape.

**geyser** *noun* (**geysers**)
 (*say* gee-zer or gy-zer)
 a natural spring that shoots up columns of
 hot water.

**ghastly** *adjective* (**ghastlier**, **ghastliest**)
 horrible; awful.

**ghetto** *noun* (**ghettos**)
 (*say* get-oh)
 an area of a city, often a slum area, where
 a group of people live who are
 discriminated against.

**ghost** *noun* (**ghosts**)
 the spirit of a dead person seen by a living
 person.
 **ghostly** *adjective*

**ghoul** *noun* (**ghouls**)
1 an evil spirit in Muslim folklore that eats dead bodies. 2 (*informal*) a person who is unpleasantly interested in death or injury, *A crowd of ghouls had gathered at the scene of the car crash.*

**giant**[1] *noun* (**giants**)
a huge man.
**giantess** *noun*

**giant**[2] *adjective*
huge.

**giddy** *adjective* (**giddier, giddiest**)
having the feeling that everything is turning round in circles; causing this feeling, *I'm feeling giddy. a giddy dance.*
**giddily** *adverb*, **giddiness** *noun*

**gift** *noun* (**gifts**)
1 a present. 2 a talent, *She has a gift for music.*

**gifted** *adjective*
having a natural ability for doing something well.

**gig** *noun* (**gigs**)
(*informal*) an occasion when a musician or band plays rock music, jazz, etc. in public.

**gigantic** *adjective*
huge.
**gigantically** *adverb*

**giggle**[1] *verb* (**giggles, giggling, giggled**)
to laugh in a silly way.

**giggle**[2] *noun* (**giggles**)
1 a silly laugh. 2 (*informal*) something amusing; a joke, *We did it for a giggle.*
**the giggles**, (*informal*) a fit of giggling.

**gild** *verb* (**gilds, gilding, gilded**)
to cover something with a thin layer of gold paint or gold.

USAGE: Do not confuse **gild** with **guild**, which is a noun meaning a society of people with similar skills.

**gill** *noun* (**gills**)
one of the parts on a fish's side that it breathes through.

gill

**gimmick** *noun* (**gimmicks**)
something unusual done or used to attract people's attention, *The comedian's funny hat was a gimmick.*
**gimmicky** *adjective*

**gin** *noun*
a colourless alcoholic drink.

**ginger** *noun*
1 a flavouring that makes food taste hot. 2 a reddish-yellow colour. 3 liveliness; energy, *Put some ginger into it!*
**ginger beer**, a sweet, fizzy drink that tastes of ginger.
**gingery** *adjective*

**gingerbread** *noun*
a cake or biscuit flavoured with ginger.

**gingerly** *adverb*
cautiously.

**gipsy** *noun* (**gipsies**)
a gypsy.

**giraffe** *noun* (**giraffes**)
a tall African animal with a very long neck.

**girder** *noun* (**girders**)
a metal beam supporting part of a building or bridge.

**girdle** *noun* (**girdles**)
a belt or piece of clothing worn around your waist.

**girl** *noun* (**girls**)
1 a young female person. 2 a daughter, *My girl's in the netball team.*
**girlhood** *noun*, **girlish** *adjective*

**girlfriend** *noun* (**girlfriends**)
1 a boy's or man's regular female friend or lover. 2 a girl's or woman's regular female friend.

**giro** noun (**giros**)
1 a system of sending money directly from one bank account or Post Office account to another. 2 a kind of cheque used to send money by this system, especially one sent to someone who is receiving a government benefit.

**girth** noun (**girths**)
1 the measurement round something. 2 a band fastened round a horse's belly to keep its saddle in place.

**gist** noun
(say jist)
the main points or general meaning of a speech, etc.

**give** verb (**gives, giving, gave, given**)
1 to let someone have something, *She has given me a sweet.* 2 to make; to do something suddenly, *He gave a laugh.* 3 to present or perform, *They gave a concert.* 4 to bend or go downwards; to collapse, *Will this branch give if I sit on it?*
**give away,** to sacrifice something; to reveal a secret, *He gave all his wealth away. They've given away our plans!*
**give in,** to surrender.
**give off,** to send out something.
**give out,** to hand out something; to become worn out, *Which government department gives out grants? I think the engine will give out soon.*
**give up,** to stop doing or trying something; to surrender, *They gave up trying to get in. Most of the soldiers gave up without a struggle.*
**give way,** to collapse; to let someone go before you, *The bridge gave way. I gave way to a woman pushing a pram.*
**giver** noun

**given** adjective
definite; stated; agreed, *Meet at a given time.*
**given to,** tending to; having a particular habit, *He is given to boasting.*

**glacial** adjective
(say glay-shăl)
1 of ice; icy. 2 formed by glaciers, *a glacial valley.*

**glaciation** noun
the action of glaciers, *This valley was formed by glaciation.*

**glacier** noun (**glaciers**)
(say glas-i-er)
a river of ice moving slowly along a valley.

**glad** adjective (**gladder, gladdest**)
pleased; happy.
**glad of something,** grateful for something.
**gladden** verb, **gladly** adverb, **gladness** noun

**gladiator** noun (**gladiators**)
in Ancient Rome, a man who fought with a sword or other weapons at public shows.

**glamorous** adjective
attractive and exciting; beautiful, *glamorous places to spend a holiday. People expect film stars to be glamorous.*

**glamour** noun
1 the attractive, exciting appearance of something, *The glamour of a career in television attracted her.* 2 a person's beauty or attractiveness.
**glamorize** verb

**glance**[1] verb (**glances, glancing, glanced**)
1 to look at something briefly. 2 to hit and slide off something, *The ball glanced off his bat.*

**glance**[2] noun (**glances**)
a brief look.

**gland** noun (**glands**)
an organ of the body that produces substances which are sent into the blood, or sent out of the body.

**glandular** adjective
of the glands.
**glandular fever,** a disease that gives you a fever and makes some of your glands painful and swollen.

**glare**[1] verb (**glares, glaring, glared**)
1 to shine with a very bright or dazzling light. 2 to look angrily at someone.

**glare**[2] noun (**glares**)
1 very strong light. 2 an angry stare.

**glaring** adjective
1 very bright, *glaring sunlight.* 2 very obvious, *That's a glaring error!*

**glass** noun (**glasses**)
1 a hard, brittle, usually clear substance, *Glass is used for making windows, mirrors, dishes, etc.* 2 a cup made of this material, usually without a handle. 3 a mirror. 4 a lens or telescope.
**glasses,** spectacles; binoculars.
**glassful** noun

**glassy** adjective (**glassier, glassiest**)
1 like glass. 2 dull; without liveliness or expression, *a glassy stare.*

**glaze** verb (**glazes, glazing, glazed**)
1 to fit or cover something with glass. 2 to give a shiny surface to pottery, etc. 3 to become glassy, *Her eyes glazed and she fainted.*

**glazier** noun (**glaziers**)
someone who fits glass into window-frames

**gleam**[1] *noun* (**gleams**)
1 a beam of soft light, especially one that comes and goes. 2 a small amount, *a gleam of hope.*

**gleam**[2] *verb* (**gleams, gleaming, gleamed**)
to shine with beams of soft light.

**glee** *noun*
delight; joy.
**gleeful** *adjective*, **gleefully** *adverb*

**glen** *noun* (**glens**)
a narrow valley, especially in Scotland.

**glide** *verb* (**glides, gliding, glided**)
1 to fly or move smoothly. 2 to fly without using an engine.

**glider** *noun* (**gliders**)
an aircraft that does not use an engine.

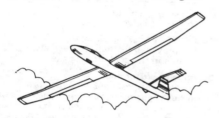

**glimmer**[1] *noun* (**glimmers**)
a faint gleam.

**glimmer**[2] *verb* (**glimmers, glimmering, glimmered**)
to gleam faintly.

**glimpse**[1] *verb* (**glimpses, glimpsing, glimpsed**)
to see something briefly.

**glimpse**[2] *noun* (**glimpses**)
seeing something briefly.

**glint** *verb* (**glints, glinting, glinted**)
to flash or sparkle.

**glisten** *verb* (**glistens, glistening, glistened**)
to shine like something wet or polished.

**glitter** *verb* (**glitters, glittering, glittered**)
to sparkle.

**gloat** *verb* (**gloats, gloating, gloated**)
to show unpleasant pleasure about your success or about harm that has happened to someone else.

**global** *adjective*
of the whole world.
**global warming,** a gradual increase in the average temperature of the earth's climate, caused by the greenhouse effect.
**globally** *adverb*

**globe** *noun* (**globes**)
1 something shaped like a ball. 2 a ball with a map of the whole world on it.
**the globe,** the world, *a company with branches all over the globe.*

**glockenspiel** *noun* (**glockenspiels**)
a musical instrument made of metal bells, tubes, or especially bars of different sizes that you hit with small hammers.

**gloom** *noun* (**glooms**)
a depressed condition or feeling.

**gloomy** *adjective* (**gloomier, gloomiest**)
1 almost dark; not lighted. 2 depressed; sad.
**gloomily** *adverb*, **gloominess** *noun*

**glorify** *verb* (**glorifies, glorifying, glorified**)
1 to praise someone highly. 2 to make something seem splendid.
**glorification** *noun*

**glorious** *adjective*
having glory.
**gloriously** *adverb*

**glory** *noun* (**glories**)
1 fame and honour; praise. 2 splendour; beauty.

**gloss** *noun* (**glosses**)
1 the shine on a smooth surface. 2 a paint that makes surfaces shiny.
**glossy** *adjective*

**glossary** *noun* (**glossaries**)
a list of words with their meanings explained, *Your Science book has a glossary at the back.*

**glove** *noun* (**gloves**)
a covering for your hand.

**glow**[1] *noun*
1 brightness and warmth without flames. 2 a cheerful or excited condition, *a glow of enthusiasm.*

**glow**[2] *verb* (**glows, glowing, glowed**)
1 to be bright and warm without flames. 2 to be in a cheerful or excited condition.

**glower** *verb* (**glowers, glowering, glowered**)
to look bad-tempered.

**glow-worm** *noun* (**glow-worms**)
an insect whose tail gives out a green light.

**glucose** *noun*
a type of sugar.

**glue**[1] *noun* (**glues**)
a thick liquid for sticking things together.
**gluey** *adjective*

**glue**[2] *verb* (**glues, gluing, glued**)
to stick something with glue.

**glum** *adjective* (**glummer**, **glummest**)
depressed; sad.
**glumly** *adverb*

**glutton** *noun* (**gluttons**)
someone who eats too much.
**gluttonous** *adjective*, **gluttony** *noun*

**gnarled** *adjective*
(*say* narld)
twisted and lumpy, like an old tree.

**gnash** *verb* (**gnashes**, **gnashing**, **gnashed**)
(*say* nash)
to strike your teeth together.

**gnat** *noun* (**gnats**)
(*say* nat)
a tiny fly that bites.

**gnaw** *verb* (**gnaws**, **gnawing**, **gnawed**)
(*say* naw)
to keep biting something that is hard, *The
dog gnawed the bone.*

**gnome** *noun* (**gnomes**)
(*say* nohm)
a kind of dwarf in fairy tales that usually
lives underground.

**go**[1] *verb* (**goes**, **going**, **went**, **gone**)
**1** to move in any direction, *Where are you
going?* **2** to leave; to set out, *We shall go in
a minute.* **3** to lead; to extend, *This road
goes to Bristol.* **4** to become, *The milk went
sour.* **5** to work properly, *My watch isn't
going.* **6** to have a proper place; to belong,
*Plates go on that shelf.* **7** to happen or
proceed, *The show went well.* **8** to make a
particular movement or sound, *The gun
went bang.* **9** to be finished or lost, *My
money has gone.* **10** to be sold, *The house
went very cheaply.*
**go back on,** not to keep a promise.
**go in for,** to do or take part in something.
**go off,** to explode; to become stale; to stop
liking someone or something, *The whole
box of fireworks went off at once. That milk
has gone off. I've gone off him ever since he
ruined my bike.*
**go on,** to happen; to do something more
than once, *What's going on? Unless you
stop him now, he'll go on stealing things.*
**go one better,** to do better than someone else.
**go out,** to leave a house, home, etc.; to go to
entertainments; to stop burning or shining,
*I went out and locked the door. We go out
twice a week to the cinema. The fire's gone
out.*
**go out with someone,** to be someone's regular
girlfriend or boyfriend.

**go**[2] *noun* (**goes**)
**1** a turn or try, *May I have a go?*
**2** (*informal*) a success, *They made a go of it.*
**3** (*informal*) energy; liveliness, *She's full of
go.*
**on the go,** always working or moving.

**go-ahead**[1] *noun*
permission to do something, *The
headteacher's given us the go-ahead to
organize a class outing.*

**go-ahead**[2] *adjective*
adventurous and keen to try out new
methods, *a modern, go-ahead company
developing new electronic products.*

**goal** *noun* (**goals**)
**1** the two posts that the ball must go
between to score a point in football, hockey,
etc. **2** a point scored in football, hockey,
netball, etc. **3** something that you try to do
or to achieve, *Her goal was to become the
Prime Minister.*

USAGE: Do not confuse **goal** with **gaol**,
which means prison.

**goalie** *noun* (**goalies**)
(*informal*) a goalkeeper.

**goalkeeper** *noun* (**goalkeepers**)
the player in football, hockey, etc. who
stands in the goal and guards it.

**goalposts** *plural noun*
the upright posts of a goal in sports.
**move the goalposts,** to change the rules or
what you thought was the correct way to
do something, *Schools were supposed to be
spending less money, but now they've
moved the goalposts and say we should
spend more.*

**goat** *noun* (**goats**)
an animal with horns, belonging to the
same family as sheep.
**to get someone's goat,** (*informal*) to annoy
someone.

**gob** *noun* (**gobs**)
(*slang*) your mouth.
**gob-stopper,** a large sweet for sucking.

**gobble** *verb* (**gobbles**, **gobbling**, **gobbled**)
to eat something quickly and greedily.

**gobbledegook** or **gobbledygook** *noun*
complicated technical or official language
that is difficult or impossible for most
people to understand.

**goblet** *noun* (**goblets**)
a glass that you drink from, with a long stem and a base.

**goblin** *noun* (**goblins**)
an evil or mischievous fairy.

**god** *noun* (**gods**)
someone or something that is worshipped. **God**, the creator of the Universe in Christian, Jewish, and Muslim belief.
**godless** *adjective*, **godlike** *adjective*

**godparent** *noun* (**godparents**)
someone who promises, when a child is baptized, to see that it is brought up as a Christian.
**godchild** *noun*, **god-daughter** *noun*, **godfather** *noun*, **godmother** *noun*, **godson** *noun*

**goggles** *plural noun*
large spectacles to protect the eyes from wind, water, dust, etc.

**going**[1] *noun*
**1** the condition of the ground for walking, riding, etc. **2** speed of working or moving, *It was good going to get there by noon.* **3** departure, *comings and goings.*

**going**[2] *adjective*
**1** working well; prosperous, *a going concern.* **2** existing, *What is the going rate for delivering newspapers?*
**going to,** ready or likely to do something.

**go-kart** *noun* (**go-karts**)
a type of very small racing car.
**go-karting** *noun*

**gold** *noun*
**1** a precious yellow metal. **2** a bright yellow colour.
**gold medal,** a medal made of gold, awarded as the first prize.
**gold-rush,** a sudden movement of people to a place where gold has been found.

**golden** *adjective*
**1** made of gold. **2** coloured like gold. **3** precious; important, *a golden opportunity.*
**golden wedding,** the 50th anniversary of a wedding.

**gold-field** *noun* (**gold-fields**)
an area where gold is found or mined.

**goldfinch** *noun* (**goldfinches**)
a small, brightly-coloured bird with yellow feathers in its wings.

**goldfish** *noun* (**goldfish**)
a small red or orange fish, often kept as a pet.

**golf** *noun*
an outdoor game played by hitting a small ball into a series of small holes, using a club.
**golfer** *noun*, **golfing** *noun*

**golf-course** *noun* (**golf-courses**)
an area of land where golf is played.

**gondola** *noun* (**gondolas**)
(*say* gon-dŏ-lă)
a boat with high pointed ends, used on the canals in Venice.
**gondolier** *noun*

**gone** past participle of **go** *verb.*

**gong** *noun* (**gongs**)
a large metal disc that makes a deep, hollow sound when it is hit.

**goo** *noun*
**1** something sticky or slimy. **2** sentimental words, poems, pictures, etc.
**gooey** *adjective*

**good**[1] *adjective* (**better, best**)
**1** of the kind that people like, want, or praise, *a good book.* **2** kind, *It was good of you to help us.* **3** well-behaved, *Be a good boy.* **4** healthy; giving benefit, *Exercise is good for you.* **5** thorough; large enough, *Have a good drink.* **6** quite large; considerable, *It's a good distance to the station.* **7** useful; suitable, *This desk is good enough for me.*
**as good as,** nearly.
**good evening,** a polite way of greeting someone in the evening.
**good morning,** a polite way of greeting someone in the morning.
**good night,** a polite way of saying goodbye to someone at night.

**good**[2] *noun*
1 something good or right, *Do good to others*. 2 benefit; profit, *I'm telling you for your own good*.
**for good**, for ever.
**no good**, useless.

**goodbye** *interjection*
a word you use when you leave someone, or at the end of a telephone call.

**Good Friday** *noun*
the Friday before Easter, when Christians remember Jesus's death on the Cross.

**good-looking** *adjective*
attractive; handsome.

**good-natured** *adjective*
kind.
**good-naturedly** *adverb*

**goodness** *noun*
1 being good. 2 the good part of something.
**goodness gracious, goodness me**, or **my goodness**, ways of expressing surprise.

**goods** *plural noun*
1 things that are bought and sold. 2 (in America, *freight*) things that are carried on trains, lorries, etc.
**someone delivers the goods**, someone does or supplies what is needed, *You can rely on her; she always delivers the goods*.

**goodwill** *noun*
1 being friendly, *They have showed us a lot of goodwill*. 2 approval, *My plan has the head teacher's goodwill*.

**goose** *noun* (**geese**)
a large bird that is kept for its meat and eggs, *Geese have webbed feet*.

**gooseberry** *noun* (**gooseberries**)
a small green fruit that grows on a prickly bush.

**goose-pimples** *plural noun*
your skin when it is covered in small bumps, with all the hairs standing on end, because you are cold or afraid.

**gore** *verb* (**gores, goring, gored**)
to wound with a horn or tusk, *The bull gored the matador*.

**gorge** *noun* (**gorges**)
a narrow valley with steep sides.

**gorgeous** *adjective*
magnificent; beautiful.
**gorgeously** *adverb*

**gorilla** *noun* (**gorillas**)
a large, strong African ape.

USAGE: Do not confuse **gorilla** with **guerrilla**, which means someone who fights by means of ambushes and surprise attacks.

**gorse** *noun*
a prickly bush with small yellow flowers.

**gory** *adjective* (**gorier, goriest**)
covered in blood; involving a lot of killing, *a gory film*.

**gosh** *interjection*
(*slang*) an exclamation of surprise.

**gosling** *noun* (**goslings**)
a young goose.

**go-slow** *noun* (**go-slows**)
a way of protesting by deliberately working slowly.

**gospel** *noun* (**gospels**)
1 the teachings of Jesus. 2 something that you can safely believe, *You can take what she says as gospel*.
**the Gospels**, the first four books of the New Testament.

**gossip**[1] *verb* (**gossips, gossiping, gossiped**)
1 to talk a lot about other people. 2 to talk a lot in a friendly way.

**gossip**[2] *noun* (**gossips**)
1 talk, especially rumours, about other people. 2 someone who likes talking about other people.

**got** past tense and past participle of **get**.

**Gothic** *adjective*
of the style of building common from the 12th to the 16th century, with pointed arches, thin pillars, and carved decoration.

**gouge** *verb* (**gouges, gouging, gouged**)
(say gowj)
to press or scoop out something.

**gourd** *noun* (**gourds**)
1 the hard-skinned fruit of a climbing plant. 2 this fruit hollowed out to make a bowl or container.

**govern** *verb* (**governs, governing, governed**)
to be in charge of a country or organization.
**governor** *noun*

**government** *noun* (**governments**)
the group of people who are in charge of a country.
**governmental** *adjective*

**gown** *noun* (**gowns**)
a loose, flowing garment, especially for a woman.

**GP** short for **general practitioner**.

**grab** *verb* (**grabs, grabbing, grabbed**)
to take hold of something suddenly, firmly, or greedily.

**grace** *noun* (**graces**)
**1** beauty, especially in movement.
**2** goodwill; favour, *They prayed, asking for God's grace.* **3** a short prayer before or after a meal.

**graceful** *adjective*
beautiful, especially in movement.
**gracefully** *adverb*, **gracefulness** *noun*

**gracious** *adjective*
**1** kind; pleasant to other people. **2** merciful.
**3** used as an exclamation of surprise, *Good gracious! Gracious me!*
**graciously** *adverb*

**grade**[1] *noun* (**grades**)
a step in a scale of quality, value, or rank; a standard, *Coal is sold in grades: Grade A coal is the best.*
**make the grade**, (*informal*) to reach the proper standard.

**grade**[2] *verb* (**grades, grading, graded**)
to sort or divide things or people according to quality, value, or rank.

**gradient** *noun* (**gradients**)
(*say* gray-di-ĕnt)
**1** a slope. **2** the amount that a road or railway slopes.

**gradual** *adjective*
happening slowly but steadily.
**gradually** *adverb*

**graduate**[1] *noun* (**graduates**)
(*say* grad-yoo-ăt)
someone who has been to a university or college and got a degree.

**graduate**[2] *verb* (**graduates, graduating, graduated**)
(*say* grad-yoo-ayt)
**1** to get a university degree. **2** to divide something into graded sections; to mark something so that it can be used for measuring, *The ruler was graduated in millimetres and centimetres.*
**graduation** *noun*

**graffiti** *plural noun*
(*say* gră-**fee**-tee)
words or drawings scribbled on a wall.

**grain** *noun* (**grains**)
**1** cereals when they are growing or after they have been harvested. **2** the seed of a cereal; a small, hard seed or piece. **3** the pattern of lines on a piece of wood.
**something goes against the grain**, something is difficult for you because it is against your beliefs or wishes, *Helping him goes against the grain because he has always been unfriendly to me.*
**grainy** *adjective*

**gram** *noun* (**grams**)
a unit of weight in the metric system, a thousandth of a kilogram.

**grammar** *noun* (**grammars**)
**1** the rules for using words. **2** a book that gives the rules for using words.
**grammar school**, a kind of secondary school.

**grammatical** *adjective*
of grammar; according to the rules of grammar, *This sentence is grammatical.*
**grammatically** *adverb*

**gramophone** *noun* (**gramophones**)
a machine for reproducing sound that has been recorded on discs.

USAGE: **gramophone** is a rather old-fashioned word; the machine is now usually called a **record-player**.

**grand** *adjective* (**grander, grandest**)
**1** great; splendid. **2** complete, *the grand total.*
**grand piano**, a large piano with horizontal strings.
**grandly** *adverb*

**grandad** *noun* (**grandads**)
(*informal*) grandfather.

**grandchild** *noun* (**grandchildren**)
a child of your son or daughter.
**granddaughter** *noun*, **grandson** *noun*

**grandeur** *noun*
greatness; splendour.

**grandfather** *noun* (**grandfathers**)
the father of your mother or father.
**grandfather clock**, a clock in a tall wooden case.

**grandma** *noun* (**grandmas**)
(*informal*) grandmother.

**grandmother** *noun* (**grandmothers**)
the mother of your mother or father.

**grandpa** *noun* (**grandpas**)
(*informal*) grandfather.

**grandparent** *noun* (**grandparents**)
a grandmother or grandfather.

**grandstand** *noun* (**grandstands**)
a structure with rows of seats for
spectators at a racecourse or sports ground.

**granite** *noun*
a very hard kind of rock.

**granny** *noun* (**grannies**)
(*informal*) grandmother.

**granny-knot** *noun* (**granny-knots**)
a reef-knot with the strings crossed the
wrong way.

**grant**[1] *verb* (**grants, granting, granted**)
to give or allow someone what he or she
has asked for.
**take something for granted,** to assume that
something is true or will always be
available.

**grant**[2] *noun* (**grants**)
something given, especially a sum of
money.

**granulated** *adjective*
in grains, *granulated sugar*.

**grape** *noun* (**grapes**)
a small green or purple fruit that grows in
bunches.

**grapefruit** *noun* (**grapefruit**)
a large, round, yellow citrus fruit with a
soft, juicy pulp.

**grapevine** *noun* (**grapevines**)
a climbing plant on which grapes grow.
**hear something on the grapevine,** to hear
something unofficially from other people
who have passed on the information from
one to another, *There's going to be a new
teacher next week; I heard it on the
grapevine.*

**graph** *noun* (**graphs**)
a diagram that shows how two amounts
are related.
**graph paper,** paper covered with small
squares, used for making graphs.

**graphic** *adjective*
1 short and lively, *a graphic account of the
race.* 2 of drawing or painting, *a graphic
artist.*
**graphically** *adverb*

**graphics** *plural noun*
diagrams, lettering, and drawings,
especially pictures that are produced by a
computer.

**graphite** *noun*
a soft kind of carbon used for the lead in
pencils, for lubricating, etc.

**grapple** *verb* (**grapples, grappling, grappled**)
1 to struggle or wrestle. 2 to hold something
firmly.
**grapple with something,** to try to deal with a
problem, etc.

**grasp**[1] *verb* (**grasps, grasping, grasped**)
1 to hold tightly. 2 to understand.

**grasp**[2] *noun*
1 the power to understand things, *She has
a good grasp of mathematics.* 2 a firm hold.

**grasping** *adjective*
greedy for money or possessions.

**grass** *noun* (**grasses**)
1 a green plant with thin stalks. 2 ground
covered with grass.
**grassy** *adjective*

**grasshopper** *noun* (**grasshoppers**)
a jumping insect that makes a shrill noise.

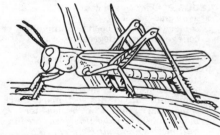

**grass snake** *noun* (**grass snakes**)
a small, harmless snake.

**grate**[1] *noun* (**grates**)
1 a metal framework that keeps fuel in the
fireplace. 2 a fireplace.

**grate**[2] *verb* (**grates, grating, grated**)
1 to shred something into small pieces, *He
grated some cheese.* 2 to make an
unpleasant noise by rubbing something,
*The chalk grated on the blackboard.*

**grateful** *adjective*
feeling glad that someone has done
something for you, *I am grateful for your
help.*
**gratefully** *adverb*

**grating** *noun* (**gratings**)
a framework of metal bars placed across an opening.

**gratitude** *noun*
being grateful.

**grave**[1] *noun* (**graves**)
the place where a corpse is buried.

**grave**[2] *adjective* (**graver, gravest**)
serious; solemn; important, *grave news*.
**gravely** *adverb*

**gravel** *noun*
small stones mixed with coarse sand, *Gravel is often used to make paths*.
**gravelled** *adjective*, **gravelly** *adjective*

**gravestone** *noun* (**gravestones**)
a stone monument over a grave.

**graveyard** *noun* (**graveyards**)
a place where corpses are buried.

**gravity** *noun*
1 the force that pulls all objects in the universe towards each other. 2 the force that pulls everything towards the earth. 3 seriousness.
**gravitation** *noun*, **gravitational** *adjective*

**gravy** *noun*
a hot brown liquid that is poured over meat before it is eaten.

**graze** *verb* (**grazes, grazing, grazed**)
1 to eat grass as it grows, *The cows were grazing in the field*. 2 to hurt your skin by rubbing against something; to scrape something as you pass it, *I grazed my arm on the wall. My bike grazed the side of the parked car*.

**grease** *noun*
thick fat or oil.
**greasy** *adjective*

**great** *adjective* (**greater, greatest**)
1 very large. 2 very important; extremely clever or talented, *a great composer*. 3 (*informal*) very good, *It's great to see you again*. 4 older by one generation, *Your great-grandfather is the grandfather of one of your parents*.
**greatly** *adverb*, **greatness** *noun*

**Grecian** *adjective*
of Greece.

**greed** *noun*
being greedy.

**greedy** *adjective* (**greedier, greediest**)
wanting more food or money than you need.
**greedily** *adverb*, **greediness** *noun*

**Greek**[1] *adjective*
of Greece.

**Greek**[2] *noun* (**Greeks**)
1 a Greek person. 2 the language spoken in Greece.

**green**[1] *adjective* (**greener, greenest**)
1 of the colour of grass, leaves, etc. 2 concerned with protecting the environment, *the green movement*.
**someone has green fingers,** someone is skilled or successful at growing plants.

**green**[2] *noun* (**greens**)
1 green colour. 2 an area of grass, especially in the middle of a village or used for a particular game, *the village green. a putting-green*.
**Green,** a person who supports the Green Party, a political party favouring a way of life which does not damage the earth or its people.

**greenery** *noun*
green leaves or plants.

**greenfinch** *noun* (**greenfinches**)
a small bird with green and yellow feathers.

**greengage** *noun* (**greengages**)
a green kind of plum.

**greengrocer** *noun* (**greengrocers**)
someone who keeps a shop that sells fruit and vegetables.
**greengrocery** *noun*

**greenhouse** *noun* (**greenhouses**)
a glass building where plants are grown.
**greenhouse effect,** the bad effect of large amounts of gases such as methane and carbon dioxide in the earth's atmosphere, trapping heat and causing the earth to become too warm.

**greenish** *adjective*
rather green.

**greens** *plural noun*
green vegetables, such as cabbage and spinach.

**greet** *verb* (**greets, greeting, greeted**)
to welcome; to receive, *The singer was greeted with applause*.

**greeting** *noun* (**greetings**)
words or actions used to greet someone.
**greetings,** good wishes.

**grenade** *noun* (**grenades**)
a small bomb usually thrown by hand.

**grew** past tense of **grow**.

**grey** *adjective* (**greyer, greyest**)
of the colour between black and white, like ashes or lead.

**greyhound** *noun* (**greyhounds**)
a fast, slim breed of dog used in racing.

**grid** *noun* (**grids**)
a framework or pattern of bars or lines crossing each other.
**grid reference** a set of figures that allows you to find a particular place on a map, *The grid reference of my house is 614790.*

**grief** *noun*
deep sadness.
**come to grief,** to have an accident or misfortune.

**grievance** *noun* (**grievances**)
something that you are discontented about.

**grieve** *verb* (**grieves, grieving, grieved**)
1 to feel very sad. 2 to make someone feel very sad.

**grievous** *adjective*
1 that causes deep sadness. 2 serious, *a grievous injury.*
**grievously** *adverb*

**grill**[1] *verb* (**grills, grilling, grilled**)
1 to cook something over or under a flame or a heated surface. 2 to question someone closely and severely, *He was grilled by the police.*

**grill**[2] *noun* (**grills**)
1 a device for grilling food. 2 grilled food. 3 a grating.

**grim** *adjective* (**grimmer, grimmest**)
1 stern; severe, *The judge looked grim.* 2 frightening; unpleasant, *a grim experience.*
**grimly** *adverb,* **grimness** *noun*

**grimace** *noun* (**grimaces**)
a strange or twisted expression on your face.

**grime** *noun*
dirt, especially in a thin layer.
**grimy** *adjective*

**grin**[1] *noun* (**grins**)
a smile showing your teeth.

**grin**[2] *verb* (**grins, grinning, grinned**)
to give a smile showing your teeth.
**grin and bear it,** to endure something without complaining.

**grind** *verb* (**grinds, grinding, ground**)
1 to crush something into tiny pieces, *The wheat was ground into flour.* 2 to sharpen or polish something by rubbing it on a rough surface. 3 to move with a harsh rubbing sound, *The bus ground to a halt.*
**grinder** *noun*

**grindstone** *noun* (**grindstones**)
a rough, round, revolving stone used for grinding things.
**keep someone's nose to the grindstone,** to make someone work hard without stopping.

**grip**[1] *verb* (**grips, gripping, gripped**)
1 to hold tightly. 2 to keep someone's attention, *The story gripped the audience.*

**grip**[2] *noun* (**grips**)
1 a way of holding tightly. 2 a handle.

**grisly** *adjective* (**grislier, grisliest**)
horrible, *the grisly remains of a dead sheep.*

**gristle** *noun*
the tough, rubbery part of meat; cartilage.
**gristly** *adjective*

**grit**[1] *noun*
1 tiny pieces of stone or sand. 2 courage; endurance.
**gritty** *adjective*

**grit**[2] *verb* (**grits, gritting, gritted**)
1 to close your teeth tightly. 2 to put grit on a road or path.

**grizzly bear** *noun* (**grizzly bears**)
a large, fierce bear of North America.

**groan**[1] *verb* (**groans, groaning, groaned**)
to make a long, deep sound of pain or distress.

**groan**[2] *noun* (**groans**)
a long, deep sound of pain or distress.

**grocer** *noun* (**grocers**)
someone who keeps a shop that sells food, drink, and other goods for the house.

**grocery** *noun* (**groceries**)
a grocer's shop.
**groceries,** goods sold by a grocer.

**groggy** *adjective* (**groggier, groggiest**)
dizzy, especially because you are ill.

**groin** *noun* (**groins**)
the place where your thighs join your body; your genitals.

**groom**[1] *noun* (**grooms**)
1 someone whose job is to look after horses. 2 a bridegroom.

**groom**[2] *verb* (**grooms, grooming, groomed**)
1 to clean and brush a horse or other animal. 2 to make neat and trim, *a well-groomed beard.*

**gruff**

**groove** *noun* (**grooves**)
a long narrow cut in the surface of
something, *Records have grooves in them.*

**grope** *verb* (**gropes, groping, groped**)
to feel about for something you cannot see.

**gross**[1] *adjective* (**grosser, grossest**)
**1** fat and ugly. **2** with bad manners; vulgar.
**3** very bad or shocking, *gross stupidity.*
**4** total; without anything deducted, *gross
income.*
**Gross Domestic Product,** the value of all the
goods produced and services provided in a
country in one year.
**grossly** *adverb*, **grossness** *noun*

**gross**[2] *noun* (**gross**)
144; twelve dozen of something.

**grotesque** *adjective*
(*say* groh-**tesk**)
very strange; ridiculous.
**grotesquely** *adverb*

**grotty** *adjective* (**grottier, grottiest**)
(*informal*) unpleasant, dirty, or useless.

**ground**[1] *noun* (**grounds**)
**1** the surface of the earth. **2** a sports field.
**grounds,** reasons, *Have you any grounds for
suspicion?*
**the grounds,** the gardens of a large house.

**ground**[2] past tense and past participle of
**grind.**

**grounded** *adjective*
**1** prevented from flying, *The aircraft were
grounded because of fog.* **2** (*informal*) kept
indoors by your parents, usually for
misbehaving.

**ground floor** *noun* (**ground floors**)
(in America, *first floor*) in a building, the
floor that is level with the ground.

**groundsheet** *noun* (**groundsheets**)
a piece of waterproof material for
spreading on the ground; the floor of a tent.

**groundsman** *noun* (**groundsmen**)
someone whose job is to look after a sports
ground.

**group**[1] *noun* (**groups**)
a number of people, animals, or things that
belong together in some way.

**group**[2] *verb* (**groups, grouping, grouped**)
to make a group; to collect people, animals,
or things together.

**grouse**[1] *verb* (**grouses, grousing, groused**)
to complain.
**grouser** *noun*

**grouse**[2] *noun* (**grouse**)
a large bird with feathered feet.

**grove** *noun* (**groves**)
a group of trees; a small wood.

**grovel** *verb* (**grovels, grovelling, grovelled**)
to act as though you were very
unimportant to try to please someone
important, or to try to prevent him or her
from being annoyed with you; to apologize
a lot.

**grow** *verb* (**grows, growing, grew, grown**)
**1** to become bigger, *He has grown a lot.* **2** to
develop, *The seeds are growing.* **3** to plant
something in the ground and look after it,
*She grows lovely roses.* **4** to become, *He
grew rich.*
**grow on,** to become more attractive or more
natural to someone, *This music grows on
you.*
**grow out of,** to get too big or too old for
something.
**grow up,** to develop; to become an adult,
*The legend grew up over the centuries. They
want to be actors when they grow up.*
**grower** *noun*

**growl**[1] *noun* (**growls**)
a deep, rough sound.

**growl**[2] *verb* (**growls, growling, growled**)
to make a deep, rough sound, *Angry dogs
growl.*

**grown-up** *noun* (**grown-ups**)
an adult.

**growth** *noun* (**growths**)
**1** growing; development. **2** something that
has grown.

**grub** *noun* (**grubs**)
**1** a tiny creature that will become an
insect. **2** (*slang*) food.

**grubby** *adjective* (**grubbier, grubbiest**)
rather dirty.

**grudge**[1] *noun* (**grudges**)
a dislike of someone because you think he
or she has harmed you, or because you are
jealous.

**grudge**[2] *verb* (**grudges, grudging, grudged**)
to resent letting someone have something.
**grudgingly** *adverb*

**gruelling** *adjective*
exhausting, *a gruelling race.*

**gruesome** *adjective*
horrible, *The dead soldiers were a
gruesome sight.*

**gruff** *adjective* (**gruffer, gruffest**)
with a rough, unfriendly voice or manner.
**gruffly** *adverb*

**grumble** *verb* (**grumbles, grumbling, grumbled**)
1 to complain continually or with a bad temper. 2 to make a deep, heavy sound, *We could hear thunder grumbling in the distance.*
**grumbler** *noun*

**grumpy** *adjective* (**grumpier, grumpiest**)
bad-tempered.
**grumpily** *adverb*, **grumpiness** *noun*

**grunt**[1] *verb* (**grunts, grunting, grunted**)
to make the sound a pig makes.

**grunt**[2] *noun* (**grunts**)
the sound a pig makes.

**guarantee**[1] *noun* (**guarantees**)
a promise to do something, especially to repair something if it goes wrong.

**guarantee**[2] *verb* (**guarantees, guaranteeing, guaranteed**)
to promise to do something, especially to repair something if it goes wrong.

**guard**[1] *verb* (**guards, guarding, guarded**)
1 to protect something or someone. 2 to prevent someone from escaping.
**guard against,** to be careful to prevent something.

**guard**[2] *noun* (**guards**)
1 protecting; preventing someone from escaping. 2 someone who protects a person or place. 3 a group of soldiers or policemen protecting something or someone, or preventing someone from escaping. 4 the person in charge of a railway train. 5 a protecting device.
**on guard,** protecting; preventing someone from escaping.

**guardian** *noun* (**guardians**)
1 someone who protects something.
2 someone who is legally in charge of a child whose parents cannot look after him or her.
**guardianship** *noun*

**guerrilla** *noun* (**guerrillas**)
(*say* gĕ-**ril**-ă)
someone who fights by means of ambushes and surprise attacks.

USAGE: Do not confuse **guerrilla** with **gorilla**, which is a kind of ape.

**guess**[1] *noun* (**guesses**)
an opinion or answer that you give about something you are not sure of.
**guesswork** *noun*

**guess**[2] *verb* (**guesses, guessing, guessed**)
to give an opinion or an answer about something you are not sure of.

**guest** *noun* (**guests**)
(*say* gest)
1 a person who is invited to visit or stay at someone's house. 2 someone staying at a hotel. 3 someone taking part in a show which he or she does not usually appear in.
**guest house,** a kind of small hotel.

**guide**[1] *noun* (**guides**)
1 someone who shows people the way, helps them, or points out interesting sights. 2 a book that tells you about a place.
**Guide,** a member of the Girl Guides Association, an organization for girls.
**guide dog,** a dog specially trained to show a blind person the way.

**guide**[2] *verb* (**guides, guiding, guided**)
to show someone the way, to help someone, or to show someone interesting sights.
**guided missile,** a kind of rocket that is controlled while it is in flight.

**guideline** *noun* (**guidelines**)
a suggestion for how something should be done, especially advice given by an official person or organization.

**guild** *noun* (**guilds**)
(*say* gild)
a society of people, especially in the Middle Ages, with similar skills or interests.

USAGE: Do not confuse **guild** with **gild**, which is a verb meaning to cover something with a thin layer of gold paint or gold.

**guillotine** *noun* (**guillotines**)
(*say* **gil**-ŏ-teen)
1 a device used in France in the past for cutting off people's heads. 2 a device with a sharp blade for cutting paper.

**guilt** *noun*
1 the fact that you have done something wrong. 2 a feeling that you have done something wrong.
**guilty** *adjective*

**guinea** *noun* (**guineas**)
21 shillings or £1.05.

**guinea-pig** *noun* (**guinea-pigs**)
1 a small furry animal without a tail, *Guinea-pigs are often kept as pets.* 2 a person who is used in an experiment, *In testing the drug, they used him as a guinea-pig.*

**guitar** *noun* (**guitars**)
a musical instrument with strings that you pluck.
**guitarist** *noun*

**Gujarati** *noun* (**Gujaratis**)
1 a person from Gujarat in western India. 2 a language spoken mainly in Gujarat.

**gulf** *noun* (**gulfs**)
1 a large bay, *the Gulf of Mexico.* 2 a great difference, *A vast gulf lies between their points of view.*

**gull** *noun* (**gulls**)
a seagull.

**gullet** *noun* (**gullets**)
the tube from the throat to the stomach.

**gullible** *adjective*
easily deceived.

**gully** *noun* (**gullies**)
a narrow channel that carries water.

**gulp** *verb* (**gulps, gulping, gulped**)
1 to swallow something quickly or greedily. 2 to make a loud swallowing noise; to gasp.

**gum**[1] *noun* (**gums**)
the fleshy part of the mouth that holds the teeth.

**gum**[2] *noun* (**gums**)
1 a sticky substance used as glue. 2 chewing-gum.
**gummy** *adjective*

**gum**[3] *verb* (**gums, gumming, gummed**)
to cover or stick something with gum.

**gum-tree** *noun* (**gum-trees**)
a eucalyptus tree.
**up a gum-tree,** (*slang*) in great difficulties.

**gun** *noun* (**guns**)
1 a weapon that fires shells or bullets from a metal tube. 2 a pistol fired to signal the start of a race. 3 a device that forces a substance out of a tube, *a grease-gun.*
**gunfire** *noun*, **gunshot** *noun*

**gunboat** *noun* (**gunboats**)
a small warship.

**gunman** *noun* (**gunmen**)
a man armed with a gun.

**gunner** *noun* (**gunners**)
someone who works with guns, especially in the army.
**gunnery** *noun*

**gunpowder** *noun*
a type of explosive.

**gurdwara** *noun* (**gurdwaras**)
a building where Sikhs worship.

**gurgle** *verb* (**gurgles, gurgling, gurgled**)
to make a bubbling sound, *The water gurgled as it flowed out of the bath.*

**guru** *noun* (**gurus**)
a Hindu religious teacher.

**Guru Granth Sahib** *noun*
the holy book of the Sikh religion.

**gush** *verb* (**gushes, gushing, gushed**)
1 to flow quickly. 2 to talk too enthusiastically or emotionally.

**gust** *noun* (**gusts**)
a sudden rush of wind, rain, smoke, etc.
**gusty** *adjective*

**gut** *verb* (**guts, gutting, gutted**)
1 to remove the insides from a dead fish or other animal. 2 to remove or destroy the inside of something, *The factory was gutted by fire.*

**guts** *plural noun*
1 the digestive system; the insides of a person or thing. 2 (*informal*) courage.

**gutter** *noun* (**gutters**)
a long, narrow channel at the side of a street or along the edge of a roof, to carry away rainwater.

**guy**[1] *noun* (**guys**)
1 a figure in the form of Guy Fawkes, burnt on or near 5 November in memory of the Gunpowder Plot. **2** (*informal*) a man.

**guy**[2] or **guy-rope** *noun* (**guys** or **guy-ropes**)
a rope used to hold something in place, *Slacken the guy-ropes of your tent at night.*

**guzzle** *verb* (**guzzles, guzzling, guzzled**)
to eat or drink greedily.
**guzzler** *noun*

**gym** *noun* (**gyms**)
(*say* jim)
(*informal*) **1** a gymnasium. **2** gymnastics.

**gymkhana** *noun* (**gymkhanas**)
(*say* jim-**kah**-nă)
a series of horse-riding contests.

**gymnasium** *noun* (**gymnasiums**)
a place designed for gymnastics.

**gymnastics** *plural noun*
exercises and movements that demonstrate strength, skill, and agility.
**gymnast** *noun*

**gypsy** *noun* (**gypsies**)
one of a community of people, also called travellers, who live in caravans or similar vehicles and often travel from place to place.
**Gypsy**, one of a race of people with dark skin and dark hair who usually live in caravans and often travel from place to place.

**gyroscope** *noun* (**gyroscopes**)
a device that keeps steady because of a heavy wheel spinning inside it.
**gyroscopic** *adjective*

# Hh

**ha** short for **hectare** or **hectares**.

**habit** *noun* (**habits**)
something that you do without thinking, because you have done it so often.
**habitual** *adjective*, **habitually** *adverb*

**habitat** *noun* (**habitats**)
where an animal or plant lives naturally.

**hack** *verb* (**hacks, hacking, hacked**)
to chop or cut roughly.

**hacker** *noun* (**hackers**)
someone who uses a computer to get access to a company's or government's computer system without permission.

**hacksaw** *noun* (**hacksaws**)
a saw for cutting metal.

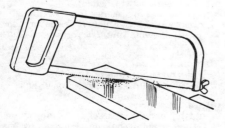

**had** past tense and past participle of **have**.

**haddock** *noun* (**haddock**)
a sea-fish that can be eaten.

**hadn't** short for *had not*.

**hag** *noun* (**hags**)
an ugly old woman.

**haggard** *adjective*
looking ill or very tired.

**haggis** *noun* (**haggises**)
a Scottish food made from parts of a sheep.

**haggle** *verb* (**haggles, haggling, haggled**)
to argue about a price or agreement.

**haiku** *noun* (**haiku**)
(*say* **hy**-koo)
a short poem, usually with three lines.

**hail**[1] *noun*
frozen drops of rain.
**hailstone** *noun*, **hailstorm** *noun*

**hail**[2] *verb* (**hails, hailing, hailed**)
(of hail) to fall, *It is hailing.*

**hail**[3] *verb* (**hails, hailing, hailed**)
to call out to someone, *She hailed the captain.*

**hair** *noun* (**hairs**)
1 a soft covering that grows on the heads and bodies of people and animals, *Her hair is black.* 2 one of the threads that makes up this soft covering, *I found a hair in the soup.*
**in your hair,** (*informal*) annoying you.
**keep your hair on!,** (*informal*) do not lose your temper.
**hairbrush** *noun*, **haircut** *noun*

**hairdresser** *noun* (**hairdressers**)
someone whose job is to cut and arrange people's hair in special ways.

**hairpin** *noun* (**hairpins**)
a pin for keeping your hair in place.
**hairpin bend,** a very sharp bend in a road.

**hair-raising** *adjective*
terrifying.

**hairy** *adjective* (**hairier, hairiest**)
1 with a lot of hair, *a hairy man.* 2 (*slang*) hair-raising; difficult, *Near the top the climb got a bit hairy.*

**hake** *noun* (**hake**)
a sea-fish that can be eaten.

**halal** *adjective*
(of food) prepared according to Muslim religious law.

**half**[1] *noun* (**halves**)
one of the two equal parts that something is or can be divided into, *Two halves make a whole.*

**half**[2] *adverb*
partly; not completely, *This meat is only half cooked.*
**not half,** (*slang*) very much, *Was she cross? Not half!*

**half-baked** *adjective*
(*informal*) not properly planned; foolish, *a half-baked idea.*

**half-hearted** *adjective*
not very enthusiastic.
**half-heartedly** *adverb*

**half-life** *noun* (**half-lives**)
the time it takes for radioactivity to fall to half the original amount.

**half-mast** *noun*
**at half-mast,** (of a flag) flying half-way down its flagpole, usually as a sign that someone important has died.

**halfpenny** *noun* (**halfpennies** or **halfpence**)
(*say* **hayp**-ni)
an old British coin that was worth half a penny.

**half-term** *noun* (**half-terms**)
a short holiday in the middle of a term.

**half-time** *noun* (**half-times**)
the time half-way through a game.

**half-way** *adverb* and *adjective*
at a point half the distance or amount between two places or times.

**halibut** *noun* (**halibut**)
a large flat sea-fish that can be eaten.

**hall** *noun* (**halls**)
1 the first room or passage inside the front door of a house. 2 a very large room for meetings, concerts, etc., *the school hall.* 3 a large, important building or house, *the Town Hall.*

**hallo** *interjection*
a word used to greet someone or to attract someone's attention.

**Hallowe'en** *noun*
the night of 31 October, when some people think that magic things happen.

**hallucination** *noun* (**hallucinations**)
thinking that you can see or hear something that is not really there.
**hallucinate** *verb*

**halo** *noun* (**haloes**)
a circle of light, especially shown round the head of a saint in a picture.

**halt**[1] *verb* (**halts, halting, halted**)
to stop.

**halt**[2] *verb* (**halts, halting, halted**)
to walk or speak slowly and uncertainly, *a halting speech.*

**halter** *noun* (**halters**)
a rope or strap put round a horse's head so that it can be controlled.

**halve** *verb* (**halves, halving, halved**)
1 to divide something into halves. 2 to reduce something to half its size, *If the shop had another checkout it would halve the queues.*

**halves** plural of **half** *noun*.

**ham** *noun* (**hams**)
1 meat from a pig's leg. 2 (*slang*) an actor or performer who is not very good. 3 (*informal*) someone who sends and receives radio messages as a hobby.

**hamburger** *noun* (**hamburgers**)
1 a fried flat cake of minced beef. 2 a bread-roll containing this.

**hammer**[1] *noun* (**hammers**)
a heavy tool used for hitting nails, breaking rocks, etc.

**hammer**<sup>2</sup> *verb* (**hammers, hammering, hammered**)
**1** to hit something with a hammer. **2** to knock loudly, *He hammered on the door.* **3** (*informal*) to treat roughly; to defeat.
**hammer out**, to agree on something after a long discussion.

**hammock** *noun* (**hammocks**)
a bed made of a strong net or piece of cloth hung up above the ground or floor.

**hamper**<sup>1</sup> *noun* (**hampers**)
a big basket with a lid, often used to carry food or picnic things.

**hamper**<sup>2</sup> *verb* (**hampers, hampering, hampered**)
to get in the way of someone or something; to make it difficult for someone to do something.

**hamster** *noun* (**hamsters**)
a small animal with brown fur, *Hamsters are often kept as pets.*

**hand**<sup>1</sup> *noun* (**hands**)
**1** the part of your body at the lower end of your arm. **2** a pointer on a clock or dial. **3** a worker. **4** one of a ship's crew, *All hands on deck!* **5** the cards held by one player in a card-game. **6** side or direction, *on the other hand.*
**at first hand**, directly from the person concerned.
**at hand**, near.
**by hand**, using your hand or hands.
**hands down**, winning easily or completely.
**in hand**, in your possession; being dealt with.
**on hand**, available.
**out of hand**, out of control.

**hand**<sup>2</sup> *verb* (**hands, handing, handed**)
to give or pass something to someone.
**hand down**, to pass something on from one generation to another, *a skill that has been handed down from father to son for centuries.*

**handbag** *noun* (**handbags**)
a woman's bag to hold her money and personal items.

**handbook** *noun* (**handbooks**)
a book that gives useful facts about something, *The school handbook began with a map of the school.*

**handcuffs** *plural noun*
a pair of metal rings joined by a chain, used for locking a person's wrists together.

**handful** *noun* (**handfuls**)
**1** what you can carry in one hand. **2** a small number of people or things. **3** (*informal*) a troublesome person, especially a child.

**handicap** *noun* (**handicaps**)
**1** a disadvantage. **2** a condition of someone's body or mind that causes them serious difficulty.

**handicapped** *adjective*
**1** suffering from a disadvantage. **2** suffering from a mental or physical handicap.

**handicraft** *noun* (**handicrafts**)
artistic work done with your hands, *Handicrafts include needlework, woodwork, and pottery.*

**handiwork** *noun*
something done or made by your hands.
**someone's handiwork**, something, especially a bad thing, that someone has done, *This is clearly the same villain's handiwork!*

**handkerchief** *noun* (**handkerchiefs**)
(*say* **hang-ker-cheef**)
a square piece of material for wiping your nose.

**handle**<sup>1</sup> *noun* (**handles**)
the part of a thing by which you can hold or control it.

**handle**<sup>2</sup> *verb* (**handles, handling, handled**)
**1** to touch or feel something with your hands. **2** to manage or deal with something.
**handler** *noun*

**handlebars** *plural noun*
the bar that steers a bicycle, motor cycle, etc., with a handle at each end.

**hand-picked** *adjective*
carefully chosen for a particular purpose, *A hand-picked squad of commandos led the raid.*

**handrail** *noun* (**handrails**)
a rail for holding on to.

**handsome** *adjective* (**handsomer, handsomest**)
**1** attractive; good-looking, *a handsome man.* **2** generous, *a handsome gift.*
**handsomely** *adverb*

**hands-on** *adjective*
involving actual experience of doing something, *a hands-on computer training course.*

**handspan** *noun* (**handspans**)
the distance across from the end of your thumb to the end of your little finger when you stretch out your fingers as wide as you can.

**handstand** *noun* (**handstands**)
balancing on your hands with your feet in the air.

**handwriting** *noun*
writing done by hand.
**handwritten** *adjective*

**handy** *adjective* (**handier, handiest**)
**1** useful. **2** conveniently placed, *His house is handy for the station.*

**handyman** *noun* (**handymen**)
someone who does small jobs or repairs.

**hang** *verb* (**hangs, hanging, hung**)
**1** to fix the top part of something to a hook, nail, etc. **2** to stick wallpaper to a wall. **3** to float in the air. **4** (in this sense, the past tense and past participle are **hanged**) to kill someone by hanging him or her from a rope that tightens around the neck.
**hang about** or **hang around**, to loiter; to wait, *A gang of youths was hanging around outside the club. Let's not hang about – we haven't much time.*
**hanging valley**, a valley that ends in a sudden drop into another valley or into the sea.
**hang on**, to hold tightly; (*informal*) to wait, *Hang on to the rope. Hang on! I'm not ready yet.*
**hang out**, (*slang*) to live in a place.
**hang up**, to end a telephone conversation; to cause someone delay or difficulty, *She hung up before I found out where she was. We were hung up in the traffic for half an hour.*

**hangar** *noun* (**hangars**)
a large shed where aircraft are kept.

USAGE: Do not confuse **hangar** with **hanger**, which is the next word in this dictionary.

**hanger** *noun* (**hangers**)
a device on which you hang things, *a coat-hanger.*

**hang-glider** *noun* (**hang-gliders**)
a device on which a person can glide through the air.
**hang-gliding** *noun*

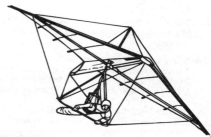

**hangman** *noun* (**hangmen**)
a man whose job is to kill people by hanging them.

**hangover** *noun* (**hangovers**)
an unpleasant feeling after drinking too much alcohol.

**hang-up** *noun* (**hang-ups**)
(*informal*) **1** a difficulty, *We had various hang-ups which made us late.* **2** something that makes you unhappy or frustrated, *He has a hang-up about his squeaky voice.*

**hank** *noun* (**hanks**)
a coil or piece of wool, thread, etc.

**hanky** *noun* (**hankies**)
(*informal*) a handkerchief.

**Hanukkah** *noun*
a Jewish festival held in December.

**haphazard** *adjective*
(*say* hap-**haz**-erd)
accidental; done or chosen at random.
**haphazardly** *adverb*

**happen** *verb* (**happens, happening, happened**)
to take place; to occur.
**happen to do something**, to do something without planning to, *I happened to see what he had written.*

**happening** *noun* (**happenings**)
something that happens; an unusual event, *We've heard of strange happenings at the deserted house.*

**happy** *adjective* (**happier, happiest**)
pleased; glad; contented; enjoying yourself.
**happily** *adverb*, **happiness** *noun*

**happy-go-lucky** *adjective*
having a cheerful attitude to life and not worrying about the future.

**harass** verb (harass, harassing, harassed)
(say ha-răs)
to annoy or trouble someone often.
**harassed** adjective, **harassment** noun

**harbour**[1] noun (harbours)
a place where ships can shelter or unload.

**harbour**[2] verb (harbours, harbouring, harboured)
to give shelter to someone, especially a
criminal, etc.

**hard**[1] adjective (harder, hardest)
1 firm; solid; not soft, hard ground.
2 difficult, hard sums. 3 severe; harsh, a
hard frost. 4 energetic; using great effort,
a hard worker.
**hard and fast**, not able to be changed, There
are no hard and fast rules about when you
should take a break.
**hard hat**, a helmet worn especially by
building workers.
**hard of hearing**, slightly deaf.
**hard shoulder**, a piece of road beside a
motorway where motorists can park in
emergencies.
**hard up**, short of money.
**hard water**, water containing minerals that
prevent soap from making much lather.
**hardness** noun

**hard**[2] adverb (harder, hardest)
1 with great effort, Work hard. 2 with
difficulty, hard-earned money. 3 so as to be
solid, The ground froze hard.

**hardboard** noun
stiff board made of compressed wood-pulp.

**hard-boiled** adjective
1 boiled until it is hard, a hard-boiled egg.
2 harsh; not sympathetic, a hard-boiled
salesman.

**hard disk** noun (hard disks)
a round, flat, rigid piece of magnetic
material, used with computers to store
information and holding more than a
floppy disk.

**harden** verb (hardens, hardening, hardened)
to make something hard; to become hard.
**hardener** noun

**hardly** adverb
only just; only with difficulty, She was
hardly able to walk.

**hardship** noun (hardships)
something that causes suffering or
discomfort.

**hardware** noun
1 metal implements and tools; machinery.
2 the machinery of a computer.

**hard-wearing** adjective
able to stand a lot of wear, Denim is a
hard-wearing cloth.

**hardwood** noun (hardwoods)
hard, heavy wood from deciduous trees,
Oak and mahogany are hardwoods.

**hardy** adjective (hardier, hardiest)
1 strong; able to endure cold or hardships.
2 able to grow outdoors all the year round,
hardy plants.

**hare** noun (hares)
an animal like a large rabbit, Hares can
run very fast.

**hark** verb (harks, harking, harked)
(old-fashioned use) to listen.
**hark back**, to return to an earlier subject.

**harm**[1] verb (harms, harming, harmed)
to hurt someone; to damage something.

**harm**[2] noun
injury; damage.
**harmful** adjective

**harmless** adjective
not dangerous or offensive.
**harmlessly** adverb

**harmonica** noun (harmonicas)
a mouth-organ.

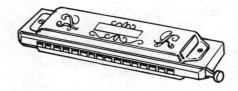

**harmonium** noun (harmoniums)
a small organ with bellows that you work
with your feet.

**harmonize** verb (harmonizes, harmonizing,
harmonized)
to produce harmony.
**harmonization** noun

**harmony** noun (harmonies)
1 a pleasant combination of musical notes.
2 agreement; friendship.
**harmonic** adjective, **harmonious** adjective,
**harmoniously** adverb

**harness**[1] noun (harnesses)
the straps put over a horse's head and
round its neck to control it.

**harness**[2] verb (harnesses, harnessing,
harnessed)
1 to put a harness on a horse. 2 to use
something to produce power, etc., They
harnessed the river to make electricity.

**haughty**

**harp**[1] *noun* (**harps**)
a musical instrument made of strings stretched across a frame and plucked by your fingers.
**harpist** *noun*

**harp**[2] *verb* (**harps, harping, harped**)
to keep on talking about something in a boring way, *He keeps harping on his misfortunes.*

**harpoon** *noun* (**harpoons**)
a spear attached to a rope, fired from a gun to catch whales and other large sea-animals.

**harpsichord** *noun* (**harpsichords**)
a musical instrument like a piano but with the strings plucked and not struck.

**harrow** *noun* (**harrows**)
a heavy device pulled over the ground to break up the soil.

**harsh** *adjective* (**harsher, harshest**)
rough and unpleasant; cruel, *harsh weather. a harsh king.*
**harshly** *adverb*, **harshness** *noun*

**harvest**[1] *noun* (**harvests**)
1 the time when farmers gather in the corn, fruit, or vegetables they have grown. 2 the crop that is gathered in.
**harvest festival**, a celebration of the harvest.

**harvest**[2] *verb* (**harvests, harvesting, harvested**)
to gather in the crops.
**harvester** *noun*

**has** 3rd person singular of **have**.

**hash** *noun* (**hashes**)
1 a mixture of small pieces of meat and vegetables, usually fried. 2 (*informal*) a mess, *You made a hash of that job.*

**hasn't** short for *has not.*

**hassle** *noun* (**hassles**)
(*informal*) a difficulty; a disagreement, *a hassle about who should borrow the car.*

**haste** *noun*
a hurry.

**hasten** *verb* (**hastens, hastening, hastened**)
to hurry; to speed something up, *What can we do to to hasten the work?*

**hasty** *adjective* (**hastier, hastiest**)
hurried; done too quickly.
**hastily** *adverb*, **hastiness** *noun*

**hat** *noun* (**hats**)
a covering for your head.
**hat trick**, getting three goals, wickets, victories, etc. one after the other or in one game.
**under your hat**, secret, *Keep it under your hat.*

**hatch**[1] *noun* (**hatches**)
an opening in a floor, wall, or door, usually with a covering.

**hatch**[2] *verb* (**hatches, hatching, hatched**)
1 to break out of an egg, *These chicks hatched this morning.* 2 to keep an egg warm until a baby bird is born. 3 to plan, *They were hatching a plot.*

**hatchback** *noun* (**hatchbacks**)
a car with a sloping back hinged at the top.

**hatchet** *noun* (**hatchets**)
a small axe.

**hate**[1] *verb* (**hates, hating, hated**)
to dislike very much.

**hate**[2] *noun* (**hates**)
1 a great dislike. 2 (*informal*) someone or something that you dislike very much.

**hateful** *adjective*
hated; very nasty.
**hatefully** *adverb*

**hatred** *noun*
(*say* **hay**-trid)
a great dislike.

**haughty** *adjective* (**haughtier, haughtiest**)
(*say* **haw**-ti)
too proud of yourself; thinking other people are inferior or worthless.
**haughtily** *adverb*, **haughtiness** *noun*

**haul**[1] *verb* (**hauls, hauling, hauled**)
　to pull something, using a lot of power or
　strength.

**haul**[2] *noun* (**hauls**)
　an amount of something that someone has
　gained, *The thieves made a haul worth over
　£20,000. The trawler brought home a large
　haul of fish.*

**haunt** *verb* (**haunts, haunting, haunted**)
　**1** to visit a place often. **2** (of ghosts) to
　appear often in a place or to a person. **3** to
　stay in your mind, *The memory haunts me.*

**have** *verb* (**has, having, had**)
　**1** to own; to possess, *We haven't any money.*
　**2** to contain, *This tin had sweets in it.* **3** to
　enjoy, *We had a good party.* **4** to experience
　or suffer, *She has had an accident.* **5** to be
　forced to do something, *We had to wash up.*
　**6** to get something done, *I'm having my
　watch mended.* **7** to receive; to get, *I had a
　letter from her.* **8** forming the past tenses of
　verbs, *She has gone. I have counted. We
　had eaten them.*
　**have someone on,** (*informal*) to fool someone.

**haven** *noun* (**havens**)
　(*say* **hay**-věn)
　**1** a harbour. **2** a safe place.

**haven't** short for *have not.*

**haversack** *noun* (**haversacks**)
　a bag carried on your back.

**hawk**[1] *noun* (**hawks**)
　**1** a bird of prey with very strong eyesight.
　**2** a warlike person.

**hawk**[2] *verb* (**hawks, hawking, hawked**)
　to go round selling things.
　**hawker** *noun*

**hawthorn** *noun* (**hawthorns**)
　a thorny tree with small red berries.

**hay** *noun*
　dried grass for feeding to animals.
　**hay fever,** irritation of the nose, throat, and
　eyes caused by pollen or dust.

**haymaking** *noun*
　spreading grass to dry after mowing it.

**haystack** *noun* (**haystacks**)
　a large, neat pile of stored hay.

**hazard** *noun* (**hazards**)
　a danger; a risk.
　**hazard warning lights,** a car's indicator lights
　arranged so that they all flash at once to
　show that the car has had to stop in a
　dangerous place.
　**hazardous** *adjective*

**haze** *noun* (**hazes**)
　thin mist.

**hazel** *noun* (**hazels**)
　**1** a type of small nut-tree. **2** a nut from this
　tree. **3** a light brown colour.

**hazy** *adjective* (**hazier, haziest**)
　**1** misty. **2** obscure; uncertain.
　**hazily** *adverb*, **haziness** *noun*

**H-bomb** *noun* (**H-bombs**)
　a hydrogen bomb.

**he**[1] *pronoun*
　the male person or animal being talked
　about.

**he**[2] *noun*
　**1** a male animal, *This cat is a he.*
　**2** (*informal*) a game in which people chase
　one another.

**head**[1] *noun* (**heads**)
　**1** the part of the body containing the
　brains, eyes, and mouth. **2** brains;
　intelligence, *Use your head!* **3** a talent or
　ability, *He has a head for sums.* **4** the side
　of a coin on which someone's head is
　shown. **5** a person, *It costs £3 per head.*
　**6** the top or front of something, *a pinhead.*
　**7** the chief; the person in charge of
　something, *She's the head of this school.* **8** a
　crisis, *Things came to a head.*
　**above your head,** too difficult for you.
　**keep your head,** to stay calm.
　**off the top of your head,** (*informal*) without
　preparation or careful thought, *He simply
　gave an estimate off the top of his head.*
　**over your head,** too difficult for you; without
　asking your opinion, *A-level mathematics is
　over my head. The decision was taken over
　my head.*

**head**[2] *verb* (**heads, heading, headed**)
　**1** to be at the top or front of something. **2** to
　hit a ball with your head. **3** to move in a
　particular direction, *They headed for the
　coast.*
　**head off,** to get in front of someone in order
　to turn them aside.

**headache** *noun* (**headaches**)
　**1** a pain in the head that goes on hurting.
　**2** (*informal*) a problem or difficulty.

**head-dress** *noun* (**head-dresses**)
　a decorative covering for the head.

**header** *noun* (**headers**)
　**1** the act of hitting the ball with your head,
　in football. **2** a dive head-first.

**head-first** *adverb*
　with your head at the front, *I dived in
　head-first.*

**heading** *noun* (**headings**)
　a word or words at the top of a piece of
　printing or writing.

**headland** *noun* (**headlands**)
a piece of high land sticking out into the sea.

**headlight** *noun* (**headlights**)
a strong light at the front of a car, railway engine, etc.

**headline** *noun* (**headlines**)
a heading in a newspaper.
**the headlines**, the main points of the news.

**headlong** *adverb* and *adjective*
1 falling head-first. 2 in a hasty or thoughtless way.

**headmaster** *noun* (**headmasters**)
the man in charge of a school.

**headmistress** *noun* (**headmistresses**)
the woman in charge of a school.

**head-on** *adverb* and *adjective*
with the front parts colliding, *a head-on collision.*

**headphone** *noun* (**headphones**)
a listening device that fits over the top of your head.

**headquarters** *noun* (**headquarters**)
the place from which an organization is controlled.

**headstand** *noun* (**headstands**)
balancing upside down on your head and hands.

**headteacher** *noun* (**headteachers**)
the person in charge of a school.

**headway** *noun*
progress, *They made no headway in their talks.*

**heal** *verb* (**heals, healing, healed**)
1 to make someone healthy; to become healthy. 2 to cure a disease.
**healer** *noun*

**health** *noun*
1 the condition of a person's body or mind, *His health is bad.* 2 being healthy, *in sickness and in health.*
**health food**, food that has been altered little from its natural condition and is thought to be good for your health.

**healthy** *adjective* (**healthier, healthiest**)
1 free from illness; having good health. 2 producing good health, *Fresh air is healthy.*
**healthily** *adverb*, **healthiness** *noun*

**heap**[1] *noun* (**heaps**)
a pile, especially an untidy pile.
**heaps**, (*informal*) a large amount, *We've got heaps of time.*

**heap**[2] *verb* (**heaps, heaping, heaped**)
1 to make into a heap. 2 to put on large amounts, *She heaped his plate with food.*

**hear** *verb* (**hears, hearing, heard**)
1 to take in sounds through the ears. 2 to receive news or information.
**hear! hear!**, I agree (said especially in Parliament).

**hearing** *noun* (**hearings**)
1 the ability to hear. 2 a chance to be heard; a trial in court.
**hearing-aid**, a device to help partially deaf people to hear.

**hearse** *noun* (**hearses**)
a vehicle for taking the coffin to a funeral.

**heart** *noun* (**hearts**)
1 the part of the body that makes the blood circulate. 2 your feelings or emotions; sympathy. 3 courage or enthusiasm. 4 the middle or most important part of something. 5 a curved shape representing a heart; a playing-card with this shape on it.
**break someone's heart**, to make someone very unhappy.
**by heart**, by using your memory.
**heart attack** or **heart failure**, a time when the heart stops working properly.

**hearth** *noun* (**hearths**)
(*say* harth)
the floor of or near a fireplace.

**heartless** *adjective*
cruel.

**hearty** *adjective* (**heartier, heartiest**)
1 strong; vigorous. 2 enthusiastic; sincere, *Hearty congratulations!*
**heartily** *adverb*, **heartiness** *noun*

**heat**[1] *noun* (**heats**)
1 being hot; great warmth. 2 a race or contest to decide who will take part in the final.
**heat wave**, a long period of hot weather.

**heat²** *verb* (**heats, heating, heated**)
to make something hot; to become hot.
**heater** *noun*

**heath** *noun* (**heaths**)
wild, flat land often covered with heather
or bushes.

**heathen** *noun* (**heathens**)
someone who does not believe in one of the
world's chief religions.

**heather** *noun*
a low bush with small purple, pink, or
white flowers.

**heave** *verb* (**heaves, heaving, heaved** or, in the
phrases given below, **hove**)
1 to lift or move something heavy.
2 (*informal*) to throw.
**heave in sight,** to appear.
**heave to,** to stop without anchoring or
mooring, *The ship hove to.*

**heaven** *noun*
1 the place where God and angels are
thought to live. 2 a very pleasant place or
condition.
**good heavens!** or **heavens!,** an exclamation
of surprise.
**the heavens,** the sky.

**heavenly** *adjective*
1 in the sky, *heavenly bodies.* 2 (*informal*)
very nice, *This cake is heavenly.*

**heavy** *adjective* (**heavier, heaviest**)
1 weighing a lot; hard to lift or carry.
2 strong; important; severe, *A heavy
emphasis is placed on practical experience.
The job carries a heavy responsibility.
Heavy rain fell.* 3 hard; difficult, *heavy
work. The book made heavy reading.*
**heavy metal,** (*in Music*) a type of loud rock
music with a strong rhythm.
**with a heavy heart,** unhappily, *I left my home
town with a heavy heart.*
**heavily** *adverb,* **heaviness** *noun*

**heavy-duty** *adjective*
able to stand hard use, *heavy-duty gloves
for gardening.*

**heavyweight** *noun* (**heavyweights**)
1 a heavy person. 2 a boxer or wrestler of
the heaviest weight.

**Hebrew** *noun*
an ancient language with a modern form
that is the official language of Israel.

**hectare** *noun* (**hectares**)
(*say* **hek**-tar)
a unit of area equal to 10,000 square
metres or nearly 2¼ acres.

**hectic** *adjective*
very active or busy, *Monday morning is a
hectic time in the office.*

**he'd** short for *he had, he should,* or *he would.*

**hedge¹** *noun* (**hedges**)
a row of bushes forming a barrier.

**hedge²** *verb* (**hedges, hedging, hedged**)
1 to make or trim a hedge. 2 to surround
something with a hedge. 3 to avoid being
too definite.

**hedgehog** *noun* (**hedgehogs**)
a small animal covered with prickles.

**hedgerow** *noun* (**hedgerows**)
a row of bushes forming a barrier,
especially between fields.

**heed¹** *verb* (**heeds, heeding, heeded**)
to pay attention to something.

**heed²** *noun*
attention given to something.
**heedless** *adjective*

**heel¹** *noun* (**heels**)
1 the back part of your foot. 2 the part of a
sock, shoe, etc. round or under the back
part of your foot.
**take to your heels,** to run away.

**heel²** *verb* (**heels, heeling, heeled**)
1 to mend the heel of a shoe. 2 to kick a ball
with your heel.

**hefty** *adjective* (**heftier, heftiest**)
big and strong.

**heifer** *noun* (**heifers**)
(*say* **hef**-er)
a young cow.

**height** *noun* (**heights**)
1 how high someone or something is. 2 a
high place. 3 the highest or most important
part of something.

**heighten** *verb* (**heightens, heightening,
heightened**)
1 to make something higher; to increase
something. 2 to become higher, *Their
excitement heightened as the kick-off
approached.*

**heir** *noun* (**heirs**)
(*say* air)
someone who inherits something.
**heiress** *noun*

**held** past tense and past participle of **hold** *verb*.

**herb**

**helicopter** *noun* (**helicopters**)
a kind of aircraft without wings, lifted by a large horizontal propeller on top.

**heliport** *noun* (**heliports**)
a place for helicopters to take off and land.

**helium** *noun*
(*say* **hee**-li-ŭm)
a light, colourless gas that does not burn.

**helix** *noun* (**helices**)
a three-dimensional spiral.

**hell** *noun*
**1** a place where people are thought to be punished after they die. **2** a very unpleasant place or condition.
**Hell!**, an exclamation of anger.
**hell for leather**, at great speed.
**hellish** *adjective*

**he'll** short for *he will*.

**hello** *interjection*
a word used to greet someone or to attract someone's attention.

**helm** *noun* (**helms**)
the handle or wheel used to steer a ship.
**helmsman** *noun*

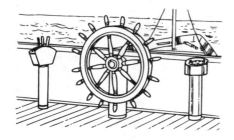

**helmet** *noun* (**helmets**)
a strong covering to protect your head.

**help**[1] *verb* (**helps, helping, helped**)
**1** to do something useful for someone. **2** to avoid doing something, *I can't help coughing*. **3** to serve food, etc. to someone.
**helper** *noun*, **helpful** *adjective*, **helpfully** *adverb*

**help**[2] *noun* (**helps**)
**1** doing something useful for someone.
**2** someone who does something, especially housework, for someone.

**helping** *noun* (**helpings**)
a portion of food.

**helpless** *adjective*
not able to do things or look after yourself.
**helplessly** *adverb*, **helplessness** *noun*

**helter-skelter** *noun* (**helter-skelters**)
a spiral slide at a fair.

**hem**[1] *noun* (**hems**)
the edge of a piece of cloth that is folded over and sewn down.

**hem**[2] *verb* (**hems, hemming, hemmed**)
to fold over and sew down the edge of something.
**hem in**, to surround a place; to restrict someone's movements.

**hemisphere** *noun* (**hemispheres**)
**1** half a sphere. **2** half of the globe, *Australia is in the southern hemisphere.*

**hemp** *noun*
a plant that produces coarse fibres from which cloth and ropes are made.

**hen** *noun* (**hens**)
**1** the ordinary female fowl kept on farms, etc. **2** any female bird.

**hence** *adverb*
**1** from this time on. **2** therefore.

**henceforth** *adverb*
from now on; from this time on.

**her**[1] *pronoun*
a word used for *she*, usually when it is the object of a sentence, or when it comes straight after a preposition, *I can see her. He took the books from her.*

**her**[2] *adjective*
of her; belonging to her, *That is her book.*

**herald**[1] *noun* (**heralds**)
**1** someone who used to make announcements or carry messages for a king or queen. **2** a person or thing that shows that something is coming.

**herald**[2] *verb* (**heralds, heralding, heralded**)
to say that someone or something is coming.

**heraldry** *noun*
the study of coats of arms.
**heraldic** *adjective*

**herb** *noun* (**herbs**)
a plant used for flavouring, or for making medicines.
**herbal** *adjective*

**herbivore** *noun* (**herbivores**)
an animal that eats plants.

**herd**[1] *noun* (**herds**)
1 a group of cattle that feed together. 2 a mass of people; a mob.

**herd**[2] *verb* (**herds, herding, herded**)
to gather animals together or move them in a large group.

**here** *adverb*
in or to this place.
**here and there**, in or to various places.

**heredity** *noun*
(*say* hi-red-i-ti)
inheriting characteristics from your parents or ancestors.
**hereditary** *adjective*

**heritage** *noun* (**heritages**)
1 what you have inherited. 2 things passed from one generation to another, *Folk music is part of our cultural heritage.*

**hermit** *noun* (**hermits**)
someone who lives alone and keeps away from everyone else.
**hermitage** *noun*

**hero** *noun* (**heroes**)
1 a man or boy who has done something very brave. 2 the most important man or boy in a story, play, etc.
**heroic** *adjective*, **heroically** *adverb*, **heroism** *noun*

**heroine** *noun* (**heroines**)
1 a woman or girl who has done something very brave. 2 the most important woman or girl in a story, play, etc.

**heron** *noun* (**herons**)
a wading bird with long legs and a long neck.

**herring** *noun* (**herring** or **herrings**)
a sea-fish that can be eaten.

**hers** *pronoun*
of her; belonging to her, *Those books are hers. That house is hers.*

**herself** *pronoun*
her and nobody else, *She hurt herself. She has good reason to feel proud of herself.*
**by herself**, on her own; alone, *She did the work all by herself. She was standing by herself at the bus-stop.*

**he's** short for *he is* and (before a verb in the past tense) *he has.*

**hesitant** *adjective*
hesitating.
**hesitantly** *adverb*

**hesitate** *verb* (**hesitates, hesitating, hesitated**)
to be slow or uncertain in speaking, moving, etc.
**hesitation** *noun*

**hexagon** *noun* (**hexagons**)
a flat shape with six sides.
**hexagonal** *adjective*

**hey** *interjection*
an exclamation used to express surprise or to call someone's attention.

**hi** *interjection*
an exclamation used to greet someone or to call someone's attention.

**hibernate** *verb* (**hibernates, hibernating, hibernated**)
(*say* hy-ber-nayt)
to sleep for a long time during cold weather, *Bats, tortoises, and hedgehogs all hibernate.*
**hibernation** *noun*

**hiccup** *noun* (**hiccups**)
a high gulping sound made when your breath is briefly interrupted.

**hide** *verb* (**hides, hiding,** *past tense* **hidden** or **hid,** *past participle* **hidden**)
1 to get into a place where you cannot be seen, *I hid behind a tree.* 2 to keep someone or something from being seen, *The gold was hidden in a cave.* 3 to keep something secret, *Are you hiding the truth from me?*

**hide-and-seek** *noun*
a game in which one person looks for others who are hiding.

**hideous** *adjective*
very ugly or unpleasant.
**hideously** *adverb*

**hide-out** *noun* (**hide-outs**)
a place where someone hides.

**hiding**[1] *noun*
being hidden, *She went into hiding.*
**hiding-place**, a place where someone or something is hidden.

**hiding**[2] *noun* (**hidings**)
a beating, *Give him a good hiding.*

**hieroglyphics** *plural noun*
(*say* hyr-ŏ-glif-iks)
pictures used especially in ancient Egypt to represent words.

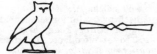

**Hindi**

**hi-fi** *noun* (**hi-fis**)
(*say* hy-fy)
(*informal*) **1** high fidelity. **2** equipment that
gives high fidelity.

**higgledy-piggledy** *adverb* and *adjective*
in disorder; completely mixed up.

**high** *adjective* (**higher, highest**)
**1** reaching a long way up, *a high building*.
**2** far above the ground or above sea-level,
*high clouds*. **3** measuring from top to
bottom, *two metres high*. **4** very important;
chief, *the high road*. **5** very large; greater
than normal, *high prices*. **6** lively; happy, *in
high spirits*. **7** made by a sound wave that
oscillates rapidly; at the top end of a
musical scale, *a high note*. **8** going bad,
*This meat is high*.
**high jump,** an athletic contest of jumping
over a horizontal bar.
**high technology,** modern, advanced
machines and knowledge such as
electronics, robots, and computers.
**high time,** when you should do something at
once, *It's high time you started work*.

**higher education** *noun*
education at a university or college.

**high explosive** *noun* (**high explosives**)
a very strong explosive.

**high fidelity** *noun*
reproducing sound with very little
distortion.

**highland** *adjective*
of or in the highlands.

**highlands** *plural noun*
mountainous country, especially in
Scotland.
**highlander** *noun*

**highlight** *noun* (**highlights**)
the most interesting part of something.

**highlighter** *noun* (**highlighters**)
a pen with bright, coloured ink that you
spread over words on paper to draw
attention to them.

**highly** *adverb*
**1** extremely, *highly amusing*. **2** favourably,
*He thinks highly of her*.

**highly-strung** *adjective*
very sensitive or nervous.

**Highness** *noun* (**Highnesses**)
a title for a prince or princess, *His Royal
Highness, the Prince of Wales*.

**high-pitched** *adjective*
high in sound.

**high-rise** *adjective*
with many storeys, *high-rise office blocks*.

**high school** *noun* (**high schools**)
a secondary school.

**high tea** *noun* (**high teas**)
a meal in the early evening.

**highway** *noun* (**highways**)
an important road or route.
**Highway Code,** a set of rules for people using
roads.

**highwayman** *noun* (**highwaymen**)
a man who robbed travellers on highways
in the past.

**hijack** *verb* (**hijacks, hijacking, hijacked**)
to seize control of an aircraft or vehicle
during a journey.
**hijacker** *noun*

**hike**¹ *noun* (**hikes**)
a long walk in the country.

**hike**² *verb* (**hikes, hiking, hiked**)
to go for a long walk in the country.
**hiker** *noun*

**hilarious** *adjective*
very funny or merry.
**hilariously** *adverb*, **hilarity** *noun*

**hill** *noun* (**hills**)
a piece of ground that is higher than the
ground around it.
**hillside** *noun*, **hilly** *adjective*

**hilt** *noun* (**hilts**)
the handle of a sword or dagger.
**to the hilt,** completely.

**him** *pronoun*
a word used for *he*, usually when it is the
object of a sentence, or when it comes
straight after a preposition, *I like him. I
gave it to him*.

**himself** *pronoun*
him and nobody else, *He hurt himself. He
ought to be ashamed of himself*.
**by himself,** on his own; alone, *He did the
work all by himself. He was sitting by
himself*.

**hind**¹ *adjective*
(*say* hynd)
at the back, *the hind legs of a donkey*.

**hind**² *noun* (**hinds**)
(*say* hynd)
a female deer.

**hinder** *verb* (**hinders, hindering, hindered**)
(*say* hin-der)
to get in someone's way; to make it difficult
for a person to do something.
**hindrance** *noun*

**Hindi** *noun*
a language spoken in northern India.

**Hindu** *noun* (**Hindus**)
someone who believes in **Hinduism**, one of
the religions of India.

**hinge**¹ *noun* (**hinges**)
a joining device on which a door, gate, or
lid swings when it opens.

**hinge**² *verb* (**hinged, hinging, hinged**)
to fix a door etc. on a hinge; (of a door etc.)
to be attached by a hinge.
**hinge on something,** to depend on something.

**hint** *noun* (**hints**)
**1** a slight indication or suggestion, *Give me
a hint of what you want.* **2** a useful idea,
*household hints.*

**hip**¹ *noun* (**hips**)
the bony part at the side of the body
between the waist and the thigh.

**hip**² *noun* (**hips**)
the fruit of the wild rose.

**hip**³ *interjection*
a word that you say when you give a cheer,
*Hip, hip, hooray!*

**hippo** *noun* (**hippos**)
(*informal*) a hippopotamus.

**hippopotamus** *noun* (**hippopotamuses**)
a very large African animal that lives near
water.

**hire** *verb* (**hires, hiring, hired**)
to pay to get the use of something.

**hire-purchase** *noun*
buying something by paying in instalments.

**his** *adjective*
of him; belonging to him.

**hiss** *verb* (**hisses, hissing, hissed**)
to make a sound like an *s*, *The snakes were
hissing.*

**histogram** *noun* (**histograms**)
a type of bar chart showing amounts as
bars of varying height and width.

**historian** *noun* (**historians**)
someone who writes or studies history.

**historic** *adjective*
famous or important in history.

**history** *noun* (**histories**)
**1** what happened in the past. **2** studying
what happened in the past. **3** a description
of important events.
**historical** *adjective*, **historically** *adverb*

**hit**¹ *verb* (**hits, hitting, hit**)
**1** to come against someone or something
with force; to knock or strike. **2** to have a
bad effect on someone or something,
*Famine hit the poor countries.* **3** to reach, *I
can't hit that high note.*
**hit it off with someone,** to become friendly
with someone the first time you meet him
or her.
**hit on something,** to think of an idea, an
answer, etc. suddenly.

**hit**² *noun* (**hits**)
**1** a knock or stroke. **2** a shot that hits the
target. **3** a success, especially a successful
song or record.

**hitch**¹ *verb* (**hitches, hitching, hitched**)
**1** to fasten with a loop, hook, etc.
**2** (*informal*) to hitch-hike.
**hitch up,** to pull something up quickly or
with a jerk, *He hitched up his trousers.*

**hitch**² *noun* (**hitches**)
**1** the movement that you make when you
hitch something up. **2** a knot. **3** a slight
difficulty or delay.

**hitch-hike** *verb* (**hitch-hikes, hitch-hiking,
hitch-hiked**)
to travel by getting lifts in other people's
vehicles.
**hitch-hiker** *noun*

**hi-tech** *adjective*
(*informal*) using high technology, such as
electronic devices, computers, and other
modern machines or knowledge, *a new
hi-tech computer system for the school office.*

**hither** *adverb*
(*old-fashioned use*) to or towards this place.
**hither and thither,** in various directions.

**hitherto** *adverb*
up to now.

**HIV** short for *human immunodeficiency virus,*
a virus that weakens a person's resistance
to disease.

**hive** *noun* (**hives**)
**1** a beehive. **2** a very busy place, *The office
was a hive of activity.*

**HMS** short for *His* or *Her Majesty's Ship.*

**ho** *interjection*
an exclamation of triumph, surprise, etc.

**hoard¹** *noun* (**hoards**)
a secret store of money, treasure, food, etc.

USAGE: Do not confuse **hoard** with **horde**, which means a large crowd, a gang, or an army.

**hoard²** *verb* (**hoards, hoarding, hoarded**)
to store things away, especially more things than you need.
**hoarder** *noun*

**hoarding** *noun* (**hoardings**)
a tall fence covered with advertisements.

**hoar-frost** *noun*
white frost.

**hoarse** *adjective* (**hoarser, hoarsest**)
with a rough or croaking voice, *He was hoarse from shouting.*
**hoarsely** *adverb*, **hoarseness** *noun*

**hoax** *noun* (**hoaxes**)
a trick played on someone.
**hoax** *verb*

**hobble** *verb* (**hobbles, hobbling, hobbled**)
to walk with difficulty; to limp.

**hobby** *noun* (**hobbies**)
something that you do for pleasure in your spare time, *Gardening and stamp-collecting are popular hobbies.*

**hockey** *noun*
an outdoor game played by two teams with curved sticks and a small hard ball.

**hoe¹** *noun* (**hoes**)
a tool for scraping up weeds.

**hoe²** *verb* (**hoes, hoeing, hoed**)
to scrape or dig with a hoe.

**hog¹** *noun* (**hogs**)
1 a male pig. 2 a greedy person.
**go the whole hog**, (*informal*) to do something completely or thoroughly.

**hog²** *verb* (**hogs, hogging, hogged**)
to take more than your fair share of something.

**Hogmanay** *noun*
New Year's Eve in Scotland.

**hoist** *verb* (**hoists, hoisting, hoisted**)
to lift something up, especially using ropes or pulleys.

**hold¹** *verb* (**holds, holding, held**)
1 to have something in your hands. 2 to have; to possess or keep, *She holds the high-jump record.* 3 to keep steady; to stop someone or something moving, *They held the thief until help arrived.* 4 to contain, *This jug holds a litre.* 5 to support, *This plank won't hold my weight.* 6 to stay unbroken; to continue, *Will this good weather hold?* 7 to believe; to value, *She holds strong opinions on animal rights.* 8 to stop, *Hold everything!*
**hold it**, (*informal*) stop; wait a minute.
**hold on**, to keep holding something; (*informal*) to wait, *Hold on as tightly as you can. Hold on! I'm not ready yet.*
**hold out**, to last or continue.
**hold up**, to hinder something or someone; to rob someone with threats or force, *Roadworks in the town centre are holding up the traffic. He was held up by a man with a knife.*

**hold²** *noun* (**holds**)
1 holding something; a way of holding something. 2 something to hold on to. 3 the part of a ship where cargo is stored.
**get hold of**, to grasp; to get; to make contact with someone, *Get hold of the handle. We couldn't get hold of any pineapples. I've phoned several times, but can't get hold of her.*

**holdall** *noun* (**holdalls**)
a large portable bag or case.

**holder** *noun* (**holders**)
a person or thing that holds something, *the holder of this job. A cigarette-holder.*

**hold-up** *noun* (**hold-ups**)
1 a delay. 2 a robbery with threats or force.

**hole** *noun* (**holes**)
1 a gap or opening made in something. 2 a burrow.
**holey** *adjective*

**Holi** *noun*
a Hindu festival held towards the end of February.

**holiday** *noun* (**holidays**)
a day or time when you do not go to work or school; a time when you go away to enjoy yourself.
**on holiday**, having a holiday.

**holidaymaker** *noun* (**holidaymakers**)
someone who is on holiday.

**hollow¹** *adjective* (**hollower, hollowest**)
with an empty space inside; not solid.

**hollow²** *verb* (**hollows, hollowing, hollowed**)
to make something hollow.

**hollow³** *noun* (**hollows**)
1 a hollow place; a hole. 2 a small valley.

**holly** *noun* (**hollies**)
an evergreen bush with shiny, prickly
leaves, *Holly often has red berries in winter.*

**holocaust** *noun* (**holocausts**)
(*say* hol-ŏ-kawst)
an immense destruction, especially by fire,
*the threat of a nuclear holocaust.*
**the Holocaust,** the murder of Jews and
others by the Nazis from the 1930s until
1945.

**hologram** *noun* (**holograms**)
an image like a photograph made by laser
beams, that appears to have depth as well
as height and width.

**holster** *noun* (**holsters**)
a leather case for a pistol, usually attached
to a belt.

**holy** *adjective* (**holier, holiest**)
1 treated with religious respect; of God,
*holy scripture.* 2 devoted to God or a
religion, *a sisterhood of holy women.*
**holiness** *noun*

**home¹** *noun* (**homes**)
1 the place where you live. 2 the place
where you were born or where you feel you
belong. 3 a place where people are looked
after, *a home for the elderly.* 4 the place
that you try to reach in a game, *The far
end of the gym is home.*
**feel at home,** to feel comfortable and happy.
**home economics,** studying how to run a
house and look after a family.
**homeless** *adjective*

**home²** *adverb*
1 to or at the place where you live, *Go
home! Is she home yet?* 2 to the place aimed
at or intended, *Push the bolt home. Try to
get the message home that smoking isn't
good for him.*
**bring something home to someone,** to make
someone realize something.

**homely** *adjective* (**homelier, homeliest**)
simple; ordinary, *a homely meal.*
**homeliness** *noun*

**home-made** *adjective*
made at home; not bought from a shop.

**homesick** *adjective*
sad because you are away from home.
**homesickness** *noun*

**homestead** *noun* (**homesteads**)
a farmhouse, usually with the land around
it.

**homeward** or **homewards** *adverb*
towards home.

**homework** *noun*
school work that a pupil has to do at home.

**homing** *adjective*
trained to fly home, *a homing pigeon.*

**homosexual** *adjective*
(*say* hoh-mŏ-**seks**-yoo-ăl or
hom-ŏ-**seks**-yoo-ăl)
loving or attracted to people of the same
sex.
**homosexual** *noun*

**honest** *adjective*
1 not stealing, cheating, or telling lies.
2 fair, *honest dealings.* 3 truthful, *an honest
reply.*
**honestly** *adverb*, **honesty** *noun*

**honey** *noun*
a sweet, sticky food made by bees.

**honeycomb** *noun* (**honeycombs**)
a wax structure made by bees to hold their
honey and eggs.

**honeymoon** *noun* (**honeymoons**)
a holiday spent together by a
newly-married couple.

**honeysuckle** *noun*
a climbing plant with sweet-smelling
yellow or pink flowers.

**honk** *noun* (**honks**)
a loud sound like the one made by a
car-horn or a wild goose.

**honour¹** *noun* (**honours**)
1 great respect for someone. 2 something
given to a deserving person. 3 good
reputation, *a person of honour.* 4 a person
or thing that brings approval and respect,
*She is an honour to the police force.*

**honour²** *verb* (**honours, honouring, honoured**)
1 to feel or show honour for someone. 2 to
accept and pay a cheque, bill, etc.

**honourable** *adjective*
honest or loyal.
**honourably** *adverb*

**hood** *noun* (**hoods**)
1 a covering of soft material for your head and neck. 2 a folding roof or cover for a car etc.
**hooded** *adjective*

**-hood** *suffix*
being in a particular state; the time when someone is in a particular state, *He has not yet reached manhood. During her childhood she lived in London.*

**hoof** *noun* (**hoofs**)
the horny part of the foot of horses, cattle, or deer, *You could hear the horses' hoofs.*

**hook**[1] *noun* (**hooks**)
a piece of bent or curved metal for hanging things on or catching hold of something.
**hooked** *adjective*

**hook**[2] *verb* (**hooks, hooking, hooked**)
1 to catch something, especially a fish, with a hook. 2 to fasten with or on a hook.

**hooligan** *noun* (**hooligans**)
a rough, noisy person.

**hoop** *noun* (**hoops**)
a large ring made of metal, wood, etc.

**hoop-la** *noun*
a game, usually played at a fair, in which you try to throw hoops so that they land on objects.

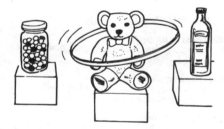

**hooray** *interjection*
a shout of joy or approval; a cheer.

**hoot**[1] *noun* (**hoots**)
1 a sound like the one made by an owl or a train-whistle. 2 a jeer.
**someone doesn't care a hoot** or **two hoots,** (*informal*) someone doesn't care at all.

**hoot**[2] *verb* (**hoots, hooting, hooted**)
to make a sound like an owl or a train-whistle.
**hooter** *noun*

**Hoover** *noun* (**Hoovers**)
(*trademark*) a vacuum cleaner.

**hoover** *verb* (**hoovers, hoovering, hoovered**)
to clean something with a vacuum cleaner.

**hop**[1] *verb* (**hops, hopping, hopped**)
1 to jump on one foot. 2 to move in jumps. 3 (*informal*) to move quickly, *Here's the car; hop in!*
**hop it,** (*slang*) go away.
**hopping mad,** (*informal*) very angry.

**hop**[2] *noun* (**hops**)
a jump made on one foot.

**hop**[3] *noun* (**hops**)
a climbing plant used to give beer its flavour.

**hope**[1] *noun* (**hopes**)
1 the feeling of wanting something to happen, and thinking that it will happen. 2 a person or thing that makes you feel like this, *A change in the weather was their only hope of survival.*

**hope**[2] *verb* (**hopes, hoping, hoped**)
to want something to happen, and to think that it will; to expect something, *I hope that she will get better. Can we hope for better weather?*

**hopeful** *adjective*
1 having hope. 2 likely to be good or successful.
**hopefully** *adverb*

**hopeless** *adjective*
1 without hope. 2 very bad at something, *I'm hopeless at cricket.*
**hopelessly** *adverb,* **hopelessness** *noun*

**hopscotch** *noun*
a game in which you hop into squares drawn on the ground.

**horde** *noun* (**hordes**)
a large crowd; a gang or army.

USAGE: Do not confuse **horde** with **hoard,** which means a secret store of something.

**horizon** *noun* (**horizons**)
(*say* hŏ-**ry**-zŏn)
the line where the sky and the land or sea seem to meet.

**horizontal** *adjective*
(*say* ho-ri-**zon**-tăl)
level; flat; going from left to right or right to left, *a horizontal line.*
**horizontally** *adverb*

**hormone** *noun* (**hormones**)
a substance made in glands in the body, sent directly into the blood, and affecting other organs in the body.

**horn** *noun* (**horns**)
1 a kind of pointed bone that grows on the heads of bulls, cows, rams, etc. 2 a brass musical instrument that you blow. 3 a device for making a warning sound.

**hornet** *noun* (**hornets**)
a large insect of the wasp family.

**horoscope** *noun* (**horoscopes**)
a forecast of future events, made by an astrologer.

**horrible** *adjective*
horrifying; nasty.
**horribly** *adverb*

**horrid** *adjective*
horrible.

**horrific** *adjective*
horrifying.
**horrifically** *adverb*

**horrify** *verb* (**horrifies, horrifying, horrified**)
to cause horror in someone.

**horror** *noun* (**horrors**)
1 great fear, dislike, or shock. 2 a horrifying person or thing.

**horse** *noun* (**horses**)
1 a four-legged animal used for riding, pulling carts, etc. 2 a framework to hang clothes on to dry. 3 a structure to jump over in gymnastics.
**look a gift horse in the mouth,** to complain about a gift or to be ungrateful for it.
**on horseback,** mounted on a horse.

**horse chestnut** *noun* (**horse chestnuts**)
1 a large tree with conical clusters of blossom, producing dark brown nuts. 2 a conker.

**horseman** *noun* (**horsemen**)
a man who rides a horse, especially a skilful rider.
**horsemanship** *noun*

**horsepower** *noun* (**horsepower**)
a unit for measuring the power of an engine, equal to 746 watts.

**horseshoe** *noun* (**horseshoes**)
a U-shaped piece of metal nailed to a horse's hoof to protect it from wear.

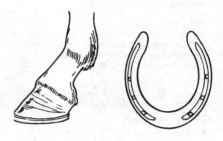

**horsewoman** *noun* (**horsewomen**)
a woman who rides a horse, especially a skilful rider.

**horticulture** *noun*
the art of planning and looking after gardens.

**hose** *noun* (**hoses**)
a long flexible tube through which liquids or gases can travel.

**hospitable** *adjective*
welcoming; liking to give hospitality, *a hospitable inn. They are a hospitable family.*
**hospitably** *adverb*

**hospital** *noun* (**hospitals**)
a place where sick or injured people are looked after.

**hospitality** *noun*
welcoming people and giving them food and entertainment.

**host**[1] *noun* (**hosts**)
someone who has guests and looks after them.
**hostess** *noun*

**host**[2] *noun* (**hosts**)
a large crowd, *a host of people.*

**hostage** *noun* (**hostages**)
someone who is held as a prisoner or is threatened with death until some demand is met.

**hostel** *noun* (**hostels**)
a place where travellers, students, etc. can stay.

**hostile** *adjective*
being an enemy; unfriendly, *a hostile climate.*
**hostility** *noun*

**hot**[1] *adjective* (**hotter, hottest**)
**1** very warm; with a high temperature.
**2** having a burning taste like pepper or
mustard. **3** excited; angry, *a hot temper*.
**hot air**, (*informal*) nonsense; boastful words.
**hot line**, a direct telephone line by which
important people can communicate with
each other, or by which you can get
information quickly.
**hot water**, (*informal*) trouble.
**hotly** *adverb*

**hot**[2] *verb* (**hots, hotting, hotted**)
**hot up**, (*informal*) to become hotter or more
exciting; to make something hotter or more
exciting.

**hot cross bun** *noun* (**hot cross buns**)
a spicy bun with a cross marked on it,
eaten at Easter.

**hot dog** *noun* (**hot dogs**)
a hot sausage in a bread-roll.

**hotel** *noun* (**hotels**)
a building where people pay to have meals
and stay for the night.

**hot-house** *noun* (**hot-houses**)
a heated greenhouse.

**hotpot** *noun* (**hotpots**)
a kind of stew.

**hot-water bottle** *noun* (**hot-water bottles**)
a container that you fill with hot water to
make a bed warm.

**hound**[1] *noun* (**hounds**)
a dog used for hunting or racing.

**hound**[2] *verb* (**hounds, hounding, hounded**)
to chase or harass someone, *The family
was hounded by newspaper reporters*.

**hour** *noun* (**hours**)
**1** one of the twenty-four parts into which a
day is divided. **2** a particular time, *Why are
you up at this hour?*

**hour-glass** *noun* (**hour-glasses**)
an old-fashioned device for telling the time,
with sand running from one glass
container into another.

**hourly** *adjective* and *adverb*
every hour; done once an hour.

**house**[1] *noun* (**houses**)
(*say* howss)
**1** a building where people live, usually
designed for one family. **2** a building used
for a special purpose, *the opera house*. **3** a
building for a government assembly; the
assembly itself, *The Houses of Parliament
consist of the House of Commons and the
House of Lords*. **4** one of the divisions in
some schools for sports competitions, etc.

**house**[2] *verb* (**houses, housing, housed**)
(*say* howz)
to provide a house or room for someone or
something.

**houseboat** *noun* (**houseboats**)
a boat that you can live in.

**household** *noun* (**households**)
all the people who live together in the
same house.

**householder** *noun* (**householders**)
someone who owns or rents a house.

**househusband** *noun* (**househusbands**)
a man who does the housekeeping for his
family.

**housekeeper** *noun* (**housekeepers**)
a person employed to look after a
household.

**housekeeping** *noun*
**1** looking after a household. **2** the money for
a household's food and other supplies.

**house-proud** *adjective*
very careful to keep a house clean and tidy.

**house-trained** *adjective*
trained not to leave faeces and urine in the
house, *This dog is not house-trained*.

**house-warming** *noun* (**house-warmings**)
a party to celebrate moving to a new home.

**housewife** *noun* (**housewives**)
a woman who does the housekeeping for
her family.

**housework** *noun*
the work like cooking and cleaning that
has to be done in a house.

**housing** *noun* (**housings**)
**1** accommodation; houses. **2** a cover or
guard for a piece of machinery.
**housing estate**, a group of houses planned
and built together.

**hove** see **heave**.

**hover** *verb* (**hovers, hovering, hovered**)
**1** to stay in one place in the air. **2** to wait
near someone or something; to loiter.

**hovercraft** *noun* (**hovercraft**)
a vehicle that travels just above the surface of water or land, supported by a strong current of air.

**how** *adverb*
1 in what way, *How did you do it?* 2 to what extent, *How sure are you?* 3 in what condition, *How are you?*
**how about,** would you like?, *How about a game of football?*
**how do you do?,** something said when you meet someone.
**how many,** what total.
**how much,** what amount; what price.
**how's that?,** the way to ask a cricket umpire if a batsman is out.

**however**[1] *adverb*
1 in whatever way; to whatever extent, *You will never catch him, however hard you try.* 2 nevertheless, *It was snowing; however, he went out.*

**however**[2] *conjunction*
in any way, *You can do it however you like.*

**howl**[1] *verb* (**howls, howling, howled**)
to make a long, loud cry like an animal in pain.

**howl**[2] *noun* (**howls**)
a long, loud cry like an animal in pain.

**howler** *noun* (**howlers**)
a silly mistake.

**h.p.** short for **hire-purchase.**

**HQ** short for **headquarters.**

**hub** *noun* (**hubs**)
the centre of a wheel.
**hub-cap,** a cover for the centre of a vehicle's wheel.

**huddle** *verb* (**huddles, huddling, huddled**)
to crowd together with other people for warmth, comfort, etc.

**hue**[1] *noun* (**hues**)
a colour.

**hue**[2] *noun*
**hue and cry,** widespread alarm or protest.

**huff** *noun* (**huffs**)
an annoyed or offended mood, *She's in a huff.*

**hug**[1] *noun* (**hugs**)
clasping someone tightly in your arms, usually lovingly.

**hug**[2] *verb* (**hugs, hugging, hugged**)
1 to clasp someone tightly in your arms. 2 to keep close to something, *The ship hugged the shore.*

**huge** *adjective* (**huger, hugest**)
extremely large.
**hugely** *adverb*

**huh** *interjection*
an exclamation of contempt or questioning.

**hulk** *noun* (**hulks**)
1 an old decaying ship. 2 a large, clumsy person or thing.
**hulking** *adjective*

**hull** *noun* (**hulls**)
the main part or framework of a ship.

**hullabaloo** *noun* (**hullabaloos**)
an uproar.

**hullo** *interjection*
a word used to greet someone or to attract someone's attention.

**hum**[1] *verb* (**hums, humming, hummed**)
1 to sing a tune with your lips closed. 2 to make a low, continuous sound like a bee.

**hum**[2] *noun* (**hums**)
a humming sound.

**human**[1] *noun* (**humans**)
any man, woman, or child.

**human**[2] *adjective*
of humans; that is a human, *a human being.*

**humane** *adjective*
(*say* hew-**mayn**)
kind; merciful.
**humanely** *adverb*

**humanitarian** *adjective*
(*say* hew-man-i-**tair**-i-ăn)
concerned with helping humanity and relieving suffering.

**humanity** *noun* (**humanities**)
1 all the people in the world. 2 being human. 3 being humane; kind-heartedness.
**humanities,** arts subjects such as history and English, not sciences.

**humble** *adjective* (**humbler, humblest**)
modest; not proud.
**humbly** *adverb*

**humid** *adjective*
(*say* **hew**-mid)
damp; moist.
**humidity** *noun*

**humiliate** *verb* (**humiliates, humiliating,
humiliated**)
to lower someone's pride or dignity.
**humiliation** *noun*

**humility** *noun*
being humble.

**humming-bird** *noun* (**humming-birds**)
a small bird that makes a humming sound
with its wings.

**humour**[1] *noun*
1 being amusing; what makes people
laugh. 2 being able to enjoy comical things,
*He has a good sense of humour.* 3 a mood,
*Keep him in a good humour.*
**humorist** *noun*, **humorous** *adjective*

**humour**[2] *verb* (**humours, humouring, humoured**)
to please someone by doing what he or she
wants.

**hump**[1] *noun* (**humps**)
a round lump, especially one on a person's
or camel's back.
**humpback** *noun*, **humpbacked** *adjective*

**hump**[2] *verb* (**humps, humping, humped**)
1 to form a round shape or lump. 2 to carry
something on your back.

**humus** *noun*
(*say* **hew**-mŭs)
rich earth made by decayed plants.

**hunch**[1] *noun* (**hunches**)
1 a feeling that you can guess what will
happen, *I have a hunch that she won't
come.* 2 a hump.

**hunch**[2] *verb* (**hunches, hunching, hunched**)
to bend something into a rounded shape,
*He hunched his shoulders.*

**hunchback** *noun* (**hunchbacks**)
a person with a hump on his or her back.
**hunchbacked** *adjective*

**hundred** *noun* (**hundreds**)
the number 100, ten times ten.
**hundreds and thousands,** tiny coloured
decorations for a cake.
**hundredth** *adjective*

**hundredweight** *noun* (**hundredweights**)
a unit of weight equal to 112 pounds or just
over 50 kilograms.

**hung** past tense and past participle of **hang.**

**Hungarian** *adjective*
of Hungary.

**hunger** *noun*
the feeling that you want to eat; a need for
food.
**hunger strike,** refusing to eat as a way of
making a protest.

**hungry** *adjective* (**hungrier, hungriest**)
feeling hunger.
**hungrily** *adverb*

**hunk** *noun* (**hunks**)
a chunk.

**hunt**[1] *verb* (**hunts, hunting, hunted**)
1 to go after a wild animal because you
want to kill it. 2 to search for something.
**hunter** *noun*, **huntsman** *noun*

**hunt**[2] *noun* (**hunts**)
1 hunting, especially for foxes. 2 a group of
people who go hunting.

**hurdle** *noun* (**hurdles**)
1 a frame that you jump over in hurdling.
2 an obstacle or difficulty.

**hurdling** *noun*
racing in which you run and jump over
obstacles.
**hurdler** *noun*

**hurl** *verb* (**hurls, hurling, hurled**)
to throw something as far as you can.

**hurrah** or **hurray** *interjection*
a shout of joy or approval; a cheer.

**hurricane** *noun* (**hurricanes**)
a very severe storm with a very strong
wind.

**hurry**[1] *verb* (**hurries, hurrying, hurried**)
1 to move quickly; to do something quickly.
2 to try to make someone be quick.
**hurriedly** *adverb*

**hurry**[2] *noun*
moving quickly; doing something quickly.
**in a hurry,** hurrying; impatient, *They were
in a hurry to catch their train. He's always
in a hurry and hates queueing.*

**hurt** *verb* (**hurts, hurting, hurt**)
to cause pain or harm to a person or
animal.

**hurtle** *verb* (**hurtles, hurtling, hurtled**)
to move very quickly, *The train hurtled
along.*

**husband** *noun* (**husbands**)
the man that a woman has married.

**hush** *verb* (**hushes, hushing, hushed**)
to make something or someone silent; to
become silent.
**hush up,** to prevent people knowing about
something.

**hush-hush** *adjective*
(*informal*) very secret, *He's researching into a new kind of fuel – it's all very hush-hush.*

**husk** *noun* (**husks**)
the dry covering of a seed.

**husky**[1] *adjective* (**huskier, huskiest**)
1 hoarse, *She has a husky voice.* 2 big and strong.
**huskily** *adverb*, **huskiness** *noun*

**husky**[2] *noun* (**huskies**)
a breed of dog used by the Inuit, especially to pull sledges.

**hustle** *verb* (**hustles, hustling, hustled**)
1 to hurry. 2 to jostle.

**hut** *noun* (**huts**)
a small house or shelter.

**hutch** *noun* (**hutches**)
a box or cage for a pet rabbit, etc.

**hyacinth** *noun* (**hyacinths**)
a sweet-smelling flower that grows from a bulb.

**hybrid** *noun* (**hybrids**)
an animal or plant that combines two different species, *A mule is a hybrid of a donkey and a mare.*

**hydrangea** *noun* (**hydrangeas**)
(*say* hy-**drayn**-jă)
a shrub with large pink, blue, or white flowers.

**hydrant** *noun* (**hydrants**)
an outdoor water-tap.

**hydraulic** *adjective*
worked by the movement of water or other liquid, *hydraulic brakes.*
**hydraulically** *adverb*

**hydrochloric acid** *noun*
a colourless acid containing hydrogen and chlorine.

**hydroelectric** *adjective*
using water-power to make electricity.

**hydrofoil** *noun* (**hydrofoils**)
a boat designed to skim over the surface of the water.

**hydrogen** *noun*
a very light gas without colour, taste, or smell.
**hydrogen bomb**, a very powerful bomb using energy from the joining of hydrogen nuclei.
**hydrogen peroxide**, a colourless liquid that is used as a bleach.

**hydrological cycle** *noun*
the circulation of water through the air, rivers, and seas, including evaporation and rain.

**hydrosphere** *noun*
all the water on the surface of the earth and in its atmosphere.

**hyena** *noun* (**hyenas**)
(*say* hy-**ee**-nă)
a wild animal that looks like a wolf and makes a shrieking howl.

**hygiene** *noun*
(*say* hy-jeen)
keeping clean and healthy.
**hygienic** *adjective*, **hygienically** *adverb*

**hymn** *noun* (**hymns**)
a religious song, especially one praising God.
**hymn-book** *noun*

**hyperactive** *adjective*
unable to relax and always moving about or doing things.

**hypermarket** *noun* (**hypermarkets**)
a very large supermarket, usually outside a town.

**hyphen** *noun* (**hyphens**)
a short dash used to join words or parts of words together, *There is a hyphen in the word 'hymn-book' but not in 'hydrogen bomb'.*
**hyphenated** *adjective*, **hyphenation** *noun*

**hypnosis** *noun*
(*say* hip-**noh**-sis)
a condition like a deep sleep in which someone's actions may be controlled by someone else.

**hypnotism** *noun*
(*say* **hip**-nŏ-tizm)
producing hypnosis.
**hypnotic** *adjective*, **hypnotist** *noun*, **hypnotize** *verb*

**hypocrite** *noun* (**hypocrites**)
(*say* **hip**-ŏ-krit)
someone who pretends to be a better person than he or she really is.
**hypocrisy** *noun*, **hypocritical** *adjective*

**hypodermic** *adjective*
(*say* hy-pŏ-**der**-mik)
injecting something under the skin, *a hypodermic syringe.*

**hypotenuse** *noun* (**hypotenuses**)
(*say* hy-**pot**-i-newz)
the side opposite the right angle in a
right-angled triangle.

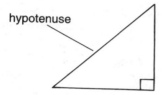

hypotenuse

**hypothermia** *noun*
the condition of having a very low body
temperature, which is harmful.

**hypothesis** *noun* (**hypotheses**)
(*say* hy-**poth**-i-sis)
a suggestion that tries to explain
something; a theory that has not been
tested or proved, *We tested John's
hypothesis to see if it was correct.*
**hypothetical** *adjective*

**hypothesize** *verb* (**hypothesizes, hypothesizing,
hypothesized**)
to put forward a hypothesis; to accept
something temporarily and use it as a
hypothesis.

**hysteria** *noun*
wild, uncontrollable excitement or emotion.
**hysterical** *adjective*, **hysterically** *adverb*,
**hysterics** *plural noun*

# Ii

**I** *pronoun*
a word used by someone to speak about
himself or herself.

**ice**[1] *noun* (**ices**)
1 frozen water. 2 an ice-cream.
**ice age**, a time in the past when ice covered
large areas of the earth.

**ice**[2] *verb* (**ices, icing, iced**)
1 to make something icy; to become icy. 2 to
put icing on a cake.

**iceberg** *noun* (**icebergs**)
a large mass of ice floating in the sea.

**ice-breaker** *noun* (**ice-breakers**)
a ship with strong bows for breaking
through ice.

**ice-cream** *noun* (**ice-creams**)
1 a sweet, creamy, frozen food. 2 a portion
of this.

**ice-hockey** *noun*
a game like hockey played on ice by skaters.

**ice lolly** *noun* (**ice lollies**)
a piece of flavoured ice or ice-cream on
a small stick.

**icicle** *noun* (**icicles**)
a thin, pointed piece of ice that hangs down.

**icing** *noun*
a sugary substance for decorating cakes.

**icy** *adjective* (**icier, iciest**)
like ice; very cold, *icy weather.*
**icily** *adverb*

**ID** *noun* (**IDs**)
something that proves who you are, such
as a passport, *The security man asked to
see my ID.*

**I'd** short for *I had, I should,* or *I would.*

**idea** *noun* (**ideas**)
something that someone has thought of;
a plan.

**ideal**[1] *adjective*
perfect.
**ideally** *adverb*

**ideal²** *noun* (**ideals**)
something or someone that you think is perfect or worth trying to be like, *Happiness for all people is an ideal that can never be reached.*

**identical** *adjective*
exactly the same.
**identically** *adverb*

**identify** *verb* (**identifies, identifying, identified**)
to discover who someone is or what something is, *The police have identified the car used in the robbery.*
**identify with,** to think that you share another person's feelings, another group's beliefs, etc.
**identification** *noun*

**identikit** *noun* (**identikits**)
a picture of someone built up from descriptions of him or her.

**identity** *noun* (**identities**)
who someone is; the typical features of a place, *He revealed his identity by signing his name. Street cafés are part of the identity of Paris.*

**idiom** *noun* (**idioms**)
(*say* id-i-ŏm)
a phrase that means something different from the meanings of the words in it, *'Jump the gun' and 'on your last legs' are idioms.*
**idiomatic** *adjective*, **idiomatically** *adverb*

**idiot** *noun* (**idiots**)
**1** (*informal*) a very stupid person. **2** a person with very limited intelligence.
**idiocy** *noun*, **idiotic** *adjective*, **idiotically** *adverb*

**idle** *adjective* (**idler, idlest**)
**1** doing nothing; lazy. **2** useless; with no particular purpose, *idle gossip.*
**idly** *adverb*

**idol** *noun* (**idols**)
a person or thing that people worship or treat as if he, she, or it were a god.
**idolatry** *noun*, **idolize** *verb*

**i.e.** short for the Latin *id est*, which means 'that is', *I like racket sports best, i.e. badminton, squash, and tennis. He was a hypocrite, i.e. someone who pretends to be better than he really is.*

**if** *conjunction*
**1** supposing that; on condition that, *I'll tell you what happened if you promise to keep it secret.* **2** although; even though, *I'll finish this job if it kills me!* **3** whenever, *I get a headache if I don't wear my glasses.* **4** whether, *Tell me if you're hungry.*
**if only,** I wish, *If only I were rich!*

**igloo** *noun* (**igloos**)
an Inuit's round house made of blocks of hard snow.

**igneous** *adjective*
(*say* ig-ni-ŭs)
formed by volcanoes, *igneous rocks.*

**ignite** *verb* (**ignites, igniting, ignited**)
to set fire to something; to catch fire.

**ignition** *noun*
**1** igniting. **2** the system that starts the fuel in an engine burning so as to drive a vehicle or machine.

**ignorant** *adjective*
not knowing about something; knowing very little.
**ignorance** *noun*, **ignorantly** *adverb*

**ignore** *verb* (**ignores, ignoring, ignored**)
to take no notice of someone or something.

**ill¹** *adjective*
**1** not well; in bad health. **2** bad; harmful, *There were no ill effects.*

**ill²** *adverb*
badly, *She was ill-treated.*

**I'll** short for *I shall* or *I will.*

**illegal** *adjective*
not legal; against the law.
**illegally** *adverb*

**illegible** *adjective*
(*say* i-lej-i-bŭl)
not clear enough to read.
**illegibly** *adverb*

**illegitimate** *adjective*
(*say* il-i-jit-i-măt)
**1** not lawful. **2** (*old-fashioned use*) born when the parents are not married to each other, *an illegitimate child.*

**illiterate** *adjective*
(*say* i-lit-er-ăt)
unable to read or write.
**illiteracy** *noun*

**illness** *noun* (**illnesses**)
**1** being ill. **2** something that makes people ill.

**illogical** *adjective*
against the rules of orderly thinking; not logical, *It is illogical to accuse her – she was nowhere near the scene of the crime.*
**illogically** *adverb*

**illuminate** *verb* (**illuminates, illuminating, illuminated**)
1 to light something up; to decorate streets, etc. with lights. 2 to make something clear; to explain something.
**illumination** *noun*

**illusion** *noun* (**illusions**)
an imaginary thing; something that you wrongly think you see.

USAGE: Do not confuse **illusion** with **delusion**, which means a false belief or opinion, or a sign of mental illness.

**illustrate** *verb* (**illustrates, illustrating, illustrated**)
1 to show something by pictures, examples, etc. 2 to put pictures in a book.
**illustrative** *adjective*, **illustrator** *noun*

**illustration** *noun* (**illustrations**)
1 a picture in a book. 2 an example that explains something. 3 explaining something by pictures, examples, etc. 4 making pictures for a book.

**illustrious** *adjective*
(*say* i-**lus**-tri-ŭs)
famous.

**I'm** short for *I am*.

**image** *noun* (**images**)
1 a picture or statue of a person or thing. 2 what you see in a mirror, through a lens, etc. 3 a person who looks very much like another. 4 the way that people think of a person or thing.

**imagery** *noun*
the skilful use of words to produce pictures in the mind of the reader.

**imaginary** *adjective*
not real; imagined.

USAGE: Do not confuse **imaginary** with **imaginative**, which means able to imagine things.

**imagination** *noun*
being able to imagine things.

**imaginative** *adjective*
able to imagine things; showing an ability to imagine things, *an imaginative design for a book of ghost stories.*

USAGE: Do not confuse **imaginative** with **imaginary**, which means imagined or not real.

**imagine** *verb* (**imagines, imagining, imagined**)
to make pictures in your mind of things and people that you cannot see.
**imaginable** *adjective*

**imbecile** *noun* (**imbeciles**)
(*say* im-bi-seel)
(*informal*) a very stupid person.

**imitate** *verb* (**imitates, imitating, imitated**)
to copy.
**imitation** *noun*, **imitator** *noun*

**immature** *adjective*
not fully grown or developed.
**immaturity** *noun*

**immediate** *adjective*
1 happening or done without any delay. 2 nearest, *our immediate neighbours.*

**immediately** *adverb*
without any delay; at once.

**immense** *adjective*
huge.
**immensely** *adverb*, **immensity** *noun*

**immerse** *verb* (**immerses, immersing, immersed**)
to put something completely into a liquid.
**be immersed in something**, to be very interested or involved in something.

**immersion** *noun*
immersing something; being immersed.
**immersion heater**, a device that heats water with an electric element immersed in the water.

**immigrant** *noun* (**immigrants**)
someone who has immigrated.

**immigrate** *verb* (**immigrates, immigrating, immigrated**)
to come into a country to live there.
**immigration** *noun*

USAGE: Do not confuse **immigrate** with **emigrate**, which means to go and live in another country.

**immobile** *adjective*
not moving.
**immobility** *noun*

**immobilize** *verb* (**immobilizes, immobilizing, immobilized**)
to stop something moving or working.

**immoral** *adjective*
not following the usual standards of right and wrong.
**immorality** *noun*

**immortal** *adjective*
living for ever; never dying.
**immortality** *noun*

**immune** *adjective*
safe from danger or attack, especially from
disease.
**immunity** *noun*

**immunize** *verb* (**immunizes, immunizing,
immunized**)
to make someone safe, especially from
disease.
**immunization** *noun*

**imp** *noun* (**imps**)
1 a small devil. 2 a naughty child.
**impish** *adjective*

**impact** *noun* (**impacts**)
1 a collision; the force of a collision. 2 a
strong influence or effect.

**impair** *verb* (**impairs, impairing, impaired**)
to harm or weaken, *The wound impaired
his health.*
**impairment** *noun*

**impale** *verb* (**impales, impaling, impaled**)
to fix something on to a sharp object; to
pierce someone or something.

**impartial** *adjective*
not favouring one side more than the other;
fair.
**impartiality** *noun*, **impartially** *adverb*

**impassable** *adjective*
that you cannot get past or through.

**impatient** *adjective*
not patient; in a hurry.
**impatience** *noun*, **impatiently** *adverb*

**imperative** *noun* (**imperatives**)
1 a command. 2 the form of a verb that
expresses a command, *'Go!' and 'stop!' are
imperatives.*

**imperceptible** *adjective*
difficult or impossible to see.
**imperceptibly** *adverb*

**imperfect** *adjective*
not perfect; not complete.
**imperfection** *noun*, **imperfectly** *adverb*

**imperial** *adjective*
of an empire or its rulers.
**Imperial**, of what used to be the British
Empire, *The country was under Imperial
rule until 1948.*
**imperial unit**, one of the official units of
weight or measurement, such as the ounce
or the gallon, used in the United Kingdom
for all goods before the introduction of the
metric system.

**impersonal** *adjective*
1 not affected by personal feelings; showing
no emotion. 2 not referring to a particular
person.
**impersonal verb**, a verb used only with 'it',
as in *It is snowing.*
**impersonally** *adverb*

**impersonate** *verb* (**impersonates,
impersonating, impersonated**)
to pretend to be someone else.
**impersonation** *noun*, **impersonator** *noun*

**impertinent** *adjective*
not respectful; rude.
**impertinence** *noun*

**implement**[1] *noun* (**implements**)
(*say* im-pli-měnt)
a tool; a device for working with.

**implement**[2] *verb* (**implements, implementing,
implemented**)
(*say* im-pli-ment)
to put a plan, idea, etc. into action.

**implore** *verb* (**implores, imploring, implored**)
to beg someone to do something.

**imply** *verb* (**implies, implying, implied**)
to suggest something without actually
saying it, *Asking what time it is implies
that you are in a hurry.*
**implication** *noun*

USAGE: Do not confuse **imply** with **infer**,
which means to guess or to reach an
opinion from something that is suggested
but not actually said.

**impolite** *adjective*
not having good manners; not respectful
and thoughtful towards other people.

**import**[1] *verb* (**imports, importing, imported**)
(*say* im-port)
to bring in goods from another country.
**importer** *noun*

**import**[2] *noun* (**imports**)
(*say* im-port)
something brought in from another
country.

**important** *adjective*
1 worth considering seriously; having a
great effect, *an important decision.*
2 powerful or influential, *an important
politician.*
**importance** *noun*, **importantly** *adverb*

**impose** *verb* (**imposes, imposing, imposed**)
1 to force something on to one or more
people, *The plans to build a motorway were
imposed on the village against everyone's
wishes.* 2 to charge a tax.
**impose on someone**, to take unfair
advantage of someone.

**imposing** *adjective*
looking important; impressive.

**imposition** *noun* (**impositions**)
something that someone is made to suffer, especially as a punishment.

**impossible** *adjective*
1 not possible. 2 (*informal*) very annoying, *He is impossible!*
**impossibility** *noun*, **impossibly** *adverb*

**impostor** *noun* (**impostors**)
someone who is not what he or she pretends to be.

**impracticable** *adjective*
that cannot be done or used, *The idea of digging a tunnel under the river proved impracticable because of its very high cost.*

USAGE: Do not confuse **impracticable** with **impractical**, which is the next word in this dictionary.

**impractical** *adjective*
1 not good at making or doing things, *He is impractical, and can't tackle any household repair jobs.* 2 not likely to work or be useful; not seeing things as they really are, *an impractical invention. Their ideas are impractical.*

**impress** *verb* (**impresses, impressing, impressed**)
to make someone think you are very good at something.
**impress something on someone,** to remind someone strongly about something.

**impression** *noun* (**impressions**)
1 a vague idea. 2 an effect on your mind or feelings. 3 an imitation of a person or a sound.

**impressive** *adjective*
impressing; having a strong effect.
**impressively** *adverb*

**imprison** *verb* (**imprisons, imprisoning, imprisoned**)
to put someone in prison.
**imprisonment** *noun*

**improbable** *adjective*
unlikely.
**improbability** *noun*, **improbably** *adverb*

**impromptu** *adjective and adverb*
(*say* im-**promp**-tew)
done without any rehearsal or preparation.

**improper** *adjective*
1 not proper; wrong. 2 indecent.
**improperly** *adverb*, **impropriety** *noun*

**improve** *verb* (**improves, improving, improved**)
to make something better; to become better.
**improvement** *noun*

**improvise** *verb* (**improvises, improvising, improvised**)
1 to do something without rehearsal or preparation, especially to play music without rehearsing, *Jazz players improvise a lot.* 2 to make something quickly with what is available.
**improvisation** *noun*

**impudent** *adjective*
not respectful; rude.
**impudence** *noun*

**impulse** *noun* (**impulses**)
1 a sudden desire to do something. 2 a push; a driving force. 3 (*in Science*) a force acting for a very short time.
**impulsive** *adjective*, **impulsively** *adverb*

**impure** *adjective* (**impurer, impurest**)
not pure.
**impurity** *noun*

**in**$^1$ *preposition*
1 at; inside, *in London.* 2 during, *in winter.* 3 into, *She has fallen in the water.* 4 arranged as; consisting of, *a serial in four parts.*
**in all,** coming to a total of, *£2 for the oranges, and £1 for the bananas – that makes £3 in all.*

**in**$^2$ *adverb*
1 inwards; inside, *Get in.* 2 at home; indoors, *Is anybody in?* 3 batting, *Which team is in?*
**in for,** likely to get, *You're in for a shock.* **in on,** taking part in something, *I want to be in on this game.*

**in-** *prefix*
not, *inefficient. independent.*

**inability** *noun*
being unable to do something.

**inaccessible** *adjective*
that you cannot reach.

**inaccurate** *adjective*
not accurate.
**inaccuracy** *noun*, **inaccurately** *adverb*

**inactive** *adjective*
not active.
**inaction** *noun*, **inactivity** *noun*

**inadequate** *adjective*
not enough.
**inadequacy** *noun*, **inadequately** *adverb*

**inanimate** *adjective*
(*say* in-an-im-ăt)
not living or moving.

**inappropriate** *adjective*
not appropriate.
**inappropriately** *adverb*

**inattention** *noun*
not being attentive; not listening.
**inattentive** *adjective*

**inaudible** *adjective*
that you cannot hear.
**inaudibility** *noun*, **inaudibly** *adverb*

**incapable** *adjective*
unable to do something, *He is incapable of work*.

**incarnate** *adjective*
having a human body, *He was so cruel he seemed like a devil incarnate*.
**incarnation** *noun*

**incendiary** *adjective*
that starts a fire, *an incendiary bomb*.

**incense**[1] *noun*
(*say* in-senss)
a substance that makes a spicy smell when it is burnt.

**incense**[2] *verb* (**incenses, incensing, incensed**)
(*say* in-senss)
to make someone very angry.

**incentive** *noun* (**incentives**)
an encouragement to do something, especially to work harder.

**incessant** *adjective*
continual; not stopping.
**incessantly** *adverb*

**inch** *noun* (**inches**)
a measure of length, one twelfth of a foot or about $2\frac{1}{2}$ centimetres.
**within an inch of his life,** so that he almost died.

**incident** *noun* (**incidents**)
an event.

**incidental** *adjective*
not important.
**incidental music,** music used to accompany a film, etc.
**incidentally** *adverb*

**incinerator** *noun* (**incinerators**)
a device in which rubbish is burnt.

**inclination** *noun* (**inclinations**)
a tendency, *He had an inclination to eat too many sweets*.

**incline**[1] *verb* (**inclines, inclining, inclined**)
(*say* in-klyn)
to lean or bend.
**be inclined to do something,** to feel like doing something; to tend to do something, *I'm not inclined to help them. He is inclined to be lazy*.

**incline**[2] *noun* (**inclines**)
(*say* in-klyn)
a slope.

**include** *verb* (**includes, including, included**)
to make or consider something as part of a group of other things.
**inclusion** *noun*

**inclusive** *adjective*
including everything; including all the things mentioned, *Stay from Monday to Thursday inclusive*.

**income** *noun* (**incomes**)
the money that you get regularly.
**income tax,** tax charged on the money that you get regularly.

**incompatible** *adjective*
**1** not able to live or exist together without trouble, *an incompatible couple*. **2** (*in Computing*) not able to be used together, *This computer and that printer are incompatible*.

**incompetent** *adjective*
unable to do a job properly.
**incompetence** *noun*, **incompetently** *adverb*

**incomplete** *adjective*
not complete.
**incompletely** *adverb*

**incomprehensible** *adjective*
that you cannot understand.

**incongruous** *adjective*
(*say* in-kong-roo-ŭs)
not suitable; out of place.
**incongruity** *noun*, **incongruously** *adverb*

**inconsiderate** *adjective*
not considerate.
**inconsiderately** *adverb*

**inconsistent** *adjective*
not consistent.
**inconsistency** *noun*, **inconsistently** *adverb*

**inconspicuous** *adjective*
not noticeable or remarkable.
**inconspicuously** *adverb*

**inconvenient** *adjective*
not convenient; awkward.
**inconvenience** *noun*, **inconveniently** *adverb*

**incorporate** *verb* (**incorporates, incorporating, incorporated**)
to include.
**incorporation** *noun*

**incorrect** *adjective*
not correct; wrong.
**incorrectly** *adverb*

**increase**[1] *verb* (**increases, increasing, increased**)
(*say* in-kreess)
to make something bigger; to become bigger.
**increasingly** *adverb*

**increase**[2] *noun* (**increases**)
(*say* in-kreess)
**1** making something bigger; becoming bigger. **2** the amount by which something is made or becomes bigger.

**incredible** *adjective*
unbelievable.
**incredibly** *adverb*

USAGE: Do not confuse **incredible** with **incredulous**, which is the next word in this dictionary.

**incredulous** *adjective*
not believing someone.
**incredulity** *noun*, **incredulously** *adverb*

**incubate** *verb* (**incubates, incubating, incubated**)
to hatch eggs by keeping them warm.
**incubation** *noun*

**incubator** *noun* (**incubators**)
**1** an apparatus for keeping alive very small babies, especially babies born sooner than usual. **2** an apparatus for hatching eggs.

**indebted** *adjective*
owing something to someone.

**indecent** *adjective*
not decent; obscene.
**indecency** *noun*, **indecently** *adverb*

**indeed** *adverb*
really; truly, *He was very wet indeed.*

**indefinite** *adjective*
not definite; vague.
**indefinite article**, the word 'a' or 'an'.

**indefinitely** *adverb*
for an indefinite or unlimited time.

**indelible** *adjective*
impossible to rub out or remove.
**indelibly** *adverb*

**indent** *verb* (**indents, indenting, indented**)
**1** to make notches or recesses in something. **2** to print or write the beginning of a line farther to the right than usual.
**indentation** *noun*

**independent** *adjective*
not controlled or influenced by any other person or thing.
**independence** *noun*, **independently** *adverb*

**index** *noun* (**indexes**)
**1** a list of names, subjects, titles, etc., especially at the end of a book. **2** a number showing how prices or wages have changed.
**index finger**, the finger next to your thumb.
**index notation**, (*in Mathematics*) using a small number after and slightly above a quantity to show that the quantity is to be multiplied by itself as many times as the number shows, *In index notation, $3 \times 3 \times 3 \times 3$ is written $3^4$.*

**Indian**[1] *adjective*
**1** of India. **2** of Native Americans.
**Indian summer**, a warm period in late autumn.

**Indian**[2] *noun* (**Indians**)
**1** an inhabitant or native of India. **2** a Native American.

**indicate** *verb* (**indicates, indicating, indicated**)
**1** to point out or show something. **2** to be a sign of something.
**indication** *noun*

**indicative** *noun* (**indicatives**)
the form of the verb used when you make a statement, *The indicative of 'to go' is 'I go', 'he goes', etc.*

**indicator** *noun* (**indicators**)
**1** something that tells you what is happening. **2** one of the lights on the corners or sides of a vehicle that are used to show which way the driver wants to turn.

**indifferent** *adjective*
**1** not caring about something; not interested. **2** not very good; ordinary, *an indifferent cricketer.*
**indifference** *noun*, **indifferently** *adverb*

**indigestible** *adjective*
not easy to digest.

**indigestion** *noun*
pain caused by difficulty in digesting food.

**indignant** *adjective*
angry at something that seems unfair or wicked.
**indignantly** *adverb*, **indignation** *noun*

**indigo** *noun*
a deep blue colour.

**indirect** *adjective*
not direct.
**indirect question,** a question reported in
indirect speech, *'She asked whether it was
time to go'* is an indirect question; the
question she actually asked was 'Is it time
to go?'
**indirect speech,** someone's words given in an
altered, reported form, instead of being
written down exactly in the way they were
said (**direct speech**), *'He said that he was
sure'* is indirect speech; *'I am sure'* is direct
speech.
**indirectly** *adverb*

**indispensable** *adjective*
essential.

**indistinct** *adjective*
not clear.
**indistinctly** *adverb*

**indistinguishable** *adjective*
1 impossible to tell apart from something
else. 2 impossible to see or hear clearly.

**individual**[1] *adjective*
1 of or for one person. 2 single; separate.
**individually** *adverb*

**individual**[2] *noun* (**individuals**)
one person.

**individuality** *noun*
the things that make one person or thing
different from another.

**indoctrinate** *verb* (**indoctrinates, indoctrinating,
indoctrinated**)
to fill someone's mind with particular ideas
or beliefs.
**indoctrination** *noun*

**indoor** *adjective*
placed or done inside a building, *indoor
sports.*

**indoors** *adverb*
inside a building.

**induce** *verb* (**induces, inducing, induced**)
1 to persuade. 2 to start the birth of a baby
artificially.
**inducement** *noun*

**indulge** *verb* (**indulges, indulging, indulged**)
to let someone have or do what he or she
wants.
**indulge in something,** to have something that
you like to eat, drink, etc.
**indulgence** *noun,* **indulgent** *adjective*

**industrial** *adjective*
of or in industry.
**industrial action,** ways for workers to
protest, such as striking or working to rule.
**Industrial Revolution,** the expansion of
industry using machines in the late 18th
and early 19th century.
**industrialist** *noun,* **industrially** *adverb*

**industrialize** *verb* (**industrializes, industrializing,
industrialized**)
to increase or develop the industry in a
country.
**industrialization** *noun*

**industrious** *adjective*
hard - working.
**industriously** *adverb*

**industry** *noun* (**industries**)
1 making things in factories; making goods
to sell. 2 working hard.
**heavy industry,** making iron, steel, large
machines, and other large or heavy
products.
**light industry,** making small or light
products.

**ineffective** *adjective*
not effective; not efficient.
**ineffectively** *adverb*

**ineffectual** *adjective*
not effective; not confident or convincing.
**ineffectually** *adverb*

**inefficient** *adjective*
not doing work well; wasteful of energy.
**inefficiency** *noun,* **inefficiently** *adverb*

**inequality** *noun* (**inequalities**)
not being equal.

**inert** *adjective*
not moving or reacting.

**inertia** *noun*
(*say* in-er-shă)
1 being inert. 2 (*in Science*) the condition
that makes things keep moving or stay
where they are.

**inevitable** *adjective*
unavoidable.
**inevitability** *noun,* **inevitably** *adverb*

**inexhaustible** *adjective*
that you cannot use up completely;
never-ending.

**inexpensive** *adjective*
not expensive; cheap.
**inexpensively** *adverb*

**inexperience** *noun*
not having experience.
**inexperienced** *adjective*

**inexplicable** *adjective*
impossible to explain.
**inexplicably** *adverb*

**infallible** *adjective*
never wrong; never-failing.
**infallibility** *noun,* **infallibly** *adverb*

**infamous** *adjective*
(*say* in-fă-mŭs)
wicked; thought to be wicked.
**infamy** *noun*

**infant** noun (**infants**)
a baby or young child.
**infancy** noun

**infantile** adjective
1 of or like babies or young children.
2 annoyingly childish.
**infantile paralysis**, poliomyelitis.

**infantry** noun
soldiers trained to fight on foot.
**infantryman** noun

**infect** verb (**infects, infecting, infected**)
to give someone a disease.

**infection** noun (**infections**)
1 infecting. 2 an infectious disease.

**infectious** adjective
that can spread from one person to
another, *an infectious disease. Her
infectious laughter soon had everyone
laughing.*

**infer** verb (**infers, inferring, inferred**)
to reach an opinion from something that is
suggested but not actually said; to guess,
*He inferred from her silence that she agreed.*
**inference** noun

USAGE: Do not confuse **infer** with **imply**,
which means to suggest something without
actually saying it.

**inferior**[1] adjective
less good or important; low or lower in
position, quality, etc.
**inferiority** noun

**inferior**[2] noun (**inferiors**)
a person who is lower in position, rank, etc.
than another.

**infernal** adjective
1 like or of hell. 2 (*informal*) awful; very
annoying, *an infernal nuisance.*
**infernally** adverb

**inferno** noun (**infernos**)
(*say* in-**fer**-noh)
a fierce fire.

**infested** adjective
full of troublesome things like insects, rats,
etc.

**infiltrate** verb (**infiltrates, infiltrating, infiltrated**)
to get into a place or organization without
being noticed.
**infiltration** noun, **infiltrator** noun

**infinite** adjective
(*say* in-fi-nit)
endless; too large to be measured or
imagined.
**infinitely** adverb

**infinitive** noun (**infinitives**)
(*say* in-fin-i-tiv)
the form of a verb that does not change to
indicate a particular tense, etc., *The
infinitive usually occurs with 'to', as in 'to
go'.*

**infinity** noun (**infinities**)
(*say* in-fin-i-ti)
an infinite number or distance.

**infirm** adjective
weak because of being old or ill.
**infirmity** noun

**infirmary** noun (**infirmaries**)
a hospital.

**inflame** verb (**inflames, inflaming, inflamed**)
1 to make a part of your body red and sore.
2 to make someone angry.
**inflammation** noun, **inflammatory** adjective

**inflammable** adjective
that can be set alight.

USAGE: The opposite of **inflammable** is
**non-flammable**. The word **flammable** means
the same as **inflammable**.

**inflate** verb (**inflates, inflating, inflated**)
1 to fill something with air or gas. 2 to raise
or expand something too much, *Inflated
claims have been made for this product.*
**inflatable** adjective

**inflation** noun
1 filling something with air or gas. 2 a
general rise in prices.
**inflationary** adjective

**inflect** verb (**inflects, inflecting, inflected**)
1 to change a word to make it fit with other
words, *'Sing' is inflected to 'sang' in the
past tense.* 2 to change the sound of your
voice when speaking.

**inflection** noun (**inflections**)
(*in grammar*) an ending on a word which
shows a grammatical relation, such as
being in the plural or being in a particular
tense, *'-ed' is the usual past tense inflection.*

**inflexible** adjective
that you cannot bend or change, *inflexible
rules.*
**inflexibility** noun, **inflexibly** adverb

**inflict** verb (**inflicts, inflicting, inflicted**)
to make someone suffer something, *She
inflicted a severe blow on him.*

**influence**[1] noun (**influences**)
the power to affect someone or something.
**influential** adjective

**influence²** *verb* (**influences, influencing, influenced**)
to have an effect on the way someone behaves; to affect something, *The tides are influenced by the moon.*

**influenza** *noun*
(*say* in-floo-**en**-ză)
an infectious disease that causes fever, soreness in your nose and throat, and pain.

**inform** *verb* (**informs, informing, informed**)
to tell someone something.
**inform against** or **on someone,** to tell the police about someone.

**informal** *adjective*
not formal; relaxed, *Words in this dictionary are marked 'informal' if you might use them when you were talking but not when you were writing formally.*
**informality** *noun*, **informally** *adverb*

**informant** *noun* (**informants**)
a person who tells you something.

**information** *noun*
facts; knowledge; what someone tells you.
**information technology,** ways of storing, arranging, and giving out information, especially the use of computers and telecommunications.

**informative** *adjective*
(*say* in-**form**-ă-tiv)
containing a lot of helpful information.

**informed** *adjective*
knowing about something.

**informer** *noun* (**informers**)
a person who tells the police about someone else.

**infrequent** *adjective*
not frequent.
**infrequency** *noun*, **infrequently** *adverb*

**infuriate** *verb* (**infuriates, infuriating, infuriated**)
to make someone very angry.

**ingenious** *adjective*
clever, especially at thinking of new ways to do things.
**ingeniously** *adverb*, **ingenuity** *noun*

**ingot** *noun* (**ingots**)
a lump of metal after it has been cast, usually shaped like a brick.

**ingrained** *adjective*
deep in the surface of something, *ingrained dirt.*

**ingredient** *noun* (**ingredients**)
(*say* in-**greed**-i-ĕnt)
**1** one of the parts of a mixture. **2** one of the things used in a recipe.

**inhabit** *verb* (**inhabits, inhabiting, inhabited**)
to live in a place.
**inhabitable** *adjective*, **inhabitant** *noun*

**inhale** *verb* (**inhales, inhaling, inhaled**)
to breathe in.
**inhaler** *noun*

**inhaler** *noun* (**inhalers**)
a device that someone uses for taking medicine, especially for asthma, into his or her lungs.

**inherent** *adjective*
(*say* in-**heer**-ĕnt)
naturally or permanently part of something.
**inherently** *adverb*

**inherit** *verb* (**inherits, inheriting, inherited**)
**1** to receive money, property, a title, etc. when its previous owner dies. **2** to get certain characteristics from your parents or ancestors.
**inheritance** *noun*, **inheritor** *noun*

**inhibited** *adjective*
resisting or holding back emotions, instincts, or impulses.

**inhospitable** *adjective*
(*say* in-**hos**-pit-ă-bŭl)
**1** unfriendly to visitors. **2** giving no shelter, *an inhospitable rocky island.*

**inhuman** *adjective*
cruel; without pity or kindness.
**inhumanity** *noun*

**initial¹** *noun* (**initials**)
the first letter of a word or name, especially of someone's forename.

**initial²** *adjective*
first; of the beginning, *the initial stages of the work.*
**initially** *adverb*

**initiate** *verb* (**initiates, initiating, initiated**)
(*say* in-**ish**-i-ayt)
**1** to start something. **2** to admit someone as a member of a society or group, often with special ceremonies.
**initiation** *noun*

**initiative** *noun* (**initiatives**)
(*say* in-**ish**-ă-tiv)
**1** the action that starts something, *He took the initiative in making peace.* **2** ability or power to start things or to get them done on your own.

**inject** *verb* (**injects, injecting, injected**)
to put a medicine or drug through someone's skin into his or her body using a hollow needle.
**injection** *noun*

**injure** *verb* (**injures, injuring, injured**)
to harm or hurt someone.
**injurious** *adjective*, **injury** *noun*

**injustice** *noun* (**injustices**)
unjust action or treatment.

**ink** *noun* (**inks**)
a black or coloured liquid used for writing
and printing.
**inky** *adjective*

**inkling** *noun*
a slight idea or suspicion, *I had an inkling
that she would win the race.*

**inland** *adverb*
in or to a place on land and away from the
coast.

**in-law** *noun* (**in-laws**)
a member of someone's husband's or wife's
family, *We're going to visit the in-laws at
Easter.*

**inlet** *noun* (**inlets**)
a strip of water reaching into the land from
a sea, river, or lake.

**inn** *noun* (**inns**)
a hotel or public house, especially in the
country.
**innkeeper** *noun*

**inner** *adjective*
inside; nearest the centre.
**inner tube,** the inflatable tube inside a tyre.
**innermost** *adjective*

**innings** *noun* (**innings**)
the time when a cricket team or player is
batting.

**innocent** *adjective*
1 not guilty; not wicked. 2 harmless.
**innocence** *noun*, **innocently** *adverb*

**innocuous** *adjective*
harmless.

**innovation** *noun* (**innovations**)
1 inventing or using new things.
2 something new that you have just
invented or started using.
**innovative** *adjective*, **innovator** *noun*

**innumerable** *adjective*
too many to be counted.

**inoculate** *verb* (**inoculates, inoculating,
inoculated**)
to inject someone as protection against a
disease.
**inoculation** *noun*

**in-patient** *noun* (**in-patients**)
someone who stays at a hospital for
treatment.

**input**[1] *noun* (**inputs**)
what you put into something, especially
data sent to a computer.

**input**[2] *verb* (**inputs, inputting, input**)
(*in Computing*) to put data or programs
into a computer, *When the symbol '?_'
appears, input the number you have chosen.*

**inquest** *noun* (**inquests**)
an official investigation to decide why
someone died.

**inquire** *verb* (**inquires, inquiring, inquired**)
1 to ask. 2 to make an official investigation.

**inquiry** *noun* (**inquiries**)
an official investigation.

**inquisitive** *adjective*
always trying to find out things, especially
about other people's business.
**inquisitively** *adverb*

**insane** *adjective* (**insaner, insanest**)
mad.
**insanely** *adverb*, **insanity** *noun*

**insanitary** *adjective*
not clean or healthy.

**inscribe** *verb* (**inscribes, inscribing, inscribed**)
to write or carve something.
**inscription** *noun*

**insect** *noun* (**insects**)
a small animal with six legs and no
backbone, *Flies, ants, butterflies, and bees
are insects.*

**insecticide** *noun* (**insecticides**)
a poison for killing unwanted insects.

**insecure** *adjective*
1 not secure or safe. 2 not feeling safe or
confident.
**insecurely** *adverb*, **insecurity** *noun*

**insensitive** *adjective*
not sensitive.
**insensitively** *adverb*, **insensitivity** *noun*

**inseparable** *adjective*
1 that cannot be separated. 2 very friendly
to each other.
**inseparably** *adverb*

**insert** verb (**inserts, inserting, inserted**)
to put a thing into something else.
**insertion** noun

**inshore** adjective and adverb
on the sea near or nearer to the shore,
*inshore boating. The storm moved inshore.*

**inside**¹ noun (**insides**)
1 the middle or centre of something; the
part nearest to the middle. 2 (*informal*)
your stomach or abdomen.
**inside out**, with the inside turned so that it
faces outwards.

**inside**² adjective
placed in or coming from the centre of
something; in or nearest to the middle, *an
inside page.*

**inside**³ preposition
in or to the middle or centre of something,
*It's inside that box.*

**inside**⁴ adverb
to the part nearest the centre of something;
indoors, *Come inside.*

**insight** noun (**insights**)
1 being able to see the truth about things.
2 an understanding of something.

**insignificant** adjective
not important; not influential.
**insignificance** noun

**insincere** adjective
not sincere.
**insincerely** adverb, **insincerity** noun

**insist** verb (**insists, insisting, insisted**)
to be very firm in asking or saying
something, *He insisted that he was
innocent.*
**insistence** noun, **insistent** adjective

**insolent** adjective
very impudent; insulting.
**insolence** noun

**insoluble** adjective
1 impossible to solve, *an insoluble problem.*
2 impossible to dissolve, *an insoluble
chemical.*
**insolubility** noun

**insomnia** noun
(*say* in-**som**-ni-ă)
not being able to sleep.

**inspect** verb (**inspects, inspecting, inspected**)
to look carefully at people or things; to
check that something is doing its work
correctly, *to inspect a school.*
**inspection** noun

**inspector** noun (**inspectors**)
1 someone employed to inspect things or
people. 2 an officer in the police.

**inspire** verb (**inspires, inspiring, inspired**)
to fill someone with good or useful
thoughts or feelings, *The applause inspired
her with confidence.*
**inspiration** noun

**install** verb (**installs, installing, installed**)
1 to put something in position and ready to
use, *They installed central heating.* 2 to put
someone into an important position with a
ceremony, *He was installed as pope.*
**installation** noun

**instalment** noun (**instalments**)
one of the parts into which something is
divided so as to spread it over a period of
time, *He is paying for his bike in monthly
instalments.*

**instance** noun (**instances**)
an example, *for instance.*

**instant**¹ adjective
1 happening immediately, *instant success.*
2 that can be made very quickly, *instant
coffee.*

**instant**² noun (**instants**)
1 a moment, *I don't believe it for an instant.*
2 an exact time, *Come here this instant!*

**instantaneous** adjective
happening or done in an instant, or
without any delay.
**instantaneously** adverb

**instantly** adverb
without any delay.

**instead** adverb
in place of something else; as a substitute,
*There were no potatoes, so we had bread
instead.*

**instep** noun (**insteps**)
the top of your foot between your toes and
your ankle.

**instinct** noun (**instincts**)
a natural tendency to do or feel something,
*Spiders spin webs by instinct.*
**instinctive** adjective, **instinctively** adverb

**institute**¹ noun (**institutes**)
1 a society or organization, *the Institute of
Civil Engineers.* 2 a building used by a
society.

**institute**² verb (**institutes, instituting, instituted**)
to establish or start something.

**institution** noun (**institutions**)
1 an institute. 2 a habit or custom; a
well-known person or thing, *Going for a
Sunday bike ride was a family institution.*

**instruct** *verb* (**instructs, instructing, instructed**)
1 to educate someone. 2 to inform someone, *My client instructs me that you have not acted upon her request.* 3 to tell someone what to do.
**instruction** *noun*, **instructional** *adjective*, **instructive** *adjective*, **instructor** *noun*, **instructress** *noun*

**instrument** *noun* (**instruments**)
1 a device for making musical sounds.
2 a device for delicate or scientific work.

**instrumental** *adjective*
1 of or using musical instruments. 2 being one of the causes of something, *She was instrumental in getting him a job.*

**instrumentation** *noun*
the use or arrangement of instruments.

**insufficient** *adjective*
not enough.
**insufficiently** *adverb*

**insulate** *verb* (**insulates, insulating, insulated**)
to cover something so as to stop the movement of heat, cold, electricity, etc.
**insulation** *noun*, **insulator** *noun*

**insulin** *noun*
a chemical that controls how much sugar you have in your blood.

**insult**[1] *verb* (**insults, insulting, insulted**)
(*say* in-**sult**)
to speak or behave in a way that hurts someone's feelings or pride.

**insult**[2] *noun* (**insults**)
(*say* **in**-sult)
a remark or action that hurts someone's feelings or pride.

**insurance** *noun*
an agreement to pay regular amounts of money to a firm which, in return, will pay you a large amount of money if you suffer a loss, injury, etc.

**insure** *verb* (**insures, insuring, insured**)
to protect yourself or your goods with insurance.

USAGE: Do not confuse **insure** with **ensure**, which means to make sure.

**intact** *adjective*
not damaged; complete, *Despite the storm our tent was still intact.*

**intake** *noun* (**intakes**)
1 taking something in. 2 the number of people or things taken in, *The school had a high intake of pupils.*

**integer** *noun* (**integers**)
(*say* **in**-ti-jer)
a negative or positive whole number, such as −2, −1, 0, 1, 2, 3, etc.

**integral** *adjective*
(*say* **in**-ti-grăl)
1 that is an essential part of something, *Your heart is an integral part of your body.*
2 whole; complete, *an integral design.*
**integrally** *adverb*

**integrate** *verb* (**integrates, integrating, integrated**)
(*say* **in**-ti-grayt)
1 to make parts into a whole; to connect things together. 2 to join people together into a single community; to get people of different races to live happily together.
**integrated circuit**, a very small piece of material with many electric circuits on it, such as a silicon chip.
**integration** *noun*

**integrity** *noun*
(*say* in-**teg**-ri-ti)
honesty.

**intellect** *noun* (**intellects**)
the ability to think.

**intellectual**[1] *adjective*
1 of or using the ability to think. 2 able to think effectively; keen to study and learn.
**intellectually** *adverb*

**intellectual**[2] *noun* (**intellectuals**)
an intellectual person.

**intelligence** *noun*
1 being intelligent. 2 information, especially of military value; the people who collect and study this information.

**intelligent** *adjective*
good at thinking and learning.
**intelligently** *adverb*

**intelligible** *adjective*
that you can understand, *The message was barely intelligible.*
**intelligibility** *noun*, **intelligibly** *adverb*

**intend** *verb* (**intends, intending, intended**)
1 to have in mind what you plan to do; to plan, *She was intending to go swimming.*
2 to have something as a plan for someone else, *I intend you to do this job.*

**intense** *adjective* (**intenser, intensest**)
1 very strong or great, *intense heat.*
2 having or showing strong feelings, *a very serious, intense woman.*
**intensely** *adverb*

**intensify** *verb* (**intensifies, intensifying, intensified**)
to make something more intense; to become more intense.
**intensification** *noun*

**intensity** *noun* (**intensities**)
how strong or great something is.

# intensive

**intensive** *adjective*
using a lot of effort; thorough, *intensive farming. We made an intensive search.*
**intensively** *adverb*

**intent**¹ *adjective*
eager; very interested.
**intent on,** eager to do something; determined to do something, *They're intent on their work. She's intent on buying her own house.*
**intently** *adverb*

**intent**² *noun* (**intents**)
intention, *with good intent.*

**intention** *noun* (**intentions**)
what you intend to do; a plan.

**intentional** *adjective*
deliberate; planned.
**intentionally** *adverb*

**inter-** *prefix*
between two or more people or things, *an inter-school tennis competition.*

**interact** *verb* (**interacts, interacting, interacted**)
to have an effect on one another, *It is interesting to watch how two boastful people interact. Observe how acids and metals interact.*
**interaction** *noun*

**interactive** *adjective*
(*in Computing*) allowing information to be sent immediately in either direction between a computer system and its user.

**intercept** *verb* (**intercepts, intercepting, intercepted**)
to stop or catch a person or thing going from one place to another.
**interception** *noun,* **interceptor** *noun*

**interchange**¹ *verb* (**interchanges, interchanging, interchanged**)
1 to put two things in each other's place. 2 to give and receive something; to exchange things.
**interchangeable** *adjective,* **interchangeably** *adverb*

**interchange**² *noun* (**interchanges**)
1 interchanging. 2 a place where you can move from one motorway, etc. to another.

**intercom** *noun* (**intercoms**)
(*informal*) a device for communicating by radio, telephone, etc.

**intercourse** *noun*
1 communication or dealings between people. 2 sexual intercourse.

**interest**¹ *verb* (**interests, interesting, interested**)
to make someone want to look, listen, help with something, etc.

**interest**² *noun* (**interests**)
1 being interested; curiosity. 2 a thing that interests someone. 3 money paid regularly in return for money loaned or deposited.

**interface** *noun* (**interfaces**)
(*in Computing*) the place where two systems or devices are connected, *My laptop computer has an interface for connecting it to the college's network.*

**interfere** *verb* (**interferes, interfering, interfered**)
1 to take part in something that has nothing to do with you. 2 to get in the way.
**interference** *noun*

**interior** *noun* (**interiors**)
the inside of something.

**interjection** *noun* (**interjections**)
an exclamation, *Interjections are words like 'ah' and 'oh'.*

**interlock** *verb* (**interlocks, interlocking, interlocked**)
to fit into one another, *The gear-wheels interlocked.*

**interlude** *noun* (**interludes**)
1 an interval. 2 music played during an interval.

**intermediate** *adjective*
coming between two things in place, order, time, etc.

**interminable** *adjective*
(*say* in-ter-min-ă-bŭl)
seeming to go on for ever.
**interminably** *adverb*

**intermission** *noun* (**intermissions**)
an interval in a play, film, etc.

**intermittent** *adjective*
happening at intervals.
**intermittently** *adverb*

**intern** *verb* (**interns, interning, interned**)
to imprison someone in a special camp or building, usually during a war.
**internee** *noun,* **internment** *noun*

**internal** *adjective*
of or in the inside of something.
**internal-combustion engine,** an engine that makes power by burning fuel inside the engine, *Cars have internal-combustion engines.*
**internally** *adverb*

**international** *adjective*
of, in, or concerning more than one country, *Interpol is an international police organization.*
**internationally** *adverb*

**interplanetary** *adjective*
between planets, *interplanetary travel.*

**interpret** *verb* (interprets, interpreting, interpreted)
1 to explain what something means. 2 to translate from one language into another.
interpretation *noun*, interpreter *noun*

**interrogate** *verb* (interrogates, interrogating, interrogated)
to question someone closely.
interrogation *noun*, interrogator *noun*

**interrogative** *adjective*
connected with a question, 'Are they here?' is an interrogative sentence.

**interrupt** *verb* (interrupts, interrupting, interrupted)
1 to stop someone talking. 2 to stop something going on.
interruption *noun*

**intersect** *verb* (intersects, intersecting, intersected)
to cross or divide something, *intersecting lines.*

**intersection** *noun* (intersections)
1 a place where lines or roads, etc. cross each other. 2 (*in Mathematics*) the items that are shared by two or more sets.

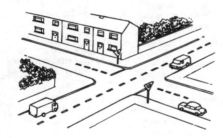

**interstellar** *adjective*
between the stars.

**interval** *noun* (intervals)
1 a time between two events or between two parts of a play, film, etc. 2 a space between two things.
at intervals, with some time or distance between each one; not continuously.

**intervene** *verb* (intervenes, intervening, intervened)
1 to come between two events, *in the intervening years.* 2 to interrupt an argument, fight, etc. and try to stop it or change its result.
intervention *noun*

**interview**[1] *noun* (interviews)
a meeting with someone to ask him or her questions or to discuss something.

**interview**[2] *verb* (interviews, interviewing, interviewed)
to have an interview with someone.
interviewer *noun*

**intestine** *noun* or **intestines** *plural noun*
the long tube along which food passes from the stomach.
intestinal *adjective*

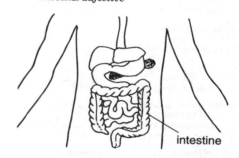

intestine

**intimate**[1] *adjective*
(*say* in-ti-măt)
1 very friendly. 2 private; personal, *intimate thoughts.* 3 detailed; close, *intimate knowledge.*
intimacy *noun*, intimately *adverb*

**intimate**[2] *verb* (intimates, intimating, intimated)
(*say* in-ti-mayt)
to tell someone or give someone a hint, *He has not yet intimated what his plans are.*
intimation *noun*

**intimidate** *verb* (intimidates, intimidating, intimidated)
to frighten someone so as to make him or her do something.
intimidation *noun*

**into** *preposition*
1 to the inside of somewhere; to a place inside, *Go into the house.* 2 to a particular condition, situation, job, etc., *He got into trouble. She got into acting.* 3 saying how many times one number is included in another, *3 into 12 goes 4 times.*

**intolerable** *adjective*
unbearable, *intolerable noise.*
intolerably *adverb*

**intolerant** *adjective*
not tolerant.
intolerance *noun*, intolerantly *adverb*

**intonation** *noun* (intonations)
1 the pitch or tone of a voice or musical instrument. 2 (*in grammar*) using the pitch of your voice to alter the meaning of what you are saying, for example when asking a question.

**intoxicate** *verb* (**intoxicates, intoxicating, intoxicated**)
1 to make someone drunk. 2 to make someone very excited.
**intoxication** *noun*

**intransitive** *adjective*
used without a direct object, *'Giggle' and 'tingle' are intransitive verbs.*
**intransitively** *adverb*

**intrepid** *adjective*
brave; fearless.
**intrepidly** *adverb*

**intricate** *adjective*
complicated.
**intricacy** *noun*, **intricately** *adverb*

**intrigue** *verb* (**intrigues, intriguing, intrigued**)
(*say* in-**treeg**)
1 to interest someone very much. 2 to make secret plans.

**introduce** *verb* (**introduces, introducing, introduced**)
1 to make someone known to other people. 2 to announce a broadcast, speaker, etc. 3 to start something being used or considered.

**introduction** *noun* (**introductions**)
1 introducing someone or something. 2 a piece at the beginning of a book, speech, etc.
**introductory** *adjective*

**intrude** *verb* (**intrudes, intruding, intruded**)
to come in or join in without being wanted.
**intrusion** *noun*, **intrusive** *adjective*

**intruder** *noun* (**intruders**)
1 someone who intrudes. 2 a burglar.

**intrusion** *noun* (**intrusions**)
1 coming in or joining in without being wanted. 2 (*in Science*) molten rock that has made its way between layers of other rock but has not reached the earth's surface.

**intuition** *noun*
(*say* in-tew-**ish**-ŏn)
the power to know or understand things without having to think hard, *His intuition told him what the next move should be.*
**intuitive** *adjective*

**Inuit** *noun* (**Inuit** or **Inuits**)
one of the people who live in very cold parts of North America.

**inundate** *verb* (**inundates, inundating, inundated**)
to flood something.
**inundation** *noun*

**invade** *verb* (**invades, invading, invaded**)
to attack and enter a country, place, etc.
**invader** *noun*

**invalid**[1] *noun* (**invalids**)
(*say* **in**-vă-leed)
someone who is ill or weakened by a long illness.

**invalid**[2] *adjective*
(*say* in-**val**-id)
not valid, *This passport is invalid.*

**invaluable** *adjective*
very valuable.

**invariable** *adjective*
that never changes.

**invariably** *adverb*
always.

**invasion** *noun* (**invasions**)
the act of attacking and entering a place.

**invent** *verb* (**invents, inventing, invented**)
to be the first person to make or think of a particular thing.
**invention** *noun*, **inventive** *adjective*, **inventor** *noun*

**inverse**[1] *adjective*
reversed; opposite, *The speed of the traffic bears an inverse relation to the number of vehicles.*
**inverse proportion,** a relation between two quantities in which one quantity grows smaller as the other grows larger.
**inversely** *adverb*

**inverse**[2] *noun* (**inverses**)
1 the opposite of something. 2 (*in Mathematics*) an operation that produces the opposite effect to another, *Division is the inverse of multiplication.*

**invert** *verb* (**inverts, inverting, inverted**)
to turn something upside down.
**inverted commas,** punctuation marks, " " or ' ', put before and after spoken words.
**inversion** *noun*

**invertebrate** *noun* (**invertebrates**)
(*say* in-**vert**-i-brăt)
an animal without a backbone, *Amoebas, worms, and jellyfish are invertebrates.*

**invest** *verb* (**invests, investing, invested**)
1 to use money so as to earn interest or make a profit. 2 to give someone an honour, medal, etc., *He was invested as Prince of Wales.*
**investment** *noun*, **investor** *noun*

**investigate** *verb* (**investigates, investigating, investigated**)
to find out as much as you can about something, especially about a crime.
**investigation** *noun*, **investigator** *noun*

**investiture** *noun* (**investitures**)
a ceremony in which someone is given an official title, *the investiture of the Prince of Wales.*

**invigilate** *verb* (**invigilates, invigilating, invigilated**)
to supervise candidates at an examination.
**invigilation** *noun*, **invigilator** *noun*

**invigorate** *verb* (**invigorates, invigorating, invigorated**)
to give someone vigour or courage.

**invincible** *adjective*
that cannot be defeated.
**invincibly** *adverb*

**invisible** *adjective*
that you cannot see.
**invisibility** *noun*, **invisibly** *adverb*

**invite** *verb* (**invites, inviting, invited**)
1 to ask someone politely to do something, especially to come to a party, etc. 2 to bring something on yourself, *You are inviting trouble by making rude jokes about the headteacher.*
**invitation** *noun*

**inviting** *adjective*
attractive; tempting.
**invitingly** *adverb*

**invoice** *noun* (**invoices**)
a list of goods sent or of work done, with the prices charged.

**involuntary** *adjective*
not deliberate; done without thinking, *an involuntary squeal of surprise.*
**involuntarily** *adverb*

**involve** *verb* (**involves, involving, involved**)
1 to mean; to result in, *The job involved great effort.* 2 to affect; to make someone part of something, *We are involved in charity work.*
**involvement** *noun*

**involved** *adjective*
complicated, *a long and involved explanation.*

**inward**[1] *adjective*
1 on the inside, especially in your mind, *inward happiness.* 2 going or facing inwards.
**inwardly** *adverb*

**inward**[2] *adverb*
inwards.

**inwards** *adverb*
towards the inside.

**iodine** *noun*
(*say* I-ŏ-deen or I-o-dyn)
a chemical used to kill germs.

**ion** *noun* (**ions**)
(*say* I-ŏn)
an electrically-charged particle.

**IOU** *noun* (**IOUs**)
(*say* I owe you)
a piece of paper on which you write that you owe someone money.

**IQ** *noun* (**IQs**)
a measure of someone's intelligence, calculated from the results of a special test.

**iris** *noun* (**irises**)
1 the coloured part of the eyeball. 2 a flower with long, pointed leaves.

**Irish** *adjective*
of Ireland.
**Irishman** *noun*, **Irishwoman** *noun*

**iron**[1] *noun* (**irons**)
1 a strong, heavy metal. 2 a device that is heated for smoothing clothes or cloth. 3 a tool made of iron, *a branding-iron.*
**Iron Curtain**, a name for the frontier that used to divide Russia and associated countries from the other countries of the world.
**irons**, chains round a prisoner's ankles.

**iron**[2] *verb* (**irons, ironing, ironed**)
to smooth clothes or cloth with an iron.
**iron out**, to solve a difficulty, *The worst faults in the program have now been ironed out.*

**Iron Age** *noun*
the time in history when iron began to be used for tools and weapons.

**ironic** *adjective*
(*say* I-ron-ik)
using irony; full of irony.
**ironical** *adjective*, **ironically** *adverb*

**ironing-board** *noun* (**ironing-boards**)
a folding table on which clothes are ironed.

**ironmonger** *noun* (**ironmongers**)
someone who keeps a shop that sells tools, nails, and other metal things.
**ironmongery** *noun*

**irony** *noun* (**ironies**)
(*say* I-rŏ-ni)
1 saying the opposite of what you mean so as to emphasize it, *You use irony if you say 'What a lovely day' when it is pouring with rain.* 2 an unexpected or strange event or situation.

**irrational** *adjective*
not rational.
**irrationality** *noun*, **irrationally** *adverb*

**irregular** *adjective*
1 not regular; not usual. 2 against the rules.
**irregularity** *noun*, **irregularly** *adverb*

**irrelevant** *adjective*
(*say* i-**rel**-i-vănt)
not relevant.
**irrelevance** *noun*, **irrelevantly** *adverb*

**irresistible** *adjective*
1 that you cannot resist, *the irresistible force of the sea.* 2 very attractive, *On such a hot day, an ice-cream is irresistible.*
**irresistibly** *adverb*

**irresponsible** *adjective*
not trustworthy; not sensible.
**irresponsibility** *noun*, **irresponsibly** *adverb*

**irreverent** *adjective*
not respectful, especially towards holy things.
**irreverence** *noun*, **irreverently** *adverb*

**irrigate** *verb* (**irrigates, irrigating, irrigated**)
to supply land with water so that crops can grow.
**irrigation** *noun*

**irritable** *adjective*
easily annoyed.
**irritability** *noun*, **irritably** *adverb*

**irritate** *verb* (**irritates, irritating, irritated**)
1 to annoy someone. 2 to make part of your body itch or feel sore.
**irritant** *noun*, **irritation** *noun*

**is** 3rd person singular present tense of **be**.

**-ish** *suffix*
somewhat; rather like something, *She has reddish hair. He is thirty-five but his manner is boyish.*

**Islam** *noun*
(*say* **iz**-lahm)
the religion of Muslims.
**Islamic** *adjective*

**island** *noun* (**islands**)
a piece of land surrounded by water.
**islander** *noun*

**isle** *noun* (**isles**)
an island.

**-ism** *suffix*
a belief or a system of thought, *Hinduism and Sikhism are two of the religions of India.*

**isn't** short for *is not.*

**isobar** *noun* (**isobars**)
(*say* **I**-sŏ-bar)
a line on a map connecting places that have the same atmospheric pressure.

**isolate** *verb* (**isolates, isolating, isolated**)
1 to separate a chemical, *Marie Curie succeeded in isolating radium.* 2 to put someone or something apart from others.
**isolation** *noun*

**isosceles** *adjective*
(*say* **I-sos**-i-leez)
(of a triangle) with two sides equal.

**isotope** *noun* (**isotopes**)
(*say* **I**-sŏ-tohp)
(*in Science*) a form of an element that is different from other forms in the structure of its nucleus, but has the same chemical properties as the other forms.

**Israeli** *adjective*
(*say* iz-**ray**-li)
of Israel.

**issue**[1] *verb* (**issues, issuing, issued**)
1 to send or give out; to supply, *They issued blankets to the refugees.* 2 to publish; to put into circulation, *The dictionary was issued in parts. These banknotes have just been issued.* 3 to come out, *Smoke was issuing from the chimney.*

**issue**[2] *noun* (**issues**)
1 sending or giving out something, *the issue of passports.* 2 something given out, published, or put into circulation, *an issue of blankets for the refugees. a Christmas issue of stamps. the latest issue of banknotes.* 3 a magazine or newspaper brought out at a particular time, *Tuesday's issue of The Guardian.* 4 a subject for discussion or concern, *What are the real issues?* 5 a result, *Await the issue.*

**-ist** *suffix*
someone who does a particular job, *An anaesthetist deals with anaesthetics.*

**isthmus** *noun* (**isthmuses**)
(*say* **iss**-mŭs)
a narrow strip of land connecting two larger pieces of land.

**it** *pronoun*
1 the thing being talked about. 2 the player in a game who has to catch other people, *You're it now!*

**Italian** *adjective*
of Italy.

**italic** *adjective*
(*say* it-**al**-ik)
printed sloping, *like this.*
**italicize** *verb*

**italics** *plural noun*
(*say* it-**al**-iks)
italic letters.

**itch**[1] *noun* (**itches**)
1 a tickling feeling in your skin that makes you want to scratch it. 2 a longing to do something, *He has an itch to go to America.*
**itchy** *adjective*

**itch**[2] *verb* (**itches, itching, itched**)
to have an itch.

**item** *noun* (**items**)
one thing in a list or group of things, especially a piece of news.

**itinerary** *noun* (**itineraries**)
(*say* I-**tin**-er-er-i)
a list of places to be visited on a journey; a route.

**-itis** *suffix*
used in names of diseases in which part of the body is inflamed, *Tonsillitis is a disease of the tonsils.*

**it'll** short for *it will.*

**its** *pronoun*
of it; belonging to it, *The cat hurt its paw.*

**it's** short for *it is* and (before a verb in the past tense) *it has, Can you see if it's raining?*

**itself** *pronoun*
it and nothing else.
**by itself,** without help, attention, etc. from anybody; alone, *This machine works by itself. His house stands by itself in a wood.*

**ITV** short for *Independent Television.*

**I've** short for *I have.*

**ivory** *noun*
**1** the hard creamy-white substance that forms elephants' tusks. **2** a creamy-white colour.
**ivories,** (*slang*) the keys of a piano.

**ivy** *noun*
a climbing evergreen plant with shiny leaves.

# Jj

**jab**¹ *verb* (**jabs, jabbing, jabbed**)
**1** to poke someone or something. **2** to stab or pierce someone or something.

**jab**² *noun* (**jabs**)
**1** a poking, stabbing, or piercing movement. **2** (*informal*) an injection.

**jabber** *verb* (**jabbers, jabbering, jabbered**)
**1** to speak quickly and not clearly. **2** to chatter, *Stop jabbering and concentrate on your work!*

**jack**¹ *noun* (**jacks**)
**1** a device for lifting something heavy off the ground. **2** a playing-card with a picture of a young man on it. **3** a small white ball that you aim at in the game of bowls.

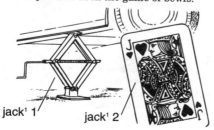

jack¹ 1          jack¹ 2

**jack**² *verb* (**jacks, jacking, jacked**)
to lift something with a jack.
**jack in,** (*slang*) to give up or abandon something.

**jackal** *noun* (**jackals**)
a wild animal rather like a dog.

**jackass** *noun* (**jackasses**)
**1** a male donkey. **2** a stupid person.
**laughing jackass,** a kookaburra.

**jackdaw** *noun* (**jackdaws**)
a bird like a small crow.

**jacket** *noun* (**jackets**)
**1** a coat which covers the top half of the body. **2** a cover for a book, water-heater, etc. **3** the skin of a potato that is baked without being peeled.

**jack-in-the-box** *noun* (**jack-in-the-boxes**)
a toy figure that springs out of a box when you lift the lid.

**jackknife** *verb* (**jackknifes, jackknifing, jackknifed**)
(of an articulated lorry) to go out of control, with the trailer skidding round towards the cab.

**jackpot** *noun* (**jackpots**)
an amount of prize-money that increases until someone wins it.

**jade** *noun*
a green stone which is carved to make ornaments.

**jaded** *adjective*
tired and bored.

**jagged** *adjective*
(*say* **jag**-id)
uneven and sharp.

**jaguar** *noun* (**jaguars**)
a large, fierce animal rather like a leopard.

**jail** *noun* (**jails**)
a prison.
**jailer** *noun*

**Jain** *noun* (**Jains**)
(rhymes with *mine*)
a believer in an Indian religion rather like Buddhism.

**jam**¹ *noun* (**jams**)
**1** a sweet food made of fruit boiled with sugar until it is thick. **2** a lot of people, cars, logs, etc. crowded together so that it is difficult to move, *a traffic jam*. **3** (*informal*) a difficult situation, *He's in a jam*. **4** (*informal*) something very easy, *Doing this job is money for jam*.

**jam**² *verb* (**jams, jamming, jammed**)
**1** to make or become fixed and difficult to move, *The door has jammed*. **2** to squeeze or wedge, *I jammed my fingers in the door*.

**jamboree** *noun* (**jamborees**)
**1** a large party or celebration. **2** a large gathering of Scouts.

**jammy** *adjective*
**1** smeared or sticky with jam. **2** (*informal*) very easy or lucky.

**jangle** *verb* (**jangles, jangling, jangled**)
to make a harsh ringing sound.

**January** *noun*
the first month of the year.

**Japanese** *adjective*
of Japan.

**jar**¹ *noun* (**jars**)
a container made of glass, baked clay, plastic, etc.

**jar**² *verb* (**jars, jarring, jarred**)
**1** to make a harsh sound or jolt. **2** to have an unpleasant effect on your feelings.

**jaundice** *noun*
a disease that makes your skin yellow.

**jaunt** *noun* (**jaunts**)
a short journey which you make for pleasure.

**jaunty** *adjective* (**jauntier, jauntiest**)
lively and cheerful.
**jauntily** *adverb*, **jauntiness** *noun*

**javelin** *noun* (**javelins**)
a light spear, especially one thrown as a sport.

**jaw** *noun* (**jaws**)
**1** the lower part of the face. **2** one of the two bones that hold the teeth.

**jay** *noun* (**jays**)
a noisy, brightly-coloured bird.

**jazz** *noun*
a kind of music with strong rhythm, often played without rehearsing.
**jazzy** *adjective*

**jealous** *adjective*
unhappy or resentful because you feel that someone rivals you or is better or luckier than you.
**jealously** *adverb*, **jealousy** *noun*

**jeans** *plural noun*
trousers made of strong, usually blue, cloth.

**Jeep** *noun* (**Jeeps**)
(*trademark*) a small, sturdy motor car used especially on rough ground.

**jeer** *verb* (**jeers, jeering, jeered**)
to laugh or shout at someone rudely or scornfully.

**jelly** *noun* (**jellies**)
**1** (in America, *jello*) a soft, sweet food that melts in your mouth. **2** any soft, slippery substance.
**jellied** *adjective*

**jellyfish** *noun* (**jellyfish**)
a sea-animal with a body like jelly.

**jerk**¹ *verb* (**jerks, jerking, jerked**)
to make a sudden sharp movement.

**jerk**² *noun* (**jerks**)
**1** a sudden sharp movement. **2** (*slang*) a fool.
**jerkily** *adverb*, **jerkiness** *noun*, **jerky** *adjective*

**jersey** *noun* (**jerseys**)
a pullover with sleeves.

**jest** *noun* (**jests**)
a joke.
**in jest,** joking; not seriously.

**jester** *noun* (**jesters**)
a professional entertainer at a king's court
in the Middle Ages.

**jet¹** *noun* (**jets**)
1 a stream of liquid, gas, flame, etc. forced
out of a narrow opening. 2 a narrow
opening from which a jet comes out, *a
gas-jet.* 3 a jet aircraft.
**jet aircraft,** an aircraft with jet engines.
**jet engine,** an engine that works by sending
out a jet of hot gas at the back.
**jet lag,** very great tiredness that someone
feels after a long air journey because he or
she has not got used to the differences in
time in different parts of the world.
**jet-propelled** *adjective,* **jet-propulsion** *noun*

**jet²** *noun*
1 a hard black mineral. 2 a deep glossy
black colour.

**jet³** *verb* (**jets, jetting, jetted**)
1 to come out in a strong stream.
2 (*informal*) to travel in a jet aircraft.

**jetty** *noun* (**jetties**)
a small landing-stage.

**Jew** *noun* (**Jews**)
1 a member of the race of people descended
from the ancient tribes of Israel. 2 someone
who believes in Judaism.
**Jewess** *noun,* **Jewish** *adjective*

**jewel** *noun* (**jewels**)
a precious stone; an ornament including
one or more precious stones.
**jewelled** *adjective*

**jeweller** *noun* (**jewellers**)
someone who sells or makes jewellery.

**jewellery** *noun*
jewels or ornaments that you wear.

**jib** *noun* (**jibs**)
1 a triangular sail stretching forward from
the mast. 2 the projecting arm of a crane.

**Jiffy bag** *noun* (**Jiffy bags**)
(*trademark*) a padded envelope for sending
breakable things.

**jig¹** *noun* (**jigs**)
1 a lively dance. 2 a device that holds
something in place while you work on it
with tools.

**jig²** *verb* (**jigs, jigging, jigged**)
1 to dance a jig. 2 to move up and down
quickly and jerkily, *Alf was jigging up and
down, trying to get warm.*

**jigsaw** *noun* (**jigsaws**)
1 a saw that can cut curved shapes. 2 a
jigsaw puzzle.
**jigsaw puzzle,** a puzzle made of shapes that
you fit together to make a picture.

**jingle¹** *verb* (**jingles, jingling, jingled**)
to make a tinkling or clinking sound.

**jingle²** *noun* (**jingles**)
1 a tinkling or clinking sound. 2 a verse or
group of words with repetitive sounds. 3 a
simple song used in an advertisement on
radio or television.

**job** *noun* (**jobs**)
1 work that someone does regularly to earn
a living, *He got a job as a postman.* 2 a
particular task, *We shall have tea when we
finish this job.* 3 (*informal*) a difficult task,
*You'll have a job to lift that box.*
4 (*informal*) a situation; a state of affairs,
*It's a good job you're here.*
**just the job,** (*informal*) exactly what you
want.

**jobcentre** *noun* (**jobcentres**)
a government office in a town centre where
you can find out what jobs are available.

**jockey** *noun* (**jockeys**)
someone who rides horses in races.

**jodhpurs** *plural noun*
(*say* **jod-perz**)
trousers for horse-riding, fitting closely
from the knee to the ankle.

**jog** *verb* (**jogs, jogging, jogged**)
1 to run slowly, especially for exercise. 2 to
give something a slight knock or push.
**jog someone's memory,** to help someone
remember something.
**jogger** *noun,* **jogging** *noun*

**jogtrot** *noun* (**jogtrots**)
a slow run with short strides.

**join¹** *verb* (**joins, joining, joined**)
1 to put things together; to come together;
to fasten or unite things. 2 to become a
member of an organization, group, etc.
**join in,** to take part in something.

**join²** *noun* (**joins**)
a place where things join.

**joiner** *noun* (**joiners**)
someone whose job is to make furniture and other things out of wood.
**joinery** *noun*

**joint**[1] *noun* (**joints**)
1 a place where things are fixed together.
2 the place where two bones fit together.
3 a large piece of meat.

**joint**[2] *adjective*
shared or done by two or more people, countries, etc.
**jointly** *adverb*

**joist** *noun* (**joists**)
a long beam supporting a floor or ceiling.

**jojoba** *noun*
(*say* hoh-**hoh**-bă)
a desert plant with seeds that give an oil used in making shampoo, skin lotion, etc.

**joke**[1] *noun* (**jokes**)
1 something said or done to make people laugh. 2 a trick.
**no joke**, something serious.

**joke**[2] *verb* (**jokes, joking, joked**)
to make jokes.
**jokingly** *adverb*

**joker** *noun* (**jokers**)
1 someone who jokes. 2 a playing-card with a picture of a jester on it, used in some games as the card having the highest value. 3 (*slang*) a person; a fool, *Who's this joker?*

**jolly**[1] *adjective* (**jollier, jolliest**)
happy; cheerful.
**jollity** *noun*

**jolly**[2] *adverb*
(*informal*) very, *That film was jolly good!*

**jolt**[1] *verb* (**jolts, jolting, jolted**)
to move something or someone suddenly and sharply; to move along with sudden sharp movements.

**jolt**[2] *noun* (**jolts**)
1 a sudden sharp movement. 2 a surprise or shock.

**jostle** *verb* (**jostles, jostling, jostled**)
to push someone roughly.

**jot** *verb* (**jots, jotting, jotted**)
to write something quickly.

**jotter** *noun* (**jotters**)
a notebook.

**joule** *noun* (**joules**)
(*in Science*) a unit of work or energy.

**journal** *noun* (**journals**)
1 a newspaper or magazine. 2 a diary.

**journalist** *noun* (**journalists**)
someone who writes for a newspaper or magazine.
**journalism** *noun*, **journalistic** *adjective*

**journey**[1] *noun* (**journeys**)
1 going from one place to another. 2 the distance you travel or the time you take to travel somewhere, *a day's journey*.

**journey**[2] *verb* (**journeys, journeying, journeyed**)
to go from one place to another.

**joust** *verb* (**jousts, jousting, jousted**)
to fight on horseback with lances, *Knights in the Middle Ages used to joust as a sport.*

**jovial** *adjective*
cheerful; good-humoured.
**joviality** *noun*, **jovially** *adverb*

**joy** *noun*
1 great happiness. 2 (*informal*) success or satisfaction, *I tried to claim my money back but I got no joy.*

**joyful** *adjective*
very happy.
**joyfully** *adverb*

**joyous** *adjective*
very happy.
**joyously** *adverb*

**joy-ride** *noun* (**joy-rides**)
(*informal*) a ride in a motor car, usually without its owner's permission.

**joystick** *noun* (**joysticks**)
1 (*informal*) the lever that controls the up-and-down and (together with the rudder) the turning movements of an aircraft. 2 a lever that controls the movements of a computer's cursor.

**jubilant** *adjective*
(*say* **joo**-bi-lănt)
rejoicing; joyful.
**jubilantly** *adverb*, **jubilation** *noun*

**jubilee** *noun* (**jubilees**)
(*say* **joo**-bi-lee)
a special anniversary, *A silver jubilee is the 25th anniversary; a golden jubilee is the 50th anniversary; and a diamond jubilee is the 60th anniversary.*

**Judaism** *noun*
(*say* **joo**-day-izm)
the religion of the Jewish people.

**judge**[1] *noun* (**judges**)
1 someone appointed to hear cases in a lawcourt and decide what should be done. 2 someone appointed to decide who has won a contest or competition. 3 someone who is good at forming opinions or making decisions about things, *She's a good judge of musical skills.*

**judge**[2] *verb* (**judges, judging, judged**)
1 to act as judge for a law case or a contest.
2 to estimate or guess something. 3 to form
an opinion about something.

**judgement** *noun* (**judgements**)
1 acting as judge for a law case or a
contest. 2 the decision made in a lawcourt.
3 ability to estimate things or to make
decisions wisely. 4 someone's opinion, *In
my judgement, the food is too salty.*
5 something considered as a punishment
from God.

**judicial** *adjective*
(*say* joo-**dish**-ăl)
of lawcourts, judges, or decisions made in
lawcourts.
**judicially** *adverb*

**judicious** *adjective*
(*say* joo-**dish**-ŭs)
having or showing good sense.
**judiciously** *adverb*

**judo** *noun*
(*say* **joo**-doh)
a Japanese method of wrestling and
self-defence.

**jug** *noun* (**jugs**)
a container for liquids, with a handle and
lip.

**juggernaut** *noun* (**juggernauts**)
a huge lorry.

**juggle** *verb* (**juggles, juggling, juggled**)
to keep a number of objects moving in the
air without dropping any.
**juggler** *noun*

**juice** *noun* (**juices**)
1 the liquid from fruit, vegetables, or other
food. 2 liquid in your body, *digestive juices.*
**juicy** *adjective*

**juke-box** *noun* (**juke-boxes**)
a machine that plays a record when you
put a coin in.

**July** *noun*
the seventh month of the year.

**jumble**[1] *verb* (**jumbles, jumbling, jumbled**)
to mix things up in a confused way.

**jumble**[2] *noun* (**jumbles**)
a confused mixture; a muddle.
**jumble sale,** (in America, *rummage sale*) a
sale of second-hand goods to raise money
for charity, etc.

**jumbo jet** *noun* (**jumbo jets**)
a huge jet aircraft.

**jump**[1] *verb* (**jumps, jumping, jumped**)
1 to move suddenly from the ground or
from a vehicle, an aircraft, etc. into the air.
2 to go over something by jumping, *The
horse jumped the fence.* 3 to move quickly
or suddenly, *He jumped out of his seat.*
**jump at something,** (*informal*) to accept
something eagerly.
**jump the gun,** to start before you should.
**jump the queue,** not to wait for your proper
turn.

**jump**[2] *noun* (**jumps**)
1 a sudden movement into the air. 2 an
obstacle to jump over.
**jump suit,** a piece of clothing made in one
piece and covering your whole body.

**jumper** *noun* (**jumpers**)
1 a person or animal that jumps. 2 a jersey.

**jumpy** *adjective* (**jumpier, jumpiest**)
nervous.

**junction** *noun* (**junctions**)
a place where roads or railway lines join.

**June** *noun*
the sixth month of the year.

**jungle** *noun* (**jungles**)
a thick, tangled forest, especially in a hot
country.
**jungly** *adjective*

**junior**[1] *adjective*
1 younger, *the junior members of the
family.* 2 for young children, *a junior
school.* 3 lower in rank or importance, *a
junior employee.*

**junior**[2] *noun* (**juniors**)
1 a younger person. 2 a person of lower
rank or importance.

**junk**[1] *noun*
1 rubbish. 2 things that are worth little or
nothing, *I'm not paying good money for
that junk!*
**junk food,** food of poor quality, usually
containing a lot of sugar and starch.
**junk mail,** advertisements that you do not
want, delivered with newspapers or with
the post.

**junk²** *noun* (**junks**)
a Chinese sailing-boat.

**junket** *noun* (**junkets**)
a sweet, runny food made from milk.

**jury** *noun* (**juries**)
a group of people appointed to make a
decision about a case in a lawcourt, *There
are usually 12 people in a jury.*
**juror** *noun*, **juryman** *noun*, **jurywoman** *noun*

**just¹** *adjective*
1 fair; right; giving proper consideration to
everybody. 2 deserved, *He got his just
reward.*
**justly** *adverb*

**just²** *adverb*
1 exactly, *It's just what I wanted.* 2 only;
simply, *I just wanted another cake.*
3 hardly; barely; by only a short distance,
*just below the belt.* 4 a very short time ago,
*She has just gone.*

**justice** *noun*
1 fairness; being just. 2 the law.
**do justice to something**, to be fair to
something; to show or use something in the
best way possible, *To do the film justice, it
had to cover a huge story in a very short
time. We did his cooking justice, and ate
every last scrap of food.*

**justify** *verb* (**justifies, justifying, justified**)
to show that something is fair, reasonable,
or acceptable, *Do you think that you were
justified in taking such a risk?*
**justifiable** *adjective*, **justifiably** *adverb*,
**justification** *noun*

**jut** *verb* (**juts, jutting, jutted**)
to stick out.

**juvenile** *adjective*
(*say* joo-vi-nyl)
of or for young people.
**juvenile delinquent**, a young person who
breaks the law.

# Kk

**kaleidoscope** *noun* (**kaleidoscopes**)
(*say* kăl-**I**-dŏs-kohp)
a tube that you look through to see
brightly-coloured patterns which change as
you turn the end of the tube.
**kaleidoscopic** *adjective*

**kangaroo** *noun* (**kangaroos**)
an Australian animal that jumps on its
strong back legs, *Female kangaroos have
pouches in which they carry their joeys, or
babies.*

**karaoke** *noun*
(*say* ka-ră-**oh**-ki)
1 a machine that plays recorded pop music
without words, so that people can sing the
words. 2 singing to music from this
machine, *We had karaoke at the party.*

**karate** *noun*
(*say* kă-**rah**-ti)
a Japanese method of self-defence using
the hands, arms, and feet.

**kayak** *noun* (**kayaks**)
(*say* **ky**-ak)
a long, thin canoe with a covering over the
top, like the kind the Inuit use.

**kebab** *noun* (**kebabs**)
1 (also called a *shish kebab*) small pieces of
meat and vegetables grilled on a skewer.
2 (usually called a *doner kebab*) slices cut
from a large cake of meat that is heated on
a vertical skewer.

**keel¹** *noun* (**keels**)
the long piece of wood or metal along the
bottom of a boat.
**on an even keel**, steady or steadily.

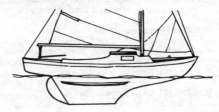

**keel**[2] *verb* (**keels, keeling, keeled**)
to tilt or overturn, *The ship keeled over.*

**keen** *adjective* (**keener, keenest**)
**1** enthusiastic; very interested, *She is keen on swimming.* **2** sharp, *a keen knife.* **3** very cold, *a keen wind.*
**keenly** *adverb*, **keenness** *noun*

**keep**[1] *verb* (**keeps, keeping, kept**)
**1** to have something and not get rid of it. **2** to stay; to remain, *Keep still!* **3** to make someone or something stay in the same position or condition, *The fire kept us warm.* **4** to stay in good condition, *Will the milk keep until tomorrow?* **5** to prevent, *How can we keep the teacher from knowing?* **6** to do something continually, *She kept laughing.* **7** to be faithful to something; not to break something, *He kept his promise.* **8** to look after; to give a home and food to people or animals, *They keep chickens.*
**keep up**, to make the same progress as others; to continue something, *They walked so fast that we couldn't keep up. Keep up the good work!*

**keep**[2] *noun* (**keeps**)
**1** the food or money that you need to live, *She earns her keep.* **2** a strong tower in a castle.
**for keeps**, (*informal*) to keep; permanently, *Is this football mine for keeps?*

**keeper** *noun* (**keepers**)
someone who looks after an animal, place, building, etc., *a lighthouse-keeper. the park-keeper.*

**keeping** *noun*
care; looking after something, *in safe keeping.*
**in keeping with something**, agreeing with or suiting something.

**keg** *noun* (**kegs**)
a small barrel.

**kennel** *noun* (**kennels**)
a small hut for a dog.

**kept** past tense and past participle of **keep** *verb.*

**kerb** *noun* (**kerbs**)
the edge of a pavement.
**kerbstone** *noun*

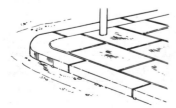

**kernel** *noun* (**kernels**)
the eatable part in the middle of a nut.

**kestrel** *noun* (**kestrels**)
a kind of falcon.

**ketchup** *noun*
a thick sauce made from tomatoes.

**kettle** *noun* (**kettles**)
a container with a spout and handle, used for boiling water in.
**another kettle of fish**, a totally different matter.
**a pretty kettle of fish**, a strange or difficult situation.

**kettledrum** *noun* (**kettledrums**)
a drum made of skin stretched over a hollow, bowl-shaped metal part.

**key** *noun* (**keys**)
**1** a piece of metal shaped so that it opens a lock. **2** a device for winding up a clockwork train, clock, etc. **3** a small lever that you press with your finger, *Typewriters and pianos have keys.* **4** a scale of musical notes related to each other, *the key of C major.* **5** a thing that explains or solves something, *Use a key to identify the tree. Detectives searched for months before finding the key to the crime.*

**keyboard** *noun* (**keyboards**)
the set of keys on a piano, typewriter, computer, etc.

**keyhole** *noun* (**keyholes**)
the hole through which a key is put into a lock.

**keynote** *noun* (**keynotes**)
**1** the note on which a key in music is based, *The keynote of C major is C.* **2** the main idea in something said, written, or done.

**kg** short for **kilogram** or **kilograms.**

**khaki** *noun*
(*say* **kah**-ki)
a dull yellowish-brown colour.

**kibbutz** *noun* (**kibbutzim**)
a group of people in Israel, sharing a home, food, etc. and working especially as farmers.

**kick**[1] *verb* (**kicks, kicking, kicked**)
**1** to hit someone or something with your foot. **2** to move your legs about vigorously. **3** (of a gun) to move backwards sharply when it is fired.
**kick off**, to start a football match; (*informal*) to start doing something.
**kick out**, to get rid of someone; to dismiss someone.
**kick up**, (*informal*) to make a noise or fuss.

**kick²** *noun* (**kicks**)
1 a kicking movement. 2 the sudden backwards movement of a gun. 3 (*informal*) a thrill; a bit of excitement or pleasure. 4 (*informal*) an interest or activity, *He's on a health kick.*

**kick-off** *noun* (**kick-offs**)
the start of a football match.

**kid¹** *noun* (**kids**)
1 a young goat. 2 (*informal*) a child.

**kid²** *verb* (**kids, kidding, kidded**)
(*informal*) to deceive or tease someone.

**kidnap** *verb* (**kidnaps, kidnapping, kidnapped**)
to take someone away and keep him or her prisoner until you get what you want.
**kidnapper** *noun*

**kidney** *noun* (**kidneys**)
one of two organs in the body that remove unwanted substances from the blood and send them out of the body in urine.
**kidney machine,** a machine that does what the kidneys should do, used by someone with kidney disease.

**kill** *verb* (**kills, killing, killed**)
1 to make someone or an animal die. 2 to destroy something; to put an end to something.
**killer** *noun*

**kiln** *noun* (**kilns**)
an oven for hardening or drying pottery, bricks, hops, etc.

**kilo** *noun* (**kilos**)
a kilogram.

**kilogram** *noun* (**kilograms**)
a unit of weight equal to 1,000 grams or about $2\frac{1}{5}$ pounds.

**kilometre** *noun* (**kilometres**)
(*say* **kil**-ŏ-mee-ter *or* kil-**om**-i-ter)
a unit of length equal to 1,000 metres or about $\frac{3}{5}$ of a mile.

**kilowatt** *noun* (**kilowatts**)
a unit of electrical power equal to 1,000 watts.

**kilt** *noun* (**kilts**)
a kind of pleated skirt worn especially by Scotsmen.
**kilted** *adjective*

**kin** *noun*
your family or relatives.
**next of kin,** your closest relative.

**kind¹** *noun* (**kinds**)
a type or sort of something, *What kind of food do you like?*
**kind of,** (*informal*) vague; vaguely, *I had a kind of idea that this would happen. We kind of hoped you would come.*

**kind²** *adjective* (**kinder, kindest**)
ready to help and love other people; friendly.
**kind-hearted** *adjective*, **kindness** *noun*

**kindergarten** *noun* (**kindergartens**)
(*say* **kin**-der-gar-tĕn)
a school or class for very young children.

**kindle** *verb* (**kindles, kindling, kindled**)
1 to set light to something. 2 to start burning.

**kindling** *noun*
small pieces of wood for lighting fires.

**kindly¹** *adverb*
1 in a kind way. 2 please, *Kindly close the door.*

**kindly²** *adjective* (**kindlier, kindliest**)
kind, *She gave a kindly smile.*
**kindliness** *noun*

**kinetic** *adjective*
(*say* kin-**et**-ik)
of or produced by movement, *A hammer makes use of kinetic energy to bang in a nail.*

**king** *noun* (**kings**)
1 a man who has been crowned as the ruler of a country. 2 a piece in chess. 3 a playing-card with a picture of a king on it.
**kingly** *adjective*

**kingdom** *noun* (**kingdoms**)
a country that is ruled by a king or queen.

**kingfisher** *noun* (**kingfishers**)
a brightly-coloured bird that lives near water and catches fish.

**king-size** *or* **king-sized** *adjective*
larger than the usual size, *a king-size packet of breakfast cereal.*

**kink** *noun* (**kinks**)
1 a short twist in a rope, wire, piece of hair, etc. 2 something peculiar or eccentric.
**kinky** *adjective*

**kiosk** *noun* (**kiosks**)
(*say* **kee**-osk)
**1** a telephone box. **2** a small hut or stall where newspapers, sweets, tobacco, etc. are sold.

**kipper** *noun* (**kippers**)
a smoked herring.

**kiss**$^1$ *noun* (**kisses**)
touching someone with your lips as a sign of affection or as a greeting or on parting.
**kiss of life,** blowing air from your mouth into someone else's to help him or her to start breathing again, especially after an accident.

**kiss**$^2$ *verb* (**kisses, kissing, kissed**)
to give someone a kiss.

**kit** *noun* (**kits**)
**1** equipment; clothes. **2** a set of parts sold to be fitted together.

**kitchen** *noun* (**kitchens**)
a room where food is prepared and cooked.

**kite** *noun* (**kites**)
a light frame covered with cloth, paper, etc. and flown in the wind at the end of a long piece of string.

**kitten** *noun* (**kittens**)
a very young cat.
**kittenish** *adjective*

**kitty**$^1$ *noun* (**kitties**)
**1** an amount of money that you can win in a game. **2** an amount of money put aside for a special purpose.

**kitty**$^2$ *noun* (**kitties**)
(*informal*) a kitten.

**kiwi** *noun* (**kiwis**)
(*say* **kee**-wee)
a New Zealand bird that cannot fly.

**kiwi fruit** *noun* (**kiwi fruits**)
a fruit with soft, juicy, green flesh and a hairy skin.

**km** short for **kilometre** or **kilometres**.

**knack** *noun* (**knacks**)
a special skill.

**knapsack** *noun* (**knapsacks**)
a bag carried by hikers, soldiers, etc. on their backs.

**knave** *noun* (**knaves**)
(*old-fashioned use*) **1** a dishonest man. **2** the jack in a pack of playing-cards.
**knavery** *noun,* **knavish** *adjective*

**knead** *verb* (**kneads, kneading, kneaded**)
to press and stretch something soft, especially dough, with your hands.

**knee** *noun* (**knees**)
the joint in the middle of your leg.

**kneecap** *noun* (**kneecaps**)
the bony part at the front of your knee.

**kneel** *verb* (**kneels, kneeling, knelt**)
to be or get into a position on your knees.

**knew** past tense of **know.**

**knickers** *plural noun*
underpants worn by women or girls.

**knife**$^1$ *noun* (**knives**)
a cutting instrument made of a short blade set in a handle.

**knife**$^2$ *verb* (**knifes, knifing, knifed**)
to stab someone with a knife.

**knight** *noun* (**knights**)
**1** a man who has been given the honour that lets him put 'Sir' before his name. **2** a warrior who had been given the rank of a nobleman, in the Middle Ages. **3** a piece in chess, with a horse's head.
**knighthood** *noun*

**knit** *verb* (**knits, knitting, knitted**)
to make something by looping together threads of wool or other material, using long needles or a machine.
**knitter** *noun,* **knitting-needle** *noun*

**knives** plural of **knife** *noun.*

**knob** *noun* (**knobs**)
**1** the round handle of a door, drawer, etc. **2** a lump or swelling. **3** a control to adjust a radio or television set, etc.
**knobbly** *adjective,* **knobby** *adjective*

**knock**$^1$ *verb* (**knocks, knocking, knocked**)
**1** to hit something hard or by accident. **2** (*informal*) to criticize something unfavourably.
**knock off,** (*informal*) to stop working; to deduct something from a price; to steal something, *Let's knock off, it's time to go home. He knocked £20 off the price because we paid in cash. They knocked off several paintings from the art gallery.*
**knock out,** to hit someone so as to make him or her unconscious.

**knock**$^2$ *noun* (**knocks**)
the act or sound of hitting something.

**knocker** *noun* (**knockers**)
a device for knocking on a door.

**knock-out** *noun* (**knock-outs**)
**1** knocking someone out. **2** a contest in which competitors have to drop out one by one. **3** (*slang*) an excellent person or thing.

**knot**[1] *noun* (**knots**)
**1** a fastening made with string, rope, ribbon, etc. **2** a tangle; a lump. **3** a round spot on a piece of wood where there was a branch. **4** a cluster of people or things. **5** a unit for measuring the speed of ships and aircraft, *One knot equals 2,025 yards (or 1,852 metres) per hour.*

**knot**[2] *verb* (**knots, knotting, knotted**)
to make a fastening with string, rope, ribbon, etc.

**knotty** *adjective* (**knottier, knottiest**)
**1** full of knots. **2** difficult; puzzling, *a knotty problem.*

**know** *verb* (**knows, knowing, knew, known**)
**1** to have something in your mind that you have learnt or discovered, *I knew she was honest.* **2** to recognize or be familiar with a person or place, *I have known him for years.*

**know-all** *noun* (**know-alls**)
someone who thinks he or she knows everything.

**know-how** *noun*
skill; ability for a particular job.

**knowing** *adjective*
showing that you know something; cunning, *He gave me a knowing look.*

**knowingly** *adverb*
**1** in a knowing way, *He winked at me knowingly.* **2** deliberately, *She would never have done such a thing knowingly.*

**knowledge** *noun*
(*say* **nol**-ij)
what someone or everybody knows.

**knowledgeable** *adjective*
(*say* **nol**-ij-ă-bŭl)
having much knowledge; clever.
**knowledgeably** *adverb*

**knuckle** *noun* (**knuckles**)
any one of the joints in your fingers.

**koala** *noun* (**koalas**)
(*say* koh-**ah**-lă)
a furry Australian animal that looks like a small bear, *Koalas climb trees.*

**kookaburra** *noun* (**kookaburras**)
(*say* **kuuk**-ă-bu-ră)
a large Australian kingfisher that makes a laughing or shrieking noise.

**Koran** *noun*
(*say* kor-**ahn**)
the holy book of the Muslims.

**kosher** *adjective*
(*say* **koh**-sher)
(of food) prepared according to Jewish religious law.

**kung fu** *noun*
(*say* kuung-**foo**)
a Chinese method of self-defence rather like karate.

# Ll

**L** short for **learner**.

**label**[1] *noun* (**labels**)
a piece of paper, cloth, etc. fixed on or beside something to show what it is, whose it is, how much it costs, or where it is going.

**label**[2] *verb* (**labels, labelling, labelled**)
to put a label on something.

**laboratory** *noun* (**laboratories**)
(*say* lă-**bo**-ră-ter-i)
a room or building where scientific work is done.

**laborious** *adjective*
needing a lot of effort; very hard, *laborious work.*
**laboriously** *adverb*

**labour** *noun*
1 hard work. 2 the movements of a woman's womb when a baby is born.
**Labour,** those who support the Labour Party, a political party representing socialist ideas.

**labourer** *noun* (**labourers**)
someone who does hard work with his or her hands, especially out of doors.

**Labrador** *noun* (**Labradors**)
a large breed of dog that is black or light brown.

**laburnum** *noun* (**laburnums**)
a tree with hanging yellow flowers.

**labyrinth** *noun* (**labyrinths**)
a complicated and confusing path, road, etc.

**lace** *noun* (**laces**)
1 thin material with decorative patterns of holes in it. 2 a piece of thin cord used to tie up a shoe or boot.
**lacy** *adjective*

**lack**[1] *noun*
being without something, *There was a lack of water for the crops.*

**lack**[2] *verb* (**lacks, lacking, lacked**)
to be without something, *He lacks intelligence.*

**lacquer** *noun*
a kind of varnish.

**lacrosse** *noun*
a game like hockey but using a stick with a net on it to catch and throw the ball.

**lad** *noun* (**lads**)
a boy; a youth.

**ladder** *noun* (**ladders**)
1 a device to help you climb up or down something, made of upright pieces of wood, metal, or rope with cross-pieces called rungs. 2 (in America, *run*) a vertical row of damaged stitches in tights or a stocking.

**laden** *adjective*
carrying a heavy load.

**ladle** *noun* (**ladles**)
a large, deep spoon used for serving soup or other liquids.

**lady** *noun* (**ladies**)
a polite name for a woman.
**Lady,** the title of a noblewoman.
**the Ladies,** a lavatory for women.
**ladylike** *adjective*, **ladyship** *noun*

**ladybird** *noun* (**ladybirds**)
(in America, *ladybug*) a small flying beetle, usually red with black spots.

**lag**[1] *verb* (**lags, lagging, lagged**)
not to make the same progress as others, because you are going too slowly, *He's lagging behind again.*

**lag**[2] *verb* (**lags, lagging, lagged**)
to wrap pipes, boilers, etc. with insulating material to keep them warm.

**lager** *noun* (**lagers**)
(*say* **lah**-ger)
a light kind of beer.

**lagging** *noun*
material wrapped around something that needs to be kept warm, such as a hot-water pipe or a boiler.

**lagoon** *noun* (**lagoons**)
1 a lake separated from the sea by sandbanks or reefs. 2 (*in Australia and New Zealand*) a pond, often a stagnant pond.

**laid** past tense and past participle of **lay** *verb*.

**lain** past participle of **lie**[1] *verb*.

**lair** *noun* (**lairs**)
the place where a wild animal lives.

USAGE: Do not confuse **lair** with **layer**, which means something that lies on or under something else.

**lake** *noun* (**lakes**)
a large area of water surrounded by land.

**lamb** *noun* (**lambs**)
1 a young sheep. 2 the meat from young sheep.

**lame** *adjective* (**lamer, lamest**)
1 unable to walk properly. 2 weak; not convincing, *a lame excuse.*
**lamely** *adverb*, **lameness** *noun*

**lament** *verb* (**laments, lamenting, lamented**)
to express grief about something.
**lamentation** *noun*

**laminated** *adjective*
1 made of layers joined together, *The knife had a laminated handle.* 2 permanently covered in a kind of plastic for protection, *a laminated wall-chart.*

**lamp** *noun* (**lamps**)
a device for producing light from electricity, gas, or oil.
**lampshade** *noun*

**lamp-post** *noun* (**lamp-posts**)
a tall post in a street, etc., with a lamp at the top.

**lance** *noun* (**lances**)
a long spear.

**lance-corporal** *noun* (**lance-corporals**)
a soldier who comes between a corporal and a private in rank.

**land**[1] *noun* (**lands**)
1 a country. 2 all the dry parts of the world's surface. 3 the ground used for farming, building, etc.

**land**[2] *verb* (**lands, landing, landed**)
1 to bring someone or something to a place by means of a ship or aircraft. 2 to arrive in a ship or aircraft. 3 to reach the ground after jumping or falling. 4 (*informal*) to bring someone or get yourself to a particular place or situation, *You've landed me in trouble again!*
**land up**, (*informal*) to get to a particular place or situation, *The ball rolled down the hill and landed up in a ditch at the bottom.*

**landing** *noun* (**landings**)
the floor at the top of a flight of stairs.

**landing-stage** *noun* (**landing-stages**)
a platform on which people and goods are landed from a ship.

**landing-strip** *noun* (**landing-strips**)
a strip of land prepared for aircraft to take off and land.

**landlady** *noun* (**landladies**)
1 a woman who lets rooms to lodgers. 2 a woman who looks after a public house.

**landlord** *noun* (**landlords**)
1 someone who rents a house or land to someone else, or lets rooms to lodgers. 2 someone who looks after a public house.

**landmark** *noun* (**landmarks**)
an object on land that you can easily see from a distance.

**landowner** *noun* (**landowners**)
someone who owns a large amount of land.

**landscape** *noun* (**landscapes**)
1 a view of a particular area of town or countryside. 2 a picture of the countryside.
**landscape gardening**, laying out large gardens so that they look beautiful.

**landslide** *noun* (**landslides**)
1 earth or rocks sliding down the side of a hill. 2 a great victory for one side, especially in an election.

**lane** *noun* (**lanes**)
1 a narrow road, especially in the country. 2 a strip of road for a single line of traffic. 3 a strip of track or water for one runner or swimmer in a race.

**language** *noun* (**languages**)
1 words spoken or written. 2 the words used in a particular country or by a particular group of people. 3 a system of signs or symbols to convey information, *a computer language.*
**language laboratory**, a room equipped with devices to help you learn languages.

**lanky** *adjective* (**lankier, lankiest**)
awkwardly tall and thin.
**lankiness** *noun*

**lantern** *noun* (**lanterns**)
a transparent box for holding a light and shielding it from the wind.

**lap**[1] *noun* (**laps**)
1 the part from the waist to the knees of a person sitting down. 2 going round a racecourse once, *The 800 metres race consisted of 2 laps.*

**lap**[2] *verb* (**laps, lapping, lapped**)
1 to drink with the tongue, *The cat lapped up the milk.* 2 to make a gentle splash, *Small waves were lapping against the rocks.*

**lapel** *noun* (**lapels**)
(*say* lă-**pel**)
the flap on either of the front edges of a
coat below the collar.

**lapse** *noun* (**lapses**)
1 a slight mistake or fault. 2 the passing of
time, *After a lapse of three months work
began again.*

**laptop** *noun* (**laptops**)
a computer small enough to be held and
used on your lap, especially while you are
travelling.

**lapwing** *noun* (**lapwings**)
a peewit.

**larch** *noun* (**larches**)
a deciduous tree that bears small cones.

**lard** *noun*
white fat from pigs, used in cooking.

**larder** *noun* (**larders**)
a cupboard or small room where food is
kept.

**large** *adjective* (**larger, largest**)
more than the ordinary or average size; big.
**largeness** *noun*

**largely** *adverb*
mainly; mostly.

**lark**[1] *noun* (**larks**)
a skylark.

**lark**[2] *noun* (**larks**)
(*informal*) something amusing; a bit of fun,
*They just did it for a lark.*

**larva** *noun* (**larvae**)
an insect in the first stage of its life, after
it comes out of the egg.

**lasagne** *noun*
(*say* la-**zan**-ya)
wide, flat sheets of flour paste cooked with
minced meat and a white sauce.

**laser** *noun* (**lasers**)
(*say* **lay**-zer)
a device that makes a very strong narrow
beam of light.

**lash**[1] *noun* (**lashes**)
1 a stroke with a whip. 2 the cord of a whip.
3 an eyelash.

**lash**[2] *verb* (**lashes, lashing, lashed**)
1 to strike someone or something with a
whip or like a whip, *Rain lashed against
the window.* 2 to tie something tightly,
*They lashed it to the mast.*

**lass** *noun* (**lasses**)
(*in dialects*) a girl.

**lasso** *noun* (**lassos**)
(*say* la-**soo**)
a rope with a loop at the end which
tightens when you pull the rope, *Cowboys
use lassos for catching cattle.*

**last**[1] *adjective*
1 coming after all the others; final, *the last
bus.* 2 most recent; the latest, *last night.*
**at last,** finally; at the end.
**the last straw,** a final or added thing that
makes something unbearable.
**lastly** *adverb*

**last**[2] *verb* (**lasts, lasting, lasted**)
1 to continue, *The journey lasts two hours.*
2 to go on without being used up, *How long
will our supplies last?*

**latch** *noun* (**latches**)
a fastener on a gate or door.

**late** *adjective* (**later, latest**)
1 coming after the proper or expected time.
2 near the end of a period of time. 3 recent,
*the latest news.* 4 no longer alive, *the late
king.*
**lateness** *noun*

**lately** *adverb*
recently.

**latent** *adjective*
(*say* **lay**-těnt)
existing but not yet active, developed, or
visible.

**lateral** *adjective*
of, at, or from the sides of something.
**lateral thinking,** thinking of unusual ways to
solve problems or achieve things.

**lathe** *noun* (**lathes**)
(*say* layth)
a machine for holding and turning pieces of
wood or metal while you shape them.

**lather** *noun* (**lathers**)
a thick, usually soapy froth.

**Latin** *noun*
the language of the ancient Romans.

**latitude** *noun* (**latitudes**)
**1** how far a place is from the equator, measured in degrees. **2** freedom, *You will have considerable latitude for making your own decisions.*

**latter**[1] *noun*
**the latter,** the second of two people or things just mentioned, *Mike and Steve came in. The latter looked worried.*

**latter**[2] *adjective*
**1** later, *In his latter years he became a monk.* **2** recent, *The most important invention of latter years has been the computer.*
**latterly** *adverb*

**lattice** *noun* (**lattices**)
a criss-cross framework.

**laugh**[1] *verb* (**laughs, laughing, laughed**)
to make sounds that show you are happy or that you think something is very funny.

**laugh**[2] *noun* (**laughs**)
**1** an act or sound of laughing. **2** (*informal*) something that makes you laugh, *Drama lessons are a good laugh.*

**laughable** *adjective*
that deserves to be laughed at.

**laughter** *noun*
laughing, *They heard laughter.*

**launch**[1] *verb* (**launches, launching, launched**)
**1** to send a ship into the water. **2** to send a rocket into space. **3** to start something new.
**launching pad** or **launch pad,** a platform or place from which rockets are sent into space.

**launch**[2] *noun* (**launches**)
**1** a large motor boat. **2** the launching of a ship or rocket.

**launder** *verb* (**launders, laundering, laundered**)
to clean and press clothes.

**launderette** *noun* (**launderettes**)
a shop with washing-machines that people pay to use.

**laundry** *noun* (**laundries**)
**1** clothes to be washed. **2** a place where clothes are sent or taken to be laundered.

**laurel** *noun* (**laurels**)
an evergreen bush with smooth, shiny leaves.

**lava** *noun*
molten rock that flows from a volcano, or the solid rock formed when it cools.

**lavatory** *noun* (**lavatories**)
a place for getting rid of waste from the body.

**lavender** *noun*
**1** a bush with pale purple flowers that smell very sweet. **2** a pale purple colour.

**lavish** *adjective*
**1** generous, *She was lavish with her gifts.* **2** plentiful, *a lavish meal.*

**law** *noun* (**laws**)
**1** a rule or set of rules that everyone must keep. **2** something that always happens, *the law of gravity.*
**-in-law,** used to distinguish someone who became your relative by marriage, *George became my brother-in-law when he and my sister were married.*

**lawcourt** *noun* (**lawcourts**)
a place where people decide whether someone has broken the law.

**lawful** *adjective*
allowed or accepted by the law.
**lawfully** *adverb*

**lawless** *adjective*
not obeying the law; without laws, *lawless bands of rebels. It was a lawless country.*
**lawlessly** *adverb*, **lawlessness** *noun*

**lawn** *noun* (**lawns**)
an area of mown grass in a garden.

**lawn-mower** *noun* (**lawn-mowers**)
a machine with revolving blades for cutting grass.

**lawsuit** *noun* (**lawsuits**)
a dispute, claim, etc. considered in a lawcourt.

**lawyer** *noun* (**lawyers**)
an expert on law; someone whose job is to
help people with the law.

**laxative** *noun* (**laxatives**)
a medicine that causes your bowels to
empty.

**lay**$^1$ *verb* (**lays, laying, laid**)
1 to put something down in a particular
place or in a particular way. 2 to arrange
things, especially for a meal, *He laid the
table.* 3 to produce an egg.
**lay off,** to stop employing someone for a
while; (*informal*) to stop doing something,
*200 workers have been laid off. Lay off
telling me what to do!*
**lay on,** to supply or provide something.
**lay out,** to arrange or prepare something; to
knock someone unconscious, *We laid out
the papers for the conference. The boxer
laid out his opponent after two rounds.*

USAGE: Do not confuse **lay** with **lie**$^1$, which
means to be in or get into a flat position, or
to stay. Remember that **lay** can also be the
past tense of **lie**$^1$, as in: *The dog lay in front
of the fire; he had been lying there all night.*

**lay**$^2$ past tense of **lie**$^1$ *verb.*

**layabout** *noun* (**layabouts**)
a lazy person.

**layer** *noun* (**layers**)
something flat that lies on or under
something else, *The cake had a layer of
icing on top and a layer of jam inside.*

USAGE: Do not confuse **layer** with **lair**,
which is the place where a wild animal
lives.

**layout** *noun* (**layouts**)
the arrangement or design of something.

**laze** *verb* (**lazes, lazing, lazed**)
to spend time in a lazy way.

**lazy** *adjective* (**lazier, laziest**)
not wanting to work; doing little work.
**lazily** *adverb*, **laziness** *noun*

**lb.** short for **pound** or **pounds** in weight, *I
bought 5 lb. of potatoes.*

**l.b.w.** short for **leg before wicket.**

**lead**$^1$ *verb* (**leads, leading, led**)
(*say* leed)
1 to guide a person or animal, especially by
going in front. 2 to be in charge of
something. 3 to be winning in a race or
contest. 4 to go; to be a way to, *This road
leads to the beach.* 5 to play the first card in
a card-game.
**lead to,** to result in, *Their carelessness led
to the accident.*

**lead**$^2$ *noun* (**leads**)
(*say* leed)
1 leading; guidance, *Give us a lead.* 2 a
leading place or position, *She took the lead.*
3 a strap or cord for leading a dog. 4 an
electric wire, *Don't trip over that lead.*

**lead**$^3$ *noun* (**leads**)
(*say* led)
1 a soft, heavy, grey metal. 2 the writing
substance in the middle of a pencil.

**leader** *noun* (**leaders**)
1 someone who leads; a chief. 2 an
important article in a newspaper.
**leadership** *noun*

**leaf** *noun* (**leaves**)
1 one of the usually green and flat growths
on trees and plants. 2 a page of a book. 3 a
very thin sheet of metal, *gold leaf.* 4 a flap
that makes a table larger.
**leafless** *adjective*, **leafy** *adjective*

**leaflet** *noun* (**leaflets**)
a piece of paper printed with information,
instructions, etc.

**league** *noun* (**leagues**)
(*say* leeg)
1 a group of teams that play matches
against each other. 2 a group of countries
that have agreed to work together for a
particular reason.
**in league with,** working or plotting together.

**leak**$^1$ *noun* (**leaks**)
1 a hole, crack, etc. through which liquid or
gas escapes. 2 the revealing of some secret
information.
**leaky** *adjective*

**leak**$^2$ *verb* (**leaks, leaking, leaked**)
1 to let something out through a hole,
crack, etc.; to get out in this way. 2 to
reveal secret information.
**leakage** *noun*

**lean**$^1$ *verb* (**leans, leaning, leaned** or **leant**)
1 to bend your body towards or over
something. 2 to put something into a
sloping position. 3 to rest against
something.

**lean**$^2$ *adjective* (**leaner, leanest**)
1 without fat, *lean meat.* 2 thin, *a lean
person.*

**lean-to** *noun* (**lean-tos**)
a building or shed with its roof leaning
against the side of a larger building.

**leap**$^1$ *noun* (**leaps**)
1 a vigorous jump. 2 a sudden increase or
advance.

**leap**$^2$ *verb* (**leaps, leaping, leapt** or **leaped**)
1 to make a vigorous jump. 2 to increase or
advance suddenly.

**leap-frog** *noun*
a game in which each player jumps with legs apart over the bended backs of the others.

**leap year** *noun* (**leap years**)
a year when February has twenty-nine days, *It is usually a leap year when you can divide the date by 4, as in 1940 and 1984.*

**learn** *verb* (**learns, learning, learnt** or **learned**)
to find out about something; to get knowledge or skill.

**learned** *adjective*
(*say* **ler**-nid)
clever; knowledgeable.

**learner** *noun* (**learners**)
someone who is learning something, especially how to drive a car.

**learning** *noun*
knowledge.

**lease** *noun* (**leases**)
an agreement to let someone pay to use a building or land for a fixed period.
**a new lease of life,** a chance to go on being active or useful.

**leash** *noun* (**leashes**)
a strap or cord for leading a dog.

**least**[1] *adjective*
smallest; less than all the others, *the least expensive bike.*
**at least,** not less than what is mentioned; anyway, *It will cost at least £30 to mend your bicycle. He doesn't mind – at least he says he doesn't.*

**least**[2] *noun*
the smallest amount.

**leather** *noun* (**leathers**)
a strong material made from animals' skins.
**leathery** *adjective*

**leave**[1] *verb* (**leaves, leaving, left**)
1 to go away from a person, place, or group. 2 to let something stay where it is or remain as it is, *I've left my book at home.* 3 to give something as a legacy, *He left me £500 in his will.*
**leave out,** not to include something or someone.
**left over,** remaining when other things have been used.

**leave**[2] *noun*
1 permission. 2 permission to be away from work; the time when you are allowed to be away from work; holiday.

**leaves** plural of **leaf.**

**lectern** *noun* (**lecterns**)
a stand to hold a Bible or other large book from which you read.

**lecture**[1] *noun* (**lectures**)
1 a talk about a subject to an audience or a class. 2 a speech telling someone off.

**lecture**[2] *verb* (**lectures, lecturing, lectured**)
to give a lecture.
**lecturer** *noun*

**led** past tense and past participle of **lead** *verb.*

**ledge** *noun* (**ledges**)
a narrow shelf.

**lee** *noun*
the sheltered side of something, away from the wind.

**leek** *noun* (**leeks**)
a white vegetable like an onion with broad leaves.

**leer** *verb* (**leers, leering, leered**)
to look unpleasantly or evilly at someone.

**leeward** *adjective*
that faces away from the wind, *the leeward side of the ship.*

**left**[1] *adjective*
1 on or near the left hand. 2 in favour of changes which would share wealth more equally, *the left wing of the party.*

**left**[2] *noun*
the left side, *In Britain, we drive on the left of the road.*

**left**[3] past tense and past participle of **leave** *verb.*

**left hand** *noun* (**left hands**)
the hand that most people use less than the other, on the same side of the body as the heart, *When they eat, most people hold the fork in their left hand and the knife in their right hand.*
**left-hand** *adjective*

**left-handed** *adjective*
using the left hand more than the right hand.

**left-overs** *plural noun*
food not eaten by the end of a meal.

**leg** *noun* (**legs**)
**1** one of the parts of a human's or animal's body on which it stands, walks, and runs. **2** the part of a piece of clothing that covers a leg. **3** one of the supports of a chair or other piece of furniture. **4** one part of a journey, championship, etc.
**leg before wicket,** when a batsman in cricket is out because of obstructing the ball with his body.
**on your last legs,** exhausted.

**legacy** *noun* (**legacies**)
something given to someone in a will.

**legal** *adjective*
**1** lawful. **2** of the law or lawyers.
**legality** *noun*, **legally** *adverb*

**legalize** *verb* (**legalizes, legalizing, legalized**)
to make something lawful.

**legend** *noun* (**legends**)
(*say* **lej**-ĕnd)
an old story handed down from the past.
**legendary** *adjective*

**legible** *adjective*
clear enough to read, *Your writing is hardly legible*.
**legibility** *noun*, **legibly** *adverb*

**legion** *noun* (**legions**)
**1** a division of the ancient Roman army. **2** a group of soldiers, or men who used to be soldiers.

**legislate** *verb* (**legislates, legislating, legislated**)
to make laws.
**legislation** *noun*, **legislator** *noun*

**legitimate** *adjective*
(*say* li-**jit**-i-măt)
lawful.
**legitimacy** *noun*, **legitimately** *adverb*

**leisure** *noun*
a time that is free from work, when you can do what you like.
**at leisure,** not at work; without hurrying, *The weekend is a time when people should be at leisure. I would like to read the details at leisure.*
**leisurely** *adjective* and *adverb*

**lemon** *noun* (**lemons**)
**1** a yellow fruit with a sour taste. **2** a pale yellow colour.
**lemon cheese** or **lemon curd,** a creamy jam made with lemons.

**lemonade** *noun* (**lemonades**)
a drink with a flavour of lemons.

**lend** *verb* (**lends, lending, lent**)
to let someone have something of yours for a short time, *She lent me her bike.*
**lend a hand,** to help someone.

**length** *noun* (**lengths**)
**1** how long something is. **2** a piece of rope, wire, cloth, etc.
**at length,** finally.

**lengthen** *verb* (**lengthens, lengthening, lengthened**)
to make something longer; to become longer.

**lengthways** or **lengthwise** *adverb*
from end to end; along the longest part of something.

**lengthy** *adjective* (**lengthier, lengthiest**)
long; too long, *a lengthy speech*.

**lenient** *adjective*
(*say* **lee**-ni-ĕnt)
merciful; not severe.
**lenience** *noun*, **leniently** *adverb*

**lens** *noun* (**lenses**)
a curved piece of glass or plastic used to focus images of things, or to concentrate light.

**Lent** *noun*
the period of about six weeks before Easter.

**lent** past tense and past participle of **lend.**

**lentil** *noun* (**lentils**)
a kind of small bean.

**leopard** *noun* (**leopards**)
(*say* **lep**-erd)
a large spotted wild animal of the cat family.

**leotard** *noun* (**leotards**)
(*say* **lee**-ŏ-tard)
a close-fitting piece of clothing worn by acrobats and dancers.

**leper** *noun* (**lepers**)
someone who has leprosy.

**leprosy** *noun*
a disease that attacks the skin and nerves, affecting the appearance and shape of the body.
**leprous** *adjective*

**less**[1] *adjective* (**lesser, least**)
smaller; not so much, *The noise eventually became less. Eat less meat.*

**less**[2] *adverb*
to a smaller extent, *It is less important.*
**no less than,** at least, *a speed of no less than thirty miles per hour.*

**less**[3] *preposition*
minus; deducting, *She earned £100, less tax.*

**-less** *suffix*
lacking something; free from something, *a useless idea. Coke is a smokeless fuel.*

**lessen** *verb* (**lessens, lessening, lessened**)
to make something smaller or not so much; to become smaller or not so much.

**lesson** *noun* (**lessons**)
**1** the time when someone is teaching you. **2** something that you have to learn. **3** a section of writing from the Bible read aloud in church.

**lest** *conjunction*
so that something should not happen; to prevent something, *He ran away lest he should be seen.*

**let** *verb* (**lets, letting, let**)
**1** to allow someone to do something. **2** to allow something to happen. **3** to allow someone to use a house, building, etc. in return for payment. **4** to leave, *Let it alone.*
**let down,** to let the air or gas out of something; to disappoint someone.
**let off,** to explode something; to excuse someone from a punishment or duty.
**let on,** (*informal*) to tell a secret, *I'll tell you the secret, but don't let on!*
**let's,** (*informal*) shall we; I suggest that we, *Let's go away for the weekend.*

**lethal** *adjective*
deadly, *a lethal gas.*
**lethally** *adverb*

**letter** *noun* (**letters**)
**1** one of the symbols used for writing words, such as a, b, or c. **2** a written message sent to another person.

**letter-box** *noun* (**letter-boxes**)
a box or slot into which letters are delivered or posted.

**lettering** *noun*
letters drawn or painted.

**lettuce** *noun* (**lettuces**)
a green vegetable used in salads.

**leukaemia** *noun*
(*say* lew-**kee**-mi-ă)
a disease in which there are too many white cells in the blood.

**level**[1] *adjective*
**1** flat; horizontal, *level ground.* **2** equal; alongside a person or thing, *He was level with the others.*
**level crossing,** a place where a road crosses a railway at the same level.

**level**[2] *verb* (**levels, levelling, levelled**)
**1** to make something flat or horizontal. **2** to make something equal, *an attempt to level incomes.* **3** to aim a gun.

**level**[3] *noun* (**levels**)
**1** height, *eye level.* **2** a device that shows if something is horizontal. **3** a flat or horizontal surface. **4** a standard or position, *She has reached level 3 in gymnastics.*
**on the level,** (*informal*) honest.

**lever** *noun* (**levers**)
a bar that is pushed or pulled to lift something heavy, force something open, or make a machine work.
**leverage** *noun*

**lexical** *adjective*
of the words of a language.

**liable** *adjective*
**1** likely to do or get something, *Parking on the yellow lines makes you liable to a fine.* **2** responsible for something.
**liability** *noun*

**liar** *noun* (**liars**)
someone who tells lies.

**liberal** *adjective*
**1** generous; ample. **2** not strict; tolerant.
**Liberal,** a supporter of the Liberal Party (now part of the Liberal Democrats).
**liberality** *noun*, **liberally** *adverb*

**liberate** *verb* (**liberates, liberating, liberated**)
to set someone free.
**liberation** *noun*

**liberty** *noun* (**liberties**)
freedom.
**take liberties,** to behave too freely or informally.

**librarian** *noun* (**librarians**)
someone who looks after or works in a library.
**librarianship** *noun*

**library** *noun* (**libraries**)
a place where books are kept for people to use or borrow.

**lice** plural of **louse.**

**licence** *noun* (**licences**)
an official document allowing someone to do, use, or own something, *a dog licence*.

USAGE: Do not confuse **licence**, which is a noun, with **license**, which is a verb and is the next word in this dictionary.

**license** *verb* (**licenses, licensing, licensed**)
to give a licence to someone; to permit, *We are licensed to sell alcoholic drinks*.
**licensee** *noun*

**lichen** *noun* (**lichens**)
(*say* **ly-kĕn**)
a dry-looking plant that grows on rocks, walls, trees, etc.

**lick**[1] *verb* (**licks, licking, licked**)
1 to move your tongue over something.
2 (*informal*) to defeat someone.

**lick**[2] *noun* (**licks**)
1 the act of moving your tongue over something. 2 (*informal*) a fast speed.

**lid** *noun* (**lids**)
1 a cover for a box, pot, etc. 2 an eyelid.

**lie**[1] *verb* (**lies, lying, lay, lain**)
1 to be in or get into a flat position, especially to rest with your body flat as it is in bed, *He lay on the grass. The cat has lain here all night*. 2 to stay; to be, *The castle was lying in ruins. The valley lay before us*.
**lie low**, to keep yourself hidden.

USAGE: Do not confuse **lie** *verb* with **lay** *verb*, which means to put something down in a particular place, to arrange things, or to produce an egg.

**lie**[2] *verb* (**lies, lying, lied**)
to say something that is not true.

**lie**[3] *noun* (**lies**)
something that is deliberately not true.

**lieutenant** *noun* (**lieutenants**)
(*say* lef-**ten**-ănt)
an officer in the army or navy.

**life** *noun* (**lives**)
1 the time between birth and death. 2 being alive. 3 living things, *Is there life on Mars?* 4 liveliness, *full of life*. 5 the story of what a person has done.
**life expectancy**, the length of time that a particular person, animal, or plant is likely to live, *Women have a longer life expectancy than men*.

**life assurance** *noun*
life insurance.

**lifebelt** *noun* (**lifebelts**)
a circle of material that will float, used to support someone's body in water.

**lifeboat** *noun* (**lifeboats**)
a boat for rescuing people at sea.

**life cycle** *noun* (**life cycles**)
the series of stages that living things go through as they develop, ending back at the first stage, *The life cycle of a butterfly is: egg, caterpillar, pupa, butterfly, egg*.

**life-guard** *noun* (**life-guards**)
someone whose job is to rescue swimmers who are in difficulty.

**life insurance** *noun*
insurance which pays someone a large amount of money if the holder of the insurance dies.

**life-jacket** *noun* (**life-jackets**)
a jacket of material that will float, used to support someone's body in water.

**lifeless** *adjective*
1 without life. 2 unconscious.

**lifelike** *adjective*
looking exactly like a real person or thing.

**lifelong** *adjective*
lasting throughout someone's life.

**lifespan** *noun* (**lifespans**)
how long a person, an animal, or a plant lives.

**lifestyle** *noun* (**lifestyles**)
the way of life of a person or a group of people, *an expensive lifestyle*.

**lifetime** *noun* (**lifetimes**)
the time for which someone is alive.

**lift**[1] *verb* (**lifts, lifting, lifted**)
1 to pick up something; to raise someone or something. 2 to rise. 3 (*informal*) to steal.

**lift**[2] *noun* (**lifts**)
1 the act of lifting. 2 (in America, *elevator*) a device for taking people or goods up and down inside a building. 3 a ride in someone else's car, lorry, etc.

**lift-off** *noun* (**lift-offs**)
the vertical take-off of a rocket.

**light[1]** *noun* (**lights**)
1 what makes things visible, the opposite of darkness, *There was not enough light to see the garden*. 2 something that provides light or a flame, especially an electric lamp, *Switch on the light*.

**light[2]** *adjective* (**lighter, lightest**)
1 full of light; not dark. 2 pale, *light blue*.

**light[3]** *adjective* (**lighter, lightest**)
1 not heavy; weighing little. 2 not large; not strong, *a light wind*. 3 not serious; not needing great thought, *light music*.
**lightly** *adverb*

**light[4]** *verb* (**lights, lighting, lit or lighted**)
1 to start something burning, *Have you lit the fire? I lit it just now. a lighted torch*. 2 to begin to burn, *The fire won't light*. 3 to give light to something, *The streets were lit by gaslamps*.
**light up**, to make something light or bright; to become light or bright; to turn lights on, especially at dusk.

**lighten** *verb* (**lightens, lightening, lightened**)
to make something lighter; to become lighter.

USAGE: Do not confuse **lightening** (which means making something lighter, or becoming lighter) with **lightning**, which means a flash of bright light in the sky during a thunderstorm.

**lighter** *noun* (**lighters**)
a device for lighting something like a cigarette or a fire.

**light-headed** *adjective*
slightly giddy.

**light-hearted** *adjective*
cheerful; free from worry; not serious.
**light-heartedly** *adverb*, **light-heartedness** *noun*

**lighthouse** *noun* (**lighthouses**)
a tower with a bright light at the top to warn ships that there are rocks or other dangers near by.

**lighting** *noun*
lamps, or the light they provide.

**lightning** *noun*
a flash of bright light in the sky during a thunderstorm.
**lightning-conductor,** a metal wire or rod fixed on a building to divert lightning into the earth.

USAGE: Do not confuse **lightning** with **lightening**, which means making something lighter, or becoming lighter.

**light-pen** *noun* (**light-pens**)
a device shaped like a pen, connected to a computer, and used to read bar-codes.

**lightship** *noun* (**lightships**)
an anchored ship with a bright light on it to warn ships that there are rocks or other dangers near by.

**lightweight** *adjective*
less than average weight, *a lightweight suit*.

**light-year** *noun* (**light-years**)
the distance that light travels in one year (about 6 million million miles).

**like[1]** *verb* (**likes, liking, liked**)
to think someone or something is pleasant or satisfactory.
**should like** or **would like,** to want, *I should like to see him*.
**likeable** *adjective*

**like[2]** *preposition*
1 resembling; similar to; in the manner of, *He cried like a baby*. 2 such as, *We need things like knives and forks*. 3 typical of, *It was like her to forgive him*.
**like anything** or **like mad,** (*informal*) very much; vigorously, *She wanted like anything to become an engineer. Run like mad!*

**like[3]** *adjective*
similar, *They are as like as two peas*.

**likely** *adjective* (**likelier, likeliest**)
probable; expected to happen or to be true, useful, etc.
**not likely!,** (*informal*) that is impossible; I refuse.

**likeness** *noun* (**likenesses**)
a resemblance.

**likewise** *adverb*
similarly.

**liking** *noun* (**likings**)
the condition of liking someone or something, *She has a great liking for chocolate*.
**something is to someone's liking,** someone likes something.

**lilac** *noun* (**lilacs**)
1 a bush with sweet-smelling purple or white flowers. 2 a pale purple colour.

**lily** *noun* (**lilies**)
a garden flower grown from a bulb.

**limb** *noun* (**limbs**)
a leg, arm, or wing.

**lime**[1] *noun*
a white, chalky powder used in making cement or as a fertilizer.

**lime**[2] *noun* (**limes**)
a green fruit rather like a lemon.
**lime-juice** *noun*

**lime**[3] *noun* (**limes**)
a tree with yellow blossom.

**limelight** *noun*
great public interest or attention, *After the newspaper wrote about us, our school was in the limelight for several weeks.*

**limerick** *noun* (**limericks**)
(*say* **lim**-er-ik)
a comical poem with five lines.

**limestone** *noun*
rock from which lime is made.

**limit**[1] *noun* (**limits**)
1 a line or point that you cannot or should not pass, *a speed limit. There are limits to how much work we can do.* 2 an edge of something, *The white line marks the limit of the road on either side.*
**limitless** *adjective*

**limit**[2] *verb* (**limits, limiting, limited**)
to restrict something or someone.
**limitation** *noun*

**limited** *adjective*
1 restricted; small. 2 that is a *limited company* or *limited liability company*, a business company whose members are responsible for only some of its debts, *'Ltd.' after the name of a business shows that it is a limited company.*

**limp**[1] *verb* (**limps, limping, limped**)
to walk with difficulty because something is wrong with your leg or foot.

**limp**[2] *noun* (**limps**)
a limping movement.

**limp**[3] *adjective* (**limper, limpest**)
not stiff or firm; without strength, *limp lettuces. a limp handshake.*

**limpet** *noun* (**limpets**)
a small shellfish that attaches itself firmly to rocks.

**linctus** *noun* (**linctuses**)
a soothing, sweet medicine for coughs or sore throats.

**line**[1] *noun* (**lines**)
1 a long, thin mark. 2 a row or series of people or things. 3 a length of rope, string, wire, etc. 4 a railway; a length of railway track. 5 a system of ships, aircraft, buses, etc. 6 a way of working, behaving, etc.
**in line**, forming a straight line; conforming.

**line**[2] *verb* (**lines, lining, lined**)
1 to mark something with lines. 2 to make an edge or border for something, *The streets are lined with trees.*
**line up**, to form lines; to cause someone or something to form lines, *The children lined up. We lined up the empty cans on top of the wall.*

**linen** *noun*
1 cloth made from flax, used to make sheets, tablecloths, handkerchiefs, etc. 2 things made of this cloth.

**liner** *noun* (**liners**)
a large ship or aircraft, usually carrying passengers.

**linesman** *noun* (**linesmen**)
an official in football, tennis, etc. who decides whether the ball has crossed a line.

**linger** *verb* (**lingers, lingering, lingered**)
1 to be slow to leave, *A few guests lingered at the end of the party.* 2 to stay somewhere for a long time, *He would linger for hours on the moors.*

**lingerie** *noun*
(*say* **lan**-zher-ee)
women's underclothes.

**linguist** *noun* (**linguists**)
an expert in languages.
**linguistic** *adjective*, **linguistics** *noun*

**lining** *noun* (**linings**)
a layer covering the inside of something.

**link**[1] *noun* (**links**)
1 one of the rings in a chain. 2 a connection.

**link**[2] *verb* (**links, linking, linked**)
to join things together.
**linking verb**, (*in grammar*) a type of verb that links parts of a clause.
**link up**, to become connected.

**linoleum** *noun*
(*say* lin-**oh**-li-ŭm)
a stiff, shiny covering for floors.

**lint** *noun*
a soft material for covering wounds.

**lion** *noun* (**lions**)
a large, light-brown wild animal of the cat family, found in Africa and India.

**lioness** *noun* (**lionesses**)
a female lion.

lioness

lion

**lip** *noun* (**lips**)
1 one of the two edges of your mouth. 2 the edge of something hollow such as a cup or a crater. 3 a projecting part at the top of a jug, saucepan, etc. to help pouring.

**lip-read** *verb* (**lip-reads, lip-reading, lip-read**)
to understand what someone is saying by watching the movements of his or her lips, not by hearing his or her voice.

**lipstick** *noun* (**lipsticks**)
a stick of a substance used especially by women for colouring their lips.

**liquid** *noun* (**liquids**)
a substance that can flow like water or oil.

**liquidizer** *noun* (**liquidizers**)
a device for making food into a pulp or a liquid.

**liquor** *noun* (**liquors**)
(*say* **lik**-er)
alcoholic drink.

**liquorice** *noun*
(*say* **lik**-er-iss)
a soft black sweet with a strong taste.

**lisp** *verb* (**lisps, lisping, lisped**)
to pronounce *s* as *th*, '*I'll thcream,*' lisped *Violet Elizabeth.*

**list**[1] *noun* (**lists**)
a number of things or names written down or printed one after another.

**list**[2] *verb* (**lists, listing, listed**)
to write down or print things one after another.

**list**[3] *verb* (**lists, listing, listed**)
to lean over to one side in the water, *The ship was listing badly.*

**listen** *verb* (**listens, listening, listened**)
to pay attention in order to hear something.
**listener** *noun*

**listless** *adjective*
too tired to be active or enthusiastic.
**listlessly** *adverb*, **listlessness** *noun*

**lit** past tense and past participle of **light** *verb*.

**literacy** *noun*
(*say* **lit**-er-ă-si)
the ability to read and write.

**literal** *adjective*
1 meaning exactly what it says. 2 precise, *a literal translation.*
**literally** *adverb*

**literary** *adjective*
(*say* **lit**-er-er-i)
of or interested in literature.

**literate** *adjective*
(*say* **lit**-er-ăt)
able to read and write.

**literature** *noun*
1 books or writings, especially those considered to have been written well. 2 printed material about a subject, *Get some literature about coach-tours.*

**lithosphere** *noun*
the solid crust of the earth, not the hydrosphere or the atmosphere.

**litmus** *noun*
a blue substance used to show whether something is an acid or an alkali.
**litmus-paper** *noun*

**litre** *noun* (**litres**)
(*say* **lee**-ter)
a measure of liquid, 1,000 cubic centimetres or about 1¾ pints.

**litter**[1] *verb* (**litters, littering, littered**)
to make a place untidy with rubbish or things left lying about.

**litter**[2] *noun*
rubbish or untidy things left lying about.

**litter**[3] *noun* (**litters**)
all the young animals born to the same mother at one time.

**little** *adjective* (**less** or **littler, least** or **littlest**)
1 small, *a little boy.* 2 not much, *We have little time.* 3 a small amount of something, *Have a little sugar.*
**little by little**, gradually.

**live**[1] *verb* (**lives, living, lived**)
(rhymes with *give*)
**1** to be alive. **2** to have your home in a
particular place, *She is living in Glasgow.*
**3** to pass your life in a certain way, *He
lived as a hermit.*
**live on**, to use something as food; to depend
upon something, *The islanders lived
mainly on fish. The whole town lives on the
tourist trade.*

**live**[2] *adjective*
(rhymes with *hive*)
**1** alive. **2** carrying electricity. **3** broadcast
while it is actually happening. **4** recorded
with an audience present.

**livelihood** *noun* (**livelihoods**)
(*say* **lyv**-li-huud)
the way in which you earn a living.

**lively** *adjective* (**livelier, liveliest**)
full of energy or cheerfulness.
**liveliness** *noun*

**liver** *noun* (**livers**)
**1** a large organ in the body that produces
bile and helps keep the blood clean. **2** this
organ from a cow, pig, lamb, etc., used as
food.

**lives** plural of **life**.

**livestock** *noun*
farm animals.

**living** *noun*
**1** the way that you live or keep alive, *What
do you do for a living?* **2** enough money for
a normal life, *He earned a living as a
salesman.*

**living-room** *noun* (**living-rooms**)
a sitting-room; a room for general use
during the day.

**lizard** *noun* (**lizards**)
a four-legged reptile with scaly skin.

**llama** *noun* (**llamas**)
(*say* **lah**-mă)
a South American animal with woolly fur.

**load**[1] *noun* (**loads**)
**1** something to be carried. **2** the quantity
that can be carried. **3** (*informal*) a large
amount, *It's a load of nonsense.*

**load**[2] *verb* (**loads, loading, loaded**)
**1** to put a load on something. **2** to put a
weight into a thing, *loaded dice.* **3** to give
someone large amounts of something, *They
loaded him with gifts.* **4** to put a bullet or
shell into a gun. **5** to put a film into a
camera.

**loaf**[1] *noun* (**loaves**)
bread in the shape it had when it was
baked.

**loaf**[2] *verb* (**loafs, loafing, loafed**)
**1** to loiter, *They spent most of the day
loafing around on the streets.* **2** to waste
time, *He's just loafing – he ought to be
helping us instead.*
**loafer** *noun*

**loam** *noun*
rich, fertile soil.
**loamy** *adjective*

**loan**[1] *noun* (**loans**)
something that has been lent to someone.

**loan**[2] *verb* (**loans, loaning, loaned**)
to lend.

**loath** *adjective*
(rhymes with *both*)
unwilling, *I was loath to go.*

USAGE: Do not confuse **loath** with **loathe**,
which is a verb and is the next word in this
dictionary.

**loathe** *verb* (**loathes, loathing, loathed**)
(rhymes with *clothe*)
to hate, *She loathed bad manners.*
**loathsome** *adjective*

**loaves** plural of **loaf** *noun*.

**lob** *verb* (**lobs, lobbing, lobbed**)
to throw or hit something high up into the
air.

**lobby** *noun* (**lobbies**)
an entrance-hall.

**lobe** *noun* (**lobes**)
the rounded part at the bottom of an ear.

**lobster** *noun* (**lobsters**)
a large shellfish with eight legs and two
claws.

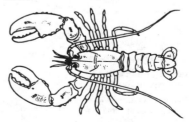

**lobster-pot** *noun* (**lobster-pots**)
a basket for catching lobsters.

**local**[1] *adjective*
1 of or belonging to a particular place or district, *local government*. 2 affecting a particular area, *a local anaesthetic*.
**local history,** events that happened in the past in a particular place; the study of these events.
**locally** *adverb*

**local**[2] *noun* (**locals**)
(*informal*) 1 someone who lives in a particular district. 2 a pub near a person's home.

**locality** *noun* (**localities**)
1 a district. 2 a location, *Where is the exact locality of the accident?*

**locate** *verb* (**locates, locating, located**)
to discover where something is, *I have located the fault.*
**located,** situated, *The cinema is located in the High Street.*

**location** *noun* (**locations**)
the place where something is.
**on location,** filmed in natural surroundings, not in a studio.

**loch** *noun* (**lochs**)
a lake in Scotland.

**lock**[1] *noun* (**locks**)
1 a fastening that is opened with a key. 2 part of a canal or river between gates where boats are raised or lowered to a different level. 3 the distance that a vehicle's front wheels can turn. 4 a piece of hair.
**lock, stock, and barrel,** completely.

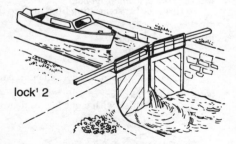

lock[1] 2

**lock**[2] *verb* (**locks, locking, locked**)
1 to fasten or secure with a lock. 2 to become fixed in one place; to jam.

**locker** *noun* (**lockers**)
a small cupboard.

**locket** *noun* (**lockets**)
a small case worn on a chain round someone's neck, often holding a photograph.

**locomotive** *noun* (**locomotives**)
a railway engine.

**locus** *noun* (**loci**)
(*in Mathematics*) the line made by a moving point or by points placed according to a particular rule.

**locust** *noun* (**locusts**)
an insect that flies in large swarms which eat all the plants in an area.

**lodge**[1] *noun* (**lodges**)
1 a small house. 2 a room or small house at the entrance to a large house, college, etc.

**lodge**[2] *verb* (**lodges, lodging, lodged**)
1 to stay somewhere as a lodger. 2 to give someone a place to sleep. 3 to become fixed, *The ball lodged in the branches.*
**lodge a complaint,** to make a complaint.
**lodging-house** *noun*

**lodger** *noun* (**lodgers**)
someone who pays to live in someone else's house.

**lodgings** *plural noun*
a room or rooms where you live in someone else's house, and for which you pay.

**loft** *noun* (**lofts**)
the room or space under the roof of a house.

**lofty** *adjective* (**loftier, loftiest**)
1 tall, *lofty trees*. 2 noble; proud, *lofty ideals*.
**loftily** *adverb*, **loftiness** *noun*

**log**[1] *noun* (**logs**)
1 a large piece of a tree that has fallen or been cut down. 2 a detailed record kept of a ship's voyage, aircraft's flight, etc.

**log**[2] *noun* (**logs**)
a logarithm.

**log**[3] *verb* (**logs, logging, logged**)
(*in Computing*)
**log in,** to gain access to a computer system, usually by inputting a secret word.
**log out,** to finish using a computer system.

**logarithm** *noun* (**logarithms**)
one of a series of numbers set out in tables, used to help you do arithmetic.

**log-book** *noun* (**log-books**)
1 a book in which a log of a ship's voyage, etc. is kept. 2 a booklet or card listing details of a motor vehicle.

**logic** *noun*
thinking in an orderly way.
**logical** *adjective*, **logically** *adverb*

**logo** *noun* (**logos**)
a symbol that stands for a company or other organization, *The Shell logo is like a sea shell.*

**loiter** *verb* (**loiters, loitering, loitered**)
to stand about with nothing to do.
**loiterer** *noun*

**loll** *verb* (**lolls, lolling, lolled**)
to sit or lie in an untidy, lazy way.

**lollipop** *noun* (**lollipops**)
a sweet on the end of a stick.
**lollipop lady** or **lollipop man,** (*informal*) an official who uses a circular sign on a stick to signal traffic to stop so that children can cross the road.

**lolly** *noun* (**lollies**)
1 (*informal*) an ice lolly. 2 (*informal*) a lollipop. 3 (*slang*) money.

**lone** *adjective*
solitary, *a lone rider.*

**lonely** *adjective* (**lonelier, loneliest**)
1 unhappy because you are on your own.
2 far from other inhabited places; not often used or visited, *a lonely village.*
**loneliness** *noun*

**long**¹ *adjective* (**longer, longest**)
1 big when measured from one end to the other, *a long river.* 2 taking a lot of time, *a long holiday.* 3 from one end to the other, *A cricket pitch is 22 yards long.*
**long division,** dividing one number by another and writing down all your calculations.
**long jump,** an athletic contest of jumping as far as you can with one leap.
**long sight,** not being able to see things clearly unless they are at a distance.
**long wave,** a radio wave of more than 1,000 metres wavelength.

**long**² *adverb* (**longer, longest**)
1 for a long time, *Have you been waiting long?* 2 a long time before or after, *They left long ago.*
**as long as** or **so long as,** provided that; on condition that.

**long**³ *verb* (**longs, longing, longed**)
**long for something,** to want something very much.

**longbow** *noun* (**longbows**)
a curved piece of springy wood used to shoot arrows, held with the ends pointing upwards and downwards (compare *crossbow*).

**longitude** *noun* (**longitudes**)
(*say* **long**-i-tewd *or* **lon**-ji-tewd)
the distance east or west, measured in degrees, from an imaginary line that passes through Greenwich, London.
**longitudinal** *adjective*

**long-playing** *adjective*
(of a record) that plays for about 20 minutes on each side.

**long-range** *adjective*
1 able to go a long distance, *a long-range transport aircraft.* 2 connected with a time that is a long way into the future, *The long-range weather forecast says that it will snow next week.*

**longshore drift** *noun*
the movement of sand, shingle, etc. along a coast by the action of waves, tides, and currents.

**long-term** *adjective*
of or for a long period of time, *Our long-term plan is to replace the car, but for now we're going to repair it.*

**loo** *noun* (**loos**)
(*informal*) a lavatory.

**look**¹ *verb* (**looks, looking, looked**)
1 to use your eyes; to turn your eyes towards something. 2 to face in a particular direction. 3 to seem; to appear, *You look sad.*
**look after,** to protect; to attend to someone's needs, *Look after my bag, will you? Can you look after Granny for the afternoon?*
**look down on,** to despise.
**look for something,** to try to find something.
**look forward to something,** to wait for something eagerly or expectantly.
**look out,** to be careful.
**look up to,** to admire or respect.

**look**² *noun* (**looks**)
1 the act of looking. 2 appearance; what something seems to be.

**look-alike** *noun* (**look-alikes**)
someone or something that looks very like another, usually more famous person or thing, *a Michael Jackson look-alike. The car is a Porsche look-alike.*

**looking-glass** *noun* (**looking-glasses**)
(*old-fashioned use*) a mirror made of glass.

**look-out** *noun* (**look-outs**)
1 a place from which you watch for something. 2 someone whose job is to keep watch. 3 watching; being watchful, *Keep a look-out for snakes as you walk through the forest.* 4 (*informal*) something you can expect or hope for, *It's your look-out if you get hurt because you were careless.*

**loom**[1] *noun* (**looms**)
a machine for weaving cloth.

**loom**[2] *verb* (**looms, looming, loomed**)
to appear large and threatening, *An iceberg loomed up through the fog.*

**loop**[1] *noun* (**loops**)
1 the shape made by a curve crossing itself; a piece of string, ribbon, wire, etc. made into this shape. 2 (*in Computing*) part of a computer program or flow chart which repeats itself.

**loop**[2] *verb* (**loops, looping, looped**)
to make into a loop.

**loophole** *noun* (**loopholes**)
1 a narrow opening. 2 a way of avoiding a law, rule, etc.

**loose**[1] *adjective* (**looser, loosest**)
1 not tight; not firm, *a loose tooth.* 2 not tied up or shut in, *The dog got loose.*
**at a loose end,** with nothing to do.
**loosely** *adverb*, **looseness** *noun*

**loose**[2] *verb* (**looses, loosing, loosed**)
to make something less tight; to untie or release something.

USAGE: Do not confuse the verb **loose** with **lose,** which is also a verb but which means to be without something, to be beaten, or to become slow.

**loose-leaf** *adjective*
with each leaf or page removable, *a loose-leaf folder.*

**loosen** *verb* (**loosens, loosening, loosened**)
to make something loose; to become loose.

**loot**[1] *noun*
stolen things.

**loot**[2] *verb* (**loots, looting, looted**)
to rob a place or an enemy, especially in a time of war or disorder.
**looter** *noun*

**lopsided** *adjective*
with one side lower than the other; uneven.

**lord** *noun* (**lords**)
a nobleman, especially one who is allowed to use the title 'Lord' in front of his name.
**Lord Mayor,** the mayor of a large city.
**Our Lord,** Jesus.
**the Lord,** God.
**lordly** *adjective*, **lordship** *noun*

**lorry** *noun* (**lorries**)
(in America, *truck*) a large motor vehicle for carrying goods.

**lose** *verb* (**loses, losing, lost**)
1 to be without something you once had, especially because you cannot find it, *I've lost my hat.* 2 to be beaten in a contest or game, *We lost last Friday's match.* 3 to become slow, *My watch loses two minutes every day.*
**be lost** or **lose your way,** not to know where you are.
**get lost!,** (*slang*) go away!
**loser** *noun*

USAGE: Do not confuse **lose** with the verb **loose,** which means to make something less tight, or to untie or release something.

**loss** *noun* (**losses**)
1 losing something. 2 something you have lost.
**at a loss,** puzzled; unable to do something.

**lot** *noun* (**lots**)
something for sale at an auction.
**a lot** or **lots,** a large amount; plenty.
**draw lots,** to choose one person or thing from a group by a method that depends on chance.
**the lot,** everything.

**lotion** *noun* (**lotions**)
a liquid that you put on your skin.

**lottery** *noun* (**lotteries**)
a way of raising money by selling numbered tickets and giving prizes to people who have the winning tickets.

**lotto** *noun*
a game like bingo.

**loud** *adjective* (**louder, loudest**)
1 noisy; easily heard. 2 bright; gaudy, *loud colours.*
**loudly** *adverb*, **loudness** *noun*

**loudspeaker** *noun* (**loudspeakers**)
a device that changes electrical impulses into sound.

**lounge**[1] *noun* (**lounges**)
a sitting-room.

**lounge**[2] *verb* (**lounges, lounging, lounged**)
to sit or stand lazily.

**louse** *noun* (**lice**)
**1** one of various small insects that suck the blood of animals or the juices of plants. **2** (*slang*) a person that you hate.

**lousy** *adjective* (**lousier, lousiest**)
**1** full of lice. **2** (*slang*) very bad.

**lout** *noun* (**louts**)
a bad-mannered or clumsy man.
**loutish** *adjective*

**love**[1] *verb* (**loves, loving, loved**)
to like someone or something very much.
**lovable** *adjective*, **lover** *noun*, **lovingly** *adverb*

**love**[2] *noun* (**loves**)
**1** a feeling of liking someone or something very much; great affection or kindness. **2** sexual feelings and great affection between two people. **3** a person that you like very much. **4** in games, a score of nothing.
**in love,** feeling strong love for another person.
**make love,** to have sexual intercourse.

**lovely** *adjective* (**lovelier, loveliest**)
**1** beautiful. **2** (*informal*) very pleasant or enjoyable.
**loveliness** *noun*

**low**[1] *adjective* (**lower, lowest**)
not high.
**lowest common denominator,** the smallest denominator into which two or more other denominators can be divided, *12 is the lowest common denominator of the fractions $\frac{1}{3}$ and $\frac{1}{4}$.*
**lowest common multiple,** the smallest number that contains an exact amount of two or more other numbers, *35 is the lowest common multiple of 5 and 7.*
**lowness** *noun*

**low**[2] *verb* (**lows, lowing, lowed**)
to make a sound like a cow.

**lower** *verb* (**lowers, lowering, lowered**)
**1** to make something less, or less high; to become less, or less high. **2** to bring something down, *He lowered the flag.*

**lower-case** *adjective*
(*in Printing*) not large; not in capital letters, *All the letters in this sentence are lower-case except the first.*

**lowland** *adjective*
of or in the lowlands.

**lowlands** *plural noun*
**1** low country. **2** the south of Scotland.
**lowlander** *noun*

**lowly** *adjective* (**lowlier, lowliest**)
humble.
**lowliness** *noun*

**loyal** *adjective*
always true to your friends; faithful.
**loyally** *adverb*, **loyalty** *noun*

**lozenge** *noun* (**lozenges**)
a small sweet tablet, especially one that contains medicine.

**LP** *noun* (**LPs**)
a long-playing record.

**L-shaped** *adjective*
shaped like the letter L, *an L-shaped room.*

**Ltd.** short for **limited**.

**lubricate** *verb* (**lubricates, lubricating, lubricated**)
to put oil or grease on something so that it moves smoothly.
**lubricant** *noun*, **lubrication** *noun*

**lucid** *adjective*
(*say* loo-sid)
**1** clear, *Though he is very old, his mind is quite lucid.* **2** easy to understand, *a lucid explanation.*
**lucidity** *noun*, **lucidly** *adverb*

**luck** *noun*
**1** the way things happen that have not been planned. **2** good things happening to you.

**lucky** *adjective* (**luckier, luckiest**)
having or bringing good luck.
**lucky dip,** a box or tub containing articles of various values, from which you pick one at random.
**luckily** *adverb*

**ludicrous** *adjective*
(*say* loo-di-krŭs)
so silly that he, she, or it makes people laugh.
**ludicrously** *adverb*

**ludo** *noun*
a game played with dice and counters on a board.

**lug** *verb* (**lugs, lugging, lugged**)
to drag, *She lugged the case up the stairs.*

**luggage** *noun*
suitcases, bags, boxes, etc. taken with you on a journey.

**lukewarm** *adjective*
slightly warm.

**lull**[1] *verb* (**lulls, lulling, lulled**)
to soothe or calm something; to send someone to sleep.

**lull**[2] *noun* (**lulls**)
a short period of quiet or rest.

**lullaby** *noun* (**lullabies**)
a song that is sung to send a baby to sleep.

**lumber[1]** *noun*
1 junk; old unwanted furniture or other things. 2 (*in America*) rough timber.

**lumber[2]** *verb* (**lumbers, lumbering, lumbered**)
1 to move along clumsily or noisily, *The elephants lumbered past*. 2 to fill a place with rubbish or worthless things.
3 (*informal*) to leave someone with a problem, unpleasant job, etc. 4 to cut down trees and get them ready to be sawn up.
**lumbering** *noun*

**lumberjack** *noun* (**lumberjacks**)
someone whose job is to cut down trees or transport them.

**luminous** *adjective*
(*say* **loo**-mi-nŭs)
that shines or glows in the dark.
**luminosity** *noun*

**lump[1]** *noun* (**lumps**)
1 a solid piece of something, *a lump of sugar*. 2 a swelling.
**lumpy** *adjective*

**lump[2]** *verb* (**lumps, lumping, lumped**)
to put or deal with things together, *Several counties were lumped together when the boundaries changed.*

**lump[3]** *verb* (**lumps, lumping, lumped**)
**lump it,** (*informal*) to put up with something you do not like, *You'll have to like it or lump it.*

**lunacy** *noun* (**lunacies**)
(*say* **loo**-nă-si)
madness.

**lunar** *adjective*
of the moon.
**lunar month,** the period between new moons; four weeks.

**lunatic** *noun* (**lunatics**)
(*say* **loo**-nă-tik)
a mad person.

**lunch** *noun* (**lunches**)
1 a meal that you eat in the middle of the day. 2 a snack.
**lunchtime** *noun*

**luncheon** *noun* (**luncheons**)
lunch.
**luncheon meat,** cold meat ready to eat, made from pressed pork or ham.

**lung** *noun* (**lungs**)
one of the two parts inside the body used for breathing.

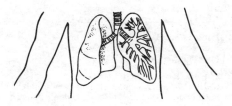

**lunge** *verb* (**lunges, lunging, lunged**)
to thrust or move forward suddenly.

**lupin** *noun* (**lupins**)
a garden plant with tall spikes of flowers.

**lurch[1]** *verb* (**lurches, lurching, lurched**)
1 to stagger, *The passengers lurched forward as the bus stopped suddenly*. 2 to lean suddenly to one side, *The table lurched to the left as one of its legs gave way.*

**lurch[2]** *noun* (**lurches**)
1 a staggering movement. 2 a sudden leaning movement.
**leave someone in the lurch,** to desert someone, leaving him or her in difficulties.

**lure** *verb* (**lures, luring, lured**)
1 to tempt a person or animal into a trap, *The cheese is supposed to lure mice into the mousetrap*. 2 to attract a person or an animal, *Thousands of people have come to the city, lured by promises of wealth.*

**lurk** *verb* (**lurks, lurking, lurked**)
to wait where you cannot be seen.

**luscious** *adjective*
tasting or smelling very pleasant.

**lush** *adjective* (**lusher, lushest**)
1 growing abundantly, *lush grass*.
2 luxurious, *lush furniture*.
**lushly** *adverb*, **lushness** *noun*

**lust** *noun* (**lusts**)
powerful desire.
**lustful** *adjective*

**lustre** *noun* (**lustres**)
(*say* **lus**-ter)
brightness; brilliance.
**lustrous** *adjective*

**lute** *noun* (**lutes**)
an old-fashioned musical instrument rather like a guitar.

**luxury** *noun* (**luxuries**)
**1** something expensive that you enjoy but do not really need. **2** having many such things, *a life of luxury*.
**luxurious** *adjective*

**lychee** *noun* (**lychees**)
a small fruit with sweet, white flesh in a thin, spiny skin.

**lycra** *noun*
(*trademark*) a thin material that can stretch a lot, used especially for sports clothing.

**lying** present participle of **lie**[1] *verb* and **lie**[2] *verb*.

**lynch** *verb* (**lynches, lynching, lynched**)
to execute someone without a proper trial, *The mob lynched the suspected thief.*

**lyre** *noun* (**lyres**)
an ancient musical instrument like a small harp.
**lyre-bird,** an Australian bird, of which the male has a fan-shaped tail.

**lyric** *noun* (**lyrics**)
(*say* li-rik)
a short poem expressing feelings and emotions.
**lyric** or **lyrics,** the words of a song.
**lyrical** *adjective*

# Mm

**m** short for **metre, metres, miles,** or **millions.**

**ma** *noun* (**mas**)
(*informal*) mother.

**mac** *noun* (**macs**)
(*informal*) a mackintosh.

**macaroni** *noun*
flour paste made into tubes and used as food.

**machine** *noun* (**machines**)
something with several parts that work together to do a job, *a washing-machine.*

**machine-gun** *noun* (**machine-guns**)
a gun that can keep firing bullets quickly one after another.

**machinery** *noun*
**1** machines. **2** mechanism, *The lift's machinery is faulty.* **3** a system for doing something, *the machinery of local government.*

**mackerel** *noun* (**mackerel**)
an edible sea-fish.

**mackintosh** *noun* (**mackintoshes**)
a raincoat.

**mad** *adjective* (**madder, maddest**)
**1** having something wrong with your mind; not sane or sensible. **2** very keen, *He's mad about football.* **3** (*informal*) very excited or annoyed.
**like mad,** (*informal*) with great speed, energy, enthusiasm, etc.
**madly** *adverb,* **madman** *noun,* **madness** *noun*

**madam** *noun*
a word sometimes used when speaking or writing politely to a woman, instead of her name, *'Can I help you, madam?' said the shopkeeper.*

**madden** *verb* (**maddens, maddening, maddened**)
**1** to make someone mad. **2** to make someone angry.

**made** past tense and past participle of **make** *verb.*

**magazine** *noun* (**magazines**)
**1** a paper-covered publication that comes out regularly. **2** the part of a gun that holds the cartridges. **3** a store for ammunition, explosives, etc. **4** a device that holds film for a camera or slides for a slide-projector.

**maggot** *noun* (**maggots**)
the larva of some kinds of fly.

**magic** *noun*
the power to do wonderful things or clever tricks that people cannot usually do.
**magic square**, a pattern of numbers arranged in a square, for example 1 to 9 written in three rows and three columns, in a special order so that all the rows, columns, and diagonal lines of numbers add up to the same total.
**magical** *adjective*, **magically** *adverb*, **magician** *noun*

**magistrate** *noun* (**magistrates**)
a judge in a local court.

**magma** *noun*
melted material beneath the earth's crust.

**magnesium** *noun*
a silvery-white metal that makes a very bright flame when it burns.

**magnet** *noun* (**magnets**)
a piece of metal that can attract iron or steel and that points north and south when it is hung in the air.
**magnetism** *noun*

**magnetic** *adjective*
having or using the powers of a magnet.
**magnetic field**, the area affected by the force from a magnet.
**magnetic tape**, a plastic strip coated with a substance that acts like a magnet, for recording sound.
**magnetically** *adverb*

**magnetize** *verb* (**magnetizes, magnetizing, magnetized**)
1 to make something into a magnet. 2 to influence someone by your attractiveness, *Felicity magnetized the audience as soon as she came on to the stage.*

**magnificent** *adjective*
1 looking grand or important. 2 excellent, *a magnificent meal.*
**magnificence** *noun*, **magnificently** *adverb*

**magnify** *verb* (**magnifies, magnifying, magnified**)
to make something look bigger than it really is.
**magnification** *noun*, **magnifier** *noun*, **magnifying glass** *noun*

**magnitude** *noun* (**magnitudes**)
how large or important something is.

**magnolia** *noun* (**magnolias**)
a tree with large white flowers.

**magpie** *noun* (**magpies**)
a black and white bird, *Magpies sometimes steal bright things and hide them.*

**mahogany** *noun*
(*say* mă-**hog**-ă-ni)
a reddish-brown wood.

**maid** *noun* (**maids**)
1 a female servant. 2 (*old-fashioned use*) a girl.

**maiden**[1] *noun* (**maidens**)
(*old-fashioned use*) a girl.

**maiden**[2] *adjective*
not married, *a maiden aunt.*
**maiden name**, a woman's name before she got married.
**maiden over**, a cricket over in which no runs are scored.
**maiden voyage**, a ship's first voyage.

**mail**[1] *noun*
letters, parcels, etc. sent by post.
**mail order**, ordering goods to be sent by post.

**mail**[2] *noun*
armour made of metal rings joined together.

**mail**[3] *verb* (**mails, mailing, mailed**)
to send something by post.

**maim** *verb* (**maims, maiming, maimed**)
to injure someone so that part of his or her body is useless.

**main**[1] *adjective*
most important; largest, *The main thing is to be accurate. They are the main suppliers of coal in this district.*
**main clause**, a clause which is a sentence and can be used by itself.

**main**[2] or **mains** *noun*
the main pipe or cable in a system carrying water, gas, or electricity to a building.

**mainframe** *noun* (**mainframes**)
(*in Computing*) a large computer that is shared by many users.

**mainland** *noun*
the main part of a country, not the islands around it.

**male**²

**mainly** *adverb*
most importantly; almost completely; usually, *We are mainly a printing company, but we do some bookbinding as well. The team was picked mainly from the girls. She is at home mainly in the afternoon.*

**maintain** *verb* (**maintains, maintaining, maintained**)
1 to keep something in good condition. 2 to have or state a belief, *I maintain that animals should not be killed or hunted.* 3 to provide money for someone.
**maintenance** *noun*

**maisonette** *noun* (**maisonettes**)
a small flat or house.

**maize** *noun*
a tall kind of corn with large seeds.

**majestic** *adjective*
imposing; dignified.
**majestically** *adverb*

**majesty** *noun* (**majesties**)
1 being imposing and dignified. 2 the title used in speaking about or to a king or queen, *Her Majesty the Queen. Yes, Your Majesty.*

**major**¹ *adjective*
1 more important; main, *major roads.* 2 of the musical scale that has a semitone between the 3rd and 4th notes and between the 7th and 8th notes.

**major**² *noun* (**majors**)
an army officer higher in rank than a captain.

**majority** *noun* (**majorities**)
(*say* mă-**jo**-rĭ-ti)
1 the greater part of a group of people or things, *The majority of the class wanted a quiz.* 2 the difference between a larger and a smaller number of votes, *She had a majority of 25 over her opponent.*

**make**¹ *verb* (**makes, making, made**)
1 to get something new, usually by putting things together, *They are making a raft out of logs.* 2 to cause something to happen, *The bang made him jump.* 3 to get or earn, *She makes £10,000 a year.* 4 to score, *He has made 20 runs so far.* 5 to reach, *The swimmer just made the shore.* 6 to estimate or reckon, *What do you make the time?* 7 to equal; to amount to, *4 and 6 makes 10.* 8 to give, *Make me an offer.* 9 to tidy or arrange for use, *Make the beds.* 10 to cause something to be successful or happy, *Her visit made my day.*
**make do**, to manage with something that is not what you really want.
**make for**, to go towards.
**make off**, to leave quickly.
**make out**, to manage to see, hear, or understand something; to pretend, *We could barely make out the inscription. She made out that she was ill.*
**make up**, to build something or put something together; to invent a story, etc.; to give someone something to make him or her feel better after losing something; to put on make-up.
**make up your mind**, to decide.

**make**² *noun* (**makes**)
1 how something is made. 2 a brand of goods; something made by a particular firm, *What make of car is that?*

**make-believe** *noun*
pretending; imagining things.

**maker** *noun* (**makers**)
the person or firm that has made something.

**makeshift** *adjective*
used because you have nothing better, *a makeshift table.*

**make-up** *noun* (**make-ups**)
1 substances for making your skin look beautiful or different. 2 a person's character.

**maladjusted** *adjective*
(of a person) not having a good relationship with the people that he or she comes into contact with; not happy in his or her surroundings.

**malaria** *noun*
(*say* mă-**lair**-i-ă)
a feverish disease spread by mosquitoes.

**male**¹ *adjective*
of the sex that does not give birth to offspring.
**male chauvinist**, a man who thinks that men are more clever, brave, etc. than women.

**male**² *noun* (**males**)
a male person or animal.

**malevolent** *adjective*
(*say* mă-**lev**-ŏ-lĕnt)
intending to harm other people.
**malevolence** *noun*, **malevolently** *adverb*

**malice** *noun*
a desire to harm other people.
**malicious** *adjective*, **maliciously** *adverb*

**mallet** *noun* (**mallets**)
a large hammer, usually made of wood.

**malnutrition** *noun*
not having enough food to eat.
**malnourished** *adjective*

**malt** *noun*
dried barley used in brewing, making
vinegar, etc.
**malted** *adjective*

**mammal** *noun* (**mammals**)
any animal of which the female can feed
her babies with her own milk, *Humans,
lions, and whales are mammals.*
**mammalian** *adjective*

**mammoth**[1] *noun* (**mammoths**)
an extinct kind of hairy elephant.

**mammoth**[2] *adjective*
huge.

**man**[1] *noun* (**men**)
**1** a grown-up male human being. **2** a
person. **3** all the people in the world. **4** one
of the pieces used in a board-game like
chess or draughts.

**man**[2] *verb* (**mans, manning, manned**)
to supply people to work something, *Man
the pumps!*

**manage** *verb* (**manages, managing, managed**)
**1** to be able to do something difficult. **2** to
be in charge of a shop, factory, etc.
**manageable** *adjective*, **management** *noun*,
**manager** *noun*, **manageress** *noun*, **managerial**
*adjective*

**mane** *noun* (**manes**)
the long hair along the back of the neck of
a horse or lion.

**manger** *noun* (**mangers**)
(*say* **mayn**-jer)
a trough for animals to feed from.

**mangle**[1] *noun* (**mangles**)
a device for squeezing water out of clothes.

**mangle**[2] *verb* (**mangles, mangling, mangled**)
**1** to crush or cut up something roughly. **2** to
squeeze wet clothes in a mangle.

**mango** *noun* (**mangoes**)
a yellowish-red tropical fruit.

**manhandle** *verb* (**manhandles, manhandling,
manhandled**)
**1** to treat someone roughly. **2** to move a
thing by human effort only.

**manhole** *noun* (**manholes**)
a hole, usually with a cover, through which
a worker can get into a sewer, boiler, etc. to
inspect or repair it.

**mania** *noun* (**manias**)
violent madness.
**maniac** *noun*, **manic** *adjective*

**manifesto** *noun* (**manifestos**)
a statement of a group's or person's policy
or principles.

**manipulate** *verb* (**manipulates, manipulating,
manipulated**)
**1** to handle something skilfully, *The
crane-driver manipulated the load with
great accuracy.* **2** to arrange something or
control someone cleverly or cunningly.
**manipulation** *noun*, **manipulator** *noun*

**mankind** *noun*
all the people in the world.

**manly** *adjective* (**manlier, manliest**)
**1** strong or brave. **2** suitable for a man,
*manly clothes.*
**manliness** *noun*

**manner** *noun* (**manners**)
the way that something happens or is done.
**manners,** how you behave with other
people; behaving politely.

**manœuvre**[1] *noun* (**manœuvres**)
(*say* mă-**noo**-ver)
**1** a clever action done to deceive or beat
someone. **2** a difficult or skilful action,
*Parking the caravan was an awkward
manœuvre.*

**manœuvre**[2] *verb* (**manœuvres, manœuvring,
manœuvred**)
**1** to make a clever action to deceive or beat
someone, *politicians manœuvring for places
in the Cabinet.* **2** to make a difficult or
skilful action, *Watch the ships manœuvring.*
**manœuvrable** *adjective*

**manor** *noun* (**manors**)
a large, important house in the country.

**mansion** *noun* (**mansions**)
a large, impressive house.

**manslaughter** *noun*
(*say* man-slaw-ter)
killing someone without meaning to do so.

**mantelpiece** *noun* (**mantelpieces**)
a shelf above a fireplace.

**mantle** *noun* (**mantles**)
a cloak.

**manual**[1] *adjective*
done with your hands, *manual work*.
**manually** *adverb*

**manual**[2] *noun* (**manuals**)
a handbook.

**manufacture** *verb* (**manufactures,
manufacturing, manufactured**)
to make things with machines.
**manufacturer** *noun*

**manure** *noun*
fertilizer, especially made from animal
waste.

**manuscript** *noun* (**manuscripts**)
something written or typed but not printed.

**Manx** *adjective*
of the Isle of Man.
**Manx cat**, a breed of cat without a tail.

**many**[1] *adjective* (**more, most**)
large in number.

**many**[2] *noun*
a large number of people or things.

**Maori** *noun* (**Maoris**)
(*say* mow-ri)
one of the original race of people who lived
in New Zealand.

**map**[1] *noun* (**maps**)
a diagram of part or all of the earth's
surface, showing towns, mountains, rivers,
etc.
**on the map**, famous or important.

**map**[2] *verb* (**maps, mapping, mapped**)
to make a map of an area.
**map out**, to arrange or organize something.

**maple** *noun* (**maples**)
a tree with broad leaves.

**mapping** *noun* (**mappings**)
(*in Mathematics*) a relationship between
two sets of numbers, or an object and its
image, that changes one into the other.

**mar** *verb* (**mars, marring, marred**)
to spoil, *The rain marred our display*.

**marathon** *noun* (**marathons**)
a long-distance race for runners, usually 26
miles long.

**marauder** *noun* (**marauders**)
someone who attacks a place and steals
things from it.
**marauding** *adjective*

**marble** *noun* (**marbles**)
1 a small glass ball used in games. 2 a hard
kind of limestone that is polished and used
for building or sculpture.

**March** *noun*
the third month of the year.

**march**[1] *noun* (**marches**)
1 the action of marching. 2 a piece of music
suitable for marching.

**march**[2] *verb* (**marches, marching, marched**)
1 to walk like soldiers, with regular steps.
2 to make someone walk somewhere.
**marcher** *noun*

**mare** *noun* (**mares**)
a female horse.

**margarine** *noun* (**margarines**)
(*say* mar-jă-reen)
a substance that looks like butter, made
from animal or vegetable fats.

**margin** *noun* (**margins**)
1 the empty space between the edge of a
page and the writing or pictures. 2 the
small difference between two scores, prices,
etc., *She won by a narrow margin*.
**marginal** *adjective*, **marginally** *adverb*

**marigold** *noun* (**marigolds**)
a yellow or orange garden flower.

**marina** *noun* (**marinas**)
(*say* mă-ree-nă)
a harbour for yachts, motor boats, etc.

**marine**[1] *adjective*
(*say* mă-reen)
of or concerned with the sea.

**marine**[2] *noun* (**marines**)
(*say* mă-reen)
a soldier trained to serve on land and sea.

**mariner** *noun* (**mariners**)
a sailor.

**marionette** *noun* (**marionettes**)
a puppet worked by strings or wires.

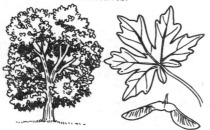

# mark¹

270

**mark¹** *noun* (**marks**)
1 a spot, dot, line, stain, etc. on something.
2 a number, letter, etc. put on a piece of
work to show how good it is. 3 a
distinguishing feature of something. 4 the
place from which you start a race.

**mark²** *noun* (**marks**)
a German unit of money.

**mark³** *verb* (**marks, marking, marked**)
1 to put a mark on something. 2 to give a
number, letter, etc. to a piece of work to
show how good it is; to correct a piece of
work. 3 to pay attention to something,
*Mark my words!*
**mark time,** to march on one spot, without
moving forward; to wait, *The soldiers
marked time. We're just marking time –
when will we get down to work?*

**market¹** *noun* (**markets**)
1 a place where things are bought and sold,
usually from stalls in the open air. 2 a
situation in which goods can be sold, *There
is hardly any market for our goods now.*
**market gardening,** (in America, *truck
farming*) growing fruit and vegetables for
sale.
**market town,** a town where a market is held
regularly.
**on the market,** available to buy.

**market²** *verb* (**markets, marketing, marketed**)
to sell something.
**marketable** *adjective*

**marksman** *noun* (**marksmen**)
an expert in shooting at a target.
**marksmanship** *noun*

**marmalade** *noun*
jam made from oranges or lemons.

**maroon¹** *verb* (**maroons, marooning, marooned**)
to abandon someone in a place far away
from other people.

**maroon²** *adjective*
brownish or dark red.

**marquee** *noun* (**marquees**)
(*say* mar-**kee**)
a very large tent.

**marriage** *noun* (**marriages**)
1 the state of being married. 2 a wedding.

**marrow** *noun* (**marrows**)
1 a large, green or yellow hard-skinned
vegetable, often cooked and eaten with
minced meat. 2 the soft substance inside
bones.

**marry** *verb* (**marries, marrying, married**)
1 to become the husband or wife of
someone. 2 to make two people into
husband and wife.

**marsh** *noun* (**marshes**)
a low-lying area of very wet ground.
**marshy** *adjective*

**marshal** *noun* (**marshals**)
1 an official who supervises a contest,
ceremony, etc. 2 a high-ranking officer,
*Field Marshal*. 3 an official in the USA like
a sheriff.

**marshmallow** *noun* (**marshmallows**)
a soft, spongy sweet.

**marsupial** *noun* (**marsupials**)
(*say* mar-**soo**-pi-ăl)
an animal such as a kangaroo or wallaby,
*Female marsupials have a pouch for
carrying their babies.*

**martial** *adjective*
of or like war.
**martial arts,** fighting sports such as karate
and judo.
**martial law,** government by the armed forces.

**Martian** *noun* (**Martians**)
a creature in stories that comes from the
planet Mars.

**martin** *noun* (**martins**)
a bird rather like a swallow.

**martyr** *noun* (**martyrs**)
(*say* **mar**-ter)
someone who is killed or suffers because of
his or her beliefs.
**martyrdom** *noun*

**marvel¹** *noun* (**marvels**)
a wonderful thing.

**marvel²** *verb* (**marvels, marvelling, marvelled**)
to be filled with wonder or astonishment.

**marvellous** *adjective*
excellent.
**marvellously** *adverb*

**Marxism** *noun*
the Communist ideas of the German writer
Karl Marx (1818–83).
**Marxist** *noun* and *adjective*

**marzipan** *noun*
a soft, sweet food made from almonds and
sugar.

**mascot** *noun* (**mascots**)
a person, animal, or object that is believed
to bring good luck.

**masculine** *adjective*
1 of, like, or suitable for men. 2 (*in
grammar*) having a grammatical form
suitable for the names of males or for
words linked with these, *a masculine noun.*
**masculinity** *noun*

**mash¹** *verb* (**mashes, mashing, mashed**)
to crush something into a soft mass,
*mashed potato.*

**mash**<sup>2</sup> *noun*
(*informal*) mashed potatoes.

**mask**<sup>1</sup> *noun* (**masks**)
a covering worn over your face to disguise or protect it.

**mask**<sup>2</sup> *verb* (**masks, masking, masked**)
1 to cover your face with a mask. 2 to hide something.

**mason** *noun* (**masons**)
someone who builds or works with stone.
**Mason,** a member of a secret society called the Freemasons.

**masonry** *noun*
the stone parts of a building.

**mass**<sup>1</sup> *noun* (**masses**)
1 a large amount, *masses of flowers*. 2 a lump; a heap. 3 (*in Science*) the amount of matter in an object.
**mass production,** producing goods in large quantities.

**mass**<sup>2</sup> *noun* (**masses**)
the Communion service in a Roman Catholic church.

**massacre** *verb* (**massacres, massacring, massacred**)
(*say* mas-ă-ker)
to kill a large number of people.

**massage** *verb* (**massages, massaging, massaged**)
(*say* mas-ahzh)
to rub and press the body to make it less stiff or less painful.
**masseur** *noun*, **masseuse** *noun*

**massive** *adjective*
huge; large and heavy, *a massive problem. Ships' engines are massive machines.*
**massively** *adverb*

**mast** *noun* (**masts**)
a tall pole that holds up a ship's sail, a flag, or an aerial.

**master**<sup>1</sup> *noun* (**masters**)
1 a man who teaches in a school. 2 someone who is in charge of something. 3 a great artist, composer, sportsman, etc.
4 something from which copies are made.
**Master,** a word used before a boy's name when addressing a letter to him.

**master**<sup>2</sup> *verb* (**masters, mastering, mastered**)
1 to learn a subject or skill. 2 to defeat something, *She succeeded in mastering her fear of heights.*

**masterly** *adjective*
very clever.

**master-mind** *noun* (**master-minds**)
1 a very clever person. 2 someone who organizes a scheme, crime, etc.

**masterpiece** *noun* (**masterpieces**)
1 an excellent piece of work. 2 someone's best piece of work.

**mastery** *noun*
1 complete control of something, *The ancient Romans achieved mastery of many countries.* 2 thorough knowledge or skill.

**mastodon** *noun* (**mastodons**)
a large extinct animal rather like an elephant.

**mat** *noun* (**mats**)
1 a small piece of material that partly covers a floor. 2 a small piece of material put on a table to protect the surface from hot or wet cups or plates.

**matador** *noun* (**matadors**)
someone who fights and kills the bull in a bullfight.

**match**<sup>1</sup> *noun* (**matches**)
a small, thin stick with a small amount of chemical at one end that gives a flame when rubbed on something rough.
**matchbox** *noun*, **matchstick** *noun*

**match**<sup>2</sup> *noun* (**matches**)
1 a game or contest between two teams or players. 2 one person or thing that is equal or similar to another. 3 a marriage.

**match**³ *verb* (**matches, matching, matched**)
1 to be equal or similar to another person or thing. 2 to put someone in competition with someone else.

**mate**¹ *noun* (**mates**)
1 a friend or companion. 2 one of a pair of animals that have come together to have offspring. 3 one of the officers on a ship.

**mate**² *noun* (**mates**)
a situation in chess when you cannot stop the king being taken.

**mate**³ *verb* (**mates, mating, mated**)
to come together so as to have offspring; to put animals together so that they will have offspring.

**material** *noun* (**materials**)
1 anything used for making something else. 2 cloth.

**materialistic** *adjective*
liking possessions, money, and comfort rather than things of the mind such as religion or art.
**materialist** *noun*

**maternal** *adjective*
of a mother or mothers; motherly, *maternal instincts. a maternal old lady.*
**maternally** *adverb*

**maternity** *noun*
having a baby.

**mathematician** *noun* (**mathematicians**)
(*say* math-ĕm-ă-**tish**-ăn)
an expert in mathematics.

**mathematics** *noun*
the study of numbers, measurements, and shapes.
**mathematical** *adjective*, **mathematically** *adverb*

**maths** *noun*
(in America, *math*) (*informal*) mathematics.

**matinée** *noun* (**matinées**)
(*say* mat-i-nay)
an afternoon performance at a theatre or cinema.

**matrimony** *noun*
(*say* mat-ri-mŏ-ni)
marriage.
**matrimonial** *adjective*

**matrix** *noun* (**matrices**)
(*in Mathematics*) a set of numbers or quantities arranged in rows and columns.

**matt** *adjective*
not shiny, *matt paint.*

**matted** *adjective*
tangled, *matted hair.*

**matter**¹ *noun* (**matters**)
1 something you need to think about or do, *a serious matter.* 2 a substance, *Peat consists mainly of vegetable matter.*
**a matter of fact,** something true.
**no matter,** it is not important.
**what's the matter?,** what is wrong?

**matter**² *verb* (**matters, mattering, mattered**)
to be important.

**matting** *noun*
mats; rough material for covering a floor.

**mattress** *noun* (**mattresses**)
a large, flat bag filled with soft or springy material and used on or as a bed.

**mature** *adjective*
fully grown or developed; grown-up, *a mature tree. She has a mature attitude.*
**maturely** *adverb*, **maturity** *noun*

**mauve** *adjective*
(*say* mohv)
pale purple.

**maximum**¹ *noun* (**maxima**)
the greatest possible number or amount, *10 out of 10 is the maximum.*
**maximum and minimum thermometer,** a device that shows the highest and the lowest temperature that has occurred over a period of time.

**maximum**² *adjective*
greatest, *maximum speed.*

**May** *noun*
the fifth month of the year.
**May Day,** 1 May.

**may**¹ *verb* (*past tense* **might**)
1 to be allowed to, *May I have a sweet?* 2 will possibly; has possibly, *He may come tomorrow. He might have missed the train.*

**may**²
hawthorn blossom.

**Mayan** *noun* (**Mayans**)
a member of a race of people who lived mainly in the Yucatan area and had an advanced civilization before the Europeans discovered America.

**maybe** *adverb*
perhaps.

**mayday** *noun* (**maydays**)
an international radio-signal calling for help.

**mayonnaise** *noun*
(*say* may-ŏn-**ayz**)
a creamy sauce made from eggs, oil, vinegar, etc.

**mayor** *noun* (**mayors**)
the person in charge of the council in a town or city.
**mayoral** *adjective*, **mayoress** *noun*

**maypole** *noun* (**maypoles**)
a decorated pole round which people dance on 1 May.

**maze** *noun* (**mazes**)
a complicated and puzzling network of paths or lines to follow.

**me** *pronoun*
a word used for *I*, usually when it is the object of a sentence or comes straight after a preposition, *She spoke to me.*

**meadow** *noun* (**meadows**)
a field of grass.

**meagre** *adjective*
(*say* **meeg**-er)
not big enough; not sufficient.

**meal** *noun* (**meals**)
1 a time when food is eaten. 2 the food eaten at breakfast, lunch, tea, dinner, or supper.
**mealtime** *noun*

**mean**[1] *verb* (**means, meaning, meant**)
1 to try to convey something; to indicate; to be the same as something, *'Maybe' means 'perhaps'.* 2 to intend, *I meant to tell him, but I forgot.*

**mean**[2] *adjective* (**meaner, meanest**)
1 not generous; selfish, *a mean man.*
2 unkind; spiteful, *a mean trick.*
**meanly** *adverb*, **meanness** *noun*

**mean**[3] *adjective*
average, *the mean temperature.*

**meander**[1] *verb* (**meanders, meandering, meandered**)
(*say* mee-**an**-der)
1 to wander, *They meandered through the town, looking in all the shop-windows.* 2 to take a winding course, *The river meandered across the plain.*

**meander**[2] *noun* (**meanders**)
one of several large bends in a river.

**meaning** *noun* (**meanings**)
what something means.
**meaningful** *adjective*, **meaningless** *adjective*

**means** *noun* (**means**)
1 a way of doing something; a method. 2 (*in plural*) money; resources, *He hadn't got the means to pay for a meal.*
**by all means**, certainly.
**by means of something**, using something; with something.
**by no means**, not at all.

**meantime**[1] *noun*
**in the meantime**, in the period of time between two events, *The taxi will be here in half an hour; in the meantime, let's pack our bags.*

**meantime**[2] *adverb*
meanwhile.

**meanwhile** *adverb*
while something else is taking place, *I cleaned the cooker; meanwhile, Jacquie mended my bike.*

**measles** *noun*
an infectious disease that causes small red spots on the skin.

**measly** *adjective* (**measlier, measliest**)
(*informal*) very small or poor, *What a measly ice-cream!*

**measure**[1] *verb* (**measures, measuring, measured**)
1 to find out how big something is. 2 to be a certain size.
**measure out**, to mark or give a particular amount.
**measurable** *adjective*, **measurement** *noun*

**measure**[2] *noun* (**measures**)
1 a unit used for measuring. 2 a device used for measuring. 3 the size of something.
4 something done for a particular purpose; a law.

**meat** *noun* (**meats**)
animal flesh used as food.
**meaty** *adjective*

**mechanic** *noun* (**mechanics**)
someone who makes, uses, or mends machines.

**mechanical** *adjective*
1 of, like, or done by machines. 2 automatic; done without thought.
**mechanically** *adverb*

**mechanics** *noun*
1 the study of force and movement. 2 the study or use of machines.

**mechanism** *noun* (**mechanisms**)
1 the moving parts of a machine. 2 the way something works, *He described the mechanism of a combine harvester.*

**medal** *noun* (**medals**)
a piece of metal shaped like a coin, star, or cross, given to someone for being brave or for achieving something.

**medallist** *noun* (**medallists**)
someone who has won a medal, *He was three times a gold medallist in the Olympics.*

**meddle** *verb* (**meddles, meddling, meddled**)
to interfere.
**meddler** *noun*, **meddlesome** *adjective*

**media** *plural noun*
(*say* **mee**-di-ă)
the plural of **medium** *noun*.
**the media**, broadcasting and newspapers, etc. which convey information and ideas to the public, *Lots of stories about the singer appeared in the media.*

**median** *noun* (**medians**)
(*in Mathematics*) the middle number in a set of numbers that have been arranged in order, *The median of 2, 3, 5, 8, 9, 14, and 15 is 8.*

**medical** *adjective*
connected with the treatment of disease.
**medically** *adverb*

**medicine** *noun* (**medicines**)
**1** a substance, usually swallowed, used to try to cure a disease. **2** the treatment of disease.
**medicinal** *adjective*

**medieval** *adjective*
(*say* med-i-**ee**-văl)
of the Middle Ages.

**mediocre** *adjective*
(*say* meed-i-**oh**-ker)
not very good.
**mediocrity** *noun*

**meditate** *verb* (**meditates, meditating, meditated**)
to think deeply and seriously.
**meditation** *noun*, **meditative** *adjective*

**Mediterranean** *adjective*
(*say* med-i-ter-ay-ni-ăn)
of or like the Mediterranean Sea or the countries round it, *a Mediterranean climate.*

**medium**[1] *adjective*
average; of middle size.
**medium wave**, a radio wave with a wavelength between 100 and 1,000 metres.

**medium**[2] *noun* (**mediums or media**)
**1** a thing in which something exists, moves, or is expressed, *Newspapers and television are media for advertising.* **2** someone who claims to communicate with the dead, *He visited several mediums.*

**meek** *adjective* (**meeker, meekest**)
humble; quiet and obedient.
**meekly** *adverb*, **meekness** *noun*

**meet**[1] *verb* (**meets, meeting, met**)
**1** to come together from different places; to come face to face, *We all met in Nottingham. I met him at the station.* **2** to get to know someone, *I met her at a friend's party.* **3** to pay a bill, solve a problem, etc., *Will he be able to meet all his debts?*

**meet**[2] *noun* (**meets**)
a gathering of riders and hounds for a hunt.

**meeting** *noun* (**meetings**)
a time when people come together for a discussion, contest, etc.

**megaphone** *noun* (**megaphones**)
a funnel-shaped device for making someone's voice sound louder.

**melancholy** *adjective*
sad; gloomy.

**mellow** *adjective* (**mellower, mellowest**)
not harsh; sweet; friendly.

**melodious** *adjective*
sounding sweet; pleasant to hear.

**melodrama** *noun* (**melodramas**)
a play full of excitement and emotion.
**melodramatic** *adjective*

**melody** *noun* (**melodies**)
a tune, especially a pleasing tune.
**melodic** *adjective*

**melon** *noun* (**melons**)
a large, round, juicy fruit with yellow or green skin.

**melt** *verb* (**melts, melting, melted**)
**1** to make something liquid by heating; to become liquid by heating. **2** to go away or disappear slowly.

**member** *noun* (**members**)
**1** someone who belongs to a society or group. **2** (*in Mathematics*) an object or number that belongs to a set.
**Member of Parliament**, someone who has been chosen by the people to act on behalf of them in the House of Commons.
**membership** *noun*

**membrane** *noun* (**membranes**)
a thin skin or covering.

**memoirs** *plural noun*
a book about events that someone has lived through or people that he or she has known.

**memorable** *adjective*
worth remembering; easy to remember, *a memorable event. He has a memorable name.*
**memorably** *adverb*

**memorial** *noun* (**memorials**)
something to remind people of a person or an event, *a war memorial.*

**memorize** *verb* (**memorizes, memorizing, memorized**)
to get something into your memory so that you do not forget it.

**memory** *noun* (**memories**)
1 the ability to remember things.
2 something that you remember. 3 the part of a computer where information is stored.
**in memory of**, as a memorial to a person or an event.

**men** plural of **man** *noun*.

**menace**¹ *verb* (**menaces, menacing, menaced**)
to threaten someone with harm or danger.
**menacingly** *adverb*

**menace**² *noun* (**menaces**)
1 something menacing. 2 an annoying person or thing.

**menagerie** *noun* (**menageries**)
(*say* min-**aj**-er-i)
a small zoo.

**mend** *verb* (**mends, mending, mended**)
to make a damaged thing as useful as it was before.
**mender** *noun*

**mending** *noun*
clothes, etc. that you are mending or about to mend.

**menstruation** *noun*
the natural flow of blood from a woman's womb, normally happening every 28 days.
**menstrual** *adjective*, **menstruate** *verb*

**-ment** *suffix*
used in making nouns, '*Amusement*' comes from the verb '*to amuse*'.

**mental** *adjective*
1 of or in the mind. 2 (*informal*) mad.
**mentally** *adverb*

**mention** *verb* (**mentions, mentioning, mentioned**)
to speak about someone or something, especially when you are talking about something else.

**menu** *noun* (**menus**)
(*say* men-yoo)
1 a list of the food that is available in a restaurant or served at a meal. 2 (*in Computing*) a list of possible actions, displayed on a screen, from which you choose what you want a computer to do.

**MEP** short for *Member of the European Parliament.*

**mercenary**¹ *adjective*
working only for money or some other reward; thinking only of money or reward, *Her interest in the sport was purely mercenary.*

**mercenary**² *noun* (**mercenaries**)
a soldier paid to fight for a foreign country.

**merchandise** *noun*
goods for buying or selling.

**merchant** *noun* (**merchants**)
someone involved in trade.
**merchant navy**, the merchant ships of a country.
**merchant ship**, a ship carrying goods for buying or selling.

**merciful** *adjective*
kind to someone instead of punishing him or her.
**mercifully** *adverb*

**merciless** *adjective*
not at all merciful; cruel.
**mercilessly** *adverb*

**mercury** *noun*
a heavy, silvery metal that is usually liquid, *Some thermometers contain mercury.*

**mercy** *noun* (**mercies**)
1 being merciful. 2 something to be thankful for, *Thank God for small mercies.*

**mere**¹ *adjective*
not more than; no better than, *He's a mere child.*
**the merest**, a very small, *The merest trace of colour.*

**mere**² *noun* (**meres**)
(*poetical use*) a lake.

**merely** *adverb*
only; simply, *She was merely joking.*

**merge** *verb* (**merges, merging, merged**)
to combine.

**merger** *noun* (**mergers**)
making two businesses or companies into one.

**meridian** *noun* (**meridians**)
(*say* mer-**rid**-i-ăn)
a line on a map or globe from one pole to the other, *the Greenwich meridian.*

**meringue** *noun* (**meringues**)
(*say* mer-**rang**)
a crisp cake made from the whites of eggs mixed with sugar and baked.

**merit**[1] *noun* (**merits**)
something that deserves praise.
**merits,** the qualities of a person or thing, *Judge it on its merits.*
**meritorious** *adjective*

**merit**[2] *verb* (**merits, meriting, merited**)
to deserve, *He merits a reward.*

**mermaid** *noun* (**mermaids**)
a mythical creature that looks like a woman but has a fish's tail instead of legs.

**merry** *adjective* (**merrier, merriest**)
happy; cheerful.
**merrily** *adverb*, **merriment** *noun*

**merry-go-round** *noun* (**merry-go-rounds**)
(in America, *carousel*) a revolving machine on which people, especially children, ride for amusement.

**mesh** *noun* (**meshes**)
**1** one of the spaces in a net, sieve, or other criss-cross structure. **2** material made like a net; a network, *wire mesh.*

**mess**[1] *noun* (**messes**)
**1** an untidy or dirty condition or thing. **2** a difficult or confused situation, *He made a mess of the job.* **3** a place where soldiers or sailors eat their meals.

**mess**[2] *verb* (**messes, messing, messed**)
**mess about,** to behave stupidly or idly.
**mess up,** to make a mess of something.

**message** *noun* (**messages**)
a question or piece of information sent from one person to another.

**messenger** *noun* (**messengers**)
someone who carries a message.

**Messiah** *noun*
(*say* mi-**sy**-ă)
**1** the person that the Jews expect to come and set them free. **2** according to Christians, Jesus.

**messy** *adjective* (**messier, messiest**)
**1** untidy or dirty. **2** difficult or complicated.
**messily** *adverb*, **messiness** *noun*

**met** past tense and past participle of **meet** *verb*.

**metal** *noun* (**metals**)
a hard substance that melts when it is hot, *Iron, steel, gold, and tin are all metals.*
**metallic** *adjective*

**metallurgy** *noun*
(*say* mi-**tal**-er-ji)
the study of metals; the craft of making and using metals.
**metallurgical** *adjective*, **metallurgist** *noun*

**metamorphic** *adjective*
(*say* met-ă-**mor**-fik)
formed or changed by heat or pressure, *metamorphic rocks.*

**metamorphosis** *noun* (**metamorphoses**)
a complete change, especially of the kind made by some living things, such as a caterpillar changing into a butterfly.

**metaphor** *noun* (**metaphors**)
(*say* met-ă-fer)
using a word or words to suggest something different from their literal meaning, *'Food for thought' and 'a heart of stone' are metaphors.*
**metaphorical** *adjective*, **metaphorically** *adverb*

**meteor** *noun* (**meteors**)
(*say* **meet**-i-er)
a piece of rock or metal that moves through space and burns up when it gets near the earth.
**meteoric** *adjective*

**meteorite** *noun* (**meteorites**)
(*say* **meet**-i-er-ryt)
a meteor that has landed on the earth.

**meteorology** *noun*
(*say* meet-i-er-**ol**-ŏ-ji)
the study of the weather.
**meteorological** *adjective*, **meteorologist** *noun*

**meter** *noun* (**meters**)
a machine for measuring something, especially for measuring how much of something has been used, *a gas meter.*

USAGE: Do not confuse **meter** with **metre**, which means a unit of length or a rhythm.

**methane** *noun*
a colourless gas produced when plants rot away, found mainly in mines and marshes.

**method** *noun* (**methods**)
**1** a way of doing something. **2** behaviour that shows good organization, *There is method in everything he does.*

**methodical** *adjective*
(*say* mi-**thod**-i-kăl)
done carefully; well organized, *methodical work. a methodical person.*
**methodically** *adverb*

**Methodist** *noun* (**Methodists**)
someone who believes in Methodism, a Christian religious movement started by John and Charles Wesley in the 18th century.

**meths** *noun*
(*informal*) methylated spirit.

**methylated spirit** or **spirits** *noun*
a liquid fuel that is a kind of alcohol.

**meticulous** *adjective*
working very carefully or precisely.
**meticulously** *adverb*

**metre** *noun* (**metres**)
(*say* **meet**-er)
**1** the main unit of length in the metric system, equal to about 39¼ inches. **2** a particular type of rhythm in poetry.

USAGE: Do not confuse **metre** with **meter**, which means a machine for measuring something.

**metric** *adjective*
**1** of or in the metric system. **2** of poetic metre.
**metric system**, a measuring system based on decimal units, *In the metric system, the metre is the unit of length, the kilogram is the unit of mass, and the litre is the unit of capacity.*
**metrically** *adverb*

**metro** *noun* (**metros**)
a name for the underground railway in some cities, *the Paris Metro.*

**metronome** *noun* (**metronomes**)
(*say* met-rŏ-nohm)
a device that makes a regular clicking noise to help you keep in time when practising music.

**mew** *verb* (**mews, mewing, mewed**)
to make a sound like a cat.

**miaow** *verb* (**miaows, miaowing, miaowed**)
(*say* mee-ow)
to mew.

**mice** plural of **mouse**.

**microbe** *noun* (**microbes**)
(*say* my-krohb)
a very tiny creature, especially one that causes disease or fermentation.

**microchip** *noun* (**microchips**)
a silicon chip.

**microcomputer** *noun* (**microcomputers**)
a small computer that uses a microprocessor as its central processing unit.

**microelectronic** *adjective*
using very small electrical circuits such as those on silicon chips.

**microfilm** *noun* (**microfilms**)
film on which something is photographed in a miniature size.

**microlight** *noun* (**microlights**)
a very small kind of aircraft, usually like a hang-glider with an engine.

**microphone** *noun* (**microphones**)
an electrical device that picks up sound waves which are then made stronger, broadcast, or recorded.

**microprocessor** *noun* (**microprocessors**)
an integrated circuit that serves as the central processing unit of a computer.

**microscope** *noun* (**microscopes**)
(*say* my-krŏ-skohp)
a device with lenses that make tiny objects appear larger.

**microscopic** *adjective*
(*say* my-krŏ-**skop**-ik)
**1** too small to be seen without a microscope; tiny. **2** using a microscope, *a microscopic examination.*

**microsurgery** *noun*
surgical operations on very tiny parts of the body, using microscopes and special small instruments.

**microwave** *noun* (**microwaves**)
**1** energy moving in very short waves.
**2** a microwave oven.
**microwave oven**, a kind of oven which heats things by using energy in very short waves.

**mid** *adjective*
in the middle of, *The holiday is from mid-July to mid-August.*

**midday** *noun*
noon.

**middle¹** *noun* (**middles**)
1 the place or part of something that is at the same distance from all its sides or edges or from both its ends. 2 someone's waist.

**middle²** *adjective*
placed in the middle.
**middle age**, the time between youth and old age.
**Middle Ages**, the period in history from about AD 1100 to about 1500.
**Middle East**, the countries roughly from Egypt to Iran.
**middle school**, a school for children aged from about 9 to 13.

**middle-aged** *adjective*
of or in middle age.

**middle class** *noun* (**middle classes**)
the class of people between the upper class and the working class.
**middle-class** *adjective*

**midge** *noun* (**midges**)
a small insect like a gnat.

**midget** *noun* (**midgets**)
an unusually short person.

**midland** *adjective*
of the middle part of a country; of the middle part of England.

**Midlands** *plural noun*
the middle part of England.

**midnight** *noun*
twelve o'clock at night.

**midst** *noun*
the middle of something.

**midsummer** *noun*
the middle of summer, coming at the end of June in the northern hemisphere.

**midway** *adverb*
half-way.

**midwife** *noun* (**midwives**)
someone trained to help when a baby is being born.
**midwifery** *noun*

**might¹** past tense of **may** *verb*.

**might²** *noun*
strength; great power.

**mighty** *adjective* (**mightier, mightiest**)
very strong or powerful.
**mightily** *adverb*, **mightiness** *noun*

**migraine** *noun* (**migraines**)
(*say* mee-grayn)
a severe kind of headache.

**migrant** *noun* (**migrants**)
(*say* my-gränt)
a person or animal that goes to live in another country.
**migrant worker**, someone who goes to live and work in another country.

**migrate** *verb* (**migrates, migrating, migrated**)
(*say* my-**grayt**)
to go to live in another country, *The birds migrated every autumn.*
**migration** *noun*, **migratory** *adjective*

**mike** *noun* (**mikes**)
(*informal*) a microphone.

**mild** *adjective* (**milder, mildest**)
gentle.
**mildly** *adverb*, **mildness** *noun*

**mile** *noun* (**miles**)
a measure of distance, equal to about 1,600 metres.

**mileage** *noun* (**mileages**)
the number of miles travelled.

**milestone** *noun* (**milestones**)
1 a stone of a kind that used to be placed beside a road to mark the distance between towns. 2 an important event.

**militant** *adjective*
prepared or wanting to fight or be aggressive.
**militancy** *noun*

**militarism** *noun*
belief in, or use of, military methods.
**militarist** *noun*, **militaristic** *adjective*

**military** *adjective*
of soldiers or the armed forces.

**milk¹** *noun*
a white liquid that female mammals produce in their bodies to feed to their babies, *People drink milk from cows and goats.*
**milk pudding**, a pudding made with milk.
**milk shake**, a drink of milk mixed with a sweet substance that usually tastes of fruit.
**milk tooth**, one of your first teeth which fall out and are replaced by the teeth you have for the rest of your life.

**milk²** *verb* (**milks, milking, milked**)
to get the milk from a cow or other animal.

**milkman** *noun* (**milkmen**)
a man who delivers milk to people's houses.

**milky** *adjective* (**milkier, milkiest**)
like milk; white.
**Milky Way**, a faintly shining band of light that you can sometimes see in the sky, that comes from the stars in our galaxy.

**mill**¹ *noun* (**mills**)
1 a building with machinery for grinding corn to make flour. 2 a factory, *a paper-mill*. 3 a grinding machine, *a coffee-mill*.

**mill**² *verb* (**mills, milling, milled**)
1 to grind grain into flour. 2 to move in a confused crowd, *The animals were milling about*.
**miller** *noun*

**millet** *noun*
a kind of cereal with tiny seeds.

**milligram** *noun* (**milligrams**)
one thousandth of a gram.

**millilitre** *noun* (**millilitres**)
one thousandth of a litre.

**millimetre** *noun* (**millimetres**)
one thousandth of a metre.

**million** *noun* (**millions**)
the number 1,000,000; a thousand thousands.
**millionth** *adjective*

**millionaire** *noun* (**millionaires**)
an extremely rich person.

**milometer** *noun* (**milometers**)
(*say* my-**lom**-it-er)
a device for measuring how far a vehicle has travelled.

**mime** *verb* (**mimes, miming, mimed**)
to tell someone something, act a story, or pretend to do something by using actions, not words.

**mimic** *verb* (**mimics, mimicking, mimicked**)
to imitate someone, especially so as to make fun of him or her.
**mimicry** *noun*

**minaret** *noun* (**minarets**)
a tall, thin tower on a mosque, with a balcony where a muezzin stands.

**mince**¹ *verb* (**minces, mincing, minced**)
to cut food into very small pieces.
**not to mince your words**, not to alter what you say just for the sake of politeness.
**mincer** *noun*

**mince**² *noun*
minced meat.
**mince pie**, a pie containing mincemeat.

**mincemeat** *noun*
a sweet mixture of currants, raisins, chopped apple, etc. used in pies.

**mind**¹ *noun* (**minds**)
1 the power to think, feel, understand, and remember; your thoughts and feelings. 2 someone's opinion, *Have you changed your mind?*
**mind's eye**, imagination.

**mind**² *verb* (**minds, minding, minded**)
1 to look after someone or something, *He was minding the baby*. 2 to be careful; to watch out for something, *Mind! I'm carrying a pan full of hot fat. Mind the doors!* 3 to be sad or upset about something; to object to something, *I don't mind missing the party*.

**mindless** *adjective*
1 done without thinking; stupid, *The film is full of mindless violence*. 2 boring, especially because it is too simple, *the mindless job of packing fruit*.

**mine**¹ *adjective* and *pronoun*
belonging to me, *That book is mine*.

**mine**² *noun* (**mines**)
1 a place where coal, metal, jewels, etc. are dug out of the ground. 2 an explosive hidden under the ground or in the sea to destroy people and things that come close to it.

**mine**³ *verb* (**mines, mining, mined**)
1 to dig something from a mine. 2 to lay explosive mines in a place.
**mining** *noun*

**miner** *noun* (**miners**)
someone who works in a mine.

**mineral** *noun* (**minerals**)
1 a hard substance that can be dug out of the ground, *Iron ore and coal are minerals*. 2 a cold fizzy drink.
**mineral water**, water from a spring.

**mingle** *verb* (**mingles, mingling, mingled**)
to mix or blend; to mix or blend things, *Salt water and fresh water mingle in the estuary. Mingle the olive oil with the vinegar*.

**mingy** *adjective* (**mingier, mingiest**)
(*say* min-ji)
(*informal*) mean; stingy.

**miniature** *adjective*
(*say* min-i-cher)
1 tiny, *A piccolo looks like a miniature flute*. 2 copying something on a very small scale, *a miniature sailing-ship*.

**minibus** *noun* (**minibuses**)
a vehicle like a small bus with seats for several people.

**minim** *noun* (**minims**)
(in America, *half note*) a musical note equal to half a semibreve, written ♩.

**minimum** *noun* (**minima**)
the smallest possible amount or number, *The teacher wants a minimum of noise*.
**minimal** *adjective*, **minimize** *verb*

**minister** *noun* (**ministers**)
1 someone in charge of a government department, *The Minister of Health decided to close the hospital.* 2 a member of the clergy.

**ministry** *noun* (**ministries**)
1 a government department. 2 the work of a minister in the church.

**mink** *noun* (**minks**)
1 a small animal rather like a stoat. 2 this animal's valuable brown fur.

**minnow** *noun* (**minnows**)
a tiny freshwater fish.

**minor** *adjective*
1 less important; not very important, *a minor operation.* 2 of the musical scale that has a semitone between the 2nd and 3rd notes.

**minority** *noun* (**minorities**)
(*say* myn-o-ri-ti)
1 the smaller part of a group of people or things, *There was a minority of votes against the decision.* 2 a small group that is different from others, *ethnic minorities.*

**minstrel** *noun* (**minstrels**)
a wandering musician in the Middle Ages.

**mint**¹ *noun*
1 a green plant with sweet-smelling leaves used for flavouring. 2 a sweet flavoured with peppermint.
**mint sauce,** chopped mint-leaves in vinegar, used as a sauce on roast lamb.

**mint**² *noun* (**mints**)
a place where coins are made.

**mint**³ *adjective*
unused and clean, *a mint stamp.*

**minus** *preposition*
reduced by subtracting; less, *Eight minus two equals six (8 − 2 = 6).*

**minute**¹ *noun* (**minutes**)
(*say* min-it)
1 one sixtieth of an hour. 2 (*informal*) a short time, *I'll be ready in a minute!*
**minutes,** a summary of what has been said at a meeting.

**minute**² *adjective*
(*say* my-newt)
1 tiny, *a minute insect.* 2 very detailed, *a minute examination.*
**minutely** *adverb*

**miracle** *noun* (**miracles**)
a wonderful or magical happening that is unexpected.
**miraculous** *adjective*, **miraculously** *adverb*

**mirage** *noun* (**mirages**)
(*say* mi-rahzh)
something that a person imagines he or she sees but which is not there at all, *The lake he thought he saw in the desert was a mirage.*

**mirror** *noun* (**mirrors**)
a glass or metal device or surface that reflects things clearly.
**mirror image,** a reflection or copy in which the right and left sides of the original are reversed.

**mirth** *noun*
a formal word for laughter or cheerfulness.

**mis-** *prefix*
wrong; wrongly, *misunderstanding. misunderstand.*

**misbehave** *verb* (**misbehaves, misbehaving, misbehaved**)
to behave badly or naughtily.
**misbehaviour** *noun*

**miscarriage** *noun* (**miscarriages**)
the birth of a baby too early, so that it dies.

**miscellaneous** *adjective*
(*say* mis-ĕl-ay-ni-ŭs)
of various kinds.
**miscellany** *noun*

**mischief** *noun*
naughty or troublesome behaviour.
**mischievous** *adjective*

**miser** *noun* (**misers**)
someone who stores money away and spends as little as he or she can.
**miserly** *adjective*

**miserable** *adjective*
unhappy; wretched, *He felt miserable. What miserable weather!*
**miserably** *adverb*

**misery** *noun* (**miseries**)
1 unhappiness; suffering. 2 (*informal*) someone who is miserable or always complaining.

**misfit** *noun* (**misfits**)
1 someone who does not fit in well with other people or with his or her surroundings. 2 a piece of clothing that does not fit.

**misfortune** *noun* (**misfortunes**)
1 an unlucky event; an accident. 2 bad luck.

**mishap** *noun* (**mishaps**)
(*say* mis-hap)
an unfortunate accident.

**mislay** *verb* (**mislays, mislaying, mislaid**)
to lose something for a short time.

**mislead** *verb* (**misleads, misleading, misled**)
to give someone a wrong idea or impression; to deceive, *I was misled into thinking he was reliable.*

**misprint** *noun* (**misprints**)
a mistake in printing.

**Miss** *noun* (**Misses**)
a word used before the name of a girl or unmarried woman when speaking or writing politely to or about her, *Dear Miss Jones.*

**miss**¹ *verb* (**misses, missing, missed**)
**1** to fail to hit, reach, catch, see, hear, or find something. **2** to be sad because someone or something is not with you, *I missed my mother when she was in hospital.* **3** to notice that something has gone, *I did not miss my gloves until I was back home; I must have left them somewhere in town.*

**miss**² *noun* (**misses**)
not hitting, reaching, or catching something, *Was that shot a hit or a miss?*

**missal** *noun* (**missals**)
a Roman Catholic prayer-book.

**missile** *noun* (**missiles**)
a weapon fired or thrown at a target.

**missing** *adjective*
**1** lost, *a missing dog.* **2** not in the proper place, *The scissors are missing; where have you put them?*

**mission** *noun* (**missions**)
**1** an important job that someone is sent to do or that someone feels he or she must do. **2** a place or building where missionaries work.

**missionary** *noun* (**missionaries**)
someone who goes to another country to spread a religion.

**misspell** *verb* (**misspells, misspelling,** *past tense* and *past participle* **misspelt** or **misspelled**)
to spell a word wrongly.

**mist** *noun* (**mists**)
**1** damp cloudy air like a thin fog. **2** condensed water-vapour on a window, mirror, etc.

**mistake**¹ *noun* (**mistakes**)
something wrong; an incorrect action or idea.
**by mistake,** by being careless, forgetful, etc.

**mistake**² *verb* (**mistakes, mistaking, mistook, mistaken**)
to misunderstand; to choose or identify wrongly.

**mistaken** *adjective*
incorrect; wrong, *a mistaken idea. You are mistaken if you believe that.*
**mistakenly** *adverb*

**mister** *noun*
**1** Mr. **2** (*informal*) sir, *Can you tell me the time, mister?*

**mistletoe** *noun*
a plant with green leaves and white berries in winter, *People kiss each other under the mistletoe that is used as a Christmas decoration.*

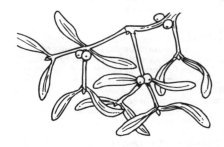

**mistreat** *verb* (**mistreats, mistreating, mistreated**)
to treat someone badly or unfairly.
**mistreatment** *noun*

**mistress** *noun* (**mistresses**)
**1** a woman who teaches in a school. **2** a woman in charge of something. **3** the woman who owns a dog or other animal. **4** a woman that a man loves and courts, even though he is married to someone else.

**mistrust** *verb* (**mistrusts, mistrusting, mistrusted**)
not to trust someone or something.

**misty** *adjective* (**mistier, mistiest**)
**1** full of mist. **2** not clear.
**mistily** *adverb*, **mistiness** *noun*

**misunderstand** *verb* (**misunderstands, misunderstanding, misunderstood**)
to get a wrong idea or impression of something, *You misunderstood what I said.*
**misunderstanding** *noun*

**misuse**¹ *verb* (**misuses, misusing, misused**)
(*say* mis-**yooz**)
to use something wrongly; to treat something badly, *You are misusing that word. Someone has been misusing that bicycle; its frame is cracked.*

**misuse**² *noun*
(*say* mis-**yooss**)
using something wrongly; treating something badly.

**mite** *noun* (**mites**)
**1** a tiny insect found in food. **2** a small child.

**mitre** *noun* (**mitres**)
(*say* **my**-ter)
1 the tall, tapering hat worn by a bishop.
2 a joint of two tapering pieces of wood,
cloth, etc.

**mitten** *noun* (**mittens**)
a glove without separate parts for the
fingers.

**mix** *verb* (**mixes, mixing, mixed**)
1 to stir or shake different things together
to make one thing; to combine. 2 to get
together with other people, *She mixes well.*
**mix up**, to confuse.
**mixer** *noun*

**mixed** *adjective*
for or containing various kinds of people or
things, especially males and females (*a
mixed school*) or people of different races or
religions (*a mixed community*).

**mixture** *noun* (**mixtures**)
something made of different things mixed
together.

**mix-up** *noun* (**mix-ups**)
a confused situation, especially one that
ruins a plan, *Owing to a mix-up in the
bookings we did not get a room at the hotel.*

**mm** short for **millimetre** or **millimetres**.

**moan**[1] *noun* (**moans**)
1 a long low sound, usually of suffering. 2 a
grumble.

**moan**[2] *verb* (**moans, moaning, moaned**)
1 to make a long low sound. 2 to grumble.

**moat** *noun* (**moats**)
a deep ditch round a castle, usually full of
water.

**mob**[1] *noun* (**mobs**)
a dangerous crowd of people.

**mob**[2] *verb* (**mobs, mobbing, mobbed**)
to crowd round someone.

**mobile**[1] *adjective*
that can or does move, *a mobile shop.*
**mobility** *noun*

**mobile**[2] *noun* (**mobiles**)
something decorative made to be hung
from a ceiling, etc. so that it moves about
in the air.

**mobilize** *verb* (**mobilizes, mobilizing, mobilized**)
to assemble people or things ready for a
particular purpose, especially for war.
**mobilization** *noun*

**moccasin** *noun* (**moccasins**)
(*say* mok-ă-sin)
a soft leather shoe like those worn by
Native Americans.

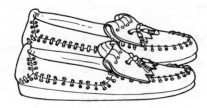

**mock**[1] *adjective*
not real; imitation, *mock cream.*

**mock**[2] *verb* (**mocks, mocking, mocked**)
to make fun of someone or something.
**mockery** *noun*

**mock-up** *noun* (**mock-ups**)
a model of something, *They made a
mock-up of the rocket.*

**mode** *noun* (**modes**)
1 the way that something is done, *a new
mode of transport.* 2 what is fashionable,
*These jackets are the latest mode.*

**model**[1] *noun* (**models**)
1 a small copy of an object, *He makes
models of aircraft.* 2 a particular version or
design of something, *We saw the new
models at the motor show.* 3 someone who
poses for an artist or photographer.
4 someone whose job is to display clothes
by wearing them. 5 an excellent person or
thing.

**model**[2] *verb* (**models, modelling, modelled**)
1 to make a small copy of something. 2 to
make something by following a pattern,
*The building is modelled on an Egyptian
temple.* 3 to work as an artist's model or a
fashion model.

**model**[3] *adjective*
1 miniature, *a model railway.* 2 being a
good example for people to follow, *She was
a model pupil.*

**modem** *noun* (**modems**)
(*in Computing*) a device that allows
computers to exchange information, using
the same wires as the telephone system.

**moderate**[1] *adjective*
(*say* mod-er-ăt)
that is not too little and not too much;
medium.
**moderately** *adverb,* **moderation** *noun*

**moderate**[2] *verb* (**moderates, moderating,
moderated**)
(*say* mod-er-ayt)
to make something less strong or severe.

**modern** *adjective*
of the kind that is normal now, *a modern house*.
**modernity** *noun*

**modernize** *verb* (**modernizes, modernizing, modernized**)
to make something modern; to change something to suit modern tastes.
**modernization** *noun*

**modest** *adjective*
1 not thinking too much of how good you are. 2 moderate, *Their needs were modest*.
**modestly** *adverb*, **modesty** *noun*

**modify** *verb* (**modifies, modifying, modified**)
to change something slightly.
**modification** *noun*

**module** *noun* (**modules**)
(*say* mod-yool)
1 an independent part of a spacecraft, building, etc. 2 a part of a course of learning, *This term I'm doing a Maths module*. 3 a unit used in measuring.

**moist** *adjective* (**moister, moistest**)
damp.
**moisture** *noun*

**moisten** *verb* (**moistens, moistening, moistened**)
(*say* moi-sĕn)
to make something moist; to become moist.

**molar** *noun* (**molars**)
(*say* moh-ler)
one of the wide teeth at the back of your mouth.

**mole** *noun* (**moles**)
1 a small, dark grey, furry animal that digs holes under the ground. 2 a small dark spot on someone's skin.

**molecule** *noun* (**molecules**)
(*say* mol-i-kewl)
1 a very small particle of matter. 2 (*in Science*) the smallest part into which you can divide a substance without changing its chemical nature; a group of atoms.
**molecular** *adjective*

**molehill** *noun* (**molehills**)
a small pile of earth thrown up by a mole.
**make a mountain out of a molehill**, to give something too much importance.

**molest** *verb* (**molests, molesting, molested**)
1 to touch someone's sexual parts in a way which upsets or hurts him or her, which is against the law. 2 to annoy or pester someone in an unfriendly or violent way.

**mollusc** *noun* (**molluscs**)
an animal with a soft body and usually a hard shell, *Snails, slugs, and oysters are molluscs*.

**molten** *adjective*
melted.

**moment** *noun* (**moments**)
1 a very short period of time, *Wait a moment*. 2 a particular time, *He arrived at the last moment*. 3 (*in Science*) a turning effect produced by a force acting at a distance on an object.
**at the moment**, now.

**momentary** *adjective*
(*say* moh-mĕn-ter-i)
lasting for only a moment.
**momentarily** *adverb*

**momentous** *adjective*
(*say* moh-**ment**-ŭs)
very important.

**momentum** *noun*
(*say* moh-**ment**-ŭm)
movement; the amount or force of movement.

**monarch** *noun* (**monarchs**)
a king, queen, emperor, or empress.
**monarchy** *noun*

**monastery** *noun* (**monasteries**)
(*say* mon-ă-ster-i)
a building where monks live and work.
**monastic** *adjective*

**Monday** *noun* (**Mondays**)
the second day of the week.

**money** *noun*
coins and notes used by people to buy things.
**money for jam** or **money for old rope**, (*informal*) profit easily made.

**Mongol** *noun* (**Mongols**)
a Mongolian person.

**Mongolian** *adjective*
of Mongolia.

**mongoose** *noun* (**mongooses**)
a small animal rather like a large weasel, that can kill snakes.

**mongrel** *noun* (**mongrels**)
  (*say* **mung-rĕl**)
  a dog of mixed breeds.

**monitor** *noun* (**monitors**)
  **1** a pupil who is given a special job to do at
  school. **2** a device used for checking how
  something is working. **3** (*in Computing*) a
  screen on which a computer displays
  information.

**monk** *noun* (**monks**)
  a member of a religious community of men.

**monkey** *noun* (**monkeys**)
  **1** an animal rather like a human, with long
  arms and a tail. **2** a mischievous person.

**mono-** *prefix*
  having one of something, *A monoplane has
  one set of wings.*

**monolingual** *adjective*
  speaking only one language; dealing with
  only one language, *a monolingual
  community. This is a monolingual
  dictionary.*

**monologue** *noun* (**monologues**)
  (*say* **mon-ŏ-log**)
  a long speech by one person or performer.

**monopoly** *noun* (**monopolies**)
  doing all the business, trade, etc. in one
  thing; controlling the supply of something,
  *The government has a monopoly in
  supplying electricity.*
  **monopolize** *verb*

**monorail** *noun* (**monorails**)
  a railway that uses only one rail.

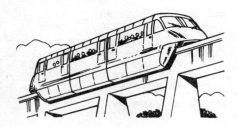

**monotonous** *adjective*
  (*say* **mŏn-ot-ŏn-ŭs**)
  boring because it does not change,
  *monotonous work.*
  **monotonously** *adverb*, **monotony** *noun*

**monsoon** *noun* (**monsoons**)
  a strong wind in and around the Indian
  Ocean, bringing heavy rain in summer.

**monster**[1] *noun* (**monsters**)
  a large, frightening creature.

**monster**[2] *adjective*
  huge.

**monstrous** *adjective*
  **1** like a monster; huge. **2** very shocking or
  cruel, *a monstrous crime.*
  **monstrosity** *noun*

**month** *noun* (**months**)
  one of the twelve parts into which a year is
  divided.

**monthly** *adjective*
  happening every month; done every month,
  *a monthly event.*

**monument** *noun* (**monuments**)
  a statue, building, column, etc. put up as a
  memorial of some person or event.

**monumental** *adjective*
  **1** of or for a monument. **2** great; huge, *a
  monumental achievement.*

**moo** *verb* (**moos, mooing, mooed**)
  to make the sound of a cow.

**mood** *noun* (**moods**)
  the way someone feels, *She's in a good
  mood.*

**moody** *adjective* (**moodier, moodiest**)
  **1** gloomy. **2** likely to become bad-tempered
  suddenly.
  **moodily** *adverb*, **moodiness** *noun*

**moon** *noun* (**moons**)
  the object which orbits the earth and
  shines in the sky at night; a similar object
  which orbits another planet.
  **moonless** *adjective*, **moonlight** *noun*, **moonlit**
  *adjective*

**moor**[1] *noun* (**moors**)
  an area of rough, high land with bushes
  but no trees.

**moor**[2] *verb* (**moors, mooring, moored**)
  **1** to tie up a boat, *You can moor upstream
  of the lock.* **2** to secure something, *The buoy
  is moored to the seabed.*
  **moorings** *plural noun*

**moorhen** *noun* (**moorhens**)
  a small water-bird.

**moose** *noun* (**moose**)
  a North American elk.

**mop**[1] *noun* (**mops**)
a piece of soft material on the end of a stick, used for cleaning floors or dishes.

**mop**[2] *verb* (**mops, mopping, mopped**)
to clean something with a mop.
**mop up,** to clear away the remains of something.

**mope** *verb* (**mopes, moping, moped**)
to be sad.

**moped** *noun* (**mopeds**)
(*say* **moh**-ped)
a small motor cycle.

**moraine** *noun* (**moraines**)
a mass of stones, earth, etc. carried down by a glacier.
**end moraine,** a terminal moraine.
**lateral moraine,** a moraine left at the sides of a glacier.
**terminal moraine,** a moraine left at the lower end of a glacier.

**moral**[1] *adjective*
**1** connected with right and wrong, *Whether it is wrong to hunt whales is a moral question.* **2** being or doing good, *Clergymen are expected to lead moral lives.*
**morality** *noun,* **morally** *adverb*

**moral**[2] *noun* (**morals**)
a lesson taught by a story or event.
**morals,** standards of behaviour; a capacity for being or doing good.

**morale** *noun*
(*say* mŏ-**rahl**)
confidence or courage.

**more**[1] *adjective*
larger in number or amount.

**more**[2] *noun*
a larger number or amount, *I want more.*

**more**[3] *adverb*
**1** again, *I'll tell you once more.* **2** to a greater extent, *You must work more.*
**more or less,** almost; approximately, *I've more or less finished the work. The repairs cost £100, more or less.*

**moreover** *adverb*
also; in addition.

**Mormon** *noun* (**Mormons**)
a member of a religious group founded in the USA.

**morning** *noun* (**mornings**)
the part of the day before noon or before lunchtime.

**moron** *noun* (**morons**)
(*informal*) a stupid person.
**moronic** *adjective*

**morphine** *noun*
(*say* **mor**-feen)
a drug made from opium, used to relieve pain.

**morris dance** *noun* (**morris dances**)
a traditional English folk-dance by people in costume with ribbons and bells.

**Morse code** *noun*
a code using dots and dashes to represent letters and numbers, *Radio operators often use Morse code to send messages.*

**morsel** *noun* (**morsels**)
a small piece of food.

**mortal** *adjective*
**1** that can die, *All men are mortal.* **2** that causes death, *a mortal wound.*
**mortally** *adverb*

**mortality** *noun*
the number of people who die over a particular period of time, *a low rate of infant mortality.*

**mortar** *noun*
a mixture of sand, cement, and water used in building to stick bricks together.

**mortgage** *noun* (**mortgages**)
(*say* **mor**-gij)
an agreement to borrow money to buy a house.

**mortuary** *noun* (**mortuaries**)
a place where dead bodies are kept before they are buried or cremated.

**mosaic** *noun* (**mosaics**)
(*say* moh-**zay**-ik)
a picture or design made from small coloured pieces of glass, stone, paper, etc.

**Moslem** *noun* (**Moslems**)
(*say* **moz**-lĕm)
a Muslim.

**mosque** *noun* (**mosques**)
(*say* mosk)
a building where Muslims worship.

**mosquito** *noun* (**mosquitoes**)
(*say* mos-**kee**-toh)
an insect that sucks blood.

**moss** *noun* (**mosses**)
a non-flowering plant that grows in damp
places.
**mossy** *adjective*

**most**¹ *adjective*
largest in number or amount.

**most**² *noun*
the largest number or amount.

**most**³ *adverb*
1 more than any other, *I liked that teacher
most.* 2 very; extremely, *It was most
amusing.*

**mostly** *adverb*
mainly.

**MOT** or **MOT test** *noun* (**MOTs** or **MOT tests**)
a safety check that has to be made every
year on vehicles that are more than a
certain age.

**motel** *noun* (**motels**)
(*say* moh-**tel**)
a hotel for motorists.

**moth** *noun* (**moths**)
an insect rather like a butterfly that
usually flies around at night.

**mother** *noun* (**mothers**)
a female parent.
**Mothering Sunday** or **Mother's Day,** the fourth
Sunday in Lent, when people often give
presents to their mothers.
**motherhood** *noun*, **motherless** *adjective*

**mother-in-law** *noun* (**mothers-in-law**)
the mother of your husband or wife.

**motherly** *adjective*
kind or tender like a mother.

**motion** *noun* (**motions**)
movement.
**go through the motions,** to do or say
something without sincere enthusiasm, or
in a way that shows you are only doing it
because you have to.
**motionless** *adjective*

**motivate** *verb* (**motivates, motivating, motivated**)
to make someone keen to achieve
something, *She is good at motivating her
team.*

**motive** *noun* (**motives**)
what makes a person do something.

**motor** *noun* (**motors**)
a machine that provides power.

**motor bike** *noun* (**motor bikes**)
(*informal*) a motor cycle.

**motor boat** *noun* (**motor boats**)
a boat driven by a motor.

**motor car** *noun* (**motor cars**)
a motor vehicle large enough to carry
several people inside it.

**motor cycle** *noun* (**motor cycles**)
a motor vehicle with two wheels.
**motor-cyclist** *noun*

**motorist** *noun* (**motorists**)
someone who drives a motor car, especially
for pleasure.

**motor vehicle** *noun* (**motor vehicles**)
a vehicle driven by a motor, for use on
roads.

**motorway** *noun* (**motorways**)
(in America, *freeway*) a wide road for fast
long-distance traffic.

**mottled** *adjective*
marked with spots or patches of colour.

**motto** *noun* (**mottoes**)
1 a short saying used as a guide for
behaviour, *His motto was 'Do your best'.*
2 a short verse, riddle, etc. found inside a
cracker.

**mould**¹ *noun* (**moulds**)
a container for making things like jelly or
plaster set in the shape that is wanted.

**mould**[2] *noun* (**moulds**)
a furry growth that appears on some moist surfaces, especially on something decaying, *There is mould on this cheese.*
**mouldy** *adjective*

**mould**[3] *verb* (**moulds, moulding, moulded**)
to make something have a particular shape or character.

**moult** *verb* (**moults, moulting, moulted**)
(*say* mohlt)
to lose feathers or hair, *Our cat is moulting.*

**mound** *noun* (**mounds**)
a pile of earth, stones, etc.; a small hill.

**mount**[1] *verb* (**mounts, mounting, mounted**)
**1** to get on to a horse or bicycle so that you can ride it. **2** to rise, *The cost of insurance is mounting.* **3** to put something firmly in place for use or display, *Mount your photos in an album.*

**mount**[2] *noun* (**mounts**)
**1** a mountain, *Mount Everest.* **2** something in or on which an object is mounted. **3** an animal on which you are riding.

**mountain** *noun* (**mountains**)
a very high hill.
**mountainous** *adjective*

**mountain bike** *noun* (**mountain bikes**)
a bicycle with a strong frame, wide tyres, and many gears, designed for use on rough ground.

**mountaineer** *noun* (**mountaineers**)
someone who climbs mountains.
**mountaineering** *noun*

**mourn** *verb* (**mourns, mourning, mourned**)
to be sad, especially because someone has died.
**mourner** *noun*

**mournful** *adjective*
sad.
**mournfully** *adverb*

**mouse** *noun* (**mice**)
**1** a small animal with a long tail and a pointed nose. **2** (*in Computing*) a device that you move around on your desk, etc. to control the movements of a computer's cursor and to choose what you want the computer to do.
**mousetrap** *noun*, **mousy** *adjective*

**mousse** *noun* (**mousses**)
(*say* mooss)
**1** a sweet flavoured pudding made with beaten egg whites and cream and served cold. **2** a frothy, creamy substance used especially for holding hair in a particular style.

**moustache** *noun* (**moustaches**)
(*say* mŭs-**tahsh**)
hair growing above a man's upper lip.

**mouth** *noun* (**mouths**)
**1** the part of the face that opens for eating and speaking. **2** the place where a river enters the sea. **3** an opening or outlet.
**mouthful** *noun*

**mouth-organ** *noun* (**mouth-organs**)
a musical instrument played by blowing and sucking.

**mouthpiece** *noun* (**mouthpieces**)
the part of a musical instrument or other device that you put to your mouth.

**movable** *adjective*
that can be moved.

**move**[1] *verb* (**moves, moving, moved**)
**1** to take or go from one place to another. **2** to affect someone's emotions, *Their story moved us deeply.*
**moving picture**, a series of photographs shown quickly one after the other to give the appearance of movement.
**moving staircase**, an escalator.

**move**[2] *noun* (**moves**)
**1** a movement. **2** someone's turn in a game.
**get a move on**, (*informal*) to hurry up.
**on the move**, moving; making progress, *Large numbers of people are on the move.*

**movement** *noun* (**movements**)
**1** the action of moving or being moved. **2** a group of people working for a particular cause. **3** one of the main parts of a piece of music, *a symphony in four movements.*

**movie** *noun* (**movies**)
a moving picture; a film.

**moving** *adjective*
causing someone to feel strong emotion, especially sadness or pity.

**mow** *verb* (**mows, mowing, mowed, mown**)
to cut grass.
**mow down**, to knock down or kill people or animals in large numbers.
**mower** *noun*

**MP** (**MPs**) short for **Member of Parliament.**

**m.p.h.** short for *miles per hour.*

**Mr** *noun* (**Messrs**)
(*say* **mis**-ter)
a word used before the name of a man when speaking or writing politely to or about him.

**Mrs** *noun* (**Mrs** or **Mesdames**)
(*say* **mis**-iz)
a word used before the name of a married woman when speaking or writing politely to or about her.

**Ms** *noun*
 (*say* miz)
 a word used before the name of a woman when speaking or writing to or about her.

**much**[1] *adjective*
 existing in a large amount, *much work.*

**much**[2] *noun*
 a large amount of something.

**much**[3] *adverb*
 1 greatly; considerably, *much to my surprise.* 2 about; approximately, *It's much the same.*

**muck**[1] *noun*
 1 dirt; filth. 2 a mess, *You have made a muck of it.*
 **mucky** *adjective*

**muck**[2] *verb* (**mucks, mucking, mucked**) (*informal*)
 **muck about** or **muck around**, to mess about.
 **muck up**, to mess up.

**mud** *noun*
 wet, soft earth.
 **muddy** *adjective*

**muddle**[1] *verb* (**muddles, muddling, muddled**)
 1 to mix things up. 2 to confuse someone.
 **muddler** *noun*

**muddle**[2] *noun* (**muddles**)
 a confusion or mess.

**mudguard** *noun* (**mudguards**)
 a device to stop mud and water being thrown up by the wheels of a vehicle.

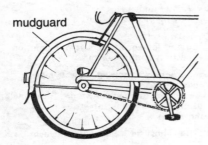
mudguard

**muesli** *noun*
 (*say* **mooz**-li)
 a food made of cereals, nuts, dried fruit, etc.

**muezzin** *noun* (**muezzins**)
 a man who calls Muslims to prayer.

**muffle** *verb* (**muffles, muffling, muffled**)
 1 to cover or wrap something up to protect it or keep it warm. 2 to deaden the sound of something, *a muffled scream.*

**mug**[1] *noun* (**mugs**)
 1 a large cup, usually used without a saucer. 2 (*slang*) a fool; someone who is easily cheated. 3 (*slang*) a person's face.

**mug**[2] *verb* (**mugs, mugging, mugged**)
 to attack and rob someone in the street.
 **mugger** *noun*

**muggy** *adjective* (**muggier, muggiest**)
 unpleasantly warm and damp, *muggy weather.*

**mule** *noun* (**mules**)
 an animal that is the offspring of a donkey and a mare.

**multi-** *prefix*
 having many of something, *a multi-purpose tool. The plant has multicoloured leaves.*

**multiple**[1] *adjective*
 having or involving many parts or elements.
 **multiple-choice test,** a test in which you are given several possible answers and have to choose the right one.

**multiple**[2] *noun* (**multiples**)
 a number that can be divided exactly by another number, *30 and 50 are multiples of 10.*

**multiply** *verb* (**multiplies, multiplying, multiplied**)
 1 to add a number to itself a given number of times, *Five multiplied by four equals twenty (5 × 4 = 20).* 2 to increase quickly in number or amount, *The rabbits were multiplying.*
 **multiplication** *noun*

**multiracial** *adjective*
 (*say* mul-ti-**ray**-shăl)
 consisting of people of many different races, *a multiracial society.*

**multitude** *noun* (**multitudes**)
 a very large number of people or things.
 **multitudinous** *adjective*

**mum** *noun* (**mums**)
 (*informal*) mother.

**mumble** *verb* (**mumbles, mumbling, mumbled**)
 to speak so that you are not easy to hear.
 **mumbler** *noun*

**mummy**[1] *noun* (**mummies**)
a dead body preserved for burial as was the custom in ancient Egypt.
**mummify** *verb*

**mummy**[2] *noun* (**mummies**)
(*informal*) mother.

**mumps** *noun*
an infectious disease that makes your neck swell up.

**munch** *verb* (**munches, munching, munched**)
to chew something noisily; to make a loud chewing sound.

**municipal** *adjective*
(*say* mew-**nis**-i-păl)
of a town or city.

**mural** *noun* (**murals**)
a picture painted on a wall.

**murder**[1] *verb* (**murders, murdering, murdered**)
to kill someone deliberately.
**murderer** *noun*, **murderess** *noun*

**murder**[2] *noun* (**murders**)
1 the deliberate killing of someone.
2 (*informal*) something very difficult or unpleasant, *Changing the car's wheel in the rain was murder.*
**murderous** *adjective*

**murky** *adjective* (**murkier, murkiest**)
dark and gloomy.

**murmur**[1] *noun* (**murmurs**)
1 a low continuous sound, *the murmur of the sea.* 2 the sound of softly spoken words, *A murmur of conversation was coming from next door.*

**murmur**[2] *verb* (**murmurs, murmuring, murmured**)
1 to make a low continuous sound. 2 to speak softly; to say something softly.

**muscle**[1] *noun* (**muscles**)
one of the parts inside the body that cause movement.
**muscular** *adjective*

**muscle**[2] *verb* (**muscles, muscling, muscled**)
**muscle in on something,** to insist on being involved in an activity in which you are not welcome, *He kept trying to muscle in on our conversation.*

**museum** *noun* (**museums**)
a place where interesting objects, especially old things, are displayed for people to see.

**mushroom**[1] *noun* (**mushrooms**)
a fast-growing edible fungus with a dome-shaped top.

**mushroom**[2] *verb* (**mushrooms, mushrooming, mushroomed**)
to grow or appear suddenly like mushrooms, *Blocks of flats mushroomed in the city.*

**music** *noun*
1 pleasant or interesting sounds made by instruments or by the voice. 2 printed or written instructions for making this kind of sound.
**music centre,** a radio, record-player, and cassette recorder combined in one cabinet.

**musical**[1] *adjective*
1 of or for music, *musical instruments.*
2 good at music; interested in music, *Are you musical?*
**musically** *adverb*

**musical**[2] *noun* (**musicals**)
a play or film containing a lot of music.

**musician** *noun* (**musicians**)
someone who plays a musical instrument.

**musket** *noun* (**muskets**)
an old type of rifle.
**musketeer** *noun*

**Muslim** *noun* (**Muslims**)
(*say* **muuz**-lim)
someone who follows the religious teachings of Muhammad.

**muslin** *noun*
thin, fine cotton cloth.

**mussel** *noun* (**mussels**)
a black shellfish, often found sticking to rocks.

**must** *verb*
1 to have to; to be forced or obliged to do something, *I must go home soon.* 2 to be sure to; to be definitely, *You must be joking!*

**mustard** *noun*
a yellow paste or powder used to give food a hot taste.
**mustard and cress,** small green plants eaten in salads.

**muster** *verb* (**musters, mustering, mustered**)
to assemble or gather together.

**musty** *adjective* (**mustier, mustiest**)
smelling or tasting mouldy or stale.
**mustiness** *noun*

**mutation** *noun* (**mutations**)
a change in the form or shape of something.

**mute**[1] *adjective*
1 unable to speak, *She had been mute from birth.* 2 silent, *They stood and stared in mute astonishment.*
**muted** *adjective*, **mutely** *adverb*

**mute**[2] *noun* (**mutes**)
1 a person who cannot speak. 2 a device fitted to a musical instrument to make it quieter.

**mutilate** *verb* (**mutilates, mutilating, mutilated**)
to damage something by breaking or cutting off part of it.
**mutilation** *noun*

**mutineer** *noun* (**mutineers**)
(*say* mew-tin-**eer**)
someone who takes part in a mutiny.

**mutiny**[1] *noun* (**mutinies**)
(*say* mew-tin-i)
a rebellion by sailors or soldiers against their officers.
**mutinous** *adjective*, **mutinously** *adverb*

**mutiny**[2] *verb* (**mutinies, mutinying, mutinied**)
(*say* mew-tin-i)
to take part in a mutiny.

**mutter** *verb* (**mutters, muttering, muttered**)
to murmur or grumble.

**mutton** *noun*
meat from a sheep.

**mutual** *adjective*
(*say* mew-tew-ǎl)
exchanged equally; shared, *mutual help.*
**mutually** *adverb*

**muzzle** *noun* (**muzzles**)
1 an animal's nose and mouth. 2 a cover put over an animal's nose and mouth so that it cannot bite. 3 the open end of a gun.

**my** *adjective*
of me; belonging to me.

**myself** *pronoun*
me and nobody else, *I'm ashamed of myself.*
**by myself,** on my own; alone, *I cooked the dinner all by myself. I walked along the beach by myself.*

**mystery** *noun* (**mysteries**)
something strange or puzzling.
**mysterious** *adjective*, **mysteriously** *adverb*

**mystify** *verb* (**mystifies, mystifying, mystified**)
to puzzle someone very much.
**mystification** *noun*

**myth** *noun* (**myths**)
1 a legend. 2 an untrue story or belief, *the myth that progress will lead to a perfect world.*
**mythological** *adjective*, **mythology** *noun*

**mythical** *adjective*
imaginary; of the sort you find in myths, *mythical beasts.*

# Nn

**nab** *verb* (**nabs, nabbing, nabbed**)
(*informal*) to catch; to grab.

**nag**[1] *verb* (**nags, nagging, nagged**)
to keep telling someone that you are not
pleased with him or her.

**nag**[2] *noun* (**nags**)
(*informal*) a horse.

**nail** *noun* (**nails**)
1 the hard covering on the end of a finger
or toe. 2 a small, sharp piece of metal used
to fix pieces of wood together.

**naïve** *adjective*
(*say* nah-**eev**)
1 innocent; not experienced, *a naïve young
child*. 2 too ready to believe what you are
told; showing a lack of experience, *He was
naïve enough to believe the crook. a naïve
remark.*
**naïvely** *adverb*, **naïvety** *noun*

**naked** *adjective*
(*say* **nay**-kid)
not wearing clothes; without any covering,
*The earth had blown away, leaving naked
rock.*
**the naked eye,** your eye when it is not
helped by a telescope, microscope, etc.
**nakedly** *adverb*, **nakedness** *noun*

**name**[1] *noun* (**names**)
what you call a person or thing.
**nameless** *adjective*

**name**[2] *verb* (**names, naming, named**)
1 to give someone or something a name.
2 to say what something or someone is
called, *Can you name these plants?*

**namely** *adverb*
that is to say, *Only one boy was absent,
namely Harry Smith.*

**nan** *noun*
a type of traditional Indian or Pakistani
bread.

**nanny** *noun* (**nannies**) (*informal*)
1 a woman whose job is to look after small
children. 2 a grandmother.

**nanny-goat** *noun* (**nanny-goats**)
a female goat.

**nap** *noun* (**naps**)
a short sleep.

**napkin** *noun* (**napkins**)
1 a serviette. 2 a nappy.

**nappy** *noun* (**nappies**)
(in America, *diaper*) a piece of cloth put
round a baby's bottom.

**narcissus** *noun* (**narcissi**)
(*say* nar-**sis**-ŭs)
a garden flower like a daffodil.

**narcotic** *noun* (**narcotics**)
(*say* nar-**kot**-ik)
a drug that makes you sleepy or
unconscious.

**narrate** *verb* (**narrates, narrating, narrated**)
to tell a story; to give an account of
something, *She narrated her adventures in
South America.*
**narration** *noun*, **narrative** *noun*, **narrator** *noun*

**narrow** *adjective* (**narrower, narrowest**)
1 not wide. 2 with only a small margin of
safety, *a narrow escape.*
**narrowly** *adverb*

**narrow-minded** *adjective*
not liking or understanding other people's
ideas.

**nasturtium** *noun* (**nasturtiums**)
(*say* nă-**ster**-shŭm)
a garden flower with round leaves.

**nasty** *adjective* (**nastier, nastiest**)
not pleasant; unkind.
**nastily** *adverb*, **nastiness** *noun*

**nation** *noun* (**nations**)
1 a large number of people who live in the
same part of the world and have the same
language, customs, etc. 2 a country and the
people who live there.

**national** *adjective*
1 of a whole country, *the national news.*
2 typical of a particular country, *the national dress of Greece.*
**National Curriculum**, directions for what should be taught in British schools that are run by the government.
**nationally** *adverb*

**national grid** *noun*
1 the cables carrying electricity from power stations all over Great Britain. 2 a pattern of numbered lines drawn all over the map of Great Britain, allowing places to be identified by sets of numbers (*grid references*).

**nationalist** *noun* (**nationalists**)
someone who loves and supports his or her country very much; someone who wants his or her nation to be independent.
**nationalism** *noun*, **nationalistic** *adjective*

**nationality** *noun* (**nationalities**)
the nation someone belongs to, *What is his nationality?*

**nationalize** *verb* (**nationalizes, nationalizing, nationalized**)
to put something under government control.
**nationalization** *noun*

**nationwide** *adjective* and *adverb*
over the whole of a country, *a nationwide fall in house prices. The fashion spread nationwide.*

**native**¹ *noun* (**natives**)
someone born in a particular place, *He is a native of Sweden.*

**native**² *adjective*
1 natural; belonging to someone from birth, *native ability.* 2 of the country where you were born, *my native language.*

**Native American**¹ *adjective*
of Native Americans.

**Native American**² *noun* (**Native Americans**)
one of the original race of people who lived in North America.

**nativity** *noun* (**nativities**)
(*say* nă-**tiv**-i-ti)
someone's birth.
**the Nativity**, the birth of Jesus.

**natural**¹ *adjective*
1 made or done by nature, not by people or machines. 2 normal; not surprising. 3 of a musical note that is not sharp or flat.
**natural gas**, gas that is found under the ground or the sea, not made from coal.
**natural history**, the study of plants and animals.
**naturally** *adverb*

**natural**² *noun* (**naturals**)
1 a natural note in music; a sign (♮) that shows a note is natural. 2 someone who is naturally good at something, *She's a natural at juggling.*

**naturalist** *noun* (**naturalists**)
someone who studies natural history.

**naturalize** *verb* (**naturalizes, naturalizing, naturalized**)
1 to make someone a full citizen of a country. 2 to make something fit into a place where it is not normally found.
**naturalization** *noun*

**nature** *noun* (**natures**)
1 everything in the universe that was not made by people. 2 the qualities or characteristics of a person or thing, *She has a loving nature.* 3 a kind or sort of thing, *He likes things of that nature.*
**nature trail**, a path in the country where you can walk and see things connected with natural history.

**naughty** *adjective* (**naughtier, naughtiest**)
not behaving as you should; disobedient or rude.
**naughtily** *adverb*, **naughtiness** *noun*

**nautical** *adjective*
connected with ships or sailors.

**naval** *adjective*
of the navy.

**nave** *noun* (**naves**)
the main central part of a church.

**navel** *noun* (**navels**)
the dimple at the front of your stomach where the umbilical cord was detached.

**navigate** *verb* (**navigates, navigating, navigated**)
1 to steer a ship on the sea, up a river, etc.
2 to make sure that an aircraft or vehicle is going in the right direction.
**navigable** *adjective*, **navigation** *noun*, **navigator** *noun*

**navy** *noun* (**navies**)
1 a fleet of ships and the people trained to use them. 2 navy blue.
**navy blue**, dark blue.

**Nazi** *noun* (**Nazis**)
(*say* nah-tsi)
a member of the German National Socialist Party in Hitler's time, with dictatorial beliefs.
**Nazism** *noun*

**near**¹ *adverb* and *adjective* (**nearer, nearest**)
not far away, *The end is near.*
**near by**, at or to a place not far away, *They live near by.*
**nearness** *noun*

**near**$^2$ *preposition*
not far away from something, *She lives near the town.*

**near**$^3$ *verb* (**nears, nearing, neared**)
to come close to something, *They were nearing the harbour.*

**nearby** *adjective*
at a place not far away, *a nearby town.*

**nearly** *adverb*
1 almost, *It was nearly midnight.* 2 closely, *nearly related.*
**not nearly,** far from; not at all, *There is not nearly enough food.*

**neat** *adjective* (**neater, neatest**)
1 tidy; simple and pleasant to look at.
2 skilfully done.
**neatly** *adverb*, **neatness** *noun*

**necessary** *adjective*
1 needed very much; essential.
2 unavoidable.
**necessarily** *adverb*, **necessity** *noun*

**neck** *noun* (**necks**)
1 the part of your body that joins your head to your shoulders. 2 a narrow part of something, especially of a bottle.
**stick your neck out,** to say or do something that you know could get you into trouble, *He stuck his neck out and complained about his boss.*

**neckerchief** *noun* (**neckerchiefs**)
a square of cloth worn round the neck, for example by Scouts and Cubs.

**necklace** *noun* (**necklaces**)
an ornament worn round your neck.

**nectar** *noun*
a sweet liquid collected by bees from flowers.

**need**$^1$ *verb* (**needs, needing, needed**)
1 to be without something that you should have. 2 to have to do something, *I needed to get a haircut.*

**need**$^2$ *noun* (**needs**)
1 something that you need. 2 a situation in which something is necessary, *There is no need to cry.*
**in need,** needing money, help, comfort, etc.
**needless** *adjective*, **needlessly** *adverb*

**needle** *noun* (**needles**)
1 a very thin, pointed piece of metal used for sewing. 2 something long, thin, and sharp, *a knitting-needle.* 3 the pointer of a meter or compass.

**needlework** *noun*
sewing or embroidery.

**needy** *adjective* (**needier, neediest**)
very poor.

**negative**$^1$ *adjective*
1 that says 'no', *a negative answer.* 2 not definite or helpful, *gloomy, negative thoughts.* 3 less than nought, *a negative number.* 4 of the kind of electric charge carried by electrons.
**negatively** *adverb*

**negative**$^2$ *noun* (**negatives**)
1 something that means 'no'. 2 a photograph or film from which prints are made.

**neglect** *verb* (**neglects, neglecting, neglected**)
not to look after or attend to something; to fail to do something, *He neglected his homework.*
**neglectful** *adjective*

**negligent** *adjective*
not taking proper care or paying enough attention, *The security staff had been negligent and had not locked all the doors.*
**negligence** *noun*

USAGE: Do not confuse **negligent** with **negligible**, which is the next word in this dictionary.

**negligible** *adjective*
(*say* neg-li-ji-bŭl)
not big enough or important enough to bother about, *The damage to my bike was negligible.*

**negotiate** *verb* (**negotiates, negotiating, negotiated**)
(*say* nig-oh-shi-ayt)
1 to try to reach agreement about something by discussion. 2 to get over or through an obstacle or difficulty.
**negotiation** *noun*, **negotiator** *noun*

**neigh** *verb* (**neighs, neighing, neighed**)
to make a high-pitched cry like a horse.

**neighbour** *noun* (**neighbours**)
someone who lives next door or near to you.
**neighbouring** *adjective*, **neighbourly** *adjective*

**neighbourhood** *noun* (**neighbourhoods**)
the surrounding district.

**neither**$^1$ *adjective* and *pronoun*
(*say* ny-*th*er or nee-*th*er)
not either, *Neither of them likes cabbage.*

**neither**$^2$ *conjunction*
**neither ... nor,** not one thing and not the other, *I neither know nor care.*

**neon** *noun*
(*say* nee-on)
a gas that glows when electricity passes through it, *Neon lights use neon in a glass tube.*

**nephew** *noun* (**nephews**)
the son of a brother or sister.

**nerve** *noun* (**nerves**)
**1** one of the fibres inside your body that
carry messages to and from your brain, so
that your body can feel and move.
**2** courage; calmness in a dangerous
situation, *Don't lose your nerve.*
**3** (*informal*) impudence, *He had the nerve
to ask for more.*
**get on someone's nerves**, to annoy him or
her.
**nerves**, nervousness, *I was suffering from
nerves before my exam.*

**nerve-racking** *adjective*
that makes you very anxious, *The
policemen spent a nerve-racking hour
trying to find out whether a bomb had been
planted.*

**nervous** *adjective*
**1** easily upset or agitated; timid. **2** of your
nerves, *the nervous system.*
**nervous breakdown**, a kind of mental illness
in which someone feels very worried and
sad, and unable to face life.
**nervously** *adverb*, **nervousness** *noun*

**nest**¹ *noun* (**nests**)
**1** the place where a bird lays its eggs.
**2** a warm place where some small animals
keep their babies.

**nest**² *verb* (**nests, nesting, nested**)
to make or have a nest, *Birds were nesting
in the roof.*

**nestle** *verb* (**nestles, nestling, nestled**)
to curl up comfortably.

**net**¹ *noun* (**nets**)
**1** something made of pieces of thread, cord,
wire, etc. joined together in a criss-cross
pattern with holes between. **2** material of
this kind. **3** (*in Mathematics*) a pattern
drawn on paper, etc. that can be cut out
and folded to make a three-dimensional
object.

**net**² *adjective*
that is left when nothing else is to be taken
away, *After tax was deducted, his net pay
was £150 a week.*

**netball** *noun*
a game in which two teams try to throw
a ball through a high net hanging from
a ring.

**nettle** *noun* (**nettles**)
a wild plant with leaves that sting.

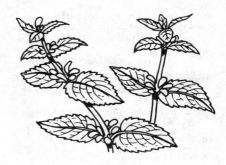

**network** *noun* (**networks**)
**1** a criss-cross arrangement. **2** a system
with many connections or parts, *a
television network.*

**neurone** *noun* (**neurones**)
(*in Science*) one of the cells making up the
fibres that carry messages to and from
your brain.

**neuter**¹ *adjective*
(*say* **new**-ter)
(*in grammar*) not masculine or feminine.

**neuter**² *verb* (**neuters, neutering, neutered**)
(*say* **new**-ter)
to operate on an animal so that it cannot
have offspring, *We had our tom-cat
neutered.*

**neutral** *adjective*
(*say* **new**-trăl)
**1** not supporting either side in a war or
quarrel. **2** not distinct or distinctive,
*neutral colours.* **3** of gears that are not
connected to the driving parts of an
engine.
**neutrality** *noun*, **neutrally** *adverb*

**neutralize** *verb* (**neutralizes, neutralizing,
neutralized**)
to take away the effect of something, *an
alkaline substance will neutralize an acid.*

**neutron** *noun* (**neutrons**)
a particle of matter with no electric charge.
**neutron bomb**, a nuclear bomb that kills
people but does little damage to buildings.

**never** *adverb*
at no time; not ever; not at all.
**the never-never**, (*informal*) hire-purchase.

**nevertheless** *conjunction* and *adverb*
in spite of this; although that is a fact.

**new** *adjective* (**newer**, **newest**)
1 not old; just bought, made, received, etc.
2 different; unfamiliar.
**new moon**, the moon when it appears as a
thin crescent.
**newly** *adverb*, **newness** *noun*

**newcomer** *noun* (**newcomers**)
someone who has recently arrived in a
place.

**news** *noun*
1 information about recent events. 2 a
broadcast report about recent events.

**newsagent** *noun* (**newsagents**)
a shopkeeper who sells newspapers and
magazines.

**newsletter** *noun* (**newsletters**)
a printed report sent regularly to members
of an organization such as a club, giving
information of interest to them.

**newspaper** *noun* (**newspapers**)
a daily or weekly publication of large
sheets of printed paper folded together,
containing news reports, articles,
advertisements, etc.

**newt** *noun* (**newts**)
a small animal rather like a lizard, that
lives near or in water.

**New Testament** *noun*
the Bible's second part, which describes
the life and teachings of Jesus.

**newton** *noun* (**newtons**)
the SI unit of force.

**next**[1] *adjective*
the nearest; following immediately after.
**next door**, in the house on one side or the
other of yours.

**next**[2] *adverb*
in the nearest place; at the nearest time,
*What comes next?*

**nib** *noun* (**nibs**)
the pointed metal part at the end of a pen
that uses ink.

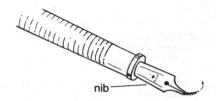

nib

**nibble** *verb* (**nibbles**, **nibbling**, **nibbled**)
to take tiny bites at something.

**nice** *adjective* (**nicer**, **nicest**)
1 pleasant; friendly; kind. 2 delicate;
precise, *There is a nice difference between
stealing and borrowing.*
**nicely** *adverb*, **niceness** *noun*

**nick**[1] *noun* (**nicks**)
1 a notch. 2 (*slang*) a prison or police
station, *in the nick*. 3 (*slang*) the condition
of something, *The car's in good nick*.
**in the nick of time**, only just in time.

**nick**[2] *verb* (**nicks**, **nicking**, **nicked**)
1 to make a notch in something. 2 (*slang*) to
steal something.

**nickel** *noun* (**nickels**)
1 a silvery-white metal. 2 (*in America*) a
5-cent coin.

**nickname** *noun* (**nicknames**)
a name given to someone instead of his or
her real name, *William Cody's nickname
was Buffalo Bill.*

**nicotine** *noun*
(*say* nik-ŏ-teen)
a poisonous substance found in tobacco.

**niece** *noun* (**nieces**)
the daughter of a brother or sister.

**night** *noun* (**nights**)
the time when it is dark, between sunset
and sunrise.
**night-time** *noun*

**night-club** *noun* (**night-clubs**)
a club or restaurant where there is
entertainment at night.

**nightfall** *noun*
the time just after sunset.

**nightingale** *noun* (**nightingales**)
a small, brown bird that sings sweetly.

**nightly** *adjective*
happening every night.

**nightmare** *noun* (**nightmares**)
a frightening dream.
**nightmarish** *adjective*

**nil** *noun*
nothing, *Our team's score was nil.*

**nimble** *adjective* (**nimbler, nimblest**)
moving quickly or easily.
**nimbly** *adverb*

**nine** *noun* (**nines**)
the number 9, one more than eight.
**ninth** *adjective* and *noun*

**nineteen** *noun* (**nineteens**)
the number 19, one more than eighteen.
**nineteenth** *adjective* and *noun*

**ninety** *noun* (**nineties**)
the number 90, nine times ten.
**ninetieth** *adjective* and *noun*

**nip**[1] *verb* (**nips, nipping, nipped**)
1 to pinch or bite someone or something
quickly. 2 (*informal*) to go quickly, *I'll just
nip into the grocer's.*

**nip**[2] *noun* (**nips**)
1 a quick pinch or bite. 2 a cold feeling,
*There's a nip in the air.*

**nipple** *noun* (**nipples**)
the small part that sticks out at the front
of a person's breast.

**nippy** *adjective* (**nippier, nippiest**)
(*informal*) 1 cold. 2 quick.

**nit** *noun* (**nits**)
1 a louse or its egg. 2 (*slang*) a stupid
person.
**nit-picking**, finding tiny faults or making
unimportant criticisms.

**nitrate** *noun* (**nitrates**)
a chemical compound that includes oxygen
and nitrogen.

**nitric** *adjective*
 (*say* ny-trik)
of nitrogen; containing nitrogen.
**nitric acid**, a very strong colourless acid.

**nitrogen** *noun*
 (*say* ny-trŏ-jĕn)
a gas that makes up about four-fifths of
the air we breathe.

**nitty-gritty** *noun*
 (*slang*) the most important details or the
true facts about something, *When you get
down to the nitty-gritty, you can travel long
distances on almost any kind of bicycle.*

**nitwit** *noun* (**nitwits**)
(*informal*) a stupid person.
**nitwitted** *adjective*

**no**[1] *adjective* and *adverb*
not any, *She had no money.*

**no**[2] *interjection*
a word used to deny or refuse something.

**noble**[1] *adjective* (**nobler, noblest**)
1 of high rank; being an aristocrat.
2 having a good, generous nature, *a noble
king.* 3 stately; impressive, *a noble
building.*
**nobility** *noun*, **nobly** *adverb*

**noble**[2] *noun* (**nobles**)
a nobleman.

**nobleman** *noun* (**noblemen**)
a man of high rank.
**noblewoman** *noun*

**nobody**[1] *pronoun*
no person; not anyone, *Nobody knows.*

**nobody**[2] *noun* (**nobodies**)
an unimportant person, *He's a nobody.*

**nocturnal** *adjective*
 (*say* nok-ter-năl)
1 active at night, *Badgers are nocturnal
animals.* 2 of or in the night, *a nocturnal
stillness lay over the countryside.*

**nod** *verb* (**nods, nodding, nodded**)
1 to move your head up and down as a way
of agreeing with someone or as a greeting.
2 to be drowsy.

**noise** *noun* (**noises**)
a loud sound, especially one that is
unpleasant or unwanted.
**noiseless** *adjective*, **noiselessly** *adverb*

**noisy** *adjective* (**noisier, noisiest**)
making a lot of noise.
**noisily** *adverb*, **noisiness** *noun*

**nomad** *noun* (**nomads**)
 (*say* noh-mad)
someone who travels from place to place
with a tribe, usually looking for pasture for
his or her animals.
**nomadic** *adjective*

**no-man's-land** *noun*
unoccupied land, especially between two
armies at war.

**nominate** *verb* (**nominates, nominating,
nominated**)
to propose that someone should be a
candidate in an election.
**nomination** *noun*

**non-** *prefix*
not, *non-powered.*

**none**[1] *pronoun*
not any; not one, *None of us went.*

**none**[2] *adverb*
not at all, *He's none too awake this
morning.*
**none the less**, nevertheless.

**non-existent** *adjective*
that does not exist.

**non-fiction** *noun*
writings that are not fiction; books about
real things and true events.

**non-flammable** *adjective*
that cannot be set alight.

**non-metal** *noun* (**non-metals**)
(*in Science*) a chemical substance that does
not behave like a metal and does not
conduct heat or electricity.

**non-renewable** *adjective*
coming from or being a fuel such as coal,
gas, or oil that cannot be replaced once it is
used, *non-renewable energy*.

**nonsense** *noun*
1 something that does not mean anything.
2 absurd or stupid ideas or behaviour.
**nonsensical** *adjective*

**non-stick** *adjective*
having a special coating to which food will
not stick, *a non-stick frying-pan*.

**non-stop** *adjective*
that does not stop.

**noodles** *plural noun*
a type of pasta made in long, narrow strips.

**noon** *noun*
twelve o'clock in the middle of the day.

**no one** *pronoun*
no person; not anyone.

**noose** *noun* (**nooses**)
a loop in a rope that gets smaller when the
rope is pulled.

**nor** *conjunction*
and not, *He cannot do it; nor can I*.

**normal** *adjective*
1 usual; typical, *It's normal to take a
holiday*. 2 sane, *He's not normal*.
**normality** *noun*, **normally** *adverb*

**north**¹ *noun*
the direction to the left of a person facing
the east.

**north**² *adjective*
1 coming from the north, *a north wind*.
2 situated in the north, *the north coast*.
**north country**, the northern part of England.
**northerly** *adjective*, **northern** *adjective*,
**northerner** *noun*

**north**³ *adverb*
towards the north.
**northward** *adjective* and *adverb*, **northwards**
*adverb*

**Norwegian** *adjective*
(*say* nor-**wee**-jăn)
of Norway.

**nose**¹ *noun* (**noses**)
1 the part of the face that is used for
breathing and smelling. 2 the front part of
something.

**nose**² *verb* (**noses, nosing, nosed**)
1 to push the nose near or into something,
*We heard cows nosing around our tent*. 2 to
pry, *I don't want him nosing around here*.
3 to go forward cautiously, *The ship nosed
through the ice*.

**nostalgia** *noun*
(*say* nos-**tal**-jă)
remembering or longing for the past.
**nostalgic** *adjective*

**nostril** *noun* (**nostrils**)
one of the two openings in your nose.

**nosy** *adjective* (**nosier, nosiest**)
(*informal*) always trying to find out things,
especially about other people's business.
**nosily** *adverb*, **nosiness** *adjective*

**not** *adverb*
a word used to change the meaning of
something to its opposite.

**notable** *adjective*
remarkable; famous, *a notable happening*.
*notable scientists*.
**notably** *adverb*

**notch** *noun* (**notches**)
a small cut or mark, usually V-shaped.

**note**¹ *noun* (**notes**)
1 something written down as a reminder or
help. 2 a short letter. 3 a single sound in
music. 4 a sound or tone that indicates
something, *a note of anger in his voice*. 5 a
banknote, *a five-pound note*. 6 notice, *Take
note of what I say*.

**note**² *verb* (**notes, noting, noted**)
1 to write down something as a reminder or
help. 2 to notice or pay attention to
someone or something.

**notebook** *noun* (**notebooks**)
a book in which you write down things.

**nothing** *noun*
not anything.

**notice**¹ *noun* (**notices**)
1 something written or printed and
displayed for people to see. 2 attention, *It
escaped my notice*. 3 a warning that
something is going to happen.

**notice**² *verb* (**notices, noticing, noticed**)
to see something; to become aware of
something.
**noticeable** *adjective*, **noticeably** *adverb*

**noticeboard** *noun* (**noticeboards**)
a piece of wood or other soft material to
which notices can be fixed with
drawing-pins, etc.

**notion** *noun* (**notions**)
an idea, especially an uncertain idea, *The notion that the earth is flat was disproved long ago.*

**notorious** *adjective*
(*say* noh-**tor**-i-ŭs)
well-known for doing something bad.
**notoriety** *noun*, **notoriously** *adverb*

**nougat** *noun*
(*say* **noo**-gah)
a chewy sweet made from nuts, sugar, etc.

**nought** *noun* (**noughts**)
(*say* nawt)
**1** the figure 0. **2** nothing.

**noun** *noun* (**nouns**)
a word that is the name of a thing or a person, *Nouns are words like 'cat', 'courage', 'Diana', 'China', and 'tent'.*
**noun phrase**, a group of words that includes a noun and is smaller than a clause, *'The large dog' is a noun phrase.*

**nourish** *verb* (**nourishes, nourishing, nourished**)
to feed someone enough good food to keep him or her alive and well.
**nourishment** *noun*

**novel**[1] *adjective*
unusual, *a novel idea.*
**novelty** *noun*

**novel**[2] *noun* (**novels**)
a story that fills a whole book.

**novelist** *noun* (**novelists**)
(*say* **nov**-ĕl-ist)
someone who writes novels.

**November** *noun*
the eleventh month of the year.

**novice** *noun* (**novices**)
a beginner; someone inexperienced.

**now**[1] *adverb*
**1** without any delay, *Do it now!* **2** at the present time, *She will be at home by now. They are here now.*
**for now**, until a later time, *Goodbye for now.*
**now and again** or **now and then**, occasionally; sometimes.

**now**[2] *conjunction*
since; as, *I do remember, now you mention it.*

**now**[3] *noun*
this moment, *I haven't seen him up to now.*

**nowadays** *adverb*
at the present time.

**nowhere** *adverb*
not anywhere; in or to no place.

**nozzle** *noun* (**nozzles**)
the part at the end of a hose or pipe from which something flows.

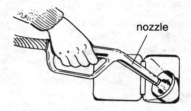
nozzle

**nuclear** *adjective*
(*say* **new**-kli-er)
**1** of a nucleus, especially of an atom. **2** of or using the energy that is created by reactions in the nuclei of atoms, *nuclear power. a nuclear weapon.*

**nucleus** *noun* (**nuclei**)
(*say* **new**-kli-ŭs)
**1** the part in the centre of something, round which other things are grouped, *The queen bee is the nucleus of the hive.* **2** the central part of an atom or cell.

**nude** *adjective*
not wearing any clothes.
**nudism** *noun*, **nudist** *noun*, **nudity** *noun*

**nudge** *verb* (**nudges, nudging, nudged**)
to touch or push someone with your elbow.

**nugget** *noun* (**nuggets**)
**1** a lump of gold. **2** a small piece of something good or valuable, *Her book contains many nuggets of information.*

**nuisance** *noun* (**nuisances**)
a person or thing that annoys you.

**numb** *adjective*
unable to feel or move.
**numbly** *adverb*, **numbness** *noun*

**number**[1] *noun* (**numbers**)
**1** a numeral. **2** a quantity of something. **3** one issue of a magazine or newspaper. **4** a song or piece of music.

**number**[2] *verb* (**numbers, numbering, numbered**)
**1** to count something. **2** to amount to, *The crowd numbered 10,000.* **3** to mark something with numbers.

**numeral** *noun* (**numerals**)
a figure or word that tells you how many of something there are.

**numerate** *adjective*
having a good basic knowledge of mathematics.

**numerator** *noun* (**numerators**)
the number above the line in a fraction, *In* ¼ the 1 is the numerator.

**numerical** *adjective*
of numbers.
**numerically** *adverb*

**numerous** *adjective*
many, *numerous kinds of cat.*

**nun** *noun* (**nuns**)
a member of a religious community of women.
**nunnery** *noun*

**nurse**¹ *noun* (**nurses**)
someone whose job is to look after people who are ill or hurt.

**nurse**² *verb* (**nurses, nursing, nursed**)
1 to look after someone who is ill. 2 to hold someone or something carefully in your arms, *He was nursing a puppy.* 3 to feed a baby.

**nursery** *noun* (**nurseries**)
1 a place where very young children are looked after or play. 2 a place where young plants are grown and usually sold.
**nursery rhyme,** a simple poem or song that young children like.

**nursing home** *noun* (**nursing homes**)
a small or private hospital.

**nurture** *verb* (**nurtures, nurturing, nurtured**)
to train or educate a child, etc.

**nut** *noun* (**nuts**)
1 a fruit with a hard shell. 2 the eatable part of this kind of fruit. 3 a hollow piece of metal for screwing on to a bolt. 4 (*slang*) someone's head. 5 (*slang*) a mad or eccentric person.
**nutty** *adjective*

**nutcrackers** *plural noun*
a device like pincers for cracking the shells of nuts.

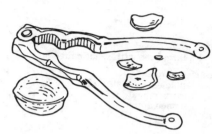

**nutmeg** *noun* (**nutmegs**)
a hard seed that is made into a powder and used as a spice.

**nutrient** *noun* (**nutrients**)
(*say* **new**-tri-ĕnt)
something nourishing.

**nutrition** *noun*
(*say* new-**trish**-ŏn)
1 food that keeps people well. 2 the study of what food keeps people well.
**nutritional** *adjective*

**nutritious** *adjective*
(*say* new-**trish**-ŭs)
nourishing, *a nutritious meal.*

**nutshell** *noun* (**nutshells**)
the shell of a nut.
**in a nutshell,** briefly.

**nuzzle** *verb* (**nuzzles, nuzzling, nuzzled**)
to rub gently against something with the nose.

**nylon** *noun*
a lightweight synthetic cloth or fibre.

**nymph** *noun* (**nymphs**)
a mythical goddess or girl living in rivers, trees, etc.

# Oo

**oak** *noun* (**oaks**)
a large tree with seeds called acorns.

**oar** *noun* (**oars**)
a pole with a flat part at one end, used for
rowing a boat.
**oarsman** *noun*

**oasis** *noun* (**oases**)
 (*say* oh-**ay**-sis)
a place with water and trees in a desert.

**oath** *noun* (**oaths**)
1 a solemn promise. 2 a swear-word.

**oatmeal** *noun*
a substance made by grinding oats.

**oats** *plural noun*
a cereal used to make food for humans and
animals, *Porridge is made from oats.*

**obedient** *adjective*
obeying; willing to obey.
**obedience** *noun*, **obediently** *adverb*

**obey** *verb* (**obeys, obeying, obeyed**)
to do what you are told to do.

**obituary** *noun* (**obituaries**)
 (*say* ŏ-**bit**-yoo-er-i)
a report that someone has died, usually
with a short account of his or her life.

**object**[1] *noun* (**objects**)
 (*say* **ob**-jikt)
1 something that can be seen or touched.
2 the purpose of something. 3 (*in grammar*)
something towards which the action of a
verb is directed, *'Him' is the object in 'I
chased him'.*

**object**[2] *verb* (**objects, objecting, objected**)
 (*say* ŏb-**jekt**)
to say that you do not like something or
that you disagree, *She objected to my
speech.*
**objection** *noun*, **objector** *noun*

**objectionable** *adjective*
unpleasant; not liked, *What do you find
objectionable about him? This chemical has
an objectionable smell.*

**objective**[1] *noun* (**objectives**)
what you are trying to reach or do.

**objective**[2] *adjective*
1 having a real existence outside someone's
mind, *No objective evidence has yet been
found to prove his claims.* 2 not influenced
by your own beliefs or ideas, *He gave an
objective account of the incident.*

**obligation** *noun* (**obligations**)
a duty.
**obligatory** *adjective*

**oblige** *verb* (**obliges, obliging, obliged**)
to help and please someone.
**obliged to do something,** forced to do
something.

**oblique** *adjective*
 (*say* ŏ-**bleek**)
1 slanting. 2 not straight or direct, *an
oblique question.*
**obliquely** *adverb*

**oblong** *noun* (**oblongs**)
a rectangle that is longer than it is wide.

**oboe** *noun* (**oboes**)
 (*say* **oh**-boh)
a high-pitched woodwind instrument.

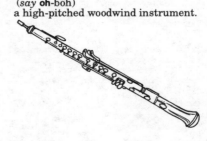

**obscene** *adjective* (**obscener, obscenest**)
(*say* ŏb-**seen**)
offensive to people's feelings, especially because of being connected with sex, violence, or cruelty.
**obscenely** *adverb*, **obscenity** *noun*

**obscure** *adjective* (**obscurer, obscurest**)
1 not clear. 2 not famous.
**obscurely** *adverb*, **obscurity** *noun*

**observance** *noun* (**observances**)
obeying a law; keeping a custom.

**observant** *adjective*
quick at noticing things.
**observantly** *adverb*

**observation** *noun* (**observations**)
1 observing; watching. 2 a remark, *He made a few observations about the weather.*

**observatory** *noun* (**observatories**)
(*say* ŏb-**zerv**-ă-ter-i)
a building equipped with telescopes for looking at the stars, planets, etc.

**observe** *verb* (**observes, observing, observed**)
1 to watch someone or something carefully. 2 to notice something. 3 to obey a law or keep a custom. 4 to make a remark, *She observed that she did not like ice in her drinks.*
**observer** *noun*

**obsessed** *adjective*
always thinking about something, *He is obsessed with his work.*
**obsession** *noun*

**obsolete** *adjective*
not used any more; out of date, *an obsolete word. Most of their machinery is obsolete.*

**obstacle** *noun* (**obstacles**)
something that gets in your way or makes it difficult for you to do something.

**obstinate** *adjective*
not ready to change your ideas or ways, even though they may be wrong.
**obstinacy** *noun*, **obstinately** *adverb*

**obstruct** *verb* (**obstructs, obstructing, obstructed**)
to stop something from getting past; to get in someone's way.
**obstruction** *noun*, **obstructive** *adjective*

**obtain** *verb* (**obtains, obtaining, obtained**)
to buy, take, or be given something.
**obtainable** *adjective*

**obtuse** *adjective* (**obtuser, obtusest**)
slow to understand; stupid.
**obtuse angle**, an angle between 90 and 180 degrees.

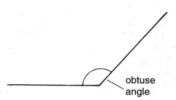

obtuse angle

**obvious** *adjective*
very easy to see or understand.
**obviously** *adverb*

**occasion** *noun* (**occasions**)
1 the time when something happens, *On this occasion, we will not take any action.* 2 a special event, *The wedding was a grand occasion.*

**occasional** *adjective*
happening from time to time, but not often and not regularly.
**occasionally** *adverb*

**occupant** *noun* (**occupants**)
someone who occupies a place.

**occupation** *noun* (**occupations**)
1 a job or hobby. 2 the occupying of territory.

**occupy** *verb* (**occupies, occupying, occupied**)
1 to live in a place. 2 to fill a space or position. 3 to capture territory in a war. 4 to keep someone busy and interested.

**occur** *verb* (**occurred, occurring, occurred**)
1 to happen; to take place. 2 to be found; to exist. 3 to come into your mind, *An idea occurred to me.*
**occurrence** *noun*

**ocean** *noun* (**oceans**)
1 the sea. 2 a large sea, *the Pacific Ocean.*

**o'clock** *adverb*
by the clock, *Lunch is at one o'clock.*

**octagon** *noun* (**octagons**)
a flat shape with eight sides.
**octagonal** *adjective*

**octave** *noun* (**octaves**)
the distance between one musical note and the next note of the same name above or below it; these two notes played together.

**October** *noun*
the tenth month of the year.

**octopus** *noun* (**octopuses**)
a sea-creature with eight arms (called *tentacles*).

**odd** *adjective* (**odder, oddest**)
1 strange. 2 not an even number, *Five and nine are odd numbers.* 3 left over; spare, *I've got an odd sock.* 4 of various kinds; occasional, *odd jobs.*
**oddity** *noun*, **oddly** *adverb*, **oddness** *noun*

**oddments** *plural noun*
small things of various kinds.

**odds** *plural noun*
1 the chances that something will happen.
2 the proportion of money that you will win if a bet is successful, *When the odds are 10 to 1, you will win £10 if you bet £1.*
**odds and ends,** small things of various kinds.

**odour** *noun* (**odours**)
a smell.
**odorous** *adjective*

**oesophagus** *noun* (**oesophagi** or **oesophaguses**)
(*say* ee-sof-ă-gŭs)
the tube from your throat to your stomach.

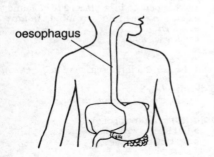

oesophagus

**of** *preposition*
1 belonging to; coming from, *a native of Italy.* 2 away from, *two miles north of the town.* 3 about; concerning, *news of peace.*
4 from; out of, *built of stone.*

**off**[1] *adverb*
1 not on; away, *His hat blew off.* 2 not working or happening, *The heating is off.*
3 behind or at the side of a stage, *There were noises off.*

**off**[2] *preposition*
1 not on; away or down from, *He fell off his chair.* 2 not taking or wanting, *She is off her food.*

**offence** *noun* (**offences**)
a crime, *When was the offence committed?*
**give offence,** to hurt someone's feelings, *I didn't mean to give offence.*
**take offence,** to be upset by what someone has said or done.

**offend** *verb* (**offends, offending, offended**)
1 to hurt someone's feelings; to be unpleasant to someone. 2 to break a law; to do wrong.
**offence** *noun*, **offender** *noun*

**offensive** *adjective*
1 that hurts someone's feelings or is unpleasant to someone. 2 used for attacking; aggressive, *offensive weapons. offensive behaviour.*
**offensively** *adverb*

**offer**[1] *verb* (**offers, offering, offered**)
1 to hold out something so that someone can take it if he or she wants it. 2 to say that you are willing to do something. 3 to say what you are willing to give for something.

**offer**[2] *noun* (**offers**)
1 the action of holding out something or saying you are willing to do something.
2 an amount of money that you are willing to pay for something.

**office** *noun* (**offices**)
1 a room or building where people do typing, accounts, business, etc. 2 a government department, *the Foreign and Commonwealth Office.* 3 an important job or position, *the office of Lord Mayor.*

**officer** *noun* (**officers**)
1 someone who is in charge of other people, especially in the armed forces; an official.
2 a policeman.

**official**[1] *adjective*
1 done or said by someone with authority.
2 connected with a job of authority or trust, *She has considerable official responsibilities.*
**officially** *adverb*

**official**[2] *noun* (**officials**)
someone who does a job of authority or trust.

---

USAGE: Do not confuse the adjective **official** with **officious**, which is the next word in this dictionary.

---

**officious** *adjective*
(*say* ŏ-**fish**-ŭs)
too ready to order people about.
**officiously** *adverb*

**offshore** *adjective and adverb*
**1** blowing away from the seashore, *an offshore breeze.* **2** on the sea at or to some distance from the shore, *offshore drilling for oil. The ship stayed offshore.*

**offside** *adjective*
(*in Sport*) in a position where you cannot move the ball without breaking the rules of the game.

**offspring** *noun* (**offspring**)
a child or young animal.

**often** *adverb* (**oftener, oftenest**)
many times; in many cases.

**ogre** *noun* (**ogres**)
a cruel giant; a frightening person.
**ogress** *noun*

**oh** *interjection*
a cry of surprise, pain, delight, etc.

**ohm** *noun* (**ohms**)
(rhymes with *home*)
a unit of electrical resistance.

**OHP** short for **overhead projector**.

**oil**[1] *noun* (**oils**)
**1** a thick, slippery liquid that does not mix with water. **2** a kind of petroleum used as fuel.
**oil rig**, a structure to support the equipment for drilling an oil well.
**oil-tanker**, a large ship made specially to carry oil.
**oil well**, a hole drilled in the ground or under the sea from which you get oil.

**oil**[2] *verb* (**oils, oiling, oiled**)
to put oil on something to make it work smoothly.

**oil-colour** *noun* (**oil-colours**)
paint made with oil.

**oilfield** *noun* (**oilfields**)
an area where oil is found under the ground or under the sea.

**oil-painting** *noun* (**oil-paintings**)
a painting done with oil-colours.

**oilskin** *noun* (**oilskins**)
a waterproof piece of clothing worn especially by fishermen.

**oily** *adjective* (**oilier, oiliest**)
**1** like oil; covered in oil. **2** unpleasantly keen to please, *She didn't like his oily manner.*

**ointment** *noun* (**ointments**)
a cream for putting on sore skin and cuts.

**OK** *adverb* and *adjective*
(*informal*) all right.

**okra** *noun*
a tropical plant with seed-pods used as a vegetable.

**old** *adjective* (**older, oldest**)
**1** not new; born or made a long time ago. **2** of a particular age, *I'm ten years old.*

**old age** *noun*
the time when a person is more than about 65 or 70 years old.
**old-age pension**, a pension paid to an old person.
**old-age pensioner**, someone who gets an old-age pension.

**old-fashioned** *adjective*
**1** of the kind that was usual a long time ago. **2** having attitudes or beliefs that were usual in past times, *He's rather old-fashioned, and never asks his children what they would like to do.*

**Old Testament** *noun*
the Bible's first part, which is the holy book of the Jewish and Christian religions.

**olive** *noun* (**olives**)
**1** an evergreen tree with a small, bitter fruit. **2** the fruit of this tree.
**olive branch**, something that shows you want to make peace.

**Olympic** *adjective*
(*say* ŏ-**lim**-pik)
of the Olympic Games or the Olympics, a series of international sports contests held every four years in different countries.

**ombudsman** *noun* (**ombudsmen**)
(*say* **om**-bŭdz-măn)
an official who investigates people's
complaints against government
departments.

**omelette** *noun* (**omelettes**)
(*say* **om**-lit)
eggs beaten together and fried, often with
a filling or flavouring.

**omen** *noun* (**omens**)
a sign that something is going to happen.

**ominous** *adjective*
threatening; suggesting that trouble is
coming.
**ominously** *adverb*

**omit** *verb* (**omits, omitting, omitted**)
**1** to miss something out. **2** to fail to do
something.
**omission** *noun*

**omnivorous** *adjective*
eating plants as well as the flesh of
animals.

**on**¹ *preposition*
**1** at or over the top or surface of something,
*Sit on the floor.* **2** at the time of, *on my
birthday.* **3** about; concerning, *a talk on
butterflies.* **4** towards; near, *They advanced
on the town.*

**on**² *adverb*
**1** so as to be on something, *Put your hat on.*
**2** forwards, *Move on.* **3** working; in action,
*Is the heater on?*
**on to,** to a position on something.

**once**¹ *adverb*
**1** at one time, *I once lived in Leeds.* **2** ever,
*They never once offered to pay.*

**once**² *conjunction*
as soon as, *We can get out once I open this
door.*

**one** *noun* (**ones**)
**1** a person on his or her own; a thing on its
own, *One of my friends is ill.* **2** the number
1, representing a person or thing alone,
*One and one make two.*
**one another,** each other.

**oneself** *pronoun*
one's own self; yourself, *One should not
always think of oneself.*

**one-sided** *adjective*
showing or considering only one person's
point of view, *He's given you a very
one-sided story of what happened.*

**one-way** *adjective*
where traffic may only go in one direction,
*a one-way street.*

**ongoing** *adjective*
continuing to exist; making progress, *an
ongoing problem. an ongoing project.*

**onion** *noun* (**onions**)
a round vegetable with a strong flavour,
*Onions make you cry when you peel them.*

**onlooker** *noun* (**onlookers**)
a spectator.

**only**¹ *adjective*
being the one person or thing of a kind,
*He's the only person we can trust.*
**only child,** a child who has no brothers or
sisters.

**only**² *adverb*
no more than, *There are only three cakes.*
**not only ... but also,** both ... and, *He not only
thanked me but also paid me.*
**only too,** extremely, *I'm only too happy to
help.*

**only**³ *conjunction*
but then; however, *I want to come, only I'm
busy that night.*

**onshore** *adjective*
blowing towards the seashore, *an onshore
breeze.*

**onward** or **onwards** *adverb*
forwards.

**ooze** *verb* (**oozes, oozing, oozed**)
to flow out slowly, especially through a
narrow opening, *Blood oozed from his
wound.*

**opaque** *adjective*
(*say* oh-**payk**)
that you cannot see through, and that does
not let light through.

**open**¹ *adjective*
**1** not shut, *an open door.* **2** not enclosed,
*open land.* **3** not folded; spread out, *with
open arms.* **4** honest; not secret or secretive,
*open government.* **5** not settled or finished,
*an open question.*
**in the open air,** not inside a house or
building.

**open**² *verb* (**opens, opening, opened**)
**1** to make something open; to become open.
**2** to start, *The jumble sale opens at 2 p.m.*
**opener** *noun*

**opening** *noun* (**openings**)
**1** a space or gap in something. **2** the
beginning of something, *Don't miss the
opening of the sale!* **3** an opportunity, *There
is an opening for experienced salespeople in
our new shop.*

**openly** *adverb*
not secretly; publicly.

**open-minded** *adjective*
ready to listen to other people's ideas and
opinions; not having fixed ideas.

**opera** *noun* (**operas**)
a play in which all or most of the words are
sung.
**operatic** *adjective*

**operate** *verb* (**operates, operating, operated**)
1 to make something work. 2 to work; to be
in action. 3 to do a surgical operation on
someone.

**operation** *noun* (**operations**)
1 making something work; working.
2 something done by a surgeon to someone
to deal with a disease or injury. 3 a
planned military activity.

**operator** *noun* (**operators**)
someone who works something, especially
a telephone switchboard.

**opinion** *noun* (**opinions**)
what you think of something; a belief.
**opinion poll,** an estimate of what people
think, made by questioning a certain
number of them.

**opium** *noun*
a drug made from poppies, used to calm
people and to make them unable to feel
pain.

**opponent** *noun* (**opponents**)
someone who is against you in a contest,
war, or argument.

**opportunity** *noun* (**opportunities**)
a time when you can do something that
you cannot do at other times.

**oppose** *verb* (**opposes, opposing, opposed**)
to be against someone or something.

**opposed** *adjective*
**as opposed to,** in contrast with, *I am
talking about deliberate damage, as
opposed to accidental damage.*
**opposed to something,** disagreeing with
something, *We are opposed to the ban on
cycles in the town centre.*

**opposite**[1] *adjective*
1 completely different, *They went in
opposite directions.* 2 facing; on the other
side, *She lives on the opposite side of the
road to me.*

**opposite**[2] *noun* (**opposites**)
something opposite, *'Happy' is the opposite
of 'sad'.*

**opposition** *noun*
opposing something; resistance.
**the Opposition,** the political party or parties
in parliament that oppose the government.

**oppress** *verb* (**oppresses, oppressing,
oppressed**)
1 to govern or treat someone cruelly or
unjustly. 2 to trouble someone with worry
or sadness.
**oppression** *noun,* **oppressive** *adjective,*
**oppressor** *noun*

**opt** *verb* (**opts, opting, opted**)
to choose, *We opted to go abroad.*
**opt for something,** to choose something, *I
opted for the cash prize.*
**opt out,** to decide not to join in.

**optical** *adjective*
of sight; of the eyes.
**optical illusion,** something you think you see
that is not really there.
**optically** *adverb*

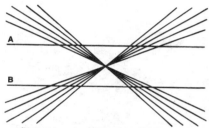

(Note: Lines **A** and **B** are straight but appear
to bend. This is an optical illusion.)

**optician** *noun* (**opticians**)
(*say* op-**tish**-ăn)
someone who tests your eyesight and
supplies spectacles.

**optimism** *noun*
expecting that things will turn out right.
**optimist** *noun,* **optimistic** *adjective*

**option** *noun* (**options**)
1 choice, *You have no option but to pay.*
2 something that is or can be chosen, *Your
options are to travel by bus or by train.*

**optional** *adjective*
that you can choose; not compulsory.
**optionally** *adverb*

**opulent** *adjective*
(*say* op-yoo-lĕnt)
1 showing wealth, *an opulent house.*
2 abundant, *a plant with green and opulent
foliage.*
**opulence** *noun,* **opulently** *adverb*

**or** *conjunction*
a word used to show that there is a choice
or alternative, *Do you want a bun or a
biscuit?*

**oral** *adjective*
1 spoken, *an oral comprehension test.*
2 using your mouth, *an oral vaccine.*
**orally** *adverb*

USAGE: Do not confuse **oral** with **aural**, which means of or using hearing.

**orange** *noun* (**oranges**)
1 a round, juicy fruit with thick reddish-yellow peel. 2 a reddish-yellow colour.

**orangeade** *noun* (**orangeades**)
a usually fizzy drink with a flavour of oranges.

**orang-utan** *noun* (**orang-utans**)
(*say* ŏ-rang-ŭ-tan)
a large kind of ape.

**orator** *noun* (**orators**)
(*say* o-ră-ter)
someone who makes speeches.
**oration** *noun*, **oratorical** *adjective*, **oratory** *noun*

**oratorio** *noun* (**oratorios**)
(*say* o-ră-tor-i-oh)
a piece of music for voices and orchestra, usually on a religious subject.

**orbit**[1] *noun* (**orbits**)
the path taken by something moving round a planet or other body in space.

**orbit**[2] *verb* (**orbits, orbiting, orbited**)
to move round a planet or other body in space, *The satellite orbited the earth.*

**orbital** *adjective*
1 of the orbit of a planet, a spacecraft, etc.
2 going round the outside of a town, *The M25 is the orbital motorway that goes round London.*

**orchard** *noun* (**orchards**)
a place where a lot of fruit trees grow.

**orchestra** *noun* (**orchestras**)
a large group of people playing musical instruments together.
**orchestral** *adjective*

**orchid** *noun* (**orchids**)
(*say* or-kid)
a brightly-coloured flower.

**ordeal** *noun* (**ordeals**)
a very hard or painful experience.

**order**[1] *noun* (**orders**)
1 a command. 2 a request for something to be supplied. 3 obedience; good behaviour.
4 tidiness; neatness. 5 the way something is arranged; condition. 6 a kind or sort of thing.
**in order that,** so that.
**in order to do something,** so as to do something; for the purpose of doing something.

**order**[2] *verb* (**orders, ordering, ordered**)
1 to tell someone to do something. 2 to ask for something to be supplied to you.
**order about,** to keep giving someone commands.

**orderly** *adjective*
1 arranged tidily or well; methodical, *an orderly desk. She is an orderly person.*
2 well-behaved; obedient.
**orderliness** *noun*

**ordinal number** *noun* (**ordinal numbers**)
a number that shows where something comes in a series; 1st, 2nd, 3rd, etc. (compare *cardinal number*).

**ordinary** *adjective*
normal; not special in any way.
**ordinarily** *adverb*

**ore** *noun* (**ores**)
rock with metal in it, *iron ore.*

**organ** *noun* (**organs**)
1 a large musical instrument with one or more keyboards. 2 a part of the body with a particular function, *the digestive organs.*

**organic** *adjective*
1 made by or found in living things. 2 not using artificial chemicals to kill pests on plants or to make plants grow bigger, *organic agriculture. These apples are organic.*

**organism** *noun* (**organisms**)
a living animal or plant.

**organist** *noun* (**organists**)
someone who plays the organ.

**organization** *noun* (**organizations**)
1 an organized group of people. 2 getting people together to do something; planning something; putting something in order.

**organize** *verb* (**organizes, organizing, organized**)
1 to get people together to do something.
2 to plan something, *She organized the picnic.* 3 to put something in order.
**organizer** *noun*

**oriental** *adjective*
of the countries east of the Mediterranean, especially China and Japan.

**orienteering** *noun*
(*say* or-i-ĕn-**teer**-ing)
the sport of finding your way across rough country with a map and compass.

**origami** *noun*
(*say* o-ri-**gah**-mi)
folding pieces of paper to make decorative shapes.

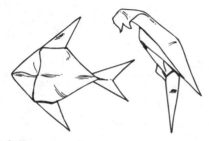

**origin** *noun* (**origins**)
the start of something; the point where something began.

**original** *adjective*
1 existing from the start; earliest, *the original inhabitants.* 2 new; not a copy or an imitation, *an original design.*
3 producing new ideas, *an original thinker.*
**originality** *noun*, **originally** *adverb*

**originate** *verb* (**originates, originating, originated**)
to start; to create something.
**origination** *noun*, **originator** *noun*

**ornament** *noun* (**ornaments**)
a thing put in or on something to make it look pretty; a decoration.
**ornamental** *adjective*, **ornamentation** *noun*

**ornithology** *noun*
(*say* or-ni-**thol**-ŏ-ji)
the scientific study of birds.
**ornithological** *adjective*, **ornithologist** *noun*

**orphan** *noun* (**orphans**)
a child whose parents are dead.

**orphanage** *noun* (**orphanages**)
a home for orphans.

**orthodox** *adjective*
having correct or generally accepted beliefs.
**Orthodox Church**, the Christian Churches of Eastern Europe.
**orthodoxy** *noun*

**oscillate** *verb* (**oscillates, oscillating, oscillated**)
to move to and fro.
**oscillation** *noun*

**ostrich** *noun* (**ostriches**)
a large, long-legged bird that can run fast but cannot fly.

**other** *adjective*
not the same as this, *The other pudding was better.*
**every other day**, every second day, *He comes here every other day; this week he'll be here on Tuesday, Thursday, and Saturday.*
**other than**, except, *They have no belongings other than what they are carrying.*
**the other day** or **the other week**, a few days or weeks ago.

**otherwise** *adverb*
1 if you do not; if things happen differently, *Write it down, otherwise you'll forget it.* 2 in other ways, *It rained a lot but otherwise the holiday was good.*

**otter** *noun* (**otters**)
a furry, long-tailed animal that lives near water.

**ouch** *interjection*
a cry of pain.

**ought** *verb*
should; must; to have a duty to, *You ought to stop fighting.*

**ounce** *noun* (**ounces**)
a unit of weight equal to $\frac{1}{16}$ of a pound or about 28 grams.

**our** *adjective*
belonging to us, *our house*.

**ours** *pronoun*
belonging to us, *This house is ours*.

**ourselves** *pronoun*
us and nobody else, *We washed ourselves*.

**out** *adverb*
1 not in; away from a place. 2 not burning,
*The fire is out*. 3 loudly, *She cried out*.
**out for something**, wanting something.
**out of**, from a place; without something.
**out of date**, old-fashioned; not used any
more.
**out of doors**, in the open air.
**out of the way**, no longer an obstacle;
distant; unusual, *Now that the exams are
out of the way I can relax. They live in a
small, out-of-the-way village. The
exhibition was nothing out of the way*.

**out-and-out** *adjective*
complete; thorough, *an out-and-out rascal*.

**outback** *noun*
the remote inland areas of Australia.

**outboard motor** *noun* (**outboard motors**)
a motor fitted to the outside of a boat's
stern.

**outbreak** *noun* (**outbreaks**)
the sudden start of a disease, war, show of
anger, etc.

**outburst** *noun* (**outbursts**)
the bursting out of steam, laughter, anger,
etc.

**outcast** *noun* (**outcasts**)
someone who has been rejected by his or
her family, friends, or society.

**outcome** *noun* (**outcomes**)
the result of something.

**outcry** *noun* (**outcries**)
a strong protest from many people, *There
was an outcry over the rise in rail fares*.

**outdoor** *adjective*
done or used outdoors, *outdoor clothes*.

**outdoors** *adverb*
in the open air, *It is cold outdoors*.

**outer** *adjective*
nearer the outside; external.
**outer space**, the universe beyond the earth's
atmosphere.

**outfit** *noun* (**outfits**)
1 clothes that are worn together. 2 a set of
things needed for doing something.

**outgrow** *verb* (**outgrows, outgrowing, outgrew,
outgrown**)
1 to grow out of clothes, habits, etc. 2 to
grow faster or taller than someone else.

**outhouse** *noun* (**outhouses**)
a small building attached to or near a
larger building.

**outing** *noun* (**outings**)
a trip to somewhere and back, made for
pleasure.

**outlaw** *noun* (**outlaws**)
a lawless person; a robber, especially one
who roams about.

**outlet** *noun* (**outlets**)
1 a way for something to come out, *The
tank has an outlet at the bottom*. 2 a way of
getting rid of something, *Running is a good
outlet for his energy*. 3 a place to sell goods,
*We need to find fresh outlets for our
products*.

**outline**¹ *noun* (**outlines**)
1 the line round the outside of something; a
line showing the shape of a thing, *the dark
outline of trees against the setting sun*. 2 a
summary.

**outline**² *verb* (**outlines, outlining, outlined**)
1 to draw a line to show the shape of
something. 2 to summarize or describe
something.

**outlook** *noun* (**outlooks**)
1 a view. 2 the way that someone looks at
and thinks about things. 3 what seems
likely to happen in the future.

**outlying** *adjective*
far from a town or city; distant, *outlying
suburbs. outlying islands*.

**outnumber** *verb* (**outnumbers, outnumbering,
outnumbered**)
to be greater in number than something
else.

**out-patient** *noun* (**out-patients**)
someone who visits a hospital for
treatment but does not stay there.

**outpost** *noun* (**outposts**)
a distant settlement.

**output** *noun* (**outputs**)
1 the amount produced, especially by a
factory etc. 2 (*in Computing*) information
sent out by a computer.

**outrage** *noun* (**outrages**)
something very shocking or cruel.
**outrageous** *adjective*

**outright** *adverb*
1 completely, *We won outright*. 2 not
gradually, *They were able to buy their
house outright*.

**outset** *noun*
**at** or **from the outset**, at or from the
beginning of something.

**outside**[1] *noun* (**outsides**)
the surface or edges of a thing; the part farthest from the middle.

**outside**[2] *adjective*
placed in or coming from the outside.
**outside broadcast,** a broadcast that is not made from a studio.

**outside**[3] *preposition*
on or to the outside of something, *The milk is outside the door.*

**outside**[4] *adverb*
on or to the outside; outdoors, *Come outside.*

**outsider** *noun* (**outsiders**)
1 someone who is not a member of a particular group of people. 2 a horse or person unlikely to win a race or contest.

**outskirts** *plural noun*
the parts on the outside edge of an area; suburbs.

**outspoken** *adjective*
speaking frankly; not tactful.

**outstanding** *adjective*
1 extremely good or distinguished, *an outstanding athlete.* 2 not yet dealt with, *outstanding debts.*

**outward** *adjective*
1 going outwards. 2 on the outside, *She displayed outward calm though she was nervous inside.*
**outwardly** *adverb*

**outwards** *adverb*
towards the outside.

**outweigh** *verb* (**outweighs, outweighing, outweighed**)
to be more important than something else, *The benefits of the plan outweigh its drawbacks.*

**outwit** *verb* (**outwits, outwitting, outwitted**)
to get an advantage over someone by being clever.

**oval**[1] *adjective*
shaped like an egg or a number 0.

**oval**[2] *noun* (**ovals**)
an oval shape.

**ovary** *noun* (**ovaries**)
1 part of a female body where egg-cells (*ova*) are produced. 2 the part of a flowering plant that produces seeds.

**oven** *noun* (**ovens**)
a closed space in which things are cooked or heated.

**over**[1] *adverb*
1 finished, *Playtime is over.* 2 left; remaining, *3 into 7 goes 2 and 1 over.* 3 sideways; into a different position, *He fell over.* 4 through; thoroughly, *Think it over.* 5 too much, *Don't get over-excited.*
**all over,** everywhere; finished, *You've spilt paint all over! The work's all over now.*
**over and over,** repeatedly; many times.

**over**[2] *preposition*
1 above; covering, *I knocked his hat over his eyes.* 2 across, *They ran over the road.* 3 more than, *There are over 20,000 kinds of insect in Britain.*

**over**[3] *noun* (**overs**)
in cricket, a series of balls bowled by one person, *There are usually 6 balls in an over.*

**over-** *prefix*
too much, *That car looks overloaded. There is no need to over-exercise.*

**overall** *adjective* and *adverb*
including everything.

**overalls** *plural noun*
a piece of clothing worn over other clothes to protect them.

**overboard** *adverb*
over the side of a boat into the water, *She jumped overboard.*

**overcast** *adjective*
covered with cloud, *The sky is grey and overcast.*

**overcoat** *noun* (**overcoats**)
a warm outdoor coat.

**overcome** *verb* (**overcomes, overcoming, overcame, overcome**)
1 to gain a victory over someone; to succeed in a struggle against something. 2 to make someone helpless, *The fumes overcame her.*

**overdo** *verb* (**overdoes, overdoing, overdid, overdone**)
1 to do something too much. 2 to cook food for too long.

**overdose** *noun* (**overdoses**)
too large a dose of a drug or medicine.

**overflow** *verb* (**overflows, overflowing, overflowed**)
1 to flow over its edges or banks, *The river overflowed.* 2 to be so full that the liquid in it spills out, *The sink is overflowing.*

**overgrown** *adjective*
covered with weeds or unwanted plants.

**overhang** *verb* (**overhangs, overhanging, overhung**)
to stick out beyond and above something else, *The second storey of the old house overhung the first.*

**overhaul** *verb* (**overhauls, overhauling, overhauled**)
1 to examine something thoroughly and repair it if necessary. 2 to overtake someone or something.

**overhead** *adjective* and *adverb*
above your head; in the sky, *overhead power lines. A few clouds floated by overhead.*
**overhead projector,** a type of projector having a flat plastic sheet on which you draw or write, and throwing a large image of the drawing, writing, etc. on to a screen.

**overheads** *plural noun*
the expenses of running a business.

**overhear** *verb* (**overhears, overhearing, overheard**)
to hear something accidentally.

**overland** *adjective* and *adverb*
over the land, not by sea.

**overlap** *verb* (**overlapped, overlapping, overlapped**)
to lie across part of something, *The tiles overlapped each other.*

**overlook** *verb* (**overlooks, overlooking, overlooked**)
1 not to notice something. 2 not to punish an offence. 3 to have a view over something.

**overnight** *adverb* and *adjective*
of or during a night, *We stayed overnight in a shepherd's hut. There will be an overnight stop in Paris.*

**overpower** *verb* (**overpowers, overpowering, overpowered**)
to overcome.
**overpowering,** very strong.

**overrun** *verb* (**overruns, overrunning, overran, overrun**)
1 to spread harmfully over an area, *The place is overrun with mice.* 2 to go on longer than it should, *The broadcast overran by ten minutes.*

**overseas** *adverb*
abroad, *They travelled overseas.*

**oversight** *noun* (**oversights**)
a mistake made by not noticing something.

**oversleep** *verb* (**oversleeps, oversleeping, overslept**)
to sleep longer than you intended to.

**overtake** *verb* (**overtakes, overtaking, overtook, overtaken**)
to pass a moving vehicle or person.

**overthrow** *verb* (**overthrows, overthrowing, overthrew, overthrown**)
to make something fall or fail; to defeat.

**overtime** *noun*
time spent working outside the normal hours.

**overture** *noun* (**overtures**)
a piece of music played at the start of a concert, opera, ballet, etc.
**overtures,** a friendly attempt to start a discussion with someone.

**overturn** *verb* (**overturns, overturning, overturned**)
1 to make something turn or fall over. 2 to turn over, *The car overturned.*

**overwhelm** *verb* (**overwhelms, overwhelming, overwhelmed**)
to overcome someone; to weigh down or bury something under a huge mass of something, *The sea overwhelmed several coastal villages.*

**overwork** *verb* (**overworks, overworking, overworked**)
1 to work too hard. 2 to use something too much, *Don't overwork the word 'nice' – find a more interesting word instead.*

**ovum** *noun* (**ova**)
(*say* oh-vŭm)
a female cell in plants and animals that can develop into offspring.

**owe** *verb* (**owes, owing, owed**)
1 to have a duty to pay or give something to someone, especially money that you have borrowed, *I owed her a pound.* 2 to have something because of someone else, *They owed their lives to the pilot's skill.*
**owing to,** because of.

**owl** *noun* (**owls**)
a bird of prey with large eyes, *Owls usually fly at night.*

**own**[1] *adjective*
belonging to yourself.
**get your own back,** (*informal*) to get revenge.
**on your own,** by yourself; alone, *I did it all on my own. I sat on my own in the empty church.*

**own**[2] *verb* (**owns, owning, owned**)
to have something that belongs to you.
**own up,** (*informal*) to confess, *Has anyone owned up to the theft yet?*

**owner** *noun* (**owners**)
the person who owns something.
**ownership** *noun*

**ox** *noun* (**oxen**)
a neutered bull kept for its meat and for pulling carts.

**oxide** *noun* (**oxides**)
a compound of oxygen and another element.

**oxidize** *verb* (**oxidizes, oxidizing, oxidized**)
to cause something to combine with oxygen; to combine with oxygen.
**oxidation** *noun*

**oxygen** *noun*
one of the gases in the air that people need to stay alive.

**oyster** *noun* (**oysters**)
a shellfish whose shell sometimes contains a pearl.

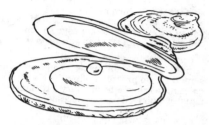

**oz.** short for **ounce** or **ounces**.

**ozone** *noun*
a colourless gas that is a form of oxygen.
**ozone-friendly,** not harmful to the ozone layer, *an ozone-friendly cleaning fluid.*
**ozone layer,** a layer of ozone in the atmosphere high above the earth, that absorbs harmful radiation from the sun.

# Pp

**p** short for **penny** or **pence**.

**pa** *noun* (**pas**)
(*informal*) father.

**pace**[1] *noun* (**paces**)
**1** one step in walking or marching. **2** speed, *She ran at a fast pace.*

**pace**[2] *verb* (**paces, pacing, paced**)
to walk with slow or regular steps.
**pace off** or **pace out,** to measure a distance in paces.

**pacemaker** *noun* (**pacemakers**)
**1** someone who sets the speed for someone else in a race. **2** a device to keep someone's heart beating.

**pacifist** *noun* (**pacifists**)
(*say* pas-i-fist)
someone who believes that war is always wrong.
**pacifism** *noun*

**pacify** *verb* (**pacifies, pacifying, pacified**)
(*say* pas-i-fy)
to make someone or something peaceful or calm.
**pacification** *noun*

**pack**[1] *noun* (**packs**)
**1** a bundle or collection of things. **2** a set of playing-cards. **3** a haversack. **4** a group of hounds, wolves, or other animals. **5** a group of people, especially a group of Brownies or Cubs.

**pack**[2] *verb* (**packs, packing, packed**)
**1** to put things into a suitcase, bag, box, etc. in order to move them or store them. **2** to fill a place, *The hall was packed.*
**packer** *noun*

**package** *noun* (**packages**)
**1** a parcel or packet. **2** a package deal.
**package deal,** a number of goods or services offered or accepted together, *a word-processing software package.*
**package holiday** or **package tour,** a holiday with everything arranged by travel agents.

**packet** *noun* (**packets**)
a small parcel.

**pad**¹ *noun* (**pads**)
  **1** a piece of soft material used to protect or shape something. **2** a device to protect your legs in cricket or other games. **3** a flat surface from which helicopters, spacecraft, etc. take off. **4** a number of sheets of paper joined together along one edge so that you can tear off a sheet when you need it.

**pad**² *verb* (**pads, padding, padded**)
  to put a piece of soft material on or in something to protect or shape it.
  **pad out**, to make a book, story, etc. longer, usually when this is not necessary.

**pad**³ *verb* (**pads, padding, padded**)
  to walk softly.

**padding** *noun*
  **1** soft material used to protect or shape something. **2** something used to make a book, story, etc. longer.

**paddle**¹ *verb* (**paddles, paddling, paddled**)
  **1** to walk about in shallow water. **2** to move a boat along with a short oar.

**paddle**² *noun* (**paddles**)
  **1** a time spent walking in shallow water. **2** a time spent moving a boat with a short oar. **3** a short oar.

**paddock** *noun* (**paddocks**)
  **1** a small field or enclosure for horses. **2** (*in Australia and New Zealand*) a field of any size.

**paddy** *noun* (**paddies**)
  a field where rice is grown.

**padlock** *noun* (**padlocks**)
  a lock with a metal loop that you can use to fasten something shut.

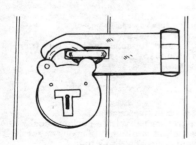

**page**¹ *noun* (**pages**)
  a piece of paper that is part of a book, magazine, etc.; one side of this piece of paper.

**page**² *noun* (**pages**)
  a boy who acts as a servant or attendant.

**pageant** *noun* (**pageants**)
  (*say* **paj**-ĕnt)
  **1** a play or entertainment about historical events and people. **2** a procession of people in costume.
  **pageantry** *noun*

**pagoda** *noun* (**pagodas**)
  (*say* pă-**goh**-dă)
  a tall religious building in the Far East.

**paid** past tense and past participle of **pay** *verb*.

**pail** *noun* (**pails**)
  a bucket.

**pain** *noun* (**pains**)
  an unpleasant feeling caused when part of your body is injured or diseased.
  **pains**, careful effort or trouble, *He took pains to do the job properly.*
  **painless** *adjective*

**painful** *adjective*
  that causes pain.
  **painfully** *adverb*

**painkiller** *noun* (**painkillers**)
  a drug that reduces pain.

**painstaking** *adjective*
  making a careful effort.

**paint**¹ *noun* (**paints**)
  a substance put on something to colour or cover it.
  **paintbox** *noun*, **paintbrush** *noun*

**paint**² *verb* (**paints, painting, painted**)
  **1** to put paint on something. **2** to make a picture with paints; to make a picture of someone or something in this way.

**painter**¹ *noun* (**painters**)
  someone who paints.

**painter**² *noun* (**painters**)
  a rope used to tie up a boat.

**painting** *noun* (**paintings**)
  **1** a painted picture, *These paintings are by Degas.* **2** using paints to make a picture, *She likes painting.*

**pansy**

**pair** *noun* (**pairs**)
1 two things or people that go together or are the same kind, *a pair of shoes*.
2 something made of two joined parts, *a pair of scissors*.

**Pakistani**[1] *adjective*
of Pakistan.

**Pakistani**[2] *noun* (**Pakistanis**)
a person from Pakistan.

**pal** *noun* (**pals**)
(*informal*) a friend.

**palace** *noun* (**palaces**)
a mansion where a king or queen or other important person lives.

**palate** *noun* (**palates**)
(*say* pal-ăt)
1 the roof of your mouth. 2 a person's sense of taste, *She has a refined palate.*

USAGE: Do not confuse **palate** with **palette**, which means a board on which an artist mixes colours.

**pale** *adjective* (**paler, palest**)
1 almost white, *a pale face*. 2 not bright in colour; faint, *a pale blue sky*.
**palely** *adverb*, **paleness** *noun*

**palette** *noun* (**palettes**)
(*say* pal-it)
a board on which an artist mixes colours.

USAGE: Do not confuse **palette** with **palate**, which means the roof of your mouth, or your sense of taste.

**paling** *noun* (**palings**)
a wooden fence.

**palisade cell** *noun* (**palisade cells**)
one of the oblong cells found just below the upper surface of a leaf.

**pallid** *adjective*
pale, especially because of illness.
**pallor** *noun*

**palm** *noun* (**palms**)
1 the inner part of your hand, between your fingers and your wrist. 2 a tropical tree with large leaves and no branches.
**Palm Sunday,** the Sunday before Easter.

**palmist** *noun* (**palmists**)
someone who claims to be able to tell, by looking at your hand, what will happen to you in the future.
**palmistry** *noun*

**pampas** *plural noun*
the grassy plains of South America.
**pampas-grass,** a tall plant with sharp-edged leaves and feathery flowers.

**pamper** *verb* (**pampers, pampering, pampered**)
to be too kind towards a person or animal, letting him or her have or do whatever he or she wants.

**pamphlet** *noun* (**pamphlets**)
a thin book with a cover of paper or thin cardboard.

**pan** *noun* (**pans**)
a pot or dish with a flat base.

**pancake** *noun* (**pancakes**)
a thin flat cake of fried batter.

**panda** *noun* (**pandas**)
a large, furry, black-and-white animal found in China.
**panda car,** a police patrol car.

**pandemonium** *noun*
a loud noise or disturbance.

**pane** *noun* (**panes**)
a sheet of glass in a window.

**panel** *noun* (**panels**)
1 a long, flat piece of wood, metal, etc. that is part of a door, wall, or piece of furniture.
2 a group of people appointed to discuss or decide something, *a panel of judges*.

**pang** *noun* (**pangs**)
a sudden feeling of guilt, sadness, or other emotion.

**panic**[1] *noun*
sudden uncontrollable fear.
**panicky** *adjective*

**panic**[2] *verb* (**panics, panicking, panicked**)
to be filled with sudden uncontrollable fear.

**pannier** *noun* (**panniers**)
a bag or basket hung on one side of a bicycle or horse.

**panorama** *noun* (**panoramas**)
a view or picture of a wide area.
**panoramic** *adjective*

**pansy** *noun* (**pansies**)
a small, brightly-coloured garden flower.

**pant** *verb* (**pants, panting, panted**)
to take short, quick breaths, usually after
running or working hard.

**panther** *noun* (**panthers**)
a leopard.

**panties** *plural noun*
(*informal*) short knickers or underpants.

**pantomime** *noun* (**pantomimes**)
a Christmas entertainment based on a
fairy tale.

**pantry** *noun* (**pantries**)
a cupboard or small room where food is
kept.

**pants** *plural noun*
**1** (*informal*) underpants. **2** (*in America*)
trousers.

**papaya** *noun* (**papayas**)
a melon-shaped tropical fruit with orange
flesh.

**paper**[1] *noun* (**papers**)
**1** a thin substance used for writing or
printing on, wrapping up things, etc.
**2** a newspaper. **3** a document.

**paper**[2] *verb* (**papers, papering, papered**)
to stick wallpaper on a wall or ceiling.

**paperback** *noun* (**paperbacks**)
a book with thin flexible covers.

**papier mâché** *noun*
(*say* pap-yay **mash**-ay)
paper made into pulp and used to make
models, ornaments, etc.

**papyrus** *noun* (**papyri**)
(*say* pă-**py**-rŭs)
**1** a kind of paper made of reeds, used in
Ancient Egypt. **2** something written on a
piece of this paper. **3** the kind of reed from
which this paper was made.

**parable** *noun* (**parables**)
a story told to teach people something,
especially one of the stories told by Jesus.

**parachute** *noun* (**parachutes**)
an umbrella-shaped device on which people
or things can float slowly down to the
ground from an aircraft.
**parachuting** *noun*, **parachutist** *noun*

**parade**[1] *noun* (**parades**)
**1** a procession that displays people or
things. **2** an assembly of troops for
inspection, etc.

**parade**[2] *verb* (**parades, parading, paraded**)
**1** to move in a procession. **2** to assemble for
inspection, drill, etc.

**paradise** *noun*
**1** heaven; a heavenly place. **2** the Garden of
Eden.

**paradox** *noun* (**paradoxes**)
(*say* pa-ră-doks)
a statement which goes against common
sense, but which may still be true, '*More
haste, less speed' is a paradox.*
**paradoxical** *adjective*, **paradoxically** *adverb*

**paraffin** *noun*
(in America, *kerosene*) an oil used as fuel.

**paragraph** *noun* (**paragraphs**)
a division of a piece of writing, starting on
a new line, *Paragraphs usually contain
several sentences.*

**parallel** *adjective*
(of lines) that are the same distance apart
for their whole length, *Railway lines are
parallel.*

**parallelogram** *noun* (**parallelograms**)
a four-sided figure with its opposite sides
parallel to each other.

**paralyse** *verb* (**paralyses, paralysing, paralysed**)
**1** to make someone unable to feel anything
or move. **2** to make something unable to
move.

**paralysis** *noun*
(*say* pă-**ral**-ĭ-sis)
being unable to move or feel anything.
**paralytic** *adjective*

**parapet** *noun* (**parapets**)
a low wall along the edge of a balcony,
bridge, roof, etc.

**paraphernalia** *noun*
(*say* pa-ră-fer-**nay**-li-ă)
numerous pieces of equipment, small
possessions, etc.

USAGE: **paraphernalia** was originally a
plural noun, but is usually treated as
singular.

**paraphrase** *verb* (**paraphrases, paraphrasing,
paraphrased**)
to give the meaning of a piece of writing in
other words.

**parasite** *noun* (**parasites**)
an animal or plant that lives in or on
another, from which it gets its food.
**parasitic** *adjective*

**parasol** *noun* (**parasols**)
a lightweight umbrella used to shade yourself from the sun.

**paratroops** *plural noun*
troops using parachutes.
**paratrooper** *noun*

**parcel** *noun* (**parcels**)
something wrapped up to be posted or carried.

**parched** *adjective*
very dry or thirsty, *parched earth. I was parched after the run.*

**parchment** *noun*
a heavy, paper-like substance made from animal skins, used for writing on.

**pardon**[1] *verb* (**pardons, pardoning, pardoned**)
to forgive or excuse someone.
**pardon me,** I apologize.
**pardonable** *adjective,* **pardonably** *adverb*

**pardon**[2] *noun*
1 forgiveness. 2 used as an exclamation to mean 'I didn't hear or understand what you said', or 'I apologize'.

**parent** *noun* (**parents**)
one of a couple who together produced a child or a young creature.
**parentage** *noun,* **parental** *adjective,* **parenthood** *noun*

**parenthesis** *noun* (**parentheses**)
(*say* pă-ren-thi-sis)
1 something extra inserted in a sentence between brackets or dashes. 2 one of a pair of brackets used in the middle of a sentence.

**parish** *noun* (**parishes**)
a district that has its own church.
**parishioner** *noun*

**park**[1] *noun* (**parks**)
1 a large garden for public use. 2 a place where vehicles may be left for a time.

**park**[2] *verb* (**parks, parking, parked**)
to leave a vehicle somewhere for a time.

**parka** *noun* (**parkas**)
a warm jacket with a hood attached.

**parking-meter** *noun* (**parking-meters**)
a device that shows how long a vehicle has been parked in a street, *When you park your car, you put a coin in the parking-meter.*

**parliament** *noun* (**parliaments**)
a group of people that meets regularly and makes a country's laws.
**parliamentary** *adjective*

**parody** *noun* (**parodies**)
a play, poem, etc. that makes fun of people or things by imitating them.

**parole** *noun*
(*say* pă-rohl)
letting a convict out of prison before his or her sentence is finished, on condition that he or she behaves well, *He was on parole.*

**parrot** *noun* (**parrots**)
a brightly-coloured bird that can learn to repeat things said to it.

**parsley** *noun*
a green plant used to flavour and decorate food.

**parsnip** *noun* (**parsnips**)
a pale yellow vegetable.

**parson** *noun* (**parsons**)
a member of the clergy.
**parsonage** *noun*

**part**[1] *noun* (**parts**)
1 anything that belongs to something bigger; a piece. 2 the character played by an actor or actress; the words spoken by a character in a play.
**part of speech,** one of the groups into which words can be divided, such as nouns, adjectives, verbs, etc.

**part**[2] *verb* (**parts, parting, parted**)
1 to separate people or things. 2 to divide hair so that it goes in two different directions.
**part with,** to give away or get rid of something.

**part-exchange** *noun* (**part-exchanges**)
giving something you own as well as some money to get something else.

**partial** *adjective*
of a part; not complete, *a partial eclipse.*
**partial to something,** fond of something.
**partially** *adverb*

**participate** *verb* (**participates, participating, participated**)
to take part or have a share in something.
**participant** *noun,* **participation** *noun*

**participle** *noun* (**participles**)
a word formed from a verb and used as part of the verb or as an adjective, *Participles are words like 'going', 'gone', 'sailed', and 'sailing'.*

**particle** *noun* (**particles**)
1 a tiny piece, *particles of dust.* 2 (*in Science*) one of the tiny simple parts, such as electrons, neutrons, and protons, of which all matter is made.

**particular**[1] *adjective*
1 only this one and no other; special; individual. 2 fussy; hard to please.
**in particular,** especially; chiefly.
**particularly** *adverb*

**particular²** *noun* (**particulars**)
a detail; a single fact.

**parting** *noun* (**partings**)
1 leaving; separation. 2 the line where your hair is parted.

**partition** *noun* (**partitions**)
1 a thin dividing wall. 2 dividing something into parts.

**partly** *adverb*
not completely; somewhat.

**partner** *noun* (**partners**)
one of a pair of people who do something together, especially in business, dancing, or playing a game.
**partnership** *noun*

**partridge** *noun* (**partridges**)
a game-bird with brown feathers.

**part-time** *adjective* and *adverb*
working for only some of the normal hours.
**part-timer** *noun*

**party** *noun* (**parties**)
1 a time when people get together to enjoy themselves, *my birthday party*. 2 a group of people working or travelling together, *a search party*. 3 an organized group of people with similar political beliefs, *the Labour Party*. 4 a person who is involved in an action or legal case, *the guilty party*.

**pascal** *noun* (**pascals**)
a unit of pressure equal to one newton per square metre.

**pass¹** *verb* (**passes, passing, passed**)
1 to go by. 2 to move or go, *They passed over the bridge*. 3 to give something to someone; to hand over, *Please pass the salt*. 4 to be successful in an examination. 5 to spend time. 6 to disappear. 7 to approve or accept, *The law was passed*.
**passable** *adjective*

**pass²** *noun* (**passes**)
1 going by something. 2 a success in an examination, *a GCSE pass*. 3 a permit to go in or out of a place. 4 a narrow way between hills.

**passage** *noun* (**passages**)
1 a corridor. 2 a way through something, *The police forced a passage through the crowd*. 3 a journey by sea or air. 4 a section of a piece of writing or music. 5 passing, *the passage of time*.
**passageway** *noun*

**passenger** *noun* (**passengers**)
someone who is driven in a car or train, flown in an aircraft, etc.

**passer-by** *noun* (**passers-by**)
someone who happens to be going past.

**passion** *noun* (**passions**)
1 strong emotion. 2 great enthusiasm.
**the Passion,** Jesus's suffering on the Cross.
**passionate** *adjective*, **passionately** *adverb*

**passive** *adjective*
1 not active; not resisting or fighting. 2 (*in grammar*) describing the type of verb which affects the subject, not the object, *The verb is passive in 'She was chased by a dog'*.
**passively** *adverb*

**Passover** *noun*
a Jewish religious festival, celebrating the escape of the Jews from Egypt.

**passport** *noun* (**passports**)
an official document that you must have if you want to travel abroad.

**password** *noun* (**passwords**)
a secret word or phrase used to distinguish friends from enemies, or to gain access to a computer system.

**past¹** *noun*
the time before now.

**past²** *adjective*
of the time before now.
**past participle,** a form of a verb used after *has, have, was, were,* etc. to describe an action that happened at a time before now, *'Done', 'overtaken',* and *'written'* are past participles.
**past tense,** a form of a verb used by itself to describe an action that happened at a time before now, *'Went' is the past tense of 'go'*.

**past**[3] *preposition*
1 beyond, *Go past the school.* 2 after, *It is past midnight.*
**past it,** (*slang*) too old to be able to do something.

**pasta** *noun*
a paste of flour, water, and often eggs, made into various shapes and used as food.

**paste**[1] *noun* (**pastes**)
a soft and moist or gluey substance.

**paste**[2] *verb* (**pastes, pasting, pasted**)
to stick something with paste.

**pastel** *noun* (**pastels**)
1 a crayon that is like a slightly greasy chalk. 2 a light, delicate colour.

**pasteurize** *verb* (**pasteurizes, pasteurizing, pasteurized**)
(*say* **pahs**-cher-ryz)
to purify milk by heating it.
**pasteurization** *noun*

**pastille** *noun* (**pastilles**)
a small flavoured sweet.

**pastime** *noun* (**pastimes**)
something done to pass time pleasantly.

**pastry** *noun* (**pastries**)
1 a mixture of flour, fat, and water rolled flat and baked. 2 something made of this kind of mixture.

**pasture** *noun* (**pastures**)
land covered with grass that cattle, sheep, or horses can eat.

**pasty**[1] *noun* (**pasties**)
(*say* **pas**-ti)
a small pie.

**pasty**[2] *adjective* (**pastier, pastiest**)
(*say* **pay**-sti)
pale or white, *a pasty face.*

**pat**[1] *verb* (**pats, patting, patted**)
to tap something or someone gently with your open hand or with something flat.

**pat**[2] *noun* (**pats**)
1 a patting movement or sound. 2 a small piece of butter.
**a pat on the back,** congratulations or praise.

**patch**[1] *noun* (**patches**)
1 a piece of material put over a hole or damaged place. 2 an area that is different from its surroundings, *a black cat with a white patch on her chest.* 3 a small area of land. 4 a small piece of something, *There are patches of ice on the road.*

**patch**[2] *verb* (**patches, patching, patched**)
to put a piece of material on something as a repair.
**patch up,** to repair something roughly; to settle a quarrel, *He's patched up his rusty old car again. We tried to patch up our disagreement.*

**patchwork** *noun*
joining small pieces of different cloth together; a piece of material made in this way, *a bedspread made of patchwork.*

**patchy** *adjective* (**patchier, patchiest**)
1 occurring in small distinct areas, *There may be patchy rain.* 2 not of the same quality throughout, *His work has been patchy in the past.*

**patent**[1] *noun* (**patents**)
(*say* **pay**-tĕnt or **pat**-ĕnt)
official authority to make something you have invented and to stop other people copying it.

**patent**[2] *adjective*
(*say* **pay**-tĕnt)
1 protected by a patent. 2 obvious, *Her statement is a patent lie.*
**patent leather,** glossy leather.
**patently** *adverb*

**patent**[3] *verb* (**patents, patenting, patented**)
(*say* **pay**-tĕnt or **pat**-ĕnt)
to get a patent for something.

**path** *noun* (**paths**)
1 a narrow way to walk or ride along. 2 the line along which something moves, *the path of the meteor.*

**pathetic** *adjective*
1 sad; pitiful, *The orphan looked pathetic.* 2 sadly or comically weak or useless, *He made a pathetic attempt to climb the tree.*
**pathetically** *adverb*

**patience** *noun*
(*say* **pay**-shĕns)
1 being patient. 2 a card-game for one person.

**patient**[1] *adjective*
(*say* **pay**-shĕnt)
1 able to wait for a long time without getting angry. 2 able to bear pain or trouble.
**patiently** *adverb*

**patient**[2] *noun* (**patients**)
(*say* **pay**-shĕnt)
someone who is ill or who is getting treatment from a doctor or dentist.

**patio** *noun* (**patios**)
(*say* **pat**-i-oh)
a paved area next to a house.

**patriot** *noun* (**patriots**)
(*say* pay-tri-ŏt or pat-ri-ŏt)
someone who loves and supports his or her country.
**patriotic** *adjective*, **patriotism** *noun*

**patrol**[1] *verb* (**patrols, patrolling, patrolled**)
to move around a place or a thing so as to guard it and see that all is well.

**patrol**[2] *noun* (**patrols**)
**1** a patrolling group of people, ships, aircraft, etc. **2** a group of Scouts or Guides.
**on patrol**, patrolling.
**patrol car**, a car in which police, etc. patrol an area.
**patrolman** *noun*

**patron** *noun* (**patrons**)
(*say* pay-trŏn)
someone who supports a person or cause with money or encouragement.
**patron saint**, a saint who is thought to protect a particular place, person, etc.
**patronage** *noun*

**patter** *noun* (**patters**)
**1** a series of light tapping sounds. **2** the quick talk of a comedian, conjuror, salesman, etc.

**pattern** *noun* (**patterns**)
**1** a decorative group of lines or shapes.
**2** a thing that you copy in order to make something, *a dress pattern*.

**pause**[1] *noun* (**pauses**)
a short stop before continuing.

**pause**[2] *verb* (**pauses, pausing, paused**)
to make a short stop before continuing.

**pave** *verb* (**paves, paving, paved**)
to make a hard surface for a road, path, etc.
**pave the way**, to prepare for something.

**pavement** *noun* (**pavements**)
(in America, *sidewalk*) a path with a hard surface, along the side of a street.

**pavilion** *noun* (**pavilions**)
a building at a sports ground for the use of players or spectators.

**paw**[1] *noun* (**paws**)
an animal's foot.

**paw**[2] *verb* (**paws, pawing, pawed**)
to touch someone or something with a paw; to touch someone or something clumsily with a hand.

**pawn**[1] *noun* (**pawns**)
**1** one of the least valuable pieces in chess.
**2** a person who is controlled by someone else.

**pawn**[2] *verb* (**pawns, pawning, pawned**)
to leave something with a pawnbroker so as to borrow money from him or her, *I pawned my watch*.

**pawnbroker** *noun* (**pawnbrokers**)
a shopkeeper who lends money to people in return for objects that they hand over to him or her and which are sold if the money is not paid back.

**pay**[1] *verb* (**pays, paying, paid**)
**1** to give money in return for something, *Have you paid for your lunch?* **2** to be profitable, *It pays to advertise*. **3** to give or make, *He paid me a compliment*. **4** to suffer for something you have done, *I'll make you pay for this!*
**Pay As You Earn**, the regular deduction of income tax from weekly or monthly earnings.
**pay back**, to pay money that you owe; to get revenge on someone, *I've paid back my debts. She is determined to pay him back for cheating her*.

**pay**[2] *noun*
wages, *Have you had your pay?*

**PAYE** short for **Pay As You Earn**.

**payment** *noun* (**payments**)
**1** the action of paying. **2** money paid.

**PC** short for **1** police constable. **2** personal computer.

**PE** short for **physical education**.

**pea** *noun* (**peas**)
a tiny, round, green vegetable that grows inside a pod.

**peace** *noun*
**1** a time when there is no war, violence, or disorder. **2** quietness; calm.

**peaceful** *adjective*
**1** having peace, *a peaceful country*. **2** liking or working for peace, *a peaceful man*.
**peacefully** *adverb*

**peach** *noun* (**peaches**)
a round, soft, juicy fruit with a large stone.

**peel**²

**peacock** *noun* (**peacocks**)
a large bird with a long, brightly-coloured tail that it can spread out like a fan.

**peak** *noun* (**peaks**)
**1** the top of a mountain. **2** the highest or best point of something, *at the peak of his career*. **3** the part of a cap that sticks out in front.
**peaked** *adjective*

**peal**¹ *verb* (**peals, pealing, pealed**)
to make a loud ringing sound.

USAGE: Do not confuse the verb **peal** with the verb **peel**, which means to remove a peel or covering, or to lose a covering or skin.

**peal**² *noun* (**peals**)
a loud ringing sound.

USAGE: Do not confuse the noun **peal** with the noun **peel**, which is the skin of fruit or vegetables.

**peanut** *noun* (**peanuts**)
a small, round nut that grows in a pod in the ground.
**peanut butter,** roasted peanuts crushed into a paste.

**pear** *noun* (**pears**)
a juicy fruit that gets narrower near the stalk.

**pearl** *noun* (**pearls**)
a small, shiny, white ball found in the shells of some oysters and used as a jewel.
**pearl barley,** grains of barley made small by grinding.
**pearly** *adjective*

**peasant** *noun* (**peasants**)
a person who belongs to a farming community, especially in poor areas of the world.
**Peasants' Revolt,** the rebellion of English peasants that took place in 1381.
**peasantry** *noun*

**peat** *noun*
rotted plant material that can be dug out of the ground and used as fuel or fertilizer.

**pebble** *noun* (**pebbles**)
a small round stone.
**pebbly** *adjective*

**peck**¹ *verb* (**pecks, pecking, pecked**)
**1** to bite or eat something with the beak, *The hens were pecking at the corn.*
**2** (*informal*) to give someone a quick kiss.

**peck**² *noun* (**pecks**)
**1** a short, sharp bite with the beak.
**2** (*informal*) a quick kiss, *She gave him a peck on the cheek.*

**peckish** *adjective*
(*informal*) hungry.

**peculiar** *adjective*
strange; unusual.
**peculiar to,** restricted to, *a custom that is peculiar to one tribe.*
**peculiarity** *noun*, **peculiarly** *adverb*

**pedal**¹ *noun* (**pedals**)
part of a machine worked by a person's foot, *A bicycle has two pedals.*

**pedal**² *verb* (**pedals, pedalling, pedalled**)
to push or turn the pedal or pedals of a device; to move something by using pedals, *You pump air for the organ by pedalling. She pedalled her bicycle right across the USA.*

**peddle** *verb* (**peddles, peddling, peddled**)
to sell things as a pedlar.

**pedestal** *noun* (**pedestals**)
the base that supports a statue, pillar, etc.
**put someone on a pedestal,** to admire someone greatly or think that he or she is perfect.

**pedestrian** *noun* (**pedestrians**)
someone who is walking.

**pedigree** *noun* (**pedigrees**)
a list of a person's or animal's ancestors, especially to show how purely an animal has been bred.

**pedlar** *noun* (**pedlars**)
someone who goes from house to house selling small things.

**peel**¹ *noun* (**peels**)
the skin of some fruit and vegetables.

USAGE: Do not confuse the noun **peel** with the noun **peal**, which means a loud ringing sound.

**peel**² *verb* (**peels, peeling, peeled**)
**1** to remove the peel or covering from something. **2** to lose a covering or skin, *My skin is peeling.*

USAGE: Do not confuse the verb **peel** with the verb **peal**, which means to make a loud ringing sound.

**peep** *verb* (**peeps, peeping, peeped**)
1 to look quickly or secretly. 2 to look through a narrow opening. 3 to show slightly or briefly, *The moon peeped out through the clouds.*
**peep-hole** *noun*

**peer**¹ *verb* (**peers, peering, peered**)
to look at something closely or with difficulty.

**peer**² *noun* (**peers**)
a nobleman.
**peeress** *noun*

**peewit** *noun* (**peewits**)
a kind of plover.

**peg**¹ *noun* (**pegs**)
1 a clip or pin for fixing things in place or for hanging things on. 2 a clothes-peg.

**peg**² *verb* (**pegs, pegging, pegged**)
1 to fix something with pegs, *We pegged out the tent.* 2 to keep something at a fixed amount, *The price was pegged at £4.*
**peg out**, (*informal*) to die.

**Pekingese** or **Pekinese** *noun* (**Pekingese** or **Pekinese**)
(*say* peek-i-**neez**)
a small breed of dog with short legs and long silky hair.

**pelican** *noun* (**pelicans**)
a large bird with a pouch in its long beak for storing fish.
**pelican crossing**, a place where you can cross a street safely by operating lights that stop the traffic.

**pellet** *noun* (**pellets**)
a tiny ball of metal, food, wet paper, etc.

**pelt**¹ *verb* (**pelts, pelting, pelted**)
1 to throw a lot of things at someone, *We pelted him with snowballs.* 2 to move very quickly. 3 to rain very hard, *The rain pelted down.*

**pelt**² *noun* (**pelts**)
an animal skin, especially with the fur or hair on it.

**pen**¹ *noun* (**pens**)
a device with a metal point for writing with ink.
**pen-friend**, someone that you write to regularly but usually do not meet.

**pen**² *noun* (**pens**)
an enclosure for cattle or other animals.

**penalize** *verb* (**penalizes, penalizing, penalized**)
1 to punish someone. 2 to give a penalty against someone in a game.

**penalty** *noun* (**penalties**)
1 a punishment. 2 an advantage given to one side in a game when a member of the other side breaks a rule. 3 a goal scored as the result of a penalty.

**pence** *plural noun*
pennies, *These sweets cost 50 pence.*

**pencil**¹ *noun* (**pencils**)
a device for drawing or writing, made of a thin stick of graphite or coloured chalk inside a cylinder of wood or metal.

**pencil**² *verb* (**pencils, pencilling, pencilled**)
to draw or write with a pencil.

**pendant** *noun* (**pendants**)
an ornament hung round your neck on a long chain or string.

**pendulum** *noun* (**pendulums**)
a rod with a weight on the end so that it swings to and fro, *Some clocks are worked by pendulums.*

pendulum

**penetrate** *verb* (**penetrates, penetrating, penetrated**)
to make or find a way through or into something.
**penetration** *noun*

**penguin** *noun* (**penguins**)
an Antarctic sea-bird that cannot fly but uses its wings as flippers for swimming.

**penicillin** *noun*
a drug obtained from fungi, that kills bacteria.

**peninsula** *noun* (**peninsulas**)
a long piece of land that is almost surrounded by water.
**peninsular** *adjective*

**penis** *noun* (**penises**)
the part of the body with which a male urinates or has sexual intercourse.

**penitence** *noun*
regret that you have done wrong.
**penitent** *adjective*

**penknife** *noun* (**penknives**)
a small folding knife.

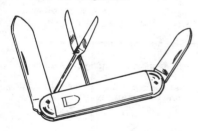

**pennant** *noun* (**pennants**)
a triangular or tapering flag.

**penniless** *adjective*
having no money; very poor.

**penny** *noun* (**pennies** or **pence**)
a British coin worth a hundredth of a pound.

**pension** *noun* (**pensions**)
regular payments made to someone who has retired.

**pensioner** *noun* (**pensioners**)
someone who receives a pension.

**pentagon** *noun* (**pentagons**)
a flat shape with five sides.
**the Pentagon,** the leaders of the American armed forces, named after their five-sided headquarters near Washington.

**peony** *noun* (**peonies**)
(*say* **pee**-ŏ-ni)
a large garden flower.

**people** *plural noun*
**1** men, women, and children. **2** the men, women, and children who live in a country.

**pepper** *noun* (**peppers**)
**1** a hot-tasting powder used to flavour food. **2** a bright green or red vegetable.
**peppery** *adjective*

**peppermint** *noun* (**peppermints**)
**1** a kind of mint used for flavouring. **2** a sweet flavoured with this mint.

**per** *preposition*
for each; in each, *The charge is £2 per person.*
**per cent,** for or in every hundred, *A pay-rise from £100 to £110 is a 10 per cent (10%) increase.*

**per annum** *adverb*
each year, *£15,000 per annum.*

**per capita** *adjective* and *adverb*
for each person, *The daily water consumption was thirty litres per capita.*

**perceive** *verb* (**perceives, perceiving, perceived**)
to notice something.
**perceptible** *adjective,* **perceptibly** *adverb,* **perception** *noun*

**percentage** *noun* (**percentages**)
the proportion out of every hundred of something, *Out of £300 he spent £60, a percentage of 20.*

**perceptive** *adjective*
quick to notice things.

**perch**[1] *noun* (**perches**)
a place where a bird sits or rests.

**perch**[2] *noun* (**perch**)
a freshwater fish that can be eaten.

**perch**[3] *verb* (**perches, perching, perched**)
to sit or stand on the edge of something or on something small.

**percolator** *noun* (**percolators**)
a device for making coffee.

**percussion** *noun*
musical instruments played by hitting or shaking, *Drums, cymbals, and chime bars are percussion instruments.*
**percussive** *adjective*

**perennial** *adjective*
1 lasting or recurring for many years, *a perennial problem*. 2 flowering for many years, *perennial plants*.
**perennially** *adverb*

**perfect**[1] *adjective*
(*say* per-fikt)
1 so good that it cannot be made any better; without any faults. 2 complete, *a perfect stranger*.
**perfection** *noun*, **perfectly** *adverb*

**perfect**[2] *verb* (**perfects, perfecting, perfected**)
(*say* per-fekt)
to make something so good that it cannot be made any better.

**perfect**[3] *noun*
a form of verb that describes a completed action or event in the past, *In English, the perfect includes the word 'has' or 'have', as in 'The letter has arrived'.*

**perforate** *verb* (**perforates, perforating, perforated**)
to make tiny holes in something, especially so that it can be torn easily.
**perforation** *noun*

**perform** *verb* (**performs, performing, performed**)
1 to do something in front of an audience, *They performed 'Macbeth' in the school hall.* 2 to do something you have to do or ought to do, *The surgeon performed the operation.*
**performance** *noun*, **performer** *noun*

**perfume** *noun* (**perfumes**)
1 a liquid with a very sweet smell. 2 a sweet smell.

**perhaps** *adverb*
it may be; possibly.

**peril** *noun* (**perils**)
danger, *She was in great peril.*
**perilous** *adjective*, **perilously** *adverb*

**perimeter** *noun* (**perimeters**)
(*say* per-im-it-er)
1 the distance round the edge of something. 2 a boundary, *A fence marks the perimeter of the airfield.*

**period** *noun* (**periods**)
1 a length of time. 2 the time every month when a woman or girl menstruates.
**periodic** *adjective*, **periodically** *adverb*

**periodical** *noun* (**periodicals**)
a magazine published regularly.

**periscope** *noun* (**periscopes**)
a device using mirrors to let you see something on a higher level than where you are.

**perish** *verb* (**perishes, perishing, perished**)
1 to die. 2 to rot, *The tyres have perished.* 3 (*informal*) to make someone very cold, *I'm perished.*
**perishable** *adjective*

**permanent** *adjective*
lasting for ever or for a very long time.
**permanent wave** or **perm**, long-lasting waves made in hair.
**permanence** *noun*, **permanently** *adverb*

**permission** *noun*
permitting something; a statement that something is permitted.

**permissive** *adjective*
letting people do what they wish; tolerant, *permissive parents. They have a permissive attitude.*
**permissively** *adverb*, **permissiveness** *noun*

**permit**[1] *verb* (**permits, permitting, permitted**)
(*say* per-mit)
to say that someone may do something; to let someone do something.
**permissible** *adjective*

**permit**[2] *noun* (**permits**)
(*say* per-mit)
a written or printed statement that something is permitted.

**perpendicular** *adjective*
1 upright, *a perpendicular cliff-face*. 2 at a right angle to the base or to another line, *a perpendicular line.*

**perpetual** *adjective*
continual; permanent.
**perpetually** *adverb*, **perpetuate** *verb*

**perplex** *verb* (**perplexes, perplexing, perplexed**)
to puzzle someone very much.
**perplexity** *noun*

**persecute** *verb* (**persecutes, persecuting, persecuted**)
to be continually cruel to someone, especially because you disagree with his or her beliefs.
**persecution** *noun*, **persecutor** *noun*

**persevere** *verb* (**perseveres, persevering, persevered**)
to go on despite difficulties.
**perseverance** *noun*

**persist** *verb* (**persists, persisting, persisted**)
**1** to keep on doing something, *She persists in slamming doors.* **2** to go on despite difficulties, *At first his experiments were unsuccessful, but he persisted.*
**persistence** *noun*, **persistent** *adjective*, **persistently** *adverb*

**person** *noun* (**persons**)
**1** a man, woman, or child. **2** (*in grammar*) the parts of a verb and the pronouns that refer to someone who is speaking (the *first person*), someone who is spoken to (the *second person*), or someone who is spoken of (the *third person*), 'I write' is the first person singular of 'to write'; 'they write' is the third person plural.

**personal** *adjective*
**1** belonging to, done by, or concerning a particular person, *The film star made a personal appearance at the gala.* **2** private, *We have personal business to discuss.*
**personal computer**, a small computer designed to be used by one person.
**personally** *adverb*

USAGE: Do not confuse **personal** with **personnel**, which means the people employed in a place.

**personality** *noun* (**personalities**)
**1** a person's nature and characteristics, *She has a friendly personality.* **2** a well-known person, *television personalities.*

**personnel** *noun*
(*say* per-sŏ-**nel**)
the people employed in a particular place.

USAGE: Do not confuse **personnel** with **personal**, which means belonging to, done by, or concerning a person.

**perspective** *noun* (**perspectives**)
the impression of depth and space in a picture or scene.
**in perspective**, in a way that gives a balanced view of things, *Look at your problems in perspective.*

**perspire** *verb* (**perspires, perspiring, perspired**)
to give off moisture through the pores of your skin.
**perspiration** *noun*

USAGE: **perspire** and **perspiration** have the same meaning as **sweat** (verb and noun), but are thought by some people to be politer words than **sweat**.

**persuade** *verb* (**persuades, persuading, persuaded**)
to get someone to agree with something.
**persuasion** *noun*, **persuasive** *adjective*

**perverse** *adjective*
(*say* per-**verss**)
obstinately being unreasonable or wicked.
**perversely** *adverb*, **perversity** *noun*

**pervert**[1] *verb* (**perverts, perverting, perverted**)
(*say* per-**vert**)
**1** to make something go wrong. **2** to make someone behave in a way that most people find unacceptable.
**perversion** *noun*

**pervert**[2] *noun* (**perverts**)
(*say* **per**-vert)
someone who behaves in a way that most people find unacceptable, especially in sexual matters.

**Pesach** *noun*
the Hebrew name for Passover.

**pessimism** *noun*
expecting that things will not happen as you want.
**pessimist** *noun*, **pessimistic** *adjective*

**pest** *noun* (**pests**)
a destructive or annoying animal or person.

**pester** *verb* (**pesters, pestering, pestered**)
to annoy someone with frequent questions, requests, etc.

**pesticide** *noun* (**pesticides**)
a chemical used to kill insects and grubs, especially on plants.

**pet** *noun* (**pets**)
**1** a tame animal kept for companionship and amusement. **2** a person treated as a favourite, *teacher's pet.*

**petal** *noun* (**petals**)
one of the separate coloured parts of a flower, *Daisies have a lot of white petals.*

**petition** *noun* (**petitions**)
a written request for something, usually signed by a large number of people.

**petrify** *verb* (**petrifies, petrifying, petrified**)
to make someone so terrified, surprised, etc. that he or she cannot act or move.

**petrochemical** *noun* (**petrochemicals**)
a chemical substance made from petroleum or natural gas.

**petrol** *noun*
(in America, *gasoline*) a liquid made from petroleum, used to drive the engines of cars, aircraft, etc.
**petrol pump,** a device for putting petrol into the tank of a motor vehicle.
**petrol station,** a place where petrol is sold.

**petroleum** *noun*
(*say* pi-**troh**-li-ŭm)
an oil found underground that is purified to make petrol, diesel oil, paraffin, etc.

**petticoat** *noun* (**petticoats**)
a piece of women's clothing worn under a skirt or dress.

**petty** *adjective* (**pettier, pettiest**)
small and unimportant, *petty regulations*.
**pettily** *adverb*, **pettiness** *noun*

**pew** *noun* (**pews**)
one of the long wooden seats in a church.

**pewter** *noun*
a grey alloy of tin and lead.

**pH** *noun*
a measure of the acidity or alkalinity of a solution, *Pure water has a pH of 7; acids have a pH between 0 and 7, and alkalis have a pH between 7 and 14.*

**phase**[1] *noun* (**phases**)
a stage in the progress or development of something.

**phase**[2] *verb* (**phases, phasing, phased**)
to carry out something in stages, *The building of the school was phased over three years.*
**phase in,** to start something gradually.
**phase out,** to stop something gradually.

**pheasant** *noun* (**pheasants**)
(*say* **fez**-ănt)
a game-bird with a long tail.

**phenomenal** *adjective*
(*say* fin-**om**-in-ăl)
amazing.
**phenomenally** *adverb*

**phenomenon** *noun* (**phenomena**)
an event or fact, especially one that is remarkable or unusual, *Thunder and lightning are strange phenomena.*

**philately** *noun*
(*say* fil-**at**-ĕl-i)
collecting postage stamps, *My hobby is philately.*
**philatelic** *adjective*, **philatelist** *noun*

**philosophical** *adjective*
1 of philosophy. 2 not upset by suffering, misfortune, etc., *He was philosophical about his illness.*
**philosophically** *adverb*

**philosophy** *noun* (**philosophies**)
(*say* fil-**os**-ŏ-fi)
1 the study of truths about life, morals, etc.
2 a way of thinking; a system of beliefs.
**philosopher** *noun*

**phobia** *noun* (**phobias**)
(*say* **foh**-bi-ă)
a great or unusual fear of something.

**phoenix** *noun* (**phoenixes**)
(*say* **fee**-niks)
a mythical bird that was said to burn itself to death on a fire and be born again from the ashes.

**phone**[1] *noun* (**phones**)
a telephone.

**phone**[2] *verb* (**phones, phoning, phoned**)
to telephone.

**phonecard** *noun* (**phonecards**)
a special plastic card that lets you use a cardphone.

**phone-in** *noun* (**phone-ins**)
a broadcast programme in which listeners or viewers telephone the studio and take part in the programme.

**phosphorescent** *adjective*
that shines or glows in the dark.
**phosphorescence** *noun*

**phosphorus** *noun*
a yellowish substance that glows in the dark.
**phosphoric** *adjective*

**photo** *noun* (**photos**)
a photograph.

**photocopier** *noun* (**photocopiers**)
a machine that makes photocopies.

**photocopy** *noun* (**photocopies**)
a copy of a document, page, etc. made by photography.

**photoelectric** *adjective*
of or using the electrical effects of light.
**photoelectric cell,** an electronic device that sends out electricity when light falls on it.

**photo-finish** *noun* (**photo-finishes**)
a very close finish of a race, photographed so that the winner can be decided.

**photograph**[1] *noun* (**photographs**)
a picture made on film, using a camera.
**photographic** *adjective*, **photography** *noun*

**photograph**[2] *verb* (**photographs, photographing, photographed**)
to take a photograph of someone or something.
**photographer** *noun*

**photosynthesis** *noun*
the process by which plants use sunlight to turn carbon dioxide and water into complex substances, giving off oxygen.

**phrase**[1] *noun* (**phrases**)
1 a small group of words; (*in grammar*) a group of words that is smaller than a clause. 2 a short part of a tune.

**phrase**[2] *verb* (**phrases, phrasing, phrased**)
to put something into words.

**physical** *adjective*
1 of or concerned with your body. 2 of things that you can touch or see.
**physical education**, gymnastics or other exercises that you do to keep healthy.
**physical geography**, the branch of geography that deals with natural features such as rivers and mountains.
**physically** *adverb*

**physician** *noun* (**physicians**)
a doctor.

**physics** *noun*
the study of energy, movement, heat, light, sound, etc.
**physicist** *noun*

**physiology** *noun*
(*say* fiz-i-ol-ŏ-ji)
the study of the bodies of people and other living things.
**physiological** *adjective*, **physiologist** *noun*

**pi** *noun*
(*say* pie)
a number roughly equal to 3.14159, shown by the symbol $\pi$ and used in calculating the circumference and area of circles, *The diameter of a circle multiplied by pi gives the circumference.*

**pianist** *noun* (**pianists**)
someone who plays the piano.

**piano** *noun* (**pianos**)
a large musical instrument with a keyboard.

**piccolo** *noun* (**piccolos**)
a small flute.

**pick**[1] *verb* (**picks, picking, picked**)
1 to choose, *Pick someone to dance with.*
2 to take something from where it is, *She picked some flowers.* 3 to steal from someone's pocket. 4 to open a lock without using a key. 5 to pull bits off or out of something.
**pick holes in something**, to find faults in something.
**pick on**, to keep criticizing or bothering a particular person.
**pick up**, to take something upwards from where it is; to collect a thing; to take someone with you in a vehicle; to manage to hear something; to improve, *I picked up a piece of litter. Can you pick up the parcel from their office? I'll drive over and pick you up. This radio can pick up messages from aircraft. Will the economy pick up?*

**pick**[2] *noun*
1 a choice, *Take your pick.* 2 the best part of something, *We got there first and had the pick of the crop.*

**pick**[3] *noun* (**picks**)
a pickaxe.

**pickaxe** *noun* (**pickaxes**)
a heavy pointed tool with a long handle, for breaking up hard ground, concrete, etc.

**picket**[1] *noun* (**pickets**)
a group of strikers who try to persuade other people not to work.

**picket**[2] *verb* (**pickets, picketing, picketed**)
to act as a picket during a strike.

**pickle**[1] *noun* (**pickles**)
1 a strong-tasting food made of vegetables, etc. preserved in vinegar. 2 (*informal*) a difficulty, *Now we're in a pretty pickle!*

**pickle**[2] *verb* (**pickles, pickling, pickled**)
to preserve something in vinegar or salt water.

**pickpocket** *noun* (**pickpockets**)
someone who steals from people's pockets.

**pick-up** *noun* (**pick-ups**)
1 an open truck for carrying small loads.
2 the part of a record-player holding the stylus.

**picnic**[1] *noun* (**picnics**)
a meal eaten in the open air away from home.

**picnic**[2] *verb* (**picnics, picnicking, picnicked**)
to have a picnic.
**picnicker** *noun*

**pictogram** *noun* (**pictograms**)
1 a picture that represents a word or a phrase. 2 a way of showing numbers, statistics, etc. as a picture.

**pictorial** *adjective*
with or using pictures.
**pictorially** *adverb*

**picture**[1] *noun* (**pictures**)
1 a painting, drawing, or photograph.
2 a film at the cinema.
**in the picture,** knowing the facts about something.

**picture**[2] *verb* (**pictures, picturing, pictured**)
1 to show someone or something in a picture. 2 to imagine someone or something.

**picturesque** *adjective*
(*say* pik-cher-**esk**)
1 attractive or charming, *a picturesque village.* 2 vivid, *a picturesque account of the battle.*

**pie** *noun* (**pies**)
meat or fruit covered with pastry and baked.
**pie chart,** a way of showing how some quantity is divided up, using a circle divided into sectors to represent the parts of the quantity.

**piece**[1] *noun* (**pieces**)
1 a part of something; a bit. 2 something written, composed, etc., *a piece of music.*
3 one of the objects used on a board to play a game, *a chess-piece.*
**in one piece,** not broken.
**piece by piece,** gradually; one part at a time.

**piece**[2] *verb* (**pieces, piecing, pieced**)
to join pieces together to make something, *The detective pieced together what had really happened.*

**piecemeal** *adverb*
piece by piece.

**pier** *noun* (**piers**)
1 a long structure built out into the sea for people to walk on. 2 a pillar supporting a bridge.

**pierce** *verb* (**pierces, piercing, pierced**)
to make a hole in or through something or someone; to make or find a way through or into something, *The torch pierced the darkness of the cave.*

**piercing** *adjective*
very strong or very loud, *a piercing shriek.*

**pig** *noun* (**pigs**)
1 a fat animal with short legs and a blunt snout, kept by farmers for its meat.
2 (*informal*) someone who is greedy, dirty, or unpleasant.
**piggy** *adjective* and *noun*

**pigeon** *noun* (**pigeons**)
1 a common grey bird with a small head and large chest. 2 (*informal*) someone's business or responsibility, *That's his pigeon.*
**homing pigeon,** a pigeon that can be taught to fly home from far away.

**pigeon-hole** *noun* (**pigeon-holes**)
a small compartment where you can put papers, letters, etc., especially for someone to collect.

**piggy-back** *noun* (**piggy-backs**)
a ride on someone's back.

**pig-headed** *adjective*
obstinate.

**piglet** *noun* (**piglets**)
a young pig.

**pigment** *noun* (**pigments**)
a substance that colours something.

**pigmy** *noun* (**pigmies**)
a pygmy.

**pigsty** *noun* (**pigsties**)
1 a building for pigs. 2 (*informal*) a very untidy room or place.

**pigtail** *noun* (**pigtails**)
a single plait of hair at the back of your head.

**pike** *noun* (**pikes**)
1 a large fish that lives in rivers and lakes.
2 a heavy spear.

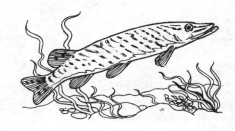

**pilchard** *noun* (pilchards)
a small sea-fish.

**pile**¹ *noun* (piles)
1 a number of things on top of one another.
2 (*informal*) a large amount of something,
especially money.

**pile**² *noun* (piles)
a heavy beam driven vertically into the
ground to support something.

**pile**³ *verb* (piles, piling, piled)
to put things on top of one another.
**pile up**, to become numerous, *Jobs were
piling up.*

**pilfer** *verb* (pilfers, pilfering, pilfered)
to steal small things.

**pilgrim** *noun* (pilgrims)
someone who goes on a journey to a holy
place.

**pilgrimage** *noun* (pilgrimages)
a journey to a holy place.

**pill** *noun* (pills)
a small pellet of medicine.
**the pill**, a special kind of pill taken by a
woman to prevent her from becoming
pregnant.

**pillar** *noun* (pillars)
a tall stone or wooden post.

**pillar-box** *noun* (pillar-boxes)
a post-box standing in a street.

**pillion** *noun* (pillions)
the seat on a motor cycle behind the
driver's seat.

**pillow** *noun* (pillows)
a cushion for a person to rest his or her
head on, especially in bed.

**pillowcase** *noun* (pillowcases)
a cover made of cotton, linen, etc. for a
pillow.

**pilot**¹ *noun* (pilots)
1 someone who flies an aircraft. 2 someone
who helps to steer a ship through narrow
or dangerous places.

**pilot**² *verb* (pilots, piloting, piloted)
to be a pilot of an aircraft or ship.

**pimple** *noun* (pimples)
a small, round swelling on the skin.
**pimply** *adjective*

**pin**¹ *noun* (pins)
1 a short piece of metal with a sharp point
and a rounded head, used to fasten pieces
of paper, cloth, etc. together. 2 a pointed
device for fixing or marking something.
**pins and needles**, a tingling feeling.

**pin**² *verb* (pins, pinning, pinned)
1 to fasten something with a pin. 2 to keep
a person or thing in one place, *He was
pinned under the wreckage.*

**pinafore** *noun* (pinafores)
a piece of clothing that you wear over the
front of your body to protect your clothes.
**pinafore dress**, a dress without collar or
sleeves.

**pincer** *noun* (pincers)
the claw of a shellfish such as the lobster.

**pincers** *plural noun*
a tool for gripping and pulling things,
especially for pulling out nails.

**pinch**¹ *verb* (pinches, pinching, pinched)
1 to squeeze something tightly between two
things, especially between your finger and
thumb. 2 (*informal*) to steal.

**pinch**² *noun* (pinches)
1 a firm squeezing movement. 2 the
amount you can pick up between the tips of
your finger and thumb, *a pinch of salt.*
**at a pinch**, if it is necessary.

**pincushion** *noun* (pincushions)
a small pad in which needles and pins are
stuck to keep them ready for use.

**pine**¹ *noun* (pines)
an evergreen tree with leaves shaped like
needles.

**pine**² *verb* (pines, pining, pined)
1 to long for someone or something. 2 to
become weak or ill through sorrow or
yearning.

**pineapple** *noun* (**pineapples**)
a large tropical fruit with prickly leaves and skin.

**ping-pong** *noun*
table tennis.

**pink**¹ *adjective* (**pinker, pinkest**)
pale red.

**pink**² *noun* (**pinks**)
a sweet-smelling garden flower.

**pint** *noun* (**pints**)
an eighth of a gallon, about 568 millilitres (British pint) or 473 millilitres (American pint).

**pioneer** *noun* (**pioneers**)
one of the first people to go to a place, do something, find out about a subject, etc.

**pious** *adjective*
very religious.
**piously** *adverb*

**pip** *noun* (**pips**)
1 a seed of an apple, orange, pear, etc. 2 one of the spots on playing-cards, dice, or dominoes. 3 a short, high-pitched sound, *She heard the 6 pips of the time-signal on the radio.*

**pipe**¹ *noun* (**pipes**)
1 a tube for carrying water, gas, etc. from one place to another. 2 a short tube with a small bowl at one end, used to smoke tobacco. 3 a tubular musical instrument.
**the pipes,** bagpipes.

**pipe**² *verb* (**pipes, piping, piped**)
1 to send something along pipes or wires. 2 to play music on a pipe or the bagpipes.
**pipe down,** (*informal*) be quiet.
**piping hot,** very hot.

**pipeline** *noun* (**pipelines**)
a pipe for carrying oil, water, etc. a long distance.

**piper** *noun* (**pipers**)
someone who plays a pipe or the bagpipes.

**pirate** *noun* (**pirates**)
a sailor who attacks and robs other ships.
**piracy** *noun*, **piratical** *adjective*

**pistil** *noun* (**pistils**)
the part of a flower that produces the seed.

**pistol** *noun* (**pistols**)
a small gun for use with one hand.

**piston** *noun* (**pistons**)
a disc that moves up and down inside a cylinder in an engine, pump, etc.

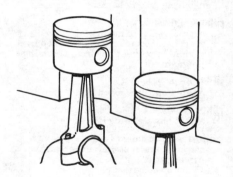

**pit**¹ *noun* (**pits**)
1 a deep hole or hollow. 2 a coal-mine. 3 the part of a race circuit where racing cars are refuelled, repaired, etc.

**pit**² *verb* (**pits, pitting, pitted**)
1 to make deep holes or hollows in something, *The ground was pitted with craters.* 2 to put someone in competition with someone else, *He was pitted against their strongest player.*

**pitch**¹ *noun* (**pitches**)
1 a piece of ground marked out for cricket, football, or another game. 2 the height of a voice or musical note. 3 intensity; strength, *Excitement was at a high pitch.*

**pitch**² *noun*
a black, sticky substance like tar.
**pitch-black** or **pitch-dark,** very black or dark; with no light at all.

**pitch**³ *verb* (**pitches, pitching, pitched**)
1 to throw. 2 to put up a tent. 3 to fall heavily, *He tripped over the doorstep and pitched headlong.* 4 to move up and down on a rough sea. 5 to set something at a particular height, *We must pitch the standard so that only the best candidates pass the test.*
**pitched battle,** a battle between troops in prepared positions.
**pitch in,** to start working or eating vigorously.

**pitcher** *noun* (**pitchers**)
a large jug, usually with two handles.

**pitchfork** *noun* (**pitchforks**)
a large fork with two prongs for lifting hay.

**pitfall** *noun* (**pitfalls**)
an unsuspected danger or difficulty.

**pitiful** *adjective*
1 causing pity, *a pitiful sight.* 2 inadequate; arousing contempt, *a pitiful attempt to make us laugh.*
**pitifully** *adverb*

**pitiless** *adjective*
having or showing no pity.
**pitilessly** *adverb*

**pitta** *noun*
a type of Greek bread made in small, flat pieces.

**pity**¹ *noun*
1 the feeling of being sorry that someone is in pain or trouble, *I feel pity for the homeless people.* 2 something that you are sorry about, *It's a pity we can't meet.*
**take pity on someone,** to help someone who is in trouble.

**pity**² *verb* (**pitied, pitying, pitied**)
to feel pity for someone.

**pivot** *noun* (**pivots**)
a point on which something turns or balances.

**pixie** or **pixy** *noun* (**pixies**)
a small fairy.

**pizza** *noun* (**pizzas**)
(*say* **peet-să**)
a layer of dough covered with cheese, vegetables, etc. and baked.

**pizzicato** *adverb* and *adjective*
(*say* pit-si-**kah**-toh)
plucking the strings of a musical instrument.

**placard** *noun* (**placards**)
a large notice or advertisement for everyone to read; a notice carried by a protester etc.

**place**¹ *noun* (**places**)
1 a particular part of space, especially where something belongs; a position or area. 2 a seat, *Save me a place.*
**from place to place,** from one place to another; travelling around.
**in place,** in the proper position.
**in place of,** instead of.
**out of place,** not in the proper position; unsuitable, *Her shoulder was out of place. That tatty jacket would look out of place in a restaurant.*
**place-name,** the name of a town, village, etc.
**take place,** to happen.

**place**² *verb* (**places, placing, placed**)
to put something in a particular place.

**placid** *adjective*
calm; peaceful.
**placidity** *noun*, **placidly** *adverb*

**plague**¹ *noun* (**plagues**)
1 a dangerous illness that spreads very quickly. 2 a large number of pests, *a plague of locusts.*

**plague**² *verb* (**plagues, plaguing, plagued**)
to pester or annoy someone, *They were plagued with enquiries.*

**plaice** *noun* (**plaice**)
a flat sea-fish that can be eaten.

**plaid** *noun* (**plaids**)
(*say* plad)
cloth with a tartan or chequered pattern.

**plain**¹ *adjective* (**plainer, plainest**)
1 not decorated. 2 not pretty. 3 easy to understand or see. 4 frank; straightforward.
**plain clothes,** civilian clothes worn instead of a uniform.
**plainly** *adverb*, **plainness** *noun*

**plain**² *noun* (**plains**)
a large area of flat country.

**plaintiff** *noun* (**plaintiffs**)
a person who brings a complaint against someone else to a lawcourt.

**plaintive** *adjective*
that sounds sad, *a plaintive cry.*
**plaintively** *adverb*

**plait**¹ *noun* (**plaits**)
(*say* plat)
a length of hair, rope, etc. with several strands twisted together.

**plait**² *verb* (**plaits, plaiting, plaited**)
(*say* plat)
to make something into a plait.

**plan**<sup>1</sup> *noun* (**plans**)
1 a way of doing something, thought out in advance. 2 a drawing showing what something should look like. 3 a map of a town or district.

**plan**<sup>2</sup> *verb* (**plans, planning, planned**)
to think out a way of doing something.
**planner** *noun*

**plane**<sup>1</sup> *noun* (**planes**)
1 an aeroplane. 2 a tool for making wood smooth. 3 a flat surface.
**plane shape,** (*in Mathematics*) a shape like a square or a triangle that has length and width only.

**plane**<sup>2</sup> *noun* (**planes**)
a tree with wide leaves.

**plane**<sup>3</sup> *verb* (**planes, planing, planed**)
to smooth wood with a plane.

**planet** *noun* (**planets**)
a large object that orbits the sun or other stars, *The main planets of the solar system are Mercury, Venus, Earth, Mars, Jupiter, Saturn, Uranus, Neptune, and Pluto.*
**planetary** *adjective*

**plank** *noun* (**planks**)
a long, flat piece of wood.

**plankton** *noun*
tiny creatures that float in the sea, lakes, etc.

**plant**<sup>1</sup> *noun* (**plants**)
1 something that grows out of the ground, *Flowers, bushes, trees, and vegetables are plants.* 2 a factory or its equipment.

**plant**<sup>2</sup> *verb* (**plants, planting, planted**)
1 to put something in the ground to grow. 2 to put something firmly in place, *He planted his feet and took hold of the rope.* 3 to hide something where it will be found, usually to cause someone trouble, *Someone planted a packet of drugs on him.*
**planter** *noun*

**plantain** *noun* (**plantains**)
a tropical tree with a fruit like a banana.

**plantation** *noun* (**plantations**)
an area of land where tobacco, tea, etc. is planted.

**plaque** *noun* (**plaques**)
(*say* plak or plahk)
1 a metal or porcelain plate fixed on a wall as a memorial or an ornament. 2 a substance that forms a thin layer on your teeth, allowing bacteria to gather.

**plasma** *noun*
(*say* plaz-mă)
the colourless liquid part of blood which carries the corpuscles.

**plaster**<sup>1</sup> *noun* (**plasters**)
1 a small covering that sticks to the skin around a wound. 2 a mixture of lime, sand, water, etc. used to cover walls and ceilings.
**plaster of Paris,** a white paste used for making moulds and cast shapes.

**plaster**<sup>2</sup> *verb* (**plasters, plastering, plastered**)
1 to cover a surface with plaster. 2 to cover something thickly, *The toddlers plastered the floor with mud.*
**plasterer** *noun*

**plastered** *adjective*
(*informal*) drunk.

**plastic**<sup>1</sup> *noun* (**plastics**)
a strong, light, synthetic substance that can be moulded into different shapes.

**plastic**<sup>2</sup> *adjective*
made of plastic, *a plastic bag.*
**plastic surgery,** work done by a surgeon to alter or mend parts of someone's body.

**Plasticine** *noun*
(*trademark*) a soft, coloured, easily shaped substance used for making models.

**plate**<sup>1</sup> *noun* (**plates**)
1 a dish that is flat or almost flat. 2 a flat sheet of metal, glass, etc. 3 one of the large areas of rock that make up the earth's crust. 4 an illustration on a separate page in a book.
**plateful** *noun*

**plate**<sup>2</sup> *verb* (**plates, plating, plated**)
to coat metal with a thin layer of gold, silver, tin, etc.

**plateau** *noun* (**plateaux**)
(*say* plat-oh)
a flat area of high land.

**platform** *noun* (**platforms**)
1 the raised area along the side of the line at a railway station. 2 a small stage in a hall. 3 the policies of a political party, *They spoke from a very right-wing platform.*

**platinum** *noun*
a silver-coloured metal that does not lose its brightness.

**platoon** *noun* (**platoons**)
a small unit of soldiers.

**plod**

**platypus** *noun* (**platypuses**)
an Australian animal with a beak and feet like those of a duck.

**play**[1] *verb* (**plays, playing, played**)
1 to take part in a game or other amusement. 2 to make music or sound with a musical instrument, record-player, etc. 3 to perform a part in a play or film.
**play about, play around,** or **play up,** to be naughty.
**player** *noun*

**play**[2] *noun* (**plays**)
1 a story acted on a stage or broadcast on radio or television. 2 playing; having fun.

**playback** *noun* (**playbacks**)
playing something that has been recorded.

**playful** *adjective*
wanting to play; full of fun; not serious.
**playfully** *adverb*, **playfulness** *noun*

**playground** *noun* (**playgrounds**)
a place out of doors where children can play.

**playgroup** *noun* (**playgroups**)
a group of children who are too young to go to school, who play together regularly, with adults to take care of them.

**playing-card** *noun* (**playing-cards**)
one of a set of cards used for playing games.

**playing-field** *noun* (**playing-fields**)
a grassy field for outdoor games.

**playmate** *noun* (**playmates**)
someone that you play games with.

**playtime** *noun* (**playtimes**)
the time when schoolchildren may go out to play.

**playwright** *noun* (**playwrights**)
someone who writes plays.

**plc** short for **public limited company**.

**plea** *noun* (**pleas**)
1 a request or appeal. 2 a statement made by or for a person charged with an offence, in a lawcourt, *a plea of not guilty*.

**plead** *verb* (**pleads, pleading, pleaded**)
to make a request or appeal.
**plead guilty,** to admit in a lawcourt that you are guilty.

**pleasant** *adjective* (**pleasanter, pleasantest**)
that pleases you; that you like.
**pleasantly** *adverb*

**please** *verb* (**pleases, pleasing, pleased**)
1 to make someone happy or satisfied, *Nothing pleases him*. 2 used when you want to make a request polite, *Shut the door, please. Please may I have a slice of cake?* 3 to wish; to choose, *Do as you please*.

**pleasure** *noun* (**pleasures**)
being pleased; something that pleases you.
**with pleasure,** gladly; willingly.
**pleasurable** *adjective*

**pleat** *noun* (**pleats**)
a fold made in the cloth of a garment.
**pleated** *adjective*

**pledge** *noun* (**pledges**)
a solemn promise.

**plentiful** *adjective*
large in amount.
**plentifully** *adverb*

**plenty** *noun*
a lot of something; more than enough, *We have plenty of chairs. You don't need to bring any food – we have plenty*.

**pliable** *adjective*
1 easy to bend, *a pliable stick*. 2 easy to influence, *He is so pliable that he will do anything his friends suggest*.
**pliant** *adjective*

**pliers** *plural noun*
a tool for gripping something or for breaking wire.

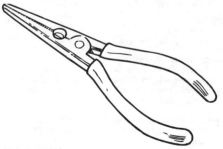

**plight** *noun* (**plights**)
a difficult situation.

**plod** *verb* (**plods, plodding, plodded**)
1 to walk slowly and heavily. 2 to work slowly but steadily.
**plodder** *noun*

**plop** *noun* (**plops**)
the sound of something dropping into water.

**plot**¹ *noun* (**plots**)
1 a secret plan. 2 what happens in a story, play, film, etc. 3 a piece of ground for a house or garden.

**plot**² *verb* (**plots, plotting, plotted**)
to make a secret plan.
**plotter** *noun*

**plough**¹ *noun* (**ploughs**)
(*say* plow)
a device used on farms for turning over the soil.

**plough**² *verb* (**ploughs, ploughing, ploughed**)
(*say* plow)
1 to turn over soil with a plough. 2 to go through something with difficulty, *He ploughed through the book.*
**ploughman** *noun*

**plover** *noun* (**plovers**)
(*say* pluv-er)
a long-legged wading bird.

**pluck**¹ *verb* (**plucks, plucking, plucked**)
1 to pull the feathers off a bird. 2 to pick a flower or fruit. 3 to pull something up or out, *She plucked out the splinter.* 4 to pull a string and let it go again.
**pluck up courage**, to overcome your fear.

**pluck**² *noun*
bravery.
**pluckily** *adverb*, **plucky** *adjective*

**plug**¹ *noun* (**plugs**)
1 something used to stop up a hole. 2 the part by which an electric wire is fitted into a socket. 3 (*informal*) a piece of publicity for something.

**plug**² *verb* (**plugs, plugging, plugged**)
1 to stop up a hole. 2 (*informal*) to publicize something.
**plug in**, to put an electric plug into a socket.

**plum** *noun* (**plums**)
a soft, juicy fruit with a stone in the middle.

**plumage** *noun*
(*say* ploo-mij)
feathers.

**plumb** *verb* (**plumbs, plumbing, plumbed**)
1 to measure how deep something is. 2 to reach the bottom of something.

**plumber** *noun* (**plumbers**)
someone who fits and mends water-pipes in a building.

**plumbing** *noun*
1 the work of a plumber. 2 the water-pipes and water-tanks in a building.

**plume** *noun* (**plumes**)
1 a large feather. 2 something shaped like a feather, *a plume of smoke.*
**plumed** *adjective*

**plump**¹ *adjective* (**plumper, plumpest**)
rounded; slightly fat, *a baby with short, plump arms and legs. You're getting a bit plump – how much exercise do you get?*

**plump**² *verb* (**plumps, plumping, plumped**)
**plump for**, to choose.

**plunder** *verb* (**plunders, plundering, plundered**)
to rob a place or an enemy, especially in a time of war or disorder.
**plunderer** *noun*

**plunge** *verb* (**plunges, plunging, plunged**)
1 to jump suddenly into water. 2 to put something suddenly into a liquid, *Plunge the jars into boiling water.* 3 to thrust something, *She plunged her spoon into the trifle.*

**plural**¹ *noun* (**plurals**)
the form of a word meaning more than one person or thing, *'Buns', 'children', 'mice', and 'teeth' are plurals.*

**plural**² *adjective*
of the plural; meaning more than one, *'Mice' is a plural noun.*

**plus** *preposition*
with the next number added, *2 plus 2 equals 4 (2 + 2 = 4).*

**plutonium** *noun*
(*say* ploo-**toh**-ni-ŭm)
a radioactive element used in nuclear weapons and reactors.

**plywood** *noun*
board made from thin sheets of wood glued together.

**p.m.** short for Latin *post meridiem* which means 'after midday'.

**pneumatic** *adjective*
(*say* new-**mat**-ik)
1 filled with air, *pneumatic tyres.* 2 using compressed air, *a pneumatic drill.*

**pneumonia** *noun*
(*say* new-**moh**-ni-ă)
a lung disease.

**poach** *verb* (**poaches, poaching, poached**)
1 to cook fish, or an egg without its shell, in or over boiling water. 2 to hunt animals illegally on someone else's land.
**poacher** *noun*

**pocket**¹ *noun* (**pockets**)
part of a garment shaped like a small bag, for keeping things in.
**pocket money**, a small amount of money given to a child to spend as he or she likes.
**your pocket**, what you can afford, *prices to suit your pocket.*
**pocketful** *noun*

**pocket**² *adjective*
small enough to carry in your pocket, *a pocket calculator.*

**pod** *noun* (**pods**)
a long seed-container on a pea or bean plant.

**podgy** *adjective* (**podgier, podgiest**)
short and fat.

**poem** *noun* (**poems**)
a piece of poetry.

**poet** *noun* (**poets**)
someone who writes poetry.

**poetry** *noun*
writing arranged in short lines, often with a particular rhythm.
**poetic** *adjective*, **poetical** *adjective*

**point**¹ *noun* (**points**)
1 the sharp end of something, *Don't hold that knife by the point.* 2 a dot or mark, *the decimal point.* 3 a particular place or time, *She gave up at this point.* 4 a detail; a characteristic, *He has some good points.* 5 purpose; advantage, *There's no point in hurrying.*
**point of view**, how you see things or think of things.
**points**, (in America, *switch*) a device for changing a railway train from one track to another.
**the point**, the main thing, *Come to the point.*

**point**² *verb* (**points, pointing, pointed**)
1 to show where something is, especially by holding out your finger towards it. 2 to aim something, *She pointed the gun at him.*
**point out**, to show or explain something.

**point-blank** *adjective*
**at point-blank range**, from a very short distance away, *The shot was fired at point-blank range.*

**pointed** *adjective*
1 with a sharp end, *a pointed stick.* 2 clearly directed at someone or his or her behaviour, *a pointed remark.*
**pointedly** *adverb*

**pointer** *noun* (**pointers**)
1 a stick, rod, mark, etc. used to point at something. 2 a breed of dog that points with its muzzle at birds which it has found by their smell. 3 an indication or hint, *She gave us a few pointers on finding bargains.*

**pointless** *adjective*
with no purpose or meaning.
**pointlessly** *adverb*

**point-to-point** *noun* (**point-to-points**)
a horse-race or series of horse-races on a course marked only at certain places.

**poise**¹ *noun*
1 balance. 2 a dignified, self-confident appearance.

**poise**² *verb* (**poises, poising, poised**)
to balance.

**poison**¹ *noun* (**poisons**)
a substance that can kill or harm you.
**poisonous** *adjective*

**poison**² *verb* (**poisons, poisoning, poisoned**)
1 to give poison to someone. 2 to put poison in something.
**poisoner** *noun*

**poke** *verb* (**pokes, poking, poked**)
to push something or someone hard with a stick, a finger, etc.
**poke out**, to stick out.

**poker** *noun* (**pokers**)
1 a metal rod for poking a fire. 2 a card-game in which the players bet on who has the best cards.

**polar** *adjective*
of or near the North or South Pole.

**polar bear** *noun* (**polar bears**)
a white Arctic bear.

**Polaroid camera** *noun* (**Polaroid cameras**)
(*trademark*) a camera that takes a picture and produces the finished photograph a few seconds later.

**Pole** *noun* (**Poles**)
a Polish person.

**pole**¹ *noun* (**poles**)
a long, round piece of wood or metal.
**up the pole**, (*slang*) mad; in difficulties, *Why did he say that? He must be up the pole. If it starts to rain we'll be up the pole.*

**pole**² *noun* (**poles**)
1 the **North Pole** or the **South Pole**, one of the two points at the ends of the earth's axis. 2 one end of a magnet.

**pole-vault** *noun* (**pole-vaults**)
a jump over a high bar done with the help of a long pole.

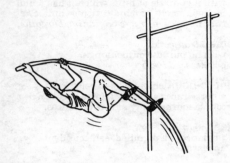

**police** *noun*
the people whose job is to catch criminals and make sure that the law is kept.
**police constable,** an ordinary member of the police.
**policeman** *noun*, **policewoman** *noun*

**policy** *noun* (**policies**)
**1** the aims and ideals of a person or group.
**2** a plan of action, *Honesty is the best policy.*

**polio** *noun*
(*say* poh-li-oh)
(*informal*) poliomyelitis.

**poliomyelitis** *noun*
(*say* poh-li-oh-my-i-ly-tis)
a disease that makes someone's body unable to move.

**Polish** *adjective*
(*say* poh-lish)
of Poland.

**polish**[1] *verb* (**polishes, polishing, polished**)
(*say* pol-ish)
to make a surface shiny or smooth.
**polish off,** (*informal*) to finish something quickly.

**polish**[2] *noun* (**polishes**)
(*say* pol-ish)
**1** a substance used in polishing. **2** a shine.

**polished** *adjective*
**1** shiny. **2** well practised or rehearsed, *a polished performance.*

**polite** *adjective* (**politer, politest**)
having good manners; respectful and thoughtful towards other people.
**politely** *adverb*, **politeness** *noun*

**political** *adjective*
connected with the governing of a country.
**politically** *adverb*

**politician** *noun* (**politicians**)
someone involved or interested in politics.

**politics** *noun*
political matters.

**polka** *noun* (**polkas**)
a lively dance.
**polka dots,** an even pattern of round dots on cloth.

**poll** *noun* (**polls**)
**1** voting at an election. **2** an opinion poll.

**pollen** *noun*
the yellow powder found inside flowers, which fertilizes the ova to make new seeds.
**pollen count,** a measurement of how much pollen there is in the air, given as a warning for people who are allergic to pollen.

**pollute** *verb* (**pollutes, polluting, polluted**)
to make a place or thing dirty or impure.
**pollution** *noun*

**polo** *noun*
a game rather like hockey, with players on horseback using mallets with long handles.
**polo-neck,** a high, round, turned-over collar.

**poltergeist** *noun* (**poltergeists**)
(*say* pol-ter-gyst)
a noisy, mischievous ghost that damages things.

**poly-** *prefix*
many, *polygon.*

**polygon** *noun* (**polygons**)
a figure or shape with many sides, *Hexagons and octagons are polygons.*

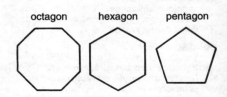

octagon    hexagon    pentagon

**polystyrene** *noun*
(*say* pol-i-**sty**-reen)
a kind of plastic used for insulating, packing, etc.

**polytechnic** *noun* (**polytechnics**)
(*say* pol-i-**tek**-nik)
a college for higher education, especially in technical or professional subjects.

USAGE: In 1992 the polytechnics changed their name to **universities**.

**polythene** *noun*
(*say* **pol**-i-theen)
a lightweight plastic used to make bags, wrappings, etc.

**pomp** *noun*
splendid, dignified display or ceremony.

**pompous** *adjective*
thinking too much of your own importance.
**pomposity** *noun*, **pompously** *adverb*

**poncho** *noun* (**ponchos**)
a piece of cloth with a hole in the middle for your head, worn as a cloak.

**pond** *noun* (**ponds**)
a small lake.

**ponder** *verb* (**ponders**, **pondering**, **pondered**)
to think seriously about something.

**ponderous** *adjective*
1 heavy. 2 not fluent; not easy to read or listen to, *He writes in a ponderous style.*
**ponderously** *adverb*

**pony** *noun* (**ponies**)
a small horse.

**pony-tail** *noun* (**pony-tails**)
a bunch of long hair tied at the back of the head.

**pony-trekking** *noun*
travelling across country on ponies for pleasure.

**poodle** *noun* (**poodles**)
a breed of dog with long, curly hair.

**pool**[1] *noun* (**pools**)
1 a pond. 2 a puddle. 3 a swimming-pool.

**pool**[2] *noun* (**pools**)
1 a fund of money. 2 a group of things shared by several people.
**the pools**, a way of gambling on the results of football matches.

**poor** *adjective* (**poorer**, **poorest**)
1 having very little money, *a poor family.*
2 bad; inadequate, *poor work.*
3 unfortunate, *Poor fellow!*

**poorly**[1] *adverb*
not adequately, *poorly dressed.*

**poorly**[2] *adjective*
unwell, *I feel poorly.*

**pop**[1] *noun* (**pops**)
1 a small explosive sound. 2 a fizzy drink.

**pop**[2] *noun*
modern popular music.

**pop**[3] *verb* (**pops**, **popping**, **popped**)
1 to make a small explosive sound.
2 (*informal*) to go quickly; to put something quickly, *I'm just popping out to the shop. She popped the pie in the oven.*

**popcorn** *noun*
maize heated till it bursts, making light, fluffy balls which are flavoured and eaten.

**Pope** *noun* (**Popes**)
the leader of the Roman Catholic Church.

**poplar** *noun* (**poplars**)
    a tall, straight tree.

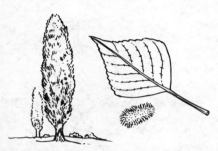

**poppadam** or **poppadom** *noun* (**poppadams** or **poppadoms**)
    a thin, crisp pancake eaten with Indian food.

**poppy** *noun* (**poppies**)
    a red flower.

**popular** *adjective*
    liked by a lot of people.
    **popular culture**, music, fashions, pastimes, television programmes, shows, etc. that a lot of people like.
    **popularity** *noun*, **popularize** *verb*, **popularly** *adverb*

**populated** *adjective*
    that has people living there, *The land is thinly populated.*

**population** *noun* (**populations**)
    the people who live in a particular place.

**populous** *adjective*
    inhabited by a lot of people.

**porcelain** *noun*
    (*say* por-sĕ-lin)
    a fine kind of china.

**porch** *noun* (**porches**)
    a small roofed area outside the door of a building.

**porcupine** *noun* (**porcupines**)
    a small animal covered with long prickles.

**pore**[1] *noun* (**pores**)
    a tiny opening in the skin through which sweat passes.

**pore**[2] *verb* (**pores, poring, pored**)
    **pore over**, to study something closely.

    USAGE: Do not confuse **pore** with **pour**, which means to make liquid flow out of a container, to flow, to rain heavily, or to come or go in large amounts.

**pork** *noun*
    meat from a pig.

**pornography** *noun*
    (*say* por-**nog**-ră-fi)
    obscene pictures, writings, etc.
    **pornographer** *noun*, **pornographic** *adjective*

**porous** *adjective*
    that allows liquid or air to pass through, *Sandy soil is porous.*
    **porosity** *noun*

**porpoise** *noun* (**porpoises**)
    (*say* por-pŭs)
    a sea-animal like a small whale.

**porridge** *noun*
    oatmeal boiled in water to make a thick paste that you can eat.

**port**[1] *noun* (**ports**)
    1 a harbour. 2 a city or town with a harbour. 3 the left side of a ship or aircraft when you are facing forward.

**port**[2] *noun*
    a strong red Portuguese wine.

**portable** *adjective*
    that you can carry, *a portable tape recorder.*

**portcullis** *noun* (**portcullises**)
    a grating that can be lowered to block the gateway to a castle.

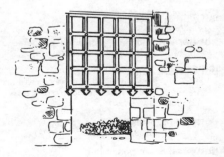

**porter**[1] *noun* (**porters**)
    someone whose job is to carry other people's luggage at railway stations, hotels, etc.

**porter**[2] *noun* (**porters**)
someone whose job is to look after the entrance to a building.

**porthole** *noun* (**portholes**)
a small round window in the side of a ship or aircraft.

**portion** *noun* (**portions**)
a part or share given to someone.

**portly** *adjective* (**portlier, portliest**)
rather fat, *a portly old gentleman*.
**portliness** *noun*

**portrait** *noun* (**portraits**)
a picture of a person.

**portray** *verb* (**portrays, portraying, portrayed**)
1 to make a portrait of someone. 2 to describe or show something, *The play portrays the king as a kind man*.
**portrayal** *noun*

**Portuguese** *adjective*
of Portugal.

**pose**[1] *noun* (**poses**)
1 a position in which someone can paint a picture or take a photograph of you.
2 a pretence; unnatural behaviour to impress people.

**pose**[2] *verb* (**poses, posing, posed**)
1 to put your body into a particular position. 2 to put someone into a particular position to be painted or photographed. 3 to pretend, *The thief posed as a Gas Board official*. 4 to present a question or problem, *Icy weather always poses a problem to motorists*.

**poser** *noun* (**posers**)
1 a puzzling question or problem.
2 someone who behaves in an unnatural way to impress people.

**posh** *adjective* (**posher, poshest**)
(*informal*) 1 very smart, *a posh hotel*. 2 of a high social class, *She doesn't approve of posh people*.

**position** *noun* (**positions**)
1 the place where something is or should be. 2 the way in which someone or something is placed or arranged, *in a sitting position*. 3 a situation or condition, *I am in no position to help you*. 4 a regular job.

**positive** *adjective*
1 sure; definite, *I am positive that my book was in my desk*. 2 that says 'yes', *a positive answer*. 3 more than nought, *positive numbers*. 4 of the kind of electric charge that lacks electrons.
**positively** *adverb*

**posse** *noun* (**posses**)
(*say* poss-i)
1 a group of people that helps a sheriff in the USA. 2 a gang.

**possess** *verb* (**possesses, possessing, possessed**)
to own something.
**possessed**, mad; controlled by an evil spirit.
**possessor** *noun*

**possession** *noun* (**possessions**)
1 something that you own. 2 owning something, *They gained possession of a piece of land*. 3 being controlled by an evil spirit, *demoniac possession*.

**possessive** *adjective*
1 wanting to get and keep things for yourself. 2 (*in grammar*) showing that someone owns something, *'His' and 'yours' are possessive pronouns*.

**possible** *adjective*
able to exist, happen, be done, or be used.
**as possible**, as can happen; as can be done, *Come as quickly as possible*.
**possibility** *noun*

**possibly** *adverb*
1 in any way, *That cannot possibly be right*. 2 perhaps, *I will arrive at six o'clock, or possibly earlier*.

**post**[1] *noun* (**posts**)
1 an upright piece of wood, concrete, metal, etc., usually fixed in the ground. 2 the post marking the start or finish of a race, *He was left at the post*.

**post**[2] *noun* (**posts**)
1 the carrying of letters, parcels, etc.
2 letters, parcels, etc. carried by post; mail.
3 a collection or delivery of mail, *The last post is at 4 p.m.*

**post**[3] *noun* (**posts**)
1 a regular job. 2 the place where a sentry stands. 3 a place occupied by soldiers, traders, etc.

**post**[4] *verb* (**posts, posting, posted**)
1 to send a letter, parcel, or card to someone. 2 to put a letter, card, etc. into a post-box.

**post**[5] *verb* (**posts, posting, posted**)
to put up a notice, poster, etc.

**post-** *prefix*
after, *the post-war years*.

**postage** *noun*
the cost of sending something by post.
**postage stamp**, a small piece of paper that you must stick on a letter, parcel, etc. before it is posted.

**postal** *adjective*
of or by the post.
**postal order**, a document bought from a post office, used for sending money by post.

**post-box** *noun* (post-boxes)
a box into which you place letters to be sent by post.

**postcard** *noun* (postcards)
a piece of card that you can write a message on and post.

**postcode** *noun* (postcodes)
(in America, *zipcode*) a group of letters and numbers included in an address to help sorting, *My postcode is OX2 7SA.*

**poster** *noun* (posters)
a large notice for everyone to read.

**postman** *noun* (postmen)
someone who delivers letters, parcels, etc.

**postmark** *noun* (postmarks)
an official mark stamped on something sent by post.

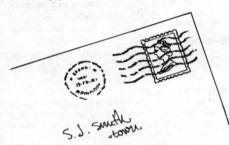

**post-mortem** *noun* (post-mortems)
an examination of a dead person to find out why he or she died.

**post office** *noun* (post offices)
a place where you can buy stamps, postal orders, etc., post letters, send parcels, etc.

**postpone** *verb* (postpones, postponing, postponed)
to decide that something will happen later than you originally intended.
**postponement** *noun*

**postscript** *noun* (postscripts)
something extra added at the end of a letter or book.

**posture** *noun* (postures)
the way that someone stands, sits, or walks.

**pot**[1] *noun* (pots)
1 a round container. 2 a chamber-pot.
**go to pot**, (*slang*) to be ruined.
**pots**, (*slang*) lots of something, *He's got pots of money.*

**pot**[2] *verb* (pots, potting, potted)
to put something into a pot.
**potted**, (*informal*) shortened, *a potted version.*

**potassium** *noun*
a soft, silvery-white metallic substance that is essential for living things.

**potato** *noun* (potatoes)
a vegetable that grows underground.

**potent** *adjective*
powerful.
**potency** *noun*, **potently** *adverb*

**potential**[1] *adjective*
capable of happening or being used sometime in the future, *potential energy.*
**potentiality** *noun*, **potentially** *adverb*

**potential**[2] *noun*
being able to do something, especially in the future.

**pot-hole** *noun* (pot-holes)
1 a deep natural hole in the ground.
2 a hole in a road.

**pot-holing** *noun*
exploring underground pot-holes.
**pot-holer** *noun*

**potion** *noun* (potions)
(*say* poh-shŏn)
a drink containing medicine, poison, or something magical.

**potter**[1] *verb* (potters, pottering, pottered)
to work in a leisurely or casual way.

**potter**[2] *noun* (potters)
someone who makes pottery.

**pottery** *noun* (potteries)
1 pots, cups, plates, etc. made of baked clay. 2 a place where a potter works.

**potty**[1] *adjective* (pottier, pottiest)
(*slang*) mad.

**potty**[2] *noun* (potties)
(*informal*) a child's chamber-pot.

**pouch** *noun* (pouches)
1 a small bag. 2 a kind of pocket that some animals have in their skin, *Kangaroos keep their babies in pouches.*

**poultry** *noun*
birds kept for their eggs and meat, *Chickens, geese, and turkeys are poultry.*

**pounce** *verb* (pounces, pouncing, pounced)
to jump on someone or something suddenly

**pound**¹ *noun* (**pounds**)
1 a unit of money, equal to 100 pence. 2 a unit of weight, equal to 16 ounces or about 454 grams.

**pound**² *verb* (**pounds, pounding, pounded**)
1 to hit something often, especially so as to crush it, *Pound the chalk into a fine powder.* 2 to hit something or someone heavily, *The boxer pounded his opponent.* 3 to make a dull, heavy sound, *We could hear large guns pounding in the distance.*

**pour** *verb* (**pours, pouring, poured**)
1 to make a liquid flow out of a container. 2 to flow. 3 to rain heavily, *It was pouring.* 4 to come or go in large amounts, *Letters poured in.*

USAGE: Do not confuse the phrase 'pour over' with **pore over**, which means to study something closely.

**pout** *verb* (**pouts, pouting, pouted**)
to stick out your lips when you are not pleased.

**poverty** *noun*
being poor.

**powder**¹ *noun* (**powders**)
1 tiny pieces of something dry, like flour or dust. 2 a dust-like coloured substance used as make-up on the face.
**powdery** *adjective*

**powder**² *verb* (**powders, powdering, powdered**)
1 to make something into powder. 2 to put powder on, *I am powdering my face.*

**power** *noun* (**powers**)
1 strength; great force, energy, or might. 2 ability; authority. 3 a powerful country. 4 electricity or other energy. 5 (*in Mathematics*) the result obtained by multiplying a number by itself one or more times, *27 is the third power of 3 (3 × 3 × 3 = 27).*
**powered** *adjective*

**powerful** *adjective*
very strong or important.
**powerfully** *adverb*

**powerhouse** *noun* (**powerhouses**)
a power station.

**powerless** *adjective*
not able to control what is happening; not able to prevent something from happening.

**power station** *noun* (**power stations**)
a building where electricity is produced.

**practicable** *adjective*
possible to do or use, *a practicable plan.*

USAGE: Do not confuse **practicable** with **practical**, which is the next word in this dictionary.

**practical** *adjective*
1 able to do or make useful things, *She is very practical and can do all kinds of repairs about the house.* 2 likely to be useful, *a practical idea.* 3 concerned with doing or making things, *He has had practical experience.*
**practical joke**, an amusing trick played on someone.

**practically** *adverb*
1 in a practical way, *She is practically skilled.* 2 almost, *It's practically ready now.*

**practice** *noun* (**practices**)
1 doing something again and again so as to get better at it, *Have you done your piano practice?* 2 actually doing something rather than thinking or talking about it, *It works well in practice.* 3 the business of a doctor or lawyer.

USAGE: Do not confuse **practice**, which is a noun, with **practise**, which is a verb and is the next word in this dictionary.

**practise** *verb* (**practises, practising, practised**)
1 to do something again and again so as to get better at it. 2 to do something, especially regularly, *He practises what he preaches.* 3 to work as a doctor, lawyer, etc.

**prairie** *noun* (**prairies**)
a large area of flat grass-covered land in North America.

**praise**¹ *verb* (**praises, praising, praised**)
to say that someone or something is very good.

**praise**² *noun* (**praises**)
words that praise someone or something.

**pram** *noun* (**prams**)
a small vehicle with four wheels, to carry a baby.

**prance** *verb* (**prances, prancing, pranced**)
to jump about in a lively or happy way.

**prank** *noun* (**pranks**)
a practical joke.

**prawn** *noun* (**prawns**)
a shellfish like a large shrimp that can be eaten.

**pray** *verb* (**prays, praying, prayed**)
1 to talk to God. 2 to ask earnestly, *He prayed to be set free.*

USAGE: Do not confuse **pray** with the noun **prey**, which means an animal hunted and eaten by another animal.

**prayer** *noun* (**prayers**)
praying; what you say when you pray.
**prayer-mat**, a small mat used by Muslims when they pray.

**pre-** *prefix*
before, *the pre-war period.*

**preach** *verb* (**preaches, preaching, preached**)
to give a talk about religion or about right and wrong.
**preacher** *noun*

**precarious** *adjective*
(*say* pri-**kair**-i-ŭs)
not secure or safe.
**precariously** *adverb*

**precaution** *noun* (**precautions**)
something done to prevent future trouble or danger.

**precede** *verb* (**precedes, preceding, preceded**)
to come or go in front of someone or something.
**precedence** *noun*

**precinct** *noun* (**precincts**)
(*say* **pree**-sinkt)
1 part of a town where traffic is not allowed, *a pedestrian precinct.* 2 the area round a cathedral.

**precious** *adjective*
very valuable.

**precipice** *noun* (**precipices**)
the steep face of a mountain, cliff, etc.

**précis** *noun* (**précis**)
(*say* **pray**-see)
a statement of the main points of a piece of writing.

**precise** *adjective*
1 exact, *Are your measurements precise?*
2 clearly stated, *precise instructions.*
**precisely** *adverb*, **precision** *noun*

USAGE: Do not confuse **precise** with **concise**, which means brief, or giving a lot of information in a few words.

**predator** *noun* (**predators**)
(*say* **pred**-ă-ter)
an animal that hunts other animals, *The heron is one of the frog's predators.*
**predation** *noun*, **predatory** *adjective*

**predecessor** *noun* (**predecessors**)
(*say* **pree**-di-ses-er)
1 an ancestor. 2 someone who did the job that you do now.

**predict** *verb* (**predicts, predicting, predicted**)
to say what is going to happen before it happens.
**predictable** *adjective*, **prediction** *noun*

**predominate** *verb* (**predominates, predominating, predominated**)
to be largest in size or number, or most important, *Girls predominate in our class.*
**predominance** *noun*, **predominant** *adjective*

**preface** *noun* (**prefaces**)
(*say* **pref**-ăss)
an introduction at the beginning of a book.

**prefect** *noun* (**prefects**)
1 a school pupil who is given certain duties to perform. 2 (in some countries) a high-ranking official.

**prefer** *verb* (**prefers, preferring, preferred**)
to like one person or thing more than another.
**preference** *noun*

**preferable** *adjective*
(*say* **pref**-er-ă-bŭl)
preferred; that you want or like more, *Living close to work is preferable to making long journeys every day.*
**preferably** *adverb*

**prefix** *noun* (**prefixes**)
a word or syllable joined to the front of a word to change or add to its meaning, as in *dis*order, *out*stretched, and *un*happy.

**pregnant** *adjective*
(of a female) having an unborn baby growing inside her body.
**pregnancy** *noun*

**prehistoric** *adjective*
of a very long time ago, before written records were kept.
**prehistory** *noun*

**prejudice** *noun* (**prejudices**)
1 making up your mind without examining the facts fairly. 2 behaviour or unfair treatment that results from a prejudice.
**prejudiced** *adjective*

**preliminary** *adjective*
coming before or preparing for something.

**prelude** *noun* (**preludes**)
(*say* prel-yood)
1 an introduction or lead-up to a play, poem, event, etc. 2 a short piece of music.

**premier** *noun* (**premiers**)
(*say* prem-i-er)
the leader of a government.

> USAGE: Do not confuse **premier** with **première**, which is the next word in this dictionary.

**première** *noun* (**premières**)
(*say* prem-yair)
the first public performance of a play or showing of a film.

**premises** *plural noun*
a building with its land.
**on the premises**, in a particular building.

**premium** *noun* (**premiums**)
(*say* pree-mi-ŭm)
an amount paid regularly to an insurance company.
**at a premium**, above the normal price; valued highly.
**premium bond**, a document showing that you have lent money to the government, and giving you a chance to win a prize of money.

**preoccupied** *adjective*
with your thoughts completely occupied by something.
**preoccupation** *noun*

**prep** *noun*
(*informal*) homework.
**prep school**, a preparatory school.

**preparation** *noun* (**preparations**)
1 the action of getting something ready.
2 a thing done in order to get ready for something, *We were making last-minute preparations*. 3 homework.

**preparatory** *adjective*
(*say* pri-pa-ră-ter-i)
in preparation for something.
**preparatory school**, a school that prepares pupils for a higher school.

**prepare** *verb* (**prepares, preparing, prepared**)
to get ready.
**be prepared to do something**, to be ready or willing to do something.

**preposition** *noun* (**prepositions**)
a word put in front of a noun or pronoun to show how the noun or pronoun is connected with another word, *In the sentence 'I stayed at the seaside from Monday to Friday with my friends', 'at', 'from', 'to', and 'with' are prepositions.*

**prescribe** *verb* (**prescribes, prescribing, prescribed**)
1 to give someone a doctor's order for a particular medicine. 2 to say what must be done.

**prescription** *noun* (**prescriptions**)
a doctor's order for a medicine to be prepared.

**presence** *noun*
being at a place, *Your presence is expected.*
**in the presence of someone**, at the place where someone is.

**present**[1] *adjective*
(*say* **prez**-ĕnt)
1 in a particular place; here, *Nobody else was present.* 2 existing now, *the present King.*
**present participle**, a form of a verb used after *am, are, is,* etc. to describe an action that is happening now, or used after *was, were,* etc. to describe an action that went on for some time in the past, *In 'I am looking' and 'you were sleeping', 'looking' and 'sleeping' are present participles.*
**present tense**, a form of a verb used on its own to describe something that is happening now, *the verbs in 'I go' and 'he sees' are in the present tense.*

**present**[2] *noun*
(*say* **prez**-ĕnt)
the time now, *Our teacher is away at present.*

**present**[3] *noun* (**presents**)
(*say* **prez**-ĕnt)
something that you give to someone.

**present**[4] *verb* (**presents, presenting, presented**)
(*say* pri-**zent**)
1 to give something to someone, especially with a ceremony. 2 to put on a play or other entertainment. 3 to show something or someone, *We are here to present our latest products.*
**presentation** *noun*, **presenter** *noun*

**presently** *adverb*
soon, *I shall be with you presently.*

**preserve** *verb* (**preserves, preserving, preserved**)
to keep something safe or in good condition.
**preservation** *noun*, **preservative** *noun*

**preside** *verb* (**presides, presiding, presided**)
(*say* pri-**zyd**)
to be in charge of a meeting, council, etc., *The mayor presided over the council.*

**president** *noun* (**presidents**)
1 the person in charge of a society,
business, etc. 2 the head of a republic,
*Roosevelt and Kennedy were American
Presidents*.
**presidency** *noun*, **presidential** *adjective*

**press**[1] *verb* (**presses, pressing, pressed**)
1 to push hard on something; to squeeze
something. 2 to make something flat and
smooth. 3 to urge someone to do or give
something; to make a demand, *They
pressed him for details. We must press for
better conditions.*

**press**[2] *noun* (**presses**)
1 the action of squeezing or pushing on
something. 2 a device for flattening and
smoothing things. 3 a device or firm that
does printing. 4 newspapers; journalists.
**press conference**, an interview with a group
of journalists.

**press-up** *noun* (**press-ups**)
an exercise in which you lie face
downwards and press down with your
hands to lift your body.

**pressure** *noun* (**pressures**)
1 continuous pushing or squeezing. 2 the
force with which something pushes against
or squeezes something. 3 an action that
persuades or forces you to do something, *If
you keep up the pressure, your opponent
will make mistakes.*

**pressurize** *verb* (**pressurizes, pressurizing,
pressurized**)
1 to keep a place, vehicle, etc. at the same
air pressure all the time, *This aircraft is
pressurized.* 2 to try to force someone to do
something.

**prestige** *noun*
(*say* pres-**tee**zh)
1 good reputation, *a politician of great
prestige.* 2 honour that comes from being
successful, rich, etc., *He wanted the
prestige of owning an expensive car.*
**prestigious** *adjective*

**presumably** *adverb*
probably; according to what you may
presume.

**presume** *verb* (**presumes, presuming, presumed**)
1 to suppose, *I presumed that he was dead.*
2 to dare, *I wouldn't presume to advise you.*
**presumption** *noun*

**presumptuous** *adjective*
too bold or confident.

**pretend** *verb* (**pretends, pretending, pretended**)
1 to behave as if something untrue or
imaginary is true. 2 to claim something
dishonestly, *They pretended that they had
not been told what to do.*
**pretence** *noun*, **pretender** *noun*

**pretty**[1] *adjective* (**prettier, prettiest**)
pleasant to look at or hear; attractive.
**prettily** *adverb*, **prettiness** *noun*

**pretty**[2] *adverb*
(*informal*) quite; moderately, *It's pretty
cold outside.*

**prevail** *verb* (**prevails, prevailing, prevailed**)
1 to be most frequent or general, *a
prevailing tendency.* 2 to be successful in
a battle, contest, or game.
**prevailing wind**, the most common wind in
a particular place, *In the British Isles the
prevailing wind is south-westerly.*
**prevalent** *adjective*

**prevent** *verb* (**prevents, preventing, prevented**)
to stop something from happening; to make
something impossible.
**prevention** *noun*, **preventive** *adjective*

**preview** *noun* (**previews**)
a showing of a film, play, etc. before it is
shown to the public.

**previous** *adjective*
coming before this; preceding, *the previous
week.*
**previously** *adverb*

**prey**[1] *noun*
(*say* pray)
an animal hunted and eaten by another
animal.
**bird of prey**, a bird that lives by killing and
eating other animals.

USAGE: Do not confuse **prey** with the verb
**pray**, which means to talk to God or to ask
earnestly.

**prey**[2] *verb* (**preys, preying, preyed**)
(*say* pray)
**prey on**, to hunt and kill an animal for food;
to make someone anxious or nervous, *Owls
prey on mice and other small animals. The
worry about not earning enough money
began to prey on her mind.*

**price**[1] *noun* (**prices**)
1 the amount of money for which
something is sold. 2 what you have to give
or do to get something, *What is the price of
peace?*
**at any price**, at any cost.

**price**[2] *verb* (**prices, pricing, priced**)
to decide the price of something.

**priceless** *adjective*
1 very valuable. 2 (*informal*) very amusing.

**prick** *verb* (**pricks, pricking, pricked**)
1 to make a tiny hole in something. 2 to
hurt someone with a pin, needle, etc.
**prick up your ears**, to start listening
suddenly.

**prickle** *noun* (**prickles**)
a thin, sharp thing like a thorn.
**prickly** *adjective*

**pride** *noun* (**prides**)
1 being proud. 2 something that makes you
feel proud. 3 a group of lions.

**priest** *noun* (**priests**)
1 a member of the clergy. 2 someone who
conducts religious ceremonies; a religious
leader.
**priestess** *noun*, **priesthood** *noun*

**prig** *noun* (**prigs**)
a self-righteous person.
**priggish** *adjective*

**prim** *adjective* (**primmer, primmest**)
not liking anything rough or rude.
**primly** *adverb*, **primness** *noun*

**primary** *adjective*
first; most important.
**primary colours,** the colours from which all
other colours can be made by mixing: red,
yellow, and blue for paint, and red, green,
and violet for light.
**primary school,** a school for children aged 5
to 11.
**primarily** *adverb*

**primate** *noun* (**primates**)
an animal of the group that includes
human beings, apes, and monkeys.

**prime**<sup>1</sup> *adjective*
1 chief; most important, *the prime cause.*
2 excellent, *prime beef.*
**prime number,** a number that can only be
divided exactly by 1 or by itself, *2, 3, 5, 7,
11, and 37 are prime numbers.*

**prime**<sup>2</sup> *noun* (**primes**)
1 the best part of a person's life, *He was in
the prime of life.* 2 (*in Mathematics*) a
prime number.

**prime**<sup>3</sup> *verb* (**primes, priming, primed**)
1 to get something ready for use, *Pour
water into the pump to prime it.* 2 to put
a first coat of paint on something.

**prime minister** *noun* (**prime ministers**)
the leader of a government.

**primer** *noun* (**primers**)
1 paint used for the first coat on an
unpainted surface. 2 a textbook dealing
with the first or simplest stages of
something.

**primeval** *adjective*
(*say* pry-mee-văl)
of the earliest times of the world; ancient.

**primitive** *adjective*
1 of or at an early stage of development or
civilization, *Primitive humans were
hunters rather than farmers.* 2 not
complicated or sophisticated, *a primitive
technology.*

**primrose** *noun* (**primroses**)
a pale yellow flower that comes out in
spring.

**prince** *noun* (**princes**)
1 the son of a king or queen. 2 a man or boy
in a royal family.
**princely** *adjective*

**princess** *noun* (**princesses**)
1 the daughter of a king or queen. 2 a
woman or girl in a royal family. 3 the wife
of a prince.

**principal**<sup>1</sup> *adjective*
chief; most important, *the principal cities
of Britain.*
**principally** *adverb*

**principal**<sup>2</sup> *noun* (**principals**)
the head of a college or school.

USAGE: Do not confuse **principal** with
**principle**, which is the next word in this
dictionary.

**principle** *noun* (**principles**)
general truth, belief, or rule, *He taught me
the principles of geometry.*
**in principle,** in general, not in details.

**print**<sup>1</sup> *verb* (**prints, printing, printed**)
1 to put words or pictures on paper with a
machine. 2 to write with letters that are
not joined together. 3 to make a
photograph from a negative.
**printed circuit,** an electric circuit made by
pressing thin metal strips on to a board.

**print**<sup>2</sup> *noun* (**prints**)
1 printed words or pictures. 2 a mark made
by something pressing on a surface, *Her
thumb left a print on the glass.* 3 a
photograph made by shining light through
a negative on to sensitive paper.

**printer** *noun* (**printers**)
1 someone whose job is to put words or pictures on paper with a machine; a company that does this work. 2 (*in Computing*) a machine that puts information stored in a computer on to paper.

**printout** *noun* (**printouts**)
sheets of printed paper produced by a computer.

**priority** *noun* (**priorities**)
(*say* pry-o-ri-ti)
1 something that is more urgent or important than other things, *Repairing the roof is a priority*. 2 the right to be considered before other things, *People in need of urgent medical help will have priority*.

**prise** *verb* (**prises, prising, prised**)
to force something open, *They prised the box open*.

**prism** *noun* (**prisms**)
1 a piece of glass that breaks up light into the colours of the rainbow. 2 (*in Mathematics*) a three-dimensional object with parallel ends that are equal triangles or polygons.
**prismatic** *adjective*

**prison** *noun* (**prisons**)
a place where criminals are kept as a punishment.
**prisoner** *noun*

**private**[1] *adjective*
1 belonging to or used by a particular person or people, *a private road*. 2 that should be kept secret, *a private letter*. 3 away from people, *a private place for a swim*.
**private school**, a school that is not given money by the government, and that charges a fee for teaching its pupils.
**privacy** *noun*, **privately** *adverb*

**private**[2] *noun* (**privates**)
a soldier of the lowest rank.
**in private**, in secret; where only particular people can see, hear, or take part.

**privet** *noun*
an evergreen shrub often used to make hedges.

**privilege** *noun* (**privileges**)
a special advantage for one person or group of people.
**privileged** *adjective*

**prize**[1] *noun* (**prizes**)
1 something won in a game, competition, etc.; an award. 2 something captured from an enemy.

**prize**[2] *verb* (**prizes, prizing, prized**)
to value something highly, *She prizes her garden more than anything else*.

**pro** *noun* (**pros**)
(*informal*) someone doing a regular job for money; a professional, *Take lessons from a golf pro*.

**pro-** *prefix*
supporting, *pro-government forces*.

**probable** *adjective*
likely to be true; likely to happen.
**probability** *noun*, **probably** *adverb*

**probation** *noun*
testing a person's character or behaviour; finding out if a person is suitable for a job, club, etc.
**on probation**, being supervised by a probation officer.
**probation officer**, an official who supervises the behaviour of a convicted criminal who is not in prison.
**probationary** *adjective*

**probe**[1] *noun* (**probes**)
1 a long, thin device used to explore wounds, etc. 2 an investigation, especially one done by a journalist.

**probe**[2] *verb* (**probes, probing, probed**)
1 to explore something with a probe. 2 to investigate something.

**problem** *noun* (**problems**)
something difficult to answer, understand, or overcome.

**procedure** *noun* (**procedures**)
1 a way of doing something. 2 (*in Computing*) a separate part of a computer program, performing an operation that is needed frequently in the program.

**proceed** *verb* (**proceeds, proceeding, proceeded**)
(*say* prŏ-**seed**)
to go on; to continue.

**proceedings** *plural noun*
1 things that happen. 2 a lawsuit.

**proceeds** *plural noun*
(*say* proh-**seedz**)
the money made from a sale, show, etc.

**process**[1] *noun* (**processes**)
a series of actions for doing something or for making something with machines.

**process**[2] *verb* (**processes, processing, processed**)
to use a process to change or deal with something, *This cheese has been processed*.

**procession** *noun* (**processions**)
a number of people, vehicles, etc. moving steadily forwards.

**proclaim** *verb* (proclaims, proclaiming, proclaimed)
to announce something officially or publicly.
**proclamation** *noun*

**prod** *verb* (prods, prodding, prodded)
to push something or someone hard with a stick, finger, etc.

**prodigal** *adjective*
wasteful; extravagant.
**prodigality** *noun*, **prodigally** *adverb*

**produce**[1] *verb* (produces, producing, produced)
(*say* prŏ-**dewss**)
1 to make or create something. 2 to bring something out so that it can be seen. 3 to organize the performance of a play or the making of a film, etc.
**producer** *noun*

**produce**[2] *noun*
(*say* **prod**-yewss)
things produced, especially by farming.

**product** *noun* (products)
1 something produced, *the products of this factory*. 2 the result of multiplying two numbers, *12 is the product of 4 and 3*.

**production** *noun* (productions)
1 the action of making or creating, *a factory engaged in car production*. 2 a thing or amount made or created, *Steel production has increased*. 3 a play or film, *the longest-running West End production. a Walt Disney production.*

**productive** *adjective*
1 producing a lot of things, *a productive farm*. 2 useful, *a productive idea*.
**productivity** *noun*

**profession** *noun* (professions)
a job for which you need special knowledge and training, *The professions include being a doctor, nurse, member of the clergy, or lawyer.*

**professional**[1] *adjective*
1 of or belonging to a profession. 2 doing a regular job for money, *a professional footballer*.
**professionally** *adverb*

**professional**[2] *noun* (professionals)
1 someone doing a regular job for money, *an amateur footballer who became a professional*. 2 someone who works in a profession.

**professor** *noun* (professors)
one of the most important teachers in a university.
**professorial** *adjective*

**proficient** *adjective*
(*say* prŏ-**fish**-ĕnt)
skilled; doing something properly, *She is proficient at welding. If you practise, you will soon be proficient.*
**proficiency** *noun*, **proficiently** *adverb*

**profile** *noun* (profiles)
1 a side view of someone's face. 2 a short description of a person's life or character.

**profit**[1] *noun* (profits)
1 the extra money got by selling something for more than it cost to buy or make. 2 an advantage or benefit.

**profit**[2] *verb* (profits, profiting, profited)
to get a profit.
**profitable** *adjective*, **profitably** *adverb*

**profound** *adjective* (profounder, profoundest)
1 very deep or great. 2 showing or needing great knowledge or thought, *That was a profound comment!*
**profoundly** *adverb*, **profundity** *noun*

**profuse** *adjective* (profuser, profusest)
(*say* prŏ-**fewss**)
large in amount, *profuse wealth*.
**profusely** *adverb*, **profusion** *noun*

**program**[1] *noun* (programs)
a coded series of actions for a computer to carry out.

**program**[2] *verb* (programs, programming, programmed)
to prepare or control a computer by means of a program.
**programmer** *noun*

**programme** *noun* (programmes)
1 a show, play, talk, etc. on radio or television. 2 a list of an organized series of events; a leaflet or pamphlet giving details of an entertainment, contest, etc.

**progress**[1] *noun*
(*say* **proh**-gress)
1 forward movement; an advance, *The procession made slow progress*. 2 development or improvement, *As progress continues, computers are becoming smaller and more powerful.*

**progress**[2] *verb* (progresses, progressing, progressed)
(*say* prŏ-**gress**)
1 to move forwards. 2 to develop or improve, *Has civilization progressed in the last century?*
**progression** *noun*, **progressive** *adjective*

**prohibit** *verb* (prohibits, prohibiting, prohibited)
to forbid, *Smoking is prohibited*.
**prohibition** *noun*

# project¹

**project¹** *noun* (projects)
(*say* proj-ekt)
1 a planned task in which you find out as much as you can about something and write about it. 2 a plan.

**project²** *verb* (projects, projecting, projected)
(*say* prŏ-jekt)
1 to stick out. 2 to show a picture on a screen.
**projection** *noun*

**projector** *noun* (projectors)
a machine for showing films or photographs on a screen.
**projectionist** *noun*

**prologue** *noun* (prologues)
(*say* proh-log)
an introduction or preface.

**prolong** *verb* (prolongs, prolonging, prolonged)
to make something last longer.

**promenade** *noun* (promenades)
(*say* prom-ĕn-ahd)
1 a place suitable for walking, especially beside the seashore. 2 a slow, relaxed walk.
**promenade concert,** a concert where some of the audience stand or walk about.

**prominent** *adjective*
1 sticking out. 2 important.
**prominence** *noun*, **prominently** *adverb*

**promise¹** *noun* (promises)
1 saying that you will definitely do or not do something. 2 an indication of future success, *She shows promise.*

**promise²** *verb* (promises, promising, promised)
to say that you will definitely do or not do something, *He promised that he would be there on time.*
**promising,** likely to be good or successful, *a promising pupil.*

**promontory** *noun* (promontories)
(*say* prom-ŏn-ter-i)
a piece of high land sticking out into the sea.

**promote** *verb* (promotes, promoting, promoted)
1 to move someone to a higher rank or position. 2 to help the progress or sale of something. 3 to organize a public entertainment.
**promoter** *noun*, **promotion** *noun*

**prompt¹** *adjective* (prompter, promptest)
without delay, *a prompt reply.*
**promptly** *adverb*, **promptness** *noun*

**prompt²** *verb* (prompts, prompting, prompted)
1 to cause or encourage someone to do something. 2 to remind an actor of the words of a play, etc. if he or she forgets them.
**prompter** *noun*

**prone** *adjective*
lying face downwards.
**prone to,** likely to do or suffer something, *He is prone to jealousy.*

**prong** *noun* (prongs)
one of the pointed spikes at the end of a fork.

**pronoun** *noun* (pronouns)
a word used instead of a noun, *Pronouns are words like 'he', 'her', 'it', 'them', and 'those'.*

**pronounce** *verb* (pronounces, pronouncing, pronounced)
1 to say a sound or word in a particular way, *'Too' and 'two' are pronounced the same.* 2 to declare formally, *I now pronounce you man and wife.*
**pronounced,** obvious; definite.
**pronouncement** *noun*

**pronunciation** *noun* (pronunciations)
(*say* prŏ-nun-si-ay-shŏn)
how you pronounce something.

**proof¹** *noun* (proofs)
1 a fact which shows that something is true. 2 a printed copy of something made for checking before other copies are printed.

**proof²** *adjective*
giving protection against something, *a bullet-proof jacket.*

**prop¹** *noun* (props)
1 a support, especially made of a long piece of wood or metal. 2 a movable object, such as a piece of furniture, used on stage during a play in a theatre.

**prop²** *verb* (props, propping, propped)
to support something by leaning it on something else, *The ladder was propped up against the wall.*

**propaganda** *noun*
publicity intended to make people believe something.

**propel** *verb* (propels, propelling, propelled)
to move something forward.
**propelling pencil,** a pencil with a lead that can be moved in and out.
**propellant** *noun*

**propeller** *noun* (**propellers**)
a device with blades that spin round to
drive an aircraft or ship.

**proper** *adjective*
1 suitable; right, *Is that screwdriver the
proper size?* 2 respectable, *prim and proper.*
3 (*informal*) complete; great, *He's in a
proper mess.*
**proper noun,** the name of a particular
person or thing, *'Mary' and 'London' are
proper nouns.*
**properly** *adverb*

**property** *noun* (**properties**)
1 things that belong to someone.
2 buildings or land belonging to someone.
3 a characteristic or quality, *Rubber has
elastic properties.*

**prophecy** *noun* (**prophecies**)
(*say* **prof**-i-si)
something that someone has said will
happen, before it actually happens; saying
what will happen in the future.

USAGE: Do not confuse **prophecy** with
**prophesy**, which is a verb and is the next
word in this dictionary.

**prophesy** *verb* (**prophesies, prophesying,
prophesied**)
(*say* **prof**-i-sy)
to say that something will happen, before
it actually happens, *She prophesied that a
war would break out.*

**prophet** *noun* (**prophets**)
1 someone who can tell what is going to
happen, before it happens. 2 a great
religious teacher.
**prophetic** *adjective*

**proportion** *noun* (**proportions**)
1 a fraction; a share. 2 a ratio. 3 the correct
relationship between the size, amount, or
importance of two things.
**proportions,** size; importance, *a ship of large
proportions.*
**proportional** *adjective*, **proportionally** *adverb*,
**proportionate** *adjective*

**propose** *verb* (**proposes, proposing, proposed**)
1 to suggest an idea or plan. 2 to ask
someone to marry you.
**proposal** *noun*

**proprietor** *noun* (**proprietors**)
(*say* prŏ-**pry**-ĕt-er)
the owner of a shop or business.

**propulsion** *noun*
propelling something.

**prose** *noun*
writing that is not in verse.

**prosecute** *verb* (**prosecutes, prosecuting,
prosecuted**)
to make someone go to a lawcourt to be
tried for a crime.
**prosecution** *noun*, **prosecutor** *noun*

**prospect**[1] *noun* (**prospects**)
(*say* **pros**-pekt)
1 a possibility; a hope, *no prospects of
success.* 2 a wide view, *A vast prospect lay
before us as we stood on the hill.*

**prospect**[2] *verb* (**prospects, prospecting,
prospected**)
(*say* prŏ-**spekt**)
to search for gold or some other mineral.
**prospector** *noun*

**prosper** *verb* (**prospers, prospering, prospered**)
to be successful; to do well.

**prosperous** *adjective*
successful; rich.
**prosperity** *noun*

**prostitute** *noun* (**prostitutes**)
someone who takes part in sexual acts for
payment.

**protect** *verb* (**protects, protecting, protected**)
to keep someone or something safe.
**protection** *noun*, **protective** *adjective*,
**protector** *noun*

**protein** *noun* (**proteins**)
(*say* **proh**-teen)
a substance in food that is necessary for
growth and good health.

**protest**[1] *noun* (**protests**)
(*say* **proh**-test)
something you say or do because you
disagree with what someone else is saying
or doing.

**protest**[2] *verb* (**protests, protesting, protested**)
(*say* prŏ-**test**)
to make a protest.
**protester** *noun*

**Protestant** *noun* (**Protestants**)
(*say* **prot**-is-tănt)
a Christian who does not belong to the
Roman Catholic or Orthodox Churches.

**proton** *noun* (**protons**)
a particle of matter with a positive electric charge.

**protoplasm** *noun*
(*say* proh-tŏ-plazm)
a colourless substance of which animal and vegetable cells are made.

**prototype** *noun* (**prototypes**)
(*say* proh-tŏ-typ)
the first example of something, used as a model for the manufacture of others.

**protractor** *noun* (**protractors**)
a device for measuring angles.

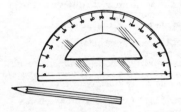

**protrude** *verb* (**protrudes, protruding, protruded**)
to stick out.
**protrusion** *noun*

**proud** *adjective* (**prouder, proudest**)
1 very pleased with yourself or with someone else who has done well, *I am proud of my sister*. 2 too satisfied because of who you are or what you have done, *He's too proud to talk to us*.
**proudly** *adverb*

**prove** *verb* (**proves, proving, proved**)
1 to show that something is true. 2 to turn out to be, *My pen proved to be useless*.

**proverb** *noun* (**proverbs**)
a short, well-known saying that states a truth, *'A stitch in time saves nine'* and *'Many hands make light work'* are proverbs.
**proverbial** *adjective*

**provide** *verb* (**provides, providing, provided**)
1 to supply something. 2 to prepare for something, *They have provided for all possible disasters*.
**provided** or **providing**, on condition; on condition that, *You can come with us providing that you pay for yourself*.

**province** *noun* (**provinces**)
a part of a country.
**the provinces**, the part of a country outside the capital.
**provincial** *adjective*

**provision** *noun* (**provisions**)
1 providing something, *the provision of free meals for old people*. 2 a statement in a document, *the provisions of the treaty*.
**provisions,** supplies of food and drink.

**provisional** *adjective*
arranged or agreed on temporarily, but possibly to be altered later.

**provoke** *verb* (**provokes, provoking, provoked**)
1 to make someone angry. 2 to arouse or stimulate something, *His statement provoked a great deal of criticism*.
**provocation** *noun*, **provocative** *adjective*

**prow** *noun* (**prows**)
the front end of a ship.

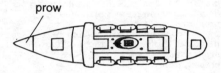

prow

**prowl** *verb* (**prowls, prowling, prowled**)
to move quietly or cautiously.
**prowler** *noun*

**prudent** *adjective*
(*say* proo-dĕnt)
careful; not reckless.
**prudence** *noun*, **prudently** *adverb*

**prune**[1] *noun* (**prunes**)
a dried plum.

**prune**[2] *verb* (**prunes, pruning, pruned**)
to cut off unwanted parts of a tree, bush, etc.

**pry** *verb* (**pries, prying, pried**)
to try often or in an annoying way to find out things about other people's business.

**PS** short for **postscript**.

**psalm** *noun* (**psalms**)
(*say* sahm)
a religious song, especially one of those in the Book of Psalms in the Bible.

**pseudonym** *noun* (**pseudonyms**)
(*say* s'yoo-dŏ-nim)
a false name used by an author.

**psychiatrist** *noun* (**psychiatrists**)
(*say* sy-ky-ă-trist)
a person trained to treat mental illness.
**psychiatric** *adjective*, **psychiatry** *noun*

**psychic** *adjective*
(*say* sy-kik)
1 supernatural. 2 having or using telepathy or supernatural powers.

**pulley**

**psychologist** *noun* (**psychologists**)
(*say* sy-**kol**-ŏ-jist)
someone who studies how the mind works.
**psychological** *adjective*, **psychology** *noun*

**PTA** short for *Parent-Teacher Association*, an
organization that arranges discussions
between teachers and parents about school
business, and raises money for the school.

**pub** *noun* (**pubs**)
(*informal*) a public house.

**puberty** *noun*
(*say* **pew**-ber-ti)
the time when a young person starts to
become an adult.

**public**[1] *adjective*
belonging or open to everyone; used or
known by everyone.
**public house,** a building where alcoholic
drinks are served to the public.
**public limited company,** a business whose
members are responsible for only some of
its debts.
**public school,** (*in England and Wales*) a
secondary school that charges fees; (*in
Scotland and America*) a school run by the
state or by the local authority.
**public works,** buildings, roads, etc.
constructed by a country's government for
its people.
**publicly** *adverb*

**public**[2] *noun*
all the people; everyone.
**in public,** openly; where anyone can see,
hear, or take part.

**publication** *noun* (**publications**)
1 printing and selling books, etc. 2 a book,
etc. that is printed and sold.

**publicity** *noun*
information or activity to make people
interested in someone or something;
advertising.

**publicize** *verb* (**publicizes, publicizing,
publicized**)
(*say* **pub**-li-syz)
to give publicity to something.

**publish** *verb* (**publishes, publishing, published**)
1 to print and sell books, etc. 2 to announce
something in public.
**publisher** *noun*

**puck** *noun* (**pucks**)
the hard rubber disc used in ice-hockey.

**pucker** *verb* (**puckers, puckering, puckered**)
to wrinkle.

**pudding** *noun* (**puddings**)
1 a food made in a soft mass, especially
with a mixture of flour and other
ingredients. 2 the sweet course of a meal.

**puddle** *noun* (**puddles**)
a small pool, usually of rainwater.

**puff**[1] *noun* (**puffs**)
1 a small amount of breath, wind, smoke,
steam, etc. 2 a soft pad for putting powder
on the skin. 3 a small cake filled with
cream.

**puff**[2] *verb* (**puffs, puffing, puffed**)
1 to blow out puffs of smoke, steam, etc.
2 to breathe with difficulty. 3 to inflate or
swell something, *He puffed out his chest.*

**puffin** *noun* (**puffins**)
a sea-bird with a large striped beak.

**pull** *verb* (**pulls, pulling, pulled**)
1 to get hold of something and make it
come towards you or follow behind you. 2 to
move, *The train pulled into the station.*
**pull a face,** to make a strange face.
**pull off,** to achieve something.
**pull out,** not to do something that you had
arranged to do, *Half the competitors pulled
out just before the race.*
**pull someone's leg,** to play a trick on
someone; to tease someone.
**pull through,** to recover from an illness.
**pull up,** (*of a vehicle*) to stop, *A car pulled
up and two men got out.*
**pull yourself together,** to become calm or
sensible.

**pulley** *noun* (**pulleys**)
a wheel with a groove round it to take a
rope, used for lifting heavy things.

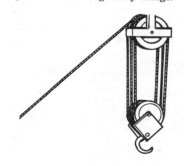

**pullover** *noun* (**pullovers**)
a knitted garment for the top half of your body.

**pulp**[1] *noun* (**pulps**)
a soft, wet mass of something, especially for making paper.

**pulp**[2] *verb* (**pulps, pulping, pulped**)
to make something into a soft, wet mass.

**pulpit** *noun* (**pulpits**)
a small enclosed platform where the preacher stands in a church.

**pulse** *noun* (**pulses**)
1 a regular movement of blood in your arteries that shows how fast your heart is beating. 2 a regular vibration.

**pulverize** *verb* (**pulverizes, pulverizing, pulverized**)
to crush something so that it becomes a powder.

**pumice** *noun*
(*say* pum-iss)
a kind of soft, sponge-like stone rubbed on things to clean or polish them.

**pump**[1] *noun* (**pumps**)
1 a device that pushes air or liquid into or out of something, or along pipes. 2 a lightweight shoe.

**pump**[2] *verb* (**pumps, pumping, pumped**)
to move air or liquid with a pump.
**pump up**, to fill something with air or gas.

**pumpkin** *noun* (**pumpkins**)
a very large, round fruit with a hard yellow skin.

**pun** *noun* (**puns**)
a joke made by using words that sound similar.
**punning** *noun*

**punch**[1] *verb* (**punches, punching, punched**)
1 to hit someone with your fist. 2 to make a hole in something; to make a hole, *The guard checked and punched our tickets. I punched a few more holes in my belt.*

**punch**[2] *noun* (**punches**)
1 a hit with the fist. 2 a device for making holes in paper, metal, or other substances. 3 force or vigour.
**punch line**, words that give the climax of a joke or story.
**punch-up**, (*informal*) a fight.

**punch**[3] *noun* (**punches**)
a hot alcoholic drink.

**punctual** *adjective*
exactly on time; not arriving late.
**punctuality** *noun*, **punctually** *adverb*

**punctuate** *verb* (**punctuates, punctuating, punctuated**)
to put punctuation in a piece of writing.

**punctuation** *noun*
marks such as commas, full stops, and brackets put into a piece of writing to make it easier to read.

**puncture** *noun* (**punctures**)
a hole in a tyre.

**punish** *verb* (**punishes, punishing, punished**)
to make someone suffer because he or she has done wrong.
**punishment** *noun*

**Punjabi** *noun* (**Punjabis**)
1 a person from the Punjab in north-western India. 2 the language spoken in the Punjab.

**punk** *noun* (**punks**)
1 someone who likes punk rock. 2 (*slang*) a rough, dirty, or worthless person.
**punk rock**, a kind of loud, simple rock music.

**punt**[1] *noun* (**punts**)
a flat-bottomed boat.

**punt**[2] *verb* (**punts, punting, punted**)
1 to use a pole to push a boat along. 2 to kick a football after dropping it from your hands, before it hits the ground.

**punter** *noun* (**punters**)
(*informal*) 1 a person who gambles or who places a bet. 2 a customer.

**puny** *adjective* (**punier, puniest**)
(*say* **pew**-ni)
small and weak.

**pup** *noun* (**pups**)
a puppy.

**pupa** *noun* (**pupae**)
(*say* **pew**-pǎ)
a chrysalis.

**pupil** *noun* (**pupils**)
1 someone who is being taught by a
teacher. 2 the opening in the centre of the
eye.

**puppet** *noun* (**puppets**)
1 a kind of doll that can be made to move
by fitting it over your hand or by working
it with strings or wires. 2 a leader or ruler
who is controlled by other people.

**puppy** *noun* (**puppies**)
a young dog.

**purchase**[1] *verb* (**purchases, purchasing,
purchased**)
to buy.
**purchaser** *noun*

**purchase**[2] *noun* (**purchases**)
1 something you have bought. 2 the action
of buying something, *Please keep the
receipt as proof of purchase.* 3 a firm hold or
grip, *It was hard to get a purchase on the
seaweed-covered rocks.*

**pure** *adjective* (**purer, purest**)
1 not mixed with anything else, *pure olive
oil.* 2 clean or clear, *a pure, cold mountain
stream.*
**purely** *adverb*, **purity** *noun*

**purge** *verb* (**purges, purging, purged**)
to get rid of unwanted people or things.

**purify** *verb* (**purifies, purifying, purified**)
to make something pure.
**purification** *noun*, **purifier** *noun*

**Puritan** *noun* (**Puritans**)
a Protestant in the 16th or 17th century
who wanted simpler religious ceremonies
and strictly moral behaviour.
**puritan**, a person with very strict morals.
**puritanical** *adjective*

**purple** *adjective* (**purpler, purplest**)
deep reddish-blue.

**purpose** *noun* (**purposes**)
what you intend to do; a plan or aim.
**on purpose**, intentionally; not by chance.
**purposeful** *adjective*, **purposeless** *adjective*

**purposely** *adverb*
on purpose.

**purr** *verb* (**purrs, purring, purred**)
to make a gentle murmuring sound like a
cat when it is pleased.

**purse** *noun* (**purses**)
a small bag to hold money.

**pursue** *verb* (**pursues, pursuing, pursued**)
1 to chase someone or something. 2 to
continue with something; to work at
something, *We cannot pursue the
investigation any further. She pursued her
studies at college.*
**pursuer** *noun*

**pursuit** *noun* (**pursuits**)
1 the action of chasing. 2 something you
spend time doing; a regular activity.

**pus** *noun*
a thick yellowish substance produced in
boils, etc. or in infected wounds.

**push**[1] *verb* (**pushes, pushing, pushed**)
to use force to move something away from
you; to press something.
**push off**, (*slang*) to go away.

**push**[2] *noun* (**pushes**)
a pushing movement.
**at a push**, in a crisis; if necessary.
**the push**, (*informal*) dismissal from a job.

**pushchair** *noun* (**pushchairs**)
a folding chair on wheels, in which a child
can be pushed along.

**puss** or **pussy** *noun* (**pusses** or **pussies**)
(*informal*) a cat.

**put** *verb* (**puts, putting, put**)
1 to move something into a place. 2 to cause
someone or something to be in a particular
condition, *Put the light out.* 3 to express
something in words, *She put it tactfully.*
**put off**, to postpone something; to stop
someone wanting something, *We'll have to
put off the Summer Fair if it rains. Eating
too much ice-cream last week seems to have
put her off ice-cream for good.*
**put out**, to stop a fire burning, light shining,
etc.
**put up**, to raise something; to give someone
a place to sleep, *Put up a tent. Can we put
him up for the night?*
**put up with**, to tolerate.

**putt** *verb* (**putts, putting, putted**)
to hit a golf-ball gently towards the hole.
**putter** *noun*, **putting-green** *noun*

**putty** *noun*
a soft paste that sets hard, used especially
for fitting windows in their frames.

**puzzle**[1] *noun* (**puzzles**)
1 a difficult question; a problem. 2 a game
where you have to solve a problem or do
something difficult.

**puzzle**[2] *verb* (**puzzles, puzzling, puzzled**)
1 to give someone a problem. 2 to think
deeply about something.

**pygmy** *noun* (**pygmies**)
(*say* **pig**-mi)
a very small person.

**pyjamas** *plural noun*
a loose jacket and trousers worn in bed.

**pylon** *noun* (**pylons**)
a metal tower that supports electric cables.

**pyramid** *noun* (**pyramids**)
1 a structure with a square base and four sloping sides coming to a point. 2 an ancient Egyptian monument shaped like this.

**pyramidal** *adjective*
like a pyramid, *a pyramidal roof.*
**pyramidal peak,** a pointed mountain peak between several corries.

**Pythagoras' theorem** *noun*
the statement that a square drawn on the longest side (*hypotenuse*) of a right-angled triangle is equal in area to the squares on the other two sides added together.

**python** *noun* (**pythons**)
a large snake that crushes its prey.

# Qq

**quack** *noun* (**quacks**)
the sound made by a duck.

**quad** *noun* (**quads**)
(*informal*) 1 a quadrangle. 2 a quadruplet.

**quadrangle** *noun* (**quadrangles**)
a rectangular courtyard.

**quadrant** *noun* (**quadrants**)
a quarter of a circle.

**quadrilateral** *noun* (**quadrilaterals**)
a four-sided figure.

**quadruple**[1] *adjective*
1 four times as much or as many. 2 having four parts.

**quadruple**[2] *verb* (**quadruples, quadrupling, quadrupled**)
to make something four times as much or as many; to become four times as much or as many.

**quadruplet** *noun* (**quadruplets**)
one of four children born to the same mother at one time.

**quail**[1] *noun* (**quails**)
a bird that looks like a small partridge.

**quail**[2] *verb* (**quails, quailing, quailed**)
to feel or show fear.

**quaint** *adjective* (**quainter, quaintest**)
attractive in an unusual or old-fashioned way.

**quake** *verb* (**quakes, quaking, quaked**)
to tremble; to shake.

**Quaker** *noun* (**Quakers**)
a member of a religious group founded by George Fox in the 17th century.

**qualify** *verb* (**qualifies, qualifying, qualified**)
1 to be suitable for a job; to make someone suitable for a job, *With her experience, she qualifies immediately for the work. His degree qualifies him to become a graphic designer.* 2 to alter a statement, etc., usually making it less strong.
**qualification** *noun*

**quality** *noun* (**qualities**)
1 how good or bad something is. 2 what something is like, *The paper had a shiny quality.*

**quantity** *noun* (**quantities**)
how much there is of something; how many things there are of one sort.

**quarantine** *noun*
(*say* **kwo**-răn-teen)
a period when a person or animal is kept apart from others to prevent a disease from spreading.

**quarrel**[1] *noun* (**quarrels**)
a strong or angry argument.
**quarrelsome** *adjective*

**quarrel**² *verb* (**quarrels, quarrelling, quarrelled**)
to have a strong or angry argument with someone.

**quarry** *noun* (**quarries**)
1 a place where stone, slate, etc. is dug out of the ground. 2 an animal that is being hunted.

**quart** *noun* (**quarts**)
a quarter of a gallon.

**quarter** *noun* (**quarters**)
1 one of four equal parts into which something is divided or can be divided.
2 three months.
**at close quarters,** close together, *They fought at close quarters.*
**quarters,** lodgings.

**quartet** *noun* (**quartets**)
(*say* kwor-**tet**)
1 a group of four musicians. 2 a piece of music for four musicians.

**quartz** *noun*
(*say* kworts)
a hard mineral.

**quaver**¹ *verb* (**quavers, quavering, quavered**)
to tremble, *His voice quavered with fear.*

**quaver**² *noun* (**quavers**)
1 a trembling sound. 2 (in America, *eighth note*) a musical note equal to half a crotchet, written ♪.

**quay** *noun* (**quays**)
(*say* kee)
a harbour wall or pier where ships tie up.

**queasy** *adjective*
feeling slightly sick.

**queen** *noun* (**queens**)
1 a woman who is the crowned ruler of a country. 2 a king's wife. 3 a female bee or ant, etc., that produces eggs. 4 an important piece in chess. 5 a playing-card with a picture of a crowned woman on it.
**queen mother,** a king's widow who is the mother of the present king or queen.

**queer** *adjective* (**queerer, queerest**)
1 strange. 2 ill, *I feel queer.* 3 (*offensive slang*) an insulting word meaning homosexual.

**quench** *verb* (**quenches, quenching, quenched**)
1 to satisfy your thirst. 2 to put out a fire.

**query** *noun* (**queries**)
(*say* **kweer**-i)
1 a question. 2 a question mark.

**quest** *noun* (**quests**)
a search, *the quest for gold.*

**question**¹ *noun* (**questions**)
1 something you ask, *I cannot answer your question.* 2 a problem; a subject, *Parliament debated the question of immigration.*
**in question,** that is being discussed.
**out of the question,** impossible.
**question mark,** the punctuation mark '?' put at the end of a question.

**question**² *verb* (**questions, questioning, questioned**)
1 to ask someone questions. 2 to be doubtful about something.
**questionable** *adjective*, **questioner** *noun*

**questionnaire** *noun* (**questionnaires**)
(*say* kwes-chŏn-**air**)
a list of questions.

**queue**¹ *noun* (**queues**)
(*say* kew)
a line of people or vehicles waiting for something.

**queue**² *verb* (**queues, queueing** or **queuing, queued**)
(*say* kew)
to wait in a queue.

**quiche** *noun* (**quiches**)
(*say* keesh)
a large pie without pastry on top, filled with savoury things such as eggs, cheese, onion, and tomato.

**quick** *adjective* (**quicker, quickest**)
**1** rapid. **2** done in a short time. **3** lively; clever, *quick-witted*. **4** (*old-fashioned use*) alive, *the quick and the dead*.
**quicken** *verb*

**quicksand** *noun* (**quicksands**)
loose, wet sand that can quickly swallow up people, animals, etc.

**quid** *noun* (**quid**)
(*slang*) a pound (£1).

**quiet** *adjective* (**quieter, quietest**)
**1** silent. **2** not loud, *a quiet voice*. **3** without much movement, *a quiet sea*.

**quieten** *verb* (**quietens, quietening, quietened**)
to make something or someone quiet; to become quiet.

**quill** *noun* (**quills**)
**1** a large feather. **2** a pen made from a large feather.

**quilt** *noun* (**quilts**)
a thick, soft cover for a bed.

**quintet** *noun* (**quintets**)
**1** a group of five musicians. **2** a piece of music for five musicians.

**quit** *verb* (**quits, quitting, quitted** or **quit**)
**1** to leave or abandon something.
**2** (*informal*) to stop doing something, *Quit pulling my leg!*
**quitter** *noun*

**quite** *adverb*
**1** completely; truly, *I am quite all right*. **2** somewhat; rather, *He's quite a good swimmer*.

**quiver**¹ *verb* (**quivers, quivering, quivered**)
to tremble, *He was quivering with excitement*.

**quiver**² *noun* (**quivers**)
a container for arrows.

**quiz** *noun* (**quizzes**)
a series of questions, especially as an entertainment or competition.

**quoit** *noun* (**quoits**)
(*say* koit)
a ring thrown at a peg in the game of **quoits**.

**quota** *noun* (**quotas**)
(*say* **kwoh**-tă)
**1** a share, *Each school was given its quota of equipment*. **2** a limited amount that is allowed, *The council has exceeded its quota of employees*.

**quotation** *noun* (**quotations**)
**1** the action of repeating words that were first written or spoken by someone else.
**2** words from someone's book, speech, etc., repeated by someone else.
**quotation marks**, inverted commas.

**quote** *verb* (**quotes, quoting, quoted**)
to repeat words that were first spoken or written by someone else.

**quotient** *noun* (**quotients**)
(*say* **kwoh**-shĕnt)
the result of dividing one number by another.

**Qur'an** *noun*
the Koran.

# Rr

**rabbi** *noun* (**rabbis**)
(*say* **rab**-I)
a Jewish religious leader.

**rabbit** *noun* (**rabbits**)
a furry animal with long ears, *Rabbits live in burrows.*

**rabid** *adjective*
(*say* **rab**-id)
**1** furious; violent. **2** affected with rabies.
**rabidly** *adverb*

**rabies** *noun*
(*say* **ray**-beez)
a disease that makes dogs go mad.

**race**¹ *noun* (**races**)
a competition to be the first to reach a particular place.

**race**² *noun* (**races**)
a group of people with the same ancestors, characteristics, or skin-colour.
**race relations,** the way in which people of different races live together in the same community.
**racial** *adjective*

**race**³ *verb* (**races, racing, raced**)
**1** to have a race against someone. **2** to move very fast, *The train raced along the track.*
**racer** *noun*

**racecourse** *noun* (**racecourses**)
a place for horse-races.

**racism** *noun*
(*say* **ray**-sizm)
**1** believing that your own race of people is better than others. **2** hostility between different races of people.
**racist** *noun* and *adjective*

**rack** *noun* (**racks**)
**1** a framework used as a shelf or container. **2** an ancient device for torturing people by stretching them.

**racket**¹ *noun* (**rackets**)
an implement for hitting the ball in tennis, badminton, etc., made of strings stretched across a wooden or metal frame.

**racket**² *noun* (**rackets**)
**1** a loud noise. **2** (*slang*) a swindle.

**racoon** *noun* (**racoons**)
a small North American meat-eating animal with greyish-brown fur and a bushy, striped tail.

**radar** *noun*
(*say* **ray**-dar)
a system that uses radio waves to find the position of objects which you cannot see because of darkness, fog, distance, etc.

**radiant** *adjective*
**1** bright; shining, *the radiant sun.* **2** looking very happy.
**radiance** *noun*, **radiantly** *adverb*

**radiate** *verb* (**radiates, radiating, radiated**)
**1** to give out heat, light, or other energy. **2** to be arranged like the spokes of a wheel, *The city's streets radiate away from the palace in the centre.*

**radiation** *noun*
**1** heat, light, or other energy given out by something. **2** radioactivity.

**radiator** *noun* (**radiators**)
**1** a device that gives out heat, especially a metal container through which steam or hot water flows. **2** the device that cools the engine of a vehicle.

**radical** *adjective*
**1** thorough, going right to the roots of something, *radical changes.* **2** wanting change in the world, *a radical politician.*
**radical** *noun*, **radically** *adverb*

**radii** plural of **radius**.

**radio** *noun* (**radios**)
1 an apparatus for receiving broadcast sound programmes. 2 sending or receiving sound by means of electrical waves.

**radioactive** *adjective*
giving out atomic energy.
**radioactivity** *noun*

**radish** *noun* (**radishes**)
a small, hard, round, red vegetable, eaten raw in salads.

**radium** *noun*
a radioactive element.

**radius** *noun* (**radii**)
1 a straight line from the centre of a circle to the circumference. 2 the distance between the centre and the circumference of a circle.

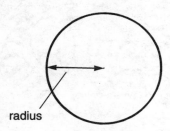

radius

**raffle** *noun* (**raffles**)
a way of raising money by selling numbered tickets which may win prizes.

**raft** *noun* (**rafts**)
a floating platform of logs, barrels, etc. fastened together.

**rafter** *noun* (**rafters**)
one of the long, sloping pieces of wood that hold up a roof.

**rag** *noun* (**rags**)
1 a torn or old piece of cloth. 2 a piece of ragtime music.

**rage**[1] *noun* (**rages**)
great or violent anger.
**all the rage,** (*informal*) very fashionable or popular.

**rage**[2] *verb* (**rages, raging, raged**)
1 to be very angry. 2 to be violent or noisy.

**ragged** *adjective*
(*say* **rag**-id)
1 torn or frayed, *ragged clothes*. 2 wearing torn or old clothes, *a ragged man*. 3 not smooth, *a ragged performance*.

**ragtime** *noun*
an old-fashioned kind of jazzy music.

**raid**[1] *noun* (**raids**)
a sudden attack.

**raid**[2] *verb* (**raids, raiding, raided**)
to attack a place suddenly; to make a surprise visit to a place where there may be law-breakers, *The police raided a night-club.*
**raider** *noun*

**rail** *noun* (**rails**)
1 a bar or rod, *a towel-rail*. 2 a long metal bar that is part of a railway track.
**by rail,** on a train.

**railings** *plural noun*
a fence made of metal bars.

**railway** *noun* (**railways**)
(in America, *railroad*) 1 the parallel metal bars that trains travel on. 2 a system of transport using rails.

**rain**[1] *noun*
drops of water that fall from the sky.
**rain forest,** a thick tropical forest with heavy rainfall.
**rain gauge,** a device for measuring how much rain has fallen.
**raindrop** *noun*, **rainwater** *noun*, **rainy** *adjective*

**rain**[2] *verb* (**rains, raining, rained**)
to come down or send something down like rain.
**it is raining,** rain is falling.

**rainbow** *noun* (**rainbows**)
an arched band of colours seen in the sky when the sun shines through rain, *The colours in a rainbow are red, orange, yellow, green, blue, indigo, and violet.*

**raincoat** *noun* (**raincoats**)
a waterproof coat.

**rainfall** *noun*
the amount of rain that falls in a particular place or time.

**rapid**

**raise** *verb* (**raises, raising, raised**)
1 to move something to a higher place or upright position. 2 to manage to get the money or people needed for something, *They raised £1,000 for the appeal. He raised an army in just ten days.* 3 to bring up young children or animals. 4 to make or cause, *He raised a laugh with his joke.* 5 to end a siege.

**raisin** *noun* (**raisins**)
a dried grape.

**rake**¹ *noun* (**rakes**)
a gardening tool with a row of short spikes fixed to a long handle.

**rake**² *verb* (**rakes, raking, raked**)
1 to move or smooth something with a rake. 2 to search, *I raked around in my desk but couldn't find the letter.*
**rake in**, (*informal*) to make money or profit.

**rally**¹ *noun* (**rallies**)
1 a large meeting. 2 a competition to test skill in driving, *the Monte Carlo Rally.* 3 a series of strokes and return strokes in tennis, etc. before a point is scored.

**rally**² *verb* (**rallies, rallying, rallied**)
1 to bring people together, or to come together, for a united effort, *The general rallied his troops. The whole village rallied to help when Mrs Brown's cottage was flooded.* 2 to revive; to recover, *The team rallied when they realized they could win.*

**RAM** short for *random-access memory,* a type of computer memory which can have information put into it or taken out of it by the user, but which does not keep the information if the computer is switched off.

**ram**¹ *noun* (**rams**)
a male sheep.

**ram**² *verb* (**rams, ramming, rammed**)
to push one thing hard against another.

**Ramadan** *noun*
(*say* ram-ă-**dan**)
the ninth month of the Muslim year, when Muslims fast during the daytime.

**ramble**¹ *noun* (**rambles**)
a long walk in the country.

**ramble**² *verb* (**rambles, rambling, rambled**)
1 to go for a long walk in the country; to wander, *I rambled through town, looking at the shops.* 2 not to keep to a subject, *The speaker kept rambling.*
**rambler** *noun*

**ramp** *noun* (**ramps**)
a slope between two levels.

**rampage** *verb* (**rampages, rampaging, rampaged**)
(*say* ram-**payj**)
to rush about wildly or destructively.

**ran** past tense of **run** *verb.*

**ranch** *noun* (**ranches**)
a large cattle-farm in America.
**rancher** *noun*

**random**¹ *noun*
**at random**, by chance; without any choice, purpose, or plan.

**random**² *adjective*
done or taken at random, *a random sample.*

**rang** past tense of **ring**² *verb.*

**range**¹ *noun* (**ranges**)
1 a line or series of things, *a range of mountains.* 2 the size of difference between first and last, or between highest and lowest in a group, *There is a large range of ages in my family.* 3 a number of different things, *a wide range of goods.* 4 the distance that a gun can shoot, an aircraft can fly, etc. 5 a place with targets for shooting-practice. 6 a large area of land. 7 a kitchen fireplace with ovens.

**range**² *verb* (**ranges, ranging, ranged**)
1 to exist between two limits; to extend, *Prices ranged from £1 to £50.* 2 to arrange, *Hundreds of people ranged themselves along the streets, hoping to see the Queen go by.* 3 to wander; to move over a wide area, *Hens ranged all over the farm.*

**ranger** *noun* (**rangers**)
1 someone who looks after a park, forest, etc. 2 a mounted policeman in a remote area.
**Ranger**, a senior Guide.

**rank** *noun* (**ranks**)
1 a line of people or things, *a taxi-rank.* 2 a position in a series of people or things, especially in society or in the armed forces, *He was promoted to the rank of captain.*

**ransack** *verb* (**ransacks, ransacking, ransacked**)
to search a place thoroughly, leaving things untidy.

**ransom** *noun* (**ransoms**)
money paid so that a prisoner can be set free.
**hold someone to ransom**, to keep someone as a prisoner and demand a ransom.

**rap**¹ *verb* (**raps, rapping, rapped**)
to knock quickly and loudly.

**rap**² *noun* (**raps**)
1 a rapping movement or sound. 2 a kind of pop music in which the words are spoken rhythmically, not sung.
**take the rap**, (*slang*) to take the blame for something.

**rapid** *adjective*
moving or working at speed.
**rapidity** *noun*, **rapidly** *adverb*

**rapids** *plural noun*
    part of a river where the water flows very
    quickly.

**rare** *adjective* (**rarer, rarest**)
    unusual; not often found or experienced,
    *She died of a rare disease.*
    **rarely** *adverb*, **rarity** *noun*

**rascal** *noun* (**rascals**)
    a dishonest or mischievous person.

**rash**[1] *adjective* (**rasher, rashest**)
    acting or done quickly without proper
    thought, *He tends to be rash. a rash
    decision.*

**rash**[2] *noun* (**rashes**)
    a red patch or red spots on the skin.

**rasher** *noun* (**rashers**)
    a slice of bacon.

**raspberry** *noun* (**raspberries**)
    a small, soft, red fruit.

**Rastafarian** *noun* (**Rastafarians**)
    (*say* ras-tă-**fair**-i-ăn)
    a member of a religious group that started
    in Jamaica.

**rat** *noun* (**rats**)
    **1** an animal like a large mouse. **2** a nasty or
    treacherous person.
    **rat-race,** a continuous competition for
    success in your career, business, etc.

**rate**[1] *noun* (**rates**)
    **1** speed, *The train moved at a great rate.*
    **2** cost; charge, *What is the rate for a letter
    to Italy?* **3** quality; standard, *first-rate.
    second-rate.*
    **at any rate,** anyway.
    **at this rate** or **at that rate,** if this is typical or
    true.
    **rates,** a tax paid in the past by
    householders to the local council.

**rate**[2] *verb* (**rates, rating, rated**)
    **1** to value something, *Drivers rated the new
    lorry very highly.* **2** to regard someone in a
    particular way, *He rated me among his
    friends.*

**rather** *adverb*
    **1** slightly; somewhat, *It was rather dark.*
    **2** preferably; more willingly, *I would rather
    not come.* **3** more truly, *He lay down, or
    rather fell, on the bed.*

**ratio** *noun* (**ratios**)
    (*say* **ray**-shi-oh)
    the relationship between two numbers;
    how often one number goes into another, *In
    a group of 2 girls and 10 boys, the ratio of
    girls to boys is 1 to 5.*

**ration**[1] *noun* (**rations**)
    (*say* **rash**-ŏn)
    an amount allowed to one person, *You have
    had your ration of sweets for today.*

**ration**[2] *verb* (**rations, rationing, rationed**)
    (*say* **rash**-ŏn)
    to share something out in fixed amounts.

**rational** *adjective*
    (*say* **rash**-ŏ-năl)
    reasonable; sane, *a rational method. No
    rational person would do such a stupid
    thing.*
    **rationalize** *verb*, **rationally** *adverb*

**rattle**[1] *verb* (**rattles, rattling, rattled**)
    **1** to make a series of short, sharp, hard
    sounds, *Dried peas rattle inside a tin.*
    **2** (*informal*) to make someone nervous and
    confused.

**rattle**[2] *noun* (**rattles**)
    **1** a series of short, sharp, hard sounds. **2** a
    baby's toy that makes this kind of sound.

**rattlesnake** *noun* (**rattlesnakes**)
    a poisonous American snake that makes
    rattling sounds with its tail.

**rave** *verb* (**raves, raving, raved**)
    to talk or behave madly or very
    enthusiastically.

**raven** *noun* (**ravens**)
    a large black bird.

**ravenous** *adjective*
    (*say* **rav**-ĕ-nŭs)
    very hungry.
    **ravenously** *adverb*

**ravine** *noun* (ravines)
(*say* rǎ-**veen**)
a very deep, narrow gorge.

**raw** *adjective* (rawer, rawest)
1 not cooked, *a raw steak*. 2 in the natural state; not processed, *raw materials*. 3 without experience, *raw beginners*. 4 with the skin removed, *a raw wound*. 5 cold and damp, *a raw wind*.
**raw deal**, (*informal*) unfair treatment.

**ray** *noun* (rays)
a thin line of light, heat, or other energy.

**razor** *noun* (razors)
a device with a very sharp blade, especially one used for shaving.

**reach**[1] *verb* (reaches, reaching, reached)
1 to get to a place or thing. 2 to stretch out your hand to get or touch something.

**reach**[2] *noun* (reaches)
1 the distance you can reach with your hand. 2 a distance that you can easily travel, *My uncle lives within reach of the sea*. 3 a straight stretch of a river or canal.

**react** *verb* (reacts, reacting, reacted)
to have a reaction.

**reaction** *noun* (reactions)
an action or feeling caused by another person or thing.

**reactor** *noun* (reactors)
an apparatus for producing nuclear power.

**read** *verb* (reads, reading, read)
to look at something written or printed, and understand it or say it aloud, *Have you read this book? I read it last year*.
**readable** *adjective*

**reader** *noun* (readers)
1 someone who reads. 2 a book that helps you learn to read.

**readily** *adverb*
1 willingly, *She readily agreed to help*. 2 quickly; without any difficulty, *The system can be installed readily by anyone who can use a screwdriver*.

**reading** *noun* (readings)
1 the action of reading a book, magazine, etc. 2 an amount shown on a measuring instrument, *Check the barometer readings every day*.

**ready** *adjective* (readier, readiest)
1 able or willing to do something or to be used at once; prepared. 2 quick, *ready answers*.
**at the ready,** ready for use or action.
**readiness** *noun*

**ready-made** *adjective*
made already, and able to be used immediately; (of clothes) made in shapes and sizes that will fit most people, and not made for one particular person.

**real** *adjective*
1 existing; true; not imaginary. 2 genuine; not a copy.

**realism** *noun*
seeing or showing things as they really are.
**realist** *noun*, **realistic** *adjective*, **realistically** *adverb*

**reality** *noun* (realities)
1 what is real. 2 something real, *Cold and hunger are the realities of homelessness*.

**realize** *verb* (realizes, realizing, realized)
to understand something clearly; to accept something as true.
**realization** *noun*

**really** *adverb*
truly; certainly; in fact.

**realm** *noun* (realms)
(*say* relm)
1 a kingdom. 2 an area of knowledge, interest, activity, etc.

**reap** *verb* (reaps, reaping, reaped)
to cut down and gather corn when it is ripe.
**reaper** *noun*

**reappear** *verb* (reappears, reappearing, reappeared)
to appear again.
**reappearance** *noun*

**rear**[1] *adjective*
placed or found at the back, *a car with a rear engine*.

**rear**[2] *noun* (rears)
1 the back of something. 2 a person's bottom.

**rear**[3] *verb* (rears, rearing, reared)
1 to bring up young children or animals. 2 to rise up on the hind legs, *The horse reared up in fright*.

**rearrange** *verb* (rearranges, rearranging, rearranged)
to arrange something differently.
**rearrangement** *noun*

**reason**[1] *noun* (**reasons**)
1 a cause for something; an explanation.
2 reasoning; common sense, *Listen to reason*.

**reason**[2] *verb* (**reasons, reasoning, reasoned**)
to think in an organized way.

**reasonable** *adjective*
1 sensible; logical. 2 fair; moderate, *reasonable prices*.
**reasonableness** *noun*, **reasonably** *adverb*

**reasoning** *noun*
thinking in an orderly way.

**reassure** *verb* (**reassures, reassuring, reassured**)
to remove someone's doubts or fears.
**reassurance** *noun*

**rebel**[1] *verb* (**rebels, rebelling, rebelled**)
(*say* ri-**bel**)
to refuse to obey someone in authority, especially the government.
**rebellion** *noun*, **rebellious** *adjective*

**rebel**[2] *noun* (**rebels**)
(*say* **reb**-ĕl)
someone who refuses to obey someone in authority.

**rebound** *verb* (**rebounds, rebounding, rebounded**)
to bounce back after hitting something.

**rebuild** *verb* (**rebuilds, rebuilding, rebuilt**)
to build something again; to put something together again.

**recall** *verb* (**recalls, recalling, recalled**)
1 to ask someone to come back. 2 to remember someone or something.

**recap** *verb* (**recaps, recapping, recapped**)
(*informal*) to state again the main points of something that has been said.

**recapture** *verb* (**recaptures, recapturing, recaptured**)
to capture something or someone again.

**recede** *verb* (**recedes, receding, receded**)
to go back, *The floods receded*.

**receipt** *noun* (**receipts**)
(*say* ri-**seet**)
1 a written statement that money has been received. 2 receiving something.

**receive** *verb* (**receives, receiving, received**)
1 to get something that is given or sent to you. 2 to greet a visitor formally, *The President was received at Buckingham Palace*.

**receiver** *noun* (**receivers**)
1 someone who receives something.
2 someone who buys and sells stolen goods. 3 an official who takes charge of a bankrupt person's property. 4 a radio or television set. 5 the part of a telephone that you hold to your ear.

**recent** *adjective*
made or happening a short time ago.
**recently** *adverb*

**receptacle** *noun* (**receptacles**)
something for holding what is put into it; a container.

**reception** *noun* (**receptions**)
1 the sort of welcome that someone gets, *We were given a friendly reception*.
2 a formal party, *a wedding reception*.
3 a place in a hotel, office, etc. where visitors are welcomed, registered, etc.
**reception-room**, a sitting-room.

**receptionist** *noun* (**receptionists**)
someone employed at the reception of a hotel, office, etc.

**recess** *noun* (**recesses**)
1 an alcove. 2 a time when work or business is stopped for a while.

**recession** *noun* (**recessions**)
a reduction in trade or in the wealth created by a country's industry.

**recipe** *noun* (**recipes**)
(*say* **ress**-i-pi)
instructions for preparing or cooking food.

**reciprocal**[1] *adjective*
(*say* ri-**sip**-rŏ-kăl)
given and received by the same person, or by two people at once; mutual, *a reciprocal greeting*.

**reciprocal**[2] *noun* (**reciprocals**)
the number by which you must multiply a number to obtain the answer 1, *0.5 is the reciprocal of 2 ($0.5 \times 2 = 1$)*.

**recital** *noun* (**recitals**)
(*say* ri-**sy**-tăl)
a concert by a small number of performers.

**recite** *verb* (**recites, reciting, recited**)
to say something aloud that you have learnt.
**recitation** *noun*

**reckless** *adjective*
doing things without thinking or caring about what might happen.
**recklessly** *adverb*, **recklessness** *noun*

**reckon** *verb* (**reckons, reckoning, reckoned**)
1 to calculate; to count. 2 to have an opinion; to think.

**reclaim** *verb* (**reclaims, reclaiming, reclaimed**)
1 to make something usable again, *reclaimed land*. 2 to claim or get something back.

**reclamation** *noun*
making something usable again, *land reclamation*.

**recline** *verb* (reclines, reclining, reclined)
to lean or lie back.

**recognize** *verb* (recognizes, recognizing, recognized)
1 to know who someone is because you have seen him or her before; to realize that you know something you have seen before. 2 to accept something; to agree with something, *We recognize that we may have acted unfairly.*
**recognition** *noun*, **recognizable** *adjective*

**recoil** *verb* (recoils, recoiling, recoiled)
to move backwards suddenly, *He recoiled in horror. Guns recoil as they are fired.*

**recollect** *verb* (recollects, recollecting, recollected)
to remember something.
**recollection** *noun*

**recommend** *verb* (recommends, recommending, recommended)
1 to say that something is good, *I recommend the Bull Hotel – it's excellent.* 2 to praise someone, saying that he or she would be a good person to do a particular job. 3 to advise doing something, *We recommend that you read the instructions thoroughly before you use the lawn-mower.*
**recommendation** *noun*

**reconcile** *verb* (reconciles, reconciling, reconciled)
1 to restore peace or friendship between people, countries, etc. 2 to persuade someone to put up with something, *He became reconciled to wearing glasses.*
**reconciliation** *noun*

**reconstruction** *noun* (reconstructions)
1 building something up again, *the reconstruction of war-damaged buildings.* 2 an object or a collection of things, buildings, etc. made to look like things that existed in the past; the acting out of an event that took place in the past, *a reconstruction of the battle of Waterloo.*

**record**[1] *noun* (records)
(*say* rek-ord)
1 a flat, round piece of plastic that makes music or other sounds when it is played on a record-player. 2 the best performance in a sport or most remarkable event of its kind, *She broke the record for swimming 100 metres.* 3 a description of things that have happened.

**record**[2] *verb* (records, recording, recorded)
(*say* ri-kord)
1 to put music or other sounds on a tape or disc. 2 to describe things that have happened.

**recorder** *noun* (recorders)
1 a tape recorder. 2 a wooden musical instrument played by blowing into one end. 3 someone who records something.

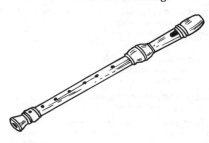

**record-player** *noun* (record-players)
a device for reproducing sound from records.

**recover** *verb* (recovers, recovering, recovered)
1 to get better after being ill. 2 to get something back that you had lost.
**recovery** *noun*

**recreation** *noun* (recreations)
a game, hobby, or other enjoyable pastime done in your spare time.
**recreation ground**, a public playground for children.
**recreational** *adjective*

**recruit** *noun* (recruits)
someone who has just joined the armed forces or a business, club, etc.

**rectangle** *noun* (rectangles)
a shape with four straight sides and four right angles.
**rectangular** *adjective*

**recur** *verb* (recurs, recurring, recurred)
to happen again.
**recurring decimal**, a decimal fraction in which the same numbers are repeated over and over.
**recurrence** *noun*, **recurrent** *adjective*

**recycle** *verb* (recycles, recycling, recycled)
to treat waste material so that it can be used again, *Waste paper can be recycled to make cardboard.*
**recycling** *noun*

**red**[1] *adjective* (redder, reddest)
1 of the colour of blood. 2 (*informal*) of Communists; favouring Communism.
**red herring**, a thing that misleads someone or diverts his or her attention.
**red tape**, excessive rules and forms in official business.
**redden** *verb*, **reddish** *adjective*

**red$^2$** *noun* (**reds**)
1 red colour. 2 (*informal*) a Communist.
**in the red**, in debt.
**see red**, to become suddenly angry.

**redeem** *verb* (**redeems, redeeming, redeemed**)
1 to save someone from sin, faults, etc. 2 to
get something back by paying for it.
**redeemer** *noun*, **redemption** *noun*

**red-handed** *adjective*
while committing a crime, *He was caught
red-handed.*

**redhead** *noun* (**redheads**)
a person with reddish-brown hair.

**Red Indian** *noun* (**Red Indians**)
a name once used for a Native American.

**reduce** *verb* (**reduces, reducing, reduced**)
1 to make something smaller or less. 2 to
force someone into a situation, *She was
reduced to borrowing the money.*
**reduction** *noun*

**redundant** *adjective*
not needed, especially for a particular job.
**redundancy** *noun*

**reed** *noun* (**reeds**)
1 a plant that grows in or near water. 2 a
thin strip that vibrates to make the sound
in a clarinet, saxophone, oboe, etc.
**reedy** *adjective*

**reef** *noun* (**reefs**)
a line of rocks near the surface of the sea.

**reef-knot** *noun* (**reef-knots**)
a symmetrical double knot for tying two
cords together.

**reek** *verb* (**reeks, reeking, reeked**)
to have a strong, unpleasant smell.

**reel$^1$** *noun* (**reels**)
1 a round device on which cotton,
fishing-line, etc. is wound. 2 a lively
Scottish dance.

**reel$^2$** *verb* (**reels, reeling, reeled**)
1 to stagger, *The drunk reeled along the
road.* 2 to be dizzy, *My head was reeling.*
**reel off**, to say something quickly.

**refer** *verb* (**refers, referring, referred**)
to pass a question, problem, etc. to
someone else.
**refer to**, to mention; to look in a book, etc.
for information; to be connected with, *Are
you referring to me? Refer to a dictionary to
find the meanings of words. The word
'equilateral' refers to a triangle with sides
of equal length.*

**referee$^1$** *noun* (**referees**)
someone who makes sure that people keep
to the rules of a game.

**referee$^2$** *verb* (**referees, refereeing, refereed**)
to act as a referee.

**reference** *noun* (**references**)
1 a mention of something. 2 a place in a
book, file, etc. where information can be
found. 3 a letter describing what work
someone has done, how well he or she did
it, etc.
**in** or **with reference to**, concerning; in
connection with.
**reference book**, a book that gives
information.

**referendum** *noun* (**referendums**)
(*say* ref-er-en-dŭm)
a vote on a particular question by all the
people in a country.

**refill** *noun* (**refills**)
a thing used to replace something that has
been used up, *My lighter needs a refill.*

**refine** *verb* (**refines, refining, refined**)
to purify.
**refined**, cultured; with good manners.
**refinement** *noun*, **refinery** *noun*

**reflect** *verb* (**reflects, reflecting, reflected**)
1 to send back light from a shiny surface; to
send back sound from a surface. 2 to show
a picture of something, as in a mirror. 3 to
think seriously about something.
**reflection** *noun*, **reflective** *adjective*, **reflector**
*noun*

**reflective** *adjective*
1 sending back light, *The traffic policeman
wore a reflective waistcoat.* 2 suggesting or
showing serious thought, *The music has a
reflective quality.*

**reflex** *noun* (**reflexes**)
(*say* **ree**-fleks)
a movement or action done without any
conscious thought.
**reflex angle**, an angle between 180 and 360
degrees.

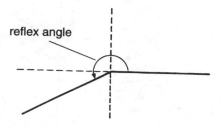

reflex angle

**reflexive** *adjective*
(*say* ri-**flek**-siv)
(*in grammar*) referring to an action whose
subject and object are the same, *In 'He
washed himself', the verb is reflexive.*

**reform**[1] *verb* (**reforms, reforming, reformed**)
to improve a person or thing by getting rid
of faults.
**reformer** *noun*

**reform**[2] *noun* (**reforms**)
changing something to get rid of faults and
to improve it; a change made for this
reason.

**Reformation** *noun*
a movement for change in the Church in
the 16th century, leading to the beginning
of the Reformed or Protestant Churches.

**refract** *verb* (**refracts, refracting, refracted**)
to cause a ray of light, a wave of sound, or
a wave of heat to change its direction.
**refraction** *noun*

**refrain**[1] *verb* (**refrains, refraining, refrained**)
to keep yourself from doing something,
*Please refrain from talking.*

**refrain**[2] *noun* (**refrains**)
the chorus of a song.

**refresh** *verb* (**refreshes, refreshing, refreshed**)
to make a tired person feel fresh and
strong again.
**refresh your memory**, to remind yourself, *I
knew the route, but glanced at the map to
refresh my memory.*

**refreshments** *plural noun*
drinks and snacks.

**refrigerate** *verb* (**refrigerates, refrigerating,
refrigerated**)
to freeze something so as to keep it in good
condition.
**refrigeration** *noun*

**refrigerator** *noun* (**refrigerators**)
a metal cupboard in which food is kept cold
and fresh.

**refuel** *verb* (**refuels, refuelling, refuelled**)
to supply a ship, aircraft, etc. with fuel.

**refuge** *noun* (**refuges**)
a place where you are safe from pursuit or
danger.

**refugee** *noun* (**refugees**)
(*say* ref-yoo-**jee**)
someone who has had to leave his or her
home or country because of war,
persecution, disaster, etc.

**refund**[1] *verb* (**refunds, refunding, refunded**)
(*say* ri-**fund**)
to pay money back.

**refund**[2] *noun* (**refunds**)
(*say* **ree**-fund)
money paid back, *I want a refund for this
bad fruit that I bought.*

**refuse**[1] *verb* (**refuses, refusing, refused**)
(*say* ri-**fewz**)
to say that you will not do or accept
something, *She refuses to help.*
**refusal** *noun*

**refuse**[2] *noun*
(*say* **ref**-yooss)
rubbish.

**regain** *verb* (**regains, regaining, regained**)
1 to get something back. 2 to reach a place
again.

**regard**[1] *verb* (**regards, regarding, regarded**)
1 to look at someone or something closely.
2 to think of someone or something in a
certain way, *I regard her as a friend.*

**regard**[2] *noun* (**regards**)
1 a gaze. 2 consideration; respect.
**regards**, kind wishes.
**with regard to**, on the subject of; about, *With
regard to the school field, there will be no
football until the snow has cleared.*

**regarding** *preposition*
on the subject of; about.

**regardless** *adjective*
paying no attention to something, *Get it,
regardless of the cost.*

**regatta** *noun* (**regattas**)
(*say* ri-**gat**-ă)
a meeting for boat or yacht races.

**reggae** *noun*
(*say* **reg**-ay)
a West Indian style of music with a strong
beat.

**regiment** *noun* (**regiments**)
an army unit consisting of two or more
battalions.
**regimental** *adjective*

**region** *noun* (**regions**)
1 a part of a country. 2 a part of the world.
**regional** *adjective*

**register**[1] *noun* (**registers**)
a book in which information is recorded,
especially of who has been present each
day at a school.

**register**[2] *verb* (**registers, registering, registered**)
1 to list in a register; to record information
officially, *Is this car registered?* 2 to
indicate; to show, *The thermometer
registered 100°.* 3 to pay extra for a letter or
parcel to be sent with special care.
**registration** *noun*

**registration number** *noun* (**registration numbers**)
the set of numbers and letters that appears
on a plate in front of and behind a motor
vehicle, *My motor cycle's registration
number was CNW 17 C.*

**regret**[1] *noun* (**regrets**)
the feeling of being sorry or sad about
something.
**regretful** *adjective*, **regretfully** *adverb*

**regret**[2] *verb* (**regrets, regretting, regretted**)
to feel sorry or sad about something.
**regrettable** *adjective*, **regrettably** *adverb*

**regular** *adjective*
1 always happening at certain times,
*regular meals.* 2 even; symmetrical, *regular
teeth.* 3 normal; correct, *the regular
procedure.* 4 of a country's permanent
armed forces, *a regular soldier.*
**regular solid**, a three-dimensional object
with all its faces the same size and shape,
and having equal angles between any face
and the one next to it.
**regularity** *noun*, **regularly** *adverb*

**regulate** *verb* (**regulates, regulating, regulated**)
to adjust or control something.
**regulator** *noun*

**regulation** *noun* (**regulations**)
1 the adjusting or controlling of something.
2 a rule or law.

**rehearse** *verb* (**rehearses, rehearsing, rehearsed**)
to practise something before it is
performed.
**rehearsal** *noun*

**reign**[1] *verb* (**reigns, reigning, reigned**)
1 to be king or queen. 2 to be the most
noticeable or important thing, *Silence
reigned.*

**reign**[2] *noun* (**reigns**)
the time when someone is king or queen.

**rein** *noun* (**reins**)
a strap used to guide a horse.

**reindeer** *noun* (**reindeer**)
a kind of deer that lives in cold countries.

**reinforce** *verb* (**reinforces, reinforcing, reinforced**)
to strengthen.
**reinforced concrete**, concrete with metal bars
or wires embedded in it.

**reinforcement** *noun* (**reinforcements**)
a thing that strengthens something.
**reinforcements**, extra troops, ships, etc. sent
to strengthen a force.

**reject**[1] *verb* (**rejects, rejecting, rejected**)
(*say* ri-jekt)
1 to refuse to accept a person or thing, *She
rejected my offer of help.* 2 to get rid of
something, *Any faulty parts are rejected at
the factory.*
**rejection** *noun*

**reject**[2] *noun* (**rejects**)
(*say* ree-jekt)
a thing that is got rid of, especially because
of being faulty or poorly made.

**rejoice** *verb* (**rejoices, rejoicing, rejoiced**)
to be very happy.

**relate** *verb* (**relates, relating, related**)
1 to connect or compare one thing with
another. 2 to tell a story.
**related**, belonging to the same family, *He
and I are related.*

**relation** *noun* (**relations**)
1 someone in your family. 2 the way that
one thing is connected or compared with
another.

**relationship** *noun* (**relationships**)
1 the way people or things are connected
with each other. 2 the way people get on
with one another, *There is a good
relationship between the teachers and the
children.* 3 a connection, especially because
of love, between two people.

**relative**[1] *noun* (**relatives**)
someone in your family.

**relative**² *adjective*
1 connected or compared with something.
2 compared with the average, *They live in relative comfort.*
**relative pronoun**, one of the words 'who', 'what', 'which', or 'that', placed in front of a clause to connect it with an earlier clause, *In 'the man who came to lunch', the relative pronoun is 'who'.*
**relatively** *adverb*

**relax** *verb* (**relaxes, relaxing, relaxed**)
1 to become less stiff or less strict. 2 to rest something.
**relaxation** *noun*

**relay**¹ *verb* (**relays, relaying, relayed**)
to pass on a message or broadcast.

**relay**² *noun* (**relays**)
1 one of a series of groups, *The firemen worked in relays.* 2 a relay race. 3 a device for passing on a broadcast. 4 a switch that is operated by electricity.
**relay race**, a race between two or more teams in which each competitor covers part of the distance.

**release**¹ *verb* (**releases, releasing, released**)
1 to set free; to unfasten. 2 to give off, *Cars release fumes.* 3 to make a film, record, etc. available to the public.

**release**² *noun* (**releases**)
1 being released. 2 something released, especially a new film, record, etc. 3 a device that unfastens something, *The seat-belt has a quick release.*

**relegate** *verb* (**relegates, relegating, relegated**)
(*say* **rel**-i-gayt)
to put something into a lower group or position than before; to put a team into a lower division of a league.
**relegation** *noun*

**relent** *verb* (**relents, relenting, relented**)
to be less angry or more merciful than you were going to be.

**relentless** *adjective*
1 pitiless, *a relentless campaign of oppression.* 2 that you cannot stop.
**relentlessly** *adverb*

**relevant** *adjective*
(*say* **rel**-i-vănt)
connected with what is being discussed or dealt with, *The weather on the day of the crime may be relevant, because the suspect's clothes were wet.*
**relevance** *noun*, **relevantly** *adverb*

**reliable** *adjective*
that you can trust or depend on.
**reliability** *noun*, **reliably** *adverb*

**relic** *noun* (**relics**)
something that has survived from an ancient time.

**relief** *noun* (**reliefs**)
1 the ending or lessening of pain, trouble, boredom, etc. 2 something that causes the ending or lessening of pain, etc. 3 a person or thing that takes over or helps with a job. 4 a method of making a map, design, etc. that stands out from a flat surface, *The model shows hills and valleys in relief.* 5 (*in Geography*) differences in height between hills and valleys, *The map shows the relief by means of different colours.*

**relieve** *verb* (**relieves, relieving, relieved**)
to end or lessen someone's pain, trouble, boredom, etc.
**relieve someone of something**, to take something from someone, *He relieved me of my watch.*

**religion** *noun* (**religions**)
what people believe about God or gods, and how they worship.
**religious** *adjective*, **religiously** *adverb*

**reluctant** *adjective*
not wanting to do something; not keen.
**reluctance** *noun*, **reluctantly** *adverb*

**rely** *verb* (**relies, relying, relied**)
**rely on** or **upon**, to trust someone or something to help or support you.
**reliance** *noun*, **reliant** *adjective*

**remain** *verb* (**remains, remaining, remained**)
1 to continue in the same place or condition. 2 to be left over, *A lot of food remained after the party.*
**remainder** *noun*

**remains** *plural noun*
1 something left over. 2 ruins; relics.
3 a corpse.

**remark**¹ *verb* (**remarks, remarking, remarked**)
to say something that you have thought or noticed.

**remark**² *noun* (**remarks**)
something said.

**remarkable** *adjective*
so unusual that you notice or remember it.
**remarkably** *adverb*

**remedial** *adjective*
(*say* ri-**mee**-di-ăl)
that helps to cure an illness or problem.

**remedy** *noun* (**remedies**)
a cure; a medicine.

**remember** *verb* (**remembers, remembering, remembered**)
**1** to keep something in your mind. **2** to bring something into your mind when you want to, *Can you remember his telephone number?*
**remembrance** *noun*

**remind** *verb* (**reminds, reminding, reminded**)
to help or make someone remember something.
**reminder** *noun*

**reminisce** *verb* (**reminisces, reminiscing, reminisced**)
(*say* rem-in-iss)
to think or talk about things you remember.
**reminiscence** *noun*, **reminiscent** *adjective*

**remnant** *noun* (**remnants**)
a small piece of something left over.

**remorse** *noun*
deep regret for having done wrong.
**remorseful** *adjective*, **remorseless** *adjective*

**remote** *adjective* (**remoter, remotest**)
**1** far away. **2** unlikely; slight, *a remote chance.*
**remote control**, controlling something from a distance, usually by means of radio or electricity.
**remotely** *adverb*, **remoteness** *noun*

**removal** *noun* (**removals**)
removing or moving something, especially moving furniture from one house to another.

**remove** *verb* (**removes, removing, removed**)
to take something away or off.

**Renaissance** *noun*
the revival of art and literature in Europe in the 14th–16th centuries.

**render** *verb* (**renders, rendering, rendered**)
**1** to put someone in a particular condition, *She was rendered speechless by the shock.* **2** to give or perform something, *a reward for services rendered.*

**rendezvous** *noun* (**rendezvous**)
(*say* ron-day-voo)
a meeting with someone; a place or appointment to meet someone.

**renew** *verb* (**renews, renewing, renewed**)
to make something as it was before or replace it with something new.
**renewal** *noun*

**renewable energy** *noun*
energy from the sun, including wind power, water power, and energy from plants.

**renown** *noun*
fame, *a man of great renown.*
**renowned** *adjective*

**rent**[1] *noun* (**rents**)
a regular payment for the use of something, especially a house, that belongs to another person.

**rent**[2] *verb* (**rents, renting, rented**)
to pay money for the use of something.

**repair**[1] *verb* (**repairs, repairing, repaired**)
to mend something.

**repair**[2] *noun* (**repairs**)
**1** mending something; the result of mending something, *The car is in for repair.* **2** condition, *His car is in good repair.*

**repay** *verb* (**repays, repaying, repaid**)
to pay back, *She has repaid her debt.*
**repayment** *noun*

**repeat**[1] *verb* (**repeats, repeating, repeated**)
to say or do the same thing again.
**repeatedly** *adverb*, **repetition** *noun*, **repetitive** *adjective*

**repeat**[2] *noun* (**repeats**)
something that is repeated, especially a radio or television programme.

**repel** *verb* (**repels, repelling, repelled**)
**1** to drive or force someone or something away, *Unlike poles of magnets attract each other, and like poles repel each other.* **2** to disgust someone.
**repellent** *adjective*

**repent** *verb* (**repents, repenting, repented**)
to be sorry for what you have done.
**repentance** *noun*, **repentant** *adjective*

**replace** *verb* (**replaces, replacing, replaced**)
**1** to put something back in its place. **2** to take the place of another person or thing. **3** to put a new thing in the place of an old one, *Replace the old engine with a new one.*
**replacement** *noun*

**replay** *noun* (**replays**)
**1** a football match played again after a draw. **2** the playing or showing again of a recording.

**replica** *noun* (**replicas**)
(*say* rep-li-kă)
an exact copy.

**reply**[1] *noun* (**replies**)
something said or written to deal with a question, letter, etc.; an answer.

**reply**[2] *verb* (**replies, replying, replied**)
to give a reply; to answer, *She replied to my letter. He replied immediately.*

**report**[1] *verb* (**reports, reporting, reported**)
**1** to describe something that has happened or something you have studied. **2** to make a complaint or accusation against someone. **3** to go to someone and say that you have arrived.

**report**[2] *noun* (**reports**)
1 a description or account of something.
2 a regular statement of how someone has worked or behaved, especially at school.
3 an explosive sound, *the report of a gun.*

**reporter** *noun* (**reporters**)
someone whose job is to collect news for a newspaper, radio, television, etc.

**repossess** *verb* (**repossesses, repossessing, repossessed**)
to claim back goods which someone has taken but has not fully paid for.

**represent** *verb* (**represents, representing, represented**)
1 to be a picture, model, or symbol of something or someone. 2 to be an example of something. 3 to help someone by speaking or acting for him or her.
**representation** *noun*, **representative** *noun*

**repress** *verb* (**represses, repressing, repressed**)
1 to keep something down or under, *The dictator tried to repress all opposition.* 2 to prevent someone or something from being free or enjoying life, *Children were repressed in Victorian times.*
**repression** *noun*, **repressive** *adjective*

**reprieve** *noun* (**reprieves**)
(*say* ri-**preev**)
postponing or cancelling a punishment, especially the death penalty.

**reprimand** *verb* (**reprimands, reprimanding, reprimanded**)
to tell someone off.

**reprisal** *noun* (**reprisals**)
(*say* ri-**pry**-zăl)
an act of revenge.

**reproach** *verb* (**reproaches, reproaching, reproached**)
to tell someone off; to find fault with someone.

**reproduce** *verb* (**reproduces, reproducing, reproduced**)
1 to make something be heard or seen again, *Sound can be reproduced by discs or magnetic tapes.* 2 to copy something. 3 to have offspring.
**reproduction** *noun*, **reproductive** *adjective*

**repromaster** *noun* (**repromasters**)
a sheet of information or drawings, especially a worksheet, that can be photocopied by a teacher for use in class.

**reptile** *noun* (**reptiles**)
an animal that creeps or crawls, *Snakes, lizards, crocodiles, and tortoises are reptiles.*
**reptilian** *adjective*

**republic** *noun* (**republics**)
a country ruled by a president and government that are chosen by the people.

**republican**[1] *adjective*
of or connected with a country ruled by a president and government that are chosen by the people.
**Republican Party,** one of the two main political parties of the USA.

**republican**[2] *noun* (**republicans**)
a person who supports a republican system of government.
**Republican,** a supporter of the American Republican Party.

**repulsive** *adjective*
disgusting.
**repulsion** *noun*

**reputation** *noun* (**reputations**)
what people think about a person or thing, *He has a reputation for being honest.*

**request**[1] *verb* (**requests, requesting, requested**)
to ask politely for something.

**request**[2] *noun* (**requests**)
1 the action of asking for something. 2 what someone asks for.

**require** *verb* (**requires, requiring, required**)
1 to need or want, *We require some paper.*
2 to make someone do something, *Drivers are required to license their cars.*
**requirement** *noun*

**reread** *verb* (**rereads, rereading, reread**)
to read something again.

**rescue** *verb* (**rescues, rescuing, rescued**)
to save someone from danger, capture, etc.
**rescue** *noun*, **rescuer** *noun*

**research** *noun* (**researches**)
careful study or investigation.
**researcher** *noun*

**resemblance** *noun* (**resemblances**)
being similar, *There is a resemblance between the brothers.*

**resemble** *verb* (**resembles, resembling, resembled**)
to look or sound like another person or thing.

**resent** *verb* (**resents, resenting, resented**)
to feel indignant or angry about something.
**resentful** *adjective*, **resentment** *noun*

**reservation** *noun* (**reservations**)
1 reserving something. 2 something reserved. 3 an area of land kept for a special purpose. 4 a doubt; a feeling of unease, *I had reservations about buying such an old car.*

**reserve**[1] *verb* (**reserves, reserving, reserved**)
to keep or order something for a particular person or for a special use.
**reserved,** shy; not sociable.

**reserve²** *noun* (**reserves**)
1 a person or thing kept ready to be used if necessary. 2 an area of land kept for a special purpose, *This island is a nature reserve.*

**reservoir** *noun* (**reservoirs**)
(*say* rez-er-vwar)
a place, especially an artificial lake, where water is stored.

**reshuffle** *noun* (**reshuffles**)
a rearrangement, especially an exchange of jobs between people in a group, *The Prime Minister announced a Cabinet reshuffle.*

**reside** *verb* (**resides, residing, resided**)
to live in a particular place.
**resident** *noun*

**residence** *noun* (**residences**)
where someone lives.
**in residence,** (*formal*) living in a particular place, especially an important house or building, *The Queen was in residence at Windsor Castle.*
**residential** *adjective*

**resign** *verb* (**resigns, resigning, resigned**)
to give up your job or position.
**resign yourself to something,** to accept something without complaining or arguing.
**resignation** *noun*

**resin** *noun* (**resins**)
(*say* rez-in)
a sticky substance that comes from plants or is made artificially.
**resinous** *adjective*

**resist** *verb* (**resists, resisting, resisted**)
to try to stop someone or something; to fight back against someone or something.
**resistant** *adjective*

**resistance** *noun* (**resistances**)
1 fighting or taking action against someone or something, *The new law met with public resistance. The troops came up against armed resistance.* 2 the way that materials hold up the passage of electric current; the amount by which a material does this.
**resistor** *noun*

**resolute** *adjective*
(*say* rez-ŏ-loot)
determined; firm.
**resolutely** *adverb*

**resolution** *noun* (**resolutions**)
1 being determined or firm. 2 something that you have decided.

**resolve** *verb* (**resolves, resolving, resolved**)
1 to make a decision. 2 to overcome disagreements, doubts, etc.

**resort** *noun* (**resorts**)
a place where people go for holidays.
**the last resort,** the only thing you can do when all else has failed.

**resound** *verb* (**resounds, resounding, resounded**)
to fill a place with sound; to echo.

**resource** *noun* (**resources**)
something that can be used, *The land is rich in natural resources.*

**respect¹** *noun* (**respects**)
1 admiration for someone's good qualities, achievement, etc. 2 consideration; concern, *Have respect for people's feelings.* 3 a detail or aspect, *In some respects, he is like his sister.*
**with respect to something,** concerning something.

**respect²** *verb* (**respects, respecting, respected**)
1 to admire someone for his or her good qualities, achievement, etc. 2 to have consideration or concern for someone.

**respectable** *adjective*
1 having good manners, character, appearance, etc. 2 of a good size or standard, *These tomatoes have reached a respectable size.*
**respectability** *noun*, **respectably** *adverb*

**respectful** *adjective*
showing respect; polite.
**respectfully** *adverb*

**respecting** *preposition*
concerning.

**respective** *adjective*
of or for each one, *We went to our respective rooms.*
**respectively** *adverb*

**respiration** *noun*
breathing.
**respirator** *noun*, **respiratory** *adjective*

**respond** *verb* (**responds, responding, responded**)
1 to reply. 2 to react.

**response** *noun* (**responses**)
1 a reply. 2 a reaction.

**responsible** *adjective*
1 looking after something and likely to take the blame if anything goes wrong. 2 that can be trusted. 3 important, *a responsible job.* 4 causing something, *His carelessness was responsible for their deaths.*
**responsibility** *noun*, **responsibly** *adverb*

**rest¹** *noun* (**rests**)
1 a time of sleep, relaxation, freedom from work, etc. 2 a support, *an arm-rest.*
**restful** *adjective*

**rest²** *noun*
the part that is left; the others, *I shall go; the rest can stay here.*

**reveal**

**rest**<sup>3</sup> *verb* (**rests, resting, rested**)
1 to sleep, relax, not work, etc. 2 to support something; to be supported, *Rest the ladder against the wall. The ladder is resting against the wall.*

**restaurant** *noun* (**restaurants**)
a place where you can buy a meal and eat it.

**restless** *adjective*
unable to rest or keep still.
**restlessly** *adverb*, **restlessness** *noun*

**restore** *verb* (**restores, restoring, restored**)
1 to put something back as it was, *We are trying to restore an ancient custom. I have restored the clock to its place on the mantelpiece.* 2 to repair something, *She restores cars as a hobby.*
**restoration** *noun*

**restrain** *verb* (**restrains, restraining, restrained**)
to hold someone or something back; to keep something under control.
**restraint** *noun*

**restrict** *verb* (**restricts, restricting, restricted**)
to keep a person or thing within certain limits.
**restriction** *noun*, **restrictive** *adjective*

**result**<sup>1</sup> *noun* (**results**)
1 a thing that happens because something else has happened. 2 the score or situation at the end of a game, competition, race, etc. 3 the answer to a sum or problem.

**result**<sup>2</sup> *verb* (**results, resulting, resulted**)
1 to happen as a result, *What resulted from their action?* 2 to have a particular result, *The game resulted in a draw.*
**resultant** *adjective*

**resume** *verb* (**resumes, resuming, resumed**)
to start again after stopping for a while.
**resumption** *noun*

**resuscitate** *verb* (**resuscitates, resuscitating, resuscitated**)
to revive someone who has been unconscious.

**retail** *adjective*
sold, usually in small quantities, to people who are not shopkeepers, etc., *retail goods.*

**retain** *verb* (**retains, retaining, retained**)
1 to keep something. 2 to hold something in place.

**retina** *noun* (**retinas**)
(*say* ret-i-nă)
a layer at the back of your eyeball that is sensitive to light.

**retire** *verb* (**retires, retiring, retired**)
1 to give up work, usually because you are getting old. 2 to retreat; to withdraw. 3 (*formal*) to go to bed.
**retirement** *noun*

**retiring** *adjective*
shy.

**retort** *verb* (**retorts, retorting, retorted**)
to reply quickly or angrily.

**retrace** *verb* (**retraces, retracing, retraced**)
to go back over something.

**retreat** *verb* (**retreats, retreating, retreated**)
to go back so as to avoid death or danger.

**retrieve** *verb* (**retrieves, retrieving, retrieved**)
to get something back; to find something.
**retrievable** *adjective*, **retrieval** *noun*

**retriever** *noun* (**retrievers**)
a dog that can find and bring back birds and other animals that have been shot.

**return**<sup>1</sup> *verb* (**returns, returning, returned**)
1 to come or go back to a place. 2 to give or send something back.
**returnable** *adjective*

**return**<sup>2</sup> *noun* (**returns**)
1 returning. 2 something given or sent back. 3 profit, *He gets a good return on his savings.* 4 a return ticket.
**return game** or **return match**, a second game between two teams.
**return ticket**, a ticket for a journey to a place and back again.

**reunion** *noun* (**reunions**)
a meeting of people who have not met for some time.

**Rev.** short for **Reverend**.

**rev**<sup>1</sup> *verb* (**revs, revving, revved**)
(*informal*) to make an engine run quickly.

**rev**<sup>2</sup> *noun* (**revs**)
(*informal*) a revolution of an engine.

**reveal** *verb* (**reveals, revealing, revealed**)
to let something be seen or known.
**revelation** *noun*

**revenge** *noun*
the action of harming someone because he or she has harmed you or your friends.

**revenue** *noun* (**revenues**)
(*say* rev-ĕ-nyoo)
income.

**revere** *verb* (**reveres, revering, revered**)
(*say* ri-**veer**)
to respect someone or something deeply or religiously.

**Reverend** *noun*
the title of a member of the clergy, *the Reverend John Smith.*

USAGE: Do not confuse **Reverend** with **reverent**, which is an adjective and is the next word in this dictionary.

**reverent** *adjective*
feeling or showing awe or respect, especially towards God or holy things.
**reverence** *noun*

**reverse**[1] *noun*
1 the opposite way or side. 2 reverse gear.
**in reverse,** going in the opposite direction.
**reverse gear,** the gear used to drive a vehicle backwards.

**reverse**[2] *verb* (**reverses, reversing, reversed**)
1 to turn something round. 2 to go backwards in a vehicle.
**reversal** *noun*, **reversible** *adjective*

**review**[1] *noun* (**reviews**)
1 an inspection or survey. 2 a published description and opinion of a book, film, play, etc.

USAGE: Do not confuse **review** with **revue**, which means an entertainment made up of several short performances.

**review**[2] *verb* (**reviews, reviewing, reviewed**)
1 to inspect or survey something. 2 to publish a description and opinion of a book, film, play, etc.
**reviewer** *noun*

**revise** *verb* (**revises, revising, revised**)
1 to get ready for an examination, etc. by studying work that you have already done.
2 to correct or change something, such as a plan or piece of writing.
**revision** *noun*

**revive** *verb* (**revives, reviving, revived**)
1 to bring someone or something back to life or strength; to come back to life or strength. 2 to start using or performing something again, *revive an old custom.*
**revival** *noun*

**revolt** *verb* (**revolts, revolting, revolted**)
1 to rebel. 2 to disgust or horrify someone.

**revolution** *noun* (**revolutions**)
1 a rebellion that overthrows the government. 2 a complete change. 3 one turn of a wheel, engine, etc.

**revolutionary** *adjective*
of or involving a revolution.

**revolutionize** *verb* (**revolutionizes, revolutionizing, revolutionized**)
to change something completely.

**revolve** *verb* (**revolves, revolving, revolved**)
to go round in a circle.

**revolver** *noun* (**revolvers**)
a pistol that has a revolving store for bullets so that it can be fired several times without having to be loaded again.

**revue** *noun* (**revues**)
an entertainment made up of several short performances such as songs, short amusing plays, or stories.

USAGE: Do not confuse **revue** with the noun **review**, which means an inspection, or a description of a book, film, or play.

**reward**[1] *noun* (**rewards**)
something given to a person because he or she has done something, behaved well, etc.

**reward**[2] *verb* (**rewards, rewarding, rewarded**)
to give someone a reward.

**rewind** *verb* (**rewinds, rewinding, rewound**)
to make a cassette tape or video tape go backwards so that it can be played again.

**rewrite** *verb* (**rewrites, rewriting, rewrote, rewritten**)
to write something again or differently.

**rheumatism** *noun*
(*say* roo-mă-tizm)
a disease that causes pain and stiffness in joints and muscles.
**rheumatic** *adjective*

**rhinoceros** *noun* (**rhinoceroses** or **rhinoceros**)
(*say* ry-**noss**-er-ŏs)
a large, heavy animal with either one or two horns on its nose.

**rhododendron** *noun* (**rhododendrons**)
(*say* roh-dŏ-**den**-drŏn)
an evergreen shrub with large flowers.

**rhombus** *noun* (**rhombuses**)
a flat shape with four straight equal sides
and with no right angles between them.

**rhubarb** *noun*
a plant with pink or green stalks used as
food.

**rhyme**[1] *noun* (**rhymes**)
1 similar sounds in the endings of words,
as in *bat* and *mat, batter* and *matter.* 2 a
short rhyming poem.

**rhyme**[2] *verb* (**rhymes, rhyming, rhymed**)
1 to have rhymes, especially at the ends of
lines, *This verse doesn't rhyme.* 2 to sound
similar to other words, *Bat rhymes with
hat.*

**rhythm** *noun* (**rhythms**)
a regular pattern of beats, sounds, or
movements, *Most poetry and music has
rhythm.*
**rhythmic** *adjective*, **rhythmical** *adjective*,
**rhythmically** *adverb*

**ria** *noun* (**rias**)
a narrow inlet of the sea, formed where
part of a river valley has become
submerged.

**rib** *noun* (**ribs**)
one of the curved bones above your waist.

**ribbon** *noun* (**ribbons**)
a strip of nylon, silk, or other material, *Her
hair was tied up with a ribbon.*
**ribbon development,** the building of houses
along a main road, extending outwards
from a town or village.

**rice** *noun*
white seeds from a kind of grass, used as
food.

**rich** *adjective* (**richer, richest**)
1 having a lot of money or property. 2 full of
goodness, quality, strength, etc. 3 costly;
luxurious, *rich furnishings.*
**richly** *adverb*, **richness** *noun*

**riches** *plural noun*
wealth.

**rick** *noun* (**ricks**)
a large, neat stack of hay or straw.

**rickety** *adjective*
unsteady; likely to fall down.

**rickshaw** *noun* (**rickshaws**)
a two-wheeled carriage pulled by one or
more people, *Rickshaws are used in the Far
East.*

**ricochet** *verb* (**ricochets, ricocheting, ricocheted**)
(*say* rik-ŏ-shay)
to bounce off something, *The bullets
ricocheted off the wall.*

**rid** *verb* (**rids, ridding, rid**)
to make a person or place free from
something unwanted, *He rid the town of
rats.*
**get rid of,** to cause someone or something to
go away; to get free of something, *I wish I
could get rid of these spots.*

**riddance** *noun*
**good riddance,** a phrase used to show that
you are glad that something or someone
has gone, *'The wasps have gone away.'
'Good riddance!'*

**riddle** *noun* (**riddles**)
a puzzling question, especially as a joke,
*Here is a riddle. Why was the farmer cross?
Because someone trod on his corn.*

**ride**[1] *verb* (**rides, riding, rode, ridden**)
1 to sit on a horse, bicycle, etc. and be
carried along on it, *I have never ridden a
pony.* 2 to travel in a car, bus, train, etc.,
*We rode to the seaside in a coach.*
**rider** *noun*

**ride**[2] *noun* (**rides**)
a journey on a horse, bicycle, etc. or in a
vehicle.

**ridge** *noun* (**ridges**)
a long, narrow part of something higher
than the rest of it, *There are special tiles
for the ridge of a roof.*

**ridicule** *verb* (**ridicules, ridiculing, ridiculed**)
to make fun of someone or something.

**ridiculous** *adjective*
so silly as to make people laugh.
**ridiculously** *adverb*

**rifle** *noun* (**rifles**)
a long gun that you hold against your
shoulder when you fire it, *Rifles have
grooved barrels and they fire bullets.*

**rift** *noun* (**rifts**)
1 a crack or split. 2 a disagreement between friends.

**rig** *verb* (**rigs, rigging, rigged**)
to provide a ship with rigging, sails, etc.
**rig out**, to provide someone with clothes, equipment, etc.
**rig up**, to make something quickly.

**rigging** *noun*
the ropes that support a ship's masts and sails.

**right**[1] *adjective*
1 on the side opposite the left. 2 correct, *Is this sum right?* 3 fair; virtuous, *Is it right to cheat?* 4 conservative; not in favour of political reforms.
**rightly** *adverb*, **rightness** *noun*

**right**[2] *noun* (**rights**)
1 the side opposite the left, *In France, cars drive on the right.* 2 what is fair or just; something that people ought to be allowed, *They protested for their rights.*

**right**[3] *adverb*
1 on or towards the right-hand side, *Turn right.* 2 completely, *Turn right round.* 3 exactly, *She stood right in the middle.* 4 straight; directly, *Go right ahead.*
**right away**, immediately.

**right**[4] *verb* (**rights, righting, righted**)
1 to make something upright, *They righted the boat.* 2 to make something correct; to avenge something, *The fault might right itself. Part of the knight's task was to right wrongs.*

**right angle** *noun* (**right angles**)
an angle of 90 degrees, *The angles in a square are right angles.*

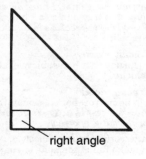
right angle

**righteous** *adjective*
being or doing good; obeying the law.
**righteously** *adverb*, **righteousness** *noun*

**rightful** *adjective*
deserved; proper, *his rightful place.*
**rightfully** *adverb*

**right hand** *noun* (**right hands**)
the hand that most people use more than the other.
**right-hand** *adjective*

**right-handed** *adjective*
using the right hand more than the left hand.

**rigid** *adjective*
(*say* **rij**-id)
1 firm; stiff, *a rigid support.* 2 strict; harsh, *rigid rules.*
**rigidity** *noun*, **rigidly** *adverb*

**rim** *noun* (**rims**)
the outer edge of a wheel or other round object.

**rind** *noun* (**rinds**)
the skin on bacon, cheese, or fruit.

**ring**[1] *noun* (**rings**)
1 a circle. 2 a thin circular piece of metal worn on a finger. 3 the space where a circus performs. 4 the place where a boxing-match or other contest is held.

**ring**[2] *verb* (**rings, ringing, rang, rung**)
1 to cause a bell to sound, *Have you rung the bell?* 2 to make a clear, musical sound like a bell. 3 to telephone, *She rang her brother last night.*

**ring**[3] *verb* (**rings, ringing, ringed**)
to put a ring round something, *Ring the answer that you think is the right one.*

**ringleader** *noun* (**ringleaders**)
someone who leads other people in rebellion, mischief, crime, etc.

**ringlet** *noun* (**ringlets**)
a curly and usually long piece of hair.

**ringmaster** *noun* (**ringmasters**)
the person who is in charge of what happens in the circus ring.

**ring road** *noun* (**ring roads**)
(in America, *beltway*) a road that goes right round a town.

**rink** *noun* (**rinks**)
a place made for skating.

**rinse** *verb* (**rinses, rinsing, rinsed**)
to wash something in clean water.

**riot**[1] *noun* (**riots**)
wild or violent behaviour by a crowd of people.
**riotous** *adjective*

**riot**[2] *verb* (**riots, rioting, rioted**)
to run wild and behave violently.

**rip**[1] *verb* (**rips, ripping, ripped**)
to tear something roughly.
**rip off,** (*slang*) to swindle someone; to steal
something, *You've been ripped off!*
*Someone's ripped off my bike.*

**rip**[2] *noun* (**rips**)
a torn place.
**rip-off,** (*slang*) a swindle.

**ripe** *adjective* (**riper, ripest**)
ready to be harvested or eaten.
**ripeness** *noun*

**ripen** *verb* (**ripens, ripening, ripened**)
to make something ripe; to become ripe.

**ripple**[1] *noun* (**ripples**)
a small wave on the surface of water.

**ripple**[2] *verb* (**ripples, rippling, rippled**)
to form small waves.

**rise**[1] *verb* (**rises, rising, rose, risen**)
1 to go upwards, *Prices have risen.* 2 to get
up, *They all rose as she came in.* 3 to rebel,
*They rose against the government.* 4 to
swell up by the action of yeast, *Let the
dough rise.*

**rise**[2] *noun* (**rises**)
1 an increase, especially in wages. 2 an
upward slope.
**give rise to something,** to cause something.

**risk**[1] *noun* (**risks**)
a chance of danger or loss.
**risky** *adjective*

**risk**[2] *verb* (**risks, risking, risked**)
to take the chance of damaging or losing
something.

**rissole** *noun* (**rissoles**)
a fried cake of minced meat.

**rite** *noun* (**rites**)
a ceremony.

**ritual** *noun* (**rituals**)
a regular ceremony or series of actions.
**ritualistic** *adjective*, **ritually** *adverb*

**rival**[1] *noun* (**rivals**)
a person or thing that competes with
another, or tries to do the same thing.
**rivalry** *noun*

**rival**[2] *verb* (**rivals, rivalling, rivalled**)
to compete with, or try to do the same
thing as someone or something.

**river** *noun* (**rivers**)
water flowing in one direction along a
channel.

**rivet**[1] *noun* (**rivets**)
a strong metal pin for holding pieces of
metal together.

**rivet**[2] *verb* (**rivets, riveting, riveted**)
1 to fasten something with rivets. 2 to fix,
*She stood riveted to the spot.* 3 to fascinate,
*The children were riveted by his story.*
**riveter** *noun*

**road** *noun* (**roads**)
a level way with a hard surface made for
traffic to go along.
**roadside** *noun*, **roadway** *noun*

**roadroller** *noun* (**roadrollers**)
a heavy motor vehicle with wide metal
wheels used to flatten surfaces when
making roads.

**roam** *verb* (**roams, roaming, roamed**)
to wander, *They roamed about the city.*

**roar**[1] *noun* (**roars**)
a loud, deep sound of the kind that a lion
makes.

**roar**[2] *verb* (**roars, roaring, roared**)
to make a loud, deep sound like a lion.
**a roaring trade,** brisk selling of something.

**roast** *verb* (**roasts, roasting, roasted**)
1 to cook something in an oven or over a
fire. 2 to make someone or something very
hot; to be very hot.

**rob** *verb* (**robs, robbing, robbed**)
to steal something from someone, *He
robbed me of my watch.*
**robber** *noun*, **robbery** *noun*

**robe** *noun* (**robes**)
a long, loose piece of clothing.

**robin** *noun* (**robins**)
a small brown bird with a red chest.

**robot** *noun* (**robots**)
(*say* roh-bot)
a machine that can move and behave in
some ways like a person.

**rock**[1] *noun* (**rocks**)
1 a large stone. 2 a large mass of stone. 3 a
hard sweet usually shaped like a stick and
sold at the seaside.
**rock plant,** a plant suitable for a rockery.
**rocky** *adjective*

**rock²** *noun* (**rocks**)
1 a backwards-and-forwards or side-to-side movement. 2 rock music.
**rock music,** popular music with a heavy beat.

**rock³** *verb* (**rocks, rocking, rocked**)
to move gently backwards and forwards or from side to side.

**rock-bottom** *adjective*
very low, *All the goods were sold off at rock-bottom prices.*

**rocker** *noun* (**rockers**)
1 a rocking-chair. 2 one of the curved bars that supports a rocking-chair.
**off your rocker,** (*slang*) mad.

**rockery** *noun* (**rockeries**)
part of a garden where flowers grow between rocks.

**rocket** *noun* (**rockets**)
1 a firework that shoots high into the air. 2 a pointed tube propelled into the air by hot gases, especially as a spacecraft or weapon.
**rocketry** *noun*

**rocking-chair** *noun* (**rocking-chairs**)
a chair which can be rocked by the person sitting in it.

**rod** *noun* (**rods**)
a long, thin stick or bar, especially one with a line attached for fishing.

**rode** past tense of **ride** *verb*.

**rodent** *noun* (**rodents**)
an animal that has large front teeth for gnawing things, *Rats, mice, and squirrels are rodents.*

**rodeo** *noun* (**rodeos**)
(*say* roh-**day**-oh or **roh**-di-oh)
a display or contest of cowboys' skill in riding, controlling cattle, etc.

**rogue** *noun* (**rogues**)
a dishonest or mischievous person.
**roguery** *noun*, **roguish** *adjective*

**role** *noun* (**roles**)
a performer's part in a play, film, etc.

**role-play** *noun*
a kind of acting in which people play the part of other people, used especially in teaching languages.

**roll¹** *verb* (**rolls, rolling, rolled**)
1 to move along by turning over and over, like a ball or wheel. 2 to move something along in this way. 3 to form something into the shape of a cylinder or ball. 4 to flatten something by moving a rounded object over it. 5 to sway from side to side, *Some ships roll more than others.* 6 to make a long vibrating sound, *The drums rolled.*

**roll²** *noun* (**rolls**)
1 a cylinder made by rolling something up. 2 a very small loaf of bread shaped like a bun. 3 a list of names. 4 a long vibrating sound, *a roll on the drums.*

**roller** *noun* (**rollers**)
1 a cylinder-shaped object, especially one used for flattening things. 2 a long sea-wave.

**roller-skate** *noun* (**roller-skates**)
a device with wheels that you can fit on your feet, making you able to move quickly and smoothly over the ground.
**roller-skating** *noun*

**rolling-pin** *noun* (**rolling-pins**)
a heavy cylinder rolled over pastry to flatten it.

**ROM** short for *read-only memory*, a type of computer memory which holds information that can be accessed but not changed by the user, and which keeps the information whether the computer is switched on or not.

**Roman¹** *noun* (**Romans**)
an inhabitant of Rome.

**Roman²** *adjective*
of Rome.
**Roman candle,** a firework that sends out coloured balls of flame.
**Roman Catholic,** a member of the Church that has the Pope as its head.
**Roman numerals,** letters that represent numbers (compare *arabic figures*), *In Roman numerals, I = 1, V = 5, X = 10, etc.*

**Romance** *adjective*
belonging to the group of languages which grew out of Latin and which includes French, Italian, Spanish, and Portuguese.

**romance** *noun* (**romances**)
1 experiences, feelings, stories, etc. connected with love. 2 a love-story.

**romantic** *adjective*
1 of or like romance. 2 connected with emotions or imagination.
**romantically** *adverb*

**romp** *verb* (**romps, romping, romped**)
to play in a lively way.

**rompers** *plural noun*
a piece of clothing for a young child, covering most of his or her body.

**roof** *noun* (**roofs**)
1 the part that covers the top of a building, shelter, or vehicle. 2 the upper part of your mouth.

**rook** *noun* (**rooks**)
1 a black bird that looks like a crow. 2 a piece in chess shaped like a castle.

**room** *noun* (**rooms**)
1 a part of a building with its own walls and ceiling. 2 enough space for someone or something, *Is there room for me?*
**roomful** *noun*

**roomy** *adjective* (**roomier, roomiest**)
with plenty of room or space.

**roost** *noun* (**roosts**)
the place where a bird rests.

**root**¹ *noun* (**roots**)
1 the part of a plant that grows under the ground. 2 a source or basis of something, *Money is the root of all evil.* 3 a number in relation to the number it produces when multiplied by itself, *9 is the root, or square root, of 81.*
**take root,** to grow roots; to become established, *The plant took root. The custom never took root in other countries.*

**root**² *verb* (**roots, rooting, rooted**)
1 to take root. 2 to fix someone in a particular spot, *Fear rooted him to the spot.*
**root out,** to get rid of something.

**rope** *noun* (**ropes**)
threads or strands twisted together.
**show someone the ropes,** to show someone how to do something.

**rose**¹ *noun* (**roses**)
a sweet-smelling flower with a thorny stem.

**rose**² past tense of **rise** *verb*.

**rosette** *noun* (**rosettes**)
a large circular badge.

**rosy** *adjective* (**rosier, rosiest**)
1 pink. 2 hopeful; cheerful.

**rot**¹ *verb* (**rots, rotting, rotted**)
to go soft or bad so that it is useless; to decay, *This wood has rotted.*

**rot**² *noun*
1 decay. 2 (*informal*) nonsense.

**rotate** *verb* (**rotates, rotating, rotated**)
1 to go round like a wheel. 2 to arrange something in a series; to happen in a series, *Rotate the jobs so that everybody has to take a turn at everything. The job of chairperson rotates.*
**rotary** *adjective*, **rotation** *noun*

**rotor** *noun* (**rotors**)
something that goes round, especially the large horizontal propeller of a helicopter.

**rotten** *adjective*
1 rotted, *rotten fruit.* 2 (*informal*) nasty; very bad, *rotten weather.*
**rottenness** *noun*

**Rottweiler** *noun* (**Rottweilers**)
a large breed of dog with short black and tan hair, often kept to protect people or buildings.

**rough** *adjective* (**rougher, roughest**)
1 not smooth; uneven, *a rough surface.* 2 not gentle, *a rough boy.* 3 not exact; done quickly, *a rough guess.*
**roughly** *adverb*, **roughness** *noun*

**roughage** *noun*
fibre in food, which helps you to digest the food.

**roughen** *verb* (**roughens, roughening, roughened**)
to make something rough; to become rough.

**round**¹ *adjective* (**rounder, roundest**)
1 shaped like a circle or ball. 2 full; complete, *a round dozen.* 3 that returns to where it started, *a round trip.*

**round**² *adverb*
1 in a circle or curve; by a longer route, *Go round to the back of the house.* 2 in all or various directions, *Hand the cakes round.* 3 in a new direction, *Turn your chair round.* 4 to someone's house, office, etc., *Come round at lunchtime.*

**round**³ *preposition*
1 on all sides of something, *a fence round the field.* 2 in a curve or circle about something, *The earth moves round the sun.* 3 to all or various parts of something, *Show them round the house.*
**round the bend** or **round the twist,** (*slang*) mad.

**round**⁴ *noun* (**rounds**)
1 a whole slice of bread; a sandwich made from two whole slices of bread. 2 a series of visits or calls made by a doctor, postman, etc. 3 one stage in a competition, *The winners go on to the next round.* 4 a shot or series of shots from a gun; a piece of ammunition. 5 a song in which people sing the same words but start at different times.

**round⁵** *verb* (**rounds, rounding, rounded**)
**1** to make something round; to become round. **2** to travel round, *The ship rounded Cape Horn.*
**round down,** to decrease a number to the nearest lower number, *123.4 may be rounded down to 123.*
**round off,** to finish something.
**round up,** to gather people, cattle, etc. together; to increase a number to the nearest higher number, *123.7 may be rounded up to 124.*

**roundabout** *noun* (**roundabouts**)
**1** (in America, *traffic circle*) a road junction where traffic has to go round a circle. **2** a merry-go-round.

**rounders** *noun*
a game in which players try to hit a ball and run round a circuit.

**Roundhead** *noun* (**Roundheads**)
an opponent of King Charles I in the English Civil War.

**rouse** *verb* (**rouses, rousing, roused**)
to make someone awake, active, or excited.

**rout¹** *verb* (**routs, routing, routed**)
(*say* rowt)
to defeat and chase away an enemy.

**rout²** *noun* (**routs**)
(*say* rowt)
a disorganized retreat from a battle.

**route** *noun* (**routes**)
(*say* root)
the way you have to go to get to a place.

**routine** *noun* (**routines**)
(*say* roo-**teen**)
a regular way of doing things.

**rove** *verb* (**roves, roving, roved**)
to wander; to travel.
**rover** *noun*

**row¹** *noun* (**rows**)
(rhymes with *go*)
a line of people or things.

**row²** *noun* (**rows**)
(rhymes with *cow*)
**1** a great noise or disturbance. **2** a quarrel; a noisy argument or scolding.

**row³** *verb* (**rows, rowing, rowed**)
(rhymes with *go*)
to use oars to make a boat move.
**rower** *noun*, **rowing-boat** *noun*

**rowdy** *adjective* (**rowdier, rowdiest**)
noisy and disorderly.
**rowdily** *adverb*, **rowdiness** *noun*, **rowdyism** *noun*

**rowlock** *noun* (**rowlocks**)
(*say* rol-ŏk)
a device on the side of a boat to hold an oar in place.

rowlock

**royal** *adjective*
of or connected with a king or queen.
**royally** *adverb*, **royalty** *noun*

**rub** *verb* (**rubs, rubbing, rubbed**)
to move something backwards and forwards while pressing it on something else, *He rubbed his hands together.*
**rub off** or **rub out,** to make something disappear by rubbing it.

**rubber** *noun* (**rubbers**)
**1** a strong elastic substance used for making tyres, balls, hoses, etc. **2** (in America, *eraser*) a piece of this substance for rubbing out pencil marks.
**rubbery** *adjective*

**rubbish** *noun*
**1** things that are not wanted or needed. **2** nonsense.

**rubble** *noun*
broken pieces of brick or stone.

**ruby** *noun* (**rubies**)
a red jewel.

**rucksack** *noun* (**rucksacks**)
a bag carried on your back.

**rudder** *noun* (**rudders**)
a flat, hinged device at the back of a ship or aircraft, used for steering.

**ruddy** *adjective* (**ruddier, ruddiest**)
**1** red and healthy-looking, *a ruddy face.*
**2** (*slang*) bloody, *a ruddy nuisance.*

**rude** *adjective* (**ruder, rudest**)
**1** not polite. **2** obscene; indecent.
**rudely** *adverb*, **rudeness** *noun*

**ruffian** *noun* (**ruffians**)
a violent, brutal person.

**ruffle** *verb* (**ruffles, ruffling, ruffled**)
to disturb the smoothness of something or the calmness of someone, *The bird ruffled its feathers. Your question seems to have ruffled her.*

**rug** *noun* (**rugs**)
1 a thick piece of material that partly covers a floor. 2 a thick blanket.

**Rugby** or **Rugby football** *noun*
a kind of football game using an oval ball that the players are allowed to touch, *There are 13 players on each side in Rugby League but 15 in Rugby Union.*

**rugged** *adjective*
(*say* **rug**-id)
1 rough; uneven, *a rugged face.* 2 rocky, *a rugged coast.*

**rugger** *noun*
(*informal*) Rugby football.

**ruin¹** *verb* (**ruins, ruining, ruined**)
to spoil something completely; to destroy something.

**ruin²** *noun* (**ruins**)
1 a building that has almost all fallen down. 2 the action of ruining; destruction.
**ruinous** *adjective*

**rule¹** *noun* (**rules**)
1 something that people have to obey; a way that people must behave. 2 governing, *a country that used to be under French rule.*
**as a rule,** usually.

**rule²** *verb* (**rules, ruling, ruled**)
1 to govern; to reign. 2 to make a decision, *The referee ruled that it was a foul.* 3 to draw a straight line with a ruler or some other straight edge.

**ruler** *noun* (**rulers**)
1 someone who governs. 2 a strip of wood, plastic, or metal with straight edges, used for measuring and drawing straight lines.

**rum** *noun* (**rums**)
a strong alcoholic drink made from sugar or molasses.

**rumble** *verb* (**rumbles, rumbling, rumbled**)
to make a deep, heavy sound like thunder.

**rummage** *verb* (**rummages, rummaging, rummaged**)
to turn things over or move them about while looking for something, *She rummaged in the wardrobe.*

**rummy** *noun*
a card-game in which players try to form sequences or sets of cards.

**rumour** *noun* (**rumours**)
something that a lot of people are saying, although it may not be true.

**rump** *noun* (**rumps**)
the hind part of an animal.

**rumpy** *noun* (**rumpies**)
a true Manx cat, with no tail at all.

**run¹** *verb* (**runs, running, ran, run**)
1 to use your legs to move quickly. 2 to go or travel; to flow, *Tears ran down his cheeks.* 3 to produce a flow of liquid, *Your nose is running.* 4 to work or function, *The engine was running smoothly.* 5 to manage or organize, *She runs a grocery shop.*
**run a risk,** to take a chance.
**run away,** to leave a place quickly or secretly.
**run into,** to hit someone or something with a vehicle; to meet someone without expecting it.
**run out,** to have used up your stock of something, *We have run out of sugar.*
**run over,** to knock someone down with your car, bicycle, etc.

**run²** *noun* (**runs**)
1 a time spent running, *Go for a run.* 2 a point scored in cricket or baseball. 3 a series of damaged stitches in a stocking or other piece of clothing. 4 a continuous series of events, *She had a run of good luck.* 5 a place for animals with a fence round it, *a chicken run.*
**on the run,** running away.

**runaway** *noun* (**runaways**)
someone who has run away.

**rung¹** *noun* (**rungs**)
one of the short crossbars on a ladder.

**rung²** past participle of **ring²** *verb*.

**runner** *noun* (**runners**)
1 a person or animal that runs, especially in a race. 2 the part of a sledge that slides along the ground.
**runner bean,** a kind of climbing bean.
**runner-up,** someone who comes second in a race or competition.

**runny** *adjective* (**runnier, runniest**)
flowing or moving like liquid.

**runway** *noun* (**runways**)
an airstrip.

**rural** *adjective*
of or like the countryside.

**rush¹** *verb* (**rushes, rushing, rushed**)
1 to hurry. 2 to attack or capture someone or something by a sudden, quick action.

**rush²** *noun* (**rushes**)
a hurry.
**rush hour,** the time when traffic is busiest.

**rush³** *noun* (**rushes**)
a plant with a thin stem that grows in wet or marshy places.

**rusk** *noun* (**rusks**)
a kind of biscuit for babies to chew.

**Russian** *adjective*
of Russia.

**rust**[1] *noun*
1 a red or brown substance formed on
metal that is exposed to air and dampness.
2 the process of forming this substance.
**rusty** *adjective*

**rust**[2] *verb* (**rusts, rusting, rusted**)
1 to cause a red or brown substance to form
on metal that is exposed to air and
dampness, *Salt water rusts steel quickly.*
2 to become covered with this substance,
*My bicycle's chain has rusted.*

**rustic** *adjective*
rural.

**rustle** *verb* (**rustles, rustling, rustled**)
1 to make a gentle sound like dry leaves
being blown by the wind. 2 to steal horses
or cattle.
**rustle up,** (*informal*) to get together or
provide a meal, helpers, etc.
**rustler** *noun*

**rut** *noun* (**ruts**)
1 a deep groove in the ground made by
wheels. 2 a boring habit or way of life, *We
are getting into a rut.*
**rutted** *adjective*

**ruthless** *adjective*
pitiless; merciless; cruel.
**ruthlessly** *adverb*, **ruthlessness** *noun*

**rye** *noun*
a cereal used to make bread, biscuits, etc.

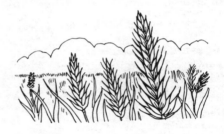

# Ss

**Sabbath** *noun* (**Sabbaths**)
a weekly day for rest and prayer, Saturday
for Jews, Sunday for Christians.

**sabotage** *noun*
(*say* sab-ŏ-tah*zh*)
deliberate damage or disruption to hinder
an enemy, employer, etc.
**saboteur** *noun*

**sac** *noun* (**sacs**)
part of an animal or plant that is shaped
like a bag.

**saccharin** *noun*
(*say* sak-ă-rin)
a sweet substance used as a substitute for
sugar.

**sachet** *noun* (**sachets**)
a small, sealed packet of something such as
shampoo.

**sack**[1] *noun* (**sacks**)
a large bag made of strong material.
**the sack,** being dismissed from a job, *They
gave me the sack.*

**sack**[2] *verb* (**sacks, sacking, sacked**)
to dismiss someone from a job.

**sacred** *adjective*
treated with religious respect; connected
with religion, *sacred places.*

**sacrifice**[1] *noun* (**sacrifices**)
1 giving or doing something that you think
will please a god. 2 giving up a thing that
you value so that something good may
happen. 3 something given or done to
please a god or to make something good
happen.
**sacrificial** *adjective*

**sacrifice**[2] *verb* (**sacrifices, sacrificing, sacrificed**)
to give something as a sacrifice.

**sad** *adjective* (**sadder, saddest**)
unhappy.
**sadly** *adverb*, **sadness** *noun*

**sadden** *verb* (**saddens, saddening, saddened**)
to make someone unhappy.

**saddle**[1] *noun* (**saddles**)
1 a seat designed to be put on the back of
a horse or other animal. 2 the seat of a
bicycle.

**saddle**[2] *verb* (**saddles, saddling, saddled**)
to put a seat on a horse's back.

**sadist** *noun* (**sadists**)
(*say* **say**-dist)
someone who likes hurting other people.
**sadism** *noun,* **sadistic** *adjective*

**safari** *noun* (**safaris**)
(*say* să-**far**-i)
an expedition to see or hunt wild animals.
**safari park,** a park where wild animals are
kept to be seen by visitors.

**safe**[1] *adjective* (**safer, safest**)
**1** free from danger; protected, *The bus
crashed, but the passengers are safe. The
child felt safe in his mother's arms.* **2** not
causing danger, *Drive at a safe speed.*
**safely** *adverb*

**safe**[2] *noun* (**safes**)
a strong cupboard or box in which valuable
things can be locked safely.

**safeguard** *noun* (**safeguards**)
a protection.

**safety** *noun*
being safe; protection.
**safety-belt,** a belt to hold someone securely
in a seat.
**safety-pin,** a curved pin made with a clip to
protect the point.

**sag** *verb* (**sags, sagging, sagged**)
to go down in the middle because
something heavy is pressing on it, *The
chair sagged under his weight.*

**saga** *noun* (**sagas**)
a long story, especially one that tells
Norwegian or Icelandic legends.

**sago** *noun*
a starchy white food used in puddings.

**said** past tense and past participle of **say**.

**sail**[1] *noun* (**sails**)
**1** a large piece of strong cloth attached to a
mast to make a boat move. **2** a short
voyage. **3** an arm of a windmill.

**sail**[2] *verb* (**sails, sailing, sailed**)
**1** to travel in a ship. **2** to start a voyage, *We
sail at noon.* **3** to control a boat. **4** to be
moved along by means of a sail or sails,
*This boat sails beautifully.*
**sailing-boat,** a boat or ship moved by sails.

**sailboard** *noun* (**sailboards**)
a type of boat like a surfboard with a mast
and sail, used for windsurfing.

**sailor** *noun* (**sailors**)
**1** a member of a ship's crew. **2** someone who
travels in a sailing-boat.

**saint** *noun* (**saints**)
a holy or very good person.
**saintly** *adjective*

**sake** *noun*
**for its own sake,** because you like doing it,
*I'm learning about music for its own sake,
not because I want to become a teacher of
music.*
**for someone's sake,** so as to help or please
someone, *She went to great trouble for his
sake.*
**for something's sake,** in order to get
something that you want, *He'll do anything
for the sake of money. I check the tyres
every day, for safety's sake.*

**salaam** *interjection*
a word used by Muslims to greet someone.

**salad** *noun* (**salads**)
a mixture of vegetables eaten cold and
often raw.
**salad cream,** a creamy sauce like
mayonnaise.

**salami** *noun* (**salamis**)
a kind of strong, spicy sausage.

**salary** *noun* (**salaries**)
a regular wage, usually paid every month.

**sale** *noun* (**sales**)
**1** the selling of something. **2** a time when
things are sold at reduced prices.
**for sale** or **on sale,** that can be bought.

**salesman** *noun* (**salesmen**)
someone whose job is to sell things.
**salesmanship** *noun*

**saline** *adjective*
salty; containing salt.

**saliva** *noun*
(*say* să-**ly**-vă)
the natural liquid in a person's mouth.

**salmon** *noun* (**salmon**)
a large fish with pink flesh that can be
eaten.

**salon** *noun* (**salons**)
the place where a hairdresser or a beauty
specialist works.

**saloon** *noun* (**saloons**)
**1** (in America, *sedan car*) a motor car with
a hard roof. **2** a room where people can sit,
drink, etc.

**salt**[1] *noun*
the white substance that gives sea-water
its taste and is used for flavouring food.
**salty** *adjective*

**salt**[2] *verb* (**salts, salting, salted**)
to use salt to flavour or preserve food.

**salute**[1] *verb* (**salutes, saluting, saluted**)
to raise your hand to your forehead as a
sign of respect or greeting, especially in the
armed forces.

**salute**[2] *noun* (**salutes**)
  **1** the act of greeting someone respectfully or politely. **2** the firing of guns as a sign of respect for someone.

**salvage** *verb* (**salvages, salvaging, salvaged**)
  to save or rescue something, especially a damaged ship, so that it can be used again.

**salvation** *noun*
  saving someone or something.

**same** *adjective*
  not different, *We are the same age.*

**samosa** *noun* (**samosas**)
  a small case of crisp pastry filled with a mixture of vegetables and spices, with or without meat.

**sample**[1] *noun* (**samples**)
  a small amount that shows what something is like, *They are giving away samples of cheese. The doctor took a blood sample.*

**sample**[2] *verb* (**samples, sampling, sampled**)
  **1** to take a sample of something, *Scientists sampled the lake water.* **2** to try part of something, *She sampled the cake.*

**sanctuary** *noun* (**sanctuaries**)
  a safe place, *a bird sanctuary.*

**sand**[1] *noun* (**sands**)
  the tiny grains of rock that you find on beaches and in deserts.
  **sands,** a sandy area.

**sand**[2] *verb* (**sands, sanding, sanded**)
  to smooth or polish something with sandpaper or some other rough material.
  **sander** *noun*

**sandal** *noun* (**sandals**)
  a lightweight shoe with straps that go round your foot.

**sandbag** *noun* (**sandbags**)
  a bag filled with sand, used to protect a place.

**sandpaper** *noun*
  strong paper with sand glued to it, rubbed on rough surfaces to make them smooth.

**sandstone** *noun*
  rock made of compressed sand.

**sandwich** *noun* (**sandwiches**)
  two slices of bread and butter with jam, meat, cheese, etc. between them.

**sandy** *adjective* (**sandier, sandiest**)
  **1** made of sand; covered with sand. **2** yellowish-red, *sandy hair.*

**sane** *adjective* (**saner, sanest**)
  not mad; with a healthy mind.
  **sanely** *adverb*

**sang** past tense of **sing.**

**sanitary** *adjective*
  free from germs and dirt.
  **sanitary towel,** an absorbent pad used by a woman during menstruation.

**sanitation** *noun*
  devices or arrangements for drainage and the disposal of sewage.

**sanity** *noun*
  having a healthy mind.

**sank** past tense of **sink** *verb.*

**sap**[1] *noun*
  the liquid inside a plant.

**sap**[2] *verb* (**saps, sapping, sapped**)
  to weaken someone's strength or energy.

**sapling** *noun* (**saplings**)
  a young tree.

**sapphire** *noun* (**sapphires**)
  a bright blue jewel.

**sarcasm** *noun*
  mocking someone or something, especially by saying the opposite of what you mean, *Saying 'Great shot!' when Jane missed the ball was a piece of sarcasm.*
  **sarcastic** *adjective*, **sarcastically** *adverb*

**sardine** *noun* (**sardines**)
  a small sea-fish, usually sold in tins.

**sari** *noun* (**saris**)
  (*say* **sar**-i)
  a long length of cloth worn as a dress, especially by Indian women and girls.

**sash** *noun* (**sashes**)
  a strip of cloth worn round the waist or over one shoulder.
  **sash window,** a window that slides up and down.

**sat** past tense and past participle of **sit.**

**satchel** *noun* (**satchels**)
a bag worn over your shoulder or on your back, especially for carrying books to and from school.

**satellite** *noun* (**satellites**)
a moon or a spacecraft that moves in an orbit round a planet.
**satellite dish,** a dish-shaped aerial for receiving television signals sent by satellite.
**satellite television,** a television system in which programmes are sent by means of an artificial satellite.

**satin** *noun*
smooth cloth that is very shiny on one side.

**satire** *noun* (**satires**)
1 using humour or exaggeration to make fun of someone or something. 2 a play, poem, etc. that does this.
**satirical** *adjective*, **satirist** *noun*, **satirize** *verb*

**satisfaction** *noun*
1 the feeling of being satisfied. 2 giving someone what he or she needs or wants. 3 something that makes you contented, *Helping people is the greatest satisfaction of his job.*

**satisfactory** *adjective*
good enough; sufficient.
**satisfactorily** *adverb*

**satisfy** *verb* (**satisfies, satisfying, satisfied**)
1 to give someone what he or she needs or wants. 2 to convince yourself or someone else, *I am satisfied that you have done your best.*

**saturate** *verb* (**saturates, saturating, saturated**)
1 to soak something, *My clothes are saturated with rain.* 2 to make something accept as much as possible of a substance or a product, *The market has been saturated with second-hand cars.*
**saturation** *noun*

**Saturday** *noun* (**Saturdays**)
the seventh day of the week.

**sauce** *noun* (**sauces**)
1 a thick liquid used to flavour food. 2 (*informal*) impudence; being cheeky.

**saucepan** *noun* (**saucepans**)
a metal cooking-pan with a handle.

**saucer** *noun* (**saucers**)
a small curved plate on which a cup is put.

**saucy** *adjective* (**saucier, sauciest**)
amusingly rude, *a saucy joke.*

**sauna** *noun* (**saunas**)
(*say* **saw**-nă or **sow**-nă)
a place where you can sit in a very hot, steamy room, and afterwards take hot or cold showers.

**saunter** *verb* (**saunters, sauntering, sauntered**)
to walk in a leisurely way.

**sausage** *noun* (**sausages**)
a tube of skin or plastic stuffed with minced meat and other ingredients.
**sausage-meat,** minced meat of the kind used in sausages.
**sausage roll,** sausage-meat in a small, short roll of pastry.

**savage**¹ *adjective*
wild and fierce; cruel.
**savagely** *adverb*, **savagery** *noun*

**savage**² *verb* (**savages, savaging, savaged**)
to attack and bite someone fiercely, *He had been savaged by a mad dog.*

**savannah** *noun* (**savannahs**)
(*say* să-**van**-ă)
a grassy plain in a hot country, with few trees.

**save** *verb* (**saves, saving, saved**)
1 to free a person or thing from danger. 2 to keep something, especially money, so that it can be used later. 3 to put information on to a computer disk so that it can be kept. 4 to stop a ball going into your goal.
**saver** *noun*

**savings** *plural noun*
money saved.
**savings certificate,** a document that you can buy at a post office to give you interest on money you save.

**saviour** *noun* (**saviours**)
a person who saves someone.
**our Saviour** or **the Saviour,** Jesus.

**savoury** *adjective*
tasty but not sweet.

**saw**¹ *noun* (**saws**)
a tool with sharp teeth for cutting wood, metal, etc.

**saw**² *verb* (**saws, sawing, sawn** or **sawed**)
to cut something with a saw, *Have you sawn that plank yet? I sawed it in half yesterday.*

**saw**³ past tense of **see**.

**sawdust** *noun*
powder that comes from wood when it is cut with a saw.

**saxophone** *noun* (**saxophones**)
a wind instrument with a reed in the mouthpiece, used especially for playing jazz music.

**say** *verb* (**says, saying, said**)
1 to make words with your voice. 2 to give an opinion.

**saying** *noun* (**sayings**)
a well-known phrase; a proverb.

**scab** *noun* (**scabs**)
1 a hard crust that forms over a cut or graze. 2 (*informal*) someone who works while other workers are on strike.

**scabbard** *noun* (**scabbards**)
a cover for the blade of a sword or dagger.

**scaffold** *noun* (**scaffolds**)
1 a platform on which criminals were executed. 2 a scaffolding.

**scaffolding** *noun*
1 a structure of poles and planks for workmen to stand on, especially when building or repairing a house. 2 the poles used to build this structure.

**scald** *verb* (**scalds, scalding, scalded**)
1 to burn yourself with very hot liquid. 2 to clean something with boiling water.

**scale**¹ *noun* (**scales**)
1 a series of units, steps, or marks for measuring something, *This ruler has one scale in centimetres and another in inches.* 2 a series of musical notes going up or down in a fixed pattern. 3 proportion; ratio, *The scale of this map is one inch to the mile.* 4 the relative size or importance of something, *They were making yoghurt on a large scale.*

**scale**² *noun* (**scales**)
1 one of the thin overlapping parts on the outside of fish, snakes, etc. 2 the coating that forms on the inside of kettles etc.
**scaly** *adjective*

**scale**³ *verb* (**scales, scaling, scaled**)
to climb up something.

**scalene** *adjective*
**scalene triangle**, a triangle with no equal sides.

**scales** *plural noun*
a weighing-machine, *bathroom scales*.

**scalp**¹ *noun* (**scalps**)
the skin on top of your head.

**scalp**² *verb* (**scalps, scalping, scalped**)
to cut off someone's scalp.

**scamper** *verb* (**scampers, scampering, scampered**)
to run quickly, *The rabbits scampered for safety*.

**scampi** *plural noun*
large prawns.

**scan** *verb* (**scans, scanning, scanned**)
1 to look at every part of something. 2 to look at a large area quickly. 3 to analyse the rhythm of a line of poetry; to have a poetic rhythm, *This line doesn't scan*. 4 to sweep a radar or electronic beam over an area in search of something; to examine part of the body using an electronic beam.
**scan** *noun*

**scandal** *noun* (**scandals**)
1 a disgraceful action. 2 gossip that damages someone's reputation.
**scandalous** *adjective*

**Scandinavian** *adjective*
of Scandinavia, *The Scandinavian countries are Norway, Sweden, Denmark, and Finland.*

**scanner** *noun* (**scanners**)
a device used to examine the body or part of it, using an electronic beam.

**scanty** *adjective* (**scantier, scantiest**)
hardly big enough; small.
**scantily** *adverb*

**scapegoat** *noun* (**scapegoats**)
someone who is blamed or punished for other people's mistakes, sins, etc.

**scar**¹ *noun* (**scars**)
the mark left on your skin by a cut or burn after it has healed.

**scar**² *verb* (**scars, scarring, scarred**)
to make a scar or scars on skin.

**scarce** *adjective* (**scarcer, scarcest**)
not available in sufficient amounts; not seen or found very often, *Wheat was scarce because of the bad harvest.*
**make yourself scarce**, (*informal*) to go away or keep out of the way.
**scarcity** *noun*

**scarcely** *adverb*
hardly.

**scare** *verb* (**scares, scaring, scared**)
to frighten.

**scarecrow** *noun* (**scarecrows**)
a figure of a man dressed in old clothes, set up to frighten birds away from crops.

**scarf** *noun* (**scarves**)
a strip of material worn round your neck or head.

**scarlet** *adjective*
bright red.
**scarlet fever,** an infectious disease which produces a scarlet rash.

**scary** *adjective* (**scarier, scariest**)
(*informal*) frightening.

**scatter** *verb* (**scatters, scattering, scattered**)
1 to throw things in various directions. 2 to move quickly in various directions, *The crowd scattered when the police arrived.*

**scene** *noun* (**scenes**)
1 the place where something happens, *the scene of the crime.* 2 part of a play or film. 3 a view. 4 a place represented on the stage by scenery; scenery. 5 an angry or noisy outburst, *She made a scene about the money.*

**scenery** *noun*
1 the natural features of an area, *They admired the scenery.* 2 painted screens, curtains, etc. put on a stage to make it look like another place.

**scent** *noun* (**scents**)
(*say* sent)
1 a perfume. 2 an animal's smell, that other animals can follow.
**scented** *adjective*

**sceptic** *noun* (**sceptics**)
(*say* **skep**-tik)
someone who is not inclined to believe things.
**sceptical** *adjective*, **scepticism** *noun*

USAGE: Do not confuse **sceptic** with **septic**, which is an adjective meaning infected with germs.

**schedule** *noun* (**schedules**)
(*say* **shed**-yool)
a list of details, things to be done, and especially times.
**on schedule,** on time; not arriving late.

**scheme**[1] *noun* (**schemes**)
1 a plan. 2 a secret plan.

**scheme**[2] *verb* (**schemes, scheming, schemed**)
to make secret plans.
**schemer** *noun*

**scholar** *noun* (**scholars**)
1 someone who studies a lot or knows a lot. 2 someone who has been given money to pay for his or her education.
**scholarly** *adjective*

**scholarship** *noun* (**scholarships**)
1 money given to someone to help pay for his or her education. 2 the knowledge that scholars have; learning or studying.

**school** *noun* (**schools**)
1 a place where children are educated. 2 the children who go there, *The whole school had a holiday.* 3 the time when children are taught things, *School begins at 9 o'clock.*
**school-leaver,** someone who is old enough to leave school, or who has just left school.
**schoolboy** *noun*, **schoolchild** *noun*, **schoolgirl** *noun*

**schooner** *noun* (**schooners**)
(*say* **skoo**-ner)
a sailing-ship with at least two masts.

**science** *noun*
studying objects and happenings which can be observed and tested; knowledge gained in this way.
**science fiction,** stories about the future.
**scientific** *adjective*, **scientifically** *adverb*

**scientist** *noun* (**scientists**)
an expert in science; someone who studies science.

**scissors** *plural noun*
a cutting device made of two movable blades joined together.

**scoff** *verb* (**scoffs, scoffing, scoffed**)
to make fun of someone; to jeer, *Many people scoffed at the inventor. Don't scoff.*

**scold** *verb* (**scolds, scolding, scolded**)
to tell someone off angrily or noisily.

**scone** *noun* (**scones**)
(*say* skon or skohn)
a small bun, usually eaten with butter, cream, and jam.

**scoop**[1] *noun* (**scoops**)
1 a deep spoon for serving ice-cream, mashed potato, etc. 2 a deep shovel. 3 (*informal*) an important piece of news published by only one newspaper.

**scoop**[2] *verb* (**scoops, scooping, scooped**)
to serve something with a deep spoon; to move something with a deep shovel.

**scooter** *noun* (**scooters**)
1 a kind of motor cycle with a small engine and small wheels. 2 a toy with two wheels and a narrow platform that you ride on.

**scope** *noun* (**scopes**)
1 opportunity; possibility, *Her job gives her scope for development.* 2 the range of something, *Chemistry is outside the scope of the syllabus for this class.*

**scorch** *verb* (**scorches, scorching, scorched**)
1 to make something go brown by heating or burning it, *He scorched the shirt he was ironing.*
**scorching,** (*informal*) very hot.

**score**[1] *noun* (**scores**)
1 the number of points or goals made in a game. 2 twenty, *He reached the age of fourscore (= 80).*

**score**[2] *verb* (**scores, scoring, scored**)
1 to get a goal or point in a game. 2 to keep a count of the score in a game. 3 to scratch a surface.
**scorer** *noun*

**scorn** *noun*
treating a person or thing as worthless or laughable.
**scornful** *adjective*, **scornfully** *adverb*

**scorpion** *noun* (**scorpions**)
a kind of spider with a poisonous sting in its tail.

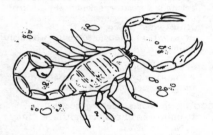

**Scot** *noun* (**Scots**)
a person from Scotland.
**Scotsman** *noun*

**Scotch** *adjective*
Scottish.
**Scotch terrier,** a small terrier with rough hair.

USAGE: Many Scots dislike the use of the word **Scotch**, and prefer to use **Scottish**.

**Scottie** *noun* (**Scotties**)
(*informal*) a Scotch terrier.

**Scottish** *adjective*
of Scotland.

**scoundrel** *noun* (**scoundrels**)
a wicked person.

**scour** *verb* (**scours, scouring, scoured**)
1 to rub something until it is clean and bright. 2 to search an area thoroughly.

**scout** *noun* (**scouts**)
someone sent out to collect information, spy on an enemy, etc.
**Scout,** a member of the Scout Association.

**scowl** *verb* (**scowls, scowling, scowled**)
to look bad-tempered.

**scramble**[1] *verb* (**scrambles, scrambling, scrambled**)
1 to move quickly and awkwardly, *We scrambled up the steep slope.* 2 to cook eggs by mixing them up and heating them in a pan.
**scramble for something,** to struggle to get something.

**scramble**[2] *noun* (**scrambles**)
1 the action of moving quickly with difficulty, *a stiff scramble over the rocks.* 2 a struggle to get something, *There was a mad scramble for the best seats.* 3 a motor-cycle race across rough country.

**scrap**[1] *noun* (**scraps**)
1 a small piece of something, *a scrap of cloth.* 2 rubbish, especially unwanted metal.
**scrap-book,** a book in which you stick newspaper cuttings, souvenirs, etc.

**scrap**[2] *noun* (**scraps**)
(*informal*) a fight.

**scrap**[3] *verb* (**scraps, scrapping, scrapped**)
to get rid of something you do not want.

**scrape**[1] *verb* (**scrapes, scraping, scraped**)
1 to rub something with something rough, hard, or sharp, *He was scraping the frying-pan.* 2 to move along or get past, touching or almost touching something, *The car scraped past.* 3 to use effort or care to get something, *They scraped together enough money for a holiday.*
**scraper** *noun*

**scrape**[2] *noun* (**scrapes**)
1 a scraping movement or sound. 2 a mark made by scraping something. 3 an awkward situation.

**scrappy** *adjective* (**scrappier, scrappiest**)
made of scraps or bits; not complete.

**scratch**[1] *verb* (**scratches, scratching, scratched**)
1 to damage a surface by rubbing something sharp over it. 2 to rub the skin with fingernails or claws because it itches.

**scratch**[2] *noun* (**scratches**)
1 a mark made by scratching. 2 the action of scratching.
**start from scratch,** to begin at the very beginning.
**up to scratch,** up to the proper standard.
**scratchy** *adjective*

**scrawl** *verb* (**scrawls, scrawling, scrawled**)
to scribble, especially big letters or marks.

**scream**[1] *noun* (**screams**)
1 a loud cry of pain, fear, etc. 2 (*informal*) something very amusing.

**scream**<sup>2</sup> *verb* (**screams, screaming, screamed**)
to give a scream.

**screech** *verb* (**screeches, screeching, screeched**)
to make a harsh, high-pitched sound, *The brakes screeched as the train came to a stop.*

**screen**<sup>1</sup> *noun* (**screens**)
**1** a flat surface on which films or television programmes are shown. **2** a movable wall or covered framework used to hide something, divide a room, or protect something from excessive heat, light, etc. **3** something that gives shelter or protection, *a smoke-screen.*

**screen**<sup>2</sup> *verb* (**screens, screening, screened**)
**1** to show a film or television programme. **2** to hide, divide, or protect something with a movable wall or covered framework. **3** to test someone to see if he or she has a disease, *The hospital can screen people for cancer.*

**screw**<sup>1</sup> *noun* (**screws**)
**1** a metal pin with a spiral ridge around it. **2** a propeller.

**screw**<sup>2</sup> *verb* (**screws, screwing, screwed**)
**1** to fix something with screws. **2** to move or fix something by turning it, *Screw the lid on to the jar. I screwed in the light-bulb.*

**screwdriver** *noun* (**screwdrivers**)
a tool for turning a screw.

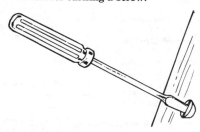

**scribble** *verb* (**scribbles, scribbling, scribbled**)
**1** to write untidily or carelessly. **2** to make meaningless marks.
**scribbler** *noun*

**script** *noun* (**scripts**)
**1** the words of a play or broadcast. **2** handwriting; something handwritten.

**scripture** *noun* (**scriptures**)
a sacred book, especially the Bible.

**scroll** *noun* (**scrolls**)
a roll of paper or parchment with writing on it.

**scrotum** *noun* (**scrotums or scrota**)
(*say* skroh-tŭm)
the pouch of skin behind the penis, containing the testicles.

**scrounge** *verb* (**scrounges, scrounging, scrounged**)
(*informal*) to get something without paying for it, *He scrounged a meal from us.*
**scrounger** *noun*

**scrub**<sup>1</sup> *verb* (**scrubs, scrubbing, scrubbed**)
**1** to rub something with a hard brush, *He scrubbed the floor.* **2** (*slang*) to cancel something, *We'll have to scrub the show.*

**scrub**<sup>2</sup> *noun* (**scrubs**)
the action of scrubbing.

**scrub**<sup>3</sup> *noun*
low trees and bushes, or land covered with them.

**scruffy** *adjective* (**scruffier, scruffiest**)
shabby and untidy.

**scrum** or **scrummage** *noun* (**scrums or scrummages**)
a group of players from each side in Rugby football pushing against each other and trying to win the ball.

**scrutinize** *verb* (**scrutinizes, scrutinizing, scrutinized**)
to examine or look at something closely.
**scrutiny** *noun*

**scuba diving** *noun*
swimming underwater, breathing air from tanks carried on your back.

**scuffle** *noun* (**scuffles**)
a confused struggle or fight.

**scullery** *noun* (**sculleries**)
in the past, a small room in some houses where the washing-up was done.

**sculptor** *noun* (**sculptors**)
someone who makes sculptures.

**sculpture** *noun* (**sculptures**)
**1** something carved or shaped out of stone, clay, metal, etc. **2** the art or work of a sculptor.

**scum** *noun*
**1** froth or dirt on the top of a liquid. **2** (*informal and offensive*) people who are thought to be worthless.

**scurry** *verb* (**scurries, scurrying, scurried**)
to run with short steps; to hurry.

**scurvy** *noun*
a disease caused by lack of fresh fruit and vegetables.

**scuttle**<sup>1</sup> *verb* (**scuttles, scuttling, scuttled**)
to sink your own ship deliberately.

**scuttle**<sup>2</sup> *verb* (**scuttles, scuttling, scuttled**)
to run with short, quick steps.

**scythe** *noun* (**scythes**)
a tool with a long curved blade for cutting grass or corn.

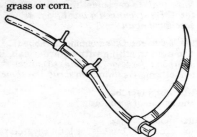

**sea** *noun* (**seas**)
1 the salt water that covers most of the earth's surface. 2 a very large area of water, *the Mediterranean Sea.* 3 a large area of something, *a sea of faces.*
**at sea**, on the sea; very puzzled, *He's completely at sea in his new job.*
**sea front**, the part of a seaside town that faces the sea, *A promenade runs along the sea front.*

**sea anemone** *noun* (**sea anemones**)
a sea-creature looking like a small mass of jelly with short tentacles around its mouth.

**seabed** *noun*
the bottom of the sea.

**sea-bird** *noun* (**sea-birds**)
a bird that lives close to the sea.

**seafaring** *adjective* and *noun*
travelling or working on the sea.
**seafarer** *noun*

**seafood** *noun*
fish or shellfish from the sea eaten as food.

**seagull** *noun* (**seagulls**)
a sea-bird with long wings.

**sea-horse** *noun* (**sea-horses**)
a small fish with a head rather like a horse's head.

**seal**¹ *noun* (**seals**)
a sea-animal that eats fish.

**seal**² *noun* (**seals**)
1 a design pressed into wax, lead, etc.
2 something designed to close an opening.
3 a small decorative sticker.

**seal**³ *verb* (**seals, sealing, sealed**)
to close something by sticking two parts together; to close tightly, *She sealed the envelope.*

**sea-level** *noun*
the level of the sea half-way between high and low tide, *The mountain rises 1,000 metres above sea-level.*

**sea-lion** *noun* (**sea-lions**)
a large kind of seal.

**seam** *noun* (**seams**)
1 the line where two edges of cloth, wood, etc. join together. 2 a layer of coal in the ground.

**seaman** *noun* (**seamen**)
a sailor.
**seamanship** *noun*

**seaplane** *noun* (**seaplanes**)
an aeroplane that can land on water.

**seaport** *noun* (**seaports**)
a port on the sea-coast.

**search**¹ *verb* (**searches, searching, searched**)
1 to look very carefully for something. 2 to examine a person, place, etc. thoroughly.
**searcher** *noun*

**search**² *noun* (**searches**)
a very careful look for someone or something.
**search-party**, a group of people looking for someone or something.

**searching** *adjective*
thorough, *Ask some searching questions.*

**searchlight** *noun* (**searchlights**)
a light with a strong beam that can be turned in any direction.

**seashore** *noun*
the land close to the sea, especially the part between high and low water marks.

**sea-sick** *adjective*
sick because of the movement of a ship.
**sea-sickness** *noun*

**seaside** *noun*
a place, town, etc. by the sea.

**season**¹ *noun* (**seasons**)
1 one of the four main parts of the year,
*The seasons are spring, summer, autumn,
and winter*. 2 a period when something
happens, *the football season*. 3 (*informal*) a
season-ticket.
**season-ticket**, a ticket that can be used as
often as you like throughout a period of
time.
**seasonal** *adjective*

**season**² *verb* (**seasons, seasoning, seasoned**)
to put salt, pepper, etc. on food to flavour it.
**seasoning** *noun*

**seat**¹ *noun* (**seats**)
something for sitting on.
**seat-belt**, a belt to hold someone securely in
a seat.

**seat**² *verb* (**seats, seating, seated**)
to have seats for a particular number of
people, *The theatre seats 3,000.*
**seat yourself**, to sit down.

**seaward** or **seawards** *adverb*
towards the sea.

**seaweed** *noun* (**seaweeds**)
plants that grow in the sea.

**secateurs** *plural noun*
(*say* sek-ă-terz)
a tool like a large pair of scissors for
pruning plants.

**secluded** *adjective*
away from large numbers of people; not
crowded, *a secluded beach.*
**seclusion** *noun*

**second**¹ *adjective*
next after the first.
**have second thoughts about something,** to
wonder whether the first decision you
made about something was really right,
*I'm having second thoughts about going
abroad; I'm not sure if I've got enough
money.*
**second nature,** behaviour that has become a
habit, *Lying is second nature to him.*
**secondly** *adverb*

**second**² *noun* (**seconds**)
1 a person or thing that is second.
2 someone who helps a fighter in a
boxing-match, duel, etc. 3 something that
is not of the best quality. 4 a very short
period of time, *60 seconds = 1 minute.*

**second**³ *verb* (**seconds, seconding, seconded**)
1 to act as a second to a fighter. 2 to
support a proposal, motion, etc.

**secondary** *adjective*
1 coming second; not original or essential,
*of secondary importance.* 2 of or for the
education of children more than about 11
years old, *a secondary school.*

**second-hand** *adjective* and *adverb*
1 bought or used after someone else has
used it, *a second-hand car.* 2 that sells used
goods, *a second-hand shop.*

**secret**¹ *adjective*
1 that must not be told or shown to other
people. 2 that is not known by everyone.
**secret agent,** a spy.
**secret service,** a government organization
that employs spies.
**secrecy** *noun*, **secretly** *adverb*

**secret**² *noun* (**secrets**)
something that must not be told or shown
to other people.
**in secret,** secretly.

**secretary** *noun* (**secretaries**)
(*say* sek-rĕ-tri)
someone whose job is to type letters,
answer the telephone, and make business
arrangements for a person, organization,
etc.
**Secretary of State,** (*in Britain*) an official in
charge of a large government department;
(*in America*) the chief government official
responsible for foreign matters.
**secretarial** *adjective*

**secrete** *verb* (**secretes, secreting, secreted**)
(*say* si-**kreet**)
1 to hide something. 2 to form a substance
in the body, *Saliva is secreted in the mouth.*
**secretion** *noun*

**secretive** *adjective*
(*say* **seek**-rĭt-iv)
liking or trying to keep things secret.
**secretively** *adverb*, **secretiveness** *noun*

**sect** *noun* (**sects**)
a group of people who have different
opinions, beliefs, etc. from the majority of
people.

**section** *noun* (**sections**)
a part of something.
**sectional** *adjective*

**sector** *noun* (**sectors**)
part of an area.

**secure**¹ *adjective* (**securer, securest**)
1 firm, *Is that ladder secure?* 2 not likely to
be lost, *a secure job.* 3 protected, *The castle
is a very secure place.* 4 tightly shut or
fixed, *Check that all the doors and
windows are secure before leaving.*
**securely** *adverb*, **security** *noun*

**secure**$^2$ *verb* (**secures, securing, secured**)
   **1** to make something secure. **2** to get hold of something, *She secured two tickets for the show.*

**sedate** *adjective*
   (*say* si-**dayt**)
   calm and dignified.
   **sedately** *adverb*

**sedative** *noun* (**sedatives**)
   (*say* **sed**-ă-tiv)
   a medicine that makes someone calm.
   **sedation** *noun*

**sediment** *noun*
   solid matter that floats in liquid or sinks to the bottom of it.

**sedimentary** *adjective*
   (*say* sed-i-**ment**-er-i)
   formed from particles that have settled on a surface, *sedimentary rocks.*

**see** *verb* (**sees, seeing, saw, seen**)
   **1** to use your eyes to get to know things, recognize people, etc., *Have you seen my brother?* **2** to meet or visit someone, *See me in my office.* **3** to understand, *She saw what I meant.* **4** to imagine, *Can you see yourself as a teacher?* **5** to experience something, *The old man had seen five reigns.* **6** to attend to something; to make sure, *See that the windows are shut.* **7** to escort or lead someone, *I'll see you to the door.*
   **see through**, not to be deceived by something or someone; to continue with something until it is finished, *I saw through his pretence. We will see the job through.*
   **see to**, to attend to something.

**seed** *noun* (**seeds**)
   a tiny part of a plant that can grow in the ground to make a new plant.

**seedling** *noun* (**seedlings**)
   a very young plant.

**seek** *verb* (**seeks, seeking, sought**)
   **1** to try to find a person or thing, *We sought him everywhere.* **2** to try to get something, *She is seeking fame.*

**seem** *verb* (**seems, seeming, seemed**)
   to give the impression of being something, *He seems clever but he is a fool.*
   **seemingly** *adverb*

**seen** past participle of **see**.

**seep** *verb* (**seeps, seeping, seeped**)
   to flow slowly through, into, or out of something, *Water was seeping into the mine.*
   **seepage** *noun*

**see-saw** *noun* (**see-saws**)
   a plank balanced in the middle so that people can sit at each end and make it go up and down.

**seethe** *verb* (**seethes, seething, seethed**)
   **1** to boil or bubble. **2** to be very angry or excited, *She seethed with anger.*

**segment** *noun* (**segments**)
   a part that is cut off or can be separated from the rest of something, *a segment of an orange.*
   **segmented** *adjective*

**segregate** *verb* (**segregates, segregating, segregated**)
   (*say* **seg**-rĭ-gayt)
   to separate people of different races, religions, etc.
   **segregation** *noun*

**seismograph** *noun* (**seismographs**)
   a device for detecting the shock-waves of earthquakes.

**seize** *verb* (**seizes, seizing, seized**)
   (*say* seez)
   to take hold of someone or something suddenly or eagerly.
   **seize up**, to become jammed or stuck.
   **seizure** *noun*

**seldom** *adverb*
   not often, *I seldom cry.*

**select**$^1$ *verb* (**selects, selecting, selected**)
   to choose a person or thing.
   **selection** *noun*, **selective** *adjective*, **selector** *noun*

**select**$^2$ *adjective*
   small and carefully chosen; exclusive, *a select group of friends.*

**self** *noun* (**selves**)
   a person as an individual; a person's particular nature, interests, etc., *He always puts self first.*

**self-centred** *adjective*
   selfish; thinking about yourself too much.

**self-confidence** *noun*
   confidence in what you can do.
   **self-confident** *adjective*

**self-conscious** *adjective*
   embarrassed or shy because you are wondering what other people are thinking of you.
   **self-consciously** *adverb*, **self-consciousness** *noun*

**self-contained** *adjective*
   **1** having all the things that a home needs; not sharing rooms with other people, *a self-contained flat.* **2** not needing the company of other people, *She is very self-contained.*

**send**

**self-control** *noun*
the ability to control your own behaviour or feelings.
**self-controlled** *adjective*

**self-defence** *noun*
1 a way of fighting back if you are attacked, *Karate is a kind of self-defence.*
2 the act of defending yourself against attack, *She stabbed the man in self-defence.*

**self-employed** *adjective*
working independently and not for an employer.

**selfish** *adjective*
only interested in yourself and what you want, *The selfish boy ate all the sweets.*
**selfishly** *adverb*, **selfishness** *noun*

**selfless** *adjective*
not selfish, *He devoted years of selfless work to helping the elderly.*

**self-raising** *adjective*
(of flour) that makes cakes, etc. rise as they are cooking.

**self-respect** *noun*
the feeling that you are behaving, thinking, etc. in the proper way.

**self-righteous** *adjective*
convinced that you are better than other people; thinking too much of your own goodness.

**self-service** *adjective*
where customers serve themselves with goods and pay a cashier for what they have taken, *a self-service shop.*

**self-sufficient** *adjective*
providing for all your own needs without help from others.
**self-sufficiency** *noun*

**sell** *verb* (**sells, selling, sold**)
to give goods or property in exchange for money, *I sold my bike yesterday.*
**sell out**, to sell all your stock of something; (*informal*) to be disloyal to something you believed in, *There are no more pineapples – the shop has sold out. He sold out and left the union.*

**Sellotape** *noun*
(*trademark*) sticky, usually clear plastic tape.

**semaphore** *noun*
a system of signalling with your arms, usually holding flags.

**semen** *noun*
(*say* **see**-men)
white liquid produced by males, containing the male sex cells.

**semi-** *prefix*
half, *semicircle.*

**semibreve** *noun* (**semibreves**)
(*say* **sem**-i-breev)
(in America, *whole note*) the longest musical note normally used, written o .

**semicircle** *noun* (**semicircles**)
half a circle.
**semicircular** *adjective*

**semicolon** *noun* (**semicolons**)
a punctuation mark (;), marking a more definite break than a comma.

**semi-detached** *adjective*
joined to the side of one other house, *a semi-detached house.*

**semi-final** *noun* (**semi-finals**)
a match played to decide who will take part in the final.
**semi-finalist** *noun*

**semitone** *noun* (**semitones**)
half a tone in music.

**semolina** *noun*
a milk pudding made with grains of wheat.

**Senate** *noun*
(*say* **sen**-ăt)
1 the higher-ranking section of the parliament in France, the USA, and some other countries. 2 the most important council in Ancient Rome.
**senator** *noun*

**send** *verb* (**sends, sending, sent**)
to make a person or thing go somewhere.
**send for**, to ask for someone or something to come to you.
**send someone mad**, to make someone become mad.
**send up**, (*informal*) to make fun of.

**senior**¹ *adjective*
1 older. 2 more important, *a senior officer in the navy.*
**senior citizen,** a person who is above the age when people usually retire.
**seniority** *noun*

**senior**² *noun* (**seniors**)
someone who is older or more important than you are.

**sensation** *noun* (**sensations**)
1 a feeling, *a sensation of warmth.* 2 a very exciting event; the excitement caused by it, *The news caused a great sensation.*
**sensational** *adjective*, **sensationally** *adverb*

**sense**¹ *noun* (**senses**)
1 the ability to see, hear, smell, touch, or taste. 2 the ability to feel or appreciate something; awareness, *a sense of humour.* 3 the power to think, make wise decisions, etc., *He hasn't got the sense to come in out of the rain.* 4 meaning, *'Reach' has several senses.*
**make sense,** to have a meaning; to be reasonable.
**senses,** sanity, *He is out of his senses.*

**sense**² *verb* (**senses, sensing, sensed**)
1 to feel; to be vaguely aware of something, *He sensed the warmth of the sun. I sensed that she did not like me.* 2 to detect something, *This device senses radioactivity.*
**sensor** *noun*

**senseless** *adjective*
1 stupid; not sensible. 2 unconscious.

**sensible** *adjective*
1 wise; having or showing common sense. 2 practical, not just fashionable, *sensible shoes.*
**sensibly** *adverb*

**sensitive** *adjective*
1 easily hurt or affected by the sun, chemicals, etc., *sensitive skin.* 2 easily offended, *She is very sensitive about her height.* 3 affected by light, *sensitive photographic paper.*
**sensitively** *adverb*, **sensitivity** *noun*, **sensitize** *verb*

**sent** past tense and past participle of **send.**

**sentence**¹ *noun* (**sentences**)
1 a group of words that belong together, starting with a capital letter and ending with a full stop, a question mark, or an exclamation mark. 2 the punishment given to a criminal in a lawcourt.

**sentence**² *verb* (**sentences, sentencing, sentenced**)
to give someone a sentence in a lawcourt, *The judge sentenced him to a year in prison.*

**sentiment** *noun* (**sentiments**)
1 a feeling; an emotion. 2 sentimental behaviour.

**sentimental** *adjective*
arousing or showing emotion, especially weak or foolish emotion, *That love-story is too sentimental.*
**sentimentality** *noun*, **sentimentally** *adverb*

**sentinel** *noun* (**sentinels**)
a sentry.

**sentry** *noun* (**sentries**)
a soldier guarding something.
**sentry-box,** a tall narrow hut to shelter a sentry.

**separate**¹ *adjective*
(*say* **sep**-er-ăt)
1 not joined to anything; on its own. 2 not together; not with other people, *They lead separate lives.*
**separately** *adverb*

**separate**² *verb* (**separates, separating, separated**)
(*say* **sep**-er-ayt)
1 to take things or people away from others; to become separate. 2 to stop living together as a married couple.
**separable** *adjective*, **separation** *noun*

**September** *noun*
the ninth month of the year.

**septic** *adjective*
infected with germs, *a septic cut.*

USAGE: Do not confuse **septic** with **sceptic**, which is a noun meaning someone who is not inclined to believe things.

**sequel** *noun* (**sequels**)
(*say* **see**-kwĕl)
1 a book, film, etc. that continues the story of an earlier one. 2 something that results from an earlier event.

**sequence** *noun* (**sequences**)
(*say* **see**-kwĕnss)
1 a series of things. 2 the order in which things happen.

**sequin** *noun* (**sequins**)
(*say* **see**-kwin)
one of the tiny bright discs sewn on clothes to decorate them.

**serene** *adjective* (**serener, serenest**)
calm; peaceful.
**serenely** *adverb*, **serenity** *noun*

**sergeant** *noun* (**sergeants**)
(*say* **sar**-jĕnt)
a soldier or policeman who is in charge of a few other soldiers or policemen.

**sergeant-major** *noun* (**sergeant-majors**)
a soldier who is one rank higher than a sergeant.

**serial** *noun* (**serials**)
a story, film, etc. that is presented in separate parts.

**series** *noun* (**series**)
a number of things following each other or connected with each other.

**serious** *adjective*
1 not funny; important, *a serious talk.*
2 thoughtful; solemn, *His face was serious.*
3 very bad, *a serious accident.*
**seriously** *adverb*, **seriousness** *noun*

**sermon** *noun* (**sermons**)
a talk about religion or right and wrong, especially one given by a priest, etc.

**serpent** *noun* (**serpents**)
a snake.

**servant** *noun* (**servants**)
a person whose job is to work in someone else's house.

**serve**[1] *verb* (**serves, serving, served**)
1 to work for someone or something. 2 to sell things to people in a shop. 3 to give food to people at a meal. 4 to be suitable for some purpose. 5 (*in tennis*) to start play by hitting the ball towards your opponent.
**it serves you right**, you deserve it.

**serve**[2] *noun* (**serves**)
the action of starting play in tennis by hitting the ball towards your opponent.

**service**[1] *noun* (**services**)
1 working for someone or something.
2 something that helps people, supplies what they want, etc., *There is a good bus service.* 3 a gathering to worship God; a religious ceremony, *a church service.*
4 providing people with goods, food, etc., *quick service.* 5 a set of plates, crockery, etc. for a meal, *a dinner service.* 6 the servicing of a vehicle, machine, etc. 7 (*in tennis*) a serve.
**the services**, the armed forces.
**service station**, a place beside the road where petrol is sold.

**service**[2] *verb* (**services, servicing, serviced**)
to repair or maintain a vehicle, machine, etc.

**serviette** *noun* (**serviettes**)
a piece of cloth or paper used to keep your clothes or hands clean at a meal.

**session** *noun* (**sessions**)
1 a time spent doing one thing, *Tennis lessons cost £6 a session.* 2 a meeting, especially of a lawcourt or a parliament.

**set**[1] *verb* (**sets, setting, set**)
1 to put or place, *Set the vase on the table.*
2 to fix or prepare, *Have you set the alarm?*
3 to become solid or hard, *The jelly has set.*
4 to go down towards the horizon, *The sun was setting.* 5 to start, *The news set me thinking.* 6 to give someone a task, problem, etc., *Has the teacher set your homework?*
**set about**, to start doing something; (*informal*) to attack someone.
**set off**, to begin a journey; to start something happening.
**set out**, to begin a journey; to display or declare something, *We set out at 7 a.m. She set out her reasons for resigning.*
**set sail**, to start a voyage.
**set up**, to place something in position; to establish something, *I've set up the ironing-board. We want to set up a playgroup.*

**set**[2] *noun* (**sets**)
1 a group of people or things that belong together. 2 an apparatus for receiving radio or television programmes. 3 (*in Mathematics*) a collection of things that have something in common, such as being odd numbers or letters of the alphabet.
4 one of the main sections of a tennis-match. 5 the scenery on a stage.

**set-square** *noun* (**set-squares**)
a triangular device for drawing parallel lines, also used to draw right angles and other angles (usually 30 degrees, 45 degrees, or 60 degrees).

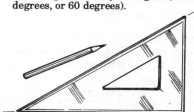

**settee** *noun* (**settees**)
a sofa.

**setting** *noun* (**settings**)
1 the land, buildings, etc. around something. 2 a set of cutlery or crockery for one person.

**settle** *verb* (**settles, settling, settled**)
1 to decide or solve something, *That settles the problem.* 2 to make or become comfortable, calm, etc., *He settled down in the armchair.* 3 to go and live somewhere, *They settled in Canada.* 4 to sink; to come to rest on something, *The dust was settling on the books.* 5 to pay a bill or debt, *She settled the bill.*
**settlement** *noun*, **settler** *noun*

**set-up** *noun* (**set-ups**)
(*informal*) the way that something is
organized or arranged.

**seven** *noun* (**sevens**)
the number 7, one more than six.
**seventh** *adjective* and *noun*

**seventeen** *noun* (**seventeens**)
the number 17, one more than sixteen.
**seventeenth** *adjective* and *noun*

**seventy** *noun* (**seventies**)
the number 70, seven times ten.
**seventieth** *adjective* and *noun*

**sever** *verb* (**severs, severing, severed**)
to cut something; to break.

**several** *adjective*
more than two but not a lot.

**severe** *adjective* (**severer, severest**)
1 strict; not gentle or kind, *Their teacher
was severe.* 2 very bad; violent, *a severe
cold.*
**severely** *adverb*, **severity** *noun*

**sew** *verb* (**sews, sewing, sewed,** *past participle*
**sewn** or **sewed**)
(*say* so)
1 to use a needle and cotton to join pieces of
cloth, etc. together. 2 to work with a needle
and thread.

**sewage** *noun*
(*say* soo-ij)
waste matter carried away in drains.

**sewer** *noun* (**sewers**)
(*say* soo-er)
a drain that carries waste matter away.

**sewing-machine** *noun* (**sewing-machines**)
a machine for sewing things.

**sex** *noun* (**sexes**)
1 one of the two groups, male or female,
that people and animals belong to. 2 the
instinct that causes members of the two
sexes to be attracted to one another.
3 sexual intercourse.

**sexism** *noun*
unfair or offensive treatment of people of a
particular sex, especially women.
**sexist** *noun* and *adjective*

**sextet** *noun* (**sextets**)
1 a group of six musicians. 2 a piece of
music for six musicians.

**sexual** *adjective*
of the sexes; of activities connected with
sexual intercourse.
**sexual intercourse,** the coming together of
two people for pleasure, to make a baby, or
for both these reasons.
**sexuality** *noun*, **sexually** *adverb*

**sexy** *adjective* (**sexier, sexiest**) (*informal*)
1 attractive to people of the opposite sex.
2 concerned with sex, *a sexy film.*

**shabby** *adjective* (**shabbier, shabbiest**)
1 very old and worn, *shabby clothes.*
2 mean; unfair, *a shabby trick.*
**shabbily** *adverb*, **shabbiness** *noun*

**shack** *noun* (**shacks**)
a roughly-built hut.

**shade**[1] *noun* (**shades**)
1 an area sheltered from bright light. 2 a
device that decreases or shuts out bright
light. 3 a colour; how light or dark a colour
is. 4 a slight difference, *This word has
several shades of meaning.*

**shade**[2] *verb* (**shades, shading, shaded**)
1 to shelter something from bright light.
2 to make part of a drawing darker than
the rest.

**shadow**[1] *noun* (**shadows**)
1 the dark shape that falls on a surface
when something is between it and the
light. 2 an area of shade.
**shadowy** *adjective*

**shadow**[2] *verb* (**shadows, shadowing, shadowed**)
1 to cast a shadow on something. 2 to follow
someone secretly.

**shady** *adjective* (**shadier, shadiest**)
1 that gives shade, *a shady tree.* 2 situated
in the shade, *a shady spot.* 3 not completely
honest, *a shady deal.*

**shaft** *noun* (**shafts**)
1 a thin pole or rod, *the shaft of an arrow.*
2 a deep, narrow hole; a vertical space, *a
mine shaft.* 3 a ray of light.

**shaggy** *adjective* (**shaggier, shaggiest**)
with long, untidy hair.
**shaggy-dog story,** a very long and usually
boring story or joke.

**shake**[1] *verb* (**shakes, shaking, shook, shaken**)
1 to move quickly up and down or from side
to side, *Have you shaken the bottle?* 2 to
shock or upset, *The news shook her.* 3 to
tremble, *His voice was shaking.*
**shake hands,** to clasp someone's hand,
usually his or her right hand, when you
meet or part or as a sign that you agree.

**shake**[2] *noun* (**shakes**)
1 the action of shaking. 2 (*in America or
New Zealand*) an earthquake. 3 (*informal*)
a moment, *I'll be there in two shakes.*

**shaky** *adjective* (**shakier, shakiest**)
1 likely to fall down. 2 that shakes, *a shaky
old man.*
**shakily** *adverb*, **shakiness** *noun*

**shall** *verb* (*past tense* **should**)
used with other verbs to refer to the future, *We shall arrive tomorrow. We told them we should arrive the next day.*

**shallow** *adjective* (**shallower, shallowest**)
not deep, *shallow water.*

**sham** *noun* (**shams**)
something that is not genuine; someone who is not what he or she pretends to be.

**shamble** *verb* (**shambles, shambling, shambled**)
to walk or run in a lazy or awkward way.

**shambles** *noun*
a scene of great disorder or bloodshed.

**shame** *noun*
1 a feeling of great sorrow or guilt because you have done wrong. 2 something that you regret.
**shameful** *adjective*, **shamefully** *adverb*, **shameless** *adjective*, **shamelessly** *adverb*

**shampoo** *noun* (**shampoos**)
liquid soap for washing hair.

**shamrock** *noun*
a small plant rather like clover.

**shandy** *noun* (**shandies**)
a mixture of beer with lemonade or some other soft drink.

**shan't** short for *shall not.*

**shanty**[1] *noun* (**shanties**)
a sailor's traditional song.

**shanty**[2] *noun* (**shanties**)
a roughly-built hut.
**shanty town**, a group of shanties, usually outside a large town, where poor people live.

**shape**[1] *noun* (**shapes**)
1 the outline of something; the way that something looks, *Books are rectangular in shape.* 2 the proper form or condition of something, *Get your essay into shape. Dry the pullover flat so that it does not go out of shape.*
**shapeless** *adjective*

**shape**[2] *verb* (**shapes, shaping, shaped**)
to give a particular shape to something.

**shapely** *adjective* (**shapelier, shapeliest**)
having an attractive shape.

**share**[1] *noun* (**shares**)
1 one of the parts into which something is divided between several people or things. 2 part of a company's money, lent by someone who is given a small part of the profits in return.

**share**[2] *verb* (**shares, sharing, shared**)
1 to divide something between several people or things, *She shared out the toffees.* 2 to use something that someone else is also using, *May I share your book? She shared her room with me.* 3 to tell someone something, *I wanted to share the news with you.*

**shark** *noun* (**sharks**)
a large sea-fish with sharp teeth.

**sharp**[1] *adjective* (**sharper, sharpest**)
1 with an edge or point that can cut or make holes, *a sharp knife.* 2 quick to learn or notice things, *sharp eyes.* 3 sudden; severe, *a sharp bend in the road.* 4 slightly sour, *This stewed apple tastes sharp.* 5 above the proper musical pitch.
**sharply** *adverb*, **sharpness** *noun*

**sharp**[2] *adverb*
1 sharply, *Turn sharp right.* 2 punctually; exactly, *at six o'clock sharp.*

**sharp**[3] *noun* (**sharps**)
the note that is a semitone above a particular musical note; the sign (#) that indicates this.

**sharpen** *verb* (**sharpens, sharpening, sharpened**)
to give something a good cutting edge or a fine point, *She sharpened her pencil.*
**sharpener** *noun*

**shatter** *verb* (**shatters, shattering, shattered**)
1 to break suddenly into tiny pieces. 2 to destroy, *Our hopes were shattered.* 3 to make someone very weak or upset, *We were shattered by the news.*

**shave**[1] *verb* (**shaves, shaving, shaved**)
1 to cut hair from the surface of your skin with a razor. 2 to cut or scrape a thin slice off something.
**shaver** *noun*

**shave**[2] *noun* (**shaves**)
the act of cutting hair from the surface of your skin.
**close shave**, (*informal*) a narrow escape.

**shavings** *plural noun*
thin strips shaved off a piece of wood.

**shawl** *noun* (**shawls**)
a piece of cloth or knitted material worn round your shoulders or head, or wrapped round a baby.

**she** *pronoun*
the female person or animal being talked about.

**sheaf** *noun* (**sheaves**)
a bundle of corn stalks tied together after reaping.

**shear** *verb* (**shears, shearing, sheared, shorn** or **sheared**)
to cut the wool off a sheep.
**shear off**, to break off.
**shearer** *noun*

USAGE: Do not confuse **shear** with **sheer**, which is an adjective meaning complete, vertical, or very thin.

**shears** *plural noun*
a tool like a very large pair of scissors for trimming bushes, shearing sheep, etc.

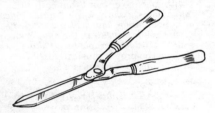

**sheath** *noun* (**sheaths**)
1 a cover for the blade of a sword or dagger. 2 a cover that fits something closely.

**sheathe** *verb* (**sheathes, sheathing, sheathed**)
1 to put a sword into its sheath. 2 to put a protective covering on something.

**shed¹** *noun* (**sheds**)
a simply-made building used for storing things, sheltering animals, etc.; a hut.

**shed²** *verb* (**sheds, shedding, shed**)
to let something fall or flow, *The caterpillar has shed its skin. We shed tears.*

**she'd** short for *she had, she should,* or *she would.*

**sheen** *noun*
a shine on a surface.

**sheep** *noun* (**sheep**)
a grass-eating animal kept by farmers for its wool and meat.

**sheep-dog** *noun* (**sheep-dogs**)
a dog trained to guard and control sheep.

**sheepish** *adjective*
shy; embarrassed.
**sheepishly** *adverb*

**sheer** *adjective* (**sheerer, sheerest**)
1 complete; thorough, *sheer stupidity.*
2 perpendicular; vertical, *a sheer drop.*
3 very thin; transparent, *sheer stockings.*

USAGE: Do not confuse **sheer** with **shear**, which is a verb meaning to cut wool off a sheep.

**sheet** *noun* (**sheets**)
1 a large piece of lightweight cloth put on a bed. 2 a whole flat piece of paper, glass, or metal. 3 a wide area of water, snow, flame, etc.

**sheikh** *noun* (**sheikhs**)
the leader of an Arab tribe or village.

**shelf** *noun* (**shelves**)
1 a board fixed to a wall or fitted in a piece of furniture so that books, ornaments, etc. may be put on it. 2 a flat, level surface that sticks out from a cliff, etc.

**shell¹** *noun* (**shells**)
1 the hard cover round or over a nut, egg, snail, tortoise, etc. 2 a long, round metal case containing explosive, shot from a large gun. 3 the walls or framework of a building, ship, etc.
**shell suit**, a kind of brightly-coloured track suit made of nylon with a cotton lining.

**shell²** *verb* (**shells, shelling, shelled**)
1 to take something out of its shell. 2 to fire explosive shells at a building, ship, town, etc.
**shell out**, (*slang*) to pay money for something.

**she'll** short for *she will.*

**shellfish** *noun* (**shellfish**)
a sea-animal that has a hard cover over its body.

**shelter¹** *noun* (**shelters**)
1 a place that protects people from rain, wind, danger, etc. 2 being protected, *We found shelter from the rain.*

**shelter²** *verb* (**shelters, sheltering, sheltered**)
1 to protect or cover, *The hill shelters the house from the wind.* 2 to find a shelter, *They sheltered under the trees.*

**shelve** *verb* (**shelves, shelving, shelved**)
1 to put something on a shelf or shelves.
2 to reject or postpone a plan, etc. 3 to slope, *The seabed shelves away from the beach.*

**shepherd** *noun* (**shepherds**)
someone whose job is to look after sheep.
**shepherd's pie**, minced meat covered with mashed potato and baked.

**sherbet** *noun* (**sherbets**)
a fizzy sweet powder or drink.

**sheriff** *noun* (**sheriffs**)
**1** (*in Britain*) the chief officer in a county or district. **2** (*in America*) the chief officer who enforces the law in a county.

**sherry** *noun* (**sherries**)
a kind of strong wine.

**she's** short for *she is* and (before a verb in the past tense) *she has*.

**shield**[1] *noun* (**shields**)
**1** a large piece of metal, wood, etc. used to protect the body, *Soldiers used to hold shields in front of them when they were fighting.* **2** a protection.

**shield**[2] *verb* (**shields, shielding, shielded**)
to protect, *I was shielded from the wind.*

**shift**[1] *noun* (**shifts**)
**1** a change of position, condition, etc. **2** a group of workers who start work as another group finishes; the time when they work, *the night shift.* **3** a woman's dress that hangs straight down from her shoulders.

**shift**[2] *verb* (**shifts, shifting, shifted**)
**1** to move or change. **2** to manage to do something; to make a living, *Shift for yourself.*

**shilling** *noun* (**shillings**)
an old British coin that was worth a twentieth of a pound.

**shimmer** *verb* (**shimmers, shimmering, shimmered**)
to shine with a quivering light, *The sea shimmered in the sunlight.*

**shin** *noun* (**shins**)
the front of your leg between your knee and your ankle.

**shine**[1] *verb* (**shines, shining, shone** or, in 'polish' sense, **shined**)
**1** to give out or reflect light; to be bright. **2** to polish, *Have you shined your shoes?* **3** to be excellent, *He does not shine in maths.*

**shine**[2] *noun*
**1** brightness, *the shine of polished brass.* **2** the act of polishing, *Give your shoes a good shine.*
**shiny** *adjective*

**shingle** *noun*
pebbles on a beach.

**ship**[1] *noun* (**ships**)
a large boat, especially one that goes to sea.

**ship**[2] *verb* (**ships, shipping, shipped**)
to send something on a ship.

**shipping** *noun*
all the ships of a country, etc., *Britain's shipping.*

**shipwreck** *noun* (**shipwrecks**)
**1** the wrecking of a ship. **2** the remains of a wrecked ship.
**shipwrecked** *adjective*

**shipyard** *noun* (**shipyards**)
a dockyard.

**shire** *noun* (**shires**)
a county.
**shire-horse**, a large, heavy kind of horse.

**shirk** *verb* (**shirks, shirking, shirked**)
to avoid doing something that you ought to do.

**shirt** *noun* (**shirts**)
a garment worn on the top half of your body, *Most shirts have sleeves, a collar, and buttons down the front.*
**in your shirt-sleeves**, not wearing a jacket over your shirt.

**shiver** *verb* (**shivers, shivering, shivered**)
to tremble with cold or fear.
**shivery** *adjective*

**shoal**[1] *noun* (**shoals**)
a large number of fish swimming together.

**shoal**[2] *noun* (**shoals**)
a shallow place.

**shock**[1] *noun* (**shocks**)
**1** a sudden unpleasant surprise. **2** a violent knock or jolt. **3** an effect caused by electric current passing through your body.

**shock**[2] *verb* (**shocks, shocking, shocked**)
**1** to give someone a shock. **2** to fill someone with disgust or outrage.

**shoddy** *adjective* (**shoddier, shoddiest**)
of poor quality, *shoddy work.*

**shoe** *noun* (**shoes**)
1 a strong covering for the foot. 2 a horseshoe.
**in someone's shoes**, in someone's place, *I'm glad I'm not in her shoes*.
**on a shoestring**, with only a small amount of money.
**shoelace** *noun*, **shoemaker** *noun*

**shone** past tense and past participle of **shine** *verb*.

**shook** past tense of **shake** *verb*.

**shoot**[1] *verb* (**shoots, shooting, shot**)
1 to fire a gun, rocket, etc. 2 to hurt or kill someone or an animal by using a gun. 3 to move or send something very quickly, *The car shot past*. 4 to kick or hit a ball at a goal. 5 to film or photograph something, *The film was shot in Africa*.
**shooting star**, a meteor.

**shoot**[2] *noun* (**shoots**)
a young branch or growth of a plant.

**shop**[1] *noun* (**shops**)
1 (in America, *store*) a building where people buy things. 2 a workshop.
**shop steward**, a trade-union official who represents his or her fellow-workers.

**shop**[2] *verb* (**shops, shopping, shopped**)
to go and buy things at shops.
**shopper** *noun*

**shopkeeper** *noun* (**shopkeepers**)
someone who owns or looks after a shop.

**shoplifter** *noun* (**shoplifters**)
someone who steals from shops.
**shoplifting** *noun*

**shopping** *noun*
1 buying things at shops, *I like shopping*.
2 what someone has bought, *Will you carry my shopping, please?*
**shopping centre**, a group of different shops in one place, often in the same large building.

**shore** *noun* (**shores**)
1 the seashore. 2 the land along the edge of a lake, etc.

**shorn** past tense of **shear**.

**short**[1] *adjective* (**shorter, shortest**)
1 not long; occupying a small distance or time, *a short walk*. 2 not tall, *a short person*. 3 not sufficient; scarce, *Water is short*. 4 bad-tempered, *He was rather short with me*. 5 rich and crumbly; containing a lot of fat, *short pastry*.
**for short**, as a shorter form of something, *Raymond is called Ray for short*.
**short circuit**, a fault in an electrical circuit when current flows along a shorter route than the normal one.
**short cut**, a route or method that is quicker than the usual one.
**short for**, a shorter form of something, *Ray is short for Raymond*.
**short sight**, not being able to see things clearly unless they are close.
**short wave**, a radio wave with a wavelength between 10 and 100 metres.
**shortish** *adjective*, **shortness** *noun*

**short**[2] *adverb*
suddenly, *She stopped short*.

**shortage** *noun* (**shortages**)
the situation when something is scarce or insufficient.

**shortbread** *noun*
a rich, sweet kind of biscuit.

**shortcake** *noun* (**shortcakes**)
1 shortbread. 2 a light cake usually served with fruit.

**shortcoming** *noun* (**shortcomings**)
a fault or failure, *He has many shortcomings*.

**shorten** *verb* (**shortens, shortening, shortened**)
to make something shorter; to become shorter.

**shorthand** *noun*
a set of special signs for writing words down as quickly as people say them.
**shorthand typist**, someone who can write shorthand and also do typing.

**shortly** *adverb*
1 soon. 2 briefly.

**shorts** *plural noun*
trousers with legs that do not go below the knee.

**short-sighted** *adjective*
unable to see distant things clearly.

**shot**[1] *noun* (**shots**)
1 the firing of a gun. 2 something fired from a gun. 3 lead pellets fired from small guns. 4 a person judged by his or her skill in shooting, *He is a good shot*. 5 a heavy metal ball thrown as a sport. 6 a stroke in tennis, cricket, etc. 7 a photograph or filmed sequence. 8 an attempt, *Have a shot at this crossword*.

**shot**[2] past tense and past participle of **shoot** *verb*.

**shotgun** *noun* (**shotguns**)
a gun for firing many small lead pellets over a short distance.

**should** *verb*
1 past tense of **shall**. 2 to have a duty or wish to; ought to, *You should come. I should like to come.* 3 used in speaking of something that will happen if something else happens first, *You should win as long as you get a good start.*

**shoulder**[1] *noun* (**shoulders**)
the part of your body between your neck and your arm.
**shoulder-blade,** one of the two large flat bones near the top of your back.

**shoulder**[2] *verb* (**shoulders, shouldering, shouldered**)
1 to put or rest something on your shoulder or shoulders, *The window-cleaner shouldered his ladder and walked over to his van.* 2 to accept responsibility or blame.

**shout**[1] *verb* (**shouts, shouting, shouted**)
to speak or call very loudly.

**shout**[2] *noun* (**shouts**)
a loud cry or call.

**shove** *verb* (**shoves, shoving, shoved**)
(*say* shuv)
to push hard.
**shove off,** (*informal*) to go away.

**shovel**[1] *noun* (**shovels**)
(*say* shuv-ĕl)
a curved spade for lifting and moving coal, earth, sand, snow, etc.

**shovel**[2] *verb* (**shovels, shovelling, shovelled**)
to move or clear something with a shovel.

**show**[1] *noun* (**shows**)
1 a display or exhibition, *a flower show.* 2 an entertainment. 3 (*informal*) something that happens or is done, *Good show!*

**show**[2] *verb* (**shows, showing, showed, shown**)
1 to let something be seen, *She showed me her new bike.* 2 to make something clear to someone, *He has shown me how to do it.* 3 to guide or lead someone, *Show him in.* 4 to be visible, *That scratch won't show.*
**show off,** to try to impress people.

**shower**[1] *noun* (**showers**)
1 a brief fall of rain or snow. 2 a lot of small things coming or falling like rain, *a shower of stones.* 3 a device to spray water on a person; a bath or wash using this device.
**showery** *adjective*

**shower**[2] *verb* (**showers, showering, showered**)
1 to fall like rain; to send a lot of something, *His father showered money on him.* 2 to wash under a shower.

**show-jumping** *noun*
a competition in which riders make horses jump over fences and other obstacles.
**show-jumper** *noun*

**showman** *noun* (**showmen**)
someone who presents entertainments; someone who is good at attracting attention or at entertaining.
**showmanship** *noun*

**showroom** *noun* (**showrooms**)
a large room where goods, especially cars, furniture, or electrical equipment, are displayed for people to look at and to buy.

**showy** *adjective* (**showier, showiest**)
likely to attract attention; bright or highly decorated.
**showily** *adverb*, **showiness** *noun*

**shrank** past tense of **shrink**.

**shrapnel** *noun*
pieces of metal scattered from an exploding shell.

**shred**[1] *noun* (**shreds**)
a tiny strip or piece torn or cut off something.

**shred**[2] *verb* (**shreds, shredding, shredded**)
to tear or cut something into shreds.
**shredder** *noun*

**shrew** *noun* (**shrews**)
1 a small animal rather like a mouse. 2 a bad-tempered woman.

**shrewd** *adjective* (**shrewder, shrewdest**)
having common sense and good judgement.
**shrewdly** *adverb*, **shrewdness** *noun*

**shriek** *noun* (**shrieks**)
a shrill scream.

**shrill** *adjective* (**shriller, shrillest**)
sounding very high, strong, and loud, *a shrill, angry voice.*
**shrillness** *noun*, **shrilly** *adverb*

**shrimp** *noun* (**shrimps**)
a small shellfish.

**shrine** *noun* (**shrines**)
a sacred place.

**shrink** *verb* (**shrinks, shrinking, shrank, shrunk**)
**1** to become smaller, *This dress has shrunk.*
**2** to make something smaller, usually by soaking it, *Their jeans have been shrunk.*
**3** to move back or avoid something because of fear, embarrassment, etc., *He shrank from meeting strangers.*
**shrinkage** *noun*

**shrivel** *verb* (**shrivels, shrivelling, shrivelled**)
to make something wrinkled and dry; to become wrinkled and dry.

**shroud**¹ *noun* (**shrouds**)
**1** a sheet in which a corpse is wrapped.
**2** one of the ropes that support a ship's mast.

**shroud**² *verb* (**shrouds, shrouding, shrouded**)
**1** to wrap a corpse in a sheet. **2** to cover or conceal something, *The countryside was shrouded in mist.*

**Shrove Tuesday** *noun*
the day before Ash Wednesday, *People often eat pancakes on Shrove Tuesday.*

**shrub** *noun* (**shrubs**)
a bush.

**shrubbery** *noun* (**shrubberies**)
an area full of shrubs.

**shrug** *verb* (**shrugs, shrugging, shrugged**)
to raise your shoulders slightly as a sign that you do not care, do not know, etc.

**shrunk** past participle of **shrink**.

**shrunken** *adjective*
that has become smaller, *a dry, shrunken pear.*

**shudder** *verb* (**shudders, shuddering, shuddered**)
to shake because you are cold or frightened.

**shuffle** *verb* (**shuffles, shuffling, shuffled**)
**1** to drag your feet along the ground as you walk. **2** to mix up playing-cards before you deal them.

**shunt** *verb* (**shunts, shunting, shunted**)
to move a railway train or wagons from one place to another.
**shunter** *noun*

**shut** *verb* (**shuts, shutting, shut**)
**1** to move a door, lid, cover, etc. in order to block up an opening; to close something, *She shut the door and drove off.* **2** to become closed, *The door shut suddenly.*
**shut down**, to stop work or business.
**shut up**, to shut securely; (*informal*) to stop talking.

**shutter** *noun* (**shutters**)
**1** a cover or screen that can be closed over a window. **2** the device in a camera that opens and closes to let light fall on the film.

**shuttle** *noun* (**shuttles**)
**1** the part of a loom that is sent to and fro, carrying a thread. **2** a vehicle that goes backwards and forwards between two places, *Take the shuttle between the airport terminals.* **3** a space shuttle.

**shuttlecock** *noun* (**shuttlecocks**)
a small rounded piece of cork or plastic with a ring of feathers fixed to it, used in the game of *badminton.*

**shy** *adjective* (**shyer, shyest**)
**1** afraid to meet or talk to other people.
**2** timid, *Deer are often shy.*
**shyly** *adverb*, **shyness** *noun*

**SI** *adjective*
belonging to the international system of units of measurement, *The kilogram is the SI unit of mass.*

**Siamese** *adjective*
of Siam (now called Thailand).
**Siamese cat**, a cat with blue eyes and short fur.
**Siamese twins**, twins whose bodies are joined together.

**sick** *adjective* (**sicker, sickest**)
**1** ill. **2** vomiting or likely to vomit, *I feel sick.*
**sick of**, tired of; fed up with.
**sickness** *noun*

**sicken** *verb* (**sickens, sickening, sickened**)
**1** to start feeling ill. **2** to disgust someone; to annoy someone very much.

**sickly** *adjective* (**sicklier, sickliest**)
**1** unhealthy; looking weak or pale, *a sickly child.* **2** that makes you feel sick, *a sickly taste.*

**side** *noun* (**sides**)
1 a flat surface, *A cube has six sides.* 2 an edge; the area near an edge, *A triangle has three sides.* 3 the outer part of something that is not the front or the back, *Paint the side of the shed.* 4 a group of people playing, arguing, or fighting against another group, *She is on my side.*

**sideboard** *noun* (**sideboards**)
a long, heavy piece of furniture with drawers and cupboards, and a flat top where things can be put.

**side-car** *noun* (**side-cars**)
a small vehicle attached to the side of a motor cycle.

**sideline** *noun* (**sidelines**)
something that you do in addition to your normal work or activity.

**sideshow** *noun* (**sideshows**)
an entertainment forming part of a large show, especially at a fair.

**sideways** *adverb* and *adjective*
1 to or from the side, *Crabs walk sideways.* 2 with one side facing forward, *We sat sideways in the bus.*

**siding** *noun* (**sidings**)
a short length of railway line leading off the main line.

**siege** *noun* (**sieges**)
(*say* seej)
1 the action of surrounding a place in order to attack it or to prevent people from leaving it. 2 being surrounded and attacked, *The castle was under siege.*

**sieve** *noun* (**sieves**)
(*say* siv)
a device made of metal or plastic mesh, or a metal or plastic sheet with many holes in it, used to separate lumps from liquid, etc.

**sift** *verb* (**sifts, sifting, sifted**)
1 to put something through a sieve. 2 to examine or select facts, evidence, etc.

**sigh**[1] *noun* (**sighs**)
a sound made by breathing out heavily when you are sad, tired, relieved, etc.

**sigh**[2] *verb* (**sighs, sighing, sighed**)
to make a sigh.

**sight**[1] *noun* (**sights**)
1 the ability to see, *She is losing her sight.* 2 something that you see, *I laughed at the sight of him in that hat.* 3 something worth seeing, *See the sights of Paris.* 4 a device that helps you to aim a gun.
**at sight** or **on sight**, as soon as you see someone or something.

**sight**[2] *verb* (**sights, sighting, sighted**)
to see or observe something.

**sightseer** *noun* (**sightseers**)
someone who goes round looking at interesting places; a tourist.
**sightseeing** *noun*

**sign**[1] *noun* (**signs**)
1 a board, notice, etc. that tells or shows people something, *a road sign.* 2 something that conveys a meaning, significance, etc., *There are signs of rust.* 3 a gesture or signal, *She made a sign to them to be quiet.*
**sign language**, a set of hand movements used for communicating with deaf people.

**sign**[2] *verb* (**signs, signing, signed**)
1 to write your signature on something. 2 to make a sign or signal. 3 to employ someone, especially a footballer; to become employed, especially as a footballer, *We have signed three new players. He signed with Leeds United.*

**signal**[1] *noun* (**signals**)
a device, gesture, sound, etc. that tells people something, *a railway signal.*

**signal**[2] *verb* (**signals, signalling, signalled**)
to wave, shout, etc. to someone to attract his or her attention or to tell him or her what to do.
**signaller** *noun*

**signal-box** *noun* (**signal-boxes**)
a building from which railway signals are controlled.

**signalman** *noun* (**signalmen**)
a person who controls railway signals.

**signature** *noun* (**signatures**)
your name written by yourself.
**signature tune**, a special tune used to introduce a particular programme, performer, etc.

**significance** *noun*
1 importance, *They attach a lot of significance to legends.* 2 what something means or is understood to mean, *What is the significance of her remark?*
**significant** *adjective*, **significantly** *adverb*

# signify

**signify** *verb* (**signifies, signifying, signified**)
to mean something.

**signpost** *noun* (**signposts**)
a sign at a road junction showing the names and distances of the places that are down each road.

**Sikh** *noun* (**Sikhs**)
(*say* seek)
someone who believes in **Sikhism**, one of the religions of India.

**silence**¹ *noun* (**silences**)
absence of sound or talk; lack of noise.

**silence**² *verb* (**silences, silencing, silenced**)
to make a person or thing silent.

**silencer** *noun* (**silencers**)
1 (in America, *muffler*) a device to make an engine quieter. 2 a device to make a gun quieter.

**silent** *adjective*
without any sound; not talking.
**silently** *adverb*

**silhouette** *noun* (**silhouettes**)
(*say* sil-oo-et)
a dark outline seen against a light background.

**silicon** *noun*
an element found in many rocks and used in the making of glass, etc.
**silicon chip**, a tiny electronic device made of a small piece of silicon with many very small electric circuits on it.

**silk** *noun*
1 fine thread made by silkworms. 2 smooth, shiny cloth made from this thread.
**silken** *adjective*, **silky** *adjective*

**silkworm** *noun* (**silkworms**)
a kind of caterpillar that covers itself with a case of fine threads when it is ready to turn into a moth.

**sill** *noun* (**sills**)
a ledge underneath a window or door.

**silly** *adjective* (**sillier, silliest**)
stupid.
**silliness** *noun*

**silver** *noun*
1 a precious shiny white metal. 2 coins made of this metal or a metal that looks like it. 3 the colour of silver.
**silver birch**, a birch with silvery bark.
**silver medal**, a medal made of silver, awarded as the second prize.
**silver paper**, paper with a thin layer of aluminium on one side, used for wrapping things.
**silver wedding**, the 25th anniversary of a wedding.
**silvery** *adjective*

**similar** *adjective*
1 of the same kind, *The two cars are exactly similar.* 2 nearly the same as another person or thing, *Your dress is similar to mine, but its collar is different.*
**similarity** *noun*, **similarly** *adverb*

**simile** *noun* (**similes**)
(*say* sim-i-li)
saying that one thing is like another, *'He is as brave as a lion'* is a simile.

**simmer** *verb* (**simmers, simmering, simmered**)
to boil very gently.
**simmer down**, to calm down.

**simple** *adjective* (**simpler, simplest**)
1 easy, *a simple question.* 2 not complicated, *a simple idea.* 3 plain, *a simple dress.* 4 stupid, *I'm not so simple.* 5 having only one part, *a simple sentence.*
**simplicity** *noun*

**simplify** *verb* (**simplifies, simplifying, simplified**)
to make something simple or easy to understand.
**simplification** *noun*

**simply** *adverb*
1 in a simple way, *She dresses simply.* 2 completely, *She looks simply lovely.* 3 only; merely, *It is simply a question of money.*

**simulate** *verb* (**simulates, simulating, simulated**)
1 to reproduce the conditions for something, *a simulated flight.* 2 to pretend.
**simulation** *noun*, **simulator** *noun*

**simultaneous** *adjective*
(*say* sim-ŭl-**tay**-ni-ŭs)
happening at the same time, *At midnight on New Year's Eve there are simultaneous celebrations all over the country.*
**simultaneously** *adverb*

**sin**¹ *noun* (**sins**)
the breaking of a religious or moral law; a very bad action.

**sin**² *verb* (**sins, sinning, sinned**)
to break a religious or moral law; to do a very bad deed.
**sinner** *noun*

**since**¹ *conjunction*
1 from the time when, *Where have you been since I last saw you?* 2 because; as, *Since you have been naughty, you must stay indoors.*

**since**² *preposition*
from the time when, *I have been here since Christmas.*

**since**³ *adverb*
from that time; before now, *He has not been seen since.*

**sincere** *adjective* (**sincerer, sincerest**)
truly felt or meant; genuine, *sincere good wishes.*
**sincerely** *adverb,* **sincerity** *noun*

**sine** *noun* (**sines**)
in a right-angled triangle, a number linked with one of the acute angles, equal to the length of the side opposite the angle divided by the length of the longest side (the *hypotenuse*).

**sinew** *noun* (**sinews**)
strong tissue that joins a muscle to a bone.

**sinful** *adjective*
wicked; very bad.
**sinfully** *adverb,* **sinfulness** *noun*

**sing** *verb* (**sings, singing, sang, sung**)
**1** to make music with your voice. **2** to make a humming or whistling sound, *A bullet went singing past his head.*
**singer** *noun*

**singe** *verb* (**singes, singeing, singed**)
(*say* sinj)
to burn something slightly; to burn the edge of something.

**single**¹ *adjective*
**1** only one; separate. **2** designed for one person, *a single bed.* **3** not married. **4** for the journey to a place but not back again, *a single ticket.*
**single file**, a line of people one behind the other.
**singly** *adverb*

**single**² *noun* (**singles**)
**1** a single person or thing. **2** a single ticket. **3** a record played at 45 revolutions per minute, usually with one tune on each side.
**singles**, a game, especially of tennis, with one player on each side.

**single**³ *verb* (**singles, singling, singled**)
**single out**, to pick out or distinguish someone or something from other people or things.

**singular**¹ *noun* (**singulars**)
the form of a word that refers to only one person or thing, *The singular of 'children' is 'child'.*

**singular**² *adjective*
**1** of the singular; referring to only one. **2** extraordinary, *a woman of singular courage.*
**singularly** *adverb*

**sinister** *adjective*
that looks or seems evil or unpleasant.

**sink**¹ *noun* (**sinks**)
a large basin with taps where you do the washing-up.

**sink**² *verb* (**sinks, sinking, sank** or **sunk, sunk**)
**1** to go under water, *The liner has sunk.* **2** to make something go under water, *They sank the ship.* **3** to go or fall down, *He sank to his knees.*
**sink in**, to penetrate; to become understood, *Let the face-cream sink in. The news was so unexpected that it only sank in gradually.*

**sinus** *noun* (**sinuses**)
(*say* sy-nŭs)
a hollow in the bones of your skull, connected with your nose, *My sinuses are blocked.*

**sip** *verb* (**sips, sipping, sipped**)
to drink a very small amount at a time.

**siphon** *verb* (**siphons, siphoning, siphoned**)
to move a liquid from a container at a high level into a lower container by letting the liquid run down a U-shaped pipe, drawing more liquid after it.
**siphon** *noun*

**sir** *noun*
a word sometimes used when speaking or writing politely to a man, instead of his name, *Can I help you, sir?*
**Sir**, the title given to a knight, *Sir Francis Bacon.*

**siren** *noun* (**sirens**)
a device that makes a loud hooting or screaming sound, usually to warn people about something.

**sister** *noun* (**sisters**)
**1** a woman or girl who has the same parents as another person. **2** a nurse who is in charge of other nurses in a hospital.
**sisterly** *adjective*

**sister-in-law** *noun* (**sisters-in-law**)
the sister of your husband or wife; the wife of your brother.

**sit** *verb* (**sits, sitting, sat**)
**1** to rest on your buttocks, as you do when you are on a chair. **2** to take up this kind of position; to put someone in this kind of position, *Sit down on that chair. Jane's father picked her up and sat her on his shoulders.* **3** to be a candidate for an examination, etc., *We sit our end-of-year exam this afternoon.* **4** to be situated; to stay, *The house sits on top of a hill. The books are still sitting on my shelves – I haven't had time to read them yet.* **5** to act as a babysitter.
**sitter** *noun*

**site** *noun* (**sites**)
**1** the place where something has been built or will be built, *a building site.* **2** the place where something happens or happened, *a camping site.*

**sit-in** *noun* (**sit-ins**)
a protest in which people stay in a building.

**sitting-room** *noun* (**sitting-rooms**)
a room with comfortable chairs for sitting in.

**situated** *adjective*
in a particular place or situation, *The town is situated in a valley.*

**situation** *noun* (**situations**)
1 a place or position; where something is.
2 the conditions affecting a person or thing. 3 a job; employment.

**six** *noun* (**sixes**)
the number 6, one more than five.
**sixth** *adjective* and *noun*

**sixpence** *noun* (**sixpences**)
an old British coin that was worth half a shilling.
**sixpenny** *adjective*

**sixteen** *noun* (**sixteens**)
the number 16, one more than fifteen.
**sixteenth** *adjective* and *noun*

**sixty** *noun* (**sixties**)
the number 60, six times ten.
**sixtieth** *adjective* and *noun*

**size**[1] *noun* (**sizes**)
1 how big a person or thing is. 2 the measurement something is made in, *a size eight shoe.*

**size**[2] *verb* (**sizes, sizing, sized**)
**size up**, (*informal*) to form an opinion or judgement about something.

**sizeable** *adjective*
fairly large.

**sizzle** *verb* (**sizzles, sizzling, sizzled**)
to make a crackling and hissing sound, *The sausages sizzled in the frying-pan.*

**skate**[1] *noun* (**skates**)
1 a boot with a steel blade attached to the sole, used for sliding smoothly over ice.
2 a roller-skate.

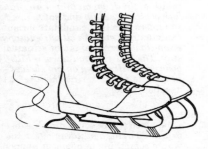

**skate**[2] *noun* (**skate**)
a large, flat sea-fish that can be eaten.

**skate**[3] *verb* (**skates, skating, skated**)
to move with skates on your feet.
**skater** *noun*

**skateboard** *noun* (**skateboards**)
a small board with wheels, on which you balance with both feet while it moves quickly over the ground.

**skeleton** *noun* (**skeletons**)
the framework of bones that is or was inside a person's or animal's body.
**skeletal** *adjective*

**sketch**[1] *noun* (**sketches**)
1 a quick or rough drawing. 2 a short amusing play.
**sketch map**, a simple map drawn quickly and not to scale.

**sketch**[2] *verb* (**sketches, sketching, sketched**)
to make a quick or rough drawing; to draw someone or something in this way.

**skewer** *noun* (**skewers**)
a pointed piece of metal or wood, used to hold meat together for cooking or used as a tent-peg to fasten down a guy-rope.

**ski**[1] *noun* (**skis**)
(*say* skee)
a long piece of wood, plastic, etc. fastened to each of your feet for moving quickly over snow.
**ski-lift**, a set of seats or handles fixed to a moving cable, pulling skiers up to the top of a slope.

**ski**[2] *verb* (**skis, skiing, skied**)
(*say* skee)
to move on skis.
**skier** *noun*

**skid** *verb* (**skids, skidding, skidded**)
to slide accidentally.

**skilful** *adjective*
having, needing, or showing skill.
**skilfully** *adverb*

**skill** *noun* (**skills**)
the ability to do something very well.
**skilled** *adjective*

**skim** *verb* (**skims, skimming, skimmed**)
1 to move quickly over a surface. 2 to remove something from the surface of a liquid, especially to take the cream off milk.

**skin**[1] *noun* (**skins**)
1 the outer covering of a person's or animal's body. 2 the outer covering of a fruit or vegetable. 3 a thin, firm layer that has formed on the surface of a liquid.

**skin**[2] *verb* (**skins, skinning, skinned**)
to take the skin off something.

**skin-diver** *noun* (**skin-divers**)
someone who swims under water without a diving-suit.
**skin-diving** *noun*

**skinny** *adjective* (**skinnier, skinniest**)
very thin.

**skint** *adjective*
(*slang*) having no money left.

**skip**[1] *verb* (**skips, skipping, skipped**)
1 to jump or move along by hopping from one foot to the other. 2 to jump over a skipping-rope. 3 to miss out or ignore something, *Skip the boring details!*

**skip**[2] *noun* (**skips**)
a large, usually open metal container used for collecting and taking away rubbish, especially waste from building work.

**skip**[3] *noun* (**skips**)
a skipping movement.

**skipper** *noun* (**skippers**)
the captain of a ship, team, etc.

**skipping-rope** *noun* (**skipping-ropes**)
a piece of rope, usually with a handle at each end, that is turned over your head and under your feet as you jump.

**skirt**[1] *noun* (**skirts**)
a woman's or girl's piece of clothing that hangs down from her waist.

**skirt**[2] *verb* (**skirts, skirting, skirted**)
to go round the edge of something.

**skirting** or **skirting-board** (**skirtings** or **skirting-boards**) *noun*
a board round the bottom of the wall of a room.

**skit** *noun* (**skits**)
a play, poem, etc. that makes fun of something by imitating it, *He wrote a skit on 'Hamlet'.*

**skittle** *noun* (**skittles**)
a piece of wood or plastic shaped like a bottle, that people try to knock down with a ball.

**skull** *noun* (**skulls**)
the framework of bones in a person's head.

**skunk** *noun* (**skunks**)
a black, furry, American animal that can make an unpleasant smell.

**sky** *noun* (**skies**)
the area above our heads when we are out of doors; the space containing the sun, moon, and stars.

**skylark** *noun* (**skylarks**)
a small brown bird that sings as it hovers high in the air.

**skylight** *noun* (**skylights**)
a window in a roof.

**skyscraper** *noun* (**skyscrapers**)
a very tall building.

**slab** *noun* (**slabs**)
1 a thick, flat piece of something. 2 (*in Australia and New Zealand*) a roughly-cut plank.

**slack** *adjective* (**slacker, slackest**)
1 not pulled tight, *The rope was slack.*
2 lazy; not busy or working hard.
**slackly** *adverb*, **slackness** *noun*

**slacken** *verb* (**slackens, slackening, slackened**)
1 to make something slack; to become slack. 2 to make something slower; to become slower, *Their speed slackened.*

**slacks** *plural noun*
trousers for informal occasions.

**slag-heap** *noun* (**slag-heaps**)
a heap of waste material from a coal-mine, etc.

**slain** past participle of **slay**.

**slam** *verb* (**slams, slamming, slammed**)
1 to shut something loudly. 2 to hit something violently, *He slammed the ball into the net.*

**slang** *noun*
a kind of colourful language not used in formal writing or speaking.
**slangy** *adjective*

**slant**[1] *verb* (**slants, slanting, slanted**)
1 to slope; to lean. 2 to present news, information, etc. from a particular point of view.

**slant**[2] *noun* (**slants**)
1 a sloping or leaning position, *The caravan's floor was at a slant.* 2 a way of presenting news, information, etc. from a particular point of view.

**slap**[1] *noun* (**slaps**)
a hit with the palm of the hand or with something flat.

**slap**[2] *verb* (**slaps, slapping, slapped**)
1 to give someone a slap. 2 to put something forcefully or carelessly, *We slapped paint on the walls.*

**slapstick** *noun*
noisy, lively comedy, with people hitting each other, falling over, etc.

**slash**[1] *verb* (**slashes, slashing, slashed**)
to make large cuts in something.

**slash**[2] *noun* (**slashes**)
1 a large cut. 2 a sloping line (/) used to separate words or letters, especially in some computer commands.

**slat** *noun* (**slats**)
a thin strip of wood, plastic, etc.

**slate** *noun* (**slates**)
1 a kind of grey rock that is easily split into flat plates. 2 a piece of this rock used as part of a roof.
**slaty** *adjective*

**slaughter** *verb* (**slaughters, slaughtering, slaughtered**)
1 to kill an animal for food. 2 to kill many people or animals.
**slaughter** *noun*

**slaughterhouse** *noun* (**slaughterhouses**)
a place where animals are killed for food.

**slave**[1] *noun* (**slaves**)
a person who has to work for someone else without being paid.
**slavery** *noun*

**slave**[2] *verb* (**slaves, slaving, slaved**)
to work very hard.

**slay** *verb* (**slays, slaying, slew, slain**)
(*old-fashioned or poetical use*) to kill.

**sled** or **sledge** *noun* (**sleds** or **sledges**)
a vehicle for travelling over snow, running on strips of metal or wood instead of wheels.

**sledge-hammer** *noun* (**sledge-hammers**)
a very large, heavy hammer.

**sleek** *adjective* (**sleeker, sleekest**)
smooth and shiny, *sleek hair.*

**sleep**[1] *noun*
1 the condition in which the eyes are closed, the body is relaxed, and the mind is unconscious, *You need some sleep.* 2 a time when you are in this condition, *Have a sleep.*
**sleepless** *adjective*

**sleep**[2] *verb* (**sleeps, sleeping, slept**)
to have a sleep.

**sleeper** *noun* (**sleepers**)
1 someone who is asleep. 2 one of the wooden or concrete beams on which a railway line rests. 3 a sleeping-car.

**sleeping-bag** *noun* (**sleeping-bags**)
a warm padded bag for sleeping in, especially when you are camping.

**sleeping-car** *noun* (**sleeping-cars**)
a railway carriage fitted with beds or berths where passengers can sleep.

**sleep-walker** *noun* (**sleep-walkers**)
someone who walks around while he or she is asleep.
**sleep-walking** *noun*

**sleepy** *adjective* (**sleepier, sleepiest**)
feeling like sleeping; wanting to sleep.
**sleepily** *adverb*, **sleepiness** *noun*

**sleet** *noun*
a mixture of rain and snow or hail.

**sleeve** *noun* (**sleeves**)
1 the part of a piece of clothing that covers your arm. 2 the cardboard cover for a record.
**sleeveless** *adjective*

**sleigh** *noun* (**sleighs**)
(*say* slay)
a sledge, especially a large one pulled by horses.

**slender** *adjective* (**slenderer, slenderest**)
1 slim, thin. 2 slight, small, *They had a slender chance of winning.*

**slept** past tense and past participle of **sleep** *verb.*

**slew** past tense of **slay.**

**slice**[1] *noun* (**slices**)
a thin, flat piece cut off something.

**slice**[2] *verb* (**slices, slicing, sliced**)
to cut something into thin, flat pieces.

**slick**[1] *adjective* (**slicker, slickest**)
quick and clever or cunning.

**slick**[2] *noun* (**slicks**)
a large patch of oil floating on water.

**slide**[1] *verb* (**slides, sliding, slid**)
1 to move smoothly over a flat, polished, or slippery surface. 2 to move quickly or secretly, *The thief slid behind the curtains.*

**slide**[2] *noun* (**slides**)
1 a sliding movement. 2 a smooth slope or a slippery surface where children can slide for fun. 3 a type of photograph that lets light through and that can be displayed on a screen by means of a projector. 4 a small glass plate on which things are examined under a microscope. 5 a device for keeping your hair tidy.

**slight** *adjective* (**slighter, slightest**)
very small; not serious or important.
**slightly** *adverb*

**slim**[1] *adjective* (**slimmer, slimmest**)
1 thin and graceful. 2 small; hardly enough, *a slim chance.*

**slim**[2] *verb* (**slims, slimming, slimmed**)
to try to make yourself thinner.
**slimmer** *noun*

**slime** *noun*
unpleasant, wet, slippery stuff, *There was slime on the pond.*
**slimy** *adjective*

**sling**[1] *verb* (**slings, slinging, slung**)
1 to throw something, especially violently or carelessly, *They slung stones at us.* 2 to hang something up; to support something so that it hangs loosely, *He had slung the bag round his neck.*

**sling**[2] *noun* (**slings**)
1 a piece of cloth tied round your neck to support an injured arm. 2 a device for throwing stones.

**slink** *verb* (**slinks, slinking, slunk**)
to move in a stealthy or guilty way, *He slunk off to bed.*

**slip**[1] *verb* (**slips, slipping, slipped**)
1 to slide without meaning to; to fall over.
2 to move quickly and quietly. 3 to escape.
**slipped disc,** part of someone's spine that causes pain because it is out of place.
**slip up,** to make a mistake.

**slip**[2] *noun* (**slips**)
1 an accidental slide or fall. 2 a mistake.
3 a small piece of paper. 4 a petticoat.
5 a pillowcase.

**slipper** *noun* (**slippers**)
a soft, comfortable shoe to wear indoors.

**slippery** *adjective*
smooth, wet, etc. so that it is difficult to stand on, hold, etc.

**slit**[1] *noun* (**slits**)
a long cut or narrow opening in something.

**slit**[2] *verb* (**slits, slitting, slit**)
to make a long cut or a narrow opening in something.

**slither** *verb* (**slithers, slithering, slithered**)
to slide; to slip as you move along.

**sliver** *noun* (**slivers**)
(*say* sli-ver)
a thin strip of wood, glass, etc.

**slog** *verb* (**slogs, slogging, slogged**)
1 to hit something hard or wildly, *He slogged the ball right past the fielders.* 2 to work hard, *She just kept slogging on until the work was done.* 3 to walk with effort, *We slogged through the snow.*

**slogan** *noun* (**slogans**)
a phrase used to advertise something or to sum up the aims of an organization, campaign, etc., *Their slogan was 'Ban the bomb!'*

**slop** *verb* (**slops, slopping, slopped**)
to spill liquid over the edge of a container.

**slope**[1] *verb* (**slopes, sloping, sloped**)
to go gradually downwards or upwards; not to be horizontal or vertical.

**slope**[2] *noun* (**slopes**)
1 a surface that is not horizontal or vertical. 2 the amount by which one edge of a surface is higher or lower than the opposite edge.

**sloppy** *adjective* (**sloppier, sloppiest**)
1 careless, *sloppy work.* 2 runny, *This porridge is sloppy.* 3 sentimental, *a sloppy story.*
**sloppily** *adverb*, **sloppiness** *noun*

**slosh** *verb* (**sloshes, sloshing, sloshed**)
1 to splash, *The bus sloshed through the puddles at the edge of the road.* 2 to slop liquid; to pour liquid carelessly. 3 (*slang*) to hit someone hard.

**slot** *noun* (**slots**)
a narrow opening to put things in,
especially money.

**sloth** *noun* (**sloths**)
(rhymes with *both*)
**1** laziness. **2** a long-haired South American
animal that lives in trees and moves slowly.

**slot-machine** *noun* (**slot-machines**)
a machine worked by putting a coin in a
slot.

**slouch** *verb* (**slouches, slouching, slouched**)
to move, stand, or sit in a lazy way,
especially with your head and shoulders
bent forwards.

**slovenly** *adjective*
(*say* sluv-ĕn-li)
careless; untidy.

**slow**[1] *adjective* (**slower, slowest**)
**1** not quick; taking more time than usual.
**2** showing a time earlier than the correct
time, *That clock is slow*.
**slowly** *adverb*, **slowness** *noun*

**slow**[2] *verb* (**slows, slowing, slowed**)
to go slower.

**slowcoach** *noun* (**slowcoaches**)
(in America, *slowpoke*) someone who moves
or works slowly.

**sludge** *noun*
thick sticky mud, oil, etc.

**slug** *noun* (**slugs**)
**1** a small animal like a snail without its
shell. **2** a pellet for firing from a gun.

**slum** *noun* (**slums**)
an area of old, dirty, crowded houses.

**slumber** *noun*
sleep.

**slump**[1] *verb* (**slumps, slumping, slumped**)
to fall heavily or suddenly.

**slump**[2] *noun* (**slumps**)
a sudden fall in prices, trade, etc.

**slung** past tense and past participle of **sling**
*verb*.

**slunk** past tense and past participle of **slink**.

**slush** *noun*
snow that is melting.
**slushy** *adjective*

**sly** *adjective* (**slyer, slyest**)
cunning; mischievous.
**slyly** *adverb*, **slyness** *noun*

**smack**[1] *verb* (**smacks, smacking, smacked**)
to slap someone, especially as a
punishment.

**smack**[2] *noun* (**smacks**)
a slap, especially as a punishment.

**small** *adjective* (**smaller, smallest**)
not big; less than the normal size.

**smallpox** *noun*
a serious disease, common in the past, that
caused a fever and produced spots that left
scars on the skin.

**smart**[1] *adjective* (**smarter, smartest**)
**1** neat; dressed well. **2** clever. **3** fast, *She
ran at a smart pace*.
**smarten** *verb*, **smartly** *adverb*, **smartness** *noun*

**smart**[2] *verb* (**smarts, smarting, smarted**)
to feel a stinging pain.

**smash**[1] *verb* (**smashes, smashing, smashed**)
**1** to break into pieces noisily and violently;
to break something in this way. **2** to hit or
move with great force, *The runaway lorry
smashed into a wall*. **3** to destroy
something or defeat someone completely,
*The Customs smashed the smuggling ring.
Our team smashed them ten–nil*.

**smash**[2] *noun* (**smashes**)
**1** the act or sound of smashing. **2** a
collision, especially one involving trains or
cars, etc.
**smash-and-grab**, describing a robbery done
by smashing a window and taking
something, *a smash-and-grab raid*.
**smash hit**, (*informal*) an extremely
successful or popular show, film, song, etc.

**smashing** *adjective*
(*informal*) excellent.

**smear** *verb* (**smears, smearing, smeared**)
**1** to rub something dirty or greasy on a
surface. **2** to try to damage someone's
reputation.
**smear** *noun*

**smell**[1] *verb* (**smells, smelling, smelt**)
**1** to use your nose to sense something, *I
bent down and smelt the rose*. **2** to give out
something that you can detect with your
nose, *This cheese smells*.

**smell**[2] *noun* (**smells**)
**1** something that you can smell, especially
something unpleasant. **2** the ability to
smell things, *the sense of smell*.
**smelly** *adjective*

**smelt** *verb* (**smelts, smelting, smelted**)
to melt ore so as to get metal from it.
**smelter** *noun*

**smile**[1] *noun* (**smiles**)
a pleased or amused expression on your
face.

**smile**[2] *verb* (**smiles, smiling, smiled**)
to have a pleased or amused expression on
your face; to look at someone while you
have this kind of expression on your face.

**smith** *noun* (**smiths**)
someone who makes things out of metal,
*a silversmith*.

**smithereens** *plural noun*
small fragments, *Smash it to smithereens*.

**smock** *noun* (**smocks**)
a loose garment like a very long shirt.

**smog** *noun*
a mixture of smoke and fog.

**smoke**[1] *noun*
1 the grey or blue gas that rises from a fire.
2 smoking tobacco, *He wants a smoke*.
**smokeless** *adjective*, **smoky** *adjective*

**smoke**[2] *verb* (**smokes, smoking, smoked**)
1 to give out smoke, *The fire is smoking*.
2 to breathe in the smoke of a cigarette,
cigar, or pipe.
**smoker** *noun*

**smooth**[1] *adjective* (**smoother, smoothest**)
1 having a surface without any lumps,
marks, roughness, etc. 2 moving without
bumps or jolts. 3 not harsh; flowing easily,
*a smooth voice*.
**smoothly** *adverb*, **smoothness** *noun*

**smooth**[2] *verb* (**smooths, smoothing, smoothed**)
to make something smooth.

**smother** *verb* (**smothers, smothering, smothered**)
1 to prevent someone from breathing. 2 to
cover something thickly, *a cake smothered
in icing*. 3 to put out a fire by covering it.

**smoulder** *verb* (**smoulders, smouldering,
smouldered**)
to burn slowly without a flame.

**smudge** *noun* (**smudges**)
a dirty mark made by rubbing something.

**smuggle** *verb* (**smuggles, smuggling, smuggled**)
to bring something into a country secretly
and illegally.
**smuggler** *noun*

**smut** *noun* (**smuts**)
1 a small piece of soot or dirt. 2 obscene
things.
**smutty** *adjective*

**snack** *noun* (**snacks**)
a small meal.

**snag** *noun* (**snags**)
an unexpected difficulty; an obstacle.

**snail** *noun* (**snails**)
a small soft animal with a shell, *Snails
move very slowly*.

**snake** *noun* (**snakes**)
a long reptile without legs, *Some snakes
give poisonous bites*.
**snaky** *adjective*

**snap**[1] *verb* (**snaps, snapping, snapped**)
1 to break suddenly with a sharp noise. 2 to
bite suddenly or quickly, *The dog snapped
at me*. 3 to say something quickly and
angrily. 4 to move or do something quickly,
*She snapped her fingers. It's time you
snapped into action!* 5 to take a snapshot of
something.

**snap**[2] *noun* (**snaps**)
1 the act or sound of snapping. 2 a
snapshot. 3 a card-game in which players
shout 'Snap!' when they see two similar
cards.

**snapshot** *noun* (**snapshots**)
a photograph taken with a simple camera.

**snare** *noun* (**snares**)
a trap for catching animals.

**snarl**[1] *verb* (**snarls, snarling, snarled**)
to growl; to say something angrily.

**snarl**[2] *verb* (**snarls, snarling, snarled**)
**snarl up**, to make something tangled or
jammed, *The traffic was snarled up*.

**snatch** *verb* (**snatches, snatching, snatched**)
to grab, *He snatched the bag from me*.

**sneak**[1] *verb* (**sneaks, sneaking, sneaked**)
1 to move quietly and secretly. 2 (*informal*)
to tell someone in authority that someone
else has misbehaved.

**sneak**[2] *noun* (**sneaks**)
(*informal*) a person who reports someone
else's misbehaviour.
**sneakily** *adverb*, **sneaky** *adjective*

**sneer** *verb* (**sneers, sneering, sneered**)
to speak or behave in a scornful way.

**sneeze**[1] *verb* (**sneezes, sneezing, sneezed**)
to push air through your nose suddenly
and uncontrollably, *She was sneezing a lot
because of her cold*.
**not to be sneezed at**, (*informal*) valuable;
important.

**sneeze**[2] *noun* (**sneezes**)
the action or sound of sneezing.

**sniff**[1] *verb* (**sniffs, sniffing, sniffed**)
1 to make a noise by drawing air in
through your nose. 2 to smell something.

**sniff**[2] *noun* (**sniffs**)
1 the action or sound of drawing air in through your nose. 2 the action or sound of smelling something.

**snigger** *verb* (**sniggers, sniggering, sniggered**)
to give a quiet, unpleasant laugh.

**snip** *verb* (**snips, snipping, snipped**)
to cut a small piece or pieces off something.

**snipe** *verb* (**snipes, sniping, sniped**)
to shoot at people from a hiding-place.
**sniper** *noun*

**snivel** *verb* (**snivels, snivelling, snivelled**)
to cry or complain in a whining way.

**snob** *noun* (**snobs**)
someone who despises people who have not got wealth, power, or particular tastes or interests.
**snobbery** *noun*, **snobbish** *adjective*

**snooker** *noun*
a game played with long sticks (called *cues*) and 22 balls on a cloth-covered table.

**snoop** *verb* (**snoops, snooping, snooped**)
to keep trying to find out secretly about someone else's business.
**snooper** *noun*

**snore** *verb* (**snores, snoring, snored**)
to breathe very noisily while sleeping.

**snorkel** *noun* (**snorkels**)
a tube that supplies air to someone swimming under water.

**snort** *verb* (**snorts, snorting, snorted**)
to make a loud noise by forcing air out of your nose.

**snout** *noun* (**snouts**)
an animal's nose, or nose and jaws, of the kind that stick out in front of its head, *The pig raised its snout*.

**snow**[1] *noun*
frozen drops of water falling from the sky as small white flakes.
**snowflake** *noun*

**snow**[2] *verb* (**snows, snowing, snowed**)
**it is snowing**, snow is falling.

**snowball** *noun* (**snowballs**)
snow pressed into the shape of a ball for throwing at someone.

**snowdrop** *noun* (**snowdrops**)
a small white flower that comes up in winter.

**snowman** *noun* (**snowmen**)
a figure made of snow.

**snow-plough** *noun* (**snow-ploughs**)
a vehicle or device for clearing snow from a road, railway, etc.

**snow-shoe** *noun* (**snow-shoes**)
a device attached to each of your feet to help you walk on deep snow without sinking in.

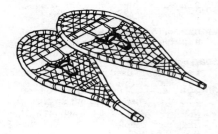

**snowstorm** *noun* (**snowstorms**)
a storm with snow falling.

**snowy** *adjective* (**snowier, snowiest**)
1 with snow falling, *snowy weather*.
2 covered with snow, *snowy roofs*.
3 brilliantly white, *snowy sheets*.

**snub** *verb* (**snubs, snubbing, snubbed**)
to treat someone in a scornful or unfriendly way.

**snub-nosed** *adjective*
with a short, thick nose.

**snuff** *noun*
powdered tobacco that is taken into someone's nose by sniffing.

**snug** *adjective* (**snugger, snuggest**)
warm and comfortable.
**snugly** *adverb*

**snuggle** *verb* (**snuggles, snuggling, snuggled**)
to curl up in a warm, comfortable place, *She snuggled down in bed*.

**so**[1] *adverb*
1 in this or that way; in such a way; to such an extent, *Why are you so cross?* 2 very, *Cricket is so boring.* 3 also, *I was wrong but so were you.*
**and so on,** and other similar things, *They took food, water, spare clothing, and so on.*
**or so,** or about that number.
**so as to,** in such a way as to; for the purpose of.
**so far,** up to now.
**so far, so good,** everything has gone well up to now.
**so long!,** (*informal*) goodbye.
**so what?,** (*informal*) what does that matter?; I don't care.

**so**[2] *conjunction*
therefore; for that reason, *They threw me out, so I came here.*

**soak** *verb* (**soaks, soaking, soaked**)
to make someone or something very wet.
**soak up,** to take in a liquid in the way that a sponge does.

**so-and-so** *noun* (**so-and-so's**) (*informal*)
1 a person or thing that need not be named, *Old so-and-so told me.* 2 an unpleasant person, *He's a real so-and-so.*

**soap** *noun* (**soaps**)
1 a substance used with water for washing and cleaning things. 2 (*informal*) a soap opera.
**soap opera,** (*informal*) a television serial about the day-to-day life of a group of imaginary people.
**soapy** *adjective*

**soar** *verb* (**soars, soaring, soared**)
1 to rise or fly high in the air. 2 to rise very high, *Prices were soaring.*

**sob** *verb* (**sobs, sobbing, sobbed**)
to make gasping noises as you cry.

**sober** *adjective* (**soberer, soberest**)
1 not drunk. 2 calm and serious, *a sober expression.* 3 not bright or showy, *sober colours.*
**soberly** *adverb*, **sobriety** *noun*

**so-called** *adjective*
named in what may be the wrong way, *This so-called mechanic couldn't mend a toy car!*

**soccer** *noun*
(*informal*) Association Football.

**sociable** *adjective*
(*say* **soh-shă-bŭl**)
liking to be with other people; friendly.
**sociability** *noun*, **sociably** *adverb*

**social** *adjective*
(*say* **soh-shăl**)
1 living in a community. 2 of or connected with society, *social science.* 3 helping the people in a community, *a social worker.* 4 helping people to meet one another, *a social club.*
**socially** *adverb*

**socialist** *noun* (**socialists**)
someone who believes that wealth should be equally shared and that the main industries and resources should be controlled by the government.
**socialism** *noun*, **socialist** *adjective*

**society** *noun* (**societies**)
1 a community; people living together in a group or nation. 2 a group of people organized for a particular purpose, *a dramatic society.* 3 people of the higher classes and their way of life, *The way you behave would not be accepted in society.*

**sociology** *noun*
(*say* **soh-si-ol-ŏ-ji**)
the study of society or societies.
**sociological** *adjective*, **sociologist** *noun*

**sock**[1] *noun* (**socks**)
a small, soft piece of clothing that covers your foot and the lower half of your leg.
**pull your socks up,** (*informal*) to try to do better.

**sock**[2] *verb* (**socks, socking, socked**)
(*informal*) to hit something forcefully; to punch someone, *He socked me on the jaw.*

**socket** *noun* (**sockets**)
a device or hole into which something fits, especially the place where an electric plug or bulb is put to make a connection.

**soda** *noun*
1 crystals dissolved in water and used for cleaning (*washing-soda*); powder used in cooking (*baking-soda*). 2 soda-water.
**soda-water,** fizzy water used in drinks.

**sodium** *noun*
(*say* **soh-di-ŭm**)
a soft, silvery-white, metallic substance.

**sofa** *noun* (**sofas**)
a long soft seat with sides and a back.

**soft** *adjective* (**softer, softest**)
1 not hard or firm; easily pressed or cut into a new shape. 2 smooth; not rough or stiff. 3 gentle; not loud, *a soft voice.*
**soft drink,** a drink that does not contain alcohol.
**softly** *adverb*, **softness** *noun*

**soften** *verb* (**softens, softening, softened**)
to make something softer; to become softer.
**softener** *noun*

**software** *noun*
(*in Computing*) things like programs and manuals, which are not part of the machinery (the *hardware*) of a computer.

**soggy** *adjective* (**soggier, soggiest**)
very wet and heavy.

**soil**[1] *noun*
the earth that plants grow in.

**soil**[2] *verb* (**soils, soiling, soiled**)
to make something dirty; to stain.

**solar** *adjective*
of or from the sun, *solar heating*.
**solar panel,** a device that collects energy, especially heat, from the sun.
**solar power,** energy from the sun.
**solar system,** the sun and the planets that revolve round it.

**sold** past tense and past participle of **sell.**

**solder** *noun*
a soft alloy that is melted to join wires, etc. together.
**solder** *verb*

**soldier** *noun* (**soldiers**)
a member of an army.

**sole**[1] *noun* (**soles**)
1 the bottom part of a shoe or foot. 2 a flat sea-fish that can be eaten.

**sole**[2] *adjective*
single; only, *She was the sole survivor*.
**solely** *adverb*

**solemn** *adjective*
serious; dignified, *a solemn face*.
**solemnity** *noun*, **solemnly** *adverb*

**solicitor** *noun* (**solicitors**)
a kind of lawyer who advises people, prepares legal documents, etc.

**solid**[1] *adjective*
1 not hollow; with no space inside. 2 that keeps its shape; not a liquid or gas.
**solidity** *noun*, **solidly** *adverb*

**solid**[2] *noun* (**solids**)
a solid thing; a solid substance.

**solidify** *verb* (**solidifies, solidifying, solidified**)
to become solid; to make something become solid.

**soliloquy** *noun* (**soliloquies**)
(*say* sŏ-lil-ŏ-kwi)
a speech in which an actor is alone and speaks his or her thoughts aloud.

**solitary** *adjective*
1 alone; on your own, *He lived a solitary life*. 2 single, *A solitary bird sang*.

**solitude** *noun*
being on your own.

**solo** *noun* (**solos**)
something sung, played, danced, or done by one person, *She sang a solo*.
**soloist** *noun*

**solstice** *noun* (**solstices**)
either of the two times in the year when the sun is at its furthest point north or south of the equator, the **summer solstice,** about 21 June, or the **winter solstice,** about 22 December.

**soluble** *adjective*
1 that can be dissolved. 2 that can be solved, *Is the problem soluble?*
**solubility** *noun*

**solution** *noun* (**solutions**)
1 something dissolved in a liquid. 2 the answer to a problem or puzzle.

**solve** *verb* (**solves, solving, solved**)
to find the answer to a problem or puzzle.

**solvent** *noun* (**solvents**)
a liquid in which other substances can be dissolved, *Some solvents can be used to remove stains*.
**solvent abuse,** using the vapour of solvents as a kind of drug.

**sombre** *adjective*
gloomy; dark.

**some**[1] *adjective*
1 a few, *some sweets*. 2 a certain amount of, *some cake*. 3 a; an unknown, *Some fool left a toffee on this chair!*

**some**[2] *pronoun*
a certain or unknown number or amount, *Some of them were late*.

**somebody** *pronoun*
someone.

**somehow** *adverb*
in some way, *We must find money somehow*.

**someone** *pronoun*
a person.

**somersault** *noun* (**somersaults**)
(*say* sum-er-solt)
a movement in which you turn head over heels in the air or on the ground, before landing on your feet.

**something** *pronoun*
a certain or unknown thing.

**sometime** *adverb*
at some time, *I saw her sometime last year*.

**sometimes** *adverb*
at some times, *Sometimes we walk to school*.

**somewhat** *adverb*
to some extent; to a certain amount, *He was somewhat annoyed*.

**somewhere** *adverb*
in or to some place.

**son** *noun* (**sons**)
a boy or man who is someone's child.

**song** *noun* (**songs**)
1 a tune for singing. 2 singing, *the song of the birds.*
**a song and dance**, (*informal*) a great fuss.

**songbird** *noun* (**songbirds**)
a bird that sings sweetly.

**sonic** *adjective*
of sound or sound-waves.
**sonic boom**, a bang caused by an aircraft flying faster than the speed of sound.

**sonnet** *noun* (**sonnets**)
a kind of poem with 14 lines.

**soon** *adverb* (**sooner, soonest**)
1 in a short time from now. 2 not long after, *She became ill, but was soon better.* 3 early; quickly, *You spoke too soon.* 4 willingly, *I'd just as soon stay at home.*
**sooner or later**, at some time in the future.

**soot** *noun*
the black powder left by smoke in a chimney, on a building, etc.
**sooty** *adjective*

**soothe** *verb* (**soothes, soothing, soothed**)
1 to make someone calm. 2 to ease a pain, ache, etc.

**sophisticated** *adjective*
(*say* sŏf-**iss**-ti-kay-tid)
1 not simple or innocent; cultured; civilized, *sophisticated people.*
2 complicated, *a sophisticated machine.*
**sophistication** *noun*

**sopping** *adjective*
very wet; soaked.

**soppy** *adjective* (**soppier, soppiest**)
(*informal*) sentimental; silly.

**soprano** *noun* (**sopranos**)
(*say* sŏ-**prah**-noh)
a woman or boy with a high singing voice.

**sorcerer** *noun* (**sorcerers**)
a man who can do magic.
**sorcery** *noun*

**sorceress** *noun* (**sorceresses**)
a woman who can do magic.

**sore**[1] *adjective* (**sorer, sorest**)
1 painful; smarting. 2 annoyed.
**sorely** *adverb*, **soreness** *noun*

**sore**[2] *noun* (**sores**)
a painful place on the body.

**sorrow** *noun* (**sorrows**)
sadness; regret.
**sorrowful** *adjective*, **sorrowfully** *adverb*

**sorry** *adjective* (**sorrier, sorriest**)
1 feeling sorrow, *I'm sorry I forgot to send you a birthday card.* 2 feeling pity, *She felt sorry for the lost child.*

**sort**[1] *noun* (**sorts**)
a group of things or people that are similar; a kind, *What sort of fruit do you like?*
**sort of**, (*informal*) rather; to some extent, *I sort of expected a present.*

**sort**[2] *verb* (**sorts, sorting, sorted**)
to arrange things into groups, kinds, etc., *I must sort these books into piles.*
**sorting office**, a place where letters are sorted before being delivered.

**SOS** *noun*
an urgent appeal for help, *The sinking ship sent out an SOS.*

**sought** past tense and past participle of **seek.**

**soul** *noun* (**souls**)
the invisible part of a person that is believed to go on living after he or she dies.

**sound**[1] *noun* (**sounds**)
something that can be heard.
**sound barrier**, the resistance of the air to objects moving at speeds near the speed of sound.
**sound effect**, a sound made artificially for use in a play, film, broadcast, etc.

**sound**[2] *verb* (**sounds, sounding, sounded**)
to make a sound; to give a particular impression by the sound that is made, *A bell sounded. He sounds angry. The car sounds as if it is about to fall to pieces.*

**sound**[3] *verb* (**sounds, sounding, sounded**)
to test the depth of water beneath a ship.
**sound out**, to try to find out what someone thinks or feels.

**sound**[4] *adjective* (**sounder, soundest**)
1 not damaged; in good condition.
2 healthy. 3 reasonable; correct, *His ideas are sound.* 4 reliable; secure, *a sound investment.* 5 thorough; deep, *a sound sleep.*
**soundly** *adverb*, **soundness** *noun*

**sound-track** *noun* (**sound-tracks**)
the sound that goes with a cinema film.

**soup** *noun* (**soups**)
a liquid food made from vegetables, meat, etc.

**sour** *adjective* (**sourer, sourest**)
having a sharp taste like vinegar or lemons.
**sourly** *adverb*, **sourness** *noun*

**source** *noun* (**sources**)
the place where something comes from; the place where a river begins.

**south¹** *noun*
the direction to the right of a person facing east.

**south²** *adjective*
1 coming from the south, *a south wind.*
2 situated in the south, *the south coast.*
**southerly** *adjective*, **southern** *adjective*,
**southerner** *noun*

**south³** *adverb*
towards the south.
**southward** *adjective* and *adverb*,
**southwards** *adverb*

**souvenir** *noun* (**souvenirs**)
(*say* soo-věn-**eer**)
something that you keep because it reminds you of a person, place, or event.

**sovereign** *noun* (**sovereigns**)
(*say* **sov**-rin)
1 a king or a queen. 2 an old British gold coin that was worth £1.

**Soviet** *adjective*
(*say* **soh**-vi-ět or **sov**-i-ět)
of the states dominated by Russia before 1991.

**sow¹** *verb* (**sows, sowing, sowed, sown** or **sowed**)
(rhymes with *go*)
to put seeds into the ground so that they will grow into plants, *Have you sown those beans? I sowed them yesterday.*
**sower** *noun*

**sow²** *noun* (**sows**)
(rhymes with *cow*)
a female pig.

**soya bean** *noun* (**soya beans**)
a kind of bean from which edible oil and flour are made.

**space¹** *noun* (**spaces**)
1 the whole area outside the earth, where the stars and planets are. 2 an area or volume, *There is plenty of space for your luggage.* 3 an empty area; a gap, *The door had spaces at the top and bottom, letting in a draught.* 4 a period of time, *They moved house twice in the space of a year.*

**space²** *verb* (**spaces, spacing, spaced**)
to arrange things with gaps or periods of time between them.

**spacecraft** *noun* (**spacecraft**)
a vehicle for travelling in space.

**spaceman** *noun* (**spacemen**)
a man who travels in a spacecraft.

**spaceship** *noun* (**spaceships**)
a spacecraft.

**space shuttle** *noun* (**space shuttles**)
a type of spacecraft that can travel into space and return to earth many times.

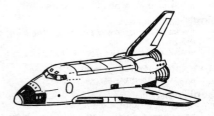

**space station** *noun* (**space stations**)
an artificial satellite used as a base for exploring space or for doing scientific experiments, etc.

**spacewoman** *noun* (**spacewomen**)
a woman who travels in a spacecraft.

**spacious** *adjective*
roomy.
**spaciously** *adverb*, **spaciousness** *noun*

**spade** *noun* (**spades**)
1 a tool with a long handle and a wide blade for digging. 2 a playing-card with a black shape, like an upside-down heart on a short stem, printed on it.

**spaghetti** *noun*
(*say* spă-**get**-i)
a type of pasta made in long, thin pieces, *Spaghetti looks like long pieces of string when it is cooked.*

**span¹** *noun* (**spans**)
1 the length from one end of something to the other, especially the distance between the tips of your thumb and little finger when your hand is spread out. 2 a part of a bridge between supports. 3 a period of time.

**span²** *verb* (**spans, spanning, spanned**)
to reach from one side or end of something to the other, *A bridge spanned the river.*

**Spaniard** *noun* (**Spaniards**)
a Spanish person.

**spaniel** *noun* (**spaniels**)
a breed of dog with long ears and silky fur.

**Spanish** *adjective*
of Spain.
**Spanish Conquest,** the discovery and conquest of South America by the Spaniards in the 16th century.

**spank** *verb* (**spanks, spanking, spanked**)
to smack someone on the bottom as a punishment.

**spanner** *noun* (**spanners**)
(in America, *wrench*) a tool for tightening or loosening a nut.

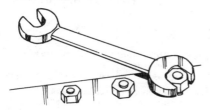

**spar**[1] *noun* (**spars**)
a strong pole, especially one used on a ship.

**spar**[2] *verb* (**spars, sparring, sparred**)
to practise boxing, *He was my sparring partner.*

**spare**[1] *verb* (**spares, sparing, spared**)
1 to afford; to give someone something, *Can you spare a penny?* 2 to be merciful towards someone; not to harm a person or thing, *Spare my feelings.* 3 to use or treat economically, *No expense will be spared.*

**spare**[2] *adjective*
1 not used but kept ready in case it is needed; extra, *a spare tyre.* 2 thin; lean.
**go spare,** (*slang*) to get very annoyed; to go mad.
**spare time,** time not needed for work or other important purposes.

**spare**[3] *noun* (**spares**)
a spare thing or part, *This garage sells spares.*

**spark** *noun* (**sparks**)
1 a tiny flash. 2 a tiny, glowing piece of something hot.

**sparkle** *verb* (**sparkles, sparkling, sparkled**)
to shine with a lot of tiny flashes of bright light.

**sparkler** *noun* (**sparklers**)
a firework that sparkles.

**spark-plug** *noun* (**spark-plugs**)
a device that makes a spark to explode the fuel in an internal-combustion engine.

**sparrow** *noun* (**sparrows**)
a small brown bird, *You often see sparrows in the garden.*

**sparse** *adjective* (**sparser, sparsest**)
small in number or amount, *a sparse population. sparse vegetation.*
**sparsely** *adverb*, **sparseness** *noun*

**spastic** *noun* (**spastics**)
someone who was born with a disability that makes it difficult for him or her to control his or her muscles.

**spat** past tense and past participle of **spit** *verb*.

**spatter** *verb* (**spatters, spattering, spattered**)
to splash; to scatter something in small drops or pieces, *My bike's front wheel has spattered mud all over my shoes.*

**spawn** *noun*
the eggs of frogs, fish, and other water-animals.

**speak** *verb* (**speaks, speaking, spoke, spoken**)
1 to say something, *Have you spoken to him? I spoke to him this morning.* 2 to be able to talk in a particular language, *Do you speak German?*
**speak up,** to say something more clearly or loudly.

**speaker** *noun* (**speakers**)
1 a person who is speaking; someone who makes a speech. 2 a loudspeaker.
**the Speaker,** the person who is in charge of debates in the House of Commons or similar parliaments.

**spear** *noun* (**spears**)
a long pole with a sharp point, used as a weapon.

**special** *adjective*
1 different from other people or things; unusual. 2 for a particular person or purpose.

**specialist** *noun* (**specialists**)
an expert in a particular subject.

**speciality** *noun* (**specialities**)
1 something that you specialize in. 2 a special product, especially a food, that you find in a particular place, *Pizza is a speciality of Italy.*

**specialize** *verb* (**specializes, specializing, specialized**)
to give particular attention to one subject or thing, *She is specializing in biology.*
**specialization** *noun*

**specially** *adverb*
especially, *I came specially to see you.*

**species** *noun* (**species**)
(*say* spee-shiz)
a group of animals or plants that are very similar, *Men and women belong to the same species.*

**specific** *adjective*
1 definite; precise. 2 referring to a particular thing, *The money was given for a specific purpose.*
**specific gravity,** the mass of something compared with the mass of the same volume of water or air.
**specifically** *adverb*

**specify** *verb* (**specifies, specifying, specified**)
to name or list things precisely, *The recipe specified brown sugar, not white.*
**specification** *noun*

**specimen** *noun* (**specimens**)
1 a small amount of something that shows what the rest is like, *This painting is a specimen of her work.* 2 an example of one kind of plant, animal, or thing, *a fine specimen of an oak.*

**speck** *noun* (**specks**)
1 a tiny piece of something. 2 a tiny mark or spot.

**speckled** *adjective*
covered with small spots.

**spectacle** *noun* (**spectacles**)
1 an impressive or exciting sight or display. 2 something that you see, especially something ridiculous.
**spectacles,** a pair of lenses in a frame to help someone see.

**spectacular** *adjective*
impressive to see.

**spectator** *noun* (**spectators**)
a person who watches a game or show, or who watches anything without joining in.

**spectre** *noun* (**spectres**)
(*say* **spek**-ter)
a ghost.

**spectrum** *noun* (**spectra**)
1 the bands of colours like those you see in a rainbow. 2 a wide range of things, ideas, etc., *The debate involved people from all parts of the political spectrum, from the far right to the left.*

**speech** *noun* (**speeches**)
1 the action or power of speaking. 2 a talk given to a group of people.

**speechless** *adjective*
unable to speak, especially because of surprise or anger.

**speed**[1] *noun* (**speeds**)
1 quickness; swiftness. 2 the rate at which something moves.
**at speed,** quickly.
**speedily** *adverb*, **speedy** *adjective*

**speed**[2] *verb* (**speeds, speeding, sped** or **speeded**)
to go very fast; to go too fast, *Drivers can be fined for speeding.*
**speed up,** to make something quicker; to become quicker.

**speedboat** *noun* (**speedboats**)
a fast motor boat.

**speedometer** *noun* (**speedometers**)
(*say* spee-**dom**-it-er)
a device that measures a vehicle's speed.

**speedway** *noun* (**speedways**)
1 motor-cycle racing. 2 a track for motor-cycle racing.

**spell**[1] *verb* (**spells, spelling, spelt** or **spelled**)
to put the right letters in the right order to make a word or name, *How is your name spelt?*

**spell**[2] *noun* (**spells**)
1 a period of time, *a cold spell.* 2 a period when something is done or happens, *a spell of work.* 3 (*in Australia and New Zealand*) a period of rest from work.

**spell**[3] *noun* (**spells**)
a saying that is supposed to have magic power.

**spelling** *noun* (**spellings**)
the way in which letters are put together to form words; how well someone does this, *Use the dictionary to check your spelling.*
**spelling-checker,** a computer program to check that words have been spelt correctly.

**spend** *verb* (**spends, spending, spent**)
1 to use money to pay for things. 2 to pass time, *He spent a year in prison.* 3 to use up, *She spends all her energy on gardening.*

**sperm** *noun* (**sperms** or **sperm**)
1 the male sex cell that joins with an ovum to produce offspring. 2 the liquid that contains these cells.
**sperm whale,** a large whale whose head contains a waxy oil.

**sphere** *noun* (**spheres**)
a globe; the shape of a ball.
**spherical** *adjective*

**spice** *noun* (**spices**)
a substance used to flavour food, *Spices are usually dried parts of plants like pepper and ginger.*
**spicy** *adjective*

**spider** *noun* (**spiders**)
a small animal with eight legs that often spins webs to catch insects.

**spied** past tense and past participle of **spy** *verb*.

**spike** *noun* (**spikes**)
a pointed piece of metal; a sharp point.
**spiky** *adjective*

**spill**[1] *verb* (**spills, spilling, spilt** or **spilled**)
1 to let something fall out of a container, *You have spilt the milk.* 2 to fall out of a container, *The coins came spilling out.*

**spill**[2] *noun* (**spills**)
a thin strip of wood or rolled paper used to light a fire, gas cooker, etc.

**spin** *verb* (**spins, spinning, spun**)
1 to turn round and round quickly; to make something turn in this way. 2 to make pieces of wool, cotton, etc. into thread by twisting them. 3 to make a web or cocoon out of threads, *The spider spun a web.*

**spinach** *noun*
a dark green vegetable.

**spindle** *noun* (**spindles**)
1 a thin rod on which you wind thread. 2 a pin or bar that turns round, or a fixed pin or bar with something turning around it.

**spin-drier** *noun* (**spin-driers**)
a machine in which clothes are dried by spinning them round and round.

**spine** *noun* (**spines**)
1 the line of bones down the middle of the back. 2 a thorn or prickle. 3 the back part of a book where the pages are joined together.
**spinal** *adjective*, **spiny** *adjective*

**spine-chilling** *adjective*
frightening but exciting, *a spine-chilling ghost story.*

**spinning-wheel** *noun* (**spinning-wheels**)
a machine for spinning thread out of wool, cotton, etc.

**spin-off** *noun* (**spin-offs**)
something useful produced when something else is developed or done, *This chemical was a spin-off from space research.*

**spinster** *noun* (**spinsters**)
a woman who has not married.

**spiral** *adjective*
that goes round and round like the shape of a spring, the thread of a screw, or the jam in a Swiss roll.

**spire** *noun* (**spires**)
a tall, pointed part on top of a church tower.

**spirit** *noun* (**spirits**)
1 the soul. 2 a being such as a ghost, an angel, a fairy, etc. that is thought by some people to exist but that cannot be seen, heard, touched, etc. in the same way that humans and animals can. 3 courage; liveliness. 4 how someone feels or thinks, *She was in good spirits.* 5 an alcoholic liquid; a strong alcoholic drink.

**spiritual**[1] *adjective*
1 of the human soul. 2 connected with religion, *the spiritual authority of the Pope.*
**spiritually** *adverb*

**spiritual**[2] *noun* (**spirituals**)
a religious song originally sung by black Americans.

**spiritualism** *noun*
the belief that the spirits of dead people can communicate with living people.
**spiritualist** *noun*

**spit**[1] *verb* (**spits, spitting, spat**)
1 to send drops of liquid forcibly out of your mouth, *He spat into the basin.* 2 (*informal*) to rain lightly, *It's only spitting.*

**spit**[2] *noun* (**spits**)
1 a long, thin spike put through meat to hold it while it is roasted. 2 a narrow strip of land sticking out into the sea.

**spite** *noun*
a desire to hurt or annoy someone.
**in spite of,** although something has happened or is happening, *They went out in spite of the rain.*
**spiteful** *adjective*

**splash**[1] *verb* (**splashes, splashing, splashed**)
1 to make liquid fly about, as you do when you jump into water. 2 to fly about in drops, *The water poured out of the hose and splashed all over me.* 3 to make someone wet by sending drops of liquid towards them, *The bus splashed us as it went past.*

**splash**[2] *noun* (**splashes**)
the action or sound of splashing.
**make a splash,** to make a big display or effect, *Her wedding made quite a splash in the village.*

**splash-down** *noun* (**splash-downs**)
the landing of a spacecraft in the sea.

**splendid** *adjective*
magnificent; very satisfying.
**splendidly** *adverb*, **splendour** *noun*

**splint** *noun* (**splints**)
a straight piece of wood, metal, etc. that is tied to a broken arm or leg to hold it firm.

**splinter** *noun* (**splinters**)
a small, sharp piece of wood, glass, etc. broken off a larger piece.

**split**¹ *verb* (**splits, splitting, split**)
1 to cut or break something into parts; to divide something. 2 (*slang*) to reveal a secret. 3 (*slang*) to leave somewhere, to go, *Let's split!*
**split up**, to divide or separate.

**split**² *noun* (**splits**)
1 the splitting or dividing of something. 2 a place where something has split.
**the splits**, a movement where you stretch out your legs in opposite directions along the floor, at right angles to the top half of your body.

**splutter** *verb* (**splutters, spluttering, spluttered**)
1 to make a quick series of spitting sounds, *The smoke from the bonfire made him cough and splutter.* 2 to speak quickly but not clearly, *Stop spluttering; I can't hear what you're saying!*

**spoil** *verb* (**spoils, spoiling, spoilt** or **spoiled**)
1 to make something less useful, pleasant, good, etc., *The rain spoilt our holiday.* 2 to make someone selfish by always giving in to his or her wishes, *Don't spoil your child.*

**spoilsport** *noun* (**spoilsports**)
a person who spoils other people's fun.

**spoke**¹ *noun* (**spokes**)
one of the rods or bars that go from the centre of a wheel to the rim.

spoke¹

**spoke**² past tense of **speak**.

**spoken** past participle of **speak**.

**spokesman** *noun* (**spokesmen**)
someone who speaks on behalf of a group of people.

**sponge**¹ *noun* (**sponges**)
1 a lump of soft material containing lots of tiny holes, used in washing. 2 a sea-creature from which you get this kind of material. 3 a soft, lightweight cake or pudding.
**spongy** *adjective*

**sponge**² *verb* (**sponges, sponging, sponged**)
1 to wash something with a sponge.
2 (*informal*) to get money or help from someone without intending to return it, *He was sponging on his relatives.*
**sponger** *noun*

**sponsor** *noun* (**sponsors**)
someone who provides money, help, etc. for a person or thing, especially someone who gives money to a charity in return for something done by another person.
**sponsorship** *noun*

**spontaneous** *adjective*
(*say* spon-**tay**-ni-ŭs)
happening or done naturally; not forced, *A spontaneous cheer greeted the local team.*
**spontaneity** *noun*, **spontaneously** *adverb*

**spooky** *adjective* (**spookier, spookiest**)
(*informal*) frighteningly strange; haunted by ghosts.

**spool** *noun* (**spools**)
a round device on which cotton, string, film, etc. is wound.

**spoon** *noun* (**spoons**)
a metal or wooden device consisting of a small bowl with a handle, used for lifting food to your mouth or for stirring or measuring.
**spoonful** *noun*

**sport** *noun* (**sports**)
1 a game that exercises your body, especially a game played out of doors, *Football, netball, swimming, and tennis are all sports.* 2 games of this sort, *Are you keen on sport?* 3 (*informal*) someone who plays or behaves fairly and unselfishly, *Come on, be a sport.*
**sports car**, a low, fast motor car, usually with two seats.
**sports coat** or **sports jacket**, a man's jacket that is not part of a suit.

**sporting** *adjective*
1 connected with sport; interested in sport.
2 behaving fairly and unselfishly.
**a sporting chance**, a reasonable chance.

**sportsman** *noun* (**sportsmen**)
1 a man who takes part in sport. 2 a person who behaves fairly and unselfishly.
**sportsmanship** *noun*

**sportswoman** *noun* (**sportswomen**)
a woman who takes part in sport.

**spot**$^1$ *noun* (**spots**)
1 a small mark that is usually round.
2 a pimple. 3 a small amount of something.
4 a place.
**on the spot**, immediately; in a difficult
situation, *We can repair your bike on the
spot. Her question really put us on the spot.*
**spotless** *adjective*, **spotty** *adjective*

**spot**$^2$ *verb* (**spots**, **spotting**, **spotted**)
1 to mark with spots. 2 to notice; to watch
for.
**spotter** *noun*

**spotlight** *noun* (**spotlights**)
a strong light that can shine on one small
area.

**spout**$^1$ *noun* (**spouts**)
1 a pipe or a shaped opening from which
liquid can pour. 2 a jet of liquid.

**spout**$^2$ *verb* (**spouts**, **spouting**, **spouted**)
1 to send out a jet of liquid; to come out in a
jet. 2 (*informal*) to speak for a long time or
in a pompous way.

**sprain** *verb* (**sprains**, **spraining**, **sprained**)
to injure an ankle, wrist, etc. by twisting it.

**sprang** past tense of **spring** *verb*.

**sprawl** *verb* (**sprawls**, **sprawling**, **sprawled**)
1 to sit or lie with your arms and legs
spread out. 2 to spread out loosely or
untidily.

**spray**$^1$ *verb* (**sprays**, **spraying**, **sprayed**)
to scatter tiny drops of liquid all over
something.

**spray**$^2$ *noun* (**sprays**)
1 tiny drops of liquid scattered on
something. 2 a device for spreading liquid
in many tiny drops.

**spray**$^3$ *noun* (**sprays**)
a small bunch of flowers.

**spread**$^1$ *verb* (**spreads**, **spreading**, **spread**)
1 to lay or stretch something out to its full
size, *The seagull spread its wings.* 2 to
make something cover a surface, *He spread
jam on his toast.* 3 to make or become
widely known, felt, heard, etc., *Spread the
news.*

**spread**$^2$ *noun* (**spreads**)
1 the action or result of spreading. 2 the
breadth or extent of something.
3 (*informal*) a huge meal.

**spreadsheet** *noun* (**spreadsheets**)
a computer program that allows you to set
out tables of figures, and to do calculations
that involve all the figures at once.

**sprightly** *adjective* (**sprightlier**, **sprightliest**)
lively; energetic.

**spring**$^1$ *verb* (**springs**, **springing**, **sprang**, **sprung**)
1 to move upwards suddenly. 2 to arise, *The
trouble has sprung from carelessness.* 3 to
start suddenly, *The engine sprang into life.*
4 to make something happen without
warning, *They sprang a surprise on us.*

**spring**$^2$ *noun* (**springs**)
1 a springy coil of metal, *This mattress
contains springs.* 2 a sudden upward
movement. 3 a place where water rises out
of the ground. 4 the season of the year
when most plants start to grow, between
winter and summer.

**springboard** *noun* (**springboards**)
a springy board from which people jump or
dive.

**spring-clean** *verb* (**spring-cleans**,
**spring-cleaning**, **spring-cleaned**)
to clean a house thoroughly, usually in
spring.

**springtime** *noun*
the season of spring, *Daffodils bloom in
springtime.*

**springy** *adjective* (**springier**, **springiest**)
that returns to its original position when
you bend it and let it go.

**sprinkle** *verb* (**sprinkles**, **sprinkling**, **sprinkled**)
to make tiny drops or pieces fall on
something, *Sprinkle the flower-bed with
water. He sprinkled sugar on his cereal.*
**sprinkler** *noun*

**sprint** *verb* (**sprints**, **sprinting**, **sprinted**)
to run very fast for a short distance.
**sprinter** *noun*

**sprout**$^1$ *verb* (**sprouts**, **sprouting**, **sprouted**)
to start to grow; to produce leaves.

**sprout**$^2$ *noun* (**sprouts**)
a Brussels sprout.

**spruce**$^1$ *noun* (**spruces**)
a kind of fir-tree.

**spruce**$^2$ *adjective* (**sprucer**, **sprucest**)
neat; smart.

**sprung** past participle of **spring** *verb*.

**spud** *noun* (**spuds**)
(*informal*) a potato.

**spun** past tense and past participle of **spin**.

**spur**$^1$ *noun* (**spurs**)
1 a sharp device worn on the heel of a
rider's boot to urge a horse to go faster.
2 (*in Geography*) a ridge that sticks out
from a mountain.
**on the spur of the moment**, without planning.

**spur**$^2$ *verb* (**spurs**, **spurring**, **spurred**)
to urge a horse to go faster; to encourage
someone.

**spurt**[1] *verb* (**spurts, spurting, spurted**)
  **1** to gush out or up, *Blood spurted from the cut*. **2** to speed up suddenly, *He spurted to catch the leader*.

**spurt**[2] *noun* (**spurts**)
  **1** a jet, especially of liquid. **2** an act of speeding up suddenly, *He put on a spurt and overtook the runner in front of him*.

**spy**[1] *noun* (**spies**)
  someone who works secretly to find out things about another country, person, etc.

**spy**[2] *verb* (**spies, spying, spied**)
  **1** to be a spy; to watch secretly, *He was spying on us*. **2** to see; to notice, *She spied a house in the distance*.

**squabble** *verb* (**squabbles, squabbling, squabbled**)
  to quarrel about something unimportant.

**squad** *noun* (**squads**)
  a small group of people working or being trained together.

**squadron** *noun* (**squadrons**)
  part of an air force, army, or navy.

**squalid** *adjective*
  dirty and unpleasant, *squalid houses*.
  **squalidly** *adverb*, **squalor** *noun*

**squall** *noun* (**squalls**)
  a sudden strong wind.
  **squally** *adjective*

**squander** *verb* (**squanders, squandering, squandered**)
  to waste money, time, etc.

**square**[1] *adjective* (**squarer, squarest**)
  **1** with four straight equal sides and four right angles; forming a right angle; having right angles, *a square piece of paper*. **2** of or using units that describe the size of an area, *A square metre is the size of a square with each side one metre long*. **3** equal; even; settled. **4** honest; fair.
  **square meal**, a good, satisfying meal.
  **square root**, the number that gives a particular number if it is multiplied by itself, *The square root of 64 is 8*.
  **squarely** *adverb*, **squareness** *noun*

**square**[2] *noun* (**squares**)
  **1** a square shape or object. **2** an area surrounded by buildings, *Leicester Square*. **3** the result of multiplying a number by itself, *9 is the square of 3*.

**square**[3] *verb* (**squares, squaring, squared**)
  **1** to make something square. **2** to multiply a number by itself, *5 squared is 25*. **3** to match; to be consistent, *His story doesn't square with yours*. **4** (*informal*) to bribe someone.

**squash**[1] *verb* (**squashes, squashing, squashed**)
  **1** to press something so that it loses its shape; to crush something. **2** to move something or yourself into a place where there is very little room, *We all squashed into Viv's small car. I'll try to squash another jumper into my suitcase*.

**squash**[2] *noun* (**squashes**)
  **1** a crowd; a crowded situation, *There was a tremendous squash outside the football ground. Both of us can sleep in my tent, though it'll be a squash*. **2** a fruit-flavoured drink. **3** a game played with rackets and a small ball in a special indoor court.

**squat**[1] *verb* (**squats, squatting, squatted**)
  **1** to sit on your heels. **2** to live in an unoccupied house without permission.
  **squatter** *noun*

**squat**[2] *adjective* (**squatter, squattest**)
  short and fat, *a squat man*.

**squaw** *noun* (**squaws**)
  a Native American woman or wife.

**squawk** *verb* (**squawks, squawking, squawked**)
  to make a loud, harsh cry.

**squeak** *noun* (**squeaks**)
  a tiny, shrill sound such as a mouse makes.
  **squeakily** *adverb*, **squeaky** *adjective*

**squeal** *noun* (**squeals**)
  a long, shrill sound.

**squeeze**[1] *verb* (**squeezes, squeezing, squeezed**)
  **1** to press something from opposite sides, especially so as to get liquid out of it. **2** to force a way into or through a place, gap, etc., *We squeezed into the car*.
  **squeezer** *noun*

**squeeze**[2] *noun* (**squeezes**)
  **1** the action of squeezing. **2** a hug. **3** a time when money is difficult to get, borrow, etc.

**squelch** *verb* (**squelches, squelching, squelched**)
  to make a sound like someone treading in thick mud.

**squid** *noun* (**squid** or **squids**)
  a sea-animal with eight short arms and two very long ones.

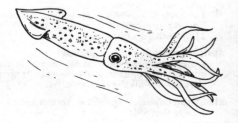

**squint** *verb* (**squints, squinting, squinted**)
**1** to be cross-eyed. **2** to peer; to look with half-shut eyes at something.

**squire** *noun* (**squires**)
**1** the man who owned most of the land in a country district. **2** a knight's young attendant in the Middle Ages. **3** (*slang*) a word sometimes used when speaking to a man, *You can't park here, squire.*

**squirm** *verb* (**squirms, squirming, squirmed**)
to wriggle; to twist your body about.

**squirrel** *noun* (**squirrels**)
a small animal that lives in trees and eats nuts, *Squirrels have very thick tails.*

**squirt** *verb* (**squirts, squirting, squirted**)
to send something out or come out in a fast-moving jet of liquid, *The grapefruit juice squirted in his eye.*

**St** short for **Saint**.

**St.** short for **Street**.

**stab** *verb* (**stabs, stabbing, stabbed**)
to pierce or wound someone with something sharp, *She stabbed him with a knife.*

**stabilize** *verb* (**stabilizes, stabilizing, stabilized**)
to make something stable; to become stable, *Prices have stabilized.*

**stabilizer** *noun* (**stabilizers**)
a device that helps keep a ship or vehicle steady.
**stabilizers,** a pair of small wheels fitted either side of a bicycle's back wheel to help someone who is learning to ride.

**stable**[1] *adjective* (**stabler, stablest**)
steady; firmly fixed.
**stability** *noun*, **stably** *adverb*

**stable**[2] *noun* (**stables**)
a building where horses are kept.

**stack**[1] *noun* (**stacks**)
**1** a neat pile. **2** a haystack. **3** a large amount of something. **4** (*in Geography*) a pillar of rock standing in the sea near cliffs.

**stack**[2] *verb* (**stacks, stacking, stacked**)
to pile things up.

**stadium** *noun* (**stadiums**)
a sports ground surrounded by seats for spectators.

**staff** *noun* (**staffs**)
**1** the people who work in an office, shop, etc. **2** the teachers in a school, college, etc. **3** a thick stick for walking with.

**stag** *noun* (**stags**)
a male deer.

**stage**[1] *noun* (**stages**)
**1** a platform for performances in a theatre or hall. **2** the point that someone or something has reached.

**stage**[2] *verb* (**stages, staging, staged**)
**1** to present a performance on a stage. **2** to organize, *They staged a show for charity.*

**stage-coach** *noun* (**stage-coaches**)
a horse-drawn coach of a kind that used to travel regularly along the same route.

**stagger** *verb* (**staggers, staggering, staggered**)
**1** to walk unsteadily. **2** to amaze or confuse someone, *I was staggered at the price.* **3** to arrange events so that they do not all happen at the same time.

**stagnant** *adjective*
not flowing or fresh, *a stagnant pond.*

**stain**[1] *noun* (**stains**)
a dirty mark on something, often caused by liquid.

**stain**[2] *verb* (**stains, staining, stained**)
**1** to make a stain on something. **2** to colour something, *The juice stained my dress.*

**stainless** *adjective*
without stains.
**stainless steel,** steel that does not rust easily.

**stair** *noun* (**stairs**)
a flat place to put your foot when walking up or down to a different level inside a building.

**staircase** *noun* (**staircases**)
a series of stairs.

**stake** *noun* (**stakes**)
**1** a thick pointed stick to be driven into the ground. **2** the thick post to which people used to be tied to execute them by burning. **3** an amount of money bet on something.

**stalactite** *noun* (**stalactites**)
a stony spike hanging from the roof of a cave, *Stalactites look like icicles.*

**stalagmite** *noun* (**stalagmites**)
a stony spike rising from the floor of a cave.

**stale** *adjective* (**staler, stalest**)
not fresh; musty, *stale bread.*

**stalk¹** *noun* (**stalks**)
1 the main part of a plant above the ground. 2 a thin branch that holds a leaf, fruit, or flower.

**stalk²** *verb* (**stalks, stalking, stalked**)
1 to hunt stealthily. 2 to walk in a stiff or dignified way.

**stall¹** *noun* (**stalls**)
1 a table or small open-fronted shop where things are sold, usually in the open air. 2 a place for one animal in a stable or shed. 3 one of the seats on the ground floor of a theatre or cinema.

**stall²** *verb* (**stalls, stalling, stalled**)
to stop suddenly, *The car engine stalled.*

**stallion** *noun* (**stallions**)
a male horse.

**stamen** *noun* (**stamens**)
(*say* **stay**-měn)
the part of a flower that bears pollen.

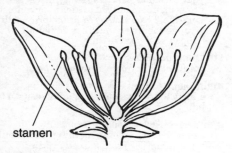

stamen

**stamina** *noun*
(*say* **stam**-in-ă)
the ability to endure physical or mental strain over a long time.

**stammer** *verb* (**stammers, stammering, stammered**)
to keep repeating the sounds at the beginning of words when you speak.

**stamp¹** *noun* (**stamps**)
1 a postage stamp. 2 the act of banging your foot on the ground. 3 a small block with raised letters, etc. for printing words or marks on something; the words or marks printed with this.

**stamp²** *verb* (**stamps, stamping, stamped**)
1 to bang your foot heavily on the ground. 2 to put a postage stamp on something; to put marks on something by means of a stamp.
**stamped addressed envelope,** an envelope with an unused postage stamp and your own address on it.

**stampede** *noun* (**stampedes**)
a sudden rush by animals or people.

**stand¹** *verb* (**stands, standing, stood**)
1 to be on your feet without moving, *She stood there like a statue.* 2 to get or put upright; to place, *Stand the vase on the table.* 3 to stay; to remain unchanged, *My offer still stands.* 4 to tolerate or endure something, *I can't stand the heat.*
**it stands to reason,** it is reasonable or obvious.
**stand by,** to be ready for action.
**stand for,** to represent; to tolerate, *'HMS' stands for His or Her Majesty's Ship. She won't stand for any disobedience.*
**stand in,** to act as a deputy for someone.
**stand out,** to stick out.
**stand up for,** to support or defend.

**stand²** *noun* (**stands**)
1 something made for putting things on, *a music-stand.* 2 a stall where things are sold or displayed. 3 a grandstand. 4 resistance to attack, *She was determined to make a stand for her rights.*

**standard¹** *noun* (**standards**)
1 how good something is, *a high standard of work.* 2 a thing used to measure or judge something else, *The metre is the standard for length.* 3 a flag. 4 an upright pole.
**standard lamp,** a lamp on a pole that stands on the floor.
**standard of living,** the sort of things that you can afford.

**standard²** *adjective*
of the ordinary kind; fitting an accepted standard, *standard English.*
**standardize** *verb*

**standstill** *noun* (**standstills**)
a stop; an end to activity.

**stank** past tense of **stink** *verb*.

**stanza** *noun* (**stanzas**)
a group of lines in a poem.

**staple¹** *noun* (**staples**)
1 a tiny piece of metal used to fix pieces of paper together. 2 a U-shaped nail.
**stapler** *noun*

**staple²** *adjective*
main; normal, *Rice is their staple food.*

**star¹** *noun* (**stars**)
1 one of the objects in space that you see at night as small points of light. 2 one of the main performers in a film, show, etc.; a famous entertainer. 3 a shape with five or six points.
**starry** *adjective*

**star²** *verb* (**stars, starring, starred**)
to be a star in a film, show, etc.; to make someone the star of a film, show, etc., *She has starred in dozens of West End shows. The film 'The Wizard of Oz' starred Judy Garland.*

**starboard** *noun*
the right-hand side of a ship or aircraft when you are facing forward.

**starch** *noun* (**starches**)
1 a white carbohydrate in bread, potatoes, etc. 2 this or a similar substance used to stiffen clothes.
**starchy** *adjective*

**stare** *verb* (**stares, staring, stared**)
to look continuously at someone or something without moving your eyes.

**starfish** *noun* (**starfish** or **starfishes**)
a small sea-animal shaped like a star with five points.

**starling** *noun* (**starlings**)
a noisy black or brown speckled bird.

**start**[1] *verb* (**starts, starting, started**)
1 to take the first steps in doing something. 2 to make something happen; to set something going. 3 to make a sudden movement, *He started at the sound of rattling chains.*
**starter** *noun*

**start**[2] *noun* (**starts**)
1 the act of starting; the beginning. 2 an advantage that someone has or is given at the beginning of something, *We gave the young ones 10 minutes' start.*

**starting-pistol** *noun* (**starting-pistols**)
a pistol fired to signal the start of a race.

**startle** *verb* (**startles, startling, startled**)
to surprise or alarm a person or animal.

**starve** *verb* (**starves, starving, starved**)
1 to suffer or die because you have not got enough food. 2 to make someone suffer or die in this way, *The prisoners had been starved to death.* 3 to deprive a person or thing of something important, *She was starved of love.* 4 (*informal*) to be very hungry, *Where's my dinner? I'm starving!*
**starvation** *noun*

**state**[1] *noun* (**states**)
1 the condition of a person or thing. 2 a nation. 3 a division of a country. 4 a government and its officials. 5 a dignified or grand style, *The King was buried in state.* 6 (*informal*) an excited or upset condition, *Don't get in a state about the burglary.*
**state school**, a school that is given money by the government, by a local authority, or both.

**state**[2] *verb* (**states, stating, stated**)
to say something clearly or formally.

**stately** *adjective* (**statelier, stateliest**)
like a king or queen; dignified.
**stately home**, a large, old house with large gardens or grounds, especially one that has been owned by a noble family for a long time and that can be visited by the public.
**stateliness** *noun*

**statement** *noun* (**statements**)
1 a sentence that says something that is either true or false, *That is not a statement, it is a question.* 2 words that someone uses to say something officially, *The witness made a statement in court.*

**statesman** *noun* (**statesmen**)
someone who is important or skilled in governing a state.
**statesmanship** *noun*

**static** *adjective*
not moving; not changing.
**static electricity**, electricity which is present in something but does not flow as a current.

**station**[1] *noun* (**stations**)
1 a set of buildings where people get on or off trains or buses. 2 a building for police, firemen, or other workers who serve the public. 3 a place from which radio or television broadcasts are made.

**station**[2] *verb* (**stations, stationing, stationed**)
to put a person somewhere for a particular purpose, *He was stationed to guard the ship.*

**stationary** *adjective*
not moving, *The car was stationary.*

USAGE: Do not confuse **stationary** with **stationery**, which is the next word in this dictionary.

**stationery** *noun*
paper, envelopes, and other things used for writing, typing, etc.

**stationmaster** *noun* (**stationmasters**)
the person in charge of a railway station.

**statistic** *noun* (**statistics**)
a piece of information expressed as a number, *The statistics show that the population has doubled.*
**statistics**, the science or study of information that is expressed as numbers.
**statistical** *adjective*, **statistically** *adverb*, **statistician** *noun*

**statue** *noun* (**statues**)
a model made of stone, metal, etc. to look like a person, animal, etc.

**status** *noun* (**statuses**)
1 a person's position or rank in relation to other people, *What is her status in the company?* 2 a good position in society; prestige.

**stave**¹ *noun* (**staves**)
a set of five parallel lines on which music is written.

**stave**² *verb* (**staves, staving,** *past tense* and *past participle* **staved** or **stove**)
to make a hole or dent in something, *The collision stove in the front of the ship.*
**stave off,** to keep something away, *They staved off hunger by drinking a lot of water.*

**stay** *verb* (**stays, staying, stayed**)
1 to remain. 2 to spend time in a place as a visitor.

**steady**¹ *adjective* (**steadier, steadiest**)
1 not shaking or moving; firm. 2 regular; continuous, *a steady pace.*
**steadily** *adverb*, **steadiness** *noun*

**steady**² *verb* (**steadies, steadying, steadied**)
to make something steady.

**steak** *noun* (**steaks**)
a thick slice of meat or fish.

**steal** *verb* (**steals, stealing, stole, stolen**)
1 to take and keep something that does not belong to you, *The money was stolen.* 2 to move stealthily, *He stole out of the room.*

**stealthy** *adjective* (**stealthier, stealthiest**)
secret and quiet, *stealthy movements.*
**stealth** *noun*, **stealthily** *adverb*, **stealthiness** *noun*

**steam**¹ *noun*
1 the vapour that comes from boiling water. 2 (*informal*) energy; power, *He ran out of steam.*
**steamy** *adjective*

**steam**² *verb* (**steams, steaming, steamed**)
1 to give out steam. 2 to move using the power of steam, *The boat steamed down the river.* 3 to cook with steam, *a steamed pudding.* 4 to cover something or be covered with mist or condensation, *The windows steamed up.*
**steamed up,** (*slang*) excited or angry, *He's got all steamed up about the broken window.*

**steam-engine** *noun* (**steam-engines**)
an engine driven by steam.

**steamer** *noun* (**steamers**)
a steamship.

**steamroller** *noun* (**steamrollers**)
a heavy vehicle with wide metal wheels, driven by steam and used to flatten surfaces when making roads.

**steamship** *noun* (**steamships**)
a ship driven by steam.

**steed** *noun* (**steeds**)
(*old-fashioned or poetical use*) a horse.

**steel** *noun*
a strong metal made from iron.
**steely** *adjective*

**steel band** *noun* (**steel bands**)
a group of musicians, especially in the West Indies, who play instruments made from oil drums.

**steep** *adjective* (**steeper, steepest**)
rising or sloping sharply.
**steeply** *adverb*, **steepness** *noun*

**steeple** *noun* (**steeples**)
a church tower with a spire.

**steeplechase** *noun* (**steeplechases**)
1 a horse-race over hedges and fences.
2 a race on foot across country.

**steeplejack** *noun* (**steeplejacks**)
someone who works on very high buildings, chimneys, etc.

**steer**¹ *verb* (**steers, steering, steered**)
to make a car, ship, bicycle, etc. go in the direction you want.

**steer**² *noun* (**steers**)
a young bull kept for its beef.

**steering-wheel** *noun* (**steering-wheels**)
a wheel for steering a car, lorry, etc.

**stem** *noun* (**stems**)
1 a stalk. 2 the thin part of a wine-glass.
3 (*in grammar*) the main part of a word, to which different endings are attached, *'Caller', 'called', and 'calling' all have the same stem.*

**stench** *noun* (**stenches**)
a very unpleasant smell.

**stencil** *noun* (**stencils**)
a piece of card, metal, etc. with pieces cut out of it, used to produce a picture, design, etc.

**step**¹ *noun* (**steps**)
**1** a movement made by your foot when walking, running, or dancing. **2** the sound of a person putting down his or her foot when walking. **3** a stair, usually out of doors. **4** one of a series of actions.
**steps**, a stepladder.
**watch your step**, be careful.

**step**² *verb* (**steps, stepping, stepped**)
to tread or walk.
**step on it**, (*slang*) to hurry.
**step up**, to increase something.

**stepchild** *noun* (**stepchildren**)
a child that someone's husband or wife has from an earlier marriage.
**stepbrother** *noun*, **stepdaughter** *noun*, **stepsister** *noun*, **stepson** *noun*

**stepfather** *noun* (**stepfathers**)
a man who is married to your mother but is not your own father.

**stepladder** *noun* (**stepladders**)
a folding ladder with flat treads that stands up without being leant against anything.

**stepmother** *noun* (**stepmothers**)
a woman who is married to your father but is not your own mother.

**steppe** *noun* (**steppes**)
a grassy plain with few trees, especially in Russia.

**stepping-stone** *noun* (**stepping-stones**)
one of a line of stones put in a river or stream to help people walk across.

**stereo**¹ *adjective*
stereophonic.

**stereo**² *noun* (**stereos**)
**1** stereophonic sound or recording. **2** a stereophonic radio or record-player, etc.

**stereophonic** *adjective*
(*say* ste-ri-ŏ-fon-ik)
of sound that comes from two different directions at the same time.

**sterile** *adjective*
**1** not fertile. **2** free from germs.
**sterility** *noun*, **sterilize** *verb*, **sterilized** *adjective*

**sterling** *noun*
British money, *Tourists paid for their meals in sterling.*

**stern**¹ *noun* (**sterns**)
the back part of a ship.

**stern**² *adjective* (**sterner, sternest**)
severe; strict; grim.
**sternly** *adverb*, **sternness** *noun*

**stethoscope** *noun* (**stethoscopes**)
(*say* steth-ŏ-skohp)
a device used by doctors for listening to patients' heartbeats, breathing, etc.

**stew**¹ *verb* (**stews, stewing, stewed**)
to cook slowly in liquid.

**stew**² *noun* (**stews**)
meat cooked slowly in liquid with vegetables.
**in a stew**, (*informal*) very worried or agitated.

**steward** *noun* (**stewards**)
**1** someone whose job is to look after the passengers of a ship or aircraft. **2** an official who looks after a public place, hotel, club, etc., *The showground stewards will show you where to park.*

**stewardess** *noun* (**stewardesses**)
a woman who looks after the passengers of a ship or aircraft.

**stick**¹ *noun* (**sticks**)
**1** a long, thin piece of wood. **2** a walking-stick. **3** the implement used to hit the ball in hockey, polo, etc. **4** a long, thin piece of something, *a stick of rock.*

**stick**² *verb* (**sticks, sticking, stuck**)
**1** to push a thing into something; to put carelessly, *She stuck a pin in her finger.* **2** to fasten or join; to glue. **3** to become fixed or jammed; not to be able to move, *The door keeps sticking.* **4** (*informal*) to stay, *We must stick together.*
**stick out**, to come or push out from a surface; to be higher than the surrounding area; to be very noticeable.
**stick up for**, (*informal*) to support or defend someone or something.
**stuck with**, (*informal*) unable to avoid a person, job, etc.

**sticker** *noun* (**stickers**)
a label or sign that you can stick on something.

**sticking-plaster** *noun* (**sticking-plasters**)
a strip of sticky material for covering
a wound.

**stick insect** *noun* (**stick insects**)
an insect whose body looks like a twig.

**stickleback** *noun* (**sticklebacks**)
a small freshwater fish with sharp spines
on its back.

**sticky** *adjective* (**stickier, stickiest**)
1 able or likely to stick to things.
2 (*informal*) unpleasant; nasty, *He came to
a sticky end.*
**stickily** *adverb*, **stickiness** *noun*

**stiff** *adjective* (**stiffer, stiffest**)
1 difficult to bend or move. 2 difficult, *a stiff
examination.* 3 formal; not friendly.
4 strong, *a stiff drink.*
**stiffly** *adverb*, **stiffness** *noun*

**stiffen** *verb* (**stiffens, stiffening, stiffened**)
to make something stiff; to become stiff.

**stifle** *verb* (**stifles, stifling, stifled**)
1 to make it difficult or impossible for
someone to breathe. 2 to suppress
something, *She stifled a yawn.*

**stile** *noun* (**stiles**)
an arrangement of steps for people to climb
over a fence.

**still**¹ *adjective* (**stiller, stillest**)
1 not moving. 2 silent, *In the night, the
streets are still.* 3 not fizzy, *still
spring-water.*
**stillness** *noun*

**still**² *adverb*
1 up to this or that time; even now, *Are you
still there? He was still there.* 2 even; yet,
*He wanted still more food.*

**still**³ *conjunction*
however, *He has been unfair; still, he is
your father.*

**stilts** *plural noun*
a pair of poles on which you can walk high
above the ground.

**stimulate** *verb* (**stimulates, stimulating,
stimulated**)
to excite or interest someone; to make
something more lively or active, *We hope
that the new book will stimulate interest in
dinosaurs.*
**stimulant** *noun*, **stimulation** *noun*

**stimulus** *noun* (**stimuli**)
something that stimulates or produces a
reaction.

**sting**¹ *noun* (**stings**)
1 the part of an insect or plant that can
cause pain. 2 a painful area or wound
caused by an insect or plant.

**sting**² *verb* (**stings, stinging, stung**)
1 to hurt someone with a sting, *She was
stung by a bee.* 2 to feel a sharp or
throbbing pain, *My back is stinging from
sunburn.* 3 (*slang*) to charge someone an
excessive price; to swindle someone, *They
stung him for £10.*
**stinging-nettle** *noun*

**stingy** *adjective* (**stingier, stingiest**)
(*say* **stin-ji**)
mean; not generous.

**stink**¹ *noun* (**stinks**)
1 a stench. 2 (*informal*) a fuss.

**stink**² *verb* (**stinks, stinking, stank** or **stunk,
stunk**)
to have a very unpleasant smell.

**stir**¹ *verb* (**stirs, stirring, stirred**)
1 to move a liquid or soft mixture round
and round, especially with a spoon. 2 to
move slightly; to start to move.
**stir up**, to excite or arouse, *They stirred up
trouble.*

**stir**² *noun* (**stirs**)
1 an act of moving something round and
round. 2 a fuss or disturbance, *The news
caused a stir.*

**stirrup** *noun* (**stirrups**)
one of the D-shaped metal rings on a strap
which hang from a horse's saddle, for
riders to put their feet into.

**stitch** *noun* (**stitches**)
1 a loop of thread made in sewing or knitting. 2 a sudden pain in your side caused by running.

**stoat** *noun* (**stoats**)
an animal rather like a weasel; an ermine.

**stock**[1] *noun* (**stocks**)
1 a number of things kept ready to be sold or used. 2 livestock. 3 a line of ancestors. 4 liquid made by stewing meat, vegetables, etc. 5 a garden flower with a sweet smell. 6 a kind of share in a company's capital. **Stock Exchange**, a place where stocks and shares are bought and sold. **Stock Market**, a Stock Exchange; the stocks and shares sold there.

**stock**[2] *verb* (**stocks, stocking, stocked**)
1 to keep a number of things ready to be sold or used. 2 to provide a place with things to be sold or used, *The explorers stocked their base camp with tinned food.*

**stockade** *noun* (**stockades**)
a fence made of large upright stakes.

**stock-car** *noun* (**stock-cars**)
an ordinary car strengthened for use in races in which bumping is allowed.

**stocking** *noun* (**stockings**)
a garment that covers the whole of someone's leg and foot.

**stockpile** *noun* (**stockpiles**)
a large stock of things kept in reserve.

**stocks** *plural noun*
a wooden framework in which people's legs used to be locked as a punishment.

**stocky** *adjective* (**stockier, stockiest**)
short and solid or strong, *a stocky man*.

**stodgy** *adjective* (**stodgier, stodgiest**)
1 thick and heavy; not easy to digest, *a stodgy pudding*. 2 boring, *a stodgy book*.

**stoke** *verb* (**stokes, stoking, stoked**)
to put fuel in a furnace or on a fire.

**stole**[1] *noun* (**stoles**)
a wide piece of material worn round your shoulders.

**stole**[2] past tense of **steal**.

**stolen** past participle of **steal**.

**stomach** *noun* (**stomachs**)
1 the part of the body where food starts to be digested. 2 the abdomen.

**stone**[1] *noun* (**stones**)
1 a hard, solid mineral which is not metal. 2 a piece of this mineral. 3 a jewel. 4 the hard seed in the middle of a cherry, plum, peach, etc. 5 a unit of weight equal to 14 pounds, *She weighs 6 stone*.

**stone**[2] *verb* (**stones, stoning, stoned**)
1 to throw stones at someone. 2 to take the stones out of fruit.

**stone-deaf** *adjective*
completely deaf.

**stony** *adjective* (**stonier, stoniest**)
1 full of stones. 2 like stone. 3 not answering or sympathizing, *a stony silence*. **stony** or **stony-broke**, (*slang*) having no money.

**stood** past tense and past participle of **stand** *verb*.

**stool** *noun* (**stools**)
a small seat without a back.

**stoop** *verb* (**stoops, stooping, stooped**)
to bend your body forwards.

**stop**[1] *verb* (**stops, stopping, stopped**)
1 to finish something. 2 to cease moving or working; to stay. 3 to prevent or obstruct something. 4 to fill a hole or gap. **stoppage** *noun*

**stop**[2] *noun* (**stops**)
1 stopping; an end. 2 a place where a bus, train, etc. stops regularly.

**stopper** *noun* (**stoppers**)
something that fits into the top of a bottle, jar, etc. to close it.

**stop press** *noun*
late news printed in a newspaper after printing has started.

**stopwatch** *noun* (**stopwatches**)
a watch that can be started or stopped as you wish, used for timing races, etc.

**storage** *noun*
the storing of things. **storage heater**, an electric heater that gives out heat which it has stored.

**store**[1] *verb* (**stores, storing, stored**)
to keep things until they are needed.

**store**[2] *noun* (**stores**)
1 a place where things are stored. 2 things kept for future use. 3 a shop, especially a large one. **in store**, that is going to happen, *There is a treat in store for you.*

**storey** *noun* (**storeys**)
one whole floor of a building; all the rooms on the same level.

USAGE: Do not confuse **storey** with **story**, which means words that tell of real or imaginary events.

**stork** *noun* (**storks**)
a large bird with very long legs and a long beak.

**storm**[1] *noun* (**storms**)
1 a very strong wind with much rain, snow, etc. 2 a violent attack or outburst, *a storm of protest.*
**storm in a teacup**, a great fuss over something unimportant.
**stormy** *adjective*

**storm**[2] *verb* (**storms, storming, stormed**)
1 to move or behave violently or angrily, *He stormed out of the room.* 2 to attack a place suddenly, *They stormed the castle.*

**story** *noun* (**stories**)
1 words that tell of real or imaginary events. 2 (*informal*) a lie, *Don't tell stories!*

USAGE: Do not confuse **story** with **storey**, which means one whole floor of a building or all the rooms on the same level.

**stout** *adjective* (**stouter, stoutest**)
1 rather fat. 2 thick and strong, *She carried a stout stick.* 3 brave, *The defenders put up a stout resistance.*
**stoutly** *adverb*, **stoutness** *noun*

**stove**[1] *noun* (**stoves**)
a device that produces heat for warming a room or cooking.

**stove**[2] past tense and past participle of **stave** *verb.*

**stow** *verb* (**stows, stowing, stowed**)
to pack or store something away.
**stow away**, to hide on a ship or aircraft so as to escape, or to travel without paying.

**stowaway** *noun* (**stowaways**)
someone who stows away on a ship or aircraft.

**straddle** *verb* (**straddles, straddling, straddled**)
to sit or stand with one leg on one side of something, and the other leg on the other side; to stand across something, *This building straddles the Welsh border.*

**straggle** *verb* (**straggles, straggling, straggled**)
1 to grow or move in an untidy way, *Brambles straggled across the path. A line of children straggled across the playing-field.* 2 to lag behind; to wander on your own.
**straggler** *noun*, **straggly** *adjective*

**straight** *adjective* (**straighter, straightest**)
1 going continuously in one direction; not curving or bending. 2 tidy; in proper order. 3 honest; frank, *Give me a straight answer.*

USAGE: Do not confuse **straight** with **strait**, which is a noun meaning a narrow stretch of water connecting two seas.

**straighten** *verb* (**straightens, straightening, straightened**)
to make something straight; to become straight.

**straightforward** *adjective*
1 easy to understand or do; not complicated. 2 honest; frank.

**strain**[1] *verb* (**strains, straining, strained**)
1 to stretch, push, or pull hard or too hard. 2 to make a great effort. 3 to put something through a sieve to separate liquid from the lumps or other things in it, *Strain the tea to get rid of the tea-leaves.*

**strain**[2] *noun* (**strains**)
1 straining; the force of straining. 2 an injury caused by straining. 3 something that uses up your strength, patience, etc.; exhaustion.

**strainer** *noun* (**strainers**)
a sieve, especially a small one for straining tea.

**strait** *noun* (**straits**)
a narrow stretch of water connecting two seas, *the Straits of Dover.*

USAGE: Do not confuse **strait** with **straight**, which is an adjective meaning going continuously in one direction, tidy, or honest.

**strand** *noun* (**strands**)
1 one of the threads or wires twisted together to make a rope, cable, etc. 2 a lock of hair.

**stranded** *adjective*
1 that has run on to the sand or rocks in shallow water, *the stranded ship.* 2 left in a difficult or lonely position, *They were stranded in the desert.*

**strange** *adjective* (**stranger, strangest**)
unusual; not known or experienced before.
**strangely** *adverb*, **strangeness** *noun*

**stranger** *noun* (**strangers**)
1 a person that you do not know. 2 a person who is in a place he or she does not know.

**strangle** *verb* (**strangles, strangling, strangled**)
to kill someone by pressing his or her throat so as to prevent breathing.
**strangler** *noun*, **strangulation** *noun*

**strap**[1] *noun* (**straps**)
a flat strip of leather, cloth, etc. for fastening things together or holding them in place.

**strap**[2] *verb* (**straps, strapping, strapped**)
to fasten something with a strap or straps.

**strategy** *noun* (**strategies**)
1 a plan or policy to achieve something. 2 planning a war, campaign, etc.
**strategic** *adjective*, **strategist** *noun*

**stratum** *noun* (**strata**)
(*say* **strah-tŭm**)
one of a series of layers or levels, *You can see several strata of rock in the cliffs.*

**straw** *noun* (**straws**)
1 dry cut stalks of corn. 2 a narrow tube for drinking through.

**strawberry** *noun* (**strawberries**)
a small, red, juicy fruit.

**stray**[1] *verb* (**strays, straying, strayed**)
to wander; to get lost.

**stray**[2] *adjective*
that has strayed, *a stray cat.*

**streak**[1] *noun* (**streaks**)
a long thin line or mark.
**streaky** *adjective*

**streak**[2] *verb* (**streaks, streaking, streaked**)
1 to mark with streaks. 2 to move very quickly. 3 (*informal*) to run naked through a public place.
**streaker** *noun*

**stream**[1] *noun* (**streams**)
1 a narrow river; a brook. 2 liquid flowing in one direction. 3 a number of things moving in the same direction. 4 a group in a school containing children of similar ability.

**stream**[2] *verb* (**streams, streaming, streamed**)
1 to move in or like a river, *Traffic streamed across the junction.* 2 to produce a flow of liquid, *Blood was streaming from her cut hand.* 3 to arrange schoolchildren in groups according to their ability.

**streamer** *noun* (**streamers**)
a long strip of paper; a long narrow ribbon.

**streamline** *verb* (**streamlines, streamlining, streamlined**)
1 to give something a smooth shape that helps it to move easily through air or water. 2 to organize something so that it works more efficiently.

**street** *noun* (**streets**)
a road in a city or town.

**strength** *noun* (**strengths**)
1 how strong a person or thing is.
2 something that makes a person or thing useful, effective, etc., *Her greatest strength is her good memory.*

**strengthen** *verb* (**strengthens, strengthening, strengthened**)
to make something or someone strong or stronger; to become strong or stronger.

**strenuous** *adjective*
needing or using great effort.
**strenuously** *adverb*

**stress**[1] *noun* (**stresses**)
1 strain, especially worry and nervous tension. 2 emphasis, especially the extra force with which you pronounce part of a word or phrase.

**stress**[2] *verb* (**stresses, stressing, stressed**)
1 to put a strain on someone. 2 to put extra force on part of a word or phrase. 3 to emphasize something, *I must stress that this is an exceptional case.*

**stretch**[1] *verb* (**stretches, stretching, stretched**)
1 to pull something so that it becomes longer, wider, or tighter. 2 to become longer or wider when pulled. 3 to extend, *The railway network stretched right across the country.*
**stretch out**, to lie down and extend your arms and legs fully.

**stretch**[2] *noun* (**stretches**)
1 the action of pulling something, making it longer, wider, or tighter; the condition of being able to become longer or wider when pulled, *This material has a lot of stretch in it.* 2 a continuous period of time or area of land.

**stretcher** *noun* (**stretchers**)
a framework with handles at each end, on which a sick or injured person is carried.

**strew** *verb* (**strews, strewing, strewed, strewn** or **strewed**)
to scatter something, *Flowers were strewn over the path.*

**stricken** *adjective*
overcome; strongly affected by something, *stricken with fear.*

**strict** *adjective* (**stricter, strictest**)
1 demanding obedience or good behaviour, *a strict teacher*. 2 complete; exact, *the strict truth*.
**strictly** *adverb*, **strictness** *noun*

**stride**[1] *verb* (**strides, striding, strode, stridden**)
to walk with long steps.

**stride**[2] *noun* (**strides**)
1 a long step when walking or running. 2 a steady way of working, *Get into your stride*.

**strides** *plural noun*
(*in Australia*) trousers.

**strife** *noun*
conflict; fighting or quarrelling.

**strike**[1] *verb* (**strikes, striking, struck**)
1 to hit, *The school was struck by lightning*. 2 to attack suddenly, *Plague struck the village*. 3 to light a match by rubbing it against something rough. 4 to sound, *The clock struck 12*. 5 to stop working until the people in charge agree to improve wages, conditions, etc. 6 to find oil, gold, etc. by drilling, mining, etc. 7 to affect someone in some way, *The film struck me as truthful*.
**striker** *noun*

**strike**[2] *noun* (**strikes**)
1 a hit. 2 refusing to work, as a way of making a protest. 3 a find of oil, gold, etc. underground.
**on strike** or **out on strike,** having stopped working, as a protest.

**striking** *adjective*
impressive; very interesting.

**string**[1] *noun* (**strings**)
1 thin rope; a piece of thin rope. 2 a piece of stretched wire, nylon, etc. used in a musical instrument to make sounds. 3 a line or series of things, *a string of buses*.
**strings,** the instruments in an orchestra that have strings; violins, cellos, etc.

**string**[2] *verb* (**strings, stringing, strung**)
1 to fasten with string. 2 to thread on a string, *I helped Frances string her pearls*. 3 to remove the tough fibre from beans. 4 to put strings into a racket, a guitar, etc.
**string out,** to spread out in a line; to extend, *The runners began to string out as the race went on. Can't we string out the work until the weekend?*

**stringed** *adjective*
having strings, *The violin and cello are stringed instruments*.

**stringy** *adjective* (**stringier, stringiest**)
1 like string. 2 containing tough fibres.

**strip**[1] *verb* (**strips, stripping, stripped**)
1 to take a covering off something. 2 to undress. 3 to deprive someone of something, *He has been stripped of his property*.

**strip**[2] *noun* (**strips**)
a long, narrow piece of something.
**strip cartoon,** a comic strip.

**stripe** *noun* (**stripes**)
1 a long, narrow band of colour, *Tigers have stripes; leopards have spots*. 2 something worn on the sleeve of a uniform to show your rank.
**striped** *adjective*, **stripy** *adjective*

**strive** *verb* (**strives, striving, strove, striven**)
to try hard; to struggle.

**strobe** *noun* (**strobes**)
a light that flashes on and off continuously.

**strode** past tense of **stride** *verb*.

**stroke**[1] *noun* (**strokes**)
1 a hit; a movement or action. 2 a sudden illness that often causes someone to be unable to move or feel anything.

**stroke**[2] *verb* (**strokes, stroking, stroked**)
to move your hand gently along something.

**stroll** *verb* (**strolls, strolling, strolled**)
to walk slowly.
**stroll** *noun*

**strong** *adjective* (**stronger, strongest**)
1 having great power, energy, or effect, *a strong horse*. 2 not easily broken or damaged, *a strong chain*. 3 with a lot of flavour or smell, *strong tea*. 4 having a particular number or size, *a crowd 20,000 strong*.
**strongly** *adverb*

**stronghold** *noun* (**strongholds**)
a fortress.

**strove** past tense of **strive**.

**struck** past tense and past participle of **strike** *verb*.

**structure** *noun* (**structures**)
1 something that has been built or put together. 2 the way that something is built or made.
**structural** *adjective*, **structurally** *adverb*

**struggle**[1] *verb* (**struggles, struggling, struggled**)
1 to move your arms, legs, etc. in fighting or trying to get free. 2 to make strong efforts to do something.

**struggle**[2] *noun* (**struggles**)
an action or time of struggling.

**strum** *verb* (**strums, strumming, strummed**)
to sound a guitar by running your finger across its strings.

**strung** past tense and past participle of **string** *verb*.

**strut**¹ *verb* (**struts, strutting, strutted**)
to walk proudly or stiffly.

**strut**² *noun* (**struts**)
a bar of wood or metal that strengthens a framework.

**stub**¹ *verb* (**stubs, stubbing, stubbed**)
**1** to knock your toe against something hard. **2** to put out a cigarette, cigar, etc. by pressing it against something hard.

**stub**² *noun* (**stubs**)
a short piece of something left after the rest has been used up or worn down, *a cigar stub.*

**stubble** *noun*
**1** the short stalks of corn left in the ground after a harvest. **2** short, stiff hairs on a man's chin.

**stubborn** *adjective*
not ready to change your ideas or ways, even though they may be wrong; resisting strongly, *as stubborn as a mule.*
**stubbornly** *adverb*, **stubbornness** *noun*

**stuck** past tense and past participle of **stick** *verb*.

**stuck-up** *adjective*
(*informal*) unpleasantly proud; despising people who have not got wealth, power, or particular tastes or interests.

**stud** *noun* (**studs**)
**1** a small curved lump or knob; a short nail with a thick head, *Football boots have studs on the bottom.* **2** a device for fastening a detachable collar to a shirt.

**student** *noun* (**students**)
someone who studies, especially at college or university.

**studio** *noun* (**studios**)
**1** a place where radio or television broadcasts are made. **2** a place where cinema or television films are made. **3** the room where a painter, photographer, etc. works.
**studio couch,** a long couch that can be converted into a bed.

**studious** *adjective*
keen on studying.
**studiously** *adverb*

**study**¹ *verb* (**studies, studying, studied**)
**1** to spend time learning about something. **2** to look at something very carefully.

**study**² *noun* (**studies**)
**1** learning about a subject. **2** a room used for reading, writing, and learning.

**stuff**¹ *noun*
**1** a substance or material. **2** things; possessions, *Do you want to move your stuff off the table?*

**stuff**² *verb* (**stuffs, stuffing, stuffed**)
**1** to fill something tightly, especially with stuffing, *She stuffed the turkey.* **2** to push something inside another thing, *He stuffed the paper into his pocket.*

**stuffing** *noun* (**stuffings**)
**1** material used to fill the inside of something. **2** a flavoured mixture put inside poultry, etc. before cooking.

**stuffy** *adjective* (**stuffier, stuffiest**)
**1** badly ventilated; without fresh air. **2** formal and boring.
**stuffily** *adverb*, **stuffiness** *noun*

**stumble** *verb* (**stumbles, stumbling, stumbled**)
**1** to lose your balance; to fall over something. **2** to speak or act hesitantly or uncertainly.
**stumble across** or **stumble on,** to find something accidentally.

**stump**¹ *noun* (**stumps**)
**1** the bottom of a tree-trunk left in the ground when the tree is cut down. **2** one of the three upright sticks put at each end of a cricket-pitch.

**stump**² *verb* (**stumps, stumping, stumped**)
**1** (*in cricket*) to get a batsman out by touching the stumps with the ball when he or she is not standing in the correct place. **2** to be too difficult for someone, *The question stumped him.*

**stun** *verb* (**stuns, stunning, stunned**)
**1** to knock someone unconscious. **2** to shock or confuse someone, *She was stunned by the news.*

**stung** past tense and past participle of **sting** *verb*.

**stunk** past tense and past participle of **stink** *verb*.

**stunt** *noun* (**stunts**)
**1** something done to attract attention, *a publicity stunt.* **2** a dangerous feat, especially one performed in making a film.

**stupendous** *adjective*
amazing; tremendous.

**stupid** *adjective* (**stupider, stupidest**)
without reason or common sense; not clever or thoughtful.
**stupidity** *noun*, **stupidly** *adverb*

**sturdy** *adjective* (**sturdier, sturdiest**)
strong and vigorous or solid.
**sturdily** *adverb*, **sturdiness** *noun*

**stutter** *verb* (**stutters, stuttering, stuttered**)
to keep repeating the sounds, especially
consonants, at the beginning of words
when you speak.

**sty** *noun* (**sties**)
1 a pigsty. 2 a sore swelling on an eyelid.

**style** *noun* (**styles**)
1 the way that something is done, made,
said, or written, *The story was written in
an old-fashioned style*. 2 a pointed stick
used in Roman times to scratch letters on
wax.

**stylish** *adjective*
fashionable; smart.
**stylishly** *adverb*

**stylus** *noun* (**styluses**)
the device like a needle that travels in the
grooves of a record to reproduce the sound.

**sub** *noun* (**subs**)
(*informal*) 1 a submarine. 2 a subscription.
3 a substitute, especially in sports.

**sub-** *prefix*
below, *substandard goods*.

**subcontinent** *noun* (**subcontinents**)
a large area of land that forms part of
a continent.

**subdue** *verb* (**subdues, subduing, subdued**)
1 to bring under control; to overcome.
2 to make quieter or gentler.

**subject**[1] *noun* (**subjects**)
(*say* **sub**-jikt)
1 the person or thing that is being talked or
written about. 2 something that is being
studied. 3 (*in grammar*) the person or thing
that is doing the action stated by the verb
in a sentence, *In 'she hit him', the subject is
'she'*. 4 someone who is ruled by a
particular king, government, etc.

**subject**[2] *adjective*
(*say* **sub**-jikt)
ruled by a king, government, etc.; not
independent.
**subject to,** having to obey; liable to;
depending upon, *The lords were all subject
to the king. Trains are subject to delays in
fog. Our decision is subject to your approval.*

**subject**[3] *verb* (**subjects, subjecting, subjected**)
(*say* sŭb-**jekt**)
1 to make a person or thing undergo
something, *They subjected him to torture.*
2 to bring a country under your control.

**subjective** *adjective*
1 that exists only in someone's mind, *a
subjective problem*. 2 influenced by your
own beliefs or ideas, *His account of the
events is rather subjective.*

**submarine** *noun* (**submarines**)
a ship that can travel under water.

**submerge** *verb* (**submerges, submerging,
submerged**)
to go under water; to put something or
someone under water.
**submergence** *noun*, **submersion** *noun*

**submit** *verb* (**submits, submitting, submitted**)
1 to surrender; to let someone rule or
control you. 2 to give something to someone
for his or her opinion, decision, etc.
**submission** *noun*, **submissive** *adjective*

**subordinate**[1] *adjective*
(*say* sŭb-**or**-din-ăt)
less important; lower in rank.
**subordinate clause,** a clause which cannot be
used by itself, but which makes a sentence
when it is joined to a *main clause*.

**subordinate**[2] *verb* (**subordinates,
subordinating, subordinated**)
(*say* sŭb-**or**-din-ayt)
to treat something as less important than
another thing.
**subordination** *noun*

**subroutine** *noun* (**subroutines**)
(*in Computing*) a separate part of a
computer program, performing an
operation that is needed frequently in the
program.

**subscribe** *verb* (**subscribes, subscribing,
subscribed**)
to pay money, especially to pay regularly
so as to be a member of a club or have the
use of a telephone, etc.
**subscriber** *noun*, **subscription** *noun*

**subsequent** *adjective*
following; later, *Subsequent events proved
that she was right.*
**subsequently** *adverb*

**subside** *verb* (**subsides, subsiding, subsided**)
1 to sink, *The house has subsided over the
years*. 2 to become quiet or normal, *The
noise subsided.*
**subsidence** *noun*

**subsidy** *noun* (**subsidies**)
money paid to keep prices low, to help an
industry, etc.
**subsidize** *verb*

        **suffocate**

**substance** *noun* (**substances**)
1 something that you can touch or see; something used for making things. 2 the essential part of something.

**substantial** *adjective*
1 large; considerable. 2 strong; solid.
**substantially** *adverb*

**substitute**¹ *verb* (**substitutes, substituting, substituted**)
to use someone or something instead of another person or thing, *In this recipe you can substitute oil for butter.*
**substitution** *noun*

**substitute**² *noun* (**substitutes**)
a person or thing used instead of another.

**subtle** *adjective* (**subtler, subtlest**)
(*say* sut-ĕl)
1 slight or faint but pleasant; delicate, *a subtle perfume.* 2 clever; ingenious, *a subtle joke.*
**subtly** *adverb*, **subtlety** *noun*

**subtract** *verb* (**subtracts, subtracting, subtracted**)
to take one amount from another, *If you subtract 2 from 7, you get 5.*
**subtraction** *noun*

**suburb** *noun* (**suburbs**)
an area of houses on the edge of a city or large town.
**suburban** *adjective*, **suburbia** *noun*

**subway** *noun* (**subways**)
an underground passage for pedestrians.

**succeed** *verb* (**succeeds, succeeding, succeeded**)
1 to do or get what you wanted or intended. 2 to come after another person or thing, especially to become king or queen after another king or queen, *She succeeded to the throne.*

**success** *noun* (**successes**)
1 doing or getting what you wanted or intended. 2 a person or thing that does well, *The plan was a great success.*

**successful** *adjective*
having success.
**successfully** *adverb*

**succession** *noun* (**successions**)
1 a series of people or things. 2 the act of following other people or things; succeeding to a throne.

**successive** *adjective*
following one after another.
**successively** *adverb*

**successor** *noun* (**successors**)
a person or thing that follows another, *The headteacher retired and handed over to her successor.*

**such** *adjective*
1 of the same kind, *sweets such as these.* 2 so great; so much of, *It gave me such a fright!*
**such-and-such**, particular but not named, *It was at such-and-such a time.*

**suck** *verb* (**sucks, sucking, sucked**)
1 to take in liquid or air through your mouth, *I sucked milk through a straw.* 2 to move something around inside your mouth, *She sucked a sweet.* 3 to draw in; to absorb, *A vacuum cleaner sucks up dirt.*

**suction** *noun*
1 producing a vacuum so that liquid, air, etc. is drawn in. 2 the action that causes something to be sucked in; the force that holds two surfaces together when some of the air has been removed from between them, *Vacuum cleaners work by suction.*

**sudden** *adjective*
happening or done quickly and unexpectedly.
**suddenly** *adverb*, **suddenness** *noun*

**suds** *plural noun*
froth on soapy water.

**sue** *verb* (**sues, suing, sued**)
to start a claim in a lawcourt to get money from someone, *I sued him for damages.*

**suede** *noun*
(*say* swayd)
soft velvety leather.

**suet** *noun*
hard fat from cattle and sheep, used in cooking.

**suffer** *verb* (**suffers, suffering, suffered**)
1 to feel pain or sadness. 2 to have to put up with something unpleasant.

**sufficient** *adjective*
enough, *Have we sufficient food?*
**sufficiency** *noun*, **sufficiently** *adverb*

**suffix** *noun* (**suffixes**)
a word or syllable joined to the end of a word to change or add to its meaning, as in forget*ful*, lion*ess*, and rust*y*.

**suffocate** *verb* (**suffocates, suffocating, suffocated**)
1 to make it impossible or difficult for someone to breathe. 2 to have difficulty in breathing. 3 to kill someone or something by cutting off the supply of oxygen; to die from lack of oxygen.
**suffocating** *adjective*, **suffocatingly** *adverb*, **suffocation** *noun*

**sugar** *noun*
 a sweet food obtained from various plants.
 **sugar beet**, a plant with a root from which
 sugar is made.
 **sugar cane**, a tropical grass with tall stems
 from which sugar is made.
 **sugary** *adjective*

**suggest** *verb* (**suggests, suggesting, suggested**)
 1 to give someone an idea that you think is
 useful. 2 to give an idea or impression of
 something, *Your smile suggests that you
 agree with me.*
 **suggestion** *noun*

**suicide** *noun* (**suicides**)
 killing yourself, *He committed suicide.*
 **suicidal** *adjective*

**suit**[1] *noun* (**suits**)
 1 a jacket and pair of trousers or skirt,
 sometimes with a waistcoat, that are
 meant to be worn together. 2 a set of
 clothes for a particular purpose, *a
 spacesuit.* 3 one of the four sets in a pack of
 playing-cards, *The four suits are spades,
 hearts, diamonds, and clubs.* 4 a lawsuit.

**suit**[2] *verb* (**suits, suiting, suited**)
 to be suitable or convenient for someone or
 something.

**suitable** *adjective*
 satisfactory or right for a particular
 person, purpose, or occasion.
 **suitability** *noun*, **suitably** *adverb*

**suitcase** *noun* (**suitcases**)
 a box with a lid and a handle, for carrying
 clothes and other things on journeys,
 holidays, etc.

**suite** *noun* (**suites**)
 (*say* sweet)
 1 a set of furniture. 2 a set of rooms. 3 a set
 of short musical pieces or dances.

**suitor** *noun* (**suitors**)
 a man who is trying to get a woman's love.

**sulk** *verb* (**sulks, sulking, sulked**)
 to be silent and bad-tempered.
 **sulkily** *adverb*, **sulkiness** *noun*, **sulky**
 *adjective*

**sullen** *adjective* (**sullener, sullenest**)
 sulking and gloomy.
 **sullenly** *adverb*, **sullenness** *noun*

**sulphur** *noun*
 a yellow chemical used in industry and
 medicine.

**sulphuric** *adjective*
 containing sulphur.
 **sulphuric acid**, a strong, colourless acid.

**sultan** *noun* (**sultans**)
 the ruler of a Muslim country.

**sultana** *noun* (**sultanas**)
 a raisin without seeds.

**sum**[1] *noun* (**sums**)
 1 the amount you get when you add
 numbers together. 2 a problem in
 arithmetic. 3 an amount of money.

**sum**[2] *verb* (**sums, summing, summed**)
 **sum up**, to give a summary of something,
 especially at the end of a discussion or talk.

**summarize** *verb* (**summarizes, summarizing,
 summarized**)
 to make or give a summary of something.

**summary** *noun* (**summaries**)
 a statement of the main points of
 something said or written.

**summer** *noun* (**summers**)
 the warm season between spring and
 autumn.
 **summer time** or **British summer time**, the time
 shown by clocks that are put forward one
 hour for the summer.

---

USAGE: Do not confuse **summer time** with
**summertime**, which is the next word in this
dictionary.

---

**summertime** *noun*
 the season of summer.

**summit** *noun* (**summits**)
 1 the top of a mountain or hill. 2 a summit
 meeting.
 **summit meeting**, a meeting between the
 most important people from various
 governments, organizations, etc.

**summon** *verb* (**summons, summoning,
 summoned**)
 to order someone to come or appear.
 **summon up**, to gather something; to bring
 back something, *She could not summon up
 the energy to get out of bed. The scent of
 jasmine summoned up memories of the
 woman he loved.*

**summons** *noun* (**summonses**)
 a command to someone to appear in a
 lawcourt.

**sun** *noun*
 1 the star from which the earth gets
 warmth and light. 2 warmth and light from
 this star.

**sunburn** *noun*
 redness of your skin caused by being in the
 sun too long.
 **sunburned** *adjective*, **sunburnt** *adjective*

**sundae** *noun* (**sundaes**)
 (*say* sun-day)
 a mixture of ice-cream with fruit, nuts,
 cream, etc.

**Sunday** *noun* (**Sundays**)
the first day of the week.
**Sunday school,** a place where children go for religious teaching on Sundays.

**sundial** *noun* (**sundials**)
a device that shows the time by a shadow made by the sun.

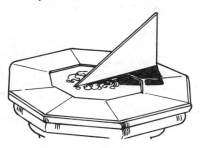

**sunflower** *noun* (**sunflowers**)
a very tall flower with a large round head.

**sung** past participle of **sing.**

**sun-glasses** *plural noun*
dark glasses to protect your eyes from the sun.

**sunk** past tense and past participle of **sink** *verb.*

**sunlight** *noun*
light from the sun.
**sunlit** *adjective*

**sunny** *adjective* (**sunnier, sunniest**)
**1** with the sun shining, *a sunny day.* **2** full of sunshine, *a sunny room.*

**sunrise** *noun* (**sunrises**)
dawn, *They left at sunrise.*

**sun-roof** *noun* (**sun-roofs**)
a panel in a car's roof that can be opened to let in air and sunlight.

**sunset** *noun* (**sunsets**)
the time when the sun sets.

**sunshade** *noun* (**sunshades**)
a device to protect people from the sun; a parasol.

**sunshine** *noun*
warmth and light that come from the sun.
**sunshiny** *adjective*

**sunspot** *noun* (**sunspots**)
**1** a dark patch on the sun's surface.
**2** (*informal*) a sunny place.

**sunstroke** *noun*
an illness caused by being in strong sun for too long.

**suntan** *noun* (**suntans**)
a brown colour of the skin caused by the sun.
**suntanned** *adjective*

**super** *adjective*
(*informal*) excellent.

**super-** *prefix*
over; beyond, *a superhuman feat of strength.*

**superb** *adjective*
magnificent; excellent.
**superbly** *adverb*

**superficial** *adjective*
**1** on the surface, *a superficial cut.* **2** not deep or thorough, *She has only superficial knowledge of the subject.*
**superficiality** *noun,* **superficially** *adverb*

USAGE: Do not confuse **superficial** with **superfluous,** which is the next word in this dictionary.

**superfluous** *adjective*
not necessary; no longer needed.

**superintend** *verb* (**superintends, superintending, superintended**)
to be in charge of something or someone and look after it, him, or her.

**superintendent** *noun* (**superintendents**)
**1** someone who is in charge of something or someone. **2** a high-ranking police officer.

**superior**[1] *adjective*
**1** higher or more important than someone else. **2** better than another person or thing. **3** conceited; proud, *I dislike his superior attitude.*
**superiority** *noun*

**superior**[2] *noun* (**superiors**)
someone of higher rank or position than another person.

**superlative** *noun* (**superlatives**)
the form of an adjective or adverb that expresses the greatest degree of something, *Superlatives are words like 'best', 'highest', 'soonest', and 'worst'.*

**supermarket** *noun* (**supermarkets**)
a large self-service shop that sells food and other goods.

**supernatural**[1] *adjective*
having no natural explanation; strange, *Ghosts are supernatural.*

**supernatural**[2] *noun*
**the supernatural,** things that have no natural explanation, such as ghosts, angels, fairies, etc.

**supersonic** *adjective*
faster than the speed of sound.

**superstition** *noun* (**superstitions**)
a belief or action that is not based on reason or evidence, *It is a superstition that it is unlucky to walk under a ladder.*
**superstitious** *adjective*, **superstitiously** *adverb*

**supervise** *verb* (**supervises, supervising, supervised**)
to be in charge of something or someone and look after it, him, or her, *He supervised the building of the dam.*
**supervision** *noun*, **supervisor** *noun*

**supper** *noun* (**suppers**)
a meal or snack eaten in the evening.

**supple** *adjective* (**suppler, supplest**)
bending easily; flexible, not stiff.
**supplely** *adverb*, **suppleness** *noun*

**supplement** *noun* (**supplements**)
1 a part added to a book, etc. to improve it or bring it up to date. 2 a magazine, usually in colour, sold as part of a newspaper, *the colour supplement.*
**supplementary** *adjective*

**supply**¹ *verb* (**supplies, supplying, supplied**)
to give or sell someone what he or she needs or wants.
**supplier** *noun*

**supply**² *noun* (**supplies**)
1 a stock of something; things kept ready to be used when needed. 2 the action of supplying something.

**support**¹ *verb* (**supports, supporting, supported**)
1 to hold something so that it does not fall down. 2 to give help, strength, or encouragement to someone or something.
**supporter** *noun*

**support**² *noun* (**supports**)
1 the action of holding something; the action of helping or encouraging someone. 2 a thing that holds something; a person or thing that helps or encourages someone.

**suppose** *verb* (**supposes, supposing, supposed**)
to think; to guess that something is true.
**supposed to,** expected or ordered to do something.
**supposedly** *adverb*, **supposition** *noun*

**suppress** *verb* (**suppresses, suppressing, suppressed**)
1 to stop something happening. 2 to keep something secret.
**suppression** *noun*, **suppressor** *noun*

**supreme** *adjective*
highest; greatest; most important.
**supremacy** *noun*, **supremely** *adverb*

**sure**¹ *adjective* (**surer, surest**)
1 confident about something; convinced. 2 that will definitely do something or happen, *The telephone is sure to ring any moment now.* 3 that is completely true, *One thing is sure: she is not here at the moment.* 4 reliable, *Visiting places is a sure way of getting to know them.*
**make sure,** to find something out or make something happen.

**sure**² *adverb*
1 (*informal*) surely. 2 (*in America*) all right; yes.
**for sure,** (*informal*) definitely.
**sure enough,** (*informal*) certainly; in fact, *I thought that he would be late, and sure enough he was.*

**surely** *adverb*
1 certainly; definitely. 2 it must be true; I believe, *Surely I met you last year.*

**surf** *noun*
waves breaking on the seashore.
**surfboard,** a board used in surfing.

**surface**¹ *noun* (**surfaces**)
1 the outside of something. 2 one of the sides of something, especially the top part.
**surface area,** the area of all the outside of something, *The surface area of a cube is six times the square of one side.*

**surface**² *verb* (**surfaces, surfacing, surfaced**)
1 to give a firm covering layer to a road, path, etc. 2 to come up to the surface of the sea, etc., *The submarine surfaced.*

**surfing** *noun*
balancing yourself on a board or small boat that is carried towards the seashore by the waves.
**surfer** *noun*

**surge** *verb* (**surges, surging, surged**)
1 to move forwards or upwards like waves. 2 to increase suddenly.
**surge** *noun*

**surgeon** *noun* (**surgeons**)
a doctor who deals with disease or injury by cutting or repairing the affected parts of the body.

**swagger**

**surgery** *noun* (**surgeries**)
1 the place where a doctor, dentist, etc. sees his or her patients. 2 the time when this place is open. 3 the work of a surgeon.

**surgical** *adjective*
dealing with disease or injury by cutting the affected parts of the body, *a surgical operation*.
**surgically** *adverb*

**surname** *noun* (**surnames**)
your last name, which is the same as your family's name.

**surpass** *verb* (**surpasses, surpassing, surpassed**)
to do or be better than others.

**surplice** *noun* (**surplices**)
a loose white garment sometimes worn by clergymen, choirboys, etc.

USAGE: Do not confuse **surplice** with **surplus**, which is the next word in this dictionary.

**surplus** *noun* (**surpluses**)
an amount left over after you have spent or used what you need.

**surprise**¹ *noun* (**surprises**)
1 something that you did not expect. 2 the feeling you have when something happens that you did not expect.

**surprise**² *verb* (**surprises, surprising, surprised**)
1 to be something that someone did not expect. 2 to catch or attack someone unexpectedly.
**surprisingly** *adverb*

**surrender** *verb* (**surrenders, surrendering, surrendered**)
1 to stop fighting someone and agree to obey him or her. 2 to give up something to someone.

**surround** *verb* (**surrounds, surrounding, surrounded**)
to be or come all round a person or thing.

**surroundings** *plural noun*
the things or conditions around a person or place.

**survey**¹ *noun* (**surveys**)
(*say* ser-vay)
1 a general look at something, *a survey of British history*. 2 a detailed inspection or examination of an area, building, etc.

**survey**² *verb* (**surveys, surveying, surveyed**)
(*say* ser-vay)
1 to take a general look at something. 2 to make a detailed inspection of an area, a building, etc.
**surveyor** *noun*

**survive** *verb* (**survives, surviving, survived**)
to stay alive; to live after someone else dies or after a disaster.
**survival** *noun*, **survivor** *noun*

**suspect**¹ *verb* (**suspects, suspecting, suspected**)
(*say* sŭ-**spekt**)
1 to think that someone is not to be trusted or has done a crime. 2 to think that something unpleasant is happening or will happen.

**suspect**² *noun* (**suspects**)
(*say* **sus**-pekt)
someone who is thought to have done something wrong.

**suspend** *verb* (**suspends, suspending, suspended**)
1 to postpone something. 2 to deprive someone of his or her job or position for a time, *He was suspended from the team*. 3 to hang something up.

**suspense** *noun*
an anxious or uncertain feeling while waiting for an event, information, etc.

**suspension** *noun* (**suspensions**)
suspending something or someone; being suspended.
**suspension bridge**, a bridge supported by cables.

**suspicion** *noun* (**suspicions**)
1 suspecting someone; being suspected. 2 a feeling that is not definite or certain.

**suspicious** *adjective*
1 that makes you suspect someone or something, *suspicious footprints*. 2 that suspects someone or something, *a suspicious policeman*.
**suspiciously** *adverb*

**sustain** *verb* (**sustains, sustaining, sustained**)
1 to keep someone alive. 2 to keep something happening, *Can he sustain this effort?* 3 to support something, *The floor should be able to sustain the weight of the new machinery*.

**swagger** *verb* (**swaggers, swaggering, swaggered**)
to walk or behave in a conceited way.

**Swahili** *noun*
a language spoken in eastern Africa.

**swallow**[1] *verb* (**swallows, swallowing, swallowed**)
to make something go down your throat.
**swallow up,** to cover or hide something.

**swallow**[2] *noun* (**swallows**)
a small bird with a forked tail and pointed wings.

**swam** past tense of **swim** *verb*.

**swamp**[1] *verb* (**swamps, swamping, swamped**)
**1** to flood something. **2** to overwhelm someone or something, *The switchboard has been swamped with people phoning in to complain.*

**swamp**[2] *noun* (**swamps**)
a marsh.
**swampy** *adjective*

**swan** *noun* (**swans**)
a large white bird with a long neck, *Swans live on or near water.*

**swank** *verb* (**swanks, swanking, swanked**)
(*informal*) to swagger or boast.
**swank** *noun*

**swap** *verb* (**swaps, swapping, swapped**)
(*informal*) to exchange, *I swapped my comic for his sweets.*

**swarm**[1] *noun* (**swarms**)
a large number of bees, birds, etc. clustering or moving about together.

**swarm**[2] *verb* (**swarms, swarming, swarmed**)
**1** to move in a large cluster. **2** to be crowded with people, insects, etc., *The town is swarming with tourists in summer.*

**swastika** *noun* (**swastikas**)
(*say* swos-ti-kă)
a sign formed by a cross with its ends bent at right angles, *The swastika was the symbol of the Nazis.*

**swat** *verb* (**swats, swatting, swatted**)
(*say* swot)
to hit or crush a fly or other insect.
**swatter** *noun*

**sway** *verb* (**sways, swaying, swayed**)
to move from side to side.

**swear** *verb* (**swears, swearing, swore, sworn**)
**1** to make a solemn promise, *She swore to tell the truth.* **2** to make someone give a solemn promise, *He was sworn to secrecy.* **3** to use curses or rude words.
**swear-word** *noun*

**sweat**[1] *verb* (**sweats, sweating, sweated**)
(*say* swet)
to give off moisture through the pores of your skin, especially when you are hot or doing exercise.

**sweat**[2] *noun*
(*say* swet)
moisture that is given off through the pores of your skin.
**sweaty** *adjective*

**sweater** *noun* (**sweaters**)
(*say* swet-er)
a jersey or pullover.

**sweatshirt** *noun* (**sweatshirts**)
a type of pullover made of thick cotton.

**Swede** *noun* (**Swedes**)
a Swedish person.

**swede** *noun* (**swedes**)
a kind of turnip.

**Swedish** *adjective*
of Sweden.

**sweep**[1] *verb* (**sweeps, sweeping, swept**)
**1** to clean or clear with a broom, brush, etc., *He swept the floor.* **2** to move, remove, or change something quickly, *The flood has swept away the bridge.* **3** to move along quickly, smoothly, or proudly, *She swept out of the room.*
**sweeper** *noun*

**sweep**[2] *noun* (**sweeps**)
**1** a sweeping action or movement, *Give this room a sweep.* **2** a chimney-sweep.

**sweet**[1] *adjective* (**sweeter, sweetest**)
**1** tasting of sugar or honey. **2** very pleasant, *a sweet smell.* **3** kind, pretty, or lovable, *a sweet little cottage. She is a sweet child.*
**sweetly** *adverb*, **sweetness** *noun*

**sweet**[2] *noun* (**sweets**)
**1** a small shaped piece of sweet food made of sugar, chocolate, etc., *a bag of sweets.* **2** a pudding; the sweet course in a meal, *There is apple pie for sweet.*
**sweet corn,** the seeds of maize.

**sweeten** *verb* (**sweetens, sweetening, sweetened**)
to make something sweet.
**sweetener** *noun*

**sweetheart** *noun* (**sweethearts**)
the person that you love very much.

**sweet pea** *noun* (**sweet peas**)
a climbing plant with sweet-smelling flowers.

**swell**[1] *verb* (**swells, swelling, swelled,** *past participle* **swollen** or **swelled**)
to get bigger or louder, *My ankle has swollen. The noise swelled as the procession got nearer.*

**swell**[2] *noun* (**swells**)
the rise and fall of the sea's surface.

**swell**[3] *adjective*
(*informal*) excellent; very good.

**swelling** *noun* (**swellings**)
a swollen place on your body.

**swelter** *verb* (**swelters, sweltering, sweltered**)
to be uncomfortably hot.

**swept** past tense and past participle of **sweep** *verb*.

**swept-back** *adjective*
(of an aircraft wing) slanting backwards from the direction in which the aircraft flies.

**swerve** *verb* (**swerves, swerving, swerved**)
to move suddenly to one side, *The car swerved to avoid the cyclist.*

**swift**[1] *adjective* (**swifter, swiftest**)
quick; moving quickly and easily.
**swiftly** *adverb*, **swiftness** *noun*

**swift**[2] *noun* (**swifts**)
a small bird that looks like a swallow.

**swill**[1] *verb* (**swills, swilling, swilled**)
to rinse or flush something.

**swill**[2] *noun*
the food and liquid given to pigs.

**swim**[1] *verb* (**swims, swimming, swam, swum**)
1 to move yourself through the water; to be in the water for pleasure, *I swam in the sea yesterday.* 2 to cross something by moving yourself through water, *She has swum the Channel.* 3 to be covered with or full of liquid, *Her eyes were swimming with tears.* 4 to feel dizzy, *His head swam.*
**swimming-bath**, a swimming-pool.
**swimming-costume**, clothing worn for swimming.
**swimming-pool**, an area of water designed for people to swim in.
**swimmer** *noun*

**swim**[2] *noun* (**swims**)
a time spent swimming, *Let's go for a swim.*

**swimsuit** *noun* (**swimsuits**)
a swimming-costume, especially one made in one piece and worn by women.

**swindle**[1] *verb* (**swindles, swindling, swindled**)
to get money or goods from someone dishonestly; to trick or cheat someone.
**swindler** *noun*

**swindle**[2] *noun* (**swindles**)
a trick to get money or goods from someone dishonestly.

**swine** *noun* (**swine** or **swines**)
1 a pig. 2 (*informal*) an unpleasant person; a difficult thing.

**swing**[1] *verb* (**swings, swinging, swung**)
1 to move to and fro; to move in a curve, *The door swung open.* 2 to turn quickly or suddenly, *He had swung the car round to avoid the bus.*

**swing**[2] *noun* (**swings**)
1 a swinging movement. 2 a seat hung on chains, ropes, etc. so that it can move backwards and forwards. 3 the amount that votes, opinions, etc. change from one side to the other.
**in full swing**, full of activity; working fully.

**swipe** *verb* (**swipes, swiping, swiped**)
1 to give someone or something a hard hit. 2 (*informal*) to steal something.

**swirl** *verb* (**swirls, swirling, swirled**)
to move around quickly in circles; to move something in this way.

**swish** *verb* (**swishes, swishing, swished**)
to make a hissing or rustling sound.

**Swiss** *adjective*
of Switzerland.
**Swiss roll**, (in America, *jelly roll*) a thin sponge-cake spread with jam or cream and rolled up.

**switch**[1] *noun* (**switches**)
1 a device that you press or turn to start or stop something working, especially something that works by electricity. 2 a sudden change of policy, methods, etc.

**switch**[2] *verb* (**switches, switching, switched**)
1 to turn an electric current on or off. 2 to change something suddenly.

**switchboard** *noun* (**switchboards**)
a panel with switches for connecting telephone lines.

**swivel** *verb* (**swivels, swivelling, swivelled**)
to turn round.

**swollen** past participle of **swell** *verb*.

**swoon** *verb* (**swoons, swooning, swooned**)
to faint, *She swooned with terror.*

**swoop** *verb* (**swoops, swooping, swooped**)
1 to dive or come down suddenly, *The eagle swooped on its prey.* 2 to make a sudden attack or raid, *The police swooped on the gangsters' hide-out.*

**swop** *verb* (**swops, swopping, swopped**)
(*informal*) to swap.

**sword** *noun* (**swords**)
(*say* sord)
a weapon like a knife with a very long blade.

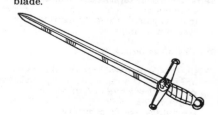

**swore** past tense of **swear**.

**sworn** past participle of **swear**.

**swot**[1] *verb* (**swots, swotting, swotted**)
(*informal*) to study hard.

**swot**[2] *noun* (**swots**)
(*informal*) someone who swots.

**swum** past participle of **swim** *verb*.

**swung** past tense and past participle of **swing** *verb*.

**sycamore** *noun* (**sycamores**)
a kind of maple-tree, *Sycamore seeds have wings, so they can be carried a long way by the wind.*

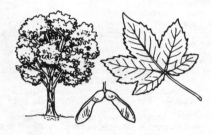

**syllable** *noun* (**syllables**)
a word or part of a word that has one separate sound when you say it, *'El-e-phant' has three syllables; 'cat' has one syllable.*
**syllabic** *adjective*

**syllabus** *noun* (**syllabuses**)
(*say* **sil**-ă-bŭs)
a list of things to be studied by a class, for an examination, etc.

**symbol** *noun* (**symbols**)
a thing that represents or suggests something, *The cross is a symbol of Christianity.*
**symbolic** *adjective*, **symbolical** *adjective*, **symbolically** *adverb*, **symbolism** *noun*

**symbolize** *verb* (**symbolizes, symbolizing, symbolized**)
to be a symbol of something, *Red symbolizes danger.*

**symmetrical** *adjective*
(*say* sim-et-rik-ăl)
that you can divide into two halves which are exactly the same but the opposite way round, *Wheels and butterflies are symmetrical.*
**symmetrically** *adverb*, **symmetry** *noun*

**sympathize** *verb* (**sympathizes, sympathizing, sympathized**)
**1** to show or feel sympathy with others, *I sympathized with her ideas.* **2** to feel sorry for someone, *I sympathized with the small boy, because he looked so sad.*
**sympathizer** *noun*

**sympathy** *noun* (**sympathies**)
**1** the sharing or understanding of other people's feelings, opinions, etc. **2** the feeling of being sorry for someone's unhappiness, pain, or bad luck.
**sympathetic** *adjective*, **sympathetically** *adverb*

**symphony** *noun* (**symphonies**)
a long piece of music for an orchestra.
**symphony orchestra**, a large orchestra.
**symphonic** *adjective*

**symptom** *noun* (**symptoms**)
one of the things that show that someone is ill, *Red spots are a symptom of measles.*
**symptomatic** *adjective*, **symptomatically** *adverb*

**synagogue** *noun* (**synagogues**)
(*say* sin-ă-gog)
a building where Jews worship.

**synchronize** *verb* (**synchronizes, synchronizing, synchronized**)
(*say* sink-rŏ-nyz)
**1** to make things happen at the same time. **2** to make watches or clocks show the same time.
**synchronization** *noun*

**syncopate** *verb* (**syncopates, syncopating, syncopated**)
(*say* sink-ŏ-payt)
to change the rhythm of a piece of music by putting stress off the beat.
**syncopation** *noun*

**synonym** *noun* (**synonyms**)
(*say* sin-ŏ-nim)
a word that means the same or almost the same as another word, *'Sufficient' and 'enough' are synonyms.*
**synonymous** *adjective*

**synthesis** *noun* (**syntheses**)
combining parts, substances, etc. into a whole thing or system.

**synthesize** *verb* (**synthesizes, synthesizing, synthesized**)
to make a whole thing out of parts.

**synthesizer** *noun* (**synthesizers**)
an electronic musical instrument that can make a large variety of sounds.

**synthetic** *adjective*
artificially made; not natural.
**synthetically** *adverb*

**syringe** *noun* (**syringes**)
a device for sucking in and squirting out a liquid.

**syrup** *noun* (**syrups**)
a thick, sticky, sweet liquid.
**syrupy** *adjective*

**system** *noun* (**systems**)
1 a set of parts, things, or ideas that work together. 2 a well-organized way of doing something, *There is system in everything she does.*
**systematic** *adjective*, **systematically** *adverb*

# Tt

**tabby** *noun* (**tabbies**)
a cat with grey or brown streaks in its fur.

**table** *noun* (**tables**)
1 a piece of furniture with a flat top supported by legs. 2 a list of facts arranged in order, especially a list of the results of multiplying a number by other numbers, *multiplication tables.*

**tablecloth** *noun* (**tablecloths**)
a cloth spread over a table.

**table d'hôte** *noun* (**tables d'hôte**)
(*say* tah-bŭl-**doht**)
a meal with a fixed menu and price ordered in a restaurant, etc.

**tablespoon** *noun* (**tablespoons**)
a large spoon used for serving food.
**tablespoonful** *noun*

**tablet** *noun* (**tablets**)
1 a pill. 2 a lump of soap. 3 a flat piece of stone, wood, etc. with words carved or written on it.

**table tennis** *noun*
a game played on a table divided in the middle by a net, over which a small ball is hit with bats.

**tack**[1] *noun* (**tacks**)
1 a short nail with a flat top, *Nail down that carpet with tacks.* 2 the action of tacking in sailing; the direction you take.

**tack**[2] *noun*
harness, saddles, etc. for horses.

**tack**[3] *verb* (**tacks, tacking, tacked**)
1 to fix something with small nails. 2 to sew something quickly with long stitches. 3 to sail a zigzag course against the wind.
**tack on**, to add something extra.

**tackle**[1] *verb* (**tackles, tackling, tackled**)
1 to try to do something that needs doing. 2 to try to get the ball from someone else in a football game, etc., or to bring down an opponent in a rugby game.

**tackle**[2] *noun*
equipment, especially for fishing.

**tacky** *adjective* (**tackier, tackiest**)
1 sticky; not quite dry, *The paint is still tacky.* 2 (*informal*) cheaply made and not beautiful, *a tacky ornament made of imitation gold.*

**tact** *noun*
skill in not offending people.

**tactful** *adjective*
having or showing skill in not offending people.
**tactfully** *adverb*

**tactics** *plural noun*
ways of organizing people or things to do something, especially organizing troops in a battle.
**tactical** *adjective*, **tactically** *adverb*

**tactless** *adjective*
likely to offend people; having no tact.
**tactlessly** *adverb*

**tadpole** *noun* (**tadpoles**)
a tiny creature, with an oval head and a long tail, that lives in water and turns into a frog or toad.

**tag**[1] *verb* (**tags, tagging, tagged**)
1 to fix a label on something. 2 to attach something extra, *She tagged on an extra paragraph at the end of her essay.*
**tag along**, to go along with other people.

**tag**² *noun* (**tags**)
1 a label. 2 the metal or plastic part at the end of a shoelace, etc.

**tag**³ *noun*
a game in which one child chases others.

**tail**¹ *noun* (**tails**)
1 the part that sticks out from the rear end of the body of an animal or bird. 2 the part at the end or rear of something, *an aircraft's tail.* 3 the side of a coin opposite the head.

**tail**² *verb* (**tails, tailing, tailed**)
1 to remove the stalks from fruit. 2 to follow a person or thing.
**tail off,** to become fewer, smaller, less successful, etc.

**tailback** *noun* (**tailbacks**)
a long queue of vehicles, *a five-mile tailback on the M25 motorway.*

**tailor** *noun* (**tailors**)
someone whose job is to make clothes.
**tailoring** *noun*

**take** *verb* (**takes, taking, took, taken**)
1 to get hold of something, *He took a bun.* 2 to carry away; to remove, *The money was taken yesterday.* 3 to guide or accompany someone, *Are you taking us to the zoo?* 4 to capture, *They took many prisoners.* 5 to have; to use, *Do you take sugar?* 6 to occupy, *Take a seat.* 7 to need; to require, *It takes two to make a quarrel.* 8 to understand; to believe, *I take it that you wish to leave.* 9 to find out; to make a note of, *Take his name.* 10 to subtract, *Take two from ten.* 11 to accept; to endure, *Can't you take a joke?* 12 to make; to get, *She took a photograph.*
**take in,** to deceive or swindle someone.
**take off,** to remove something; to begin a flight.
**take over,** to take control of something.
**take part,** to share in doing something.
**take place,** to happen.
**take up,** to start something; to occupy a place, time, etc., *I've taken up yoga. That car takes up a lot of space.*

**take-away** *noun* (**take-aways**)
a place where you can buy cooked food to take away with you.

**takings** *plural noun*
money that has been received, especially by a shopkeeper.

**talc** or **talcum powder** *noun*
a perfumed powder put on the skin to dry it or make it smell pleasant.

**tale** *noun* (**tales**)
a story.

**talent** *noun* (**talents**)
a natural ability to do something well, *She has a talent for singing.*
**talented** *adjective*

**talk**¹ *verb* (**talks, talking, talked**)
to speak; to have a conversation.
**talk down to,** to talk to someone as though he or she were unimportant or unintelligent.
**talker** *noun*

**talk**² *noun* (**talks**)
1 a conversation or discussion. 2 a lecture.

**talkative** *adjective*
that talks a lot, *a talkative boy.*

**tall** *adjective* (**taller, tallest**)
1 higher than the average, *a tall pine tree.* 2 measured from the bottom to the top, *The bookcase is two metres tall.*
**tall story,** a story that is hard to believe.

**tally** *verb* (**tallies, tallying, tallied**)
to correspond or agree with something else, *Does your list tally with mine?*

**talon** *noun* (**talons**)
the claw of a bird of prey.

**tambourine** *noun* (**tambourines**)
a round musical instrument like a small drum with metal discs fixed around the edge so that it jingles when you shake or hit it.

**tame**¹ *adjective* (**tamer, tamest**)
1 not wild or dangerous, *The deer are very tame.* 2 dull; uninteresting, *The football match was very tame.*
**tamely** *adverb*, **tameness** *noun*

**tame**² *verb* (**tames, taming, tamed**)
to make an animal used to humans and not afraid of or dangerous to them.
**tamer** *noun*

**tamper** *verb* (**tampers, tampering, tampered**)
**tamper with something,** to interfere with something; to change something so that it will not work properly.

**tan**¹ *noun* (**tans**)
1 a suntan. 2 a yellowish-brown colour.

**tan**² *verb* (**tans, tanning, tanned**)
1 to make your skin brown with suntan.
2 to make the skin of a dead animal into leather.

**tandem** *noun* (**tandems**)
a bicycle for two riders, one behind the other.

**tangent** *noun* (**tangents**)
(*say* **tan**-jĕnt)
(*in Mathematics*) 1 a straight line that touches the outside of a curve or circle. 2 in a right-angled triangle, a number linked with one of the acute angles, equal to the length of the side opposite the angle divided by the length of the shorter side next to the angle.

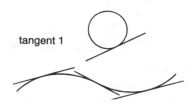

tangent 1

**tangerine** *noun* (**tangerines**)
(*say* tan-jer-**een**)
a kind of small orange.

**tangle** *verb* (**tangles, tangling, tangled**)
to make something twisted or muddled; to become twisted or muddled, *My fishing-line has tangled.*

**tank** *noun* (**tanks**)
1 a large container for a liquid or gas.
2 a heavy armoured vehicle used in war.

**tankard** *noun* (**tankards**)
a large, heavy mug for drinking from.

**tanker** *noun* (**tankers**)
1 a large ship for carrying oil. 2 a large lorry for carrying a liquid.

**tantalize** *verb* (**tantalizes, tantalizing, tantalized**)
to torment someone by showing him or her something that he or she cannot have.

**tantrum** *noun* (**tantrums**)
an outburst of bad temper.

**tap**¹ *noun* (**taps**)
(in America, *faucet*) a device for controlling the flow of a liquid or gas.

**tap**² *noun* (**taps**)
1 a quick, light hit, *I gave him a tap on the shoulder.* 2 tap-dancing.

**tap**³ *verb* (**taps, tapping, tapped**)
1 to take liquid out of something, *Tap the barrel.* 2 to fix a device to a telephone wire, etc. so that you can hear someone else's conversation.

**tap**⁴ *verb* (**taps, tapping, tapped**)
to hit a person or thing quickly and lightly.

**tap-dancing** *noun*
dancing in which you wear hard shoes that make tapping sounds on the floor.
**tap-dance** *noun*, **tap-dancer** *noun*

**tape**¹ *noun* (**tapes**)
1 a narrow strip of cloth, paper, plastic, etc.
2 a narrow plastic strip coated with a magnetic substance and used for making recordings.

**tape**² *verb* (**tapes, taping, taped**)
1 to fix, cover, or surround something with tape. 2 to record sound on magnetic tape.
**get** or **have something taped**, to know, understand, or be able to deal with something.

**tape-measure** *noun* (**tape-measures**)
a long strip marked in inches or centimetres for measuring lengths.

**taper**¹ *verb* (**tapers, tapering, tapered**)
to get narrower towards one end.

**taper**² *noun* (**tapers**)
a piece of string thinly coated with wax, *Light the gas with a taper.*

**tape recorder** *noun* (**tape recorders**)
a device for recording sound on magnetic tape and playing it back.
**tape recording** *noun*

**tapestry** *noun* (**tapestries**)
(*say* **tap**-i-stri)
a piece of strong cloth with pictures or patterns woven on it.

**tapioca** *noun*
a starchy substance consisting of white grains used for making milk puddings.

**tar**¹ *noun*
a thick, black, sticky liquid made from coal or wood and used in making roads.
**tarry** *adjective*

**tar**² *verb* (**tars, tarring, tarred**)
to coat something with tar.

**tarantula** *noun* (**tarantulas**)
(*say* tă-**ran**-tew-lă)
a large hairy spider found in warm countries, *A tarantula bite is painful but not deadly.*

**target** *noun* (**targets**)
something that you aim at and try to hit or reach.
**target language,** the language that you translate something into.

**Tarmac** *noun*
(*trademark*) a mixture of tar and broken stone, used for surfacing roads, paths, playgrounds, etc.

**tarnish** *verb* (**tarnishes, tarnishing, tarnished**)
1 to lose brightness; to cause something to lose its brightness, *Dampness tarnishes some metals.* 2 to spoil something, *The scandal tarnished his reputation.*

**tarpaulin** *noun* (**tarpaulins**)
a large piece of waterproof canvas.

**tart**[1] *noun* (**tarts**)
a pie containing fruit or jam.

**tart**[2] *adjective* (**tarter, tartest**)
sour, *The apples are tart.*

**tartan** *noun* (**tartans**)
Scottish woollen cloth with a criss-cross pattern, *Each clan has its own design of tartan.*

**task** *noun* (**tasks**)
a piece of work to be done.
**take someone to task**, to tell someone off for doing wrong.

**tassel** *noun* (**tassels**)
a bundle of threads tied together at the top and used to decorate something, *Dressing-gown cords often have tassels at each end.*

**taste**[1] *verb* (**tastes, tasting, tasted**)
1 to eat a little bit of food or sip a drink to see what it is like. 2 to have a particular flavour.

**taste**[2] *noun* (**tastes**)
1 the flavour something has when you taste it, *This milk has a strange taste.* 2 the ability to taste things. 3 the ability to appreciate beautiful things, *Her choice of clothes shows her good taste.* 4 a tiny amount of food, *Can I have a taste of your pudding?*
**tasteful** *adjective*, **tastefully** *adverb*, **tasteless** *adjective*, **tastelessly** *adverb*

**tasty** *adjective* (**tastier, tastiest**)
having a taste that you like.

**tattered** *adjective*
badly torn; in rags, *a tattered figure dressed in cast-off clothes.*

**tatters** *plural noun*
rags; badly torn pieces, *My coat was in tatters.*

**tattoo**[1] *verb* (**tattoos, tattooing, tattooed**)
to make a picture or pattern on someone's skin using a needle and some dye.

**tattoo**[2] *noun* (**tattoos**)
a picture or pattern made on someone's skin with a needle and some dye.

**tattoo**[3] *noun* (**tattoos**)
1 a drumming sound, *He beat a tattoo on the table with his fingers.* 2 an entertainment consisting of military music, marching, etc.

**tatty** *adjective* (**tattier, tattiest**)
ragged or shabby; untidy, *a tatty old coat. The paintwork is looking tatty.*

**taught** past tense and past participle of **teach**.

**taunt** *verb* (**taunts, taunting, taunted**)
to jeer at or insult someone, especially by making fun of his or her weaknesses.

**taut** *adjective* (**tauter, tautest**)
stretched tightly.
**tautly** *adverb*, **tautness** *noun*

**tavern** *noun* (**taverns**)
(*old-fashioned use*) a public house; an inn.

**tawny** *adjective* (**tawnier, tawniest**)
brownish-yellow.

**tax**[1] *noun* (**taxes**)
money that people have to pay to the government.
**taxpayer** *noun*

**tax**[2] *verb* (**taxes, taxing, taxed**)
1 to charge someone a tax. 2 to charge a tax when someone buys, owns, or uses something, *The government taxes alcohol, tobacco, and petrol.* 3 to pay the tax on something, *The car is taxed until June.*
**taxable** *adjective*, **taxation** *noun*

**taxi**[1] or **taxi-cab** *noun* (**taxis** or **taxi-cabs**)
a car with a driver which you can hire for journeys, *Most taxis have meters to record the fare.*

**taxi**[2] *verb* (**taxis, taxiing, taxied**)
to move along the ground or on the water before or after flying, *The plane taxied towards the hangar.*

**tea** *noun* (**teas**)
1 a drink made by pouring hot water on the dried leaves of an evergreen shrub. 2 the dried leaves of this shrub. 3 a meal eaten in the afternoon.
**teacup** *noun*, **tea-leaf** *noun*, **tea-table** *noun*, **teatime** *noun*

**teach** *verb* (**teaches, teaching, taught**)
1 to educate someone. 2 to give lessons in a particular subject, *She taught history last year.*

**teacher** *noun* (**teachers**)
someone who teaches others, especially in a school.

**tea cloth** *noun* (**tea cloths**)
1 a tea towel. 2 a cloth for a tea-table.

**teak** *noun*
a hard, strong wood from Asia.

**team** *noun* (**teams**)
1 a group of people who play on the same side in a game. 2 a group of people who work together.

USAGE: Do not confuse **team** with **teem**, which is a verb meaning to be full of something or to rain very hard.

**teapot** *noun* (**teapots**)
a pot in which tea is made.

**tear**[1] *verb* (**tears, tearing, tore, torn**)
(*say* tair)
1 to pull something apart, away, or into pieces. 2 to become torn, *Tissue paper tears easily.* 3 to move very quickly, *He tore down the street.*

**tear**[2] *noun* (**tears**)
(*say* teer)
a drop of water that comes from your eye when you cry.
**in tears**, crying.
**tear-gas**, a gas that makes your eyes water painfully.
**tearful** *adjective*, **tearfully** *adverb*

**tear**[3] *noun* (**tears**)
(*say* tair)
a hole or split made by pulling something apart or away.

**tease** *verb* (**teases, teasing, teased**)
to amuse yourself by annoying someone or saying humorous things about him or her.

**teaspoon** *noun* (**teaspoons**)
1 a small spoon. 2 the amount that this spoon holds.
**teaspoonful** *noun*

**teat** *noun* (**teats**)
1 the part of a female animal through which her babies suck milk. 2 the rubber top of a baby's feeding-bottle.

**tea towel** *noun* (**tea towels**)
a cloth used for drying washed dishes, cutlery, etc.

**tech** *noun* (**techs**)
(*informal*) a technical college.

**technical** *adjective*
to do with machinery or the way that things work.
**technical college**, a college where technical subjects are taught.
**technically** *adverb*, **technician** *noun*

**technique** *noun* (**techniques**)
(*say* tek-**neek**)
the method of doing something skilfully.

**technology** *noun* (**technologies**)
1 the study of machinery and the way things work. 2 the machinery, methods, and ideas used in a particular activity, *computer technology.*
**technological** *adjective*, **technologically** *adverb*, **technologist** *noun*

**teddy bear** *noun* (**teddy bears**)
a soft, furry, toy bear.

**tedious** *adjective*
(*say* **tee**-di-ŭs)
boring; annoyingly slow or long.
**tediously** *adverb*, **tediousness** *noun*, **tedium** *noun*

**teem** *verb* (**teems, teeming, teemed**)
1 to be full of something, *The river was teeming with fish.* 2 to rain very hard.

USAGE: Do not confuse **teem** with **team**, which is a noun meaning a group of people who play or work together.

**teenage** *adjective*
of teenagers.
**teenaged** *adjective*

**teenager** *noun* (**teenagers**)
a person between 13 and 19 years old.

**teens** *plural noun*
the time of your life between the ages of 13 and 19, *He started playing chess in his teens.*

**teeth** plural of **tooth**.

**teetotaller** *adjective*
someone who never drinks alcoholic drink.
**teetotal** *adjective*

**telecommunications** *plural noun*
sending news, messages, etc. over long distances by telephone, telegraph, fax, television, etc.

**telegram** *noun* (**telegrams**)
a message sent by telegraph, usually delivered as words on paper.

**telegraph** *noun* (**telegraphs**)
a way of sending messages by using electric current along wires or by radio.
**telegraph pole**, a pole that supports telephone wires.
**telegraphic** *adjective*, **telegraphy** *noun*

**telepathy** *noun*
(*say* til-**ep**-ă-thi)
communication from one person's mind to another without speaking, writing, or gestures.
**telepathic** *adjective*

## telephone[1] *noun* (telephones)
a device using electric wires, radio, etc. to enable someone to speak to another person who is some distance away.
**on the telephone,** using a telephone to speak to someone; having a telephone in your house, office, etc.
**telephone book,** a telephone directory.
**telephone box,** a small enclosed place containing a telephone for the public to use.
**telephone directory,** a book containing the telephone numbers of all the people in a district.
**telephone number,** a number given to a particular telephone and used in making connections to it.

## telephone[2] *verb* (telephones, telephoning, telephoned)
to speak or try to speak to someone on the telephone.

## telephonist *noun* (telephonists)
(*say* til-ef-ŏn-ist)
someone who operates a telephone switchboard.

## telescope *noun* (telescopes)
a tube with lenses at each end, through which you can see distant things more clearly, *Portable telescopes have sections that slide inside one another.*
**telescopic** *adjective*

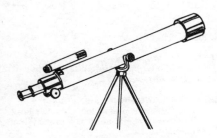

## teletext *noun*
a system for getting information from a database and displaying it on a screen, using a special television set.

## televise *verb* (televises, televising, televised)
to send out a programme by television.

## television *noun* (televisions)
1 a system using radio waves to reproduce a picture on a screen. 2 a television set. 3 televised programmes.
**television set,** an apparatus for receiving pictures sent by television.

## tell *verb* (tells, telling, told)
1 to pass on a story, news, instructions, etc. to someone by speaking, *He told us a joke.*
2 to reveal a secret, *Promise you won't tell.*
3 to recognize, *Can you tell the difference between butter and margarine?* 4 to count, *There are ten of them all told.*
**tell off,** to speak severely to someone who has done wrong.
**tell tales,** to report that someone else has done wrong.

## telling *adjective*
meaningful, *It was a telling reply.*

## telltale[1] *noun* (telltales)
a sneak.

## telltale[2] *adjective*
that shows or tells something, *He had a telltale spot of jam on his chin.*

## telly *noun* (tellies)
(*informal*) 1 television. 2 a television set.

## temper *noun* (tempers)
1 the mood you are in, *Your good behaviour has put him in a good temper.* 2 an angry mood, *Now she's in a temper.*
**lose your temper,** to become very angry.

## temperate *adjective*
neither extremely hot nor extremely cold; mild; moderate, *Britain has a temperate climate.*

## temperature *noun* (temperatures)
1 how hot or cold someone or something is. 2 an unusually high body-temperature.

## tempest *noun* (tempests)
(*old-fashioned use*) a violent storm.
**tempestuous** *adjective*

## temple[1] *noun* (temples)
a building where a god is worshipped.

## temple[2] *noun* (temples)
part of your head between your forehead and your ear.

## tempo *noun* (tempos)
the speed or rhythm of something, especially of a piece of music.

## temporary *adjective*
lasting, or intended to last, for only a short time, *a temporary classroom.*
**temporarily** *adverb*

## tempt *verb* (tempts, tempting, tempted)
1 to try to make someone do wrong or do something he or she would not normally do. 2 to attract someone to do something, *I am tempted to try the chocolate cake.*
**temptation** *noun*, **tempter** *noun*, **temptress** *noun*

## ten *noun* (tens)
the number 10, one more than nine.
**tenth** *adjective* and *noun*

**tenant** *noun* (**tenants**)
someone who rents a house, building, piece of land, etc.
**tenancy** *noun*

**tend**[1] *verb* (**tends, tending, tended**)
to be inclined or likely to do something, *Prices are tending to rise.*

**tend**[2] *verb* (**tends, tending, tended**)
to look after something, *The shepherds were tending their sheep.*

**tendency** *noun* (**tendencies**)
wanting or being likely to do something; a habit, *She has a tendency to be lazy.*

**tender**[1] *adjective* (**tenderer, tenderest**)
1 not tough or hard; easy to chew, *tender meat.* 2 delicate; sensitive, *tender plants.* 3 gentle; loving, *a tender smile.*
**tenderly** *adverb*, **tenderness** *noun*

**tender**[2] *noun* (**tenders**)
a truck attached to a steam locomotive to carry its coal and water.

**tender**[3] *verb* (**tenders, tendering, tendered**)
to give; to offer, *She tendered her resignation.*

**tendon** *noun* (**tendons**)
strong tissue that joins a muscle to a bone.

**tendril** *noun* (**tendrils**)
the part of a climbing plant that twists round something to support itself.

**tennis** *noun*
a game played with rackets and a ball on a court with a net across the middle.

**tenor** *noun* (**tenors**)
a male singer with a high voice.

**tenpin bowling** *noun*
a game in which you knock down sets of ten skittles with a ball.

**tense**[1] *adjective* (**tenser, tensest**)
1 tightly stretched. 2 nervous; excited or exciting.
**tensely** *adverb*, **tension** *noun*

**tense**[2] *noun* (**tenses**)
a form of a verb that shows when something happens, *The past tense of 'come' is 'came'.*

**tent** *noun* (**tents**)
a kind of shelter made of cloth supported by a pole or poles.

**tentacle** *noun* (**tentacles**)
a long, snake-like part of an animal's body, *An octopus has eight tentacles.*

**tepid** *adjective*
only just warm, *tepid water.*

**term** *noun* (**terms**)
1 the period of weeks when a school or college is open. 2 a definite period, *a term of imprisonment.* 3 a word or expression, *'Decimal point' is a mathematical term.* 4 a condition offered or agreed, *terms of surrender.*
**to be on good, bad, etc. terms**, to be in a good, bad, etc. relationship with someone, *They are on good terms.*

**terminal** *noun* (**terminals**)
1 the place where something ends; a terminus. 2 a building where air passengers arrive or depart. 3 a place where a wire is connected to a battery, etc. 4 a device by which you can make contact with a computer.

**terminate** *verb* (**terminates, terminating, terminated**)
to end; to stop.
**termination** *noun*

**terminus** *noun* (**termini**)
the station at the end of a railway or bus route.

**terrace** *noun* (**terraces**)
1 a row of houses joined together. 2 a level area on a slope or hillside. 3 a raised flat place next to a house or in a garden.

**terrapin** *noun* (**terrapins**)
a kind of tortoise that lives in water.

**terrible** *adjective*
awful.
**terribly** *adverb*

**terrier** *noun* (**terriers**)
one of various breeds of strong, lively, usually small dog.

**terrific** *adjective*
(*informal*) 1 very great, *a terrific speed.* 2 very good; excellent, *a terrific idea.*
**terrifically** *adverb*

**terrify** *verb* (**terrifies, terrifying, terrified**)
to make a person or animal very frightened.

**territory** *noun* (**territories**)
an area of land, especially an area that belongs to a country or person.
**territorial** *adjective*

**terror** *noun* (**terrors**)
great fear.

**terrorist** *noun* (**terrorists**)
someone who uses violence for a political cause.
**terrorism** *noun*

**terrorize** *verb* (**terrorizes, terrorizing, terrorized**)
to fill someone with terror.

**tessellation** *noun* (**tessellations**)
an arrangement of shapes, usually of the same shape and size, to cover a surface without gaps or overlapping, *Hexagons can form a tessellation, but octagons cannot.*

**test**[1] *noun* (**tests**)
**1** a short set of questions to check someone's knowledge, especially in school. **2** a series of questions, experiments, etc. to get information about someone or something, *a computer aptitude test. They gave her a test for diabetes.* **3** (*informal*) a test match.

**test**[2] *verb* (**tests, testing, tested**)
to make a test on a person or thing.

**testament** *noun* (**testaments**)
a written statement.
**Testament,** one of the two main parts of the Bible, the *Old Testament* or the *New Testament.*

**testicle** *noun* (**testicles**)
one of the two glands in the scrotum where semen is produced.

**testify** *verb* (**testifies, testifying, testified**)
to give evidence; to swear that something is true.

**testimonial** *noun* (**testimonials**)
a letter describing someone's abilities, character, etc., *Send two testimonials when you apply for the job.*

**testimony** *noun* (**testimonies**)
evidence; what someone testifies.

**test match** *noun* (**test matches**)
a match between teams from different countries, especially in cricket and Rugby.

**test-tube** *noun* (**test-tubes**)
a glass tube, closed at one end, used for experiments in chemistry.

**tether**[1] *verb* (**tethers, tethering, tethered**)
to tie an animal so that it cannot move far.

**tether**[2] *noun* (**tethers**)
a rope for tying an animal.
**at the end of your tether,** unable to endure something any more.

**text** *noun* (**texts**)
**1** the words of a book, speech, etc. **2** a short extract from the Bible.

**textbook** *noun* (**textbooks**)
a book that teaches you about a subject.

**textiles** *plural noun*
kinds of cloth; fabrics.

**texture** *noun* (**textures**)
the way that the surface of something feels, *Silk has a smooth texture.*

**than** *conjunction*
compared with another person or thing, *Fred is taller than Jim.*

**thank** *verb* (**thanks, thanking, thanked**)
to tell someone you are grateful for something he or she has given you or done for you.
**thank you,** words that you say when thanking someone.

**thankful** *adjective*
feeling glad that someone has done something for you.
**thankfully** *adverb*

**thanks** *plural noun*
**1** saying that you are glad that someone has done something for you. **2** (*informal*) a short way of saying 'Thank you'.
**thanks to,** because of, *Thanks to you, we succeeded.*

**that**[1] *adjective* and *pronoun*
the one there, *Whose is that book? That is mine.*

**that**[2] *conjunction*
**1** with the result, *He was such a liar that nobody believed him.* **2** used to introduce a fact, thought, wish, hope, etc., *I hope that you are well. Do you know that it is one o'clock?*

**that**[3] *pronoun*
which; who, *This is the record that I wanted.*

**thatch**[1] *noun*
straw or reeds used to make a roof.

**thatch**[2] *verb* (**thatches, thatching, thatched**)
to make a roof with straw or reeds.
**thatcher** *noun*

**thaw** *verb* (**thaws, thawing, thawed**)
to melt; to stop being frozen, *The ice has thawed. How long will it take for the frozen fish to thaw?*

**the** *adjective* (called the *definite article*)
a particular one; that or those.

**theatre** *noun* (**theatres**)
**1** a place where people go to see plays or shows. **2** a special room where surgical operations are done.

**theatrical** *adjective*
of plays or acting.
**theatrically** *adverb*

**thee** *pronoun*
(*old-fashioned use*) you, *I gave thee my commands.*

**theft** *noun* (**thefts**)
stealing, *the theft of the jewels.*

**their** *adjective*
belonging to them, *Their coats are over there.*

**theirs** *pronoun*
belonging to them, *Those cakes are theirs, not ours.*

**them** *pronoun*
a word used for *they* when it is the object of the sentence, or when it comes straight after a preposition, *We can hand them round. We went on holiday with them.*

**theme** *noun* (**themes**)
1 a subject. 2 a short melody.
**theme park,** a place with exciting things to do and machines to ride on, all connected with a particular subject, *a Wild West theme park.*

**themselves** *plural noun*
them and nobody else.
**by themselves,** on their own; alone, *They built the house by themselves. Rosa, Joshua, and Salim were standing by themselves.*

**then**[1] *adverb*
1 after that; next, *Then there were nine.* 2 at that time, *She was happy then.* 3 in that case; therefore, *It isn't here. It must be lost, then.*

**then**[2] *noun*
that time, *Have you seen him since then?*

**theology** *noun*
the study of religion.
**theologian** *noun*, **theological** *adjective*

**theorem** *noun* (**theorems**)
a statement that can be proved or needs to be proved.

**theory** *noun* (**theories**)
1 an idea or set of ideas suggested to explain something. 2 the principles of a subject; the non-practical part of a subject or process, *In theory, this printer should run automatically, but in practice it needs to be adjusted by hand.*
**theoretical** *adjective*, **theoretically** *adverb*

**therapy** *noun* (**therapies**)
a way of treating an illness of the mind or the body, usually without using surgery or artificial medicines.
**therapist** *noun*

**there** *adverb*
1 in or to that place. 2 a word that you say to call attention to someone or something, *There's a good boy!*

**thereabouts** *adverb*
near there, *They live in Swindon or thereabouts.*

**therefore** *adverb*
for that reason; and so.

**thermal** *adjective*
of heat; using or operated by heat, *a thermal power station.*

**thermometer** *noun* (**thermometers**)
a device for measuring temperature.

**Thermos** *noun* (**Thermoses**)
(*trademark*) a kind of vacuum flask.

**thermostat** *noun* (**thermostats**)
a device that automatically keeps temperature steady.
**thermostatic** *adjective*, **thermostatically** *adverb*

**thesaurus** *noun* (**thesauri** or **thesauruses**)
a book giving sets of words arranged according to their meanings, *Use a thesaurus to find another word for 'enough'.*

**these** *adjective* and *pronoun*
the people or things here.

**they** *pronoun*
the people or things that someone is talking about.

**they'd** short for *they had, they should,* or *they would.*

**they'll** short for *they will.*

**they're** short for *they are.*

**they've** short for *they have.*

**thick** *adjective* (**thicker, thickest**)
1 measuring a lot from one side to the other, *a thick book.* 2 measured from one side to the other, *a wall ten centimetres thick.* 3 crowded; dense, *thick fog.* 4 (*informal*) stupid, *Don't be so thick.*
**thickly** *adverb*, **thickness** *noun*

**thicken** *verb* (**thickens, thickening, thickened**)
to make something thicker; to become thicker.

**thicket** *noun* (**thickets**)
a group of trees and shrubs growing close together.

**thief** *noun* (**thieves**)
someone who steals things.

**thigh** *noun* (**thighs**)
the part of your leg above your knee.

**thimble** *noun* (**thimbles**)
a metal or plastic cover to protect the end of your finger when you are sewing.

**thin**[1] *adjective* (**thinner, thinnest**)
not fat; not thick.
**thinly** *adverb*, **thinness** *noun*

**thin**[2] *verb* (**thins, thinning, thinned**)
1 to make something less thick or less crowded, *Thin the seedlings once they are an inch high.* 2 to become less thick or less crowded, *The crowds had thinned by the late afternoon.*

**thine** *adjective*
(*old-fashioned use*) yours.

**thing** *noun* (**things**)
an object; anything that can be touched, seen, thought about, etc.

**think** *verb* (**thinks, thinking, thought**)
1 to use your mind. 2 to have an idea or opinion, *I think that's a good plan.*
**thinker** *noun*

**third**[1] *adjective*
next after the second.
**Third World**, the countries of the world whose industry is less developed than that of America, Europe, and the countries that used to have Communist governments.
**thirdly** *adverb*

**third**[2] *noun* (**thirds**)
one of three equal parts into which something is divided or could be divided.

**thirst** *noun*
the feeling that you want to drink.
**thirsty** *adjective*

**thirteen** *noun* (**thirteens**)
the number 13, one more than twelve.
**thirteenth** *adjective* and *noun*

**thirty** *noun* (**thirties**)
the number 30, three times ten.
**thirtieth** *adjective* and *noun*

**this** *adjective* and *pronoun*
the one here, *Is this the man? This is the one.*

**thistle** *noun* (**thistles**)
a wild plant with prickly leaves and purple flowers.

**thorn** *noun* (**thorns**)
a small pointed growth on the stem of a plant, *Roses have thorns.*

**thorny** *adjective* (**thornier, thorniest**)
1 full of thorns; prickly. 2 difficult; causing argument or disagreement, *a thorny problem.*

**thorough** *adjective*
1 done properly and carefully, *thorough work.* 2 absolute; complete, *a thorough mess.*
**thoroughly** *adverb*, **thoroughness** *noun*

**those** *adjective* and *pronoun*
the ones there, *Where are those cards? Those are the ones I want.*

**thou** *pronoun*
(*old-fashioned use*) you, *Thou art a friend of Robin Hood, I hear.*

**though**[1] *conjunction*
and yet; in spite of the fact that, *It is not true, though he believes it.*

**though**[2] *adverb*
however; all the same, *She said she would come; she didn't, though.*

**thought**[1] *noun* (**thoughts**)
1 something that you think; an idea or opinion. 2 thinking, *Give the problem some thought.*

**thought**[2] past tense and past participle of **think**.

**thoughtful** *adjective*
1 thinking a lot. 2 thinking of other people and what they would like.
**thoughtfully** *adverb*, **thoughtfulness** *noun*

**thoughtless** *adjective*
not thinking of other people and what they would like; reckless.
**thoughtlessly** *adverb*, **thoughtlessness** *noun*

**thousand** *noun* (**thousands**)
the number 1,000, ten hundreds.
**thousandth** *adjective* and *noun*

**thrash** *verb* (**thrashes, thrashing, thrashed**)
1 to keep hitting a person or animal very hard. 2 to defeat a person, team, etc. 3 to move your arms and legs wildly.

**thread**[1] *noun* (**threads**)
1 a long piece of cotton, wool, nylon, etc. used for sewing, weaving, etc. 2 a long, thin piece of something. 3 the spiral ridge round a screw or bolt.

**thread**[2] *verb* (**threads, threading, threaded**)
1 to put thread through the eye of a needle.
2 to put beads, pearls, etc. on a piece of
cotton, nylon, etc.

**threat** *noun* (**threats**)
1 a warning that you will punish or harm
someone if he or she does not do what you
want. 2 a danger.

**threaten** *verb* (**threatens, threatening, threatened**)
1 to make threats to someone. 2 to be a
danger to someone or something.

**three** *noun* (**threes**)
the number 3, one more than two.
**three-piece**, consisting of three separate
parts, *A three-piece suit comprises a jacket,
a pair of trousers, and a waistcoat.*

**three-dimensional** *adjective*
that has depth as well as height and width.

**thresh** *verb* (**threshes, threshing, threshed**)
to beat corn so as to get the grain out of it.

**threshold** *noun* (**thresholds**)
1 the stone, board, etc. under the doorway
of a house, building, etc.; the entrance.
2 the beginning of something, *We are on the
threshold of a new discovery in science.*

**threw** past tense of **throw** *verb*.

**thrift** *noun*
being careful with money.
**thriftily** *adverb*, **thrifty** *adjective*

**thrill**[1] *verb* (**thrills, thrilling, thrilled**)
to give someone a sudden excited feeling.

**thrill**[2] *noun* (**thrills**)
1 a sudden excited feeling. 2 something
that gives you a sudden excited feeling.

**thriller** *noun* (**thrillers**)
an exciting story, usually about crime.

**thrive** *verb* (**thrives, thriving, throve, thrived**)
to prosper; to grow strongly.

**throat** *noun* (**throats**)
1 the front of the neck. 2 the tube in the
neck that takes food and air into the body.

**throb** *verb* (**throbs, throbbing, throbbed**)
to beat or vibrate with a strong rhythm.

**throne** *noun* (**thrones**)
1 a special chair for a king or queen. 2 the
position of being king or queen, *Henry VIII
came to the throne when he was a young
man.*

**throng** *noun* (**throngs**)
a crowd of people.

**throttle**[1] *verb* (**throttles, throttling, throttled**)
to strangle someone.
**throttle back** or **throttle down**, to reduce speed
while driving a car, motor cycle, etc.

**throttle**[2] *noun* (**throttles**)
a device to control the flow of fuel to an
engine; an accelerator.

**through**[1] *preposition*
1 from one end or side to the other, *Climb
through the window.* 2 because of; by
means of, *We sold our car through an
advertisement.*

**through**[2] *adverb*
1 from one end or side to the other, *Can we
get through?* 2 (*informal*) finished, *I'm
through with this job.*

**through**[3] *adjective*
that goes somewhere by the most direct
route, or without stopping, *a through train.
a through road.*

**throughout** *preposition* and *adverb*
all the way through.

**throve** past tense of **thrive**.

**throw**[1] *verb* (**throws, throwing, threw, thrown**)
1 to make a person or thing move through
the air; to put something somewhere
casually or carelessly, *'Who has thrown
that stick into the water?' 'He threw it.'* 2 to
move your body about wildly. 3 to shape a
pot on a potter's wheel.
**throw away**, to get rid of something.

**throw**[2] *noun* (**throws**)
a throwing action or movement.

**thrush** *noun* (**thrushes**)
a bird that has a white front with brown
spots on it.

**thrust** *verb* (**thrusts, thrusting, thrust**)
to push hard, *He thrust his hands into his
pockets.*

**thud** *noun* (**thuds**)
the dull sound of something heavy falling
on to something softer.

**thumb** *noun* (**thumbs**)
the short, thick finger at the side of each
hand.
**under someone's thumb**, controlled or ruled
by him or her.

**thump** *verb* (**thumps, thumping, thumped**)
1 to hit something heavily. 2 to punch
someone. 3 to make a dull, heavy sound.

**thunder** *noun*
1 the loud noise that follows lightning.
2 a loud, heavy noise.
**thunderous** *adjective*, **thunderstorm** *noun*

**Thursday** *noun* (**Thursdays**)
the fifth day of the week.

**thus** *adverb*
in this way, *She did it thus.*

**thy** *adjective*
(*old-fashioned use*) your.

**tick**¹ *noun* (**ticks**)
1 a small mark, usually ✓, made next to something when checking it. 2 the high, short, sharp sounds that a traditional clock or watch makes when it is working; one of these sounds.

**tick**² *verb* (**ticks, ticking, ticked**)
1 to mark something with a tick, *She ticked the correct answers.* 2 to make the sound of a traditional clock or watch, *His watch was still ticking.*
**tick off**, (*informal*) to speak severely to someone who has done wrong.

**ticket** *noun* (**tickets**)
a piece of paper or card that allows you to see a show, travel on a bus or train, etc.

**tickle** *verb* (**tickles, tickling, tickled**)
1 to keep touching someone's skin lightly so as to make him or her laugh or feel irritated. 2 to have a tickling or itching feeling, *My throat is tickling; perhaps I'm catching a cold.* 3 to please or amuse someone.

**ticklish** *adjective*
1 likely to laugh or wriggle when tickled, *Are you ticklish?* 2 awkward; difficult, *a ticklish situation.*

**tidal** *adjective*
of the tide or tides.
**tidal power**, power from the movement of the tides.
**tidal wave**, an unusually large sea-wave.

**tiddler** *noun* (**tiddlers**)
(*informal*) a tiny fish, child, etc.

**tiddly-wink** *noun* (**tiddly-winks**)
a small counter flipped by another counter into a cup, etc. in the game of **tiddly-winks**.

**tide**¹ *noun* (**tides**)
the rising or falling of the sea which usually happens twice a day.

**tide**² *verb* (**tides, tiding, tided**)
**tide over**, to provide someone with what he or she needs, especially money, during a time of shortage, *Here's £5 to tide you over until you get the rest of your pocket money.*

**tidy** *adjective* (**tidier, tidiest**)
1 looking clean and orderly, *a tidy room.* 2 fairly large; considerable, *a tidy sum of money.*
**tidily** *adverb*, **tidiness** *noun*

**tie**¹ *verb* (**ties, tying, tied**)
1 to fasten something with string, ribbon, etc. 2 to make a knot or bow in something. 3 to finish a game or competition with an equal score or position.
**tied up**, very busy, *I'm tied up until late this afternoon.*

**tie**² *noun* (**ties**)
1 a thin strip of material tied round the collar of a shirt. 2 the situation where there is an equal score or position in a game or competition. 3 one of the matches in a competition, *a cup-tie.*

**tiger** *noun* (**tigers**)
a large wild animal of the cat family, with yellow fur and black stripes.
**tigress** *noun*

**tight** *adjective* (**tighter, tightest**)
1 fitting very closely; firmly fastened. 2 fully stretched. 3 (*informal*) drunk; intoxicated.
**tightly** *adverb*, **tightness** *noun*

**tighten** *verb* (**tightens, tightening, tightened**)
to make something tighter; to become tighter.

**tightrope** *noun* (**tightropes**)
a tightly stretched rope above the ground, for acrobats to balance on.

**tights** *plural noun*
a piece of clothing that fits tightly over the parts of your body below your waist.

**tile** *noun* (**tiles**)
a thin piece of baked clay or other hard material used to cover roofs, walls, or floors.
**tiled** *adjective*

**till**¹ *preposition* and *conjunction*
until.

**till**² *noun* (**tills**)
a drawer or box for money in a shop; a cash register.

**till**³ *verb* (**tills, tilling, tilled**)
to cultivate land.

**tiller** *noun* (**tillers**)
a long handle used to turn a boat's rudder.

**tilt** *verb* (**tilts, tilting, tilted**)
1 to slope or lean. 2 to make something slope; to tip, *The whole caravan suddenly tilted sideways.*

**timber** *noun* (**timbers**)
1 wood for building or making things.
2 a beam of wood.

**time**[1] *noun* (**times**)
1 years, months, weeks, days, hours, minutes, and seconds; the way that these pass by. 2 a particular moment or period; an occasion. 3 a period suitable or available for something, *Is there time for another cup of tea?* 4 the rhythm and speed of a piece of music.
**times,** multiplied by, *5 times 3 is 15 (5 × 3 = 15).*
**at times** or **from time to time,** occasionally.
**in time,** not late; eventually, *In time, water can wear away rock.*
**on time,** not late.
**time after time** or **time and again,** often; on many occasions.
**time-limit,** a limited amount of time for doing something; the time by which something must be done.

**time**[2] *verb* (**times, timing, timed**)
1 to measure how long something takes.
2 to note the time when something happens or starts. 3 to arrange the time when something happens.
**timer** *noun*

**time-scale** *noun* (**time-scales**)
the length of time taken by something or allowed for something, *What time-scale do you foresee for the rebuilding work?*

**timetable** *noun* (**timetables**)
1 a list of the times when buses, trains, etc. depart and arrive. 2 a list showing the time of school lessons in each subject.

**timid** *adjective* (**timider, timidest**)
fearful; easily frightened.
**timidity** *noun*, **timidly** *adverb*

**timpani** *plural noun*
(*say* timp-ă-ni)
kettledrums.

**tin**[1] *noun* (**tins**)
1 a soft, white metal. 2 a metal container for food.
**tin-opener,** a tool for opening tins.

**tin**[2] *verb* (**tins, tinning, tinned**)
to put something into tins.

**tingle** *verb* (**tingles, tingling, tingled**)
to have a slight stinging or tickling feeling, *Her ears were tingling with the cold.*

**tinker**[1] *verb* (**tinkers, tinkering, tinkered**)
to try to mend or improve something unskilfully.

**tinker**[2] *noun* (**tinkers**)
(*old-fashioned use*) someone who travelled around mending pots and pans.

**tinkle** *verb* (**tinkled, tinkling**)
to make a gentle ringing sound.

**tinsel** *noun*
strips of glittering material used for decorations.

**tint** *noun* (**tints**)
a shade of colour, especially a pale one.
**tinted** *adjective*

**tiny** *adjective* (**tinier, tiniest**)
very small.

**tip**[1] *noun* (**tips**)
1 the part right at the end of something.
2 a small present of money given to someone who has helped you. 3 a piece of advice. 4 a place where rubbish is left.

**tip**[2] *verb* (**tips, tipping, tipped**)
1 to turn something upside down; to move something on to one edge. 2 to leave rubbish somewhere. 3 to give a small present of money to someone who has helped you.
**tipper** *noun*

**tiptoe** *verb* (**tiptoes, tiptoeing, tiptoed**)
to walk on your toes very quietly or carefully.

**tire** *verb* (**tires, tiring, tired**)
to make someone tired; to become tired.

**tired** *adjective*
feeling that you need to sleep or rest.
**tired of,** bored with, *I am tired of doing the housework.*

**tiresome** *adjective*
1 annoying, *The flies buzzed around my face constantly, which was tiresome.*
2 boring, *a long, tiresome speech.*

**tissue** *noun* (**tissues**)
1 very thin, soft paper; a piece of this. 2 the substance of which an animal or plant is made.
**tissue-paper** *noun*

**tit** *noun* (**tits**)
a kind of small bird.

**title** *noun* (**titles**)
1 the name of a book, film, piece of music, etc. 2 a word that shows a person's position or profession, such as *Sir, Lady, Dr,* and *Mrs.*

**titter** *verb* (**titters, tittering, tittered**)
to laugh in a silly way.

**to**¹ *preposition*
1 towards, *They set off to London.* 2 as far as; so as to reach, *I am wet to the skin.* 3 compared with; rather than, *She prefers cats to dogs.* 4 used before a verb to show that it is the infinitive, *To be or not to be, that is the question.*

**to**² *adverb*
to or in the proper or closed position or situation, *Push the door to.*
**to and fro,** backwards and forwards.

**toad** *noun* (**toads**)
an animal like a big frog, *Toads usually live on land.*

**toad-in-the-hole** *noun*
sausages baked in batter.

**toadstool** *noun* (**toadstools**)
a fungus that looks like a mushroom, *Most toadstools are poisonous.*

**toast**¹ *verb* (**toasts, toasting, toasted**)
1 to cook something by heating it under a grill, in front of a fire, etc. 2 to have a drink as a way of honouring a person or thing.
**toaster** *noun*

**toast**² *noun* (**toasts**)
1 toasted bread. 2 drinking to honour a person or thing; the person or thing honoured in this way.

**tobacco** *noun*
the dried leaves of certain plants prepared for smoking in cigarettes, cigars, or pipes.

**tobacconist** *noun* (**tobacconists**)
someone who keeps a shop that sells tobacco and other things for smoking.

**toboggan** *noun* (**toboggans**)
a small sledge.
**tobogganing** *noun*

**today**¹ *noun*
this day; the present time, *Today is Monday.*

**today**² *adverb*
on this day; nowadays, in the present time, *I saw him today. Today we do not allow children to work in factories and mines.*

**toddler** *noun* (**toddlers**)
a young child just learning to walk.

**toe** *noun* (**toes**)
1 one of the five separate parts at the end of each foot. 2 the part of a shoe or sock that covers the toes.

**toffee** *noun* (**toffees**)
a sticky sweet made from butter and sugar.
**toffee-apple,** an apple coated with toffee and fixed on a small stick.
**toffee-nosed,** (*informal*) despising people who have not got a high social position.

**toga** *noun* (**togas**)
a long, loose piece of clothing worn by men in Ancient Rome.

**together** *adverb*
1 with another person or thing; with each other, *They went to school together.* 2 so as to join one with another, *Tie the ends together.*

**toil** *verb* (**toils, toiling, toiled**)
1 to work hard. 2 to move slowly and with difficulty.

**toilet** *noun* (**toilets**)
a lavatory.
**toilet-paper,** paper for use in a lavatory.
**toilet-roll,** a roll of toilet-paper.

**token** *noun* (**tokens**)
1 a card, piece of plastic, etc. used instead of money to pay for something, *a record token.* 2 a sign or signal of something, *A white flag is a token of surrender.*

**told** past tense and past participle of **tell**.

**tolerant** *adjective*
that tolerates things, especially other people's beliefs, behaviour, etc.
**tolerance** *noun,* **tolerantly** *adverb*

**tolerate** *verb* (**tolerates, tolerating, tolerated**)
to allow something; not to oppose something.
**tolerable** *adjective,* **tolerably** *adverb,* **toleration** *noun*

**toll**¹ *noun* (**tolls**)
a payment charged for using a bridge, road, etc.

**toll**² *verb* (**tolls, tolling, tolled**)
to ring a bell slowly.

**tom** *noun* (**toms**)
a male cat.
**tom-cat** *noun*

**tomahawk** *noun* (**tomahawks**)
an axe used by Native Americans.

**tomato** *noun* (**tomatoes**)
a soft, round, red fruit with seeds inside it, *Tomatoes are eaten raw in salads.*

**tomb** *noun* (**tombs**)
(*say* toom)
a place where a corpse is buried; a grave.
**tombstone** *noun*

**tomboy** *noun* (**tomboys**)
a girl who likes doing things that boys usually do.

**tommy-gun** *noun* (**tommy-guns**)
a small machine-gun.

**tomorrow** *noun* and *adverb*
the day after today.

**tom-tom** *noun* (**tom-toms**)
a drum used in jazz and modern rock music.

**ton** *noun* (**tons**)
1 a unit of weight equal to 2,240 pounds or about 1,016 kilograms. 2 (*informal*) a large amount, *tons of money*. 3 (*slang*) a speed of 100 miles per hour, *This motor bike can do a ton*.

**tone** *noun* (**tones**)
1 a sound, especially in music. 2 one of the five larger intervals between two notes in a musical scale. 3 a shade of a colour. 4 the quality or character of something.
**tonal** *adjective*, **tonally** *adverb*

**tongs** *plural noun*
a tool that is used for picking up things, *coal tongs*.

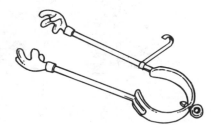

**tongue** *noun* (**tongues**)
1 the long, soft part that moves about inside the mouth. 2 a language. 3 the strip of material under the laces of a shoe. 4 the part inside a bell that makes it ring.
**tongue-tied**, too shy to speak.
**tongue-twister**, something that is very difficult to say.

**tonic** *noun* (**tonics**)
something that makes a person healthier or stronger.
**tonic water**, a kind of clear fizzy drink.

**tonight** *adverb* and *noun*
this evening or night.

**tonne** *noun* (**tonnes**)
a unit of weight equal to 1,000 kilograms.

**tonsillitis** *noun*
a disease that makes your tonsils sore.

**tonsils** *plural noun*
two small masses of soft flesh inside your throat.

**too** *adverb*
1 also, *I know the answer too*. 2 more than is wanted, allowed, safe, etc., *Don't drive too fast*.

**took** past tense of **take**.

**tool** *noun* (**tools**)
a device that you use to help you do a particular job, *Hammers and saws are tools*.

**tooth** *noun* (**teeth**)
1 one of the hard, white, bony parts that grow in your gums, used for biting and chewing. 2 one of a row of sharp parts, *the teeth of a saw*.
**fight tooth and nail**, to fight very fiercely.
**toothache** *noun*, **toothbrush** *noun*, **toothed** *adjective*

**toothpaste** *noun* (**toothpastes**)
a creamy paste for cleaning your teeth.

**top**¹ *noun* (**tops**)
1 the highest part of something. 2 the upper surface of something. 3 the covering or stopper of a jar, bottle, etc. 4 a piece of clothing that a girl or woman wears on the upper part of her body.

**top**² *noun* (**tops**)
a toy that spins round and round.

**top**³ *adjective*
highest; most important.

**top**⁴ *verb* (**tops, topping, topped**)
1 to put a top on something, *a cake topped with icing*. 2 to be at the top of something.
**top up**, to fill a container to the top.

**top hat** *noun* (**top hats**)
a tall, stiff, black or grey hat worn with formal clothes.

**topic** *noun* (**topics**)
a subject to write, talk, or learn about.

**topical** *adjective*
to do with things that are happening now, *a topical film*.
**topicality** *noun*, **topically** *adverb*

**topless** *adjective*
not wearing any clothes over the top half of your body.

**topple** *verb* (**topples, toppling, toppled**)
1 to overturn something; to remove someone from power, *The army had toppled the President.* 2 to fall over, *That pile of books is about to topple.*

**top secret** *adjective*
extremely secret, *top secret military research.*

**topsy-turvy** *adverb* and *adjective*
upside-down; muddled.

**torch** *noun* (**torches**)
1 (in America, *flashlight*) a small portable electric lamp. 2 burning material tied to a stick, giving light.

**tore** past tense of **tear** *verb*.

**toreador** *noun* (**toreadors**)
a bullfighter.

**torment** *verb* (**torments, tormenting, tormented**)
1 to make someone or an animal feel great pain. 2 to keep annoying someone deliberately.
**tormentor** *noun*

**torn** past participle of **tear** *verb*.

**tornado** *noun* (**tornadoes**)
(*say* tor-**nay**-doh)
a violent storm or whirlwind.

**torpedo** *noun* (**torpedoes**)
a long, tubular bomb sent under water to destroy ships and submarines.

**torrent** *noun* (**torrents**)
a very strong stream or fall of water.
**torrential** *adjective*

**tortoise** *noun* (**tortoises**)
(*say* **tor**-tŭs)
a slow-moving animal with a shell over its body.

**torture** *verb* (**tortures, torturing, tortured**)
to make someone feel great pain, especially in order to make him or her tell a secret.
**torture** *noun*, **torturer** *noun*

**Tory** *noun* (**Tories**)
a Conservative.

**toss** *verb* (**tosses, tossing, tossed**)
1 to throw, especially up into the air. 2 to spin a coin so as to decide something from the way it lies after falling. 3 to move about restlessly in bed.

**total**[1] *noun* (**totals**)
the amount you get by adding everything together.

**total**[2] *verb* (**totals, totalling, totalled**)
1 to add up, *Total the scores of all the players.* 2 to make a particular total, *Sales totalled over £50,000 this month.*

**total**[3] *adjective*
complete; including everything.
**totally** *adverb*

**totalitarian** *adjective*
(*say* toh-tal-i-**tair**-i-ăn)
of or like a government with only one political party.

**totem-pole** *noun* (**totem-poles**)
a large pole carved or painted by Native Americans.

**totter** *verb* (**totters, tottering, tottered**)
to walk unsteadily; to wobble, *The toddler tottered across the room. The chair on which I was standing tottered, and I nearly fell off.*

**touch**[1] *verb* (**touches, touching, touched**)
1 to feel something with your hand or fingers. 2 to come into contact with something; to hit something gently. 3 to be next to something so that there is no space in between. 4 to interfere with something, *Leave the engine alone; don't touch anything.* 5 to reach, *His temperature touched 104 degrees.* 6 to affect someone's emotions, *We were touched by his sad story.*
**touch down**, to land, *The aircraft touched down.*
**touch up**, to improve something by making small changes or additions.

**touch**[2] *noun* (**touches**)
1 the action of touching. 2 the ability to feel things by touching them. 3 a small amount of something; a small action or piece of work, *the finishing touches*.
4 communication with someone, *We have lost touch with them*. 5 the part of a football-field outside the playing area.
**touch-and-go,** uncertain; risky.

**touchy** *adjective* (**touchier, touchiest**)
easily or quickly offended.

**tough** *adjective* (**tougher, toughest**)
1 strong; hard to break or damage, *tough shoes*. 2 hard to chew, *tough meat*. 3 firm; stubborn; rough or violent, *tough criminals*. 4 difficult, *a tough job*.
**toughly** *adverb*, **toughness** *noun*

**toughen** *verb* (**toughens, toughening, toughened**)
1 to become or to make something stronger or more difficult to break, *The glass in the door was specially toughened*. 2 to make someone or become more resistant to discomfort or suffering, *His time in the army toughened him*.

**tour** *noun* (**tours**)
a journey visiting several places.

**tourist** *noun* (**tourists**)
someone making a tour or visit for pleasure.
**tourism** *noun*

**tournament** *noun* (**tournaments**)
a series of contests, *a chess tournament*.

**tow** *verb* (**tows, towing, towed**)
(rhymes with *go*)
to pull a vehicle, boat, etc. along behind you, *They towed our car to a garage*.

**toward** or **towards** *preposition*
1 in the direction of, *She walked towards the sea*. 2 in relation to, *He behaved badly towards his children*. 3 as a contribution to, *Put the money towards a new bicycle*.

**towel** *noun* (**towels**)
a piece of soft cloth used for drying things.
**towelling** *noun*

**tower**[1] *noun* (**towers**)
1 a tall, narrow building, *Blackpool Tower*. 2 a tall, flat-topped part of a building, *the church tower*.
**tower block,** a tall building containing offices or flats.
**tower crane,** a crane on top of a tall metal tower, used for lifting materials on building sites.

**tower**[2] *verb* (**towers, towering, towered**)
to be very high, *The skyscrapers towered above the city*.

**town** *noun* (**towns**)
a place where there are many houses near to each other, with shops, schools, offices, factories, etc.

**town hall** *noun* (**town halls**)
a building with offices for the local council and usually a hall for public events.

**towpath** *noun* (**towpaths**)
a path beside a canal or river.

**toxic** *adjective*
poisonous.

**toy** *noun* (**toys**)
something to play with.
**toyshop** *noun*

**trace**[1] *noun* (**traces**)
1 a mark left by a person or thing; a sign, *There was no trace of the thief*. 2 a very small amount of something, *They found traces of poison in his stomach*.

**trace**[2] *verb* (**traces, tracing, traced**)
1 to find someone or something after a search; to follow the marks left by a person or thing. 2 to copy a picture, map, etc. by drawing over it on tracing-paper.

**tracing-paper** *noun*
special paper that you can see through, used for copying pictures, maps, etc.

**track**[1] *noun* (**tracks**)
1 a path made by people or animals.
2 marks left by a person or thing. 3 a set of rails for trains, trams, etc. 4 a road or area of ground prepared for racing. 5 a metal belt used instead of wheels on a tank, tractor, etc.
**keep track of,** to know where something is, what someone is doing, etc.

**track**[2] *verb* (**tracks, tracking, tracked**)
1 to follow the marks left by a person or animal. 2 to follow or observe something as it moves.
**tracker** *noun*

**track suit** *noun* (**track suits**)
a warm, loose suit of a kind worn by athletes.

**tract**[1] *noun* (**tracts**)
1 an area of land. 2 a series of connected parts in the body, *the digestive tract*.

**tract**[2] *noun* (**tracts**)
a short pamphlet or essay, often about religion.

**traction** *noun*
1 the ability to grip the ground, *The car's wheels lost traction in the mud*. 2 a medical treatment in which an injured arm, leg, etc, is pulled gently for a long time.
**traction-engine,** a heavy vehicle, usually driven by steam, for pulling a heavy load.

**tractor** *noun* (**tractors**)
a motor vehicle used on farms for pulling heavy machines or loads.

**trade**[1] *noun* (**trades**)
1 buying, selling, or exchanging things.
2 a job; an occupation, especially a craft.
**trademark**, a sign or name used by only one manufacturer.
**trade name**, a name used by only one manufacturer.
**trade wind**, one of the winds that blow continually towards the equator from the tropics.

**trade**[2] *verb* (**trades, trading, traded**)
to buy, sell, or exchange things.
**trade in**, to give a thing to pay part of the cost of something new, *He traded in his motor cycle for a car.*
**trader** *noun*, **tradesman** *noun*

**trade union** *noun* (**trade unions**)
an organized group of workers.
**trade-unionism** *noun*, **trade-unionist** *noun*

**tradition** *noun* (**traditions**)
1 the passing down of beliefs, customs, habits, etc. from one generation to another.
2 something passed on in this way.

**traditional** *adjective*
passed down from one generation to another; of a kind that has existed for a long time, *a traditional rocking-chair.*
**traditionally** *adverb*

**traffic** *noun*
1 cars, buses, lorries, bicycles, etc. travelling on the road. 2 trade, *the drug traffic.*
**traffic-light**, a light that controls traffic.
**traffic warden**, someone whose job is to control the movement and parking of vehicles.

**tragedy** *noun* (**tragedies**)
1 a serious play about sad events, *Shakespeare's 'Hamlet' is a tragedy.* 2 a very sad event, *Her death was a tragedy.*
**tragic** *adjective*, **tragically** *adverb*

**trail**[1] *noun* (**trails**)
1 a path through the countryside or a forest. 2 the scent and marks left behind an animal as it moves. 3 marks left behind by someone or something.

**trail**[2] *verb* (**trails, trailing, trailed**)
1 to follow the scent or marks left by a person or animal. 2 to drag something behind you; to be dragged along in this way. 3 to follow someone at a distance or at a slower speed, *A few walkers trailed behind the others.* 4 to hang down or float loosely, *She wore a long, trailing scarf.*

**trailer** *noun* (**trailers**)
1 a vehicle that is pulled along by a car or lorry. 2 a short film advertising a film or television programme that will soon be shown.

**train**[1] *noun* (**trains**)
1 a group of railway coaches or trucks joined together and pulled by an engine.
2 a number of people or animals making a journey together, *a camel train.* 3 a series, *a train of events.* 4 a long part of a dress that trails on the ground.

**train**[2] *verb* (**trains, training, trained**)
1 to give someone skill or practice in something. 2 to practise, *She was training for the race.* 3 to make something grow in a particular direction, *Roses can be trained on trellises.* 4 to aim a gun, *He trained his rifle on the bridge.*
**trainer** *noun*

**trainers** *plural noun*
special shoes with a soft sole to hold and protect the foot, worn for running and jogging and also as part of a fashionable set of clothes.

**traitor** *noun* (**traitors**)
someone who betrays his or her country or friends.
**traitorous** *adjective*

**tram** *noun* (**trams**)
(in America, *streetcar*) a bus that runs along rails set in the road.

**tramp**[1] *noun* (**tramps**)
1 someone without a home or job who walks from place to place. 2 a long walk.
3 the sound of heavy footsteps.
**tramp steamer**, a steamship carrying cargo.

**tramp**[2] *verb* (**tramps, tramping, tramped**)
1 to walk with heavy footsteps. 2 to walk for a long distance.

**trample** *verb* (**tramples, trampling, trampled**)
to tread heavily on something; to crush something with your feet.

**trampoline** *noun* (**trampolines**)
(*say* tramp-ŏ-leen)
a large piece of canvas joined to a frame by springs, used for bouncing up and down on.

**trance** *noun* (**trances**)
an unconscious condition like sleep.

**tranquil** *adjective*
peaceful; quiet; calm.
**tranquillity** *noun*, **tranquilly** *adverb*

**tranquillizer** *noun* (**tranquillizers**)
a drug used to make someone feel calm.

**trans-** *prefix*
across, *a transcontinental train*.

**transaction** *noun* (**transactions**)
a piece of business.
**transact** *verb*

**transatlantic** *adjective*
1 across the Atlantic Ocean, *a transatlantic voyage*. 2 American, *a transatlantic accent*.

**transfer**[1] *verb* (**transfers, transferring, transferred**)
(*say* trans-fer)
to move a person or thing to another place.
**transference** *noun*

**transfer**[2] *noun* (**transfers**)
(*say* trans-fer)
1 the moving of a person or thing to another place. 2 a piece of paper with a picture or design that can be applied to a surface by soaking or heating the paper.

**transform** *verb* (**transforms, transforming, transformed**)
to make a great change in a person or thing, *The caterpillar is transformed into a butterfly*.
**transformation** *noun*

**transformer** *noun* (**transformers**)
a device to change the voltage of electric current.

**transfusion** *noun* (**transfusions**)
putting blood from one person into another person's body.

**transistor** *noun* (**transistors**)
1 a tiny electronic device that controls a flow of electricity. 2 a portable radio that uses transistors to strengthen the signal it receives.

**transition** *noun* (**transitions**)
a change from one thing to another.
**transitional** *adjective*

**transitive** *adjective*
used with a direct object, '*Damage*' and '*release*' are transitive verbs.
**transitively** *adverb*

**translate** *verb* (**translates, translating, translated**)
to put something into another language, *This German book has been translated into English*.
**translation** *noun*, **translator** *noun*

**translucent** *adjective*
that allows light to shine through, but which you cannot see through, *Frosted glass is translucent but not transparent*.

**transmission** *noun* (**transmissions**)
1 the transmitting of something. 2 the gears, clutch, etc. that transmit power from the engine to the wheels of a vehicle.

**transmit** *verb* (**transmits, transmitting, transmitted**)
1 to broadcast something. 2 to send or pass from one person or place to another.
**transmitter** *noun*

**transparency** *noun* (**transparencies**)
1 being transparent. 2 a type of photograph that lets light through and that can be displayed on a screen by means of a projector.

**transparent** *adjective*
that you can see through.

**transpire** *verb* (**transpires, transpiring, transpired**)
1 to become known, *It transpired that she had been secretly hoarding money for years*. 2 (of plants or animals) to emit moisture through the leaves, skin, etc.

**transplant** *verb* (**transplants, transplanting, transplanted**)
to move a plant, part of a human body, etc. from one place to another.
**transplant** *noun*, **transplantation** *noun*

**transport**[1] *verb* (**transports, transporting, transported**)
(*say* trans-port)
to take people, animals, or things from one place to another.
**transportation** *noun*, **transporter** *noun*

**transport**[2] *noun*
(*say* trans-port)
1 the action of moving people, animals, or things from one place to another. 2 vehicles, ships, or planes.

**trap**[1] *noun* (**traps**)
1 a device to catch animals or people. 2 a plan to capture, detect, or cheat someone. 3 a two-wheeled carriage pulled by a horse. 4 (*slang*) a person's mouth, *Shut your trap!*

**trap**[2] *verb* (**traps, trapping, trapped**)
1 to catch a person or animal in a trap. 2 to capture, detect, or cheat someone.
**trapper** *noun*

**trapdoor** *noun* (**trapdoors**)
a door in a floor, ceiling, or roof.

**trapeze** *noun* (**trapezes**)
a bar hanging from two ropes, used by acrobats.

**trapezium** *noun* (**trapeziums**)
a four-sided figure that has only two parallel sides, which are of different length.

**trapezoid** *noun* (**trapezoids**)
a four-sided figure with no two sides parallel.

**trash** *noun*
rubbish; nonsense.
**trashy** *adjective*

**travel**[1] *verb* (**travels, travelling, travelled**)
to move from one place to another.

**travel**[2] *noun*
the action of travelling.
**travel agent**, someone whose job is to arrange travel and holidays for people.

**traveller** *noun* (**travellers**)
1 someone who is making a journey or who often makes journeys. 2 a commercial traveller. 3 a gypsy; a person who does not settle in one place.
**traveller's cheque**, a cheque for a fixed amount of money that is sold by banks and that can be exchanged for money in foreign countries.

**trawler** *noun* (**trawlers**)
a fishing-boat that pulls a large net behind it.

**tray** *noun* (**trays**)
a flat piece of wood, metal, or plastic, usually with raised edges, used for carrying food, cups, plates, etc.

**treacherous** *adjective*
1 not loyal. 2 dangerous, *treacherous quicksands.*
**treacherously** *adverb*, **treachery** *noun*

**treacle** *noun*
a thick, sweet, sticky liquid.

**tread**[1] *verb* (**treads, treading, trod, trodden**)
to walk or put your foot on something, *Who has trodden on the flowers? He trod on them.*

**tread**[2] *noun* (**treads**)
1 a sound or way of walking. 2 the part of a staircase or ladder that you put your foot on. 3 the part of a tyre that touches the ground.

**treason** *noun*
the action of betraying your own country.

**treasure**[1] *noun* (**treasures**)
1 valuable things, like jewels or money. 2 a precious thing.
**treasure hunt**, a search for hidden valuable things; a game in which you try to find something that is hidden.

**treasure**[2] *verb* (**treasures, treasuring, treasured**)
to think that something is very precious.

**treasurer** *noun* (**treasurers**)
the person in charge of the money of a club, association, etc.

**treasury** *noun* (**treasuries**)
a place where treasure is stored.
**the Treasury**, the government department in charge of a country's money.

**treat**[1] *verb* (**treats, treating, treated**)
1 to behave towards someone or something in a certain way; to deal with something, *She treats her dog badly. How should we treat this problem?* 2 to give medical attention to a person or animal, *He was treated for rheumatism.* 3 to pay for someone else's food, drink, or entertainment, *I'll treat you to an ice-cream.*
**treatment** *noun*

**treat**[2] *noun* (**treats**)
1 something special that gives someone pleasure. 2 the action of paying for someone else's food, drink, or entertainment, *You're not to pay; this is my treat.*

**treaty** *noun* (**treaties**)
an agreement between two or more countries.

**treble**[1] *adjective*
three times as many; three times as much.

**treble**[2] *noun* (**trebles**)
1 a boy with a high singing voice. 2 an amount that is three times the usual size.

**tree** *noun* (**trees**)
a tall plant with leaves, branches, and a thick wooden stem.
**tree diagram**, a diagram that has pairs of lines like the branches of a tree to show results of actions where one of two things may happen, such as the results of tossing a coin several times.

**trek** *verb* (**treks, trekking, trekked**)
to make a long journey, often on foot and usually in a remote part of the world, *We spent our summer holidays trekking through the Himalayas.*
**trek** *noun*

**trellis** *noun* (**trellises**)
a framework of crossing wooden or metal bars, used to support climbing plants.

**tremble** *verb* (**trembles, trembling, trembled**)
to shake gently, especially with fear.

**tremendous** *adjective*
**1** very large. **2** excellent.
**tremendously** *adverb*

**tremor** *noun* (**tremors**)
a shaking or trembling.

**trench** *noun* (**trenches**)
a long hole dug in the ground; a ditch.
**the Trenches,** the fighting that took place in trenches during the First World War.

**trend** *noun* (**trends**)
the general direction in which something is going; a tendency.

**trendy** *adjective* (**trendier, trendiest**)
(*informal*) fashionable; trying to be up to date.
**trendily** *adverb*, **trendiness** *noun*

**trespass** *verb* (**trespasses, trespassing, trespassed**)
to go on someone's land or property without permission.
**trespasser** *noun*

**trestle** *noun* (**trestles**)
one of a set of supports on which you place a board to make a table.
**trestle-table,** a table made in this way.

**trial** *noun* (**trials**)
**1** trying something to see how well it works. **2** examining the charges against someone in a lawcourt.
**by trial and error,** by trying out different methods until you find one that works.
**on trial,** being tried out; being examined in a lawcourt.

**triangle** *noun* (**triangles**)
**1** a flat shape with three straight sides and three corners. **2** a chiming percussion instrument made from a metal rod bent into this shape.
**triangular** *adjective*

**tribe** *noun* (**tribes**)
a group of families living together, ruled by a chief.
**tribal** *adjective*, **tribesman** *noun*

**tributary** *noun* (**tributaries**)
a river or stream that flows into a larger one or a lake.

**tribute** *noun* (**tributes**)
a speech, gift, etc. to show that you like or respect someone.

**trick**[1] *noun* (**tricks**)
**1** something done to deceive or fool someone. **2** a clever action. **3** the winning of one round of a card-game like whist.

**trick**[2] *verb* (**tricks, tricking, tricked**)
to deceive or fool someone.
**trickery** *noun*, **trickster** *noun*

**trickle**[1] *verb* (**trickles, trickling, trickled**)
to flow slowly and in small quantities, *Tears trickled down her face.*

**trickle**[2] *noun* (**trickles**)
a small amount of flowing liquid; a very small amount, *The flood of customers dropped to a trickle by 5 o'clock.*

**tricky** *adjective* (**trickier, trickiest**)
**1** difficult; that needs skill, *a tricky job.*
**2** deceitful; cunning, *a tricky salesman.*

**tricycle** *noun* (**tricycles**)
a vehicle like a bicycle with three wheels.

**tried** past tense and past participle of **try** *verb.*

**trifle** *noun* (**trifles**)
**1** a pudding made of sponge-cake covered with custard, fruit, cream, etc. **2** a very small amount of something. **3** something that has little importance or value.

**trigger** *noun* (**triggers**)
the lever that you pull to fire a gun.

**trillion** *noun* (**trillions**)
**1** a million millions (1,000,000,000,000).
**2** (*old-fashioned use*) a million million millions (1,000,000,000,000,000,000).

**trim**[1] *adjective* (**trimmer, trimmest**)
neat; tidy.

**trim**[2] *verb* (**trims, trimming, trimmed**)
**1** to cut the edges or unwanted parts off something. **2** to decorate a piece of clothing. **3** to arrange sails to suit the wind. **4** to balance a boat or aircraft by arranging its cargo or passengers.

**Trinity** *noun*
**the Trinity,** God regarded as Father, Son, and Holy Spirit.

**trio** *noun* (**trios**)
1 three people or things. 2 a group of three musicians. 3 a piece of music for three musicians.

**trip**[1] *verb* (**trips, tripping, tripped**)
1 to fall over something. 2 to make someone fall over. 3 to move with quick, gentle steps.

**trip**[2] *noun* (**trips**)
1 a journey, usually a short one. 2 the action of falling over something; the action of making someone fall over.

**tripe** *noun*
1 part of the stomach of an ox used as food. 2 (*informal*) nonsense.

**triple** *adjective*
consisting of three parts.
**triple jump,** an event in athletics in which you run up to a line on the ground and then do a hop, a step, and a jump.

**triplet** *noun* (**triplets**)
one of three children or animals born at the same time from the same mother.

**tripod** *noun* (**tripods**)
(*say* try-pod)
a support with three legs, *Fix the camera on a tripod.*

**triumph** *noun* (**triumphs**)
1 a great success; a victory. 2 a celebration of a victory.
**triumphal** *adjective*, **triumphant** *adjective*, **triumphantly** *adverb*

**trivial** *adjective*
not important; not valuable.
**triviality** *noun*, **trivially** *adverb*

**trod** past tense of **tread** *verb*.

**trodden** past participle of **tread** *verb*.

**troll** *noun* (**trolls**)
a kind of dwarf in Scandinavian stories.

**trolley** *noun* (**trolleys**)
1 a small table on wheels. 2 a small cart or truck. 3 a kind of large basket on wheels, used in supermarkets.

**trombone** *noun* (**trombones**)
a large brass musical instrument with a sliding tube.

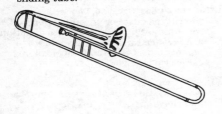

**troop**[1] *noun* (**troops**)
an organized group of soldiers, Scouts, etc.

**troop**[2] *verb* (**troops, trooping, trooped**)
to move along in large numbers.

**troops** *plural noun*
soldiers.

**trophy** *noun* (**trophies**)
a prize or souvenir for a victory or success, *Silver cups were given to the winners as trophies.*

**tropic** *noun* (**tropics**)
a line of latitude about 23½° north of the equator (*Tropic of Cancer*) or about 23½° south of the equator (*Tropic of Capricorn*).
**the tropics,** the hot regions between these two latitudes.
**tropical** *adjective*

**trot**[1] *verb* (**trots, trotting, trotted**)
to run but not to canter or gallop, *The horse trotted along.*

**trot**[2] *noun* (**trots**)
a trotting run.
**on the trot,** (*informal*) one after another; continually busy, *He worked ten days on the trot.*

**trouble**[1] *noun* (**troubles**)
something that upsets, worries, or bothers you; something difficult or unpleasant.
**take trouble,** to take great care in doing something.

**trouble**[2] *verb* (**troubles, troubling, troubled**)
1 to cause trouble to someone. 2 to make an effort to do something, *Nobody ever troubled to check our tickets.*

**troublesome** *adjective*
that causes trouble.

**trough** *noun* (**troughs**)
(*say* trof)
1 a long, narrow box for cattle, horses, etc. to eat or drink from. 2 an area of low pressure between two areas of high pressure.

**trousers** *plural noun*
(in America, *pants*) a piece of clothing worn over the lower half of your body, with two parts to cover your legs.

**trout** *noun* (**trout**)
a freshwater fish.

**trowel** *noun* (**trowels**)
1 a tool for digging small holes, lifting plants, etc. 2 a tool with a flat blade for spreading cement, mortar, etc.

**truant** *noun* (**truants**)
a child who stays away from school without permission.
**play truant**, to stay away from school without permission.
**truancy** *noun*

**truce** *noun* (**truces**)
an agreement to stop fighting for a while.

**truck** *noun* (**trucks**)
**1** a railway wagon for carrying goods. **2** a lorry. **3** a cart.

**trudge** *verb* (**trudges, trudging, trudged**)
to walk slowly and heavily.

**true** *adjective* (**truer, truest**)
**1** real; correct; factual, *a true story*. **2** loyal; faithful, *a true friend*.
**truly** *adverb*

**trump** *noun* (**trumps**)
a playing-card that is of higher value than cards in other suits, *For this game of whist, hearts are trumps*.

**trumpet** *noun* (**trumpets**)
a brass musical instrument.
**trumpeter** *noun*

**truncheon** *noun* (**truncheons**)
a short, thick stick carried by a policeman.

**trundle** *verb* (**trundles, trundling, trundled**)
to move along noisily or awkwardly; to move something in this way.

**trunk** *noun* (**trunks**)
**1** the main stem of a tree. **2** an elephant's long nose. **3** a large box for carrying or storing clothes, etc. **4** the human body except for the head, legs, and arms.
**trunk call**, a long-distance telephone call.
**trunk road**, a main road.

**trunks** *plural noun*
shorts worn for swimming, athletics, etc.

**trust**¹ *verb* (**trusts, trusting, trusted**)
**1** to believe that a person or thing is good, truthful, or strong. **2** to hope, *I trust that you are well*.
**trust someone with something**, to let him or her use it or look after it.

**trust**² *noun*
**1** the feeling that a person or thing can be trusted. **2** responsibility; being trusted.
**trustful** *adjective*, **trustfully** *adverb*

**trustworthy** *adjective*
that can be trusted; reliable.

**truth** *noun* (**truths**)
something that is true; the quality of being true.
**truthful** *adjective*, **truthfully** *adverb*, **truthfulness** *noun*

**try**¹ *verb* (**tries, trying, tried**)
**1** to attempt. **2** to use or do something to see if it works, *Try sleeping on your back*. **3** to attempt to find out, in a lawcourt, whether someone is guilty or not. **4** to annoy someone, *You really do try me with your constant complaining*.
**try it on**, (*informal*) to see how annoying, cheeky, etc. you can be without getting into trouble.
**try on**, to put on clothes to see if they fit.
**try out**, to use or do something to see if it works.

**try**² *noun* (**tries**)
**1** an attempt. **2** in Rugby football, putting the ball down on the ground behind your opponents' goal so as to score points.

**T-shirt** *noun* (**T-shirts**)
a shirt or vest with short sleeves.

**tub** *noun* (**tubs**)
a round container, *a tub of ice-cream*.

**tuba** *noun* (**tubas**)
(*say* **tew**-bă)
a large brass musical instrument with a deep sound.

**tube** *noun* (**tubes**)
**1** a long, thin, hollow piece of metal, plastic, rubber, glass, etc. **2** a long, hollow container, *a tube of toothpaste*. **3** the underground railway in London, *She goes to work by tube*.
**tubing** *noun*

**tubular** *adjective*
shaped like a tube.

**tuck**[1] *verb* (**tucks, tucking, tucked**)
to push the loose end of something into a tidy place.
**tuck in,** (*informal*) to eat vigorously.
**tuck up,** to put the bedclothes snugly round someone.

**tuck**[2] *noun* (**tucks**)
**1** a flat fold stitched in a garment.
**2** (*slang*) food, especially the kind which children enjoy eating.
**tuck-shop,** (*slang*) a shop that sells tuck to children.

**Tudor** *noun* (**Tudors**)
a member of a royal family that ruled England from 1485 to 1603, *Henry VIII and Elizabeth I were Tudors.*
**Tudor** *adjective*

**Tuesday** *noun* (**Tuesdays**)
the third day of the week.

**tuft** *noun* (**tufts**)
a bunch of threads, grass, hair, feathers, etc. held or growing together.

**tug**[1] *noun* (**tugs**)
**1** a hard or sudden pull. **2** a powerful boat used for towing ships.
**tug of war,** a contest between two teams pulling a rope from opposite ends.

**tug**[2] *verb* (**tugs, tugging, tugged**)
to pull hard.

**tulip** *noun* (**tulips**)
a brightly-coloured flower that grows from a bulb in springtime.

**tumble** *verb* (**tumbles, tumbling, tumbled**)
to fall over or down.

**tumble drier** *noun* (**tumble driers**)
a machine that dries washed clothes, etc. by turning them over many times in heated air.

**tumbler** *noun* (**tumblers**)
**1** a drinking-glass with no stem or handle.
**2** an acrobat.

**tummy** *noun* (**tummies**)
(*informal*) the stomach.

**tumour** *noun* (**tumours**)
(*say* **tew**-mer)
a diseased growth on or in the body.

**tumult** *noun* (**tumults**)
(*say* **tew**-mult)
an uproar.
**tumultuous** *adjective*

**tuna** *noun* (**tuna** or **tunas**)
(*say* **tew**-nă)
a large sea-fish used as food.

**tundra** *noun*
a large area of flat land in northern Canada and Siberia with no trees and with soil that is frozen for most of the year.

**tune**[1] *noun* (**tunes**)
a short piece of music; a pleasant series of musical notes.
**in tune,** at the correct musical pitch.
**tuneful** *adjective*, **tuneless** *adjective*

**tune**[2] *verb* (**tunes, tuning, tuned**)
**1** to put a musical instrument in tune. **2** to adjust a radio or television set so as to receive a particular programme. **3** to adjust an engine so that it works smoothly.
**tuner** *noun*

**tunic** *noun* (**tunics**)
(*say* **tew**-nik)
a long or close-fitting jacket.

**tunnel**[1] *noun* (**tunnels**)
a long hole made under the ground or through a hill, especially for a railway.

**tunnel**[2] *verb* (**tunnels, tunnelling, tunnelled**)
to make a tunnel.

**turban** *noun* (**turbans**)
a covering for your head made by wrapping a long strip of cloth round it.

**turbine** *noun* (**turbines**)
a motor that is driven by a flow of water or gas.

**turbo** *noun* (**turbos**)
a turbocharger; a car fitted with a turbocharger.

**turbocharger** *noun* (**turbochargers**)
a device driven by a turbine fitted to a vehicle's exhaust, supplying the vehicle's engine with air under pressure.

**twice**

**turbulent** *adjective*
 violent; not controlled, *turbulent waves*.
 **turbulence** *noun*

**turf** *noun* (**turfs** or **turves**)
 **1** short grass and the soil it is growing on.
 **2** a piece of grass and soil cut out of the ground.

**Turk** *noun* (**Turks**)
 a Turkish person.

**turkey** *noun* (**turkeys**)
 a large bird used for its meat.

**Turkish** *adjective*
 of Turkey.
 **Turkish bath**, a bath in steam or hot air.
 **Turkish delight**, a sweet consisting of lumps like jelly covered in powdered sugar.

**turmoil** *noun* (**turmoils**)
 a great disturbance; confusion.

**turn**¹ *verb* (**turns, turning, turned**)
 **1** to move round; to move to a new direction. **2** to become, *He turned pale*. **3** to change, *The frog turned into a prince*. **4** to make something change, *She turned the milk into cheese*. **5** to move a switch, tap, etc. to control something, *Turn on the radio*.
 **turn down**, to reduce the volume, flow, etc.; to reject something.
 **turn out**, to happen; to put out; to empty a place or thing so as to clean or search it, *Wait and see how things turn out. Turn out the cat before you go to bed. I'm going to turn out the cupboard under the stairs.*
 **turn up**, to appear or arrive; to increase the volume, flow, etc., *He always turns up when you least expect him. Turn up the heating.*

**turn**² *noun* (**turns**)
 **1** the action of turning. **2** a place where a road bends; a junction. **3** the proper time for something to happen, *It's your turn to wash up*. **4** a short performance in a show. **5** (*informal*) an attack of illness; a nervous shock, *It gave me a nasty turn*.
 **good turn**, a helpful action.
 **in turn**, first one and then the other; following one after another.

**turnip** *noun* (**turnips**)
 a plant with a large, round, white root used as a vegetable.

**turnover** *noun* (**turnovers**)
 a small pie made of pastry folded over fruit, jam, etc.

**turnstile** *noun* (**turnstiles**)
 a revolving gate that lets through one person at a time.

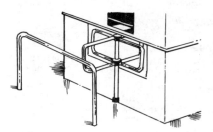

**turntable** *noun* (**turntables**)
 the revolving part of a record-player that you put the record on.

**turpentine** *noun*
 (*say* ter-pĕn-tyn)
 an oil used to make paint thinner and to clean paintbrushes.

**turquoise** *noun*
 (*say* ter-kwoiz)
 **1** sky-blue or greenish-blue. **2** a blue jewel.

**turret** *noun* (**turrets**)
 **1** a small tower in a castle. **2** a revolving structure containing a gun.

**turtle** *noun* (**turtles**)
 a sea-animal that looks like a tortoise.
 **turn turtle**, to capsize.

**tusk** *noun* (**tusks**)
 a long pointed tooth that sticks out of the mouth of an elephant, walrus, or boar.

**tutor** *noun* (**tutors**)
 a teacher, especially one who teaches one person at a time.

**TV** short for **television**.

**tweed** *noun*
 a thick, rough woollen cloth.

**tweezers** *plural noun*
 a small tool for gripping or picking up small things like stamps and hairs.

**twelve** *noun* (**twelves**)
 the number 12, one more than eleven.
 **twelfth** *adjective* and *noun*

**twenty** *noun* (**twenties**)
 the number 20, one more than nineteen.
 **twentieth** *adjective* and *noun*

**twice** *adverb*
 **1** two times; on two occasions. **2** double the amount.

**twiddle** *verb* (**twiddles, twiddling, twiddled**)
to turn something round or over and over
in an idle way, *He just twiddled his
thumbs*.

**twig** *noun* (**twigs**)
a short, thin branch.

**twilight** *noun*
the time just before sunrise or just after
sunset; the dim light at these times.

**twin** *noun* (**twins**)
1 one of two children or animals born at the
same time from one mother. 2 one of two
things that are exactly alike.

**twine** *noun*
strong, thin string.

**twinkle** *verb* (**twinkles, twinkling, twinkled**)
to sparkle.

**twirl** *verb* (**twirls, twirling, twirled**)
to turn round and round quickly; to cause
something to turn in this way.

**twist**[1] *verb* (**twists, twisting, twisted**)
1 to turn something round, *He twisted my
arm*. 2 to turn round or from side to side,
*The river twisted along the valley*. 3 to bend
out of its proper shape, *My bicycle's front
wheel is twisted*.

**twist**[2] *noun* (**twists**)
a twisting movement or action.
**round the twist**, (*slang*) mad.

**twister** *noun* (**twisters**)
(*informal*) 1 someone who swindles people.
2 (*in America*) a tornado.

**twitch** *verb* (**twitches, twitching, twitched**)
to jerk; to move suddenly and quickly, *The
rabbit was twitching its nose*.

**twitter** *verb* (**twitters, twittering, twittered**)
to make quick chirping sounds, *The
sparrows twittered*.

**two** *noun* (**twos**)
the number 2, one more than one.
**in two minds**, undecided.
**two-piece**, consisting of two separate parts,
*a two-piece suit*.

**tying** present participle of **tie** *verb*.

**type**[1] *noun* (**types**)
1 a group or class of similar people or
things; a kind or sort. 2 letters, figures, etc.
designed and made for use in printing,
*Movable type was invented in Germany*.

**type**[2] *verb* (**types, typing, typed**)
to write something with a typewriter; to
use a typewriter.
**typist** *noun*

**typewriter** *noun* (**typewriters**)
a machine with keys that you press to
print letters or figures on a sheet of paper.
**typewritten** *adjective*

**typhoon** *noun* (**typhoons**)
a violent windy storm.

**typical** *adjective*
1 belonging to a particular type of person
or thing, *a typical saloon car has seats for
four people*. 2 usual in a particular person
or thing, *She worked with typical
thoroughness*.
**typically** *adverb*

**tyranny** *noun* (**tyrannies**)
(*say* ti-ră-ni)
a cruel or unjust way of ruling people.
**tyrannical** *adjective*, **tyrannous** *adjective*

**tyrant** *noun* (**tyrants**)
(*say* ty-rănt)
someone who rules people cruelly or
unjustly.

**tyre** *noun* (**tyres**)
a circle of rubber round the rim of a wheel,
*Tyres are usually hollow tubes filled with
air*.

# Uu

**udder** *noun* (**udders**)
the part of a cow, goat, etc. from which milk is taken.

**UFO** *noun* (**UFOs**)
(short for *unidentified flying object*)
a flying object that cannot be explained, and is thought to be a spacecraft from a planet other than Earth.

**ugly** *adjective* (**uglier, ugliest**)
1 not beautiful; unpleasant to look at.
2 threatening; dangerous, *an ugly crowd*.
**ugliness** *noun*

**ulcer** *noun* (**ulcers**)
a sore on the surface of the body or on one of its organs, *a stomach ulcer*.

**ultimate** *adjective*
last; final, *the ultimate weapon*.
**ultimately** *adverb*

**ultra-** *prefix*
beyond, *ultraviolet light*.

**ultraviolet** *adjective*
(of light) beyond the violet end of the spectrum.

**umbilical cord** *noun* (**umbilical cords**)
the tube connecting the bodies of a mother and her baby until the baby is born.

**umbrella** *noun* (**umbrellas**)
a mushroom-shaped piece of cloth stretched over a folding frame, used to protect yourself from rain or snow.

**umpire** *noun* (**umpires**)
a referee in cricket, tennis, and some other games.

**un-** *prefix*
not, *uncommon*.

**unable** *adjective*
not able, *She was unable to hear*.

**unanimous** *adjective*
(*say* yoo-**nan**-i-mŭs)
that everyone agrees to, *a unanimous decision*.
**unanimity** *noun*, **unanimously** *adverb*

**unavoidable** *adjective*
that you cannot avoid; bound to happen.
**unavoidably** *adverb*

**unbearable** *adjective*
that you cannot bear or endure.
**unbearably** *adverb*

**unbelievable** *adjective*
1 that you cannot believe. 2 amazing.
**unbelievably** *adverb*

**uncanny** *adjective* (**uncannier, uncanniest**)
1 strange and rather frightening, *Hyenas make an uncanny sound like laughter*.
2 difficult to explain, *The computer forecast the results of the election with uncanny accuracy*.

**uncertain** *adjective*
1 not certain, *He is uncertain about what to do*. 2 not reliable, *uncertain weather*.
**uncertainly** *adverb*, **uncertainty** *noun*

**uncle** *noun* (**uncles**)
the brother of your father or mother; your aunt's husband.

**uncomfortable** *adjective*
not comfortable.
**uncomfortably** *adverb*

**unconscious** *adjective*
1 not conscious. 2 not aware, *I was unconscious of doing anything wrong*.
**unconsciously** *adverb*, **unconsciousness** *noun*

**uncontrollable** *adjective*
that you cannot control or stop.
**uncontrollably** *adverb*

**uncountable** *adjective*
that cannot be counted.
**uncountable noun**, a type of noun which is the name of something that cannot be counted, and which is used with 'a lot of', *'Happiness'* and *'information'* are uncountable nouns.

**uncover** *verb* (**uncovers, uncovering, uncovered**)
1 to take the cover or top off something. 2 to reveal something, *The police have uncovered a huge fraud*.

**undecided** *adjective*
not decided; uncertain.

**under**[1] *preposition*
1 lower than; below, *under the desk*. 2 less than, *under 5 years old*. 3 ruled or controlled by, *under his command*. 4 in the process of; undergoing, *The road is under repair*. 5 using; moving by means of, *under its own steam*.

**under**[2] *adverb*
in or to a lower place, *The diver went under*.

**underclothes** *plural noun*
underwear.
**underclothing** *noun*

**underdeveloped** *adjective*
not fully developed; not rich; not yet modernized, *an underdeveloped country.*

**underfoot** *adverb*
1 on the ground, *There was a thick carpet of leaves underfoot.* 2 under someone's feet, *The flag fell to the ground and was trampled underfoot.*

**undergo** *verb* (**undergoes, undergoing, underwent, undergone**)
to experience or suffer something; to pass through something, *The coffee beans undergo a process of drying and roasting.*

**undergraduate** *noun* (**undergraduates**)
a student at a university who has not yet taken a degree.

**underground**[1] *noun* (**undergrounds**)
(in America, *subway*) a railway that runs through tunnels under the ground.

**underground**[2] *adverb* and *adjective*
1 under the ground. 2 done or working in secret.

**undergrowth** *noun*
bushes and other plants growing under tall trees.

**underhand** *adjective*
secret and deceitful.

**underlay** *noun* (**underlays**)
a floor covering underneath a carpet.

**underlie** *verb* (**underlies, underlying, underlay, underlain**)
1 to be or lie under something. 2 to be the basis or explanation for something, *Hard work underlies the team's success this season.*

**underline** *verb* (**underlines, underlining, underlined**)
1 to draw a line under a word. 2 to show something clearly, *John's accident underlines what I was saying about being careful.*

**undermine** *verb* (**undermines, undermining, undermined**)
1 to make a hollow or tunnel beneath something. 2 to weaken something gradually.

**underneath** *preposition* and *adverb*
below; under.

**underpants** *plural noun*
underwear worn under trousers.

**underpass** *noun* (**underpasses**)
a place where one road or path goes under another.

**understand** *verb* (**understands, understanding, understood**)
1 to know what something means, what it is, or how it works, *She understood what the Frenchman said.* 2 to learn; to have heard, *I understand he has measles.*
**understandable** *adjective*, **understandably** *adverb*

**understanding**[1] *noun*
1 the power to understand or think; intelligence. 2 agreement; harmony. 3 sympathy; tolerance.

**understanding**[2] *adjective*
sympathetic and tolerant, *He was very understanding when I was ill.*

**undertake** *verb* (**undertakes, undertaking, undertook, undertaken**)
to agree or promise to do something.

**undertaker** *noun* (**undertakers**)
someone whose job is to arrange funerals.

**underwater** *adjective*
placed, used, or done under water.

**underwear** *noun*
clothes worn next to the skin, under other clothes.

**underworld** *noun*
1 in legends, the place for the spirits of the dead; hell. 2 criminals, *The London underworld.*

**undesirable** *adjective*
not wanted; not liked.

**undeveloped** *adjective*
1 not developed. 2 not rich or up to date, *an undeveloped country.*

**undo** *verb* (**undoes, undoing, undid, undone**)
1 to unfasten something, *I undid the knot. Your shoe is undone.* 2 to destroy the effect of something, *He has undone our good work.*

**undoubted** *adjective*
definite; certain.
**undoubtedly** *adverb*

**undress** *verb* (**undresses, undressing, undressed**)
to take your clothes off; to take someone's clothes off.

**unearth** *verb* (**unearths, unearthing, unearthed**)
1 to dig up something. 2 to find something by searching.

**unearthly** *adjective*
supernatural; strange and frightening, *the unearthly sound of an owl in the night.*

**uneasy** *adjective*
uncomfortable; worried.
**uneasily** *adverb*, **uneasiness** *noun*

**unemployed** *adjective*
without a job.
**unemployment** *noun*

**uneven** *adjective*
1 not level, *an uneven playing-field.* 2 not regular, *an uneven row of teeth.*
**unevenly** *adverb*, **unevenness** *noun*

**unexpected** *adjective*
not expected; surprising.
**unexpectedly** *adverb*, **unexpectedness** *noun*

**unfair** *adjective*
not fair; unjust.
**unfairly** *adverb*, **unfairness** *noun*

**unfamiliar** *adjective*
not familiar.

**unfasten** *verb* (**unfastens, unfastening, unfastened**)
to open something that has been fastened.

**unfavourable** *adjective*
not helpful; not approving.
**unfavourably** *adverb*

**unfinished** *adjective*
not finished.

**unfold** *verb* (**unfolds, unfolding, unfolded**)
1 to open; to spread something out. 2 to make something known slowly; to become known slowly, *as the story unfolds.*

**unforgettable** *adjective*
that you cannot forget.

**unforgivable** *adjective*
that you cannot forgive.

**unfortunate** *adjective*
1 unlucky. 2 that you regret, *an unfortunate argument.*
**unfortunately** *adverb*

**unfreeze** *verb* (**unfreezes, unfreezing, unfroze, unfrozen**)
to stop being frozen; to cause something to stop being frozen.

**unfriendly** *adjective*
not friendly.
**unfriendliness** *noun*

**ungrateful** *adjective*
not grateful.
**ungratefully** *adverb*

**unhappy** *adjective* (**unhappier, unhappiest**)
1 not happy. 2 that you regret, *an unhappy remark.*
**unhappily** *adverb*, **unhappiness** *noun*

**unhealthy** *adjective* (**unhealthier, unhealthiest**)
not healthy.

**unheard** *adjective*
not heard.
**unheard-of,** never known or done before; extraordinary.

**unicorn** *noun* (**unicorns**)
(*say* **yoo**-ni-korn)
an imaginary animal like a horse with a long, straight horn growing out of the front of its head.

**uniform**[1] *noun* (**uniforms**)
the special clothes worn by members of an army, organization, school, etc.
**uniformed** *adjective*

**uniform**[2] *adjective*
always the same; not changing.
**uniformity** *noun*, **uniformly** *adverb*

**unify** *verb* (**unifies, unifying, unified**)
to make several things, especially countries, into one thing; to join together.
**unification** *noun*

**unimportant** *adjective*
not important.
**unimportance** *noun*

**uninhabited** *adjective*
where nobody lives.

**unintentional** *adjective*
not deliberate.
**unintentionally** *adverb*

**uninterested** *adjective*
not interested.

> USAGE: Do not confuse **uninterested** with **disinterested**, which means not prejudiced or not favouring one side more than the other.

**uninteresting** *adjective*
not interesting.

**union** *noun* (**unions**)
1 the joining of things together; a united thing. 2 a trade union.
**Union Jack**, the British flag.

**unique** *adjective*
(*say* yoo-**neek**)
that is the only one of its kind; very unusual, *This jewel is unique.*
**uniquely** *adverb*, **uniqueness** *noun*

**unisex** *adjective*
for either men or women; designed to suit men or women, *a unisex bicycle. A sweatshirt is a unisex piece of clothing.*

**unison** *noun*
(*say* **yoo**-ni-sŏn)
**in unison**, making the same sound together; agreeing.

**unit** *noun* (**units**)
1 an amount used in measuring or counting, *Centimetres are units of length, and pence are units of money.* 2 a single person or thing. 3 a group of people or things that belong together.

**unite** *verb* (**unites, uniting, united**)
to form into one thing; to join together.

**unity** *noun* (**unities**)
1 being united; agreement. 2 a complete thing.

**universal** *adjective*
concerning or including everyone and everything.
**universal joint**, a joint which allows movement in all directions.
**universally** *adverb*

**universe** *noun*
everything that exists; the whole of space and the stars, etc. in it.

**university** *noun* (**universities**)
a place where people go to study for degrees after they have left school.

**unjust** *adjective*
not fair; not just.
**unjustly** *adverb*

**unkind** *adjective* (**unkinder, unkindest**)
not kind, *an unkind remark.*
**unkindly** *adverb*, **unkindness** *noun*

**unknown** *adjective*
not known, *He is unknown to me.*

**unleaded** *adjective*
not containing lead, *This car runs on unleaded petrol.*

**unless** *conjunction*
except when; if not, *We shall not go unless we have to. You cannot come into this club unless you are a member.*

**unlike**[1] *preposition*
differently from, *Unlike me, she enjoys sport.*

**unlike**[2] *adjective*
not similar; different, *The two children are unlike.*

**unlikely** *adjective* (**unlikelier, unlikeliest**)
not likely to happen or be true.

**unload** *verb* (**unloads, unloading, unloaded**)
to take off the things carried by a car, lorry, boat, etc.

**unlock** *verb* (**unlocks, unlocking, unlocked**)
to open a door, box, etc. with a key.

**unlucky** *adjective* (**unluckier, unluckiest**)
not lucky.
**unluckily** *adverb*

**unmistakable** *adjective*
obvious; definite.
**unmistakably** *adverb*

**unnecessary** *adjective*
not necessary.
**unnecessarily** *adverb*

**unoccupied** *adjective*
not occupied; empty.

**unpack** *verb* (**unpacks, unpacking, unpacked**)
to take things out of a suitcase, box, etc.

**unpleasant** *adjective*
not pleasant.
**unpleasantly** *adverb*, **unpleasantness** *noun*

**unplug** *verb* (**unplugs, unplugging, unplugged**)
to disconnect an electrical device by taking its plug out of the socket.

**unpopular** *adjective*
not popular.
**unpopularity** *noun*

**unravel** *verb* (**unravels, unravelling, unravelled**)
to undo a piece of knitting, or something that is tangled.

**unrest** *noun*
1 riots, revolts, etc. 2 a discontented feeling, *There was unrest among the workers.*

**unroll** *verb* (**unrolls, unrolling, unrolled**)
to open something that has been rolled up.

**unruly** *adjective* (**unrulier, unruliest**)
(*say* un-**roo**-li)
difficult to control; behaving badly.
**unruliness** *noun*

**unscrew** *verb* (**unscrews, unscrewing, unscrewed**)
to undo something that has been screwed up.

**unseen** *adjective*
not seen; invisible.

**unselfish** *adjective*
not selfish.
**unselfishly** *adverb*, **unselfishness** *noun*

**unskilled** *adjective*
1 (of a person) not having special training for a job. 2 (of a job) not needing workers with special training.

**unsteady** *adjective* (**unsteadier, unsteadiest**)
not steady.
**unsteadily** *adverb*, **unsteadiness** *noun*

**unsuccessful** *adjective*
not successful.
**unsuccessfully** *adverb*

**unsuitable** *adjective*
not suitable.
**unsuitably** *adverb*

**untidy** *adjective* (**untidier, untidiest**)
not tidy.
**untidily** *adverb*, **untidiness** *noun*

**untie** *verb* (**unties, untying, untied**)
to undo something that has been tied.

**until** *preposition* and *conjunction*
1 up to a particular time, *The shop is open until 8 o'clock.* 2 up to the time when, *We will help them until they are able to look after themselves.*

**unto** *preposition*
(*old-fashioned use*) to.

**untold** *adjective*
not able to be counted or measured, *untold wealth.*

**untrue** *adjective*
not true.

**untruthful** *adjective*
not telling the truth.
**untruthfully** *adverb*

**unused** *adjective*
(*say* un-**yoozd**)
not used, *an unused stamp.*
**unused to something,** (*say* un-**yoost**) not familiar with something, *He is unused to eating meat.*

**unusual** *adjective*
not usual; strange or rare.
**unusually** *adverb*

**unwaged** *adjective*
not earning a wage, *a reduced fee for unwaged people.*

**unwanted** *adjective*
not wanted.

**unwell** *adjective*
not well; ill.

**unwilling** *adjective*
not willing.
**unwillingly** *adverb*, **unwillingness** *noun*

**unwind** *verb* (**unwinds, unwinding, unwound**)
(rhymes with *find*)
1 to unroll something; to become unrolled. 2 (*informal*) to relax.

**unwrap** *verb* (**unwraps, unwrapping, unwrapped**)
to take something out of what it is wrapped in.

**unzip** *verb* (**unzips, unzipping, unzipped**)
to undo something that has a zip.

**up**[1] *adverb*
1 in or to a standing or upright position.
2 in or to a high or higher place.
3 completely, *Eat up your carrots.* 4 out of bed, *It's time to get up.* 5 finished, *Your time is up.* 6 (*informal*) happening, *Something is up.*
**up against something,** faced with difficulties, dangers, etc.
**up and down,** backwards and forwards; to and fro.
**up to,** until; busy with; capable of; needed from, *We'll be at home up to 9 p.m. What's she up to at the moment? He's up to winning the race. It's up to you to do it.*
**up to date,** suiting what is now needed, known, or fashionable; modern.

**up**[2] *preposition*
in or to a higher position on something, *Climb up the mountain.*

**upgrade** *verb* (**upgrades, upgrading, upgraded**)
to improve something, especially a machine, by replacing some or all of it with something better or more modern, *Alec has just upgraded his music centre by adding a CD player.*

**upheaval** *noun* (**upheavals**)
a sudden or violent change or disturbance.

**uphill** *adjective*
1 sloping upwards. 2 difficult, *an uphill job.*

**uphold** *verb* (**upholds, upholding, upheld**)
to support a decision, statement, or belief, *The headmistress upheld the teacher's version of the story.*

**upholster** *verb* (upholsters, upholstering, upholstered)
to provide furniture with covers, padding, springs, etc.
**upholstery** *noun*

**upkeep** *noun*
the cost of looking after something and keeping it in good condition.

**upland** *noun* (uplands)
a high district.

**upon** *preposition*
on.

**upper** *adjective*
higher.

**upper-case** *adjective*
(*in Printing*) large; in capital letters, '*BBC*' *is in upper-case letters*.

**upper class** *noun* (upper classes)
the people in society who have the highest privileges and titles, etc.
**upper-class** *adjective*

**upright** *adjective*
1 erect; vertical. 2 honest.

**uprising** *noun* (uprisings)
a situation in which people refuse to obey someone in authority, especially the government; a rebellion.

**uproar** *noun*
a loud noise or disturbance.

**upset**[1] *verb* (upsets, upsetting, upset)
(*say* up-**set**)
1 to make someone unhappy. 2 to knock something over; to overturn.

**upset**[2] *noun* (upsets)
(*say* up-**set**)
1 a slight illness, *a stomach upset*. 2 an unexpected result or setback, *Their plans suffered an upset when the holiday was cancelled*.

**upshot** *noun* (upshots)
a result of something happening, *The upshot of it was that they were both given detention*.

**upside down** *adverb*
1 so that the top is at the bottom. 2 into disorder.

**upside-down** *adjective*
1 turned over so that the top is at the bottom. 2 very untidy; in disorder.

**upstairs** *adverb* and *adjective*
to or on a higher floor.

**upstart** *noun* (upstarts)
someone who quickly reaches a position of power even though he or she is relatively young or inexperienced.

**upstream** *adjective*
in the direction opposite to the way a river or stream flows.

**uptight** *adjective*
(*informal*) upset; annoyed; nervous.

**upward**[1] *adjective*
moving or directed upwards, *an upward glance*.

**upward**[2] or **upwards** *adverb*
towards a higher place; up.

**uranium** *noun*
(*say* yoor-**ay**-ni-ŭm)
a valuable metal used as a source of atomic energy.

**urban** *adjective*
of, in, or like a town or city.

**urbanize** (urbanizes, urbanizing, urbanized)
to change a place into a town-like area.
**urbanization** *noun*

**urchin** *noun* (urchins)
a poor or mischievous boy.

**Urdu** *noun*
one of the official languages of Pakistan, related to Hindi and spoken also in India.

**urge**[1] *verb* (urges, urging, urged)
1 to try to make someone do something. 2 to drive people or animals forward.

**urge**[2] *noun* (urges)
a sudden strong desire or wish, *She felt an urge to dive into the cool water*.

**urgent** *adjective*
that must be done or dealt with immediately.
**urgency** *noun*, **urgently** *adverb*

**urinate** *verb* (urinates, urinating, urinated)
(*say* **yoor**-i-nayt)
to pass urine out of the body.
**urination** *noun*

**urine** *noun*
(*say* **yoor**-in)
waste liquid that collects in the bladder and is passed out of the body.
**urinary** *adjective*

**urn** *noun* (**urns**)
1 a large metal container in which water is heated. 2 a kind of vase.

**US** or **USA** short for *United States of America.*

**us** *pronoun*
a word used for *we,* usually when it is the object of a sentence, or comes straight after a preposition, *We thanked him and he thanked us.*

**usable** *adjective*
that you can use.

**usage** *noun* (**usages**)
(*say* **yoo**-sij)
the way that something is used, especially the way that a language is used.

**use**[1] *verb* (**uses, using, used**)
(*say* yooz)
to do a job with something, *Have you used my pen? I am using it now.*
**use-by date,** a date marked on a package of food, showing how long the food can be kept.
**used to,** (*say* **yoost**-too) did in the past; having the habit of doing something, *I used to like her. He's not used to hard work.*
**use up,** to use all of something.
**user** *noun*

**use**[2] *noun* (**uses**)
(*say* yooss)
1 the action of using something; being used. 2 the purpose or value of something, *That money is no use to us.*

**used** *adjective*
(*say* yoozd)
second-hand, *a used car.*

**useful** *adjective*
that can be used a lot; helpful.
**usefully** *adverb,* **usefulness** *noun*

**useless** *adjective*
not useful.
**uselessly** *adverb,* **uselessness** *noun*

**user-friendly** *adjective* (**user-friendlier, user-friendliest**)
designed to be easy to use for someone who does not have technical knowledge, *a user-friendly computer system.*

**usher** *noun* (**ushers**)
someone who shows people to their seats in a theatre, church, etc.

**usherette** *noun* (**usherettes**)
a female usher, especially in a cinema.

**usual** *adjective*
such as happens often or all the time; expected.
**usually** *adverb*

**utensil** *noun* (**utensils**)
(*say* yoo-ten-sil)
a device used in the house, especially in the kitchen.

**uterus** *noun* (**uteri**)
the womb.

**utilize** *verb* (**utilizes, utilizing, utilized**)
to use something.
**utilization** *noun*

**utmost** *adjective*
greatest, *Change the fuse with the utmost care.*

**utter**[1] *verb* (**utters, uttering, uttered**)
to say something; to make a sound with your mouth, *She uttered a scream.*
**utterance** *noun*

**utter**[2] *adjective*
complete; absolute, *He is an utter fool.*
**utterly** *adverb*

**U-turn** *noun* (**U-turns**)
turning a vehicle round in one movement so that it faces in the opposite direction, *This traffic sign means no U-turns:*

# Vv

**vacant** *adjective*
1 empty; available. 2 not thoughtful; not
intelligent, *a vacant stare.*
**vacancy** *noun*, **vacantly** *adverb*

**vacation** *noun* (**vacations**)
(*say* vă-**kay**-shŏn)
a holiday, especially between the terms at
a university.

**vaccinate** *verb* (**vaccinates, vaccinating,
vaccinated**)
(*say* **vak**-si-nayt)
to inject someone with a medicine,
especially against smallpox.
**vaccination** *noun*

**vaccine** *noun* (**vaccines**)
(*say* **vak**-seen)
a type of medicine injected into people to
protect them from disease.

**vacuum** *noun* (**vacuums**)
1 a completely empty space; a space
without any air in it. 2 (*informal*) a vacuum
cleaner.
**vacuum cleaner,** a device that sucks up dust
and dirt.
**vacuum flask,** a container with a vacuum
between its two walls, to keep the contents
at an unchanging temperature.

**vagina** *noun* (**vaginas**)
(*say* vă-**jy**-nă)
the passage in the female body between
the vulva and the womb.

**vague** *adjective* (**vaguer, vaguest**)
not definite; not clear.
**vaguely** *adverb*, **vagueness** *noun*

**vain** *adjective* (**vainer, vainest**)
1 too proud of yourself, especially of how
you look. 2 useless, *They made vain
attempts to save her.*
**in vain,** with no result; uselessly.
**vainly** *adverb*

**valentine** *noun* (**valentines**)
1 a card sent on St Valentine's Day (14
February) to someone you love. 2 the
person you send a valentine to.

**valiant** *adjective*
courageous.
**valiantly** *adverb*

**valid** *adjective*
that can be accepted or used; legal, *This
passport is not valid.*
**validity** *noun*

**valley** *noun* (**valleys**)
an area of low land between hills.

**valour** *noun*
bravery, especially in fighting.

**valuable** *adjective*
1 worth a lot of money. 2 of great
usefulness or importance, *a valuable
lesson. She gave me some valuable advice.*

**valuables** *plural noun*
things that are worth a lot of money.

**value**[1] *noun* (**values**)
1 the amount of money that something
could be sold for. 2 how useful or important
something is.
**value-added tax,** a tax on the value of goods
or services.
**valueless** *adjective*

**value**[2] *verb* (**values, valuing, valued**)
1 to think that something is valuable. 2 to
estimate the value of a thing, *The estate
agent valued our house.*
**valuation** *noun*, **valuer** *noun*

**valve** *noun* (**valves**)
1 a device used to control the flow of gas or
liquid. 2 a device that controls the flow of
electricity.

**vampire** *noun* (**vampires**)
a mythical creature that sucks people's
blood.

**van** *noun* (**vans**)
a small lorry with a covered area for goods
at the back.

**vandal** *noun* (**vandals**)
someone who deliberately breaks or spoils
things, *Vandals broke the seats in the park.*
**vandalism** *noun*

**vane** *noun* (**vanes**)
1 a pointer that shows which way the wind
is blowing. 2 a blade or surface that moves,
or is moved by, air or water, *Windmills
and propellers have vanes.*

**vanilla** *noun*
the flavouring used for white ice-cream.

**vanish** *verb* (**vanishes, vanishing, vanished**)
to disappear.

**vanity** *noun*
being too proud of yourself.

**vanquish** *verb* (**vanquishes, vanquishing, vanquished**)
to gain a victory over someone.

**vapour** *noun* (**vapours**)
a visible gas produced by heat; steam or mist.

**variable**[1] *adjective*
that varies or changes.

**variable**[2] *noun* (**variables**)
(*in Mathematics*) a quantity that can have various values, represented by a symbol, *In the formula to find the circumference of a circle, $c=2\pi r$, c and r are variables.*

**variation** *noun* (**variations**)
**1** varying; alteration. **2** something that has changed or been changed. **3** the difference between individuals in the same family, race, or species.

**varied** *adjective*
of various kinds.

**variety** *noun* (**varieties**)
**1** a number of different kinds of things, *There was a variety of sweets.* **2** a particular kind of something, *rare varieties of butterflies.* **3** change; a situation where things are not always the same, *a life full of variety.*
**variety show,** an entertainment including items of various kinds.

**various** *adjective*
**1** of different kinds, *for various reasons.*
**2** several, *He uses various names.*

**varnish** *noun* (**varnishes**)
a transparent paint that gives a hard, shiny surface.

**vary** *verb* (**varies, varying, varied**)
**1** to change; to keep changing. **2** to be different, *These cars are the same, though the colours vary.*

**vase** *noun* (**vases**)
(*say* vahz)
a jar used for holding flowers or as an ornament.

**vast** *adjective*
very large; very wide.
**vastly** *adverb,* **vastness** *noun*

**VAT** short for **value-added tax.**

**vat** *noun* (**vats**)
a very large container for liquid.

**vault**[1] *verb* (**vaults, vaulting, vaulted**)
to jump over something, especially with the help of your hands or a pole.

**vault**[2] *noun* (**vaults**)
**1** a vaulting jump. **2** an arched roof. **3** an underground room.

**VCR** short for **video cassette recorder.**

**VDU** short for **visual display unit.**

**veal** *noun*
calf's flesh used as food.

**vector** *noun* (**vectors**)
(*in Mathematics*) a quantity that has size and direction.

**Vedas** *plural noun*
the holy books of the Hindu religion.

**veer** *verb* (**veers, veering, veered**)
to swerve; to change direction.

**vegan** *noun* (**vegans**)
(*say* vee-găn)
someone who neither uses nor eats any products from animals.

**vegetable** *noun* (**vegetables**)
a plant that can be used as food.

**vegetarian** *noun* (**vegetarians**)
(*say* vej-i-**tair**-i-ăn)
someone who does not eat meat.

**vegetation** *noun*
plants that are growing.

**vehicle** *noun* (**vehicles**)
a device for carrying people or things on land or in space, *Cars, lorries, buses, and carts are all vehicles.*

**veil** *noun* (**veils**)
a piece of thin material to cover your face or head.

**vein** *noun* (**veins**)
**1** one of the tubes in the body through which blood flows towards the heart. **2** a line or streak on a leaf, rock, insect's wing, etc. **3** a long deposit of a mineral in the middle of rock.

vein 2

**velocity** *noun* (**velocities**)
(*say* vil-**os**-ĭ-ti)
**1** speed. **2** (*in Science*) speed in a particular direction, *The astronomer calculated the velocity of the meteor.*

**velvet** *noun*
a kind of thick, soft material, *She wore a velvet skirt.*
**velvety** *adjective*

**venereal** *adjective*
(*say* vin-**eer**-i-ăl)
**venereal disease,** a disease that is passed on by sexual intercourse.

**venetian blind** *noun* (**venetian blinds**)
a type of blind for a window, made of thin, horizontal slats which you can move to control the amount of light that comes through.

**vengeance** *noun*
revenge.
**with a vengeance,** very strongly or effectively.

**venison** *noun*
deer's flesh used as food.

**Venn diagram** *noun* (**Venn diagrams**)
(*in Mathematics*) a diagram that shows relations between sets of things, drawn as circles.

**venom** *noun*
**1** the poison of snakes. **2** hatred; a very bitter feeling towards someone.
**venomous** *adjective*

**vent** *noun* (**vents**)
an opening in something, especially to let out smoke, gas, etc.
**give vent to,** to express your feelings openly, *He gave vent to his anger.*

**ventilate** *verb* (**ventilates, ventilating, ventilated**)
to let air move freely in and out of a place.
**ventilation** *noun*

**ventilator** *noun* (**ventilators**)
a device that lets air move into and out of a place.

**ventriloquist** *noun* (**ventriloquists**)
(*say* ven-**tril**-ŏ-kwist)
an entertainer who makes his or her voice seem to come from a dummy, or from another place.
**ventriloquism** *noun*

**venture**¹ *noun* (**ventures**)
something you decide to do that is dangerous or adventurous.

**venture**² *verb* (**ventures, venturing, ventured**)
to do something or go somewhere which is dangerous, *They ventured into the lion's cave.*

**veranda** *noun* (**verandas**)
(*say* vĕ-**ran**-dă)
a long, open place with a roof and floor along the outside of a house.

**verb** *noun* (**verbs**)
a word that says what someone or something is doing, feeling, etc., *Verbs are words like 'bring', 'eat', 'sit', 'suffer', 'enjoy', 'seem', 'be', 'have', and 'need'.*
**verb phrase,** a group of words that includes a verb and is shorter than a clause, '*Has been running*' *is a verb phrase.*

**verdict** *noun* (**verdicts**)
the decision made by a judge or jury.

**verge** *noun* (**verges**)
a strip of grass beside a road or path.

**verify** *verb* (**verifies, verifying, verified**)
to find or show the truth of something.
**verification** *noun*

**vermin** *noun*
animals, birds, or insects that damage crops or food, or carry diseases, *Rabbits are considered as vermin by some farmers.*

**verruca** *noun* (**verrucas**)
(*say* ver-**oo**-kă)
a wart on the sole of someone's foot.

**versatile** *adjective*
(*say* **ver**-să-tyl)
able to do or be used for many different things.
**versatility** *noun*

**verse** *noun* (**verses**)
**1** poetry. **2** a group of lines in a poem or song. **3** one of the numbered parts of a chapter in the Bible.

**version** *noun* (**versions**)
**1** someone's account of something that has happened, *His version of the accident is different from mine.* **2** something translated or rewritten, *a new version of the Bible.* **3** a particular form of a thing, *a new version of this car.*

**versus** *preposition*
against; competing with, *Arsenal versus Aston Villa.*

**vertebra** *noun* (**vertebrae**)
(*say* **ver**-ti-bră)
one of the bones that form the backbone.

**vertebrate** *noun* (**vertebrates**)
(*say* **ver**-ti-brăt)
an animal with a backbone.

**vertex** *noun* (**vertices**)
(*in Mathematics*) one of the points of a triangle, square, etc.

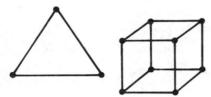

**vertical** *adjective*
at a right angle to a flat surface; directed or moving straight up; upright.
**vertically** *adverb*

**very**[1] *adverb*
extremely, *Ice is very cold.*

**very**[2] *adjective*
exact; actual, *That's the very thing we need!*

**vessel** *noun* (**vessels**)
1 a boat; a ship. 2 a container. 3 a tube inside an animal or plant, carrying blood or some other liquid.

**vest** *noun* (**vests**)
(in America, *undershirt*) a piece of underwear worn on the top half of your body.

**vestry** *noun* (**vestries**)
a room in a church where the priest, etc. or the choir get ready for a service.

**vet** *noun* (**vets**)
a veterinary surgeon.

**veteran** *noun* (**veterans**)
a person with long experience, especially as a soldier.
**veteran car**, a car made before 1917.

**veterinary** *adjective*
(*say* vet-rin-ri)
concerned with the diseases of animals.
**veterinary surgeon**, a person trained to heal sick animals.

**veto** *noun* (**vetoes**)
(*say* vee-toh)
a refusal to let something happen; the right to prohibit something.

**vex** *verb* (**vexes, vexing, vexed**)
to annoy someone; to cause someone worry.
**vexation** *noun*, **vexatious** *adjective*

**VHF** short for *very high frequency*.

**via** *preposition*
(*say* vy-ă)
going through; stopping at, *This train goes to London via Leeds.*

**viaduct** *noun* (**viaducts**)
(*say* vy-ă-dukt)
a long bridge with many arches.

**vibrate** *verb* (**vibrates, vibrating, vibrated**)
to move quickly to and fro; to make a quivering sound.
**vibration** *noun*

**vicar** *noun* (**vicars**)
a member of the clergy who is in charge of a parish.

**vicarage** *noun* (**vicarages**)
the house of a vicar.

**vice**[1] *noun* (**vices**)
1 evil; wickedness. 2 a bad habit or bad feature of someone, *His only vice is eating between meals.*

**vice**[2] *noun* (**vices**)
a device for holding something in place while you work on it.

**vice-president** *noun* (**vice-presidents**)
a deputy for a president.

**vice versa** *adverb*
(*say* vy-si-**ver**-să)
the other way round, 'We talk about them and vice versa' means 'We talk about them and they talk about us'.

**vicinity** *noun* (**vicinities**)
the neighbourhood; the surrounding district, *There are shops in the vicinity of their house.*

**vicious** *adjective*
(*say* vish-ŭs)
cruel; dangerously wicked or strong.
**viciously** *adverb*, **viciousness** *noun*

**victim** *noun* (**victims**)
1 a person who suffers from something, *a polio victim.* 2 someone who is killed, injured, robbed, etc., *The murderer lay in wait for his victim.*

**victor** *noun* (**victors**)
the winner of a battle or contest.

**Victorian** *adjective*
of the time when Queen Victoria reigned (1837–1901).

**victory** *noun* (**victories**)
 success in a battle, contest, or game.
 **victorious** *adjective*

**video**[1] *noun* (**videos**)
 (*say* **vid**-i-oh)
 **1** the recording on tape of pictures and
 sound. **2** a video recorder. **3** a television
 programme or a film recorded on a video
 cassette, *Have you got a video of 'Robin
 Hood'?*
 **video cassette**, a sealed case containing
 videotape.
 **video cassette recorder**, a machine for
 recording pictures and sound on
 videotape.
 **video game**, a game in which you use
 joysticks, etc. to move around pictures
 produced by a computer program and
 shown on a VDU screen.
 **video recorder**, a video cassette recorder.

**video**[2] *verb* (**videoes, videoing, videoed**)
 to record something on videotape.

**videotape** *noun* (**videotapes**)
 magnetic tape suitable for video recording.

**view**[1] *noun* (**views**)
 **1** what you can see from one place, *What a
 lovely view!* **2** someone's opinion, *She has
 strong views about teaching.*
 **in view** or **on view**, that you can see.
 **in view of**, because of.
 **with a view to**, with the intention of.

**view**[2] *verb* (**views, viewing, viewed**)
 to look at something; to consider
 something, *They viewed the paintings. He
 views smoking as a nasty habit.*
 **viewer** *noun*

**vigilant** *adjective*
 (*say* **vij**-i-lănt)
 watchful.
 **vigilance** *noun*, **vigilantly** *adverb*

**vigorous** *adjective*
 full of vigour.
 **vigorously** *adverb*

**vigour** *noun*
 energy; liveliness; strength.

**Viking** *noun* (**Vikings**)
 (*say* **vy**-king)
 one of the Scandinavian pirates or traders
 that sailed to various parts of Europe
 between the 8th and 10th centuries.

**vile** *adjective* (**viler, vilest**)
 disgusting, *a vile smell.*

**village** *noun* (**villages**)
 a group of houses and other buildings in
 the country, *Villages are smaller than
 towns.*
 **villager** *noun*

**villain** *noun* (**villains**)
 a wicked person.
 **villainous** *adjective*, **villainy** *noun*

**vine** *noun* (**vines**)
 a plant on which grapes grow.

**vinegar** *noun*
 a sour liquid used to flavour food, *Do you
 want vinegar on your fish and chips?*

**vineyard** *noun* (**vineyards**)
 (*say* **vin**-yard)
 an area of land where vines are grown to
 produce grapes.

**vintage** *noun* (**vintages**)
 **1** all the grapes that are harvested in one
 season; wine made from these grapes. **2** the
 period in history from which something
 comes, *This furniture is of 1960s vintage.*
 **vintage car**, a car made between 1917 and
 1930.

**vinyl** *noun*
 (*say* **vy**-nil)
 a kind of plastic.

**viola** *noun* (**violas**)
 (*say* vee-**oh**-lă)
 a stringed instrument rather like a violin
 but slightly larger and with a lower pitch.

**violate** *verb* (**violates, violating, violated**)
 **1** to break something like a promise or a
 law. **2** to treat a person or place without
 respect.
 **violation** *noun*, **violator** *noun*

**violence** *noun*
 force that does harm or damage.
 **violent** *adjective*, **violently** *adverb*

**violet** *noun* (**violets**)
 **1** purple. **2** a small plant that usually has
 purple flowers.

**violin** *noun* (**violins**)
a musical instrument with four strings played by a bow.
**violinist** *noun*

**VIP** short for *very important person.*

**viper** *noun* (**vipers**)
a small poisonous snake; an adder.

**virgin** *noun* (**virgins**)
a person, especially a girl or woman, who has not yet had sexual intercourse.
**the Virgin**, Mary, the mother of Jesus.
**virginity** *noun*

**virtual** *adjective*
actual; as good as the real thing, *His silence was a virtual admission that he was guilty.*
**virtually** *adverb*

**virtue** *noun* (**virtues**)
**1** goodness; excellence. **2** a particular kind of goodness, *Honesty is a virtue.*
**virtuous** *adjective*, **virtuously** *adverb*

**virus** *noun* (**viruses**)
(*say* vy-rŭs)
a microscopic creature that can cause disease.

**visa** *noun* (**visas**)
an official mark put on someone's passport by officials of a foreign country to show that the holder of the passport has permission to enter that country.

**visible** *adjective*
that you can see, *The ship was visible on the horizon.*
**visibility** *noun*, **visibly** *adverb*

**vision** *noun* (**visions**)
**1** the power to see. **2** something that you see or imagine, especially in a dream. **3** imagination; understanding, *a leader with vision.*

**visit** *verb* (**visits, visiting, visited**)
to go to see a person or place; to stay somewhere for a while.
**visiting-card**, a card with your name and address printed on it.
**visit** *noun*, **visitor** *noun*

**visor** *noun* (**visors**)
(*say* vy-zer)
the part of a helmet that closes over your face.

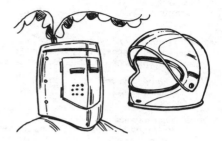

**visual** *adjective*
of or used in seeing.
**visual aids**, pictures, films, etc. used by teachers or people giving talks.
**visual display unit**, a screen on which a computer displays information.
**visually** *adverb*

**visualize** *verb* (**visualizes, visualizing, visualized**)
to imagine something.

**vital** *adjective*
**1** that you need so that you can live; connected with living. **2** extremely important; essential.
**vitally** *adverb*

**vitality** *noun*
liveliness; energy.

**vitamin** *noun* (**vitamins**)
(*say* vit-ă-min or vyt-ă-min)
a substance in food that you need to stay healthy.

**vivid** *adjective*
bright; clear; lively, *She gave a vivid description of the storm.*
**vividly** *adverb*, **vividness** *noun*

**vivisection** *noun*
surgical experiments on live animals, or other painful treatment of them, done as part of scientific research.

**vixen** *noun* (**vixens**)
a female fox.

**vocabulary** *noun* (**vocabularies**)
(*say* vŏ-kab-yoo-lă-ri)
**1** a list of words used in a particular book, language, etc. **2** the words that a person knows and uses.

**vocal** *adjective*
of or to do with your voice, *The sound of your voice is made by your vocal cords.*
**vocally** *adverb*

**vocalist** *noun* (**vocalists**)
a singer.

**vocational** *adjective*
that gives someone the skills needed for a particular job, *vocational training*.

**vodka** *noun* (**vodkas**)
a strong alcoholic drink especially popular in Russia.

**voice**[1] *noun* (**voices**)
1 the sound of speaking or singing. 2 the power to speak or sing, *She lost her voice*.

**voice**[2] *verb* (**voices, voicing, voiced**)
to say something, *He voiced their objections to the plan*.

**volcano** *noun* (**volcanoes**)
a mountain with a hole at the top formed by molten lava which has burst through the earth's crust.
**volcanic** *adjective*

**vole** *noun* (**voles**)
a small animal rather like a rat.

**volley** *noun* (**volleys**)
1 a number of bullets or shells fired at the same time. 2 in tennis and some other games, hitting back the ball before it bounces.

**volleyball** *noun*
a game in which two teams hit a large ball to and fro over a net with their hands.

**volt** *noun* (**volts**)
a unit for measuring the strength of an electric current.
**voltage** *noun*

**volume** *noun* (**volumes**)
1 the amount of space filled by something. 2 an amount, *The volume of work has increased*. 3 the power of sound; how loud something is, *Turn down the volume!* 4 a book, especially one of a set, *Shakespeare's plays in 3 volumes*.

**voluntary** *adjective*
done or working without payment, *voluntary work. The youth club has several voluntary workers*.
**voluntarily** *adverb*

**volunteer**[1] *verb* (**volunteers, volunteered, volunteering**)
1 to offer to do something that you do not have to do. 2 to give something willingly or freely, *Several people generously volunteered their time*.

**volunteer**[2] *noun* (**volunteers**)
someone who volunteers to do something.

**vomit** *verb* (**vomits, vomiting, vomited**)
to bring food back from the stomach through the mouth.

**vote**[1] *verb* (**votes, voting, voted**)
1 to show which person or thing you prefer by putting up your hand, making a mark on paper, etc. 2 to say what you would prefer to do, *I vote we go away this weekend*.
**voter** *noun*

**vote**[2] *noun* (**votes**)
1 the act of voting. 2 the right to vote.

**voucher** *noun* (**vouchers**)
a piece of paper showing that you have paid something or that you can receive something, *This gift voucher can be exchanged for clothes*.

**vow**[1] *noun* (**vows**)
a solemn promise.

**vow**[2] *verb* (**vows, vowing, vowed**)
to make a vow.

**vowel** *noun* (**vowels**)
any of the letters a, e, i, o, u, and sometimes y.

**voyage** *noun* (**voyages**)
a journey by ship, especially a long journey.
**voyager** *noun*

**vulgar** *adjective*
rude; without good manners.
**vulgar fraction**, a fraction shown by numbers above and below a line, not a decimal fraction, $\frac{3}{10}$ *is a vulgar fraction*.
**vulgarity** *noun*, **vulgarly** *adverb*

**vulture** *noun* (**vultures**)
a large bird that eats dead animals.

**vulva** *noun* (**vulvas**)
the outer parts of the female genitals.

# Ww

**wad** *noun* (**wads**)
a pad or bundle of soft material, pieces of paper, etc.

**waddle** *verb* (**waddles, waddling, waddled**)
to walk like a duck, with short steps, rocking from side to side.

**wade** *verb* (**wades, wading, waded**)
to walk through water.

**wafer** *noun* (**wafers**)
a very thin kind of biscuit, often eaten with ice-cream.

**wag** *verb* (**wags, wagging, wagged**)
to move quickly to and fro; to move something in this way, *The dog wagged its tail.*

**wage¹** *noun* or **wages** *plural noun*
the money paid to someone for the job he or she does.

**wage²** *verb* (**wages, waging, waged**)
to carry on a war or campaign.

**wager** *noun* (**wagers**)
(*say* **way**-jer)
a bet.

**waggle** *verb* (**waggles, waggling, waggled**)
to wag, *He waggled his finger.*

**wagon** *noun* (**wagons**)
**1** a cart with four wheels, pulled by a horse or ox. **2** an open railway truck.

**wagtail** *noun* (**wagtails**)
a kind of bird with a long tail that moves up and down constantly when the bird is standing still.

**wail** *verb* (**wails, wailing, wailed**)
to make a long, sad cry; to moan or howl, *The wind wailed among the chimney-pots.*

**waist** *noun* (**waists**)
the narrow part in the middle of your body.

**waistcoat** *noun* (**waistcoats**)
(in America, *vest*) a close-fitting jacket without sleeves, usually worn under a loose jacket.

**wait** *verb* (**waits, waiting, waited**)
**1** to remain in a place or situation until something happens. **2** to be a waiter.
**waiting-list**, a list of people waiting for something to become available.
**waiting-room**, a room for people who are waiting for something, such as catching a train or seeing a doctor.

**waiter** *noun* (**waiters**)
a man whose job is to serve people with food in a restaurant or hotel.

**waitress** *noun* (**waitresses**)
a woman whose job is to serve people with food in a restaurant or hotel.

**waive** *verb* (**waives, waiving, waived**)
not to insist on having something, *She waived her right to travel first class.*

USAGE: Do not confuse **waive** with **wave**, which means to move your hand to and fro, to move to and fro, or to make hair curved or curly.

**wake¹** *verb* (**wakes, waking, woke, woken**)
**1** to stop sleeping, *Wake up! I woke when I heard the bell. Has he woken up yet?* **2** to make someone stop sleeping, *You have woken the baby.*

**wake²** *noun* (**wakes**)
**1** the trail left on the water by a ship.
**2** what is left when something is gone, or when something unusual has happened, *The storm left a lot of damage in its wake.*
**in the wake of**, following.

**waken** *verb* (**wakens, wakening, wakened**)
to wake.

**walk¹** *verb* (**walks, walking, walked**)
to move along on your feet at an ordinary speed.
**walker** *noun*

**walk²** *noun* (**walks**)
**1** a journey on foot. **2** the way that someone walks, *He has a funny walk.* **3** a path or route for walking, *There are some lovely walks near here.*
**walk of life**, your job or occupation.
**walk-over**, an easy victory.

**walkie-talkie** *noun* (**walkie-talkies**)
a small portable radio transmitter and receiver.

**walking-stick** *noun* (**walking-sticks**)
a stick carried or used as a support when you walk.

**Walkman** *noun* (**Walkmans**)
(*trademark*) a portable stereo cassette-player.

**wall** *noun* (**walls**)
1 one of the sides of a building or room.
2 a barrier of bricks or stone surrounding a garden, field, etc.
**up the wall,** (*informal*) mad.
**wall-to-wall,** (of a carpet) covering the whole floor of a room.
**walled** *adjective*

**wallaby** *noun* (**wallabies**)
(*say* wol-ă-bi)
a kind of small kangaroo.

**wallet** *noun* (**wallets**)
(in America, *billfold*) a small, flat, folding case for holding banknotes, documents, etc.

**wallflower** *noun* (**wallflowers**)
a sweet-smelling garden plant.

**wallop** *verb* (**wallops, walloping, walloped**)
(*informal*) to give something a hard hit; to thrash or beat someone or an animal.

**wallow** *verb* (**wallows, wallowing, wallowed**)
1 to roll about in water, mud, etc. 2 to get great pleasure from something, *wallowing in luxury*.

**wallpaper** *noun* (**wallpapers**)
paper used to cover the walls of rooms.

**walnut** *noun* (**walnuts**)
a kind of nut with a wrinkled surface.

**walrus** *noun* (**walruses**)
a large Arctic sea-animal with two long tusks.

**waltz** *noun* (**waltzes**)
a dance with three beats to a bar.

**wand** *noun* (**wands**)
a short, thin stick, especially used by a conjurer.

**wander** *verb* (**wanders, wandering, wandered**)
1 to go about without trying to reach a particular place. 2 to get lost, *Do not let the sheep wander*.
**wanderer** *noun*

**wane** *verb* (**wanes, waning, waned**)
to become less or smaller, *His popularity was waning*.

**wangle** *verb* (**wangles, wangling, wangled**)
(*informal*) to get or arrange something by trickery or persuasion.

**want**¹ *verb* (**wants, wanting, wanted**)
1 to feel that you would like to have something. 2 to need something. 3 to be without something; to lack. 4 to be poor, *Waste not, want not*.

**want**² *noun* (**wants**)
1 a desire or need. 2 a lack of something.

**wanted** *adjective*
that the police wish to find or arrest, *He was a wanted man*.

**war** *noun* (**wars**)
1 fighting between nations or armies; a long period of such fighting. 2 a serious struggle or effort, *the war on poverty*.

**warble** *verb* (**warbles, warbling, warbled**)
to sing gently, like some birds.

**warbler** *noun* (**warblers**)
a kind of small bird.

**ward**¹ *noun* (**wards**)
1 a room for patients in a hospital. 2 a child looked after by a guardian. 3 an area of a town or city represented by a councillor.

**ward**² *verb* (**wards, warding, warded**)
**ward off,** to keep something away.

**-ward** or **-wards** *suffix*
in a particular direction, *She stood on the shore, looking seaward. The birds are flying southwards.*

**warden** *noun* (**wardens**)
1 the person in charge of a hostel, college, etc.; a supervisor. 2 a traffic warden.

**warder** *noun* (**warders**)
someone in charge of prisoners in a prison.

**wardrobe** *noun* (**wardrobes**)
1 a cupboard to hang clothes in. 2 a stock of clothes or costumes.

**ware** *noun* (**wares**)
manufactured goods, especially pottery.
**wares,** goods offered for sale.

**warehouse** *noun* (**warehouses**)
a large building where goods are stored.

**warfare** *noun*
making war; fighting, *guerrilla warfare*.

**warhead** *noun* (**warheads**)
the explosive head of a missile.

**warlike** *adjective*
that likes fighting; ready for war, *a warlike tribe. warlike preparations.*

**warm**[1] *adjective* (**warmer, warmest**)
**1** fairly hot; not cold. **2** enthusiastic; kind, *a warm welcome.* **3** (*informal*) close to the right answer, or to something hidden, *Try again; you're getting warm!*
**warmly** *adverb*, **warmth** *noun*

**warm**[2] *verb* (**warms, warming, warmed**)
to make something or someone warm; to become warm.

**warn** *verb* (**warns, warning, warned**)
to tell someone about a danger or future event.
**warning** *noun*

**warp** *verb* (**warps, warping, warped**)
(*say* worp)
**1** to bend or twist because of dampness, heat, etc., *The rain warped the boards.* **2** to distort something; to make something unnatural, *Her ideas are warped.*

**warrant** *noun* (**warrants**)
a document that entitles you to do something, especially to arrest someone or search a place.

**warren** *noun* (**warrens**)
a piece of ground where there are many rabbit burrows.

**warrior** *noun* (**warriors**)
someone who fights in battles; a soldier.

**warship** *noun* (**warships**)
a ship designed for use in war.

**wart** *noun* (**warts**)
a small, hard lump on the skin.

**wary** *adjective* (**warier, wariest**)
(*say* **wair**-i)
cautious; careful.
**warily** *adverb*, **wariness** *noun*

**was** 1st and 3rd person singular past tense of **be**.

**wash**[1] *verb* (**washes, washing, washed**)
**1** to clean something with water. **2** to flow, *Waves washed over the deck.* **3** to carry along by means of moving liquid, *The sailor was washed overboard.* **4** (*informal*) to be accepted or believed, *That story won't wash.*
**wash up**, to wash dishes and cutlery after a meal.
**washable** *adjective*

**wash**[2] *noun* (**washes**)
**1** the action of washing. **2** the disturbed water or air behind a moving ship or aircraft.

**wash-basin** *noun* (**wash-basins**)
a small basin with taps, holding water for washing yourself.

**washer** *noun* (**washers**)
**1** a small ring of metal, rubber, etc. placed between two surfaces, especially under a bolt or screw. **2** a washing-machine.

**washing** *noun*
clothes that need washing, are being washed, or have been washed.

**washing-machine** *noun* (**washing-machines**)
a machine for washing clothes, etc.

**washing-up** *noun*
the action of washing dishes after a meal, etc.; dishes that need to be washed or are being washed, *Will you do the washing-up? The sink is full of washing-up.*

**wash-out** *noun* (**wash-outs**)
(*slang*) a complete failure.

**wasn't** short for *was not.*

**wasp** *noun* (**wasps**)
a flying insect that can sting.

**waste**[1] *verb* (**wastes, wasting, wasted**)
**1** to use more of something than you need to; to use something without getting much value from it. **2** to make no use of something, *You are wasting a lot of your talent.* **3** to make something weak or useless; to become weak or useless, *The illness had wasted his muscles.*
**wastage** *noun*

**waste**[2] *adjective*
**1** not wanted; thrown away, *waste paper.* **2** not used or usable; not cultivated, *waste land.*
**waste-paper basket**, a container for waste paper.

**waste**[3] *noun* (**wastes**)
**1** the action of wasting something, *It's a waste of time.* **2** things that are not wanted or rubbish. **3** an area of desert or frozen land, *the wastes of Alaska.*
**wasteful** *adjective*, **wastefully** *adverb*, **wastefulness** *noun*

**watch**[1] *verb* (**watches, watching, watched**)
1 to look at a person or thing for some while. 2 to be on guard or ready for something to happen. 3 to take care of something, *His job is to watch the sheep.*
**watcher** *noun*

**watch**[2] *noun* (**watches**)
1 a device like a small clock, usually worn on your wrist. 2 the action of watching. 3 a period of duty on a ship.

**watchful** *adjective*
alert; careful.
**watchfully** *adverb*, **watchfulness** *noun*

**watchman** *noun* (**watchmen**)
someone whose job is to guard a building or other place, especially at night.

**water**[1] *noun*
1 a transparent, colourless liquid that is a compound of hydrogen and oxygen. 2 the tide, *at high water.* 3 urine, *The doctor asked if I had passed water.*

**water**[2] *verb* (**waters, watering, watered**)
1 to sprinkle something with water, *Have you watered the plants?* 2 to give water to an animal. 3 to produce water, tears, or saliva, *The smell of bacon makes my mouth water.*
**water down**, to dilute.

**water-colour** *noun* (**water-colours**)
1 a paint that can be mixed with water. 2 a painting done with this kind of paint.

**watercress** *noun*
a kind of cress that grows in water.

**water cycle** *noun*
the circulation of water through the air, rivers, and seas, including evaporation and rain.

**waterfall** *noun* (**waterfalls**)
a place where a river or stream flows over a cliff or large rock.

**watering-can** *noun* (**watering-cans**)
a container with a long spout, for watering plants.

**waterlogged** *adjective*
completely soaked or filled with water.

**water polo** *noun*
a game played by swimmers with a ball like a football.

**waterproof** *adjective*
that keeps water out, *a waterproof coat.*

**water-ski** *noun* (**water-skis**)
one of a pair of skis on which someone stands for **water-skiing**, skimming over the surface of water while being towed by a motor boat.

**watertight** *adjective*
1 that water cannot get into, *watertight boots.* 2 that cannot be changed or questioned, *a watertight agreement.*

**waterway** *noun* (**waterways**)
a route that ships can travel on.

**waterworks** *noun* (**waterworks**)
the place from which water is supplied to a district.

**watery** *adjective*
1 of or like water. 2 full of water, *watery eyes.*

**watt** *noun* (**watts**)
a unit of electric power.

**wave**[1] *verb* (**waves, waving, waved**)
1 to move your hand to and fro, usually to say hello or goodbye to someone. 2 to move something to and fro or up and down. 3 to make hair curved or curly.

USAGE: Do not confuse **wave** with **waive**, which means not to insist on having something.

**wave**[2] *noun* (**waves**)
1 a moving ridge on the surface of water, especially on the sea. 2 a curving piece of hair; a curl. 3 a sudden build-up of something strong, *a wave of anger.* 4 (*in Science*) one of the to-and-fro movements in which sound, light, etc. travel. 5 the action of waving your hand.

**waveband** *noun* (**wavebands**)
the wavelengths between certain limits.

**wavelength** *noun* (**wavelengths**)
the size of a radio wave or electric wave.

**waver** *verb* (**wavers, wavering, wavered**)
1 to be unsteady or uncertain, *They wavered between two choices.* 2 to move unsteadily, *He wavered as the force of the wind hit him.*
**waverer** *noun*

**wavy** *adjective* (**wavier, waviest**)
full of waves or curves.

**wax**[1] *noun* (**waxes**)
a slippery substance that melts easily, *Wax is used for making candles, crayons, and polish.*
**waxy** *adjective*

**wax**[2] *verb* (**waxes, waxing, waxed**)
**wax and wane,** (of the moon) to grow bigger and then smaller.

**waxwork** *noun* (**waxworks**)
a model of a person, etc. made of wax.

**way** *noun* (**ways**)
**1** a road or path. **2** a route; the direction or distance to a place. **3** how something is done; a method. **4** a respect, *It's a good idea in some ways.* **5** a condition or state, *Things are in a bad way.*
**no way,** (*informal*) that is impossible; that is not true.

**WC** short for *water-closet*, used especially on a plan or a sign showing where a lavatory is.

**we** *pronoun*
a word used by someone to mean 'I and someone else' or 'I and others'.

**weak** *adjective* (**weaker, weakest**)
not strong; easy to break, bend, defeat, etc.
**weakly** *adverb*, **weakness** *noun*

**weaken** *verb* (**weakens, weakening, weakened**)
to become weak or weaker; to make something or someone become weak or weaker.

**weakling** *noun* (**weaklings**)
a weak person.

**wealth** *noun*
**1** a lot of money or property. **2** a large quantity, *This book has a wealth of illustrations.*

**wealthy** *adjective* (**wealthier, wealthiest**)
having a lot of money or property.

**weapon** *noun* (**weapons**)
something used to hurt other people in a battle or fight.

**wear**[1] *verb* (**wears, wearing, wore, worn**)
**1** to be dressed in something, *I wore that dress last night.* **2** to have something attached to your clothes, *He often wears that badge.* **3** to damage something by rubbing or using it; to become damaged like this, *Your sleeve has worn thin.* **4** to last, *This cloth wears well.*
**wear off,** to become less; to disappear.
**wear out,** to become weak or useless; to make something or someone become weak or useless.
**wearer** *noun*

**wear**[2] *noun*
**1** clothes, *men's wear.* **2** gradual damage done by rubbing or using something.

**weary** *adjective* (**wearier, weariest**)
not wanting to make any more effort; tired.
**wearily** *adverb*, **weariness** *noun*

**weasel** *noun* (**weasels**)
a small, fierce animal with a slender body.

**weather**[1] *noun*
the rain, snow, wind, sunshine, etc. at a particular time or place.
**under the weather,** feeling ill or depressed.
**weather forecast,** a report saying what the weather is expected to be like in the near future.

**weather**[2] *verb* (**weathers, weathering, weathered**)
**1** to become dried, worn, etc. because of being exposed to the rain, sun, etc., *The rocks have weathered over the centuries.* **2** to wear down buildings, rocks, etc., *The wind and rain have weathered the cliffs.* **3** to come through something successfully, *They weathered the storm.*

**weathercock** *noun* (**weathercocks**)
a pointer, often shaped like a cockerel, showing which way the wind is blowing.

**weathering** *noun*
the action of the weather on materials, especially rock, exposed to it, *The rocks have taken on strange shapes through weathering.*

**weave** *verb* (**weaves, weaving, wove, woven**)
**1** to make something by passing threads or strips over and under other threads or strips, *This basket was woven from straw.* **2** to twist and turn, *He wove through the traffic.*
**weaver** *noun*

**web** *noun* (**webs**)
**1** a cobweb. **2** something like a net, *caught up in a web of lies.*

**webbed** or **web-footed** *adjective*
with toes joined by pieces of skin, *Ducks have webbed feet. They are web-footed.*

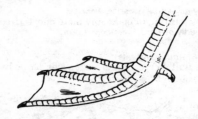

**wed** *verb* (**weds, wedding,** *past tense and past participle* **wedded** or **wed**)
to marry.

**we'd** short for *we had, we should,* or *we would.*

**wedding** *noun* (**weddings**)
the ceremony when a man and woman get married.

**wedge**[1] *noun* (**wedges**)
a piece of wood, metal, etc. that is thick at one end and thin at the other.
**the thin end of the wedge,** a situation which does not seem serious now, but which will quickly get worse.

**wedge**[2] *verb* (**wedges, wedging, wedged**)
to put or keep something firmly in place, especially with a wedge.

**Wednesday** *noun* (**Wednesdays**)
the fourth day of the week.

**weed**[1] *noun* (**weeds**)
a wild plant that grows where it is not wanted.

**weed**[2] *verb* (**weeds, weeding, weeded**)
to remove weeds from the ground.

**weedy** *adjective* (**weedier, weediest**)
1 full of weeds. 2 weak; thin.

**week** *noun* (**weeks**)
a period of seven days, especially from Sunday to the following Saturday.

**weekday** *noun* (**weekdays**)
any day except Saturday and Sunday.

**weekend** *noun* (**weekends**)
Saturday and Sunday.

**weekly** *adjective* and *adverb*
done or happening once a week.

**weep** *verb* (**weeps, weeping, wept**)
to cry; to shed tears.
**weeping willow,** a kind of willow tree that has drooping branches.

**weigh** *verb* (**weighs, weighing, weighed**)
1 to find out how heavy something is. 2 to have a certain weight, *The melon weighs two kilograms.*
**weigh anchor,** to raise the anchor and start a voyage.
**weigh down,** to hold something down; to depress or trouble someone.
**weigh up,** to estimate something; to consider something.

**weight** *noun* (**weights**)
1 how heavy something is. 2 a piece of metal of known heaviness, used on scales to weigh things. 3 a heavy object, *I used a stone as a weight to keep my papers from blowing away.*
**weights,** discs of known heaviness, fixed to the ends of a bar and lifted as a sport or for exercise.
**weightless** *adjective*

**weightlifting** *noun*
lifting heavy weights as a sport or for exercise.

**weighty** *adjective* (**weightier, weightiest**)
1 heavy. 2 important.

**weir** *noun* (**weirs**)
(*say* weer)
a small dam across a river or canal to control the flow of water.

**weird** *adjective* (**weirder, weirdest**)
(*say* weerd)
very strange; not natural.
**weirdly** *adverb,* **weirdness** *noun*

**welcome**[1] *adjective*
1 that you are glad to get or see, *a welcome gift.* 2 allowed or free to do or take something, *You are welcome to use my bicycle.*

**welcome**[2] *verb* (**welcomes, welcoming, welcomed**)
to show that you are pleased when a person or thing arrives.

**weld** *verb* (**welds, welding, welded**)
to join two pieces of metal or plastic together by heat or pressure.
**welder** *noun*

**welfare** *noun*
people's health, happiness, or comfort.

**well**[1] *noun* (**wells**)
a deep hole dug or drilled to get water or
oil out of the ground.

**well**[2] *adverb* (**better, best**)
1 in a good or right way, *He swims well.*
2 actually; probably, *It may well be our last
chance.*
**well off,** fairly rich; lucky.

**well**[3] *adjective*
1 in good health, *She is not well.* 2 good;
satisfactory, *All is well.*

**we'll** short for *we shall* or *we will.*

**well-being** *noun*
health or happiness.

**well-disposed** *adjective*
**be well-disposed towards,** to have a friendly
feeling for someone; to support or be in
favour of something.

**wellington boots** or **wellingtons** *plural noun*
rubber or plastic boots that reach up to
your knee.

**well-known** *adjective*
known by many people.

**well-mannered** *adjective*
with good manners.

**Welsh** *adjective*
of Wales.
**Welsh rabbit** or **Welsh rarebit,** melted cheese
on a piece of toast.
**Welshman** *noun*

**went** past tense of **go** *verb.*

**wept** past tense and past participle of **weep.**

**were** plural and 2nd person singular past
tense of **be.**

**we're** short for *we are.*

**werewolf** *noun* (**werewolves**)
in stories, a person who sometimes
changes into a wolf.

**Wesak** *noun*
a Buddhist festival held at the time of the
full moon at the end of April or the
beginning of May.

**west**[1] *noun*
the direction in which the sun sets.
**the West,** a name that used to be given to
the countries of Europe and America that
were not Communist.

**west**[2] *adjective*
1 coming from the west, *a west wind.*
2 situated in the west, *the west coast.*
**westerly** *adjective*

**west**[3] *adverb*
towards the west.
**westward** *adjective* and *adverb,* **westwards**
*adverb*

**western**[1] *adjective*
of or in the west.

**western**[2] *noun* (**westerns**)
a film or story about cowboys, American
Indians, etc.

**West Indian**[1] *adjective*
of the West Indies.

**West Indian**[2] *noun* (**West Indians**)
a West Indian person.

**wet**[1] *adjective* (**wetter, wettest**)
1 covered or soaked in water or other
liquid. 2 not dry, *wet paint.* 3 rainy, *wet
weather.*
**wet blanket,** (*informal*) someone who is
gloomy and who prevents other people
from enjoying themselves.
**wet suit,** a suit made from a kind of rubber
and worn by skin-divers, windsurfers, etc.
to keep them warm.
**wetly** *adverb,* **wetness** *noun*

**wet**[2] *verb* (**wets, wetting, wetted**)
to make something wet.

**we've** short for *we have.*

**whack** *verb* (**whacks, whacking, whacked**)
to hit someone or something hard,
especially with a stick.

**whale** *noun* (**whales**)
a very large sea-animal.
**a whale of a,** (*informal*) a very great or good,
*We had a whale of a time.*

**whaler** *noun* (**whalers**)
a person or ship that hunts whales.
**whaling** *noun*

**wharf** *noun* (**wharfs**)
(*say* worf)
a quay where ships are loaded or unloaded.

**what**[1] *adjective*
1 used to ask the amount or kind of
something, *What food have you got?* 2 used
to say how strange or great a person or
thing is, *What a fool you are!*

**what**[2] *pronoun*
> the thing that; which thing or things, *What did you say? This is what I said.*
> **what's what,** (*informal*) what is important or useful, *She knows what's what.*

**whatever**[1] *pronoun*
> no matter what; anything or everything that, *Whatever happens. Do whatever you like.*

**whatever**[2] *adjective*
> of any kind or amount, *Get whatever help you can.*

**wheat** *noun*
> a cereal from which flour is made.

**wheel**[1] *noun* (**wheels**)
> 1 a round device that turns on an axle.
> 2 a horizontal revolving disc on which clay is made into a pot.

**wheel**[2] *verb* (**wheels, wheeling, wheeled**)
> 1 to push along a bicycle, cart, etc. 2 to move in a curve or circle, *The column of soldiers wheeled to the right.*

**wheelbarrow** *noun* (**wheelbarrows**)
> a small cart with one wheel at the front and two handles at the back.

**wheelchair** *noun* (**wheelchairs**)
> a chair on wheels for someone who cannot walk easily, which can be moved and steered by the person in it or by someone pushing it.

**wheel clamp** *noun* (**wheel clamps**)
> a device that can be locked around a vehicle's wheel to stop it from moving, used especially on cars that have been parked illegally.

**wheeze** *verb* (**wheezes, wheezing, wheezed**)
> to make a whistling or gasping noise as you breathe.

**whelk** *noun* (**whelks**)
> a shellfish that looks like a snail.

**when**[1] *adverb*
> at what time, *When can you come to tea?*

**when**[2] *conjunction*
> 1 at the time that, *The bird flew away when I moved.* 2 because; considering that, *Why do you smoke when you know it is dangerous?*

**whenever** *conjunction*
> at any time; every time, *Whenever I see him, he's asleep.*

**where** *adverb* and *conjunction*
> 1 in or to what place, *Where is he? Where have you put the glue?* 2 in or to that place, *Leave the cat where it is.*

**whereabouts** *adverb*
> roughly where, *'Whereabouts are the Turks and Caicos Islands?' 'They're somewhere east of Cuba.'*

**whereas** *conjunction*
> but, *Some people like sailing whereas others hate it.*

**whereupon** *adverb*
> after that; and then.

**wherever** *adverb* and *conjunction*
> in or to whatever place; no matter where.

**whether** *conjunction*
> used to introduce more than one possibility, *I don't know whether she is here or not.*

**whey** *noun*
> (*say* way)
> the watery liquid left when milk forms curds.

**which**[1] *adjective*
> what particular, *Which way did he go?*

**which**[2] *pronoun*
> the thing spoken about; what person or thing, *Which is your teacher?*

**whichever** *pronoun* and *adjective*
> that or those which; any which, *Take whichever you like.*

**whiff** *noun* (**whiffs**)
> a puff or slight smell of smoke, gas, etc.

**while**[1] *conjunction*
> 1 during the time that; as long as, *Whistle while you work.* 2 but; although, *She was dressed in black, while I was in white.*

**while**[2] *noun*
> a period of time, *We have waited all this while.*

**while**[3] *verb* (**whiles, whiling, whiled**)
> **while away,** to pass time, *We whiled away the time by playing cards.*

**whilst** *conjunction*
> while.

**whimper** *verb* (**whimpers, whimpering, whimpered**)
to make feeble crying sounds, *The dog whimpered while I bathed its injured leg.*

**whine** *verb* (**whines, whining, whined**)
1 to make a long, high, piercing sound, *The electric drill whined.* 2 to complain in a feeble, miserable voice, *'It's just not fair', he whined.*

**whinny** *verb* (**whinnies, whinnying, whinnied**)
to neigh gently or happily.

**whip¹** *noun* (**whips**)
a cord or strip of leather fixed to a handle and used for hitting people or animals.

**whip²** *verb* (**whips, whipping, whipped**)
1 to hit a person or animal with a whip. 2 to beat cream, eggs, etc. into a froth. 3 to move or take something suddenly, *He whipped out a gun.* 4 (*informal*) to steal something.

**whirl** *verb* (**whirls, whirling, whirled**)
to turn or spin very quickly; to cause something to move in this way.

**whirlpool** *noun* (**whirlpools**)
a strong current of water going round in a circle and often drawing floating objects towards it.

**whirlwind** *noun* (**whirlwinds**)
a very strong wind that whirls around or blows in a spiral.

**whirr** *verb* (**whirrs, whirring, whirred**)
to make a continuous buzzing sound.

**whisk¹** *verb* (**whisks, whisking, whisked**)
1 to move something very quickly, *A waiter whisked away my plate as soon as I had finished my meal.* 2 to stir something briskly.

**whisk²** *noun* (**whisks**)
1 a device for whisking eggs, cream, etc. 2 a whisking movement.

**whisker** *noun* (**whiskers**)
a hair growing on the face of a person or animal.

**whisky** *noun* (**whiskies**)
a kind of very strong alcoholic drink.

**whisper¹** *verb* (**whispers, whispering, whispered**)
1 to speak very softly. 2 to talk secretly.

**whisper²** *noun* (**whispers**)
a whispering voice or sound.

**whist** *noun*
a card-game usually for four people.

**whistle¹** *verb* (**whistles, whistling, whistled**)
to make a shrill or musical sound by blowing through your lips.
**whistler** *noun*

**whistle²** *noun* (**whistles**)
1 a whistling sound. 2 a device that makes a shrill sound when you blow into it.

**white¹** *adjective* (**whiter, whitest**)
1 of the very lightest colour, like snow or milk. 2 with light-coloured skin.
**white coffee,** coffee with milk or cream.
**white elephant,** something useless.
**white-hot,** extremely hot.
**whiteness** *noun*, **whitish** *adjective*

**white²** *noun* (**whites**)
white colour.
**White,** a white person.

**whiten** *verb* (**whitens, whitening, whitened**)
to make something white; to become white.

**whitewash** *noun*
a liquid painted on walls and ceilings to make them white.

**Whitsun** *noun*
Whit Sunday, or the period around it.

**Whit Sunday** *noun*
the 7th Sunday after Easter.

**whiz** *verb* (**whizzes, whizzing, whizzed**)
1 to move very quickly. 2 to sound like something rushing through the air.

**whiz-kid** *noun* (**whiz-kids**)
(*informal*) a brilliant or very successful young person, *a nine-year-old computer whiz-kid.*

**who** *pronoun*
1 which person; which people, *Who threw that?* 2 the person or people spoken about, *the boys who did it.*

**whoever** *pronoun*
the person who; any person who.

**whole¹** *adjective*
complete; not broken or damaged.
**whole number,** a number without any fractions.

**whole²** *noun* (**wholes**)
a complete thing.
**on the whole,** considering everything; mainly.

**wholemeal** *adjective*
made from the whole grain of wheat, etc.,
*wholemeal bread.*

**wholesale** *adjective* and *adverb*
1 sold in large quantities, usually to
shopkeepers. 2 on a large scale; including
everybody or everything, *wholesale
destruction.*

**wholesome** *adjective*
good for health; healthy, *wholesome food.*

**wholly** *adverb*
completely; entirely.

**whom** *pronoun*
a word used for *who* when it is the object of
a sentence, or comes straight after a
preposition, *the lawyer whom I consulted.
Whom did you see? To whom did you give
the parcel?*

**whoop** *noun* (**whoops**)
(*say* woop)
a loud excited cry.

**whoopee** *interjection*
(*say* **wuup**-ee)
a joyful exclamation, *It's a holiday!
Whoopee!*

**whooping-cough** *noun*
(*say* **hoop**-ing-kof)
an illness that makes you cough and gasp.

**who's** short for *who has* or *who is, Who's
coming for a swim?*

**whose** *adjective* and *pronoun*
1 belonging to what person, *Whose bike is
that?* 2 of which; of whom, *The house whose
roof is red. The boy whose mother died.*

**why** *adverb*
for what reason or purpose.

**wick** *noun* (**wicks**)
1 the string that goes through the middle of
a candle. 2 the strip of material that you
light in a lamp or heater that uses oil.

**wicked** *adjective* (**wickeder, wickedest**)
1 very bad or cruel; doing things that are
wrong or spiteful, *a wicked deed. He was a
wicked and dangerous man.* 2 (*slang*) very
good or impressive, *That's a wicked bike!*
**wickedly** *adverb,* **wickedness** *noun*

**wicker** or **wickerwork** *noun*
things made of reeds or canes woven
together.

**wicket** *noun* (**wickets**)
1 the set of three stumps with two bails on
top of them in cricket. 2 the part of a
cricket ground between or near the
wickets.
**wicket-keeper,** the fielder in cricket who
stands behind the batsman's wicket.

**wide**[1] *adjective* (**wider, widest**)
1 measuring a lot from one side to the
other, *a wide river.* 2 from one side to the
other, *The room is 4 metres wide.*
3 covering a great area, *wide knowledge.*
**widely** *adverb,* **wideness** *noun*

**wide**[2] *adverb* (**wider, widest**)
1 completely; fully, *wide awake.* 2 far from
the target, *His shot went wide.* 3 over a
large area, *She travelled far and wide.*

**widen** *verb* (**widens, widening, widened**)
to make something wider; to become wider.

**widespread** *adjective*
existing in many places; common.

**widow** *noun* (**widows**)
a woman whose husband has died.

**widower** *noun* (**widowers**)
a man whose wife has died.

**width** *noun* (**widths**)
how wide something is.

**wield** *verb* (**wields, wielding, wielded**)
(*say* weeld)
to hold something and use it, *He wielded
a sword.*

**wife** *noun* (**wives**)
the woman that a man has married, *Henry
VIII had six wives.*

**wig** *noun* (**wigs**)
a covering of false hair worn on someone's
head.

**wiggle** *verb* (**wiggles, wiggling, wiggled**)
to move from side to side.

**wigwam** *noun* (**wigwams**)
the tent of a Native American.

**wild** *adjective* (**wilder, wildest**)
1 not tame; not looked after by people,
*a wild dog.* 2 not grown by people; not
cultivated, *a wild flower.* 3 not controlled;
violent, *wild behaviour.*
**Wild West,** the western parts of America in
the 19th century, when Europeans were
settling there.
**wildly** *adverb,* **wildness** *noun*

**wilderness** *noun* (**wildernesses**)
an area of wild country; a desert.

**wildlife** *noun*
wild animals.

**wilful** *adjective*
1 obstinate, *a wilful child.* 2 deliberate,
*wilful disobedience.*
**wilfully** *adverb,* **wilfulness** *noun*

**will**[1] *verb* (*past tense* **would**)
shall; is or are going to, *She will like this.*

**will**[2] *noun* (**wills**)
1 the power to use your mind to decide and control what you do. 2 what someone chooses or wants, *The people's will must be done.* 3 a legal document saying what is to be done with someone's possessions after he or she dies.

**willing** *adjective*
ready and happy to do what is wanted.
**willingly** *adverb*, **willingness** *noun*

**willow** *noun* (**willows**)
a tree with thin, flexible branches, *Willows often grow near water.*

**wilt** *verb* (**wilts, wilting, wilted**)
1 to lose freshness and to droop; to cause a plant to do this, *The plants have wilted.*
2 to lose strength, *The team began to wilt after half-time.*

**wily** *adjective* (**wilier, wiliest**)
crafty; cunning.

**wimp** *noun* (**wimps**)
(*informal*) a feeble, easily frightened person.

**win** *verb* (**wins, winning, won**)
1 to do best in a contest, game, battle, etc.
2 to get something by using effort, skill, etc., *She won the prize.*

**wince** *verb* (**winces, wincing, winced**)
to make a slight movement because you are in pain, unhappy, etc.

**winch** *noun* (**winches**)
a device for lifting or pulling things, using a rope or cable that goes round a wheel.

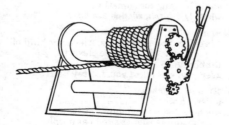

**wind**[1] *noun* (**winds**)
(rhymes with *tinned*)
1 a current of air. 2 gas in the stomach that makes you uncomfortable. 3 breath used for a purpose. 4 the wind instruments of an orchestra.
**get** or **have the wind up,** (*slang*) to be scared.
**wind instrument,** a musical instrument that you blow into.
**wind power,** energy from the wind.
**wind turbine,** a machine like a windmill but with blades like an aircraft's wings, used mainly for generating electricity.
**wind vane,** a device that shows which way the wind is blowing.

**wind**[2] *verb* (**winds, winding, wound**)
(rhymes with *find*)
1 to turn or go in twists, curves, or circles.
2 to wind up a watch or clock.
**wind up,** to make a watch, clock, etc. work by turning a key; to close a business; (*informal*) to end in a place or condition; (*informal*) to tease someone, *I have wound up my watch. The company has been wound up. He wound up in gaol. Stop saying that – you're winding me up!*

**windfall** *noun* (**windfalls**)
1 a fruit blown down from a tree. 2 a piece of unexpected good luck, especially getting a sum of money.

**windmill** *noun* (**windmills**)
a mill with four long arms called *sails* which are turned by the wind.

**window** *noun* (**windows**)
1 an opening in a wall, roof, etc. to let in light and air, usually filled with glass; this piece of glass. 2 (*in Computing*) an area on a VDU screen used for a particular purpose, *You can display different pieces of text in separate windows.*
**window-shopping,** looking at things in shop-windows but not buying anything.

**windpipe** *noun* (**windpipes**)
the tube through which air reaches the lungs.

**windscreen** *noun* (**windscreens**)
(in America, *windshield*) the window at the front of a motor vehicle.

**windsurfing** *noun*
a type of sailing in which you use a sailboard.
**windsurfer** *noun*

**windward** *adjective*
that faces the wind, *the windward side of the ship*.

**windy** *adjective* (**windier, windiest**)
with much wind, *a windy night*.

**wine** *noun* (**wines**)
1 an alcoholic drink made from grapes or other plants. 2 a dark red colour.

**wing** *noun* (**wings**)
1 one of the parts of a bird or insect that it uses for flying. 2 one of the long, flat parts that support an aircraft in the air. 3 part of a building that extends from the main part. 4 (in America, *fender*) the part of a motor vehicle's body above a wheel. 5 one of the players in football, hockey, etc. whose place is at the side of the pitch.
**on the wing**, flying.
**take wing**, to fly away.
**wings**, the sides of a theatre stage.
**winged** *adjective*, **wingless** *adjective*

**wingspan** *noun* (**wingspans**)
the distance across the wings of an insect, a bird, or an aeroplane.

**wink**[1] *verb* (**winks, winking, winked**)
1 to close and open your eye quickly. 2 to flicker or twinkle, *a sky full of stars that winked and twinkled*.

**wink**[2] *noun* (**winks**)
1 the action of winking. 2 a short period of sleep, *I didn't sleep a wink*.

**winkle** *noun* (**winkles**)
a shellfish that can be eaten.

**winner** *noun* (**winners**)
1 a person who wins something.
2 something very successful, *Her book is a winner*.

**winnings** *plural noun*
money won by betting, in a game, etc.

**winter** *noun* (**winters**)
the coldest season of the year, between autumn and spring.
**wintry** *adjective*

**wintertime** *noun*
the season of winter.

**wipe** *verb* (**wipes, wiping, wiped**)
to dry or clean something by rubbing it.
**wipe out**, to destroy someone or something; to remove something, *wipe out a debt*.
**wiper** *noun*

**wire**[1] *noun* (**wires**)
1 a very thin length of metal, especially used to carry electric current. 2 (*informal*) a telegram.

**wire**[2] *verb* (**wired, wiring, wired**)
1 to connect objects with wires so that electricity can flow between them. 2 to fix something with wire.

**wireless** *noun* (**wirelesses**)
(*old-fashioned use*) 1 radio. 2 a radio set.

**wiring** *noun*
the system of wires carrying electricity in a building or in an electrical device.

**wiry** *adjective* (**wirier, wiriest**)
1 like wire, *Terriers have wiry hair*. 2 lean and strong, *a tanned, wiry man*.

**wisdom** *noun*
1 being wise. 2 wise sayings or writings.
**wisdom tooth**, a molar that may grow at the back of your jaw much later than the other teeth.

**wise** *adjective* (**wiser, wisest**)
knowing or understanding many things.
**someone is none the wiser**, someone knows no more about something than before, *He tried to explain his theory to me, but I'm afraid I'm none the wiser*.
**wisely** *adverb*

**wish**[1] *verb* (**wishes, wishing, wished**)
1 to think or say that you would like something. 2 to say that you hope someone will get something, *We wish you a merry Christmas*.

**wish**[2] *noun* (**wishes**)
1 something you want. 2 the action of wishing, *Make a wish. We send you our best wishes*.

**wishbone** *noun* (**wishbones**)
a forked bone from a bird like a chicken, *Two people break the wishbone and the person who gets the bigger piece can make a wish*.

**wisp** *noun* (**wisps**)
a thin piece of hair, straw, smoke, etc.
**wispy** *adjective*

**wistful** *adjective*
sadly longing for something.
**wistfully** *adverb*, **wistfulness** *noun*

**wit** *noun* (**wits**)
1 intelligence; cleverness. 2 a clever kind of humour; the ability to be cleverly humorous. 3 a witty person.
**keep your wits about you**, to stay alert.

**witch** *noun* (**witches**)
a person who is believed to use magic.
**witch-doctor**, a magician who belongs to a tribe and is thought to heal people.

**witchcraft** *noun*
using magic, especially to make bad things happen.

**with** *preposition*
**1** having, *a man with a wooden leg*. **2** in the company of; accompanied by, *I came with a friend*. **3** using, *Hit it with a hammer*. **4** against, *They fought with each other*. **5** because of, *He shook with laughter*. **6** towards; concerning, *Be patient with me*.

**withdraw** *verb* (**withdraws, withdrawing, withdrew, withdrawn**)
**1** to take away or back; to remove, *She withdrew money from the bank*. **2** to retreat; to leave, *They have withdrawn from the frontier*.
**withdrawal** *noun*

**wither** *verb* (**withers, withering, withered**)
to shrivel; to wilt, *The old apples had withered. The seedlings will wither unless you water them.*

**withhold** *verb* (**withholds, withholding, withheld**)
to refuse to give something to someone, *He withheld his permission*.

**within** *preposition* and *adverb*
inside; not beyond something, *Stay within the city boundaries*.

**without** *preposition*
not having; free from, *They were without food. They would like a life without worry.*

**withstand** *verb* (**withstands, withstanding, withstood**)
to resist something; to put up with something successfully, *She withstood her disappointment*.

**witness** *noun* (**witnesses**)
**1** a person who sees something happen, *There were no witnesses to the accident*. **2** someone who gives evidence in a lawcourt.

**witty** *adjective* (**wittier, wittiest**)
clever and amusing.
**wittily** *adverb*, **wittiness** *noun*

**wizard** *noun* (**wizards**)
**1** a man who can do magic things. **2** an amazing person, *He's a wizard on the accordion*.
**wizardry** *noun*

**wobble** *verb* (**wobbles, wobbling, wobbled**)
to move unsteadily from side to side; to shake, *The jelly was wobbling*.
**wobbly** *adjective*

**woe** *noun* (**woes**)
sorrow; misfortune.
**woeful** *adjective*, **woefully** *adverb*

**wok** *noun* (**woks**)
a deep, round-bottomed frying-pan used in Chinese cookery.

**woke** past tense of **wake** *verb*.

**woken** past participle of **wake** *verb*.

**wolf** *noun* (**wolves**)
a wild animal like a large, fierce dog.

**woman** *noun* (**women**)
a grown-up female human being.

**womb** *noun* (**wombs**)
(*say* woom)
the part of a female's body where babies develop before they are born.

**won** past tense and past participle of **win**.

**wonder**[1] *noun* (**wonders**)
**1** a feeling of surprise and admiration. **2** something that makes you feel surprised and admiring; a marvel.
**no wonder**, it is not surprising.

**wonder**[2] *verb* (**wonders, wondering, wondered**)
**1** to feel that you want to know or decide about something, *I wonder what to do next*. **2** to feel surprise and admiration at something, *The tourists stood and wondered at the temple*.

**wonderful** *adjective*
**1** astonishing. **2** excellent.
**wonderfully** *adverb*

**won't** short for *will not*.

**wood** *noun* (**woods**)
**1** the substance of which trees are made. **2** a lot of trees growing together.

**wooded** *adjective*
covered with growing trees.

**wooden** *adjective*
**1** made of wood, *a wooden leg*. **2** stiff; awkward, *His movements were wooden*.

**woodland** *noun* (**woodlands**)
wooded country.

**woodlouse** *noun* (**woodlice**)
a small crawling creature with seven pairs of legs, living in rotten wood or damp soil and rolling itself up into a ball if it is alarmed.

**woodpecker** *noun* (**woodpeckers**)
a bird that makes holes in trees with its beak, to find insects to eat.

**woodwind** *noun*
wind instruments that are usually made of wood or plastic, such as the clarinet and oboe.

**woodwork** *noun*
1 making things with wood. 2 things made out of wood.

**woodworm** *noun* (**woodworm** or **woodworms**)
the larva of a beetle that bores into wood.

**woody** *adjective* (**woodier, woodiest**)
1 like wood. 2 full of trees.

**wool** *noun*
1 the thick, soft hair of sheep, goats, etc. 2 thread or cloth made from this hair.

**woollen** *adjective*
made of wool.

**woollens** *plural noun*
clothes made of wool.

**woolly** *adjective* (**woollier, woolliest**)
1 covered with wool. 2 of or like wool. 3 not clear; vague, *He had woolly ideas.*
**woolliness** *noun*

**word** *noun* (**words**)
1 a letter or group of letters that means something when you write it. 2 a sound or group of sounds that means something when you say it. 3 a promise, *He cannot keep his word.* 4 a command; an order, *Run when I give the word.* 5 a message; information, *We sent word that we had arrived safely.*

**word-blindness** *noun*
dyslexia.

**word processor** *noun* (**word processors**)
a computer system designed specially to allow you to store, alter, arrange, and print pieces of writing.

**wordy** *adjective* (**wordier, wordiest**)
using too many words, *a wordy speech.*

**wore** past tense of **wear** *verb.*

**work¹** *noun* (**works**)
1 something that you have to do that needs effort or energy, *Weeding is hard work.* 2 a person's job, *Has Dad gone to work yet?* 3 something produced by work, *The teacher marked our work.* 4 (*in Science*) the result of applying a force to move an object.
**at work**, working; functioning.
**work of art**, a painting, sculpture, etc.
**works**, a factory; the moving parts of a machine.

**work²** *verb* (**works, working, worked**)
1 to do work. 2 to have a job; to be employed, *She works in a bank.* 3 to act or operate correctly or successfully, *Is the lift working?* 4 to make something act or operate, *Can you work the lift?* 5 to become gradually, *The screw had worked loose.*
**work out**, to find an answer by working or calculating; to have a particular result.
**work to rule**, to make a protest or delay by following strictly the rules of your work.

**workable** *adjective*
that can be used or done, *a workable plan.*

**worker** *noun* (**workers**)
1 someone who works. 2 a member of the working class. 3 a bee, ant, etc. that does the work in a hive or colony.

**working** *noun* (**workings**)
a mine or quarry.
**working** or **workings**, the way that something works.

**working class** *noun* (**working classes**)
those who work for wages, especially in industry; the poorest group of people.
**working-class** *adjective*

**workman** *noun* (**workmen**)
a man who does a job, especially for pay.

**workmanship** *noun*
skill in working, or the result of such skill.

**workout** *noun* (**workouts**)
a session of physical exercise or training.

**worksheet** *noun* (**worksheets**)
a sheet of paper with a set of questions about a subject for students, often intended to be used with a textbook, *The museum has produced a series of worksheets for pupils studying dinosaurs.*

**workshop** *noun* (**workshops**)
a place where things are made or mended.

**world** *noun* (**worlds**)
1 the planet that we live on, with all its peoples; the earth. 2 the universe. 3 everything to do with a particular subject or activity, *the world of sport.*
**world war**, a war in which countries all over the world are involved, especially the *First World War* (1914–18) and the *Second World War* (1939–45).

**worldly** *adjective* (**worldlier, worldliest**)
of or interested in money, possessions, etc.
**worldliness** *noun*

**worldwide** *adjective* and *adverb*
over the whole of the world, *Global warming could bring a worldwide rise in temperature. Electricity is used worldwide.*

**worm**¹ *noun* (**worms**)
1 a small, thin, wriggling animal without legs, especially an earthworm. 2 an unimportant or disliked person.

**worm**² *verb* (**worms, worming, wormed**)
to move by wriggling or crawling.

**worn** past participle of **wear** *verb.*

**worry**¹ *verb* (**worries, worrying, worried**)
1 to trouble someone; to make someone think of something bad that may happen. 2 to think of something bad that may happen. 3 (of an animal) to hold something in its teeth and shake it, *The dog was worrying the rat.*
**worrier** *noun*

**worry**² *noun* (**worries**)
1 being worried. 2 something that worries you.

**worse** *adjective* and *adverb*, comparative of **bad** and **badly**.
more bad or more badly; less good or less well.

**worsen** *verb* (**worsens, worsening, worsened**)
to make something worse; to become worse.

**worship**¹ *verb* (**worships, worshipping, worshipped**)
to give praise or respect to God or a god.
**worshipper** *noun*

**worship**² *noun*
worshipping; religious ceremonies or services.

**worst** *adjective* and *adverb*, superlative of **bad** and **badly**.
most bad or most badly; least good or least well.

**worth**¹ *adjective*
1 having a certain value, *This stamp is worth £100.* 2 that deserves; good enough for, *That book is worth reading.*

**worth**² *noun*
value, *a book of little worth.*

**worthless** *adjective*
with no value; useless.

**worthwhile** *adjective*
important or good enough to do; useful.

**worthy** *adjective* (**worthier, worthiest**)
that deserves respect or support; good, *The jumble sale is for a worthy cause.*
**worthy of something**, that deserves something; good enough for something, *This charity is worthy of support.*
**worthily** *adverb*, **worthiness** *noun*

**would** *verb*
1 past tense of **will** *verb*. 2 to be willing or likely to do something, *He would come if he could.*

**wouldn't** short for *would not.*

**wound**¹ *noun* (**wounds**)
(*say* woond)
an injury done to a body or to someone's feelings.

**wound**² *verb* (**wounds, wounding, wounded**)
(*say* woond)
to give someone a wound.

**wound**³ past tense and past participle of **wind** *verb*.
(*say* wownd)

**wove** past tense of **weave**.

**woven** past participle of **weave**.

**WPC** short for *woman police constable.*

**wrap** *verb* (**wraps, wrapping, wrapped**)
to put paper, cloth, etc. round something.

**wrapper** *noun* (**wrappers**)
a piece of paper or cloth wrapped round something.

**wrath** *noun*
(rhymes with *cloth*)
(*old-fashioned use*) anger.
**wrathful** *adjective*, **wrathfully** *adverb*

**wreath** *noun* (**wreaths**)
(*say* reeth)
flowers, branches, etc. bound together to make a circle, *wreaths of holly.*

**wreathe** *verb* (**wreathes, wreathing, wreathed**)
(*say* reeth)
1 to surround or decorate something with a wreath. 2 to cover, *Her face was wreathed in smiles.*

**wreck**¹ *verb* (**wrecks, wrecking, wrecked**)
to damage something, especially a ship, so badly that it cannot be used again.
**wrecker** *noun*

**wreck**² *noun* (**wrecks**)
a wrecked ship, car, building, etc.

**wreckage** *noun*
the pieces of a wreck.

**wren** *noun* (**wrens**)
a very small, brown bird.

**wrench**[1] *verb* (**wrenches, wrenching, wrenched**)
to pull or twist something suddenly or
violently, *He wrenched the door open*.

**wrench**[2] *noun* (**wrenches**)
1 a wrenching movement. 2 a tool for
gripping and turning bolts, nuts, etc.

**wrestle** *verb* (**wrestles, wrestling, wrestled**)
1 to struggle with someone and try to
throw him or her to the ground. 2 to
struggle with a difficulty, problem, etc.
**wrestler** *noun*, **wrestling** *noun*

**wretch** *noun* (**wretches**)
someone who is unhappy, poor, or disliked.

**wretched** *adjective*
(*say* rech-id)
1 unhappy; miserable; poor, *a wretched
beggar*. 2 not satisfactory or pleasant, *This
wretched car won't start*.

**wriggle** *verb* (**wriggles, wriggling, wriggled**)
to twist and turn your body around.
**wriggler** *noun*, **wriggly** *adjective*

**wring** *verb* (**wrings, wringing, wrung**)
1 to squeeze or twist a wet thing to get the
water out of it, *Have you wrung out your
swimsuit?* 2 to squeeze or twist something,
*I'll wring your neck!*
**wringing wet**, very wet; soaked.

**wrinkle**[1] *noun* (**wrinkles**)
a small crease or line in the skin or on
a surface.

**wrinkle**[2] *verb* (**wrinkles, wrinkling, wrinkled**)
to make wrinkles.

**wrist** *noun* (**wrists**)
the thin part of your arm where it joins
your hand.
**wrist-watch**, a watch that you wear on your
wrist.

**write** *verb* (**writes, writing, wrote, written**)
1 to put words or signs on paper or some
other surface so that people can read them,
*Who wrote these words on the wall?* 2 to be
the author or composer of something,
*'Hamlet' was written by Shakespeare*. 3 to
send a letter to someone.
**write off**, to damage a vehicle so badly that
it is not worth repairing.
**writing** *noun*

**writer** *noun* (**writers**)
a person who writes books, etc.; an author.

**writhe** *verb* (**writhes, writhing, writhed**)
(*say* ryth)
to twist your body about because you are in
pain or discomfort.

**wrong**[1] *adjective*
1 not fair; not moral, *Is it wrong to swear?*
2 incorrect, *Your answer is wrong*. 3 not
working properly, *There's something wrong
with the engine*.
**wrongly** *adverb*

**wrong**[2] *noun* (**wrongs**)
something that is wrong.
**in the wrong**, having done or said something
wrong.

**wrote** past tense of **write**.

**wrung** past tense and past participle of **wring**.

**wry** *adjective* (**wryer, wryest**)
twisted; showing disgust or
disappointment, *a wry smile*.

# Xx

**Xmas** *noun* (**Xmases**)
(*say* kris-măs or eks-măs)
(*informal*) Christmas.

**X-ray**[1] *noun* (**X-rays**)
1 a ray that can pass through something
solid. 2 a photograph of the inside of
something, especially part of the body,
made by means of these rays.

**X-ray**[2] *verb* (**X-rays, X-raying, X-rayed**)
to make an X-ray photograph of
something.

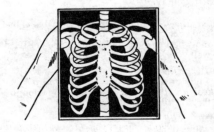

**xylophone** *noun* (**xylophones**)
(*say* **zy**-lŏ-fohn)
a musical instrument made of wooden bars
of different lengths, that you hit with small
hammers.

# Yy

**yacht** *noun* (**yachts**)
(*say* yot)
**1** a sailing-boat used for racing or cruising.
**2** a private ship.
**yachting** *noun*, **yachtsman** *noun*,
**yachtswoman** *noun*

**yam** *noun* (**yams**)
a tropical vegetable that grows
underground.

**yank** *verb* (**yanks, yanking, yanked**)
to pull something strongly and suddenly.

**yap** *verb* (**yaps, yapping, yapped**)
to make a shrill barking sound, *a yapping
dog.*

**yard**[1] *noun* (**yards**)
a measure of length, 36 inches or about 91
centimetres.

**yard**[2] *noun* (**yards**)
a piece of ground surrounded by or next to
walls or buildings.

**yarn** *noun* (**yarns**)
**1** thread. **2** (*informal*) a story.

**yawn**[1] *verb* (**yawns, yawning, yawned**)
**1** to open your mouth wide and breathe in
deeply when you are tired or bored. **2** to
form a wide opening, *The chasm yawned
beneath them.*

**yawn**[2] *noun* (**yawns**)
the action of yawning.

**ye** *pronoun*
(*old-fashioned use*) you, *O ye of little faith!*

**year** *noun* (**years**)
the time that the earth takes to go right
round the sun; twelve months.
**yearly** *adjective* and *adverb*

**yearn** *verb* (**yearns, yearning, yearned**)
to long for something.

**yeast** *noun*
a substance used in making bread, beer,
wine, etc.

**yell** *noun* (**yells**)
a loud cry; a shout.

**yellow**[1] *noun*
the colour of lemons or buttercups.

**yellow**[2] *adjective* (**yellower, yellowest**)
**1** yellow in colour. **2** (*informal*) cowardly.
**yellow fever,** a tropical disease that makes
your skin yellow.
**Yellow Pages,** a special telephone directory
giving addresses and numbers of
businesses, arranged according to what
services they provide.
**yellowish** *adjective*

**yelp** *verb* (**yelps, yelping, yelped**)
to make a shrill bark or cry.

**yen** *noun* (**yen**)
a Japanese unit of money.

**yeoman** *noun* (**yeomen**)
(*say* **yoh**-măn)
(*old-fashioned use*) a man who runs a small
farm.
**Yeoman of the Guard,** a guard at the Tower
of London; a beefeater.

**yes** *interjection*
a word used for agreeing to something.

**yesterday** *noun* and *adverb*
the day before today.

**yet**[1] *adverb*
**1** up to now; by this time, *Has the postman
called yet?* **2** eventually, *I'll get even with
him yet.* **3** in addition; even; still, *She
became yet more excited.*

**yet**$^2$ *conjunction*
nevertheless, *It is strange, yet it is true.*

**yeti** *noun* (**yetis**)
(*say* yet-i)
a huge animal thought to live in the Himalayas.

**yew** *noun* (**yews**)
an evergreen tree with dark leaves like needles.

**yield**$^1$ *verb* (**yields, yielding, yielded**)
1 to surrender; to give in, *He yielded to persuasion.* 2 to produce a crop, profit, etc., *These trees yield good apples.*

**yield**$^2$ *noun* (**yields**)
an amount produced by something, *What is the yield of milk per cow?*

**yippee** *interjection*
a shout of joy.

**yodel** *verb* (**yodels, yodelling, yodelled**)
to sing or shout with your voice often going from low to high notes, *The Swiss mountaineer was yodelling.*
**yodeller** *noun*

**yoga** *noun*
(*say* yoh-gă)
a method of meditation and self-control.

**yoghurt** *noun* (**yoghurts**)
(*say* yog-ert)
sour fermented milk, *Yoghurt is often flavoured with fruit.*

**yoke** *noun* (**yokes**)
a curved piece of wood put across the necks of animals pulling a cart.

**yolk** *noun* (**yokes**)
(rhymes with *coke*)
the yellow part of an egg.

**Yom Kippur** *noun*
an important religious day for Jews.

**yonder** *adverb* and *adjective*
(*old-fashioned use*) that is over there, *Yonder peasant, who is he?*

**Yorkshire pudding** *noun* (**Yorkshire puddings**)
a pudding made of batter and usually eaten with roast beef.

**you** *pronoun*
1 the person or people someone is speaking to, *Who are you?* 2 people; everyone; anyone, *You can never be too sure.*

**you'd** short for *you had, you should,* or *you would.*

**you'll** short for *you will.*

**young**$^1$ *adjective* (**younger, youngest**)
born not long ago; that has existed for a short time; not old.

**young**$^2$ *noun*
children or young animals, *The hen defended its young.*

**youngster** *noun* (**youngsters**)
a young person.

**your** *adjective*
belonging to you; of you.

**you're** short for *you are.*

**yours** *pronoun*
belonging to you; the things belonging to you, *This pen is yours. I've found this pen of yours.*
**yours faithfully, yours sincerely, yours truly,** formal ways of ending a letter before you sign it.

**yourself** *pronoun* (**yourselves**)
you and no one else.
**by yourself,** on your own.

**youth** *noun* (**youths**)
1 being young; the period when you are young, *She was a swimmer in her youth.* 2 a young person, especially a young man, *a youth of 16.* 3 young people, *a youth club.*
**youth hostel,** a hostel, often in the countryside, where people can stay cheaply when they are on holiday.
**youthful** *adjective*

**you've** short for *you have.*

**yo-yo** *noun* (**yo-yos**)
a round wooden or plastic toy that moves up and down on a string which you hold.

**yuppie** *noun* (**yuppies**)
(*informal*) a young, usually middle-class person with a professional job, who earns a lot of money and spends it on expensive things.

# Zz

**zany** *adjective* (**zanier, zaniest**)
funny in a crazy kind of way.

**zap** *verb* (**zaps, zapping, zapped**)
(*slang*) **1** to attack or destroy something
forcefully; to shoot someone. **2** to change
quickly from one section of a videotape, etc.
to another.

**zeal** *noun*
keenness, especially in doing what you
believe to be right.
**zealous** *adjective*, **zealously** *adverb*

**zebra** *noun* (**zebras**)
(*say* zeb-ră)
an animal like a horse with black and
white stripes, *Zebras are found in Africa.*
**zebra crossing**, part of a road marked with
broad white stripes for pedestrians to cross.

**zero** *noun* (**zeros**)
nought; the figure 0; nothing.
**zero hour**, the time when something is
planned to start.

**zest** *noun*
**1** enthusiasm. **2** great enjoyment or
interest, *The risk added zest to the
adventure.*

**zigzag**[1] *noun* (**zigzags**)
a line or route full of sharp turns from one
side to the other.

**zigzag**[2] *verb* (**zigzags, zigzagging, zigzagged**)
to move in a zigzag.

**zinc** *noun*
a white metal.

**zip**[1] *noun* (**zips**)
**1** a device with two rows of small teeth that
fit together to join two pieces of material.
**2** a sharp sound like a bullet going through
the air. **3** liveliness; energy.

**zip**[2] *verb* (**zips, zipping, zipped**)
**1** to fasten something with a zip. **2** to move
quickly with a sharp sound.

**zodiac** *noun*
(*say* **zoh**-di-ak)
(*in Astrology*) an area of the sky divided
into twelve equal parts called signs, *Pisces
and Sagittarius are signs of the zodiac.*

**zombie** *noun* (**zombies**)
(*informal*) someone who seems to be doing
things without thinking, as if he or she
were very tired.

**zone** *noun* (**zones**)
a district; an area, *a parking zone.*

**zoo** *noun* (**zoos**)
a place where wild animals are kept so
that people can look at them.

**zoology** *noun*
(*say* zoo-**ol**-ŏ-ji or zoh-**ol**-ŏ-ji)
the scientific study of animals.
**zoological** *adjective*, **zoologist** *noun*

**zoom** *verb* (**zooms, zooming, zoomed**)
to move very quickly, especially upwards.

**zoom lens** *noun* (**zoom lenses**)
a camera lens that can be adjusted quickly
to focus on things that are close up or far
away.

# APPENDICES

## Some common Prefixes

| Prefix | Meaning | Example |
| --- | --- | --- |
| ant(i)- | against | anti-aircraft |
| arch- | chief | archbishop |
| auto- | self | autobiography |
| com-; con- | together; with | compare; connect |
| contra- | against | contradict |
| de- | removing something | debug |
| dis- | not; taking away | dishonest; disarm |
| em-; en- | in; into | embark; encircle |
| ex- | that used to be | ex-husband |
| extra- | more; outside | extra-special; extraterrestrial |
| fore- | before | foresee |
| il-, im-, in-, ir- | not | illegal; impossible |
| il-, im-, in-, *etc.* | in; into | illuminate; import |
| inter- | between | international |
| mis- | wrong | misbehave |
| mono- | one | monorail |
| multi- | many | multiracial |
| non- | not | nonsense |
| over- | too much | overdo |
| poly- | many | polygon |
| post- | after | postpone |
| pre- | before | prehistoric |
| pro- | supporting | pro-government |
| re- | again | reappear |
| semi- | half | semicircle |
| sub- | below | submarine |
| super- | over; beyond | supersonic |
| tele- | at a distance | television |
| trans- | across | transport |
| ultra- | beyond | ultraviolet |
| un- | not | uncertain |

# Some common Suffixes

| Suffix | Meaning | Example |
|--------|---------|---------|
| -able, -ible, -uble | able (to be . . .) | eatable; edible; soluble |
| -ant; -ent | a doer | attendant |
| -dom | condition; rank; territory | freedom; kingdom |
| -ee | one who is . . . | employee |
| -er | a doer | baker; miner |
| -er | more | harder; higher |
| -esque | in the style of | picturesque |
| -ess | used to make feminine forms of words | lioness |
| -est | most | hardest; highest |
| -fold | times | threefold; fourfold |
| -ful | full of | trustful |
| -hood | state of | childhood; manhood |
| -ic | belonging to | historic |
| -ize; -ise | used to make verbs | publicize |
| -ish | rather like | reddish; boyish |
| -ism | belief; system of thought | Hinduism; Communism |
| -ist | a doer | artist |
| -itis | inflammation of | tonsillitis |
| -less | lacking; free from | useless; smokeless |
| -let | small | piglet |
| -ly | used to make adverbs and adjectives | bravely; kindly |
| -ment | used to make nouns | amusement |
| -ness | state of being | kindness |
| -oid | like | cuboid |
| -or | a doer | sailor; tailor |
| -ous | used to make adjectives | dangerous |
| -ship | state of being | friendship |
| -some | full of | troublesome |
| -ty | showing condition | cruelty; loyalty |
| -ward(s) | in a particular direction | seaward(s) |

# Grammar

Words can be put into sets called word classes, or parts of speech. The main ones are:
**noun   pronoun   verb   adjective   adverb   preposition   conjunction   interjection**

## Nouns

Nouns are words that are the names of things or persons, such as **child, danger, tree**.
Nouns divide up into names (or **proper nouns**) and descriptions (or **common nouns**).

|  |  |
|---|---|
| proper nouns: | {James, Africa, Dickens, Concorde . . .} |
| common nouns: | {dog, stream, mystery, bone, fire, danger . . .} |

Common nouns divide into those which stand for objects (**concrete nouns**), and those which stand for ideas (**abstract nouns**).

|  |  |
|---|---|
| concrete nouns: | {dog, stream, bone, fire, steel, bread, car . . .} |
| abstract nouns: | {mystery, danger, happiness, beauty . . .} |

Nouns also divide into those which can be made plural (**countables**), and those which cannot (**uncountables**).

|  |  |
|---|---|
| countables: | {dog, stream, bone, car . . .} |
| uncountables: | {bread, steel, air, clothing . . .} |

## Pronouns

Pronouns are words used instead of a noun, such as **it**, **me**, **they**.

## Verbs and their tenses

Some verbs express actions or feeling. For example,

I **came**.   She **ate**.   They **know**.

Other verbs connect words or phrases in a sentence.

It **is** late.   I **am** coming.   You **have** eaten.   They **must** not know.

Verbs have several different forms, depending on their **tense**. For example:

Present tense: I speak, she speaks, they are speaking.
Past tenses:  I spoke, she has spoken, you had spoken, they have been speaking.
Future tense: I will be speaking, they will be speaking.

The forms of verbs are given in the dictionary in the same order every time:

**speak**  *verb* (**speaks, speaking, spoke, spoken**)
speak: present tense after I, you, and they.
speaks: present tense after he, she, or it.
speaking: present participle (used after is, are, was, has been, etc.).
spoke: simple past tense.
spoken: past participle (used after has, had, etc.).

You will see that some verbs are *regular* which means that they follow a rule in the way they form their tenses. For example:

**kick**  *verb* (**kicks, kicking, kicked**)

But many verbs are *irregular* and have rules of their own! For example:

**throw** *verb* (**throws, throwing, threw, thrown**)

The connecting verb, **be**, is the most irregular of all:

**be** *verb* (*present tense: singular, 1st person* **am**, *2nd person* **are**, *3rd person* **is**, *plural* **are**; *present participle* **being**; *past tense: singular, 1st and 3rd persons* **was**, *2nd person* **were**, *plural* **were**; *past participle* **been**)

## Adjectives

Adjectives are words that describe a noun and add to its meaning, such as **happy, important, old**.

## Adverbs

Adverbs are words that tell you how, when, where, or why something happens, such as **quickly, again, here, together**.

### Comparison of adjectives and adverbs

Adjectives and adverbs can be made **comparative** or **superlative** in the following ways:

| positive | comparative | superlative |
|----------|-------------|-------------|
| stiff | stiffer | stiffest |
| quick | quicker | quickest |
| funny | funnier | funniest |
| late | later | latest |

(For general rules about adding -er and -est, see **Spelling**, p503)

For longer adjectives, and for most adverbs, the comparative and superlative are formed by putting **more** or **most** in front of them.

| positive | comparative | superlative |
|----------|-------------|-------------|
| terrible | more terrible | most terrible |
| quickly | more quickly | most quickly |

But watch out for exceptions:

| | | |
|----------|-------------|-------------|
| bad | worse | worst |
| badly | worse | worst |

If in doubt, look them up in the dictionary.

## Prepositions

Prepositions are words put in front of nouns or pronouns to show how the nouns and pronouns are connected with other words, such as **against, in, on**.

## Conjunctions

Conjunctions are joining words, such as **and, but, whether**.

## Interjections

Interjections are words that express surprise, pain, delight, etc., such as **oh, ouch, hooray**.

# **Spelling** – Some useful rules

## To make a noun plural:

Normally, just add **-s**:   *skirts, socks, ties, pianos, pieces, stars.*

> But watch out for some words ending in -o, that need **-es**:
> *echoes, heroes, potatoes, tomatoes, volcanoes*, etc.

To words ending in **-ch, -s, -sh, -x, or -z**, add **-es**:
*dress – dresses, box – boxes, stitch – stitches.*

To some words ending in **-f** and **-fe**, change to **-ves**:
*scarf – scarves, life – lives, half – halves.*

> But watch out for the exceptions: *beliefs, proofs, roofs*, etc.

To words ending in a consonant followed by **-y**, change the **y** to **i** and add **-es**:
*copy – copies, cry – cries, party – parties.*

## Adding **-ing** and **-ed** to verbs

Normally just add **-ing** or **-ed**:
*load – loading – loaded; open – opening – opened; stay – staying – stayed.*

For short words ending in **-e**, usually leave off the **e**:
*race – raced – racing; blame – blamed – blaming.*

For many short words that end with one consonant, double the last consonant:
*slam – slamming – slammed; tip – tipping – tipped.*

For longer words ending with one consonant and having the stress on the last syllable, double the last consonant:
*compel – compelling – compelled; prefer – preferring – preferred.*

For words ending in **-y** after a consonant, change the **y** to an **i** before **-ed**:
*try – trying – tried.*

For words ending in **-ie**, change the **ie** to **y** before adding **-ing**:
*lie – lying – lied; tie – tying – tied.*

> Watch out for these exceptions:  *lay – laid; pay – paid; say – said.*

## Adding -er and -est to adjectives

Normally just add **-er** and **-est**, unless the word already ends in **-e**:
*cold – colder – coldest; wide – wider – widest.*

For many short words that end with one consonant, change to a double consonant:
*wet – wetter – wettest; dim – dimmer – dimmest.*

If the word has two syllables and ends in **-y**, change the **y** to an **i**:
*dirty – dirtier – dirtiest; happy – happier – happiest.*
(See also **Grammar**, p501, on adjective and adverb forms.)

## Adding -ly

Adding **-ly** to an adjective makes it into an adverb:
*slowly, badly, awkwardly.*

If the word ends in **-ll**, just add **-y**:
*full – fully.*

For words ending in **-y** and with more than one syllable, leave off the **-y** and add **-ily**:
*happy – happily; hungry – hungrily.*

For words ending in **-le**, leave off the e:
*idle – idly; simple – simply.*

For adjectives ending in **-ic**, you usually add **-ally**:
*basic – basically; drastic – drastically.*

---

But watch out for these special ones: *public – publicly.*

---

# Punctuation

Punctuation marks are signs that help to make the writer's meaning clear to the reader. They mark where sentences end, and where pauses come. They also give clues to the kind of expression we should use when we are reading aloud.

.  A **full stop** is used to mark the end of a sentence. It is also used to mark abbreviations:
*My name is John Henry Maxwell.*
*J.H. Maxwell, 14 London Rd. Tel. 459346*

,  **Commas** mark pauses, for instance when there is a break or interruption in a sentence:
*When you cross a road, you should stop, look, listen, and think.*
*Driving fast, especially in wet weather, is dangerous.*
*Peter, take care crossing the road.*

;  A **semicolon** marks a more definite break than a comma. For instance it can be used, instead of a full stop, between short sentences that follow one another closely:
*The sun was getting low; the air was getting colder; it was time to head for home.*

:  A **colon** is used before a list of examples, or before a sentence which helps to explain the sentence before:
*Bring the following: sleeping bag, change of clothing, washing kit, and a towel.*
*Pack everything in a rucksack: it's much easier to carry than a suitcase.*

?  A **question mark** is used at the end of a *direct* question:
*What is your name? Where do you live?*
(**Note**: there is no question mark after an *indirect* question:
*She asked me what my name was and where I lived.*)

!  An **exclamation mark** is used at the end of a sentence expressing surprise or anger, or after a sentence that gives a strong or urgent command:
*How stupid of you to show your face here! Hide quickly before anyone sees you!*

( )  **Brackets** are used to enclose extra information, explanation, or examples:
*Quadrilaterals (rectangles, parallelograms, squares, etc.) always have four sides.*

'. . .' or ". . ." **Speech marks** are used to enclose all words that are direct speech:
*"I can handle this," she said. "Leave it to me."*

**Quotation marks** look like speech marks and are used to enclose a word or saying that has been borrowed or that is being quoted (i.e. mentioned):
*Winning, we are told, is 'the name of the game'.*
*Speech marks and quotation marks are also known as 'inverted commas'.*

'  An **apostrophe** marks where one or more letters have been missed out of a word:
*I'm (= I am)   haven't (= have not)   cont'd (= continued)   '62 (= 1962)*

An apostrophe is also used with an **s** to show *belonging*:
*A shark's fin appeared above the water. Soon there were sharks' fins all around the boat.*

**Note**: It is a mistake to put apostrophes in other, ordinary words that happen to end in **s:**
*Some sharks are harmless. A shark will attack if it smells blood.*

# Pronunciation and stress

There are no clear, simple rules that tell you how to pronounce English words from the way they are written. To help with the pronunciation of difficult or unfamiliar words the dictionary gives a guide in brackets, e.g. **mirage** *noun* (*say* **mi**-rahzh).

It tells you that the word has two syllables, **mi**-rage and that the **stress** is on the first syllable, the one in **bold** type. Putting stress on a syllable means pronouncing it more strongly than the rest of the word. Here is a full list of the way sounds are given in the pronunciation guide, with examples to explain them:

| | | | |
|---|---|---|---|
| a | as in **a**nd, b**a**t, c**a**t | nk | as in tha**nk**, pi**nk**, ta**nk** |
| ă | as in **a**bove, **a**go, centr**a**l | o | as in g**o**t, t**o**p, **o**n |
| ah | as in c**a**lm, f**a**ther, l**au**gh | ŏ | as in lem**o**n, c**o**rrect, t**o**gether |
| air | as in f**air**, c**are**, th**ere** | oh | as in m**o**st, b**oa**t, g**o** |
| ar | as in **ar**m, b**ar**, **are** | oi | as in j**oi**n, v**oi**ce, b**oy** |
| aw | as in l**aw**, p**aw**, s**aw** | oo | as in s**oo**n, b**oo**t, **oo**ze |
| ay | as in pl**ay**, **a**ge, f**a**ce | oor | as in p**oor**, m**oor**, t**our** |
| b | as in **b**at, ha**b**it, ro**b** | or | as in f**or**, m**ore**, h**or**se |
| ch | as in **ch**in, **ch**ur**ch**, whi**ch** | ow | as in c**ow**, h**ow**, **ou**t |
| d | as in **d**ay, un**d**er, ha**d** | p | as in **p**en, **p**ig, hi**p** |
| e | as in b**e**d, t**e**n, **e**gg | r | as in **r**ed, **r**oad, t**r**y |
| ĕ | as in tak**e**n, rott**e**n, sil**e**nt | s | as in **s**it, **s**o, ye**s** |
| ee | as in m**ee**t, s**ee**, **ea**ch | sh | as in **sh**op, **sh**e, fi**sh** |
| eer | as in b**eer**, ch**eer**, n**ear** | t | as in **t**op, in**t**o, no**t** |
| er | as in h**er**, b**ir**d, p**ur**se | th | as in **th**in, me**th**od, bo**th** |
| ew | as in f**ew**, d**ew**, b**eau**ty | *th* | as in **th**is, ei**th**er, **th**ose |
| ewr | as in c**ure**, p**ure**, end**ure** | u | as in b**u**n, c**u**p, **u**p |
| f | as in **f**at, le**f**t, i**f** | ŭ | as in circ**u**s, bon**u**s, prec**iou**s |
| g | as in **g**et, wa**g**on, do**g** | uu | as in b**oo**k, l**oo**k, p**u**ll |
| h | as in **h**at, **h**is, **h**ow | v | as in **v**an, ri**v**er, ha**v**e |
| i | as in p**i**n, s**i**t, **i**s | w | as in **w**as, **w**ill, **w**ish |
| ĭ | as in penc**i**l, bas**i**n, commun**i**ty | y | as in **y**ard, **y**es, **y**ou or when it follows a |
| I | as in **eye**, cr**y**, l**igh**t | | consonant = I as in cr**y** |
| j | as in **j**am, **j**ob, en**j**oy | yoo | as in **you**, **u**nit, v**iew** |
| k | as in **k**ing, see**k**, **c**at | yoor | as in **Eu**ropean, man**ure**, d**ur**able |
| l | as in **l**eg, a**l**so, wi**ll** | yr | as in f**ire**, w**ire**, sp**ire** |
| m | as in **m**an, **m**e, fro**m** | z | as in **z**oo, la**z**y, rai**s**e |
| n | as in **n**ot, ha**n**d, o**n** | zh | as in divi**si**on, vi**si**on, mea**s**ure |
| ng | as in si**ng**, fi**ng**er, thi**ng** | | |

# List of Countries

| Country | People | Country | People |
|---------|--------|---------|--------|
| Afghanistan | Afghans | Djibouti | Djiboutians |
| Albania | Albanians | Dominica | Dominicans |
| Algeria | Algerians | Dominican Republic | Dominicans |
| Andorra | Andorrans | Ecuador | Ecuadoreans |
| Angola | Angolans | Egypt | Egyptians |
| Antigua and Barbuda | Antiguans, Barbudans | El Salvador | Salvadoreans |
| Argentina | Argentinians | England | English |
| Armenia | Armenians | Equatorial Guinea | Equatorial Guineans |
| Australia | Australians | Estonia | Estonians |
| Austria | Austrians | Ethiopia | Ethiopians |
| Azerbaijan | Azerbaijanis | Falkland Islands | Falkland Islanders |
| Bahamas | Bahamians | Fiji | Fijians |
| Bahrain | Bahrainis | Finland | Finns |
| Bangladesh | Bangladeshis | France | French |
| Barbados | Barbadians | Gabon | Gabonese |
| Belarus | Belorussians | Gambia | Gambians |
| Belgium | Belgians | Georgia | Georgians |
| Belize | Belizians | Germany | Germans |
| Benin | Beninese | Ghana | Ghanaians |
| Bhutan | Bhutanese | Gibraltar | Gibraltarians |
| Bolivia | Bolivians | Great Britain | British or Britons |
| Bosnia-Herzegovina | Bosnians | Greece | Greeks |
| Botswana | Batswana | Grenada | Grenadians |
| Brazil | Brazilians | Guatemala | Guatemalans |
| Brunei Darussalam | People of Brunei | Guinea | Guineans |
| Bulgaria | Bulgarians | Guinea-Bissau | People of Guinea-Bissau |
| Burkina Faso | Burkinans | Guyana | Guyanese |
| Burma (now called Myanmar) | Burmese | Haiti | Haitians |
| Burundi | People of Burundi | Honduras | Hondurans |
| Cambodia | Cambodians | Hong Kong | Inhabitants of Hong Kong |
| Cameroon | Cameroonians | Hungary | Hungarians |
| Canada | Canadians | Iceland | Icelanders |
| Central African Republic | People of the Central African Republic | India | Indians |
| Chad | Chadians | Indonesia | Indonesians |
| Chile | Chileans | Iran | Iranians |
| China, People's Republic of | Chinese | Iraq | Iraqis |
| | | Ireland, Republic of | Irish |
| | | Israel | Israelis |
| | | Italy | Italians |
| China, Republic of | Taiwanese | Ivory Coast | People of the Ivory Coast |
| Colombia | Colombians | Jamaica | Jamaicans |
| Congo | Congolese | Japan | Japanese |
| Costa Rica | Costa Ricans | Jordan | Jordanians |
| Croatia | Croats | Kazakhstan | Kazakhs |
| Cuba | Cubans | Kenya | Kenyans |
| Cyprus | Cypriots | Kirgyzstan | Kirgyz |
| Czech Republic | Czechs | Kuwait | Kuwaitis |
| Denmark | Danes | Laos | Laotians |

| Country | People | Country | People |
|---------|--------|---------|--------|
| Latvia | Latvians | St Vincent and the | St Vincentians, |
| Lebanon | Lebanese | Grenadines | Grenadines |
| Lesotho | Basotho | São Tomé and Príncipe | People of São Tomé and |
| Liberia | Liberians | | Príncipe |
| Libya | Libyans | Saudi Arabia | Saudi Arabians |
| Liechtenstein | Liechtensteiners | Scotland | Scots |
| Lithuania | Lithuanians | Senegal | Senegalese |
| Luxembourg | Luxembourgers | Sierra Leone | Sierra Leoneans |
| **M**acedonia | Macedonians | Singapore | Singaporeans |
| Madagascar | Malagasies | Slovakia | Slovaks |
| Malawi | Malawians | Slovenia | Slovenes |
| Malaysia | Malaysians | Solomon Islands | Solomon Islanders |
| Mali | Malians | Somalia | Somalis |
| Malta | Maltese | South Africa | South Africans |
| Mauritania | Mauritanians | South Korea | South Koreans |
| Mauritius | Mauritians | Spain | Spaniards |
| Mexico | Mexicans | Sri Lanka | Sri Lankans |
| Moldavia, Moldova | Moldavians | Sudan | Sudanese |
| Monaco | Monégasques | Suriname | Surinamers |
| Mongolia | Mongolians | Swaziland | Swazis |
| Montserrat | Montserratians | Sweden | Swedes |
| Morocco | Moroccans | Switzerland | Swiss |
| Mozambique | Mozambicans | Syria | Syrians |
| Myanmar (until 1989 | | **T**ajikistan | Tajiks |
| called *Burma*) | | Tanzania | Tanzanians |
| | | Thailand | Thais |
| **N**amibia | Namibians | Togo | Togolese |
| Nauru | Nauruans | Trinidad and Tobago | Trinidadians and |
| Nepal | Nepalese | | Tobagans |
| Netherlands | Dutch | | |
| New Zealand | New Zealanders | Tunisia | Tunisians |
| Nicaragua | Nicaraguans | Turkey | Turks |
| Niger | Nigeriens | Turkmenistan | Turkmens |
| Nigeria | Nigerians | **U**ganda | Ugandans |
| North Korea | North Koreans | Ukraine | Ukrainians |
| Norway | Norwegians | United Arab Emirates | People of the United Arab |
| **O**man | Omanis | | Emirates |
| **P**akistan | Pakistanis | United Kingdom | British |
| Panama | Panamanians | United States of America | Americans |
| Papua New Guinea | Papua New Guineans | Uruguay | Uruguayans |
| Paraguay | Paraguayans | Uzbekistan | Uzbeks |
| Peru | Peruvians | **V**anuatu | People of Vanuatu |
| Philippines | Filipinos | Venezuela | Venezuelans |
| Poland | Poles | Vietnam | Vietnamese |
| Portugal | Portuguese | **W**ales | Welsh |
| **Q**atar | Qataris | Western Samoa | Western Samoans |
| **R**omania | Romanians | **Y**emen, Republic of | Yemenis |
| Russia (Russian | Russians | Yugoslavia (Montenegro | Yugoslavs (Montenegrins |
| Federation) | | and Serbia) | and Serbians) |
| Rwanda | Rwandans | **Z**aïre | Zaïreans |
| **S**t Kitts-Nevis | People of St Kitts-Nevis | Zambia | Zambians |
| St Lucia | St Lucians | Zimbabwe | Zimbabweans |

# Weights and Measures

## Metric

### LENGTH
| | | |
|---|---|---|
| 1 millimetre (mm) | | 0.04 inch |
| 1 centimetre (cm) | = 10 mm | 0.39 inch |
| 1 metre (m) | = 100 cm | 39.4 inches |
| 1 kilometre (km) | = 1000 m | 0.62 mile |

### SQUARE MEASURE
| | | |
|---|---|---|
| 1 square centimetre (cm$^2$) | | 0.155 square inch |
| 1 square metre (m$^2$) | = 10 000 cm$^2$ | 1.2 square yards |
| 1 hectare (ha) | = 10 000 m$^2$ | 2.47 acres |
| 1 square kilometre (km$^2$) | = 100 ha | 247 acres (0.39 square mile) |

### CAPACITY
| | | |
|---|---|---|
| 1 millilitre (ml) | | 0.002 pints |
| 1 litre (l) | = 1000 ml | 1.76 pints |

### MASS (WEIGHT)
| | | |
|---|---|---|
| 1 milligram (mg) | | 0.015 grain |
| 1 gram (g) | = 1000 mg | 0.035 ounces |
| 1 kilogram | = 1000 g | 2.2 pounds |
| 1 tonne | = 1000 kg | 0.98 ton |

## British

### LENGTH
| | | |
|---|---|---|
| 1 inch (in.) | | 25.4 millimetres |
| 1 foot (ft.) | = 12 inches | 0.3 metre |
| 1 yard (yd.) | = 3 feet | 0.91 metre |
| 1 mile | = 1760 yards | 1.61 kilometres |

### SQUARE MEASURE
| | | |
|---|---|---|
| 1 square inch (sq. in.) | | 6.45 square centimetres |
| 1 square foot (sq. ft.) | = 144 sq. ins. | 0.09 square metre |
| 1 square yard (sq. yd.) | = 9 sq. ft. | 0.84 square metre |
| 1 acre | = 4840 sq. yds. | 0.405 hectare |
| 1 square mile | = 640 acres | 259 hectares (2.6 square kilometres) |

### CAPACITY
| | | |
|---|---|---|
| 1 pint (pt.) | = 20 fluid ounces | 0.57 litre |
| 1 quart (qt.) | = 2 pts. | 1.14 litres |
| 1 gallon (gal.) | = 8 pts. | 4.55 litres |

(NB: 1 American pint = 16 fluid ounces = 0.47 litres. Therefore 1 American gallon = 3.79 litres.)

### MASS (WEIGHT)
| | | |
|---|---|---|
| 1 ounce (oz) | | 28.35 grams |
| 1 pound (lb) | = 16 ozs. | 0.45 kilogram |
| 1 stone (st.) | = 14 lbs. | 6.35 kilograms |
| 1 ton | = 2240 lbs. | 0.91 tonne |